D1192426

DISCARD - WEEDED

A TREASURY OF OPERA LIBRETTOS

A TREASURY OF OPERA LIBRETTOS

EDITED WITH AN INTRODUCTION BY

DAVID G. LEGERMAN

782.12
L
c.2

DOUBLEDAY & COMPANY, INC.
GARDEN CITY, NEW YORK

~~MISSISSIPPI LIBRARY COMMISSION~~
~~405 State Office Building, Jackson~~

LIBRARY OF CONGRESS CATALOG CARD NUMBER: 61–13329
COPYRIGHT © 1962 BY DOUBLEDAY & COMPANY, INC.
ALL RIGHTS RESERVED
PRINTED IN THE UNITED STATES OF AMERICA
FIRST EDITION

CONTENTS

HOW THIS BOOK CAME TO BE

The idea for this book came to the editor some twenty years ago as he sat in at NBC studios on a radio broadcast of *The Barber of Seville,* performed from the English translation by Stewart Robb, who took his text from the Beaumarchais play in French. Rossini's music was used.

Mr. Blevins Davis, producer of the *Great Plays* series for NBC, had assigned Welbourne Kelly to adapt the Robb translation for a one-hour presentation with full orchestra, chorus, and soloists, including Felix Knight, a tenor with a fine but light voice, who took the role of Count Almaviva. The other leading roles were sung by young American singers whose names do not come readily to mind.

It was a thoroughly enjoyable performance and incidentally my first experience with opera in English, and I dare say the first opera in English for several million radio listeners.

After the performance, the possibility of more operas being translated and perhaps included in a book was discusssed with Mr. Robb, who had already begun to translate the opening scenes of Wagner's *Siegfried.* Thus the seed was planted.

Some two years later, the Metropolitan Opera produced *The Magic Flute* in English for the first time, in a version prepared by Ruth and Thomas Martin. John Brownlee, Australian baritone, and Charles Kullman, American tenor, starred in a cast of singers whose native tongues for the most part were not English—and quite a variety of accents resulted. The performance was, however, a complete success, and today this version is still performed to appreciative audiences.

Some years later, your editor finally met the Martins through the good offices of Mr. John White, associate director of the New York City Opera. The Martins, in the meantime, had translated into English all the other Mozart operas that appear in this book; Verdi's *Rigoletto* and *La Traviata,* Puccini's *Bohème* and *Madama Butterfly,* and other operas for performance at the Met and other leading opera houses here and abroad. This was still before the day of NBC opera on television, where several Martin translations have been performed, outstandingly *Così Fan Tutte.*

At a memorable conference with the Martins it was decided that there were in existence enough good, singable translations in English of the great operas in the standard repertory to go ahead with plans for a book.

Consultation with such people as Messrs. Hans Heinsheimer of G. Schirmer, Inc., Drs. Franco Colombo and Carlo Ricordi of G. Ricordi & Company, George F. Handel of Rullman & Company, as well as John Gutman and Boris Goldovsky of the Met, brought the field of selection to twenty-one operas and seven translators whose versions are being sung in leading opera houses, on radio and TV, and elsewhere. The entire list appears in the Table of Contents.

The presentation of the foreign-language librettos in juxtaposition with the English translation was a happy thought of the publishers. While this meant additional technical responsibilities for the editor, the obvious advantages of a single book containing the most complete collection of popular foreign-language opera librettos available today will be clear to every opera lover and student.

The bilingual arrangement on each page of the text should also make the book of great value for the casual opera listener to radio broadcasts or records.

Translations of *Siegfried* and *Parsifal* were commissioned for the book, and Mr. Robb, whose previous contribution to the book has been acknowledged, went on to translate the entire *Ring*, which E. P. Dutton & Company published in their Everyman's series in 1960. The translations of *Otello, Falstaff, Faust, The Barber of Seville, Don Giovanni,* and a new version of *Pelléas and Mélisande,* while previously performed, had not yet appeared in any book or published libretto when they were included in this volume. Needless to say, the translators of the above-named operas reserve all rights, with the exception of the last, *Pelléas,* where G. Schirmer controls rights as agent for Durand et Fils of Paris.

As translator of *Boris Godunov* we were fortunate to obtain Mr. John Gutman, assistant to the general manager of the Metropolitan Opera, Mr. Rudolph Bing. Mr. Gutman's translation was made from the Russian language version found in the Lamm edition of Moussorgsky's works. The original Russian in the Lamm score has been compared with Mr. Gutman's translation for this book by Mme. Nadia Vouki, librettist of G. Ricordi & Company, and herself of Russian birth. However, for technical reasons, the Russian language libretto of *Boris* has been omitted.

It is the editor's sincere hope that numerous future performances of opera in English, as well as frequent use of this book by those who will find their enjoyment and appreciation of opera enhanced considerably thereby, will justify his labors as well as those of the translators and others who have made this book possible. Not least among those are Messrs. Mel Evans and George de Kay, of M. Evans & Company, and Mr. Harold Kuebler, of Doubleday & Company, whose encouragement and cooperation were indispensable in bringing about its publication.

New York

DAVID G. LEGERMAN

OPERA IN ENGLISH

Every generation has its own tune for its language, hence each generation must have its own translations. And in the field of opera particularly, where the existing translations are admittedly outdated and in many cases absurd to the modern reader, there has long been a need for fresh, singable, and readable translations from the original language of the composer into English.

"A translation is no translation," says Synge in *The Aran Islands,* "unless it will give you the music of a poem along with the words." This then is the problem faced by the translator of an opera libretto from the original language into English. Not only must he get the meaning into musical language, but he must also fit the English words to the music language of the composer, keeping in mind the problems of the singers. In other words he must write musical words to fit music. Not an easy task. Yet we feel that the translators whose work appears here are among the best practitioners of the art today.

Opera in English has been the subject of so much discussion that any essay such as this must necessarily reflect many opinions. The author therefore has attempted to bring together a body of such opinion from the translators themselves, critics and musicologists, singers and the operagoing public.

The question will naturally arise as to why none of Edward Dent's translations are used in this book. The answer is that, although his translations of the Mozart operas among others and their performance in England far antedated those in America, for some reason British English does not hit the American ear as does American English and as a consequence the Dent versions are not performed in America. On the other hand, the Martins' translations of Mozart's operas and indeed of Bizet's *Carmen,* as well as many others in this volume, have won increasingly wide performance. At the time of this writing it is noted with satisfaction that the Martin version of *Così Fan Tutte* is being performed for New York City school children right in the schools by Metropolitan Opera Association casts and conductors under the title *Women Are Like That!*

Can it be, then, that the Martins have eminently succeeded in accomplishing the goals set for translators of opera by W. H. Auden, translator with Chester Kallman of *The Magic Flute,* first performed by NBC Opera on TV, January 15, 1956? Mr. Auden wrote: "In his relation to the composer, the translator is in a different position from the original librettist. The latter writes his verses without any notion of the music to which they are going to be set, but the translator knows the music already and probably knows it better than the text.

"If, as one assumes, he is a complete versifier, he can, without too much difficulty copy the form of the original verses, their metres, rhymes, etc., and know that, if he does this accurately, his words will conform to the notes. It does not necessarily follow, however, that he should be content with this. The ideal goal he should set himself, whether attainable or not, is to make the audience believe, when his version is performed, that *his are the words that the composer actually set!*" (Editor's italics.)

However, let the Martins speak for themselves concerning translators' problems: "I would like to answer some of the questions most frequently put to me and my wife. How do you proceed in making a translation? By what principles are you guided? This is a complex question and not easily answered. First of all it depends on who the composer and the librettists are, on the style of the work, on the period in which it plays. As a guiding principle I would say that at all times the English must fit the musical line and notation perfectly. The slightest unevenness and misaccentuation will already cause trouble for both the singer and the listener.

"At musical climaxes, particularly on high notes, the original vowel is preferable, since its tone color influences the sound of the place in question. At the same time it will be easier to manage by the singer, who often knows the role in the original language and is used to producing that particular vowel.

"The selection of words depends greatly on their singability, but here again one must proceed with consideration. There are soft and mellow passages where round words with soft and few consonants are appropriate; at other times we have chatty patterns where words with short vowels and explosive consonants are preferable.

"A great deal of dissenting opinion exists as to the necessity of rhyming. Eliminating rhymes entirely makes the task of translating much easier, but we feel strongly that such a procedure is wrong where a work in verse form is concerned. Often, however, the composer has removed two rhyming lines far from each other, or hidden the rhyme in the pattern of the music. Then, of course, it would be senseless to force a rhyme, particularly at the expense of straightforward English.

"The question of how close to the original a translation should be must also be left to the individual case. At times the composition reflects so much of the word that it must be translated as literally as possible. At other times a freer treatment is advisable or necessary.

"At all times the tempo of the music must be taken into account. It would be useless to write nice, even poetic words which read well on paper but, when sung at the speed the tempo dictates, become unpronounceable. I consider it most important that the opera translator be a musician who has a thorough and practical knowledge of the work and of all its vocal and scenic problems.

"At no time do we permit ourselves inverted lines and the use of what Olin Downes once called 'translationese.' I am referring to the filling in with small, meaningless words like 'just,' 'then,' 'there,' 'now,' 'oh,' 'so,' etc., which the amateur translator squeezes in invariably when things won't come out otherwise. Verse lines must sound like original lyrics, and prose lines like good dialogue, which would hold water if only spoken, without any music. While the music should not be changed in order to accommodate the words, there are occasions where it cannot be helped, where an additional note has to be used, or a tie be eliminated.

"We try to avoid this as much as possible, out of respect for the music. There are cases, though, where it is better to add an up-beat or make two sixteenths of one eighth note, if this is the only way of making the sentence right. We have found, however, that another attempt and some more thinking generally produce a solution without change of the music."

In answering these questions before a meeting of the National Opera Association, Mr. Thomas P. Martin succeeded in stating some sound principles of translation, at least principles that have guided him and his wife in their work. That they are right and that their methods have won the approval of their fellow translators are attested in the following rules of thumb for translators as laid down by Fred Merkling, editor of *Opera News* and a translator of *Carmen* for the Metropolitan and Offenbach for television:

"*Select words that echo the original.* This is desirable at least in works where there is some evidence that the composer was sensitive to the musical question of language. Thus the Martins' happy rendition of Butterfly's '*Un bel dì vedremo*' by 'Soon, as we are waiting,' which did little violence to the vowels audiences have come to expect."

Mr. Merkling also in the same breath included the work of some of the other contributors to this volume and, in commenting on the use of the open-throated vowels on all high notes, found disagreement among translators. He wrote: "John Gutman points out that Richard Strauss, master orchestrator of all instruments, voice included, as often as not assigned short 'i's' or long 'e's' to top notes. Gutman personally is more careful with terminal consonants. He relates that although Kirsten Flagstad liked his 'Alestis' in English, she said, 'There's one thing, Mr. Gutman. I can't sing love on a high A!'—because of the 'v' and not the vowel. The experience of George Mead has been that many male singers have had to learn to sing all vowels at all pitches anyway.

"*Respect rhymes!*" cautioned Mr. Merkling further. "This is a vexed question. There are translators who favor a scrupulous observance of the rhyme pattern, even in recitatives. There are others who feel it is essential to preserve only those rhymes which lead to important cadences. Here again the individual opera must determine the treatment. Phyllis Mead believes that unrhymed translations, due to the very latitude of choice they permit, are more difficult to execute in an unprosaic way than versions in 'verse.' This may surprise anyone who has ever struggled with a rhyming dictionary. Mrs. Mead, however, knows whereof she speaks, having tried her hand at an English version of 'Tristan and Isolde' from which she rigorously excluded all rhymes except in a few numbers, such as the sailor's song and the love duet. Furthermore, she confined herself as far as possible to words with Saxon roots. She points out that the case endings of certain Romance languages—the '–ato' and '–ate' of Italian are an example—are largely responsible for the high frequency, or toleration, of rhymes in librettos written in those languages. Translated into English, which lacks these case endings, such endless rhyming sounds stilted at best. It can also sound unintentionally comic. In preparing 'Tosca' in English for television, John Gutman translated the moment when Scarpia shows the jealous heroine her supposed rival's fan as follows:

TOSCA: That fatal obsession.

SCARPIA: I have made an impression.

It had to go, admirable though it looks on paper, because the TV producer feared that a rhyme at this point might produce laughter.

"Look out for laughs," cautions Mr. Merkling further. With or without rhymes, unintentional humor is a recurring problem in translation. The Martins discovered that Sharpless' question to Butterfly, rendered by them as "Do you have any sisters?" drew sharp male guffaws night after night. The difficulty was solved by substituting "Have you sisters and brothers?"

Finally, Mr. Merkling advises, *"Keep yourself out of your translation.* The Meads, for example, go out of the way to avoid a bad pun or obvious cleverness. (The most that they will permit themselves is to translate *'E una donna od è castrato?'* by 'Are you a female or an ex-male?' which they did in Wolf-Ferrari's 'The Inquisitive Women' and have not subsequently regretted.)"

Before turning to the larger question of opera in English and counting noses of those for or against it, it seems in order to consider the stories and sources of some of our great operatic works and to permit comment by those of our translators who have given the matter thought upon our request. Chiefly we find six categories or types of opera books:

1) A book originally written for the composition of an opera, e.g., *Der Rosenkavalier,* Menotti's books, etc.
2) A novel dramatized for the theatre: *Manon,* Prévost; *Carmen,* Mérimée; *Bohème,* Murger; *Traviata,* Dumas *fils; Mignon,* Goethe; and countless others.
3) Adaptations from plays already written for the stage: *Le Nozze di Figaro, Barber of Seville, Otello, Don Carlos, Faust, Tosca, Rigoletto.*
4) A play so appropriate for composition that it was taken in its original form or at least only slightly adjusted: *Salome, Pelléas et Mélisande, Wozzeck.*
5) Historical events or mythological material. Almost all of the Wagnerian works fit into this category, and of course a great number of earlier classic works too numerous to mention.
6) The fairy tale with its magical background: Hansel and Gretel, Undine, Oberon, Koenigskinder, etc.

Thomas Martin, to whom we are indebted for the above summary, has also commented tellingly on the important factor of librettist-and-composer relationship. He writes: "An opera plot must possess the same qualities as the successful stage play: a dramatic plot, characters whose fate and personality appeal. It must never fail to move or amuse as the case may be. In other words, it must have literary qualities and all the virtues of a theatrical play.

"And how does this welding of the two facets, the book and the music, come about? Most of the time, there are two artists at work, the librettist and the composer. It requires a close co-operation of the two if the end product is to be satisfactory. We have such a collaboration in letter exchanges between Richard Strauss and

Hugo von Hofmannsthal, who incidentally was a great lyricist in his own right; and Verdi, particularly in his letters to Ghislanzoni, the librettist of *Äida.*

"Occasionally, and this is the ideal case, a composer is also his own poet and possesses the additional talent for writing his own libretto. Such composer poets were Wagner, who attributed such importance to his opera books that he called his works music dramas; Berlioz; Boito, whom we know as his own as well as Verdi's librettist for *Otello* and *Falstaff;* and in our own day Gian-Carlo Menotti and others."

With the chemical reaction complete and the result proven and tested by performance, what operas should translators tackle and producers put on? Howard Taubman, of the New York *Times,* wrote, on February 12, 1956: "One does not ask for all opera in English. It would not be easy to get a batch of fine translations overnight, and it is questionable whether one would wish to have some operas with their thick plots and turgid philosophies translated at all. But good translations can be made.

"The comic operas cry out for performance in English. 'Der Rosenkavalier,' with its saltiness and poetry, would be more enjoyable than it is. Mozart's 'Marriage of Figaro,' with its radiant laughter, is another case in point. It would be difficult to match in English the effervescence of Da Ponte's tripping Italian, but if we come close, audiences would derive fresh pleasure from a marvelous work."

So a note of hope for opera in English was sounded as the plan for this book was taking form. So a challenge to the translators was thrown down in this letter to the *Times* a week or two later: "While performed predominantly in an unintelligible language, it [opera] is doomed to remain—and justifiably so—a foreign body in our artistic and cultural life. Only when meaningful words of the mother tongue can be *integrated* [editor's italics] with the music into an organic and inseparable psychological entity will it become assimilated and begin to permeate our cultural consciousness."

An argument for this book if not for opera in English performance was put forth at this time by Olin Downes, late master of modern music critics, who wrote: "I am congenitally opposed to opera sung in any language other than the one in which it was written. Only then can the magic communication of the word when it is wedded to the enhancing tone be fully understood, and the secret of the eternal appeals of music drama to be fully grasped.

"It's customary, in famous lyric theatres of our land, for the operagoer to read his libretto or find out in some way the 'story' of the opera before he attends its performance; or failing that, to listen to the outlines of the music and plot and enjoy the fine sounds and general effect of the mixture. This is the way to get half or two-thirds of an opera's significance in performance."

Thomas Martin recently commented: "It is encouraging to see that we have an ever-growing number of institutions pursuing the goal of making operas more popular and accessible to wider circles of people, especially the younger generation, by performing them in the English language. It removes the stigma from so-called 'Grand Opera' as being long-hair, high brow, or, in one word, a bore. I am speaking of our university opera departments, the local companies in many cities, the touring companies like the Grass Roots Opera of Raleigh, N.C., televised opera, and opera companies like the New York City Opera, whose repertory is given in English to a large degree.

"Looking at a Metropolitan Opera playbill you might see: Monday: *Boris Godunov,* in English; Tuesday: *Eugen Onegin,* in English; Wednesday: *Die Fledermaus,* in English; and next week, Wednesday: *Vanessa,* in English; Friday: *The Magic Flute,* in English; Saturday: *Die Fledermaus,* in English. This sounds encouraging indeed."

This program presented in the 1958–59 season did sound encouraging for the future of opera in English. However, polls taken of the audiences at the Met and in Covent Garden in London did not reflect this trend. At five performances of *Le Nozze di Figaro,* over nine thousand cards returned showed that only 2952 preferred an English version while 6129 liked the original Italian best. British audiences at Covent Garden seem to prefer foreign languages, a poll of the Wagner Society, for example, showing an overwhelming majority for German performances of his works. Sadler's Wells operagoers, on the other hand, less sophisticated musically and certainly less well heeled than their compatriots, preferred English versions of the standard repertory, performed as they are by native English singers for the most part, who are considered less capable than their foreign-born colleagues who sing at the top British opera house.

And what of the singers themselves? What do they think of singing opera in English? James Pease, American bass-baritone, who has sung Hans Sachs (in English) in New York and London; Wotan (in German) in London; and a variety of Italian and German roles, in German, at Hamburg, wrote: "The clamor for original language performances stemming from the 'public' may be resolved to snobs for the greater part, or to that very small circle of real opera students . . . the specialists who are as devoted to the medium as a true philatelist to his hobby. One must assume that the critics who beat the drum for the original more or less belong to that persuasion too.

"But this does not apply to the great mass of mankind, and as long as a foreign language is combined with a strange art form, there will be no true operatic culture in either England or America. For that reason I left my native shore to sing in Germany in German for a German audience. To sing opera for an audience, which the majority cannot follow, for my feeling is perpetrating a fraud.

"But even as important as reaching the true public is the question of the performer singing basically in his own tongue. How many of the great artists one still remembers made their profound impression in a language they could not speak? How many British or American singers, even though we are required in our own lands to perform in every known tongue, can color and express in all those varied languages in competition with the Italian who sings nothing but Italian or the German who knows nothing but Deutsch? When we sing in English we are at our best, and that is aside from the question of the quality of certain translations . . . *they can and must be improved.* [Editor's italics.] To decry the beauty of the English language, the home ground of Shelley and Keats and Shakespeare, is laughable. And if we can speak it, we can sing it better than any other."

What an eloquent plea from an American singer for opera in his native tongue! But listen to Lotte Lehmann, great German soprano: "I am nowadays against singing opera in the original tongue unless it is the language of the place where it is being performed. To make opera really popular it is better to do it in the language of the audience."

Readers of *Opera* magazine, a British publication, have also contributed some cogent arguments pro and con on the subject of opera in English. An American opera lover wrote: "A point from Bernard Berenson may be apropos. He declares that a key function not only of the visual arts, but also of the drama, the opera, and all the other arts which stir the emotions is life enhancement. This 'life enhancement' makes the spectator or recipient of the artist's message feel more hopefully and zestfully alive . . . Without claiming Berenson to be on the side of opera in English, one can certainly state that 'life enhancement' is endangered by the inferiority one feels at a performance of an opera in a foreign language one does not know too well."

On the other hand consider this unequivocal vote against opera in English, by a Britisher: "We in the audience should be given as nearly as possible what the composer intended us to hear: in other words, we should be given not only the notes the composer had in mind, but also the words he set them to, since they are his point of departure, his springboard into music, and as such, part of his score . . . Respect for a composer's intentions should be our only criterion, and there can therefore be no alternative to opera in the language in which it was written and intended to be performed. Anything else is, to a greater or less degree, travesty."

Coming in between the extremes of the immediately foregoing, and sounding perhaps the most farsighted of all the views on opera in English here presented, let us consider finally the thoughts of Virgil Thomson, American composer and critic:

"In a majority of cases trained American singers are more distinct and finished in their enunciation of a foreign language than they are of their own native English. Why? The basis of his training was usually that of a foreign tongue. He was taught to vocalize on Italian syllables, upon which, when he arrived at the interpretive stage, were usually imposed vocalizations according to the requirements of foreign languages, not his own and not making the same demands upon his tonal mechanism.

"This is particularly true of those who train for opera, and perfectly logical, because there is not a single serious opera in English in the current international repertory. The singer who prepares for a career in serious opera must do so with especial attention to foreign languages. This influences not only his diction but his vocalism, in addition to the fact that he has less and less awareness, as he proceeds, of the actual life of the word in the tone and its poetic and emotional significance. When he sings he is, as it were, transplanted to foreign soil, and that is not the soil from which native poetry and eloquence in communication arise.

"We believe that the American singer's training, which is usually after foreign models, must be changed before we can expect English to be given its full significance in song. There is both the physical and the intellectual approach to be taken into consideration. No one nation uses its language in the same phonetical ways. The throat and vocal organs operate from different angles. Correct technical bases of tone and breath control are mechanically the same, but the ways of heredity and environment, where speech and therefore song is concerned, vary very much.

"A French tenor does not sing in the Italian manner nor with the Italian character of tone, nor does a German have the throat or vocal predisposition of a Latin artist. Race and soil are present here as in every field of art. Americans should sing in ways that are basic to the physical formation and use of the vocal organs, as they are predisposed to make tone from birth. And when an American poet and composer can mate song and text as indissolubly as these are welded so beautifully and eloquently —and vocally—together in our Negro spirituals, we will have songs and singing in English of a kind that we have not yet evolved.

"In the meantime, we have what for the present is a vicious circle, where the upper intellectual brackets of our music are concerned: the lack of the native consciousness in our cultured music, consequent largely upon the lack of a deep-seated awareness of the wonder and eloquence of our native tongue to be transmuted into the miracle of music. Slowly the forces which will produce this development are moving—more slowly in America, with its great mixture of races and its brief, tumultuous past, than elsewhere. But the day will come when a genuinely American opera will be composed, equivalent in its realization of the national consciousness to the appearance of a *Freischuetz* in German opera . . . Then the problems of singing in English will disappear. We have only to see what follows such dramatically insufficient but but idiomatically and melodically native productions as the Gershwin 'Porgy and Bess' which has gone everywhere, or 'Showboat,' 'Oklahoma!' and other offerings of the popular musical theatre which flourish as they do, not merely because they are tuneful, but because of their native authenticity of language and song. But we should not wait for that to happen before learning to sing more naturally, distinctly and eloquently in English."

There you have it.

Opera has been successfully translated into singable English, as this book, we hope, proves. The genuine American opera of Mr. Thomson's dream is yet to be composed. But in the meantime opera in English is in the hands of the producers, the singers and you—the opera audience.

And there we leave it. D.G.L.

A TREASURY OF OPERA LIBRETTOS

AIDA

by Giuseppe Verdi (1813–1901)

LIBRETTO BY ANTONIO GHISLANZONI

Translated by MARY ELLIS PELTZ.

Based on a sketch by Mariette Bey that was later used as a basis for a prose drama written by Camille du Locle in collaboration with Verdi.

CHARACTERS

THE KING OF EGYPT	*Bass*
AMNERIS, *his daughter*	*Mezzo-soprano*
AÏDA, *an Ethiopian girl and slave to Amneris*	*Soprano*
RADAMES, *an Egyptian captain of the guard*	*Tenor*
RAMFIS, *a high priest of Isis*	*Bass*
AMONASRO, *King of Ethiopia and father of Aïda*	*Baritone*
MESSENGER	*Tenor*
PRIESTESS	*Soprano*

PRIESTS AND PRIESTESSES, GUARDS, SLAVES, DANCERS, SOLDIERS, EGYPTIANS, PRISONERS

Place: Memphis and Thebes in ancient Egypt
Time: The dynasty of the Pharaohs
First performance: Cairo Opera House, Cairo, Egypt, December 24, 1871

COPYRIGHT © 1962 BY MARY ELLIS PELTZ

ACT I

Scene 1

The brief prelude musically introduces two of the protagonists of the drama: first, there is the romantic and gentle theme of the Ethiopian princess AÏDA, *who is held in captivity by the Egyptians as a slave of the princess* AMNERIS, *then the ponderous music later to be associated with the Egyptian priests.*

The curtain rises on a hall in the palace of the KING OF EGYPT *at Memphis, where the young warrior,* RADAMES, *is trying, in talk with the high priest,* RAMFIS, *to gain information about a new Ethiopian invasion. His ambitious nature is roused by the hope that he may be called to command the army.*

RAMFIS
Yes, it is known to us that Ethiopia
Again has risen, and has threatened our valley,
The Nile and also Thebes.
And soon a messenger will bring the news.

RADAMES
Have you consulted the goddess Isis?

RAMFIS
She has made known to us the man
Who shall lead us
As supreme commander.

RADAMES
O happy soldier!

RAMFIS (*looking significantly at* RADAMES)
He is young and valiant also.
Her sacred order
I now must tell the King.
(*exit* RAMFIS)

RADAMES
If I could be that warrior!
If my dream could be accomplished!
With an army of the brave at my disposal
How I would triumph!
All Memphis would sing my praises.
To you, my sweet Aïda,
I'd come with all my laurels,
Saying: for you I've battled,
For you I've conquered!

Aria

Heavenly Aïda, wonderful maiden,
Mystical garland, bright as a flower,
With love for your beauty my life is laden,
Over my spirit I feel your power.

RAMFIS
Sì: corre voce che l'Etiope ardisca
Sfidarci ancora, e del Nilo la valle
E Tebe minacciar. Fra breve un messo
Recherà il ver.

RADAMES
La sacra
Iside consultasti?

RAMFIS
Ella ha nomato
Delle Egizie falangi
Il condottier supremo.

RADAMES
Oh, lui felice!

RAMFIS
Giovane e prode è desso. Ora del Nume
Reco i decreti al Re.

RADAMES
Se quel guerrier
Io fossi! se il mio sogno
Si avverasse! . . . Un esercito di prodi
Da me guidato . . . e la vittoria e il plauso
Di Menfi tutta! E a te, mia dolce Aïda,
Tornar di lauri cinto . . .
Dirti: per te ho pugnato e per te ho vinto!

Celeste Aïda, forma divina,
Mistico serto di luce e fior;
Del mio pensiero tu sei regina,
Tu di mia vita sei lo splendor.
Il tuo bel cielo vorrei ridarti,

Le dolci brezze del patrio suol,
Un regal serto sul crin posarti,
Ergerti un trono vicino al sol, ah!
Celeste Aïda, forma divina,
Mistico raggio di luce e fior;
Del mio pensiero tu sei regina,
Tu di mia vita sei lo splendor.
Il tuo bel cielo vorrei ridarti,
Le dolci brezze del patrio suol,
Un regal serto sul crin posarti,
Ergerti un trono vicino al sol,
Un trono vicino al sol, un trono vicino al sol.

Would I could set your fair skies around you,
Gather you breezes when day is done.
How I would gladly with gold have crowned you,
Built you a throne near the shining sun!
Heavenly Aïda, wonderful maiden,
Mystical garland, bright as a flower,
With love for your beauty my life is laden,
Over my spirit I feel your power.
Would I could set your fair skies around you,
Gather you breezes when day is done.
How I would gladly with gold have crowned you,
Built you a throne near the shining sun!
A throne near the shining sun!
(*enter* AMNERIS)

AMNERIS
Quale insolita gioia
Nel tuo sguardo! Di quale
Nobil fierezza ti balena il volto!
Degna d'invidia, oh! quanto
Saria la donna il cui bramato aspetto
Tanta luce di gaudio in te destasse!

AMNERIS
Do I find in your face
New signs of gladness? Can it be pride
That I see is flashing through your glances?
How enviable is she
And lucky, this woman by whose beloved presence
You are kindled to joyous appearance of rapture!

RADAMES
D'un sogno avventuroso
Si beava il mio cuore. Oggi, la Diva
Profferse il nome del guerrier che al campo
Le schiere Egizie condurrà . . . S'io fossi
A tal onor prescelto . . .

RADAMES
My spirits were elated
By a dream of adventure. Isis today
Has revealed the warrior who shall lead the army
Of the Egyptians in the field.
Ah, what honor!
If I were only chosen!

AMNERIS
Nè un altro sogno mai
Più gentil . . . più soave . . .
Al cuore ti parlò? . . . Non hai tu in Menfi
Desiderii . . . speranze? . . .

AMNERIS
And is no other vision
Sweeter far and more tender
Reflected in your heart?
Are there in Memphis
No attractions? No fancies?

RADAMES
Io! . . . (quale inchiesta!)

RADAMES
Fancies? (*aside*) What a question!

Duet

(Forse . . . l'arcano amore
Scoprì che m'arde in core . . .)

Can she perhaps be learning
What love in me is burning?

AMNERIS
(Oh! guai se un altro amore
Ardesse a lui nel core! . . .)

AMNERIS (*aside*)
Alas, he may be spurning
My love and to another turning!

RADAMES
(Della sua schiava il nome
Mi lesse nel pensier!)

RADAMES (*aside*)
Can she have read my secret
And guessed I love her slave?

AMNERIS
(Guai se il mio sguardo penetra
Questo fatal mister!
Guai se il mio sguardo penetra
Questo fatal mister!
Oh! guai, oh, guai!

AMNERIS (*aside*)
Ah, alas, I cannot penetrate
The secret of his heart!
Alas, I cannot bear to penetrate
The secret of his heart!
Alas! Alas! Alas!

RADAMES (*aside*)
Perhaps she reads it in my mind!
She reads it in my mind!
(AÏDA *enters;* RADAMES *suddenly notices her*)
See her!

RADAMES
(Forse mi lesse nel pensier,
mi lesse nel pensier!)
Dessa!

AMNERIS (*aside*)
He is troubled.
Ah, how he watches to catch her eye!
Aïda!—Is she my rival?
Can it indeed be she?
(*turning to* AÏDA)
Hither my dear, draw near to me.
None of us can resist her;
Not as a slave or a waiting maid
See how I call you sister . . .
Tell me! Oh tell me why you are weeping in secret.
Tell me your secret woes.

AMNERIS
(Ei si turba . . . e quale
Sguardo rivolse a lei!
Aïda! . . . a me rivale . . .
Forse saria costei?)
Vieni, o diletta, appressati . . .
Schiava non sei nè ancella
Qui dove in dolce fascino
Io ti chiamai sorella . . .
Piangi? . . . delle tue lacrime
Svela il segreto,
Svela il segreto a me.

AÏDA
Alas! I hear the sounds of war!
I see the troops assemble
For my unhappy fatherland, for me, for you
I tremble.

AÏDA
Ohimè! di guerra fremere
L'atroce grido io sento . . .
Per l'infelice patria,
Per me . . . per voi pavento.

AMNERIS
Is this the truth? And are there not more sorrows in your heart?
(*aside, glancing at* AÏDA)

AMNERIS
Favelli, il ver?
Nè s'agita più grave cura in te?

Trio

Tremble, you guilty servant!

Trema, o rea schiava.

RADAMES (*aside, glancing at* AMNERIS)
Her glance is hot with anger—

RADAMES
(Nel volto a lei balena . . .)

AMNERIS (*aside*)
Yes, tremble, you guilty servant.

AMNERIS
(Ah! trema, rea schiava, trema.)

RADAMES (*aside*)
With scorn and with suspicion.

RADAMES
(Lo sdegno ed il sospetto.)

AMNERIS (*aside*)
Deep in your heart I feel you tremble.

AMNERIS
(Ch'io nel tuo cor discenda!)

RADAMES (*aside*)
Ah, she will read the secret
And learn of our devotion.

RADAMES
(Guai se l'arcano affetto
A noi leggesse in cor!)

AMNERIS (*aside*)
Do you suppose you can dissemble
Your blushes and your tears?

AMNERIS
(Trema che il ver ni apprenda
Quel pianto e quel rossor!)

RADAMES (*aside*)
She knows our secret love!

RADAMES
(Guai se leggesse in cor.)

AÏDA (*aside*)
Ah, no!
Over my country
I do not repine. My heart in sorrow
Weeping, ever weeping in sorrow,
I must weep ever in pain with a broken heart!

AÏDA
(No, sull' afflitta patria
Non geme il cor soltanto;
Quello ch'io verso e pianto
Di sventurato amor.)

AMNERIS
(Rea schiava, trema,
Ch'io nel tuo cor discendo.
Ah, trema che il ver
Ah, trema che il ver m'apprenda
Quel pianto e quel rossor.)

AMNERIS (*aside*)
You guilty servant, tremble,
For in your heart you tremble.
Ah, do you not suppose
That you may at last dissemble
Your blushes and your tears!

RADAMES
(Nel volto a lei balena
Non geme il cor sottanto;
Quello ch'io verso e pianto
Di sventurato amor.)

RADAMES (*aside*)
Her glance is hot with rage
And anger, disdaining the
love within our heart.
Ah, she will learn our secret
And read it in our heart.

The KING *enters, preceded by his guards and followed by* RAMFIS *and the priests, the ministers of state, and officers. A palace official indicates the arrival of a messenger from Ethiopia.*

IL RE
Alta cagion v'aduna,
O fidi Egizii, al vostro Re d'intorno.
Dai confin d'Etiòpia un Messaggiero
Dianzi giungea; gravi novelle ei reca . . .
Vi piaccia udirlo . . .
Il Messaggier s'avanzi!

THE KING
Mighty the cause that calls you to your king,
O loyal men of Egypt!
There has come a messenger with news
From far Ethiopia.
Grave is the tale he brings us.
I beg you hear him. (*turning to the official*)
The messenger may enter.

MESSAGGIERO
Il sacro suolo dell'Egitto è invaso
Dai barbari Etiòpi; i nostri campi
Fur devastati . . . arse le messi . . . e baldi
Della facil vittoria i predatori
Già marciano su Tebe . . .

MESSENGER
The savage men of Ethiopia
Harass the borders of Egypt.
They all lay waste the fields of our country.
They burn our harvest.
Encouraged by so easy a conquest,
They march on Thebes in pursuit of rape and pillage.

TUTTI
Ed osan tanto!

ALL
How bold and daring!

MESSAGGIERO
Un guerriero indomabile, feroce,
Li conduce: Amonasro.

MESSENGER
They are led by a warrior ferocious
And unconquered: Amonasro!

TUTTI
Il Re!

ALL
The King!

AÏDA
(Mio padre!)

AÏDA (*aside*)
My father!

MESSAGGIERO
Già Tebe è in armi e dalle cento porte
Sul barbaro invasore
Prorompera, guerra recando e morte.

MESSENGER
The rising Thebans, from all the hundred portals,
Are bursting out to meet them,
A savage band, crying battle and murder.

IL RE
Sì: guerra e morte il nostro grido sia!

THE KING
Yes, we shall rally with our cry of battle!

RADAMES and RAMFIS
Battle!

ALL
Battle! Battle!

RADAMES, RAMFIS, and CHORUS
Battle! Tremendous, and unrelenting!

THE KING (*addressing* RADAMES)
Isis, the holy goddess,
Revered by all our forces,
Has signified the man who shall command them;
Radames!

ALL
Radames!

RADAMES
Ah, ye gods! I thank you,
For you have heard my prayers.

AMNERIS (*aside*)
Our leader!

AÏDA (*aside*)
I tremble!

PRIESTS
Radames!

THE KING
Now to the shrine of Vulcan
You must proceed. He will gird you
With sacred arms to win our battles.
Up the Nile, the sacred valley,
Hasten, heroes of our land.
From your hearts proclaim the rally:
Battle and death to every hostile band.

RAMFIS
Praise to heaven, praise be to Isis!
God alone controls the crisis;
In the power wielded by heaven,
Every warrior's fate must stand.

Chorus

MINISTERS and OFFICERS
Up the Nile, the sacred valley,
All our men will guard the country.
With one cry the host will rally:
Battle and death to every hostile band!

THE KING
Up! Up the Nile, the sacred valley,
Hasten, heroes of our country.
From all your hearts proclaim the rally:
War and death on every hand.

RAMFIS
Praise be to Isis!
In the power of heaven,
In heaven's power the fate of every man must stand.

RADAMES e RAMFIS
Guerra!

TUTTI
Guerra! Guerra!

RADAMES, RAMFIS e CORO
Guerra! Tremenda! Inesorata!

IL RE
Tremenda, inesorata . . .
Iside venerata
Di nostre schiere invitte
Già designava il condottier
supremo:
Radames

TUTTI
Radames!

RADAMES
Ah!—Sien grazie ai Numi!
I miei voti fur paghi.

AMNERIS
(Ei duce!)

AÏDA
(Io tremo!)

SACERDOTI
Radames!

IL RE
Or, di Vulcano al tempio
Muovi, o guerrier. Le sacre
Armi ti cingi e alla vittoria vola.
Su! del Nilo al sacro lido
Accorrete, Egizii eroi;
Da ogni cor prorompa il grido:
Guerra e morte allo stranier!

RAMFIS
Gloria ai Numi! ognun rammenti
Ch'essi reggono gli eventi,
Che in poter de' Numi solo
Stan le sorti del guerrier.

MINISTRI e CAPITANI
Su! del Nilo al sacro lido
Sien barriera i nostri petti;
Non echeggi che un sol grido:
Guerra e morte allo stranier!

IL RE
Su! Su! de Nilo al sacro lido
Accorrete, Egizii eroi,
Da ogni cor prorompa il grido;
Guerra e morte allo stranier!

RAMFIS
Ognun rammenti
Che in poter dei Numi—
De' Numi solo stan
Le sorti del guerrier!

AÏDA
(Per chi piango? per chi prego? . . .
Qual poter m'avvince a lui!)

RADAMES
Sacro fremito di gloria
Tutta l'anima m'investe
Su! corriamo alla vittoria!
Guerra e morte allo stranier!

AÏDA
(Deggio amarlo . . . ed è costui
Un nemico . . . uno stranier!)

AMNERIS
Di mia man ricevi, o duce,
Il vessillo glorioso;
Ti sia guida, ti sia luce
Della gloria sul sentier.

TUTTI
Guerra! guerra! sterminio all'invasor!
Va, Radames, ritorna vincitor!

AÏDA
(Deggio amarlo . . . ed è costui
Un nemico . . . uno stranier!)

AMNERIS
Ritorna vincitor!

TUTTI
Ritorna vincitor!

AÏDA
Ritorna vincitor! . . . E dal mio labbro
Uscì l'empia parola! Vincitor
Del padre mio . . . di lui che impugna l'armi
Per me . . . per ridonarmi
Una patria, una reggia! e il nome illustre
Che qui celar m'è forza! Vincitor
De' miei fratelli . . . ond'io lo vegga tinto
Del sangue amato, trionfar nel plauso
Dell'Egizie coorti! . . . E dietro il carro,
Un Re . . . mio padre . . . di catene avvinto! . . .
L'insana parola,
O Numi, sperdete!
Al seno d'un padre
La figlia rendete;
Struggete le squadre
Dei nostri oppressor!
Ah! Sventurata! che dissi? . . . e l'amor mio? . . .
Dunque scordar poss'io
Questo fervido amor che, oppressa e schiava,

AÏDA (*aside*)
Who is this for whom I'm praying, whom I weep for?
Who is master of my prison?

RADAMES
Sacred ecstasy of glory
Moves my heart and stirs my senses.
We shall write a deathless story,
Battle, battle to every warring foe!

AÏDA (*aside*)
In my heart has love arisen
For a stranger and a foe?

AMNERIS
From my hand accept as leader
This the standard of our country,
She will guide you, if you heed her,
To the ambush of the foe.

ALL (*except* AÏDA)
Battle! Battle! Battle! Battle! Battle!
Battle! Battle! Destruction!
Destruction on every hand!

AÏDA (*aside*)
Can I love him when I know him
As a foe of my fatherland!

AMNERIS (*to* RADAMES)
And may you win the war!

ALL
And may you win the war!
(*exeunt all but* AÏDA)

AÏDA
And may you win the war!
What are these wicked words my lips are saying?
Win the war and slay my father!
The one who wages battle for me,
Winning me back to my country,
To my kingdom,
Winning the title which now I keep in hiding.
Win the war and slay my brothers!
Yes, I can see him,
Stained with their blood so precious,
In the noisy triumph of the army of Egypt.
Behind his chariot a king, my father,
In his chains a captive.
Forget what I pray you, O gods, stem the slaughter!
Return to her father his heartbroken daughter.
Destroy them, destroy them,
Destroy all the legions that persecute our race.
What do I say in my anguish?
The man I cherish—
How can his memory perish?
His devotion consoles me when griefs oppress me.
And like a ray of light I feel it bless me!

Can I invoke the death of Radames,
For whom I love and languish?
Ah, in the whole wide world,
There never was a heart in wilder anguish!
The holy names of my lover and father
I do not dare remember, I dare not say.
Confused and trembling, from one to the other,
I turn and weep for both and long to pray.
Yet all my prayers seem to turn to blaspheming,
A crime it is to weep, a sin to sigh,
With gloomy terrors my spirit is teeming,
In my cruel affliction I would die!
Merciful gods, dwelling on high,
There is no hope for my distress.
Fatal the power love can possess,
Break my poor heart, then let me die.
Merciful gods, dwelling on high,
Oh, hear my cry,
Oh, hear my prayer, Oh, hear my cry!

Come raggio di sol qui mi beava?
Imprecherò la morte
A Radames . . . a lui ch'amo pur tanto!
Ah! non fu in terra mai
Da più crudeli angoscie un core affranto!
I sacri nomi di padre . . . d'amante
Nè profferir poss'io, nè ricordar . . .
Per l'un . . . per l'altro . . . confusa . . . tremante.
Io piangere vorrei, vorrei pregar.
Ma la mia prece in bestemmia si muta . . .
Delitto è il pianto a me . . . colpa il sospir . . .
In notte cupa la mente è perduta . . .
E nell'ansia crudel vorrei morir.
Numi, pietà del mio soffrir!
Speme non v'ha pel mio dolor
Amor fatal,—tremendo amor,
Spezzami il cor,—fammi morir!
Numi, pietà del mio soffrir,
Ah! pietà, Numi, pietà del mio soffrir,
Numi, pietà del mio soffrir,
Pietà, pietà del mio soffrir!

Scene 2

The interior of the Temple of Vulcan in Memphis. A mysterious light falls on the altar. Shadowy columns vanish in the darkness. Statues of deities and sacred emblems are wreathed in the incense that rises from golden tripods. RAMFIS *stands near the altar, while the voice of an unseen priestess is heard, accompanied by a harp.*

PRIESTESS (*from within*)
Almighty Phta,
The spirit of life in the world,
Ah! Ah!

SACERDOTA
Possente, possente Fthà . . . del mondo spirito animator, ah! ah!

PRIESTESSES
Hear us invoke you!

SACERDOTESSE
Noi t'invochiamo!

RAMFIS and PRIESTS
You, who have made of nothing
Heaven and earth and sea,
Hear us invoke you!

RAMFIS, SACERDOTI
Tu che dal nulla hai tratto
L'onde, la terra, il ciel,
Noi t'invochiamo!

PRIESTESSES
Almighty, almighty Phta,
The spirit who makes all the world grow—
Ah! Hear us invoke you!

SACERDOTESSE
Immenso, immenso Fthà, del mondo
Spirito fecondator, ah! ah!
Noi t'invochiamo!

RAMFIS, PRIESTS
God of the dual nature,
Father as well as son,
Hear us invoke you!

RAMFIS, SACERDOTI
Nume che del tuo spirito
Sei figlio e genitor
Noi t'invochiamo!

SACERDOTESSE
Fuoco increato, eterno,
Onde ebbe luce il sol, ah! ah!
Noi t'invochiamo!

PRIESTESSES
Spirit of fire eternal,
Source of the light of the sun, ah! ah!
Hear us invoke you!

RAMFIS, SACERDOTI
Vita dell' Universo,
Mito d'eterno amor,
Noi t'invochiam!

RAMFIS, PRIESTS
Life of the whole creation,
Source of eternal love,
We call your name!

SACERDOTESSE
Immenso Phtà!

PRIESTESSES
Almighty Phta!

RAMFIS, SACERDOTI
Noi t'invochiam!

RAMFIS, PRIESTS
We call your name!

(*as the priestesses execute a sacred dance,* RADAMES *enters, unarmed, and approaches the altar, where a silver veil is placed on his head*)

SACERDOTESSE
Immenso Fthá

PRIESTESSES
Almighty Phta!

RAMFIS, SACERDOTI
Noi t'invochiam!

RAMFIS and PRIESTS
We call your name!

RAMFIS
Mortal, diletto ai Numi, a te fidate
Son d'Egitto le sorti. Il sacro brando
Dal Dio temprato, per tua man diventi
Ai nemici terror, folgore, morte.

RAMFIS (*to* RADAMES)
O youth, beloved of heaven,
To you the fate of Egypt now is confided.
The sacred weapon, by God created,
In your hand shall bring to our foemen
Dismay, massacre, murder!

RAMFIS, SACERDOTI
Il sacro brando dal Dio temprato,
Per tua man diventi ai nemici terror,
Folgore, morte.

RAMFIS and PRIESTS
The sacred weapon, by God created,
In your hand shall bring to our foemen
Dismay, massacre, murder!

RAMFIS
Folgore, morte.
Nume, custode e vindice
Di questa sacra terra,
La mano tua distendi
Sovra, sovra l'Egizio suol.

RAMFIS (*turning to the god*)
. . . massacre, murder . . .
Hear us, avenging deity,
You who defend our country,
Keep your control extending
Over, over Egyptian soil.

RADAMES
Nume, che duce ed arbitro
Sei d'ogni umana guerra,
Proteggi tu, difendi
D'Egitto il sacro, il sacro suol.

RADAMES
Hear us, O God, who rules the world,
Turning the fate of battle,
Keep watch, our land defending,
Safeguard our sacred Egyptian soil!

RAMFIS
La mano tua, la mano tua distendi
Sovra l'Egizio, l'Egizio suol.

RAMFIS
Keep your control; keep your control extending
Over Egyptian soil.

(*while* RADAMES *is invested with the sacred arms, the priests and priestesses resume their ritual hymns and dances*)

Chorus

SACERDOTI
Nume, custode e vindice
Di questa sacra terra,

PRIESTS
Hear us, avenging deity,
You who defend our country!

Keep your control, keep your control extending
Over Egyptian soil.

RAMFIS
Hear us, avenging arbiter,
You who defend our country,
Keep your control extending
Over Egyptian soil.

RADAMES
Keep watch, our land defending,
Safeguard our sacred Egyptian soil!

PRIESTESSES
Almighty, almighty Phta—

RADAMES, RAMFIS, and PRIESTS
Almighty Phta—

PRIESTESSES
You who have made the world,
Ah! Ah!

RADAMES, RAMFIS, and PRIESTS
Spirit of life, creating
Out of nothing the world around us,
Hear us invoke you!
You, who created the endless ocean,
The earth, the heavens,
Hear us invoke you!
You, who from nothing created all things,
Hear us invoke you!

PRIESTESSES
Almighty Phta!
Spirit, bringing life to all,
Spirit, hear when we call—
Almighty Phta!

RADAMES, RAMFIS, and PRIESTS
Hear as we call, hear as we call,
Hear as we call!

RADAMES and RAMFIS
Almighty Phta!

ALL
Almighty Phta!

La mano tua, la mano tua distandi
Sovra l'Egizio, sovra l'Egizio suol.

RAMFIS
Nume, custode ed arbitro
Di questa sacra terra,
La mano tua distendi
Sovra, sovra l'Egizio suol.

RADAMES
Proteggi tu,
Proteggi tu, difendi d'Egitto
il sacro, il sacro suol.

SACERDOTESSE
Possente, possente Fthà.

RADAMES, RAMFIS, SACERDOTI
Possente Fthà!

SACERDOTESSE
Del mondo creator,
Ah! ah!

RADAMES, RAMFIS, SACERDOTI
Spirito fecondator,
Tu che dal nulla hai tratto il mondo,
Noi t'invochiamo!
Tu che dal nulla hai tratto l'onde
La terra, il cielo,
Noi t'invochiamo,
Tu che dal nulla hai tratto il mondo,
Noi t'invochiamo.

SACERDOTESSE
Possente Fthà!
Spirito animator,
Spirito fecondator
Immenso Fthà!

RADAMES, RAMFIS, SACERDOTI
Noi t'invochiam! Noi t'invochiam!
Noi t'invochiam!

RADAMES, RAMFIS
Immenso Fthà!

TUTTI
Immenso Fthà!

ACT II

Scene 1

A room in the apartments of AMNERIS. *The princess is surrounded by her slave girls, who are adorning her for the triumphal feast. The fragrance of perfume arises from the tripods about her couch. Young Moorish slaves wave tall feather fans.*

SCHIAVE
Chi mai fra gl'inni e i plausi
Erge alla gloria il vol,
Al par d'un Dio terribile,
Fulgente al par del sol?
Vieni: sul crin ti piovano
Contesti ai lauri i fior;
Suonin di gloria i cantici
Coi cantici d'amor.

SLAVE GIRLS
What man has won our hymns and praises?
Whose glorious fame has risen high,
And like a god so terrible,
Outshines the dazzling sky?
Oh, bind the garlands in your hair,
Entwined with laurel and flowers above,
While we are singing canticles
In praise of love.

AMNERIS
Ah, vieni, amor mio,
m'inebbria . . .
Fammi beato il cor!

AMNERIS
Ah, come, love, again and move me,
Bring blessings to my heart!

SCHIAVE
Or dove son le barbare
Orde dello stranier?
Siccome nebbia sparvero
Al soffio del guerrier.
Vieni: di gloria il premio
Raccogli, o vincitor;
T'arrise la vittoria,
T'arriderà l'amor.

SLAVE GIRLS
Ah where are they, the enemy?
Where have the foemen gone?
Afar they've scattered through the land,
Like clouds before the sun.
Now take the crown of triumph,
Receive the victor's due,
For victory has blessed you,
And love will bless you too.

AMNERIS
Ah, vieni, amor mio, ravvivami
D'un caro accento ancor!

AMNERIS
Ah come, love, and wake my heart again
With words of love from you.

SCHIAVE
Vieni: sul crin ti piovano
Contesti ai lauri,
Ai lauri i fior;
Suonin di gloria i cantici,
coi cantici d'amor,
coi cantici d'amor.

SLAVE GIRLS
Oh, bind the garland in your hair,
Entwined with laurel
And flowers above,
While we are singing canticles,
Our canticles of love,
Our canticles of love.

AMNERIS
Ah, vieni, vieni amor mio,
m'inebbria
Fammi beato il cor,
Fammi beato il cor!
Silenzio! Aïda verso noi
s'avanza . . .
Figlia dei vinti, il suo dolor
m'è sacro.
Nel rivederla, il dubbio
Atroce in me si desta . . .
Il mistero fatal si squarci alfine!

AMNERIS
Ah, come, love, again and move me,
Bring blessings to my heart,
Bring blessings to my heart!
Be silent! Aïda comes at last to join us.
Child of the conquered, to me her grief is sacred.
(*the slaves retire.* AÏDA *enters*)
But when I see her,
I feel again a dark suspicion.
I shall learn it at last, her fatal secret.
(*turns to* AÏDA *with simulated affection*)

In the chances of battle you were unlucky,
Wretched Aïda!
But you must not be lonely, I share in your affliction.
I offer you my friendship—
I'll give you all you wish of me.
You will be happy.

AÏDA
Ah, how can I be happy,
Far from my native country, where I shall never
Know the fate of my father and my brothers!

AMNERIS
Deeply you move me. Yet they're not enduring:
Our sorrows here below.
Time brings its healing to sorrows of the spirit.
Yet one is stronger: a god, to help you.
The god of love.

Duet

AÏDA (*aside, much moved*)
O love, I hail you, sublime desire,
Sweetest of raptures, cruel delight.
In all your torment I feel the fire,
When you are smiling, all heaven is bright,
When you are smiling, all heaven is bright,
In all your torment I feel the fire,
When you are smiling, all heaven is bright.

AMNERIS (*aside*)
Ah, what a pallor I can inspire,
This is her passion, secret, apart.
How can I ask her? Can I inquire?
I share her torment and read all her heart.
(*to* AÏDA)
But now what new emotion torments you, gentle Aïda?
Reveal your secret thoughts to me,
Trusting your new friend, who's ready when you need her.
Among the heroes who have died, fighting against your nation,
There was one who, with emotion,
Perhaps has aroused your heart?

AÏDA
Your meaning?

AMNERIS
It is not everyone whom fortune's hand will cherish.
The fearless leader in the field may fall
Wounded and perish.

AÏDA
What are you saying?
Misery! Misery!

Fu la sorte dell'armi a' tuoi funesta,
Povera Aïda! Il lutto
Che ti pesa sul cor teco divido.
Io son l'amica tua . . .
Tutto da me tu avrai, vivrai felice!

AÏDA
Felice esser poss'io
Lungi dal suol natio . . . qui dove ignota
M'è la sorte del padre e dei fratelli? . . .

AMNERIS
Ben ti compiango! pure hanno un confine
I mali di quaggiù . . . Sanerà il tempo
Le angoscie del tuo core . . .
E più che il tempo, un Dio possente . . . amore.

AÏDA
(Amore, amore! gaudio . . . tormento . . .
Soave ebbrezza, ansia crudel . . .
Ne' tuoi dolori la vita io sento . . .
Un tuo sorriso mi schiude il ciel.
Un tuo sorriso mi schiude il ciel!
Ne' tuoi dolori la vita io sento,
Un tuo sorriso mi schiude il ciel!)

AMNERIS
(Ah, quel pallore . . . quel turbamento
Svelan l'arcana febbre d'amor . . .
D'interrogarla quasi ho sgomento . . .
Divido l'ansie del suo terror . . .)
Ebben: qual nuovo fremito
T'assal, gentil Aïda?
I tuoi segreti svelami,
All'amor mio, all'amor mio t'affida . . .
Tra i forti che pugnarono
Della tua patria a danno . . .
Qualcuno . . . un dolce affanno . . .
Forse . . . a te in cor destò? . . .

AÏDA
Che parli?

AMNERIS
A tutti barbara
Non si mostrò la sorte . . .
Se in campo il duce impavido
Cadde trafitto a morte . . .

AÏDA
Che mai dicesti! misera! misera! . . .

AMNERIS
Sì . . . Radames da' tuoi
Fu spento . . . E pianger puoi?

AÏDA
Per sempreio piangerò!

AMNERIS
Gli Dei t'han vendicata . . .

AÏDA
Avversi sempre
A me furo i Numi . . .

AMNERIS
Trema! in cor ti lessi! . . .
Tu l'ami . . .

AÏDA
Io . . .

AMNERIS
Non mentire! . . .
Un detto ancora e il vero
Saprò . . . Fissami in volto . . .
Io t'ingannava . . . Radames vive . . .

AÏDA
Vive!
Ah grazie, o Numi!

AMNERIS
E ancor mentir tu speri?
Si . . . tu l'ami . . . Ma l'amo
Anch'io . . . intendi tu? . . .
Son tua rivale . . .
Figlia de' Faraoni.

AÏDA
Mia rivale! . . .
Ebben, sia pure . . . Anch'io . . .
Son tal . . .
Che dissi mai? . . . pietà! perdono! Ah!
Pietà ti prenda del mio dolor . . .
È vero . . . io l'amo d'immensa amor . . .
Tu sei felice . . . tu sei possente
Io vivo solo per questo amor!

AMNERIS
Trema, vil schiava! spezza il tuo core . . .
Segnar tua morte può quest' amore . . .
Del tuo destino arbitra sono
D'odio e vendetta le furie ho in cor.
Alla pompa che s' appresta,
Meco, o schiava, assisterai;
Tu prostrata nella polvere,
Io sul trono, accanto al Re.

AMNERIS
Yes, Radames by yours was slaughtered—
And you can mourn him?

AÏDA
My tears will forever flow.

AMNERIS
The gods—they will avenge you!

AÏDA
The gods are hostile to me in their fury.

AMNERIS
(*crying out with violence*)
Tremble! I know your secret.
You love him.

AÏDA
Love him?

AMNERIS
You were lying.
A single sentence
Will tell me the truth.
Look at me closely,
For you may see him:
Radames, living!

AÏDA (*kneeling, enraptured*)
Living!
Gods, I thank you!

AMNERIS
And still you would deceive me?
Yes, you love him,
But so do I, you hear my words?
Behold your rival, daughter of all the Pharaohs.

AÏDA (*drawing herself up with pride*)
You, my rival! What if it were so?
For I—I too—
(*checking herself and falling at* AMNERIS' *feet*)
Ah! What do I say?
Forgive, forgive me! Ah!
You are so happy, you have such power,
All that I have is my love alone.
Forgive, forgive,
And pity my despair.

AMNERIS
Tremble, vile servant,
Your heart may break indeed.
Do I not hold you in my power?
My heart is hot with the vengeance and rage,
I will not spare!
In the triumph that is coming
You, the slave, will be in waiting.
In the dust Aïda sits alone.
I shall stand beside the throne.

CHORUS (*in the distance*)
Up the Nile, the sacred valley,
All our men will guard the country.
With one cry the host will rally:
Battle and death to every hostile band!

AÏDA
Ah! my life is bleak and empty, so have pity on my sorrow;
You may live and reign in glory,
Rage will not disturb your breast,
Curb your anger, for tomorrow,
In the tomb I'll be at rest.

AMNERIS
Follow now and I will show you
Whether you may vie with me.

AÏDA
Ah forgive, for my love I shall bury within the tomb.
Forgive, forgive!

CHORUS
Death and battle to the foe.

AÏDA
Merciful gods dwelling on high,
There is no hope,
There is no hope for my distress.
Oh hear my prayer! Oh hear my cry!
Oh, hear my prayer!
Oh, hear my cry!

CORO
Su! del Nilo al sacro lido
Sien barriera i nostri petti;
Non eccheggi che un sol grido:
Guerra, guerra e morte allo stranier!

AÏDA
Ah! pieta! che più mi resta? Un deserto e la mia vita;
Vivi regna, il tuo furore.
Io tra breve placherò.
Quest'amore che t'irrita
Nella tomba spegnerò.

AMNERIS
Vien, mi segui, apprenderai
Se lottar tu puoi con me.

AÏDA
Ah! pietà!
Quest'amor
Nella tomba spegnerò,
Pietà, pietà!

CORO
Guerra e morte allo stranier!

AÏDA
Numi, pietà del mio martir,
Speme non v'ha pel mio dolor;
Numi, pietà! del mio soffrir,
Numi, pietà! pietà! pietà!

Scene 2

An avenue at the gates of Thebes. On one side stands the Temple of Ammon, on the other a throne hung with purple. A triumphal gate is seen at the rear. The stage is crowded with people gathered to celebrate the glorious victory over the Ethiopians. The KING *enters, followed by his ministers, priests, and standard bearers, and later by* AMNERIS *with* AÏDA *and her other slaves. The* KING *takes his seat on the throne with* AMNERIS *beside him.*

THE PEOPLE
Glory to Isis, whom we hail,
She is our true defender.
And to our King we render,
To Egypt's King we sing our hymns and festal songs.
Glory, O King! Glory! Glory!

WOMEN
The laurel and the lotus
Our heroes' heads are wreathing;

POPOLO
Gloria all'Egitto e ad Iside
Che il sacro suol protegge;
Al Re che il Delta regge
Inni festosi alziam!
Gloria! Gloria! Gloria! Gloria al Re!

DONNE
S'intrecci il loto al lauro
Sul crin dei vincitori;

Nembo gentil di fiori
Stenda sull'armi un vel.
Danziam, fanciulle Egizie,
Le mistiche carole,
Come d'intorno al sole
Danzano gli astri in ciel!

The flowers, sweet perfume breathing,
Veil all their armor bright.
Oh, dance, you girls of Egypt,
In mystic jubilation,
As round the sun in heaven
The stars dance their way with delight.

SACERDOTI
Della vittoria agl'arbitri
Supremi il guardo ergete;
Grazie agli Dei rendete
Nel fortunato dì.

PRIESTS
Raise your eyes, oh, raise them
To the gods that won the battle.
Praise to the gods, oh praise them
For this triumphant day!
(the Egyptian troops, preceded by trumpeters, defile before the KING *to the music of the famous Grand March. A group of dancing girls also appears, bearing the spoils of the vanquished)*

POPOLO
Vieni, o guerriero vindice,
Vieni a gioir con noi,
Sul passo degli eroi,
I lauri, i fior versiam!
Grazie agli Dei rendete
Nel fortunato dì.
Vieni, o guerrier,
A gioir con noi,
Sul passo degli eroi
I lauri e i fior versiam.

THE PEOPLE
Here come the victors glorious!
All of us hail your name.
We scatter wreaths of laurel!
Over your path to fame!
Thanks to the gods we worship on this triumphant day.
Hail, o hero, hail. Come and rejoice with us,
We scatter wreaths of laurel over your path to fame.

SACERDOTI
Agli arbitri supremi,
Il guardo ergete.
Grazie agli Dei
Agli Dei rendete
Nel fortunato dì.

PRIESTS
Raise your eyes, oh, raise them
To the gods that won the battle.
Praise to the gods, oh praise them
For this triumphant day!
(sacred statues and emblems are carried in the great procession. Dances of triumph are executed before the KING. *Last to appear is* RADAMES, *hero of the day, borne aloft by his officers)*

POPOLO
Gloria, gloria, gloria!
Gloria all'Egitto!

THE PEOPLE
Glory! Glory! Glory!
Glory to Egypt!

IL RE
Salvator della patria, io ti saluto.
Vieni; e mia figlia di sua man ti porga
Il serto trionfale.
Ora a me chiedi
Quanto più brami. Nulla a te negato
Sarà in tal dì; lo giuro
Per la corona mia, pei sacri Numi.

THE KING *(descending from his throne to embrace* RADAMES*)*
To the man who has saved our land, salutation!
Come then, and my daughter will herself bestow on your head
The crown of triumph.
*(*RADAMES *kneels before* AMNERIS, *who places the wreath on his head)*
Now you may ask us
What you desire.
We deny you nothing on such a day.
We pledge our word by the crown of Egypt!
We swear by heaven!

RADAMES
Concedi in pria che innanzi a te sien tratti
I prigionier . . .

RADAMES
Will you at first command that all the captives shall appear!

(*under guard the Ethiopian prisoners stumble in,* AMONASRO, *in the uniform of an officer, the last of them*)

RAMFIS and PRIESTS
Thanks to the gods that we worship
And praise for this triumphant,
For this triumphant day.
Praises! Praises to the gods!

AÏDA (*rushing toward* AMONASRO)
I see him! It is—my father!

ALL
Her father!

AMNERIS
And in our power!

AÏDA (*embracing her father*)
You are in chains!

AMONASRO (*whispering to* AÏDA)
Say not a word!

THE KING (*to* AMONASRO)
Come forward. Who then—are you?

AMONASRO
Her father. I, too, have fought.
And we were conquered. Death I sought in vain.
(*points to his uniform*)

Aria

From my garments you know it already,
That I fought for my king and my nation.
But your warriors were daring and steady,
Our ill luck we could never defy.
And still greater was our desperation,
For our monarch had perished beside us;
If the love of our country is denied us
We are guilty—and ready to die.
(*turns to the* KING *in supplication*)
But, O King, who can wield mighty power,
On these people your mercy may shower;
Though today we are stricken by fortune,
Ah, on another day your fortune may fail.

AÏDA
But, O King, who can wield mighty power,
On these people your mercy may shower;
Though today we are stricken by fortune—

AÏDA and AMONASRO
Ah, on another day your fortune may fail.

PRISONERS and SLAVES
Yes, our people the gods have forsaken,
May your mercy and pity awaken,
May your life never know such ill fortune
As is causing our painful distress.

RAMFIS, SACERDOTI
Grazie agli Dei rendete,
Nel fortunato,
Nel fortunato dì.
Grazie, grazie agli Dei.

AÏDA
Che veggo! . . . Egli? . . . mio padre!

TUTTI
Suo padre!

AMNERIS
In poter nostro! . . .

AÏDA
Tu! Prigionier!

AMONASRO
Non mi tradir!

IL RE
T'appressa . . .
Dunque . . . Tu sei? . . .

AMONASRO
Suo padre . . . Anch'io pugnai . . .
Vinti noi fummo e morte invan cercai.

Quest' assisa ch'io vesto vi dica
Che il mio Re, la mia patria ho difeso:
Fu la sorte a nostr'armi nemica . . .
Tornò vano de'forti l'ardir.
Al mio piè nella polve disteso
Giacque il Re da più colpi trafitto;
Se l'amor della patria è delitto
Siam rei tutti, siam pronti a morir!
Ma tu, Re, tu signore possente,
A costoro ti volgi clemente.
Oggi noi siam percossi dal fato, ah!
Doman voi potria il fato colpir.

AÏDA
Ma tu, Re, tu signore possente,
A costoro ti volgi clemente.
Oggi noi siam percossi dal fato.

AÏDA, AMONASRO
Doman voi potria il fato colpir.

PRIGIONIERI, SCHIAVE
Si: dai Numi percossi noi siamo;
Tua pietà, tua clemenza imploriamo;
Ah! giammai di soffrir vi sia dato
Ciò che in oggi n'è dato soffrir!

RAMFIS, SACERDOTI
Struggi, o Re, queste ciurme feroci,
Chiudi il cor alle perfide voci.

AÏDA, PRIGIONIERI
Pietà!

RAMFIS, SACERDOTI
Fur dai Numi votati alla morte . . .

AÏDA, PRIGIONIERI
Pietà!

RAMFIS, SACERDOTI
Si compisca dei Numi il voler!

AÏDA, PRIGIONIERI
Pietà!

AÏDA
Ma tu, o Re, tu signor possente
A costoro ti mostra clemente.
Oggi noi siam percossi dal fato,
Ah, doman voi potria il fato colpir.
Pietà! Pietà! Tua pietà imploro!

AMONASRO
Oggi noi siam percossi dal fato,
Voi doman potria il fato colpir.
Tua pietà, tua clemenza imploriamo;
Ma tu, o Re, tu signore possente,
A costoro ti mostra clemente,
Oggi noi siam percossi dal fato
Ah, doman voi potria il fato colpir.

PRIGIONIERI
Si: dai Numi percossi noi siamo;
Tua pietà, tua clemenza imploriamo;
Ah! giammai di soffrir vi sia dato
Ciò che in oggi n'e dato soffrir.

RAMFIS, SACERDOTI
Struggi, o Re, queste ciurme feroci,
Chiudi il core alle perfide voci,
Fur dai Numi votati alla morte,
Si compisca dei Numi il voler.
A morte! A morte! A morte!

POPOLO
Sacerdoti, gli sdegni placate,
L'umil prece de' vinti ascoltate;
E tu, o Re, tu possente, tu forte,
A clemenza dischiudi il pensier.

RADAMES
(Il dolor che in quel volto favella
Al mio sguardo la rende più bella;
Ogni stilla del pianto adorato
Nel mio petto ravviva l'amor.)

RAMFIS and PRIESTS
Mighty King, see these villains before us,
Close your heart to their criminal chorus—

AÏDA and PRISONERS
Forgive!

RAMFIS and PRIESTS
It is death that the gods have decided—

AÏDA and PRISONERS
Forgive!

RAMFIS and PRIESTS
And the gods we are bound to obey!

AÏDA and PRISONERS
Forgive!

AÏDA
But, O King, who can wield mighty power,
On these people your mercy may shower;
Though today we are stricken by fortune,
Ah, on another day your fortune may fail.
Forgive! Forgive!
I implore your mercy.

AMONASRO
Though today we are stricken by fortune,
On another day your fortune may fail.
We implore that you grant us your mercy.
You, O King, who can wield mighty power,
On these people your mercy may shower;
Though today we are stricken by fortune,
On another day your fortune may fail.

PRISONERS
Yes, our people the gods have forsaken,
May your mercy and pity awaken,
May your life never know such ill fortune
As is causing our painful distress.

RAMFIS and PRIESTS
Mighty King, see these villains before us,
Close your heart to their criminal chorus;
It is death that the gods have decided,
And the gods we are bound to obey.
Destroy them! destroy them! destroy them!

THE PEOPLE
Holy priests, may your violence waver,
Hear us, pleading your favor.
Mighty King, you, whose power is stronger,
May your mercy hold sway in your heart.

RADAMES (*aside, watching* AÏDA)
Sign of grief that I see in her glances
To my mind all her beauty enhances.
Every drop of the tears she is shedding
In my heart wakens utter delight.

AMNERIS (*aside*)
Oh, what glances he has turned upon her!
With what passion his eye flashes on her!
And I only am rejected and slighted
While revenge is on fire in my heart.

THE KING
Now that all things go so well in our city,
Let us show them our mercy and pity.
To be kind is a virtue in heaven,
And increases the power of the King.

RADAMES (*to the* KING)
O King, by God in heaven,
And by your crown and its royal splendor,
You swore an oath to grant my wishes.

THE KING
I swore.

RADAMES
Then hear me!
And free all of the Ethiopians.
I ask their freedom and their life.

AMNERIS
The prisoners!

PRIESTS
Death to the foes that fought our fatherland!

THE PEOPLE
Oh, spare the wretched captives!

RAMFIS
Hear me, O King!
(*to* RADAMES)
And you, O brave young commander!
Listen to words of prudence!
They are foes and they are ardent,
They are unrelenting men.
They'll be bolder if they're pardoned,
They will take to arms again.

RADAMES
But Amonasro, their warrior king,
Is dead and they have no leader.

RAMFIS
At least then, as a precaution for our peace,
Keep one hostage: Aïda's father.

THE KING
I yield to your suggestion.
For our security and peace a better pledge I give you:
Radames, to you our land is indebted,
As reward I offer my child, Amneris.
Monarch of Egypt,
One day you will share the throne with her.

AMNERIS
(Quali sguardi sovr'essa ha rivolti!
Di qual fiamma balenano i volti!
Ed io sola, avvilita, rejetta?
La vendetta mi rugge nel cor.)

IL RE
Or che fausti ne arridon gli eventi
A costoro mostriamci clementi;
La pietà sale ai Numi gradita
E rafferma de' prenci il poter.

RADAMES
O Re: pei sacri Numi,
Per lo splendore della tua corona,
Compier giurasti il voto mio . . .

IL RE
Giurai.

RADAMES
Ebbene: a te pei prigionieri Etiopi
Vita domando e libertà.

AMNERIS
(Per tutti!)

SACERDOTI
Morte ai nemici della patria!

POPOLO
Grazia per gl'infelici!

RAMFIS
Ascolta, o Re.
Tu pure giovine eroe,
Saggio consiglio ascolta:
Son nemici e prodi sono . . .
La vendetta hanno nel cor,
Fatti audaci dal perdono
Correranno all'armi ancor!

RADAMES
Spento Amonasro, il re guerrier, non resta
Speranza ai vinti.

RAMFIS
Almeno
Arra di pace e securtà, fra noi
Resti col padre Aïda . . .

IL RE
Al tuo consiglio io cedo.
Di securtà, di pace un miglior pegno
Or io vo' darvi. Radames, la patria
Tutto a te deve. D'Amneris la mano
Premio ti sia. Sovra l'Egitto un giorno
Con essa regnerai . . .

AMNERIS
(Venga la schiava
Venga a rapirmi l'amor mio
. . . se l'osa!)

AMNERIS (*aside*)
Now for my handmaid!
Now let her dare to try and steal my lover!

IL RE, POPOLO
Gloria all'Egitto e ad Iside
Che il sacro suol difende,
S'intrecci il loto al lauro
Sul crin del vincitor!

THE KING and THE PEOPLE
Glory to Isis whom we hail,
She is our true defender!
With lotus and with laurel
Our hero's head we'll crown with joy,
For he has won the war!

PRIGIONIERI
Gloria al clemente Egizio
Che i nostri ceppi ha sciolto,
Che ci ridona ai liberi
Solchi del patrio suol!

PRISONERS
Glory to Egypt's gracious king!
He has destroyed our fetters!
It is his mercy makes us free
So we can till our soil!

RAMFIS, SACERDOTI
Inni leviamo ad Iside
Che il sacro suol difende;
Preghiam che i fati arridano
Fausti alla patria ognor.

RAMFIS and PRIESTS
Praise be to Isis whom we hail,
She is our true defender!
And pray that the fates may smile on us,
Blessing our fatherland.

AMONASRO
Fa cor: della tua patria
I lieti eventi aspetta:
Per noi della vendetta
Già prossimo è l'albor.
Fa cor, fa cor, fa cor,
Ah! fa cor!
Fa cor! della tua patria
I lieti eventi aspetta:
Per noi della vendetta
Già prossimo è l'albor.

AMONASRO (*to* AÏDA)
Take heart, a happy future
Is waiting for our country,
And soon the day of vengeance
Will dawn for us again.
Take heart, take heart, take heart.
Ah! Take heart,
Take heart, a happy future
Is waiting for our country,
And soon the day of vengeance
Will dawn for us again.

RADAMES
(D'avverso Nume il folgore
Sul capo mio discende . . .
Ah! no! d'Egitto il soglio
Non val d'Aïda il cor.)

RADAMES (*aside*)
A burst of lightning on my head,
On my head has now descended.
All Egypt's wealth and treasure
Are not Aïda's love.

AMNERIS
(Dall'inatteso giubilo
Inebbriata io sono;
Tutti in un dì si compiono
I sogni del mio cor.)

AMNERIS (*aside*)
One day alone has brought to me
All that I wish, all that I long!
In the new joy that fills my heart
All of my pain means naught to me!

AÏDA
(Qual speme omai più
restami?)
A lui la gloria e il trono . . .
A me l'oblio . . . le lacrime
Di disperato amor.)

AÏDA (*aside*)
I must forget him in my tears of love.
Ah, what hope, alas, is left for me?
For him the glory and triumph,
For me but tears to mourn my hopeless love.

IL RE, POPOLO
Gloria all'Egitto e ad Iside
Che il sacro suol difende!
S'intrecci il loto al lauro
Sul crin del vincitor!

THE KING and THE PEOPLE
Glory to Isis whom we hail,
She is our true defender!
With lotus and with laurel
Our hero's head we'll crown with joy,
For he has won the war!

RAMFIS and PRIESTS
Praise be to Isis whom we hail,
She is our true defender!
And pray that the fates may smile on us,
Blessing our fatherland.

PRISONERS
Glory to Egypt's gracious king!
He has destroyed our fetters!
It is his mercy makes us free
So we can till our soil!

(the KING *descends from his throne, and all exit joyfully.* AÏDA *and* AMONASRO *are left alone in their despair)*

RAMFIS, SACERDOTI
Inni leviamo ad Iside
Che il sacro suol difende;
Preghiam che i fati arridano
Fausti alla patria ognor.

PRIGIONIERI
Gloria al clemente Egizio
Che i nostri ceppi ha sciolto,
Che ci ridona ai liberi
Solchi del patrio suol!

ACT III

Scene 1

The banks of the Nile, flooded in moonlight; great rocks of granite, among which grow palm trees. On the summit of the rocks is the Temple of Isis, half hidden in the trees. As the priests and priestesses invoke the aid of the goddess, a bark bearing AMNERIS *and* RAMFIS *glides up among the rushes. The* HIGH PRIEST *conducts the princess, veiled for her vigil, into the temple, where she is to spend the night praying for her marriage on the morrow. They are followed by the others.*

CORO
O tu che sei d'Osiride
Madre immortale e sposa,
Diva che i casti palpiti
Desti agli uomini in cor
Soccorri a noi pietosa,
Madre d'eterno amor.
Soccorri a noi,
Soccorri a noi.

CHORUS
Goddess whom great Osiris loves,
Mother and wife immortal,
Goddess who moves the human heart,
Pulsing with chaste delight.
Aid, aid us who seek you tonight,
Aid us who seek your blessing,
Mother of mighty love,
We seek you, seek you tonight.

RAMFIS
Vieni d'Iside al tempio; alla vigilia
Delle tue nozze, implora
Della Diva il favore. Iside legge
Dei mortali nel cuore; ogni mistero
Degli umani è a lei noto.

RAMFIS
Come to the shrine of Isis,
And on the eve before you are married,
Invoke the favors granted by Isis.
She knows what mortals suffer when in a crisis,
She knows the secrets of our nature, for she has wisdom.

AMNERIS
Sì; io pregherò che Radames mi doni
Tutto il suo cor, come il mio core a lui
Sacro è per sempre . . .

AMNERIS
Yes, here I will pray that Radames may give me all his heart,
Just as my own is given to him forever.

RAMFIS
Entriamo.
Pregherai fino all'alba; io sarò teco.

RAMFIS
Now enter. You shall pray till the morning.
I shall be with you.

CORO
Soccorri a noi pietosa,
Madre d'immenso amor.

CHORUS
Aid us who seek you tonight,
Mother of mighty love!

(AÏDA *enters cautiously, heavily veiled for her secret tryst with* RADAMES)

Recitative

AÏDA
—Qui Radames verrà . . . Che vorrà dirmi?
Io tremo . . . Ah! se tu vieni
A recarmi, o crudel, l'ultimo addio,
Del Nilo i cupi vortici
Mi daran tomba . . . e pace forse . . . e oblio.
O patria mia, mai più, mai più ti rivedrò!
Mai più, mai più ti rivedrò!

AÏDA
Here Radames will come. What will he tell me?
I tremble. Ah, if you come,
Cruel man, to insist that you must leave me,
I'll go too, and in the gloomy Nile
I'll seek destruction.
Peace I will find there, peace and perhaps oblivion.
My native land,
No more shall I see you again,
No more shall I return!

Aria

O azure sky of home and gentle breezes,
Where in my happy childhood I could remain,
O verdant hillsides, whose fragrant perfume pleases,
O native country, when shall we meet again?
O native country, no more, ah, no more to meet again!
O lovely valleys, cool as an oasis,
Telling of love for which the heart can yearn,
Gone is that dream and scattered are all its traces,
My native country, no more, shall I return!
My native country, no more, ah, no more shall I return.
(*enter* AMONASRO, *stealthily*)
Heaven! My father!

AMONASRO

I'm here, prompted by solemn thoughts, Aïda.
There is little escapes me.
You are in love with young Radames.
He loves you. You are waiting.
The daughter of the Pharaohs is your rival.
How I hate them! Wicked people! Wishing us evil!

AÏDA

And I am in her power—
Amonasro's daughter!

AMONASRO

You are in her power? No, if you wish it
You may vanquish her power, outdo your rival!
Your country, your scepter, your love: all may be yours.

Duet

You may see once again our fragrant forests,
Our lovely valleys, our temples built of gold.

AÏDA (*happily musing*)

I may see once again our fragrant forests,
Our lovely valleys, our temples built of gold!

AMONASRO

A happy life beside the man you treasure,
There is no joy that fate will not supply.

AÏDA (*rapturously*)

A single day of such enchanting pleasure,
A single hour of such delight—and then to die!

AMONASRO

Egypt's record with cruelty is laden:
Our dwellings, our temples, our altars they profane;
Bind with fetters each helpless captive maiden;
Mothers, old men and children they have slain!

O cieli azzurri . . . o dolci aure native
Dove sereno il mio mattin brillò . . .
O verdi colli . . . o profumate rive . . .
O patria mia, mai più ti rivedrò!
O fresche valli . . . o queto asil beato
Che un dì promesso dall'amor mi fu . . .
Or che d'amore il sogno è dileguato . . .
O patria mia, non ti vedrò mai più!
Cielo! mio padre!

AMONASRO

A te grave cagione
Mi adduce, Aïda. Nulla sfugge al mio sguardo. D'amor ti struggi
Per Radames . . . ei t'ama . . . e qui lo attendi.
Dei Faraon la figlia è tua rivale . . .
Razza infame, abborrita e a noi fatale!

AÏDA

E in suo potere io sto! . . . Io d'Amonasro figlia!

AMONASRO

In poter di lei! . . . No! . . . se lo brami
La possente rival tu vincerai.
E patria, e trono, e amor, tutto tu avrai.

Rivedrai le foreste imbalsamate,
Le fresche valli . . . i nostri templi d'ôr! . . .

AÏDA

Rivedrò le foreste imbalsamate,
Le nostre valli . . . i nostri templi d'ôr! . . .

AMONASRO

Sposa felice a lui che amasti tanto,
Tripudii immensi ivi potrai gioir . . .

AÏDA

Un giorno solo di sì dolce incanto . . .
Un'ora di tal gaudio . . . e poi morir!

AMONASRO

Pur rammenti che a noi l'Egizio immite,
Le case, i templi e l'are profanò . . .
Trasse in ceppi le vergini rapite . . .
Madri . . . vecchi fanciulli ei trucidò.

AÏDA
Ah! ben rammento
quegl'infausti giorni!
Rammento i lutti che il mio cor soffrì . . .
Deh! fate, o Numi, che per noi ritorni
L'alba invocata de' sereni dì.

AMONASRO
Non fia che tardi. In armi ora si desta
Il popol nostro; tutto pronto è già . . .
Vittoria avrem . . . Solo a saper mi resta
Qual sentier il nemico seguirà . . .

AÏDA
Chi scoprirlo potria? chi mai?

AMONASRO
Tu stessa!

AÏDA
Io!

AMONASRO
Radames so che qui attendi
. . . Ei t'ama . . .
Ei conduce gli Egizii . . .
Intendi? . . .

AÏDA
Orrore!
Che mi consigli tu? No! no! giammai!

AMONASRO
Su, dunque! sorgete,
Egizie coorti;
Col fuoco struggete
Le nostre città . . .
Spargete il terrore,
Le stragi, le morti . . .
Al vostro furore
Più freno non v'ha.

AÏDA
Ah padre! padre! . . .

AMONASRO
Mia figlia
Ti chiami! . . .

AÏDA
Pietà! Pietà! Pietà!

AMONASRO
Flutti di sangue scorrono
Sulle città dei vinti . . .
Vedi? dai negri vortici
Si levano gli estinti . . .
Ti additan essi e gridano:
Per te la patria muor!

AÏDA
Pietà! . . . Pietà! Padre, pietà!

AÏDA
Well I remember all those days of sorrow,
All of the anguish that my heart has known.
Gods, high in heaven, bring a happier morrow,
Once more may peace to our dear land be shown!

AMONASRO
Remember! And we must hasten.
Our men-at-arms are panting,
And alerted when to strike the blow.
Success is sure, only one thing is wanting:
By which route they will come we do not know.

AÏDA
Who can tell us the answer? Can you?

AMONASRO
Aïda!

AÏDA
I?

AMONASRO
Radames knows you are waiting.
He loves you.
He commands the Egyptians.
You hear me?

AÏDA
Oh, horror!
What do you ask of me? No, I will not!

AMONASRO (*with savage fury*)
Arise then, Egyptians,
And spur on your warriors!
And all of our cities
Commit to the flames!
Unbridle your terrors,
Your murders, your harriers,
There is no resistance
To hinder your claims.

AÏDA
Ah, father! Father!

AMONASRO (*repulsing her*)
You call yourself daughter?

AÏDA (*begging on her knees*)
I beg, I pray for mercy!

AMONASRO
Torrents of crimson blood shall flow
Over the towns they've taken
See them? From inky depth below
Corpses arise, forsaken,
Pointing at you, as well they know
Through you your country falls!

AÏDA
I beg—I pray. Father, I pray!

AMONASRO
There one dreadful ghost I see,
Standing in phantom vesture,
Tremble! Its bony gesture—

AÏDA
Ah!

AMONASRO
Over your head is raised.

AÏDA
Father!

AMONASRO
Your mother's ghost.

AÏDA
No!

AMONASRO
I see her now, coming to curse you.

AÏDA (*terrified*)
Ah, no! O father, pity me,

AMONASRO (*repulsing her*)
You're not my daughter!
You are the servant of all the Pharaohs!

AÏDA
Ah, no! I pray! Ah, no!
(*dragging herself to her father's feet*)
Father, not their servant, servant no longer.
No, do not curse me; your words appall me.
I'm still your daughter. This you can call me.
I love my country. I shall be worthy to love my land.

AMONASRO
Think that a people, overcome and tortured,
Through you alone now may rise again.

AÏDA
Beloved country, how much you cost me!
Beloved land, how much you cost me!

AMONASRO
Have courage. He's coming.
There—I will hear.
(*he hides himself among the palm trees*)

RADAMES (*entering joyously*)
Again I see you, my lovely Aïda!

AÏDA
Begone now. Leave me. There is no hope.

RADAMES
When in your presence my love is leader.

AÏDA
A marriage waits for you, another love:
Amneris' bridal.

AMONASRO
Una larva orribile
Fra l'ombre a noi s'affaccia . . .
Trema! le scarne braccia.

AÏDA
Ah!

AMONASRO
Sul capo tuo levò.

AÏDA
Padre!

AMONASRO
Tua madre ell'è.

AÏDA
No! . . .

AMONASRO
Ravvisala
Ti maledice!

AÏDA
Ah! No! O padre, pietà!

AMONASRO
Non sei mia figlia!
Dei Faraoni tu sei la schiava!

AÏDA
Ah! pietà! pietà! pietà!
Padre, a costoro schiava io non sono . . .
Non maledirmi . . . non imprecarmi . . .
Ancor tua figlia potrai chiamarmi,
Della mia patria degna sarò.

AMONASRO
Pensa che un popolo vinto, straziato,
Per te soltanto risorger può . . .

AÏDA
O patria! o patria . . . quanto mi costi!
O patria! quanto mi costi!

AMONASRO
Coraggio, ei giunge . . . là tutto udrò . . .

RADAMES
Pur ti riveggo, mia dolce Aïda . . .

AÏDA
T'arresta, vanne . . . che speri ancor?

RADAMES
A te dappresso l'amor mi guida.

AÏDA
Te i riti attendono d'un altro amor.
D'Amneris sposo . . .

RADAMES
Che parli mai? . . .
Te sola, Aïda, te deggio amar.
Gli Dei m'ascoltano . . . tu mia sarai . . .

AÏDA
D'uno spergiuro non ti macchiar!
Prode t'amai, non t'amerei spergiuro.

RADAMES
Dell'amor mio dubiti, Aïda?

AÏDA
E come
Speri sottrarti d'Amneris ai vezzi,
Del Re al voler, del tuo popolo ai voti,
Dei sacerdoti all'ira?

RADAMES
Odimi, Aïda.
Nel fiero anelito di nuova guerra
Il suolo Etiope si ridestò . . .
I tuoi già invadono la nostra terra,
Io degli Egizii duce sarò.
Fra il suon, fra i plausi della vittoria,
Al Re mi prostro, gli svelo il cor . . .
Sarai tu il serto della mia gloria,
Vivrem beati d'eterno amor.

AÏDA
Nè d'Amneris paventi
Il vindice furor? la sua vendetta,
Come folgor tremenda,
Cadrà su me, sul padre mio, su tutti.

RADAMES
Io vi difendo.

AÏDA
Invan, tu nol potresti . . .
Pur . . . se tu m'ami . . . ancor s'apre una via
Di scampo a noi . . .

RADAMES
Quale?

AÏDA
Fuggir . . .

RADAMES
Fuggire!

AÏDA
Fuggiam gli ardori inospiti
Di queste lande ignude;
Una novella patria
Al nostro amor si schiude . . .

Là . . . tra foreste vergini,
Di fiori profumate,

RADAMES
What do you say?
You are Aïda, my only love.
The gods can hear when I swear that you'll be mine.

AÏDA
Do not swear falsely and stain your soul.
You once were brave. I cannot love a falsehood.

RADAMES
And do you doubt my love, dear Aïda?

AÏDA
How can you hope to outwit them: the love of Amneris,
The will of the King, all the prayers of your people,
And all the wrath of the priesthood?

RADAMES
Hear me, Aïda!
The Ethiopians, roused by their orders,
Are panting eagerly, ready they stand.
Your men again invade our country's borders,
Armies of Egypt I must command.
When shouts declare us ever victorious
I'll greet our monarch, baring my heart,
You'll be my garland, glowing and glorious,
We'll live in blessedness, never to part again,
We'll live in joy, nevermore to part.

AÏDA
Do you not fear Amneris,
Her fury and revenge? Her royal vengeance,
Like a bolt shot from heaven,
Will fall on me, upon my father, my country!

RADAMES
I will defend you.

AÏDA
In vain you would attempt it.
Yet, if you love me, there is one way
That we may still escape.

RADAMES
Name it!

AÏDA
To flee.

RADAMES
Aïda!

AÏDA
To flee this arid desert sand,
Where every breath is burning;
Seeking another fatherland,
With love and joy returning.

Duet

There in the virgin woods we'll find
Flowers their fragrance lending.

In ecstasy unending
The world we may forget.
In ecstasy unending,
The world we may forget.

In estasi beate
La terra scorderem.
In estasi, in estasi
La terra scorderem.

RADAMES
You call me to a strange land and with you bid me go,
To leave my native country, altars of gods I know.
The land where first I gathered the leaves of bay around me,
The land where first you found me—
How can my heart forget?

RADAMES
Sovra una terra estrania
Teco fuggir dovrei!
Abbandonar la patria,
L'are de' nostri Dei!
Il suol dov'io raccolsi
Di gloria i primi allori,
Il ciel de' nostri amori
Come scordar potrem?

AÏDA
There in the virgin woods we'll find
Flowers their fragrance lending
In ecstasy unending, the world we may forget.
Beneath our skies the room for love is granted free and ample,
And in our holy temple
The selfsame gods we'll find.
Ah, let us fly!
You don't love me? Go. Go.

AÏDA
Là . . . tra foreste vergini,
Di fiori profumate,
In estasi beate la terra scorderem.
Sotto il mio ciel, più libero
L'amor ne fia concesso;
Ivi nel tempio istesso
Gli stessi Numi avrem.
Tu non m'ami . . . Va! Va!

RADAMES
Not love you?
No man or god in rapture
Burned with a love so strong as that which burns me.

RADAMES
Non t'amo?
Mortal giammai nè Dio
Arse d'amor al par del mio possente.

AÏDA
Go! go!
Amneris must be waiting.

AÏDA
Va . . . va . . . t'attende all'ara
Amneris . . .

RADAMES
No! In vain!

RADAMES
No! giammai!

AÏDA
In vain you're saying.
Then let the ax fall on me and on my father.

AÏDA
Giammai, dicesti?
Allor piombi la scure
Su me, sul padre mio . . .

RADAMES
Ah, no, we'll flee then!

RADAMES
Ah no! fuggiamo!

Duet

We will leave the royal palace
And we'll hasten to the desert.
In this land is only malice,
There we'll make a home some day.
Distant deserts with gloomy shadows
And the branches for our cover.
While the shining stars will hover
Over us in bright array.

Sì, fuggiam da queste mura,
Al deserto insiem fuggiamo;
Qui sol regna la sventura,
Là si schiude un ciel d'amor.
I deserti interminati
A noi talamo saranno,
Su noi gli astri brilleranno
Di più limpido fulgor.

AÏDA
In the country of our future
Earth and heaven alike await us:
Fragrant breezes, smiling nature,
Fertile earth and flowers gay.
Cooler valleys, verdant meadows,
With the branches for our cover,

AÏDA
Nella terra avventurata
De' miei padri, il ciel ne attende;
Ivi l'aura è imbalsamata,
Ivi il suolo è aromi e fior.
Fresche valli e verdi prati
A noi talamo saranno,
Su noi gli astri brilleranno
Di più limpido fulgor.

While the shining stars will hover
Over us in bright array.

RADAMES
Il ciel de' nostri amori
Come scordar potrem?

RADAMES
The land where first you found me—
How can my heart forget?

AÏDA
Sotto il mio ciel, più libero
L'amor ne fia concesso;
Ivi nel tempio istesso
Gli stessi Numi avrem.
Ivi nel tempio istesso
Gli stessi Numi avrem.

AÏDA
Beneath our skies the room for love
Is ever free and ample,
And in our holy temple
The selfsame gods we'll find.
And in our holy temple
The selfsame gods we'll find.

RADAMES
Abbandonar la patria,
L'are de' nostri Dei!
Il ciel de' nostri amori
Come scordar potrem.

RADAMES
To leave my native country,
Altars of gods I know!
The land where first you found me—
How can my heart forget?

AÏDA
Fuggiam! fuggiam!

AÏDA
Ah, let us fly!

RADAMES
Aïda!

RADAMES (*hesitating*)
Aïda!

AÏDA, RADAMES
Vieni meco, insiem fuggiamo
Questa terra di dolor.
Vieni meco, io t'amo, io t'amo!
A noi duce fia l'amor.

RADAMES, AÏDA
Come with me, and I'll restore you,
Leave this land of pain and woe,
Come with me for I adore you!
Love will lead us as we go
(*they start to go, then* AÏDA *hesitates*)

AÏDA
Ma, dimmi: per qual via
Eviterem le schiere
Degli armati?

AÏDA
But tell me, by what path shall we avoid the forays of the soldiers?

RADAMES
Il sentier scelto dai nostri
A piombar sul nemico fia deserto
Fino a domani . . .

RADAMES
By the path that we have chosen to strike at the foe, no one will use it until tomorrow.

AÏDA
E quel sentier? . . .

AÏDA
Which is the path?

RADAMES
Le gole
Di Nàpata . . .

RADAMES
The gorges of Napata.

AMONASRO
Di Nàpata le gole!
Ivi saranno i miei . . .

AMONASRO
By Napata they're marching! There will I send my men!

RADAMES
Oh! chi ci ascolta? . . .

RADAMES
Who was it listening?

AMONASRO
D'Aïda il padre e degli Etiopi il Re.

AMONASRO
Aïda's father, Ethiopia's King!

RADAMES
Iu Amonasro! . . . tu, il Re?
Numi! che dissi?
No! . . . non è ver! . . .
sogno . . . delirio è questo . . .

RADAMES (*overcome with surprise*)
You, Amonasro! You . . . the King? Heavens! You're saying? No!—It is false, it is false, no, no, no,
It is false! No! Surely I'm dreaming. I'm dreaming!

Trio

AÏDA
Ah, no! Be calm and listen now.
To my love you must yield you.

AMONASRO
The love she has revealed you—
Will raise you to a throne.

RADAMES
I'm branded as a traitor!
I'm branded as a traitor!
For you I've sold the fatherland!

AÏDA
Be quiet!

AMONASRO
No! Blame can never fall on you,
For it was fate that led you.
No! No! No blame can fall on you.

RADAMES
I'm branded as a traitor!
For you I've sold the fatherland!

AÏDA
Ah, no! Ah, no! Be quiet!

AMONASRO
Come where beyond the river Nile
Our gallant men are standing.
Ask what you will, all the world demanding,
And it will crown your love.
(*pulling* RADAMES)
Hasten!
(*enter* AMNERIS *from the temple, followed by* RAMFIS, *priests, and guards*)

AMNERIS
Radames!

AÏDA
My rival here!

AMONASRO
(*approaching* AMNERIS *with drawn dagger*)
You have come to bring us ruin!
Die, then!

RADAMES (*rushing between them*)
Give over, you madman!

AMONASRO
Oh, fury!

RAMFIS
Soldiers, advance!

RADAMES (*to* AÏDA *and* AMONASRO)
Hurry! Escape them!

AMONASRO (*dragging* AÏDA)
Hasten, my daughter!
(*they rush out*)

AÏDA
Ah no! ti calma . . . ascoltami,
All'amor mio t'affida.

AMONASRO
A te l'amor d'Aïda
Un soglio innalzerà.

RADAMES
Io son disonorato . . .
Io son disonorato!
Per te tradii la patria!

AÏDA
Ti calma!

AMONASRO
No: tu non sei colpevole,
Era voler del fato . . .
No, tu non sei colpevole.

RADAMES
Io son disonorato,
Per te tradii la patria!

AÏDA
Ah, no! Ah, no! Ti calma!

AMONASRO
Vieni: oltre il Nil ne attendono
I prodi anoi devoti;
Là del tuo core i voti
Coronerà l'amor.

Vieni!

AMNERIS
Traditor!

AÏDA
La mia rivale! . . .

AMONASRO
L'opra mia a strugger vieni!
Muori! . . .

RADAMES
Arresta, insano! . . .

AMONASRO
Oh rabbia!

RAMFIS
Guardie, olà!

RADAMES
Presto! fuggite! . . .

AMONASRO
Vieni, o figlia!

MISSISSIPPI LIBRARY COMMISSION
405 State Office Building, Jackson

RAMFIS
L'inseguite!

RADAMES
Sacerdote, io resto a te.

RAMFIS (*to the guards*)
Go, pursue them!

RADAMES
(*to* RAMFIS, *dramatically surrendering his sword*)
Priest of Isis, I shall remain!

ACT IV

Scene 1

A hall in the palace of the KING. *At the left is a large portal leading to the subterranean judgment hall; on the right, the passage to* RADAMES' *prison.*

AMNERIS (*mournfully crouched before the portal*)
The detested Aïda has escaped me.
And Radames waits for the doom
The priests demand for his crime as traitor.
Yet a traitor he is not.
Though he revealed the weighty secrets of battle,
Flight was his only purpose, to flee beside her.
All of them are traitors!
And many should perish! What am I saying?
I love him, love him always.
In the love that ruins all my life
I'm mad with desperation.
Oh, if he only could love me!
I wish to save him. How can I?
I'll try it. Soldiers!
Radames bring hither!
(RADAMES *is led in by the guards.* AMNERIS *addresses him*)
Now are the priests prepared to judge
All that you once committed;
Yet from the dreadful charge of crime
You still may be acquitted.
When you have earned your pardon
I will address my father,
And he will forgive you rather
Than sacrifice his daughter,
Pleading to make you mine.

AMNERIS
L'abborrita rivale a me sfuggia . . .
Dai sacerdoti Radames attende
Dei traditor la pena.—Traditor
Egli non è . . . Pur rivelò di guerra
L'alto segreto . . . egli fuggir volea . . .
Con lei fuggire . . . Traditori tutti!
A morte! A morte! . . .
Oh! che mai parlo?
Io l'amo . . .
Io l'amo sempre . . .
Disperato, insano
È quest'amor che la mia vita strugge.
Oh! s'ei potesse amarmi! . . .
Vorrei salvarlo. E come?
Si tenti! . . . Guardie:
Radames qui venga.
Già i sacerdoti adunansi
Arbitri del tuo fato;
Pur dell' accusa orribile
Scolparti ancor t'è dato;
Ti scolpa e la tua grazia
Io pregherò dal trono,
E nunzia di perdono,
Di vita, a te sarò.

RADAMES
The judges will not hear from me
Deeds I admit were faulty;
Before the sight of gods and men
I am not vile or guilty.
I told a fatal secret,
I should have kept it nameless;
My thoughts were pure and blameless,
And honor still is mine.

RADAMES
Di mie discolpe i giudici
Mai non udran l'accento;
Dinanzi ai Numi, agl'uomini
Nè vil, nè reo mi sento.
Profferse il labbro incauto
Fatal segreto, è vero,
Ma puro il mio pensiero
E l'onor mio restò.

AMNERIS
Then save your life and clear yourself.

AMNERIS
Salvati dunque e scolpati.

RADAMES
No!

RADAMES
No.

AMNERIS
Would you die?

AMNERIS
Tu morrai . . .

RADAMES
La vita
Abborro! d'ogni gaudio
La fonte inaridita,
Svanita ogni speranza,
Sol bramo di morir.

AMNERIS
Morire! . . . ah! . . . tu dei vivere! . . .
Sì, all'amor mio vivrai;
Per te le angoscie orribili
Di morte io già provai;
T'amai . . . soffersi tanto,
Vegliai le notti in pianto . . .
E patria, e trono, e vita
Tutto darei per te.

RADAMES
Per essa anch'io la patria
E l'onor mio tradia . . .

AMNERIS
Di lei non più! . . .

RADAMES
L'infamia
M'attende e vuoi ch'io viva? . . .
Misero appien mi festi,
Aïda a me togliesti;
Spenta l'hai forse . . . e in dono
Offri la vita a me?

AMNERIS
Io . . . di sua morte origine!
No! . . . vive Aïda . . .

RADAMES
Vive!

AMNERIS
Nei disperati aneliti
Dell'orde fuggitive
Sol cadde il padre . . .

RADAMES
Ed ella? . . .

AMNERIS
Sparve, nè più novella
S'ebbe . . .

RADAMES
Gli Dei l'adducano
Salva alle patrie mura,
E ignori la sventura
Di chi per lei morrà!

AMNERIS
Ma s'io ti salvo, giurami
Che più non la vedrai . . .

RADAMES
No! posso!

RADAMES
My life is hateful,
For the wellspring of happiness is arid;
My hopes have come to nothing,
I wish that I could die.

AMNERIS
And dying? Ah, you shall live again,
You shall live for my caresses;
For you I've looked at death
And I have felt its bitternesses.
For you, love, at night unsleeping,
For you, love, my eyes are weeping.
My country, my title, my power and life, too,
All I'd surrender, all I'd freely give for you.

RADAMES
For her I too have given up my well-beloved country,
And my honor, and my honor for her has gone.

AMNERIS
No more of her!

RADAMES
Dishonor awaits me
And you would save me?
All of my hopes are shaken,
Aïda, my love, is taken.
You may have slain her,
And yet you would preserve my life?

AMNERIS
I—for her death responsible?
No, she is living.

RADAMES
Living?

AMNERIS
When all the foe were put to flight
In violent disorder,
Death claimed her father.

RADAMES
Aïda?

AMNERIS
Vanished!
We've heard no further tidings.

RADAMES
The gods will guide her in safety
To find her dwelling,
And let no man be telling
That I have died for her.

AMNERIS
But if I save you,
Swear to see her face never again.

RADAMES
I cannot!

AMNERIS
If you will leave her forever,
Life shall be yours!

RADAMES
I cannot!

AMNERIS
My word is final.
Will you renounce her?

RADAMES
No, never!

AMNERIS
You wish to die then, madman?

RADAMES
I am prepared to die.

AMNERIS
Who will save you, wretched being,
From the fate which you are courting?
You have lost it, little-seeing
Love, whose equal is not known.
I can hear the gods retorting—
Only sorrow can atone.

RADAMES
But my dying is my good fortune,
If I die for her I cherish;
In the hour that I perish
Endless delight my heart will own.
Mortal anger I fear no more,
Pity I must fear alone.

AMNERIS
Ah, who will save you?
I can hear the gods retorting—
Only sorrow can atone!

Alas, his death approaches! Now who will save him?
He is now in their power. I myself am the cause.
Oh, how I curse my wicked, jealous nature,
That has destroyed him,
And has condemned my heart to endless sorrow.
Here come the judges, ruthless, vindictive,
The doom of the dying.
Oh, I will not look at those pallid specters.
He is now in their power and I have sealed his fate.
I only, I only, I alone! He is now in their power
And I sealed his fate.

RAMFIS and CHORUS
Spirit of heaven, hear us now and bless us.
Kindle in us a ray of light eternal.
In our decrees may your own wisdom possess us.

AMNERIS
A lei rinunzia
Per sempre . . . e tu vivrai! . . .

RADAMES
Nol posso!

AMNERIS
Anco una volta:
A lei rinunzia . . .

RADAMES
È vano . . .

AMNERIS
Morir vuoi dunque, insano?

RADAMES
Pronto a morir son già.

AMNERIS
Chi ti salva, sciagurato,
Dalla sorte che t'aspetta?
In furore hai tu cangiato
Un amor ch'egual non ha.
De' miei pianti la vendetta
Or dal ciel si compirà.

RADAMES
È la morte un ben supremo
Se per lei morir m'è dato;
Nel subir l'estremo fato
Gaudii immensi il cor avrà;
L'ira umana più non temo,
Temo sol la tua pietà.

AMNERIS
Ah! chi ti salva?
De' miei pianti la vendetta
Or dal ciel si compirà.
Ohimè! . . . morir mi sento . . . Oh! chi lo salva?
E in poter di costoro
Io stessa lo gettai! . . . Ora, a te impreco,
Atroce gelosia, che la sua morte
E il lutto eterno del mio cor segnasti!
Ecco i fatali,
Gli inesorati ministri di morte! . . .
Oh! ch'io non vegga quelle bianche larve!
E in poter di costoro io stessa lo gettai.
Io stessa! io stessa! lo gettai! e in poter di costoro.
Io stessa lo gettai!

RAMFIS, CORO
Spirito del Nume sovra noi discendi!
Ne avviva al raggio dell'eterna luce;
Pel labbro nostro tua giustizia apprendi.

AMNERIS
Numi, pietà del mio straziato core . . .
Egli è innocente, lo salvate, o Numi!
Disperato, tremendo è il mio dolore!

RAMFIS, CORO
Spirito del Numi sovra noi discendi!

AMNERIS
Oh! chi lo salva? Mi sento morir!
Ohimè! ohimè! mi sento morir!

RAMFIS
Radames! Radames! Radames! tu rivelasti
Della patria i segreti allo straniero . . .

RAMFIS, CORO
Discolpati! Egli tace! Traditor!

AMNERIS
Ah! pietà! egli è innocente!
Numi, pietà! Numi, pietà!

RAMFIS
Radames! Radames! Radames! tu disertasti
Dal campo il dì che precedea la pugna.

RAMFIS, CORO
Discolpati! Egli tace! Traditor!

AMNERIS
Ah pietà! ah! lo salvate,
Numi, pietà, Numi pietà!

RAMFIS
Radames! Radames! Radames!
Tua fè violasti, alla patria spergiuro, al Re, all'onor.

RAMFIS, CORO
Discolpati! Egli tace! Traditor!

AMNERIS
Ah! lo salvate—Numi, pietà.
Numi, pietà!

RAMFIS, CORO
Radames: è deciso il tuo fato;
Degli infami la morte tu avrai;
Sotto l'ara del Nume sdegnato
A te vivo fia schiuso l'avel.

AMNERIS
A lui vivo . . . la tomba . . . oh! gl'infami!
Nè di sangue son paghi giammai . . .
E si chiaman ministri del ciel!

RAMFIS, CORO
Traditor! traditor! traditor!

AMNERIS
Pity the heart, oh heaven, so sorely wounded . . .
The man is guiltless and the gods can save him.
But my sorrow and grief remain unbounded!

RAMFIS and CHORUS
Spirit of heaven, hear us now and bless us!

AMNERIS
Oh, who will save him? I feel I shall die.
Alas, alas, I feel I shall die.

RAMFIS
Radames! Radames! Radames!
You have revealed your country's innermost secrets to our opponents.

RAMFIS and CHORUS
Defend yourself . . . He is silent . . . It is true!

AMNERIS
Ah, have mercy! He is not guilty.
Oh gods in heaven, oh, spare his life!

RAMFIS
Radames! Radames! Radames!
You have deserted the army the very day before the battle.

RAMFIS and CHORUS
Defend yourself . . . He is silent . . . It is true!

AMNERIS
Ah, have mercy! If you can spare him, oh gods in heaven,
Spare his life.

RAMFIS
Radames! Radames! Radames!
And you have broken your faith to your country, your king and your honor.

RAMFIS and CHORUS
Defend yourself . . . He is silent . . . It is true!

AMNERIS
Ah, you can save him, oh gods in heaven,
Oh gods, save his life!

RAMFIS and CHORUS
Radames, now your guilt is decided.
You shall suffer the fate of your sin.
Near the altar whose gods you derided
We shall seal you alive in your tomb.

AMNERIS
In a tomb for the living? Oh, you blackguards,
Is his death not sufficient to win?
Are you priests or the regents of doom?

RAMFIS and CHORUS
It is true. It is true. He shall die.

AMNERIS

Oh, you priests, what you do is an outrage.
You are tigers, for prey ever thirsting,
Through the limits of hell your will is bursting,
You have punished an innocent man.

RAMFIS and CHORUS

He is condemned, he dies.

AMNERIS

Oh, you priests, do you know that your victim
Is a man I have ardently cherished,
Hear the curse of a heart whose hope has perished,
As you slay him, on you may it fall!

RAMFIS and CHORUS

He is condemned. He dies.

AMNERIS

You have outraged the laws of earth and heaven;
You are punishing the one who is guiltless of crime.
Ah no, not he. We pray.

RAMFIS and CHORUS

A traitor's death he dies.
He shall die.

AMNERIS

Evil priesthood, hear my curses on you all.
May the vengeance of heaven descend on you all!
Hear my curse on you all.

AMNERIS

Sacerdoti: compiste un delitto . . .
Tigri infami di sangue assetate . . .
Voi la terra ed i Numi oltraggiate . . .
Voi punite chi colpe non ha.

RAMFIS, CORO

È traditor! morrà!

AMNERIS

Sacerdote: quest'uomo che uccidi,
Tu lo sai . . . da me un giorno fu amato . . .
L'anatèma d'un core straziato
Col suo sangue su te ricadrà!

RAMFIS, SACERDOTI

È traditor! morrà!

AMNERIS

Voi la terra ed i Numi oltraggiate.
Voi punite, punite chi colpe non ha!
Ah no, non è, pietà!

RAMFIS, CORO

È traditor! morrà.
Traditor!

AMNERIS

Empia razza! anatema! su voi
La vendetta del ciel scenderà!
Anatema su voi!

Scene 2

The scene is divided into two levels. Above, the Temple of Vulcan is resplendent with gold and glittering light. Below is a small, dark crypt, where RADAMES *is standing on one of the steps descending from the temple. Two priests are letting down the stone that seals the crypt from above.*

RADAMES

The fatal stone is closing now upon me.
This is my tomb forever.
I shall not see the daylight again
I shall not see Aïda.
Aïda, where are you now?
May you in life at least find contentment!
And may you never know my horrible fate!
Was that a groan or a phantom!
Perhaps a ghost. No, for the shade is human.
Heavens! Aïda!

RADAMES

La fatal pietra sovra me si chiuse . . .
Ecco la tomba mia. Del dì la luce
Più non vedrò . . . Non rivedrò più Aïda . . .
Aïda, ove sei tu? Possa tu almeno
Viver felice e la mia sorte orrenda
Sempre ignorar!—Qual gemito! . . . Una larva . . .
Una vision . . . No! forma umana è questa . . .
Ciel! . . . Aïda!

AÏDA
Son io . . .

RADAMES
Tu . . . in questa tomba!

AÏDA
Presago il core della tua condanna
In questa tomba che per te s'apriva
Io penetrai furtiva . . .
E qui lontana da ogni umano sguardo
Nelle tue braccia desiai morire.

RADAMES
Morir! sì pura e bella!
Morir per me d'amore . . .
Degli anni tuoi nel fiore
Fuggir la vita!
T'avea il cielo per l'amor creata,
Ed io t'uccido per averti amata!
No, non morrai!
Troppo t'amai! . . .
Troppo sei bella!

AÏDA
Vedi? . . . di morte l'angelo
Radiante a noi s'appressa . . .
Ne adduce a eterni gaudii
Sovra i suoi vanni d'ôr.
Già veggo il ciel dischiudersi . . .
Ivi ogni affanno cessa . . .
Ivi comincia l'estasi
D'un immortale amor.

SACERDOTI, SACERDOTESSE
Ah! Immenso, immenso Fthà!
Del mondo spirito animator,
noi t'invochiamo.

AÏDA
Triste canto!

RADAMES
Il tripudio
Dei sacerdoti . . .

AÏDA
Il nostro inno di morte . . .

RADAMES
Nè le mie forti braccia
Smuovere ti potranno, o fatal pietra!

AÏDA
Invan! . . . tutto è finito
Sulla terra per noi . . .

AÏDA
Aïda!

RADAMES (*in the utmost despair*)
You? And buried with me!

AÏDA (*sadly*)
My heart foretold the nature of the sentence.
I tried to learn the tomb that they assigned you,
And here I crept to find you.
And here, so far from any other being,
Within your arms I've come to die beside you.

RADAMES
To die—so pure and lovely!
To die for love like ours!
Your youth is filled with flowers,
Yet you are dying.
It was for heaven's love your mother bore you,
And I am killing you though I adore you!
You shall not die,
My love, for I,
I love your beauty.

AÏDA (*as in a trance*)
Look now: The angel of death
Has come with radiant pinion,
And beckons us to heaven's joys.
All golden it will soar
Where heaven's gates are open wide,
Where pain has no dominion.
There only joy and bliss abide
And love forevermore.
(*in the temple above, the priests and priestesses begin a solemn chant and sacred dancing*)

PRIESTS and PRIESTESSES
Ah! Almighty Phta,
The spirit of life in the world,
Hear us invoke you!

AÏDA
Mournful voices!

RADAMES
Hear the priests as they sing their triumph!

AÏDA
For us a requiem sounding.

RADAMES (*trying to displace the stone closing the vault*)
If with my lusty sinews
I could dislodge the keystone!
It is too heavy!

AÏDA
In vain! All, all is over
On the earth for us both.

RADAMES (*with sad resignation*)
I know it, I know it.

Duet

AÏDA
Farewell to earth; farewell, oh, vale of sorrow!
A dream of joy which now must fade away.
For us all heaven, all heaven is wide.
In heaven waits a brighter morrow,
When we shall find us in eternal day.

AÏDA and RADAMES
Farewell to earth; farewell, oh, vale of sorrow!
A dream of joy which now must fade away.
For us all heaven, all heaven is wide.
In heaven waits a brighter morrow,
When we shall find us in eternal day.
Ah, all heaven is wide.

PRIESTS and PRIESTESSES
Almighty Phta, hear us invoke you!

AÏDA and RADAMES
Farewell to earth; farewell, oh, vale of sorrow!
A dream of joy which now must fade away.
For us all heaven, all heaven is wide.
In heaven waits a brighter morrow,
When we shall find us in eternal day.

AMNERIS
For peace I pray you—
Beloved spirit—
Isis, relenting, receive his soul!
For peace I pray you, for peace, for peace, for peace.

PRIESTS and PRIESTESSES
Almighty Phta!

RADAMES
È vero! È vero! . . .

AÏDA
O terra, addio; addio, valle di pianti . . .
Sogno di gaudio che in dolor svanì . . .
A noi si schiude il cielo e l'alme erranti
Volano al raggio dell'eterno dì.

AÏDA, RADAMES
O terra, addio; addio, valle di pianti . . .
Sogno di gaudio che in dolor svanì . . .
A noi si schiude il cielo e l'alme erranti
Volano al raggio dell'eterno dì.
Ah, si schiude il ciel.

SACERDOTI, SACERDOTESSE
Immenso Fthà, noi t'invochiamo!

AÏDA, RADAMES
O terra, addio; addio, valle di pianti . . .
Sogno di gaudio che in dolor svanì . . .
A noi si schiude il cielo e l'alme erranti
Volano al raggio dell'eterno dì.

AMNERIS
Pace t'imploro,—salma adorata . . .
Isi placata—ti schiuda il ciel!
Pace t'imploro, pace, pace!

SACERDOTI, SACERDOTESSE
Immenso Fthà!

THE BARBER OF SEVILLE

(Il Barbiere di Siviglia)

by Gioacchino Antonio Rossini (1792–1868)

LIBRETTO BY CESARE STERBINI

Translated by GEORGE MEAD

Based on the comedy *Le Barbier de Séville* by the French dramatist Pierre Augustin Caron de Beaumarchais.

CHARACTERS

FIORELLO, *Count Almaviva's servant*	*Baritone*
COUNT ALMAVIVA	*Tenor*
FIGARO, *a barber*	*Baritone*
ROSINA, *ward of Dr. Bartolo*	*Soprano*
DR. BARTOLO	*Bass*
DON BASILIO, *a music teacher*	*Bass*
BERTA, *Dr. Bartolo's housemaid*	*Soprano*
AMBROGIO, *Dr. Bartolo's servant*	*Bass*

A MAGISTRATE, A NOTARY, AN OFFICER, MUSICIANS, AND SOLDIERS

Place: Seville
Time: Seventeenth century
First performance: Teatro Argentina, Rome, February 20, 1816

COPYRIGHT © 1962 BY GEORGE MEAD

ACT I

Introduction

A square in Seville. At the left DR. BARTOLO'S *house.* FIORELLO, *carrying a lantern, leads in a band of musicians with their instruments. Later* COUNT ALMAVIVA *enters wearing a cloak.*

FIORELLO
Piano, pianissimo, no one must hear.
All are asleep, nothing to fear.

CHORUS
Piano, pianissimo, no one must hear.

FIORELLO
Where is my lord?

CHORUS
He should be here.
Softly, softly, soon he'll appear.

FIORELLO
Now all is silent, no one in sight!
We'll serenade her, here in the night.
Although the neighbors may be awake
We'll serenade her till daybreak.

COUNT (*sotto voce*)
Fiorello! You there?

FIORELLO
Good sir, right here.

COUNT
And now, your comrades?

FIORELLO
They're here, no fear.

COUNT
Bravo, bravissimo, no one must hear you,
Piano, pianissimo, let not a word be overheard!

CHORUS
Piano, pianissimo!

FIORELLO
Let not a word . . .

CHORUS
Never a word!

FIORELLO
Be overheard. Come gather 'round . . .

COUNT, FIORELLO, CHORUS
Without a sound!

(*The musicians tune their instruments. They accompany the* COUNT *as he sings his serenade beneath the closed windows of* DR. BARTOLO'S *house*)

Cavatina

FIORELLO
Piano, pianissimo
Senza parlar,
Tutti con me
Venite qua.

CORO
Piano, pianissimo,
Eccoci qua.

FIORELLO
Venite qua?

CORO
Eccoci qua.
Piano, piano, venite qua.

FIORELLO
Tutto è silenzio;
Nessun qui sta,
Che i nostri canti
Possa turbar.

CONTE
Fiorello . . . Olà . . .

FIORELLO
Signor, son qua.

CONTE
Ebben! . . . gli amici?

FIORELLO
Son pronti già.

CONTE
Bravi, bravissimi,
Fate silenzio;
Piano, pianissimo,
Senza parlar.

CORO
Piano, pianissimo!

FIORELLO
Senza parlar . . .

CORO
Senza parlar.

FIORELLO
Senza parlar.
Venite qua.

CONTE, FIORELLO, CORO
Senza parlar.

CONTE
Ecco ridente in cielo
Spunta la bella aurora,
E tu non sorgi ancora
E puoi dormir così?
Sorgi, mia dolce speme,
Vieni, bell'idol mio;
Rendi men crudo, oh Dio,
Lo stral che mi ferì.
Oh sorte! già veggo
Quel caro sembiante:
Quest'anima amante
Ottenne pietà.
Oh istante d'amore!
Felice momento!
Oh dolce contento!
Che eguale non ha!
Ehi, Fiorello? . . .

FIORELLO
Mio Signore . . .

CONTE
Di', la vedi?

FIORELLO
Signor, no.

CONTE
Ah, ch'è vana ogni speranza!

FIORELLO
Signor Conte, il giorno avanza . . .

CONTE
A che penso! che farò?
Tutto è vano . . . buona gente! . . .

CORO
Mio signor . . .

CONTE
Avanti, avanti.
Più di suoni, più di canti
Io bisogno ormai non ho.

FIORELLO
Buona notte a tutti quanti,
Più di voi che far non sò.
Buona notte, buona notte,
Più di voi che far non sò.

CORO
Mille grazie . . . mio signore . . .
Del favore . . . dell'onore.

CONTE
Basta, basta, non parlate . . .
Ma non serve, non gridate . . .

COUNT
Now all the world is waking,
Dawn through the darkness is breaking,
Why do you lie a-sleeping?
Oh when will you arise!
Wake, oh wake, my lady,
Rise to the song I render.
Come like the sun in splendor
With light to blind my eyes.
Oh dearest, oh fairest,
Do you doubt that I adore you?
I stand enraptured before you,
My one guiding star!
Ah, to know you; ah, to show you,
Ah to tell you how I love you!
Ah, what maiden can excel you,
The fairest by far.
My guiding star,
My bright and shining star!
Ho, Fiorello!

FIORELLO
At your service!

COUNT
Say! D'you see her?

FIORELLO
Not at all.

COUNT
Ah, my hopes are dashed to pieces!

FIORELLO
Noble master, day is approaching.

COUNT
What a failure, all is lost!
All is over! Gather round me!

CHORUS OF MUSICIANS
Here we are . . .

COUNT
Come closer, come closer. No more music, no more singing! All is over! For your music I have no need.

FIORELLO
Now diminish, this is the finish.
What's the use, she will not heed!
Now diminish, it's the finish.
There's no need, she will not heed!

CHORUS (*gathering noisily around the* COUNT, *kiss his hands and the hem of his cloak*)
We are happy if you treasure
Music's measure for your pleasure.

COUNT (*annoyed, trying to chase them away*)
Quiet! Quiet! Stop your chatter;
What a riot, what a clatter!

FIORELLO
What a bother!

COUNT
What a bother!

FIORELLO
What a riot!

COUNT
I say, be quiet!

FIORELLO
Stop your chatter!

COUNT
What a clatter!

FIORELLO
Stop your noise!

COUNT
Stop your noise!

CHORUS OF MUSICIANS
Since your honor is so gracious,
Since your bounty is so spacious,
We would hardly be audacious
To expect a fair reward!

COUNT, FIORELLO
For your labors rouse the neighbors,
All your noise is overheard!

CHORUS OF MUSICIANS
What a patron, what a payday,
He's a noble, a noble lord!

COUNT, FIORELLO
Stop your shattering clattering chattering!
What a clatter! Stop your noise!

CHORUS OF MUSICIANS
Yes, a really noble lord!

FIORELLO
Oh, you rascals, stop your noise!

CHORUS OF MUSICIANS
Oh, thank you, thank you, thank you, thank you!
He's a really noble lord!

Recitative

COUNT
Noisy musicians!

FIORELLO
They really gave you more than you had paid for. All the neighbors are wondering what was the matter. Oh well, at last it's quiet.

COUNT
She will not see me. What use is it to stay? But I'll remain here in the hope that I'll see her here. In the morning early I've often seen her open her window to welcome in the sunlight. Lucky sunlight! My friend, better go now. I wish to be alone.

FIORELLO
Zitti, zitti!

CONTE
Maledetti!

FIORELLO
Che rumore!

CONTE
Andate via!

FIORELLO
Maledetti!

CONTE
Ah canaglia!

FIORELLO
Via di qua!

CONTE
Via di qua!

CORO
Ah, di tanta cortesia,
Ah, di tanta cortesia,
Obbligati, obbligati,
Obbligati in verità!

CONTE, FIORELLO
Tutto quanto il vicinato,
Questo chiasso sveglierà.

CORO
(Ah, che incontro fortunato,
È un signore di qualità.)

CONTE, FIORELLO
Maledetti, andate via,
Ah canaglia, via di qua!

CORO
(Si, è un signor di qualità!)

FIORELLO
Via di qua! Via di qua!

CORO
(Si, grazie, grazie, grazie, grazie!
È un signor di qualità!)

CONTE
Gente indiscreta! . . .

FIORELLO
Ah, quasi
Con quel chiasso importuno
Tutto quanto il quartiere han risvegliato.
Alfin sono partiti!

CONTE
E non si vede!
È inutile sperar
(Eppur qui voglio
Aspettar di vederla. Ogni mattina
Ella su quel balcone

A prender fresco viene sull'-
aurora.
Proviamo.) Olà, tu ancora
ritirati, Fiorel.

FIORELLO
Vado. Là in fondo
Attenderò suoi ordini.

CONTE
Con lei
Se parlar mi riesce,
Non voglio testimoni. Che a
quest'ora
Io tutti i giorni qui vengo per
lei
Dev'essersi avveduta. Oh, vedi,
amore
A un uomo del mio rango
Come l'ha fatta bella! Eppure,
eppure
Oh, dev'essere mia sposa . . .
Chi è mai quest'impor-
tuno? . . .
Lasciamolo passar; sotto quegli
archi
Non veduto, vedrò quanto
bisogna;
Già l'alba appare e amor non si
vergogna.

FIORELLO
Quite so, I'm leaving. Just call me when you need me.

COUNT
Perhaps she will come to the window. Why should we have a witness? Need I tell her, show her that I love her? She knows how I've wasted each morning at her window. I love her, I love her. Romance defies discretion. Let me but live to love her, to woo her, to marry! Ah, to share our love together!
(FIGARO *is heard singing off-stage*)
But who is this intruder? I'd better stand aside. I will take refuge in the archway. I'll have a chance to see him. Daylight is breaking, but love is never weary.
(FIGARO *enters gaily, with a guitar*)

Cavatina

FIGARO
Largo al factotum
Della, città, largo!
Presto a bottega,
Chè l'alba è già, presto!
Ah, che bel vivere,
Che bel piacere,
Che bel piacere,
Per un barbiere
Di qualità, di qualità!
Ah bravo Figaro!
Bravo bravissimo;
Fortunatissimo
Per verità!
Pronto a far tutto,
La notte, il giorno
Sempre d'intorno,
In giro sta.
Miglior cuccagna
Per un barbiere,
Vita più nobile,
No, non si dà.
Rasori e pettini,
Lancette e forbici,
Al mio comando
Tutto qui sta.
V'è la risorsa,
Poi, del mestiere
Colla donnetta . . .
Col cavaliere . . .
Tutti mi chiedono,
Tutti mi vogliono,
Donne, ragazzi,
Vecchi, fanciulle,
Qua la parrucca . . .
Presto la barba . . .

FIGARO
I am the cleverest fellow in all Seville!
I can do anything if you can pay the bill!
When folks of quality,
Full of frivolity,
With plenty of money,
Call for a barber,
I am the one, I am the one.
Ah, bravo, Figaro, bravo, bravissimo, bravo!
Smartest and busiest fellow I know. Bravo!
Nighttime and daytime,
Busy and playtime,
There you will find me, keeping my shop.
I'd never change it,
Nor rearrange it,
Once you're a barber you never can stop!
Brushing the dust o' my very best customer
There with my razor, ready I stand,
Ready to tidy the frizziest whisker,
I stand at attention, scissors in hand.
Sometimes I cover matters romantic,
Soothing a maiden, soothing a lover
Country-and-citified wish to be prettified,
Men who are gallant call for my talent,
Wanting a waving, craving a shaving,
Needing a bleeding, ranting and raving.
Maybe a lady is wanting a waving
Or maybe a gent has a note to be sent,

Or it's cleaning a wig,
Or it's dancing a jig
Or a gallant is wanting a gal!
Figaro! Alas, they always demand my counsel.
One at a time, sir, you are the next,
Just wait your turn, you're sure to be next.
Figaro! Now here . . . Eh, Figaro! Now there!
Figaro there, Figaro here, Figaro there, Figaro here!
Figaro up, Figaro down, Figaro low, Figaro high!
Where is a happier, snappier chap, and all-over-the-mappier fellow than I!
Happy as I, snappy as I, happy as I, snappy as I!
Ah, bravo, Figaro, bravo, bravissimo!
Where is a luckier, where is a pluckier, where is a luckier fellow than I!
Where is a downier, do-it-up-brownier, full-of-renownier, round-the-townier fellow than I!
I'm a jack of every trade in the town,
A jack of each and every trade in all the town!

Recitative

Ah yes, my life is happy with time to work and leisure for enjoyment. I always have some cash to line my pockets, the profits of a man of reputation. It's like this. When a debutante of Seville wants a husband, Figaro finds one. Or maybe a widow who wants another husband! Daytimes, when in trouble, they find they need a barber, and my guitar at night calls out their secrets. A fellow of discretion, I am their friend. They know I want to please them. Life is pleasant, amusing. What could be finer! I must hurry. Time for business!

Qua la sanguigna . . .
Presto il biglietto . . .
Figaro . . . Figaro . . .
Son qua, son qua.
Figaro . . . Figaro . . .
Eccomi qua.
Ahimè, ahimè, che furia!
Ahimè, che folla!
Una alla volta,
Per carità!
Pronto prontissimo
Son come il fulmine;
Sono il factotum
Della città, della città!
Ah bravo Figaro!
Bravo, bravissimo!
Fortunatissimo
Per verità.
Ah, ah! che bella vita! . . .
Faticar poco, divertirsi assai,
E in tasca sempre aver qualche doblone
Gran frutto della mia riputazione.
Ecco qua: senza Figaro
Non si accasa in Siviglia una ragazza;
A me la vedovella
Ricorre pel marito: io colla scusa
Del pettine di giorno,
Della chitarra col favor la notte,
A tutti onestamente,
Non fo per dir, m'adatto a far piacere.
Oh che vita! che vita! Oh che mestiere!
Orsù, presto a bottega . . .

COUNT
This fellow, I seem to know him.

CONTE
(È desso, o pur m'inganno?)

FIGARO
Who is this early riser?

FIGARO
(Chi sarà mai costui? . . .)

COUNT
Can it be the barber, Figaro?

CONTE
Oh è lui senz' altro. Figaro!

FIGARO
Your servant. Oh, my goodness, it's Your Lordship!

FIGARO
Mio padrone . . .
Oh, chi veggo! . . .
Eccellenza! . . .

COUNT
Keep it quiet. These people! Someone may overhear you. I prefer my incognito. The reason . . . you have no need to question.

CONTE
Zitto, zitto, prudenza!
Qui non son conosciuto,
Nè vo' farmi conoscere. Per questo
Ho le mie gran ragioni.

FIGARO
Oh no, sir. Quite so, sir. I'd best be on my way.

FIGARO
Intendo, intendo,
La lascio in libertà.

COUNT
Wait!

CONTE
No . . .

FIGARO
Why so, sir?

FIGARO
Che serve?

CONTE
No, dico; resta qua;
Forse ai disegni miei
Non giungi inopportuno . . .
Ma cospetto,
Dimmi un po', buona lana,
Come ti trovo qua? . . . poter del mondo!
Ti veggo grasso e tondo . . .

FIGARO
La miseria, signore!

CONTE
Ah birbo!

FIGARO
Grazie.

CONTE
Hai messo ancor giudizio?

FIGARO
Oh! e come . . . Ed ella
Come in Siviglia? . . .

CONTE
Or te lo spiego. Al *Prado*
Vidi un fior di bellezza, una fanciulla
Figlia d'un certo medico barbogio
Che qua da pochi dì s'è stabilito.
Io, di questa invaghito,
Lasciai patria e parenti, e qua men venni,
E qui la notte e il giorno
Passo girando a que' balconi intorno.

FIGARO
A que' balconi? . . . un medico? . . . Oh cospetto!
Siete ben fortunato;
Sui maccheroni il cacio v'è cascato.

CONTE
Come?

FIGARO
Certo. Là dentro
Io son barbiere, parrucchier, chirurgo,
Botanico, spezial, veterinario,
Il faccendier di casa.

CONTE
Oh che sorte! . . .

FIGARO
Non basta. La ragazza
Figlia non è del medico.
È soltanto
La sua pupilla!

CONTE
Oh che consolazione!

FIGARO
Perciò . . . Zitto! . . .

COUNT
I ask you, will you stay?
(*aside*)
Maybe he'll think of something to clear away my troubles.
(*to* FIGARO)
But how is it that you're here when I need you. Maybe you'll bring me luck. By all that's holy, you're looking very prosperous!

FIGARO
I have plenty . . . of nothing.

COUNT
You rascal!

FIGARO
Thank you!

COUNT
And are you just as clever?

FIGARO
Quite and more so. But you, sir, why in Seville?

COUNT
Come, let me tell you. I saw her, this enchanting young maiden, out on the Prado. She is the daughter of a certain doctor who moved into that house not long ago. On the day that I saw her, I forgot every other. She's all I live for. I hope that I will meet her. Daytime and nighttime I wait beneath her window.

FIGARO
You mean that window? The balcony of the doctor? How exceedingly lucky! That little pigeon . . . you'll have her for your dinner!

COUNT
Really?

FIGARO
Surely. Inside there, I am their barber, their coiffeur, their bleeder. I cure them all . . . their dogs, their little kittens . . . I handle all their business!

COUNT
How delightful!

FIGARO
And listen! Your beloved . . . she is his ward in chancery. She's not really the doctor's daughter.

COUNT
Oh, how happy you've made me!

FIGARO
Perhaps.
(*someone starts to open the window at the balcony*)
Quiet!

COUNT
What's up?

FIGARO
Look at the window.
(*they hide under the portico*)

ROSINA (*on the balcony*)
Perhaps he is not coming. Shall I . . . ?

COUNT
Oh my darling, my goddess, my beloved. Can I be dreaming? This moment . . . !
(BARTOLO *appears at the window*)

ROSINA
Oh, what a bother. What to do with my letter?

BARTOLO (*joins* ROSINA)
My child, good morning. How is the weather? But what are you hiding?

ROSINA
Not a thing, really nothing. It is the words of an aria! From "The Scheme That Came to Nothing."

COUNT
How clever! . . . from "The Scheme That Came to Nothing"!

FIGARO
How foxy!

BARTOLO
I remember! "The Scheme That Came to Nothing."

ROSINA
You know it, of course you do. It is an opera, a comedy.

BARTOLO
An opera, so you call it. But when I was young, they handled these things better. Do you think a thing like that is really opera? It's just a lot of nonsense. Howling horseplay. Just to please the public.
(ROSINA *drops the letter from the balcony*)

ROSINA
How very stupid! I seem to have dropped it. Will you please go and get it?

BARTOLO
Just a moment, I will try to.

ROSINA
St! st!

COUNT
I'm listening . . .

ROSINA
Hurry!
(*the* COUNT *picks up the letter*)

COUNT
Don't you worry!
(BARTOLO *comes out of the house*)

BARTOLO
I'm here. Where is it?

CONTE
Cos' è?

FIGARO
S'apre il balcone.

ROSINA
Non è venuto ancora. Forse . . .

CONTE
Oh mia vita! mio nume! mio tesoro! vi veggo alfine, alfine . . .

ROSINA
Oh che vergogna! vorrei dargli il biglietto?

BARTOLO
Ebben, ragazza? Il tempo è buono. Cos' è quella carta?

ROSINA
Niente, niente, signore: son le parole dell'aria dell'*inutil precauzione.*

CONTE
Ma brava—Dell'*inutil precauzione!*

FIGARO
Che furba!

BARTOLO
Cos' è questa *inutil precauzione?*

ROSINA
Oh bella! è il titolo del nuovo dramma in musica.

BARTOLO
Un dramma! Bella cosa! sarà al solito un dramma semiserio, un lungo, malinconico, noioso, poetico strambotto.
Barbaro gusto! secolo corrotto!

ROSINA
Oh me meschina! L'aria m'è caduta. Raccoglietela presto.

BARTOLO
Vado, vado.

ROSINA
St! st!

CONTE
T'ho inteso.

ROSINA
Presto.

CONTE
Non temete.

BARTOLO
Son qua. Dov'è?

ROSINA
Ah il vento l'ha portata via. Guardate.

BARTOLO
Io non la veggo. Eh signorina, non vorrei—(Cospetto! costei m'avesse preso!) In casa, in casa, animo, su. A chi dico? In casa, presto.

ROSINA
Vado, vado, Che furia!

BARTOLO
Quel balcone voglio far murare: Dentro, dico!

ROSINA
Ah che vita da crepare!

CONTE
Povera disgraziata! Il suo stato infelice sempre più m'interessa.

FIGARO
Presto, presto; vediamo cosa scrive.

CONTE
Appunto. Leggi.

FIGARO
"Le vostre assidue premure hanno eccitata la mia curiosità. Il mio tutore è per uscire di casa; appena si sarà allontanato, procurate con qualche mezzo ingegnoso d'indicarmi il vostro nome, il vostro stato, e le vostre intenzioni. Io non posso giammai comparire al balcone, senza l'indivisible compagnia del mio tiranno. Siate però certo, che tutto è disposta a fare, per rompere le sue catene, la sventurata Rosina . . ."

CONTE
Sì, sì, le romperà! Su, dimmi un poco: che razza d'uomo è questo suo tutore?

FIGARO
È un vecchio indemoniato, avaro, sospettoso, brontolone, avrà cent'anni indosso e vuol fare il galante. Indovinate! per mangiare a Rosina tutta l'eredità, s'è fitto in capo di volerla sposare. Aiuto!

ROSINA
The wind might easily have moved it back farther.

BARTOLO
I do not see it. No, little lady, I don't see it.
(*to himself*)
I wonder, perhaps she wants to fool me.
(*to* ROSINA, *brusquely*)
Inside there! Go in there! Go right away, I command you! I tell you hurry!

ROSINA
All right, all right. I'm going!

BARTOLO
That reminds me. I must wall up that balcony. Get inside there!

ROSINA
Oh, good heaven, what a torment!
(*she leaves the balcony.* BARTOLO *returns into the house*)

COUNT
Poor little troubled lady! When I see how she suffers, how my ardor increases.

FIGARO
Will you hurry! Let's see what's in the letter!

COUNT
You're right!
(*he gives* FIGARO *the letter*)
Read it!

FIGARO (*reading the letter*)
"Your assiduous attentions have attracted my notice. My guardian is going out. As soon as he is gone, contrive some means to let me know your name, your condition, and your intentions. I can never appear at the balcony without my inevitable tyrant. Be assured, however, that every effort will be made to break her chains by the unfortunate Rosina . . ."

COUNT
Yes, yes, she must escape. But will you tell me what kind of person is this disgusting doctor!

FIGARO
An overbearing maniac. He's vicious, avaricious, and suspicious. His age must be a hundred, but he acts like a youngster. It's his ambition to inherit both Rosina and all her worldly goods. He's quite determined that he'll marry her money.
(*the door of the house starts to open*)

Watch out there!

COUNT

Why?

FIGARO

I think he's coming.

BARTOLO

(talking to ROSINA, *who is still in the house)*

That is final. I warn you, don't admit any callers. If Don Basilio should want me while I'm absent, let him enter.

(talking to himself as he locks the door)

She will marry me soon. I'll not be sorry. As her husband, I'll have no further worry.

Recitative

COUNT

A marriage! My Rosina and that satyr, that ancient Casanova! I'm eager to know just who is Don Basilio.

FIGARO

He's a snake full of guile. He makes his living arranging weddings. A truly clever swindler always borrowing money. Still, he goes into Rosina's house instructing her in music.

COUNT

That will help us. I am glad to hear it.

FIGARO

Now, let me ask you. When you answer Rosina, what are are you going to tell her?

COUNT

We shall not tell her that I'm a count, a noble. I must discover her feelings. Does she love me, me only, and truly, not merely what would come to her as Countess Almaviva? Ah, you must help me.

FIGARO

Help you? Not at all! Why should I? It's your job!

COUNT

Without you, how may I . . .

FIGARO

Be quiet, I think I see her. Take a look, sir. My eyes do not deceive me. Standing behind that curtain I see a lady. Here's a chance to besiege her. Now's the moment for you to serenade her. Some canzonetta will get her. I'll lend you my guitar.

COUNT

I? Serenade her?

FIGARO

Surely. That's what she's expecting. Start the music.

COUNT

I really—

CONTE

Che?

FIGARO

S'apre la porta.

BARTOLO

Fra momenti io torno.
Non aprite a nessuno. Se Don Basilio
Venisse a ricercarmi, che m'aspetti.
Le mie nozze con lei meglio è affrettare.
Sì, dentr'oggi finir vo' quest'affare.

CONTE

Dentr'oggi le sue nozze con Rosina!
Ah vecchio rimbambito!
Ma dimmi, or tu! chi è questo Don Basilio? . . .

FIGARO

È un solenne imbroglion di matrimoni,
Un collo torto, un vero disperato,
Sempre senza un quattrino . . .
Già, è maestro di musica;
Insegna alla ragazza.

CONTE

Bene, bene;
Tutto giova saper.

FIGARO

Ora pensate della bella Rosina a soddisfar le brame.

CONTE

Il nome mio non le vo' dir, nè il grado; assicurarmi vo' pria ch'ella ami me, me solo al mondo, non le ricchezze e i titoli del Conte Almaviva. Ah, tu potresti.

FIGARO

Io? no, signor; voi stesso dovete.

CONTE

Io stesso? E come?

FIGARO

Zi zitto. Eccoci a tiro, osservate: per bacco, non mi sbaglio. Dietro la gelosia sta la ragazza; presto, presto, all'assalto, niun ci vede. In una canzonetta così alla buona il tutto spiegatele, signor.

CONTE

Una canzone?

FIGARO

Certo. Ecco la chitarra; presto, andiamo.

CONTE

Ma io . . .

FIGARO
Oh che pazienza!

CONTE
Ebben, proviamo.
Se il mio nome saper voi bramate,
Dal mio labbro il mio nome ascoltate.
Io son Lindoro,
Che fido v'adoro,
Che sposa vi bramo,
Che a nome vi chiamo,
Di voi sempre parlando così
Dall'aurora al tramonto del dì.

ROSINA
Segui, o caro; deh, segui così!

FIGARO
Sentite! Ah! che vi pare?

CONTE
Oh me felice!

FIGARO
Da bravo, a voi, seguite.

CONTE
L'amoroso e sincero Lindoro
Non può darvi, mia cara, un tesoro.
Ricco non sono,
Ma un core vi dono,
Un'anima amante,
Che fida e costante
Per voi sola sospira così
Dall'aurora al tramonto del dì.

ROSINA
L'amorosa sincera Rosina
Del suo core Lindo . . .

CONTE
Oh cielo!

FIGARO
Nella stanza
Convien dir che qualcuno entrato sia.
Ella si è ritirata.

CONTE
Ah cospettone!
Io già deliro . . . avvampo! . . .
Oh, ad ogni costo
Vederla io voglio . . . Vo' parlarle . . . Ah tu,
Tu mi devi aiutar.

FIGARO
Ih, ih, che furia!
Sì, sì, v'aiuterò.

CONTE
Da bravo: entr'oggi
Vo' che tu m'introduca in quella casa.
Dimmi, come farai? . . . via! . . . del tuo spirito
Vediam qualche prodezza.

FIGARO
Don't be so modest!

COUNT
All right, I'll try it.

Canzone

If you wonder whose voice is repeating
Tender hopes of a lover's meeting,
I am Lindoro and how I adore you!
My longing has led me
To ask you to wed me.
Ah, could ever a lover do more!
Day and night 'tis you I adore.

ROSINA
Serenade me a little bit more!

FIGARO
By heaven! She gave an answer.

COUNT
Oh happy moment!

FIGARO
Continue, continue, she likes it!

COUNT
I have nothing to offer a maiden
Save Lindoro with hope overladen.
All I can measure to add to my treasure
Is my heart's devotion, with fond love's emotion,
Ah, could ever a lover do more!
Day and night 'tis you I adore.

ROSINA
If so true is your love for Rosina, ah my Lindoro, why do . . .
(*she suddenly disappears from the balcony*)

Recitative and Duet

COUNT
By heaven!

FIGARO
She's gone back into the room. There was someone who interrupted.
Someone is in there with her.

COUNT
How can I bear it! I am distracted, delirious. You must assist me. We must be together. What's your answer, my friend? Can you think of a plan?

FIGARO
My, my, such ardor! Yes, yes, I'll help you out.

COUNT
I thank you. But listen! Can you get me inside there so I may see her? Tell me, how shall we do it? Surely with your genius you're sure to think of something.

FIGARO
Such a genius! Well now, let's see. Perhaps I—
(*he hesitates, doubtfully*)

COUNT
What ails you? You're speechless. Oho, I think I know. Now don't you worry. You will be paid a-plenty.

FIGARO
I will!

COUNT
I promise!

FIGARO
Plus the money for all my expenses?

COUNT
All you can squander. Now my friend, answer!

FIGARO
I'm ready. How can I tell you how the mention of money starts me going, how all my talents enlist for the duration! Just mention gold . . . my mind begins to function.
For the very thought of money sets my genius in rapid motion.
Like the tide upon the bosom of the ocean,
When the most attractive moon exerts her sway.
Ah yes, the very thought of money sets my genius into motion
Like the tide 'neath the moon's bright ray.
So like the tide, so like the tide,
When the most attractive moon exerts her sway.

COUNT
Let this tidal wave be full to overflowing.
Let Diana set this mighty tide in motion,
Fish us up a pearl of wisdom from the ocean
For we must devise a plan without delay!
Ah yes, with the wisdom of Minerva let's devise a plan without delay.
Ah yes, with the wisdom of Minerva
Let us plan without delay.

FIGARO
Let's decide how to disguise you. For example, you're a soldier!

COUNT
I'm a soldier?

FIGARO
Be a soldier!

COUNT
Me a soldier? What good is that? What's the game?

FIGARO
There's a regiment of soldiers that arrives this very morning . . .

FIGARO
Del mio spirito! . . .
Bene . . . vedrò . . . ma in oggi . . .

CONTE
Eh via! t'intendo.
Va là, non dubitar; di tue fatiche
Largo compenso avrai.

FIGARO
Davver?

CONTE
Parola.

FIGARO
Dunque, oro a discrezione?

CONTE
Oro a bizzeffe.
Animo, via.

FIGARO
Son pronto. Ah, non sapete
I simpatici effetti prodigiosi
Che, ad appagare il mio signor Lindoro,
Produce in me la dolce idea dell'oro.
All'idea di quel metallo
Portentoso, onnipossente,
Un vulcano la mia mente
Già comincia a diventar.

CONTE
Su, vediam di quel metallo
Qualche effetto sorprendente,
Del vulcan della tua mente
Qualche mostro singolar.

FIGARO
Voi dovreste travestirvi,
Per esempio . . . da soldato.

CONTE
Da soldato?

FIGARO
Sì, signore.

CONTE
Da soldato? . . . e che si fa?
Che si fa?

FIGARO
Oggi arriva un reggimento,
oggi arriva un reggimento.

CONTE
Sì, è mio amico il Colonello,
è mio amico il Colonello.

COUNT
Yes, and the Colonel is a friend of mine. He told me they were coming.

FIGARO
Va benon.

FIGARO
Splendid luck!

CONTE
Ma e poi?

COUNT
You think so?

FIGARO
Cospetto!
Dell'alloggio col biglietto
Quella porta s'aprirà.
Che ne dite, mio signore?
Non vi par? No l'ho trovata?

FIGARO
By heavens! By a military order you'll be quartered in this house. There's a sample of my genius! As a plan, how does it strike you? I am so endowed with genius I amaze myself.

CONTE
Che invenzione!

COUNT
You amaze me!

CONTE, FIGARO
Che invenzione prelibata!
Bravo, bravo, in verità!
Bella, bella, in verità!

COUNT, FIGARO
How ingenious, how ingenious, how amazing!
Bravo, bravo, that is all that I can say.

FIGARO
Piano, piano . . . ul'altra idea!
Veda l'oro cosa fa.
Ubbriaco . . . sì, ubbriaco,
Mio signor, si fingerà.

FIGARO
Quiet, quiet! a new idea! Ah, how money always helps to find a way! You've been drinking, yes, you've been drinking and it makes you very gay.

CONTE
Ubbriaco?

COUNT
I've been drinking?

FIGARO
Sì, signore.

FIGARO
You've been drinking.

CONTE
Ubbriaco? . . . Ma perchè?
Ma perchè? Ma perchè?

COUNT
I've been drinking. Why is that? What's the game? What's the game?

FIGARO
Perchè d'un ch'è poco in sè,
Che dal vino casca già,
Il tutor, credete a me,
Il tutor si fiderà.
Che invenzione prelibata!
Bravo, bravo, in verità!
Bella, bella, in verità!

FIGARO
When a man is in his cups, when he's fuller than a keg,
He's a man no one suspects. He may pull the doctor's leg!
Such a man, believe me, believe me, my friend, he may pull the doctor's leg!
I am so endowed with genius I amaze myself,
Bravo, bravo, that is all that I can say.

CONTE
Dunque . . .

COUNT
Now then . . .

FIGARO
All'opra.

FIGARO
To business!

CONTE
Andiamo.

COUNT
To business!

FIGARO
Da bravo.

FIGARO
To victory!

CONTE
Vado . . . Oh, il meglio mi scordavo!
Dimmi un po', la tua bottega,
Per trovarti, dove sta?

COUNT
Good-by! Wait! A most important point, a most important question. When we meet, where shall I find you, Master Barber? Where's your shop?

FIGARO
La bottega? . . . Non si sbaglia;
Guardi bene; eccola là.

FIGARO
Don't you worry, you will find it. I'll direct you. Here is the way.

Look for the barbershop just down the street there,
Fifteen's the number, we two will meet there.
Look for the lantern right in the entry,
Look for my motto "I shave the gentry."
Just as you enter there is a statue
Right in the center, looking straight at you.
Look for a barber, that's where I'll be,
Fifteen's the number, look in the entry,
There is a motto "I shave the gentry."
Just as you enter there is a statue
Right in the center looking straight at you.
Look for a barber, that's where I'll be,
Look for a barber, that will be me.

Numero quindici a mano manca,
Quattro gradini, facciata bianca,
Cinque parrucche nella vetrina,
Sopra un cartello « *Pomata fina* »,
Mostra in azzurro alla moderna,
V'è per insegna una lanterna . . .
Là senza fallo mi troverà.

COUNT
That will be easy . . .

FIGARO
Sir, you must hurry!

COUNT
How will you manage?

FIGARO
You need not worry.

COUNT
All of my secrets . . .

FIGARO
I will not mention.

COUNT
My trusty Figaro . . .

FIGARO
You have my attention.

COUNT
I shall be bringing . . .

FIGARO
Plenty of money.

COUNT
I will stand by you, I will supply you . . .

FIGARO
I have no doubt of it. Happen what may,
You're sure to find your love today!

COUNT
Love is a garden shining and sunny
Life is a paradise, full of milk and honey,
Love that I never knew rises within me,
All of my darkness turns into day.

FIGARO
I hear a tinkle, can it be money?
Last night a poor man, wealthy today!
I hear a tinkle, can it be money?

CONTE
Ho ben capito . . .

FIGARO
Or vada presto.

CONTE
Tu, guarda bene . . .

FIGARO
Io penso al resto.

CONTE
Di te mi fido . . .

FIGARO
Colà l'attendo.

CONTE
Mio caro Figaro . . .

FIGARO
Intendo, intendo.

CONTE
Porterò meco . . .

FIGARO
La borsa piena.

CONTE
Sì, quel che vuoi, ma il resto poi . . .

FIGARO
Oh non si dubiti, che bene andrà . . .
Che bene, bene, bene andrà.

CONTE
Ah, che d'amore
La fiamma io sento,
Nunzia di giubilo
E di contento!
Ecco propizia
Che in sen mi scende;
D'ardore insolito
Quest'alma accende,
E di me stesso
Maggior mi fa.

FIGARO
Delle monete
Il suon già sento!
L'oro già viene,
Viene l'argento;
Eccolo, eccolo,

Che in tasca scende;
E di me stesso
Maggior mi fa.

CONTE, FIGARO
E di me stesso
Maggior mi fa.

FIORELLO
Evviva il mio padrone! Due ore, fitto in piè, là come un palo mi fa aspettare e poi mi pianta e se ne va. Corpo di bacco! brutta cosa servir un padron come questo. Nobile, giovinotto e innamorato, questa vita, cospetto! è un gran tormento! ah durarla così non me la sento!

ROSINA
Una voce poco fa
Qui nel cor mi risuonò;
Il mio cor ferito è già,
E Lindor fu che il piagò.
Sì, Lindoro mio sarà;
Lo giurai, la vincerò.
Il tutor ricuserà,
Io l'ingegno aguzzerò.
Alla fin s'accheterà
E contenta io resterò . . .
Sì, Lindoro mio sarà;
Lo giurai, la vincerò.
Io son docile,—son rispettosa,
Sono obbediente,—dolce, amorosa;
Mi lascio reggere,—mi fo guidar.
Ma se mi toccano—dov'è il mio debole,
Sarò una vipera—e cento trappole
Prima di cedere—farò giocar.
Sì, sì, la vincerò. Potessi almeno
Mandargli questa lettera. Ma come!
Di nessun qui mi fido;
Il tutor ha cent'occhi . . . basta, basta;
Sigilliamola intanto.
Con Figaro, il barbier, dalla finestra
Discorrer l'ho veduto più d'un'ora;
Figaro è un galantuomo,
Un giovin di buon cuore . . .

Think of it! Look at me, a simple barber, I'm in the money!
Think of it! Look at me, a man with pockets full of pay!
Love that I never knew rises within me!
All of my darkness turns into day!

COUNT, FIGARO
All of my darkness turns into day!

(FIGARO *enters the* DOCTOR'S *house. The* COUNT *goes out the other way*)

Recitative

FIORELLO
My high and mighty master! I've been standing on my feet more than two hours. He keeps me waiting while he goes unthinking upon his way! Ah, what a life! It is slavery to serve such a lord as this. Noble, young and unheeding, and so in love!

He has money and power,
But I never share it;
I must work like a slave!
Why do I bear it?

(*A room in* DR. BARTOLO'S *house.* ROSINA *alone, holding a letter*)

Cavatina

ROSINA
When a lover's tender voice fills the heart and will not fade,
Then a maid must make her choice lest he woo some other maid.
Yes, Lindoro is my choice. No one shall stop me, my plans are made.
If my guardian should object I shall hardly be afraid,
For he never need detect that his little lamb has strayed.
I am quite well behaved, as sweet as honey,
My disposition is bright and sunny,
For I am gently bred when I am gently led,
It all depends on what you do.
But if you push me round then I will stand my ground,
I can be very nasty too.
I'll get you in the end,
I'll have the laugh, my friend,
The final joke will be on you.
No matter what you say,
I'll get my own sweet way,
I'll have the last laugh on you.

Recitative

Oh yes, I'll have my way. What of this letter? I need someone to carry it. I've no one who will keep it a secret, and the doctor would get it. What a nuisance! Just the same, I will seal it. (*she seals it at the writing table*) I think that I know a way. Maybe that barber.

Yes, Figaro was with him, right beside him. He is a gallant fellow, a person of discretion. I wonder if he'll help us. Love will persuade him!

(*enter* FIGARO)

Chi sa ch'ei non protegga il nostro amore!

FIGARO

Oh, good day, señorita.

FIGARO

Oh buon dì, signorina!

ROSINA

How are you, Señor Figaro?

ROSINA

Buon giorno, signor Figaro.

FIGARO

Your servant, if I may . . .

FIGARO

Ebbene, che si fa?

ROSINA

I'm unhappy.

ROSINA

Si muor di noia.

FIGARO

Confound it all, a pretty girl should be like a wineglass, shapely and full of spirits.

FIGARO

Oh diavolo! Possibile!
Una ragazza bella e spiritosa . . .

ROSINA

Ah, ah, you're so encouraging. What good are my spirits with no one here to see me, secluded in this house. It's like a dungeon . . . might as well be a prison or yet a graveyard.

ROSINA

Ah, ah, mi fate ridere!
Che mi serve lo spirito,
Che giova la bellezza,
Se chiusa io sempre sto fra quattro mura,
Che mi par d'esser proprio in sepoltura? . . .

FIGARO

Or yet a graveyard!

(*He hears someone coming. He talks hurriedly to* ROSINA)

Oh dear, now listen. There's something . . .

FIGARO

In sepoltura? . . . ohibò!
Sentite: io voglio . . .

ROSINA

He's coming back!

ROSINA

Ecco il tutor.

FIGARO

Your guardian?

FIGARO

Davvero?

ROSINA

Yes, he's coming. That's his footstep.

ROSINA

Certo, certo; è il suo passo . . .

FIGARO

Now for cover! I'll have to talk with you later. There is something I must tell you.

FIGARO

Salva, salva; fra poco
Ci rivedremo: ho a dirvi qualche cosa.

ROSINA

I too have something we must talk about.

ROSINA

E ancor io, signor Figaro.

FIGARO

You'll tell me all later.

FIGARO

Bravissima.
Vado.

ROSINA

(*as* FIGARO *leaves*) He's quite a fellow!

(*She goes backstage.* FIGARO *hides himself but peeps out occasionally during the scene that follows.* DR. BARTOLO *enters*)

ROSINA

Quanto è garbato!

BARTOLO

Oh that infernal Figaro. The devil! Oh what a rascal! Oh what a scoundrel!

BARTOLO

Ah! disgraziato Figaro,
Ah, indegno! ah, maledetto! ah, scellerato!

ROSINA (*at the back*)

He's complaining just as usual.

ROSINA

Ecco qua: sempre grida.

BARTOLO

He's stealing all my business. His patients keep increas-

BARTOLO

Ma si può dar di peggio!

Un'ospedale ha fatto
Di tutta la famiglia
A forza d'oppio, sangue e stranutiglia.
Signorina, il barbiere
Lo vedeste?

ROSINA
Perchè?

BARTOLO
Perchè lo vo' sapere.

ROSINA
Forse anch'egli v'adombra?

BARTOLO
E perchè no?

ROSINA
Ebben, ve lo dirò. Sì, l'ho veduto,
Gli ho parlato, mi piace, m'è simpatico
Il suo discorso, il suo gioviale aspetto . . .
(Crepa di rabbia, vecchio maledetto.)

BARTOLO
Vedete che grazietta!
Più l'amo, e più mi sprezza, la briccona.
Certo, certo è il barbiere
Che la mette in malizia.
Chi sa cosa le ha detto!
Chi sa! Or lo saprò. Ehi, Berta, Ambrogio!

BERTA
Eccì . . .

AMBROGIO
Ah! che comanda?

BARTOLO
Dimmi.

BERTA
Eccì . . .

BARTOLO
Il barbiere parlato ha con Rosina?

BERTA
Eccì . . .

BARTOLO
Rispondi almen tu, babbuino!

AMBROGIO
Ah, ah!

BARTOLO
Che pazienza!

AMBROGIO
Ah, ah! che sonno!

BARTOLO
Ebben!

BERTA
Venne, ma io . . .

ing, but mine are quite exhausted, what with his bleeding, cupping, dosing, and rubbing. Señorita, where's the barber? Have you seen him?

ROSINA
But why?

BARTOLO
Because I wish to know.

ROSINA
Would it add to your troubles?

BARTOLO
It surely would.

ROSINA
Then I will tell you all. Yes, I have seen him. We were talking. He's charming. He appeals to me. His conversation, his most delightful manner . . . (Now, you old buzzard, go and lose your temper!)
(ROSINA *goes out*)

BARTOLO
A charming little vixen. I love her. I love her even when she's naughty. But I'm certain that this barber put her up to this mischief. Now what could he have told her? Who knows? Let us find out. Hey, Berta, Ambrogio!

BERTA (*sneezing*)
Attchee!

AMBROGIO (*yawning*)
Aah! Did you want me?

BARTOLO
Tell me . . .

BERTA
Attchee!

BARTOLO
Was the barber alone with my Rosina?

BERTA
Attchee!

BARTOLO
You idiot! Do you hear? Give an answer!

AMBROGIO
Aah! Aah!

BARTOLO
Lord in heaven!

AMBROGIO
Aah! I'm sleepy.

BARTOLO
Speak up!

BERTA
Well now, he came here . . .

BARTOLO
Rosina . . .

AMBROGIO
Aah!

BERTA
Attchee!

AMBROGIO
Aah!

BERTA
Attchee!

BARTOLO
You numbskulls! Acting like this! You'll drive me crazy! Get out, you!

AMBROGIO
Aah!

BERTA
Attchee!

BARTOLO
And may the devil take you!

Recitative and Aria

Ah, I'll make him regret it, that most infernal barber.
(*enter* DON BASILIO)
Ah, Don Basilio! You shall assist me. Oh, I'll win her with kisses or with clouts! One way or the other, I'll marry her tomorrow. You understand me?

BASILIO
You put it most succinctly, sir. Allow me to reveal my latest tidings. But it's a secret. I've seen him, the Count of Almaviva.

BARTOLO
Who? Is he the fellow who courts Rosina?

BASILIO
Yes, he's the fellow.

BARTOLO
Oh damn it all! We've got to stop his nonsense.

BASILIO
Surely. But . . . with great discretion . . .

BARTOLO
What's in your mind?

BASILIO
A plan that will delight you. We must invent some story that reflects on his character to lower him in people's estimation, ruin his reputation. Hint at some secret, some dark or dirty scandal! I'll help as best I can. Four days will do it. Take my advice, I'll gladly make a wager. Scandal will chase him home, back where he came from.

BARTOLO
Rosina . . .

AMBROGIO
Ah!

BERTA
Eccì . . .

AMBROGIO
Aah!

BERTA
Eccì!

BARTOLO
Che serve! Eccoli qua, son
mezzo morti.
Andate.

AMBROGIO
Ah!

BERTA
Eccì . . .

BARTOLO
Eh, il diavolo che vi porti!

Ah! Barbiere d'inferno . . .
Tu me la pagherai . . . Qua,
Don Basilio;
Giungete a tempo! Oh! Io
voglio,
Per forza o per amor, dentro
domani
Sposar la mia Rosina. Avete
inteso?

BASILIO
Eh, voi dite benissimo
E appunto io qui veniva ad
avvisarvi . . .
Ma segretezza! . . . È giunto
Il Conte d'Almaviva.

BARTOLO
Chi? l'incognito amante
Della Rosina?

BASILIO
Appunto quello.

BARTOLO
Oh diavolo!
Ah, qui ci vuol rimedio!

BASILIO
Certo; ma . . . alla sordina.

BARTOLO
Sarebbe a dir? . . .

BASILIO
Così, con buona grazia
Bisogna principiare
A inventar qualche favola
Che al pubblico lo metta in
mala vista.
Che comparir lo faccia
Un uomo infame, un'anima
perduta . . .
Io, io vi servirò: fra quattro
giorni,

Credete a me, Basilio ve lo giura,
Noi lo farem sloggiar da queste mura.

BARTOLO
E voi credete?

BASILIO
Oh certo! È il mio sistema.
E non sbaglia.

BARTOLO
E vorreste?
Ma una calunnia . . .

BASILIO
Ah, dunque
La calunnia cos'è voi non sapete?

BARTOLO
No, davvero.

BASILIO
No? Uditemi e tacete.

La calunnia è un venticello,
Un'auretta assai gentile
Che insensibile, sottile,
Leggermente, dolcemente,
Incomincia a sussurrar.
Piano piano, terra terra,
Sotto voce, sibilando,
Va scorrendo, va ronzando;
Nelle orecchie della gente
S'introduce destramente,
E le teste ed i cervelli
Fa stordire e fa gonfiar.
Dalla bocca fuori uscendo
Lo schiamazzo va crescendo,
Prende forza a poco a poco,
Vola già di loco in loco;
Sembra il tuono, la tempesta,
Che nel sen della foresta
Va fischiando, brontolando
E ti fa d'orror gelar.
Alla fin trabocca e scoppia,
Si propaga, si raddoppia
E produce un'esplosione
Come un colpo di cannone,
Un tremuoto, un temporale,
Un tumulto generale,
Che fa l'aria rimbombar.
E il meschino calunniato,
Avvilito, calpestato,
Sotto il pubblico flagello
Per gran sorte va a crepar.
Ah! che ne dite?

BARTOLO
Can I believe that?

BASILIO
I'm certain. I have a system. Sir, it's perfect!

BARTOLO
Is it really? Still, to start a slander . . .

BASILIO
Don't worry. Have you ever stopped to think who starts a scandal?

BARTOLO
No, no, never.

BASILIO
No? Attention please, you just listen!

Slander Song

Start a rumor, light as a feather,
Watch that rumor float on the breezes,
How it tickles how it teases!
Oh how shyly, or how slyly!
Watch it find its way to every hidden place.
First a whisper, then a murmur,
Little voices all a-tremble
As the little words assemble,
Round and round the rumor reaches
Ears will open to its speeches,
Ears will listen to the lesson that it teaches
And the mind will pay attention
To whatever it will mention.
Who will drop it, who can stop it,
As it runs its rapid race!
Never stopping, never slowing,
Still increasing, ever growing,
Now it gathers and converges,
And a mighty wind emerges,
Now it shatters the foundation
Of a shaky reputation.
Tears asunder like the thunder,
Shouting insults into space.
And the end of this corrosion
Is a very fine explosion
Of a most destructive powder.
Like a cannon only louder!
Like a cannon, only louder!
Let us say it's like a cannon
Like an overheated cannon,
Like an old mistreated cannon
That's exploding in your face.

Oh it's very like a cannon,
Like an old and dated cannon,
Like an antiquated cannon
That's exploding in your face.
So you ruin some poor devil
With a tiny breath of evil,
So they beat him and mistreat him
Till he's buried in disgrace!

Recitative

Well, what's the verdict?

BARTOLO

You may be right. However, what must be done must be done in a hurry. No, I think we'll do it my way. Let's get on with it. Come on, we two together will draw up a contract this very moment. As soon as we are married I'll finish all her wooing and her cooing. I'll keep her safely. Trust me. She'll forget him.

BASILIO (*aside*)

He thinks he'll keep her. I wonder if she'll let him.
(*they leave together*)

Recitative and Duet

FIGARO

The rascals! Am I lucky! I overheard them! Confusion to the doctor! What a disgusting person! Her husband? The devil! He'll have some competition. While they work on the contract I suppose I had better tell Rosina.
(ROSINA *enters*)
Ah, señorita!

ROSINA

Ah, tell me what's happening.

FIGARO

I hardly dare to tell you.

ROSINA

Yes, what is it?

FIGARO

Hurry up with your trousseau!

ROSINA

What do you mean by that?

FIGARO

I mean a wedding! Your guardian has decided you're to be married, with himself as the groom, tomorrow morning!

ROSINA

You're joking.

FIGARO

I am in earnest. He's making out the contracts with your teacher, Don Basilio. They're in this thing together.

BARTOLO

Eh! sarà ver, ma intanto
Si perde tempo e qui stringe il bisogno.
No: vo' fare a modo mio:
In mia camera andiam. Voglio che insieme
Il contratto di nozze ora stendiamo.
Quando sarà mia moglie,
Da questi zerbinotti innamorati
Metterla in salvo sarà pensier mio.

BASILIO

(Vengan danari: al resto son qua io.)

FIGARO

Ma bravi! ma benone!
Ho inteso tutto. Evviva il buon Dottore.
Povero babbuino!
Tua sposa? Eh via! Pulisciti il bocchino.
Or che stanno là chiusi
Procuriam di parlare alla ragazza:
Eccola appunto.

ROSINA

Ebbene, signor Figaro?

FIGARO

Gran cose, signorina.

ROSINA

Sì, davvero?

FIGARO

Mangerem dei confetti.

ROSINA

Come sarebbe a dir?

FIGARO

Sarebbe a dire
Che il vostro bel tutore ha stabilito
Esser dentro doman vostro marito.

ROSINA

Eh, via!

FIGARO

Oh, ve lo giuro;
A stender il contratto
Col maestro di musica
Là dentro or s'è serrato.

ROSINA
Sì? oh, l'ha sbagliata affè!
Povero sciocco! L'avrà a far con me.
Ma dite, signor Figaro,
Voi poco fa sotto le mie finestre
Parlavate a un signore . . .

FIGARO
A, un mio cugino,
Un bravo giovinotto; buona testa,
Ottimo cor; qui venne
I suoi studi a compire,
E il poverin cerca di far fortuna.

ROSINA
Fortuna? oh, la farà.

FIGARO
Oh, ne dubito assai: in confidenza
Ha un gran difetto addosso.

ROSINA
Un gran difetto? . . .

FIGARO
Ah grande,
È innamorato morto.

ROSINA
Sì, davvero?
Quel giovine, vedete,
M'interessa moltissimo.

FIGARO
Per bacco!

ROSINA
Non ci credete?

FIGARO
Oh sì!

ROSINA
E la sua bella,
Dite, abita lontano?

FIGARO
Oh no! . . . cioè. . . .
Qui! . . . due passi . . .

ROSINA
Ma è bella? . . .

FIGARO
Oh, bella assai!
Eccovi il suo ritratto in due parole:
Grassotta, genialotta,
Capello nero, guancia porporina,
Occhio che parla, mano che innamora . . .

ROSINA
E il nome? . . .

FIGARO
Ah, il nome ancora?
Il nome . . . Ah, che bel nome! . . .
Si chiama . . .

ROSINA
Ebben, si chiama? . . .

ROSINA
Oh? That's what they mean to do! The silly idiots! They'll have to deal with me. But tell me, Señior Figaro, a while ago here underneath my window you were speaking to someone.

FIGARO
Ah, that was my cousin, a brave and handsome fellow. He is brainy, he has a heart, he's here to get a real education. The silly lad! He hopes to make a fortune.

ROSINA
A fortune? I think he will!

FIGARO
Oh, I am not too certain, for just between us there's one thing that may stop him.

ROSINA
And is it serious?

FIGARO
Yes, fatal. He is in love with someone.

ROSINA
Yes, that's fatal. I feel for him. Believe me, he's enlisted my sympathy.

FIGARO
Not really.

ROSINA
Don't you believe me?

FIGARO
Oh yes!

ROSINA
And is his sweetheart here or someplace far away?

FIGARO
Ah no! She lives here . . . quite nearby.

ROSINA
Is she pretty?

FIGARO
Oh, is she pretty? Listen and let me tell you if she is pretty! She's graceful, she's delightful, oh what a maiden! Hair as dark as midnight, a lovely figure, eyes that smile so sweetly.

ROSINA
Her name is?

FIGARO
Must I reveal it? Her name is . . . it's like a flower. They call her . . .

ROSINA
Come on! They call her?

FIGARO

Pretty darling—they call her R, O, Ro, S, I, si, Rosi, N, A, na, Rosina!

FIGARO

Poverina! . . .
Si chiama r . . . o . . . ro . . . s . . . i . . . si . . . rosi . . . n . . . a . . . na . . . Rosina.

ROSINA

Then it's I! I, his beloved!
Then it's he who is my lover!
This can hardly bowl me over
Since I knew it first of all!

ROSINA

Dunque io son . . . tu non m'inganni?
Dunque io son la fortunata! . . .
(Già me l'ero immaginata:
Lo sapevo pria di te.)

FIGARO

Your Lindoro loves you truly,
He will worship you forever,
Can't resist you, can't forget you,
How could he ever!
(*aside*)
If you ask me, she's too clever!
(*to* ROSINA)
You are very very clever,
He will come if you but call.

FIGARO

Di Lindoro il vago oggetto
Siete voi, bella Rosina.
(Oh, che volpe sopraffina,
Ma l'avrà da far con me.)

ROSINA

Dear Lindoro. Shall I see him?
Is it really, really true?

ROSINA

Senti, senti . . . m'a Lindoro
Per parlar come si fa?

FIGARO

I assure you that Lindoro
Craves to have a word with you.

FIGARO

Zitto, zitto, qui Lindoro
Per parlarvi or or sarà.

ROSINA

Sweet Lindoro! Heaven help me!
Here's another cause to worry.
When a maiden's in a hurry,
What's a maiden to decide?

ROSINA

Per parlarmi? . . . Bravo! bravo!
Venga pur, ma con prudenza;
Io già moro d'impazienza!
A che tarda? . . . ma che fa?

FIGARO

Pray, have a pity, have compassion
On a man in his condition.
He's awaiting your permission,
You just send a little note
And he will hasten to your side,
Yes, he'll hasten here to your side.
What's your answer?

FIGARO

Egli attende qualche segno,
Poverin, del vostro affetto;
Sol due righe di biglietto
Gli mandate, e qui verrà.
Che ne dite?

ROSINA

Can I bear to . . .

ROSINA

Non vorrei . . .

FIGARO

Come, why worry?

FIGARO

Su, coraggio.

ROSINA

Do I dare to . . .

ROSINA

Non saprei . . .

FIGARO

Write the letter!

FIGARO

Sol due righe . . .

ROSINA

I don't care to . . .

ROSINA

Mi vergogno . . .

FIGARO
Ma di che? ma di che? . . .
si sa.
Presto, presto; qua un biglietto.

ROSINA
Un biglietto? . . . eccolo qua.

FIGARO
Già era scritto? ve', che
bestia!
Il maestro faccio a lei!

ROSINA
Fortunati affetti miei!
Io comincio a respirar.

FIGARO
Ah che in cattedra costei
Di malizia può dettar.

ROSINA
Ah, tu solo, amor, tu sei
Che mi devi consolar!

FIGARO
Donne donne, eterni Dei
Chi v'arriva a indovinar?

ROSINA
Ah tu solo, amor, tu sei
Che mi devi consolar.
Ora mi sento meglio. Questo
Figaro

È un bravo giovinotto.

BARTOLO
Insomma, colle buone,
Potrei sapere dalla mia Rosina
Che venne a far colui questa
mattina?

ROSINA
Figaro? Non so nulla.

BARTOLO
Ti parlò?

ROSINA
Mi parlò.

BARTOLO
Che ti diceva?

ROSINA
Oh! mi parlò di certe
bagattelle . . .
Del figurin di Francia,
Del mal della sua figlia
Marcellina.

BARTOLO
Davvero! . . . Ed io
scommetto . . . que porto
la risposta al tuo biglietto

ROSINA
Qual biglietto?

FIGARO
Tell me why, tell me why, my dear.
Quickly, quickly write the letter.

ROSINA
Why be bothered? I have it here!

FIGARO
Ah, what a woman! I'm a blockhead!
She is way ahead of me.

ROSINA
Now I'm sure my note will reach him.
I have nothing more to fear.

FIGARO
You have taught me quite a lesson.
I am at your feet, my dear.

ROSINA
Now my heart is filled with gladness
For my love will soon be here.

FIGARO
When a woman makes her mind up,
Nothing ever can distract her,
Nothing else can interfere.

ROSINA
He will banish all my sadness,
All my sorrow, all my fear.
(*exit* FIGARO)

Recitative and Aria

I am feeling better, now that Figaro is coming to the rescue.

BARTOLO (*entering*)
One moment, my Rosina. I meant to ask you what you have been doing and what you were discussing with the barber?

ROSINA
Figaro? That was nothing.

BARTOLO
Did you speak?

ROSINA
Yes, we spoke.

BARTOLO
What did you speak of?

ROSINA
Of this and that, the latest news from Paris. And we spoke of his daughter; his little Marcellina has the measles.

BARTOLO
Oh really? Now let me ask you, did he bring you an answer to your letter?

ROSINA
To what letter?

BARTOLO
Why bother! The aria from "The Scheme That Came to Nothing" that you dropped from your hand only this morning. Now you are blushing!
(*aside*)
I knew I had guessed her secret!
(*to* ROSINA)
What's that stain on your finger? Did you fall in the inkwell?

BARTOLO
Che serve! L'arietta dell'*Inutil precauzione* che ti cadde staman giù dal balcone. Vi fate rossa? (Avessi indovinato!)
Che vuol dir questo dito così sporco d'inchiostro?

ROSINA
Inkwell? Oh, that one. That's where I burned my finger and someone told me that ink would surely heal it.

ROSINA
Sporco? oh, nulla.
Io me l'avea scottato,
E coll'inchiostro or or l'ho medicato.

BARTOLO (*at the writing table*)
Blast it all! These sheets of paper. There were seven. One is missing.

BARTOLO
(Diavolo!) E questi fogli . . .
Or son cinque . . . eran sei.

ROSINA
That paper? That's easy. I used a sheet of paper when I wrapped up a present for Marcellina.

ROSINA
Que fogli? . . . è vero.
D'uno mi son servita
A mandar de' confetti a Marcellina.

BARTOLO
Bravissima! And this pen point? What tricks has it been up to?

BARTOLO
Bravissima! E la penna
Perchè fu temperata?

ROSINA (*aside*)
Now he's got me!
(*to* BARTOLO)
That pen point? I drew a pretty flower on my embroidery.

ROSINA
(Maledetto!) La penna! . . .
Per disegnare un fiore sul tamburo.

BARTOLO
A flower?

BARTOLO
Un fiore!

ROSINA
A flower.

ROSINA
Un fiore.

BARTOLO
A flower. Ah, how brazen!

BARTOLO
Un fiore!
Ah! fraschetta!

ROSINA
It's true!

ROSINA
Davver.

BARTOLO
Silence!

BARTOLO
Zitta!

ROSINA
Believe me.

ROSINA
Credete.

BARTOLO
That's quite enough.

BARTOLO
Basta così.

ROSINA
Señor!

ROSINA
Signor . . .

BARTOLO
No more! Be quiet!

BARTOLO
Non più . . . tacete.

When you try to fool the doctor,
I advise you, little lady,
When you're lying to a doctor,
I advise you, little lady,
When you're trying something shady,

A un dottor della mia sorte
Queste scuse, signorina!
Vi consiglio, mia carina,
Un po' meglio a imposturar.
I confetti alla ragazza!
Il ricamo sul tamburo!

Vi scottaste: eh via! eh via!
Ci vuol altro, figlia mia,
Per potermi corbellar.
Perchè manca là quel foglio?
Vo' saper cotesto imbroglio.
Sono inutili le smorfie;
Ferma là, non mi toccate!
No, figlia mia, non lo sperate
Ch'io mi lasci infinocchiar.
A un dottor della mia sorte
Queste scuse, signorina!
Vi consiglio mia carina,
Un po' meglio a imposturar.
Via, carina, confessate;
Son disposto a perdonar.
Non parlate? Vi ostinate?
So ben io quel che ho da far.
Signorina, un'altra volta
Quando Bartolo andrà fuori,
La consegna ai servitori
A suo modo far saprà.
Signorina, un' altra volta
Quando Bartolo andrà fuori,
La consegna ai servitori
A suo modo far saprà.
Ah, non servono le smorfie,
Faccia pur la gatta morta.
Cospetton! per quella porta
Nemmen l'aria entrar potrà.
E Rosina innocentina,
Sconsolata, disperata,
Ah! non servono le smorfie,
Faccia pur la gatta morta!
Cospetton! per quella porta
Nemmen l'aria entrar potrà!
E Rosina innocentina,
Sconsolata, disperata,
In sua camera serrata
Fin ch'io voglio star dovrà,
Sì, sì, sì. . . .
In sua camera serrata
Fin ch'io voglio star dovrà,
Sì, sì. . . . sì!
Signorina, un'altra volta
Quando Bartolo andrà fuori,
La consegna ai servitori
A suo modo far saprà.
Signorina, un'altra volta
Quando Bartolo andrà fuori,
La consegna ai servitori
A suo modo far saprà.
Ah! non servono le smorfie,
Faccia pur la gatta morta!
Cospetton! per quella porta
Nemmen l'aria entrar potrà.
E Rosina innocentina,
Sconsolata, disperata . . .
Un dottor della mia sorte
Non si lascia infinocchiar!

You had better make it good.
Better, better tell a good one!
I advise you, little lady,
You had better make it good.
When you try to tell a lie,
You had better make it good!
First, it's candy for his daughter,
Then a flower on your embroidery!
Burned your finger! What rot! What rot!
When you ask me to believe you
Do you really think I should?
I am wise to all your capers
With the pen and with the papers,
I am wise to all your capers,
And you'd better not forget it!
Don't you dare attempt to fool me,
Have a care for you'll regret it!
No, don't you try to fool the doctor,
Just in case you think you could.
I entreat you, don't deny me,
I am willing to let it pass!
Won't you answer? Still persisting?
Still resisting? You defy me?
You're a very stubborn lass,
You're a naughty, stubborn lass!
If you try it once again,
You'll find me getting even madder,
Just attempt it once again,
And you will find yourself a sadder
And a wiser little lady
Than you ever were before.
Your excuses will not move me
Nor your alibis persuade me,
If I find you've disobeyed me,
I will lock you in your chamber,
And in spite of all your sighing
And your sobbing and your crying,
I will lock you in your chamber
With a bar across the door.
Your excuses will not move me,
Nor your alibis persuade me.
If I find you've disobeyed me,
Then your crying will begin.
And in spite of all your sighing
And your sobbing and your crying,
No excuses will persuade me
If I find you've disobeyed me,
And in spite of all your crying,
As a punishment for lying
And denying and defying,
I will have to lock you in.

Oh yes, I will lock you in your chamber
And your troubles will begin.
Don't you try to fool the doctor,
That's a thing I won't allow!
No, no, don't attempt to fool the doctor,
That's a thing I won't allow!
And in spite of all your crying,
All your sobbing, all your sighing,
I will lock you in your chamber,
And I think I'll do it now!
(*exits*)

ROSINA

Rant and rave all you want to! Bar the doors and the windows! You make me laugh. All normal women find this a challenge. It brings out their cleverness and calls forth all their spirit and their genius. Lock them in with a key! That's when they'll fool you.
(*exits*)

ROSINA
Brontola quanto vuoi, chiudi porte e finestre, io me ne rido; già di noi femmine alla più marmotta per aguzzar l'ingegno e farla spiritosa tutto a un tratto basta chiuderla a chiave e il colpo è fatto!

Recitative

BERTA (*entering*)

I thought I heard a noise in here. Someone was in here. That's the doctor, no doubt, having a quarrel with my mistress again. These modern women should be taught to behave.
(*there is a loud knock on the door*)
Who is that?

BERTA
Finora in questa camera
Mi parve di sentir un mormorio;
Sarà stato il tutor; colla pupilla
Non ha un'ora di ben . . . Queste ragazze
Non la voglion capir.
Battono.

COUNT (*outside*)

Come on there!

CONTE
Aprite.

BERTA

Coming! Atchee! I'm always sneezing, but that snuff I've been taking eases my wheezing.

BERTA
Vengo . . . Ecci . . . Ancora dura;
Quel tabacco m'ha posto in sepoltura.

Finale 1

(*enter* COUNT ALMAVIVA *disguised as a cavalry soldier*)

COUNT

May I enter? Am I welcome? Am I welcome? Hi! No one answers, none to greet me, none to meet me. Hi! (*he is pretending to be tipsy*)

CONTE
Ehi, di casa! . . . buona gente! . . .
Ehi, di casa! . . . niun risponde! Ehi!

BARTOLO

Who's this fellow? Some brutish rascal. He's been drinking! What goes on? What goes on?

BARTOLO
Chi è costui? . . . che brutta faccia!
È ubbriaco! chi sarà? chi sarà?

COUNT

What an entrance, what a welcome, what a greeting! Hi!

CONTE
Ehi di casa? . . . maledetti! . . .
Maledetti, ehi!

BARTOLO

What have I to do with soldiers?
(*as the* COUNT *sees* BARTOLO, *he reaches for something in his pocket*)

BARTOLO
Cosa vuol, signor soldato? . . .

COUNT

Ah! Ah! Yes, now let me thank you.

CONTE
Ah! . . . sì, . . . sì, . . . bene obbligato.

BARTOLO (*aside*)

What can be his little game?

BARTOLO
(Qui costui che mai vorrà?)

CONTE
Siete voi . . . Aspetta un poco . . .
Siete voi . . . dottor Balordo?

BARTOLO
Che Balordo? che Balordo?

CONTE
Ah, ah, Bertoldo?

BARTOLO
Che Bertoldo? che Bertoldo? Eh, andate al diavolo!
Dottor Bartolo, dottor Bartolo, dottor Bartolo!

CONTE
Ah, bravissimo;
Dottor Barbaro; benissimo,
Dottor Barbaro!

BARTOLO
Un corno!

CONTE
Va benissimo; già v'è poca,
Già v'è poca, già v'è poca differenza!

BARTOLO
(Io già perdo la pazienza.)

CONTE
(Non si vede! che impazienza!
Quanto tarda! dove sta?)

BARTOLO
(Qui prudenza ci vorrà.)

CONTE
Dunque voi . . . siete dottore?

BARTOLO
Son dottore . . . sì, signore.

CONTE
Va benissimo; un abbraccio,
Qua, collega.

BARTOLO
Indietro!

CONTE
Qua.
Sono anch'io dottor per cento,
Maniscalco al reggimento.
Dell'alloggio sul biglietto
Osservate, eccolo qua.
(Ah, venisse il caro oggetto)

BARTOLO
Dalla rabbia e dal dispetto
Io già crepo in verità!

CONTE
(Della mia felicità!)

BARTOLO
Ah, ch'io fo, se mi ci metto,
Qualche gran bestialità!

COUNT (*taking a paper from his pocket and looking at it*)
May I ask you . . . I think I have it . . . Do they call you Dr. Balordo?

BARTOLO
What's Balordo? Who's Balordo?

COUNT (*consulting the paper again*)
No, No. Bertoldo?

BARTOLO
What's Bertoldo? Who's Bertoldo? May the devil take you, sir! My name's Bartolo, Dr. Bartolo, Dr. Bartolo!

COUNT
Howdy-do to you! Dr. Barbaro; I bow to you, Dr. Barbaro!

BARTOLO
You half-wit!

COUNT
My regards to you. What's the difference, little Doctor, I forgive you!

BARTOLO (*aside*)
I've a notion I'm about to lose my temper.

COUNT (*aside*)
My Rosina, my Rosina! Where the devil can she be?

BARTOLO (*aside*)
I must try to keep my head.

COUNT
I must ask you, are you a doctor?

BARTOLO
Yes, indeed, sir. I'm a doctor.

COUNT
My regards to you. I embrace you! Hi! My comrade!

BARTOLO
Get back there!

COUNT (*embracing* BARTOLO)
There! Your indifference does not jar me, I'm a doctor in the army
(*he shows* BARTOLO *the paper*)
And your house will have the pleasure
Of providing me with quarters.
I've the order here in my hand.
It's a command! It's a command!
(*aside, in case* ROSINA *is listening*)
Come, my love, delay no longer!

BARTOLO
You're a low insulting bandit,
That is what I think of you!

COUNT (*aside*)
Let me speak of love to you!

BARTOLO
I suppose I've got to stand it

Since there's nothing else to do!
What to do, what to do?
What on earth am I to do?

COUNT (*aside*)
Now my love for you grows stronger
Till I know not what to do.

CONTE
(Vieni, vieni; il tuo diletto
Pien d'amor t'attende già.)

(ROSINA *enters and stops short on seeing a stranger*)

ROSINA
Who's the soldier? With my guardian?
Are they up to something new?
What am I supposed to do?

ROSINA
Un soldato ed il tutore!
Cosa mai faranno qua?
Cosa mai faranno qua?

COUNT
Here's Rosina! Now I am happy!

CONTE
(È Rosina; or son contento.)

ROSINA
Oh, the soldier, he's advancing!

ROSINA
(Ei mi guarda, e s'avvicina.)

COUNT (*to* ROSINA)
I'm Lindoro!

CONTE
(Son Lindoro.)

ROSINA
Oh how alarming! Oh my goodness, oh my darling, oh my dear!

ROSINA
(Oh ciel! che sento!
Ah, giudizio, per pietà!)

BARTOLO (*to* ROSINA)
So, you thought you'd come a-prowling.
This is not the place for women!

BARTOLO
Signorina, che cercate?
Presto, presto, andate via.

ROSINA
Won't you ever stop your growling!

ROSINA
Vado, vado, non gridate.

BARTOLO
Hurry, hurry out of here!

BARTOLO
Presto, presto, via di qua . . .

COUNT
Wait, my lady, I'll escort you.

CONTE
Ehi, ragazza, vengo anch'io.

BARTOLO
Where the devil are you going?

BARTOLO
Dove, dove, signor mio?

COUNT
To my bedroom.

CONTE
In caserma.

BARTOLO
To your bedroom?

BARTOLO
In caserma?

COUNT
This way, my pretty!

CONTE
Oh, questa è bella!

BARTOLO
To his bedroom. Very witty!

BARTOLO
In caserma? . . . bagattella!

COUNT
Darling!

CONTE
Cara! . . .

ROSINA
My goodness!

ROSINA
Aiuto!

BARTOLO
Get back, you ruffian!

BARTOLO
Olà, cospetto!

COUNT
Now I'm going . . .

CONTE
Dunque vado . . .

BARTOLO
Not on your life, sir.
There is no place for you here.
I will never have you here!

BARTOLO
Oh, non signore,
Qui d'alloggio non può star,
Qui d'alloggio non può star.

CONTE
Come? Come?

BARTOLO
Eh, non v'è replica:
Ho il brevetto d'esenzione.

CONTE
Il brevetto? . . .

BARTOLO
Mio padrone,
Un momento e il mostrerò.

CONTE
(Ah, se qui restar non posso,
Deh, prendete . . .)

ROSINA
(Ahimè, ci guarda!)

BARTOLO
(Ah, trovarlo ancora non posso.)

ROSINA
(Prudenza!)

BARTOLO
(Ma, sì, sì, lo troverò.)

ROSINA, CONTE
(Cento smanie io sento addosso.
Ah, più reggere non so.)

BARTOLO
Ah! Ecco qua!
Colla presente
Il Dottor Bartolo, etcetera.
Esentiamo . . .

CONTE
Eh, andate al diavolo!
Non mi state più a seccar.

BARTOLO
Cosa fa, signor mio caro?
Cosa fa, signor mio caro?

CONTE
Zitto là, Dottor somaro.
Il mio alloggio è qui fissato,
E in alloggio qui vo' star.

BARTOLO
Vuol restar?

CONTE
Restar, sicuro.

BARTOLO
Oh, son stufo, mio padrone;
Presto fuori, o un buon bastone
Lo farà di qua sloggiar.

CONTE
Dunque lei . . . lei vuol battaglia?
Ben! Battaglia le vo' dar.

COUNT
Come now, come now!

BARTOLO
I am a doctor, sir,
I am not obliged to do it.

COUNT
Can you prove it?

BARTOLO
I've an order of exemption.
Just a moment, I will get it out for you.
(*he goes to the writing table*)

COUNT
Then I guess I cannot stay here.
(*holding out a note toward* ROSINA)
Here, my darling!

ROSINA
Oh dear, he's watching!

BARTOLO (*searching among his papers*)
Now wherever did I put it?

ROSINA
He's looking . . .

BARTOLO
Yes, indeed. I left it here.

ROSINA and COUNT
Now we've got to think of something,
What in heaven shall we do?

BARTOLO
Ah, here it is!
(*he reads*)
"Be it known by these presents that Dr. Bartolo is exempted from . . ."

COUNT (*knocking the paper up in the air*)
I say to hell with it!
I've been waiting much too long.

BARTOLO
You are acting like a flunky,
Like a brazen little monkey . . .

COUNT
Do be quiet, Dr. Donkey! If you think I am leaving
You are very, very wrong.

BARTOLO
Won't you go?

COUNT
I mean to stay here.

BARTOLO
I shall never let you stay, sir.
Now pray be going on your way, sir,
Or I'll have to throw you out.

COUNT
Are you serious? You want to fight me?
Fine! I'm spoiling for a fight.

It will help me to keep in practice
How to take a strong redoubt.
Right before you are the breastworks,
You will make a splendid target!
On your guard, fellow soldiers
(aside to ROSINA, *showing her the letter)*
Now drop your handkerchief.
(he drops the letter. ROSINA *lets her handkerchief fall upon it)*
Now my comrades to the fray. On your guard!

Bella cosa una battaglia!
Ve la voglio qui mostrar.
Osservate! . . . questo è il fosso . . .
L'inimico voi sarete . . .
Attenzione gli amici (giù il fazzoletto.)
E gli amici stan di qua.
Attenzione!

BARTOLO *(sensing that something is going on)*
Stop it, stop it!

BARTOLO
Ferma, ferma! . . .

COUNT
What ails you? Ah.
(he pretends to catch sight of the letter, and picks it up, along with the handkerchief)

CONTE
Che cos'è? . . . ah! . . .

BARTOLO
Let me see it!

BARTOLO
Vo' vedere.

COUNT
Ah, it looks like a prescription!
Wait, it's a letter. It's for Rosina.
It's for her without a doubt.

CONTE
Sì, se fosse una ricetta!
Ma un biglietto . . . è mio dovere . . .
Mi dovete perdonar.

ROSINA
Thank you, thank you.

ROSINA
Grazie, grazie!

BARTOLO
Give it here, you brazen wanton,
Or I'll make you hand it over.
For I mean to have my way!

BARTOLO
Grazie un corno! qua quel foglio
Qua quel foglio; impertinente!
A chi dico? Presto qua.

COUNT
Would you fight, sir? On your guard! Hi!

CONTE
Vuol battaglia?
Attention! Ih!

ROSINA
Must it put you in a quandary
When I drop a piece of paper?
Just the list of last week's laundry . . .

ROSINA
Ma quel foglio che chiedete,
Per azzardo m'è cascato;
È la lista del bucato.

BARTOLO
You deceitful little devil. Hand it over, I command you! Hand it over right away!
(he grabs a paper from ROSINA*'s hand, but she has managed to substitute another paper for the letter)*
Oh my goodness!
(enter BASILIO, *carrying a document; enter* BERTA *from the opposite side)*

BARTOLO
Ah, fraschetta! Presto qua.
Presto, presto, presto qua!
Ah, che vedo!

BERTA
Here's the barber.

BERTA
Il barbiere!

BARTOLO
She was not lying. It's the laundry!

BARTOLO
Ho preso abbaglio! È la lista!

BERTA
Crazy people!

BERTA
Quanta gente!

BARTOLO
I surrender.

BARTOLO
Son di stucco!

CONTE
Bravo, bravo il mammalucco,
Che nel sacco entrato è già!

COUNT
Now the snare has caught its maker,
Now the hunter's in the trap!

ROSINA, BERTA, BARTOLO
Che nel sacco entrato è già.

ROSINA, BERTA, BARTOLO
Now the snare has caught its maker.

BARTOLO
Oh che gran bestialità!

BARTOLO
I'm a most unlucky chap!

BERTA
Qualche
imbroglio qui ci sta! Qui ci sta!

BERTA
What a scrap! What a most infernal scrap!

ROSINA
Ecco qua! . . . sempre un'istoria;
Sempre oppressa e maltrattata;
Ah, che vita disperata!
Non la so più sopportar.

ROSINA
All my life the same old story.
Always thwarted and suspected and defeated,
Always cheated, badly treated, since my dreary life began.

BARTOLO
Ah, Rosina . . . poverina . . .

BARTOLO (*approaching her*)
Ah, Rosina, do forgive me!

CONTE
Tu vien qua, cosa le hai fatto?

COUNT
Get away or I will make you!

BARTOLO
Ah, fermate . . . niente affatto . . .

BARTOLO
Get away, sir, devil take you!

CONTE
Ah, canaglia, traditore!

COUNT (*holding* BARTOLO *by the arm*)
Take your hands off, or you'll get it!

ROSINA, BERTA, BARTOLO, BASILIO
Via, fermatevi, signore.

ROSINA, BERTA, BARTOLO, BASILIO (*holding back the* COUNT)
Don't be rash or you'll regret it.

CONTE
Io ti voglio subissar!

COUNT
Come and fight if you're a man,
If you call yourself a man!

ROSINA, BERTA, BARTOLO, BASILIO
Gente! aiuto, soccorrete {mi! / lo!}

ROSINA, BERTA, BARTOLO, BASILIO
Come and help us, help to quiet him!

CONTE
Lasciatemi, lasciatemi!

COUNT
Let go of me, let go of me!

ROSINA, BERTA, BARTOLO, BASILIO
Gente! aiuto, per pietà!

ROSINA, BERTA, BARTOLO, BASILIO
Help us hold him if you can!
(FIGARO *enters, carrying a basin*)

FIGARO
Alto là!
Che cosa accadde,
Signori miei?
Che chiasso è questo?
Eterni Dei!
Già sulla piazza
A questo strepito
S'è radunata
Mezza città.
(Signor, giudizio,
Per carità.)

FIGARO
What goes on?
What's all the trouble? Where is the riot?
Merciful heaven. Can't you be quiet.
What a commotion, rousing the neighborhood!
I came a-running 'way down the street.
(*to the* COUNT)
Señor, be careful, be more discreet!

BARTOLO
Quest'è un birbante . . .

BARTOLO (*pointing to the* COUNT)
He is a bandit!

CONTE
Quest'è un briccone . . .

COUNT (*pointing to* BARTOLO)
He is a cutthroat!

BARTOLO
Ah, disgraziato! . . .

BARTOLO
He's an assassin!

COUNT
He is a villain!

FIGARO
Now Mr. Soldier, be more respectful,
You are neglectful of decent manners.
Here is a basin and I declare to you,
You'll get the contents upon your head.
(*aside*)
Señor, be careful, be more discreet!

COUNT (*to* BARTOLO)
Oh, what a dumb ox!

BARTOLO (*to the* COUNT)
Oh, what a lummox!

ROSINA, BERTA, FIGARO, BASILIO
Doctor, be quiet!

BARTOLO
Please let me hit him!

ROSINA, BERTA, FIGARO, BASILIO
Don't let him try it!

COUNT
Please let me slit him!

ROSINA, BERTA, FIGARO, BASILIO
Don't rouse the neighbors! Be more discreet!

COUNT
When I have murdered him, then I'll retreat.

ROSINA, BERTA, FIGARO, BASILIO
Do be more quiet! Be more discreet!
(*a heavy knock is heard on the street door*)

ROSINA, BERTA, FIGARO
We have a visitor . . .

ROSINA, BERTA, COUNT, FIGARO, BARTOLO, BASILIO
Out on the street.

BARTOLO
Who's there?

OFFICER OF THE GUARD (*outside*)
Hola!

CHORUS OF GUARDSMEN (*outside*)
Come on there! The guard's here! The guard won't wait!

ALL
The guard's here! Oh blast it all!

FIGARO, BASILIO
Now you have done it!

COUNT, BARTOLO
They will arrest us! They will not wait!

BARTOLO, BASILIO
Heaven preserve us!

ROSINA
Heaven preserve us, I am so nervous!

CONTE
Ah, maledetto! . . .

FIGARO
Signor soldato,
Porti rispetto,
O questo fusto,
Corpo del diavolo,
Or la creanza
Le insegnerà.
(Signor, giudizio,
Per carità.)

CONTE
Brutto scimmiotto! . . .

BARTOLO
Birbo malnato!

ROSINA, BERTA, FIGARO, BASILIO
Zitto, dottore . . .

BARTOLO
Voglio gridare . . .

ROSINA, BERTA, FIGARO, BASILIO
Fermo, signore . . .

CONTE
Voglio ammazzare . . .

ROSINA, BERTA, FIGARO, BASILIO
Fate silenzio,
Per carità.

CONTE
No, voglio ucciderlo,
Non v'è pietà.

ROSINA, BERTA, FIGARO, BASILIO
Fate silenzio,
Per carità.

ROSINA, BERTA, FIGARO
Zitti, chè bussano!

ROSINA, BERTA, CONTE, FIGARO, BARTOLO, BASILIO
Che mai sarà?

BARTOLO
Chi è?

UFFICIALE
Olà!

CORO
La forza, la forza,
Aprite qua!

TUTTI
La forza! Oh diavolo!

FIGARO, BASILIO
L'avete fatta!

CONTE, BARTOLO
Niente paura.
Venga pur qua.

BARTOLO, BASILIO
Quest'avventura!

ROSINA
Quest'avventura! Quest'avventura!

ROSINA, BERTA
Quest'avventura! Quest'avventura!

ROSINA, BERTA
They will molest us when they arrest us!

TUTTI
Quest'avventura,
Ah, come diavolo
Mai finirà!

ALL
Heaven preserve us. Where do we go from here?
What shall be our fate?

CORO
Fermi tutti. Nessun si muova.
Miei signori, che si fa?
Questo chiasso donde è nato?
La cagione presto qua!

CHORUS OF GUARDSMEN
What goes on here? What's all the trouble?
Keep your places, if you please.
What's the cause of all the trouble,
Of such goings on as these?

BARTOLO
Questa bestia di soldato,
Mio signor, m'ha maltrattato.
Sì, signor, sì signor, sì signor, m'ha maltrattato,
Questa bestia di soldato,
Mio signor, m'ha maltrattato,
Sì signor, sì signor,
Sì signor, m'ha maltrattato.

BARTOLO
This intruder was attempting to mistreat me, I assure you.
Cross my heart, he had just begun to beat me,
He was trying to mistreat me.
He had just begun to beat me.
Cross my heart and hope to die,
He has murder in his eye!

FIGARO
Io qua venni, mio signore,
Questo chiasso ad acquetar.

FIGARO
I was trying to be helpful, I was just a passer-by,
Cross my heart and hope to die!

CONTE
In alloggio quel briccone, non mi volle qui accettar.
Sì signor, non mi volle qui accettar,
Sì signor, sì signor.

COUNT
I am ordered to be quartered here but he will not comply.
Cross my heart, he refuses to comply.
Cross my heart, hope to die!

ROSINA
Perdonate, poverino,
Tutto effetto fu del vino,
Tutto effetto fu del vino.
Sì signor, sì signor.

ROSINA
Oh, no matter what you're thinking,
You can see that he's been drinking.
You can see how such a lot'll
Happen when there is a bottle!
Cross my heart, hope to die!

BERTA
Fa un inferno di rumore,
Parla sempre d'ammazzare.
Sì signor, sì signor.

BERTA
All I know was that I heard a
Lot of people yelling murder,
Cross my heart, hope to die!

UFFICIALE
Ho inteso.
Galantuom, siete in arresto.
Fuori presto,
Via di qua!

OFFICER
All right now, don't fight now!
Ah, my friend, I must arrest you,
Let's be going off to jail!

CONTE
In arresto? In arresto? Io?
. . . Fermi, olà.

COUNT
I'm arrested? Just a moment! Stand back! Stop where you are!
(*the* COUNT *waves the* GUARD *away and takes the* OFFICER *aside. He shows him a paper. The* OFFICER, *astonished and impressed, orders the* GUARD *to move back. The* OFFICER *stands at their head. All on stage stand frozen in position*)

Sextet

ROSINA
Freddo ed immobile

ROSINA
Fright leaves me all undone,

Dumb and helpless as a stone,
Quite takes my breath away.
What can I say!

Come una statua
Fiato non restami
Da respirar.

COUNT
Fright leaves her all undone,
Dumb and helpless as a stone,
Quite takes her breath away.
What can I say!

CONTE
Freddo ed immobile
Come una statua,
Fiato non restagli
Da respirar.

BARTOLO
Fright leaves me all undone,
Dumb and helpless as a stone,
Quite takes my breath away.
What can I say!

BARTOLO
Freddo ed immobile
Come una statua,
Fiato non restami
Da respirar.

FIGARO
Look at Don Bartolo,
He stands there like a stone!
There's not a single word that he can say.
Poor Dr. Bartolo!

FIGARO
Guarda Don Bartolo!
Sembra una statua!
Ah! ah! dal ridere
Sto per crepar!

BASILIO
Fright leaves me all undone, like a stone,
Takes my breath all away.
What can I say!

BASILIO
Freddo ed immobile
Fiato non restami
Da respirar.

BERTA
This takes my breath away!
What can I say!

BERTA
Fiato non restami.
Da respirar.

FIGARO
He's more amusing than a funny play, I say!

FIGARO
Ah, ah, dal ridere sto per crepar.

BARTOLO
Let me say . . .

BARTOLO
Ma, signor . . .

GUARDSMEN
Don't you dare . . .

CORO
Zitto tu!

BARTOLO
If I may . . .

BARTOLO
Ma un dottor . . .

GUARDSMEN
Have a care!

CORO
Oh non più!

BARTOLO
When you've heard . . .

BARTOLO
Ma se lei . . .

GUARDSMEN
That will do!

CORO
Non parlar . . .

BARTOLO
What occurred,

BARTOLO
Ma vorrei . . .

GUARDSMEN
Not from you!

CORO
Non gridar.

BARTOLO, BASILIO
Just a word!

BARTOLO, BASILIO
Ma se noi? . . .

GUARDSMEN
Not a word!

CORO
Zitti voi!

ROSINA, BARTOLO, BASILIO
How absurd!

ROSINA, BARTOLO, BASILIO
Ma se noi!

UFFICIALE
Pensiam noi!

ROSINA, BARTOLO, BASILIO
Ma se poi.

UFFICIALE
Zitto tu!

ROSINA, BARTOLO, BASILIO
Ma se noi.

UFFICIALE
Non parlar!
Vada ognun pei fatti suoi,
Si finisca d'altercar,
Sì, d'altercar!

CONTE, FIGARO
Zitto su!

ROSINA, BERTA, BASILIO
Zitto su!

BARTOLO
Ma sentite!

CONTE, FIGARO
Zitto giù.

ROSINA, BERTA, BASILIO
Zitto giù.

BARTOLO
Ma sentite, ma sentite,
ascoltate.

CONTE, FIGARO
Zitto qua.

ROSINA, BERTA, BASILIO
Zitto qua.

BARTOLO
Ma sentite, ascoltate.

CONTE, FIGARO
Zitto là.

ROSINA, BERTA, BASILIO
Zitto là.

CONTE, FIGARO
Zitto su.

ROSINA, BERTA, BASILIO
Zitto giù.

CONTE, FIGARO
Zitto giù.

ROSINA, BERTA, BASILIO
Zitto su.

BARTOLO
Ascoltate, ascoltate,
Ascoltate, ascoltate.

ROSINA, BERTA, CONTE, FIGARO, BASILIO
Zitto qua! Zitto là!

TUTTI
Mi par d'esser con la testa

GUARDSMEN
Just be still!

ROSINA, BARTOLO, BASILIO
If you will . . .

GUARDSMEN
That will do!

ROSINA, BARTOLO, BASILIO
But it's true . . .

GUARDSMEN
Never mind!
Now we quickly shall discover
If there's anything to find.
What shall we find!

COUNT, FIGARO (*to the others*)
Just be dumb!

ROSINA, BERTA, BASILIO
We'll be dumb.

BARTOLO
Won't you listen?

COUNT, FIGARO
Dumb and blind!

ROSINA, BERTA, BASILIO
Dumb and blind.

BARTOLO
I have many things to tell. Oh won't you listen!

COUNT, FIGARO
Not a thought . . .

ROSINA, BERTA, BASILIO
Not a thought . . .

BARTOLO
Won't you listen, my good fellow!

COUNT, FIGARO
On our mind!

ROSINA, BERTA, BASILIO
On our mind.

COUNT, FIGARO
Keeping mum . . .

ROSINA, BERTA, BASILIO
Keeping mum.

COUNT, FIGARO
Just be still!

ROSINA, BERTA, BASILIO
That we will.

BARTOLO
There is something I could say to you
If you will be so kind . . .

ROSINA, BERTA, COUNT, FIGARO, BASILIO
We shall see what they find!

ROSINA, BERTA, COUNT, FIGARO, BARTOLO, BASILIO
As the blacksmith strikes the anvil

So these sounds beat down upon me,
My poor head is like the anvil,
Where my woes strike down and stun me.
Never ceasing, still increasing,
Like a thousand pounding hammers,
Every sound affects my brain!
Like the beating of a hammer,
Hear them yammer, yammer, yammer!
Like a hammer, hear them yammer . . . !

ROSINA, BERTA, BARTOLO
Such commotion will occasion
An alarming situation!

GUARDSMEN, BASILIO
Such commotion, how alarming!

COUNT, FIGARO, BARTOLO
Such a dissonant vibration
Is affecting the foundation.

GUARDSMEN
Such vibration, it's affecting . . .

BASILIO
Such vibration!

ROSINA, BERTA, COUNT, FIGARO, BARTOLO, BASILIO
Oh the very walls are shaking
And the very halls are quaking!
Oh the house itself is shaking,
It will never bear the strain!
Oh such commotion will occasion
An alarming situation,
For the house itself is shaking,
It will never bear the strain.

GUARDSMEN
Like the hammer on the anvil, like a hammer on the anvil . . .

ROSINA, BERTA, COUNT, FIGARO, BARTOLO, BASILIO, THE GUARD
Such a clamor like a hammer
Now my battered brain is shattered,
Since my system can't resist 'em,
I will surely go insane!
I'll go insane!
Yes, I will surely, positively,
Absolutely go insane!

In un'orrida fucina,
Parmi esser con la testa,
In un'orrida fucina,
Dove cresce e mai non resta,
Dell'incudini sonore,
L'importuno strepitar.
Alternando questo e quello
Pesantissimo martello.
Alternando questo e quello.

ROSINA, BERTA, BARTOLO
Alternando questo e quello
pesantissimo martello.

BASILIO, UFFICIALE
Alternando, questo e quello.

CONTE, FIGARO, BARTOLO
Alternando questo e quello
Pesantissimo martello.

UFFICIALE
Alternando questo e quello.

BASILIO
Alternando!

ROSINA, BERTA, CONTE, FIGARO, BARTOLO, BASILIO
E il cervello, poverello,
già stordito, sbalordito,
Non ragiona, si confonde,
Muri e vôlte rimbombar.
Sì, alternando questo e quello
Pesantissimo martello,
Fa con barbara armonia
Muri e vôlte rimbombar.

UFFICIALE
Alternando, alternando, alternando questo e quello.

TUTTI
E il cervello, poverello,
Già tordito, sbalordito,
Non ragiona, si confonde,
Si riduce ad impazzar.
Non ragiona, si confonde,
Si riduce ad impazzar.

BARTOLO
Ma vedi il mio destino! Quel soldato,
Per quanto abbia cercato,
Niun lo conosce in tutto il reggimento.
Io dubito . . . eh, cospetto!
Che dubitar? Scommetto
Che dal conte Almaviva
È stato qui spedito quel signore
Ad esplorar della Rosina il core.
Nemmeno in casa propria
Sicuri si può star! Ma io . . . Chi batte?
Ehi, chi è di là . . . Battono, non sentite!
In casa io son; non v'è timore, aprite.

CONTE
Pace e gioia sia con voi.

BARTOLO
Mille grazie, non s'incomodi.

CONTE
Gioia e pace per mill'anni.

BARTOLO
Obbligato in verità.

CONTE
Pace e gioia sia con voi.

BARTOLO
Mille grazie, non s'incomodi.

CONTE
Gioia e pace per mill'anni!

BARTOLO
Obbligato in verità.
(Questo volto non m'è ignoto,)

CONTE
(Ah se un colpo è andato a vuoto)

BARTOLO
(Non ravviso, non ricordo—)

CONTE
(A gabbar questo balordo,)

BARTOLO
(Ma quel volto, ma quel volto?)

CONTE
(Un novel travestimento,)

BARTOLO
(Non capisco chi sarà?)

CONTE
(Più propizio a me sarà.
Sì, sì, propizio a me sarà.)
Gioia e pace, pace e gioia.

ACT II

The library in DR. BARTOLO's *house, with chairs and a piano, from which there is music.*

BARTOLO

My life is full of trouble. That soldier, about whom I've inquired, is not known at all throughout the whole regiment. I'm wondering . . . Ah, why wonder! I'm very sure, certain that the Count Almaviva arranged for him to come here as a spy to find out if my Rosina loves him. A man is never safe, not even in his own house. But I will . . . (*a knock is heard*) Who's knocking? Hey, who is there? Somebody come and answer! This is my own house; why need I worry? I'll open it.

Recitative and Duet

(*enter the* COUNT, *disguised as a music master*)

COUNT
May your days be full of gladness!

BARTOLO
Sir, I thank you. Very kind of you . . .

COUNT
Free from every thought of sadness . . .

BARTOLO
Sir, I thank you with all my heart.

COUNT
May your days be even brighter . . .

BARTOLO
Sir, I thank you, very kind of you.

COUNT
May your cares be ever lighter . . .

BARTOLO
Sir, I thank you with all my heart.
(*aside*)
Does this fellow think I've met him?

COUNT (*aside*)
My appearance has upset him.

BARTOLO
How I wish that I could place him . . .

COUNT
I am not afraid to face him.

BARTOLO
This is really most confusing . . .

COUNT
This is really quite amusing.

BARTOLO
Shall I try to make a guess?

COUNT
My disguise is a success!
Oh yes I am really a success.
May your days be ever brighter . . .

BARTOLO (*aside*)
Why repeat it, the silly blighter!

COUNT
May your cares be ever lighter . . .

BARTOLO
Stop it, stop it!
I am weary of your talk. I must confess.

COUNT
Brighter . . .

BARTOLO
Brighter . . .

COUNT
Lighter . . .

BARTOLO
Lighter . . . Why repeat it, the silly blighter!

COUNT
May your days be full of gladness . . .

BARTOLO
This is madness! Stop it, stop it! Heaven, what a mess!
Do I always have to suffer?

COUNT
I have fooled the poor old duffer!

BARTOLO
Do you wonder that I'm whining?

COUNT
Now the sun is really shining!

BARTOLO
Do I always have to suffer.
Do you wonder that I'm whining.
For what else am I to do, since
Every damned unpleasant nuisance
Brings intrusion and confusion,
So my house is in a mess!

COUNT (*aside*)
Ah, Rosina! I've come to tell you
Words of love and happiness.
Now, my dear, the sun is shining,
Dawning with our happiness.
Now my dear the sun is shining,
Now my dear my heart is singing,
Ah Rosina, I am bringing
Tidings of our happiness!

BARTOLO
Every damned unpleasant nuisance
Turns my house into a mess.

COUNT (*aside*)
Oh my dear, I am here my devotion to confess,
But I fear, oh my dear,
That my tongue cannot express
My happiness!

BARTOLO
Ho capito. (Oh ciel! che noia!)

CONTE
Gioia e pace, ben di core.

BARTOLO
Basta, basta!
Basta, basta, basta, basta, per pietà!

CONTE
Gioia . . .

BARTOLO
Gioia . . .

CONTE
Pace . . .

BARTOLO
Pace . . . Ho capito. (Oh ciel! che noia!)

CONTE
Ben di core, pace e gioia.

BARTOLO
Pace e gioia, basta, basta, basta per pietà.
(Ma che perfido destino!)

CONTE
(Il vecchion non mi conosce!)

BARTOLO
(Ma che barbara giornata!)

CONTE
(Oh mia sorte fortunata!)

BARTOLO
(Ma che perfido destino!
Ma che barbara giornata!
Tutti quanti a me davanti!
Tutti quanti a me davanti.
Tutti quanti a me davanti!
Che crudel fatalità!)

CONTE
(Ah mio ben! fra pochi istanti
Parlerem con libertà!
Ah mio ben, fra pochi istanti
Parlerem con libertà!
Ah mio ben, fra pochi istanti,
Ah mio ben, fra pochi istanti,
Parleremo, parleremo,
Parlerem con libertà!)

BARTOLO
Tutti quanti a me davanti!
Che crudel fatalità!

CONTE
(Parlerem, parlerem, parlerem con libertà!
Parlerem, parlerem, parlerem con libertà!
Con libertà!)

BARTOLO
Che crudel, che crudel
che crudel fatalità!
Che crudel, che crudel,
Che crudel fatalità!

BARTOLO
Me oh my! How I try
To get out of all this mess,
But I'm in it every minute,
Yes, I'm in it nonetheless!
I'm in a mess!

Recitative

Insomma, mio signore,
Chi è lei si può sapere? . . .

Permit me, sir, one question. Who are you and what's your business?

CONTE
Don Alonso,
Professore di musica ed allievo
Di Don Basilio.

COUNT
Don Alonso, a professor of music, sir, and a pupil of Don Basilio.

BARTOLO
Ebbene?

BARTOLO
Go on, sir . . .

CONTE
Don Basilio
Sta male, il poverino, ed in sua vece . . .

COUNT
Don Basilio was stricken with a fever. I'm to replace him.

BARTOLO
Sta mal? . . . Corro a vederlo . . .

BARTOLO
He's ill? I'll go to see him.

CONTE
Piano, piano.
Non è un mal così grave.

COUNT
Don't you worry. His complaint is a slight one.

BARTOLO
(Di costui non mi fido.)
Andiamo, andiamo.

BARTOLO (*aside*)
I'm not sure that I trust him. (*to* COUNT) We'll see him together.

CONTE
Ma signore . . .

COUNT
Just a moment . . .

BARTOLO
Che c'è?

BARTOLO
What now?

CONTE
Voleva dirvi . . .

COUNT (*drawing him aside, speaking very softly*)
I know a secret.

BARTOLO
Parlate forte.

BARTOLO
I cannot hear you.

CONTE
Ma . . .

COUNT
Well . . .

BARTOLO
Forte, vi dico.

BARTOLO (*loud and angry*)
Louder, d'you hear me!

CONTE
Ebben, come volete,
Ma chi sia Don Alonso apprenderete.
Vo' dal conte Almaviva . . .

COUNT (*also angry*)
All right, you have it your way. You'll regret that you trifled with Don Alonso (*he pretends to go away*) When the Count Almaviva . . .

BARTOLO
Piano, piano.
Dite, dite, v'ascolto.

BARTOLO (*holding him back*)
Just a moment. Won't you please say it softly!

CONTE
Il conte . . .

COUNT (*loudly*)
The count . . .

BARTOLO
Piano,
Per carità.

BARTOLO
Soft, for heaven's sake!

CONTE
Stamane
Nella stessa locanda

COUNT
This morning when the count was not present, I dropped in for a visit. As I was waiting, just by a stroke of luck,

I found a letter to the Count Almaviva from your Rosina. (*he shows him a letter*)

BARTOLO
Let's see it. (*takes it*) That is her writing.

COUNT
Don Basilio does not know of the letter, and since I knew that I would give a lesson to Rosina, it had occurred to me that maybe it would please you . . . I mean, I had a notion . . . if I showed it . . .

BARTOLO
If what, sir?

COUNT
My idea was to show her this letter, if you'll permit me. To show her, if you let me, that her lover is known to be in love with some other woman. I could contrive to prove it. I'd say he showed the letter to his mistress as a joke!

BARTOLO
Say it softly, for that is slander! Oh, bravo! You have the subtle mind of Don Basilio! I'll reward you quite handsomely for what you've done. I'll follow your suggestion. I shall call my Rosina. I am greatly obliged. I am your servant. You'll find me not ungrateful.

COUNT
That will be splendid!
(BARTOLO *goes off into another room*)
Remembering that letter was a chance in a million. I was desperate. What could I do? If I had not done it, he would soon have remembered where he had seen me. I only want to tell her all that is in my heart. If she will take me, my cup is overflowing. (BARTOLO *returns, bringing* ROSINA) There she is, my heart! How I have longed to see her!

BARTOLO (*leading* ROSINA)
Come with me, señorita. Now Rosina, here's Don Alonso. He's come to give your lesson.

ROSINA (*recognizing the* COUNT *as* LINDORO *in disguise*)
Ah!

BARTOLO
What's the trouble?

Era meco d'alloggio, ed in mie mani
Per caso capitò questo biglietto
Della vostra pupilla a lui diretto.

BARTOLO
Che vedo! . . . è sua scrittura!

CONTE
Don Basilio
Nulla sa di quel foglio: ed io, per lui
Venendo a dar lezione alla ragazza,
Voleva farmene un merito con voi . . .
Perchè . . . con quel biglietto . . .
Si potrebbe . . .

BARTOLO
Che cosa? . . .

CONTE
Vi dirò . . .
S'io potessi parlare alla ragazza,
Io creder . . . verbigrazia . . . le farei
Che me lo diè del Conte un'altra amante,
Prova significante
Che il Conte di Rosina si fa giuoco.
E perciò . . .

BARTOLO
Piano un poco.
Una calunnia! . . . Oh bravo!
Degno e vero scolar di Don Basilio!
Io saprò come merita
Ricompensar sì bel suggerimento.
Vo a chiamar la ragazza,
Poichè tanto per me v'interessate;
Mi raccomando a voi.

CONTE
Non dubitate.
L'affare del biglietto
Dalla bocca m'è uscito non volendo.
Ma come far? Senza un tal ripiego
Mi toccava andar via come un baggiano.
Il mio disegno a lei
Ora paleserò; s'ella acconsente,
Io son felice appieno.
Eccola. Ah, il cor sento balzarmi in seno.

BARTOLO
Venite, signorina. Don Alonso,
Che qui vedete, or vi darà lezione.

ROSINA
Ah! . . .

BARTOLO
Cos'è stato?

ROSINA
È un granchio al piede.

CONTE
Oh nulla:
Sedete a me vicino, bella fanciulla.
Se non vi spiace, un poco di lezione,
Di Don Basilio in vece, vi darò.

ROSINA
Oh, con mio gran piacere la prenderò.

CONTE
Che volete cantar?

ROSINA
Io canto, se le aggrada,
Il rondò dell'*Inutil Precauzione.*

BARTOLO
E sempre, sempre in bocca
L'*Inutil Precauzione!*

ROSINA
Io ve l'ho detto:
È il titolo dell'opera novella.

BARTOLO
Or bene, intesi; andiamo.

ROSINA
Eccola qua.

CONTE
Da brava, incominciamo.

ROSINA
Contro un cor che accende amore
Di verace invitto ardore,
S'arma invan poter tiranno
Di rigor, di crudeltà.
D'ogni assalto vincitore
Sempre amor trionferà.
Ah Lindoro, mio tesoro,
Se sapessi, se vedessi!
Questo cane di tutore,
Ah, che rabbia che mi fa!
Caro, a te mi raccomando,
Tu mi salva per pietà, sì, sì, sì, sì.

CONTE
Non temer, ti rassicura;
Non temer, ti rassicura
Sorte amica a noi sarà.

ROSINA
Dunque spero?

CONTE
A me t'affida.

ROSINA
E il mio cor?

ROSINA
Twisted my ankle.

COUNT
Don't worry. Just take your place beside me, lovely lady. Now let me hear you. It is my pleasant duty, replacing Don Basilio, who is ill.

ROSINA
I'm really very grateful. Now I'll begin.

COUNT
What's the name of the song?

ROSINA
A new one I've been learning, from "The Scheme That Came to Nothing."

BARTOLO
That's all she keeps repeating, "The Scheme That Came to Nothing"!

ROSINA
That's just the title. The opera is really very clever.

BARTOLO
Let's hear it! I'm listening. Let's hear it!

ROSINA
Here is the song.

COUNT
I thank you. Now let's begin it.

Aria

ROSINA
What can stay the power of love,
Love that is blest by the gods above,
Though the tyrant seems all glorious,
At the last his power shall fail!
Love alone shall be victorious,
Love is mighty and shall prevail!
(*to the* COUNT)
Ah Lindoro, my beloved,
Won't you take me away.
Only you can make me happy,
Darling why must we delay!
Ah, beloved, save me, save me,
Take me away, I pray.

COUNT
Yes, my darling, I will save you,
Oh, I swear that I will save you,
Never fear, I'll find a way.

ROSINA
Do you mean it?

COUNT
Trust in me.

ROSINA
Can it be?

COUNT
I'll set you free.

ROSINA
Ah, what joy to see my beloved,
Ah, what torture that we must be apart!
When I am near you to see you and hear you,
Ah, what gladness fills my heart!

CONTE
Giubilerà.

ROSINA
Cara immagine ridente,
Dolce idea d'un lieto amor,
Tu m'accendi in petto il core,
Tu mi porti a delirar.

Recitative and Arietta

COUNT
How enchanting! Bravissima!

CONTE
Bella voce! Bravissima!

ROSINA
Oh, did you like it?

ROSINA
Oh! mille grazie!

BARTOLO
Yes, yes, you were charming. If you ask my opinion, that song is stupid. Composers knew their business back in the old days. There used to be an aria, it was sung by Caffariello. How well he used to do it . . . la ra la la . . . Just listen, Don Alonso. Here's how it goes . . . "Sweeter than sweet verbena, my neat petite Rosina." (Really it says Giannina, I change it to Rosina.) (*enter* FIGARO, *basin under his arm. He stands behind* BARTOLO *and mimics him*)
Sweeter than sweet verbena,
My neat, petite Rosina!
I never will forget-o
That graceful minuetto!

BARTOLO
Certo, bella voce;
Ma quest'aria, cospetto! è assai noiosa;
La musica a' miei tempi era altra cosa.
Ah! quando per esempio
Cantava Caffariello
Quell'aria portentosa la, ra, la . . .
Sentite, Don Alonso; eccola qua.
Quando mi sei vicina,
Amabile Rosina . . .
L'aria dicea Giannina,
Ma io dico Rosina . . .
Quando mi sei vicina,
amabile Rosina,
Il cor mi brilla in petto,
Mi balla il minuetto.

Recitative

BARTOLO (*seeing* FIGARO)
Bravo, my clever barber. Oh, bravo!

BARTOLO
Bravo, signor barbiere,
Ma bravo!

FIGARO
Oh please excuse me. Pardon, I could not help it.

FIGARO
Eh, niente affatto:
Scusi, son debolezze.

BARTOLO
And now you rascal, what are you here for?

BARTOLO
Ebben, guidone,
Che vieni a fare?

FIGARO
Today, sir, is the time we appointed for me to shave you.

FIGARO
Oh bella!
Vengo a farvi la barba: oggi vi tocca.

BARTOLO
Shave me tomorrow.

BARTOLO
Oggi non voglio.

FIGARO
Suppose I can't? Tomorrow I'm very busy. (*takes out a notebook and looks in it*)

FIGARO
Oggi non vuol? . . . Domani
Non potrò io.

BARTOLO
How so?

BARTOLO
Perchè?

FIGARO
Tomorrow morning the regiment expects me. Their hair will need attention, likewise their whiskers; the Marchesa Andronica has just sent me her wig, and I must dress it; and the young Count Bombé—his hair needs cutting; and then there is the lawyer Bernardone, he's

FIGARO
Perchè ho da fare.
A tutti gli Ufficiali
Del nuovo reggimento barba e testa, . . .
Alla marchesa Andronica
Il biondo perrucchin coi maroné . . .

Al Contino Bombé
Il ciuffo a campanile . . .
Purgante all'avvocato Bernardone
Che ieri s'ammalò d'indigestione . . .
E poi . . . e poi . . . che serve?
Doman non posso.

BARTOLO
Orsù, meno parole.
Oggi non vo' far barba.

FIGARO
No? Cospetto!
Guardate che avventori!
Vengo stamane: in casa v'è l'inferno . . .
Ritorno dopo pranzo: oggi non voglio . . .
Ma che? M'avete preso
Per un qualche barbier da contadini?
Chiamate pur un altro, io me ne vado.

BARTOLO
Che serve? . . . a modo suo;
Vedi che fantasia!
Va in camera a pigliar la biancheria.
No, vado io stesso.

FIGARO
(Ah, se mi dava in mano
Il mazzo delle chiavi, ero a cavallo.)
Dite: non è fra quelle
La chiave che apre quella gelosia?

ROSINA
Sì, certo; è la più nuova.

BARTOLO
(Oh, son pur buono
A lasciar qua quel diavolo di barbiere!)
Animo, va tu stesso
Passato il corridor, sopra l'armadio,
Il tutto troverai.
Bada, non toccar nulla . . .

FIGARO
Oh, non son matto.
(Allegri!) Vado e torno. (Il colpo è fatto.)

BARTOLO
È quel briccon, che al Conte
Ha portato il biglietto di Rosina.

CONTE
Mi sembra un imbroglion di prima sfera.

BARTOLO
Eh, a me non me la ficca . . .
Ah, disgraziato me!

just taken ill and needs some medicine. So then, tomorrow . . . Why bother? I'm much too busy.

BARTOLO
All right, we won't discuss it.

FIGARO
That's the limit! This house will drive me crazy. First, it's this morning. The place is in an uproar. This afternoon you tell me, "Shave me tomorrow." Am I some village barber who must beg for my trade? My time is precious. Go find yourself another! Now, sir, I'll be going.
(*he takes his basin and pretends to start off*)

BARTOLO (*aside*)
These artists! They must be humored. Why should I try to stop him. (*to* FIGARO) The keys are here on this ring. (*gives them to* FIGARO) Bring me a towel . . . No, I don't trust you!
(*he takes back the keys and goes out*)

FIGARO
Just let me get that key ring for just a single moment. Nothing could stop us. (*to* ROSINA) Listen, those keys he's holding . . . now tell me, is the key to your room among them?

ROSINA
Yes, surely. It is the new one.
(BARTOLO *returns*)

BARTOLO
No, it is safer not to leave such a girl with such a rascal. (*to* FIGARO) You shall fetch me the towel. The first door on your left, just as you enter. You'll find what you are seeking. Go now. Don't start exploring.

FIGARO
Me? (*aside*) We've done it! (*to* BARTOLO) Now, sir, I'm going. (*aside*) We've done it! We've done it!

BARTOLO (*to the* COUNT)
That is the scamp who carried the letter of Rosina to the count.

COUNT
He seems to be a master of deception.

BARTOLO
Well, here's one who can outwit him.
(*a crash of breaking crockery offstage*)

Ah, what's he up to now!

ROSINA

What can have happened?

BARTOLO

The clumsy lout! I never should have sent him! (BARTOLO *goes out*)

COUNT (*to* ROSINA)

Figaro is a genius. Now that they've left us, answer me, my darling!

Oh, would you consent to marry a fellow such as I am? I beg you . . .

ROSINA

Ah, my Lindoro, I'll marry no one but you!

COUNT

You will!

(BARTOLO *and* FIGARO *return*)

BARTOLO

Help me, I'm ruined! My china! My lovely goblets! Even the soup bowl!

FIGARO

You're lucky it wasn't worse.

(*he shows the key of the balcony to the* COUNT, *who takes the key off the bunch*)

Forget your dishes! I too could have been hurt had they not warned me. The clatter made me stop myself just in time. What a hallway! So dark I nearly stumbled and dashed my brains out. Why must you close your shutters. Moreover—

BARTOLO

That will do.

(FIGARO *prepares to shave* DR. BARTOLO)

FIGARO

Here we go! Be careful!

BARTOLO

I'm ready. (*he settles himself to be shaved*)

(DON BASILIO *enters*)

Quintet

ROSINA

Don Basilio!

COUNT

Heaven help us!

FIGARO

What a mixup!

BARTOLO

Look who's here!

BASILIO

My respects, I'm your most obedient servant.

BARTOLO

This is looking rather queer.

ROSINA

Ah, che rumore!

BARTOLO

Oh, che briccon! Me lo diceva
il core.

CONTE

Quel Figaro è un grand'uomo.
Or che siam soli,
Ditemi, o cara: il vostro al mio destino
D'unir siete contenta?
Franchezza! . . .

ROSINA

Ah, mio Lindoro,
Altro io non bramo . . .

CONTE

Ebben?

BARTOLO

Tutto m'ha rotto;
Sei piatti, otto bicchieri, una terrina.

FIGARO

Vedete che gran cosa! Ad una chiave
Se io non m'attaccava per fortuna,
Per quel maledettissimo
Corridor così oscuro,
Spezzato mi sarei la testa al muro.
Tiene ogni stanza al buio, e poi . . . e poi . . .

BARTOLO

Oh, non più.

FIGARO

Dunque andiam. Giudizio.

BARTOLO

A noi.

ROSINA

Don Basilio!

CONTE

(Cosa veggo!)

FIGARO

(Quale intoppo!)

BARTOLO

Come qua?

BASILIO

Servitor, servitor di tutti quanti.

BARTOLO

(Che vuol dir tal novità?)

ROSINA
(Di noi che mai sarà?)

CONTE
(Qui franchezza ci vorrà.)

FIGARO
(Qui franchezza ci vorrà.)

BARTOLO
Don Basilio, come state?

BASILIO
Come sto? . . .

FIGARO
Or che s'aspetta?
Que barba benedetta
La facciamo sì o no?
Questa barba la facciamo,
La facciamo sì o no?

BARTOLO
Ora vengo, ora vengo.
E . . . il Curiale?

BASILIO
Il Curiale? . . .

CONTE
Io gli ho narrato
Che già il tutto è combinato.
Non è ver? . . .

BARTOLO
Sì, sì, tutto io so, tutto io.

BASILIO
Ma, Don Bartolo, spiegatevi . . .

CONTE
Ehi, Dottore, una parola.
Don Basilio, son da voi.
Ascoltate un poco qua.
Ascoltate un poco qua.
Fate un po' ch'ei vada via,
Ch'ei ci scopra ho gran timore.

ROSINA
(Io mi sento il cor tremar!)

FIGARO
(Non vi state a disturbar.)

CONTE
(Della lettera, signore, ei
l'affare ancor non sa.)

BASILIO
Ah, qui certo v' è un pasticcio,
Non s'arriva a indovinar.

CONTE
(Ch'ei ci scopra ho gran timore:
ei l'affare ancor non sa.
L'affar non sa, l'affar non sa,
l'affare non sa.)

ROSINA
This queers it all I fear.

COUNT
We must keep the doctor's ear.

FIGARO
There are things he must not hear.

BARTOLO
Don Basilio, how's your fever?

BASILIO (*astonished*)
My fever?

FIGARO (*breaking in on* DON BASILIO, *to* DR. BARTOLO)
I'm apprehensive,
Lest your beard become offensive.
Your appearance is a fright,
For you bristle like a thistle,
And your whiskers are a sight.

BARTOLO
Just a moment, I'll be with you.
(*to* BASILIO) So—what of the lawyer?

BASILIO
What about him?

COUNT (*interrupting, to* BASILIO)
I told the doctor that arrangements were concluded, did I not?

BARTOLO
Yes, yes, so you said, so you said!

BASILIO (*to* DR. BARTOLO)
I'm not sure I understand you, sir.

COUNT
Listen, Doctor, just a moment,
There is something I must tell you,
Don Basilio, just a moment,
(*to* DR. BARTOLO) Let me whisper in your ear.
This is something you should hear.
Chase him out without delay, sir,
He is really in the way, sir.

ROSINA
Now disaster's getting near.

FIGARO
I'll prevent it, never fear.

COUNT (*to* BARTOLO)
Don Basilio does not know about the note I brought you here.

BASILIO
I am drifting in a fog without a notion how to steer.

COUNT
He knows nothing of the letter I delivered to you here,
He does not know about the note I brought you here.

BARTOLO
Be specific, my good fellow, or I'll have to throw you out.
Be specific my good fellow or it's bound to cost you dear,
Yes indeed, 'twill cost you dear.

COUNT (*to* BASILIO)
Don Basilio, what about your raging fever?
What could make you leave your bed with such a fever?

BASILIO (*mystified*)
Such a fever?

COUNT
You have a color like a dead man.
Go to bed, man!

BASILIO
Like a dead man?

FIGARO (*feeling* BASILIO'*s pulse*)
As I told you, getting worse!
Look at him shiver, see him quiver,
See him shiver, see him shaking!
How he's quaking! It's a case of scarlet fever!

BASILIO
Scarlet fever?
(*the* COUNT *gives a purse to* BASILIO)

COUNT, FIGARO
Here is something that will cure it,
That will help you to endure it
When you're fighting the disease.

FIGARO
Go to bed without delay, sir,

COUNT
Let me help you on your way, sir.

ROSINA
Better do just as they say, sir.

BARTOLO
Go to bed, oh, won't you please!

ROSINA, COUNT, FIGARO, BARTOLO
Go to bed, oh won't you please!

BASILIO (*aside*)
This is funny. He gave me money!
Why should everyone agree to such a story?

FIGARO
Go to bed till you recover,

ROSINA, FIGARO
Go to bed until it's over!

ROSINA, COUNT, FIGARO, BARTOLO
Go to bed, oh won't you please!

BASILIO
I am not deaf, nor am I dumb
To good suggestions such as these.

FIGARO
This is serious . . .

BARTOLO
Dite bene, mio signore, or lo mando via di qua,
Dite bene, mio signore, or lo mando via di qua.
Or lo mando via di qua.

CONTE
Colla febbre, Don Basilio,
Chi v'insegna colla febbre a passeggiar? . . .

BASILIO
Colla febbre?

CONTE
E che vi pare?
Siete giallo come un morto.

BASILIO
Come un morto?

FIGARO
Bagattella!
Cospetton! Che tremarella!
Bagatella! bagatella!
Tremarella! tremarella!
Questa è febbre scarlattina! . . .

BASILIO
Scarlattina!

CONTE, FIGARO
Via, prendete medicina,
Via, prendete medicina,
Non vi state a rovinar.

FIGARO
Presto, presto andate a letto . . .

CONTE
Voi paura in ver mi fate . . .

ROSINA
Dice bene, andate a letto.

BARTOLO
Presto andate a riposar.

ROSINA, CONTE, FIGARO, BARTOLO
Presto, andate a riposar.

BASILIO
(Una borsa! . . . Andate a letto! . . .
Ma che tutti sian d'accordo!)

FIGARO
Presto a letto, presto a letto!

ROSINA, FIGARO
Presto a letto, presto a letto!

ROSINA, CONTE, FIGARO, BARTOLO
Presto a letto, presto a letto!

BASILIO
Eh, non son sordo.
Non mi faccio più pregar.

FIGARO
Che color! . . .

CONTE
Che brutta cera! . . .

BASILIO
Brutta cera? . . .

CONTE, FIGARO, BARTOLO
Oh, brutta assai! . . .

BASILIO
Dunque vado.

ROSINA, CONTE, FIGARO, BARTOLO
Vada, vada!

BASILIO
Vado!

CONTE
Buona sera, mio signore.

FIGARO
Buona sera, buona sera.

CONTE
Buona sera, mio signore,
Presto andata via di qua.

FIGARO
Buona sera, mio signore.

CONTE
Buona sera, buona sera.

ROSINA
Buona sera, mio signore,
Buona sera, mio signore,
Presto andate via di qua.

BASILIO
Buona sera, mio signore.

ROSINA, CONTE, FIGARO, BARTOLO
Buona sera, buona sera.

BASILIO
Buona sera, ben di core
Poi doman si parlerà.

ROSINA, FIGARO
Maledetto seccatore!

BASILIO
Non gridate, non gridate.

ROSINA, CONTE, FIGARO, BARTOLO
Vada, vada!
Buona sera, mio signore,
Pace, sonno e sanità
(Maledetto seccatore!)
Presto, andate via di qua.

BASILIO
Buona sera . . . ben di core . . .
Poi doman si parlerà
Non gridate, ho inteso già
Non gridate, per pietà!

COUNT
Maybe delirious . . .

BASILIO
I'm delirious?

COUNT, FIGARO, BARTOLO
He is delirious!

BASILIO
I must leave you.

ROSINA, COUNT, FIGARO, BARTOLO
Leave us, leave us!

BASILIO
Farewell!

COUNT
As we send you on your way, sir . . .

FIGARO
On your way, sir, don't delay sir . . .

COUNT
Health attend you, God befriend you,
Only if you leave us now!

FIGARO
As we send you on your way, sir . . .

COUNT
On your way, sir, don't delay, sir! . . .

ROSINA
As we send you on your way,
Health attend you, God befriend you,
Yes, 'twere best you leave us now.

BASILIO (*delaying and bowing to all*)
Health attend you, God befriend you!

ROSINA, COUNT, FIGARO, BARTOLO
On your way, sir, don't delay, sir!

BASILIO
On my way then, no delay, then,
Fleeting time will not allow . . .

ROSINA, FIGARO
There's a place I'd like to send you . . .

BASILIO
Why so noisy? I can hear you.

ROSINA, COUNT, FIGARO, BARTOLO
Health attend you, heal and mend you,
Soon as nature will allow.
Go to healthy slumber now.
It will cool your fevered brow
If you'll only do it now!

BASILIO
Health attend you, God befriend you,
More our time will not allow.
For I must be leaving now,
Yes I must be leaving now,

Oh, I must be leaving now!
(*exit* BASILIO)

FIGARO
At last, Señor Don Bartolo!
(BARTOLO *sits down*)

BARTOLO
At last! . . . Proceed! (FIGARO *ties a napkin around his neck*)
Tighter . . . You're choking me!
(FIGARO *stands so that he shields the lovers*)

COUNT
Rosina, Rosina dear. Are you listening?

ROSINA
I'm listening! I'm listening. Now let me hear!
(*both sit at the piano and pretend to be studying the music*)

COUNT
We'll come for you at midnight, the very stroke of midnight.
We have the key to free you, you have no need to fear.

FIGARO (*trying to keep* BARTOLO'S *attention*)
Oh me! Oh my!

BARTOLO
What is the trouble?

FIGARO
It is my eye. I think there's something in it. Assist me.
Do not touch it. Just blow it, I think I feel it here.

ROSINA (*to the* COUNT)
I'll wait for you at midnight, yes, on the stroke of midnight.
With all my heart's devotion, I'll wait for you, my dear.

COUNT
When he began to doubt me, I kept my wits about me.
I had to use your letter. It helped me to deceive him.

BARTOLO (*overhearing*)
It helped you to deceive me? Aha!
Let me applaud you, Don Alonso! Splendid! Splendid!
You robbers! You rascals! You devils,
You tried to deceive me,
But you just believe me, you ungrateful devils.
I know you too well!
I'll make you regret it,
You'll never forget it.
If I can arrange it,
I'll see you in hell!

ROSINA, COUNT, FIGARO
Now don't overdo it,
You're sure to regret it!
Oh, don't overdo it
You're sure to regret it,

FIGARO
Orsù, signor Don Bartolo . . .

BARTOLO
Son qua, son qua.
Stringi, bravissimo!

CONTE
Rosina, Rosina, deh, ascoltatemi.

ROSINA
V'ascolto, v'ascolto; eccomi qua

CONTE
A mezzanotte in punto
A prendervi qui siamo:
Or che la chiave abbiamo
Non v'è da dubitar.

FIGARO
Ahi! . . . ahi!

BARTOLO
Che cosa è stato? . . .

FIGARO
Un non sò che nell'occhio!
Guardate . . . non toccate . . .
Soffiate per pietà.

ROSINA
A mezzanotte in punto,
Anima mia, t'aspetto.
Io già l'istante affretto
Che a te mi stringerà.

CONTE
Ora avvertir vi voglio,
Cara, che il vostro foglio,
Perchè non fosse inutile
Il mio travestimento . . .

BARTOLO
Il suo travestimento?
Ma bravi, ma bravissimi,
Ma bravi in verità!
Bricconi, birbanti!
Ah, voi tutti quanti
Avete giurato
Di farmi crepar!
Su, fuori, furfanti,
Vi voglio accoppar.
Di rabbia, di sdegno
Mi sento crepar.

ROSINA, CONTE, FIGARO
L'amico delira,
La testa gli gira.
Ma zitto, Dottore,
Vi fate burlar.
Tacete, tacete,
Non serve gridar.

(Intesi già siamo,
Non vo' replicar.)

BARTOLO
Su fuori, furfanti,
Vi voglio accopar!

ROSINA, CONTE, FIGARO
Tacete, tacete,
Non serve gridar.

BARTOLO
Bricconi! birbanti!
Bricconi! birbanti!
Avete giurato
Di farmi crepar.
Vi voglio, vi voglio,
Vi voglio accoppar.
Di rabbia, di sdegno
Mi sento crepar.
Di rabbia, di sdegno,
Di rabbia, di sdegno,
Di rabbia, di sdegno.
Mi sento crepar,
Mi sento crepar.

ROSINA, CONTE, FIGARO
Tacete, tacete,
Non serve gridar.
L'amico delira,
L'amico delira,
(Intesi già siamo,
Intesi, già siamo.
Non vo'replicar,
Non vo' replicar!)
Ma zitto, Dottore,
Vi fatte burlar.
Vi fatte burlar.
Non serve gridar.
Vi voglio accoppar.
Non vo' replicar.

BARTOLO
Si, accoppar,
Si, accoppar,
Vi voglio accoppar,
Vi voglio accoppar!

BARTOLO
Ah! disgraziato me! ma come? ed io non mi accorsi di nulla! Ah! Don Basilio sa certo qualche cosa. Ehi! chi è di là? Chi è di là? Senti, Ambrogio: corri da Don Basilio qui rimpetto, digli ch'io qua l'aspetto, che venga immantinente, che ho

Your anger will choke you
To death if you let it.
Oh Doctor, relax!

BARTOLO
You plotted and schemed it,
How nicely you planned it.

ROSINA, COUNT, FIGARO
Oh, Doctor, be careful,
Your nerves will not stand it!

BARTOLO
(*to* ROSINA) You vixen! (*to* FIGARO) You bleeder!
(*to the* COUNT) You musical bandit!
I'd cut off your head
Only there is no ax!
I'm out of control,
Oh my body and soul!
I am out of control
And my senses are hazy,
I'm out of control,
Oh my body and soul,
I am out of control,
Can it be that I'm crazy!
I am heading for one
Of my awful attacks!

ROSINA, COUNT, FIGARO
You're heading for one
Of your awful attacks!
This really is serious,
He's really delirious!
The poor man is crazy,
His senses are hazy,
He's heading for one
Of his awful attacks!
Oh, Doctor, Oh Doctor, just relax!
Stop throwing a fit,
'Twon't help you a bit.
Why don't you relax?

BARTOLO
I'll see you dead,
I'll have your head,
I'd cut off your head,
Just give me an ax!
(*all go off except* BARTOLO)

BARTOLO
Ah, what am I to do! He fooled me, he fooled me, and I suspected nothing! Ah! Don Basilio knows more than he has told me. (*noise of people approaching*) Ha! Who's there? Who's there?
(AMBROGIO *and* BERTA *appear*)
Listen, Ambrogio, you must go and bring me Don Basilio. Tell him that I must see him. I have many things to tell

him, many things that will surprise him. I cannot go myself because it is best for me to stay here. Go quickly! (*exit* AMBROGIO) You, Berta, you go and watch the doorway and tell me . . . No, no, I do not trust you. I'll have to go myself. (*exit* BARTOLO)

BERTA

He thinks we mean to trick him. "Watch the doorway. Never mind, I do not trust you." Such suspicion makes us all suspect one another. What bitterness! What wrangling! What confusion! Ah, for just one peaceful moment! He's selfish and unkind and so unforgiving. What a household! What a wretched life to be living!

Here's a man whose years afflict him,
Here's a lady who has tricked him,
Each is equally the victim
Of the very same disease.
How sad! They are both a trifle mad.
When they do such things as these,
It's the very same disease.
They are slowly going mad.
Something seems to drive him foolish,
Just what does it, can you say?
She is obstinate and mulish,
Just how did they get that way?
It is love that makes them do it,
I must know for I've been through it,
All the sighing, all the burning,
All the crying, all the yearning!
I can feel it all returning,
All the burning and the yearning,
I can feel what she is feeling,
For that splendid-looking lad.
He's as nice a looking lad
As a lady ever had.
When a woman's getting older,
All the men are getting colder,
No one ever wants to hold her,
No one wants to drive her mad.
Ah me, no one wants to drive me mad!
Ah me, not a lover to be had,
Not a man to drive me mad,
Not a fellow to be had.
When a woman's getting old,
There's not a fellow to be had.
Life is very, very sad.
When the men are getting cold
And no one wants to drive me mad,
Things are very, very bad.

(*she goes out*)

(*room as in the first act, with barred windows. Enter* BARTOLO, *ushering in* BASILIO)

gran cose da dirgli, e ch'io non vado, perchè, perchè, perchè, perchè ho di gran ragioni. Va subito. Di guardia tu piantati alla porta, e poi no, no (Non me ne fido) Io stesso ci starò.

BERTA

Che vecchio sospettoso! Vada pure
E ci stia finchè crepa . . .
Sempre gridi e tumulti in questa casa;
Si litiga, si piange, si minaccia . . .
Sì non v'è un'ora di pace
Con questo vecchio avaroe brontolone!
Oh, che casa! Oh, che casa in confusione!
Il vecchiotto cerca moglie,
Vuol marito la ragazza;
Quello freme, questa è pazza.
Tutti e due son da legar.
Ma che cosa è quest'amore
Che fa tutti delirar?
Egli è un male universale,
Una smania, un pizzicore . . .
Un solletico, un tormento . . .
Poverina, anch'io lo sento,
Nè sò come finirà.
Oh! vecchiaia maledetta!
Son da tutti disprezzata . . .
E vecchietta disperata.
Mi convien così crepar.

Recitative

BARTOLO
Dunque voi Don Alonso
Non conoscete affatto?

BASILIO
Affatto.

BARTOLO
Ah, certo
Il Conte lo mandò.
Qualche gran tradimento
Qui si prepara.

BASILIO
Io poi
Dico quell'amico
Era il Conte in persona.

BARTOLO
Il Conte? . . .

BASILIO
Il Conte.
(La borsa parla chiaro).

BARTOLO
Sia chi si vuole . . . amico, dal notaro
Vo' in questo punto andare; in questa sera
Stipular di mie nozze io vo' il contratto.

BASILIO
Il notar? . . . siete matto?
Piove a torrenti, e poi
Questa sera il notaro
È impiegato con Figaro; il barbiere
Marita sua nipote.

BARTOLO
Sua nipote?
Che nipote? . . . Il barbiere
Non ha nipoti. Ah, qui v'è qualche imbroglio.
Questa notte i bricconi
Me la vogliono far; presto, il notaro
Qua venga sull'istante.
Ecco la chiave del portone: andate,
Presto, per carità.

BASILIO
Non temete; in due salti io torno qua.

BARTOLO
Per forza o per amore
Rosina avrà da cedere. Cospetto!
Mi vien un'altra idea. Questo biglietto
Che scrisse la ragazza ad Almaviva
Potria servir . . . che colpo da maestro!
Don Alonso, il briccone,
Senza volerlo mi diè l'armi in mano.
Ehi, Rosina, Rosina, avanti, avanti;

BARTOLO
And this man, Don Alonso, you say you do not know him?

BASILIO
Oh no, sir!

BARTOLO
I'm certain he's in the count's employ. They are planning some new way to betray us.

BASILIO
There is something that I should tell you. This Alonso *is* the count!

BARTOLO
You're certain?

BASILIO (*fingering the purse that the* COUNT *gave him*)
I'm certain. He speaks a noble language.

BARTOLO
Now that we know it, go summon me my lawyer and see that he gets here quickly to draw a contract to arrange all the legal matters of my wedding.

BASILIO
Are you mad? It is raining, raining in buckets. Moreover, he's engaged for this evening. An appointment with Figaro, with the barber, his niece is getting married.

BARTOLO
You must be crazy! The barber, devil take him, has no nieces! This smells a trifle fishy. These deceivers are attempting some other nasty trick. Hurry, get the lawyer and do not lose a moment. Here is the key to get back in here, and if you love me, go while there's time.

BASILIO
Don't you worry. I'll be back as soon as I can.
(BASILIO *leaves*)

BARTOLO
By heaven, I'll stand no nonsense. I'll make Rosina marry me. I have it! This will solve my problem! (*he takes from his pocket the letter that the* COUNT *gave to him*) This charming letter, the letter from Rosina to Almaviva! 'Twill do the trick. Oh this is really brilliant! Don Alonso, though a rascal, hands me a weapon that will cause his finish. Hey there, Rosina, Rosina! Come in here! (ROSINA *enters*) Your charming lover seems to be a dirty scoundrel. How can I bear to tell you! It makes me sad when I say that he's trifled with your affections. He counts your love as nothing. Now I will prove it.

This he left with his mistress just to amuse her. (*gives the letter to* ROSINA)

ROSINA

Oh heavens, it is my letter!

BARTOLO

Don Alonso and the barber are hired by Almaviva. You'll be the victim when the count weds another pretty woman. That's how they make their money.

ROSINA

Heaven help me, can I bear it? Oh, Lindoro. What an awakening! You wretch! I'll fix you. I'll show you! You will be sorry you ever saw me. Tell me, my doctor. Do you want me? Do I still attract you?

BARTOLO

I should say so!

ROSINA

All right! We'll do it. Yes, sir, we'll be married. Yes, right this moment! But listen, that man Lindoro will be here at midnight. The barber's coming too. He has decided that we'd run away together.

BARTOLO

Worse than I dreamed of! Now I must lock the doors.

ROSINA

No, Señor Doctor. Watch for them at my window. They have a key.

BARTOLO

Then I'll stay here with you. Wait, they may try to attack us. Dear Rosina, since now I know that you will not betray me, this is my plan. Lock yourself up in your room. I'll call the guard to help us. I'll say that they are burglars. They'll go to prison. Merciful heaven, I think we've really got them! Sweetheart, lock yourself in there. I'll get the soldiers.

ROSINA

Heaven! How shall I bear all my misfortune!
(*they both go off*)
(*a storm has been brewing. Thunder is heard, and flashes of lightning appear. As the storm subsides, the shutters are opened from outside.* FIGARO *and the* COUNT

Del vostro amante io vi vo' dar novella.
Povera sciagurata! In verità
Collocaste assai bene il vostro affetto!
Del vostro amor sappiate
Ch'ei si fa giuoco in sen d'un altra amante.
Ecco la prova.

ROSINA

(Oh cielo! il mio biglietto!)

BARTOLO

Don Alonso e il barbiere
Congiuran contro voi; non vi fidate.
Nelle braccia del Conte d'Almaviva
Vi vogliono condurre.

ROSINA

(In braccio a un altro!
Che mai sento . . . ah, Lindoro! . . . ah, traditore!
Ah sì! . . . vendetta! e vegga,
Vegga quell'empio chi è Rosina). Dite . . .
Signore, di sposarmi
Voi bramavate.

BARTOLO

E il voglio.

ROSINA

Ebben, si faccia!
Io . . . son contenta! . . . ma, all'istante. Udite:
A mezzanotte qui sarà l'indegno
Con Figaro il barbier; con lui fuggire
Per sposarlo io voleva . . .

BARTOLO

Ah, scellerati!
Corro a sbarrar la porta.

ROSINA

Ah mio signore!
Entran per la finestra. Hanno la chiavo.

BARTOLO

Non mi muovo di qui.
Ma . . . e se fossero armati? . . . Figlia mia,
Poichè ti sei sì bene illuminata,
Facciam così. Chiuditi a chiave in camera,
Io vo' a chiamar la forza;
Dirò che son due ladri, e come tali,
Corpo di bacco! l'avremo da vedere!
Figlia, chiuditi presto; io vado via.

ROSINA

Quanto, quanto è crudel la sorte mia!

enter through the window. They are wrapped in cloaks. FIGARO *carries a lantern*)

Recitative and Trio

FIGARO
Alfin, eccoci qua.

CONTE
Figaro, dammi man. Poter del mondo!
Che tempo indiavolato!

FIGARO
Tempo da innamorati.

CONTE
Ehi, fammi lume.
Dove sarà Rosina?

FIGARO
Ora vedremo . . .
Eccola appunto.

CONTE
Ah, mio tesoro!

ROSINA
Indietro,
Anima scellerata; io qui di mia
Stolta credulità venni soltanto
A riparar lo scorno, a dimostrarti
Qual sono, e quale amante
Perdesti, anima indegna e sconoscente!

CONTE
Io son di sasso!

FIGARO
Io non capisco niente.

CONTE
Ma per pietà . . .

ROSINA
Taci. Fingesti amore
Per vendermi alle voglie
Di quel tuo vil Conte Almaviva . . .

CONTE
Al Conte! Ah sei delusa! O me felice!
Adunque tu di verace amore ami Lindoro? rispondi!

ROSINA
Ah sì! T'amai pur troppo!

CONTE
Ah! non è tempo di più celarsi, anima mia: ravvisa colui che si gran tempo seguì tue traccie, che per te sospira, che sua ti vuole; mirami, o mio tesoro, Almaviva son io, non son Lindoro!

ROSINA
(Ah! qual colpo inaspettato!

FIGARO
It's midnight and here we are.

COUNT
Figaro, lend a hand. Angels protect us! A lovely night for murder!

FIGARO
Also a night for lovers!

COUNT
Hey, light your lantern. Where is my sweet Rosina?
(FIGARO *strikes a light and looks around*)

FIGARO
We soon shall see her. (ROSINA *appears*) What did I tell you?

COUNT
My dearest angel!

ROSINA
Get back there, you treacherous deceiver! Because of my simple and trusting heart I thought you loved me. My heart is disillusioned. I hope to make you regret it. You will find out what you're losing. Oh, what a scoundrel! Oh, what a pity!

COUNT
This leaves me speechless!

FIGARO
I do not understand it.

COUNT
Give me a chance . . .

ROSINA
Silence! Oh what a villain! You thought you could abduct me to sell to that devil Almaviva!

COUNT
So, that's it? Ah, how you wrong me! Look in my eyes, Rosina. What of this poor Lindoro? Tell me the truth. Do you love him?

ROSINA
Oh yes! I love him dearly.

COUNT (*aside*)
Ah, why deceive her? This is the moment I've long awaited.
(*to* ROSINA) Rosina, this lover who adores you, this ardent swain who loves the ground you walk on, kneels here before you. Look in my eyes, beloved. Though you call me Lindoro, I'm Almaviva!
(*he throws off his cloak and appears in his proper dress as Count Almaviva*)

ROSINA (*aside*)
Could I ever have imagined such a moment!

Now my darkness is turned to daylight,
Life is glowing with a gladsome gay light,
All creation has smiled at me.

FIGARO (*aside*)
Now the lovers are enchanted
For their prayers have all been granted,
They are getting what they wanted
Since they put their trust in me.

COUNT
I could never have imagined such a moment,
For my darkness is turned to daylight,
Love is glowing with a gladsome gay light,
All creation has smiled at me!

FIGARO
Now the lovers are enchanted,
So enchanted,
All their darkness and their sorrow
Turned to daylight!
Did you ever see a fellow
Quite as clever?
No, you never, never saw a man like me!

ROSINA
Oh my lord, sir. Shall I—your lordship—

COUNT
Oh my dear, what a solemn name to call me.
Call me "dearest," "best beloved."
After all you are my bride.

ROSINA
Ah my dearest, my beloved,
Let me keep you at my side!

COUNT
Are you happy?

ROSINA
Oh yes, beloved, Ah, best beloved,
I am happy!

FIGARO
Happy!

ROSINA
As flowers in sunlight!
Ah, so happy!

FIGARO
Oh, hurry!

ROSINA
My heart is singing!

COUNT
I am happy!

FIGARO
Happy! Now then let's hurry!

COUNT
As flowers in sunlight,
Ah so happy my heart must sing.

Egli stesso? o ciel, che sento!
Di sorpresa e di contento
Son vicina a delirar.)

FIGARO
(Son rimasti senza fiato:
Ora muoion di contento.
Guarda, guarda il mio talento
Che bel colpo seppe far!)

CONTE
(Qual trionfo inaspettato!
Me felice! oh bel momento!
Ah! d'amore e di contento
Son vicino a delirar.)

FIGARO
(Son rimasti senza fiato,
senza fiato:
Ora muoion di contento,
Di contento.
Guarda, guarda, guarda, guarda
il mio talento,
Che bel colpo, che bel colpo
seppe far!)

ROSINA
Mio signor! . . . ma voi . . .
ma io . . .

CONTE
Ah, non più, non più, ben mio.
Il bel nome di mia sposa,
Idol mio, t'attende già.

ROSINA
Il bel nome di tua sposa,
Oh, qual gioia al cor mi dà!

CONTE
Sei contenta!

ROSINA
Ah! mio signore! Dolce nodo!

FIGARO
Nodo.

ROSINA
Avventurato,
Che fai paghi.

FIGARO
Andiamo!

ROSINA
I miei desiri!

CONTE
Dolce nodo.

FIGARO
Nodo. Presto, andiamo!

CONTE
Avventurato,
Che fai paghi i miei desir!

FIGARO
(Paghi!) Vi sbrigate!

ROSINA
Alla fin de' miei martiri
Tu sentisti, amor, pietà.

CONTE
Alla fi de' miei martiri
Tu sentisti, amor, pietà.

FIGARO
Presto andiamo, vi sbrigate;
Via, lasciate quei sospiri.
Presto, andiam, per carità!
Se si tarda, i miei raggiri
Fanno fiasco in verità.
Ah! cospetto! che ho veduto
Alla porta una lanterna . . .
Due persone . . . che si fa?

CONTE
Hai veduto.

FIGARO
Sì, signor.

CONTE
Due persone?

FIGARO
Sì, signor.

CONTE
Una lanterna?

FIGARO
Alla porta, alla porta, sì, signor.

ROSINA, CONTE, FIGARO
Che si fa? che si fa?
Zitti, zitti piano, piano,
Non facciamo confusione;
Per la scala del balcone
Presto andiamo via di qua.

FIGARO
Ah, disgraziati noi! come si fa?

CONTE
Che avvenne mai? . . .

FIGARO
La scala . . .

CONTE
Ebben?

FIGARO
La scala non v'è più.

CONTE
Che dici?

FIGARO
Happy! Let's be starting!

ROSINA
Flinging all my care and sorrow
To the shadows of the past.

COUNT
All our care and sorrow flinging
To the shadows of the past!

FIGARO
Come along and let's get started if you hope to get away!
Ah, I knew it! Now it's happened, I knew it. I can see it.
At the doorway there is a lantern. At the doorway, I see a lantern!
There's a fellow with a lantern. There's another. There are two!

COUNT
Someone's coming!

FIGARO
There are two!

COUNT
They will catch us!

FIGARO
Very true!

COUNT
They have a lantern . . .

FIGARO
Can you offer a suggestion what to do?

ROSINA, COUNT, FIGARO
What to do? What to do!
There's a ladder at the window,
We will leave them here behind us,
Not a sound or they will find us,
Let's escape without delay.
By the ladder at the window
Let us fly while yet we may.
Softly, softly! Careful! Quiet!
Fly away, while we may!
(*they are about to go*)

Recitative

FIGARO
Ah, but we spoke too soon. What shall we do?

COUNT
What is the trouble?

FIGARO
The ladder—

COUNT
Go on!

FIGARO
The ladder is not there!

COUNT
You're joking!

FIGARO
Now who could have removed it?

COUNT
Our elopement is off.

ROSINA
I might have known it!

FIGARO
Be quiet! Someone's coming. Will someone give me some suggestion what to do?

COUNT
My dear Rosina. Don't worry! (*he wraps himself in his cloak*)

FIGARO
Oh, here they come.
(*they withdraw to the side; enter* DON BASILIO *with a notary*)

BASILIO (*softly*)
Don Bartolo, Don Bartolo!

FIGARO (*softly*)
It's Basilio!

COUNT (*softly*)
Who's the other?

FIGARO
Well, well, it's my own lawyer! All will be well! Just leave it all to me. Ah, Mr. Lawyer, you remember the contract that we spoke of this evening? Your agreement to marry my niece to Almaviva without delay? They're waiting, ready to sign. I hope you've got it in your pocket. That's wonderful! (*the notary takes a document from his pocket*)

BASILIO
One moment. Is Bartolo around?

COUNT
Hey, Don Basilio. (*he takes* BASILIO *aside, bids him be silent, and gives him a ring that he takes from his finger*) Here is something to persuade you!

BASILIO
But listen . . .

COUNT
You take it, you take that ring or else I'll have to shoot you right in the head!

BASILIO
Oh lord, I s'pose I'll have to. (*he takes the ring*) Who signs it?

COUNT (*signing*)
We that are here. You two shall witness, Figaro and Don Basilio.

FIGARO
Chi mai l'avrà levata? . . .

CONTE
Quale inciampo crudel! . . .

ROSINA
Me sventurata!

FIGARO
Zi . . . zitti . . . sento gente.
Ora ci siamo.
Signor mio, che si fa?

CONTE
Mia Rosina, coraggio.

FIGARO
Eccoli qua.

BASILIO
Don Bartolo! Don Bartolo! . . .

FIGARO
Don Basilio.

CONTE
E quell'altro?

FIGARO
Ve', ve' il nostro notaro.
Allegramente.
Lasciate fare a me. Signor notaro:
Dovevate in mia casa
Stipular questa sera
Un contratto di nozze
Fra il conte Almaviva e mia nipote.
Gli sposi eccoli qua. Avete indosso
La scrittura?
Benissimo!

BASILIO
Ma piano.
Don Bartolo . . . dov'è? . . .

CONTE
Ehi, Don Basilio,
Questo anello è per voi.

BASILIO
Ma io . . .

CONTE
Per voi
Vi sono ancor due palle nel cervello
Se v'opponete.

BASILIO
Oibò, prendo l'anello.
Chi firma? . . .

CONTE
Eccoci qua.
Son testimoni
Figaro e Don Basilio.

Essa è mia sposa.

FIGARO
Evviva!

CONTE
Oh, mio contento!

ROSINA
Oh, sospirata mia felicità!

TUTTI
Evviva!

BARTOLO
Fermi tutti. Eccoli qua.

FIGARO
Colle buone, signor.

BARTOLO
Signor, son ladri;
Arrestate, arrestate!

UFFICIALE
Mio signore,
il suo nome?

CONTE
Il mio nome? È quel d' un uomo d'onere;
Lo sposo io son di questa—

BARTOLO
Eh, andate al diavolo!
Rosina esser deve mia, non è vero?

ROSINA
Io sua sposa?
Oh nemmeno per pensiero.

BARTOLO
Come, come, fraschetta!
Arrestate, vi dico:
E un ladro!

FIGARO
Or, or l' accoppo.

BARTOLO
È un birbante, è un briccone.

UFFICIALE
Signore?

CONTE
Indietro!

UFFICIALE
Il nome—

CONTE
Indietro, dico; indietro!

UFFICIALE
Ehi, mio signor, basso quel tuono;—
E chi è lei?

CONTE
Il Conte d' Almaviva io sono.

I take this woman . . . (ROSINA *and the* COUNT *are married*)

FIGARO
We've done it!

COUNT
Now I am happy!

ROSINA
Ah, what a blessed answer to all my prayers!

ALL
We've done it!
(*the* COUNT *kisses* ROSINA's *hand and* FIGARO *comically hugs* BASILIO. DON BARTOLO *enters with an officer and some soldiers*)

BARTOLO
Just a moment! These are the men!

FIGARO
At your service, my friend!

BARTOLO
These two are burglars. Now arrest them, they deserve it!

OFFICER
First, you tell me, what's your name?

COUNT
It's a good one, a name of virtue and honor. This lady is my wife.

BARTOLO
The devil take you, sir! Rosina has agreed to be *my* wife. You just ask her.

ROSINA
Me, your wife? I'm afraid you must be crazy!

BARTOLO
Crazy? Dare you deny it? (*points to the* COUNT) Now you've got to arrest him. He's a robber!

FIGARO
Now just a moment!

BARTOLO
He's a bandit. He's a thief!

OFFICER (*to the* COUNT)
Come on, you!

COUNT
How dare you!

OFFICER
Then tell me . . .

COUNT
Don't be familiar! Get back there!

OFFICER
That tone of voice is disrespectful. Who are you?

COUNT (*throwing aside his cloak*)
The Count of Almaviva in person!

Recitative and Finale 2

BARTOLO
It's my fault, really, that they are married.

FIGARO
Yes, you're right, sir, you're to blame.

BARTOLO (*to* BASILIO)
And you betrayed me! You signed the contract that made them man and wife.

BASILIO
Oh, my friend, forgive me. Count Almaviva has such persuasive reasons. Who could resist them! He took them from his pocket.

BARTOLO
And I moved the ladder, and so they were married here in my house. My plan was not a very good one!

FIGARO
Why don't you call it "The Scheme That Came to Nothing"?

BARTOLO
What of her dowry? I'm not wealthy . . .

COUNT
Forget it! Forget it! Keep it all for yourself. I do not need it.

FIGARO (*to* BARTOLO)
Aha! That makes you smile! Bravissimo, Don Bartolo! Since you don't have to pay, you are contented. Now your ferocious face is quite serene. Thus, in a world such as this, the wicked always prosper.

ROSINA
So then, Señor Don Bartolo?

BARTOLO
Ah yes, you expect my blessing.

COUNT
Why not, dear Doctor?

BARTOLO
Ah yes, why not? What is done is done. Go on your way! May Heaven bless you always!

FIGARO
Bravo, bravo, noble Doctor! Come to my arms; embrace me!

ROSINA
Now to be happy!

COUNT
Now to be happy, Rosina!

FIGARO
Goodnight, my faithful lantern,
To darkness now returning!
The light of love is burning,
To shine forevermore!

BERTA, BARTOLO, BASILIO, CHORUS
May love and joy attend you.

BARTOLO
Insomma, io ho tutti i torti.

FIGARO
Pur troppo è così.

BARTOLO
Ma tu briccone—
Tu pur tradirmi, e far da testimonio!

BASILIO
Ah Dottore Bartolo mio,
Quei Signor Conte certe ragioni
Ha in tasca; certi argomentri
A cui non si risponde.

BARTOLO
Ed io bestia solenne, per meglio assicurare il matrimonio,
Portai via la scala dal balcone.

FIGARO
Ecco che fa un'*Inutil Precauzione.*

BARTOLO
Ma e la dote? io non posso.

CONTE
Eh via; di dote io bisogno non ho: te la dono.

FIGARO
Ah! ah! ridete adesso? Bravissimo, Don Bartolo, ho veduto
alla fin rasserenarsi quel vostro ceffo amaro e furibondo.
Eh! i bricconi han fortuna in questo mondo.

ROSINA
Dunque, signor Don Bartolo?

BARTOLO
Sì, sì, ho capito tutto.

CONTE
Ebben, Dottore?

BARTOLO
Sì, sì, che servo? quel ch'è fatto è fatto. Andate pur,
che il ciel vi benedica!

FIGARO
Bravo, bravo, un abbraccio, venite qua, Dottore.

ROSINA
Ah noi felici!

CONTE
Oh, fortunato amore!

FIGARO
Di sì felice innesto,
Serbiam memoria eterna,
Io smorzo la lanterna,
Qui più non ha che far!

BERTA, BARTOLO, BASILIO, CORO
Amore e fede eterna,
Si vegga in voi regnar.

Amore e fede eterna
Si vegga in voi regnar.

May sorrow pass your door,
May smiling heaven send you
Bright skies forevermore!

ROSINA
Costò sospiri e pene,
Un sì felice istante,
Alfin quest' alma amante
Comincia a respirar!

ROSINA
And so my woes are over,
My joyful days have started.
I'm free and happy-hearted
Today and ever more!

CONTE
Dell' umile Lindoro,
La flamma a te fu accetta
Più bel destin t'aspetta—
Su, vieni a giubilar!

COUNT
You loved me as Lindoro
With no thought of hesitating;
And now a nobler name is waiting
For you whom I adore!

TUTTI
Amore e fede eterna,
Si vegga in voi regnar!
Amore e fede eterna
Si vegga in voi regnar.

ROSINA, COUNT, *and the* OTHERS
May love and joy attend us,
May sorrow pass our door.
May smiling heaven send us
Bright skies forevermore!

LA BOHÈME

by Giacomo Puccini (1858–1924)

LIBRETTO BY GIUSEPPE GIACOSA AND LUIGI ILLICA

Translated by RUTH and THOMAS MARTIN.

Based on Henri Murger's novel *Scènes de la Vie de Bohème.*

CHARACTERS

MARCELLO, *a painter*	*Baritone*
RODOLFO, *a poet*	*Tenor*
COLLINE, *a philosopher*	*Bass*
SCHAUNARD, *a musician*	*Baritone*
BENOIT, *a landlord*	*Bass*
MIMI, *a seamstress*	*Soprano*
PARPIGNOL, *a vendor of toys*	*Tenor*
MUSETTA, *a girl of the Latin Quarter*	*Soprano*
ALCINDORO, *an admirer of Musetta*	*Bass*
CUSTOMS GUARD	*Bass*

HABITUÉS OF THE LATIN QUARTER, MERCHANTS, SHOPGIRLS, STUDENTS, VENDORS, SOLDIERS, WAITERS

Place: Latin Quarter of Paris
Time: About 1830
First performance: Teatro Reggio, Turin, February 1, 1896

COPYRIGHT, 1958, BY G. SCHIRMER, INC. BY PERMISSION OF G. RICORDI & CO.

ACT I

A garret. A large window, with a view of an expanse of snow-covered roofs. A stove, left. A table, a cupboard, a small bookcase, four chairs, an easel, a bed; some books, many bundles of paper, two candlesticks. Center, a door; left another.

Curtain rises quickly. RODOLFO *and* MARCELLO *on-stage.* RODOLFO *looks thoughtfully out the window.* MARCELLO *works on his painting,* The Passage of the Red Sea, *though his hands are numb with cold. He warms his hands now and then by blowing on them, and often changes his position because of the cold.*

MARCELLO (*continuing to paint*)
Whatever made me paint this old Red Sea today!
Even the sight of so much water chills me!
(*stands back from the easel to look at his painting*)
But in revenge a Pharoah has to drown!
(*turns to his work; to* RODOLFO)
Rodolfo!

MARCELLO
Questo Mar Rosso—mi ammollisce e assidera
come se addosso—mi piovesse in stille.
Per vendicarmi, affogo un Faraone.
Che fai?

RODOLFO (*turning slightly*)
I am admiring millions of chimneys smoking
On all the roofs of Paris,
(*pointing to the fireless stove*)
And thinking how that stove there,
That lazy, good-for-nothing piece of hardware,
Won't do a single thing to earn his board!

RODOLFO
Nei cieli bigi
guardo fumar dai mille comignoli Parigi,
e penso a quel poltrone
d'un vecchio caminetto ingannatore
che vive in ozio come un gran signor!

MARCELLO
Well, it must have been ages
Since last we paid his wages!

MARCELLO
Le sue rendite oneste
da un pezzo non riceve.

RODOLFO
And as much as we need him,
We're not able to feed him.

RODOLFO
Quelle sciocche foreste
che fan sotto la neve?

MARCELLO
Rodolfo I must make you
A most sincere confession: (*blowing on his fingers*)
It's freezing cold here.

MARCELLO
Rodolfo, io voglio dirti un mio pensier profondo:
ho un freddo cane.

RODOLFO (*approaching* MARCELLO)
And I will grant you this concession,
That I am not exactly perspiring.

RODOLFO
Ed io, Marcel, non ti nascondo
che non credo al sudor della fronte.

MARCELLO
All my fingers are frozen,
Just as cold and devoid of all feeling
As that enormous iceberg,
The heart of Musetta!
(*heaves a long sigh, and stops painting; puts down his palette and brushes*)

MARCELLO
Ho diacciate
le dita quasi ancora le tenessi immollate
giù in quella gran ghiacciaia
che è il cuore di Musetta.

RODOLFO
Yes, love is like a stove that is burning fiercely.

RODOLFO
L'amor è un caminetto che sciupa troppo . . .

MARCELLO
. . . and quickly!

MARCELLO
e in fretta!

RODOLFO dove l'uomo è fascina.	RODOLFO Where the man is the tinder
MARCELLO e la donna è l'alare . . .	MARCELLO Which the woman ignited . . .
RODOLFO l'uno brucia in un soffio . . .	RODOLFO While he burns to a cinder . . .
MARCELLO e l' altro sta a guardare.	MARCELLO She never gets excited.
RODOLFO Ma intanto qui si gela . . .	RODOLFO But meanwhile we are freezing . . .
MARCELLO e si muore d'inedia! . . .	MARCELLO Almost dead of starvation!
RODOLFO Fuoco ci vuole . . .	RODOLFO We need a fire . . .
MARCELLO Aspetta . . . sacrifichiam la sedia!	MARCELLO All right, then, this chair will be our salvation! *(grasping a chair, as if to break it up)*
RODOLFO *Eureka!*	RODOLFO *(energetically resists* MARCELLO*'s plan)* Eureka! *(joyous at an idea that has struck him)*
MARCELLO Trovasti?	MARCELLO You found it?
RODOLFO Sì. Aguzza l'ingegno. L'idea vampi in fiamma.	RODOLFO Yes! *(runs to the table and takes a bulky manuscript from below)* My genius is burning, aflame with inspiration!
MARCELLO Bruciamo il Mar Rosso?	MARCELLO *(pointing to his painting)* To burn my new painting?
RODOLFO No. Puzza la tela dipinta. Il mio dramma, l' ardente mio dramma ci scaldi.	RODOLFO No, who could endure the aroma! But my drama, Its passionate ardor will warm us both!
MARCELLO Vuoi leggerlo forse? Mi geli.	MARCELLO *(with comic terror)* You don't mean to read it? How awful!
RODOLFO No, in cener la carta si sfaldi e l' estro rivoli ai suoi cieli. Al secol gran danno minaccia . . . Ea Roma è in periglio . . .	RODOLFO No, the paper will crumble to ashes, The Muse will return to Olympus, *(importantly)* A masterpiece goes to perdition! The loss is prodigious!
MARCELLO Gran cor!	MARCELLO *(exaggeratedly)* How true!
RODOLFO A te l' atto primo.	RODOLFO *(gives* MARCELLO *part of the manuscript)* Begin with the first act.
MARCELLO Qua.	MARCELLO Right!
RODOLFO Straccia.	RODOLFO Tear it!
MARCELLO Accendi.	MARCELLO You light it.

(RODOLFO *lights a candle, and goes to the stove with* MARCELLO; *together they set fire to a part of the manuscript thrown into the grate, then both draw up their chairs and sit down, warming themselves with exquisite delight*)

RODOLFO
How cozy and bright.

MARCELLO
A heart-warming sight!
(*the door at the back is flung open noisily, and* COLLINE *enters, stiff and numb with cold, stamping his feet; angrily throws on the table a bundle of books tied with a handkerchief*)

COLLINE
Could it be that Judgment Day is dawning!
On Christmas Eve the broker shops won't do any pawning!
(*stops in surprise on seeing the fire in the stove*)
I must be dreaming!

RODOLFO (*to* COLLINE)
Quiet! There goes my drama.

COLLINE
To blazes.
It seems to be enlightening!

RODOLFO
Brilliant!
(*the fire dies down*)

COLLINE
And very short.

RODOLFO
Brevity is an asset.

COLLINE (*takes the chair from* RODOLFO)
I have your kind permission!

MARCELLO
I cannot stand a boring intermission! Hurry!

RODOLFO (*takes another part of the manuscript*)
Here is the second act!

MARCELLO
Don't breathe a whisper!
(RODOLFO *tears up the manuscript and throws it into the stove; the fire revives.* COLLINE *moves his chair closer and warms his hands;* RODOLFO *stands near the two with the rest of the manuscript*)

COLLINE
What words of wisdom!

MARCELLO
Right to the point!

RODOLFO
Amid these bluish flickering flames
A passionate love scene goes up in smoke!

RODOLFO
Che lieto baglior.

MARCELLO
Che lieto baglior.

COLLINE
Già dell' Apocalisse appariscono i segni.
In giorno di Vigilia non si accettano pegni! . . .
Una fiammata!

RODOLFO
Zitto, si dà il mio dramma . . .

COLLINE
. . . al fuoco.
Lo trovo scintillante.

RODOLFO
Vivo.

COLLINE
Ma dura poco.

RODOLFO
La brevità, gran pregio.

COLLINE
Autore, a me la sedia.

MARCELLO
Quest' intermezzi fan morir d'inedia. Presto.

RODOLFO
Atto secondo.

MARCELLO
Non far susurro.

COLLINE
Pensier profondo!

MARCELLO
Giusto color!

RODOLFO
In quell' azzurro—guizzo languente
sfuma un' ardente scena d'amor.

COLLINE
Scoppietta un foglio.

MARCELLO
Là c' eran baci!

RODOLFO
Tre atti or voglio d' un colpo
udir.

COLLINE
Tal degli audaci l' idea
s'integra.

TUTTI
Bello in allegra vampa svanir.

MARCELLO
Oh! Dio . . . già s'abbassa la
fiamma.

COLLINE
Che vano, che fragile dramma!

MARCELLO
Già scricchiola, increspasi,
muor.

MARCELLO, COLLINE
Abbasso, abbasso l' autor.

RODOLFO
Legna!

MARCELLO
Bordò!

COLLINE
Sigari!

RODOLFO
Legna!

MARCELLO
Sigari!

TUTTI
Le dovizie d' una fiera
il destin ci destinò.

SCHAUNARD
La Banca di Francia
per voi si sbilancia.

COLLINE
Raccatta, raccatta!

MARCELLO
Son pezzi di latta! . . .

SCHAUNARD
Sei sordo? . . . Sei lippo?
Quest' uomo chi è?

COLLINE
It pops and crackles!

MARCELLO
There! Those were kisses!

RODOLFO (*throws the rest of the manuscript into the fire*)
Acts three to five at a single stroke!

COLLINE
Thus is a poet's dream accomplished.

ALL THREE
Nothing so gay as death on the pyre!
(*they applaud enthusiastically. The fire dies down*)

MARCELLO
Already the drama is ending.

COLLINE
It's finished, there's no use pretending!

MARCELLO
It shrivels and crumbles away!
(*the fire goes out*)

MARCELLO and COLLINE
Fiasco! Fiasco! Down the play!
(*from the center door two boys enter, one carrying food, bottles of wine, and cigars, the other a fagot of wood. At the noise the three at the stove turn around and, with a cry of wonder, fall upon the food brought by the boys and put it on the table.* COLLINE *takes the wood and carries it near the stove. Darkness begins to fall*)

RODOLFO
Firewood!

MARCELLO
Burgundy!

COLLINE
Cigars!

RODOLFO
Firewood!

MARCELLO
Cigars!

ALL THREE (*enthusiastically*)
Well, it looks as if we'll celebrate this Christmas after all!

SCHAUNARD (*enters with an air of triumph*)
I herewith provide us
With all the gold of Midas!
(*throws some coins on the floor. The two boys leave*)

COLLINE
We're rolling in money!

MARCELLO (*picking up the coins, incredulously*)
You're not very funny!

SCHAUNARD (*showing* MARCELLO *a coin, shouting*)
You stupid! Look closer!
You notice this face?

RODOLFO (*bowing*)
We bow to His Majesty's bountiful grace.

ALL FOUR
Why, King Louis Philippe in our lowly place!
(*they place the coins on the table*)

SCHAUNARD (*continues to recount his good luck, but the others do not listen to him; they continue busying themselves with placing the things on the table*)
Now you must hear,
This gold here, or better silver . . .
Has quite a striking story.

MARCELLO (*putting wood in the stove*)
I must tend to my stoking!

COLLINE
Get the poor fellow smoking!

SCHAUNARD
Seems a rich English peer,
Lord, or Milord or something,
Required a musician . . .

MARCELLO (*pushing* COLLINE'S *books off the table, shouting*)
Off! Let's prepare the festivities!

SCHAUNARD
I fly there.

RODOLFO
Where is the flint?

COLLINE
There!

MARCELLO
Here!
(*they build up a great fire in the stove*)

SCHAUNARD
I make my entrance,
I ask him, "How about it . . . ?"
(*they arrange the food on the table, while* RODOLFO *lights the other candle*)

MARCELLO
Delicious pastry!

COLLINE
Excellent roast beef!

SCHAUNARD
"When shall we start the lessons?"
I make my entrance,
I ask him, "How about it,
When shall we start the lessons?"
He answers,
(*imitating an English accent in the words in italics*)
"*Right away!*"
"*Look here,*" says he, and points to a parrot in a cage;
Then he added, "*Just keep right on playing*
Till he expires!"

RODOLFO
Luigi Filippo!
M' inchino al mio Re!

TUTTI
Sta Luigi Filippo ai nostri piè!

SCHAUNARD
Or vi dirò: quest' oro, o meglio, argento
ha la sua brava storia . . .

MARCELLO
Riscaldiamo
il camino!

COLLINE
Tanto freddo ha sofferto!

SCHAUNARD
Un inglese . . . un signor . . . lord o milord
che sia, cercava un musicista . . .

MARCELLO
Via!
Prepariamo la tavola!

SCHAUNARD
Io? volo!

RODOLFO
L' esca dov' è?

COLLINE
Là.

MARCELLO
Qua.

SCHAUNARD
E mi presento.
M'accetta, gli domando.

MARCELLO
Pasticcio dolce!

COLLINE
Arrosto freddo!

SCHAUNARD
A quando le lezioni? . . .
Mi presento
M'accetta e gli domando:
A quando le lezioni?
Risponde: "Incominciamo!"
"Guardare!" (e un pappagallo m'addita al primo pian),
poi soggiunge: "Voi suonare finchè quello morire!" E fu così:
Suonai tre lunghi dì . . .

RODOLFO
Fulgida folgori la sala splendida.

MARCELLO
Or le candele!

COLLINE
Pasticcio dolce!

SCHAUNARD
Allora usai l'incanto
di mia presenza bella,
di mia presenza bella . . .
Affascinai l'ancella . . .

MARCELLO
Mangiar senza tovaglia?

RODOLFO
Un' idea! . . .

MARCELLO, COLLINE
Il Costituzional!

RODOLFO
Ottima carta . . .
Si mangia e si divora un' appendice!

SCHAUNARD
Gli propinai prezzemolo . . .
Lorito allargò l'ali,
Lorito allargò l'ali,
Lorito il becco aprì,
Un poco di prezzemolo,
Da Socrate morì!

COLLINE
Chi?!

SCHAUNARD
Che il diavolo vi porti tutti quanti!
Ed or che fate?
No! Queste cibarie
sono la salmeria
pei dì futuri
tenebrosi e oscuri.
Pranzare in casa il dì della Vigilia.
Mentre il Quartier Latino le sue vie
addobba di salsiccie e leccornie?
Quando un olezzo di frittelle imbalsama
le vecchie strade?
Là le ragazze cantano contente . . .

And so it was; I played for three whole days.

RODOLFO
Let's have a festival illumination!

MARCELLO (*places two lighted candles on the table*)
Here are the candles!

COLLINE
Delicate pastry!

SCHAUNARD
But then I started to flirt
With the parlor Cinderella,
The parlor Cinderella.
Sub rosa, a capella . . .

MARCELLO
A bare table to eat on?

RODOLFO (*taking a newspaper out of his pocket and unfolding it*)
Here you are!

MARCELLO, COLLINE
The Paris Evening Star!

RODOLFO
What could be better!
You eat as you digest the latest gossip!

SCHAUNARD
I treat the bird to arsenic.
(*they spread the newspaper like a tablecloth.* RODOLFO *and* MARCELLO *bring the four chairs to the table while* COLLINE *continues to busy himself with the food*)
My polly spreads his pinions,
My polly spreads his pinions,
His beak he opened wide.
A little pinch of arsenic—
Like Socrates, he died!
(*seeing that nobody pays attention, grasps* COLLINE *as he passes with a plate*)

COLLINE
Who?

SCHAUNARD (*irritably*)
I hope the devil takes you altogether!
(*seeing the others get ready to eat the cold pie*)
What are you doing? No! (*shouted*)
All these provisions
We'll put inside our larder,
(*extends his hand with a solemn gesture over the pie and prevents his friends from eating it, then he lifts the food from the table and puts it in the small cupboard*)
They will be welcome
When the times are harder.
On Christmas Eve we cannot linger indoors,
While all the markets of the Latin Quarter

Are filled with food that makes your palate water!
When the aroma of baked apples
Deliciously pervades the alleys!
(RODOLFO, MARCELLO, *and* COLLINE *encircle* SCHAUNARD, *laughing*)
Where all the young girls merrily are singing

RODOLFO, MARCELLO, COLLINE
Christmas carols through the night!

RODOLFO, MARCELLO, COLLINE
La vigilia di Natal!

SCHAUNARD
Each has a student following her footsteps!
(*solemnly*)
No more of this blaspheming,
My friends, I beg you.
We're drinking indoors,
But we're dining out!
(RODOLFO *locks the door, then all return to the table and pour the wine. Two knocks are heard at the door*)

SCHAUNARD
Ed han per eco ognuna uno studente!
Un po' di religione, o miei signori:
Si beva in casa, ma si pranzi fuor!

BENOIT
Permit me?
(*All stop in amazement*)

BENOIT
Si può?

MARCELLO
Who is there?

MARCELLO
Chi è là?

BENOIT
Benoit!

BENOIT
Benoit.

MARCELLO
Oh good heavens, the landlord!
(*they put down their glasses*)

MARCELLO
Il padrone di casa!

SCHAUNARD
Lock the door quickly!

SCHAUNARD
Uscio sul muso.

COLLINE (*calling toward the door*)
Nobody's home!

COLLINE
Non c' è nessuno.

SCHAUNARD
It's bolted!

SCHAUNARD
È chiuso.

BENOIT (*back-stage*)
One word only!

BENOIT
Una parola.

SCHAUNARD (*after consulting his friends, goes to open the door*)
One!

SCHAUNARD
Sola!

BENOIT (*enters, smiling, and shows a paper to* MARCELLO)
Rent!

BENOIT
Affitto!

MARCELLO (*receiving him with great cordiality*)
Hello! Won't you sit down, sir?

MARCELLO
Olà!
Date una sedia.

RODOLFO
Quickly.

RODOLFO
Presto.

BENOIT
Please don't bother, I only . . .
(*excusing himself*)

BENOIT
Non occorre. Vorrei . . .

SCHAUNARD (*gently insisting that he sit down*)
Be seated.

SCHAUNARD
Segga.

MARCELLO (*offers* BENOIT *a glass of wine*)
A drink?

MARCELLO
Vuol bere?

BENOIT
Grazie.

RODOLFO, COLLINE
Tocchiamo!

SCHAUNARD
Beva!

RODOLFO
Tocchiam!

BENOIT
Quest'
è l' ultimo trimestre . . .

MARCELLO
N'ho piacere.

BENOIT
E quindi . . .

SCHAUNARD
Ancora un sorso.

BENOIT
Grazie.

RODOLFO
Tocchiam!

COLLINE
Tocchiam!

I QUATTRO
Alla sua salute!

BENOIT
A lei ne vengo
perchè il trimestre scorso
mi promise . . .

MARCELLO
Promisi ed or mantengo.

RODOLFO
Che fai? . . .

SCHAUNARD
Sei pazzo?

MARCELLO
Ha visto? Or via
resti un momento in nostra compagnia.
Dica: quant' anni ha,
caro signor Benoit

BENOIT
Gli anni? . . . Per carità!

RODOLFO
Su e giù la nostra età.

BENOIT
Thank you!

RODOLFO, COLLINE
Good health, sir.
(BENOIT, RODOLFO, MARCELLO, *and* SCHAUNARD *seated,* COLLINE *standing*)
(*they all drink*)

SCHAUNARD
Another!

RODOLFO
Your health!

BENOIT (*puts down his glass and turns to* MARCELLO, *showing him the paper*)
I have come here to remind you . . .

MARCELLO (*innocently*)
Yes, I know it.

BENOIT
And therefore . . .

SCHAUNARD (*interrupting him*)
Let's have another!

BENOIT
Thank you!

RODOLFO (*raising his glass*)
A toast!

COLLINE
A toast!

RODOLFO, MARCELLO, SCHAUNARD, COLLINE (*rising, they all touch glasses with* BENOIT)
Here's to Mr. Benoit!
(*they sit and drink;* COLLINE *takes the stool near the easel and sits down also*)

BENOIT (*aside to* MARCELLO)
I came because when your last month's rent was owing . . .
You had promised . . .

MARCELLO (*showing* BENOIT *the money on the table*)
I never break a promise.

RODOLFO (*amazed, aside to* MARCELLO)
What's this?

SCHAUNARD (*aside to* MARCELLO)
You're crazy?

MARCELLO (*to* BENOIT, *disregarding the two*)
You saw it? And now just stay a moment
In our congenial circle.
(*resting his elbows on the table*)
Tell me how old you are—
Dear Mr. Benoit?

BENOIT
How old? For heaven's sake!

RODOLFO
Our own age, more or less?

BENOIT (*half spoken, protesting*)
Much more, very much more.
(*while they make* BENOIT *chatter, they fill up his glass as soon as he has emptied it*)

COLLINE
He only made a guess.

MARCELLO (*lowering his voice, and with a sly inflection*)
Sunday evening, at a certain tavern,
You were seen making love!

BENOIT (*uneasily*)
I?

MARCELLO
No one else.
With my own eyes I saw you. Admit it!

BENOIT
It's true, but . . .

MARCELLO (*flattering him*)
Gorgeous woman!

BENOIT (*suddenly half drunk*)
A darling!

SCHAUNARD (*slaps him on the shoulder*)
You rascal!

RODOLFO
You Don Juan!

COLLINE (*does the same on the other shoulder*)
He's a smart one!

SCHAUNARD
Seducer!

RODOLFO
Seducer!

MARCELLO (*elaborating*)
You should see her! What a woman!

BENOIT (*laughing*)
Ha! Ha!

RODOLFO
He is an expert.

MARCELLO
A veritable Venus!

SCHAUNARD
Old fox!

MARCELLO
With youthful fire he returned her ardent kisses.

BENOIT (*preening himself*)
I'm old, but don't show it.

RODOLFO, SCHAUNARD, COLLINE (*with mock seriousness*)
With youthful fire he answered her caresses.

MARCELLO
He made her yield, the lovely child of joy!

BENOIT
I was a timid boy,
(*confiding fully*)

BENOIT
Di più, molto di più.

COLLINE
Ha detto su e giù.

MARCELLO
L'altra sera al Mabil.
L'han colto
in peccato d'amor!

BENOIT
Io?

MARCELLO
Al Mabil, l'altra sera
l'han colto. Neghi!

BENOIT
Un caso.

MARCELLO
Bella donna!

BENOIT
Ah! molto!

SCHAUNARD
Briccone!

RODOLFO
Briccone!

COLLINE
Seduttore!

SCHAUNARD
Briccone!

RODOLFO
Briccone!

MARCELLO
Una quercia! . . . un cannone!

BENOIT
Eh! Eh!

RODOLFO
L' uomo ha buon gusto.

MARCELLO
Il crin ricciuto e fulvo.

SCHAUNARD
Briccon!

MARCELLO
Ei gongolava arzillo, pettoruto.

BENOIT
Son vecchio, ma robusto.

RODOLFO, SCHAUNARD, COLLINE
Ei gongolava arzuto e pettorillo.

MARCELLO
E a lui cedea, la femminil virtù.

BENOIT
Timido in gioventù
Ora me ne ripago! Si sa,
È uno svago qualche . . .

Donnetta allegra . . .
E un po' . . .
Non dico una balena
O un mappamondo
O un viso tondo
Da luna piena,
Ma magra, proprio magra,
No, poi no!
Le donne magre
Son grattacapi
E spesso sopracavi . . .
E son piene di doglie,
Per esempio: mia moglie . . .

MARCELLO
Quest'uomo ha moglie
e sconcie voglie
ha nel cor!

SCHAUNARD, COLLINE
Orror!

RODOLFO
E ammorba, e appesta
la nostra onesta
magion!

SCHAUNARD, COLLINE
Fuor!

MARCELLO
Si abbruci dello zucchero!

COLLINE
Si discacci il reprobo!

SCHAUNARD
È la morale offessa . . .

BENOIT
Io di, io di . . .

COLLINE
Silenzio!

SCHAUNARD
Che vi scaccia!

MARCELLO
Silenzio!

RODOLFO
Silenzio!

BENOIT
Miei signori . . .

MARCELLO, SCHAUNARD, COLLINE, RODOLFO
Silenzio! Via, signore! Via di qua!

Now I am getting even! You know
I've a certain weakness.
For certain ladies . . .
(*nodding for emphasis*)
You see . . .
Not that I like them portly
Or downright tubby,
Or even chubby,
A blooming full moon.
But skinny, lean and skinny,
No, sir, no!
When they are skinny,
They are malicious,
And sometimes even vicious.
I don't care for their kisses,
Least of all for—my Missus! . . .

MARCELLO (*pounds the table with his fist and rises. The others follow his example.* BENOIT *looks at them in confusion*)
This man is married and leads a scandalous life!

SCHAUNARD, COLLINE
Disgrace!

RODOLFO
This man infects and corrupts our impeccable home!

SCHAUNARD, COLLINE
Out!
(BENOIT, *staggering, rises, and tries in vain to speak*)

MARCELLO
We'll have to disinfect the place!

COLLINE
Drive the wretched sinner out!

SCHAUNARD
Our morals are offended!

BENOIT
One word . . . I say . . .

COLLINE
Keep quiet!

SCHAUNARD
We expel you!

MARCELLO
Be quiet!

RODOLFO
Be quiet!
(*they surround* BENOIT *and gradually push him toward the door*)

BENOIT (*more and more bewildered*)
Only listen . . .

MARCELLO, SCHAUNARD, COLLINE, RODOLFO
Be quiet! Quickly out of here!
(*pushing* BENOIT *out the door*)

Out you go!
(*all at the door, looking toward the landing of the staircase*)
And give your lady our very best regards.
(*laughing, returning to center stage*)
Ha, ha, ha, ha!

MARCELLO
Go and look for your money!
(*shuts the door*)

SCHAUNARD
Now it's time to be off for Café Momus!

MARCELLO
Spending our money!

SCHAUNARD
Let's divide all the spoils.
(*they divide the money on the table*)

RODOLFO
Right away!

COLLINE
Right away!

MARCELLO (*holding up a cracked mirror to* COLLINE)
There you will find girls,
Heavenly creatures.
Now that you're wealthy,
Bow before convention!
Bear! Get yourself a trimming.
(*takes off his smock and puts on his jacket*)

COLLINE
I shall for the first time receive attention
From a barber's scissors.
Escort me to the ludicrous excesses of the razor.
Come on!

SCHAUNARD (*humorously*)
Let's go!

MARCELLO (*humorously*)
Let's go!

SCHAUNARD
Let's go!

COLLINE (*humorously*)
Let's go!

RODOLFO
I'm staying, I have to write
A critical report for next month's "Beaver."

MARCELLO
Then hurry.

RODOLFO
I will be with you in no time at all . . .

COLLINE
We'll wait for you downstairs in the hall.

E buona sera a vostra signori . . .
Ah! ah! ah! ah!

MARCELLO
Ho pagato il trimestre!

SCHAUNARD
Al Quartiere Latin ci attende Momus.

MARCELLO
Viva chi spende!

SCHAUNARD
Dividiamo il bottin!

RODOLFO
Dividiam!

COLLINE
Dividiam!

MARCELLO
Là ci son beltà scese dal cielo.
Or che sei ricco, bada alla decenza!
Orso, ravviati il pelo.

COLLINE
Farò la conoscenza
la prima volta d'un barbitonsore.
Guidatemi al ridicolo
oltraggio d'un rasoio.
Andiam!

SCHAUNARD
Andiam!

MARCELLO
Andiam!

SCHAUNARD
Andiam!

COLLINE
Andiam!

RODOLFO
Io resto
per terminar l'articolo di fondo del *Castoro*.

MARCELLO
Fa presto.

RODOLFO
Cinque minuti. Conosco il mestier.

COLLINE
T' aspetterem dabbasso dal portier.

MARCELLO
Se tardi, udrai che coro!

RODOLFO
Cinque minuti.

SCHAUNARD
Taglia corta la coda al tuo *Castor*.

MARCELLO
Occhio alla scala. Tienti alla ringhiera.

RODOLFO
Adagio.

COLLINE
È buio pesto!

SCHAUNARD
Maledetto portier!

COLLINE
Accidenti!

RODOLFO
Colline, sei morto?

COLLINE
Non ancor!

MARCELLO
Vien presto.

RODOLFO
Non sono in vena.
Chi è là?

MIMÌ
Scusi.

RODOLFO
Una donna!

MIMÌ
Di grazia, mi s'è spento il lume.

RODOLFO
Ecco.

MIMÌ
Vorrebbe . . . ?

MARCELLO
If you are late you'll hear us!

RODOLFO (*takes a light from the table and goes to open the door;* MARCELLO, SCHAUNARD, *and* COLLINE *go out and descend the staircase*)
Five minutes only.

SCHAUNARD (*leaving*)
Better shorten your Beaver's wordy tale!

MARCELLO (*off-stage*)
Look where you're going,
Keep along the railing.

RODOLFO (*on the landing, near the open door, raising the candle*)
Be careful!
(*the voices of* MARCELLO, SCHAUNARD, *and* COLLINE *fade into the distance*)

COLLINE (*off-stage*)
Infernal darkness!

SCHAUNARD (*off-stage*)
I am risking my neck!
(*noise of someone falling*)

COLLINE (*crying out*)
I have done it!

RODOLFO
Colline, are you dead?

COLLINE (*in the distance, from the bottom of the stairs*)
No, not quite.

MARCELLO (*farther away*)
Come soon!
(RODOLFO *closes the door, puts the candle down, clears a corner of the table, places pen and paper on it, then sits down and prepares to write, after having extinguished the other candle, which had remained burning. Writes, breaks off, thinks, writes again. He is restless, tears up what he has written, and throws the pen down*)

RODOLFO (*disconsolately*)
I'm not inspired.
(*a timid knock at the door*)
Who's there?

MIMI (*off-stage*)
Excuse me.

RODOLFO (*rising*)
It's a lady!

MIMI
Forgive me. Will you light my candle?

RODOLFO (*runs to open the door*)
There now.

MIMI (*at the door, holding an extinguished candle and a key*)

Allow me . . .

RODOLFO

Won't you stay a moment?

MIMI

Please don't bother.

RODOLFO (*insistently*)

Come in please, won't you?

MIMI (*enters, but suddenly is seized with a coughing spell*)

RODOLFO (*concerned*)

You're feeling ill?

MIMI (*coughing*)

No . . . nothing.

RODOLFO

But you are trembling.

MIMI

Oh, these stairs, they exhaust me . . .

(*faints, and* RODOLFO *hardly has time to support her and lead her to a chair, while the candlestick and key drop from her hand*)

RODOLFO (*embarrassed*)

What can I do to help her?

I know!

(*goes to get water, and sprinkles it on her face; looking at her with deep interest*)

How pale and wan her face is!

Do you feel better?

MIMI (*revives*)

Yes!

RODOLFO

It is very cold here.

Warm yourself by the fire.

(MIMI *declines with a gesture*)

One moment . . .

A little wine now . . .

MIMI

Thank you!

RODOLFO

To you!

(*gives her a glass and pours out some wine*)

MIMI

Just a little!

RODOLFO

Like this?

MIMI

Thank you!

(*she drinks*)

RODOLFO (*admiring her*)

She really is lovely!

MIMI (*rising, she looks for her candlestick*)

Now may I ask you to light my candle.

I feel much better.

RODOLFO

S' accomodi un momento.

MIMÌ

Non occorre.

RODOLFO

La prego, entri.

RODOLFO

Si sente male?

MIMÌ

No . . . nulla.

RODOLFO

Impallidisce!

MIMÌ

Il respir . . . Quelle scale . . .

RODOLFO

Ed ora come faccio? . . .

Così.

Che viso d'ammalata!

Si sente meglio?

MIMÌ

Sì.

RODOLFO

Qui c'è tanto freddo. Segga vicino al fuoco.

Aspetti . . . un po' di vino.

MIMÌ

Grazie.

RODOLFO

A lei.

MIMÌ

Poco, poco.

RODOLFO

Così.

MIMÌ

Grazie.

RODOLFO

(Che bella bambina!)

MIMÌ

Ora permetta

che accenda il lume. È tutto passato.

RODOLFO
Tanta fretta?

MIMÌ
Sì.
Grazie. Buona sera.

RODOLFO
Buona sera.

MIMÌ
Oh! sventata, sventata!
La chiave della stanza!
Dove l' ho lasciata?

RODOLFO
Non stia sull' uscio; il lume, vacilla al vento.

MIMÌ
Oh Dio! Torni ad accenderlo.

RODOLFO
Oh Dio! . . . anche il mio s' è spento.

MIMÌ
Ah!
E la chiave?
Ove sarà?

RODOLFO
Buio pesto!

MIMÌ
Disgraziata!

RODOLFO
Ove sarà?

MIMÌ
Importuna è la vicina . . .

RODOLFO
Ma le pare!

MIMÌ
Importuna è la vicina

RODOLFO
Cosa dice, me le pare!

MIMÌ
Cerchi!

RODOLFO
Cerco!

RODOLFO
Such a hurry?

MIMI
Yes.
(RODOLFO *sees the candlestick on the floor, picks it up, lights it, and hands it to* MIMI *without speaking. She is ready to go*)
Thank you! And good evening.

RODOLFO (*accompanies her to the door*)
You are welcome.
(*returns at once to the table*)

MIMI (*off-stage*)
Oh! How dreadful, how dreadful,
(*re-entering and stopping on the threshold of the door, which remains open*)
I cannot find my door key,
Where could I have left it?

RODOLFO
Don't stay so near the doorway;
The wind is too strong for your candle.
(MIMI's *light goes out*)

MIMI
Good heavens! Light it once more for me.

RODOLFO (*runs with his candle, but as he approaches the door his light goes out too; the room is in darkness*)
Oh my! Now I have none either!

MIMI (*groping about, she finds the table and places her candlestick on it*)
Ah! And my key, where can it be?

RODOLFO (*finds himself near the door and shuts it*)
And it's dark here!

MIMI
I am sorry!

RODOLFO
Where can it be?

MIMI (*apologetically, still advancing cautiously*)
Oh, what trouble I am causing!

RODOLFO (*turns in the direction of* MIMI's *voice*)
It is nothing . . .

MIMI
Oh, what trouble I am causing!
(*looks for the key by sliding her foot over the floor*)

RODOLFO
It is nothing, I assure you!

MIMI
Help me!

RODOLFO
Gladly!
(*knocks against the table, puts his candlestick down, and searches for the key with his hands on the floor*)

MIMI
Where can it be?

MIMÌ
Ove sarà?

RODOLFO (*finds the key and lets an exclamation escape, then suddenly checks himself and puts the key in his pocket*)
Ah!

RODOLFO
Ah!

MIMI
Did you find it?

MIMÌ
L'ha trovata?

RODOLFO
No!

RODOLFO
No!

MIMI
I thought you . . .

MIMÌ
Mi parve . . .

RODOLFO
I thought so too!

RODOLFO
In verità!

MIMI (*searches with her fingers*)
Nowhere?

MIMÌ
Cerca?

RODOLFO (*pretends to search but, guided by* MIMI's *voice and movements, tries to get near her*)
Nowhere!

RODOLFO
Cerco!

MIMI (*stoops to the floor, continuing to search for the key; at this moment* RODOLFO *reaches her, and as he also stoops his hand encounters hers*)
Ah!
(*surprised*)

MIMÌ
Ah!

RODOLFO (*holding* MIMI's *hand, with a voice full of emotion*)
How cold your little hand is!
Let me warm it in my own.
Your key, don't mind it,
It's far too dark to find it.
A little later the moon will be rising,
And very soon then, the light will be stronger.
(MIMI *tries to withdraw her hand*)
So stay a little longer,
And we'll talk a while together,
So you may know my vocation,
My ambitions.
Won't you?
(MIMI *is silent.* RODOLFO *releases her hand; drawing back, she finds a chair, into which she sinks, overcome by emotion*)
I am, well who?
I am a poet. What am I doing?
Writing! How do I live then?
Somehow!
I have no worldly riches;
Ev'ry poetic measure
Holds a fabulous treasure.
In dreams and flights of fantasy
And castles in the air,
I am indeed a millionaire!
And now two eyes have stolen
Ev'ry priceless possession

RODOLFO
Che gelida manina,
se la lasci riscaldar.
Cercar che giova?
Al buio non si trova.
Ma per fortuna è una notte di luna,
e qui la luna l'abbiamo vicina.
Aspetti signorina,
le dirò con due parole
chi son, chi son e che faccio,
come vivo.
Vuole?
Chi son, chi son?
Sono un poeta. Che cosa faccio?
Scrivo. E come vivo?
Vivo.
In povertà mia lieta
scialo da gran signore
rime ed inni d'amore.
Per sogni e per chimere
e per castelli in aria,
l'anima ho milionaria.
Talor dal mio forziere
ruban tutti i gioielli
due ladri: gli occhi belli.
V'entrar con voi pur ora,
ed i miei sogni usati
e i bei sogni miei
tosto si dileguar!
Ma il furto non m'accora
poichè, poichè v'ha preso stanza
la dolce speranza!
Or che mi conoscete,
parlate voi,
deh! parlate. Chi siete?
Vi piaccia dir!

MIMÌ
Sì.
Mi chiamano Mimì,
ma il mio nome è Lucia.
La storia mia è breve.
A tela o a seta ricamo in casa e fuori.
Son tranquilla e lieta
ed è mio svago far gigli e rose.
Mi piaccion quelle cose
che han sì dolce malìa,
che parlano d'amor,
di primavere,
che parlano di sogni e di chimere,
quelle cose che han nome poesia.
Lei m'intende?

RODOLFO
Sì.

MIMÌ
Mi chiamano Mimì,
il perchè non so.
Sola, mi fo il pranzo da me stessa.
Non vado sempre a messa
ma prego assai il Signor.
Vivo sola, soletta,
là in una bianca cameretta:
guardo sui tetti e in cielo,
ma quando vien lo sgelo
il primo sole è mio.
Il primo baccio dell'aprile
è mio!
il primo sole è mio!
Germoglia in un vaso una rosa . . .
Foglia a foglia la spiro!
Così gentil il profumo d'un fior!
Ma i fior ch'io faccio, ahimè!
i fior ch'io faccio, ahimè, non hanno odore!
Altro di me non le saprei narrare:
sono la sua vicina che la vien fuori
d'ora a importunare.

Of my esteemed profession.
Their charming gentle glances
Captured my thoughts and visions,
And my daydreams and fancies
Swiftly as clouds depart.
However, I don't mind it,
Because they have suddenly brought me
New hope and revelation!
Now I feel that you know me,
So let me ask you:
Won't you tell me who you are?
Please say you will!

MIMI (*hesitates, then decides to speak; still seated*)
Yes.
I'm always called Mimi,
But my name is Lucia.
My story is a brief one:
I earn my living by sewing and embroidering.
Working gives me pleasure;
In leisure hours I make lilies and roses.
I dearly love those flowers,
They delight and enchant me,
They speak to me of love,
Of love and springtime,
They speak to me of dreams and of illusions,
Of those wonders the world would call poetic.
You understand me?

RODOLFO (*moved*)
Yes.

MIMI
I'm always called Mimi,
I don't know just why!
Doing my work the daytime passes fairly,
I go to Mass but rarely,
Though ev'ry night I pray.
I live all by myself.
There from my lofty garret window
Over the rooftops I see the sky.
(*she rises*)
But, when the snow is thawing,
But, when the snow is thawing,
Spring's first caress belongs to me,
To me!
The spring's first sunshine is mine!
When rosebuds are starting to blossom
Then I watch them unfolding.
How sweet the scent of a blooming flower!
But those I make myself,
Embroidered flowers, alas, they have no fragrance.
I'm afraid my life is not too exciting,

I am merely a neighbor who intruded
And interrupted your writing.

SCHAUNARD (*from the courtyard*)
Eh! Rodolfo!

COLLINE
Rodolfo!

MARCELLO
Hello! Do you hear us?
(*at the shouts of his friends,* RODOLFO *is annoyed*)
You slowpoke!

COLLINE
What is keeping you?

SCHAUNARD
Are you writing a novel?

RODOLFO (*getting more annoyed,* RODOLFO *gropes his way to the window and opens it, leaning out a bit to answer his friends in the courtyard. From the open window rays of moonlight enter, which brighten the room*)
Three more lines and I'll be ready.

MIMI (*approaching the window a little*)
Who's there?

RODOLFO (*turning to her*)
My colleagues.

SCHAUNARD
We will tell you plenty!

MARCELLO
Aren't you very lonely?

RODOLFO
I'm not lonely, someone's with me.
Why don't you go ahead,
Reserve a table, we will follow quickly.
(*remains at the window to make sure that his friends are going.* MIMI *goes still nearer the window. The moonlight is falling upon her*)

MARCELLO, SCHAUNARD, COLLINE (*more and more in the distance*)
Momus, Momus, Momus
Now it is time we tactfully retired,

SCHAUNARD, COLLINE
Momus, Momus,

MARCELLO (*far off, as though shouting*)
The poets are inspired!

SCHAUNARD, COLLINE
Momus, Momus, Momus!

RODOLFO (*turning, sees* MIMI *with the light like a halo around her; he contemplates her ecstatically*)
O adorable angel,
O gentle vision,
Surrounded by the moonlight's silver glow,
In your sweet person

SCHAUNARD
Ehi! Rodolfo!

COLLINE
Rodolfo!

MARCELLO
Olà. Non senti?
Lumaca!

COLLINE
Poetucolo!

SCHAUNARD
Accidenti
al pigro!

RODOLFO
Scrivo ancor tre righe a volo.

MIMÌ
Chi son?

RODOLFO
Amici.

SCHAUNARD
Sentirai le tue.

MARCELLO
Che te ne fai lì solo?

RODOLFO
Non son solo. Siamo in due.
Andate da Momus, tenete il posto,
ci saremo tosto.

MARCELLO, SCHAUNARD, COLLINE
Momus, Momus, Momus,
zitti e discreti andiamocene via.

SCHAUNARD, COLLINE
Momus, Momus,

MARCELLO
Trovò la poesia!

SCHAUNARD, COLLINE
Momus, Momus, Momus!

RODOLFO
O soave fanciulla,
o dolce viso
di mite circonfuso alba lunar,
in te, ravviso
il sogno ch'io vorrei sempre sognar!
Fremon già nell'anima

le dolcezze estreme.
Fremon nell'anima
dolcezze estreme,
fremon dolcezze estreme,
nel baccio freme amor!

I realize my fondest dreams of long ago!
Never have I known before
So divine a rapture!
(*putting his arm around* MIMI)
Radiant with happiness
My heart is glowing,
Now at last I have found you,
My one and only love!

MIMÌ
Ah! tu sol comandi, amor!
tu sol comandi, amore!
Oh! come dolci scendono
le sue lusinghe al core . . .
tu sol comandi, amor!

MIMI (*much moved*)
Ah! I've never known before,
A love so tender and glowing!
(*on the verge of yielding*)
Oh, how its soothing power
Overcomes my heart with gladness,
How sweet to be in love!
(RODOLFO *kisses* MIMI)

MIMÌ
No, per pietà!

MIMI (*withdrawing*)
No, please don't.

RODOLFO
Sei mia!

RODOLFO
My sweetheart!

MIMÌ
V'aspettan gli amici

MIMI
Your friends are waiting . . .

RODOLFO
Già mi mandi via?

RODOLFO
You're sending me away, then?

MIMÌ
Vorrei dir . . . ma non oso . . .

MIMI (*hesitating*)
I would say . . . but I dare not . . .

RODOLFO
Di'.

RODOLFO (*gently*)
What?

MIMÌ
Se venissi con voi?

MIMI (*coquettishly*)
Would you take me along?

RODOLFO
Che? . . . Mimì!
Sarebbe così dolce restar qui.
C' è freddo fuori.

RODOLFO (*surprised*)
You, Mimi?
(*insinuatingly*)
Would you not rather stay at home with me?
Out there it's freezing . . .

MIMÌ
Vi starò vicina! . . .

MIMI (*with great abandon*)
I'll stay close beside you!

RODOLFO
E al ritorno?

RODOLFO (*lovingly helps* MIMI *put on her shawl*)
And later?

MIMÌ
Curioso!

MIMI (*archly*)
I wonder!

RODOLFO
Dammi il braccio, mia
piccina . . .

RODOLFO (*with tender gallantry*)
Take my arm, my little darling.

MIMÌ
Obbedisco, signor!

MIMI (*gives her arm to* RODOLFO)
I obey you, My Lord!
(*they go arm in arm to the door*)

RODOLFO
Che m' ami dì.

RODOLFO
Your love is mine?

MIMI (*with abandon*)
I love you! (*exit*)
BOTH (*off-stage*)
My love, my love!
My love!

MIMÌ
Io t'amo!

MIMÌ, RODOLFO
Amor! Amor!
Amor!

ACT II

The Latin Quarter. A square at the intersection of several streets: shops of all kinds; on one side, the Café Momus.
It's Christmas eve. A milling crowd of various people: townspeople, soldiers, servants, children, boys and girls, students, working girls, gendarmes, etc. In front of their shops vendors are shouting their wares, looking for prospective customers. On one side, away from the crowd, RODOLFO *and* MIMI *are strolling up and down.* COLLINE *is near the seamstress's shop:* SCHAUNARD *is buying a pipe and horn at the* IRONMONGER'S; MARCELLO *is caught up in the movements of the crowd. A group of townspeople are seated at an outside table in front of the Café Momus. It is evening. The shops are lit by little lamps: the street lights are also burning: and a large lantern illumines the entrance of the café.*

VENDITORI
Aranci, datteri!
Caldi i marroni!
Ninnoli, croci! Torroni!
Panna montata!
Oh! la crostata!

VENDORS (*in front of their shops*) (*shouted*)
Bananas, apricots!
Hot roasted chestnuts!
Cabbages, carrots, tomatoes!
Pastry and fruitcake!
Say, what will you take?
(*pushing through the crowd and offering their different wares*)

STUDENTI
Quanta folla! Che chiasso!

STUDENTS
Merry Christmas! Hello there!

DONNE
Ah! Ah!

WORKING GIRLS
Ah! Ah!

RAGAZZI
Aranci, ninnoli!
Caldi i marroni!
e caramelle. Torroni!

STREET URCHINS
Bananas, apricots!
Hot roasted chestnuts!
Necklaces, carrots, potatoes!

VENDITORI
Caramelle!
Fiori alle belle!
La crostata!
Panna montata!
Fringuelli, passeri!
Datteri!
Caldi marroni!
Panna, torroni!
Latte di cocco!
Oh! la crostata!
Panna montata!
Ninnoli, torroni!
Aranci, fiori!
Datteri, torroni!

VENDORS
Macaroni!
More for your money!
Lower prices!
Candies and ices!
Tobacco, licorice!
Necklaces!
Hot roasted chestnuts!
Strawberry ices!
Coconut taffy!
Ginger and spices!
Coconut taffy!
Gingerbread and spices!
Oranges, apples!
Reasonable prices!

(*At Café Momus*)

LA FOLLA

GUESTS (*shouting and calling to the waiters, who are busy hurrying here and there*)

Hurry up!
Let me pass!
Bring a glass!
Hurry!
Waiter!
A beer!
Bring me a beer!
A beer!
And a glass!
Ho there!

Presto qua!
Camerier!
Un bicchier!
Corri!
Birra!
Da ber!
Dunque? Un caffè!
Da ber!
Camarier!
Olà!

VENDORS
Coconut kisses,
Cabbage and carrots!
Necklaces, carrots, potatoes!

VENDITORI
Latte di cocco!
Giubbe! Carote!
E caramelle. Torroni!

GIRLS (*still walking*)
What confusion!

DONNE
Quanta folla!

STUDENTS
Come let's run!

STUDENTI
Su, corriam!

GIRLS
Hold on to me, it's crowded!

DONNE
Stringiti a me, che chiasso!

STUDENTS
Hold on to me! This is fun!

STUDENTI
Stringiti a me. Su, corriam!

URCHINS
Try and catch me, this is fun!

RAGAZZI
Su, corriamo, su, corriam!

GIRLS, STUDENTS
Look at the holiday crowd!
Let's go with them, come along!

DONNE e STUDENTI
Date il passo, corriam!
Quanta folla! su partiam!

URCHINS
Oranges, apples! Coconut slices!
Hot roasted chestnuts!
Gingerbread and spices!

RAGAZZI
Datteri, aranci! Latte di cocco!
Caldi i marroni!
Ninnoli, torroni!

GIRLS, STUDENTS
Ah!

DONNE e STUDENTI
Ah!

GIRLS
Merry Christmas!
Ah, what an uproar!

DONNE
Date il passo!
Ah! quanta folla!

GIRLS, STUDENTS
Hold on to me, let's go!

DONNE e STUDENTI
Stringiti a me, corriam!

TWO MOTHERS
Emma! Come when I call you!

DUE MADRE
Emma, quando ti chiamo!

GIRLS, STUDENTS
Be careful! Hold on to me!

DONNE e STUDENTI
Che chiasso, stringiti a me!

STUDENTS
It's too noisy, come along!
(*they move on*)

STUDENTI
Quanta folla, su partiam!

URCHINS
Pastry and chocolate, Turkish delight!

RAGAZZI
Fringuelli e passeri, caldi i marron!

SOME URCHINS
I want some candy!

ALCUNI RAGAZZI
Voglio una lancia!

TUTTI RAGAZZI
Aranci, caldi i marron!
Datteri! ninnoli, aranci e fior!

ALL URCHINS
A bag of hot roasted nuts!
(*moving on*)
Oranges, necklaces, flowers, and nuts!

SCHAUNARD
Falso questo *Re!*
falso questo *Re!*
Pipa e corno quant'è?

SCHAUNARD (*after blowing the horn several times, tries to strike a bargain with the ironmonger*)
Listen to this E!
It is out of key!
You can take it from me!
(*he pays the bill.* RODOLFO *and* MIMI, *arm in arm, push their way through the crowd to get near a hat shop*)

COLLINE
È un poco usato . . .
ma è serio e a buon mercato . . .

COLLINE (*to the seamstress, who has been mending the hem of his coat*)
A trifle shiny, but old and very worthy . . .
(*pays, then carefully distributes the books in the many pockets of his coat.* MARCELLO *is all alone in the middle of the crowd, a bundle under his arm, eying the girls who brush past him*)

RODOLFO
Andiam.

RODOLFO
Let's go! . . .

MIMÌ
Andiam per la cuffietta?

MIMI
To buy a pretty bonnet?

RODOLFO
Tienti al mio braccio stretta . . .

RODOLFO
Stay close to me, my darling.

MIMÌ
A te mi stringo.
Andiam.

MIMI
I'm right beside you. Let's go.

RODOLFO
Andiam.

RODOLFO
Let's go.
(*they enter the hat shop*)

MARCELLO
Io pur mi sento in vena di gridar:
Chi vuol, donnine allegre, un po' d'amor!
Facciamo insieme . . .
facciamo a vendere a comprar!

MARCELLO
Among so many young and lovely girls
There surely must be one or two left for me!
(*approaching a young girl*)
You, too, look lonely.
I think we'd make a handsome pair!

VENDITORI
Datteri!
Trote!

VENDORS
Oranges!
Lobster!

UN VENDITOR
Prugne di Tours!

STROLLING VENDOR (*crossing the stage*) (*shouted*)
Hot lemonade!
(*a group of salesgirls enters*)

MARCELLO
Io dò ad un soldo il vergine mio cuor!

MARCELLO
That you should come with me is only fair!
(*the young girl runs away, laughing*)

SCHAUNARD
Fra spintoni e pestate accorrendo, affretta
la folla e si diletta
nel provar gioie matte insoddisfatte.

SCHAUNARD (*wanders about in front of the Café Momus, looking for his friends. Armed with his huge pipe and hunting horn, he watches the crowd with philosophic curiosity*)
I can never see why people crowd like herds of cattle
In all this noise and prattle,

How they find satisfaction
In such distraction!
(*looks sympathetically over* COLLINE's *shoulder*)

SALESGIRLS
Souvenirs and laces!
Caramels and choc'late kisses!

DONNE
Ninnoli, spillette!
Datteri e caramelle!

URCHINS
Ah!

RAGAZZI
Ah!

VENDORS
Flow'rs for the misses!

VENDITORI
Fiori alle belle!

COLLINE (*comes to meet his friend, triumphantly waving in his hand a rare book*)
This rare book is the theory
Of an ancient philosophy!

COLLINE
Copia rara, anzi unica:
la grammatica Runica!

SCHAUNARD
Quite a bargain!

SCHAUNARD
Uomo onesto! . . .

MARCELLO (*on arriving at the Café Momus, shouts to* COLLINE *and* SCHAUNARD)
To dinner!

MARCELLO
A cena!

SCHAUNARD, COLLINE
Rodolfo!

SCHAUNARD, COLLINE
Rodolfo!

MARCELLO
He went into that hat shop!

MARCELLO
Entrò da una modista.

RODOLFO (*leaving the hat shop with* MIMI)
Come, dear, our friends are waiting there.

RODOLFO
Vieni, gli amici aspettano.

MIMI (*showing off her little bonnet*)
Do you think this bonnet is becoming?
(MARCELLO, SCHAUNARD, *and* COLLINE *look for a free table outside the café, but they see only one, which is ocupied by several townspeople. The three friends glare at the townspeople contemptuously, and then go into the café*)

MIMÌ
Mi sta ben questa cuffietta rosa?

VENDORS
Strawberry ices!

VENDITORI
Panna montata!

URCHINS
Coconut slices!

RAGAZZI
Latte di cocco!

VENDORS
Gingerbread spices!
Strawberry ices!

VENDITORI
Oh! la crostata!
Panna montata!

THE CROWD (*from the café*)
Waiter here!
One more beer!
Hurry up!
Aquavit!

LA FOLLA
Camerier!
Un bicchier!
Presto, olà!
Ratafià!

RODOLFO
In anything you would look lovely!

RODOLFO
Sei bruna
e quel color ti dona.

MIMI (*looking admiringly at the window display of a shop*)
Oh, what a lovely bracelet!

MIMÌ
Bel vezzo
di corallo!

RODOLFO
My old uncle who has millions

RODOLFO
Ho un zio milionario

Se fa senno il buon Dio
voglio comprarti un vezzo assai più bel.

Soon will leave for greener pastures.
Then I shall buy you twenty strings of pearls!
(RODOLFO and MIMI, talking tenderly together, move to stage rear, where they are lost in the crowd)
(a vendor in front of his shop at stage rear stands on a chair and with grand gestures tries to sell some lingerie, nightcaps, etc. Young girls in a group gather around his shop and burst into gay giggles)

RAGAZZI
Ha, ha, ha, ha, ha! ha! ha! ha! ha! ha!

URCHINS
Ha! ha! ha! ha! ha! ha! ha! ha! ha! ha!

DONNE, STUDENTI
Ha, ha!

GIRLS, STUDENTS
Ha! ha! *(running to stage rear, to the street urchins)*

RAGAZZI, DONNE, STUDENTI
Ha! ha! ha! ha! ha! ha! ha! ha! ha!

URCHINS, GIRLS, STUDENTS
Ha! ha! ha! ha! ha! ha! *(they run to another shop)*

BORGHESI
Facciam coda alla gente!
Raggaze, state attente!
Che chiasso! Quanta folla!
Pigliam via Mazzarino!
Io soffoco, partiamo!
Vedi, il caffè e vicin!
Andiam, là da Momus!

TOWNSPEOPLE
Let's see where they are going!
Look how the crowd is growing!
How noisy! What an uproar!
They're turning around the corner!
(moving toward Rue Mazarin)
They're tearing me to pieces!
Let's try Café Momus!
All right, Café Momus!
(they enter the café)

VENDITORI
Oh! la crostata!

VENDORS *(from the shops)*
Coconut slices!

RAGAZZI
Oh! la crostata!

URCHINS
Coconut slices!

VENDITORI
Panna montata!

VENDORS
Gingerbread spices!

RAGAZZI
Panna montata!

URCHINS
Gingerbread spices!

VENDITORI
Fiori alle belle!

VENDORS
Flow'rs for the ladies!

RAGAZZI
Ninnoli, datteri, caldi marron!

URCHINS
Oranges, apples, and hot roasted nuts!

VENDITORI
Aranci, datteri, ninnoli, fior!
Fringuelli, passeri, panna, torron!

VENDORS
Oranges, apricots, ginger and spice
Pastry and chocolate, Turkish delight!
(a large crowd gathers on the square, coming from all directions; gradually they work their way to the back of the stage. COLLINE, SCHAUNARD, and MARCELLO come out of the café, carrying a table; followed by a waiter bringing the chairs: the townspeople at the next table are annoyed by the noise the three friends are making, and in a little while they get up and leave. RODOLFO and MIMI come forward again: she watches a group of students)

RODOLFO
Chi guardi? . . .

RODOLFO *(reproving her gently)*
You're flirting?

MIMI
Are you jealous?

MIMÌ
Sei geloso?

RODOLFO
A man in love is bound to be suspicious.

RODOLFO
All' uom felice sta il sospetto accanto.

MIMI
Do you love me?

MIMÌ
Sei felice?

RODOLFO
Ah, forever!
And you?

RODOLFO
Ah! sì, tanto. E tu?

MIMI
I love you!

MIMÌ
Sì, tanto.

GIRLS AND STUDENTS
There is Momus!
Go in!
Go in!
(they enter the café. RODOLFO *and* MIMI *come into the Café Momus)*

DONNE, STUDENTI
Là da Momus!
Andiam!
Andiam!

COLLINE
I cannot stand a vulgar crowd of people.

COLLINE
Odio il profano volgo al par d'Orazio.

SCHAUNARD
And I, when I am dining,
Must have room for reclining.

SCHAUNARD
Ed io quando mi sazio
vo' abbondanza di spazio.

MARCELLO *(to the waiter)*
We must have a very special supper!
Hurry!

MARCELLO
Vogliamo una cena prelibata.
Lesto!

SCHAUNARD
And plenty!

SCHAUNARD
Per molti!

MARCELLO, SCHAUNARD, COLLINE *(to the waiter, who runs frantically back into the café, while another waiter dashes out to set the table)*
Hurry!

MARCELLO, SCHAUNARD, COLLINE
Lesto!

PARPIGNOL *(faintly, from a distance)*
Come, buy some Christmas toys from Parpignol!

PARPIGNOL
Ecco i giocattoli
di Parpignol!

RODOLFO
Two places!
(meets his friends and presents MIMI *to them)*

RODOLFO
Due posti.

COLLINE
Here's our poet!

COLLINE
Finalmente!

RODOLFO
Yes, here we are.
This is Mimi, she is an artist.
With her our chosen circle
Now at last is completed.
You see, although I am the poet,
She is the purest poetry!
Here in my mind blossom the verses,
And from her fingers blossom the flow'rs,
Two joyous hearts united
Blossom in love, blossom in love!

RODOLFO
Eccoci qui.
Questa è Mimì
gaia fioraia.
Il suo venir completa
la bella compagnia,
perchè, perchè son io il poeta,
essa la poesia.
Dal mio cervel sbocciano i canti
dalle sue dita sbocciano i fior
dall' anime esultanti
sboccia l'amor, sboccia l'amor!

MARCELLO, SCHAUNARD, COLLINE
Ah, ah, ah, ah!
MARCELLO
Dio, che concetti rari!

COLLINE
Digna est intrari.

SCHAUNARD
Ingrediat si necessit.

COLLINE
Io non dò che un: *accessit.*

PARPIGNOL
Ecco i giocattoli
di Parpignol!
COLLINE
Salame . . .

RAGGAZZI, BAMBINE
Parpignol, Parpignol,
Parpignol, Parpignol!

RAGAZZI, BAMBINE
Ecco Parpignol! Parpignol!
Parpignol!
Col carretto tutto fior!
Ecco Parpignol!
Parpignol! Parpignol! Parpignol!
Voglio la tromba, il cavallin,
Il tambur, tamburel,
Voglio il cannon, voglio il frustin.
Dei soldati i drappel.

SCHAUNARD
Cervo arrosto!

MARCELLO
Un tacchino!

SCHAUNARD
Vin del Reno!

MARCELLO, SCHAUNARD, COLLINE
Ha! Ha! Ha! Ha!

MARCELLO (*ironically*)
That was a flow'ry oration!
COLLINE (*seriously bowing to* MIMI)
Worthy presentation!
SCHAUNARD (*comically, as if passing judgment*)
She passes my inspection!
COLLINE
Then I make no objection!
(*they all take their places at the table as the waiter returns*)
PARPIGNOL (*now much nearer*)
Come, buy your Christmas toys from Parpignol!
COLLINE (*seeing the waiter, shouts loudly*)
Salami!
(*from Rue Dauphin a cart is seen, all decorated with greens and flowers, and lit by Chinese lanterns: the man who is pushing the cart is* PARPIGNOL, *the popular peddler of toys: a crowd of children follow him on-stage, skipping merrily, and gathering around the little cart to admire the toys*)
CHILDREN (*off-stage*)
Parpignol, Parpignol, Parpignol, Parpignol!
(*the waiter presents the menu, which is handed from one to the other of the four friends and studied with admiration and serious analysis*)
CHILDREN (*entering*)
Follow Parpignol, Parpignol, Parpignol!
With his cart all filled with toys!
Follow Parpignol,
Parpignol, Parpignol, Parpignol!
I want a trumpet and a ball!
Buy a nice little ship!
I want a carriage and a doll!
Buy a horse and a whip!
(*the boys and girls have surrounded* PARPIGNOL'S *little cart and gesticulate with great vivacity: some of their mothers come running in to look for their children, and, finding them with* PARPIGNOL, *start scolding them: one mother takes her little boy by the hand, another tries to lead her little girl away by threatening and scolding, but all in vain, as the children do not want to leave*)
SCHAUNARD
Mushroom omelet!
MARCELLO (*studying the menu, and giving the order to the waiter in a loud voice*)
Roasted capon!
SCHAUNARD
I want Rhine wine!

COLLINE
Sparkling Burgundy!

SCHAUNARD
And a casserole of lobster!

MOTHERS (*shrieking and threatening*)
You naughty children are an awful bother!
Why don't you stop your fighting and your shouting!
Go home at once, or I will tell your father,
And he will give you all a thorough clouting!
Go home now, you naughty pack of little rascals!
It's bedtime!
(*one mother takes her little boy by the ear, and he starts to whine and whimper*)

BOY (*whimpering*)
Want a trumpet and a horse!

RODOLFO
And you, Mimi, you wish?

MIMI
Some pastry!
(*the mothers, relenting, decide to buy from* PARPIGNOL: *the children jump for joy*)

SCHAUNARD (*with an air of great importance to the waiter, who writes down what they have just ordered*)
Bring the best one, for the lady!
(PARPIGNOL *starts down Rue Vieille Comédie: the boys and girls follow him gaily, marching, and pretending to play their new toy instruments*)

CHILDREN
Follow Parpignol, Parpignol, Parpignol, Parpignol!
(*off-stage*)
Tarata, taratam!
(*farther away*)
Dadadum, dadadum!

MARCELLO (*continuing their conversation*)
May I ask, Miss Mimi, what special present
Has your Rodolfo bought you?

MIMI (*showing him her little bonnet, which she takes out of the paper wrapping*)
He bought me a delightful little
Hand-embroidered bonnet.
Against my hair its shade is so becoming.
As long as I remember
I had set my heart upon it.
He read my mind without my even saying.
A man who reads the heart's concealed ambition
Is no novice,
He knows what love is!

SCHAUNARD
A clever definition!

COLLINE (*following* SCHAUNARD'*s thought*)
He has experience,

COLLINE
Vin da tavola!

SCHAUNARD
Aragosta senza crosta!

MAMME
Ah! razza di furfanti
indemoniati,
che ci venite a fare in questo
loco?
A casa, a letto! Via brutti
sguaiati,
gli scappellotti vi parranno
poco!
A casa, a letto, razza di furfanti,
a letto!

RAGAZZO
Vo' la tromba, il cavallin.

RODOLFO
E tu Mimì, che vuoi!

MIMÌ
La crêma.

SCHAUNARD
E gran sfarzo, c'è una dama!

RAGAZZI
Viva Parpignol, Parpignol,
Parpignol, Parpignol!
Il tambur, tamburel!
dei soldati, il drappel!

MARCELLO
Signorina Mimì, che dono raro
le ha fatto il suo Rodolfo?

MIMÌ
Una cuffietta a pizzi tutta
Rosa ricamata.
Coi miei cappelli bruni ben si
fonde.
Da tanto tempo tal cuffietta
È cosa desiata.
Ed egli ha letto quel che il core
asconde.
Ora colui che legge dentro a un
cuore.
Sa l'amore ed è lettore.

SCHAUNARD
Esperto professore!

COLLINE
Che ha già diplomi e

Non son armi prime
Le sue rime.

SCHAUNARD
Tanto che sembra ver
Ciò ch'egli esprime.

MARCELLO
O bella età d'inganni e d'utopie!
Si crede, spera e tutto bello
appare.

RODOLFO
La più divina delle poesie
È quella, amico, che c'insegna
amare!

MIMÌ
Amare è dolce ancora più del
miele,
Più del miele!

MARCELLO
Secondo il palato
è miele o fiele!

MIMÌ
O Dio, l'ho offeso!

RODOLFO
È in lutto, o mia Mimì.

SCHAUNARD, COLLINE
Allegri e un toast!

MARCELLO
Qua del liquor!

MIMÌ, RODOLFO, MARCELLO
E via i pensier,
alti bicchier!
Beviam!

TUTTI
Beviam!

MARCELLO
Ch'io beva del tossico! Essa!

RODOLFO, SCHAUNARD, COLLINE
Oh! Musetta!

LE DAMME BOTTEGGIE
To'! Lei! Sì!
To'! Lei! Musetta!
Siamo in auge!
Che toeletta!

ALCINDORO
Come un facchino . . .
Correr di qua . . . di là . . .
No! no! non ci stà! . . .

And for years rehearses,
Writing verses!

SCHAUNARD (*interrupting him*)
All that he says sounds true
As he converses.

MARCELLO (*watching* MIMI)
O lovely state of dreams and admiration!
You hope, believe, and see the world in sunshine.

RODOLFO
The most divine of poet's inspiration
Is that, my friend, which teaches us to love!

MIMI
To be in love is very close to heaven,
Close to heaven!

MARCELLO (*angrily*)
For some it is heaven,
For others, damnation!

MIMI (*surprised, to* RODOLFO)
O dear, did I hurt him?

RODOLFO
He mourns his former love.

SCHAUNARD, COLLINE
It's time for a toast!

MARCELLO (*to the waiter*)
Fill up my glass!

MIMI, RODOLFO, MARCELLO (*rising*)
Down with despair!
Life is so fair!
A toast!

ALL FIVE
A toast!

MARCELLO (*stops, having seen* MUSETTA *approaching*) (*shouting*)
Bring me a dose of arsenic! She's here!
(*he slumps down in his chair; from the corner of Rue Mazarin a beautiful young lady enters, a gay coquette with a provocative smile. She is accompanied by a pompous old man, pretentious both in manner and in dress*)

RODOLFO, SCHAUNARD, COLLINE (*surprised, seeing* MUSETTA)
Look! Musetta!

SHOPWOMEN (*seeing* MUSETTA)
Look! Where? There!
What? She! Musetta!
Bold as ever!
To the letter!

ALCINDORO (*out of breath*)
Just like a porter . . .
Running around like mad . . .
No, no! not for me!

(MUSETTA *enters, walking rapidly and looking around, as if trying to find someone in particular, followed by* ALCINDORO, *peevishly huffing and panting*)

MUSETTA (*as if calling her puppy*)
Come, Fifi! Come, Fifi!

MUSETTA
Vien, Lulù! Vien, Lulù!

ALCINDORO
It's too much for me!
It's too much for me!

ALCINDORO
Non ne posso più . . .
non ne posso più!

(MUSETTA *sees the table where the friends are sitting outside the Café Momus, and signals* ALCINDORO *to reserve the table that the townspeople have just left*)

SCHAUNARD
Now the old codger will start to suffer!

SCHAUNARD
Quel brutto coso mi par che sudi!

ALCINDORO
Sit here? In the open? No!

ALCINDORO
Come! qui fuori? qui?

MUSETTA
Stop it, Fifi!

MUSETTA
Siedi, Lulu!

(ALCINDORO, *testy and irritated, sits down and turns up his coat collar*)

ALCINDORO (*grumbling*)
Please do not use any pet names
In public when talking to me!

ALCINDORO
Tali nomignoli prego
serbateli al tu per tu!

(*a waiter enters and sets the table*)

MUSETTA
Don't take that tone with me!

MUSETTA
Non farmi il Barbablù!

(*sits down at the table, facing the café*)

COLLINE (*scrutinizing the old man*)
A dangerous seducer!

COLLINE
È il vizio contegnoso!

MARCELLO (*disdainfully*)
With his chaste little pigeon!

MARCELLO
Colla casta Susanna!

MIMI (*to* RODOLFO)
But her dress is lovely!

MIMÌ
È pur ben vestita!

RODOLFO
Angels must do without them.

RODOLFO
Gli angeli vanno nudi.

MIMI (*with curiosity*)
Do you know who she is?

MIMÌ
La conosci! Chi è?

MARCELLO
Let me answer you this.
Her first name is Musetta.
Her last one is Temptation!
By way of vocation,
Like a reed in the breezes,
She will change in her love
And her lovers very often,
Exactly like the raven,
She's callous and malicious,
And her fav'rite of dishes
Is heart blood!
Ravenous prey bird!
And she ate my heart, too!
Please pass me the ragout!

MARCELLO
Domandatelo a me.
Il suo nome: Musetta;
cognome: Tentazione!
Per sua vocazione
fa la rosa dei venti;
gira e muta soventi
e d' amanti e d' amore
E come la civetta,
è uccello sanguinario;
il suo cibo ordinario
è il cuore . . .
Mangia il cuore! . . .
Per questo io non ne ho più . . .
Passatemi il ragù!

MUSETTA
(Marcello . . . mi vide . . .
e non mi guarda il vile!
Quel Schaunard che ride!
Mi fan tutti una bile!
Se potessi picchiar!
se potessi graffiar!
Ma non ho sotto man
che questo pellican.
Aspetta!)
Ehi! Camerier!
Ehi! Camerier! Questo piatto
ha una puzza di rifritto!

ALCINDORO
No. Musetta . . .
zitto, zitto!

MUSETTA
(Non si volta!)

ALCINDORO
Zitto, zitto, zitto!
Modi, garbo!

MUSETTA
(Ah non si volta!)

ALCINDORO
A chi parli?

MUSETTA
(Ora lo batto, lo batto!)

ALCINDORO
Con chi parli?

COLLINE
Questo pollo e un poema!

SCHAUNARD
Il vino è prelibato.

MUSETTA
Al cameriere!
Non seccar!
Voglio fare il mio piacere.

ALCINDORO
Parla pian, parla pian!

MUSETTA
Vo' far quel che mi pare!
Non seccar!

DONNE
Guarda, guarda chi si vede,
proprio lei, Musetta!

MUSETTA (*irritated on seeing that her friends at the next table are not watching her*)
(Marcello has seen me,
But he ignores me, the scoundrel! (*getting angrier*)
That Schaunard is laughing!
One's as bad as the other!
I would blacken their eyes!
If I just had a chance!
And I am here alone
With this ridiculous dunce!
I'll show you!) (*shouting*)
Hey, waiter, here! (*sniffing at her plate, while the waiter runs to her*)
Hey! waiter, here!
The smell of this plate is too distasteful!
(*throws the plate to the ground. The waiter picks up the pieces*)

ALCINDORO (*trying to restrain her*)
Stop! Musetta!
Don't be wasteful!

MUSETTA (*seeing that* MARCELLO *has not turned around*)
(He's not looking!)

ALCINDORO (*with comic despair*)
Quiet, quiet, quiet!
Hold your temper!

MUSETTA
(Still he ignores me!)

ALCINDORO
What's the trouble?

MUSETTA (*furious*)
(If I could tear him to pieces!)

ALCINDORO
What's the trouble?

COLLINE
The soufflé is delicious!

SCHAUNARD
The wine is simply perfect!

MUSETTA
This stupid waiter!
That's enough!
I'll do just what I feel like doing!

ALCINDORO
Not so loud! Not so loud!
(*takes the menu from the waiter and starts to order dinner*)

MUSETTA
I don't need you to tell me!
And I want to be left alone!

WORKING GIRLS (*crossing the stage, stop a moment to watch* MUSETTA)
Look who's here on exhibition,

Mad'moiselle Musetta!

STUDENTS (*crossing the stage*)
What a priceless proposition,

BOTH GROUPS
That's just like Musetta!
Ha ha ha ha ha ha ha!

MUSETTA
(Could he be jealous of such a mummy?
Let's see if my power over his heart
Is strong enough to make him yield!)

ALCINDORO (*interrupting his ordering to calm* MUSETTA, *who is still raging*)
Your reputation . . . your virtue.
My good name!

SCHAUNARD
This is simply stupendous!

MUSETTA (*facing* MARCELLO; *at the top of her voice*)
You still ignore me!

ALCINDORO (*believing that* MUSETTA *had meant him, still does not comply, and replies seriously*)
Don't you see I am ordering?

SCHAUNARD
It is simply stupendous!

COLLINE
Stupendous!

RODOLFO (*to* MIMI)
If you should ever
Treat me like that I never,
Never would forgive you!

SCHAUNARD
She speaks to one
And knows the other listens.

MIMI
Darling, I love you
For now and ever after!
So why talk about forgiving?

COLLINE (*to* SCHAUNARD)
The other one pretends
But he's a piece of putty in her hands!

MUSETTA
But your heart throbs and hammers.

ALCINDORO
Softer, softer!

MUSETTA (*still seated, and obviously directing her attentions to* MARCELLO, *who is beginning to feel uneasy*)
Day after day,
When I am strolling by on promenade,
The people turn admiringly,
Praising my dazzling beauty,
With eager eyes they gaze at me
Wherever I go!

STUDENTI
Con quel vecchio che balbetta.

DONNE, STUDENTI
Proprio lei, Musetta!
Ah, ah, ah, ah, ah, ah, ah!

MUSETTA
(Che sia geloso di questa mummia?
Vediam se mi resta tanto poter
su lui da farlo cedere!)

ALCINDORO
La convenienza . . . il grado . . .
la virtù . . .

SCHAUNARD
La commedia è stupenda!

MUSETTA
Tu non mi guardi!

ALCINDORO
Vedi bene che ordino! . . .

SCHAUNARD
La commedia è stupenda!

COLLINE
Stupenda!

RODOLFO
Sappi per tuo
governo che non darei
perdono in sempiterno.

SCHAUNARD
Essa all'un parla
perchè l'altro intenda.

MIMÌ
Io t'amo tanto,
e sono tutta tua!
Che mi parli di perdono?

COLLINE
E l'altro invan crudel,
finge di non capir, ma sugge miel!

MUSETTA
Ma il tuo cuore martella.

ALCINDORO
Parla piano!

MUSETTA
Quando me'n vo',
quando me'n vo soletta per la via
la gente sosta e mira,
e la bellezza mia
tutta ricerca in me
ricerca in me
da capo a piè.

MARCELLO
Legatemi alla seggiola!

ALCINDORO
Quella gente che dirà?

MUSETTA
Ed assaporo allor
la bramosia sottil,
che da gl'occhi traspira
e dai palesi vezzi intender sa
alle occulte beltà.
Così l'effluvio del desio
tutta m'aggira
felice mi fa,
felice mi fa!

ALCINDORO
Quel canto scurrile
mi muove la bile!
mi muove la bile!

MUSETTA
E tu che sai
che memori e ti struggi,
da me tanto rifuggi?
So ben: le angoscie tue non le vuoi dir,
non le vuoi dir, so ben
ma ti senti morir!

MIMÌ
Io vedo ben
che quella poveretta,
tutta invaghita ell'è!
Tutta invaghita di Marcel,
tutta invaghita ell'è!

ALCINDORO
Quella gente che dirà?

RODOLFO
Marcello un dì l'amò.
La fraschetta l'abbandonò,
per poi darsi a miglior vita!

SCHAUNARD
Ah! Marcello cederà!

COLLINE
Chi sa mai quel che avverrà!

MARCELLO
Will someone please hold on to me?

ALCINDORO (*on pins and needles*)
What will people think of you?

MUSETTA
And then I savor keenly
That intense desire,
Which is burning in their glances,
And proudly show my ravishing attire,
In a charming display.
(*rising*)
And when the wave of fervent longing
Invites romances,
How happy I feel,
How happy I feel!

ALCINDORO (*coming closer to* MUSETTA *and trying to stop her*)
This meaningless ditty
Begins to annoy me!
Begins to annoy me!

MUSETTA
You must remember,
Your passion still must burn for me,
Why do you not return to me?
I know, you fight your tortured heart in vain,
You fight your heart in vain,
For you love me again!

MIMI (*to* RODOLFO)
It's plain to see
The beautiful Musetta
Adores your friend Marcel,
She is in love with your Marcel,
Head over heels in love!
(SCHAUNARD *and* COLLINE *rise and stand at one side, observing the little drama with interest, while* RODOLFO *and* MIMI, *now alone at the table, continue quietly talking to each other.* MARCELLO, *his uneasiness increasing, leaves his seat; he would like to leave but cannot resist the sound of* MUSETTA'S *voice*)

ALCINDORO
What will people think of you?

RODOLFO (*to* MIMI)
She loved him once, you know,
But one day she let him go,
Went in search for something better.
(ALCINDORO *tries in vain to persuade* MUSETTA *to return to the table, where their dinner is now ready*)

SCHAUNARD
Ah, Marcello soon will bow!

COLLINE
Anything may happen now!

SCHAUNARD
(Both the victor and the victim
Seem to like the parts they play.)

COLLINE
From the clutches of a woman
I, Colline, must keep away!

MUSETTA
(Ah! Marcello loves me,
Marcello will surrender!)

ALCINDORO
Not so loud! Softly, softly!

MIMI
(I do feel sorry for that unhappy girl!)
Darling! (*cuddling close to* RODOLFO)

RODOLFO (*with his arm around* MIMI'S *waist*)
Mimi!

COLLINE
There's no doubt that she is pretty!

SCHAUNARD
Now it won't be long until he will give in!
The game is most exciting!

MUSETTA (*turns to* MARCELLO)
And yet your anguished heart you fight in vain!
Ah! and you love me again!
(*obstreperously, to* ALCINDORO)
I'll do just what I feel like doing!
I'll do only what I like, let me go!
Let me go, let me go!

MIMI
I do feel sorry for that most unhappy girl!
A selfish love is a dreary affair!
It makes me feel sad,
Ah, what a pity, a pity and a shame!

RODOLFO
It is a miserable love that won't defend itself!
You can't revive a love that is dead!
It is a stale love, gone is all its brilliance,
And its burning flame!

SCHAUNARD (*to* COLLINE)
Marcello won't resist!
If such a lovely lady should ever cast her eyes on you,
You would burn your books on science, and behave as others do!

COLLINE
But I prefer my pipe and my comfortable slippers,
And Greek philosophers!
There's no doubt that she is pretty,
But I prefer my pipe and my comfortable slippers!

SCHAUNARD
(Trovan dolce al pari il laccio
chi lo tende e chi ci dà.)

COLLINE
Santi numi, in simil briga
mai Colline intopperà!

MUSETTA
(Ah! Marcello smania,
Marcello è vinto!)

ALCINDORO
Parla pian! Zitta, zitta!

MIMÌ
(Quell' infelice mi muove a pietà!)
T'amo!

RODOLFO
Mimì!

COLLINE
Essa è bella io non son cieco!

SCHAUNARD
(Quel bravaccio a momenti cederà!)
Stupenda è la commedia!

MUSETTA
So ben, le angoscie tue non le vuoi dir,
ah! ma ti senti morir.
Io voglio fare il mio piacere!
Voglio far quel che mi par, non seccar,
non seccar, non seccar!

MIMÌ
Quell' infelice mi muove a pietà!
l'amor ingeneroso è tristo amor!
Quell' infelice,
ah! ah! mi muove, mi muove a pietà!

RODOLFO
È fiacco amor quel che le offese vendicar non sa!
Non risorge spento amor!
È fiacco amore, quel che le offese
vendicar non sa!

SCHAUNARD
Marcello cederà!
Se tal vaga persona, ti trattasse a tu per tu,
la tua scienza brontolona manderesti a Belzebù!

COLLINE
Ma piaccionmi assai più una pipa e un testo greco!
mi piaccion assai più!
Essa è bella, non son cieco,
ma piaccionmi assai più una pipa e un testo greco!

ALCINDORO
Modi, garbo!
Zitta, zitta!

MUSETTA
(Or convien liberarsi del vecchio!)
Ahi! qual dolore, qual bruciore!

ALCINDORO
Che c'è? Dove?

MUSETTA
Al piè!

MARCELLO
Gioventù mia,
tu non sei morta
nè di te morto è il sovvenir!
Se tu battessi alla mia porta
t'andrebbe il mio core ad aprir, ad aprir!

MUSETTA
Sciogli, slaccia!
rompi, straccia!
Te ne imploro . . .
Laggiù c'è un calzolaio!
Corri, presto!
Ne voglio un altro paio.
Ahi! che fitta,
maledetta scarpa stretta!
Or la levo!
Eccola qua!
Corri, va, corri!
Presto, va! va!

ALCINDORO
Imprudente!
Quella gente che dirà?
Ma il mio grado! Vuoi ch'io comprometta?
Aspetta! Musetta! Vo'!

SCHAUNARD
La commedia è stupenda!
La commedia è stupenda!

COLLINE
La commedia è stupenda!
La commedia è stupenda!

MUSETTA
Marcello!

ALCINDORO
Manners, manners!
Quiet, quiet!

MUSETTA
(Now it's time to get rid of my pet here!)
(*sits down again, pretending to feel a terrible pain in her foot*)
Ow! This is awful, it will kill me!

ALCINDORO
What now? What's wrong?

MUSETTA (*coyly showing her foot*)
My foot!
(ALCINDORO *stoops down to untie* MUSETTA'*s shoe*)

MARCELLO (*deeply moved, goes toward* MUSETTA)
Lovely Musetta,
How could I have forgotten,
I find myself in love again!
No matter what has come between us,
My heart is forever yours alone,
Yours alone!

MUSETTA (*shouting*)
Slash the laces!
Rip the leather!
Strip the shoe off!
Nearby there is a shoestore,
Hurry, quickly!
And get another pair.
Ah, this slipper fits so tight
It drives me crazy!
Off it comes!
(*takes off the shoe and puts it on the table*)
So there you are!
(*impatiently*)
Hurry, go quickly!
Hurry on! Go!

ALCINDORO
What imprudence!
What will all the people say?
(*trying to restrain* MUSETTA)
My position! You provoke a scandal!
How dare you? Musetta! No!
(*quickly hides* MUSETTA'*s shoe under his coat, which he then buttons up, runs off-stage*)

SCHAUNARD
The performance is amazing,
I declare it's amazing!

COLLINE
The performance is amazing!
The performance is amazing!

MUSETTA
Marcello!

MARCELLO
Musetta!
(*MUSETTA and MARCELLO embrace each other passionately*)

SCHAUNARD
Now the drama is ending!
(*a waiter brings in the bill*)

RODOLFO, SCHAUNARD, COLLINE (*amazed*)
The bill?

SCHAUNARD
Not already?
(*drums are in the distance off-stage*)

COLLINE
Did someone ask for it?

SCHAUNARD (*to the waiter*)
Let's see!
(*after looking at the bill, he passes it to his friends; the tattoo, first heard from a great distance, is gradually getting louder as the soldiers approach*)

RODOLFO, COLLINE (*studying the bill*)
Expensive!

RODOLFO, SCHAUNARD, COLLINE (*emptying their pockets*)
Empty your pockets!

SCHAUNARD
Rodolfo, Marcel, and you, Colline?

STREET URCHINS (*running on-stage from the right*)
There are the bugles!

MARCELLO
We are insolvent!

SCHAUNARD
Really?

RODOLFO
I haven't got a penny!

GIRLS, STUDENTS (*hurriedly leaving the Café Momus*)
There are the bugles!
(*the tattoo is still quite a distance away, and the people run in from all directions, looking about to see from which road the soldiers will enter*)

TOWNSPEOPLE
There are the bugles!

MARCELLO, SCHAUNARD, COLLINE
Really! Nothing at all?

SCHAUNARD
Has someone seen my purse?
(*they turn their pockets inside out; they are empty; no one can explain the strange disappearance of SCHAUNARD's purse; they look at one another in amazement*)

STREET URCHINS
Do you think they come from here?
(*trying to find their bearings*)

MARCELLO
Sirena!

SCHAUNARD
Siamo all' ultima scena!

RODOLFO, SCHAUNARD, COLLINE
Il conto!

SCHAUNARD
Così presto?

COLLINE
Chi l' ha richiesto?

SCHAUNARD
Vediam!

RODOLFO, COLLINE
Caro!

RODOLFO, SCHAUNARD, COLLINE
Fuori il danaro!

SCHAUNARD
Colline, Rodolfo e tu Marcel?

RAGAZZI
La Ritirata!

MARCELLO
Siamo all' asciutto!

SCHAUNARD
Come?

RODOLFO
Ho trenta soldi in tutto!

DONNE, STUDENTI
La Ritirata!

BORGHESI
La Ritirata!

MARCELLO, SCHAUNARD, COLLINE
Come? Non ce n'è più?

SCHAUNARD
Ma il mio tesoro ov'è!

RAGAZZI
S'avvicinan per di qua?

MUSETTA
Il mio conto date a me.

DONNE, STUDENTI
No! di là!

RAGAZZI
S'avvicinan per di là!

DONNE, STUDENTI
Vien di qua!

RAGAZZI
No! vien di là!

MUSETTA
Bene!

VENDITORI, BORGHESI
Largo! largo!

RAGAZZI
Voglio veder!
voglio sentir!

MUSETTA
Presto sommate quello con questo!

MAMME
Lisetta, vuoi tacer!
Tonio, la vuoi finir!

RAGAZZI
Mamma, voglio veder!
Papà, voglio sentir!

MUSETTA
Paga il signor che stava qui con me!

RODOLFO, MARCELLO, SCHAUNARD, COLLINE
Paga il signor!

MAMME
Vuoi tacer, la vuoi finir!

RAGAZZI
Vuò veder la Ritirata!

DONNE, BORGHESI
S'avvicinano di qua!

TUTTI
Sì di qua!

MUSETTA (*to the waiter*)
Give the bill right here to me.

GIRLS, STUDENTS
No! From there!

STREET URCHINS (*still uncertain, they point in the opposite direction*)
They are coming from the right!

GIRLS, STUDENTS
No, from left!
(*several windows on the square are opened. Some mothers with their children lean out of the windows; others go out on their balconies. All speculate excitedly about the arrival of the soldiers*)

URCHINS
No, from the right!

MUSETTA (*to the waiter, who hands her the bill*)
Thank you!

VENDORS, TOWNSMEN
Clear the roadway!
(*running forward from the back, and trying to clear the streets of the crowd*)

BOYS (*from the windows*)
They're coming near!
Soon they'll be here!

MUSETTA
Take the two bills and add them together!
(*the waiter adds the two amounts together*)

MOTHERS (*from the windows*)
Don't go too far away!
I told you not to stay!

BOYS
Mommy, please let me stay!
Papa, I want to play!

MUSETTA
And the man who came with me will pay!

RODOLFO, MARCELLO, SCHAUNARD, COLLINE (*pointing in the direction where* ALCINDORO *left; with comic emphasis*)
Yes, he will pay!

MOTHERS
Why can't you for once obey!

BOYS
Let us see the men parading!
(*the crowd has by now filled the entire stage. The soldiers are heard approaching from the left*)

GIRLS, TOWNSPEOPLE
They are coming up the street!

ALL
Here they come!

STREET URCHINS
When the parade comes past us
Let's fall in step behind it!
(the shopkeepers and vendors close their shops and move into the streets)

COLLINE *(aside, with comic emphasis)*
Yes, he will pay!

SCHAUNARD
Yes, he will pay!

MARCELLO
He will pay!
(the waiter presents the two bills, now added together, to MUSETTA*)*

MUSETTA *(takes the two bills together and puts them at* ALCINDORO's *place at the table)*
And all my pains and trouble
Will cost him more than double!

VENDORS *(speaking to a group of townspeople they meet on the street)*
In this majestic music our country's glory shines!

RODOLFO, MARCELLO, SCHAUNARD, COLLINE
And all her pains and trouble
Will cost him more than double!
(everybody looks to the left; the soldiers are about to enter the square; the crowd draws back and some go to the right, others to the left, while the friends, with MUSETTA *and* MIMI, *form a group on the side near the café)*

CROWD
Here they come right up the street!
Let's follow!

MARCELLO
Here comes the whole procession.

MARCELLO, COLLINE
Be sure our benefactor can't see us steal his angel!

MARCELLO, SCHAUNARD, COLLINE
Such a crowd is ideal,
It won't be hard to dodge him!

RODOLFO
Here comes the whole procession!
(the soldiers' procession enters from the left, led by a huge drum major, who handles his baton with skill and seriousness, and indicates the course of march)

CROWD *(pointing in admiration)*
The flags are gaily flying!
May ever so proudly they wave!
Hear the fife and drum!
Hear the fife and drum!

MIMI, MUSETTA, RODOLFO, MARCELLO, SCHAUNARD, COLLINE
Hurry, hurry, hurry!

RAGAZZI
Come sarà arrivata
la seguiremo al passo!

COLLINE
Paga il signor!

SCHAUNARD
Paga il signor!

MARCELLO
Il signor!

MUSETTA
È dove s'è seduto
ritrovi il mio saluto!

VENDITORI
In quel rullio tu senti la patria maestà!

RODOLFO, MARCELLO, SCHAUNARD, COLLINE
E dove s'è seduto
ritrovi il suo saluto!

LA FOLLA
Largo, largo, eccoli qua!
in fila!

MARCELLO
Giunge la ritirata!

MARCELLO, COLLINE
Che il vecchio non ci veda
fuggir colla sua preda!

MARCELLO, SCHAUNARD, COLLINE
Quella folla serrata
il nascondiglio appresti!

RODOLFO
Giunge la ritirata!

LA FOLLA
Ecco il tambur maggiore!
Più fier d'un antico guerrier!
Il tambur maggior!
Il tambur maggior!

MIMÌ, MUSETTA, RODOLFO, MARCELLO, SCHAUNARD, COLLINE
Lesti, lesti, lesti!

LA FOLLA
I Zappator, I Zappatori olà!
Ecco il tambur maggior!
La ritiratata è qua!

CROWD
There they are now!
See how they march along!
(the soldiers' procession crosses the stage, and moves off, right)
See how they march along!
The guards are marching by!
(MUSETTA, not able to walk, because she has only one shoe on, is lifted onto the shoulders of MARCELLO and COLLINE, who get ready to join the procession following the soldiers. The crowd, seeing MUSETTA carried off triumphantly, bursts into noisy ovations. MARCELLO and COLLINE, with MUSETTA, join the line at the end of the procession, while RODOLFO and MIMI, their arms linked with SCHAUNARD with his horn in his mouth, follow. Then come the students and working girls, skipping about merrily, followed by children, townspeople, and women, all of them marching in time. All the crowd goes off-stage, following the retiring soldiers' procession)

Eccolo là!
Il bel tambur maggior!
La canna d'or,
tutto splendor!
Che guarda, passa, va!
Tutto splendor!
Di Francia è il più bell'uom!
Il bel tambur maggior!
Eccolo là!
Che guarda, passa, va!

See them parade!
The guards are marching by!
Their heads held high,
The pennants fly!
The sabers gleam and shine!
See them pass by!
They march in perfect line!
While pennants proudly fly!
The sabers shine!
The guards are passing by!

RODOLFO, MARCELLO, SCHAUNARD, COLLINE
Viva Musetta! Cuor biricchin!
Gloria ed onor!
onor e gloria del quartier latin!

RODOLFO, MARCELLO, SCHAUNARD, COLLINE
Viva Musetta! Queen of our heart!
Glory and pride,
The joy and glory of the whole Montmartre!
(at this moment, ALCINDORO, with a new pair of shoes wrapped up in paper, enters and goes toward the Café Momus, looking for MUSETTA. The waiter, standing by the table, takes the bill left by the friends and presents it ceremoniously to ALCINDORO, who, seeing the amount and not finding anyone else around, slumps into a chair, stunned and dumfounded)

ACT III

The Barrière d'Enfer. Beyond the tollgate, the outer boulevard, and in the extreme rear, the Orléans Road, which loses itself in the distance, among old houses, and in the February mist. At the left there is a tavern and the small yard in front of the tollgate.

At the right, Boulevard d'Enfer, at the left, Boulevard St. Jacques.

At the left is the entrance to Rue d'Enfer, which leads into the very heart of the Latin Quarter. As its sign the tavern displays Marcello's painting The Passage of the Red Sea, *but beneath is inscribed in large letters "At the Port of Marseilles."*

On each side of the entrance is a fresco, one of a Turk, the other of a Zouave with an enormous laurel crown around his fez. The wall of the tavern that faces the tollgate has a ground-floor window from which light is shining.

Flanking the tollgate yard are tall, gray plane trees that separate diagonally in long lines toward the two boulevards. Between each two trees stands a marble bench. It is the end of February. Snow is everywhere.

As the curtain rises, the scene is plunged into the uncertainty of dawn's first light. Seated in front of a brazier are the customs officers, dozing. From the tavern, at intervals, one hears loud voices, clinking glasses, laughter. A customs officer comes out of the tavern, carrying wine. The tollgate barrier is closed.

Behind the closed tollgate stand the street sweepers, stamping their feet with the cold and blowing into their stiff hands.

STREET SWEEPERS (*shouting*)
Wake up! You keepers! Admit us!
(*the customs officers remain motionless. The sweepers knock on the closed gate with brooms and shovels shouting louder*)
Hey, there!
We have to go to work!
We are the sweepers!
(*stamping their feet*)
Don't keep us waiting!
Hurry up! We are freezing!

SPAZZINI
Ohè, là le guardie . . .
Aprite! . . . Ohè, là!
Quelli di Gentilly! . . . Siam gli spazzini! . . .
Fiocca la neve! Ohè, là! Qui s'agghiaccia!

TOLLGATE OFFICIAL (*rising sleepily and stretching his arms*)
Coming!
(*goes to open the gate. The street sweepers enter and leave by Rue d'Enfer. The tollgate official closes the barrier again*)

DOGANIERE
Vengo!

NINE WOMEN (*from the tavern; they accompany their singing by clinking their glasses*)
All the joys of life combine
In love and wine, in love and wine—Ah!

VOCI INTERNE
Chi nel ber trovò il piacer,
nel suo bicchier, nel suo bicchier, ah!
d'una bocca nell'ardor,
trovò l'amor, trovò l'amor!

Glowing lips and glowing wine
Make life divine, make life divine!

MUSETTA
Ah!
Se nel bicchiere sta il piacer
in giovin bocca sta l'amor!

MUSETTA'S VOICE (*from the tavern*)
Ah!—
In glowing lips and glowing wine
All pleasures in this world combine!

VOCI DAL CABARET
Tralleralè, tralleralè!
Eva e Noè!

NINE MEN (*from the tavern*)
Trallerallay, trallerallay!
Ever and aye!
(*all laugh noisily*)

LATTIVENDOLE
Hopp-là! Hopp-là!

SIX MILK SELLERS (*girls, off-stage shouting*)
Hoopla! Hoopla!

DOGANIERE
Son già le lattivendole!

CUSTOMS OFFICER
(*from the guardhouse comes the sergeant of the customs office, who gives orders to open the gate*)
The peasant girls are coming in!
(*tinkling of cart bells*)

CARRETTIERI
Hopp-là!
Hopp-là!

CARTERS (*off-stage*)
Giddap! (*shouted*)
(*on the outer boulevard carts pass by with large lanterns hanging between the wheels; cracking of whips*)
Giddap! (*very near; shouted*)
(*the mist has risen and day begins to dawn*)

LATTIVENDOLE
Buon giorno!
Buon giorno!
Buon giorno!

SIX MILK SELLERS (*entering, to the customs officers, who examine and let them pass*)
Good morning!
Good morning!
Good morning!
(*they leave in different directions; it stops snowing;*)

CONTADINE
Burro e cacio!
Polli ed ova!
Voi da che parte andate?
A San Michele!
Ci troverem più tardi?
A mezzodì,
A mezzodì!

SIX PEASANT WOMEN (*entering with boxes on their arms; to customs officers*)
Cheese and butter!
Eggs and chicken!
(*they pay and go on*)
(*from the crossroad*)
Where are you people going?
St. Michael's market!
Then will you see us later?
At twelve o'clock!
At twelve o'clock!
(*they disappear in different directions; the customs officers take away the benches and the brazier;* MIMI *enters from Rue d'Enfer, looking around carefully, trying to recognize the surroundings, but, arriving at the first plane tree, she is stricken by a violent attack of coughing. Then she recovers and, seeing the* SERGEANT, *goes up to him*)

MIMÌ
Sa dirmi, scusi, qual è
l'osteria . . .
Dove un pittor lavora?

MIMI (*to the* SERGEANT)
Excuse me, sir—which is the tavern . . .
(*not able to remember the name*)
Where an artist is painting?

SERGEANT (*pointing to the tavern*)
There it is.

MIMI
Thank you.
(*coughs; a servant maid comes out of the tavern.* MIMI *goes up to her*)
Please may I ask you to do me a favor.
Could you find me the painter Marcello?
I have to see him.
It's very urgent.
Quietly tell him that Mimi is waiting.
(*the woman re-enters the tavern*)

SERGEANT (*to someone who is passing by*)
Eh, what's in the basket!

CUSTOMS OFFICER (*after having examined the basket*)
Empty!

SERGEANT
Pass it.
(*from the gate enter other people, who proceed in various directions. From the Maria Teresa Hospice the matin sounds. It is full daylight; a winter day, sad and dark; from the tavern emerge a few couples, homeward bound*)

MARCELLO (*comes from the tavern, surprised*)
Mimi!

MIMI
I am so glad I found you here.

MARCELLO
Yes, for a month we're staying
At this inn without paying.
Musetta sings her songs for the patron's enjoyment;
And I found employment
Painting these murals.
It's cold here. Come in now.

MIMI
Is Rodolfo there?

MARCELLO
Yes.

MIMI
Then I cannot go in.
(*bursts into tears*)

MARCELLO
Why not?

MIMI (*in despair*)
Oh dear Marcello, help me!
I beg you!

MARCELLO
Tell me what happened?

MIMI
Rodolfo, Rodolfo loves me,
And yet he deeply distrusts me,

SERGENTE
Eccola.

MIMÌ
Grazie.
O buona donna, mi fate il favore
di cercarmi il pittore Marcello?
Ho da parlargli.
Ho tanta fretta.
Ditegli, piano, che Mimì l'aspetta.

SERGENTE
Ehì, quel paniere!

DOGANIERE
Vuoto!

SERGENTE
Passi!

MARCELLO
Mimì?!

MIMÌ
Speravo di trovarvi qui.

MARCELLO
È ver, siam qui da un mese
di quell' oste alle spese.
Musetta insegna il canto ai passeggieri,
io pingo quei guerrieri
sulla facciata.
È freddo. Entrate.

MIMÌ
C' è Rodolfo?

MARCELLO
Sì.

MIMÌ
Non posso entrar, no, no!

MARCELLO
Perchè?

MIMÌ
O buon Marcello, aiuto!
aiuto!

MARCELLO
Cos' è avvenuto?

MIMÌ
Rodolfo, Rodolfo m'ama,
Rodolfo m'ama e mi fugge,
il mio Rodolfo si strugge

per gelosia.
Un passo, un detto . . .
un vezzo, un fior . . .
lo mettono in sospetto.
Onde corrucci ed ire.
Talor la notte fingo di dormire
e in me lo sento fiso
spiarmi i sogni in viso.
Mi grida ad ogni istante:
"non fai per me,
ti prendi un altro amante,
non fai per me!"
Ahimè! Ahimè!
In lui parla il rovello, lo so,
ma che rispondergli, Marcello?

He makes me suffer unjustly,
He is so jealous.
A chance admission,
A step, a word,
Awaken his suspicion
And start his fury sweeping.
At night, when I pretend that I am sleeping,
I feel that he is scheming
To know what I am dreaming.
So many times he told me:
"Our love is gone,
Go find another lover,
We can't go on!"
It breaks my heart!
He does not really mean it, it's true,
But what on earth am I to do?

MARCELLO
Quando s'è come voi
non si vive in compagnia.

MARCELLO
If you're both so unhappy,
Then you should not live together.

MIMÌ
Dite ben, dite bene.
Lasciarci conviene.
Aiutateci,
Aiutateci voi;
noi s'è provato più volte
ma invano.
Dite ben, dite ben
lasciarci convien!

MIMI
You are right, I must leave him,
I have to confess it.
All I ask of you,
Will you help us decide?
Though we have tried it so often,
It is hopeless!
It is hard, sad and hard
For lovers to part.

MARCELLO
Son lieve a Musetta
ell'è lieve a me
perchè ci amiamo in allegria . . .
Canti e risa, ecco il fior
d'invariabile amor!

MARCELLO
Take me and my Musetta,
She's ideal for me,
Because she always takes me lightly.
Song and laughter are keeping
Our love firm and strong!

MIMÌ
Fate voi per il meglio.

MIMI
Will you promise to help us?

MARCELLO
Sta ben, sta ben!
Ora lo sveglio.

MARCELLO
All right, all right!
I'll go and wake him.

MIMÌ
Dorme?

MIMI
Wake him?

MARCELLO
È piombato qui un' ora avanti l'alba,
s'assopì sopra una panca.
Guardate . . .
Che tosse!

MARCELLO
He came here very early in the morning
And fell asleep exhausted.
I'll show you.
(*motions* MIMI *to look through the window into the tavern;* MIMI *coughs persistently*)
(*compassionately*)
You are ill!

MIMÌ
Da ieri ho l'ossa rotte.

MIMI
I'm weary to exhaustion.

Last night, Rodolfo left me,
And said to me:
"It's the end."
That's why I need your help now,
You have always been our friend.

Fuggì da me stanotte
dicendomi: "È finita."
A giorno sono uscita
e me ne venni a questa volta.

MARCELLO (*watching* RODOLFO *inside the tavern*)
He's waking, rising, and calls me.
He's coming . . .

MARCELLO
Si desta . . .
s' alza, mi cerca . . .
viene . . .

MIMI
Don't let him see me!

MIMÌ
Ch' ei non mi veda!

MARCELLO
Then it is better, Mimi,
If you go home!
I'll speak to him alone.
(MARCELLO *leads* MIMI *gently toward the corner of the tavern, where, however, she lingers and eavesdrops with interest.* MARCELLO *goes to meet* RODOLFO)

MARCELLO
Or rincasate,
Mimì . . . per carità!
Non fate scene qua!

RODOLFO (*comes out of the tavern and rushes toward* MARCELLO)
Marcello, I'll confide it,
Why should I hide it,
I cannot go on living with Mimi!

RODOLFO
Marcello. Finalmente!
Qui niun ci sente.
Io voglio separarmi da Mimì.

MARCELLO
Then you want to be free?

MARCELLO
Sei volubil così?

RODOLFO
Once more I thought
That our love was faded and past,
But now I know, my love for her will last,
Always and always
Oh, it drives me insane!

RODOLFO
Già un' altra volta
credetti morto il mio cor,
ma di quegl'occhi azzurri allo
splendor
esso è risorto.
Ora il tedio l'assal!

MARCELLO
And you want to renew it all again?
(MIMI, *who has been unable to hear the words, choosing the proper moment, re-enters, unobserved, and moves behind a plane tree near where the friends are conversing*)

MARCELLO
E gli vuoi rinnovare il funeral?

RODOLFO
Forever!

RODOLFO
Per sempre!

MARCELLO
Change your tune then.
A love that's drear and mirthless
Is dull indeed and worthless.
Love without happy laughter,
Is always stale and brittle.
I think you're jealous.

MARCELLO
Cambia metro.
Dei pazzi è l' amor tetro
che lacrime distilla.
Se non ride e sfavilla,
l' amore è fiacco e roco.
Tu sei geloso.

RODOLFO
A little.

RODOLFO
Un poco.

MARCELLO
Cantankerous, belligerent,
Full of prejudice and suspicion,
Annoying and stubborn!

MARCELLO
Collerico, lunatico,
imbevuto di pregiudizi,
noioso, cocciuto!

MIMÌ
Or lo fa incollerir!
Me poveretta!

RODOLFO
Mimì è una civetta
che frascheggia con tutti.
Un moscardino
di Viscontino le fa l'occhi di triglia.
Ella sgonnella e scopre la caviglia
con un far promettente e lusinghier.

MARCELLO
Lo devo dir?
Non mi sembri sincer.

RODOLFO
Ebbene, no, non lo son.
Invan, invan nascondo
la mia vera tortura.
Amo Mimì sovra ogni cosa al mondo,
io l'amo.
Ma ho paura,
ma ho paura!
Mimì è tanto malata!
Ogni dì più declina.
La povera piccina
è condannata!

MARCELLO
Mimì?

MIMÌ
Che vuol dire?

RODOLFO
Una terribil tosse
l'esil petto le scuote
già le smunte gote
di sangue ha rosse . . .

MARCELLO
Povera Mimì!

MIMÌ
Ahimè, morire?!

RODOLFO
La mia stanza è una tana
squallida . . . il fuoco ho spento.
V'entra e l'aggira il vento
di tramontana.
Essa canta e sorride,
e il rimorso m'assale.
Me cagion del fatale
mal che l'uccide!

MIMI (*to herself*)
Now his temper will flare!
He is so pettish!

RODOLFO (*with ironical bitterness*)
Mimi is so coquettish,
So inanely flirtatious.
(*with irony*)
Some silly highbrow,
Some titled dandy makes his leering advances.
(*with growing irony*)
And she responds with inviting hints and glances
In a promising way that's all too clear.

MARCELLO
Shall I speak out?
You are not quite sincere.

RODOLFO
All right then, no, I am not!
In vain I have been lying,
I unjustly accuse her!
I love Mimi, my love for her is stronger
Than ever!
(MIMI *is moved*)
But I will lose her,
But I will lose her.
(MIMI, *surprised, comes even nearer, always hidden behind the trees*)
Mimi is dreadfully ailing.
Day by day she is failing.
I fear the spark of life has lost its power!

MARCELLO (*surprised, in a low voice*)
Mimi?

MIMI (*to herself*)
Can he mean it?

RODOLFO
Terrible fits of coughing
Shake her fragile existence,
And her brave resistance
Can't last much longer!

MARCELLO
And I never knew!

MIMI (*weeping*)
Must I die so soon then?

RODOLFO
And my room is a den of poverty,
No fire is going,
Fiercely the wind is blowing,
Ice-cold, relentless!
She is always so cheerful,
But remorse overcomes me.
I have aided the fearful ill
Which destroys her!

MARCELLO (*tries to lead* RODOLFO *away*)
What to do now?
MIMI (*in desolation*)
It is true then?
RODOLFO
Mimi is like a flower,
Lacking water and sunshine,
But you can't revive a blossom
By love alone, by love alone.
MIMI (*anguished*)
All is ended!
All is ended!
All I lived for!
All is ended!
I must say good-by to all I love.
MARCELLO
Oh wretched fate!
What a pity!
Must she really die?
Must she really die?
(*her cough and violent sobs reveal her presence*)
RODOLFO (*rushing to* MIMI)
You, Mimi! You here?
You overheard me?
MARCELLO
Then she overheard you!
RODOLFO
Darling, you must not mind me,
There is no need to worry.
Here, come and get warm!
(*tries to lead her into the tavern*)
MIMI
No, the smoke there would smother me!
RODOLFO
Ah, Mimi!
(*presses* MIMI *lovingly into his arms and caresses her. From the tavern* MUSETTA'*s brazen laugh is heard*)
MARCELLO (*running to the window*)
I can tell it's Musetta.
Who is with her?
Wait till I catch you!
This time I'll show you!
(*stormily enters the tavern*)
MIMI (*freeing herself from* RODOLFO)
Good-by then!
RODOLFO (*astonished*)
Mimi! You're leaving!
MIMI
Once again I'll return
To my own scentless flowers,
Lonely as once before

MARCELLO
Che far dunque?
MIMÌ
O mia vita!
RODOLFO
Mimì di serra è fiore.
Povertà l'ha sfiorita,
per richiamarla in vita
non basta amor, non basta amor.
MIMÌ
Ahimè, ahimè!
È finita!
O mia vita!
È finita!
Ahimè morir, ahimè morir!
MARCELLO
Oh qual pietà!
Poveretta!
Povera Mimì!
Povera Mimì!
RODOLFO
Chè! Mimì! Tu qui?
M'hai sentito?
MARCELLO
Ella dunque ascoltava?
RODOLFO
Facile alla paura
per nulla io m'arrovello.
Vien là nel tepor.
MIMÌ
No, quel tanfo mi soffoca.
RODOLFO
Ah, Mimì!
MARCELLO
È Musetta
che ride.
Con chi ride? Ah la civetta!
Imparerai.
MIMÌ
Addio.
RODOLFO
Che! Vai?
MIMÌ
Donde lieta uscì
al tuo grido d'amore,
torna sola Mimì
al solitario nido.

Ritorna un' altra volta
a intesser finti fior.
Addio, senza rancor.
Ascolta, ascolta.
Le poche robe aduna che lasciai sparse.
Nel mio cassetto stan chiusi
quel cerchietto d'or,
e il libro di preghiere.
Involgi tutto quanto
in un grembiale e manderò il portiere . . .
Bada . . . sotto il guanciale
c'è la cuffietta rosa.
Se vuoi, se vuoi,
se vuoi serbarla a ricordo d'amor!
Addio,
addio senza rancor.

RODOLFO
Dunque è proprio finita!
Te ne vai, te ne vai,
la mia piccina.
Addio sogni d'amor!

MIMÌ
Addio dolce svegliare
alla mattina!

RODOLFO
Addio sognante vita
che un tuo sorriso acqueta!

MIMÌ
Addio rabbuffi e gelosie.
Addio sospetti . . .

RODOLFO
Baci!

MIMÌ
Pungenti amarezze.

RODOLFO
Ch' io da vero poeta
Rimavo con: carezze!

MIMÌ
Soli l'inverno . . .

MIMÌ, RODOLFO
è cosa da morire!

MIMÌ
Soli!

MIMÌ, RODOLFO
Mentre a primavera
c'è compagno il sol.

MIMÌ
C'è compagno il sol!

To live with all my mem'ries
Through solitary hours
Where longing never ends!
Good-by then, we part as friends.
One thing I ask you!
Gather together the few keepsakes I treasure.
There in a box is my locket
And the little cross,
Together with my prayerbook.
Collect the other things I own
And I'll send someone to get them tomorrow . . .
Listen—under the pillow
I left my little bonnet.
It's yours, it's yours,
A souvenir of love you'll always recall!
Good-by then
Good-by for good and all!

RODOLFO
Then you really will leave me,
Dear Mimi, sweet Mimi,
My own beloved,
Farewell to my dream of love.

MIMI
Farewell awaking together
When dawn is ascending!

RODOLFO
Farewell to romantic dreaming
Which had a happy ending!

MIMI (*smiling*)
Farewell distrust and jealous quarrels!
Farewell suspicions,

RODOLFO
Kisses . . .

MIMI
The sharp sting of sadness,

RODOLFO
Which, like ev'ry true poet,
I rhymed with "love" and "gladness"!

MIMI
How sad and hopeless

BOTH
To be alone in winter!

MIMI
Lonely!

BOTH
But when spring returns,
The sun will be our friend.

MIMI
Our consoling friend!
(*inside the tavern the clatter of broken plates and glasses is heard*)

MARCELLO (*from within*)
What the devil is the meaning——
MUSETTA (*from within*)
That's enough!
MARCELLO
Of your giggling and your gushing?
MUSETTA
That's enough!
(*comes out running*)
MIMI
No one's lonely in spring.
MARCELLO (*stopping in the doorway of the tavern, turning to* MUSETTA)
When I came in I saw how deeply you were blushing.
MUSETTA (*with a provocative attitude*)
That nice gentleman was saying:
"Shall we dance now, Miss Musetta?"
RODOLFO
The roses and lilies are blooming!
MIMI
In ev'ry tree the birds are gaily singing.
RODOLFO
In the glory of the springtime
MIMI
In the glory of the springtime
RODOLFO
No one is alone!
MIMI
No one is alone!
RODOLFO
Brooklets and fountains murmur,
MIMI
Brooklets and fountains murmur,
MIMI, RODOLFO
The tender evening breezes
Calmly descending
Soothe our grief and sorrow,
We'll part when spring is
with us once again!
MUSETTA
And I was blushing when I answered
"There is nothing I'd like better!"
MARCELLO
Sure as fate I know you're up to
something shady!
MUSETTA
Liberty is what I want!
MARCELLO (*almost hurling himself upon* MUSETTA)
You'll be sorry, my dear lady.
MUSETTA
Why this shouting?

MARCELLO
Che facevi? Che dicevi?

MUSETTA
Che vuoi dir!

MARCELLO
Presso al fuoco a quel signore?

MUSETTA
Che vuoi dir!

MIMÌ
Niuno è solo l'april.

MARCELLO
Al mio venire hai mutato di
colore.

MUSETTA
Quel signore mi diceva:
ama il ballo, signorina?

RODOLFO
Si parla coi gigli e le rose.

MIMÌ
Esce dai nidi un cinguettio
gentile.
RODOLFO
Al fiorir di primavera.

MIMÌ
Al fiorir di primavera.

RODOLFO
C'è compagno il sol!

MIMÌ
C'è compagno il sol!

RODOLFO
Chiacchieran le fontane.

MIMÌ
Chiacchieran le fontane.

MIMÌ, RODOLFO
La brezza della sera
balsami stende
sulle doglie umane.
Vuoi che aspettiam
la primavera ancor?

MUSETTA
Arrossendo rispondeva:
ballerei sera e mattina.

MARCELLO
Quel discorso asconde mire
disoneste.

MUSETTA
Voglio piena libertà!

MARCELLO
Io t'acconcio per le feste!

MUSETTA
Chè mi canti?

MARCELLO
Se ti colgo a incivettire!

MUSETTA
Chè mi gridi? Chè mi canti?
All' altar non siamo uniti!

MARCELLO
Bada sotto il mio cappello
non ci stan certi ornamenti.

MUSETTA
Io detesto quegli amanti
Che la fanno da—ah! ah! ah!
mariti

MARCELLO
In non faccio da zimbello
ai novizi intraprendenti.

MUSETTA
Fo' all'amor con chi mi piace!
non ti garba?
fo' all'amor con chi mi piace!

MARCELLO
Ve n'andate? Vi ringrazio:
or son ricco divenuto.
Vana frivola civetta!

MUSETTA
Musetta se ne va, si, se ne va!

MUSETTA, MARCELLO
Vi saluto.

MUSETTA
Signor, addio.
Vi dico con piacer!

MARCELLO
Son servo e me ne vò!

MUSETTA
Pittore da bottega!

MARCELLO
Vipera!

MUSETTA
Rospo!

MARCELLO
Strega!

MIMÌ
Sempre tua per la vita.

RODOLFO
Ci lascieremo . . .

MIMÌ
Ci lascieremo
alla stagion dei fior . . .

MARCELLO
If I catch you gallivanting!

MUSETTA
Stop your raving! Stop your ranting!
We are not yet married people!

MARCELLO
Do you think you can deceive me
With that feeble-minded fellow!

MUSETTA
I detest that sort of lover
Who behaves just like, ha ha ha, a
husband!

MARCELLO
I am on to you, believe me,
You don't know your friend Marcello.

MUSETTA
I'll behave the way I want to!
Don't you like it?
I'll behave the way I want to!

MARCELLO
Are you leaving? I am grateful!
What a lucky stroke of fortune!
Shameless superficial hussy!

MUSETTA
Musetta says good day, and goes away!

MUSETTA, MARCELLO (*ironically*)
I'm delighted.

MUSETTA
Good-by, sir.
The pleasure's mine, good-by!

MARCELLO
The pleasure's mine, good-by!

MUSETTA (*goes away, furious, then suddenly stops, shouting*)
You vulgar shanty painter.

MARCELLO (*from stage center*)
Jezebel!

MUSETTA
Bullfrog!
(*exits*)

MARCELLO
Hell-cat!
(*enters the tavern*)

MIMI (*slowly starting to go with* RODOLFO)
I am yours forever!

RODOLFO
We'll wait till springtime.

MIMI
We'll wait till spring
Before we say good-by . . .

RODOLFO
Before we say good-by.

MIMI
If only winter would last forever.
(the curtain begins to fall slowly)

BOTH *(off-stage)*
We'll part when spring is here again!
(the curtain closes completely)

RODOLFO
Alla stagion dei fior.

MIMÌ
Vorrei che eterno durasse il verno!

MIMÌ, RODOLFO
Ci lascierem alla stagion dei fior!

ACT IV

Same as Act I. MARCELLO *again is standing before his easel, and* RODOLFO *is seated at his table. One tries to convince the other that he is working hard, while they actually do nothing but chat.*

MARCELLO In un coupè?	MARCELLO (*continuing the conversation*) Was that today?
RODOLFO Con pariglia e livree. Mi salutò ridendo: "Tò! Musetta!" Le dissi: "e il cuor?" "Non batte o non lo sento grazie al velluto che il copre."	RODOLFO In a handsome coupé. Smiling, she waved a greeting. "Well! Musetta," I asked her. "How's your heart?" "It's not beating, or I can't feel it, Buried so deeply in velvet."
MARCELLO Ci ho gusto davver, ci ho gusto davver.	MARCELLO (*forcing a laugh*) I'm happy to hear that, I'm happy indeed!
RODOLFO (Loiola va! Ti rodi e ridi.)	RODOLFO (*to himself*) (A brazen lie! He's trying to fool me!) (*resumes his work*)
MARCELLO Non batte? Bene! Io pur vidi . . .	MARCELLO Not beating? Splendid! (*paints with long strokes of his brush*) Guess whom I saw!
RODOLFO Musetta?	RODOLFO Musetta?
MARCELLO Mimì.	MARCELLO Mimi.
RODOLFO L' hai vista? Oh guarda!	RODOLFO (*startled, stops writing*) You saw her? (*collects himself*) Oh, really!
MARCELLO Era in carrozza vestita come una regina.	MARCELLO (*stops working*) Dressed like a princess And riding in a smart-looking carriage.
RODOLFO Evviva! Ne son contento.	RODOLFO That's splendid! I'm glad to hear it!
MARCELLO (Bugiardo, si strugge d'amor.)	MARCELLO (*to himself*) (Not one word he's saying is true.)
RODOLFO Lavoriam.	RODOLFO Let us work!
MARCELLO Lavoriam.	MARCELLO Let us work! (*both resume their work*)
RODOLFO Che penna infame!	RODOLFO This pen is dreadful! (*throws it away*)
MARCELLO Che infame pennello!	MARCELLO Impossible paint brush!

(throws it away; RODOLFO *always seated and very much lost in thought;* MARCELLO *looking at his painting, then, without* RODOLFO *noticing it, he takes a ribbon from his pocket and kisses it)*

RODOLFO
Ah, Mimi, I can't forget you,
Oh golden mem'ry, joys shared together!
Glorious days departed . . .

RODOLFO
O Mimì tu più non torni.
O giorni belli,
piccole mani—odorosi capelli . . .

MARCELLO *(puts the ribbon back and looks again at his painting)*
Somehow lately my paint brush
Has become so capricious
And does as it wishes
All against my will.

MARCELLO
Io non so come sia che
il mio pennello lavori
e impasti colori
contro voglia mia.

RODOLFO
Gone forever! Ah, Mimi!
My fleeting dream of love!

RODOLFO
Collo di neve! Ah! Mimì!
Mia breve gioventù!

MARCELLO
Whenever I begin to paint a sunset,
The sky, or changing season,
I find it tracing
For some unknown reason,
Two dark eyes and two mocking lips,
The likeness of Musetta, time again!

MARCELLO
Se pingere mi piace o cieli,
o terre,
o inverni, o primavere,
egli mi traccia
due pupille nere,
e una bocca procace.
E n'esce di Musetta il viso
ancor . . .

RODOLFO *(takes* MIMI's *bonnet from the table drawer)*
Ah—dear little bonnet
She once gave to me,
As parting remembrance,
You know all, our moments of blinding joy!
Come to my heart, console my sorrow,
Ah, come, console my lonely heart,
Console my lonely heart!

RODOLFO
E tu, cuffietta lieve,
che sotto il guancial
partendo ascose,
tutta sai la nostra felicità.
Vien sul mio cuor, sul mio cuor
morto,
ah vien, ah vien sul mio cuor;
poichè è morto amor.

MARCELLO
Ah, vision of Musetta
With all her charming grace,
So lovely and faithless.
While she enjoys her pleasure,
My forsaken heart keeps calling her name,
My lonely heart,
My sad and lonely heart!

MARCELLO
E n' esce di Musetta
il viso tutto vezzi
e tutto frode.
Musetta intanto gode
e il mio cuor vile la chiama,
la chiama,
e aspetta il vil mio cuor.

RODOLFO *(presses the bonnet to his heart, then, trying to hide his emotion from* MARCELLO, *he turns to him, asks casually:)*
What is the time?

RODOLFO
Che ora sia?

MARCELLO *(who had remained sunk in thought, is aroused by* RODOLFO's *question and answers him gaily)*
Time for our yesterday's dinner!

MARCELLO
L' ora del pranzo di ieri.

RODOLFO
Not a sign of Schaunard?

RODOLFO
E Schaunard non torna?

*(*SCHAUNARD *and* COLLINE *enter. The former carries four rolls, the latter a paper bag)*

SCHAUNARD Eccoci.	SCHAUNARD Here we are.
RODOLFO Ebben?	RODOLFO What's that?
MARCELLO Ebben?	MARCELLO Let's see! (SCHAUNARD *puts the rolls on the table*)
MARCELLO Del pan?	MARCELLO (*disdainfully*) Just bread? (COLLINE *opens the bag and extracts a herring from it, which he likewise places on the table*)
COLLINE È un piatto degno di Demostene: un' aringa . . .	COLLINE A platter worthy of Demosthenes! Have a herring!
SCHAUNARD . . . salata.	SCHAUNARD It's pickled!
COLLINE Il pranzo è in tavola.	COLLINE To tempt an epicure.
MARCELLO Questa è cuccagna da Berlingaccio.	MARCELLO (*sitting down at the table, pretending to have a splendid meal*) This is a banquet fit for a Caesar.
SCHAUNARD Or lo Sciampagna mettiamo in ghiaccio.	SCHAUNARD (*puts* COLLINE's *hat on the table and places a bottle of water in it*) Put the champagne to cool in the freezer.
RODOLFO Scelga, o Barone, Trota o salmone?	RODOLFO (*to* MARCELLO, *offering him bread*) Choose, worthy lordship, oysters or salmon?
MARCELLO Duca, una lingua di pappagallo?	MARCELLO (*thanks him, accepts, then turns to* SCHAUNARD *and offers him a slice of bread*) Baron, will you sample this breast of parrot?
SCHAUNARD Grazie, m'impingua. Stasera ho un ballo.	SCHAUNARD (*refuses politely, pours a glass of water, then gives it to* MARCELLO) No, sir, it's fatt'ning. I'm sorry, I dare not. (*the one and only glass is passed from one to another.* COLLINE, *who has gulped down his bread in a great hurry, rises*)
RODOLFO Già sazio?	RODOLFO (*to* COLLINE) All finished?
COLLINE Ho fretta. Il Re m'aspetta.	COLLINE (*with importance and dignity*) I'm rushing. The King expects me!
MARCELLO C'è qualche trama?	MARCELLO (*concerned*) The King expects you?
RODOLFO Qualche mister?	RODOLFO What do you mean?
SCHAUNARD Qualche mister?	SCHAUNARD (*rises, goes up to* COLLINE, *and asks him with comical curiosity*) What do you mean?
MARCELLO Qualche mister?	MARCELLO What do you mean? (COLLINE *struts around with an air of great importance*)

COLLINE
The King has named me Lord Premier!
(they surround COLLINE, *bowing low to him)*

COLLINE
Il Re mi chiama
al minister.

SCHAUNARD
Splendid!

SCHAUNARD
Bene!

MARCELLO
Splendid!

MARCELLO
Bene!

RODOLFO
Splendid!

RODOLFO
Bene!

COLLINE *(patronizingly)*
This is the start of my career!

COLLINE
Però
vedrò, vedrò . . . Guizot!

SCHAUNARD *(to* MARCELLO*)*
Drink to his meeting!

SCHAUNARD
Porgimi il nappo!

MARCELLO *(gives him the glass)*
You do it, I'm eating!

MARCELLO
Sì! bevi, io pappo!

SCHAUNARD *(pompously, jumps from his seat, lifting his glass)*
Have I permission
To drink to your commission?

SCHAUNARD
Mi sia permesso
al nobile consesso . . .

RODOLFO, COLLINE *(interrupting him, shouting)*
Stop it!

RODOLFO, COLLINE
Basta!

COLLINE
Silly asses!

COLLINE
Che decotto!

MARCELLO *(shouting)*
Idiot! Stop this nonsense!

MARCELLO
Fiacco! Leva il tacco.

COLLINE *(taking the glass from* SCHAUNARD*)*
Pass the glasses!

COLLINE
Dammi il gotto.

SCHAUNARD *(inspired, motions to his friends to let him continue)*
I know a thrilling serenade
Which I'm anxious to offer!

SCHAUNARD
M'ispira irresistibile
l'estro della romanza . . .

RODOLFO *(howling)*
No!

RODOLFO
No!

MARCELLO
No!

MARCELLO
No!

COLLINE
No!

COLLINE
No!

SCHAUNARD *(yielding)*
Perhaps the classic dance would amuse you?

SCHAUNARD
Azione coreografica
allora? . . .

RODOLFO, MARCELLO, COLLINE
That's it!
(applauding, they surround SCHAUNARD *and make him come down from his chair)*

RODOLFO, MARCELLO, COLLINE
Sì! sì! . . .

SCHAUNARD
Some dances with vocal orchestrations!

SCHAUNARD
La danza con musica vocale!

COLLINE
But first the preparations!
(carrying table and chairs out of the way, they get ready to dance; proposing various dances)
Gavotte.

COLLINE
Si sgombrino le sale!
Gavotta.

MARCELLO
Minuetto.

RODOLFO
Pavanella.

SCHAUNARD
Fandango.

COLLINE
Propongo la quadriglia.

RODOLFO
Mano alle dame.

COLLINE
Io detto.

SCHAUNARD
Lal-le-ra, lal-le-ra!

RODOLFO
Vezzosa damigella,

MARCELLO
Rispetti la modestia.
La prego.

SCHAUNARD
Lallera, lallera, lallera!

MARCELLO
Lallera, lallera, lallera!

COLLINE
Balancez.

SCHAUNARD
Prima c' è il *Rond.*

COLLINE
No, bestia!!

SCHAUNARD
Che modi da lacchè!

COLLINE
Se non erro lei m' oltraggia.
Snudi il ferro!

SCHAUNARD
Pronti. Assaggia.
Il tuo sangue io voglio ber!

COLLINE
Un di noi qui si sbudella.

MARCELLO
Minuet.

RODOLFO
Pavenella.

SCHAUNARD (*imitating a Spanish dance*)
Fandango!

COLLINE
And now quadrille positions.
(*the others approve*)

RODOLFO
Please choose your ladies.

COLLINE
Get ready.
(*improvising, he beats the time with comical importance*)

SCHAUNARD
Lal-le-ra, lal-le-ra, lal-le-ra, lá, lal-le-ra, lal-le-ra, lal-le-ra, lá.

RODOLFO (*accosting* MARCELLO, *he bows very low, offering his arm, and gallantly saying to him*)
Permit me, gracious lady,

MARCELLO (*modestly, imitating a woman's voice*)
Oh dear, I'm so embarrassed.
(*with his natural voice*)
With pleasure.

SCHAUNARD
Lallera, lallera, lallera, la.
(RODOLFO *and* MARCELLO *are dancing the quadrille*)

MARCELLO
Lallera, lallera, lallera, la.

COLLINE (*speaking, calls the dance figures*)
Balancez!

SCHAUNARD (*protesting*)
First comes the round.

COLLINE (*shouting*)
No! Jackass!
(RODOLFO *and* MARCELLO *continue dancing*)

SCHAUNARD (*with exaggerated disdain*)
You dance just like a clod!

COLLINE (*offended*)
I believe you slur my honor.
Here's my challenge!
(*runs to the stove and grabs the tongs*)

SCHAUNARD (*takes the palette from the fireplace; speaking*)
Ready! On guard!
(*going into dueling position*)
I shall tear you limb from limb!

COLLINE
One of us must die this moment!
(RODOLFO *and* MARCELLO *stop dancing; laughing*)

SCHAUNARD
Get a hearse for my opponent.

SCHAUNARD
Apprestate una barella.

COLLINE
Better dig a grave for him.
(SCHAUNARD *and* COLLINE *are dueling*)

COLLINE
Apprestate un cimiter.

RODOLFO, MARCELLO (*gaily*)
While the duel is advancing
Let's continue with our dancing.
(*the blows become more frequent. The duelists pretend to become more and more infuriated, stamp their feet, and shout: There! Take that! You wretch! Die! The door opens wide and* MUSETTA *enters in a state of great agitation*)

RODOLFO, MARCELLO
Mentre incalza
la tenzone
gira e balza
Rigodone.

MARCELLO (*noticing her*)
Musetta!
(*all gather anxiously around her*)

MARCELLO
Musetta!

MUSETTA (*with choked voice*)
It's Mimi.
It's Mimi, she came with me and is ill.

MUSETTA
C'è Mimì . . .
C'è Mimì che mi segue e che sta male.

RODOLFO
Mimi?

RODOLFO
Ov' è?

MUSETTA
The many stairs were too great an effort.
(*through the open door* MIMI *is seen sitting on the highest step of the stairs*)

MUSETTA
Nel far le scale
più non si resse.

RODOLFO
Ah!
(*rushes toward* MIMI. MARCELLO *follows him*)

RODOLFO
Ah!

SCHAUNARD (*to* COLLINE)
Move the bed a little nearer.
(*both move the bed forward*)

SCHAUNARD
Noi
accostiamo quel lettuccio.

RODOLFO
There. Some water.
(RODOLFO *and* MARCELLO *support* MIMI *and lead her to the bed*)

RODOLFO
Là.
Da bere.

MIMI
Rodolfo!
(MUSETTA *hurries to bring a glass of water and makes* MIMI *take a sip*)

MIMÌ
Rodolfo!

RODOLFO (*gently places* MIMI *on the bed*)
Careful, that's better.

RODOLFO
Zitta, riposa.

MIMI (*embraces* RODOLFO)
Oh, my Rodolfo!
May I stay here with you?

MIMÌ
O mio Rodolfo,
Mi vuoi
qui con te?

RODOLFO
Ah, dear Mimi,
Now and always!

RODOLFO
Ah! mia Mimì,
Sempre, sempre!

MUSETTA (*pulls the others away and says softly to them*)
I heard the rumor
That Mimi deserted her wealthy Count,

MUSETTA
Intesi dire che Mimì fuggita
dal Viscontino, era in fin di vita.

Dove stia? Cerca, cerca . . .
la veggo
passar per via . . .
trascinandosi a stento.
Mi dice: "Più non reggo . . .
Muoio, lo sento . . .
Voglio morir con lui! forse
m' aspetta . . ."

And now was nearly dying.
I went out, hoping, searching . . .
I found her at last today.
(RODOLFO *persuades* MIMI *to stretch out on the bed, covers her with the blanket, then he adjusts the pillow under her head with greatest care*)
Pale and weak with exhaustion,
She whispered, "I can't bear it . . .
I'm dying! I feel it,
(*forgetting herself, raising her voice*)
I want to die near him,
He may be waiting . . ."

MARCELLO
Sst.

MARCELLO (*to* MUSETTA, *so she will lower her voice*)
Hush!
(MUSETTA *moves far away from* MIMI)

MIMÌ
Mi sento assai meglio . . .
lascia ch' io guardi intorno.

MIMI
I'm feeling much better.
Just let me look around a little.

MUSETTA
"M'accompagni, Musetta?" . . .

MUSETTA
"Will you take me, Musetta?"

MIMÌ
Ah come si sta bene qui!
Si rinasce, si rinasce.
Ancor sento la vita qui.
No, tu non mi lasci più!

MIMI (*with a sweet smile*)
Ah, it is good to be with you!
(*rising a little and embracing* RODOLFO *again*)
I am happy, I am happy.
At last I am with you again!
Ah, my love stay close to me!

RODOLFO
Benedetta bocca
Tu ancor mi parli!

RODOLFO!
Just to hear your voice again,
To have you near me!

MUSETTA
Che ci avete in casa?

MUSETTA (*aside to the other three*)
Could we give her something?

MARCELLO
Nulla!

MARCELLO
Nothing!

MUSETTA
Non caffè? Non vino?

MUSETTA
Any wine or coffee?

MARCELLO
Nulla! Ah! miseria!

MARCELLO (*with great despondency*)
Nothing! Only mis'ry!

SCHAUNARD
Fra mezz' ora è morta!

SCHAUNARD (*observing* MIMI *carefully; sadly to* COLLINE, *taking him aside*)
She won't live an hour.

MIMÌ
Ho tanto freddo!
Se avessi un manicotto!
Queste mie mani riscaldare
non si potranno mai?

MIMI
How cold I am!
I wish I had a muff.
When will these ice cold hands of mine
Ever get warm again?
(*coughs*)

RODOLFO
Qui, nelle mie! Taci!
Il parlar ti stanca.

RODOLFO (*takes* MIMI'*s hands into his, warming them*)
Come, let me warm them,
Don't try to speak, my darling.

MIMI
You must not worry!
I'm used to coughing.
(*seeing the friends of* RODOLFO, *calling them by name; they rush to her eagerly*)
How are you, Marcello,
Schaunard, Colline, how are you?
(*smiling*)
Here you are, all you three
Smiling welcome to me.

RODOLFO
You must rest, do not talk.

MIMI
Only softly, I promise.
(*making a sign to* MARCELLO *to come nearer*)
Marcello, let me tell you:
Your Musetta is good.

MARCELLO
I know, I know.
(SCHAUNARD *and* COLLINE *move away.* SCHAUNARD *sits at the table, his face buried in his hands.* COLLINE *remains preoccupied in thought*)

MUSETTA (*leads* MARCELLO *far away from* MIMI, *takes off her earrings. Handing them to him, she says softly:*)
Take these, sell them,
And buy whatever will help.
Go for the doctor!

RODOLFO
Lie quiet.

MIMI
You will not leave me?

RODOLFO
No! No!
(MIMI *gradually becomes drowsy.* RODOLFO *takes a chair and sits down near the bed.* MARCELLO *is about to leave;* MUSETTA *stops him and leads him farther away from* MIMI)

MUSETTA
Marcello!
This may be the last time
That Mimi ever expresses a desire!
I'll go and buy the muff.
You come with me.

MARCELLO
How good you are, Musetta.
(MUSETTA *and* MARCELLO *leave hurriedly*)

COLLINE (*while* MARCELLO *and* MUSETTA *are talking he takes off his overcoat; with growing emotion*)
Faithful companion, listen,
I must remain, you journey to higher, better regions,
Take my grateful allegiance.

MIMÌ
Ho un po' di tosse!
Ci sono avvezza.
Buon giorno Marcello,
Schaunard, Colline . . . buon giorno.
Tutti qui, tutti qui
sorridenti a Mimì.

RODOLFO
Non parlar, non parlar.

MIMÌ
Parlo pian,
non temere. Marcello date retta:
è assai buona Musetta.

MARCELLO
Lo so, lo so.

MUSETTA
A te, vendi, riporta
qualche cordial—manda un dottore! . . .

RODOLFO
Riposa.

MIMÌ
Tu non mi lasci?

RODOLFO
No. No.

MUSETTA
Ascolta!
Forse è l' ultima volta
che espresso ha un desiderio, poveretta!
Pel manicotto io vo. Con te verrò.

MARCELLO
Sei buona, o mia Musetta.

COLLINE
Vecchia zimarra, senti,
io resto al pian, tu ascendere
il sacro monte or devi.
Le mie grazie ricevi.
Mai non curvasti il logoro

dorso ai ricchi ed ai potenti.
Passar nelle tue tasche
come in antri tranquilli
filosofi e poeti.
Ora che i giorni lieti
fuggir, ti dico addio
fedele amico mio,
addio, addio.
Schaunard, ciascuno per diversa via
mettiamo insieme due atti di pietà;
io . . . questo!
E tu . . .
lasciali soli là! . . .

Neither to wealth nor temporal power
Have you ever yielded.
Hidden deep in your pockets,
Cozily there have rested
Philosophers and poets.
Now that our happy days have gone by,
I bid you farewell,
(*with emotion*)
Ever faithful old companion.
Farewell, farewell.
(*he rolls up his coat, puts it under his arm, and starts to leave, but, seeing* SCHAUNARD, *he goes to him, pats his shoulder, and says sadly:*)
Schaunard,
(SCHAUNARD *raises his head*)
Each of us in a diff'rent way
Can now accomplish a kindness of his own,
(*pointing to his overcoat*)
I this one. And you . . .
Let them stay here alone.
(SCHAUNARD *rises*)

SCHAUNARD
Filosofo, ragioni!
È ver! . . . Vo via!

SCHAUNARD (*moved*)
A logical conclusion!
(*looks toward the bed*)
You're right. I'll go.
(SCHAUNARD *looks around and in order to justify his leaving he takes the water bottle and leaves after* COLLINE, *gently closing the door.* MIMI *opens her eyes, seeing that all have left, extends her hand toward* RODOLFO, *which he kisses lovingly*)

MIMÌ
Sono andati? Fingevo di dormire
perchè volli con te sola restare.
Ho tante cose che ti voglio dire
o una sola, ma grande come il mare,
come il mare profonda ed infinita . . .
Sei il mio amor e tutta la mia vita.
Sei il mio amore e tutta la mia vita.

MIMI
Have they gone now?
(RODOLFO *nods "yes"*)
I was not really sleeping.
To make them leave us,
I only was pretending.
So many things are in my heart to tell you,
Or just one, which is true and never-ending.
(*lifting herself a little on the bed.* RODOLFO *rises and helps her*)
As the sky is eternal there above you,
So is my love, and I will always love you,
(*clasping her arms around* RODOLFO'*s neck*)
So is my love, and I will always love you!

RODOLFO
Ah! Mimì,
mia bella Mimì.

RODOLFO
Ah, Mimi, my lovely Mimi!

MIMÌ
Son bella ancora?

MIMI (*letting her arms fall back*)
Am I really still lovely?

RODOLFO
Bella come un' aurora.

RODOLFO
Fair as sunshine at dawning!

MIMI
A mistaken defining!
You should have said:
Fair as sunset declining.
"I'm always called Mimi,
(*like an echo*)
I'm always called Mimi,
But I don't know why . . ."

MIMÌ
Hai sbagliato il raffronto.
Volevi dir: bella come un tramonto.
"Mi chiamano Mimì
mi chiamano Mimì
il perchè non so."

RODOLFO (*in a tender and caressing tone*)
Home to her nest came the weary little swallow.
(*he takes the bonnet from where he had kept it, close to his heart, and gives it to* MIMI)

RODOLFO
Tornò al nido la rondine e cinguetta.

MIMI (*cheerfully, turns her head to* RODOLFO. *He puts the bonnet on it*)
My little bonnet, my little bonnet!
Ah! . . .
(MIMI *makes* RODOLFO *sit down near her and rests her head on his breast*)
Do you remember how by chance I came here
The first time that we met?

MIMÌ
La mia cuffietta, la mia cuffietta . . . Ah!
Te lo rammenti quando sono entrata
la prima volta, là?

RODOLFO
Do I remember!

RODOLFO
Se lo rammento!

MIMI
The wind blew out the candles . . .

MIMÌ
Il lume si era spento . . .

RODOLFO
And you were so embarrassed!
Then your door key was missing.

RODOLFO
Eri tanto turbata!
Poi smarristi la chiave . . .

MIMI
You tried to find it
In spite of the darkness!

MIMÌ
E a cercarla
tastoni ti sei messo!

RODOLFO
We looked, and looked . . .

RODOLFO
E cerca, . . . cerca . . .

MIMI
Now my young Lothario,
You may as well admit it,
You found it soon, but you hid it.

MIMÌ
Mio bel signorino
posso ben dirlo adesso,
lei la trovò assai presto.

RODOLFO
I improved the scenario.

RODOLFO
Aiutavo il destino.

MIMI (*remembering her first meeting with* RODOLFO *on Christmas Eve*)
In the dark, you could not see how I was blushing.
(*in a very faint voice, repeating* RODOLFO'*s voice*)
"How cold your little hand is . . .
Let me warm it in my own!"
It was dark, and you took my hand in yours.
(*gripped by a spasm of coughing, she lets her head fall back, exhausted*)

MIMÌ
Era buio, e il mio rossor non si vedeva . . .
"Che gelida manina . . .
Se la lasci riscaldar! . . ."
Era buio, e la man tu mi prendevi . . .

RODOLFO (*terrified, supporting her*)
Oh God, Mimi!

RODOLFO
Oh Dio! Mimì.

SCHAUNARD (*at this moment returning, runs to* MIMI, *at the outcry of* RODOLFO)

SCHAUNARD
Che avvien?

What's wrong?

MIMÌ
Nulla. Sto bene.

MIMI (*opens her eyes and smiles, reassuring* RODOLFO *and* SCHAUNARD)
Nothing . . . I'm better.

RODOLFO
Zitta per carità.

RODOLFO (*letting her lie back on the pillow*)
Careful, for heaven's sake!

MIMÌ
Sì, sì, perdona.
Or sarò buona.

MIMI
Yes, yes, forgive me,
I'll be good now . . .
(MUSETTA *and* MARCELLO *enter quickly.* MUSETTA *carries a muff,* MARCELLO *a medicine bottle*)

MUSETTA
Dorme?

MUSETTA (*to* RODOLFO)
How is she?

RODOLFO
Riposa.

RODOLFO (*going closer to* MARCELLO)
She's resting.

MARCELLO
Ho veduto il dottore!
Verrà; gli ho fatto fretta.
Ecco il cordial.

MARCELLO
I have called at the doctor's.
He'll come. I made it urgent.
Meanwhile, take this . . .
(*gives him the medicine bottle, takes a spirit lamp, puts it on the table, and lights it*)

MIMÌ
Chi parla?

MIMI
Who is it?

MUSETTA
Io, Musetta.

MUSETTA (*goes to* MIMI, *and gives her the muff*)
I, Musetta.

MIMÌ
Oh come è bello e morbido.
Non più, non più
le mani allividite.
Il tepore l' abbellirà.
Sei tu che me lo doni?

MIMI (*helped by* MUSETTA, *she sits up in bed, and with almost childlike joy takes the muff*)
Oh, it's so soft and beautiful!
At last, at last,
My hands will get warm now.
This will keep them . . .
So nice and soft . . .
(*to* RODOLFO)
Did you do this for me?

MUSETTA
Sì.

MUSETTA (*quickly*)
Yes.

MIMÌ
Tu! Spensierato!

Grazie. Ma costerà. Piangi?
Sto bene . . .
Pianger così perchè? . . .
Qui . . . amor . . . sempre con te! . . .
Le mani . . . al caldo . . . e . . . dormire.

MIMI (*stretching out her arms to* RODOLFO)
You! What a spendthrift!
Thank you! It cost a lot!
(RODOLFO *bursts into tears*)
You're crying?
I'm better . . .
Why do you weep like this?
(*with a very weak voice*)
I'm here . . .
Always with you! . . .
(*fading away more and more, puts her hands into the muff—by and by getting drowsy, she gracefully bends down on the muff, as if about to fall asleep*)
My hands are . . .
So warm now . . . I . . .

Am tired . . .

RODOLFO (*after having made sure that* MIMI *has fallen asleep, he leaves his place near her, carefully motioning the others to make no noise. He approcahes* MARCELLO)

What did the doctor say?

RODOLFO
Che ha detto
il medico?

MARCELLO

He'll come.

MARCELLO
Verrà.

MUSETTA (*meanwhile, on the burner she has warmed up the medicine* MARCELLO *brought, and while she is busily engaged in this action she murmurs a prayer as if subconsciously*)

Oh, gracious Virgin Mary,
Bless her, I beg you,
With your boundless mercy,
So she won't have to die.

(RODOLFO, MARCELLO, *and* SCHAUNARD *are talking in a low voice among themselves.* RODOLFO *steps again to the bed, watching* MIMI, *then goes back to his friends*)

MUSETTA (*interrupts herself, motions to* MARCELLO, *who comes to her and puts a book upright on the table, shading the lamp*)

We must fasten a shade there,
Because the flame is flickering,
Like this . . .
(*resuming her prayer*)
Oh, please let her recover;
Mother most holy,
I am unworthy of your pardon,
But Mimi is just like an angel from heaven.

MUSETTA
Madonna benedetta,
fate la grazia a questa poveretta
che non debba morire.
Qui ci vuole un riparo
perchè la fiamma sventola.
Così.
E che possa guarire.
Madonna santa, io sono
indegna di perdono,
mentre invece Mimì è un angelo
del cielo.

RODOLFO (*goes to* MUSETTA, *while* SCHAUNARD *goes on tiptoe to watch* MIMI, *makes a gesture of sorrow, and returns to* MARCELLO)

I think she's better.
You do not think it's hopeless?

RODOLFO
Io spero ancora. Vi pare che sia
grave?

MUSETTA

Of course not.

MUSETTA
Non credo.

SCHAUNARD

Marcello, she's dead . . .

(MARCELLO *in turn goes to the bed and shrinks back, terrified*)

SCHAUNARD
Marcello, è spirata.

COLLINE (*enters discreetly, putting the money on the table, near* MUSETTA)

Musetta, for you!

(*a ray of sunshine falls on* MIMI's *face through the window.* RODOLFO *notices it and looks for a way to put up a curtain.* MUSETTA *points to her cloak.* RODOLFO *thanks her with a look, takes the cloak, climbs on a chair, and tries to find a way to drape it across the window*)

COLLINE (*rushes to* RODOLFO *to help him spread the cloak, and asks him for news about* MIMI)

COLLINE
Musetta, a voi!
Come va?

How is she?

RODOLFO
Vedi! . . . È tranquilla.
Che vuol dire
quell' andare e venire . . .
quel guardarmi così? . . .

RODOLFO (*turning, sees* MUSETTA, *who motions to him that the medicine is ready. He descends from the chair, but while approaching* MUSETTA *he becomes aware of the strange behavior of* MARCELLO *and* SCHAUNARD)
Look, she is asleep.
(*with a voice, hoarse from fear*)
What is wrong?
You are acting so strangely.
(*stupefied, looking from one to another*)
Why look at me like that?

MARCELLO
Coraggio.

MARCELLO (*can't contain himself any longer, rushes to* RODOLFO, *and exclaims, embracing him*)
Rodolfo!

RODOLFO
Mimì! . . . Mimì! . . .

(RODOLFO *rushes to the bed, grasps* MIMI, *and cries out in the utmost despair*)
Mimi!
(*weeping, throws himself upon the lifeless body of* MIMI)
Mimi!
(MUSETTA, *terrified, rushes to the bed, with an anguished outcry. Kneeling in tears at the feet of* MIMI *opposite* RODOLFO. SCHAUNARD *sinks into a chair, despondent;* COLLINE *stands at the foot of the bed, remaining stunned by the suddenness of the tragedy;* MARCELLO, *sobbing, stands with his back to the audience*)

BORIS GODUNOV

by Modest Petrovich Moussorgsky
(1839–81)

LIBRETTO BY THE COMPOSER

Translated by JOHN GUTMAN

Based on the drama of the same name by Aleksandr Pushkin.

CHARACTERS

POLICE OFFICER	*Bass*
MITYUKH, *a Russian peasant*	*Bass*
PRINCE VASSILI IVANOVICH SHUISKI, *court adviser to Boris Godunov*	*Tenor*
ANDREI SHCHELKALOV, *Secretary of the Duma*	*Baritone*
PIMEN, *a monk and historian*	*Bass*
GRIGORI, *a novice* (*later Dimitri the Pretender*)	*Tenor*
BORIS GODUNOV	*Bass*
HOSTESS OF THE INN	*Mezzo-soprano*
MISSAIL } MENDICANT FRIARS	*Tenor*
VARLAAM } MENDICANT FRIARS	*Bass*
XENIA, *daughter of Boris*	*Soprano*
FYODOR, *son of Boris*	*Mezzo-soprano*
NURSE TO XENIA	*Contralto*
MARINA MNISHEK, *daughter of a Polish land-owner*	*Mezzo-soprano*
RANGONI, *a Jesuit priest*	*Bass*
KHRUSHCHOV, *a boyar*	*Tenor*
THE SIMPLETON	*Tenor*
LAVITSKI } *Jesuit priests*	*Tenor*
CHERNIKOVSKI } *Jesuit priests*	*Baritone*

RUSSIAN PEOPLE, SOLDIERS, GUARDS, BOYARS, PILGRIMS, CHILDREN, LADIES AND GENTLEMEN OF THE POLISH COURT

Place: Russia and Poland
Time: 1598–1605
First performance: Marinsky Theater, St. Petersburg, Feb. 8, (Russian-style January 24), 1874.

COPYRIGHT 1953, BY JOHN GUTMAN

ACT I

Scene 1

(*Outside a monastery near Moscow. A* GUARD *appears at the door. The people stand motionless.*)

GUARD

You loafers—
have you turned to wooden statues?
Down there—on your knees!
Faster! go down!
You're the devil's sons and daughters!
(*the people go down on their knees, reluctantly*)

PEOPLE

Lord in heaven, do not reject us, oh Father.
Lord, we beseech You that You protect us, oh Father.
We are all orphans without You—
help your children, Lord!
And with tears we ask You, Lord in Heaven:
hear our wailing—hear our bitter cries . . .
Help, Father—Lord in the skies above.
Oh Father, Benefactor, don't leave us—
Help, Father!
(GUARD *exits*)

MEN

Mityukh—say, Mityukh: why do we cry?

MITYUKH

I can't tell you.

MEN

We must find a tsar to govern Russia. . . .

A WOMAN

To hell with it! I'm hoarse from shouting.
I ask you, my darling dove—have you a drop of water?

ANOTHER WOMAN

Wait—I'll serve you in a moment.
Just do not shout so much,
so you won't be so thirsty.

MEN

Women, stop your silly chatter. Quiet!

WOMEN

And who are you to tell us?
Don't think that you can bully us!

MITYUKH

Oh, you witches, keep your mouths shut!

WOMEN

Listen to that little devil.

VARIOUS GROUPS OF WOMEN

He's a fool—he's only boasting.
He's a heathen—he'll be roasting.
God have mercy on this sinner.
Let us run and look for shelter.

MEN

If this nickname does not please you,
if you feel he shouldn't tease you,
we regret it, we regret it.

WOMEN

If we stay, it won't be healthy,
so we'd better run for shelter.

MEN

See the witches—how they're running.
(*the* GUARD *appears again*)

GUARD

What's this? so silent? you spare your voices . . .
I'll show you . . . maybe that your backs
are longing for a thrashing?
I will teach you, you loafers. . . .

WOMEN

Don't be mad, Nikitich; don't be mad, beloved.

MEN

Let us do some breathing—then we'll do some praying.

ANOTHER GROUP

He won't let us breathe, the bastard.

GUARD

Shut up—use your voices as you're told. Well?

MEN

Ready.

CHORUS

Lord in heaven, do not reject us, oh Father, we beseech
You that You protect us, oh Father . . .
We are lost without You.
Lord in heaven: hear our wailing, hear our bitter cries.
Help, Father!—Lord in the skies above: oh Father,
Oh Father in heaven, oh Father . . . ah . . .
(*during the last outcries of the people* SHCHELKALOV *has appeared at the door of the monastery*)

GUARD

Quiet—and listen. Hear what he has to say.
(SHCHELKALOV *lifts his cap and bows to the people*)

SHCHELKALOV

Hear me, citizens.
Boris has not relented.
He pays no heed to his advisers, nor to the Duma.
He does not want to hear of his accession.
What sorrow and grief has come to this holy land,
fellow-citizens . . .
Right has been wronged in this country.
Let's pray to the Lord in His mercy
that He may grace us by His divine consolation
and to Boris may grant His guidance,
and waken his weary soul.
(*from afar the song of the pilgrims is heard. The people listen in silence*)

PILGRIMS

Glory to Him who is the Mightiest in this world,
Glory, Glory to all His powers and His saints,
eternally glory . . . praise to Him.
Glory to You, Almightiest—glory!
Thus spoke the Angel to this world—:
Up, you clouds, and run your stormy way.
Spread your wings across the heavens' dome,
over Russia wake, you clouds of God.
Over Russia wake, you clouds of God.

(the pilgrims have arrived at the monastery, with images of saints, and amulets. The people greet them with reverence)

CHORUS

Slay and kill that evil dragon—
dragon spewing poisoned flames from its
thousand heads. . . . Slay that dragon,
Russia's misery, and its unending feud.
And to all who have the true belief
say: they will be saved.
Now rejoice and don your festive gowns,
show the Mother of God on Her heavenly throne.
And from the corners of this holy land
united, you greet a mighty tsar.
Sing hymns to God, our Father.
Glory, glory to His holy saints.
Sing hymns to praise Him,
glory, glory to His holy saints.
Glory to Him who rules all the world,
glory, glory to God, the Lord.

(the pilgrims disappear)

MEN

Mityukh—say: did you hear what they were singing?

MITYUKH

I did . . . "from the corners of this holy land . . ."

MEN

Well . . . ?

MITYUKH

". . . from the corners of this holy land . . . you will greet him . . . from the corners of this. . ."

MEN

Go on . . .
Right!

CHORUS

Now rejoice and don your festive gowns.
From all the corners of this holy land
reunited, you greet a mighty tsar.

(the GUARD, *who has accompanied the pilgrims, returns)*

CHORUS I

What tsar?—which tsar do they mean?

CHORUS II

Stupid question: Tsar Boris.

GUARD

Listen—listen,
you bunch of donkeys . . . Pay attention!
Listen to what I say:
tomorrow after dawn
you'll gather at the Kremlin.
That is all.
(*exits*)

CHORUS

Kremlin?
And what are we to do there?

VARIOUS GROUPS OF PEOPLE

It's all the same.
They tell us "cry"—
and so we cry some more.
More crying?
That's not very hard. . . .
Well, it's time for sleeping.

Scene 2

(*The square in the Kremlin. The people, on their knees. The sound of many bells is heard.* SHUISKI *appears with* SHCHELKALOV.)

SHUISKI

Long may he live,
Tsar Boris Feodorovich.

CHORUS

Long life and glory—
Our Tsar and Father.

SHUISKI

G l o r y . . .

CHORUS

As the sun is to heaven
its highest glory,—glory
to this country, to Russia
Tsar Boris is glory—g l o r y .
Long life and glory—
Long life and glory. . . .
Long live Tsar Boris.
Long live Tsar Boris.
Long life and glory—
Long live Tsar Boris.
Long life and glory. . . .
Be happy, friends.
Jubilate, and be happy, friends.

Let's be happy, friends.
Let us praise our Tsar, Boris Godunov.

BOYARS

Long life to him! Tsar Boris Feodorovich. . . .

CHORUS

Long may he live.
(BORIS *appears.* SHUISKI *motions to the crowd to end their jubilation*)
To the mightiest of tsars, Boris,
be glory—glory—glory—glory—
GLORY!
(BORIS *stands in front of the cathedral; beside him his children,* FYODOR *and* XENIA)

BORIS

My heart is sad—
a strange and fearful omen
invades all my being with its dark foreboding.
My Lord and God—You, my Eternal Father,
from heaven's throne in mercy look on us,
and send to me, and to the power of my reign,
Your holy blessing.
Let me be kind and merciful like You—
let me bring glory to the Throne.
And now we bend our knees
before the mighty tsars who governed Russia.
And then I'll call you to a feast!
All—from boyar down to the lowly poor,
All be my guests. . . .
All will be dearly welcome. . . .
(BORIS, *with* SHUISKI *and his retinue, enters the cathedral*)

CHORUS

Glory—glory—glory.
Long life and glory—
Our Tsar and Father—long may he reign,
the mighty ruler!!
As to heaven the sun is its glory—glory,
so to Russia her great Tsar Boris is glory—
(BORIS *appears in the door of the cathedral*)
Glory—and long may he reign.
GLORY——GLORY!

Scene 3

(*A cell in a monastery. It is night.* PIMEN, *writing.* GRIGORI *sleeps*)

PIMEN

Just one more page—

the last of all my stories,
and this will end the chronicle I wrote.
The work is done, entrusted to this sinner
by God, the Lord.
And not in vain have I been called for many years
to be a witness:
there'll come a day,
a monk will read these papers,
and he will reap the fruits of all my toiling.
Then he will light, like me, his lamp at midnight,
and shake the dust of all too many years
to tell again the legends of the fathers.
And thus the true believers will remember
all that befell in long-forgotten times.
Though I am old, my memories are young,
the olden times I often see before me,
like waves that stir the quiet of the sea. . . .
How stormy was it once with great adventures,
how still is now the ocean, and how silent!
The dawn of day is near—my lamp is but a flicker . . .
Just one more page, the last of all my stories. . . .

CHORUS (*from afar*)
Lord in heaven, Father, have mercy on Your slaves!
Merciful God.
From the flock of true believers
turn away all evil thoughts, merciful God!

GRIGORI (*wakes up*)
That dream again! Once again I dreamed that dream!
How it haunts me, that cursed dream.
Still at work, the worthy father,
and no slumber has touched his eyes all through
the weary night.
It warms my heart to see this peaceful scene
when he is steeped in thoughts of ancient glory—
so quiet—so untiring: he writes the book of time.

PIMEN
Awake so soon?

GRIGORI
I beg you, worthy man: give me your blessing.

PIMEN
May God the Lord protect you, Son—
today, and always, and forever!

CHORUS
Lord—Almighty God—do not abandon me!

GRIGORI
All through the night you never ceased your writing.
I was asleep—and yet I am not rested:
an evil dream has stirred my tortured heart.
I mounted on a mighty stairway
that led me to a tower
and I saw

all Moscow from on high.
Like in an ant heap
the crowds below
were running to and fro.
At me they laughed,
and pointed with their fingers . . .
it frightened me,
and I began to tremble . . .
I tumbled down the stairs,
and I awakened.

PIMEN

Dreams of a youthful sinner!
Chastise yourself with fasting and with prayers—
and every dream you may be dreaming
will be pleasant.
Believe me: even now
when in the evening
slumber overcomes me,
before I find the time
to say my prayer,
unquiet is my sleep,
and even sinful.
And in those nights,
I dream of stormy feasts,
of fights and valiant battles
and all the vain pursuits
of thoughtless youth!

GRIGORI

How cheerful was your youth,
how full of ventures!
Down at Kazan
you fought and won a battle
and you were there,
when Shuiski beat the foe
and Tsar Ivan you saw
in all his splendor.
But I have always been condemned
to wander from one cloister to another.
Why was not I
allowed to fight a war,
to see the Tsar
and join him at his banquet?

PIMEN

Consider, Son,
the fate of Russia's rulers:
great are the tsars! yet often . . .
many times it happened
that they abandoned
the regal sceptre
and the purple
and with the crown

their power,
to don a monk's most humble vestment,
to find their peace of soul
within a holy cloister.

(GRIGORI *has listened to* PIMEN *with increasing interest*)

GRIGORI

But now, I want to ask a question that is on my mind:
Who killed young Dimitri, our Tsarevich?
You, I am told, were present that frightful day?

PIMEN

Yes, I was. Our Lord and God had destined me
to see and witness a bloody deed. I was in Uglich . . .
they sent me there to do a term of penance . . .
I came at night . . . next morning dawn awoke me—
there was a noise, the sound of tolling bells—
screams—shouts—we all ran to the palace—
What a sight we saw!
A sea of blood, and in it the Tsarevich . . .
his hapless mother unconscious by his side.
His faithful nurse was crazed with fear,
and sobbed in desperation.
And then, quite suddenly, the crowd cried out in wrath
and dragged in the servant who betrayed her helpless master.
Wailing . . . moaning. . . .
But then they find a man, his face distorted,
his eyes aghast: Yehuda Bityagovski.
"Hold him—he killed the boy,"
they're shouting, all at once.
Then the crowd started to pursue
the three who did the murder—
and finally they caught them and made them stand
before the lifeless body. Oh wonder!
He who died began to tremble!
"Confess the deed," they shouted in the crowd.
The murderers, in fear of death, admitted
they killed the boy . . . by order of Boris!

GRIGORI

How old was he, Dimitri, the Tsarevich?

PIMEN

Seven years . . . but no . . . how many years have passed since?
was it ten?—or twelve years?
Yes, yes—twelve years ago. He would be as old
as you are—and Tsar today!
But God did not allow it, and thus the crime
that Tsar Boris committed
will conclude the chronicle I write.
You, Grigori, by learning you have formed an
eager mind: to you I want to leave my work;
in humbleness continue what I started, and

describe whatever life may show you:
both war and peace, the reign of future rulers,
the prophecies and signs that come from heaven.
My time has come—it's time for me to rest.
This is the matin bell. . . .
Do give your blessing, Lord, to all Your slaves.
—I need my stick, Grigori.

CHORUS

Lord, have mercy on us, have mercy, God, on us all!
Heavenly, mighty Father—ever just, eternal—
have mercy, Lord!

(exit PIMEN. GRIGORI *accompanies him but remains standing at the door)*

GRIGORI

Boris, Boris—you make the country tremble,
and no one ever dares remember
the fate you meted out to the Tsarevich.
Yet in this quiet cell
a monk recorded all that he knew
of this most heinous murder.
You will be called before your earthly judges,
nor can you flee
the judgment of the Lord.

Scene 4

(An inn near the Lithuanian border.)

INNKEEPER

In a pond quite near
lives a gander here,
oh—you my gander, dear!
my beloved gander, dear!
Now you must stay here,
lovely gander, dear.
Likes to swim in every pond,
of the willows he is fond.
Fold your little wings,
darling gander mine!
Don't fly away from me,
stay and keep me company.
You will be my love—
like a turtle dove. . . .
and this love will have no end,
you, my sweetheart gander friend!
Come and sit with me,

(the voices of passers-by are heard in the distance)

close as close can be . . .
Hug me, give me one more kiss,
in my arms you will find bliss—

What is this? I heard a voice.
Guests are always welcome! Hey, there. . . .
No one. It seems they passed us by. . . .
Kiss me once again—
hold me very tight—
Oh—you my gander, dear,
my beloved gander, dear.
Come, console my heart,
console my lonely heart!
Say, we will never part.

MISSAIL, VARLAAM (*approaching*)
Brothers and Christians,
friends and honest people,
for the church we're building
we ask you for a modest gift.
Bread on the waters—
you'll be rewarded!

INNKEEPER
Wandering monks they are—two worthy pilgrims.
Here I am, singing that stupid song—
stupid and sinful, that's too much!
Here are they! two monks, two worthy pilgrims!
(*she opens the door.* VARLAAM *and* MISSAIL *enter, followed by* GRIGORI, *disguised as a peasant*)

VARLAAM
The Lord may bless this house of yours!

INNKEEPER
Would you like to eat something, Reverend Fathers?

MISSAIL
We take whatever God may send. . . .

VARLAAM
No wine today?

INNKEEPER
Why, of course! I'll bring you some.
Sit down—rest a while.
(VARLAAM *watches* GRIGORI, *who has sat down at the table, brooding*)

VARLAAM (*to* GRIGORI)
What are you so glum about, companion?
Here we are close to the border now: Lithuania!
And that's where you asked us to take you.

GRIGORI
I'll never really be safe till I'm over the border!

VARLAAM
And what's so good about Lithuania?
Take us—my friend Missail, and I, wicked sinner:
since we escaped from the cloister walls,
we don't care a single rap what country we're in—
Russia—Lithuania—what do we care?
If there's some wine!
Ah, there is some now.

INNKEEPER
This is the best I have—may it keep you healthy!

MISSAIL, VARLAAM
We thank you a thousand times—God the Lord will bless your heart.

VARLAAM
Near Kazan—near the famous olden fortress
sat Ivan—making merry at a banquet.
Tartars got from him no pity—
they were told to leave the city,
and not to come again!
But one day he had enough, and in the dark of the night
asked his men to put a lot of mines all over the town.
But the Tartars kept on acting like the owners of the place,
when they saw Ivan, they simply laughed right in his face—
That's the way they are!
And the Tsar was sad by day and night,
hung his head
to the left, but later also to the right.
Then he called for all his cannoneers,
and he ordered them to be prepared—every one of them.
As the fuses began to smolder merrily,
one young man threw a light into a powder keg—
they exploded every single mine that could be found. Hey!
One could hear the blast for miles around—
What a noise it was!
And the Tartars yelled and shouted and shed bitter tears,
such a noise as this one seldom hears. . . .
Most of them would never yell or shout again:
forty thousand Tartars lay there—slain!
Even forty-three!
That's how it went—
in Kazan, the famous city!

VARLAAM (*to* GRIGORI)
Tell me: don't you drink anything?
And it seems you don't even sing?

GRIGORI
I don't drink—

MISSAIL
Each to his own taste!

VARLAAM
. . . and mine is for wine! Come on, Missail,
let us drink a toast to our charming host. . . .
(*to* GRIGORI)
Now listen, you—I do not care for those that
don't like wine!
Drinking may be piggish—
soberness is priggish!
If you are like us, we'll always love you,

but, if you're a kill-joy, get out of here!

GRIGORI

Drink—but don't forget who you were, my friend Varlaam!

VARLAAM

Who I was? Remember? But I want to forget!
Phew!
(*he is quite drunk, and slowly falling asleep.* MISSAIL *dozes*)
There was a man—
a darling man—
spurred his horse so it ran.
He wore a cap—he did not care a rap:
he was filthy, that chap!

GRIGORI (*to the* INNKEEPER)

Please tell me: this road out there—
where does it lead to?

INNKEEPER

Into Lithuania.

GRIGORI

Is the border very far?

INNKEEPER

No, it isn't . . . if you hurry you can still get there
tonight . . . if they do not stop you!

GRIGORI

Me? Why should they?

INNKEEPER

Somebody must have escaped . . .
police have been ordered everywhere to look out for him!

GRIGORI

Eh! This does not seem to be my lucky day!

VARLAAM

Horse ran and ran—
threw down the man—
he'll get up . . . if he can . . .

GRIGORI

What's the charge against him?

INNKEEPER

How would I know? Maybe some robber or thief.
But if he's smart enough, he has a chance to fool them!
Do they always get them? No—they don't!
It might be desperate, if there were no other road
than just the high road, but
let me tell you:
If you cross the main street, you'll find a footpath—
keep on walking—you'll come to a chapel,
nearby a brook. . . .
and from there to Khlopino—and then to Zaitsero—
From there on you cannot miss it:
you are almost at the border.
Police are everywhere—therefore be careful!
They are out to fleece us, and rob us of our last kopeck!

VARLAAM

Came to a door—
he made: knock—knock—
(a knock at the door)
and then he knocked again: knock—knock—knock. . . .
(another knock at the door, louder)

INNKEEPER

Who is it now? them again; Oh, darn it all!
(she goes to the window)
They're always snooping around. . . .
(she opens the door. Enter two POLICE OFFICERS*)*

VARLAAM *(waking up for a moment)*

There was a man . . . a darling man . . .
spurred his horse so it . . .

OFFICER

Who are these two men?
*(*VARLAAM *and* MISSAIL *jump up from their chairs, frightened)*

VARLAAM, MISSAIL

We are two lay brothers—we are poor and honest—
wandering through the villages,
begging for a kopeck, or two!

OFFICER *(to* GRIGORI*)*

And you—who are you?

VARLAAM, MISSAIL

Our companion.

GRIGORI

A peace-loving friend of the law!
I have come with these worthy old men,
I'm on my way home now.

OFFICER

Try to get milk from a stone! That case is hopeless.
Let's try the old ones . . . Hm. . . .
How is everything? Tell me: how are they treating you?

VARLAAM

Oh, very badly—very! Everybody seems so stingy—
fond of money . . . and they hide it!
God is last on their list. This world is so sinful,
and it's chock-full of heathens. . . .
Walk your feet off . . . begging . . . praying . . .
and they'll give you half a kopeck . . .
that is all!
It is so little, it's just enough for some wine!
I'm afraid Judgment Day cannot be very far. . . .
(during VARLAAM*'s last speech the* OFFICER *has looked at him very closely.* VARLAAM *gets upset)*

INNKEEPER

Lord above—have mercy on us sinners!

VARLAAM

Why d'you look at me—so long and so closely?

OFFICER

I'll tell you!
Alyokha: have you got that sheet?
Let's have a look. Listen—:
From his cell escaped some unworthy monk: Grishka Otrepyev—
Have you heard about it?

VARLAAM

No—never.

OFFICER

Well, the Tsar has ordered us to find that man,
to arrest him and hang him!
I'm sure you have heard that?

VARLAAM

I have not!

OFFICER

Are you a reader?

VARLAAM

No—sorry. I was not meant to be.

OFFICER

Come, have a look at this.

VARLAAM

What is the use?

OFFICER

That man who escaped—whom we must find—you're the one!

VARLAAM

Good Lord! Who gave you that idea?

INNKEEPER

God above! The poor old man . . . he's never hurt a spider. . . .

OFFICER

Who can read? somebody?

GRIGORI

Yes—I can read.

OFFICER

Take this. Hurry up. Read aloud!

GRIGORI

"Be it known to every one:
that a heretic, named Grigori Otrepyev, has run away from a Moscow monastery.
After he listened to the Evil One, he set out
to tempt his brethren with visions of sin—
Now he may be trying to reach Lithuania.
The Tsar orders you to arrest this man . . ."

OFFICER

". . . and to hang him!"

GRIGORI

It says nothing here of hanging!

OFFICER

Fool! You ought to learn to read between the lines. . . .

Again: ". . . to arrest and to hang him."

GRIGORI

". . . and to hang him. As for his age . . . he is . . .
(looking at VARLAAM*)*
He's about fifty two. . . .
. . . has a rather red nose . . .
is of medium height, but heavy. . . .

OFFICER

That's him all right: let's catch him, children!

VARLAAM

Hands off! I warn you—don't lay hands on me!
you picked the wrong man. . . . Who says I am Grishka?
(he takes the warrant from GRIGORI*)*
No, friends—I don't care for such jokes!
My reading may be halting—I don't say it is fluent. . . .
but I can try—let me try—
it seems my life may hang on my reading. . . .
"his age . . . age . . . his age is twen . . . twenty!"
Who says "fifty-two"? Liar!
"Of medium height . . . he has reddish hair . . .
and on his nose there is . . .
on his nose there is one little wart. . . .
Furthermore—one of his arms . . .
his arms . . . is shorter . . .
one of his arms is. . . ."
I think it might be. . . .
*(*GRIGORI *brandishes a knife and jumps out of the window)*
It's him—
don't let him get away!
It's him!

OFFICER

It's him!

MISSAIL

Get hold of him!

ACT II

Scene 1

(a room in the Tsar's palace in the Kremlin)

XENIA

Where are you—
love of mine?
You, for whom I'm longing.
Resting under the greensward,
far from all who love you,
you must be so lonely,
there under your tombstone.
You don't see my sorrow—
You don't hear my crying—
Why did you leave me?
Like you
I am lonely.
(*she cries*)

FYODOR

Xenia, don't cry,
I beg you!
Cruel is your suffering,
but all your weeping
and sighing
cannot bring back to you
your bridegroom—

XENIA

Oh—Fyodor . . .
I loved and adored him,
yet my love did not save him.
All my happiness left me—
I will mourn him forever.

FYODOR

Do not cry, I implore you,
Xenia, my darling.
(*pointing at the big clock*)
The clock starts!
Come, have a look.
The carillon is playing—
it's a very old, famous clock:
once an hour
it shows its wonders to us—
a herald first—
after him come two that play the trumpet—
two soldiers,
and one with a banner!
Please look at them—
aren't they pretty?
just like live ones—
look!

XENIA

My dearly beloved!
You had promised
to love me—
my heart is aching—
I am yours—forever!

NURSE

My child, darling Tsarevna—
You must not cry!
All this weeping
will make you ugly!

XENIA

I'm suffering, Mamushka—
I'm suffering. . . .

NURSE

Yes—yes, I know, my child.
Maiden tears
are like the morning dew:
comes the sun
and the grass is dry anew.
Think, dear, how wide the world is:
you'll find another prince—
he'll be handsome, too,
and he'll love only you—
and you will soon forget
the bitter tears you cried.

XENIA

Oh no—no—Mamushka!
No! I want to be
faithful to him alone.

NURSE

Stubborn!
Love was much too brief
for so long a grief!
To a man a maiden gave her heart,
And they swore that they would never part,
but one day he left her all the same,
and she said: I don't recall his name!
Yes, my darling:
that's the way it happens!
Please, wipe your tears away,
and listen to my song:

Gnat and Bug
were friends, you see,
the Gnat went and cut a tree,
while the Bug baked the bread—
what a lovely meal they had!
While they sat there,
had a talk,
came a cricket,

on a walk,
to the Gnat's and Bug's dismay,
started stirring up the hay!
Bug said: this is bad!
and the Gnat got mad,
for he thought that this was wicked,
with a stick he chased the cricket!
But the cricket
was too quick—
so the Gnat
just threw the stick!
But the stick
would not obey him,
turned around and
tried to slay him!
In the morning's
early light,
Bug came running—
what a sight!
With a shovel
and a spade
to the Gnat
he offered aid.
Tried to lift him . . .
all in vain:
by his own stick he was slain!
Parting from
what he loved most,
Bug himself
gave up the ghost.

FYODOR

Oh—what wonderful story,
Mamushka—
and very funny!
but what gruesome end!

NURSE

Tell me, Tsarevich:
don't you know another?
Let's hear it, child!
And I'll be very patient,
I'm pretty good at that,
for Tsar Ivan
taught us all
how to be patient!
Well then?

FYODOR

I'll sing one,
and you will join me soon.
I know your patience!
Here's a tale
that you'll like to hear:

a hen, one day,
gave birth to a steer,
and a suckling pig
laid twenty eggs.
Fools think I'm lying—
I'm not even trying!
Cock-a-doodle,
Cock-a-doo—
Little cock, how do you do?
May I ask
what brought you here?
I have come from Kiev, dear!
And in Kiev town,
on an old tree,
sits an owl
with a frown—
for that owl
can't see!

FYODOR and NURSE

Owl thinks
that is wrong.
Owl blinks,
sings a song—
Ping—ping—
double ping—
cut my feather,
hell for leather—
Pong—pong—
double pong—
if you love me,
love my song.
All five fingers—
no one lingers!
In the middle
of the night
little sparrow
saw the light.
He had
narrow eyes—
real
sparrow eyes!
and a beak
like a wedge
with a neat
cutting edge.
Sparrow flew
from his nest,
to the owl
as his guest.
'Cause the night
was so long

they sang
a song.
There was a sexton,
his corn he was thrashing—
it sounded
like thunder—
the flail broke
asunder!
The flames caught
the hayloft,
there was
no hay left!
Sexton got scared—
through the window
he stared.
He was so frightened,
he hid
in the larder
and cried
all the harder!
So he lay there—
it was not gay there!
His wife
all the same
baked a cake
on the flame—
many guests
she would invite
and they feasted
all the night.
And the sexton
ate alone
five hundred pigs—
then he ate
a bull—
after that
he was full!
Clap!

(*enter* BORIS; *the* NURSE, *on seeing him, curtsies in reverence*)

BORIS

What's this?
What wolf has stirred
the hen amid her brood?

NURSE

Mightiest Tsar, forgive me:
but I am old,
and everything upsets me.

BORIS (*embracing his daughter*)

My Xenia,
my much-beloved daughter!

You shed a widow's tears
before your wedding—
for he who was betrothed to you
is dead.

XENIA

Father and Tsar,
please do not heed
the tears that I am shedding,
for all my grief
must seem so unimportant
compared to your afflictions.

BORIS

My dearest child—
My darling daughter—
now in a kindly talk
with friends and dear companions,
try to forget
your grief and sorrow.
Good-by, my child.

(XENIA *and* NURSE *leave the room;* BORIS, *turning to his son*)

And you, my son—
my Fyodor—
What is this?

FYODOR

This is a map of Russia,
of our country—
from East to West
Look, Father:
Moscow—here!
there Novgorod!
and here Kazan.
Astrakhan!
Here mountains,
there Siberia.
And here
the old mysterious woods
of Perm.
The Caspian Sea!

BORIS

All this is beautiful!
As from the clouds
you see our country—
this great and mighty realm
before you:
the borders,
rivers—cities.
Go on, and study!
The time will come,
perhaps it will be soon,
when you

will be the Tsar
of this holy land.
Good-by—my son.
(*exit* FYODOR)
Mine is the highest power!
Year after year
my reign was calm
and peaceful—
and yet my heart
has never known
a moment's peace.
How often have I
heard it prophesied:
my power
and my glory
would be endless!
But life,
and fame,
the heady wine of power,
the people's applause—
all that
has lost its lure.
I hoped
I might be happy
with my loved ones—
and I prepared
a splendid wedding
for my child,
for my Tsarevna,
my darling daughter.
Like lightning,
death sweeps down
and takes the groom!
How heavy
lies on me
the hand of the Lord!
And every sinful soul
must fear His verdict.
In vain I strive
to flee from this darkness—
oh, for a ray of hope
to guide me!
My weary heart is aching
with longing,
it cries to God for mercy.
At times I hear around me
a secret whisper . . .
I begged and pleaded—
my arms raised to heaven—
I hoped
that the saints might hear my prayer.

In splendor I reigned,
my power *is* unending—
the Tsar of Russia!
For tears I begged
that might console me—
I am betrayed,
the nobles hate me—
open revolt
is rife in Lithuania—
hungry crowds . . .
and plague . . .
and devastation!
Like an angry beast
on the prowl
are the people—
in hunger
and poverty—
Russia moans . . .
For all the sorrows
that heaven has sent us,
to punish the sins we committed,
they blame the Tsar!
For all their misfortunes
they curse my very name—
curse and despise it!
I cannot sleep
at night—
and yet
I have nightmares!
The child—appears to me . . .
its bloody head. . . .
eyes red with crying . . .
begging and pleading . . .
pleading for mercy—
no answer to its crying!
Gaping the wound in its body—
piercing the shriek
it cried in dying. . . .
Oh—Lord above!
God! My Lord!

(*the* NURSES *are heard shouting off-stage*)

NURSES (*off-stage*)

Ah—shush!

(FYODOR *returns*)

BORIS

What has happened?

NURSES

Ah—shush—shush! Quiet!

BORIS (*to* FYODOR)

Find out
what's going on there!

NURSES
Shush—shush—ahh!

BORIS
Ah—
how they yell!

NURSES
Shush—shush—shush—ah—
(*as* BOYAR *enters and greets* BORIS)

BORIS
Well—what now?

NURSES
Shush—shush—

BORIS
Well—speak up! Speak!

BOYAR
Almighty Lord and Tsar—
it is, asking you to see him,
Prince Shuiski. . . .

BORIS
Shuiski? He's here?
Tell him
We shall be glad to see him,
to listen to his message!

BOYAR (*approaching* BORIS *and whispering into his ear*)
Last night
one of Pushkin's servants
came to tell us
that Shuiski and Mstislavski,
and some others,
and even Pushkin,
held a meeting
in the middle of the night:
a man, it seems,
arrived from Cracow,
to report . . .

BORIS
Arrest that man!
It's just as I thought!
My son,
what happened to these stupid women?

FYODOR
The parrot's fault . . .

BORIS
Parrot?

FYODOR
Yes—but there's no reason
why the mighty Tsar
should waste his time
to hear
a silly parrot story—

BORIS

No! no! My son,
let's hear it,
as it happened!

FYODOR

Like every afternoon
Popinka, the parrot,
sitting among the maids,
talked away and chattered.
Then, for a bit of change,
he looked for some caresses—
flying from maid to maid,
he asked to have his head scratched.
First came Nastasya—
she did not feel like scratching!
Popinka—he got mad,
called her "stupid woman."
That was too much for her,
and *he* got a spanking!
Popka began to shriek,
ruffled up his feathers.
Well—then the maids got scared,
and they brought him lots of sugar,
coaxed him with loving words,
to pacify the parrot!

BORIS

Stupid women!

FYODOR

. . . But no,
he would not listen!
He sat there with a scowl,
shoulders raised in anger. . . .

BORIS

I see him!

FYODOR

He would not even look
at the sweets they brought him—
then, turning on the one
who did not feel like scratching,
he pecked her in her face—
and the poor maid cried and fainted.
That's where the noise began:
all the maids were yelling—
and chasing through the room,
Popinka they tried to capture—
but all in vain—
every one got pecked by Popka!
This, Father dear and Tsar,
is why you heard an uproar:
just a bunch of maids, frightened by a parrot!

That is all there was—
that's the story.

BORIS

My son—
my dear, beloved Fyodor,
cleverly and like an artist,
you told me a truthful story.
In simple and well-chosen pictures
you clearly described
all that had happened.
Such are the fruits
of learning—
Trust is the beacon
that shines in the darkness!
Lord,
let me see the day
when they as Tsar acclaim him—
the rightful lord of holy Russia!
Oh—how I would gladly,
renouncing all my powers,
for such a blessing
exchange my scepter
and the purple!
When you are the Tsar
you always must endeavor
to have around you, child,
a group of trusted counsels.
Don't trust Shuiski—
he's a cunning intriguer,
he's full of knowledge,
but he's sly—and false. . . .

SHUISKI (*enters*)

Almighty Tsar and Lord
I greet you!

BORIS

Oh! It's you, my worthy prince!
the man who's proud to lead
the brainless masses—
a master in the noble art of treason!
You—the evil spirit of the throne—
every oath that you swore
you've broken threefold—
cunning hypocrite—wheedling flatterer—
a traitor disguised as a boyar.
Deceiver! Snake!

SHUISKI

When Ivan ruled Russia
(may he rest in peace, now and ever)
Shuiski was a name
that used to be received with honors!

BORIS

Yes—but Tsar Ivan,
were he alive now,
it would be his delight
to see you burn to death.
Yes, and he himself,
the Tsar and master,
would fan the raging flames,
fan them ever higher,
a holy psalm upon his lips.
But I am kinder:
it gives me pleasure
to forgive my haughty servants!

SHUISKI

Tsar . . .

BORIS

Well, what do you have to say?

SHUISKI

Tsar—please listen:
I bring you news
of great importance to the throne.

BORIS

Is this perhaps the news
that you and Pushkin heard
when you received a message
from all your noble friends
that I have banished?

SHUISKI

Yes, mighty Tsar.
The rumor speaks of a usurper;
the Poles—the Pope—
they *all* are on his side!

BORIS

But—who is the man?
Whose name has he usurped,
the scoundrel?
Yes—first I want to know
his name! You know it?

SHUISKI

Believe me, Tsar:
your power is tremendous.
Your charity, your kindness, and your bounty
have won the love
of every humble slave;
and they have vowed their faith
to you and to your throne.
Yet, I must warn the Tsar,
my master and my lord,
although with sorrow and with grief
my heart is bleeding—

you *must* be told
that this may happen:
if he should drive so far
his criminal intentions
to enter Russia
and to march on us,
and if he tries to captivate the crowds,
Dimitri's name
may be a mighty weapon!

BORIS

Dimitri's name?
Tsarevich, leave us, please.

FYODOR

Please let me stay
and let me be
beside my father
when he must hear
the fearful news
that threatens Russia's throne.

BORIS

No–no–
you must not stay!
You heard me–
obey me:
go! Tsarevich!
(FYODOR *exists*)
Take measures–
don't delay:
have soldiers guard
all Lithuanian frontiers at once,
that not a single soul
can enter Russia any more!
That's all.
No! Stay here–
stay here, Shuiski.
I ask you:
have you ever heard
that children who are dead
return from where they slumber,
to prosecute the Tsar–
the Tsar,
the ruler
elected by the people,
and crowned in solemn ritual
by the Patriarch . . . ?
Ha–ha–ha–ha
What? You laugh?
Why don't you laugh, then?

SHUISKI

Forgive me,
Almighty Tsar and Lord.

BORIS

Tell me, Prince:
That day in Uglich,
where the murder was committed,
and when Dimitri, the Tsarevich,
was killed—
I know that you were there:
you must have seen the lifeless body
while the people of Uglich
were shouting in the streets
to vent their deep despair,
crying out for vengeance . . .
are you *quite* sure
the victim . . . was . . . Dimitri?

SHUISKI

Quite.

BORIS

Vassili Ivanovich!
By all that you hold holy
I beseech you
be frank with me—
Truth—
truth is all I want!
I shall be magnanimous:
the past is past—
and even your betrayal
I can forget.
But—
if you cheat me now,
and lie to me,
I shall devise
a punishment,
so devilish
that Tsar Ivan himself
would tremble in his grave
with horror . . .
Now answer me!

SHUISKI

You don't believe me, Tsar.
You even doubt that I have
always been your faithful slave—
you speak of punishment
to scare me—
no death I fear,
I only fear your anger!
Everyone in Uglich
had seen the body:
five days and nights
it lay outside the old cathedral,
and with the child
another thirteen corpses,

disfigured terribly,
in rags, and blood-bespattered.
One could see
how all of them
had slowly started rotting . . .
but then I saw
Dimitri's face
was peaceful, pure, and radiant.
But bloody red,
frightfully,
his wound was gaping—
yet on his lips,
so chaste and so guileless,
a child's contented smile was playing—
he looked as if he were asleep
and dreaming a happy dream . . .
and in his right hand
he clutched a little toy,
as though defending it.

BORIS

No more—Prince!
(*exit* SHUISKI)
Ah—for some air!
I'm suffocating here—
I feel how all my blood
is rushing to my head,
it's raging in my temples.
A guilty conscience
is a cruel punishment.
(*it is getting darker; the carillon begins to play*)
If you did
but once in life
an evil deed,
and though it was your fate
that made you do it—
your soul is doomed,
your heart is drowned in poison—
The furies
haunt and mock you—
like hammer blows
falls on your ears
the thunder
of damnation.
My head is reeling—
reeling—
and all my strength has left me—
I see . . . the child . . .
I see it lying there . . .
(*the clock strikes eight. A ray of moonlight falls on the moving figures*)
What . . . is this . . . over there . . .

in the dark . . . ?
It threatens me . . .
it grows . . . closes in . . .
it moans and trembles . . .
Go–go–
not I–
I did not . . . murder you–
go–go, my child!
It was–not I–
It was the people–
go! my child . . .
Hear me–Lord!
You, so great
and ever merciful–
forgive me, Father!
Have mercy on
Boris, the sinner.

ACT III

Scene 1

(a castle in Poland. MARINA'S *room; friends of* MARINA*)*

FOUR GIRLS

How blue is the river
how shady the willow—
See there: a flower,
whiter than snow-white,
and down in the water
it looks at its picture:
how lovely the flower
admiring its beauty.

CHORUS

And over the flower
so gay in the sunshine
a swarm of
enchanted butterflies
is dancing.

FOUR GIRLS

They all are
madly
in love with the flower—
longing
to touch it—
and yet they
do not dare.
They all are
in love
with its beauty.
So blue is the river
so lovely the flower
and down in the water
it looks at its picture.

MARINA

I want my golden band.

CHORUS

But here in
the castle
there, too, is beauty—
a beauty
much greater
than that
of flowers:
no flower ever
has been
so enchanting!
A glory,
a treasure
to all
who love Poland:

a woman—
a queen.

FOUR GIRLS

And many daring men—
so proud and
so noble,
in awe
they bend their knees
before her
regal beauty.

CHORUS

A smile
and a greeting
is all they
are craving.
For this
they would gladly
forget
all the others!
The beauty
is silent.
It seems she
is smiling
at all they are saying
of love
and of passion—

FOUR GIRLS

The longing
the pining
of their hearts:
she gives them . . .
no answer.

MARINA

How charming!
The lovely lady answers:
"Thank you."
I thank you
for your kindness,
and for comparing me
to flowers
that are whiter still
than snow-white . . .
But what you're saying
does not please me.
Your words are meant to flatter
and you speak of daring men
who pay me homage,
young and noble heroes
who bend their knees before me.
"A smile is all they're craving
they pine away in longing . . ."

These are not the words to please me,
my companions:
do not speak to me of beauty,
of admirers.
Sing to me the olden ballads
that my dear old nurse once sang me—
Songs of greatness—
songs of battle—
of the glory
that was Poland.
Songs of Poland's
mighty maidens—
songs of foes that
ask for mercy. . . .
Yes, these are the songs
that please me,
lovely ballads
of my childhood.
(*dismissing them*)
. . . till later.
You, Ruzya, I do not need you, darling—
go and rest—
(MARINA, *remaining alone*)
Life is so boring—oh! how boring—
All my days
are dull and empty—
I am sad and weary,
life is meaningless,
a wasteland.
All the noble counts and princes
with their wealth and power
can't relieve this frightful boredom . . .
And yet,
from far horizons
comes a ray of hope
that blinds me—
there, from Moscow,
comes a stranger,
fills my doubting heart
with wonder.
My Dimitri,
great avenger,
show no mercy!
In the name of
God Almighty,
you'll avenge
our poor Tsarevich,
who was slain
by lust for power,
and the Tsar
whose hands are guilty

of bloody murder
you will punish!
I'll awake
my noble countrymen,
and with dreams
of gold and booty
I will lure
their greedy hearts!
You, my friend,
my valiant hero,
you'll be mine forever,
for with tears of
burning passion
I'll enslave you!
My Tsarevich,
my Dimitri,
You were meant
to love me. . . .
and with words of
tender longing
I will tie
your heartstrings.
Not for me
the love of courtiers,
all their wooing
only bores me—
to their fervent protestations
my contempt will be my answer.
What I want is
fame and glory—
What I want is—might and power!
On the throne
of Russia's rulers
the Tsarina I shall be,
and enwrapped in gold and purple
I'll be shining
like a sun.
With my charms,
my radiant beauty,
I will conquer
all of Moscow.
The boyars,
so proud and haughty,
they will bow to me,
and greet me!
And in ballads,
songs and legends
they will praise me.
Yes—the dullest men in Moscow
yet will praise
their proud Marina!—

(she suddenly sees RANGONI, *who is standing by the door humbly)*
Ah! It is you, holy man?

RANGONI
In humbleness,
as servant of the Lord, our Father,
I crave that I may ask
the beautiful Marina
to lend an ear to me?

MARINA
My father, you must not even ask!
I am, and will be
an obedient daughter
of the faith.
I'm serving
the Church that is forever
great and undivided.

RANGONI
But, my child,
the holy Church
is now forsaken:
and the pictures of the saints
have faded—
Where is our faith?
Its sources flow no longer . . .
and where do you find
the scent of incense?
And bleeding—gaping—
the wounds of the martyrs.
All you hear in the temples
is moaning . . .
all the priests
shed tears of desperation.

MARINA
My father! I . . .
I am confused by what you say . . .
all your bitter words
sound to my faithful heart
like a knoll of sorrow
and of mourning.

RANGONI
Hear me, child—Marina!
You have been called
to bring the unbelieving
back to faith and church
and to lead them to their salvation,
to destroy all this sinful dissension.
And your name will be holy forever,
and the angels of God, the Almighty—
they will sing your praises!

MARINA

. . . And my name will be holy forever
and the angels of God, the Almighty,
they will sing my praises . . .
Oh!—sinful words!
My father . . .
with what temptation
you try to lure the weak and fickle heart
of one who has no knowledge of the world!
I'm young, I'm fond of pleasures,
I want a life in joy and splendor—
I am not the one who's chosen
to serve the Church in glory—
please—forgive me.

RANGONI

Enslave with your beauty
the heart of Dimitri!
Tell him you love him,
be tender and passionate,
try to beguile and enchant him.
Flames in your glances
and smiles on your lovely lips,
make him forget who he is!
Dismiss all your futile and groundless fears
and defy
all the pangs of your conscience.
Pay no attention
to empty old legends
of maidenly modesty
and all such nonsense.
One day
you show him your anger,
you prod him with moods and caprices—
the next,
you're loving and longing,
and try to deceive him—
always tempt his heart,
and bewitch his mind . . .
And when finally vanquished,
he's kneeling before you,
in wordless enchantment,
waiting for your orders,
ask him to swear
that he'll serve the Church forever!

MARINA

I shall never do that!

RANGONI

What? The Church demands it,
and you dare deny it?
Whatever may redound to its glory

your duty will bid you surrender,
unfearing, and without asking—
even your honor!

MARINA

That . . . is not true!
I curse every word you have said to me.
You have a wicked and vicious heart.
My curse on you!
I've only contempt for you.
Go—go—I say!

RANGONI

Marina!
How your eyes sparkle
with diabolical passion—
your face is distorted,
and you are trembling—
a breath of hell and its pestilence
has blown all your charms away.

MARINA

Oh, heaven, save your helpless child!
Heaven, tell me what to do!

RANGONI

You can't flee
the powers of darkness,
the demon of pride
fills your mind with his poison
and on the wings
with which hell has endowed him,
Satan himself
is hovering above you.

MARINA

Ah!

RANGONI

To me who comes from the Lord
entrust your soul—and surrender.
With every thought—with every dream you're dreaming
you will become . . . my slave!

Scene 2

(*A hall in the castle. A fountain is seen through the windows. It is a moonlit night.*)

GRIGORI

This is the night . . .
I am trembling—
Oh, my beloved,
you have enchanted my heart.
I'm yours forever!

Oh come, my love,
I long for you—
I'm waiting . . .
I'm waiting for you in the dark of night!
Why don't you hear my plea?
Have you forgotten me?
I have no dream but you—
all my life is yours . . .
a loving word from you
and a tender smile
alone can heal all the sorrows
of my weary heart.
Marina! Marina!
I beg you give me answer.
Oh come, oh come . . . I love you so!
No—no one answers!
(RANGONI *appears suddenly*)

RANGONI
Tsarevich—Dimitri!

GRIGORI
Who are you?

RANGONI
I warn you, go and hide
before Marina's guests come nearer.
Beware, Tsarevich—I beseech you, beware!

GRIGORI
Let them come—
I'm ready to receive them
with all the honor that is due them!

RANGONI
I've warned you, Tsarevich,
you will perish yourself—
endanger Marina!—
They must not find you.
(*he drags* GRIGORI *away with him.* MARINA *enters with her guests,* MARINA *herself on the arm of an old Polish nobleman*)

MARINA
Do not speak to me of love and passion,
all your solemn oaths, I fear, will not convince me—
Yes, my friend, your case is hopeless . . .
(MARINA *and her escort disappear*)

CHORUS
Moscow's haughty power
will yet yield to Poland.

MEN
And her mighty soldiers,
they will rot in prison.
And Boris, their ruler,
we will beat forever!

WOMEN
Yes, it sounds enchanting—
but why don't you do it?
Show the Russians: you're the stronger.
And Boris is Tsar no longer!

MEN
For Poland's greater glory
first we must destroy
the might of Moscow!

WOMEN
Marina cannot help us:
her beauty is too cold
she's haughty—proud . . .
(MARINA *returns and joins her guests*)

MARINA
And now—let's drink, my friends!

CHORUS
And here's to you, Marina!

MEN
Drink with us to fame and beauty!
A glass of wine to toast Marina!
The crown of Tsars
will yet adorn Marina!

CHORUS
To her!
To fame!
To might!
The crown of Tsars for her!
(*they all leave.* GRIGORI *enters*)

GRIGORI
There was no escaping!
In his cursed claws
the wily priest had caught me!
And yet—I saw her—fleetingly.
I saw my love, the beautiful
Marina . . .
and like a thief
at night
I stole a glance
from radiant eyes—
enchantment!
. . . and as my heart beat louder,
I lost my patience
and I felt I must be free
to kneel before her—
I had to rid myself of my protector,
whose help I never wanted!
I had enough
(I told him so)
of all his talk,
his sly insinuations!

And then I saw a sight
that made me shudder—
I saw the proud and beautiful Marina
escorted by a toothless Polish ruin—
she smiled at him and whispered
of tender feelings,
of love and passion
of happiness and marriage,
to him—
to that toothless, tottering monster!
And yet I know
there's waiting for her
the splendor of glory:
the golden crown,
the scepter,
and the purple!
Oh—damn it all!
I want my sword—
I want my helmet—
my horse,
and on to glory!
The time has come—
my friends:
it's fame or death!
Fighting for me,
an army of heroes
will be victorious,
will win the day—
Glory to him who dares!
The throne will be mine!
(MARINA *enters*)

MARINA

Dimitri! Tsarevich! Dimitri!

GRIGORI

It's you—Marina!
You have come, beloved,
most beautiful of all.
How the days are long,
and lonely, dearest,
when I must be without you.
Doubting,
my heart is suffering tortures.
All that I cherish,
all that my longing heart ever has hoped for—
the dream of love and passion that I dreamed—
now is shattered.

MARINA

I know—you suffer.
No sleep at night
and yet you dream;
for day and night

you always dream
about Marina!
But not for words of passion,
not for a lover's empty ravings
did I come to you!
When you're alone and lonely,
you may do all the dreaming
that your heart desires!

GRIGORI

Marina!

MARINA

Yet there's no sacrifice,
however great,
that you won't bring for me,
if love demands it so!
but when
will you . . .
take Moscow
as the Tsar?

GRIGORI

The Tsar!—Marina!
All your words offend me.
How can the throne,
the heady wine of power,
a swarm of servile men
who flatter and betray you,
how can all this make up to you
for what you're losing:
for love requited—
for true devotion—
for passion
and wild embraces—
for all that a woman
can only find in loving?

MARINA

I know that!
Yes, I know, we could be happy
as a tender loving pair—
What is glory—what is power?
If we are in love, what do we care?
I say no, Tsarevich!
If love is all you're craving,
in Moscow you will find
a thousand enchanting women—
the youngest, the fairest,
they all are made for love!

GRIGORI

Don't speak of them to me!
In beds of luxury
they look for pleasure . . .
Love indeed!

A friendly word
and they are yours—
Don't call that love,
don't call that passion!
It's you—
it's you alone,
Marina,
it's you I worship!
Yes, I adore you—
With all my love,
with all my passion.
Hear me—
I beg you!
Have pity
on my wounded heart—
Do not reject my love!

MARINA

You love Marina?
But do you love her
only as a woman?
Win the throne for me
in Moscow—
win the purple
and the golden crown—
that alone,
my friend,
can tempt me . . .

GRIGORI

How cruel you can be,
invincible Marina,
in all your words I feel
the chilly wind of winter.
See me lying at your feet,
a humble slave, I beg of you:
do not deny me,
and my ardent passion!

MARINA

No—my tender hero,
do not waste your words
in vain endeavors!
Up, my pining martyr,
I pity you!
Poor darling,
how he suffers,
how he weakens
out of love for his Marina!
Day and night
you dream of loving—
the mighty throne
of Holy Russia
and Boris

you have forgotten!
No, you never loved me!

GRIGORI

Marina—hear me first!

MARINA

Serve your Polish masters, you slave!

GRIGORI

Hear me first!
No, Marina!
I will not have you
throw into my face
the bitter lot
of times that are behind me—
Lies!
and you know you're lying—
I *am* the Tsar
and one day soon
from Russia's farthest regions
a host of valiant men
will heed the call of duty—
I will lead them all!
We will march on Moscow
and conquer the throne
that fate has willed to me!
Yes, and then,
as Tsar and master,
enthroned in lonely splendor,
I shall sit above you,
laughing and jeering at you!
I shall be happy
seeing you humbled at last—
and you, in abject obedience,
bewailing the glory
that could have been yours,
will be crawling
up to the throne
on which I sit.
Everyone
Will point a mocking finger at you,
and deride you!

MARINA

Deride me?
My Tsarevich!
I beseech you,
do forgive me
for the evil words that I spoke.
If I blamed you,
if I scorned you,
believe me, Dimitri:
love inspired all my words—
love for your glory,

a deep, abiding love for you
my master,
My Lord and Tsar!
You may put all your trust
in your Marina,
forget,
yes, forget me now!
Let fame be
your only love,
and conquer
the throne of the Tsar!

GRIGORI

Marina!
Oh, how I wish
that your words were true—
do not betray
a love that is holy!

MARINA

I love you, Tsar!
Yes, I love you—
You are my hero!

GRIGORI

Oh—let me hear it again, Marina—
Yes, this deep delight
that you promise me
will bring peace
to my tortured heart—
forever and ever
you are mine!

MARINA

My Tsar!

GRIGORI

You, Tsarina,
you will be forever mine!
Come,
and embrace
the man you love.

MARINA

You have conquered my heart,
and I love you.
I'm forever yours.
Oh, my Dimitri—
heroes are waiting
to march with you
to fame:
the Tsar you will be!

(RANGONI *reappears; he sees* MARINA *and* GRIGORI *embracing, and shows his delight over the victory he has won*)

GRIGORI

You, my Marina!

Oh, how impatiently
I'm longing to be happy—
the day of love must dawn!

RANGONI

What an enchanting sight:
lovers so sweet and so tender!
You may embrace her
with passionate kisses
but *I* have won
the game you played!

ACT IV

Scene 1

(*Outside a convent near Moscow. A crowd of poor people. A group of men enters, among them* MITYUKH)

MEN

Say—is the service over?
Yes, and once again he was cursed!
What do you mean?
Once more they cursed
Grishka Otrepyev's name.
Grishka?

MITYUKH

Listen, Brothers, let me tell you
how the deacon, the fat one,
started yelling:
"Grishka Otrepyev—
Anathema!"

MEN

This is very funny—
why should Dimitri care
if they are cursing Grishka?
He is not Grishka!

OTHERS

That's certain.

CHORUS

Some have seen him in the Kromy woods.
They say he can't be very far.
And soon he will destroy
Boris and all his might.
Triumphant, he will mount the golden steps
to the throne
that rules over Russia.
He'll save us all.
Through him
Boris and all his henchmen
will be doomed.

OLD ONES

Will you shut up?
Stupid devils,
or are you longing
for the torture chamber?

(*the* SIMPLETON *comes running, followed by a group of boys*)

BOYS

Trr, trr, trr, tr . . .
his hat is of tin
it makes such a din!
Trr, trr, trr, tr . . .
his hat is of tin—

it makes such a din!
U - lu - lu - lu - eh
Trrrr!

THE SIMPLETON

Moon is shining—
a kitten whining—
get up, you stupid fool,
pray to God above you,
ask that He should love you,
praise Lord Jesus!
Lovely weather . . . lovely moonlight—
lovely weather—moonlight . . .

BOYS

Greetings!
Greetings—
dear simpleton Ivanich,
get up and greet us!
Bow to show us your respect
and take off your cap—
such a heavy cap . . .

SIMPLETON

I have a coin—
I'm hiding it here!

BOYS

Liar!
Do not try to fool us, fool!

SIMPLETON

Here!

BOYS

There!

SIMPLETON

Ah—ah—
Why did you take my kopeck away?
Ah—ah—
Come and give it back to me—
Ah—ah—

(the retinue of the Tsar appears; BOYARS *are distributing alms)*

CHORUS

Please, in the name of Christ,
do save us from hunger!
Tsar—Father—
in the name of the Saviour!

OTHERS

Look,
there's the Tsar.
Tsar—
in the name of Jesus, our Saviour
you are our father, Tsar:
have mercy on us,
for we all are your children!

In the name of Lord Jesus,
our Saviour.
(BORIS *has entered, accompanied by* SHUISKI)

CHORUS
Your people cry—
we're hungry—
We are hungry!
Give us bread to eat!
Tsar, give us bread to eat!
We are hungry—
Tsar—give us bread to eat!
In the name of Lord Jesus.

SIMPLETON
Ah—ah—ah—!
Boris—hear, Boris!
Those wicked boys
are nasty to me.

BORIS
Why does he cry so?

SIMPLETON
Those boys—
they took my only coin away.
Why don't you have them murdered,
the way you murdered long ago
our Tsarevich!

SHUISKI
Be silent, fool!
Arrest the stupid fool!

BORIS (*restraining him*)
Don't touch him!
Go, pray for your Tsar,
poor idiot. . . .
(*exit* BORIS)

SIMPLETON
No, Boris—
I cannot pray for you.
"Don't pray for Herod"
our Lady ordered me—
no, I must not pray
for Boris.

Scene 2

(*The Great Hall in the Kremlin. The Duma is in session.*)

SHCHELKALOV
May I ask for your attention—
The ruler of this land,
Tsar Boris Feodorovich,

with all the blessings
of the Very Holy Patriarch,
and all the highest powers
of Russia's Church,
has ordered me to say:
"An outlaw,
thief,
and fugitive from prison,
with mutinous intent
has gathered to his ranks
a crowd of hunger-ridden hirelings,
and dares pretend to be
the late Tsarevich,
the rightful Tsar of Russia.
In his plotting
he is abetted
by some exiled noblemen
and by some Lithuanian rabble!
He wants to overthrow
law and order,
and you, boyars,
he hopes to win as his supporters.
He even openly
proclaims his evil plans!"
You're requested,
friends and boyars,
to weigh his crime
and pass an honest judgment!

BOYARS

Yes, let's take a vote on it.
What say you?

ANOTHER GROUP

First, tell us
what you think about him?

OTHERS

Well—our opinion is,
and always has been:
(take notes, Andrei Mikhailich)

VARIOUS GROUPS OF BOYARS

The scoundrel
must be condemned to death!
Wait a moment!
You'd better catch him first,
before you execute him.
Obvious!
We're not so sure
it's obvious!
You must be silent
till your turn comes!
The scoundrel,

whoever he may be,
once he's caught,
he shall be tortured,
and then we'll kill him,
and we'll hang his body—
Let him be
food for the hungry crows!
No! The flames
shall burn his body,
and all the people
shall be present
to witness his death
and curse his ashes.
And the winds
that storm in anger
will disperse
his cursed ashes,

ALL BOYARS

wiping out the last remembrance
of the life of this usurper!

VARIOUS GROUPS

And everyone who sides
with this impostor
shall die!
His corpse
be fastened
to the pole of shame!
His name
shall be proclaimed
in all parts of Russia—

ALL BOYARS

in all the cities,
towns, and smallest hamlets—
and everywhere it shall be read,
in every church,
and in the market places!
And, falling on our knees,
we'll pray
and ask the Lord
to have mercy
on our country,
this land of suffering.
But . . .
Shuiski is not with us?
though he's a traitor,
when he is not with us
we miss him in our council.
(SHUISKI *enters*)

SHUISKI

Boyars! I ask your pardon!

BOYARS
Why,
speaking of the devil!

SHUISKI
If I am late,
forgive me—
and do believe me
that I have my reasons!
My mind
is full of gloomy thoughts—
my task is heavy!

BOYARS
Oh, shame on you,
Vassili Ivanovich!
A man your age,
to get involved
in treason and sedition,
to make the fickle crowds believe
that he, Dimitri, is alive!

SHUISKI
What?
Surely, my brothers,
you are not serious?
How could I,
in these days of our misfortune,
when in my heart I share
all Russia's sorrow,
how could I think
of treason and sedition?
My enemies are spreading
these slanderous lies,
out of bitter hatred!
But as a friend, boyars,
I am compelled to tell you
a strange and fearful tale.
Last week
I saw the Tsar,
and when I left him,
my heart was heavy
with pity for his soul's affliction . . .
A secret door
was open . . .
and I saw . . .
Oh, what a frightful scene
I witnessed!
Ashen . . .
his forehead moist with perspiration,
his body shaking . . .
and mumbling to himself
some strange and incoherent phrases—
eyes throwing

daggers of fury—
a secret pain
distorting his features . . .
I saw
the Tsar
of all the Russias!
Then . . .
he began
to stare into a corner,
he started to moan
and to shiver.

BOYARS
Lies! Liar!

SHUISKI
. . . and, crying out,
he called the dead Dimitri . . .
Seeing his ghost,
he raised his hands
to chase it . . .
(BORIS *appears, in a state of great agitation, as if trying to escape from a ghost*)
"Go—go," he begged.

BORIS
Go! Go!

SHUISKI
Go, my child!

SHCHELKALOV
Heaven! It's . . . he!

BORIS
Go! Go! Go, my child!

BOYARS
Help us, Lord—
Almighty God:
have mercy and protect us!

BORIS
Go!—go!
Who says that I
have killed him?
It is not true:
He lives! Dimitri—
And Shuiski—
I will have him
drawn and quartered
for all his lies!

SHUISKI
May the heaven's blessing
be with you!

BORIS
What! ?
(*awakening from his trance, addresses the* BOYARS)
I called for you, my counsels,

because I always
trust your wisdom—
In times of danger
and bitter trials
you are
the guardians of my power!

SHUISKI

Almighty Lord and Tsar!
You know I am
your humble slave,
yet duty bids me speak:
here's what happened—
Tsar,
a man came to your door—
he's very old
and humbly hopes
he might be allowed
to stand before his sovereign.
A man of truth and wisdom—
his life was pure and blameless—
he says he knows a secret
that he must tell you . . .

BORIS

Yes, Prince,
admit the man!
Perhaps his story
will be a welcome balsam
for all that secret fear
that tortures me so much . . .
(SHUISKI *returns with* PIMEN)

PIMEN

My name is Pimen,
a peaceful monk,
oblivious of the world
and yet I ask
the Tsar should hear me.

BORIS

You're speaking to the Tsar:
tell your story—
tell your secret.

PIMEN

My story will be brief
and truthful:
it simply is a story
of God—
and all His wondrous blessings . . .
One evening,
close on the night,
a shepherd came to me . . .
his face was old with wrinkles . . .
he sat with me—

and this is what he told me!
"From early childhood"
he started
"I was blind—
I'd never seen the dark of night
nor daylight,
my eyes were dead!
In vain I tried
to heal them
with herbs and roots,
by secret incantation . . .
I wandered far
to find a holy well
and wash my eyes with soothing waters . . .
that blindness!
I grew so used
to being blind
that, when I dreamed at night,
I did not even see
what I was dreaming—
my dreams were
only voices.
Once . . . I heard a voice
in dreaming,
soft and childish
it called my name . . .
I still hear that voice . . .
Come! Get up at once,
find out where Uglich is—
go there
and enter the cathedral.
And then you kneel
and pray
where I am resting—
I'm buried there . . .
Dimitri—
your Tsarevich!
But I am now
among the angels of the Lord
and am endowed with all the blessed gifts of healing!
Next morning I
remembered
and set out for Uglich,
together with my grandson.
I found the grave,
and as I knelt in prayer,
I felt a strange elation:
my weary heart grew light,
and tears were streaming
down my face—
and of a sudden

I saw the light,
my grandson
and the grave!"

(BORIS, *who has listened to* PIMEN *with great attention, cries out and falls into the arms of the* BOYARS. PIMEN *has left.*)

BORIS

I'm choking—choking!
Help me!
I want to see my son
I . . . cannot breathe . . .
cannot . . .

(FYODOR *enters and throws his arm around his father*)

Leave us alone—
my son and me!
Farewell, my son,
I am dying . . .
from now on
you will be the Tsar!
Don't ever ask . . .
don't ask how I
ascended to this throne,
my son . . .
you need not know. . . .
Tsar you shall be,
and rightful ruler—
as my successor,
my son,
my first-begotten.
Hear me!
My child,
the regal purple
will weigh upon your shoulders:
these are times of danger.
That man—
that vile usurper,
the name he stole
appeals to foolish crowds.
Where you may look,
you see
rebellion—
a traitorous army,
hunger,
plague!
Hear me, Fyodor!
Do not trust the boyars
and their words,
they're liars!
Never forget
that some are traitors

in league with Lithuania—
and treason must always be punished.
Be strong,
and merciless!
Yet, to be just in your judgment,
listen to your people.
Always fight for the faith,
defend the true belief,
and revere the saints,
and ask them to bless you.
Never lose
your own integrity,
my Fyodor:
in it you'll find your greatness—
a mind at rest
is a heart's salvation!
And Xenia,
protect her,
and be kind to her,
for now you are
her brother and her father.
Love and treasure her,
so pure,
so tender . . .
God above! Merciful—
look down, my Lord,
upon a sinful father's tears.
Not for myself I pray,
not for myself I beg You!
Father!
See my children—
send to them
the light
of Your unending love—
Protect them both,
forever.
They are guiltless.
Angels of God the Lord:
You who guard
the eternal throne—
unfold your shining wings
to give him shelter,
to save my son, my Fyodor,
from every ill,
and from temptation.
Hear
those sepulchral sounds!

CHORUS (*off-stage*)
Mortal brothers,
weep and cry:

for his end is near—
forever
his lips will close
in eternal silence—
Mercy! Hallelujah!

BORIS
The plaint of death . . .
give me . . .
the cloister's vestments—
the Tsar
withdraws to God!

FYODOR
Mighty Tsar—
do have courage—
the Lord will help you—

BORIS
No, no, Fyodor—
this is the end.

CHORUS
Dying, a child appears
before our eyes—
we lament it,
poor child,
it struggles,
it moans and sobs
and cries and begs for mercy—
but death
will show no mercy!

BORIS
Heaven! Heaven!
I am lost.
Oh Lord—
forgive me
for my sins!
Oh fearful death,
how cruel
is your torture—
It is not time yet—
I still am Tsar—
I still am Tsar . . .
Heaven—
death—
forgive me, all—
He . . .
he now is . . .
Tsar!
Forgive me—
forgive me.
(*dies*)

BOYARS (*in a whisper*)
The Tsar!

Scene 3

(*A forest near Kromy. A crowd of milling people, carrying the boyar* KHRUSHCHOV *in their midst.*)

CHORUS

Let's set him down—

MEN

. . . right here,
let's make him comfortable.
Sit down!
And so that he won't yell,
and that his noble throat
won't suffer damage,
let's stop his mouth!
That's it!

WOMEN

But, listen:
here sits a boyar,
and you do not
pay him homage.

MEN

What?
No one greets him?

WOMEN

That's a scandal!
Friends of Boris
deserve more honor!

MEN

Boris, the robber Tsar,
he stole the throne of Russia,
but then
this robber
robbed the thief!
So—let's honor him for that,
like any decent thief—
Heh! come on—
Fomka—Epiklan,
be his bodyguard.
That's it.

WOMEN

How can I
trust my eyes?
Whoever saw
an elegant boyar
without a sweetheart?

OTHER WOMEN

We will not have it!

Boyars who have no sweethearts
are like thorns
without roses.
What can we do?

GROUPS OF WOMEN

Afimya—come, help us!
We've heard it rumored
that you are
more than ninety years old—
If that's true,
then you're the one.
Come here,
and sacrifice your youth to him!
Sit down!

CHORUS

Ha—ha—ha!

MEN

Now then,
Let's sing a song for him
You, women—you are first!
Come on, women,
you are first!

WOMEN

He is not like an eagle
with wings soaring—
he is not like a steed,
with his mane flowing—
he sits and sits—
dear darling boyar,
he is deep in thoughts.

CHORUS

Long live the proud boyar!
Lickspittle of the Tsar!
Long live the proud boyar,
Lickspittle of the Tsar!
Glory!

MEN

Wait, women:
don't leave the poor boyar
without his horsewhip!

OTHER MEN

Who speaks of horsewhips?
Cat-o'-nine-tails
for him!
On with the song!

WOMEN

He sits,
and sits,
he is pondering
how a boyar
can oblige his Tsar—

CHORUS
How to please
and how to help him
torture and beat
decent folk?
Long live the proud boyar,
Lickspittle of the Tsar!
Long live the proud boyar,
Lickspittle of the Tsar!
Glory!
You have honored us
when we deserved honor,
and in darkest night
you have enlightened us:
Yes! By whipping
you have improved our mind—
thank you, master.
You are so kind!
Long live the proud boyar,
Lickspittle of the Tsar—
Long live the proud boyar,
Lickspittle of the Tsar.
Glory shall be your reward
forever,
Glory shall be your reward
forever more!
Glory—
praise to you!

(MISSAIL *and* VARLAAM *are heard singing in the distance*)

MISSAIL, VARLAAM
Dim in the sky
are sun and moon—
and all the stars
will have vanished soon—
the day of final reckoning
has begun
for all the evil deeds
Boris has done.
Beasts roam the fields,
unknown to the sight,
and beast breeds beast
by day and by night.
And they slay
and devour
man and woman and child,
to punish the world
for all his sins!

MISSAIL
Those who are true
to God, the Lord,

must suffer pain
through Boris, the Tsar.

VARLAAM

He has bowed
to Hell's infernal ghost,

MISSAIL, VARLAAM

to the glory of Satan
and his fearful host.
(*they enter*)
Deep is the grief
of this holy land,
and heavy is the hand
of him who scorned the Lord,
that threefold cursed hand
of him who killed a tsar—
for his sins
he will pay
in all eternity!

CHORUS

Who is singing?
Pious monks,
who come to us from Moscow—
Can you hear them?
They sing a song
of your Tsar Boris—
and of all the cruel tortures
. . . they sing of all the tortures
that are our lot,
. . . that he has meted out
to decent people!
To arms!
Free and daring
we will fight them—
valor always wins the day!
Free and daring
we will fight them!
valor always
wins the day!
We will fight them—
daring—
In this fight
we will gladly
shed our blood,
gladly shed our blood!
In this fight we will
gladly shed our blood!
And in glory rises,
and in glory rises
all our force and might,
rises all our force and might.
And in glory rises,

and in glory rises,
all our never-ending might.
All our glory,
all our might!
Eternal Russia's might.
Fight!
Might that guides
our fate—lead us!
Might that stems
from the Lord—lead us!
Don't betray your sons ever,
valiant men
who fight for us.
Might—might!
Might that rules all the universe,
great and eternal might!
Might!
Don't betray those,
who fight for you.
Don't betray
all those valiant men!
Might!
Might eternal
unending might!
We sing a hymn to life power—
there's joy among your worshipers!
Eternal might,
great life power!
Might!

VARLAAM, THREE MEN
Bid him welcome,
dearest friends,
the one and only Tsar!

MISSAIL, THREE MEN
Bid him welcome,
him whom the Lord has saved
from the evil hands
of his vilest foe!

MISSAIL, VARLAAM, THREE MEN
Bid him welcome,
dearest friends,
and greet
Dimitri,
noble son of Ivan!

CHORUS
Everywhere
Boris has his henchmen,
who torture
innocent people!
Everywhere
Boris has his henchmen,

torturing
innocent people!
Torture most frightful,
hanging and beating—
the true believers must suffer
Torture most cruel. . . .
Hanging and beating
innocent people,
innocent people.
Death!
Death!
Death!
Death!
Death for him—
Death—
Kill the killer!
Death!—Kill the killer!
Kill Boris the Killer. Death!
Kill the Killer!
He who has killed
must die!

LAVITSKI, CHERNIKOVSKI

Domine, Domine, salvum fac Regem,
Regem Demetrium Moscoviae, Regem
Demetrium omnis Russiae, salvum fac
Regem Demetrium!

CHORUS

And who are those?
What devil brought them here?
Like the wolves
they're howling.
What infernal noise!

VARLAAM

Nasty ravens,
both of them.
It seems
they also are defending
the rightful Tsar—
We won't have it!
My friend Missail.

VARLAAM, MISSAIL

We won't have it!

(LAVITSKI *and* CHERNIKOVSKI *appear*)

VARLAAM, MISSAIL

Let's kill the cursed ravens!

CHORUS

A tree—
A tree!
A rope!
Yes! We will hang you—
threefold cursed enemies!

VARLAAM

Yes, dearest friends,
we will hang them
on the highest tree!

VARLAAM, MISSAIL

There they can pray
for the universe
in eternity!

CHORUS

A rope!
(the crowd ties the two Jesuits together)

LAVITSKI, CHERNIKOVSKI

Sanctissima Virgo, juva servos tuos.

VARLAAM

Let's tie them fast—
and that will make an end
to their praying!
Let them beg and cry—
no one shall help them!

CHORUS

A tree!
Come on,
let us hang them!
(the crowd drags them away. The followers of DIMITRI *enter)*

VARLAAM, MISSAIL

Glory to you,
our Tsar and Lord—
saved by the grace of God!
Glory to you, our Tsar and Lord,
saved by the Lord on high!

CHORUS

Glory
our Tsar and Lord
saved by the grace of God—
you whom the Lord has saved
Glory to you—
saved by the grace of God.
Great be your power
Dimitri Ivanovich!
(the crowd, VARLAAM, MISSAIL, LAVITSKI, CHERNIKOVSKI, *and the* SIMPLETON *all greet the new ruler,* DIMITRI*)*
Glory—glory—glory!
*(*GRIGORI *(now under the name of* DIMITRI*) appears with his retinue)*

DIMITRI

We, Dimitri Ivanovich,
by the grace of God, the Lord,
Tsarevich of all the Russias,
Prince of the blood
of noble forebears,

We assure you of our kindness.
To those
whom Godunov made suffer
we will grant protection!

KHRUSHCHOV

Mighty Lord,
our Tsar Dimitri,
glory to you!

DIMITRI

On to glory!
I lead you—
fight with me
to free
the land of our fathers!
With me
march on to Moscow!

(the tocsin is heard from afar. DIMITRI *leaves, followed by the entire crowd. The* SIMPLETON *remains all alone)*

CHORUS

Hail!
Victory!
Hail,
mighty Tsar!

LAVITSKI, CHERNIKOVSKI *(off-stage)*

Deo gloria—Deo gloria!

CHORUS *(from afar)*

Hail—
mighty Tsar,
Dimitri Ivanovich!

(a great fire is seen in the distance. The SIMPLETON *sits on a stone)*

SIMPLETON

Eyes are burning,
bitter tears flowing—
cry, faithful heart,
cry in deep anguish:
soon the foe will come—
and the dark will fall—
night will blind us all
and no hope of dawn.
Russia's sorrow
is great—
Cry—cry—
Russian land—
hungry people—
cry. . . .

(the sound of the tocsin continues. The SIMPLETON *trembles, and gazes at the fire on the horizon)*

CARMEN

By Georges Bizet (1838–75)

LIBRETTO BY HENRI MEILHAC AND LUDOVIC HALÉVY

Translated by RUTH and THOMAS MARTIN.

Based on the story of the same name by the French novelist, Prosper Mérimée.

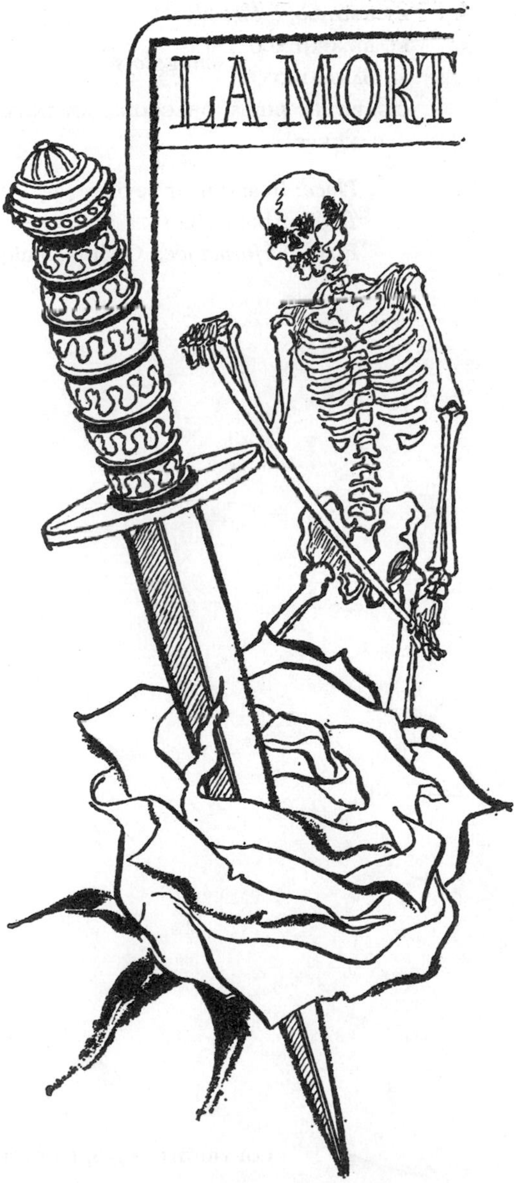

CHARACTERS

MORALES, *an officer*		*Bass*
MICAELA, *a peasant girl*		*Soprano*
ZUNIGA, *a lieutenant of dragoons*		*Bass*
DON JOSÉ, *a corporal of dragoons*		*Tenor*
CARMEN, *a gypsy girl*		*Soprano*
MERCEDES	*gypsy companions of Carmen*	*Mezzo-soprano*
FRASQUITA		*Mezzo-soprano*
ESCAMILLO, *a toreador*		*Baritone*
EL REMENDADO	*smugglers*	*Tenor*
EL DANCAIRO		*Baritone*

CIGARETTE GIRLS, DRAGOONS, AN INNKEEPER, SMUGGLERS, DANCERS

Place: In and near Seville
Time: About 1820
First performance: Opéra-Comique, Paris, March 3, 1875

COPYRIGHT, 1958, BY G. SCHIRMER, INC.

ACT I

Prelude

Scene and Chorus

(A square in Seville. On the right, the door of a tobacco factory; on the left, a guardhouse; at the back, a bridge. When the curtain rises, CORPORAL MORALES *and the soldiers are grouped in front of the guardhouse. People are coming and going on the square.)*

CHORUS OF DRAGOONS
Lazy people, crazy people,
Old and young, bold and shy;
Strolling along or hustling by,
Nobody knows the reason why.
Neither do I!

CHOEUR DES SOLDATS
Sur la place
Chacun passe,
Chacun vient, chacun va;
Drôles de gens que ces gens-là.

MORALES *(nonchalantly)*
Lolling idly about and smoking,
Playing dice and cards,
We pass the time in talk and joking
With our fellow guards.
Lazy people, crazy people,
Old and young, bold and shy.

MORALES
A la porte du corps de garde,
Pour tuer le temps,
On fume, on jase, l'on regarde
Passer les passants.

CHORUS
Lazy people, crazy people,
Old and young, bold and shy;
Strolling along or hustling by,
Nobody knows the reason why.
Neither do I!
*(*MICAELA *enters)*

CHOEUR
Sur la place
Chacun passe,
Chacun vient, chacun va;
Drôles de gens que ces gens-là.

MORALES
Now, there's a pretty girl approaching;
She seems to be shy and afraid.
Perhaps, but no!
She's too bashful, she needs coaching.

MORALES
Regardez donc cette petite
Qui semble vouloir nous parler.
Voyez, elle tourne, elle hésite.

CHORUS
You do it then; go to her aid!

LES SOLDATS
A son secours il faut aller.

MORALES *(to* MICAELA*)*
Young lady, may I help you?

MORALES
Que cherchez-vous, la belle?

MICAELA *(with simplicity)*
Yes, I'd like to speak to a guard.

MICAELA
Moi, je cherche un brigadier.

MORALES *(with gallantry)*
You're in luck, I'm here!

MORALES
Je suis là! Voilà!

MICAELA
No, I am looking for a soldier named Don José.
Do you know him too?

MICAELA
Mon brigadier, à moi, s'appelle
Don José, le connaissez-vous?

MORALES
Don José? Oh yes, of course we do.

MORALES
Don José, nous le connaissons tous.

MICAELA *(animatedly)*
You do? Perhaps you can tell me where to find him?

MICAELA
Vraiment! Est-il avec vous, je vous prie?

MORALES
Il n'est pas brigadier dans notre compagnie.

MICAELA
Alors il n'est pas là?

MORALES
Non, ma charmante, il n'est pas là,
Mais tout à l'heure il y sera.
Il y sera quand la garde montante
Remplacera la garde descendante.

MORALES, CHOEUR
Il y sera quand la garde montante
Remplacera la garde descendante.

MORALES
Mais en attendant qu'il vienne,
Voulez-vous, la belle enfant,
Voulez-vous prendre la peine
D'entrer chez nous un instant?

MICAELA
Chez vous?

LES SOLDATS
Chez nous.

MICAELA
Chez vous?

LES SOLDATS
Chez nous.

MICAELA
Non pas, non pas.
Grand merci, messieurs les soldats.

MORALES
Entrez sans crainte, mignonne,
Je vous promets qu'on aura,
Pour votre chère personne,
Tous les égards qu'il faudra.

MICAELA
Je n'en doute pas; cependant
Je reviendrai, c'est plus prudent.
Je reviendrai quand la garde montante
Remplacera la garde descendante.

MICAELA, MORALES, CHOEUR
Je reviendrai quand } la garde
Il faut rester car } montante
Remplacera } la garde
Va remplacer } descendante.

MORALES
Vous resterez.

MICAELA
Non pas! non pas!

MORALES
The company he's serving with has not arrived yet.

MICAELA (*with disappointment*)
I see. Then he's not here?

MORALES
No, I am sorry, but don't you worry.
For very soon he will be here,
My pretty dear.
It won't be long, the bugle will be blowing.
His company will come and we'll be going.

MORALES, CHORUS
It won't be long, the bugle will be blowing.
His company will come and we'll be going.

MORALES (*very gallantly*)
But may I suggest at present,
Since you have to wait, my dear,
You will find it far more pleasant
Inside the guardhouse than out here.

MICAELA
In there?

CHORUS
Why not?

MICAELA
With you?

CHORUS
With us!

MICAELA (shyly)
I'd better not.
All the same, I thank you a lot!

MORALES
You may enter without fear.
We will show you all respect,
And in ev'ry way, my dear,
We're most polite and correct.

MICAELA
I don't doubt your word.
Nonetheless, I'd rather go and then return.
(*gently mocking*)
For very soon the bugle will be blowing.
His company will come and you'll be going.

MICAELA, MORALES, CHORUS
For, very soon the bugle will be blowing.
His company will come and you'll be going.
(*the soldiers surround* MICAELA. *She tries to evade them*)

MORALES
Why don't you stay?

MICAELA
No, no, I can't!

CHORUS
Why don't you stay?

MICAELA
No, no, I can't, no, no! I cannot!
Now good-by. Some other day!
(she escapes)

CHORUS
Why don't you stay, don't go away.
Stay a little while, don't go away!

MORALES *(resignedly)*
Farewell to beauty,
Back to our duty.
Let's resume where we stopped before,
And watch the passing crowd once more.

CHORUS
Lazy people, crazy people,
Old and young, bold and shy;
Strolling along or hustling by,
Nobody knows the reason why.
Neither do I!
(a bugle call is played. A military march is heard at a distance. The soldiers form in line in front of the guardhouse. The relief appears; first a bugler and fifer, then a crowd of street boys. Lieutenant Zuniga and Corporal Don José follow, then the dragoons. During the streetboys' chorus the relief forms in front of the guard going off duty)

CHILDREN
We are soldiers marching proudly,
Here we come to change the guard.
Boys, blow your bugles loudly!
Ta ra tatata ratata.
See us march in perfect manner,
We are never out of step.
Follow the waving banner,
One two, one two, hep, hep!
Straight in line beside our neighbors,
Shoulders back and heads up high,
We raise our trusty sabers
And salute you going by.
We are soldiers marching proudly,
Here we come to change the guard.
Boys, blow your bugles loudly!
Ta ra tatata ratata.
Company halt! Stand at ease!
Tarata tarata tarata tatata, taratata!
Recitative

MORALES *(to* DON JOSÉ*)*
I have a message for you from a young and charming girl

LES SOLDATS
Vous resterez.

MICAELA
Non pas! non pas!
Au revoir, messieurs les soldats.

LES SOLDATS
Vous resterez, vous resterez,
Oui, vous resterez, vous resterez!

MORALES
L'oiseau s'envole,
On s'en console.
Reprenons notre passe-temps,
Et regardons passer les gens.

CHOEUR
Sur la place.
Chacun passe,
Chacun vient, chacun va;
Drôles de gens que ces gens-là.

CHOEUR DES GAMINS
Avec la garde montante,
Nous arrivons, nous voilà.
Sonne, trompette éclatante,
Ta ra ta ta, ta ra ta ta;
Nous marchons, la tête haute
Comme de petits soldats,
Marquant sans faire de faute
Une, deux, marquant le pas.
Les épaules en arrière
Et la poitrine en dehors,
Les bras de cette manière
Tombant tout le long du corps;
Avec la garde montante
Nous arrivons, nous voilà.
Sonne, trompette éclatante,
Ta ra ta ta, ta ra ta ta.

MORALES
Une jeune fille charmante
Vient de nous demander

Si tu n'étais pas là. Jupe
Bleue et natte tombante.

JOSÉ
Ce doit être Micaela.

CHOEUR
DES GAMINS
Et la garde descendante
Rentre chez elle et s'en va.
Sonne, trompette éclatante,
Ta ra ta ta, ta ra ta ta.
Nous marchons la tête haute
Comme de petits soldats,
Marquant, sans faire de faute,
Une . . . deux . . . marquant le pas.
Ta ra ta ta, ta ra ta ta.

ZUNIGA
C'est bien là, n'est ce pas, dans ce grand bâtiment
Que travaillent les cigarières?

JOSÉ
C'est là, mon officier, et bien certainement
On ne vit nulle part, filles aussi légères.

ZUNIGA
Mais au moins sont-elles jolies?

JOSÉ
Mon officier, je n'en sais rien,
Et m'occupe assez peu de ces galanteries.

ZUNIGA
Ce qui t'occupe ami,
Je le sais bien,
Une jeune fille charmante,
Qu'on appelle Micaela,
Jupe bleue et natte tombante.
Tu ne réponds rien à celà?

JOSÉ
Je réponds que c'est vrai,
Je réponds que je l'aime!
Quant aux ouvrières d'ici,
Quant à leur beauté, les voici!
Et vous pouvez juger vous-même.

JEUNES GENS
La cloche a sonné, nous, des ouvrières
Nous venons ici guetter le retour;
Et nous vous suivrons, brunes cigarières,

who asked to speak to you . . .
Light blue skirt and very long braids.

JOSÉ
I am sure that was Micaela!

(exit guard going off duty. The boys march off behind the bugler and fifer of the retiring guard, in the same manner as they followed those of the relief)

CHILDREN
We are soldiers marching proudly,
Leaving with the changing guard.
Boys, blow your bugles loudly!
Taratatata ratata.
See us march in perfect manner.
We are never out of step.
Follow the waving banner,
One, two, one two, hep, hep!

Recitative

ZUNIGA
Don José, is it true that in that factory, there,
Many pretty women are working?

JOSÉ
Indeed, sir, that is so; and ev'rybody knows
That these cigarette girls are of very easy virtue.

ZUNIGA
Are they also easy to look at?

JOSÉ
Sir, I don't know much about that,
For I am not concerned with women of that nature.

ZUNIGA
What concerns you, my friend, I think I know.
You're in love with one charming girl. Micaela is her name.
"Light blue skirt and very long braids."
Well, am I right about that?

JOSÉ
I admit you are right! I confess, she's the girl I love.
And as for the factory girls, when you hear the bell
They'll be here. Then you can judge their looks quite well.

(the factory bell rings. José sits down busying himself with repairing the chain of his saber and pays no attention to the young men and the townspeople entering. The bell stops ringing)

TOWNSPEOPLE, YOUNG MEN
Ev'ry day at noon
You will find us here,
Waiting for the time
When the girls appear,

Charming to the eye,
How we love to court them
Hoping that our fond wishes may come true
As all lovers do.
(*the cigarette girls enter, smoking*)
Here they are, the bright-eyed coquettes,
Keen and audacious,
Idly smoking their cigarettes,
And so flirtatious!

En vous murmurant des propos d'amour.
Voyez-les! Regards impudents,
Mines coquettes,
Fumant toutes du bout des dents
La cigarette.

CIGARETTE GIRLS
Smoke rings make their lazy way,
Softly curling.
Skyward they stray,
In a fragrant cloud unfurling.
Their perfume pervades the air,
Gently stealing,
Soothing our mind
To a mellow pleasant feeling.
Those tender words you lovers say every day
Fade away!
Your promises, too, like the smoke in the blue,
Fade away.
Smoke rings rise and float away
In the blue of the sky.
See them curling and rising
And vanish at last in the blue of the sky.
See them rise,
To the skies!

LES CIGARIÈRES
Dans l'air, nous suivons des yeux
La fumée,
Qui vers les cieux
Monte, monte parfumée.
Dans l'air nous suivons des yeux
La fumée.
Cela monte gentiment
A la tête,
Tout doucement cela vous met
L'âme en fête!
Le doux parler des amants,
C'est fumée!
Leurs transports et leurs serments
C'est fumée!
Dans l'air nous suivons des yeux la fumée
qui monte en tournant
vers les cieux.
La fumée,
La fumée!

SOLDIERS
But where's Carmen today?
Why is she missing?
(CARMEN *enters*)

LES SOLDATS
Mais nous ne voyons pas la Carmencita.

CIGARETTE GIRLS, YOUNG MEN
There she is!
Look at her!
Where she is, there is always excitement!

LES CIGARIÈRES, LES JEUNES GENS
La voilà
La voilà,
Voilà la Carmencita.

YOUNG MEN (*to* CARMEN)
At last! We've been anxiously waiting for you!
We men want at least an answer from you.
Oh Carmen, why must you tease us this way?
When will you give your love?
Won't you name the day?

LES JEUNES GENS
Carmen, sur tes pas, nous nous pressons tous;
Carmen, sois gentille, au moins réponds-nous
Et dis-nous quel jour tu nous aimeras!

CARMEN (*after a swift glance at* JOSÉ)
When I'll give you my love?
Who knows, it's hard to tell!
Perhaps not at all,
Perhaps very soon!
(*resolutely*)
But one thing I'll say:
Not today.

CARMEN
Quand je vous aimerai? Ma foi, je ne sais pas.
Peut-être jamais, peut-être demain;
Mais pas aujourd'hui, c'est certain.

L'amour est un oiseau rebelle
Que nul ne peut apprivoiser,
Et c'est bien en vain qu'on
l'appelle,
S'il lui convient de refuser.
Rien n'y fait; menace ou prière,
L'un parle bien, l'autre se tait;
Et c'est l'autre que je préfère,
Il n'a rien dit mais il me plait.
L'amour! l'amour!
L'amour! l'amour!
L'amour est enfant de Bohême,
Il n'a jamais connu de loi;
Si tu ne m'aimes pas, je t'aime;
Si je t'aime, prends garde à toi.
L'oiseau que tu croyais
surprendre
Battit de l'aile et s'envola;
L'amour est loin, tu peux
l'attendre;
Tu ne l'attends plus—il est là.
Tout autour de toi, vite, vite,
Il vient, s'en va, puis il revient;
Tu crois le tenir, il t'évite,
Tu crois l'éviter, il te tient.
L'amour, l'amour!
L'amour, l'amour!
L'amour est enfant de Bohême,
Il n'a jamais connu de loi;
Si tu ne m'aimes pas, je t'aime;
Si je t'aime, prends garde à toi.

Habanera
Love is free as the wayward breeze,
It can be shy, it can be bold.
Love can fascinate, love can tease,
Its whims and moods are thousandfold.
All at once it arrives and lingers,
For just how long can't be foretold.
Then it deftly slips through your fingers,
For love's a thing no force can hold.
That's love for you,
That's love for you!
A heart in love is quickly burned,
It knows no law except its own desire.
If I should love you and you spurn me,
I'm warning you, you play with fire!
If I'm in love with you,
Don't ever, ever try to spurn me.
My friend, remember, if I love you, you play with fire!
Wait for love and you wait forever,
Don't wait at all, it comes to you.
Try to grasp it, it's far too clever,
It flies away into the blue.
Love has so many forms and shapes,
Each day it wears a new disguise.
Think you've caught it and it escapes
To catch you later by surprise.
That's love for you,
That's love for you!

JEUNES GENS
Carmen, sur tes pas, nous nous pressons tous;
Carmen, sois gentille, au moins réponds-nous.

YOUNG MEN (*to* CARMEN)
Say when! Carmen, do not torment us this way!
We men want a word of promise today!
Carmen, please, do not tease!
Say, at least, which one you will choose!
(*spoken over music*)

CARMEN
Eh! compère, qu'est-ce que tu fais là?

JOSÉ
Je fais une chaîne avec du fil de laiton, une chaîne pour attacher mon épinglette.

CARMEN
Ton épinglette, vraiment! Ton épinglette—épinglier de mon âme.

CARMEN
Hey, soldier, what are you doing here?

JOSÉ
I'm repairing the chain that holds my saber.

CARMEN
Repairing the chain that holds your saber!
Really! Is that *all* you want to hold?
(*the young men surround* CARMEN; *she looks first at them, then at* JOSÉ; *hesitates; turns as if going to factory, then retraces her steps and goes straight to* JOSÉ, *who is still occupied with his saber chain*)
Look! Here's something to hold on to!
(CARMEN *takes a flower from her bodice and throws it at* JOSÉ. *She runs away*)
Recitative

(there is a burst of laughter. The factory bell begins to ring again. Exit workingmen, young men. The soldiers enter the guardhouse. JOSÉ *is left alone; he picks up the flower, which has fallen at his feet)*

JOSÉ
What outrageous, scandalous behavior! And the way she threw that flower at me! It came like a dart! But its fragrance is sweet and the flower is lovely. And the woman . . . if it is true there are witches, she is one! There can be no doubt.
(MICAELA *enters*)

JOSÉ
Quels regards! Quelle effronterie!
Cette fleur là m'a fait
L'effet d'une balle qui m'arrivait!
Le parfum en est fort et la fleur est jolie!
Et la femme . . .
S'il est vraiment des sorcières,
C'en est une certainement.

MICAELA
José!

MICAELA
José!

JOSÉ (*joyously*)
What a surprise!

JOSÉ
Micaela!

MICAELA
There you are!

MICAELA
Me voici!

JOSÉ
Micaela!

JOSÉ
Quelle joie!

MICAELA
I bring a message from your mother!

MICAELA
C'est votre mère qui m'envoie!

Duet

JOSÉ (*agitated*)
So you come from my mother?
Tell me, how is my mother?

JOSÉ
Parle-moi de ma mère.

MICAELA (*with simplicity*)
She sends me with a message that will make you happy,
And a letter . . .

MICAELA
J'apporte de sa part, fidèle messagère,
Cette lettre.

JOSÉ (*joyfully*)
A letter!

JOSÉ
Une lettre!

MICAELA
And then some money, too,
To help along until your pay is due.
(*hesitating*)
And then . . .

MICAELA
Et puis un peu d'argent
Pour ajouter à votre traitement,
Et puis—

JOSÉ
Go on . . .

JOSÉ
Et puis?

MICAELA
And then . . . How can I tell you . . .
And then I also have another message
Which is of greater worth,
And, for a loving son,
Means more than all the gold on earth.

MICAELA
Et puis—vraiment je n'ose,
Et puis—encore une autre chose
Qui vaut mieux que l'argent et qui, pour un bon fils,
Aura sans doute plus de prix.

JOSÉ
That other message from my mother, won't you say?

JOSÉ
Cette autre chose, quelle est-elle?
Parle donc.

MICAELA
You shall have it, too.
I promised to obey.

MICAELA
Oui, je parlerai;
Ce que l'on m'a donné, je vous le donnerai.

Votre mère avec moi sortait de la chapelle,
Et c'est alors qu'en m'embrassant,
"Tu vas," m'a-t-elle dit, "t-en aller à la ville;
La route n'est pas longue, une fois à Séville,
Tu chercheras mon fils, mon José, mon enfant.
Et tu lui diras que sa mère
Songe nuit et jour à l'absent,
Qu'elle regrette et qu'elle espère,
Qu'elle pardonne et qu'elle attend;
Tout cela, n'est-ce pas? mignonne,
De ma part tu le lui diras,
Et ce baiser que je te donne
De ma part tu le lui rendras."

JOSÉ
Un baiser de ma mère!

MICAELA
Un baiser pour son fils!

José, je vous le rends, comme je l'ai promis.

JOSÉ
Ma mère, je la vois, oui, je revois mon village.
O souvenirs d'autrefois! Doux souvenirs du pays!
O souvenirs chéris!
Vous remplissez mon coeur de force et de courage
O souvenirs chéris,
Ma mère je la vois,
Je revois mon village!

MICAELA
Sa mère il la revoit!
Il revoit son village!
O souvenirs d'autrefois!
Souvenirs du pays!
Vous remplissez son coeur
De force et de courage,
O souvenirs chéris!
Sa mère il la revoit,
Il revoit son village!

JOSÉ
Qui sait de quel démon j'allais être la proie!
Même de loin, ma mère me défend,

I'll pass it on to you.
After church I was walking homeward with your mother,
When she embraced me like her own child:
"My dear," she said to me,
"Make a trip to Seville.
You don't have far to travel,
And once you reach the city,
You'll go and find your way to José, my dear son.
You'll go and find my son, my beloved José.
Then say I implore God Almighty
To watch over him night and day.
Say that I'll never cease to love him;
That I forgive him, hope and pray."
Then she kissed me and said sincerely
As she sent me upon my way,
"Give this fond kiss he'll value dearly
From my heart to my son, José."

JOSÉ (*deeply moved*)
A kiss from my mother!

MICAELA
Yes, a kiss for her son.
(*with simplicity*)
I give it now to you
As I was asked to do.
(*she kisses* JOSÉ)

JOSÉ (*with emotion*)
My heart is all aglow
With loving thoughts of my mother.
I see her dear beloved face,
I see my village and home.
Through all the years dear to me,
Mem'ries of long ago.
As I recall, my heart is all aglow,
My hope is bright and strong,
My soul restored with courage.
My heart is all aglow
As I recall my home and my beloved mother.

MICAELA
His heart is all aglow
With loving thoughts of his mother.
He sees her dear, beloved face,
He sees his village and home.
His hope is bright and strong,
His soul restored with courage.
His heart is all aglow
As he recalls his home
And his beloved mother.

JOSÉ (*absorbedly*)
Who knows what turn of fate might have shattered my hopes?
Even from far my mother shields her son,

(raptly)
And with the kiss she sent to me
Has turned away the danger
And has made me strong.

MICAELA *(animatedly)*
Turn of fate, did you say?
Some danger you don't know?
Is there anything wrong?

JOSÉ
No, no! Let's speak of you, dear Micaela.
When do you intend to go home?

MICAELA
Soon, this very evening.
Tomorrow, I'll be with your mother.

JOSÉ *(animatedly)*
I'm so glad! And please, tell her for me:
Tell her my thoughts are always near her,
And say I repent what I've done.
And say that I shall not fail her,
She'll be proud of her son!
Now I bid you good-by
As I send you upon your way.
Give her this kiss she'll value dearly
From the heart of her son, José.
(JOSÉ *kisses* MICAELA)

MICAELA *(with simplicity)*
I'll tell her all you say,
That I promise to do,
And I'll give her from you
This kiss, my dear José.

Recitative

JOSÉ
Let me see what she wrote, while you stay here with me.

MICAELA
Oh no, I'd rather go and later I will come back.

JOSÉ
But why should you go?

MICAELA
I'd prefer it. I'd rather you read it without me.
Good-by, until later on.

JOSÉ
You won't be long?

MICAELA
Not long at all.
(exit MICAELA*)*

JOSÉ *(after having read the letter)*
I'll obey, dear Mother.
You need not be afraid.
I'll obey with a happy heart.

Et ce baiser qu'elle m'envoie
Écarte le péril et sauve son enfant.

MICAELA
Quel démon? Quel péril? Je ne comprends pas bien.
Que veut dire cela?

JOSÉ
Rien! Rien!
Parlons de toi, la messagère.
Tu vas retourner au pays?

MICAELA
Oui, ce soir même, demain je verrai votre mère.

JOSÉ
Tu la verras!
Eh bien, tu lui diras
Que son fils l'aime et la vénère,
Et qu'il se repent aujourd'hui.
Il veut que là-bas sa mère
Soit contente de lui!
Tout cela, n'est-ce pas, mignonne,
De ma part tu le lui diras;
Et ce baiser que je te donne,
De ma part tu le lui rendras.

MICAELA
Oui je vous le promets, de la part de son fils.
José je le rendrai comme je l'ai promis.

JOSÉ
Reste là maintenant,
Pendant que je lirai.

MICAELA
Non pas, lisez d'abord,
Et puis je reviendrai.

JOSÉ
Pourquoi t'en aller?

MICAELA
C'est plus sage,
Cela me convient d'avantage.
Lisez! puis je reviendrai.

JOSÉ
Tu reviendras?

MICAELA
Je reviendrai!

JOSÉ
Ne crains rien, ma mère, ton fils t'obéira,
Fera ce que tu lui dis; j'aime Micaela,

Je la prendrai pour femme,
Quant à tes fleurs, sorcière
infâme!

LE LIEUTENANT
Que se passe-t-il donc là-bas?

SOPRANES
Au secours! n'entendez-vous
pas?

MEZZOS
Au secours, messieurs les
soldats!

SOPRANES
C'est la Carmencita.

MEZZOS
Non, non, ce n'est pas elle!

SOPRANES
C'est elle.

MEZZOS
Pas du tout.

SOPRANES
Si fait! C'est elle
Elle a porté les premiers coups.

TOUTES LES FEMMES
Ne les écoutez pas, monsieur,
Écoutez-nous,
Écoutez-nous!

MEZZOS
La Manuelita disait
Et répétait à voix haute
Qu'elle achèterait sans faute
Un âne qui lui plaisait.

SOPRANES
Alors la Carmencita,
Railleuse à son ordinaire,
Dit: "un âne, pourquoi faire?
Un balai te suffira."

MEZZOS
Manuelita riposta
Et dit à sa camarade:
"Pour certaine promenade
Mon âne te servira!"

SOPRANES
"Et ce jour-là tu pourras
A bon droit faire la fière;
Deux laquais suivront derrière,
T'émouchant à tour de bras."

I give my solemn word
To marry Micaela,
In spite of you! You and your flowers!

Chorus

(*the girls are heard screaming behind the scene*)

LIEUTENANT ZUNIGA
Say, what is going on in there?

SOPRANOS (*on-stage*)
Hurry up, hurry up.
Can't somebody hear?

MEZZOS (*on-stage*)
Hurry up, hurry up!
Someone interfere!

SOPRANOS
Carmen began the fight!

MEZZOS
No, no, she didn't do it!

SOPRANOS
She did it!

MEZZOS
Not at all!

SOPRANOS
I tell you, Carmen did it!
She was the first to strike a blow!

ALL THE WOMEN
They're telling you a lie!
They're telling you a lie!
Of course, it is a lie!
It is a lie, it is a shameful lie,
They are telling a lie!

MEZZOS (*drawing the* LIEUTENANT *to their side*)
This is how it came to pass:
Our Manuela kept talking
That she had enough of walking,
She would go and buy an ass.

SOPRANOS (*also drawing the* LIEUTENANT *to their side*)
Carmen shouted through the room,
(Maybe she tried to be funny):
"You would only waste your money,
You'd look better on a broom!"

MEZZOS
Manuela shouted back:
"You cat, you are only jealous!
You don't even have to tell us,
We know all your gypsy pack!"

SOPRANOS
"You can't buy a pair of shoes,
Let alone donkeys to ride on,
So why put that air of pride on?
And watch out whom you attack!"

ALL THE WOMEN
And in just one moment more,
Both of them rolled on the floor,
And then and there
We saw the pair
Pulling at each other's hair!

LIEUTENANT (*impatiently*)
The devil with this female squalling!
(*to* DON JOSÉ)
Listen, José, you go and take two men.
Go inside and find out what's the cause of this brawling.
(JOSÉ *enters the factory, followed by two soldiers*)

SOPRANOS
Carmen began the fight!

MEZZOS
No, no, she didn't do it!

LIEUTENANT
Enough!
Somebody take all these females away!

ALL THE WOMEN
But, sir!
But, sir!
Don't listen to their lies
We swear it isn't true,
It isn't true, it isn't true,
It isn't true at all!

SOPRANOS
Carmen began the fight.
She was the first to attack.

MEZZOS
No, she was in the right!
She only tried to hit back!

SOPRANOS
Carmen is to blame!

MEZZOS
Absolutely not!

SOPRANOS
Yes, yes, yes, yes, yes, yes!

MEZZOS
No, no, no, no, no, no!

ALL THE WOMEN
It was she who struck the first blow!

SOPRANOS
Carmen began the fight!

MEZZOS
No, no, that isn't right!
(*the soldiers clear the square.* CARMEN *appears at the factory door, led by* JOSÉ *and followed by the two soldiers*)

Song and Melodrama

TOUTES LES FEMMES
Là-dessus toutes les deux
Se sont prises aux cheveux.

LE LIEUTENANT
Au diable tout ce bavardage!
Prenez, José, deux hommes avec vous
Et voyez là-dedans qui cause ce tapage.

SOPRANES
C'est la Carmencita!

MEZZOS
Non, non, écoutez, nous, etc., etc.

LE LIEUTENANT
Holà! holà!
Éloignez-moi toutes ces femmes-là.

TOUTES LES FEMMES
Écoutez-nous! écoutez-nous!
Ne les écoutez pas!
Monsieur, écoutez-nous!
Écoutez-nous, écoutez-nous!
Monsieur, écoutez-nous!

SOPRANES
C'est la Carmencita
Qui porta les premiers coups!

MEZZOS
C'est la Manuelita
Qui porta les premiers coups!

SOPRANES
La Carmencita!

MEZZOS
La Manuelita!

SOPRANES
Si! Si! Si! Si! Si! Si!

MEZZOS
Non! Non! Non! Non! Non! Non!

TOUTES LES FEMMES
Elle a porté les premiers coups!

SOPRANES
C'est la Carmencita!

MEZZOS
C'est la Manuelita!

JOSÉ Mon officier, c'était une querelle; Des injures d'abord, puis à la fin des coups, Une femme blessée.	JOSÉ Sir, it is true, two girls started a quarrel. Only insults at first, later it came to blows. One of them has been wounded.
LE LIEUTENANT Et par qui?	LIEUTENANT And by whom?
JOSÉ Mais par elle.	JOSÉ This one here, sir.
LE LIEUTENANT Vous entendez, que nous répondrez-vous?	LIEUTENANT (*to* CARMEN) You heard the report. What have you got to say?
CARMEN Tra la la la la la la la, Coupe-moi, brûle-moi, Je ne te dirai rien; Tra la la la la la la la, Je brave tout, le feu, le fer, et le ciel même!	CARMEN Tra lalalalalalala! You can burn me alive, I won't tell you a thing. Tra lalalalalalala! You may flog me or torture me, It doesn't matter!
LE LIEUTENANT Fais-nous grâce de tes chansons, Et puisque l'on t'a dit de répondre, réponds!	LIEUTENANT Do us a favor and kindly stop. I told you to answer my question. Speak up!
CARMEN Tra la la la la la la la, Mon secret, je le garde et je le garde bien! Tra la la la la la la la, J'en aime un autre et meurs en disant que je l'aime!	CARMEN (*staring impudently at the Lieutenant*) Tra lalalalalalala, I will never betray What I keep in my heart! Tra lalalalalalala. There's one man I adore, And he knows that I love him.
LE LIEUTENANT Puisque tu le prends sur ce ton, Tu chanteras ton air aux murs de la prison.	LIEUTENANT Since you are disposed to rebel, You may practice your arias inside of a cell.
CHOEUR En prison! en prison!	CHORUS OF WOMEN Off with her, off to jail! (CARMEN *strikes a woman who happens to be near her*)
LE LIEUTENANT La peste! Décidément vous avez la main leste!	LIEUTENANT (*to* CARMEN) Confound you! You are a menace to all those around you!
CARMEN Tra la la la la la la la!	CARMEN (*with the utmost impertinence*) Tra lalalalalalala. . . .
LE LIEUTENANT C'est dommage, C'est grand dommage, Car elle est gentille vraiment! Mais il faut bien la rendre sage, Attachez ces deux jolis bras.	LIEUTENANT It's a shame, though, She's such a wildcat! For she has spirit and wit! But we must tame her just a bit. Tie her hands behind her back! (*he goes into the guardhouse*)
CARMEN Où me conduirez vous?	CARMEN Where are you going to take me?
JOSÉ A la prison; et je n'y puis rien faire.	JOSÉ You go to jail, and no one can prevent it.

CARMEN
Indeed, no one can prevent it?

JOSÉ
That's right. I must do as I'm told.

CARMEN
Even so, I will bet that no matter how strict the order,
You will help me to escape. You know why? Because you love me.

JOSÉ
I, love you?

CARMEN
Yes, José! The flower I gave you today, the flower you hid there in your jacket,
You might as well throw it away, it has done its duty.

JOSÉ
You're going too far! Once and for all, you must not talk. That's a command!

CARMEN (*speaks, while music goes on*)
Very well, General, very well!
You forbid me to talk, so I won't talk.

Seguidilla

Close to the wall of Sevilla,
I know a certain old tavern.
I go there to dance Seguidilla
And to drink Manzanilla,
At the inn of Señor Lillas Pastia.
But when a girl goes out to dance,
She wants to have some company.
So I don't want to take a chance,
I'll take the man I love with me.
(*laughing*)
The man I love?
What am I saying?
I told him yesterday we're through.
My heart is free, longing for someone,
Eager for love with someone new.
There are so many who adore me
But I don't care for any one.
With one whole Sunday free before me,
Who wants my love? He'll be the one.
Who wants my heart?
Who comes to claim it?
Here is your chance, it still is free.
You can have it for the asking.
With my new love I'm on my way.
Close to the wall of Sevilla,
I know a certain old tavern.
I go there to dance Seguidilla
And drink Manzanilla.
I will meet my love at Lillas Pastia's inn!

CARMEN
Vraiment? tu n'y peux rien faire?

JOSÉ
Non, rien! j'obéis à mes chefs.

CARMEN
Eh bien moi, je sais bien qu'en dépit de tes chefs eux-mêmes
Tu feras tout ce que je veux,
Et cela parce-que tu m'aimes!

JOSÉ
Moi, t'aimer?

CARMEN
Oui, José.
La fleur dont je t'ai fait présent,
Tu sais, la fleur de la sorcière,
Tu peux la jeter maintenant,
Le charme opère!

JOSÉ
Ne me parle plus! Tu m'entends!
Ne parle plus. Je le défends!

CARMEN

Près des remparts de Séville,
Chez mon ami Lillas Pastia,
J'irai danser la Séguedille
Et boire du Manzanilla! . . .
J'irai chez mon ami Lillas Pastia
Oui, mais toute seule on s'ennuie,
Et les vrais plaisirs sont à deux . . .
Donc pour me tenir compagnie,
J'emmènerai mon amoureux.
Mon amoureux! . . . il est au diable . . .
Je l'ai mis à la porte hier . . .
Mon pauvre coeur très consolable,
Mon coeur est libre comme l'air . . .
J'ai des galants à la douzaine
Mais ils ne sont pas à mon gré;
Voici la fin de la semaine.
Qui veut m'aimer? je l'aimerai!
Qui veut mon âme? elle est à prendre!
Vous arrivez au bon moment,
Je n'ai guère le temps d'attendre,
Car avec mon nouvel amant . . .
Près des remparts de Séville,
Chez mon ami Lillas Pastia,
J'irai danser la Séguedille
Et boire du Manzanilla.
Oui, j'irai chez mon ami Lillas Pastia!

JOSÉ
Tais-toi, je t'avais dit de ne pas me parler!

CARMEN
Je ne te parle pas,
Je chante pour moi-même
Et je pense . . . il n'est pas défendu de penser,
Je pense à certain officier,
A certain officier qui m'aime,
Et qu'à mon tour je pourrais bien aimer . . .

JOSÉ
Carmen! . . .

CARMEN
Mon officier n'est pas un capitaine,
Pas même un lieutenant, il n'est que brigadier:
Mais c'est assez pour une Bohémienne,
Et je daigne m'en contenter!

JOSÉ
Carmen, je suis comme un homme ivre,
Si je cède, se je me livre,
Ta promesse, tu la tiendras . . .
Ah! Si je t'aime, Carmen,
Carmen, tu m'aimeras? . . .

CARMEN
Oui.

JOSÉ
Chez Lillas Pastia.

CARMEN
Nous danserons la Séguedille.

JOSÉ
Tu le promets?

CARMEN
En buvant du Manzanilla.

JOSÉ
Tu le promets?

CARMEN
Ah! Près des remparts de Séville,
Chez mon ami Lillas Pastia,
Nous danserons la Séguedille
Et boirons du Manzanilla.
Tra la la la la la la la . . .

JOSÉ
Le lieutenant! . . . Prenez garde.

JOSÉ (*with severity*)
Enough! For the last time, I forbid you to talk!

CARMEN (*with simplicity*)
I do not talk to you. I sing for my own pleasure,
And I'm thinking!
And ev'rybody knows thoughts are free.
I'm thinking of one certain man,
An officer who might be you,
Who loves me, and, I am sure,
Yes, I confess that I could love him, too.

JOSÉ
Carmen!

CARMEN (*pointedly*)
This certain soldier is not of high standing;
Really, his rank is quite low.
To tell you the truth, he's a corp'ral.
But why should I be demanding?
I'll be happy with him, I know.

JOSÉ (*agitated*)
Carmen, I can bear it no longer!
If I free you, if I surrender,
Will you promise to keep your word?
And if I love you, Carmen,
Will you return my love?

CARMEN
Yes.

JOSÉ
At Lillas Pastia's—

CARMEN
We both will dance the Seguidilla,

JOSÉ
I have your word?

CARMEN
And we will drink Manzanilla.

JOSÉ
(*untying the rope*)
You'll keep your word!

CARMEN
Ah!
Close to the wall of Sevilla,
I know a certain old tavern.
Together we'll dance Seguidilla
And we'll drink Manzanilla!
Tra lalalalalalalala!

Finale

(ZUNIGA *comes out of the guardhouse*)

JOSÉ
The lieutenant—be careful!

LIEUTENANT (*to José*)
Here's the order, José.
Now go and do your duty.

ZUNIGA
Voici l'ordre, partez et faites bonne garde.

CARMEN (*aside to* JOSÉ)
You pretend to lead me away.
Stay in back of me
(*making a backward gesture with her head*)
And I'll give you a heavy push.
Turn around, as you fall,
The rest I will take care of.

CARMEN
En chemin je te pousserai aussi fort que je le pourrai . . .
Laisse-toi renverser . . . le reste me regarde!

(*in a different tone; singing and laughing in* ZUNIGA'S *face*)
A heart in love is quickly burned,
It knows no law except its own desire.
If I should love you and you spurn me,
I'm warning you, you play with fire!

L'amour est enfant de Bohême.
Il n'a jamais connu de loi;
Si tu ne m'aimes pas, je t'aime
Si je t'aime, prends garde à toi.

(*she marches off with* JOSÉ. *At the bridge* CARMEN *pushes him. He falls down and she escapes, laughing loudly*)

ACT II

Lillas Pastia's Inn. When the curtain rises, CARMEN, FRASQUITA, *and* MERCEDES *are discovered seated at a table with the officers. The gypsy girls dance, accompanied by gypsies playing the guitar and tambourine. At the end of the dance the song begins.*

Gypsy Song

CARMEN

Les tringles des sistres tintaient
Avec un éclat métallique,
Et sur cette étrange musique
Les Zingarellas se levaient.
Tambours de basque allaient
leur train,
Et les guitares forcenées
Grinçaient sous des mains
obstinées
Même chanson, même refrain,
Tra la la la la la.

CARMEN

The stillness at the end of day
Is broken by a lazy jingle,
The sleepy air begins to tingle.
The gypsy dance is under way!
And soon the tambourines of Spain
And strumming of guitars competing,
Continue on and on, repeating
The same old song, the same old strain,
The same old song, the same refrain.
Tra lalalalalala!

FRASQUITA, MERCEDES

Tra la la la la la la la

FRASQUITA, MERCEDES

(*the dance continues*)
Tra lalalalalalala!
(*the dance ceases*)

CARMEN

Les anneaux de cuivre et
d'argent
Reluisaient sur les peaux
bistrées;
D'orange ou de rouge zébrées
Les étoffes flottaient au vent.
La danse au chant se marait,
D'abord indécise et timide,
Plus vive ensuite et plus rapide,
Cela montait, montait,
montait! . . .
Tra la la la la la.

CARMEN

The copper rings the gypsies wear
Against their dusky skins are gleaming,
With red and orange colors streaming,
Swirling skirts billow through the air!
The music guides the dancing feet
With ever more compelling beat.
Quite timid first, but soon the master,
It drives them on, and growing faster,
It starts to rise and rise to fever heat!
Tra lalalalalalala!

FRASQUITA, MERCEDES

Tra la la la la la la la.

FRASQUITA, MERCEDES

(*the dance continues*)
Tra lalalalalalala!
(*the dance ceases*)

CARMEN

Les Bohémiens à tour de bras,
De leurs instruments faisaient
rage,
Et cet éblouissant tapage,
Ensorcelait les Zingaras!
Sous le rhythme de la chanson,
Ardentes, folles, enfiévrées,
Elles se laissaient, enivrées,
Emporter par le tourbillon!
Tra la la la la la.

CARMEN

The gypsy men play on with fire!
Their tambourines loudly whirring!
The pulsing rhythm fiercely stirring,
Inflames the gypsy girls' desire.
Their passion carries them away,
Their agile bodies turn and sway
In burning frenzy and abandon.
On and on they dance, madly driven,
Like a whirlwind no force can stay!
Tra lalalalalalala!

CARMEN, FRASQUITA, MERCEDES
(*the dance continues*)
Tra lalalalalalala!
(CARMEN, FRASQUITA, MERCEDES *join the dance*)
Recitative

FRASQUITA
My friends, Pastia just said . . .

LIEUTENANT
What is it that he said, Lillas Pastia?

FRASQUITA
He said that the chief of police told him the inn should be closing.

LIEUTENANT
All right, then, let us go. You girls will come with us.

FRASQUITA
We can't. We have to stay.

LIEUTENANT
But Carmen, you? You'll come with us? You're silent.
I think I know why: you are cross.

CARMEN
I should be cross! But why?

LIEUTENANT
On account of the boy who went to jail for you.

CARMEN
What has happened to the poor lad?

LIEUTENANT
They released him today.

CARMEN
They released him? I'm glad!
And now, to all of you, good night!

CARMEN, FRASQUITA, MERCEDES
And now, to all of you, good night!

CHORUS OF MEN (*off-stage*)
Hurrah, hurrah, the torero!
Hurrah, hurrah, Escamillo!

LIEUTENANT
They're having a torchlight parade!
They're going wild cheering Escamillo!
(*toward the street*)
We all would be proud, torero, if you would join us.
We'll toast your former triumphs, and all the ones to come!
(ESCAMILLO *enters*)

CHORUS, SOLOISTS (*on-stage*)
Hurrah, hurrah, the torero!
Hurrah, hurrah, Escamillo!
Hurrah!

LES TROIS VOIX
Tra la la la la la la la!

FRASQUITA
Messieurs, Pastia me dit—

LE LIEUTENANT
Que nous veut-il encore, maître Pastia?

FRASQUITA
Il dit que le Corrégidor veut que l'on ferme l'auberge.

LE LIEUTENANT
Eh bien! nous partirons.
Vous viendrez avec nous?

FRASQUITA
Non pas! nous, nous restons.

LE LIEUTENANT
Et toi, Carmen, tu ne viens pas?
Écoute! Deux mots dits tout bas:
Tu m'en veux.

CARMEN
Vous en vouloir! pourquoi?

LE LIEUTENANT
Ce soldat, l'autre jour, emprisonné pour toi.

CARMEN
Qu' a-t-on fait de ce malheureux?

LE LIEUTENANT
Maintenant il est libre!

CARMEN
Il est libre! tant mieux.
Bonsoir, messieurs nos amoureux!

CARMEN, FRASQUITA, MERCEDES
Bonsoir messieurs nos amoureux!

CHOEUR
Vivat! vivat le toréro!
Vivat! vivat Escamillo!

LE LIEUTENANT
Une promenade aux flambeaux!
C'est le vainqueur des courses de Grenade,
Voulez-vous avec nous boire mon camarade?
A vos succès anciens, à vos succès nouveaux!

CHOEUR
Vivat! vivat! le toréro! Vivat! vivat! Escamillo!

ESCAMILLO
Votre toast . . . je peux vous le rendre,
Señors, car avec les soldats
Oui, les toréros peuvent s'entendre,
Pour plaisirs ils ont les combats.
Le cirque est plein, c'est jour de fête,
Le cirque est plein du haut en bas.
Les spectateurs perdant la tête,
Les spectateurs s'interpellent à grand fracas;
Apostrophes, cris et tapage
Poussés jusques à la fureur,
Car c'est la fête du courage,
C'est la fête des gens de coeur!
Allons, en garde, ah
Toréador, en garde,
Toréador, Toréador!
Et songe bien, oui, songe en combattant
Qu'un oeil noir te regarde
Et que l'amour t'attend.

TOUT LE MONDE
Toréador, en garde!
Toréador! Toréador!
Et songe bien, oui, songe en combattant,
Qu'un oeil noir te regarde
Et que l'amour t'attend,
Toréador, Toréador!
L'amour, l'amour t'attend!

ESCAMILLO
Tout d'un coup, on fait silence . . .
On fait silence, ah que se passe-t-il?
Plus de cris, c'est l'instant!
Le taureau s'élance
En bondissant hors du Toril!
Il s'élance! Il entre, il frappe!
Un cheval roule, entraînant un Picador,
"Ah! bravo! Toro!" hurle la foule,
Le taureau va . . . il vient . . . et frappe encor!
En secouant ses banderilles,
Plein de fureur, il court!
Le cirque est plein de sang!
On se sauve . . . on franchit les grilles!
C'est ton tour maintenant!
Allons! en garde! ah!
Toréador, en garde!

Toreador Song

ESCAMILLO
Thank you all, you gallant soldier heroes,
And in return I drink to you tonight!
Long may you soldiers and we toreros
Live to share a common joy,
The thrill of the fight!
Crowds are swarming in the great arena,
Excitement fills the atmosphere.
Ev'ryone waiting, loudly debating,
Wild with impatience,
They raise a thunderous cheer!
Shouts and stamping become contagious,
Till at last it's like a thunderstorm.
Day of fame for men of soul courageous,
Day of fame for men of heart!
It's time, torero, come on! On guard! Ah!
Toreador, fight well and hard,
Proud as a king,
Yours is the ring!
And, after you have won the victor's crown,
Earn your sweet reward,
Your señorita's love!
Toreador, your sweet reward is love!

ALL
Toreador, fight well and hard,
Proud as a king,
Yours is the ring!
And, after you have won the victor's crown,
Earn your sweet reward,
Your señorita's love!
Toreador, your sweet reward is love!

ESCAMILLO
All at once, the crowd is silent.
What are they waiting for?
And what is happening?
Breathless expectancy
Hushes the gallery.
Through the gate the bull is leaping out into the ring!
Rushing on, he charges madly,
A horse goes under, dragging down a picador.
"Come on, torero!"
They roar like thunder.
Then, like a flash, the bull turns round,
Charging once more!
The lances stab his bleeding shoulder,
And blind with rage he runs.
The sand is red with blood!
Clear the ring, ev'ryone take cover!
Just one man stands sword in hand!

It's time, torero, come on! On guard!
Ah!
Toreador, fight well and hard,
Proud as a king,
Yours is the ring!
And, after you have won the victor's crown,
Earn your sweet reward,
Your señorita's love!
Toreador, your sweet reward is love!

Toréador, Toréador!
Et songe bien, oui, songe en combattant,
Qu'un oeil noir te regarde
Et que l'amour t'attend!

Recitative

Señorita, one word. I'd like to know your name. And when I fight again, it shall be on my lips.

La belle, un mot:
Comment t'appelle-t-on?
Dans mon premier danger
Je veux dire ton nom!

CARMEN
My name? It's Carmen. Or else, Carmencita.

CARMEN
Carmen, Carmencita!
Cela revient au même.

ESCAMILLO
And if I would say that I love you?

ESCAMILLO
Si l'on te disait que l'on t'aime?

CARMEN
Then I would say you are wasting your time.

CARMEN
Je répondrais qu'il ne faut pas m'aimer.

ESCAMILLO
That does not sound very inviting. And I've no other choice but to hope and keep waiting.

ESCAMILLO
Cette réponse n'est pas tendre;
Je me contenterai d'espérer et d'attendre.

CARMEN
I can't stop you from waiting, and to hope is always sweet.

CARMEN
Il est permis d'attendre, il est doux d'espérer.

LIEUTENANT
Since you have decided to stay, I shall come back.

LE LIEUTENANT
Puisque tu ne viens pas Carmen, je reviendrai.

CARMEN
That would be a mistake!

CARMEN
Et vous aurez grand tort.

LIEUTENANT
Bah! That risk I will take!

LE LIEUTENANT
Bah! je me risquerai!

Recitative

FRASQUITA (*calling* EL REMENDADO *and* EL DANCAIRO)
Tell us quickly, what are you planning?

FRASQUITA
Eh bien vite, quelles nouvelles?

EL DANCAIRO (*entering with* EL REMENDADO)
We're handling goods coming from England. I'm sure we'll get them through in the usual way. But you three girls must go along.

LE DANCAIRO
Pas trop mauvaises les nouvelles,
Et nous pouvons encore faire quelques beaux coups!
Mais nous avons besoin de vous.

CARMEN, FRASQUITA, MERCEDES
We'll go along?

CARMEN, FRASQUITA, MERCEDES
Besoin de nous!

EL DANCAIRO
I must be sure nothing goes wrong.

LE DANCAIRO
Oui, nous avon besoin de vous.

Quintet

This is a superb proposition.

Nous avons en tête une affaire.

MERCEDES, FRASQUITA
Another deal in contraband?

MERCEDES, FRASQUITA
Est-elle bonne, dites-nous?

EL DANCAIRO
We will earn a nice fat commission,
But we need you to lend a hand.

LE DANCAIRO
Elle est admirable, ma chère;
Mais nous avons besoin de vous.

LE REMENDADO
Oui, nous avons besoin de vous!

LES DEUX HOMMES
Car nous l'avouons
humblement
Et très respectueusement,
Quand il s'agit de tromperie,
De duperie, de volerie,
Il est toujours bon, sur ma foi,
D'avoir les femmes avec soi,
Et sans elles,
Mes toutes belles,
On ne fait jamais rien de bien.

CARMEN, FRASQUITA, MERCEDES
Quoi! sans nous jamais rien
de bien?

LES DEUX HOMMES
N'êtes-vous pas de cet avis?

LES TROIS FEMMES
Si fait, je suis de cet avis.

LE DANCAIRO
C'est dit alors, vous partirez?

FRASQUITA, MERCEDES
Quand vous voudrez.

LE DANCAIRO
Mais tout de suite.

CARMEN
Ah! permettez.
S'il vous plaît de partir, partez,
Mais je ne suis pas du voyage,
Je ne pars pas, je ne pars pas!

LE REMENDADO, LE DANCAIRO
Carmen, mon amour, tu
viendras,
Et tu n'auras pas le courage
De nous laisser dans l'embarras.

CARMEN
Je ne pars pas, je ne pars pas.

FRASQUITA, MERCEDES
Ah! ma Carmen,
Tu viendras!

LE DANCAIRO
Mais au moins la raison, Carmen, tu la diras?

CARMEN
Je la dirai certainement.

LES AUTRES
Voyons! Voyons!

CARMEN
La raison, c'est qu'en ce
moment.

LES DEUX HOMMES
Eh bien? Eh bien?

EL REMENDADO
Yes, we need you to lend a hand.

EL REMENDADO, EL DANCAIRO
We might as well admit as much,
This bus'ness needs a woman's touch.
When it's a case of double dealing,
Lying or stealing,
Better concealing,
It happens time and time again,
Women are more subtle than men.
In addition,
Their intuition
Can turn a guess to sure success!

CARMEN, FRASQUITA, MERCEDES
Yes, you might as well confess,
We turn a guess to sure success.

EL REMENDADO, EL DANCAIRO
Now don't you girls agree with me?

CARMEN, FRASQUITA, MERCEDES
Of course, why should we disagree?

EL DANCAIRO
All right, agreed. We'll go today.

FRASQUITA, MERCEDES
Just as you say.

EL DANCAIRO
Then let us hurry.

CARMEN
Wait, not so fast. I say no.
If you all want to go, then go!
But this time our plans seem to vary.
I'm staying here.

EL REMENDADO, EL DANCAIRO
Please say you'll join us, Carmen dear.
You do not want to be contrary.
The plans are made, why interfere?

CARMEN
You heard it all, I'm staying here.

FRASQUITA, MERCEDES
Say you will come, Carmen dear.

EL DANCAIRO
But, at least, tell us why.

CARMEN
I'll tell you what you want to know.

THE OTHERS
Go on! Go on!

CARMEN
The reason I refuse to go . . .

EL REMENDADO, EL DANCAIRO
Is what?

CARMEN
That I am in love again!

EL REMENDADO, EL DANCAIRO
Did I hear right?

FRASQUITA, MERCEDES
She merely said she is in love.

EL REMENDADO, EL DANCAIRO
She's in love!

FRASQUITA, MERCEDES
She's in love!

CARMEN
Yes, I'm in love!

EL DANCAIRO
Come on, my dear, say you don't mean it!

CARMEN
I'm in love as never before!

EL REMENDADO, EL DANCAIRO
We must admit we are astounded,
Because you've shown us more than once
How easy you have always found it
To combine your duty with love.
You know well, very well,
How to combine your duty with love!

CARMEN
You know that I would join you gladly
In this new plan you've spoken of!
Though I may disappoint you badly,
Just this once, love comes first.
This evening duty must yield to love!

EL DANCAIRO
You mean you will not change your mind?

CARMEN
No, I will not.

EL REMENDADO
But look, you simply cannot leave us so!

ALL
Say you will go, be nice, say you will go!
We need you there—
To do your share.
You know it's true!

FRASQUITA, MERCEDES
You know it's true!

CARMEN
In that respect, I will agree with you.

Recitative

EL DANCAIRO
Who is the lucky man?

CARMEN
If you must know, it's a soldier of the guard, who, in order to help me, went to prison for me.

CARMEN
Je suis amoureuse.

LES DEUX HOMMES
Qu'a-t-elle dit?

FRASQUITA, MERCEDES
Elle dit qu'elle est amoureuse.

LES DEUX HOMMES
Amoureuse!

LES DEUX FEMMES
Amoureuse!

CARMEN
Oui! Amoureuse!

LE DANCAIRO
Voyons, Carmen, sois sérieuse.

CARMEN
Amoureuse à perdre l'esprit!

LES DEUX HOMMES
La chose certes nous étonne,
Mais ce n'est pas le premier jour
Où vous aurez su, ma mignonne,
Faire marcher de front le devoir et l'amour.

CARMEN
Mes amis, je serais fort aise
De partir avec vous ce soir;
Mais cette fois, ne vous déplaise,
Il faudra que l'amour passe avant le devoir.

LE DANCAIRO
Ce n'est pas là ton dernier mot?

CARMEN
Absolument!

LE REMENDADO
Il faut
Que tu te laisses attendrir.

TOUS LES QUATRE
Il faut venir, Carmen, il faut venir.
Pour notre affaire,
C'est nécessaire,
Car entre nous—

LES DEUX FEMMES
Car entre nous—

CARMEN
Quant à cela, je l'admets avec vous.

LE DANCAIRO
Mais qui donc attends tu?

CARMEN
Presque rien, un soldat qui l'autre jour pour me rendre service
S'est fait mettre en prison.

LE REMENDADO
Le fait est délicat.

LE DANCAIRO
Il se peut qu'après tout ton soldat réfléchisse.
Es-tu bien sûre qu'il viendra?

JOSÉ
Halte-là!
Qui va là?
Dragon d'Alcala!

CARMEN
Ecoutez! Le voilà!

JOSÉ
Où t'en vas-tu par là,
Dragon d'Alcala?
Moi je m'en vais faire,
Mordre la poussière
A mon adversaire.
S'il en est ainsi,
Passez mon ami,
Affaire d'honneur
Affaire de coeur,
Pour nous tout est là,
Dragon d'Alcala.

FRASQUITA
C'est un beau dragon!

MERCEDES
Un très beau dragon!

LE DANCAIRO
Qui serait pour nous un fier compagnon.

LE REMENDADO
Dis-lui de nous suivre.

CARMEN
Il refusera.

LE REMENDADO
Mais, essaye, au moins.

CARMEN
Soit! on essayera.

JOSÉ
Halte là!
Qui va là!
Dragon d'Alcala!
Où t'en vas-tu par là,
Dragon d'Alcala?
Exact et fidèle,
Je vais ou m'appelle
L'amour de ma belle.
S'il en est ainsi,
Passez, mon ami.
Affaire d'honneur,
Affaire de coeur,

EL REMENDADO
A most beautiful thought!

EL DANCAIRO
It may be that your man has become less obliging.
How do you know that he will come?

Song
(*behind the scene, far away*)

JOSÉ
"Who are you?
Someone new?
Soldier, who goes there?"

CARMEN
Do you hear?
I was right!

JOSÉ (*as before*)
"Where are you going to?
Soldier, tell me where?"
"Looking for my rival,
I intend to meet him,
Fight him and defeat him."
"Since the case is so,
Freely you may go.
Honor's stern command,
Affairs of the heart,
Those are things apart.
Soldiers understand."

FRASQUITA
That's a handsome boy!

MERCEDES
A very handsome boy!

EL DANCAIRO
Men like that we need to have on our side!

EL REMENDADO
Tell him to join us!

CARMEN
That he'll never do.

EL REMENDADO
It is worth a try.

CARMEN
Good, at least I'll try.
(*the voice approaches little by little*)

JOSÉ
"Who are you?
Someone new?
Soldier, who goes there?
Where are you going to?
Soldier, tell me where?"
"Faithful to my sweetheart,
Mine's a lover's mission
In the old tradition."
"Since the case is so,

Freely you may go.
Honor's stern command,
Affairs of the heart,
Those are things apart.
Soldiers understand."
(*enter* DON JOSÉ)

Pour nous tout est là,
Dragons d'Alcala!

Recitative

CARMEN
You're here at last!

CARMEN
Enfin c'est toi.

JOSÉ
Carmen!

JOSÉ
Carmen!

CARMEN
You had to go to jail?

CARMEN
Et tu sors de prison?

JOSÉ
For all of two months.

JOSÉ
J'y suis resté deux mois.

CARMEN
You complain?

CARMEN
Tu t'en plains!

JOSÉ
Not a bit!
And, if it were for your sake, they could have kept me longer.

JOSÉ
Ma foi non!
Et si c'était pour toi, j'y voudrais être encore.

CARMEN
Then you love me?

CARMEN
Tu m'aimes donc?

JOSÉ
Love you? I adore you!

JOSÉ
Je t'adore!

CARMEN
We have been visited by your superiors. They had us sing and dance.

CARMEN
Vos officiers sont venus tout à l'heure,
Ils nous ont fait danser.

JOSÉ
Not you, too?

JOSÉ
Comment? Toi?

CARMEN (*ironically*)
Bless my soul, I'll bet that you are jealous!

CARMEN
Que je meure si tu n'es pas jaloux!

JOSÉ
Of course! And why not?

JOSÉ
Eh oui, je suis jaloux.

CARMEN
Calm down, my friend, calm down.

CARMEN
Tout doux, monsieur, tout doux,

Duet

(*gaily*)
Now that you're here, I'll dance for you,
For you alone, señor.
And even more than that, I'll sing and play my music.
(*she makes* JOSÉ *sit down*)
You sit right here, Don José.
(*with a serio-comic air*)
You're the audience!
(*she dances, accompanying herself with the castanets. Near the end of the dance bugles are heard behind the scenes*)

Je vais danser en votre honneur,
Et vous verrez, Seigneur,
Comment je sais moi-même accompagner ma danse.
Mettez-vous là, Don José, je commence.

JOSÉ (*stopping* CARMEN)
Just one moment, wait,
Only one moment, I beg you!

JOSÉ
Attends un peu, Carmen, rien qu'un moment, arrête.

CARMEN
Et pourquoi, s'il te plaît?

JOSÉ
Il me semble, là-bas . . .
Oui, ce sont nos clairons qui sonnent la retraite
Ne les entends-tu pas?

CARMEN
Bravo! j'avais beau faire . . .
Il est mélancolique
De danser sans orchestre. Et vive la musique
Qui nous tombe du ciel!
La la la la la.

JOSÉ
Tu ne m'as pas compris . . .
Carmen, c'est la retraite, . . .
Il faut que moi, je rentre au quartier pour l'appel.

CARMEN
Au quartier! pour l'appel!
Ah! j'ètais vraiment trop bête!
Je me mettais en quatre et je faisais des frais
Pour amuser monsieur! Je chantais,
Je dansais . . .
Je crois, Dieu me pardonne,
Qu'un peu plus, je l'aimais . . .
Ta ra ta ta, c'est le clairon qui sonne!
Ta ra ta ta!
Il part! il est parti!
Va-t'en donc, canari.
Tiens! prends ton shako, ton sabre, ta giberne.
Et va-t'en, mon garçon, retourne à ta caserne.

JOSÉ
C'est mal à toi, Carmen, de te moquer de moi;
Je souffre de partir . . . car jamais femme,
Jamais femme avant toi
Aussi profondément n'avait troublé mon âme.

CARMEN (*surprised*)
And just why, may I ask?

JOSÉ
In the distance I hear . . .
Yes, our bugles are blowing,
Sounding the retreat.
Now, don't you hear them, too?

CARMEN (*gaily*)
Bravo, bravo! That's even better!
It's not an easy thing to sing and dance without music,
But now we have some music which has dropped from the sky.
(*she resumes her dancing. The sound of the bugles dies away*)
Lalalalalalala.

JOSÉ (*again stopping* CARMEN)
You do not understand, my love!
That was the signal,
I must be back, in camp,
In my quarters by night.

CARMEN (*stupefied*)
Back in camp? For the night?
(*with an outburst*)
Ah, how could I be so stupid!
I took no end of pains,
I tried my very best,
My very, very best
To entertain my guest!
So I sang and I danced,
Thinking (may God forgive me)
I was almost in love!
Taratata!
He hears the blasted bugle!
Taratata!
Dear me, and off he goes!
Back to camp, stupid fool!
Here!
(*throwing his shako at him*)
Take your belt, your saber and your helmet,
And go back to your camp, my boy!
Hurry back to your quarters!

JOSÉ (*sadly*)
You're very wrong, you know,
To mock me as you do!
I do not want to go!
You must believe me, Carmen,
And I confess to you,
No one before has thrilled my heart like you,
No woman on this earth
Has stirred my heart so deeply!

CARMEN
Taratata! "My God, retreat is sounding!"
Taratata! "I'm going to be late!
Oh my God, there are the bugles,
I'm afraid I'll be late!"
So he forgets me, runs off.
That's the end of his love!

JOSÉ
And so, you don't believe my love is real!

CARMEN
I don't!

JOSÉ
Well then, you do not know!

CARMEN
What more is there to know?

JOSÉ
Listen to me!

CARMEN
You are keeping them waiting!

JOSÉ (*violently*)
Listen to me!
Yes, I say you will!

CARMEN
No, no, no, no!

JOSÉ
I want it so!
(*he draws, from the vest of his uniform, the flower that* CARMEN *threw at him and shows it to her*)
Through ev'ry long and lonely hour
In prison there, I kept your flower,
And though its bloom was swiftly gone,
Its haunting fragrance lingered on.
In the darkness, as I lay dreaming,
Its perfume consoling, redeeming,
Recalled your image night and day,
And my despair would fade away.
Another time, I would berate you,
I swore to detest and to hate you!
Of what nemesis am I the prey?
What whim of fate sent you my way?
Then I realized I was lying;
There could be no doubt, no denying,
One burning hope was all I knew,
One sole desire inflamed my heart!
Carmen, I longed for you,
I longed for you!
Carmen, the magic of your glances
Cast a spell around my heart.
Luring me on like an enchantress,

CARMEN
Ta ra ta ta, mon Dieu!
c'est la retraite,
Je vais être en retard.
Il perd la tête, il court,
Et voilà son amour.

JOSÉ
Ainsi tu ne crois pas
A mon amour?

CARMEN
Mais non!

JOSÉ
Eh bien! tu m'entendras.

CARMEN
Je ne veux rien entrendre . . .

JOSÉ
Tu m'entendras!

CARMEN
Tu vas te faire attendre.

JOSÉ
Tu m'entendras, oui, tu
m'entendras!

CARMEN
Non, non, non, non!

JOSÉ
Je le veux, Carmen

Tu m'entendras!
La fleur que tu m'avais jetée,
Dans ma prison m'était restée.
Flétrie et sèche, cette fleur
Gardait toujours sa douce odeur
Et pendant des heures entières,
Sur mes yeux fermant mes
paupières,
De cette odeur je m'enivrais
Et dans la nuit je te voyais!
Je me prenais à te maudire,
A te détester, à me dire:
Pourquoi faut-il que le destin
L'ait mise là sur mon chemin?
Puis je m'accusais de blasphème
Et je ne sentais en moi même
Qu'un seul désir, un seul espoir,
Te revoir, Carmen, te
revoir! . . .
Car tu n'avais eu qu'à paraître,
Qu'à jeter un regard sur moi
Pour t'emparer de tout mon
être,
O ma Carmen!
Et j'étais une chose à toi!
Carmen, je t'aime!

You ruled my soul! You took possession of my heart!
Carmen, I love you!

CARMEN
Non! tu ne m'aimes pas!

CARMEN
No, I don't call that love!

JOSÉ
Que dis tu?

JOSÉ
What did you say?

CARMEN
Non, tu ne m'aimes pas, non, car si tu m'aimais,
Là-bas, là-bas, tu me suivrais.

CARMEN
No, you do not love me,
No, no, for if you did, you see,
You'd come with me!

JOSÉ
Carmen!

JOSÉ
Carmen!

CARMEN
Oui! Là-bas, là-bas dans la montagne,
Là-bas, là-bas tu me suivrais!
Sur ton cheval tu me prendrais,
Et comme un brave, à travers la compagne,
En croupe, tu m'emporterais.
Là-bas, là-bas dans la montagne.

CARMEN
People in love belong together,
They cannot bear to be apart.
Carry me off and far away,
Over the highest hills and deepest valleys.
I would know that you love me then!
Carry me far across the mountains,

JOSÉ
Carmen!

JOSÉ (*disconcerted*)
Carmen!

CARMEN
Là-bas, là-bas tu me suivrais!
Tu me suivrais, si tu m'aimais.
Point d'officier à qui tu doives obéir,
Tu n'y dépendrais de personne;
Et point de retraite qui sonne
Pour dire l'amoureux qu'il est temps de partir!
Le ciel ouvert, la vie errante,
Pour pays l'univers, pour loi sa volonté,
Et surtout la chose enivrante:
La liberté! la liberté!

CARMEN
Sharing adventures day by day.
Take me away and prove your love!
At liberty coming and going,
No silly rules or officers there to obey.
No stupid retreat ever blowing,
Bidding the lovers part at the end of the day.
Happy to roam the open spaces,
All the world for our home,
We obey our will alone!
Best of all, a priceless possession.
Our life is free!

JOSÉ
Mon Dieu!

JOSÉ
My God!

CARMEN
Oui, n'est-ce pas,
Là-bas, là-bas, tu me suivras,
Tu m'aimes et tu me suivras.

CARMEN
People in love belong together,
They cannot bear to be apart.

JOSÉ
Hélas! hélas! pitié!
Carmen, pitié!
O mon Dieu! hélas!
Ah! tais-toi! tais-toi!
Non, je ne veux plus t'écouter . . .
Quitter mon drapeau . . . déserter . . .
C'est la honte, c'est l'infamie!
Je n'en veux pas!

JOSÉ (*in painful resolution*)
Carmen, please,
No more! I beg of you, no more!
No, Carmen, no, no more!
Oh have pity, Carmen!
(*wresting himself away from* CARMEN'S *embraces*)
No, I cannot do what you say!
Deserting my flag and betray . . .
That's dishonor, that's degradation.
That I won't do!

CARMEN (*harshly*)
Well, then, go!
JOSÉ (*imploringly*)
Carmen, please have mercy!
CARMEN
No, I'm finished with you!
JOSÉ
I beg you!
CARMEN
How I hate you! Good-by!
It's good-by once for all!
JOSÉ (*grievingly*)
So then once for all, good-by!
CARMEN
At last!
JOSÉ
Farewell! Good-by, once for all!
CARMEN
Good-by!
(JOSÉ *goes toward the door; as he is about to open it, someone knocks. Silence*)

Finale

LIEUTENANT (*from outside*)
Hello, Carmen, hello, hello!
JOSÉ
Who is it? Who is there?
CARMEN
Be still, be still!
LIEUTENANT (*enters after forcing the door*)
What's going on there, I ask you!
(*he sees* JOSÉ; *to* CARMEN)
Oh, shame, my lovely Carmen,
Your taste is rather poor!
When there's an officer
Who offers so much more,
It's a private you prefer!
(*to* JOSÉ)
Get out, and hurry!
JOSÉ (*calmly but resolutely*)
No!
LIEUTENANT (*sternly*)
Get out, there is the door!
JOSÉ (*firmly*)
I don't intend to go!
LIEUTENANT (*menacing* JOSÉ)
Scoundrel!
JOSÉ (*seizing his saber*)
Damnation! I'll show you who will go!

CARMEN
Eh bien, pars!
JOSÉ
Carmen, je t'en prie . . .
CARMEN
Non! je ne t'aime plus, je te hais!
JOSÉ
Carmen!
CARMEN
Adieu! mais adieu pour jamais!
JOSÉ
Eh bien, soit . . . adieu pour jamais!
CARMEN
Va t'en!
JOSÉ
Carmen! adieu! adieu pour jamais!
CARMEN
Adieu!

LE LIEUTENANT
Holà Carmen!
Holà! Holà!
JOSÉ
Qui frappe? qui vient là?
CARMEN
Tais-toi! Tais-toi!
LE LIEUTENANT
J'ouvre moi-même et j'entre.
Ah! fi, la belle,
Le choix n'est pas heureux; c'est se mésallier,
De prendre le soldat quand on a l'officier.
Allons! décampe.
JOSÉ
Non.
LE LIEUTENANT
Si fait, tu partiras!
JOSÉ
Je ne partirai pas!
LE LIEUTENANT
Drôle!
JOSÉ
Tonnerre! il va pleuvoir des coups!

CARMEN
Au diable le jaloux!

A moi! a moi!

CARMEN *(throwing herself between them)*
You're mad, you jealous fool!
(calls toward the adjoining room)
Come here, come here!
(the gypsies appear from every side. At a sign from CARMEN, EL DANCAIRO, *and* EL REMENDADO *seize* ZUNIGA *and disarm him)*

CARMEN
Bel officier, l'amour
Vous joue en ce moment un assez vilain tour,
Vous arrivez fort mal et nous sommes forcés,
Ne voulant être dénoncés,
De vous garder au moins pendant une heure.

CARMEN *(to the* LIEUTENANT *in a mocking tone)*
It's a shame,
My gallant captain!
Love has played a nasty trick on you!
Your call was badly timed.
Too bad! And so we must resort,
For we cannot risk being caught,
To keep you here with us for our protection!

LE DANCAIRO, LE REMENDADO
Mon cher monsieur,
Nous allons, s'il vous plait,
Quitter cette demeure,
Vous viendrez avec nous . . .

EL DANCAIRO, EL REMENDADO
(to the LIEUTENANT, *pistols in hand, with the utmost politeness)*
It breaks my heart,
But you and I are going in the same direction.
You'll come along with us?

CARMEN
C'est une promenade!

CARMEN *(laughing)*
Consider the diversion!

LE DANCAIRO, LE REMENDADO
Répondez, camarade,
Consentez-vous?

EL DANCAIRO, EL REMENDADO
We'll go on this excursion.
What do you say?

LE LIEUTENANT
Certainement,
D'autant plus que votre argument
Est un de ceux auxquels on ne résiste guère,
Mais gare à vous plus tard!

LIEUTENANT *(accepting the situation with good grace)*
Why, yes, of course, I accept!
For as matters stand,
Your invitation is a most convincing one!
(in a merry tone)
But, later on, watch out!

LE DANCAIRO
La guerre, c'est la guerre!
En attendant, mon officier,
Passez devant sans vous faire prier!

EL DANCAIRO *(philosophically)*
I'm sorry, such is life, sir!
Let's think of that some other day!
You have the honor of leading the way!

CHORUS
Passez devant sans vous faire prier!

EL REMENDADO, MEN
You have the honor of leading the way!

CARMEN
Es-tu des nôtres maintenant?

CARMEN *(to* JOSÉ*)*
Have you at last made up your mind?

JOSÉ
Il le faut bien.

JOSÉ *(sighing)*
I have no choice!

CARMEN
Ah! le mot n'est pas galant,
Mais qu'importe, tu t'y feras
Quand tu verras
Comme c'est beau la vie errante
Pour pays l'univers, pour loi sa volonté,
Et surtout la chose enivrante!
La liberté! la liberté!

CARMEN
Ah, that does not sound too kind,
But, no matter! For soon you will see
What life can be!
Happy to roam the open spaces,
All the world for our home,
We obey our will alone.
Best of all, a priceless possession,
Our life is free!

ALL

Happy to roam the open spaces,
All the world for a home,
We obey our will alone.
Best of all, a priceless possession,
Our life is free!

TOUS

Le ciel ouvert! la vie errante,
Pour pays l'univers, pour loi sa volonté,
Et surtout la chose enivrante!
La liberté! la liberté!

ACT III

A wild spot in the mountains. As the curtain rises a few of the smugglers are seen lying about, enveloped in their cloaks. The gypsies enter.

Sextet and Chorus

CHOEUR
Écoute, compagnon, écoute,
La fortune est là-bas, là-bas,
Mais prends garde pendant la route,
Prends garde de faire un faux pas.

FRASQUITA, MERCEDES, CARMEN, JOSÉ, LE REMENDADO, LE DANCAIRO
Notre métier est bon, mais pour le faire il faut
Avoir une âme forte,
Et péril est en haut, le péril est en bas,
Il est partout, qu'importe?
Nous allons devant nous, sans souci du torrent,
Sans souci de l'orage,
Sans souci du soldat qui là-bas nous attend,
Et nous guette au passage.
Sans souci nous allons en avant!

LE DANCAIRO
Reposons-nous une heure ici mes camarades;
Nous, nous allons nous assurer
Si le chemin est libre,
Et que sans algarades
La contrebande peut passer.

CARMEN
Que regardes-tu donc?

JOSÉ
Je me dis que là-bas
Il existe une bonne et brave vieille
Femme qui me croit honnête homme.
Elle se trompe, hélas!

CARMEN
Qui donc est cette femme?

JOSÉ
Ah! Carmen sur mon âme, ne raille pas—
Car c'est ma mère.

CARMEN
Eh bien! va la retrouver tout de suite!

SMUGGLERS
Be cautious, be cautious,
Ev'ryone remember,
There before us gold and riches loom;
But remember, the path is dang'rous,
A faulty step may be your doom!

FRASQUITA, MERCEDES, CARMEN, JOSÉ, EL REMENDADO, EL DANCAIRO
This is the life, the life we want to lead,
But he who leads it must possess
The courage of the fearless!
We must be keen, alert and unafraid,
For danger lies at ev'ry turn,
At ev'ry hour it's near us!
On our way, unconcerned,
Come what may, we prevail
Through the hazardous storm,
While the thunder is rolling!
Toward our goal, undeterred,
We proceed without fail,
Never minding the vigilant soldier patrolling!
We will get to our goal, come what may!

Recitative

EL DANCAIRO
You all may take a little rest, while you can get it. Meanwhile I want to make quite sure that there'll be no surprises. We can't take any chances, our merchandise must get through!

CARMEN (*to* JOSÉ)
Why do you stare like that?

JOSÉ
I was thinking that there in the valley lives a kind and God-fearing woman who believes me to be honest. I have not kept her faith!

CARMEN
And who is that sweet lady?

JOSÉ
I am warning you, Carmen, watch what you say; she is my mother!

CARMEN
I see. Then you should go home to your mother. The kind

of life we lead is not for you. And you might as well leave us, the sooner the better.

JOSÉ

You say that I should leave?

CARMEN

Precisely!

JOSÉ

And go away from you? I warn you, if you say that once more . . .

CARMEN

You mean that you would kill me?
How fierce you look!
You don't say a word. It is all in the cards, we have no way to change it!

Trio

(FRASQUITA *and* MERCEDES *spread cards before them*)

FRASQUITA, MERCEDES

Shuffle, shuffle!
Now then, now then!
Come, let us try! Come, let us try!
Three cards to the right.
Three cards to the left.
Four above,
Four below.
The cards will say what joy or sorrow
They hold in store, what luck we'll have tomorrow,
Which lover will be treacherous,
And which one will be true to us.
We want to know
Which one we should be wary of,
Which man will be our own true love.
Let's see! Let's see!

FRASQUITA

See, my man is youthful and bold,
One lover with daring and courage.

MERCEDES

And my suitor is very old,
But he's rich and offers me marriage.

FRASQUITA (*haughtily*)

Then he lifts me up on his horse
And speeds me away to the mountains!

MERCEDES

We live in a palace, of course,
With gardens and statues and fountains.

FRASQUITA

And his ardor never grows cold,
Every day unending embraces.

MERCEDES

I've barrels and barrels of gold,
Diamonds, pearls, satins and laces!

Notre métier vois-tu, ne te vaut rien.
Et tu ferais fort bien de partir au plus vite.

JOSÉ

Partir, nous séparer?

CARMEN

Sans doute.

JOSÉ

Nous séparer, Carmen?
Écoute, si tu redis ce mot—

CARMEN

Tu me tuerais peut-être?
Quel regard,
Tu ne réponds rien—
Que m'importe? Après tout, le destin est le maître.

FRASQUITA, MERCEDES

Mêlons. Mêlons!
Coupons! Coupons!
Bien, c'est cela! Bien, c'est cela!
Trois cartes ici, trois cartes ici!
Quatre là! Quatre là!
Et maintenant, parlez, mes belles,
De l'avenir donnez-nous des nouvelles;
Dites-nous qui nous trahira,
Dites-nous qui nous aimera.
Parlez! Parlez!

FRASQUITA

Moi, je vois un jeune amoureux
Qui m'aime on ne peut davantage.

MERCEDES

Le mien est très riche et très vieux,
Mais il parle de mariage.

FRASQUITA

Il me campe sur son cheval
Et dans la montagne il m'entraîne.

MERCEDES

Dans un château presque royal
Le mien m'installe en souveraine.

FRASQUITA

De l'amour à n'en plus finir,
Tous les jours nouvelles folies.

MERCEDES

De l'or tant que j'en puis tenir,
Des diamants . . . des pierreries.

FRASQUITA
Le mien devient un chef fameux,
Cent hommes marchent à sa suite.

MERCEDES
Le mien, en croirai-je mes yeux . . . ?
Il meurt. Ah! je suis veuve et j'hérite!

FRASQUITA, MERCEDES
Parlez encor, parlez, mes belles,
De l'avenir donnez-nous des nouvelles.
Dites-nous qui nous trahira,
Dites-nous qui nous aimera.

MERCEDES
Fortune!

FRASQUITA
Amour!

CARMEN
Voyons, que j'essaie à mon tour.
Carreau, pique . . . la mort!
J'ai bien lu . . . moi d'abord.
Ensuite lui . . . pour tous les deux la mort. . . .
En vain pour éviter les réponses amères,
En vain tu mêleras,
Cela ne sert à rien, les cartes sont sincères
Et ne mentiront pas!
Dans le livre d'en haut si ta page est heureuse,
Mêle et coupe sans peur,
La carte sous tes doigts se tournera joyeuse,
T'annonçant le bonheur.
Mais si tu dois mourir, si le mot redoutable
Est écrit par le sort,
Recommence vingt fois—la carte impitoyable
Répétera: la mort!
Encor! Toujours la mort.

Eh bien? . . .

LE DANCAIRO
Eh bien! nous essayerons de passer et nous passerons!
Reste là-haut, José, garde les marchandises.

FRASQUITA
La route est-elle libre?

FRASQUITA
My goodness, this is a surprise!
My man is a powerful pirate.

MERCEDES (*joyfully*)
And mine, and mine . . . can I credit my eyes?
He . . . he dies! Ah, I'm his widow and heiress.

BOTH
Let's try again, we may discover
Important traits about our future lover.
Which suitor will be treacherous,
And which one will be true to us.

MERCEDES
An heiress!

FRASQUITA
True love!

CARMEN
Let's see what the cards hold for me.
(*she turns up the cards, on her side*)
Diamonds! Spades!
It's death! It is plain.
First for me, then for him,
But all the same, it's death!
You can't evade the truth the cards are saying clearly,
No matter how you try.
No use to deal again, they're telling you sincerely,
The cards will never lie!
If Fate saved you a happy page within its book,
No need for anxiousness.
You know you'll get a lucky card before you look,
Your fate is happiness.
But if your time has come and you are evil-starred,
And if the end is near,
You can try twenty times, the unrelenting card
Will reappear once more; if you are evil-starred,
If there is death in store
The unrelenting card will reappear once more!
(*turning up the cards*)
Once more, once more,
There's death in store . . .

Recitative

What news?

EL DANCAIRO
Quite good! We might as well move on, we have an even chance.
And you, José, stay here.
You will shoot on sight if need be.

FRASQUITA
You think we'll have clear sailing?

EL DANCAIRO
Yes, except for one spot. Close to the pass, three guards are on patrol.
That might mean trouble.
We must get them out of the way.

CARMEN
This is an assignment for us.
We must get through and so we shall!

Ensemble with Chorus

CARMEN, FRASQUITA, MERCEDES, WOMEN
All men are weak and fond of women,
So are the guards, they're only human.
They're eager and anxious to be nice,
So we'll go ahead and break the ice.

ALL
It won't be hard!

MERCEDES
And they're eager to be nice.

CARMEN
We will catch the guards off-guard!

ALL
They will be nice.

MERCEDES
Yes, to us women they will be more than nice!

THE THREE WOMEN, CHORUS
All men are weak and fond of women,
So are the guards, they're only human.
They're eager and anxious to be nice.
We must succeed at any price!

CARMEN, FRASQUITA, MERCEDES
It won't be hard, there's nothing to it,
Just keep the guards happy awhile.
They like to flirt, we let them do it.
No one gets hurt giving a smile.
And if we add one or two kisses
For our success, it's worth a try!

ALL
Here's the answer, it never misses,
Our contraband always gets by!

CHORUS OF WOMEN
All men are weak and fond of women
So are the guards, they're only human
And are anxious to be nice
So we will succeed at any price.
We'll clear the way
For you all.
(*they all leave*)

Air

MICAELA (*entering*)
Here's where the smugglers hide

LE DANCAIRO
Oui, mais gare aux surprises!
J'ai sur la brèche où nous devons passer vu trois douaniers.
Il faut nous en débarrasser.

CARMEN
Prenez les ballots et partons.
Il faut passer, nous passerons.

TOUTES LES TROIS, LES FEMMES
Quant au douanier, c'est notre affaire,
Tout comme un autre il aime à plaire,
Il aime à faire le galant,
Laissez-nous passer en avant.

TOUS
Il est galant!

MERCEDES
Le douanier sera clément.

CARMEN
Le douanier sera charmant.

TOUS
Il aime à plaire.

MERCEDES
Oui, le douanier sera même entreprenant! . . .

TOUTES LES FEMMES
Quant au douanier c'est notre affaire,
Tout comme un autre il aime à plaire,
Il aime à faire le galant,
Laissez-nous passer en avant.

CARMEN, MERCEDES, FRASQUITA
Il ne s'agit plus de bataille,
Non, il s'agit tout simplement
De se laisser prendre la taille
Et d'écouter un compliment.
S'il faut aller jusqu'au sourire,
Que voulez-vous? on sourira!

TOUT LE MONDE
Et d'avance, je puis le dire,
La contrebande passera.

LES FEMMES
Quant au douanier c'est leur affaire,
Tout comme un autre, il aime à plaire,
Il aime à faire le galant,
Laissons-les passer en avant.

MICAELA
C'est des contrebandiers le

refuge ordinaire. Il est ici, je le verrai . . . Et le devoir que m'imposa sa mère sans trembler je l'accomplirai.
Je dis que rien ne m'épouvante,
Je dis, hélas, que je réponds de moi,
Mais j'ai beau faire la vaillante,
Au fond du cœur, je meurs d'effroi!
Seule en ce lieu sauvage,
Toute seule j'ai peur, mais j'ai tort d'avoir peur;
Vous me donnerez du courage,
Vous me protégerez, Seigneur.
Je vais voir de près cette femme
Dont les artifices maudits
Ont fini par faire un infâme
De celui que j'aimais jadis;
Elle est dangereuse, elle est belle,
Mais je ne veux pas avoir peur,
Ah! Siegneur je parlerai haut devant elle,
Seigneur, vous me protégerez! Ah!
Protégez-moi! O Seigneur!
Donnez-moi du courage!
Protégez-moi! O Seigneur!
Protégez-moi! Seigneur!

With their contraband booty;
So it is here I'll find José,
And for his mother's sake I'll do my duty,
For her sake conquer ev'ry fear.
I thought I could master my terror.
I was so sure I would be brave and strong.
But now, too late, I see my error!
Deep in my heart I know I was wrong!
Here in this dread surrounding
I'm alone and afraid,
But I will not despair!
God in His kindness all-abounding
Will make me strong and hear my prayer.
I'll be face to face with that woman
Who, with the blackest arts of hell,
Made a lawless man and a traitor
Of him I used to love so well.
She's dangerous, too, and alluring,
But she can't hurt me any more!
No, no, she can't hurt me any more!
I will speak to José right before her!
Ah! I place my hope and faith in Thee,
O Lord, dear God, watch over me! Ah!
Make me strong and protect me!
Watch over me, God above!
Watch over me,
My Lord!

Recitative

Je ne me trompe pas . . . c'est lui sur ce rocher. A moi José, José! Je ne puis approcher. Mais que fait-il? . . . Il ajuste . . . il fait feu . . . Ah! j'ai trop présumé de mes forces, mon Dieu!

High up there on the rocks, it's he!
That's José. José, come here, José!
He has not heard me yet!
He has a gun! He is aiming!
Don José!
(JOSÉ *fires a shot*)
Dear God, what shall I do?
I don't know where to turn.
(*she disappears behind the rocks*)

ESCAMILLO
Quelques lignes plus bas . . .
Et tout était fini.

ESCAMILLO (*entering*)
Just one inch further down
And all would have been over.

JOSÉ
Votre nom, répondez!

JOSÉ
Who are you? What's your name?

ESCAMILLO
Eh . . . doucement! l'ami!

ESCAMILLO
Hey, easy now, my boy!

Duo

ESCAMILLO
Je suis Escamillo, Toréro de Grenade!

ESCAMILLO
My name is Escamillo,
Toreador of Granada.

JOSÉ
Escamillo!

JOSÉ
Escamillo!

ESCAMILLO
That's right.
JOSÉ
Then I welcome you here.
You have a famous name.
But really, you were foolish to take so great a risk!
ESCAMILLO (*carelessly*)
Yes, there you may be right.
But you see, I'm in love, my friend,
And love takes chances;
(*gaily*)
And any man, indeed, would not be worth his salt,
Who would not risk his life pursuing his romances.
JOSÉ
Then the one you love must be here?
ESCAMILLO
Right you are.
A most exciting gypsy girl!
JOSÉ
What is her name?
ESCAMILLO
Carmen.
JOSÉ (*aside*)
Carmen?
ESCAMILLO
It is. That's her name.
The way the rumor goes
She loved another man,
A soldier who deserted his brigade to please her.
JOSÉ (*aside*)
Carmen!
ESCAMILLO
A mad affair, but that of course was once,
For the loves of a Carmen do not last six months.

JOSÉ
You don't mind that at all?
ESCAMILLO
I love her, yes, I do.
I love her, my friend,
I love her madly!
JOSÉ
But when anyone takes a gypsy from her people,
You know, of course, he has to pay?
ESCAMILLO (*gaily*)
Good, then I'll pay, yes, I will pay.
JOSÉ (*threateningly*)
The price is to be paid with knives to the finish!
ESCAMILLO (*surprised*)
With knives to the finish?

ESCAMILLO
C'est moi.

JOSÉ
Je connais votre nom,
Soyez le bienvenu; mais vraiment, camarade,
Vous pouviez y rester.

ESCAMILLO
Je ne vous dis pas non,
Mais je suis amoureux, mon cher, à la folie,
Et celui-là serait un pauvre compagnon,
Qui, pour voir ses amours, ne risquerait sa vie.

JOSÉ
Celle que vous aimez est ici?

ESCAMILLO
Justement.
C'est une zingara, mon cher.

JOSÉ
Elle s'appelle?

ESCAMILLO
Carmen.

JOSÉ
Carmen!

ESCAMILLO
Carmen! Oui, mon cher.
Elle avait pour amant
Un soldat qui jadis a déserté pour elle.

JOSÉ
Carmen!

ESCAMILLO
Ils s'adoraient, mais c'est fini, je crois.
Les amours de Carmen ne durent pas six mois.
JOSÉ
Vous l'aimez cependant . . .

ESCAMILLO
Je l'aime, oui mon cher,
Je l'aime à la folie!

JOSÉ
Mais pour nous enlever nos filles de Bohème, savez-vous bien qu'il faut payer?
ESCAMILLO
Soit! on paiera; soit! on paiera!

JOSÉ
Et que le prix se paie à coups de navaja!
ESCAMILLO
À coups de Navaja?

JOSÉ
Comprenez-vous?

ESCAMILLO
Le discours est très net.
Ce déserteur, ce beau soldat qu'elle aime,
Ou du moins qu'elle aimait.
C'est donc vous?

JOSÉ
Oui, c'est moi-même.

ESCAMILLO
J'en suis ravi, mon cher, et le tour est complet!

JOSÉ
Enfin ma colère trouve à qui parler!
Le sang, je l'espère, va bientôt couler.

ESCAMILLO
Quelle maladresse j'en rirais vraiment!
Chercher la maîtresse et trouver l'amant!

ENSEMBLE
Mettez-vous en garde,
Et veillez sur vous!
Tant pis pour qui tarde
A parer les coups!
Allons! En garde!
Ah! Seigneur
Veillez sur vous!
Veillez sur vous!

CARMEN
Holà, José! . . .

ESCAMILLO
Vrai, j'ai l'âme ravie
Que ce soit vous, Carmen, qui me sauviez la vie.

Quant à toi, beau soldat,
Nous sommes manche à manche, et nous jouerons la belle,

JOSÉ
You understand?

ESCAMILLO (*ironically*)
Why, of course, now I do!
That fine dragoon deserter she's in love with,
Or rather *was* in love with . . .
That is you!

JOSÉ (*menacingly*)
Yes, I'm the one!

ESCAMILLO
Oh, what a treat, my boy,
I'm overcome with joy.
Now I know where I stand.

BOTH
What stroke of good fortune
Brought my rival here.

JOSÉ
His blood will flow before his sweetheart.
This will cost him dear.

ESCAMILLO
I look for his sweetheart
And find her cavalier.

BOTH
Man to man, I dare you,
Defend your life!

JOSÉ
We'll fight to the end
At the point of the knife!

ESCAMILLO
I welcome the challenge
To draw my knife!

BOTH
One of us must fall,
Defend your life!
Now draw your knife. On guard.
Defend your life!
(*they fight.* ESCAMILLO *slips and falls.* JOSÉ *is about to strike him when* CARMEN *enters*)

Finale

CARMEN (*arresting* JOSÉ's *arm*)
Hold on, hold on, José!

ESCAMILLO (*to* CARMEN)
Ah, the thought is enchanting!
I am a lucky man to owe my life to Carmen!
(*to* JOSÉ, *jauntily but haughtily*)
As for you, soldier friend,
The fight is undecided,
But we'll renew the duel.

Whatever day you choose,
I'll be at your command.

EL DANCAIRO (*interposing*)
No more of that, and no more quarrels.
Come, we're anxious to leave!
Let's go, and you go, too, my friend!

ESCAMILLO
Just one thing more, and then I shall be on my way:
May I invite you all
To the bullfight in Seville.
I'll do my very best to do honor to you.
All my friends will be there,
(*with a look at* CARMEN)
All my friends will be there.
(*coolly to* JOSÉ, *who makes a menacing gesture*)
And you, not so ferocious!
(*gazing at* CARMEN)
Time will tell, yes, time will tell.
So till we meet again,
I bid you all farewell!
(ESCAMILLO *exits slowly.* JOSÉ *tries to attack him but is held back by* EL DANCAIRO *and* EL REMENDADO)

JOSÉ (*to* CARMEN, *menacingly but restrainedly*)
This is enough, you hear!
Do not drive me too far!

EL DANCAIRO
Get ready, companions, it's time to start.

CHORUS
Get ready, get ready, companions, it's time to start!

EL REMENDADO
Stop! Someone is hiding there behind the rocks! (*he brings* MICAELA *forward*)

CARMEN
It's a woman!

EL DANCAIRO
What luck! We have caught her in time!

JOSÉ (*recognizing* MICAELA)
You! Micaela!

MICAELA (*joyously*)
Don José!

JOSÉ
Micaela! What folly brings you here?

MICAELA
I, I came here to find you!
I came here to remind you
Of someone dear to you.
A lonely mother is waiting sadly,
Longing for her son.

Le jour où tu voudras reprendre le combat.

LE DANCAIRO
C'est bon, plus de querelle,
Nous, nous allons partir.
Et toi, l'ami, bonsoir!

ESCAMILLO
Souffrez au moins qu'avant de vous dire au revoir,
Je vous invite tous aux courses de Séville.
Je compte pour ma part y briller de mon mieux,
Et qui m'aime y viendra.
Et qui m'aime y viendra.
L'ami, tiens-toi tranquille,
J'ai tout dit et je n'ai plus ici qu'à faire mes adieux . . .

JOSÉ
Prends garde à toi, Carmen . . . je suis las de souffrir . . .

LE DANCAIRO
En route . . . en route . . . il faut partir . . .

TOUS
En route . . . en route . . . il faut partir . . .

LE REMENDADO
Halte! . . . quelqu'un est là qui cherche à se cacher.

CARMEN
Une femme!

LE DANCAIRO
Pardieu, la surprise est heureuse!

JOSÉ
Micaela! . . .

MICAELA
Don José! . . .

JOSÉ
Malheureuse!
Que viens-tu faire ici?

MICAELA
Moi, je viens te chercher . . .
Là-bas est la chaumière
Où sans cesse priant,
Une mère, ta mère,
Pleure, hélas, sur son enfant . . .
Elle pleure et t'appelle,
Elle pleure et te tend les bras;

Tu prendras pitié d'elle,
José, tu me suivras,
Tu me suivras!

She is grieving for you and needs you.
She is kind and she will forgive.
Go to her, I implore you.
José, ah, José,
Come home with me,
Come home with me!

CARMEN
Va-t'en! va-t'en! Tu feras bien,
Notre métier ne te vaut rien!

CARMEN (*to* JOSÉ)
Go on, go on, it's better thus,
You never did belong to us!

JOSÉ
Tu me dis de la suivre?

JOSÉ (*to* CARMEN)
So you want me to leave you?

CARMEN
Oui, tu devrais partir.

CARMEN
Yes, you had better go.

JOSÉ
Tu me dis de la suivre!
Pour que toi, tu puisse courir
Après ton nouvel amant!
Non! non vraiment!
Dût-il m'en coûter la vie,
Non, Carmen je ne partirai pas,
Et la chaîne qui nous lie
Nous liera jusqu'au trépas . . .

JOSÉ
So you want me to leave you
So that you can quickly run off,
Into Escamillo's arms!
No, that you won't!
(*resolutely*)
I swear, I won't leave you ever.
I won't go, I swear I never will,
You and I belong together,
Till the end for good or ill!
I swear I won't leave you ever,
I won't leave until the day I die.

MICAELA
Écoute-moi, je t'en prie,
Ta mère te tend les bras,
Cette chaîne qui te lie,
José, tu la briseras.

MICAELA (*to* JOSÉ)
Hear what I say, I implore,
José, do not tempt your fate.
If you stay, it will be folly;
José, it is not too late.

CHOEUR
Il t'en coutera la vie!
José, si tu ne pars pas,
Et la chaîne qui vous lie
Se rompra par ton trépas.

ALL (*to* JOSÉ)
This may cost you very dearly,
José, you're tempting your fate.
If you stay, it will be folly.
You must go before it's too late.

JOSÉ
Laisse-moi!
Car je suis condamné!

JOSÉ (*to* MICAELA)
Let me go!
There is no turning back!

MICAELA
Hélas! José!

MICAELA
You must give in!
(*he seizes* CARMEN *in a transport of passion*)

TOUS
José! prends garde!

ALL
José, we warn you!

JOSÉ
Ah! je te tiens, fille damnée,
Et je te forcerai bien
A subir la destinée
Qui rive ton sort au mien!
Dût-il m'en coûter la vie,
Non je ne partirai pas!

JOSÉ
You are mine, and mine you stay.
You are mine, and I'll never let you go!
I will force you to obey,
Our destiny willed it so!
I swear, I won't let you leave me,
No, I won't until my dying day!

ALL
Stop! Go easy, we warn you, Don José!

MICAELA (*authoritatively*)
Just one more word I'll say,
And then I shall leave!
(*sadly*)
You see, José, your mother is ill,
She is dying. You must not let her die without blessing her son!

JOSÉ
My mother, she is dying!

MICAELA
Yes, Don José!

JOSÉ
Then come, let us go!
(*he takes a few steps, then stops and speaks to* CARMEN)
Have your way then, I'll go.
But, we shall meet again!
(JOSÉ *leads* MICAELA *away; hearing* ESCAMILLO'S *voice, he pauses, hesitating*)

ESCAMILLO (*behind the scenes*)
Toreador, fight well and hard,
Proud as a king,
Yours is the ring.
(CARMEN *rushes toward him:* JOSÉ *threateningly bars the way*)
And after you have won the victor's crown,
Earn your sweet reward,
Your señorita's love.
Toreador, your prize is love!
(*His voice fades away in the distance*)

TOUS
Ah! prends garde, Don José!

MICAELA
Une parole encor, ce sera la dernière!
Hélas! José, ta mère, se meurt, et ta mère
Ne voudrait pas mourir sans t'avoir pardonné.

JOSÉ
Ma mère se meurt?

MICAELA
Oui, Don José.

JOSÉ
Partons ah, partons!
Sois contente . . . je pars, mais nous nous reverrons!

ESCAMILLO
Toréador en garde,
Toréador! Toréador!
Et songe en combattant,
Qu'un œil noir te regarde
Et que l'amour t'attend,
Toréador, l'amour t'attend!

ACT IV

Chorus

A square in Seville: at the back, the walls of an ancient amphitheater; the entrance is closed by a long awning.

CHOEUR
A deux cuartos, à deux cuartos
Des éventails pour s'éventer!
Des oranges pour grignotter!
Le programme avec les détails!
Du vin! De l'eau!
Des cigarettes!
A deux cuartos,
Des éventails pour s'éventer!
Des oranges pour grignotter!
Le programme avec les détails!
Du vin! De l'eau!
Des cigarettes!
A deux cuartos, à deux cuartos
Señoras et caballeros . . .

VENDORS, PEDDLERS
Get your program for the bullfight!
Just a quarter, just a quarter!
Buy a trinket for the ladies!
Wine and water, wine and water!
Who wants to buy a souvenir?
Cigarettes and cigarros here!
Pretty combs to wear in your hair!
Sweet wine! And beer!
A jug of water!
Toys for the children and balloons!
Coconuts, dates, and macaroons!
Colored beads for ladies to wear! Perfume!
So cheap! At the lowest prices!
Get your program for the bullfight!
Just a quarter, just a quarter!
Ladies and gentlemen!
Señoras and caballeros!

LE LIEUTENANT
Des oranges, vite!

LIEUTENANT
I'll take oranges, hurry!

PLUSIEURS MARCHANDS
En voici.
Prenez, prenez, mesdemoiselles.

GIRLS
Buy from me, señor, for you and your ladies.

UN MARCHAND
Merci, mon officier, merci.

GIRL (*to* LIEUTENANT, *who pays her*)
I thank you very much, señor!

LES AUTRES MARCHANDS
Celles-ci, señor, sont plus belles.
Des éventails pour s'éventer!
Des oranges pour grignotter!
Le programme avec les détails!
A deux cuartos,
A deux cuartos,
Señoras et caballeros.

OTHERS (*to* LIEUTENANT)
Buy a shawl, señor, for the lady!
Who wants to buy a souvenir?
Cigarettes and cigarros here?
Pretty fans to give you some air!
Sweet wine! And beer!
A jug of water!

LE LIEUTENANT
Hola! Des éventails!

LIEUTENANT
Hey, there! I want two fans!

MARCHAND DE PROGRAMME
Voulez-vous aussi des lorgnettes?
Le programme avec les détails.

A MAN (*to* LIEUTENANT)
Will you buy a fine pair of glasses?
Buy a program for the bull fight.

CHOEUR
A deux cuartos! a deux cuartos!
A deux cuartos! a deux cuartos!
Voyez! A deux cuartos!
Señoras et caballeros!

ALL
Just a quarter, just a quarter!
Ladies and gentlemen!
Señoras and caballeros!

Version II

(*If a ballet is introduced, the following words are sung.*)

CHOEUR
Dansez, dansez,
Dansez, dansez, tournez, tournez,

CHORUS
Choose your partner,
Take your places for the dancing!

Dance to the ring of tambourines,
To the twang of the mandolins,
Castanets are clicking away,
Come on!
Let's dance!
You señoritas,
Look for a partner, join the fun,
The fandango and the bolero,
Seguidilla and farandole.
Come on!
Let's dance!
You señoritas,
Choose your partner,
Take your places for the dancing!
Ladies and gentlemen,
Señoras and caballeros!
Ev'ryone has happy smiles upon their faces!
We'll dance till it is time to see the toreros
Take over our places!
Dance to the ring of tambourines,
To the twang of the mandolins
Let's dance!
Let's dance till the moment's arrived
To admire the great toreros.
Take your places for the dancing!
Ladies and gentlemen,
Señoras and caballeros!
Ole, Ole!

Au joyeux bruit du tambourin,
Au joyeux bruit du tambourin!
Dansez! Allons, prenez-vous par
La main.
Beaux garçons
Et jeunes fillettes.
Danseuses et danseurs, tournez
Au joyeux bruit du tambourin,
Au joyeux bruit du tambourin!
Dansez!
Allons,
Prenez-vous par la main.
Beaux garçons et jeunes fillettes,
Allons prenez-vous la main!
Dansez, dansez, dansez
jeunes garçons et jeunes
fillettes!
De la vigueur, de la vigueur,
et de la grace.
Après vous céderez la place
aux toreros!
Danseuses et danseurs, tournez
Au joyeux bruit du tambourin,
Au joyeux bruit du tambourin!
Dansez!
Dansez, dansez, dansez, dansez,
Dansez, dansez, dansez, dansez,
Dansez, jeunes garçons,
Oui, dansez jeunes fillettes!
Dansez, dansez, dansez, dansez!
Tournez, tournez!

March and Chorus

CHILDREN (*entering*)
The parade, the parade,
Here comes the procession!

LES ENFANTS
Les voici! les voici!
Voici la quadrille!

CHORUS
Here they come! Yes, here they come!
Yes, here they are.
Here comes the procession!
Look at them, so handsome and dashing!
We salute the brave toreros!
In the sun their lances are flashing,
Hurrah, hurrah, hurrah!
Let's give them a rousing welcome,
Toss our hats and wave the sombreros.
We salute the brave toreros,
Here they come, here they come!
(*the procession begins*)

CHOEUR
Les voici, voici la quadrille,
La quadrille des Toréros,
Sur les lances le soleil brille!
En l'air toques et sombreros!
Les voici, voici la quadrille,
La quadrille des Toréros.

CHILDREN
Now it's time for booing and hissing.
There's the sheriff, mean as can be,
No one is as nasty as he.
On holidays he's never missing!
Away, go home, away, go home!

LES ENFANTS
Voici, débouchant sur la place,
Voici d'abord, marchant au pas,
L'alguazil à vilaine face!
À bas, à bas!

CHOEUR
À bas, à bas!
Et puis saluons au passage,
Saluons les hardis chulos!
Bravo! vivat! gloire au courage!
Voici les hardis chulos.
Voyez les banderilleros!
Voyez quel air de crânerie,
Voyez quels regards et de quel éclat
Étincelle la broderie
De leur costume de combat.
Voici les banderilleros!

LES ENFANTS
Une autre quadrille s'avance!

CHOEUR
Une autre quadrille s'avance!
Voyez les picadors! comme ils sont beaux!
Comme ils vont du fer de leur lance,
Harceler le flanc des taureaux.
L'espada! Escamillo!
C'est l'espada, la fine lame
Celui qui vient terminer tout,
Qui paraît à la fin du drame
Et qui frappe le dernier coup!
Vive Escamillo, ah bravo!
Les voici! voici la quadrille,
La quadrille des Toréros!
Sur les lances le soleil brille!
En l'air toques et sombreros!
Les voici! voici la quadrille,
La quadrille des Toréros!
Vive Escamillo! Ah bravo!

ESCAMILLO
Si tu m'aimes, Carmen, tu pourras tout à l'heure être fière de moi.

CHORUS
We don't want you here, go home!
Down! Go home, away, go home!
See them march along, proud and hardy!
Give a cheer for the chulos, too!
Bravo! Bravo!
Hail to the worthy!
Let us cheer the chulos, too!
Oh look, the banderilla men!
See how they swagger in their finery.
Hurrah, hurrah, hurrah!
See there, how proud they are
As they display the lace and sparkling
Gold embroid'ry upon their gala dress array!
Hello, you banderilla men!

CHILDREN
Another quadrille is approaching!

CHORUS
Another quadrille is approaching!
They are the picadors,
Ah, what handsome men!
So full of pride!
What a thrill to see how their lances
Pierce the raging bull in the side!
The hero! The champion!
Torero, torero!
(ESCAMILLO *enters: beside him* CARMEN, *radiant with delight and brilliantly dressed*)
Escamillo, Escamillo!
Hail Escamillo, hail the torero!
Proud as a king, yours is the ring!
One and all, we applaud our hero.
Ev'ryone's looking up to you,
Hail, Escamillo, hail, Escamillo!
Ah! Bravo!
Look at him, so handsome and dashing!
We salute the brave torero!
On his sword the sunlight is flashing,
Hurrah, hurrah, hurrah!
Let's give him a rousing welcome,
Toss your caps and wave your sombrero.
We salute the brave torero.
Hail, Escamillo! Ah!
Bravo, bravo, viva, bravo!

ESCAMILLO (*to* CARMEN)
If you love me, Carmen,
Then today, of all days,
You will be proud of me,
If you love me, if you love me.

CARMEN
I am yours, Escamillo,
And may God be my witness,
I never loved a man with such passion before!

BOTH
How I love you, how I love you!

SEVERAL MEN
Back there, back there,
Ev'ryone greet the mayor!
(*the mayor appears accompanied by guards; he enters the amphitheater followed by the cuadrilla, the crowd*)

FRASQUITA
Carmen, do not stay here,
Please follow my advice.

CARMEN
And why, may I ask?

MERCEDES
He is here!

CARMEN
José?

MERCEDES
Yes. Over there, in the crowd he is hiding.
You can see him.

CARMEN
Yes, I can see him.

FRASQUITA
Be careful!

CARMEN
I am not afraid of a soul in the world.
I will stay, and I'll wait for him here.

MERCEDES
I beg you, believe me, don't stay here!

CARMEN
I'm not afraid!

FRASQUITA
Be careful!
(*the crowd has entered the amphitheater.* FRASQUITA *and* MERCEDES *also go in.* CARMEN *and* JOSÉ *are left alone*)

Duet and Final Chorus

CARMEN
So you came back?

JOSÉ
I did.

CARMEN
Frasquita and Mercedes both told me you were near,
That you would look for me.
And they even believe my life will be in danger.
But I have courage and decided to stay.

CARMEN
Ah! je t'aime, Escamillo, je t'aime et que je meure
Si j'ai jamais aimé quelqu'un autant que toi!

TOUS LE DEUX
Ah, je t'aime!
Oui, je t'aime.

LES ALGUAZILS
Place, place, place au seigneur alcade!

FRASQUITA
Carmen, un bon conseil, ne reste pas ici.

CARMEN
Et pourquoi, s'il te plaît?

MERCEDES
Il est là.

CARMEN
Qui donc?

MERCEDES
Lui, Don José.
Dans la foule il se cache; regarde.

CARMEN
Oui, je le vois.

FRASQUITA
Prends garde!

CARMEN
Je ne suis pas femme à trembler devant lui, je l'attends—et je vais lui parler.

MERCEDES
Carmen, crois-moi, prends garde!

CARMEN
Je ne crains rien!

FRASQUITA
Prends garde!

CARMEN
C'est toi?

JOSÉ
C'est moi.

CARMEN
L'on m'avait avertie,
Que tu n'étais pas loin, que tu devais venir,
L'on m'avait même dit de craindre pour ma vie,
Mais je suis brave et n'ai pas voulu fuir.

JOSÉ
Je ne menace pas, j'implore, je supplie,
Notre passé, Carmen, notre passé, je l'oublie,
Oui, nous allons tous deux
Commencer une autre vie,
Loin d'ici, sous d'autres cieux.

JOSÉ (*gently*)
I do not mean you harm,
I beg you, I implore you.
What used to be is done,
The past is dead, it is over.
Yes, we'll start life anew.
It will be a new existence,
Far away, for me and you.

CARMEN
Tu demandes l'impossible,
Carmen jamais n'a menti,
Son âme reste inflexible.
Entre elle et toi, c'est fini.
Jamais je n'ai menti;
Entre nous, tout est fini.

CARMEN
You are talking like a dreamer.
I won't lie, I won't pretend!
What was between us is over;
Once and for all this is the end!
You know, I never lie,
Once and for all, this is good-by!

JOSÉ
Carmen, il en est temps encore,
Oui, il est temps encore
O ma Carmen, laisse-moi
Te sauver, toi que j'adore,
Et me sauver avec toi!

JOSÉ
Carmen, oh let me persuade you,
Yes, life is still before you.
I beg of you, please, come away with me,
For I adore you.
(*passionately*)
Ah Carmen, come away with me,
We both can be happy still!

CARMEN
Non, je sais bien que c'est l'heure,
Je sais bien que tu me tueras.
Mais que je vive ou que je meure,
Non, je ne te céderai pas!

CARMEN
No, I have made my decison,
And I know that this is the hour.
But come what may, I do not care, no, no!
No, I will not give in to you!

JOSÉ
Carmen, il est temps encore,
Oui, il est temps encore
O ma Carmen, laisse-moi
Te sauver, toi que j'adore,
Et me sauver avec toi.

JOSÉ
Carmen, life is still before you,
Yes, life is still before you.
I beg of you, please come away with me,
For I adore you.

CARMEN
Pourquoi t'occuper encore
D'un cœur qui n'est plus à toi?
Non, ce coeur n'est plus à toi.
En vain tu dis: je t'adore,
Tu n'obtiendras rien, non, rien de moi.
Ah! c'est en vain.
Tu n'obtiendras rien, rien de moi!

CARMEN
There's no use at all imploring,
My heart holds no love for you.
No, my love for you is dead.
I will not hear what you say.
There's no hope for you.
My love is dead, you hope in vain.
I won't go with you,
Never will!

JOSÉ
Tu ne m'aimes donc plus?
Tu ne m'aimes donc plus?

JOSÉ (*anxiously*)
You don't love me any more?
You don't love me any more?

CARMEN
Non, je ne t'aime plus.

CARMEN (*tranquilly*)
No, not any more.

JOSÉ
Mais moi, Carmen, je t'aime encore;
Carmen, hélas, mois je t'adore!

JOSÉ
But I, I love you more than ever,
You know, I worship and adore you!

CARMEN
Why do you tell me that?
You waste your words on me!

JOSÉ (*passionately*)
I love you, Carmen, I adore you!
All right, I will remain an outlaw,
I'll rob and steal for you.
I will do anything, yes, all you ask.
If only you will come with me again!
Those golden days, have you forgotten them?
How much we loved each other!
(*with desperation*)
Oh Carmen, do not leave me now!

CARMEN
I won't give in, this is good-by!
Free I was born, and free I shall die!
(*Hearing the cries of the crowd in the amphitheater applauding* ESCAMILLO, CARMEN *makes a gesture of delight.* JOSÉ *keeps his eyes fixed on her. When* CARMEN *attempts to enter the amphitheater* JOSÉ *steps in front of her*)

CHORUS (*behind scenes*)
Now the fighting is getting exciting.
See the bull is raging madly,
Running wildly, he charges forward.
Hurrah, hurrah, hurrah!
Hurrah, it's a marvelous fight!
With lightning speed he charges again!
Escamillo, now show your skill,
Hurrah, hurrah, hurrah!
Toréro!

JOSÉ
Is it he?

CARMEN
Let me go!

JOSÉ
That is your fine new lover
Applauded by the mob!

CARMEN
Let me go, let me go!

JOSÉ
Never, never, you will not run to him!
I swear, I'll make you follow me!

CARMEN
Let me go, Don José, I'll never go with you!

JOSÉ
You're on the way to him, Carmen.
(*furiously*)
You love this man?

CARMEN
A quoi bon tout cela? que de mots superflus!

JOSÉ
Carmen, je t'aime, je t'adore!
Eh bien, s'il le faut, pour te plaire,
Je resterai bandit, tout ce que tu voudras.
Tout, tu m'entends, mais ne me quitte pas, ah ma Carmen,
Ah, souviens-toi du passé, nous nous aimons naguère!
Ah! ne me quitte pas, Carmen!

CARMEN
Jamais Carmen ne cédera!
Libre elle est née et libre elle mourra!

CHOEUR ET FANFARES
Viva! la course est belle,
Viva sur le sable sanglant
Le taureau, le taureau s'élance!
Le taureau qu'on harcèle
En bondissant s'élance . . .
Voyez, voyez, voyez!
Frappé juste en plein cœur,
Voyez, voyez!
Victoire!

JOSÉ
Où vas-tu?

CARMEN
Laisse-moi!

JOSÉ
Cet homme qu'on acclame,
C'est ton nouvel amant!

CARMEN
Laisse-moi! laisse-moi!

JOSÉ
Sur mon âme,
Tu ne passeras pas,
Carmen, c'est moi que tu suivras!

CARMEN
Laisse-moi, Don José! . . . je ne te suivrai pas.

JOSÉ
Tu vas le retrouver, dis . . . tu l'aimes donc?

CARMEN
Je l'aime,
Je l'aime, et devant la mort même,
Je répéterai que je l'aime!

CHOEUR
Viva! viva! la course est belle.
Viva! sur le sable sanglant,
Le taureau, le taureau s'élance!
Voyez, voyez, voyez!
Le taureau qu'on harcèle
En bondissant s'élance, voyez!

JOSÉ
Ainsi, le salut de mon âme,
Je l'aurai perdu pour que toi,
Pour que tu t'en ailles, infâme!
Entre ses bras, rire de moi.
Non, par le sang, tu n'iras pas,
Carmen, c'est moi que tu suivras!

CARMEN
Non! non! jamais!

JOSÉ
Je suis las de te menacer.

CARMEN
Eh bien! frappe-moi donc ou laisse-moi passer.

CHOEUR
Victoire!

JOSÉ
Pour la dernière fois, démon,
Veux-tu me suivre?

CARMEN
Non! non!
Cette bague autrefois tu me l'avais donnée,
Tiens!

JOSÉ
Eh bien, damnée . . .

CHOEUR
Toréador, en garde,
Toréador! Toréador!
Et songe bien en combattant
Qu'un œil noir te regarde
Et que l'amour t'attend.
Toréador, l'amour t'attend!

CARMEN
I love him!
And even in the face of death,
With my dying breath,
I shall love him!
(CARMEN *again tries to enter the amphitheater but is stopped by* JOSÉ)

CHORUS (*behind scenes*)
Bravo, bravo, this is exciting.
Now the bull is raging madly,
Running wildly, pierced by the lances!
Hurrah, hurrah, hurrah!
This time it's the end of the fight.
The bull is down, he staggers and falls!

JOSÉ (*violently*)
And so I have lost my salvation.
I am damned to hell, so that you
May run to your lover, you harlot,
And in his arms jeer at my despair!
I swear to God you shall not go.
I say, you are coming with me!

CARMEN
No, no, I won't!

JOSÉ
Once again, time is getting short!

CARMEN (*angrily*)
Go ahead, kill me right here,
Or let me go my way!

CHORUS (*behind scenes*)
Escamillo!

DON JOSÉ (*madly*)
For the very last time, answer,
Will you come with me?

CARMEN
No, no!
(*tearing a ring from her finger and throwing it away*)
And here, take your ring,
The ring you once gave me!
There!

JOSÉ (*rushing toward* CARMEN)
By God, then die!
(CARMEN *attempts to escape, but* JOSÉ *catches up with her at the entrance of the amphitheater. He stabs her; she falls and dies.* JOSÉ, *distracted, falls on his knees beside her*)

CHORUS (*behind scenes*)
Toreador, fight well and hard,
Proud as a king,
Yours is the ring.
And after you have won the victor's crown,

Earn your sweet reward,
Your señorita's love.
(*the crowd re-enters the stage*)
Toreador, your prize is love!

JOSÉ (*in utter despair*)
I have killed my own love!
I killed the one I loved!
She is dead!
Oh my Carmen, how I loved you!

JOSÉ
Vous pouvez m'arrêter . . .
c'est moi qui l'ai tuée!
Ah Carmen! ma Carmen
adorée!

CAVALLERIA RUSTICANA

by Pietro Mascagni (1863–1945)

LIBRETTO BY GIOVANNI TARGIONI-TOZZETTI AND GUIDO MENASCI

Translated by GEORGE MEAD

Based on a short story *Cavalleria Rusticana* written and later dramatized by the Italian novelist, Giovanni Verga.

CHARACTERS

SANTUZZA, *a beautiful peasant girl*	*Soprano*
LUCIA, *mother of Turiddu*	*Contralto*
ALFIO, *a village teamster*	*Baritone*
TURIDDU, *a young soldier*	*Tenor*
LOLA, *the young wife of Alfio*	*Mezzo-soprano*
VILLAGERS AND PEASANTS	

Place: A Sicilian village
Time: Nineteenth century
First performance: Teatro Costanzi, Rome, May 17, 1890

COPYRIGHT 1958, 1959 BY GEORGE MEAD. PERFORMANCE RIGHTS RESERVED

Scene 1

(A public square in a Sicilian village. On one side is a church opening on the square, on the other side, the inn and cottage of MAMMA LUCIA. *It is the morning of Easter Day. Before the curtain rises,* TURIDDU *is heard singing.)*

Siciliana

TURIDDU
O Lola, fair as flowers in the springtime,
Lola with shining eyes brighter than sunlight,
He who has known the rapture of your kisses
Never shall find any other fairer than Lola!
Danger may wait for him who hopes to possess you,
Still I would gladly give my life to caress you.
If I were dead, and God took me to heaven,
Heaven could never hold me without my Lola!

TURIDDU
O Lola c'hai di latti la cammisa
Si bianca e russa comu la cirasa,
Quannu t'affacci fai la vucca a risa,
Biatu pi lu primu cu ti vasa!
Ntra la puorta tua lu sangu è sparsu,
Ma nun me mpuorta si ce muoru accisu—
E si ce muoru e vaju'n paradisu
Si nun ce truovo a ttia, mancu ce trasu.*

O Lola, bianca come fior di spino,
Quando t'affacci te, s'affaccia il sole;
Chi t' ha baciato il labbro porporino
Grazia più bella a Dio chieder non vôle.
C'è scritto sangue sopra la tua porta,
Ma di restarci a me non me n'importa;
Se per te mojo e vado in paradiso,
Non c'entro se non vedo il tuo bel viso.

CHORUS OF WOMEN
Now all the flowers of the meadow are blossoming,
Larks are arising to welcome the spring.
Now that the winter's past,
Now that the blessings of springtime have come at last,
Every heart must sing.

CORO DONNE
Gli aranci olezzano
Sui verdi margini,
Cantan le allodole
Tra i mirti in fior;
Tempo è si mormori
Da ognuno il tenero
Canto che i palpiti
Raddoppia al cor.

CHORUS OF MEN
The golden corn is shining in the sunlight,
The birds of spring are singing up above us,
We rest a while and listen to your voices,
We rest a while and think of those who love us.
We come to be at your side, O dearest and best,
Like the birds flying homeward, home to the nest.

UOMINI
In mezzo al campo tra le spiche d'oro
Giunge il rumore delle vostre spole,
Noi stanchi riposando dal lavoro
A voi pensiamo, o belle occhi-di-sole.
O belle occhi-di-sole, a voi corriamo,
Come vola l'augello al suo richiamo.

CHORUS OF WOMEN
Put all your troubles away,
The Virgin is smiling,

DONNE
Cessin le rustiche
Opre: la Vergine
Serena allietasi

* Since the setting of the opera is Sicily, Turiddu's serenade is often sung in the Sicilian dialect. Both versions are given here, the Sicilian first.

Del Salvator;
Tempo è si mormori
Da ognuno il tenero
Canto che i palpiti
Raddoppia al cor.

The Saviour is risen today.
Now that the winter's past,
Now that the blessings of springtime have come at last,
Every heart must sing.

UOMINI
In mezzo al campo tra le spiche d'oro
Giunge il rumore delle vostre spole,
Noi stanchi riposando dal lavoro
A voi pensiamo, o belle occhi-di-sole.
O belle occhi-di-sole, a voi corriamo,
Come vola l'augello al suo richiamo.

CHORUS OF MEN
The golden corn is shining in the sunlight,
The birds of spring are singing up above us,
We rest awhile and listen to your voices,
We rest a while and think of those who love us.
We come to be at your side, O dearest and best,
Like the birds flying homeward, home to the nest.
(*the people cross the scene and go off*)

Scene 2

SANTUZZA
Dite, mamma Lucia—

SANTUZZA (*entering*)
Tell me, Mamma Lucia—

LUCIA
Sei tu?—che vuoi?

LUCIA
Is it you, Santuzza. What do you want?

SANTUZZA
Turiddu ov'è?

SANTUZZA
Where is Turiddu?

LUCIA
Fin qui vieni a cercare
Il figlio mio?

LUCIA
What now! Why are you looking for my son?

SANTUZZA
Voglio saper soltanto,
Perdonatemi voi, dove trovarlo.

SANTUZZA
Is it too much to ask you?
I must speak with Turiddu. Where may I find him?

LUCIA
Non lo so, non lo so, non voglio brighe!

LUCIA
I don't know, I don't know. I want no trouble.

SANTUZZA
Mamma Lucia, vi supplico piangendo,
Fate come il Signore a Maddalena,
Ditemi per pietà, dov'è Turiddu!

SANTUZZA
Mamma Lucia, I beg you to forgive me!
Did not our blessed Lord forgive the Magdalen?
Tell me, in pity's name, where is Turiddu?

LUCIA
È andato per il vino a Francofonte.

LUCIA
He went to get some wine in Francofonte.

SANTUZZA
No!—l'han visto in paese ad alta notte.

SANTUZZA
No! . . . Last night he was seen in the village.

LUCIA
Che dici?—se non è tornato a casa!
Entra—

LUCIA
Who said so? Who told you? I know he has not come home.
Come in.

SANTUZZA
Non posso entrare in casa vostra—
Sono scomunicata!

SANTUZZA
I'm not allowed inside your door.
Ah, no one can befriend me! I am excommunicated.

LUCIA
E che ne sai
Del mio figliuolo?

LUCIA
What has all this to do with my Turiddu?

SANTUZZA
I am trying to tell you.

SANTUZZA
Quale spina ho in core!

Scene 3

(Enter ALFIO *and people of the village)*

ALFIO
With my horses running free,
Harness jingling merrily,
Crack goes the whip, and away!
Though the raindrops round us fly,
Though the icy wind goes by,
Never a care have I!

ALFIO
Il cavallo scalpita,
I sonagli squillano,
Schiocci la frusta.—Ehi là!—
Soffi il vento gelido,
Cada l'acqua e nevichi,
A me che cosa fa?

CHORUS
Racing on the highways,
Pacing through the byways,
His life is bright and gay!

CORO
O che bel mestiere
Fare il carrettiere
Andar di quà e di là!

ALFIO
Now I've come home to Lola,
My loving, faithful Lola,
Lola, my pretty wife.
With my own roof above me,
And Lola there to love me,
Ah, what a happy life!
It's Easter, and here am I!

ALFIO
M'aspetta a casa Lola
Che m'ama e mi consola,
Ch'è tutta fedeltà.
Il cavallo scalpita,
I sonagli squillano,
È Pasqua, ed io son quà!

CHORUS
Racing on the highways,
Pacing through the byways,
His life is bright and gay!

CORO
O che bel mestiere
Fare il carrettiere
Andar di quà e di là.

LUCIA
Welcome home, neighbor Alfio! You always seem to be happy and gay.

LUCIA
Beato voi, compar Alfio, che siete
Sempre allegro così!

ALFIO
Mamma Lucia, do you still have some of that good wine?

ALFIO
Mamma Lucia,
N'avete ancora di quel vecchio vino?

LUCIA
Not now. Turiddu has gone to town to buy it.

LUCIA
Non so; Turiddu è andato a provvederne.

ALFIO
But he's still here. I saw him only this morning,
I saw him near my cottage.

ALFIO
Se è sempre qui!—L'ho visto stamattina vicino a casa mia.

LUCIA *(surprised)*
What?

LUCIA
Come?

SANTUZZA *(quickly)*
Be silent!
(the sound of music comes from the church)

SANTUZZA
Tacete.

ALFIO
Now I must leave you. You should be going to church.
(he goes out)

ALFIO
Io me ne vado, ite voi altri in chiesa.

CORO INTERNO
Regina cœli, lætare—Alleluja!
Quia, quem meruisti portare—
Alleluja!
Resurrexit sicut dixit—Alleluja!

SANTUZZA, CORO ESTERNO
Inneggiamo, il Signor non è
morto,
Ei fulgente ha dischiuso l'avel,
Inneggiamo al Signore risorto
Oggi asceso alla gloria del Ciel!

CORO INTERNO
Ora pro nobis Deum—Alleluja!
Gaude et lætare, Virgo Maria
—Alleluja!
Quia surrexit Dominus vere—
Alleluja!

CORO ESTERNO
Dall' altare ora fu benedetto
Quest' olivo che amava il Si-
gnor;
Porti e accresca nell'umile tetto
La domestica pace e l'amor!

CHORUS (*in the church*)
O Queen of Heaven, rejoice!
For He whom you were worthy to bear
Is risen, as He said!

SANTUZZA, CHORUS (*outside the church*)
Alleluia! The Lord has arisen,
Now the Angel of Death passes by,
Christ has broken the bonds of his prison,
Now in glory He reigns from on high!

CHORUS (*in the church*)
Pray for us to God, Alleluia!
Rejoice and be glad, O Virgin Mary, Alleluia!
For the Lord has truly arisen, Alleluia!

CHORUS (*outside the church*)
These olive branches which the Lord loved
Were blessed at the altar.
Let us hang them at our doors
To bring peace and love to our homes!
(*the people leave the scene*)

Scene 4

LUCIA
Perchè m'hai fatto segno di
tacere?

SANTUZZA
Voi lo sapete, o mamma, prima
d'andar soldato
Turiddu aveva a Lola eterna
fè giurato.
Tornò, la seppe sposa; e con
un nuovo amore
Volle spegner la fiamma che gli
bruciava il core:
M'amò, l'amai ah! l'amai!
Quell'invidia d'ogni delizia
mia,
Del suo sposo dimentica, arse
di gelosia—
Me l'ha rapito. Priva dell'onor
mio rimango:
Lola e Turiddu s'amano, io
piango, io piango!

LUCIA
Miseri noi, che cosa vieni a
dirmi
In questo santo giorno?

SANTUZZA
Io son dannata—
Andate, o mamma, ad im-
plorare Iddio,
E pregate per me.—Verrà
Turiddu,

LUCIA
Santuzza, why did you tell me to be silent?

SANTUZZA
You know that your Turiddu, when he became a soldier,
Was engaged to marry Lola, pledging his faith and honor,
And Lola said she'd wait for him forever.
He returned. Lola was married. He had to find a new
love
Who would help him forget her, someone to soothe his
sorrow.
He found me! I loved him. She envied me, envied my
newfound happiness.
Filled with desire and envy, burning with jealous fury,
She stole Turiddu, my love. Now I have nothing to live
for,
Nothing but shame and dishonor.
Lola and he are lovers again, and I must weep.

LUCIA
God in heaven! What a thing to be hearing upon this
holy day!

SANTUZZA
My soul is damned.
Go into church now and ask God to forgive me,
Say a prayer for my soul. I'll see Turiddu

And I will beg my love to take me back,
That once again we two may be together.

LUCIA

Now be with her and help her, O blessed Mary!
(*she goes into the church*)

Vo' supplicarlo un'altra volta ancora!

LUCIA

Ajutatela voi, Santa Maria!

Scene 5

(TURIDDU *enters*)

TURIDDU

You here, Santuzza!

SANTUZZA

I had to see you.

TURIDDU

It's Easter. Should you not be in church now?

SANTUZZA

Oh no! I want to talk with you.

TURIDDU

Where is my mother?

SANTUZZA

I want to talk with you.

TURIDDU

Not here, not here!

SANTUZZA

Where have you been?

TURIDDU

Why do you ask me?
To Francofonte.

SANTUZZA

That is a lie!

TURIDDU

You must believe me.

SANTUZZA

No, you are lying. I saw you coming here from the other road.
This morning very early you were seen standing at Lola's door.

TURIDDU

Ah! You were spying!

SANTUZZA

No, I swear! I heard her husband Alfio say that he had seen you there today.

TURIDDU

You listen to him, yet you say that you love me!
D'you want him to kill me!

SANTUZZA

Ah, do not speak of killing!

TURIDDU

Tu qui, Santuzza?

SANTUZZA

Qui t'aspettavo.

TURIDDU

È Pasqua, in chiesa non vai?

SANTUZZA

Non vo.
Debbo parlarti—

TURIDDU

Mamma cercavo.

SANTUZZA

Debbo parlarti—

TURIDDU

Qui no! Qui no!

SANTUZZA

Dove sei stato?

TURIDDU

Che vuoi tu dire?—
A Francofonte!

SANTUZZA

No, non è ver!

TURIDDU

Santuzza, credimi—

SANTUZZA

No, non mentire;
Ti vidi volgere giù dal sentier.
E stamattina, all' alba, t'hanno scorto
Presso l'uscio di Lola.

TURIDDU

Ah! mi hai spiato!

SANTUZZA

No, te lo giuro. A noi l'ha raccontato
Compar Alfio, il marito, poco fa.

TURIDDU

Così ricambi l'amor che ti porto?
Vuoi che m'uccida?

SANTUZZA

Oh! questo non lo dire—

TURIDDU
Lasciami dunque, lasciami.
Invan tenti sopire
Il giusto sdegno colla tua pietà.

TURIDDU
Why do you plague me! Let me be!
At first you make me angry, then try to soothe me by talking like a fool!

SANTUZZA
Tu l'ami dunque?

SANTUZZA
That means you love her?

TURIDDU
No—

TURIDDU
No.

SANTUZZA
Assai più bella è Lola.

SANTUZZA
You find her more attractive.

TURIDDU
Taci, non l'amo.

TURIDDU
Stop it! I don't love her.

SANTUZZA
L'ami—
Oh! maledetta!

SANTUZZA
You love her. You have betrayed me.

TURIDDU
Santuzza!

TURIDDU
Santuzza!

SANTUZZA
Quella cattiva femmina ti tolse a me.

SANTUZZA
That lying, scheming girl has stolen you from me.

TURIDDU
Bada, Santuzza, schiavo non sono
Di questa vana tua gelosia!

TURIDDU
Santuzza, remember, I'm not a slave
For you to command whenever you please!

SANTUZZA
Battimi, insultami, t'amo e perdono,
Ma è troppo forte l'angoscia mia.

SANTUZZA
Beat me, insult me and still I will love you,
But how can I bear it if you desert me!

Scene 6

LOLA
Fior di giaggiolo,
Gli angeli belli stanno a mille in cielo,
Ma bello come lui ce n'è uno solo.
Oh! Turiddu—È passato Alfio?

LOLA (*outside*)
O best beloved!
Were I in heaven with angels all about me,
Still it would not be heaven in heaven without thee.
(*entering*)
Oh! Turiddu, has Alfio passed this way?

TURIDDU
Son giunto ora in piazza. Non so—

TURIDDU (*impatiently*)
I have not been here long. I don't know.

LOLA
Forse è rimasto dal maniscalco, ma non può tardare.
E—voi—sentite le funzioni in piazza?—

LOLA
He may have waited to see the blacksmith. But I must not linger.
And you (*ironically*) I suppose you came to hear the service?

TURIDDU
Santuzza mi narrava—

TURIDDU
Santuzza just was saying . . .

SANTUZZA
Gli dicevo che oggi è Pasqua e il Signor vede ogni cosa!

SANTUZZA
That today is the feast of Easter, and the Lord sees all our sins.

LOLA
Non venite alla messa?

LOLA (*ironically*)
Are you not going to Mass today?

SANTUZZA
Not I. No one may go but those who know they're free from sin.

LOLA
Then I thank the Almighty and bow before him.

SANTUZZA
Oh, you be careful, Lola!

TURIDDU
Come on then, come on then!
Why stay around all day!

LOLA (*to* TURIDDU, *ironically*)
Oh! You should stay here.

SANTUZZA
Yes, stay here, stay here! I still have more to say to you.

LOLA
And may heaven be with you! Now I must leave you.
(*goes into church*)

SANTUZZA
Io no, ci deve andar chi sa di non aver peccato.

LOLA
Io ringrazio il Signore e bacio in terra!

SANTUZZA
Oh! fate bene, Lola!

TURIDDU
Andiamo! andiamo!
Qui non abbiam che fare.

LOLA
Oh! rimanete!

SANTUZZA
Sì, resta, resta, ho da parlarti ancora!

LOLA
E v'assista il Signore, io me ne vado.

Scene 7

TURIDDU
Now, you fool, you have insulted her!

SANTUZZA
I said it because I mean it.

TURIDDU
Now, by God—

SANTUZZA
O my Turiddu!

TURIDDU
No!

SANTUZZA
Turiddu, I beg you—

TURIDDU
Go!

SANTUZZA
Ah, my Turiddu! I beg of you, do not desert me.
Oh, Turiddu, how can you leave me?

TURIDDU
Why do you follow me? Why do you plague me
Before the door of the holy church?

SANTUZZA
How can you leave me!
No, no, Turiddu, I beg of you, do not desert me,
No, Turiddu, you shall not desert me now!

TURIDDU
Oh, why do you plague me and spy on me!

TURIDDU
Ah! lo vedi, che hai tu detto—?

SANTUZZA
L'hai voluto, e ben ti sta.

TURIDDU
Ah! per Dio!

SANTUZZA
Squarciami il petto—

TURIDDU
No!

SANTUZZA
Turiddu, ascolta!

TURIDDU
Va!

SANTUZZA
No, no, Turiddu—rimani, rimani ancora,
Abbandonarmi dunque tu vuoi?

TURIDDU
Perchè seguirmi—perchè spiarmi
Sul limitare fin della chiesa?

SANTUZZA
Rimani ancora!
No, no, Turiddu—rimani ancora,
No Turiddu, Turiddu, rimani ancora!

TURIDDU
Perchè seguir.

SANTUZZA
La tua Santuzza piange e t'implora;
Come cacciarla così tu puoi?
TURIDDU
Va, ti ripeto—va non tediarmi,
Pentirsi è vano dopo l'offesa.

SANTUZZA
Bada!—
TURIDDU
Dell' ira tua non mi curo!

SANTUZZA
A te la mala Pasqua, spergiuro!

SANTUZZA
I am your Santuzza, how can you break my heart?
Have you forgotten how I have loved you?
TURIDDU
Do not annoy me! How can I love you,
How can I forgive you when you insult me?
SANTUZZA
I've had enough!
TURIDDU
I'm sick and tired of all your nagging!
(*he throws her down and goes into church*)
SANTUZZA (*at the height of anger*)
A black Easter to you, you betrayer!

Scene 8

Oh! il Signore vi manda, compar Alfio.
ALFIO
A che punto è la messa?
SANTUZZA
È tardi ormai, ma per voi: Lola è andata con Turiddu!
ALFIO
Che avete detto?
SANTUZZA
Che mentre correte all'acqua e al vento a guadagnarvi il pane,
Lola v'adorna il tetto in malo modo!
ALFIO
Ah! nel nome di Dio, Santa, che dite?
SANTUZZA
Il ver. Turiddu mi tolse l'onore,
E vostra moglie lui rapiva a me!
ALFIO
Se voi mentite, vo' schiantarvi il core!
SANTUZZA
Uso a mentire il labbro mio,
Il labbro mio non è!
Per la vergogna mia pel mio dolore
La trista verità vi dissi, ahimè, ahimè!
Per la vergogna mia pel mio dolore!
Turiddu mi tolse, mi tolse, l'onore,
E vostra moglie lui rapiva a me.

(*enter* ALFIO)
Oh! The good Lord has sent you, neighbor Alfio!
ALFIO
At what point is the Mass?
SANTUZZA
It's nearly over. Neighbor Alfio, Lola is going with Turiddu.
ALFIO
What do you mean?
SANTUZZA
That while you are working in the wind and rain, trying to make a living,
Lola has found another way of living.
ALFIO
Ah! In the name of heaven, what are you telling me!
SANTUZZA
The truth. Turiddu, my love, has deceived and betrayed me.
It was your Lola who stole him away from me.
ALFIO
If I find that you're lying, Santuzza, I will kill you!
SANTUZZA
I was never one to be a liar. You must believe what I say.
Alfio, I swear to you, by all my sorrow, by all my shame,
By all I've suffered I swear it's true.
By everything I've lost I swear that Turiddu, my lover, betrayed me,
And that your wife stole him away from me.

ALFIO
Thank you for telling me, for now I know the truth.

SANTUZZA
I'm ashamed that I have had to tell you this.

ALFIO
The shame is theirs! For them there's no forgiveness,
For them there is no pardon. I'll have revenge before the day is done.

SANTUZZA
What have I done! I never should have told you this.

ALFIO
And blood shall flow before the day is over,
For all my love is turned to hatred now.

ALFIO
Comare Santa, allor grato vi sono.

SANTUZZA
Infame io son che vi parlai così!

ALFIO
Infami loro! Ad essi non perdono,
Vendetta avrò pria che tramonti il dì.

SANTUZZA
Infame io son, infame io son,
Che vi parlai così.

ALFIO
Io sangue voglio, all'ira m'abbandono,
In odio tutto l'amor mio finì!

Scene 9

(The people come out of the church. LUCIA *goes into her house.* LOLA, TURIDDU, *and* CHORUS*)*

CHORUS OF MEN
Good neighbors, we should be leaving now.
Our wives are waiting, come on!
Today is Easter, let's enjoy our happiness
And forget all our cares!

CHORUS OF WOMEN
Good neighbors, we must be leaving now.
Our men are waiting, come on!
Today is Easter, let's enjoy our happiness,
And forget all our cares!
(the people go off)

TURIDDU *(to* LOLA, *as she is leaving)*
My pretty Lola, is there something wrong?
Why do you pretend not to see me?

LOLA
I'm going home. I have not yet seen Alfio.

TURIDDU
He will be here, never fear!
(to the crowd)
My friends, come gather round! Let's all have a drink together!
(they all go to the tables of the tavern and take up wine cups)

TURIDDU
When the wine is sparkling brightly,
Then it is the heart beats lightly,
For the wine is like a maiden in the dawn of love and spring.
Let your troubles all forsake you,
Let the glowing grape awake you,

UOMINI
A casa, a casa, amici, ove ci aspettano
Le nostre donne, andiam.
Or che letizia rasserena gli animi
Senza indugio corriam.—

DONNE
A casa, a casa, amiche, ove ci aspettano
I nostri sposi, andiam.
Or che letizia rasserena gli animi
Senza indugio corriam.

TURIDDU
Comare Lola, ve ne andate via
Senza nemmeno salutare?

LOLA
Vado a casa: non ho visto compar Alfio!

TURIDDU
Non ci pensate, verrà in piazza.
Intanto amici, qua, beviamone un bicchiere.

TURIDDU
Viva il vino spumeggiante
Nel bicchiere scintillante
Come il riso dell' amante
Mite infonde il giubilo!
Viva il vino ch' è sincero
Che ci allieta ogni pensiero,
E che affoga l'umor nero
Nell' ebbrezza tenera.

Drink it down, and it will make you
Want to dance and play and sing!
Drink, drink! Wine will make you jolly,
Drown, drown care and melancholy,
Drink, drink! Frowning is but folly,
Drink the wine of love and spring!

TURIDDU
Ai vostri amori!

TURIDDU (*to* LOLA)
To those who love you!

LOLA
Alla fortuna vostra!

LOLA (*to* TURIDDU)
Good luck to you, Turiddu!

CORO
Beviam! Rinnovisi la giostra!

CHORUS
It's time to have another!

PRIMO DEL CORO
Un bicchiere!

ONE OF THE CHORUS
A drink!

SECONDO DEL CORO
Un bicchiere!

ANOTHER OF THE CHORUS
A drink!

TERZO DEL CORO
Un altro!

A THIRD
Another!

QUARTO DEL CORO
Un altro!

A FOURTH
Another!

PRIMO DEL CORO
Al più felice!

THE FIRST
To the happiest!

TURIDDU
Alla bella!

TURIDDU
To the fairest!

LOLA
Al più scaltro!

LOLA
To the smartest!

TUTTI
Viva il vino spumeggiante,
Nel bicchiere scintillante
Come il riso dell' amante
Mite infonde il giubilo!
Viva il vino ch' è sincero
Che ci allieta ogni pensiero,
E che affoga l'umor nero
Nell' ebbrezza tenera.

ALL
When the wine is sparkling brightly,
Then it is the heart beats lightly,
For the wine is like a maiden in the dawn of love and spring.
Let your troubles all forsake you,
Let the glowing grape awake you,
Drink it down, and it will make you
Want to dance and play and sing!
Drink, drink! Wine will make you jolly,
Drown, drown care and melancholy,
Drink, drink! Frowning is but folly,
Drink the wine of love and spring!

Scene 10

(*enter* ALFIO)

ALFIO
A voi tutti salute!

ALFIO
Easter greetings to all!

CORO
Compar Alfio, salute!

CHORUS
Happy Easter to you!

TURIDDU
Welcome, Alfio! You're just in time to join us.
Alfio, here is a drink.

ALFIO
Thank you. I cannot swallow your politeness, nor the wine that you offer.
It might be poison.

TURIDDU
Just as you please.

LOLA
Has Alfio found us out?

WOMEN (*to* LOLA)
O neighbor Lola, you'd better come with us.
(*they take* LOLA *out with them*)

TURIDDU
Have you anything more to say to me?

ALFIO
Me? Nothing.

TURIDDU
Suit yourself. I'll be here when you want me.

ALFIO
Right now?

TURIDDU
Right now!
(*they embrace.* TURIDDU *bites* ALFIO'*s right ear*)

ALFIO
Neighbor Turiddu, your teeth are very sharp.
(*meaningfully*)
We both understand what we are doing!

TURIDDU
Neighbor Alfio, I know that I have wronged you,
And I confess, as the Lord is my judge,
That I deserve to die for what I've done to you.
But if you kill me, what of poor Santuzza? Her future?
She will be deserted, no one will befriend her.
(*suddenly changing*)
Why speak like that when I shall kill you first!

ALFIO (*coldly*)
Turiddu, you may do just as you please.
I'll be waiting outside in the garden.
(*he goes out*)

TURIDDU
Benvenuto! con noi dovete bere:
Ecco, pieno è il bicchiere.

ALFIO
Grazie. Ma il vostro vino io non l'accetto,
Diverrebbe veleno entro il mio petto!

TURIDDU
A piacer vostro!

LOLA
Ahimè! che mai sarà?

ALCUNE DONNE
Comare Lola, andiamo via di qua.

TURIDDU
Avete altro a dirmi?

ALFIO
Io? nulla!

TURIDDU
Allora sono agli ordini vostri.

ALFIO
Or ora!

TURIDDU
Or ora!

ALFIO
Compar Turiddu, avete morso a buono—
C'intenderemo bene, a quel che pare!

TURIDDU
Compar Alfio, lo so che il torto è mio;
E ve lo giuro nel nome di Dio
Che al par d'un cane mi farei sgozzar,
Ma—s'io non vivo, resta abbandonata—
Povera Santa!—lei che mi s'è data, povera Santa!
Vi saprò in core il ferro mio piantar!

ALFIO
Compare, fate come più vi piace;
Io v'aspetto qui fuori, dietro l'orto.

Scene 11

TURIDDU (*to* LUCIA, *who enters*)
Mamma . . . that wine . . . I'm sorry, Mamma . . .
I must have drunk more than was good for me.
I will walk in the garden—

TURIDDU
Mamma, quel vino è generoso, e certo
Oggi troppi bicchier ne ho trancannati—

Vado fuori all' aperto—
Ma prima voglio che mi benedite
Come quel giorno che partii soldato.
E poi—mamma—sentite—
S'io non tornassi—voi dovrete fare
Da madre a Santa, ch'io le avea giurato
Di condurla all'altare.—

Before I leave you, Mamma, will you bless me
As once you blessed me when I became a soldier—
Oh listen, Mamma, I beg you—
If I should never, never return—
You must be a mother to Santuzza,
I gave her my promise that we would be married.

LUCIA
Perchè parli così, figliolo mio?

LUCIA
What makes you talk like this, my poor Turiddu?

TURIDDU
Oh! nulla!—È il vino che m' ha suggerito!
Per me pregate Iddio! per me pregate Iddio!
Un bacio, mamma—un altro bacio—addio!

TURIDDU
Oh! Nothing! It's all because I have been drinking.
Oh, pray to God in heaven that I may be forgiven!
Oh, kiss me, Mamma, kiss me—kiss me again! Good-by!
(*he embraces her and runs out*)
(SANTUZZA *enters*)

LUCIA
Oh Turiddu?! che vuoi dire?
Turiddu! Santuzza!—

LUCIA (*terrified, running after* TURIDDU)
Turiddu! What is wrong? Turiddu! Santuzza!

SANTUZZA
Oh! madre mia!—

SANTUZZA (*throws her arms around* LUCIA)
Mamma Lucia!
(*sound of voices outside*)

DONNE
Hanno ammazzato compare Turiddu!

WOMEN (*running in*)
Turiddu has been murdered!
(*there is a scream of terror from the crowd. The curtain falls*)

COSÌ FAN TUTTE

by Wolfgang Amadeus Mozart (1756–1791)

LIBRETTO BY LORENZO DA PONTE.

Translated by RUTH and THOMAS MARTIN.

CHARACTERS

FERRANDO, *a young officer in love with Dorabella*	*Tenor*
GUGLIELMO, *a young officer in love with Fiordiligi*	*Bass*
DON ALFONSO, *an elderly bachelor*	*Baritone*
FIORDILIGI, *a lady of Ferrara*	*Soprano*
DORABELLA, *her sister*	*Mezzo-soprano*
DESPINA, *their maid*	*Soprano*

TOWNSPEOPLE, SOLDIERS, SINGERS, MUSICIANS, LADIES AND GENTLEMEN, SERVANTS

Place: Naples
Time: Eighteenth century
First performance: Burgtheater, Vienna, January 26, 1790

COPYRIGHT, 1951, 1952, BY G. SCHIRMER, INC.

ACT I

Scene 1

(*A room in a café.* FERRANDO, GUGLIELMO, *and* DON ALFONSO)

Trio

FERRANDO
To doubt Dorabella is simply absurd,
Completely absurd!
She'll always be faithful and true to her word!

GUGLIELMO
To doubt Fiordiligi would no more be right,
Would no more be right
Than trying to tell you the sun shines at night!

DON ALFONSO
I'm well over sixty, I speak from experience,
But since you won't heed the advice of a friend,
At least let us bring this dispute to an end.

FERRANDO, GUGLIELMO
With no shred of proof you declared them unfaithful.
An insult like that we could never ignore.

DON ALFONSO
Don't ask me to prove it.

FERRANDO, GUGLIELMO (*putting their hands on their swords*)
That's just what we ask you,
We want satisfaction,
Or else choose your weapon to settle the score.

DON ALFONSO
You both must be crazy!
I only was trying to save you some trouble,
And warn you of what is in store.

FERRANDO, GUGLIELMO
I can't take it lightly!
You slander unrightly
The high-minded woman I worship,
Admire, and adore.
My honor is slighted,
Our friendship is blighted,
You wounded my pride to the core!

Recitative

GUGLIELMO
Choose your weapon! You'll render us complete satisfaction.

DON ALFONSO (*calmly*)
I'm a peace-loving bachelor, and get my satisfaction when I'm dining.

FERRANDO
Either fight with me or apologize for casting all those slurs upon our sweethearts and their good reputation.

FERRANDO
La mia Dorabella
capace non è,
fedel quanto bella
il cielo la fè.

GUGLIELMO
La mia Fiordiligi
tradirmi non sa,
uguale in lei credo
costanza e beltà.

DON ALFONSO
Ho i crini già grigi,
ex cathedra parlo,
ma tali litigi
finiscano quà.

FERRANDO, GUGLIELMO
No, detto ci avete
che infide esser ponno,
provar cel' dovete,
se avete onestà.

DON ALFONSO
Tai prove lasciamo.

FERRANDO, GUGLIELMO
No, no le vogliamo:
o fuori la spada,
rompiam l'amistà.

DON ALFONSO
O pazzo desire!
cercar de scoprire
quel mal che trovato
meschini ci fa.

FERRANDO, GUGLIELMO
Sul vivo mi tocca,
chi lascia di bocca
sortire un accento
che torto le fa.

GUGLIELMO
Fuor la spada! Sciegliete qual di noi più vi piace.

DON ALFONSO
Io son uomo di pace, e duelli non fo, se non a mensa.

FERRANDO
O battervi, o dir subito, perchè d'infedeltà le nostre amanti sospettate capaci.

DON ALFONSO
Cara semplicità, quanto mi piaci!

FERRANDO
Cessate di scherzar, o giuro al cielo—

DON ALFONSO
Ed io, giuro alla terra, non scherzo, amici miei: solo saper vorrei che razza d'animali son queste vostre belle, se han come tutti noi carne, ossa, e pelle, se mangian come noi, se veston gonne, alfin, se dee, se donne son.

FERRANDO, GUGLIELMO
Son donne: ma son tali, son tali—

DON ALFONSO
E in donne pretendete di trovar fedeltà? Quanto mi piaci mai, semplicità!

DON ALFONSO
È la fede delle femmine
come l'araba Fenice,
che vi sia, ciascun lo dice,
dove sia,
nessun lo sa.

FERRANDO
La fenice è Dorabella.

GUGLIELMO
La fenice è Fiordiligi.

FERRANDO
Dorabella,

GUGLIELMO
Fiordiligi,

FERRANDO, GUGLIELMO
la fenice è {Dorabella! / Fiordiligi!}

DON ALFONSO
Non è questa, non è quella,
non fu mai, non vi sarà.
E la fede delle femmine
come l'araba fenice!

FERRANDO, GUGLIELMO
La fenice è {Dorabella, Dorabella / Fiordiligi, Fiordiligi}
è la fenice.

DON ALFONSO
Che vi sia, ciascun lo dice.

FERRANDO
Dorabella,

DON ALFONSO
How can you be so blind! You make me laugh!

FERRANDO
This joke has gone too far! I will not stand for it!

DON ALFONSO
My friends, I can assure you, I spoke in bitter earnest. May I ask one question: What strange, uncommon species do your ladyloves belong to? Would you say they are goddesses, boneless, and bloodless, or do they eat and drink like us poor mortals? Are they angels or are they women?

FERRANDO, GUGLIELMO
They're women—but what women!

DON ALFONSO
They're women, and faithful? That you really believe?
Are you so inexperienced, or just naïve?

Trio

DON ALFONSO
Woman's famous faith and constancy
Is a myth and fabrication.
Though it makes good conversation,
Who can prove it?
Name me one name!

FERRANDO
I have proof in Dorabella!

GUGLIELMO
I have proof in Fiordiligi!

FERRANDO
Dorabella!

GUGLIELMO
Fiordiligi!

FERRANDO, GUGLIELMO
No one else but {Dorabella! / Fiordiligi!}

DON ALFONSO
Fiddle-faddle, fiddle-faddle,
You are wrong, they're all the same.
I repeat that woman's constancy
Is the purest sort of fiction.

FERRANDO, GUGLIELMO
I believe in {Dorabella, / Fiordiligi}
You can't
weaken my conviction!

DON ALFONSO
Is that all you have to offer?

FERRANDO
Dorabella!

GUGLIELMO
Fiordiligi!

DON ALFONSO
Are you serious?

GUGLIELMO
Fiordiligi!

DON ALFONSO
Can you prove it?

FERRANDO
Dorabella!

DON ALFONSO
No, no, you can't!

FERRANDO
Dorabella!

GUGLIELMO
Fiordiligi!

DON ALFONSO
I say you can't!

GUGLIELMO
Fiordiligi,

DON ALFONSO
Dove sia,

GUGLIELMO
Fiordiligi,

DON ALFONSO
Dove sia,

FERRANDO
Dorabella,

DON ALFONSO
Nessun lo sa,

FERRANDO
Dorabella,

GUGLIELMO
Fiordiligi.

DON ALFONSO
Nessun lo sa.

Recitative

FERRANDO
Theoretical bombast!

GUGLIELMO
The talk of senile cynics!

DON ALFONSO
I'm flattered! However, you say that they are virtuous. Today that may be true, but will it be tomorrow? How can you be so certain? Have you any guarantee that the love they profess is eternal?

FERRANDO
Impeccable morals.

GUGLIELMO
Old-fashioned principles.

FERRANDO
Lofty ideals.

GUGLIELMO
High-minded way of life.

FERRANDO
Utter unselfishnes.

GUGLIELMO
The firmest of characters!

FERRANDO
Her promise!

GUGLIELMO
Her honor!

FERRANDO
Her devotion!

DON ALFONSO
Kisses and tears, caresses, fits of swooning! What could be more ridiculous!

FERRANDO
Scioccherie di Poeti!

GUGLIELMO
Scompiaggini di vecchi!

DON ALFONSO
Or bene; udite, ma senza andar in collera: qual prova avete voi, che ognor costanti vi sien le vostre amanti; chi vi fè sicurtà, che invariabili sono i lor cori?

FERRANDO
Lunga esperienza—

GUGLIELMO
Nobil educazion—

FERRANDO
Pensar sublime—

GUGLIELMO
Analogia d'umor—

FERRANDO
Disinteresse—

GUGLIELMO
Immutabil carattere—

FERRANDO
Promesse—

GUGLIELMO
Proteste—

FERRANDO
Giuramenti—

DON ALFONSO
Pianti, sospir, carezze, svenimenti. Lasciatemi un po' ridere—

FERRANDO
Cospetto! finite di deriderci?

DON ALFONSO
Pian piano: e se toccar can mano oggi vi fo che come l'altre sono?

GUGLIELMO
Non si pùo dar!

FERRANDO
Non è.

DON ALFONSO
Giochiam.

FERRANDO
Giochiamo.

DON ALFONSO
Cento zecchini.

GUGLIELMO
E mille, se volete.

DON ALFONSO
Parola.

FERRANDO
Parolissima.

DON ALFONSO
E un cenno, un motto, un gesto, giurate, di non far di tutto questo alle vostre Penelopi.

FERRANDO
Giuriamo.

DON ALFONSO
Da soldati d'onore.

GUGLIELMO
Da soldati d'onore.

DON ALFONSO
E tutto quel farete ch'io vi dirò di far.

FERRANDO
Tutto!

GUGLIELMO
Tuttissimo!

DON ALFONSO
Bravissimi!

FERRANDO, GUGLIELMO
Bravissimo! Signor Don Alfonsetto! A spese vostre or ci divertiremo. E de' cento zecchini, che faremo?

FERRANDO
Una bella serenata
far io voglio alla mia dea.

FERRANDO
Damnation! When will there be an end to this?

DON ALFONSO
Be patient! What if I could convince you this very day that they're like all the others?

GUGLIELMO
That is a lie!

FERRANDO
Of course!

DON ALFONSO
Will you bet?

FERRANDO
I'm willing.

DON ALFONSO
One hundred sovereigns!

GUGLIELMO
A thousand, if you wish!

DON ALFONSO
Agreed?

FERRANDO
On my honor!

DON ALFONSO
But promise: no inkling, no mention, not even a suggestion of our wager to your glorious paragons.

FERRANDO
We promise.

DON ALFONSO
On your honor as soldiers?

GUGLIELMO
On our honor as soldiers!

DON ALFONSO
And till tomorrow evening you will do what I say?

FERRANDO
Gladly!

GUGLIELMO
Most willingly!

DON ALFONSO
Your hand on it!

FERRANDO, GUGLIELMO
My hand on it! You connoisseur of women!
To see you beaten will be extremely funny!
Let us plan how to spend all that money!

Trio

FERRANDO
I shall serenade my goddess,
With a dozen fine musicians,
Sing her praises
In the honored old traditions.

GUGLIELMO
As the sure and happy winner
Of the bet we made before,
I shall give a gala dinner
For the sweetheart that I adore.

GUGLIELMO
In onor di Citerea
un convito io voglio far.

DON ALFONSO
May I also join the party?

DON ALFONSO
Sarò anch'io de' convitati?

FERRANDO, GUGLIELMO
Why of course, that's only fair!
Don Alfonso, you'll be there.

FERRANDO, GUGLIELMO
Ci sarete, si, Signor!

FERRANDO, DON ALFONSO, GUGLIELMO
While the sound of clinking glasses
Echoes gaily through the air,
We shall sing the endless praises
Of true women everywhere.
(they leave)

FERRANDO, DON ALFONSO, GUGLIELMO
E che brindis replicati
far vogliamo al Dio d'amor.

Scene 2

(A garden at the seashore. FIORDILIGI *and* DORABELLA, *gazing at the portraits of their lovers in the little lockets they each wear.)*

Duet

FIORDILIGI
See here, Dorabella,
Guglielmo, my lover!
Tell me, Sister,
Where could you discover
So great a nobility
As shows in his face?

FIORDILIGI
Ah guarda, sorella,
ah guarda, sorella,
se bocca più bella
se aspetto più nobile
si può ritovar.

DORABELLA
This one of Ferrando,
I love it!
What light in his glances!
It sparkles, and dances,
And lends him such grace!

DORABELLA
Osserva tu un poco,
osserva che foco ha ne' sguardi,
se fiamma, se dardi non sembran scoccar.

FIORDILIGI
The face of a hero,
Audacious, yet disarming!

FIORDILIGI
Si vede un sembiante
guerriero ed amante.

DORABELLA
His face is expressive,
So gracious, so kindly and charming.
Yet he's manly and possessive, so possessive!

DORABELLA
Si vede una faccia,
che alletta, che alletta,
e minaccia.

BOTH
I'm ever so happy, contented and happy!
If this love of mine ever fails in affection,
Or turns in another direction,

FIORDILIGI, DORABELLA
Felice son io, felice son io!
Se questo mio core
mai cangia desio,

Amore, Amore
mi faccia vivendo penar.

My darling, my darling,
May Fate take revenge on my heart!

DORABELLA
Amore, mi faccia vivendo penar.

DORABELLA
Beloved, may Fate take revenge on my heart.

FIORDILIGI
Se questo mio core mai cangia desio,
Amore mi faccia vivendo penar.

FIORDILIGI
If ever my feelings should waver or alter,
If ever a discord should tear us apart,

DORABELLA
Se questo mio core mai cangia desio,
Amore mi faccia vivendo penar.

DORABELLA
If ever my candor should weaken or falter,
If ever my fervor should fail or depart,

FIORDILIGI, DORABELLA
Amore mi faccia vivendo penar.

BOTH
My darling, may Fate take revenge on my heart!

Recitative

FIORDILIGI
Mi par, che stamattina volontieri farei la pazzarella: ho un certo foco, un certo pizzicor entro le vene—quando Guglielmo viene—se sapessi, che burla gli vo far.

FIORDILIGI
On such a lovely morning I can't help feeling just a little roguish. I can't explain it, but somehow I could do some harmless mischief. When my Guglielmo gets here, how I'd love to tease him just a bit!

DORABELLA
Per dirti il vero, qualche cosa di nuovo anch'io nell'alma provo: io giurerei, che lontane non siam da gli Imenei.

DORABELLA
To be quite honest, I myself have a feeling that something's bound to happen. I almost think we are soon to be married to our sweethearts.

FIORDILIGI
Dammi la mano: io voglio astrologarti: uh, che bell' Emme! e questo è un Pì: va bene: Matrimonio Presto.

FIORDILIGI
Give me your hand, dear, I want to read your future. Look at that M there! And here a P! That's easy: Matrimony Pending.

DORABELLA
Affè, che ci avrei gusto.

DORABELLA
That's one thing I would welcome!

FIORDILIGI
Ed io non ci avrei rabbia.

FIORDILIGI
I would not mind it either.

DORABELLA
Ma che diavol vuol dir che i nostri sposi ritardano a venir? son già le sei—

DORABELLA
But where in the world are our two sweethearts? What's keeping them so long? It's getting late.
(*enter* DON ALFONSO)

FIORDILIGI
Eccoli.

FIORDILIGI
There they are!

DORABELLA
Non son essi: è Don Alfonso, l'amico lor.

DORABELLA
You're mistaken, it's Don Alfonso, our mutual friend.

Scene 3

FIORDILIGI
Ben venga il Signor Don Alfonso.

FIORDILIGI
Good morning to you, Don Alfonso.

DON ALFONSO
Riverisco.

DON ALFONSO
G-good morning!

DORABELLA

Dear me! you're out of breath and excited. For heaven's sake, what's wrong? Can't you speak faster? Ferrando—?

FIORDILIGI

Guglielmo—?

DON ALFONSO

What a disaster!

Aria

How I hate to break the news!
It's so awful my lips refuse.
I must talk, I have no choice,
But it seems I've lost my voice.
How explain it? What to say?
Oh accursed, tragic day!
When you know, you will agree,
Nothing worse could ever be!
All your joys are done and past.
Poor dear boys, the die is cast.

Recitative

FIORDILIGI

Goodness! What can it be, dear Don Alfonso? Do not keep us in suspense.

DON ALFONSO

You must have courage, be prepared for a shock.

DORABELLA

Good heavens! What happened to our fiancés? Are they in trouble? Is my Ferrando dead?

FIORDILIGI

Or my Guglielmo?

DON ALFONSO

Dead—they are not, but not much less than that.

DORABELLA

In prison?

DON ALFONSO

No.

FIORDILIGI

Are they ill?

DON ALFONSO

No, no.

FIORDILIGI

What could it be then?

DON ALFONSO

By royal order they must leave for the front.

FIORDILIGI, DORABELLA

Oh dear! How dreadful!

FIORDILIGI

When do they leave?

DON ALFONSO

At once!

DORABELLA

Cos' è? perchè qui solo? voi piangete? parlate per pietà! che cosa è nato? d'amante—

FIORDILIGI

L'idol mio—

DON ALFONSO

Barbaro fato!

Vorrei dir, e cor non ho, e cor non ho—
balbettando il labbro va—
fuor la voce uscir non può—
ma mi resta mezza quà.
Che farete?
Che farò?
oh che gran fatalità!
dar di peggio non si può, ah non si può,
ho di voi, di lor pietà.

FIORDILIGI

Stelle! per carità, Signor Alfonso, non ci fate morir.

DON ALFONSO

Convien armarvi, figlie mie, di costanza.

DORABELLA

Oh Dei! qual male è addivenuto mai, qual caso rio? forse è morto il mio bene?

FIORDILIGI

È morto il mio?

DON ALFONSO

Morti non son, ma poco men che morti.

DORABELLA

Feriti?

DON ALFONSO

No.

FIORDILIGI

Ammalati?

DON ALFONSO

Neppur.

FIORDILIGI

Che cosa dunque?

DON ALFONSO

Al marzial campo ordin regio li chiama.

FIORDILIGI, DORABELLA

Ohimè! che sento!

FIORDILIGI

E partiran?

DON ALFONSO

Sul fatto.

DORABELLA
E non v'è modo d'impedirlo?

DON ALFONSO
Non v'è.

FIORDILIGI
Ne un solo addio?

DON ALFONSO
Gli infelici non hanno coraggio di vedervi; ma se voi lo bramate, son pronti—

DORABELLA
Dove son?

DON ALFONSO
Amici, entrate!

DORABELLA
And is there no way to exempt them?

DON ALFONSO
No way.

FIORDILIGI
And no good-bys?

DON ALFONSO
Wretched fellows, they don't have the courage to face you. But if you both can bear it, I'll call them.

DORABELLA
Oh, please do!

DON ALFONSO
Come in now, my heroes!
(*enter* FERRANDO *and* GUGLIELMO *in traveling clothes*)

Scene 4

Quintet

GUGLIELMO
Sento, o Dio!
che questo piede
è restio nel girle avante.

FERRANDO
Il mio labbro palpitante
non può detto pronunziar.

DON ALFONSO
Nei momenti i più terribili
sua virtù l'eroe palesa.

FIORDILIGI, DORABELLA
Or che abbiam la nuova intesa,
or che abbiam la nuova intesa,
a voi resta a fare il meno;
fate core, fate core,
a entrambe in seno
immergeteci l'acciar.

FERRANDO, GUGLIELMO
Idol mio! la sorte incolpa
se ti deggio abbandonar!

DORABELLA
Ah no, no, non partirai!

FIORDILIGI
No crudel, non tene andrai,

DORABELLA
Voglio pria cavarmi il core.

FIORDILIGI
Pria ti vo morire ai piedi.

FERRANDO
(Cosa dici?)

GUGLIELMO
(Te n'avveddi?)

GUGLIELMO
All is over, the blow has fallen,
All my hopes destroyed and shattered.

FERRANDO
I am speechless, shocked and battered!
You behold a broken man!

DON ALFONSO
In the face of this catastrophe,
Steel your heart and be courageous!

FIORDILIGI, DORABELLA
Now that all has been decided,
You must do me one last favor:
Be a stoic, be heroic,
Without a waver
Plunge your sword right through my heart.

FERRANDO, GUGLIELMO
Dearest angel! The worst has happened!
Fate decrees that we must part.

DORABELLA
No, no, no, I cannot bear it!

FIORDILIGI
I will die of grief, I swear it!

DORABELLA
Let me perish, I implore you!

FIORDILIGI
Let me die right here before you!

FERRANDO
(Are we winning?)

GUGLIELMO
(Are we losing?)

DON ALFONSO
(The beginning is amusing,
But tomorrow comes the sorrow!)

DON ALFONSO
(Saldo amico, saldo amico,
finem lauda, finem lauda!)

FIORDILIGI, DORABELLA
So does Fate take away the joy of living,
End forever all the hopes and dreams we cherished.

FERRANDO, DON ALFONSO, GUGLIELMO
So the sudden hand of Fate
Will take away the joy of living,
All the hopes and dreams we cherished.

ALL
Bowed by grief, all alone in sorrow,
Who would care to live at all?

FIORDILIGI, DORABELLA, FERRANDO, DON ALFONSO, GUGLIELMO
Il destin così defrauda,
le speranze, de' mortali.
Ah chi mai fra tanti mali,
chi mai può la vita amar?

Recitative

GUGLIELMO
Take courage, my beloved!

GUGLIELMO
Non piangere, idol mio!

FERRANDO
My little sweetheart, do not yield to despair.

FERRANDO
Non disperarti, adorata mia sposa!

DON ALFONSO
My friends, you must be patient, do not console them, let them have a good cry.

DON ALFONSO
Lasciate lor tal sfogo: è troppo giusta la cagion di quel pianto.

FIORDILIGI
Perhaps we part forever!

FIORDILIGI
Chi sa s'io più ti veggio?

DORABELLA
How can I live without you!
(they embrace tenderly)

DORABELLA
Chi sa se più ritorni?

FIORDILIGI
Lend me your sword, I beg you, to end my torture. Since fortune is so cruel, only death can console me!

FIORDILIGI
Lasciami questo ferro: ei mi dia morte, se mai barbara sorte in quel seno a me caro—

DORABELLA
I'll die of grief, I shall not need a weapon.

DORABELLA
Morrei di duol, d'uopo non ho d'acciaro.

FERRANDO, GUGLIELMO
Forget these ominous fancies, and remember, I love you! Trust to the gods above you, to cheer your grieving heart, and guide me safely.

FERRANDO, GUGLIELMO
Non farmi, anima mia, quest' infausti presagi! proteggeran gli Dei la pace del tuo cor ne'giorni miei.

Duet

FERRANDO, GUGLIELMO
Your love is a power,
An ally beside us;
A beacon, a tower,
A star that will guide us;
The barbarous fates too must bow to its reign.
So wait and be patient;
No space can divide us.
We'll soon be united and happy again.

FERRANDO, GUGLIELMO
Al fato dan legge
quegli occhi vezzosi;
Amor li protegge
nè i loro riposi
le barbare stelle ardiscon turbar.
Il ciglio sereno,
mio bene, a me gira;
felice al tuo seno
io spero tornar.

Recitative

DON ALFONSO
(The performance is charming! The way they're acting exceeds my expectations!)
(a drum is heard)

DON ALFONSO
(La comedia è graziosa, e tutti due fan ben la loro parte.)

FERRANDO
O cielo! questo è il tamburo funesto, che a divider mi vien dal mio tesoro.

FERRANDO
Oh heavens! That is the ominous signal, which will tear me away from my beloved.

DON ALFONSO
Ecco amici, la barca.

DON ALFONSO
And the boat is arriving.

FIORDILIGI
Io manco.

FIORDILIGI
Guglielmo!

DORABELLA
Io moro.

DORABELLA
Ferrando!

Scene 5

(*Enter soldiers, village men and women. The military march is heard in the distance. A boat arrives at the landing.*)

CORO
Bella vita militar!
Ogni dì si cangia loco,
oggi molto, doman poco,
ora in terra ed or sul mar.
Il fragor di trombe e pifferi,
la sparar di schioppi, e bombe,
forza accresce al braccio, e all' anima
vaga sol di trionfar.
Bella vita militar!

CHORUS
On to glory, on to war!
We are free of care and sorrow,
Here today and there tomorrow!
Over land and over sea!
We are marching on to victory
With the flags and banners flying
For our country's honor,
While trumpets are sounding
And our spirits soar.
On to glory, on to war!

Recitative

DON ALFONSO
Non v'è più tempo, amici, andar conviene, ove il destino, anzi il dover v'invita.

DON ALFONSO
My friends, it's time you started. You must be going, duty is calling, destiny has decided.

FIORDILIGI
Mio cor—

FIORDILIGI
My love—

DORABELLA
Idolo mio—

DORABELLA
My dear beloved—

FERRANDO
Mio ben—

FERRANDO
My life—

GUGLIELMO
Mia vita—

GUGLIELMO
My treasure—

FIORDILIGI
Ah per un sol momento—

FIORDILIGI
Stay just a moment longer!

DON ALFONSO
Del vostro reggimento già è partita la barca, raggiungerla convien coi pocchi amici che su legno più lieve attendendo vi stanno.

DON ALFONSO
The first one of the barges has already departed. Hurry to meet the soldiers who are waiting to escort you on board. They are getting impatient.

FERRANDO, GUGLIELMO
Abbracciami, idol mio!

FERRANDO, GUGLIELMO
Just one last kiss, my darling!

FIORDILIGI, DORABELLA
I cannot bear it!

FIORDILIGI, DORABELLA
Muojo d'affano.

Quintet

FIORDILIGI (*weeping*)
Be sure to write me daily,
Ev'ry day, will you promise?
Swear you'll always be true!

FIORDILIGI
Di scrivermi ogni giorno!
giurami, vita mia!

DORABELLA (*weeping*)
You write me twice a day.
Twice daily, please, will you?

DORABELLA
Due volte ancora tu
scrivimi, se puoi.

FERRANDO
Of course, dear, I promise, dear angel.

FERRANDO
Sii certa, sii certa,
o cara!

GUGLIELMO
Of course I will.
I promise, my dear angel.

GUGLIELMO
Non dubitar,
non dubitar, mio bene!

DON ALFONSO (*aside*)
This really is too silly!

DON ALFONSO
Io crepo se non rido.

FIORDILIGI
Swear you'll always be true!

FIORDILIGI
Sii costante a me sol!

DORABELLA
Think of me always!

DORABELLA
Serbati fido!

FERRANDO
I promise!

FERRANDO
Addio!

GUGLIELMO
I promise!

GUGLIELMO
Addio!

FIORDILIGI, DORABELLA
Farewell, then!

FIORDILIGI, DORABELLA
Addio!

FIORDILIGI, DORABELLA, FERRANDO, GUGLIELMO
How I shall grieve and mourn
When we are parted!
I love you,
Forever, forever!

FIORDILIGI, DORABELLA
FERRANDO, GUGLIELMO
Mi si divide il cor,
bell' idol mio!
Addio!

(FERRANDO *and* GUGLIELMO *board the boat. The two women stand at the landing, motionless. The boat gradually recedes in the distance, to the sound of drums.* CHORUS *exits singing.*)

Scene 6

Recitative

DORABELLA (*as if awakening from a trance*)
Are they gone?

DORABELLA
Dove son?

DON ALFONSO
They are gone.

DON ALFONSO
Son partiti.

FIORDILIGI
This separation is a terrible blow!

FIORDILIGI
Oh dipartenza crudelissima
amara!

DON ALFONSO
Be courageous, it's not as bad as that. Look there, now;

DON ALFONSO
Fate core, carissime figliuole;

guardate, da lontano vi fan cenno con mano i cari sposi.

FIORDILIGI
Buon viaggio. Mia vita!

DORABELLA
Buon viaggio!

FIORDILIGI
Oh Dei! come veloce se ne va quella barca! già sparisce! già non si vede più. Deh faccia il cielo ch'abbia prospero corso.

DORABELLA
Faccia che al campo giunga con fortunati auspici.

DON ALFONSO
E a voi salvi gli amanti, e a me gli amici.

FIORDILIGI, DORABELLA, DON ALFONSO
Soave sia il vento,
tranquilla sia l'onda,
ed ogni elemento
benigno risponda
ai nostri desir!

in the distance, on the ship you can see your sweethearts waving.

FIORDILIGI
God keep you, my treasure!

DORABELLA
Safe journey!

FIORDILIGI
How rapidly the vessel disappears in the distance! In one moment they will be out of sight. Heaven protect them on their perilous journey!

DORABELLA
How I will miss my darling, away in foreign lands!

DON ALFONSO
I will miss them no less—my two best friends.

Trio

FIORDILIGI, DORABELLA, DON ALFONSO
May breezes blow lightly,
May fair winds betide you,
May stars shimmer brightly
And faithfully guide you,
Beloved so dear.
May Fortune direct you
And journey beside you,
Watch over and protect you,
Benign and responsive
To love so sincere.
(FIORDILIGI *and* DORABELLA leave)

Scene 7

Recitative

DON ALFONSO
Non son cattivo comico! va bene; al concertato loco i due campioni di Ciprigna, e di Marte mi staranno attendendo; or senza indugio, raggiungerli conviene. Quante smorfie, quante buffonerie! Tanto meglio per me, cadran più facilmente: questa razza di gente è la più presta a cangiarsi d'umore. Oh poverini! per femmina giocar cento zecchini?
Nel mare solca,
e nell' arena semina,
e il vago vento
spera in rete accogliere
chi fonda sue speranze
in cor di femmina.

DON ALFONSO
I have a flair for comedy! My acting, to judge from my success, has been convincing. But Ferrando and Guglielmo, can they equal my performance? I'll go and meet them to coach them for their roles. And the ladies! Much ado about nothing. That means only one thing: they'll weaken so much sooner. They're the kind of women who are quickest to reverse their affection. Oh you poor fellows! You risk a hundred sov'reigns on two women!
A man in danger,
Lost in the jungle's wilderness
Or in a shipwreck,
Is safer than the simpleton
Who founds his hopes on Woman
And her fidelity.

Scene 8

(*a pretty room, with several chairs, a little table, three doors.* DESPINA *alone.*)

Recitative

DESPINA

There's nothing quite so thankless as being a perfect maid. From morning till midnight you work, you slave, do your best, and when you're finished, you have nothing to show for it. For example, I have to serve my mistresses' breakfast and all I get is the wonderful aroma of fresh coffee. Do they want me to live on mere aroma? Just where is it written that they should have the egg and I the shell? For once I think I'll try some. How delicious!
(*she wipes her mouth*)
The ladies! That was a narrow escape!

DESPINA

Che vita maledetta è il far la cameriera! dal mattino alla sera si fa, si suda, si lavora, e poi di tanto, che si fa, nulla è per noi. E mezza ora, che sbatto, il cioccolatte è fatto, ed a me tocca restar ad odorarlo a secca bocca? mon è forse la mia come la vostra? o garbate Signore, che a voi dessi l'essenza e a me l'odore? per Bacco, vo assagiarlo: com' è buono! Vien gente! oh ciel! son le padrone.

Scene 9

(*enter* FIORDILIGI *and* DORABELLA, *distraught.*)

DESPINA

My ladies, I've already brought your breakfast. Bless my soul! What has happened?

DESPINA

Madame, ecco la vostra collazione. Diamine! cosa fate?

FIORDILIGI

Ah!

FIORDILIGI

Ah!

DORABELLA

Ah!

DORABELLA

Ah!

DESPINA

What's the matter?

DESPINA

Che cosa è nato?

FIORDILIGI

Find me a dagger!

FIORDILIGI

Ov' è un acciaro?

DORABELLA

And some poison for me!

DORABELLA

Un veleno, dov è?

DESPINA

My ladies, easy!

DESPINA

Padrone, dico!

Recitative and Aria

DORABELLA

Away from here! For in my state of frenzy I might do something desperate. You must draw all the curtains—I hate the sunlight, hate the air I am breathing, even myself! Who would mock my despair? Who dares console me? Away from me at once! Hurry, hurry! Far from where I am! Leave me alone here!

Come, endless agony,
Come and possess me,

DORABELLA

Ah scostati! paventa il tristo effetto d'un disperato affetto. Chiudi quelle fenestre—odio la luce, odio l'aria, che spiro, odio me stessa! Chi schernisce il mio duol? chi mi consola? Deh fuggi, per pietà! fuggi, lasciami sola.

Smanie implacabili,
che m'agitate,

entro quest' anima
più non cessate,
finchè l'angoscia
mi fa morir.

Enter this heart of mine,
Burn and obsess me,
Torment and goad me
Until I die.

Esempio misero
d'amor funesto,
darò all' Eumenidi,
se viva resto
col suono orribile
de' miei sospir.

My love is tragedy.
With none to share it.
Should cruel destiny
Force me to bear it,
Till death releases me,
I'll mourn and sigh.

Smanie implacabili,
che m'agitate,
entro quest' anima
più non cessate,
finchè l'angoscia
mi fa morir.

Come, hopeless misery,
Deride and taunt me,
Enter this soul of mine,
Pursue and haunt me,
Pierce and corrode me
Until I die.

Esempio misero
d'amor funesto,
darò all' Eumenidi,
se viva resto
col suono orribile
de' miei sospir.

My love is martyrdom,
A storm that rages.
Should Fate prolong my life
Through countless ages,
I'll grieve the years away
Until I die.

(*both women collapse in their chairs, in utter despair*)

Recitative

DESPINA
Signora Dorabella, Signora Fiordiligi, ditemi, che cosa è stato?

DESPINA
Dear Mistress Dorabella, dear Mistress Fiordiligi, tell me, what has happened?

DORABELLA
Oh terribil disgrazia!

DORABELLA
A terrible disaster!

DESPINA
Sbrigatevi in buon' ora.

DESPINA
Please tell me about it.

FIORDILIGI
Da Napoli partiti sono gli amanti nostri.

FIORDILIGI
Our fiancés left Naples and we are both deserted!

DESPINA
Non c'è altro? ritorneran.

DESPINA (*laughing*)
Oh, is that all? They will be back.

DORABELLA
Chi sa!

DORABELLA
Who knows?

DESPINA
Come, chi sa? dove son iti?

DESPINA
Why do you say that? Where have they gone?

DORABELLA
Al campo di battaglia.

DORABELLA
They have both gone to war.

DESPINA
Tanto meglio per loro: li vedrete tornar carchi d'alloro.

DESPINA
So much the better! In that case they'll return covered with laurels.

FIORDILIGI
Ma ponno anche perrir.

FIORDILIGI
But if they should die?

DESPINA
Well, what about it? All the better for you!

FIORDILIGI (*rises in rage*)
How dare you say that!

DESPINA
I merely tell the truth. What if you lose them? There still are all the others.

FIORDILIGI
Ah, without my Guglielmo I could not go on living!

DORABELLA
Ah, if I would lose Ferrando, then for me also death would be more than welcome.

DESPINA
Well spoken indeed, but you are wrong. I've never heard of a woman dying of love. To die for a man, when a thousand others can be had for the asking!

DORABELLA
You really mean to tell me that there are men comparing even vaguely with a Guglielmo, a Ferrando?

DESPINA
They are no better, nor are they worse than the others. Today you're loving one man, tomorrow another. One's worth the others, because they are all worthless! Why waste your time on tears? They're still alive, and will be for some time. But they're away and rather than lament in sackcloth and ashes, forget them and be gay.

FIORDILIGI (*furiously*)
Forget them?

DESPINA
Exactly! By far the best cure for lonely hearts is a new romance. What else do you think your sweethearts are doing while they're away?

DORABELLA
You dare to offend those noble spirits, models of faith and paragons of virtue?

DESPINA
You think that men are stable? That's no more than an old woman's fable!

Aria

DESPINA
Stability in a soldier
And virtue in a man?
Who ever saw it since the world began?
Give me one good example if you can,
If you can!
(*laughing*)
Who'd believe such a sentimental tale
Of the perfect and ever-loving male!

DESPINA
Allora poi tanto meglio per voi.

FIORDILIGI
Sciocca, che dici?

DESPINA
La pura verità: due ne perdete, vi restan tutti gli altri.

FIORDILIGI
Ah, perdendo Guglielmo, mi pare ch'io morrei!

DORABELLA
Ah, Ferrando perdendo, mi par, che viva a sepellirmi andrei.

DESPINA
Brave, vi par, ma non è ver: ancora non vi fu donna, che d'amor sia morta. Per un uomo morir! altri, ve n'hanno, che compensano il danno.

DORABELLA
E credi che potria altro uom amar, chi s'ebbe per amante un Guglielmo, un Ferrando?

DESPINA
Han gli altri ancora tutto quello ch'han essi, un uom adesso amate, un altro n'amerete, uno val l'altro, perchè nessun val nulla; ma non parliam di ciò, sono ancor vivi, e vivi torneran; ma son lontani, e più tosto che in vani pianti perdere i tempo, pensate a divertivi.

FIORDILIGI
Divertirci?

DESPINA
Sicuro e quel ch'è meglio far all' amor come assassine, e come faranno al campo i vostri cari amanti.

DORABELLA
Non offender così quelle alme belle, di fedeltà, d'intatto amore esempi.

DESPINA
Via, via, passaro i tempi da spacciar queste favole ai bambini.

DESPINA
In uomini, in soldati,
sperare fedeltà?
in uomini sperare fedeltà?
in soldati sperare fedeltà,
non vi fate sentir per carità!
Di pasta simile son tutti quanti:
le fronde mobili, l'aure incostanti
han più degli uomini stabilità.
Mentite lagrime,
fallaci sguardi,

voci ingannevoli,
vezzi bugiardi,
son le primarie
lor qualità.
In noi non amano che il cor diletto,
poi ci dispregiano, neganci affetto,
nè val da' barbari chieder pietà.
Paghiam, o femmine, d'ugual moneta
questa malefica razza indiscreta;
amiam per comodo, per vanità.
La ra la, la ra la
la ra la la,
amiam per comodo
per vanità.

Dealing with womankind, all men are brothers,
One like the others!
Don't be a featherbrain
Ever to trust them.
Even a weather-vane changes much less.
All men's duplicity
Passes believing.
Feigning simplicity,
Lying, deceiving,
And when they fool you, oh what finesse!
Let him be glamorous,
Clever and handsome,
Gallant and amorous,
Stronger than Samson!
Do not be gullible,
Trusting his lies!
He wants to pull the wool
Over your eyes,
Your trusting eyes!
Pay them in kind when they flirt and philander.
Sauce for the goose is the same for the gander!
Even the best of them,
'Neath his veneer,
Is like the rest of them,
Never you fear!
Perish the thought of a man who is true,
La ra la la ra la la ra la la
Do unto them as they do unto you!
(*exit. Enter* DON ALFONSO)

Scene 10

Recitative

DON ALFONSO
Che silenzio! che aspetto di tristezza spirano queste stanze! Poverette! non han già tutto il torto: bisogna consolarle; infin che vanno i due creduli sposi, com' io loro commisi, a mascherarsi, pensiam cosa può farsi—temo un po' per Despina,—quella furba potrebbe riconoscerli; potrebbe rovesciarmi le macchine, vedremo—se mai farà bisogno un regaletto a tempo, un zechinetto per una cameriere è un gran scongiuro. Ma per esser sicuro, si potria metterla in parte a parte del secreto. Eccellente è il progetto—la sua camera è questa—Despinetta!

DON ALFONSO
Not a sound! This atmosphere of sadness! Graver than a graveyard! Poor girls! They must be very downcast! I cannot really blame them. Meanwhile, I'll go and meet my two friends. In their present disguise I'm optimistic my strategy is foolproof! But that rascal Despina! She is clever—she might see through the masquerade. She even might upset the whole apple-cart! However . . . I know just how to handle a girl like Despina. A little money always goes a long way in such a case. But to further my purpose, I could even ask her to be a partner in my project. Without losing a minute I will knock at her door.
(*knocks*)
Despinetta!

DESPINA
Who's knocking?

DON ALFONSO
I!

DESPINA (*entering*)
Oh!

DON ALFONSO
My dear Despina, I want to ask a favor.

DESPINA
I don't give any favors!

DON ALFONSO
Won't you listen to my offer?

DESPINA
To girls of my age, a man of your vintage offers very little.

DON ALFONSO (*shows her a gold piece*)
This might change your opinion.

DESPINA
A gold piece?

DON ALFONSO
Yes. It's yours for the asking.

DESPINA
What are you asking? For gold I might do it.

DON ALFONSO
The merest trifle—your goodwill and your help.

DESPINA
Is that all? Go on!

DON ALFONSO
Well, then, here's my problem. Doubtlessly you have heard what has happened to your ladies?

DESPINA
I have.

DON ALFONSO
Then you have noticed that they are overcome by desperation.

DESPINA
What about it?

DON ALFONSO
Now then: suppose, in order to distract them, or, as the saying goes, make the best of a bad bargain, you help me to persuade them to meet two nice young men with romantic intentions, who are here from abroad. You understand me, if you make them successful, I shall give you a most generous reward.

DESPINA
That sounds appealing. It's an attractive proposition. But those two silly females!—Tell me—your visitors, these foreigners, are they handsome? And, more important, have they well-lined pockets—these two prospective lovers?

DESPINA
Chi batte?

DON ALFONSO
Oh!

DESPINA
Ih!

DON ALFONSO
Despina mia, di te bisogno avrei.

DESPINA
Ed io niente di voi.

DON ALFONSO
Ti vo fare del ben.

DESPINA
A una fanciulla un vecchio come lei non può far nulla.

DON ALFONSO
Parla piano ed osserva.

DESPINA
Me lo dona?

DON ALFONSO
Sì, se meco sei buona.

DESPINA
E che vorebbe? è loro il mio giulebbe.

DON ALFONSO
Ed oro avrai; ma ci vuol fedeltà.

DESPINA
Non c'è altro? son quà.

DON ALFONSO
Prendi ed ascolta. Sai, che le tue padrone han perduti gli amanti.

DESPINA
Lo so.

DON ALFONSO
Tutti i lor pianti, tutti deliri loro ancor tu sai.

DESPINA
So tutto.

DON ALFONSO
Or ben; se mai per consolarle un poco, e trar, come diciam, chiodo per chiodo, tu ritrovassi il modo, da metter in lor grazia due soggetti di garbo che vorrieno provar, già mi capisci. C'e una mancia per te di venti scudi, se li fai riuscir.

DESPINA
Non mi dispiace questa proposizione. Ma con quelle buffone—basta, udite: son giovani? son belli? e sopra tutto hanno una buona borsa i vostri concorrenti?

DON ALFONSO
Han tutto quello che piacer può alle donne di giudizio. Li vuoi veder?

DESPINA
E dove son?

DON ALFONSO
Son lì: li posso far entrar?

DESPINA
Direi di sì.

DON ALFONSO
They are the most eligible young men any woman could dream of! Is that enough?

DESPINA
Where are they now?

DON ALFONSO
Right here. May I ask them in?

DESPINA
A good idea!
(DON ALFONSO *opens the door and the disguised lovers step in*)

Scene 11

Sextet

DON ALFONSO
Alla bella Despinetta
vi presento, amici miei;
non dipende che da lei,
consolar il vostro cor.

FERRANDO, GUGLIELMO
Per la man,
che lieto io bacio,
per quei rai di grazia pieni,
fa che volga a me sereni
i begli occhi il mio tesor.

DESPINA
Che sembianze!
che vestiti!
che figure!
che mustacchi!
Io non so, se son Vallacchi?
o se Turchi son costor?
Vallacchi, Turchi,
Turchi, Vallacchi?

DON ALFONSO
Che ti par di quell' aspetto?

DESPINA
Per parlarvi schietto, schietto,
hanno un muso fuor dell' uso,
vera antidoto d'amor.
Che figure, che mustacchi!
Io non so se son Vallacchi
O se Turchi son costor,
Io non so se son Vallacchi
O se Turchi son costor,
Io non so se son Vallacchi
O se Turchi son costor?

FERRANDO, DON ALFONSO, GUGLIELMO
Or la cosa è appien decisa,

DON ALFONSO
I present Miss Despinetta,
A discreet and charming person.
There is no one who knows better
How to help you reach your goal.

FERRANDO, GUGLIELMO
I am pleased and deeply honored
At the compliment you paid me,
Being kind enough to aid me
Win the goddess of my soul.

DESPINA (*laughing to herself*)
Goodness gracious!
How loquacious!
That regalia! Those mustaches!
Did they come here from Patagonia
Or perhaps from Timbuctoo?
The Congo? China? Turkey? Malaya?

DON ALFONSO (*softly to* DESPINA)
Don't you think they have some virtue?

DESPINA
Though I do not like to hurt you,
They're fantastic,
Far too drastic,
And as lovers, they won't do!
Too outlandish, too exotic,
Positively Don Quixotic.
I am quite surprised at you.
Don Alfonso, just between us,
Did you find them on the moon
Or perhaps on Mars or Venus,
Did they land in a balloon?

FERRANDO, DON ALFONSO, GUGLIELMO
She is fooled by our (their) disguises!

Barring unforeseen surprises,
There is nothing more to fear.

FIORDILIGI, DORABELLA (*from within*)
Eh, Despina! Come here, Despina!

DESPINA
I am coming!

DON ALFONSO (*to* DESPINA)
Now, you take over, and remember,
I'll join you later.
(*he retires. Enter* FIORDILIGI *and* DORABELLA)

FIORDILIGI, DORABELLA
I must say this is the limit!
You're forgetting your position.
Who has given you permission
To indulge in silly babble
With total strangers and common rabble?
Put the creatures out the door,
Nothing less and nothing more!

DESPINA, FERRANDO, GUGLIELMO (*all three kneel down*)
Ah, dear ladies, how unfeeling!
Here before your feet are kneeling
Two poor slaves, begging your mercy,
That is all we're asking for.

FIORDILIGI, DORABELLA
What an outrage! What pretensions!
Who would force unwished attentions
On us now, amid our woe?
Who would dare descend so low?

DESPINA, FERRANDO, GUGLIELMO
Dearest ladies, they (we) are gentle,
Sentimental!

FIORDILIGI, DORABELLA
Now I'm thoroughly disgusted,
You are brazen and revolting!
Stop molesting us and go!

DESPINA, DON ALFONSO (*the latter from the doorway*)
I've a certain strong suspicion
That their fury is all for show.

FERRANDO, GUGLIELMO
I am certain their opposition
And their fury are not for show.

FIORDILIGI, DORABELLA
Ah, dear love, the pangs I suffer
You will never, never know.
You are brazen and revolting
With the insults you propose.

DESPINA, DON ALFONSO
I am sure they won't stay faithful
And their fury is a pose.

se costei non ci ravvisa,
non c'è più nessun timor.

FIORDILIGI, DORABELLA
Ehi, Despina! olà Despina!

DESPINA
Le padrone.

DON ALFONSO
Ecco l'istante!
fa con arte:
io quì m'ascondo.

FIORDILIGI, DORABELLA
Ragazzaccia tracotante!
Ragazzaccia tracotante!
Che fai li con simil gente.
Con simil gente, con simil gente.
Falli uscire immantinente,
Immantinente, immantinente,
O ti so pentir con lor,
O ti so pentir con lor,
O ti so pentir con lor.

DESPINA, FERRANDO, GUGLIELMO
Ah, Madame! perdonate!
al bel piè languir mirate
due meschin, di vostro merto,
spasimanti adorator.

FIORDILIGI, DORABELLA
Giusti numi! cosa sento?
dell' enorme tradimento,
chi fu mai l'indegno autor?

DESPINA, FERRANDO, GUGLIELMO
Deh calmate, quello sdegno.

FIORDILIGI, DORABELLA
Ah, che più non ho ritegno!
tutta piena ho l'alma in petto
di dispetto e di terror!

DESPINA, DON ALFONSO
Mi da un poco di sospetto,
quella rabbia e quel furor!

FERRANDO, GUGLIELMO
Qual diletto è a questo petto,
quella rabbia e quel furor!

FIORDILIGI, DORABELLA
Ah, perdon mio bel diletto,
innocente è questo cor.
Tutta piena ho l'alma in petto
di dispetto e di terror!

DESPINA, DON ALFONSO
Mi da un poco di sospetto,
Quella rabbia e quel furor!

FERRANDO, GUGLIELMO
Qual diletto è a questo petto,
Quella rabbia e quel furor!

FIORDILIGI, DORABELLA
Ah, che più non ho ritegno!

DESPINA, DON ALFONSO, FERRANDO, GUGLIELMO
Mi da poco di sospetto,
Quella rabbia e quel furor!

FIORDILIGI, DORABELLA
Tutta piena ho l'alma in petto,
Di dispetto e di terror!

DESPINA, DON ALFONSO
Mi da un poco di sospetto,
Quella rabbia e quel furor!

FERRANDO, GUGLIELMO
Qual diletto è a questo petto,
Quella rabbia e quel furor!

FIORDILIGI, DORABELLA
Ah, perdon, mio bel diletto,
Innocente è questo cor.

FERRANDO, GUGLIELMO
Qual diletto è a questo petto,
Quella rabbia e quel furor!

DESPINA, DON ALFONSO
Mi da un poco di sospetto,
Quella rabbia e quel furor!

FIORDILIGI, DORABELLA
Tutta piena ho l'alma in petto,
Di dispetto e di terror!

DESPINA, DON ALFONSO
Quella rabbia e quel furor!

FERRANDO, GUGLIELMO
Quella rabbia e quel furor!

TUTTI
Quella rabbia e quel furor!

DON ALFONSO
Che susurro! che strepito, che scompiglio è mai questo! siete pazze, care le mie ragazze? volete sollevar il vicinato? cosa avete? ch'è nato?

DORABELLA
Oh ciel! mirate uomini in casa nostra?

DON ALFONSO
Che male c'è?

FIORDILIGI
Che male? in questo giorno? dopo il caso funesto?

FERRANDO, GUGLIELMO
I am certain they are faithful
And their fury is no pose.

FIORDILIGI, DORABELLA
We are thoroughly disgusted.

DESPINA, DON ALFONSO, FERRANDO, GUGLIELMO
Their resentment can't (can) be trusted
And this fury is a (no) pose.

FIORDILIGI, DORABELLA
I refuse to stay and listen
To the insults you propose.

DESPINA, DON ALFONSO
I've a certain strong suspicion
That this fury is all a pose.

FERRANDO, GUGLIELMO
How I relish the opposition
That this fury so clearly shows.

FIORDILIGI, DORABELLA
What a shameless imposition!
Your offensive proposition
Only adds to all our woes.

FERRANDO, GUGLIELMO
Their behavior is an admission
They are faithful as we suppose.

DESPINA, DON ALFONSO
I am nursing a suspicion
They're pretending as we suppose.

FIORDILIGI, DORABELLA
Stop molesting us and go,
We will spite you until you go,

DESPINA, DON ALFONSO
They will spite you until you go.

FERRANDO, GUGLIELMO
They will spite us until we go.

ALL
And the answer will be No!

Recitative

DON ALFONSO (*re-entering*)
What commotion! What excitement! And why all this confusion? My dear ladies, have you lost your minds? You're liable to rouse all the neighbors! What has happened, I ask you?

DORABELLA (*furiously*)
Good Lord! An outrage! Men in a house like ours!

DON ALFONSO
Is that so bad?

FIORDILIGI (*enraged*)
So bad? It is unheard of—on this tragic occasion!

DON ALFONSO

Bless me! It can't be! Am I dreaming? I can't believe it! My two very best friends! You here? Really? How so? You here! Of all people! Tell me, when did you get here? (*softly*) (Play along with me!)
(*They rapturously embrace each other*)

FERRANDO

I'm overjoyed to see you!

GUGLIELMO

My benefactor!

DON ALFONSO

What a very small world!

DESPINA

You've seen these men before?

DON ALFONSO

Oh, have I seen them! I have known them since they were babies! I love them like a father, and you will love them also.

FIORDILIGI

What do they want in my house?

GUGLIELMO

Two humble creatures, two slaves, two wretched wretches, lie at your feet here, and love—

FIORDILIGI

Heavens! How dare you!
(*The women draw back, weakly, followed by the persistent lovers*)

FERRANDO

And Love, our idol, leads us onward to you, into your power.

GUGLIELMO

Overcome by your beauty, the devastating splendor of your eyes—

FERRANDO

Like two fluttering butterflies—

GUGLIELMO

Irresistibly drawn into your orbit—

FERRANDO

Like two bees by two rosebuds—

GUGLIELMO

There we hover, adoring,

BOTH

And humbly ask for mercy and consolation!

FIORDILIGI

That is enough!

DORABELLA

O sister, what to do now?

Recitative and Aria

DON ALFONSO

Stelle! sogno, o son desto? amici miei, miei dolcissimi amici! Voi quì? come? perchè? quando! in qual modo? Numi! quanto ne godo! (Secondatemi.)

FERRANDO

Amico Don Alfonso!

GUGLIELMO

Amico caro!

DON ALFONSO

Oh, bella improvisata!

DESPINA

Li conoscete voi?

DON ALFONSO

Se li conosco! questi sono i più dolci amici ch'io m'abbia in questo mondo, e vostri ancor saranno.

FIORDILIGI

E in casa mia che fanno?

GUGLIELMO

Ai vostri piedi due rei, due delinquenti, ecco Madame! Amor—

FIORDILIGI

Numi! che sento?

FERRANDO

Amor, il nume, si possente per voi, qui ci conduce.

GUGLIELMO

Vista appena la luce di vostre fulgidissime pupille—

FERRANDO

che alle vive faville—

GUGLIELMO

farfallette amorose e agonizzanti—

FERRANDO

vi voliamo davanti—

GUGLIELMO

ed ai lati ed a retro

FERRANDO, GUGLIELMO

per implorar pietade in flebil metro!

FIORDILIGI

Stelle! che ardir!

DORABELLA

Sorella! che facciamo?

FIORDILIGI
Temerari, sortite fuori di questo loco! e non profani l'alito infausto degli infami detti nostro cor, nostro orecchio, e nostri affetti! Invan per voi, per gli altri invan si cerca le nostre alme sedur: l'intatta fede che per noi già si diede ai cari amanti saprem loro serbar infino a morte, a dispetto del mondo e della sorte.
Come scoglio immoto resta
contra i venti e la tempesta, e la tempesta,
così ognor quest'alma è forte
nella fede e nell' amor.
Con noi nacque quella face,
che ci piace e ci consola,
e potrà la morte sola, la morte sola,
far che cangi affetto il cor,
far che cangi, far che cangi affetto il cor.
Come scoglio immoto resta
contra i venti e la tempesta,
così ognor quest'alma è forte
nella fede e nell'amor,
nella fede e nell'amor.
Rispettate, anime ingrate,
questo esempio di costanza,
e una barbara speranza
non vi renda audaci ancor.

FERRANDO
Ah, non partite!

GUGLIELMO
Ah, barbara restate! (Che vi pare?)

DON ALFONSO
(Aspettate!) Per carità ragazze, non mi fate più far trista figura.

DORABELLA
E che pretendereste?

DON ALFONSO
Eh nulla; ma mi pare che un pocchin di dolcezza—alfin son galantuomini e sono amici miei.

FIORDILIGI
Come! e udire dovrei?

FIORDILIGI
Bold intruders, leave this house this very instant.
(DESPINA *becomes alarmed*)
We will not let you profane our ears, our spirits' inmost reaches, with your vile, sacrilegious, disgusting speeches! Do not attempt to win our love or ever find the way to our hearts. Our faith is lasting and belongs now and always to our beloveds, till the day of our death, pure and unfailing, in the face of misfortune ever prevailing.
Strongly founded, a marble tower,
Safely guarded from ev'ry foe and hostile power,
So my heart, forever faithful,
Bears an armor no force can rend.
It is love, complete, unfailing,
Bringing joy and sweetest comfort,
Over evil force prevailing,
Forever prevailing,
Love that only death can end.
Strongly founded, a marble tower,
Safely guarded from ev'ry foe and hostile power,
So my heart, forever faithful,
Bears an armor no force can rend,
Bears an armor no force can rend.
You will never win our favor.
Bear the truth with resignation.
We are proof against temptation,
We are deaf when you implore.
Cast your idle hopes away.
There is nothing more to say.
We are faithful evermore,
Forevermore! Forevermore!
(*the women start to leave.* FERRANDO *and* GUGLIELMO *try to detain them*)

Recitative

FERRANDO
Please do not leave us!

GUGLIELMO (*to* DORABELLA)
How can you be so cruel! (*to* ALFONSO)
(See, I told you!)

DON ALFONSO
(Wait till later.) Dear ladies, I implore, your outbursts embarrass me severely.

DORABELLA (*angrily*)
Just what are you suggesting?

DON ALFONSO
Quite simply: there's no reason to become so offensive. They are not only gentlemen, but also friends of mine.

FIORDILIGI
Really! And why should we listen?

GUGLIELMO

Because we're suffering and deserve to be heard. The heavenly radiance of your beauty has thrown us into misery for which there is no remedy except the balm of love. Just for one moment bestow on us the favor of your merciful pity! You see us lying abjectly before you. Our passion is undying!

Aria

How can you refuse us
The light of your gazes,
The glow that suffuses
And dazes our hearts?
We promise you happiness
Untroubled by sadness,
A life that is paradise,
All sunshine and gladness!
Have patience, consider our qualifications:
We're strong and athletic,
Romantic, poetic,
We're just over twenty,
With money aplenty,
And so sympathetic,
Good-natured and healthy,
Well balanced and wealthy,
And before you forgo us—
We want you to know us—
Two models of manhood!
And then these mustaches,
So rightly notorious,
What could be more glorious
A symbol of love?
(*the women leave*)
They make us victorious
And peerless in love!
(*laughing*)
What glorious, victorious mustaches!

GUGLIELMO

Le nostre pene e sentirne pietà! La celeste beltà degli occhi vostri la piaga aprì nei nostri cui rimediar può solo il balsamo d'amore: un solo istante il core aprite o bella a sue dolci facelle, a voi davanti spirar vedrete i più fedeli amanti.

Non siate ritrosi
occhietti vezzosi,
due lampi amorosi
vibrate un po' quà.
Felici rendeteci
amate con noi,
e noi felicissimi
faremo anche voi.
Guardate, toccate,
Il tutto osservate:
siam forti e ben fatti,
e come ognun vede,
sia merto, sia caso,
abbiamo bel piede,
bell' occhio, bel naso,
guardate bel piede,
osservate bell'occhio,
toccate bel naso,
il tutto osservate:
e questi mustacchi
chiamare si possono
trionfi degli uomini,
penacchi d'amor,
trionfi,
penacchi, mustacchi!

Scene 12

Trio

DON ALFONSO
What is so funny?

FERRANDO, GUGLIELMO (*trying to suppress their laughter*)
We won your money!

DON ALFONSO
You are conceited!

FERRANDO, GUGLIELMO
You are defeated!

DON ALFONSO
E voi ridete?

FERRANDO, GUGLIELMO
Certo, ridiamo.

DON ALFONSO
Ma cosa avete?

FERRANDO, GUGLIELMO
Già lo sappiamo.

DON ALFONSO
Ridete piano.

FERRANDO, GUGLIELMO
Parlate invano.

DON ALFONSO
Ridete piano, piano, piano, piano!

FERRANDO, GUGLIELMO
Parlate invano.

DON ALFONSO
Se vi sentissero,
se vi scoprissero,
si guasterebbe tutto l'affar,
si guasterebbe
tutto l'affar.

FERRANDO, GUGLIELMO
Ah che dal ridere,

DON ALFONSO
Mi fa da ridere

FERRANDO, GUGLIELMO
l'alma dividere,
ah, ah, ah, ah, ah, ah, ah, ah,
che le viscere,
sento scoppiar.

DON ALFONSO
questo lor ridere,
ma so che in piangere
dee terminar.

FERRANDO, GUGLIELMO
Ah, che dal ridere.

DON ALFONSO
Mi fa da ridere.

FERRANDO, GUGLIELMO
Ah, che dal ridere,
L'alma dividere
Ah, che le viscere
Sento scoppiar.

DON ALFONSO
Mi fa da ridere
Questo lor ridere
Ma so che in piangere
Dee terminar.

DON ALFONSO
Si può sapere un poco la cagion di quel riso?

GUGLIELMO
Oh cospettaccio, non vi pare che abbiam giusta ragione, il mio caro padrone?

FERRANDO
Quanto pagar volete, e a monte è la scommessa?

DON ALFONSO
Can't you be quiet?

FERRANDO, GUGLIELMO
You can't deny it!

DON ALFONSO
Will you be quiet, quiet, quiet, quiet!

FERRANDO, GUGLIELMO
You can't deny it, you can't deny it!

DON ALFONSO
How inconsiderate!
Why not cooperate,
Try to be patient another day.

FERRANDO, GUGLIELMO
This is hilarious!

DON ALFONSO
It's too precarious!

FERRANDO, GUGLIELMO
I can't be serious!
Ha, ha, ha, ha, ha, ha.
What a comedy,
What a display!

DON ALFONSO
You are delirious!
There'll be a tragedy,
Sorry to say.
Control yourself,
Don't be so gay!

FERRANDO, GUGLIELMO
It is ridiculous!

DON ALFONSO
You're too meticulous!

FERRANDO, GUGLIELMO
This is too much for me,
Past my capacity,
Of all the laughs I had
This is the best.

DON ALFONSO
Laugh in your innocence,
Happy in ignorance,
But he who laughs the last
Still laughs the best.

Recitative

DON ALFONSO
May I ask in all politeness, what's so terribly funny?

GUGLIELMO
How can you ask us? I should think we have more than ample reason, most reverend benefactor.

FERRANDO (*jokingly*)
Pay us each fifty sov'reigns and admit that you are beaten!

GUGLIELMO
Or pay us at least one half!

FERRANDO
I'll even settle for a mere twenty sov'reigns.

DON ALFONSO
Poor, inexperienced children. Just wait a bit and I will make you eat your words!

GUGLIELMO
You want to tell us you still will not give up?

DON ALFONSO
Tomorrow morning we'll talk again.

FERRANDO
I'll be delighted.

DON ALFONSO
But meanwhile, our bet is still valid up to tomorrow morning.

GUGLIELMO
We are soldiers and gave our word of honor.

DON ALFONSO
All right! I'll go ahead then and await you behind the little garden, and there you shall receive my further orders.

GUGLIELMO
And what about our dinner?

FERRANDO
What's the diff'rence? Once the battle is over, it will taste that much better to the winner!

Aria

My love is a flower,
All fragrant before me,
To soothe and restore me
With wonderful art.
Its charm and its power,
So sweet and alluring
And always enduring,
Will grow in my heart.
A spirit I nourish
With tender devotion
Forever will flourish
In glory apart.
(*exit* FERRANDO *and* GUGLIELMO)

GUGLIELMO
Pagate la metà.

FERRANDO
Pagate solo venti quattro zecchini.

DON ALFONSO
Poveri innocentini! venite quà, vi voglio porre il ditino in bocca.

GUGLIELMO
E avete ancora coraggio di fiatar?

DON ALFONSO
Avanti sera ci parlerem.

FERRANDO
Quando volete.

DON ALFONSO
Intanto silenzio e ubbidienza fino a doman mattina.

GUGLIELMO
Siamo soldati, e amiam la disciplina.

DON ALFONSO
Or bene: andate un poco ad attendermi entrambi in giardinetto, colà vi manderò gli ordini miei.

GUGLIELMO
Ed oggi non si mangia?

FERRANDO
Cosa serve: a battaglia finita fia la cena per noi più saporita.

Un' aura amorosa
del nostro tesoro
un dolce ristoro
al cor porgerà.
Un' aura amorosa
del nostro tesoro
un dolce ristoro
al cor porgerà.
Al cor che nudrito
da speme, d'amore,
d'un esca migliore
bisogna non ha.

Scene 13

Recitative

DON ALFONSO
That would be too ridiculous! I've never found a woman who's faithful in this world and now I should find two! That is impossible.

DON ALFONSO
Oh la saria da ridere: sì poche son le donne costante in questo mondo e quì ve ne son due! non sarà nulla—vieni,

vieni, fanciulla, e dimmi un poco dove sono e che fan le tue padrone?

(*enter* DESPINA)

There you are, my Despina. Your precious ladies, where are they? Are we making any progress?

DESPINA

Le povere buffone stanno nel giardinetto a lagnarsi coll' aria e colle mosche d'aver perso gli amanti.

Those simple-minded creatures, they're in the little garden and are telling the birds and bees of the loss of their lovers.

DON ALFONSO

E come credi che l'affar finirà? vogliam sperare che faranno giudizio?

What's your opinion on just how this will end? What can we do to achieve our objective?

DESPINA

Io lo farei; e dove piangon esse io riderei, disperarsi, strozzarsi perchè parte un amante: guardate che pazzia. Se ne pigliano due, s'uno va via.

Don't you worry! The more they will lament, the more I'll cheer them. All this ranting and raving for their former two lovers—I call that downright foolish. For each man who is gone, two more are waiting.

DON ALFONSO

Brava! questa è prudenza. (Bisogna impuntigliarla.)

Splendid! You are a wizard! (It never hurts to flatter.)

DESPINA

E legge di natura, e non prudenza sola: amor cos' è? piacer, comodo, gusto, gioja, divertimento, passatempo, allegria: non è più amore se incomodo diventa, se invece di piacer nuoce e tormenta.

It doesn't take much wisdom, it's female intuition. For what is love? It's fun, pleasantry, gaiety, laughter, entertainment, merely pastime or a whim: once it gets serious, it is no longer love, because it is a burden and a nuisance.

DON ALFONSO

Ma intanto queste pazze.

Let's think about our ladies.

DESPINA

Quelle pazze? faranno a modo nostro. E buon che sappiano d'esser amate da color.

That is simple. They'll do what we tell them. But do they realize how much they mean to our friends?

DON ALFONSO

Lo sanno.

They do.

DESPINA

Dunque riameranno. Diglielo si suol dire e lascia fare il diavolo.

Then let's prepare the groundwork. Expose them to temptation and leave the rest to nature.

DON ALFONSO

E come far vuoi perchè ritornino or che partiti sono, e che li sentano e tentare si lasciano queste tue bestioline?

And tell me, your two indignant mistresses, now that they are so angry, how will you manage to calm them sufficiently, make them reconsider?

DESPINA

A me lasciate la briga di condur tutta la macchina. Quando Despina macchina una cosa, non può mancar d'effetto: ho già menati mill' uomini pel naso, saprò menar due femmine. Son ricchi i due monsieurs mustacchi?

Leave it to me. In such matters, there is no one who can equal me. When Despina manages a romance, she does not miss a chance. I have succeeded in fooling a thousand men—I can fool two women. You said your friends are very wealthy?

DON ALFONSO

Son richissimi.

Lots of money!

DESPINA

Dove son?

Where are they?

DON ALFONSO
They are waiting to receive further orders.

DESPINA
Splendid! Then I ask you to lead them to my room through the little garden door. I'll be ready. And I know my course of action. If both of them are willing to follow my advice, then by tomorrow your two friends will lap milk and honey, and you will win your wager, and I your money.

DON ALFONSO
Sulla strada attendandomi stanno.

DESPINA
Ite, e sul fatto per la picciola porta a me riconduceteli: v'aspetto, nella camera mia. Purchè tutto facciate quel ch'io v'ordinerò pria di domani i vostri amici canteran vittoria; ed essi avranno il gusto ed io la gloria.

Scene 14

(*a flower garden. Two grassy seats on either side.* FIORDILIGI *and* DORABELLA.)

FIORDILIGI, DORABELLA
Ah, how sad and unrelenting
Is the fate that I must suffer,
Endless grief, cruelly tormenting,
Makes my life too hard to bear.
All was happiness and gladness
Till the moment we were parted.
Not a thought of grief or sadness,
Not a trouble, not a care,
Life was sweet and life was fair, ah—
Now the lovely dream is ended
And my joy destroyed forever.
All alone and unbefriended,
I shall die of dark despair.

FIORDILIGI, DORABELLA
Ah! che tutta in un momento
si cangiò la sorte mia,
ah, che un mar pien di tormento,
è la vita omai per me.
Finchè meco il caro bene
mi lasciar le ingrate stelle,
non sapea cos' eran pene,
non sapea languir cos' è—
Non sapea languir cos' è—no!
Ah! che tutta in un momento
si cangiò la sorte mia,
ah che un mar pien di tormento
è la vita omai per me.

Scene 15

FERRANDO, GUGLIELMO (*back-stage*)
A double dose of poison,
That is the one solution!

FERRANDO, GUGLIELMO
Si mora, sì, si mora,
onde appagar le ingrate.

DON ALFONSO
I beg you reconsider
So grim a resolution.

DON ALFONSO
C'è una speranza ancora,
non fate, oh dei, non fate!

FIORDILIGI, DORABELLA
Heavens, that noise is horrible!

FIORDILIGI, DORABELLA
Stelle, che grida orribili!

FERRANDO, GUGLIELMO
Don't hinder me!

FERRANDO, GUGLIELMO
Lasciatemi!

DON ALFONSO
Not so hasty!
(FERRANDO *and* GUGLIELMO *enter, each carrying a little flask, followed by* DON ALFONSO)

DON ALFONSO
Aspettate!

FERRANDO, GUGLIELMO
With arsenic upon our lips
We leave the world behind.

FERRANDO, GUGLIELMO
L'arsenico mi liberi
di tanta crudeltà.

(they drink, then throw their flasks to the ground; turning, they see the two women)

FIORDILIGI, DORABELLA
Stelle, un velen fu quello?

FIORDILIGI, DORABELLA
Goodness, they've taken poison?

DON ALFONSO
Veleno buono e bello,
che ad essi in pocchi istanti
la vita toglierà.

DON ALFONSO
The strongest kind of poison,
Some arsenic and henbane
And strychnine all combined.

FIORDILIGI, DORABELLA
Il tragico spettacolo
gelare il cor mi fa!

FIORDILIGI, DORABELLA
O tragic, woeful spectacle,
It makes my blood run cold!

FERRANDO, GUGLIELMO
Barbare, avvicinatevi:
d'un disperato affetto
mirate il tristo effetto
e abbiate almen pietà.

FERRANDO, GUGLIELMO
Heartless, unfeeling womankind,
Our will to live is undermined.
You have disdained our wooing,
Brought on our sad undoing,
We cannot be consoled!

FIORDILIGI, DORABELLA
Il tragico spettacolo
gelare il cor mi fa!

FIORDILIGI, DORABELLA
I'm terrified by suicide,
It frightens me to death!

FIORDILIGI, DORABELLA
FERRANDO, DON ALFONSO,
GUGLIELMO
Ah! che del sole il raggio
fosco per me diventa.
Tremo, le fibre e l'anima
par che mancar si senta,
nè può la lingua o il labbro
accenti articolar.

ALL FIVE
All I can see is blackness,
Horror has stunned my feeling!
Trembling and shaking and shivering,
Giddy and faint and reeling,
I cannot utter a whisper,
I cannot draw a breath.
(FERRANDO *and* GUGLIELMO *fall down on the grass*)

DON ALFONSO
Giacchè a morir vicini
sono quei meschinelli
pietade almeno a quelli
cercate di mostrar.

DON ALFONSO
Frozen in rigor mortis
See how their muscles tighten!
Their handsome faces whiten
Upon the brink of death.

FIORDILIGI, DORABELLA
Gente, accorrete, gente!
Nessuno, o dio, ci sente!
Despina! Despina!

FIORDILIGI, DORABELLA
Help us, somebody come and help us!
We're powerless to save them!
Despina, Despina!

DESPINA
Chi mi chiama?

DESPINA *(back-stage)*
Did you call me?

FIORDILIGI, DORABELLA
Despina! Despina!

FIORDILIGI, DORABELLA
Despina, Despina!

DESPINA
Cosa vedo!
morti i meschini io credo,
o prossimi a spirar.

DESPINA *(entering)*
What has happened?
How did they come to lie here
In such a helpless state?

DON ALFONSO
Ah che pur troppo è vero:
furenti, disperati
si sono avvelenati,
oh amore singolar!

DON ALFONSO
Driven by hopeless passion,
Despondent and melancholic,
They swallowed pure carbolic!
All help might come too late.

DESPINA
How can you see them lying there,
With no attention paid them?
We all must try to aid them.

FIORDILIGI, DORABELLA, DON ALFONSO
Tell us what you suggest!

DESPINA
We all must try to aid them!

FIORDILIGI, DORABELLA, DON ALFONSO
Tell us what you suggest!

DESPINA
There still are signs of life left.
Raise their heads just slightly,
Stroke their foreheads lightly,
(*to* DON ALFONSO)
Let's run and get a doctor.
I know of one who's marvelous
With people who are ill.
He's known for working miracles
Without a knife or pill.
He's famous for his skill.
Perhaps he'll save them still.
(*exit* DESPINA *and* DON ALFONSO)

FIORDILIGI, DORABELLA
What can we do, I wonder?
We made a fatal blunder
And brought about their death!

FERRANDO, GUGLIELMO (*aside*)
This is so very funny,
I'll laugh myself to death!
(*aloud, moaning*)
Ah!

FIORDILIGI, DORABELLA
Poor fellows, they are sighing!

FIORDILIGI (*standing at quite a distance from the two lovers*)
Are they suff'ring?

DORABELLA
What do you think?

FIORDILIGI
Hear them moaning,
Loudly groaning!
Who could disregard such pain?

DORABELLA (*coming a little closer*)
They have quite distinguished faces.

FIORDILIGI (*also coming closer*)
Let's advance a few more paces.

DORABELLA
This one's head is simply frigid.

FIORDILIGI
This one's arms are very rigid.

DESPINA
Abbandonar i miseri
saria per voi vergogna,
soccorrerli bisogna.

FIORDILIGI, DORABELLA
DON ALFONSO
Cosa possiam mai far?

DESPINA
Soccorrerli bisogna.

FIORDILIGI, DORABELLA
DON ALFONSO
Cosa possiam mai far?

DESPINA
Di vita ancor dan segno,
colle pietose mani
fate un po lor sostegno.
E voi con me correte:
un medico un antidoto
voliamo a ricercar.
Un medico un antidoto
voliamo a ricercar,
voliamo a ricercar.

FIORDILIGI, DORABELLA
Dei! che cimento è questo!
Evento più funesto
non si potea trovar!

FERRANDO, GUGLIELMO
Più bella comediola
non si potea trovar!
Ah!

FIORDILIGI, DORABELLA
Sospiran gl'infelici!

FIORDILIGI
Che facciamo?

DORABELLA
Tu che dici?

FIORDILIGI
In momenti si dolenti
chi potria li abbandonar?

DORABELLA
Che figure interessanti!

FIORDILIGI
Possiam farci un poco avanti.

DORABELLA
Ha fredissima la testa.

FIORDILIGI
Fredda, fredda è ancora questa.

DORABELLA
Ed il polso?

FIORDILIGI
Io non gliel' sento.

DORABELLA
Questo batte lento, lento.

FIORDILIGI
Ah se tarda ancor l'aita,

FIORDILIGI, DORABELLA
speme più non v'è di vita.

FERRANDO, GUGLIELMO
Più domestiche e trattabili
sono entrambe diventate.

FIORDILIGI, DORABELLA
Poverini, poverini!
la lor morte
mi farebbe lagrimar.

FERRANDO, GUGLIELMO
Sta a veder
che lor pietade
va in amore a terminar.

DORABELLA
Is he breathing?

FIORDILIGI
He is, but rarely.

DORABELLA
This one's pulse is beating barely.

FIORDILIGI
Help must come this very minute!

FIORDILIGI, DORABELLA
Their endurance reached the limit!

FERRANDO, GUGLIELMO (*softly*)
They have lost their proud relentlessness,
Getting tamer by the minute.

FIORDILIGI, DORABELLA
Oh so helpless, so pathetic!
If they die now,
I am sure that I will cry.

FERRANDO, GUGLIELMO
I'm afraid that they may weaken,
That's a thought I can't deny,
A dreadful thought I can't deny.
(*enter* DESPINA, *disguised as a doctor*)

Scene 16

DON ALFONSO
Eccovi il medico,
signore belle.

FERRANDO, GUGLIELMO
(Despina in maschera, che trista pelle!)

DESPINA
Salvete amabiles
bones puelles.

FIORDILIGI, DORABELLA
Parla un linguaggio che non sappiamo.

DESPINA
Come comandano dunque parliamo,
So il greco e l'arabo, so il turco e il vandalo,
lo sveco e il tartaro so ancor parlar.

DON ALFONSO
Tanti linguaggi per se conservi:
quei miserabili per ora osservi:
Preso hanno il tossico; che si può far?

FIORDILIGI, DORABELLA
Signor Dottore, che si può far?

DON ALFONSO
May I present to you Dr. Fatalis?

FERRANDO, GUGLIELMO (*to themselves*)
That is Despina, just as we have planned it!

DESPINA
Salve ad libitum cum grano salis.

FIORDILIGI, DORABELLA
That may be so, but we don't understand it.

DESPINA
If you insist on it, I will translate it,
But the vernacular
Sounds less spectacular,
Completely flavorless, not recherché.

DON ALFONSO
Who cares for flavor? Do us a favor,
Make a suggestion.
These frantic gentlemen have taken poison,
They swallowed arsenic.
What do you say?

FIORDILIGI, DORABELLA
What are their chances?
What do you say?

DESPINA (*feels their pulses and puts her hand to their foreheads*)
That will necessitate
Knowing the hist'ry,
I must investigate,
Study this myst'ry.
For instance, this suicide,
What caused it? The potion,
Have you a notion
If it was brown?

DESPINA
Saper bisognami
pria la cagione,
E quinci l'indole
della pozione,
se calda, o frigida,
se poca, o molta,
se in una volta,
ovvero in più.

FIORDILIGI, DORABELLA, DON ALFONSO
They both took arsenic,
A double potion.
Love caused their suicide.
They had a bottle and with a swallow
They gulped it down.

FIORDILIGI, DORABELLA, DON ALFONSO
Preso han l'arsenico,
Signor Dottore
Qui dentro il bebbero.
La causa è amore
Ed in un sorso
sel mandar giù.

DESPINA
I am delighted!
Don't get excited,
I'll make them well again,
As good as new.
Just let me show you
What I can do.

DESPINA
Non vi affannate,
non vi turbate,
non vi affannate
non vi turbate,
Ecco una prova
di mia virtù.

FIORDILIGI, DORABELLA, DON ALFONSO
He is producing a giant magnet!

FIORDILIGI, DORABELLA, DON ALFONSO
Egli ha di un ferro
la man fornita.

DESPINA (*touches the foreheads of the two imaginary invalids with the magnet, then gently strokes the whole length of their bodies*)
Old Dr. Mesmer
Was my professor
Over in Germany.
Using his principles
Based on magnetics,
I now will demonstrate
My art to you.

DESPINA
Questo è quel pezzo
di calamita
pietra Mesmerica,
ch' ebbe l'origine
nell' Alemagna,
che poi sì celebre
là in Francia fù.

FIORDILIGI, DORABELLA, DON ALFONSO
See them gesticulate,
Oscillate, palpitate,
And their convulsions are really desperate!

FIORDILIGI, DORABELLA, DON ALFONSO
Come si muovono,
torcono, scuotono,
in terra il cranio
presto percuotono.

DESPINA
Help me support them.
They are still weak.

DESPINA
Ah lor la fronte
tenete sù.

FIORDILIGI, DORABELLA (*putting their hands to the foreheads of the two lovers*)
We'll do it gladly.

FIORDILIGI, DORABELLA
Eccoci pronte.

DESPINA
You're doing nicely.
That's it precisely!
They soon will be fully recovered.

DESPINA
Tenete forte,
coraggio!
or liberi
siete da morte.

FIORDILIGI, DORABELLA, DON ALFONSO
Attorno guardano:
forze riprendono:
ah questo medico vale un Perù.

FERRANDO, GUGLIELMO
Dove son!
che loco è questo?
Chi è colui? color chi sono?
son di Giove innanzi al trono?
Sei tu Palla, o Citerea?
No tu sei l'alma mia dea;
ti ravviso al dolce viso:
e alla man ch'or ben conosco
e che sola è il mio tesor.

DESPINA, DON ALFONSO
Son effetti acor del tosco,
Non abbiate alcun timor.

FIORDILIGI, DORABELLA
Sarà ver, ma tante smorfie
fanno torto al nostro onor.
Sarà ver, ma tante smorfie
fanno torto al nostro onor.

DESPINA, DON ALFONSO
Son effetti ancor del tosco.
Non abbiate alcun timor.

FERRANDO, GUGLIELMO
(Dalla voglia ch'ho di ridere,
il polmon mi scoppia oror.)
Per pietà, bell' idol mio!
volgi a me le luci liete!

FIORDILIGI, DORABELLA
Più resister non poss' io!

DESPINA, DON ALFONSO
In poch' ore lo vedrete
per virtù del magnetismo
finire quel parossismo,
torneranno al primo umor.

FERRANDO, GUGLIELMO
Dammi un bacio, o mio tesoro,
Un sol bacio, o qui mi moro!

FIORDILIGI, DORABELLA
Stelle, un bacio?

DESPINA, DON ALFONSO
Secondate
per effetto di bontate.

FIORDILIGI, DORABELLA
Ah, che troppo si richiede

FIORDILIGI, DORABELLA, DON ALFONSO
See them revive again,
Fully alive again,
Thanks to the doctor's amazing technique!

FERRANDO, GUGLIELMO (*slowly raising themselves*)
Am I dead? Or am I dreaming?
Is this Eden or Valhalla?
Or the garden realm of Allah?
Are you Venus?
Or Cleopatra?
(*to* FIORDILIGI *and* DORABELLA)
No, you are my dear beloved!
Even death can't come between us.
Here's the hand I love so dearly
And would kiss with all respect.
(*they embrace the women tenderly and kiss their hands*)

DESPINA, DON ALFONSO
If they talk a little queerly,
It's the magnet's strong effect.

FIORDILIGI, DORABELLA
That may be, but such effusions
Mar the honor of my name.
Make them see that these delusions
Are a scandal and a shame.

DESPINA, DON ALFONSO
Please forgive them for their effusions,
Their condition is to blame.

FERRANDO, GUGLIELMO (*softly*)
(Though it's really too ridiculous,
I enjoy it just the same.)
(*aloud*)
Take my heart and my devotion!
Do not spurn my burning ardor!

FIORDILIGI, DORABELLA
Who could hear without emotion?

DESPINA, DON ALFONSO
We are certain they'll recover.
Only wait a little longer
Till they feel a trifle stronger.
It is too much to expect.

FERRANDO, GUGLIELMO
Kiss me, darling, I implore you,
Or I'll die right here before you!

FIORDILIGI, DORABELLA
Kiss you? Good heavens!

DESPINA, DON ALFONSO
Better do it out of kindness!
Nothing to it.

FIORDILIGI, DORABELLA
What a shameless imposition

On good faith and true devotion,
Forcing us to give permission
For an outrage we abhor!

da una fida onesta amante
oltraggiata è la mia fede,
oltraggiato è questo cor.

DESPINA, DON ALFONSO, FERRANDO, GUGLIELMO
Since the dawning of creation
Was there ever a like flirtation?
This has been the gayest comedy
I have ever seen before.

DESPINA, DON ALFONSO, FERRANDO, GUGLIELMO
Un quadretto più giocondo
non si vide in tutto il mondo,
quel che più mi fa da ridere
è quell' ira e quel furor.

FIORDILIGI, DORABELLA
Go away, you wicked madmen,
With your kisses and embraces!
Shameless, evil-minded badmen,
Never dare to show your faces anymore!
There is the door!

FIORDILIGI, DORABELLA
Disperati, attossicati,
ite al diavol quanti siete;
tardi inver vi pentirete
se più cresce il mio furor,
Il mio furor.

FERRANDO, GUGLIELMO
Kiss me, darling, I implore you,
Or I'll die right here before you!

FERRANDO, GUGLIELMO
Dammi un bacio, o mio tesoro,
Un sol bacio, o qui mi moro.

FIORDILIGI, DORABELLA
Go away, you wicked madmen,
With your kisses and embraces,
We don't want to see your faces
For a single minute more!

FIORDILIGI, DORABELLA
Disperati, attossicati,
ite al diavol quanti siete;
tardi inver vi pentirete
se più cresce il mio furor.

FERRANDO, GUGLIELMO
Darling, kiss me!

FERRANDO, GUGLIELMO
Un sol bacio.

FIORDILIGI, DORABELLA
Never! How dare you!

FIORDILIGI, DORABELLA
Stelle, un bacio?

DESPINA, DON ALFONSO
Better do it
Out of kindness.
Nothing to it!

DESPINA, DON ALFONSO
Secondate
per effetto di bontate.

FIORDILIGI, DORABELLA
Ah, how dare you stand and face us,
After such a bold proposal?
Are you trying to disgrace us?
Never dare to show your face!
Don't come back here any more!
Do not make our anger greater,
We disdain and spurn your love!

FIORDILIGI, DORABELLA
Ah, che troppo si richiede
da una fida onesta amante
oltraggiata è la mia fede,
oltraggiato è questo cor,
oltraggiato è questo cor.
Tardi inver vi pentirete,
se più cresce il mio furor.

DESPINA, DON ALFONSO
I'm convinced that soon or later
Their disdain will turn to love.

DESPINA, DON ALFONSO
Ch'io ben so che tanto foco
cangerassi in quel d'amor.

FERRANDO, GUGLIELMO
I'm afraid that soon or later
Their disdain may turn to love.

FERRANDO, GUGLIELMO
Ch'io ben so che tanto foco
terminasse in quel d'amor.

ACT II

Scene 1

(*A room in the sisters' home.* FIORDILIGI, DORABELLA, *and* DESPINA)

Recitative

DESPINA
Andate là, che siete due bizarre ragazze!

DESPINA
For heaven's sake, how can you be so unrealistic?

FIORDILIGI
Oh cospettaccio! cosa pretenderesti?

FIORDILIGI
You little devil! What is it you want?

DESPINA
Per me nulla.

DESPINA
Nothing for me.

FIORDILIGI
Per chi dunque?

FIORDILIGI
For whom then?

DESPINA
Per voi.

DESPINA
For you.

DORABELLA
Per noi?

DORABELLA
For us?

DESPINA
Per voi. Siete voi donne, o no?

DESPINA
That's right. Are you both women or not?

FIORDILIGI
E per questo?

FIORDILIGI
Can you doubt it?

DESPINA
E per questo dovere far da donne.

DESPINA
Yes, I doubt it; you act like little schoolgirls.

DORABELLA
Cio è?

DORABELLA
How so?

DESPINA
Tratter l'amore en bagatelle. Le occasioni belle non negliger giammai! cangiar a tempo, a tempo esser costanti, coquettizar con grazia, prevenir la disgrazia sì comune a chi si fida in uomo, mangiar il fico, e non gittare il pomo.

DESPINA
Because you think that love is serious. You must be ready when opportunity knocks. You must be equal to every new occasion, be frank or coquettish, all depending upon the man in question. That way you're always winner, and have your bread buttered on both sides.

FIORDILIGI
(Che diavolo!) tai cose falle tu, se n'hai voglia.

FIORDILIGI
(What deviltry!) You may do things like that, if you want to.

DESPINA
Io già le faccio. Ma vorrei che anche voi per gloria del bel sesso faceste un po' lo stesso; per esempio: i vostri Ganimedi son andati alla guerra; infin che tornano fate alla militare: reclutate.

DESPINA
I've always done them. But I wish that you both, for the sake of all womanhood, would follow my example. Let me tell you, now that your two Romeos have become valiant warriors, do as they did, seek your own adventures, and do it quickly.

DORABELLA
Il cielo ce ne guardi.

DORABELLA
May heaven preserve me!

DESPINA
Eh! che noi siamo in terra, e non in cielo! Fidatevi al mio zelo. Giacchè questi forestieri v'adorano lasciatevi adorar. Son ricchi, belli, nobili, generosi come fede fece a voi Don Alfonso;

DESPINA
Eh, be glad we are not yet in heaven, but very much on earth. You have met two nice young suitors. They worship you! Then why not let them do so? They're wealthy, handsome, generous, well bred, Don Alfonso told you everything about them. They had the courage

to die for your sake—is that not proof that they mean what they're saying? And aren't you both young, lovable women who deserve to be loved and adored? (Seems I am making headway!)

FIORDILIGI

I am inclined to think you want to lead us into mischief. Are you really proposing that we become the topic for gossip? And what about our lovers—do you think we would ever betray them?

DESPINA

And who said that you should? Where would be the betrayal?

DORABELLA

In my opinion, it would be bad enough if anybody heard that we met other men.

DESPINA

That is no problem. Let me take care of that for you. I'll simply spread a rumor they came to visit me.

DORABELLA

Who would believe it?

DESPINA

Why not? Any average lady's maid has a lover—why couldn't I have two? Don't let that worry you!

FIORDILIGI

No, no! I could not do it! Those two men are so reckless! They even had the daring to beg us for kisses!

DESPINA

(Isn't that awful!) I give you my assurance that your suitors' behavior was due to the influence of poison—all their tantrums, their ravings, their fits, and all their antics. Get to know them as they really are. They are modest and decent, very polished. You'll see it for yourselves.

DORABELLA

And then?

DESPINA

And then: ask yourself! That's your business! (I knew that I could handle them.)

FIORDILIGI

What do you suggest?

DESPINA

Follow your heart. Are you made of flesh and blood, or just what are you?

Aria

Any girl fifteen or over
Must pursue a woman's mission,
And with feminine intuition

avean corraggio di morire per voi; questi son merti che sprezzar non si denno da giovani qual voi belle e galanti, che pon star senza amor, non senza amanti. (Par che ci trovin gusto!)

FIORDILIGI

Per Bacco ci faresti far delle belle cose; credi tu che vogliamo favola diventar degli oziosi? ai nostri cari sposi credi tu che vogliam dar tal tormento?

DESPINA

E chi dice, che abbiate a far loro alcun torto?

DORABELLA

Non ti pare, che sia torto bastante, se noto si facesse, che trattiamo costor?

DESPINA

Anche per questo c'è un mezzo sicurissimo, io voglio sparger fama, che vengono da me.

DORABELLA

Chi vuol che il creda?

DESPINA

Oh bella! non ha forse merto una cameriera d'aver due cicisbei? di me fidatevi.

FIORDILIGI

No, no, son troppo audaci questi tuoi forestieri, non ebber la baldanza fin di chieder dei baci.

DESPINA

(Che disgrazia!) io posso assicurarvi che le cose che han fatto furo effetti del tossico, che han preso, convulsioni, deliri, follie, vaneggiamenti; ma or vedrete, come son discreti, manierosi, modesti, e mansueti, lasciateli venir.

DORABELLA

E poi?

DESPINA

E poi: caspita! fate voi. (L'ho detto che cadrebbero.)

FIORDILIGI

Cosa dobbiamo far?

DESPINA

Quel che volete. Siete d'ossa, e di carne, o cosa siete?

Una donna a quindici anni
dee saper ogni gran moda,
dove il diavolo ha la coda,
cosa è bene, e mal cos' è,

dee saper le maliziette,
che innamorano gli amanti,
finger riso, finger pianti,
inventar i bei perchè.
Dee in un momento
dar retta a cento,
colle pupille
parlar con mille,
dar speme a tutti,
sien belli o brutti,
saper nascondersi,
senza confondersi,
senza arrossire
saper mentire,
e qual regina
dall' alto soglio
col posso e voglio
farsi ubbidir.
Par ch'abbian gusto
di tal dottrina,
viva Despina
che sa servir.
Dee in un momento
dar retta a cento,
colle pupille
parlar con mille,
dar speme a tutti,
sien belle o brutti,
saper nascondersi,
senza confondersi,
senza arrossire
saper mentire,
e qual regina
dall' alto soglio
col posso e voglio
farsi ubbidir.

Be an expert managing men.
She must know a thousand ruses
To attract the man she chooses.
Laugh or chatter,
Weep or flatter,
Know the moment where and when.
When to amuse them,
When to confuse them,
When she should tease them,
When she should please them.
She must act slyly,
Clever and wily,
In all the ritual,
New or habitual,
Never revealing
Her inner feeling.
Love is the kingdom
She rules in splendor.
Men must surrender,
Serve her and bow.
Life can be keener,
Love can be greener.
Come to Despina,
She'll tell you how!
She'll answer questions,
Give you suggestions
How you can handle
Gossip or scandal.
She can direct you,
She can perfect you
In all formalities
And technicalities,
Never revealing
Her inner feeling.
Love is the kingdom
She rules in splendor.
Men must surrender,
Serve her and bow!

(*exit* DESPINA)

Scene 2

Recitative

FIORDILIGI
Sorella, cosa dici?

DORABELLA
Io son stordita dallo spirto
infernal di tal ragazza.

FIORDILIGI
I never heard such nonsense!

DORABELLA
I am speechless at the girl's unbelievable badness!

FIORDILIGI
Her theories are sheerest madness! For self-respecting women they are quite out of question!

DORABELLA
Not quite so out of question if we treat it as a joke.

FIORDILIGI
In my opinion, such a joke could be dangerous. Or do you think it proper for two ladies engaged to be married to harbor such ideas?

DORABELLA
But she assured us we'd be doing no harm.

FIORDILIGI
If people gossip, that would be harm enough!

DORABELLA
But she has offered to claim them as her suitors!

FIORDILIGI
My, what a nice, convenient type of conscience! Think of our lovers! What would they say?

DORABELLA
Nothing! Either they will not know it—in that case it is simple. Or, if by chance they should hear it, then we will tell them they are Despina's friends.

FIORDILIGI
And our engagements?

DORABELLA
They will remain unbroken. An innocent diversion to pass away the tedious time of waiting can't be called a breach of faith—don't you think so?

FIORDILIGI
That is true.

DORABELLA
Well then?

FIORDILIGI
Do as you please. But remember I warned you, if something should go wrong.

DORABELLA
And what could possibly happen if we do not go too far? Just one more thing: let me ask you one question. Which of them is your choice for your admirer?

FIORDILIGI
No, you decide, dear sister.

DORABELLA
I have decided!

Duet

I will choose the handsome dark one
If it's all the same to you.

FIORDILIGI
Ma credimi è una pazza. Ti par che siamo in caso di seguir suoi consigli?

DORABELLA
Oh certo se tu pigli pel rovescio il negozio.

FIORDILIGI
Anzi io lo piglio per il suo vero dritto: non credi tu delitto per due giovani omai promesse spose il far di queste cose?

DORABELLA
Ella non dice che facciamo alcun mal.

FIORDILIGI
E mal che basta il far parlar di noi.

DORABELLA
Quando si dice che vengon per Despina!

FIORDILIGI
Oh, tu sei troppo larga di coscienza! e che diranno gli sposi nostri?

DORABELLA
Nulla: o non sapran l'affare ed è tutto finito: o sapran qualche cosa e allor diremo che vennero per lei.

FIORDILIGI
Ma i nostri cori?

DORABELLA
Restano quel che sono; per divertirsi un poco, e non morire della malinconia non si manca di fè, sorella mia.

FIORDILIGI
Questo è ver.

DORABELLA
Dunque?

FIORDILIGI
Dunque fa un po tu: ma non voglio aver colpa, se poi nasce un imbroglio.

DORABELLA
Che imbroglio nascer deve con tanta precauzion, per altro ascolta, per intenderci bene, qual vuoi scieglier per te de' due Narcisi.

FIORDILIGI
Decidi tu, sorella.

DORABELLA
Io già decisi.

Prenderò quel brunettino,
che più lepido mi par.

FIORDILIGI
Ed intanto io col biondino
vo un po ridere e burlar.

DORABELLA
Scherzosetta ai dolci detti
io di quel risponderò.

FIORDILIGI
Sospirando i sospiretti
io dell' altro imiterò.

DORABELLA
Mi dirà, ben mio, mi moro.

FIORDILIGI
Mi dirà, mio bel tesoro!

FIORDILIGI, DORABELLA
Ed intanto che diletto
che spassetto io proverò! ah!

DORABELLA
Mi dirà, ben mio, mi moro.

FIORDILIGI
Mi dirà, mio bel tesoro!

DORABELLA, FIORDILIGI
Ed intanto che diletto,
ed intanto che diletto,
che spassetto io proverò!
Io proverò!

FIORDILIGI
I myself prefer the blond one.
He is gay and winning too!

DORABELLA
I'll delight in his lovelorn phrases
With a most engaging smile.

FIORDILIGI
If he sighs and moons and gazes,
I will echo him in style.

DORABELLA
Mine will say, "My soul is burning!"

FIORDILIGI
Mine will say, "My heart is yearning!"

FIORDILIGI, DORABELLA
How romantic, how enchanting!
How amusing it will be! Ah!

DORABELLA
Mine will say, "I love you only!"

FIORDILIGI
Mine will say, "My heart is lonely!"

BOTH
How romantic, how enchanting!
It may be a little naughty,
But at least it will be fun,
A lot of fun!
(*they start to leave, and run into* DON ALFONSO)

Scene 3

Recitative

DON ALFONSO
Ah, correte al giardino, le mie care ragazze! che allegria! che musica! che canto! che brillante spettacolo! che incanto! Fate presto, correte!

DORABELLA
Che diamine esser può?

DON ALFONSO
Tosto vedrete.

DON ALFONSO
Ah, I'm glad that I found you! You must come into the garden! Such a frolic, with music and singing! You'll enjoy it enormously. Don't miss it! It is simply delightful!

DORABELLA
I can hardly wait to see!

DON ALFONSO
Then come with me!
(*they leave*)

Scene 4

(*A garden at the seashore, with grass seats and two little stone tables. A boat decorated with flowers, and a band of musicians. Servants in elaborate costumes.* DESPINA, FERRANDO, *and* GUGLIELMO *on-stage. Then* DON ALFONSO, FIORDILIGI *and* DORABELLA.)

Duet and Chorus

FERRANDO, GUGLIELMO
Friendly breezes, bear my message
To the one I love so dearly!
Ask her favor, beg her to hear me,
Lovely goddess that I adore!
Go and tell her, friendly breezes,
How my lonely heart is breaking,
Ever longing, ever aching!
Say I love her more and more!

FERRANDO, GUGLIELMO
Secondate, aurette amiche,
Secondate i miei desiri,
E portate i miei sospiri
Alla dea di questo cor.
Voi, che udiste mille volte
Il tenor delle mie pene;
Ripetete al caro bene,
tutto quel che udiste allor.

CHORUS
(*During this chorus,* FERRANDO *and* GUGLIELMO, *decked with chains of flowers, rise.* DON ALFONSO *and* DESPINA *lead them to the two women, who look at them astonished and speechless.*)
Friendly breezes, bear their message
To the dear ones they adore.

CORO
Secondate, aurette amiche,
il desir di sì bei cor.

Recitative

DON ALFONSO (*to the servants who are bringing vases with flowers*)
Just leave all the flowers over there on the tables, and then go back to your boat, my good friends.

DON ALFONSO
Il tutto deponete sopra quei tavolini, e nella barca ritiratevi, amici.

FIORDILIGI, DORABELLA
Why all the decorations?

FIORDILIGI, DORABELLA
Cos' è tal mascherata?

DESPINA (*to* GUGLIELMO *and* FERRANDO)
Here is your chance. Don't miss it! Can't you speak up—or has the cat got your tongue?

DESPINA
Animo, via, coraggio: avete perso l'uso della favella?

FERRANDO
I'm willing, but somehow I'm a victim of stage fright.

FERRANDO
Io tremo, e palpito dalla testa alle piante.

GUGLIELMO
It seems I have forgotten all my lines.

GUGLIELMO
Amor lega le membra a vero amante.

DON ALFONSO
Dear ladies, please encourage them.

DON ALFONSO
Da brave incorraggiteli.

FIORDILIGI (*to the lovers*)
We're list'ning!

FIORDILIGI
Parlate!

DORABELLA
Don't be afraid to say what's on your mind!

DORABELLA
Liberi dite pur quel che bramate!

FERRANDO
My lady . . .

FERRANDO
Madama . . .

GUGLIELMO
Say, "Fairest ladies . . ."

GUGLIELMO
Anzi madame . . .

FERRANDO
You make the speech.

FERRANDO
Parla pur tu.

GUGLIELMO
No, you, you're so much better!

GUGLIELMO
No, no, parla pur tu.

DON ALFONSO
Why, this is too ridiculous! The way you are behaving

DON ALFONSO
Oh! cospetto del diavolo! lasciate tali smorfie del

secolo passato: Despinetta, terminiam questa festa, fa tu con lei, quel ch'io farò con questa.
La mano a me date,
movetevi un pò!
Se voi non parlate,
per voi parlerò.
Perdono vi chiede
un schiavo tremante,
v'offese, lo vede,
ma solo un istante;
or pena, ma tace . . .

FERRANDO, GUGLIELMO
Tace . . .

DON ALFONSO
Or lasciavi in pace . . .

FERRANDO, GUGLIELMO
In pace . . .

DON ALFONSO
Non può quel che vuole,
vorrà, quel che può.

FERRANDO, GUGLIELMO
Non può quel che vuole,
vorrà quel che può.

DON ALFONSO
Su! via! rispondete!
guardate, e ridete?

DESPINA
Per voi la risposta
a loro darò, per
voi la risposta
a loro darò.
Quello ch'è stato, è stato,
scordiamci del passato.
Rompasi omai quel laccio,
segno di servitù;
A me porgete il braccio:
nè sospirate più.

DESPINA, DON ALFONSO
Per carità partiamo,
quel che san far veggiamo,
Per carità partiamo,
quel che san far veggiamo.
Le stimo più
del diavolo,
s'ora non cascan giù,
s'ora non cascan giù.

is hopelessly old-fashioned. Despinetta, if they can't talk themselves, I'll do it for them. You do it for the ladies.

Quartet

(*takes* DORABELLA *by the hand*)
Step forward a little and do as I do.
(DESPINA *takes* FIORDILIGI'S *hand*)
If you are too timid,
I will speak for you.
"If we have displeased you,
We truly lament it.
If we have disturbed you,
We deeply repent it.
Two slaves who adore you . . ."

FERRANDO, GUGLIELMO (*imitating* DON ALFONSO)
—dore you . . .

DON ALFONSO
"Have come to implore you . . ."

FERRANDO, GUGLIELMO
Implore you . . .

DON ALFONSO
"Whatever you ask us, we gladly will do."

FERRANDO, GUGLIELMO (*in one big breath*)
"Whatever you ask us, we gladly will do."

DON ALFONSO
And now you must answer, my ladies!
You are silent? You are laughing?

DESPINA (*stands in front of the two women*)
Since they are so bashful,
So modest and shy,
I'll venture to give you my ladies' reply.
"Let us forget what happened
And think about the future.
(DESPINA *takes* DORABELLA'S *hand,* DON ALFONSO FIORDILIGI'S; *the two ladies break the flower chains around the two lovers*)
All former ties are broken.
Now we shall be good friends.
Let's join our hands in token
That all your suff'ring ends."

DESPINA, DON ALFONSO (*aside*)
And now that we have spoken,
Let's watch it from a distance.
I think the ice is broken.
They need no more assistance.
I'm absolutely positive
The battle has been won,
Completely won!
The comedy is on!

(*Exit* DESPINA *and* DON ALFONSO. GUGLIELMO *arm in arm with* DORABELLA. FERRANDO *and* FIORDILIGI *more distant to each other. A short pantomime scene, in which the four look at each other, sigh, giggle in embarrassment*)

Scene 5

Recitative

FIORDILIGI
What a beautiful morning!

FIORDILIGI
Oh che bella giornata!

FERRANDO
I think it's a trifle too warm.

FERRANDO
Caldetta anzi che no.

DORABELLA
Oh, what beautiful flowers!

DORABELLA
Che vezzosi arboscelli!

GUGLIELMO
That's what I say. However they could smell a little stronger.

GUGLIELMO
Certo, certo: son belli: han più foglie che frutti.

FIORDILIGI
In the garden there are nice shady alleys. Do you wish to promenade?

FIORDILIGI
Quei viali come sono leggiadri; volete passeggiar?

FERRANDO
With greatest pleasure! It's good for your health.

FERRANDO
Son pronto, o cara, ad ogni vostro cenno.

FIORDILIGI
I agree with you.

FIORDILIGI
Troppa grazia!

FERRANDO (*passing by* GUGLIELMO)
(Now we are at the crossroads.)

FERRANDO
(Eccoci alla gran crisi.)

FIORDILIGI
What was it that you told him?

FIORDILIGI
Cosa gli avete detto?

FERRANDO
Oh, I only was saying there's moss on the road.

FERRANDO
Eh gli raccomandai di divertirla bene.

DORABELLA
Shall we, too, take a walk?

DORABELLA
Passeggiamo anche noi.

GUGLIELMO
I am all for it!
(*they walk*)
Good Lord!

GUGLIELMO
Come vi piace.
Ahimè!

DORABELLA
Is something wrong?

DORABELLA
Che cosa avete?

GUGLIELMO
All at once I feel dreadful—perhaps it's some kind of fever—I may even be dying.

GUGLIELMO
Io mi sento sì male, sì male, anima mia, che mi par di morire.

DORABELLA
(I don't believe a word of it.) You still are feeling effects from the poison you've taken.

DORABELLA
(Non otterà nientissimo.) Saranno rimasagli del velen che beveste.

GUGLIELMO
There is a far more deadly poison, a far more fatal danger, in the flame of your two glorious eyes.
(FIORDILIGI *strolls off with* FERRANDO)

GUGLIELMO
Ah che un veleno assai più forte io bevo in que' crudi e focosi mongibelli amorosi!

DORABELLA
Sarà veleno calido; fatevi un poco fresco.

GUGLIELMO
Ingrata, voi burlate, ed intanto io mi moro! (Son spariti: dove diamin son iti?)

DORABELLA
Eh voi non fate.

GUGLIELMO
Io mi moro, crudele, e voi burlate?

DORABELLA
Io burlo? io burlo?

GUGLIELMO
Dunque datemi qualche segno, anima bella, della vostra pietà.

DORABELLA
Due, se volete; dite quel che far deggio, e lo vedrete.

GUGLIELMO
(Scherza, o dice davvero?) Questa picciola offerta d'accettare degnatevi.

DORABELLA
Un core?

GUGLIELMO
Un core: è simbolo di quello ch'arde, languisce e spasima per voi.

DORABELLA
(Che dono prezioso!)

GUGLIELMO
L'accettate?

DORABELLA
Crudele, di sedur non tentate un cor fedele.

GUGLIELMO
(La montagna vacilla: mi spiace ma impegnato è l'onor di soldato.) V'adoro!

DORABELLA
Per pietà!

GUGLIELMO
Son tutto vostro!

DORABELLA
Oh Dei!

GUGLIELMO
Cedete, o cara!

DORABELLA
Mi farete morir.

GUGLIELMO
Morremo insieme, amorosa mia speme. L'accettate?

DORABELLA
L'accetto.

DORABELLA
A flattering comparison! You ought to write a poem!

GUGLIELMO
You really should not tease me, when you know how I'm suff'ring. (I can't see them. Are they hiding on purpose?)

DORABELLA
Don't be so silly!

GUGLIELMO
You are heartless and cruel to go on joking!

DORABELLA
I'm joking? You think so?

GUGLIELMO
Won't you show me a sign of pity, fairest of ladies, to uphold my morale?

DORABELLA
Only too gladly. Merely say what you wish and you shall have it!

GUGLIELMO
(She's fooling, or could she have meant it?) Will you do me one favor? Let me give you this locket.

DORABELLA
A heart?

GUGLIELMO
Yes, darling! A most appropriate symbol to reassure you of my everlasting love.

DORABELLA
(Oh dear, it is charming!)

GUGLIELMO
You accept it?

DORABELLA
I'd like to, but my heart is not free, as you well know.

GUGLIELMO
(The iceberg is melting. I'm sorry, but my soldierly word can't be broken.) I love you!

DORABELLA
Please don't!

GUGLIELMO
I love you madly!

DORABELLA
Don't say it!

GUGLIELMO
Do not reject me!

DORABELLA
I insist that you go!

GUGLIELMO
If you reject me I'm determined to perish! You'll accept it?

DORABELLA (*after a short hesitation, with a sigh*)
I will then!

GUGLIELMO
(What a blow for Ferrando!) I am delirious!
Duet
This heart is for you, dear,
My only beloved!
Give me yours to treasure
As long as I live!

DORABELLA
I take it with pleasure,
But one thing I'll tell you:
The heart that you ask for
Is not here to give.

GUGLIELMO
Whose heart do I hear then,
If your heart is gone?

DORABELLA
Whose heart is so near then,
If I have your own?

GUGLIELMO
What is beating, beating loud and clear?

DORABELLA
What is throbbing, throbbing in my ear?

BOTH
What is beating, beating loud and clear?
It must be my own heart,
My loving and lone heart,
A heart which is yours now
For ever and ever!
A heart true as gold,
To have and to hold!

GUGLIELMO (*wants to put the heart where she keeps the portrait of her lover*)
And now you must wear it!

DORABELLA
I really don't dare.

GUGLIELMO
You rascal, I know you!
Just wait till I show you!

DORABELLA
What is it?

GUGLIELMO (*he gently turns her face the other way, then takes away the portrait and puts the heart in its place*)
Don't look yet.

DORABELLA (*to herself*)
I feel so excited,
Aglow and on fire,
So strangely delighted
And filled with desire.

GUGLIELMO (*to himself*)
(Ferrando, poor fellow!
His future looks dire.)

GUGLIELMO
(Infelice Ferrando!) Oh che diletto!
Il core vi dono,
bell' idolo mio;
ma il vostro vo' anch'io,
via datelo a me.

DORABELLA
Mel date, lo prendo,
ma il mio non vi rendo,
invan mel' chiedete,
più meco ei non è.

GUGLIELMO
Se teco non l'hai,
perchè batte quì?

DORABELLA
Se a me tu lo dai,
che mai balza lì?

GUGLIELMO
Perchè batte, batte, batte quì?

DORABELLA
Che mai balza, balza, balza lì?

DORABELLA, GUGLIELMO
Perchè batte, batte, batte quì?
È il mio coricino,
che più non è meco,
ei venne a star teco,
ei batte così.

GUGLIELMO
Quì lascia che il metta.

DORABELLA
Ei quì non può star.

GUGLIELMO
T'intendo furbetta,
t'intendo furbetta.

DORABELLA
Che fai?

GUGLIELMO
Non guardar.

DORABELLA
Nel petto un Vesuvio d'avere mi par,
nel petto un Vesuvio d'avere mi par.

GUGLIELMO
(Ferrando meschino!
possibil non par.)
L'occhietto a me gira.

(*aloud*)
And now you may see it.

DORABELLA
Che brami?

DORABELLA
Oh, may I?

GUGLIELMO
Rimira, rimira,
se meglio può andar.

GUGLIELMO
Look here, dear,
Now what do you say?

DORABELLA, GUGLIELMO
Oh cambio felice,
di cori e d'affetti!
che nuovi diletti,
che dolce penar!
Oh cambio felice,
di cori e d'affetti!
che nuovi diletti,
che dolce penar!

BOTH
How joyful a union
Of hearts and affection,
The noblest perfection
That love can attain!
How joyful a union
Of thought and of feeling,
So sweetly revealing
The wonder of love!
(*they leave, arm in arm*)

Scene 6

(*enter* FERRANDO *and* FIORDILIGI)
Recitative

FERRANDO
Barbara! perchè fuggi?

FERRANDO
You torture me! Why do you leave me?

FIORDILIGI
Ho visto un aspide, un' idra, un basilisco!

FIORDILIGI
I've seen monstrosities, a hydra, a writhing serpent!

FERRANDO
Ah! crudel, ti capisco! L'aspide, l'idra, il basilisco, e quanto i Libici deserti han di più fiero, in me solo tu vedi.

FERRANDO
Now I grasp the allusion! All of them, the hydra, the writhing serpent, and all the horrifying monsters you could imagine you have seen in my person.

FIORDILIGI
È vero, è vero. Tu vuoi tormi la pace.

FIORDILIGI
It's true, I admit it. You have caused me such anguish.

FERRANDO
Ma per farti felice.

FERRANDO
For your happiness only.

FIORDILIGI
Cessa di molestarmi!

FIORDILIGI
If you would only leave me!

FERRANDO
No ti chiedo ch'un guardo.

FERRANDO
All I ask is one glance.

FIORDILIGI
Partiti!

FIORDILIGI
Never!

FERRANDO
Non sperarlo, se pria gli occhi men fieri a me non giri. O ciel! ma tu mi guardi e poi sospiri?

FERRANDO
You dismiss me, abandon me to grief and desperation! Dear God! Is there no hope, no consolation?

Aria

(*happily*)

Ah! lo veggio quell' anima bella
al mio pianto resister non sà:

Though you try to be deaf to my pleading,
I am sure you will yield in the end.

You're not meant to be cold and unheeding
To the love of so faithful a friend.
All your glances, so demure and appealing,
Make my heart glow with soft, radiant light.
You will yield to the force of my feeling,
To its boundless endurance and might.
You'll surrender to its endless delight!
But you spurn me, disdainful, uncaring,
Coldly leave me to languish and sigh!
Ah, I'm hopeless, abandoned, despairing,
For you cruelly condemn me to die!
(*exit*)

non è fatta per esser rubella
agli affetti di amica pietà.
In quel guardo, in quei cari sospiri,
dolce raggio lampeggia al mio cor:
già rispondi a miei caldi desiri,
già tu cedi al più tenero amor.
Ma tu fuggi,
spietata tu taci,
ed invano mi senti languir?
Ah, cessate speranze fallaci,
la crudel mi condanna a morir.

Scene 7

Recitative

FIORDILIGI

I hurt him! . . . Should I . . . ? Ah, no! It's better this way. At least I will not see him, the wretched person who has caused me to weaken. What grievous anguish the cruel man has brought me! But I deserve it for my shameless behavior! At such a moment how could I ever listen to a new lover's plea? Should I have treated his proposal more lightly? Yes, I am guilty. I am punished quite justly. O dear Guglielmo! This stranger, he has aroused my heart to passion, not to love, true and perfect. This passion is restless, disturbing, and deceitful, superficial! It's wicked, faithless betrayal!

FIORDILIGI

Ei parte . . . senti . . . Ah no! partir si lasci, si tolga ai sguardi miei l'infausto oggetto della mia debolezza. A qual cimento il barbaro mi pose! un premio è questo ben dovuto a mie colpe! In tale istante dovea di nuovo amante, i sospiri ascoltar? l'altrui querele dovea volger in gioco? Ah, questo core a ragione condanni, o giusto amore! Io ardo e l'ardor mio non è più effetto d' un amor virtuoso: è smania, affano, rimorso, pentimento, leggerezza, perfidia, è tradimento!

Rondo

Dearest love, I beg your pardon
For the faith that I have broken.
May my error remain unspoken,
Stay forgotten, unknown and past.
May my honest, true devotion,
Glowing love, and deep repentance
Purge my heart of all remembrance,
Make me worthy of you at last.
Dearest love, I beg your pardon
For the faith that I have broken.
Why did I embrace temptation;
Break the tender vows I swore,
When it was my aspiration
To be faithful evermore?
Dearest love, I beg your pardon
For the faith that I have broken.
Heaven grant me one kind favor,

Per pietà, ben mio, perdona
all' error d'un alma amante
fra quest' ombre, e queste piante
sempre ascoso, oh Dio, sarà!
Svenerà quest' empia voglia
l'ardir mio la mia costanza,
perderà la rimembranza,
che vergogna e orror mi fa.
Per pietà, ben mio, perdona
all' error d'un alma amante.
A chi mai mancò di fede
questo vano ingrato cor?
si dovea miglior mercede,
caro bene, al tuo candor.
Per pietà, ben mio perdona
all' error d'un alma amante.
A chi mai mancò di fede
questo vano ingrato cor?
si dovea miglior mercede,
caro bene, al tuo candor.

Let my secret remain unknown.
With unfailing endeavor
For my fault I shall atone.
(*exit*)

Scene 8

(*enter* FERRANDO *and* GUGLIELMO)

Recitative

FERRANDO
Amico, abbiamo vinto!

GUGLIELMO
Un ambo, o un terno?

FERRANDO
Una cinquina, amico; Fiordiligi è la modestia in carne.

GUGLIELMO
Niente meno?

FERRANDO
Nientissimo; sta attento e ascolta come fù.

GUGLIELMO
T'ascolto; di pur sù.

FERRANDO
Pel giardinetto come eravam d'accordo, a passeggiar mi metto; le do il braccio; si parla di mille cose indifferenti; alfine viensi all'amor.

GUGLIELMO
Avanti.

FERRANDO
Fingo labbra tremanti, fingo di pianger, fingo di morir al suo piè.

GUGLIELMO
Brava assai per mia fè! Ed ella?

FERRANDO
Ella da prima ride, scherza, mi burla—

GUGLIELMO
E poi?

FERRANDO
E poi finge d'impietosirsi—

GUGLIELMO
Oh cospettaccio!

FERRANDO
Alfin scoppia la bomba: "pura come colomba al suo caro Guglielmo ella si serba" mi dissaccia superba, mi maltratta, mi fugge, testimonio rendendomi e messaggio, che una femmina ell' è senza paraggio.

FERRANDO (*deliriously happy*)
Guglielmo, it can't go better!

GUGLIELMO
I knew it, I knew it!

FERRANDO
Yes, you have your wager. Fiordiligi is the rock of Gibraltar!

GUGLIELMO
Nothing less?

FERRANDO
No, nothing! Now listen: I'll tell you how it went.

GUGLIELMO
I'm listening. Go ahead.

FERRANDO
As we agreed, both of us went strolling together in the garden, arm in arm, just chatting. At first we talked about the weather and then we talked about love.

GUGLIELMO
Go on, friend.

FERRANDO
I said all I could think of, swore that I loved her, threatened to die at her feet.

GUGLIELMO
My dear boy, you did well! And she?

FERRANDO
At the beginning she was laughing and joking.

GUGLIELMO
And then?

FERRANDO
For a moment I thought she wavered.

GUGLIELMO
That little vixen!

FERRANDO
But then, bang! went the bombshell. "Dare you question my virtue? I will always be faithful to my Guglielmo." She began to abuse me, called me names, and left me. So you see from her attitude there's no doubt. Fiordiligi is one woman in a million.

GUGLIELMO

Good for you, good for me, good for my faithful sweetheart! You're a friend in a million, bringer of happy tidings. I'm deliriously happy!
(*they embrace*)

FERRANDO

And my dear Dorabella? How did you fare with her? Why do I even ask you! (*enthusiastically*) I know your answer! How could I even doubt it?

GUGLIELMO

A little doubting, my dear undoubting Thomas, might be advisable at times.

FERRANDO

How so?

GUGLIELMO

Oh, it was just a thought. (I wish I knew how to sweeten his cup of bitterness!)

FERRANDO

Braggart! Are you implying she yielded to your advances? No, it can't be! I will never suspect her!

GUGLIELMO

You would be wiser to leave a little room for some suspicion.

FERRANDO

What do you mean? Speak up! If you must poison me, must it be drop by drop? But no! It can't be! Tell me that you are joking! I am her love and she loves only me.

GUGLIELMO

Surely! And to prove the fact beyond any question, she gave me this delightful little portrait.

FERRANDO (*raging*)

Gave you my portrait! Ah, shame on her!
(*starts to leave*)

GUGLIELMO

Are you raving?

FERRANDO (*furiously*)

No, I am not, but she will pay me dearly for her misdeed. How could she dare betray me?

GUGLIELMO

Calm yourself!

FERRANDO (*determined*)

No, I cannot!

GUGLIELMO

This is madness! Why do you want to wreck yourself for a woman so completely worthless? (If I could just prevent him from doing something foolish.)

FERRANDO

Think of it! Her deep devotion, her promises, her affec-

GUGLIELMO

Bravo tu! bravo io! brava la mia Penelope! lascia un po ch'io ti abbracci per sì felice augurio, o mio fido Mercurio!

FERRANDO

E la mia Dorabella? come s'è diportata? Oh non ci ho neppur dubbio! assai conosco quella sensibil alma.

GUGLIELMO

Eppur un dubbio, parlando di quattr' occhi, non saria mal, se tu l'avessi!

FERRANDO

Come?

GUGLIELMO

Dico così per dir! (avre piacere d'indorargli la pillola.)

FERRANDO

Stelle! cesse ella forse alle lusinghe tue? ah, s'io potessi sospettarlo soltanto!

GUGLIELMO

E sempre bene il sospettare un poco in questo mondo.

FERRANDO

Eterni Dei! favella: a foco lento non mi far quì morir; ma no, tu vuoi prenderti meco spasso: ella non ama, non adora che me.

GUGLIELMO

Certo! anzi in prova di suo amor, di sua fede questo bel ritrattino ella mi diede.

FERRANDO

Il mio ritrato! Ah perfida!

GUGLIELMO

Ove vai!

FERRANDO

A trarle il cor dal scellerato petto, e a vendicar, il mio tradito affetto.

GUGLIELMO

Fermati!

FERRANDO

No, mi lascia!

GUGLIELMO

Sei tu pazzo? vuoi tu precipitarti per una donna, che non val due soldi? (Non vorrei, che facesse qualche corbelleria!)

FERRANDO

Numi! tante promesse e lagrime, e sospiri, e giuramenti

in sì pochi momenti come l'empia obliò!

GUGLIELMO
Per Bacco io non lo so!

FERRANDO
Che fare or deggio! a qual partito, a qual idea m'appiglio? Abbi di me pietà, dammi consiglio!

GUGLIELMO
Amico, non saprei qual consiglia a te dar!

FERRANDO
Barbara! ingrata! in un giorno! in poch'ore!

GUGLIELMO
Certo un caso quest'è da far stupore.

Donne mie, la fate a tanti! a
tanti, a tanti, a tanti, a tanti!
che se il ver vi deggio dir,
se si lagnano gli amanti,
li commincio a compatir.
Io vo bene al sesso vostro,
lo sapete, ognun lo sà,
ogni giorno ve lo mostro,
ve lo mostro, ve lo mostro,
vi do segno d'amistà.
ve lo mostro, ve lo mostro
vi do segno d'amistà,
vi do segno d'amistà.
Ma quel farla a tanti e tanti, a
tanti e tanti,
m'avvilisce in verità.
Mille volte il brando presi,
per salvar il vostro onor,
mille volte, mille volte,
mille volte vi difesi
colla bocca, e più col cor.
Ma quel farla a tanti e tanti, a
tanti e tanti,
è un vizietto seccator.
Siete vaghe, siete amabili,
più tesori il ciel vi diè;
e le grazie vi circondano,
dalla testa sino ai piè.
Ma, ma, ma la fate a tanti e
tanti, a
tanti e tanti,
che credibile non è.
Io vo bene al sesso vostro
ve lo mostro, mille volte il
brando presi,
vi difesi, gran tesori il ciel vi
diè.
Ma, ma, ma la fate a tanti e
tanti,
a tanti e tanti, a tanti,
la fate a tanti e tanti, a tanti e
tanti,
che se gridano gli amanti,
hanno certo un gran perchè.

tion and protestations—all forgotten entirely in the wink of an eye!

GUGLIELMO
That seems to be the case.

FERRANDO
My life is ruined! What shall I do now? What use is there in living? I'm in a dreadful state! Help me, I beg you!

GUGLIELMO
I wish I could advise you, but I really don't know.

FERRANDO
Horrible! My future! All in shambles! Torn asunder!

GUGLIELMO
This is really a case that makes you wonder!

Aria

I would like a word with all you lovely,
Lovely, lovely women.
I have something on my mind.
It's a basic human problem
And it touches all mankind.
Like my fellow men and brothers,
I have worshiped before your shrine.
Like a million others,
I believed you were divine.
I've respected
And protected
Your good name in ev'ry way,
Yes, in each and ev'ry way.
But, you thankless, lovely, lovely, lovely women
Fill my soul with deep dismay.
With my sword I saved your virtue,
I have fought a fearless fight.
I've discovered
And uncovered
Ev'ry plot designed to hurt you.
I have been your peerless knight.
But, you wicked, lovely, lovely, lovely women
Put my chivalry to flight.
You're delightful, you're adorable,
You are precious, you are sweet,
You are gracious, fair, and lovable,
And we men are at your feet.
But, but, but,
You thankless, lovely, lovely, lovely women
Shock my heart with your deceit.
In the most poetic phrases
I have sung your sex's praises,
I have lauded
And applauded
And extolled you to the sky.

But, but, but, you wicked, lovely women,
When I see how you mistreat us
I begin to wonder why.
(*exit*)

Scene 9

Recitative

FERRANDO

I can scarcely imagine that I myself have become the prey of a woman's ruthless deception! I'm so stunned by misfortune, so disillusioned, I feel helpless, defeated, totally dazed and hopeless! Alfonso, Alfonso! You were right after all! Now you will be triumphant! But I shall be avenged! I'll tear her image from my heart and my mem'ry, and shall not regret her! Not regret her? No, dear God, I cannot! I can't forget her!

FERRANDO

In qual fiero contrasto, in qual disordine di pensieri e di affetti io mi ritrovo? Tanto insolito e novo è il caso mio, che non altri, non io basto per consigliarmi . . . Alfonso! Alfonso! quanto rider vorrai della mia stupidezza! Ma, mi vendicherò! saprò dal seno cancellar quell' iniqua . . . saprò cancellarla—cancellarla? troppo, oh Dio! questo cor per lei mi parla.

Cavatina

Defeated, mistreated,
Despairing, forlorn!
I'll never forget her,
I'll always adore her
And ever regret her,
The love that I mourn.
Rejected, neglected,
My heart grieved and sore!
(DON ALFONSO *enters with* GUGLIELMO. *They stay in the background, listening to* FERRANDO)
I still love her dearly,
Forever sincerely.
My love is as great
And as strong as before.
(DON ALFONSO *and* GUGLIELMO *step forward*)

Tradito, schernito dal perfido cor,
io sento, che ancora
quest' alma l'adora,
io sento per essa le voci d'amor.
Tradito, schernito dal perfido cor,
io sento, che ancora
quest' alma l'adora,
io sento per essa le voci d'amor.

Recitative

DON ALFONSO

Bravo. That's how it should be.

FERRANDO

Stay away from me! You have caused all my misery!

DON ALFONSO

Learn how to bear it calmly, and you will be so much the wiser. The fact is, Fiordiligi was faithful, at least up to now, but Dorabella was too weak to resist.

FERRANDO

Yes, to my shame.

GUGLIELMO

Dear Ferrando, you must be able to see a thing in its true aspect. Where would you find a woman who would

DON ALFONSO

Bravo! questa è costanza.

FERRANDO

Andate, o barbaro, per voi misero sono.

DON ALFONSO

Via se sarete buono vi tornerò l'antica calma. Udite: Fiordiligi a Guglielmo si conserva fedel, e Dorabella infedel a voi fù.

FERRANDO

Per mia vergogna.

GUGLIELMO

Caro amico, bisogna far delle differenze in ogni cosa. Ti pare che una sposa mancar possa a un Guglielmo? un picciol calcolo, non parlo per lodarmi; se facciamo tra noi . . . tu vedi, amico, che un poco di più merto.

fail a Guglielmo? If you compare us—I say it in all modesty—you will have to admit, if you are honest, I have a slight advantage.

DON ALFONSO
Eh anch'io lo dico!

DON ALFONSO
He's got a point there.

GUGLIELMO
Intanto mi darete cinquanta zecchinetti.

GUGLIELMO
And now, suppose you pay me half of the wager.

DON ALFONSO
Voluntieri: pria però di pagar vo che facciamo qualche altra esperienza.

DON ALFONSO
I'll be glad to, but before I shall do it, permit me to try one more test.

GUGLIELMO
Come?

GUGLIELMO
You mean?

DON ALFONSO
Abbiate pazienza: Infin domani siete entrambi miei schiavi: a me voi deste parola da soldati, di far quel, ch'io dirò. Venite; io spero mostrari ben che folle è quel cervello, che sulla frasca ancor vende l'uccello.

DON ALFONSO
I'm not yet defeated. Until tomorrow you are bound to our wager, and just remember, you gave your word of honor to obey my command. Till then, I will not give up the ship, and I am still competing, for the proof of the pudding is in the eating!

Scene 10

(*A room with several doors, a mirror, and a little table.* DORABELLA *and* DESPINA *on-stage*)

Recitative

DESPINA
Ora vedo che siete una donna di garbo.

DESPINA
Now at last you are acting like a woman of the world.

DORABELLA
Invan, Despina, di resister tentai: quel demonietto ha un artifizio, un eloquenza, un tratto, che ti fà cader giù se sei di sasso.

DORABELLA
I was not able to resist the temptation. That charming devil is so persuasive, he is so clever, so gentle, he would even succeed in melting millstones.

DESPINA
Corpo di satanasso, questo vuol dir saper! tanto di raro noi povere ragazze abbiamo un po di bene, che bisogna pigliarlo allor ch'ei viene. Ma ecco la sorella, che ceffo!

DESPINA
Now you are talking logic and really showing sense! Only too seldom are we poor girls permitted to snatch a bit of pleasure, so it is up to us to make hay while the sun shines! Who's coming? It's your sister! She's raving!

FIORDILIGI
Sciagurate! ecco per colpa vostra in che stato mi trovo!

FIORDILIGI (*entering*)
How disgraceful! It's on account of you that I am in this dilemma.

DESPINA
Cosa è nato, cara Madamigella?

DESPINA
What has happened? Why are you so excited?

DORABELLA
Hai qualche mal, sorella?

DORABELLA
Is something wrong, dear sister?

FIORDILIGI
Ho il diavolo, che porti me, te, lei, Don Alfonso, i forestieri e quanti pazzi ha il mondo.

FIORDILIGI
I hope the devil takes you all, you, and her, Don Alfonso, those two intruders! And all the fools in this world!

DORABELLA
Hai perduto il giudizio?

DORABELLA
Are you out of your mind?

FIORDILIGI
Worse than that! Dare I admit it? I love him! And worst of all is, I do not mean Guglielmo!

DESPINA
Sounds exciting!

DORABELLA
Do you mean that you've also started yielding, and you love your new suitor?

FIORDILIGI (*sighing*)
Ah, yes, only too much!

DESPINA
Delightful!

DORABELLA
Sister, I simply have to kiss you. Then we both will be married! What could be more romantic!

FIORDILIGI
But how can we? Just think of our poor soldiers who have gone to the wars! Have you no feeling for those two faithful men, the grief we'd cause them? How could we deceive them? What has come over you, that you want to commit such a betrayal?

DORABELLA
Wait a bit! How do we know that the worst might not happen? Suppose they fell in battle? In that case, what would become of us? Wouldn't we be the losers? You know the saying: A bird in the hand is worth two in the bush!

FIORDILIGI
But if they should return?

DORABELLA
In that event, it's their loss! By that time we'll be married, and what's more, we'll be living abroad.

FIORDILIGI
I am still at a loss to understand this sudden change of heart.

DORABELLA
That is downright ridiculous! We're women! After all, what did you do?

FIORDILIGI
But I'm not surrendering!

DESPINA
There you are quite mistaken!

FIORDILIGI
I won't! I'll never do it!

DORABELLA
Come, dearest sister, you must, or you will rue it.

Aria

DORABELLA
I know a naughty fellow,
A wily thief called Love.

FIORDILIGI
Peggio, peggio, inorridisci: io amo! e l'amor mio non è sol per Guglielmo.

DESPINA
Meglio, meglio!

DORABELLA
E che si, che anche tu se' innamorata del galante biondino?

FIORDILIGI
Ah, pur troppo per noi.

DESPINA
Ma brava!

DORABELLA
Tieni, settanta mille baci: tu il biondino, io'l brunetto, eccoci entrambe spose!

FIORDILIGI
Cosa dici? non pensi agli infelici, che stamane partir? ai loro pianti, alla lor fedeltà tu più non pensi? Così barbari sensi, dove, dove apprendesti? sì diversa da te come ti festi?

DORABELLA
Odimi: sei tu certa, che non muojano in guerra i nostri vecchi amanti? e allora? entrambe resterem colle man piene di mosche: tra un bon certo e un incerto c'è sempre un gran divario.

FIORDILIGI
E se poi torneranno?

DORABELLA
Se torneran lor danno! noi saremo allor mogli, noi saremo lontane mille miglia.

FIORDILIGI
Ma non so, come mai si può cangiar in un sol giorno un core.

DORABELLA
Che domanda ridicola! siam donne! e poi tu com' hai fatto!

FIORDILIGI
Io saprò vincermi.

DESPINA
Voi non saprete nulla.

FIORDILIGI
Farò, che tu lo veda.

DORABELLA
Credi sorella, è meglio che tu ceda.

DORABELLA
È amore un ladroncello,
un serpentello è amor,
ei toglie e dà la pace,

come gli piace ai cor.
Per gli occhi al seno appena,
un varco aprir si fa,
che l'anima in catena,
e toglie libertà.
È amore un ladroncello,
un serpentello è amor,
ei toglie e dà la pace,
come gli piace ai cor.
Porta dolcezza,
dolcezza e gusto,
se tu lo lasci far,
ma t'empie di disgusto,
se tenti di pugnar.
È amore un ladroncello,
un serpentello è amor,
ei toglie e dà la pace,
come gli piace ai cor.
Se nel tuo petto ei siede,
s'egli ti becca quì,
fa tutto quel ch'ei chiede,
che anch'io farò così.
Se nel tuo petto ei siede,
s'egli ti becca quì
fa tutto quel ch'ei chiede,
che anch'io farò così.
Fa tutto quel ch'ei chiede,
ch'ei chiede
che anch'io farò così,
così,
che anch'io farò così.

He slyly steals your calmness,
Sweet as a turtledove.
The moment he has found you,
He wounds you with his dart—
He ties his chains around you
And rules your helpless heart.
I know a naughty fellow,
A wily rogue called Love,
He slyly steals your calmness,
Sweet as a turtledove.
He can be charming, divine, delightful,
If he's allowed his way,
But also cruel and spiteful,
Malevolent and spiteful,
If you should disobey.
I know a naughty fellow,
A wily thief called Love.
He slyly steals your calmness,
Sweet as a turtledove.
Each time his fire brands you,
Raging inside your breast,
Do all that he commands you
And better not protest.
If he should come and seize you,
Pulling your heartstrings tight,
Just let the rascal tease you
And do not try to fight.
Just let him seize you,
And tickle and tease you!
Just let the rascal seize you and tease you,
As I intend to do,
I too,
As I intend to do.

(DESPINA *leaves with* DORABELLA)

Scene 11

Recitative

FIORDILIGI

Come tutto conguira a sedurre il mio cor! ma no! si mora, e non si ceda! errai quando alla suora io mi scopersi ed alla serva mia. Esse a lui diran tutto, ed ei più audace, fia di tutto capace, agli occhi miei mai più non comparisca! a tutti i servi minacierò il congedo, se lo lascian passar, veder nol voglio quel sedut-tor.

FIORDILIGI

How they're plotting together to make me break my word! But no! I will not! I'd rather die. I never should have talked to Dorabella, or even to Despina. They might tell him my secret, and thus encouraged, I could never control him. I must avoid him, not even let him see me. I will give orders that any of my servants will be dismissed on the spot if they should dare to let him come near me.

GUGLIELMO (*listening at the door, unseen by* FIORDILIGI)
(By Jupiter! What a model of virtue! Let's hear more!)

FIORDILIGI
I'm afraid Dorabella cannot be persuaded. Wait! An idea! Now I know what to do! By some good fortune Guglielmo and Ferrando left some uniforms behind. That's lucky! Despina, Despina!

DESPINA (*enters*)
My lady called?

FIORDILIGI
Go up to the attic, and without questioning and without contradiction, open your masters' trunks and bring me two helmets, two sabers, and two complete uniforms they left there.

DESPINA
What for, if I may ask you?

FIORDILIGI
Go, do as I told you!

DESPINA
(What a high and mighty tone! It is disgusting.)
(*leaves*)

FIORDILIGI
I am determined. Now my problem is getting Dorabella to consent to go with me. The sooner, the better. It's the only solution to preserve our integrity.

DON ALFONSO (*at the door to* DESPINA, *who returns*)
(I see what she's up to. Better do what she says.)

DESPINA
There you are.

FIORDILIGI
Thank you. Now order us horses and a man we can trust. Tell Dorabella that I want her at once.

DESPINA
I'm at your service. (This to-do and commotion is beyond me!)
(*exit*)

FIORDILIGI
This uniform of Ferrando's should be just about my size, and Dorabella can wear one of Guglielmo's. Disguised as soldiers, we two can go and find our sweethearts. If it must be, we shall fight beside them. Even death shall not part us!
(*throws off her headdress*)
Off with this headgear, this insane decoration! Oh, how I hate it!

GUGLIELMO (*to himself*)
Her devotion and courage are astounding!

GUGLIELMO
Bravissima! la mia casta Artemisia! la sentite?

FIORDILIGI
Ma potria Dorabella senza saputa mia—piano! un pensiero per la mente mi passa: in casa mia restar molte uniformi di Guglielmo e di Ferrando, ardir! Despina! Despina!

DESPINA
Cosa c'è!

FIORDILIGI
Tieni un po questa chiave, e senza replica, senza replica alcuna, prendi nel guardaroba, e quì mi porta due spade, due cappelli, e due vestiti de' nostri sposi.

DESPINA
E che volete fare?

FIORDILIGI
Vanne, non replicare.

DESPINA
(Comanda in abregè donna Arroganza.)

FIORDILIGI
Non c'è altro; ho speranza che Dorabella stessa seguirà il bell' esempio: al campo, al campo, altra strada non resta per serbaci innocenti.

DON ALFONSO
(Ho capito abbastanza: vanne pur non temer.)

DESPINA
Eccomi.

FIORDILIGI
Vanne: sei cavalli di posta, voli un servo ordinar, di a Dorabella che parlarle vorrei.

DESPINA
Sarà servita. (Questa donna mi par di senno uscita.)

FIORDILIGI
L'abito di Ferrando sarà buono per me; può Dorabella prender quel di Guglielmo; in questi arnesi raggiungerem gli sposi nostri, a loro fianco pugnar potremo e morir se fa d'uopo: ite in malora, ornamenti fatali, io vi detesto.

GUGLIELMO
Si può dar un amor simile a questo?

FIORDILIGI
Di tornar non sperate alla mia fronte pria ch'io qui torni col mio ben; in vostro loco porrò questo cappello; oh come ei mi trasforma le sembianze e il viso! come appena io medesma or mi ravviso!

Fra gli amplessi, in pochi istanti,
Giungerò del fido sposo,
Sconosciuta a lui davanti
In quest' abito verrò.
Oh che gioja il suo bel core
Proverà nel ravvisarmi!

FERRANDO
Ed intanto di dolore
meschinello, io mi morrò!

FIORDILIGI
Cosa veggio!
son tradita!
Deh, partite!

FERRANDO
Ah no, mia vita:
con quel ferro di tua mano
questo cor tu ferirai,
e se forza oh Dio non hai,
io la man ti reggerò.

FIORDILIGI
Taci, ahimè! son abbastanza
tormentata ed infelice!

FERRANDO
Ah che omai la sua costanza,

FIORDILIGI
Ah, che omai la mia costanza,

FIORDILIGI, FERRANDO
A quei sguardi, a quel che dice,
Incomincia a vacillar.

FIORDILIGI
Sorgi, sorgi—

FERRANDO
Invan lo credi.

FIORDILIGI
Per pietà, da me che chiedi?

FERRANDO
Il tuo cor, o la mia morte.

FIORDILIGI
Ah non son, non son più forte!
Ah non son, non son più forte?

FIORDILIGI
Not until I return with my beloved shall it adorn my head again! And, in its stead, this helmet will disguise me! Now off to war and adventure! I'll be lucky, I'm certain! Not a soul will suspect that I'm a woman!

Duet

By tomorrow we'll be united!
I will join you, dear Guglielmo!
Unexpected, your Fiordiligi
Will appear in her disguise.
What a wonderful surprise!
You'll be joyful and so delighted
When you see your faithful sweetheart!

FERRANDO (*stepping forward*)
And I'll die here, unrequited,
Right before your very eyes!

FIORDILIGI
Why are you here? Oh, how dreadful!
Spare my feelings!

FERRANDO
Before you leave me,
(*takes his sword from the table, and draws it from its sheath*)
Take this sword and plunge it through me,
Through this loving heart you wounded!
Take this sword and pierce my heart!

FIORDILIGI
Never! Please go! I have endured too much unhappiness already!

FERRANDO
Her resistance starts to weaken.

FIORDILIGI
My resistance starts to weaken.

BOTH
Now my (her) courage is less steady,
And my (her) will is failing fast.

FIORDILIGI
Do not tempt me!

FERRANDO
I beg you, hear me!

FIORDILIGI
Why on earth must you pursue me?

FERRANDO
Take my life or say you love me!
(*he takes her hand and covers it with kisses*)

FIORDILIGI
He is strong and so appealing!
I will yield, I have a feeling.

FERRANDO
Dearest angel, say you love me!
Don't resist me any longer!

FIORDILIGI
God above me!

FERRANDO (*with great tenderness*)
Always obey your heart's true feeling,
Yield to love sincere and tender.
Dearest, I beg you, you must surrender!
Do not let me plead in vain!

FIORDILIGI (*trembling*)
Gracious Lord! Gracious Lord!
I am frail! I fail!
Have pity! I have fought my love in vain!
(GUGLIELMO *wants to rush in, but* DON ALFONSO *holds him back*)

BOTH
I'm so happy, it's past believing!
All our tortured hours of grieving
Are forgotten now forever!
We shall never part again!
Dearest heart,
We shall never part again!
(*exit* FIORDILIGI *and* FERRANDO)

FERRANDO
Cedi cara, cedi cara!
cedi cara, cedi cara!

FIORDILIGI
Dei, consiglio!

FERRANDO
Volgi a me pietoso il ciglio,
in me sol trovar tu puoi
sposo, amante, a più, se vuoi,
idol mio, più non tardar.

FIORDILIGI
Giusto ciel!
crudel! hai vinto.
Fa di me quel che ti par!

FIORDILIGI, FERRANDO
Abbracciamci, o caro bene,
e un conforto a tante pene
sia languir di dolce affetto,
di diletto sospirar.
Sospirar,
di diletto sospirar.

Scene 12

Recitative

GUGLIELMO
This should happen to me! To a Guglielmo! Victimized by a woman!

DON ALFONSO
Compose yourself, I beg you!

GUGLIELMO
The devil with composing! I'm madder than a hornet! I feel like flying through the ceiling! So that is Fiordiligi! Model of virtue! My rock of Gibraltar! That vixen, that hyena, that serpent, tigress, viper!

DON ALFONSO (*unruffled*)
Let him get it off his mind.

FERRANDO (*entering*)
What now?

GUGLIELMO
Where is she?

GUGLIELMO
Oh poveretto me! cosa ho veduto! cosa ho sentito mai!

DON ALFONSO
Per carità! silenzio!

GUGLIELMO
Mi pelerei la barba! mi graffierei la pelle! e darei colle corna entro le stelle, fu quella Fiordiligi? la Penelope, l'Artemisia del secolo! briccona, assassina furfante, ladra, cagna!

DON ALFONSO
Lasciamolo sfogar—

FERRANDO
Ebben!

GUGLIELMO
Dov' è!

FERRANDO
Chi? la tua Fiordiligi?

GUGLIELMO
La mia Fior, Fior di diavolo, che strozzi lei prima e dopo me!

FERRANDO
Tu vedi bene, v'han delle differenze in ogni cosa, un poco di più merto—

GUGLIELMO
Ah cessa! cessa di tormentarmi, ed una via piuttosta studiam di castigarle sonoramente.

DON ALFONSO
Io so, qual è: sposarle.

GUGLIELMO
Vorrei sposar piuttosto la barca di Caronte.

FERRANDO
La grotta di Vulcano.

GUGLIELMO
La porta dell' Inferno.

DON ALFONSO
Dunque restate celibi in eterno.

FERRANDO, GUGLIELMO
Mancheran forse donne ad uomin come noi?

DON ALFONSO
Non c'è abbondanza d'altro. Ma l'altre, che faran, se ciò fer queste? in fondo voi le amate queste vostre cornacchie spennacchiate.

GUGLIELMO
Ah pur troppo!

FERRANDO
Pur troppo.

DON ALFONSO
Ebben pigliatele com' elle son, natura non potea fare l'eccezzione, il privilegio, di creare due donne d'altra pasta, per i vostri bei musi; in ogni cosa, ci vuol filosofia. Venite meco; di combinar le cose, studierem la maniera: vo che ancor questa sera doppie nozze si facciano. Frattanto un' ottava ascoltate: felicissimi voi, se la imparate.

Tutti accusan le donne,
ed io le scuso,
se mille volte al dì cangiano amore,
altri un vizio lo chiama,
ed altri un uso,
ed a me par necessità del core.
L'amante che si trova al fin deluso,
non condanni l'altrui, ma il proprio errore:

FERRANDO
Who? Your good Fiordiligi?

GUGLIELMO
My good Fior—good for nothing! The devil may take her, and me with her!

FERRANDO
Do you remember? I say it without the least bit of conceit, "I have a slight advantage!"

GUGLIELMO
Keep quiet! This is no time for joking. We'd better think of some way to punish those two hussies most severely.

DON ALFONSO
I'll tell you how. Marry them!

GUGLIELMO
I'd much rather marry the devil's grandmother!

FERRANDO
And I an ugly ogress!

GUGLIELMO
Or any female dragon!

DON ALFONSO
Then you will end your days as lonely bachelors.

FERRANDO
For men of our kind there are women a-plenty!

DON ALFONSO
I do not deny that. However, do you think they would be diff'rent? You might as well admit it, you love your unfaithful little sweethearts.

GUGLIELMO
Yes, we love them!

FERRANDO
We love them!

DON ALFONSO
Why don't you marry them just as they are? What gives you the right to demand of nature to make exceptions and create two superhuman women, just because you would like it? We cannot alter what has already happened. There's only one way to make your future happy. I will make the arrangements, and before it is evening you shall both wear a wedding ring. And now let me tell you an adage. If you take it to heart, it's to your advantage.

Women cannot be faithful,
But I don't mind it,
For I can see the principle behind it.
You are wrong to upbraid them.
You have to take them as they are,
As Mother Nature made them.
You lovers, don't complain of disillusion.
What you need is to reach the wise conclusion:
All your ancestors, fathers, and brothers went through it.

Women always betray!
That's how they do it!

giacchè giovani, vecchie, e belle e brutte,
ripetete con me:
Così fan tutte!

ALL THREE
"Così fan tutte!"

FERRANDO, DON ALFONSO, GUGLIELMO
Così fan tutte.

Scene 13

Recitative

DESPINA (*enters*)
Hurrah for our two winners! The ladies have decided to consent to the wedding, and shortly after, according to your wishes, they will be prepared to depart from the city. They gave me orders to arrange all the details. The notary is ready. So are the witnesses. You may go now to see them. Well, are you pleased and happy?

DESPINA
Vittoria padroncini! a sposarvi disposte son le care madame: a nome vostro loro io promisi, che in tre giorni circa partiranno con voi: l'ordin mi diero, di trovar un notajo, che stipuli il contratto: alla lor camera attendendo vi stanno. Siete così contenti?

FERRANDO, GUGLIELMO, DON ALFONSO
Overwhelmingly!

FERRANDO, GUGLIELMO, DON ALFONSO
Contentissimi.

DESPINA
In affairs of this kind depend upon Despina's mastermind!

DESPINA
Non è mai senza effetto, quand' entra la Despina in un progetto.

Scene 14

(*A hall, richly decorated and illuminated. An orchestra at the back. Table set for four people, with silver candlesticks. Four servants in rich costumes.* DESPINA, *the servants and musicians.*)

DESPINA
Go ahead and light the candles
And complete the decorations.
Make the final preparations.
Soon the couples will be here!
We must do our ladies honor
At their wedding celebration.
(*to the musicians*)
Let us plan a great ovation
When the brides and grooms appear.

DESPINA
Fate presto, o cari amici,
alle faci il foco date,
e la mensa preparate
con ricchezza e nobiltà!
Delle nostre padroncine
gl'imenei son già disposti:
e voi gite ai vostri posti
finchè i sposi vengon quà.

SERVANTS, MUSICIANS
Go ahead and light the candles
And complete the decorations.
Make the final preparations.
Soon the couples will be here.

CORO
Facciam presto, o cari amici,
Alle faci il foco diamo,
e la mensa preparate
con ricchezza e nobiltà.

DON ALFONSO
Bravi, bravi!
ottimamente!
che abbondanza, che eleganza!
una mancia conveniente
l'un e l'altro a voi darà.
Le due coppie omai si avvanzano,
fate plauso al loro arrivo,
lieto canto e suon giulivo
empia il ciel d'ilarità.

DON ALFONSO (*while he sings, the musicians tune their instruments*)
This is perfect! I am delighted!
This is splendid, simply splendid!
I shall see that you're commended
In a most substantial way.
When the couples make their entrances,
At my signal gather near them.
Wish them luck and loudly cheer them.
Clap your hands and shout hurray.

DESPINA, DON ALFONSO
La più bella comediola
non s'è vista, o si vedrà.
La più bella comediola
non s'è vista, o si vedrà.

DESPINA, DON ALFONSO
I am absolutely certain
That the ev'ning will be gay!
Very soon we'll raise the curtain
On the play within the play.
(*exit* DESPINA *and* DON ALFONSO *through different doors*)

Scene 15

(*As the two sets of lovers enter, the chorus sings and the orchestra begins a march.*)

CORO
Benedetti i doppi conjugi,
e le amabili sposine:
benedetti i doppi conjugi,
e le amabili sposine.
Splenda lor il ciel benefico,
ed a guisa di galline
sien di figli ognor prolifiche
che le agguaglino in beltà,
che le agguaglino in beltà.

CHORUS
Heaven bless you with prosperity
And success in each endeavor.
With our heartfelt, true sincerity
May we wish you joy forever.
May you live in perfect harmony,
Carefree, peaceful, and untroubled,
And attain redoubled happiness
With your children at your side.
Hail the bridegroom and the bride!

FIORDILIGI, DORABELLA, FERRANDO, GUGLIELMO
Come par che qui prometta
tutto gioja e tutto amore!
FIORDILIGI, DORABELLA
Della cara Despinetta
FERRANDO, GUGLIELMO
certo il merito sarà.
TUTTI
Radoppiate il lieto suono,
replicate il dolce canto,
e noi qui seggiamo intanto
in maggior giovialità.

FIORDILIGI, DORABELLA, FERRANDO, GUGLIELMO
Fortune showers us with favor!
Life can hold no greater promise!
FIORDILIGI, DORABELLA
Thank you, dearest Despinetta,
FERRANDO, GUGLIELMO
For our happiness tonight!
ALL FOUR
Dearest friends, continue singing
In your bright and merry chorus!
Sing to happy days before us
And a life of new delight!
(*the betrothed couples eat*)

CORO
Beneditti i doppi conjugi,
e le amabili sposine:
benedetti i doppi conjugi,
e le amabili sposine.

CHORUS
Heaven bless you with prosperity
And success in each endeavor.
With our heartfelt, true sincerity

May we wish you joy forever.
May you live in perfect happiness,
Carefree, peaceful, and untroubled,
And attain redoubled happiness
With your children at your side.
Hail the bridegroom and the bride!

FERRANDO, GUGLIELMO
Happy, happy end of sorrow,
Bright new promise of joy hereafter!

FIORDILIGI, DORABELLA
Glowing hope for life tomorrow,
Filled with tender love and laughter!

FERRANDO, GUGLIELMO
You're my angel!

FIORDILIGI, DORABELLA
You're my hero!

FERRANDO, GUGLIELMO
Say you love me!

FIORDILIGI, DORABELLA
I'll always love you!

FERRANDO, CUCLIELMO
Here's to gladness!

FIORDILIGI, DORABELLA
Let's be happy!
Drink a toast to happy days together!
(*they clink their glasses*)

FERRANDO, GUGLIELMO
Drink to happiness together!

FIORDILIGI, DORABELLA, FERRANDO
May the glow of wine's contentment
Heal our woe and drown all resentment.
May our sorrow and our sadness
Swiftly vanish from our mem'ry forevermore.

GUGLIELMO
Ah, just to think of their dishonesty
Makes me wish there had been poison in their wine.
(*enter* DON ALFONSO)

Splenda lor il ciel benefico,
ed a guisa di galline
sien di figli ognor prolifiche
che le agguaglino in beltà,
che le agguaglino in beltà.

FERRANDO, GUGLIELMO
Tutto, tutto, o vita mia,
al mio foco, or ben rispende!

FIORDILIGI, DORABELLA
Pel mio sangue l'allegria
cresce, cresce e si diffonde!

FERRANDO, GUGLIELMO
Sei pur bella!

FIORDILIGI, DORABELLA
Sei pur vago!

FERRANDO, GUGLIELMO
Che bei rai!

FIORDILIGI, DORABELLA
Che bella bocca!

FERRANDO, GUGLIELMO
Tocca e bevi,

FIORDILIGI, DORABELLA
Bevi e tocca,

FERRANDO, GUGLIELMO
tocca, bevi, bevi tocca!

FIORDILIGI, DORABELLA, FERRANDO
E nel tuo, nel mio bicchiero
si sommerga ogni pensiero,
E non resti più memoria
del passato ai nostri cor.

CUCLIELMO
Ah, bevessero del tossico
queste volpi senza cor.

Scene 16

DON ALFONSO
Now it's time that we proceeded
With the signing of the contract.
We have ev'rything that's needed,
And the couples both are here.

BOTH COUPLES
We are ready, call the notary!

DON ALFONSO
Miei Signori, tutto è fatto;
col contratto nuziale
il notajo è sulle scale
e ipso facto qui verrà.

FIORDILIGI, DORABELLA, FERRANDO, GUGLIELMO
Bravo, bravo! passi subito.

DON ALFONSO
Vò a chiamarlo:
eccolo quà.

DESPINA
Augurandovi ogni bene,
il notajo Beccavivi
coll' usata a voi sen viene
notariale dignità!
È il contratto stipulato
colle regole ordinarie,
nelle forme giudiziarie,
pria tossendo, poi sedendo
clara voce leggerà.

FIORDILIGI, DORABELLA,
FERRANDO, GUGLIELMO
Bravo, bravo, in verità!

DESPINA
Per contratto da me fatto
si congiunge in matrimonio
Fiordiligi con Sempronio,
e con Tizio Dorabella,
sua legitima sorella,
quelle dame ferraresi,
questi nobili albinesi,
e per dote e contradote—

FIORDILIGI, DORABELLA,
FERRANDO, GUGLIELMO
Cose note, cose note!
vi crediamo,
ci fidiamo, soscriviam,
date pur quà!

DESPINA, DON ALFONSO
Bravi, bravi, in verità!

CORO
Bella vita militar,
ogni dì si cangia loco,
oggi molto, e doman poco,
ora in terra ed or sul mar.

FIORDILIGI, DORABELLA,
DESPINA, FERRANDO, GUGLIELMO
Che rumor! che canto è questo!

DON ALFONSO
State cheti; io vò a guardar.
Misericordia!
Numi del cielo!
Che caso orribile!
io tremo! io gelo!
gli sposi vostri—

FIORDILIGI, DORABELLA
Lo sposo mio!

DON ALFONSO
Honored Counselor Illegalis,
Kindly come in.
(*enter* DESPINA, *disguised as a notary*)

DESPINA
"Cornucopia verborum,"
As we always say in Latin.
Since we have a legal quorum,
I suggest that we proceed.
Here's the bona fide agreement
With the statement of the causes
And the modifying clauses.
With decorum,
Harum, horum,
I shall now begin to read.

THE COUPLES
Very well, proceed, proceed!

DESPINA (*with a nasal tone*)
Marriage is the sworn intention
Of the parties I now mention.
Fiordiligi and Sempronio,
Dorabella and Antonio,
Ladies hereby called "the sisters,"
To the designated misters,
Latter nobles of Albania,
Dowry, gifts, and miscellanea . . .

THE COUPLES
Never mind it, never mind it,
We will read it when we've signed it
Later on! Hand us a pen!
(*only the two women sign the contract*)

DESPINA, DON ALFONSO
Happy ladies, lucky men!
(DON ALFONSO *takes the contract. The sound of drums and singing is heard.*)

CHORUS (*off-stage*)
On to glory, on to war!
We are free of care and sorrow,
Here today and there tomorrow
Over land and over sea!

COUPLES, DESPINA
Hear that song! It sounds familiar!

DON ALFONSO
Wait a moment, let me look! (*he goes to the window*)
O boundless misery! Heaven preserve us!
What a catastrophe! How awful! How dreadful!
Your former sweethearts!

FIORDILIGI, DORABELLA
Our former sweethearts!

DON ALFONSO
I see them landing down at the mooring.
I hate to say so, but it is true!

COUPLES
O this is shocking! How can we stay them?
At least delay them,
What can we do?
(the servants take the table away, and the musicians hurry off)

FIORDILIGI, DORABELLA *(to* FERRANDO *and* GUGLIELMO*)*
You cannot stay here!
Either you hide yourselves or run away!

THE OTHER FOUR
If they discover you (us), what will they do to you (us)?
(FIORDILIGI *and* DORABELLA *hide their lovers in one room.* DON ALFONSO *leads* DESPINA *to another room)*

FIORDILIGI, DORABELLA *(frantically)*
Heaven protect us! Heaven preserve us!
Who will advise us in our dismay?
Who?

DON ALFONSO
Do not get panicky!
My ladies, calm yourselves!
Just put your trust in me!
I'll save the day!

FIORDILIGI, DORABELLA
I have never been so frightened,
So upset and so bewildered.
If they learn how we deceived them,
Heaven knows what we can say!

DON ALFONSO
In questo istante
tornaro, o Dio, ed alla riva
sbarcano già!

FIORDILIGI, DORABELLA, FERRANDO, GUGLIELMO
Cosa mai sento!
Barbare stelle! in tal momento,
che si farà?

FIORDILIGI, DORABELLA
Presto partite!
Presto fuggite!
Là, là celatevi, per carita!

DESPINA, FERRANDO, DON ALFONSO, GUGLIELMO
Ma se li veggono?
Ma se li incontrano?

FIORDILIGI, DORABELLA
Numi! soccorso!
Numi consiglio!
Chi dal periglio ci salverà?
chi?

DON ALFONSO
Rasserenatevi,
Ritranquillatevi!
In me fidatevi
ben tutto andrà.

FIORDILIGI, DORABELLA
Mille barbari pensieri
tormentando il cor mi vanno,
se discoprono l'inganno,
ah, di noi che mai sarà!

Last Scene

(FIORDILIGI *and* DORABELLA *on-stage.* FERRANDO *and* GUGLIELMO *enter, in their soldier uniforms and hats.)*

FERRANDO, GUGLIELMO
We are home, safe and sound from our journey,
Our perilous journey!
How we've longed for a glimpse of your faces!
How we've yearned for your tender embraces,
For your love so sincere to the end!

DON ALFONSO
Well, I never! Guglielmo! Ferrando!
This is marvelous!
You! Back here? So quickly!

FERRANDO, GUGLIELMO
Our commander has altered his strategy.

FERRANDO, GUGLIELMO
Sani e salvi agli amplessi amorosi,
delle nostre fidissime amanti,
ritorniamo di gioja esultanti,
per dar premio alla lor fedeltà.

DON ALFONSO
Giusti Numi! Guglielmo! Ferrando!
o che giubilo! qui,
come,
e quando?

FERRANDO, GUGLIELMO
Richiamati da regio contrordine,

pieni il cor di contento e di
 gaudio,
ritorniamo alle spose adorabili,
ritorniamo alla vostro amistà.

To our joy we were called back to Naples.
With our hearts full of wonderful happiness
We return to our sweethearts and friend.

GUGLIELMO
Ma cos' è quel pallor, quel
 silenzio?

GUGLIELMO (*to* FIORDILIGI)
Dearest love, why so pale and so silent?

FERRANDO
L'idol mio, perchè mesto si stà?

FERRANDO
Dearest heart, why this sorrowful air?

DON ALFONSO
Dal diletto confuse ed attonite,
confuse ed attonite,
Mute, mute si restano là.

DON ALFONSO
They are totally speechless from happiness.
You took them unaware,
That should show you how deeply they care!

FIORDILIGI, DORABELLA
Ah, che al labbro le voci mi
 mancano,
Se non moro, un prodigio sarà.

FIORDILIGI, DORABELLA (*aside*)
I am speechless with terror and misery!
I am ready to die of despair!

GUGLIELMO
Permettete che sia posto
quel baul in quella stanza.
Dei! che veggio! un uom
 nascosto?
un notajo? qui che fa?

GUGLIELMO
If you ladies will permit us,
We will put away our baggage.
What does this mean? Is someone hiding?
An attorney? Who is this?

DESPINA
Non Signor non è un notajo,
è Despina mascherata,
che dal ballo or è tornata,
e a spogliarsi, venne quà.

DESPINA (*enters, without wearing her notary's hat*)
I am neither man nor lawyer
But Despina pure and simple.
I was trying on my costume
For tomorrow's masquerade.

FIORDILIGI, DORABELLA
La Despina, la Despina!
Non capisco come và.

FIORDILIGI, DORABELLA
How she fooled us so completely
Is a mystery to me.
It's Despina! How on earth could it be she?

FERRANDO, GUGLIELMO
Una furba uguale a questa,
dove mai si troverà?

FERRANDO, GUGLIELMO
There is no one like Despina,
That is plain enough to see!
(DON ALFONSO *discreetly lets the contract signed by the ladies fall to the floor*)

DESPINA
Una furba che m'agguagli
dove mai si troverà!

DESPINA
There is no one like Despina,
There is no one else like me.

DON ALFONSO
Già cader lasciai le carte,
raccoglietele con arte.

DON ALFONSO (*softly to the lovers*)
Here's the evidence you needed!
Take this document and read it.

FERRANDO
Ma che carte sono queste?

FERRANDO
May I ask what's in this paper?

GUGLIELMO
Un contratto nuziale?

GUGLIELMO
Are you willing to explain it?
Can it be a marriage contract?

FERRANDO, GUGLIELMO
Giusto ciel! voi quì scriveste,
contradirci omai non vale,
tradimento, tradimento,
ah si faccia il scoprimento;
e a torrenti, a fiumi, a mari
indi il sangue scorrerà!

FERRANDO, GUGLIELMO
What a crime! And you have signed it!
To deny your guilt is useless!
To my horror I discover
You betrayed your faithful lover!

You will not escape my vengeance!
Streams of guilty blood will flow!
(they try to go into the other room, but the ladies hold them back)

FIORDILIGI, DORABELLA
Ah, I beg of you to kill me!
I am guilty, as you declare me.
Show no pity, do not spare me!
Take your saber and do your duty.
I will welcome it, for I deserve it so!

FIORDILIGI, DORABELLA
Ah! Signor son rea di morte
e la morte io sol vi chiedo,
il mio fallo tardi vedo,
con quel ferro un sen ferite
che non merita pietà!

FERRANDO, GUGLIELMO
Tell the truth!

FERRANDO, GUGLIELMO
Cosa fù?

FIORDILIGI, DORABELLA *(point to* DESPINA *and* DON ALFONSO*)*
These are the traitors!
All we did was their suggestion.

FIORDILIGI, DORABELLA
Per noi favelli
il crudel, la seduttrice.

DON ALFONSO
That is true without a question.
I can prove it very well.
(shows them the room where the lovers had gone to hide. FERRANDO *and* GUGLIELMO *go into the room for a moment, then come out, without the hats, coats, and beards, but with the outer clothing of their former disguise, in the comic manner they had formerly affected)*

DON ALFONSO
Troppo vero è quel che dice,
e la prova è chiusa lì!

FIORDILIGI, DORABELLA
What a dreadful trick to play on us!
Oh, why did he have to tell?

FIORDILIGI, DORABELLA
Dal timor io gelo, io palpito:
perchè mai li discoprì!

FERRANDO *(with an exaggerated bow to* FIORDILIGI*)*
You are my goddess! I kneel before you!
I am your hero who wants to adore you!

FERRANDO
A voi s'inchina
bella damina!
il Cavaliere dell' Albania.

GUGLIELMO *(to* DORABELLA*)*
Here is a portrait I know you treasure.
Give me my heart now, measure for measure.

GUGLIELMO
Il ritrattino
pel coricino,
ecco io le rendo
Signora mia.

FERRANDO, GUGLIELMO *(to* DESPINA*)*
Let us congratulate Dr. Fatalis,
Master of Magnets, the paragon!

FERRANDO, GUGLIELMO
Ed al magnetico
Signor Dottore
rendo l'onore
che meritò.

FIORDILIGI, DORABELLA, DESPINA
Gracious! Amazing!
Stunning and dazing!

FIORDILIGI, DORABELLA, DESPINA
Stelle! che veggo!
Al duol non reggo!

FERRANDO, DON ALFONSO, GUGLIELMO
They're struck by thunder!
Speechless with wonder!

FERRANDO, DON ALFONSO, GUGLIELMO
Son stupefatte!
Son mezze matte!

FIORDILIGI, DORABELLA *(pointing to* DON ALFONSO*)*
Here is the guilty one
Who led us on!

FIORDILIGI, DORABELLA
Ecco là il barbaro che
c'ingannò.

DON ALFONSO
Yes, I did, but my deception
Was to undeceive your lovers
And to prove there's no exception

DON ALFONSO
V'ingannai, ma fu l'inganno
disinganno ai vostri amanti,
che più saggi omai saranno
che faran quel ch'io vorrò.

Quà le destre, siete sposi,
abbracciatevi e tacete.
Tutti quattro ora ridete,
Chi'io già risi e riderò.

To a rule that's always true.
Learn your lesson, heed the moral!
Let's be friends again! End your quarrel!
Laugh about what's past and over
And I'll laugh along with you.

FIORDILIGI, DORABELLA
Idol mio, se questo è vero,
colla fede e coll' amore
compensar saprò il tuo core,
adorarti ognor saprò!

FIORDILIGI, DORABELLA
Dear beloved, please forgive me!
Oh, my sweetheart, I hope to show you
All the loving faith I owe you!
I will prove my worth to you.
(*the lovers join hands and embrace each other*)

FERRANDO, GUGLIELMO
Te lo credo, gioja bella,
ma la prova io far non vò.

FERRANDO, GUGLIELMO
You don't have to, my beloved,
I shall ask no proof from you.

DESPINA
Io non so se questo è sogno,
mi confondo, mi vergogno:
manco mal se a me l'han fatta,
che a molt' altri
anch'io la fò.

DESPINA
I who was the master schemer
Find myself a baffled dreamer.
I have learned a useful lesson,
Something that I never knew.
Tricks you play on other people,
Other people play on you!

TUTTI
Fortunato l'uom, che prende
ogni cosa pel buon verso,
e tra i casi, e le vicende
da ragion guidar si fà.
Quel che suole altrui far
piangere
fia per lui cagion di riso,
e del mondo in mezzo i turbini,
bella calma troverà.

ALL
Happy is the man of reason
Who can face the world in season.
Firm and steadfast
And uncomplaining,
He will go his cheerful way.
Things that make his brothers sorrowful,
He will answer with knowing laughter.
He has learned that life's adversities
Turn to joy another day.

DON GIOVANNI

by Wolfgang Amadeus Mozart (1756–1791)

LIBRETTO BY LORENZO DA PONTE.

Translated by RUTH and THOMAS MARTIN

CHARACTERS

DON GIOVANNI, *a licentious young nobleman*	*Baritone*
DON PEDRO, *Commendatore of Seville*	*Bass*
DONNA ANNA, *Don Pedro's daughter*	*Soprano*
DON OTTAVIO, *Donna Anna's fiancé*	*Tenor*
DONNA ELVIRA, *a noble lady of Burgos*	*Soprano*
LEPORELLO, *servant of Don Giovanni*	*Bass*
ZERLINA, *a peasant girl*	*Soprano*
MASETTO, *a peasant, Zerlina's fiancé*	*Bass*
PEASANTS, DANCERS, MUSICIANS, AND DEMONS	

Place: In and near Seville
Time: Eighteenth century
First performance: National Theater, Prague, October 29, 1787

COPYRIGHT © 1951 BY RUTH AND THOMAS MARTIN

ACT I

Overture and Scene 1

(*A street with the house of the* COMMENDATORE; LEPORELLO *is discovered keeping watch before the house.*)

Introduction

LEPORELLO
Slave and toil, no sleep at all,
At my master's beck and call
Ev'ry hour in twenty-four,
I can't bear it any more!
I won't stand it any longer,
I resign as of today,
I don't care what he will say,
No, no, no, no, no,
I resign as of today!
My dear master takes no chances:
While he courts the female gentry,
I stand here to play the sentry,
And guard the entry!
He has pleasures and romances
While the troubles all are mine,
I won't stand it, I resign,
But it seems there's someone coming.
I hear cries and angry voices.
I will hurry out of sight,
I don't want to have a fight.
(*he hides;* DON GIOVANNI *enters from the house struggling with* DONNA ANNA)

LEPORELLO
Notte e giorno faticar,
Per chi nulla sa gradir;
Piova e vento sopportar,
Mangiar male e mal dormir.
Voglio far il gentiluomo
E non voglio più servir;
No, no, no, non voglio più servir.
Oh che caro galantuomo:
Vuol star dentro colla bella,
Ed io far la sentinella!
Voglio far il gentiluomo,
E non voglio più servir,
No, no, no, non voglio più servir.
Ma mi par, che venga gente,
Non mi voglio far sentir.

DONNA ANNA
Wicked man, you won't escape me,
I'll discover who you are!

DONNA ANNA
Non sperar, se non m'uccidi,
Ch'io ti lascio fuggir mai.

DON GIOVANNI
Foolish woman, your insistence
Will not get you very far!

DON GIOVANNI
Donna folle, indarno gridi!
Chi son io tu non saprai.

LEPORELLO
What a master! A new disaster!
I'm afraid he went too far.

LEPORELLO
(Che tumulto! oh, ciel, che gridi)
Il padron in nuovi guai!

DONNA ANNA
Help me! Hurry to my rescue!

DONNA ANNA
Gente! servi! al traditore!

DON GIOVANNI
Do not try my patience further!

DON GIOVANNI
(Taci, e trema al mio furore.)

DONNA ANNA
Vile seducer!

DONNA ANNA
Scellerato!

DON GIOVANNI
Foolish woman!

DON GIOVANNI
Sconsigliata!

DONNA ANNA
Desperado!

DONNA ANNA
Scellerato!

DON GIOVANNI
What bravado!

DON GIOVANNI
Sconsigliata!

DONNA ANNA
Gente! servi!

DONNA ANNA
Help me, help me!

DON GIOVANNI
Taci e trema!

DON GIOVANNI
You'll repent this!

DONNA ANNA
Come furia disperata
Ti saprò perseguitar.
Come furia disperata
Ti saprò perseguitar.

DONNA ANNA
With the force of desperation I will never cease to fight,
And with grim persistence and determination,
I'll prevent you from your flight!

DON GIOVANNI
(Questa furia disperata
Mi vuol far precipitar.
Questa furia disperata
Mi vuol far precipitar.)

DON GIOVANNI
With the force of desperation
She is hindering my flight,
And with grim determination
She has spoiled my plan tonight!

LEPORELLO
(Sta a veder che il libertino
Mi farà precipitar.)
Che tumulto!
Oh ciel, che gridi!

LEPORELLO
If my master is not careful,
He will not escape tonight.
What an uproar! And what confusion!
(exit DONNA ANNA*)*

Scene 2

(DON GIOVANNI, COMMENDATORE, *and* LEPORELLO)

COMMENDATORE
Lasciala, indegno;
Battiti meco.

COMMENDATORE
Coward, release her!
Fight or surrender!

DON GIOVANNI
Va, non mi degno
Di pugnar teco.

DON GIOVANNI
You are unworthy as her defender!

COMMENDATORE
Così pretendi
Da me fuggir?

COMMENDATORE
With such pretensions you hide your fear?

LEPORELLO
(Potessi almeno
Di quà partir.)

LEPORELLO
If I could only escape from here!

DON GIOVANNI
Va, non mi degno, no!
Misero! Misero!

DON GIOVANNI
I will not fight you, no!
Foolishness! Stubbornness!

COMMENDATORE
Battiti!

COMMENDATORE
I challenge you!

DON GIOVANNI
Misero! attendi,
Se vuoi morir.

DON GIOVANNI
Well then, so be it!
Prepare to die!
(they fight—the COMMENDATORE *falls)*

TRIO

COMMENDATORE
Ah soccorso! son tradito.
L'assassino m'ha ferito,
E dal seno palpitante
Sento l'anima partir.

COMMENDATORE
Ah, God help me, I am wounded!
Helpless, at my victor's mercy!
I can feel that I am dying.
Very soon, I'll breathe my last!
(he dies)

DON GIOVANNI
Ah, the foolish man has fallen,
And his feeble heart is failing.
Very soon, he'll breathe his last!

DON GIOVANNI
Ah! già cade il sciagurato
Affannoso e agonizzante;
Già dal seno palpitante
Veggo l'anima partir.

LEPORELLO
What a villain!
I am mute with stupefaction
At his shameful, wicked action.
I can only stand aghast
At a crime so black and vast!

LEPORELLO
(Qual misfatto! qual eccesso!
Entro il sen dallo spavento
Palpitar il cor mi sento—
Io non so che far, che dir!)

Recitative

DON GIOVANNI (*in a low voice*)
Leporello, where are you?

DON GIOVANNI
Leporello, ove sei?

LEPORELLO
I'm here, much to my sorrow! And you, sir?

LEPORELLO
Son quì per mia disgrazia, e voi?

DON GIOVANNI
I'm here.

DON GIOVANNI
Son quì.

LEPORELLO
Who's dead, you or her father?

LEPORELLO
Chi è morto, voi, o il vecchio?

DON GIOVANNI
A ridiculous question! Her father!

DON GIOVANNI
Che domanda da bestia! il vecchio!

LEPORELLO
Really, a successful adventure! To rape the daughter, and then to kill the father!

LEPORELLO
Bravo! due imprese leggiadre: sforzar
la figlia, ed ammazzar il padre!

DON GIOVANNI
Well, he got what he asked for!

DON GIOVANNI
L'ha voluto suo danno.

LEPORELLO
And Donn' Anna, what did she ask for?

LEPORELLO
Ma Donn'Anna cos'ha voluto?

DON GIOVANNI (*threatening him*)
Quiet, that is enough! Come with me, unless you're asking for something, too.

DON GIOVANNI
Taci,
Non mi seccar, vien meco; se non vuoi qualche cosa ancor tu.

LEPORELLO
I don't ask for a thing!
I'll come with you.
(*they leave*)

LEPORELLO
Non vo' nulla, Signor! non parlo più.

Scene 3

(DONNA ANNA, DON OTTAVIO *and* SERVANTS *with torches*)

DONNA ANNA
Quick, let us hasten to help him, we may still be in time!

DONNA ANNA
Ah! del padre in periglio in soccorso voliam.

DON OTTAVIO
I shall defend him with my life, if need be.
Where is the fiend who attacked him?

DON OTTAVIO
Tutto il mio sangue verserò, se bisogna.
Ma dov'è il scellerato?

DONNA ANNA
This is the place.

DONNA ANNA
In questo loco.

Recitative and Duet

Ma qual mai s'offre, oh Dei!
spettacolo funesto agli occhi
Il padre, miei! padre mio! mio
caro padre!

(*sees the body of her father*)
What a heartbreaking sight unfolding here before me!
Oh God in heaven!
My Father, dearest Father!
Speak to your daughter!

DON OTTAVIO
Signore!

DON OTTAVIO
Commendatore!

DONNA ANNA
Ah, l'assassino mel trucidò!
Quel sangue, quella piaga—
quel volto tinto e coperto del
color di morte! Ei non
respira più—fredde le membra! Padre mio! caro padre!
padre amato! Io manco—io
moro!

DONNA ANNA
Ah, the assassin stabbed him to death!
He lies here, still and silent, so lonely—
Shrouded in death's irrevocable pallor.
The spark of life is gone,
Cruelly extinguished!
How I loved you, dearest Father!
Father, I loved you!
I falter . . . dear Father . . .
(*she faints*)

DON OTTAVIO
Ah soccorrete, amici, il mio
tesoro! Cercatemi, recatemi
qualche odor, qualche spirto.
Ah non tardate! Donn'Anna,
sposa, amica! Il duolo estremo la meschinella uccide.

DON OTTAVIO
Friends, lend me your assistance and help your mistress!
Go find for me some remedy,
We must try to revive her!
I beg you, hurry!
Beloved! Anna! My dearest!
This great disaster seems to have overwhelmed her.

DONNA ANNA
Ahi!

DONNA ANNA
Ah!

DON OTTAVIO
Già riviene! Datele nuovi ajuti.

DON OTTAVIO
She's reviving! Do all you can to aid her.

DONNA ANNA
Padre mio!

DONNA ANNA
Where's my father?

DON OTTAVIO
Celate, allontanate agli occhi
suoi quell'oggetto d'orrore.
Anima mia! consolati, fa core!

DON OTTAVIO
Act swiftly, remove the body of your master.
We must spare her the sight.
Dearest beloved, I grieve with you! Believe me!

Duet

DONNA ANNA
Fuggi, crudele, fuggi!
Lascia che mora anch'io!
Ora ch'è morto, oh Dio!
Chi a me la vita diè!

DONNA ANNA
No, do not try to cheer me.
Death is my one desire.
Now that I lost my father,
What else is left for me?

DON OTTAVIO
Senti cor mio, deh senti!
Guardami un solo istante!
Ti parla il caro amante.
Che vive sol per te!

DON OTTAVIO
Hear me, beloved, oh hear me!
How can you doubt or fear me,
I love you so sincerely
And live for you alone.

DONNA ANNA
Tu sei, perdon! mio bene!
L'affanno mio, le pene!
Ah, il padre mio dov'è?

DONNA ANNA
Dear love, forgive, forgive me . . .
The shock I suffered, my anguish . . .
My father, where is he?

DON OTTAVIO
Your father?
Dearest Anna, banish the bitter mem'ry.
Your husband and father I shall be.

DONNA ANNA
Ah, my father, he's gone forevermore.

DON OTTAVIO
Dearest Anna, banish the bitter mem'ry.
As husband, and father I'm near you,
So place your trust in me.

DONNA ANNA
Swear that you will avenge him,
Swear to the one you love.

DON OTTAVIO
I swear it, I swear it,
By all the love I bear you,
I swear by God above!

BOTH
We swear by God in Heaven
To find the brutal slayer,
Seducer and betrayer,
Justice demands it so . . .

DONNA ANNA
You'll avenge the murder, swear it!

DON OTTAVIO
I swear it, by God in Heaven,
By all our love.

BOTH
His act of force and fury,
His deed of desperation,
Demands a vindication,
That is our solemn vow,
Revenge and vindication,
That is our solemn vow.

DON OTTAVIO
Il padre? Lascia, o cara!
La rimembranza amara:
Hai sposo e padre in me!

DONNA ANNA
Ah! il padre, il padre mio dov'è?

DON OTTAVIO
Lascia, o cara,
La rimembranza, amara!
Hai sposo e padre, hai sposo
E padre in me.

DONNA ANNA
Ah! vendicar, se il puoi,
Giura quel sangue ognor!

DON OTTAVIO
Lo giuro, lo giuro,
Lo giuro agli occhi tuoi.
Lo giuro al nostro amor!

DONNA ANNA, DON OTTAVIO
Che giuramento oh Dei!
Che barbaro momento!
Tra cento affetti e cento
Vammi ondeggiando il cor!

DONNA ANNA
Vendicar quel sangue, giura!

DON OTTAVIO
Lo giuro agli occhi tuoi,
Al nostro amor.

DONNA ANNA, DON OTTAVIO
Che giuramento, oh Dei,
Che barbaro momento!
Tra cento affetti, e cento
Vammi ondeggiando il cor,
Tra cento affetti e cento,
Vammi ondeggiando il cor.

Scene 4

(*street*—DON GIOVANNI *and* LEPORELLO)

Recitative

DON GIOVANNI
Speak up, I'm in a hurry, what's the matter?

LEPORELLO
What I have got to say is most important.

DON GIOVANNI
Undoubtedly.

LEPORELLO
Of utmost gravity.

DON GIOVANNI
Orsù spicciati presto—cosa vuoi?

LEPORELLO
L'affar di cui si tratta è importante.

DON GIOVANNI
Lo credo.

LEPORELLO
È importantissimo.

DON GIOVANNI
Meglio ancora. Finiscila.

LEPORELLO
Giurate di non andar in collera.

DON GIOVANNI
Lo giuro sul mio onore, purchè non parli del Commendatore.

LEPORELLO
Siamo soli?

DON GIOVANNI
Lo vedo.

LEPORELLO
Nessun ci sente?

DON GIOVANNI
Via!

LEPORELLO
Vi posso dire tutto liberamente.

DON GIOVANNI
Sì.

LEPORELLO
Dunque quand'è così, caro signor padrone, la vita che menate è da briccone!

DON GIOVANNI
Temerario! in tal guisa!

LEPORELLO
E il giuramento.

DON GIOVANNI
Non sò di giuramento, taci o ch'io—

LEPORELLO
Non parlo più! non fiato, o padron mio.

DON GIOVANNI
Così saremo amici. Or odi un poco. Sai tu perchè son qui?

LEPORELLO
Non ne so nulla. Ma essendo l'alba chiara, non sarebbe qualche nuova conquista: io lo devo saper per porla in lista.

DON GIOVANNI
Va là che sei 'l grand'uom! Sappi ch'io sono innamorato d'una bella dama, e son certo che m'ama. La vidi, le parlai: meco al casino questa notte verrà; zitto! Mi pare sentir odor di femmina.

LEPORELLO
Cospetto! che odorato perfetto!

DON GIOVANNI
All'aria mi par bella.

LEPORELLO
E che occhio, dico!

DON GIOVANNI
So much the better, let's hear it.

LEPORELLO
But promise me that you won't be furious.

DON GIOVANNI
I swear upon my honor, with one proviso: not a word of the Commendatore.

LEPORELLO
We're alone here?

DON GIOVANNI
That's obvious.

LEPORELLO
No one will hear us?

DON GIOVANNI
No.

LEPORELLO
Then I am free to speak without reservation?

DON GIOVANNI
Yes.

LEPORELLO
Well, if that is the case—my noble lord and master, the life you are leading—is simply scandalous!

DON GIOVANNI
Why, you devil, how dare you!

LEPORELLO
Where's your promise?

DON GIOVANNI
When did I make that promise? Quiet, or I'll . . . (*threatening him*)

LEPORELLO
I shall be still, as quiet as a mouse.

DON GIOVANNI
Then our friendship will continue. Now let me ask you: Why do you think I'm here?

LEPORELLO
How should I know? But since it's early morning, could it be for another new conquest? Better tell me at once for my statistics.

DON GIOVANNI
That's right, keep up-to-date. Let me inform you: I fell in love with a charming lady, we made friends and she will come to the castle tonight. Quiet! That perfume! I scent a woman's presence.

LEPORELLO (*aside*)
Amazing! He has the nose of a beagle!

DON GIOVANNI
It seems that she is lovely.

LEPORELLO (*aside*)
And the eyes of an eagle!

DON GIOVANNI
Let us quickly retire and find out where we stand.

LEPORELLO
(He is on fire!)

DON GIOVANNI
Ritiriamoci un poco, e scopriamo terren.

LEPORELLO
(Già prese fuoco.)

Scene 5

(DONNA ELVIRA; DON GIOVANNI *and* LEPORELLO *concealed*)

Trio

DONNA ELVIRA
Shall I at last discover
Wherever he may be,
That false and heartless lover
Who broke his faith to me!
Though he so deeply wronged me,
Gladly I would forgive;
But if again he scorns me
I swear he shall not live.

DONNA ELVIRA
Ah! chi mi dice mai
Quel barbaro dov'è,
Che per mio scorno amai,
Che mi mancò di fè?
Ah se ritrovo l'empio,
E a me non torna ancor,
Vo' farne orrendo scempio,
Gli vo' cavar il cor.

DON GIOVANNI (*to* LEPORELLO)
You heard it, it's a lady,
Abandoned by her lover.

DON GIOVANNI
Udisti? Qualche bella del vago abbandonata.

DONNA ELVIRA
But if again he scorns me,
I swear he shall not live!

DONNA ELVIRA
Vo' farne orrendo scempio
Gli vo' cavar il cor.

DON GIOVANNI
What a pity, what a pity!
Perhaps I can console her and restore her.

DON GIOVANNI
Poverina! poverina! cerchiam di consolar il suo tormento.

LEPORELLO (*aside*)
Just like the eighteen hundred girls before her.

LEPORELLO
Così ne consolò mille e ottocento.

DONNA ELVIRA
Shall I at last discover
That evil man again,
That false and heartless lover
Who caused me so much pain?
Oh, gracious God above me,
Help me attain my goal,
To make the traitor love me,
Or crush him heart and soul!

DONNA ELVIRA
Ah! chi mi dice mai
Quel barbaro dov'è?
Che per mio scorno amai,
Che mi mancò di fè.
Ah se ritrovo l'empio,
E a me non torna ancor,
Vo' farne orrendo scempio,
Gli vo' cavar il cor.

DON GIOVANNI
It is tragic, really tragic!
I must console this girl, I can't ignore her.

DON GIOVANNI
Poverina! poverina!
Cerchiam di consolare
Il suo tormento.

LEPORELLO
Just like the eighteen hundred more before her.

LEPORELLO
Così ne consolò mille e ottocento.

DON GIOVANNI
Señorita, Señorita!

DON GIOVANNI
Signorina! signorina!

Recitative

DONNA ELVIRA
Who's there?

DONNA ELVIRA
Chi è là!

DON GIOVANNI
Stelle! che vedo?

LEPORELLO
Oh bella! Donna Elvira!

DONNA ELVIRA
Don Giovanni! Sei quì? Mostro, fellon, nido d'inganni!

LEPORELLO
(Che titoli cruscanti! Manco male che lo conosce bene.)

DON GIOVANNI
Via, cara Donna Elvira, calmate quella collera! sentite, lasciatemi parlar!

DONNA ELVIRA
Cosa puoi dire dopo azion sì nera? In casa mia entra furtivamente, a forza d'arte, di giuramenti e di lusinghe arrivi a sedurre il cor mio! m'innamori, o crudele! Mi dichiari tua sposa, e poi,—mancando della terra e del ciel al santo dritto,—con enorme delitto, dopo tre dì da Burgos t'allontani. M'abbandoni, mi fuggi—e lasci in preda al rimorso ed al pianto per pena forse che t'amai cotanto!

LEPORELLO
(Pare un libro stampato!)

DON GIOVANNI
Oh, in quanto a questo ebbi le mie ragioni.
È vero?

LEPORELLO
(È vero. E che ragioni forti!)

DONNA ELVIRA
E quali sono, se non la tua perfidia, la leggerezza tua? Ma il giusto cielo volle, ch'io ti trovassi per far le sue, le mie vendette.

DON GIOVANNI
Eh via, siate più ragionevole! (Mi pone a cimento costei.) Se non credete al labbro mio, credete a questo galantuomo.

LEPORELLO
Salvo il vero?

DON GIOVANNI
Via, dille un poco.

LEPORELLO
E cosa devo dirle?

DON GIOVANNI
Sì, sì, dirle pur tutto.

DON GIOVANNI
Heaven preserve me!

LEPORELLO
Surprise! Donna Elvira!

DONNA ELVIRA
Don Giovanni! It's you? Criminal brute! Heartless betrayer!

LEPORELLO (*aside*)
An excellent description. She's expressing herself with great precision.

DON GIOVANNI
Please, dearest Donn' Elvira, your outburst is not justified. Consider, permit me to explain.

DONNA ELVIRA
What explanation could absolve an outrage? One fatal night you entered my house in secret, and you succeeded, by means of flattery and by promising marriage, in seducing my virtue. Like a fool I believed you, when you said we would marry and then, you scoundrel, since no rites had sanctioned our union, you felt free to desert me after three days and went away from Burgos. You departed uncaring and left me sick with remorse and hopeless longing. Thus you rewarded me for my devotion.

LEPORELLO (*aside*)
What a recitativo!

DON GIOVANNI
As far as that's concerned, there were urgent reasons. (*to* LEPORELLO) You know them!

LEPORELLO (*aside*)
I know them. Yes, all-embracing reasons.

DONNA ELVIRA
What other reasons, besides your bad intentions and vicious inclinations? But heaven heard my prayer and let me find you, so my revenge would be accomplished.

DON GIOVANNI
Come on now, you must not be hysterical. (This female will never give up.) Since you won't listen to me, at least listen to Leporello.

LEPORELLO
That's a good one.

DON GIOVANNI
Go on and tell her.

LEPORELLO
What story shall I tell her?

DON GIOVANNI
The whole truth, what's the diff'rence.
(*he escapes unnoticed*)

DONNA ELVIRA
Well then, but hurry.

LEPORELLO
My Lady, it is this way, you know the saying; Though you may lead a horse to water, you cannot make him drink.

DONNA ELVIRA
How dare you! In such a callous way you mock my sorrow? And you? Heavens! He has fled again! Where has he gone? Tell me, where's he hiding?

LEPORELLO
Be glad that he's gone. He's not deserving of your love or affection.

DONNA ELVIRA
The wretched man has deceived me again!

LEPORELLO
Take my word for it, you're by no means the first one, nor the second, and you won't be the last one. I'll show you: This quite impressive booklet contains a faithful account of his adventures. Ev'ry village, ev'ry province, yes ev'ry nation, can furnish proof, of Don Giovanni's occupation.

Aria

LEPORELLO
Señorita! Here are valid statistics
Of his conquests from border to border
In the best alphabetical order.
They are listed from A down to Z,
If you want to, go through them with me.
There in Italy, three hundred and forty—
One hundred in Greece, which is plenty.
Germany's share is two hundred and twenty—
But look at Spain here,
Spain supplied him a thousand and three.
There are peasants by the dozens,
Here's a queen and all her cousins,
Here's a countess and a duchess
Who have fallen in his clutches—
Ev'ry type of female gender,
Stern or tender, warm or cold,
Plump or slender, young or old.
Little Sicily compares well with Turkey—
Eighty-seven, if added together;
England has fifty in spite of the weather,
But Spain still is leading,
Spain is leading with thousand and three.
From Toledo to Gibraltar
Without blessing from the altar,
He has lured a thousand beauties
From their homes and moral duties;
Whether destitute or wealthy,

DONNA ELVIRA
Ebben, fa presto.

LEPORELLO
Madama—veramente—in questo mondo conciossia cosa quando fosse che il quadro non è tondo—

DONNA ELVIRA
Sciagurato! Così del mio dolor gioco ti prendi? Ah voi— Stelle! l'iniquo fuggì! Misera me! dove? In qual parte . . .

LEPORELLO
Eh, lasciate che vada! Egli non merta che di lui ci pensiate.

DONNA ELVIRA
Il scellerato m'ingannò, mi tradì!

LEPORELLO
Eh consolatevi! Non siete voi, non foste, e non sarete nè la prima, nè l'ultima. Guardate, questo non picciol libro tutto pieno dei nomi di sue belle. Ogni villa, ogni borgo, ogni paese, è testimon di sue donnesche imprese.

LEPORELLO
Madamina!
Il catalogo è questo,
Delle belle, che amò il padron mio!
Un catalogo egli è ch'ho fatto io:
Osservate, leggete con me!
In Italia seicento e quaranta,
In Almagna duecento trent'una;
Cento in Francia, in Turchia novant'una,
Ma, ma in Ispagna, son già mille e tre!
V'han fra queste contadine,
Cameriere cittadine;
V'han contesse, baronesse,
Marchesane, principesse,
E v'han donne d'ogni grado,
D'ogni forma, d'ogni età.
In Italia seicento e quaranta,
In Almagna duecento trent'una;
Cento in Francia, in Turchia novant'una,
Ma, ma in Ispagna, son già mille e tre!
V'han fra queste contadine,
Cameriere cittadine;
V'han contesse, baronesse,
Marchesane, principesse,
E v'han donne d'ogni grado,
D'ogni forma, d'ogni età.
Di lodar la gentilezza,
Nella bianca la dolcezza!
Nella bionda, egli ha l'usanza

Nella bianca la dolcezza!
Vuol d'inverno la grassotta
Vuol d'estate la magrotta;
È la grande, maestosa;
La piccina è ognor vezzosa.
Delle vecchie fa conquista
Pel piacer di porle in lista:
Sua passion predominante
È la giovin principiante
Non si picca, se sia ricca
Se sia brutta, se sia bella!
Purchè porti la gonnella,
Voi sapete quel che fa!

Weak or healthy,
Short or tall—
Don Giovanni loves them all!
His affections change with the season,
His selections have rhyme and season—
Nordic goddess, dark Eurasian,
All depending on the occasion.
He likes round ones when it's wintry,
And in summer, slim and splint'ry.
Comes the autumn, then my patron
Likes a large, imposing matron.
But in springtime, in the springtime,
He prefers them very tiny,
Pink and shiny, clinging-viny,
Very tiny, very tiny, very tiny!
He likes the sweet ones
And the petite ones!
Haggard spinsters, gray-haired donnas
In his favor share equal honors.
He adores the adolescent—
Innocent and acquiescent.
Marguerita, Bess or Lily
Or Conchita—willy-nilly—
Rich or poor receive the same caresses,
Just as long as they wear dresses.
You should know it best of all!
(*he goes out*)

Recitative

DONNA ELVIRA
In questa forma dunque mi tradì il scellerato? è questo il premio che quel barbaro rende all'amor mio? Ah vendicar vogl'io l'ingannato mio cor! Pria ch'ei mi fugga, si ricorra—Si vada; io sento in petto sol vendetta parlar, rabbia, e dispetto!

DONNA ELVIRA (*alone*)
So I am one of many, and the scoundrel betrayed me! Thus Don Giovanni has rewarded my love and my devotion. Ah, I shall seek for vengeance for the anguish he caused. Though he is clever and resourceful, I'll brave him. I shall pursue him and exact my revenge. Nothing can save him.
(*she goes into the house*)

Scene 6

(*The country, with a view of* DON GIOVANNI'S *palace; enter* ZERLINA, MASETTO, *and chorus of villagers.*)

Duet and Chorus

ZERLINA
Giovinette, che fate all'amore,
Non lasciate che passi l'et ì;
Se nel seno vi bulica il core,
Il rimedio vedetelo quà!

ZERLINA
We are carefree and young only once, you must always remember,
Time is fleeting and flying away, is flying away.

Since the flowers that blossom in springtime are gone in December,
Make good use of your time while you may.

CHORUS
Make good use of your time while you may,
Lalalalala, lalalalala.

MASETTO
Do not squander your youth on philand'ring and foolish romances,
They are fancies that never will last,
If you're planning to marry, good fellows, don't take any chances,
Find a sweetheart and marry her fast.

CHORUS
Find a sweetheart and marry her fast.
Lalalalala, lalalalala.

ZERLINA, MASETTO
Come, my darling, let's sing and be happy,
There'll be dancing and wedding orations,
Altogether a great celebration.
What a beautiful, beautiful day!

CHORUS
Ah, what a beautiful, beautiful day!
Lalalalala, lalalalala.

La la la, la la la!
Che piacer, che piacer,
Che sarà!

CORO
Ah, che piacer che sarà,
La la lera la, la la lera la.

MASETTO
Giovinetti leggieri di testa,
Non andate girando quà e là.
Poco dura de' matti la festa,
Ma per me cominciata non ha!
Che piacer, che piacer, che sarà!
La la lera la, la la lera la!

CORO
Che piacer! che piacer che sarà!
La la lera la, la la lera la!

ZERLINA, MASETTO
Vieni, vieni, carino / carina godiamo
E cantiamo, e balliamo, e suoniamo!
Vieni, vieni, carino / carina godiamo,
Che piacer, che piacer, che sarà!

CORO
Che piacer che piacer che sarà!
La la lera la, la la lera la!

Scene 7

(*the same*—DON GIOVANNI, LEPORELLO)

DON GIOVANNI
God be praised, she is gone! But look here, what's this? What beauty and what charm, what youth and gaiety!

LEPORELLO
(As far as I can see, in this crowd there should be one left for me.)

DON GIOVANNI
Dear friends, let me greet you! Carry on with your celebration, and continue your music and dancing. This seems to be a wedding?

ZERLINA
Yes, Your Lordship, and I am the bride.

DON GIOVANNI
I am delighted! The bridegroom?

MASETTO
I, at your service.

DON GIOVANNI
Manco male è partita! Oh guarda, guarda, che bella gioventù! Che belle donne!

LEPORELLO
(Tra tante per mia fè, vi sarà qualche cosa anche per me.)

DON GIOVANNI
Cari amici, buon giorno! Seguitate a stare allegramente; —seguitate a suonar, o buona gente. C'è qualche sposalizio!

ZERLINA
Sì, signore; e la sposa son io.

DON GIOVANNI
Me ne consolo. Lo sposo?

MASETTO
Io, per servirla.

DON GIOVANNI
Oh bravo! per servirmi! Questo è vero parlar da galantuomo.

LEPORELLO
Basta che sia marito.

ZERLINA
Oh, il mio Masetto è un uom d'ottimo core!

DON GIOVANNI
Oh anch'io, vedete: voglio che siamo amici.
Il vostro nome?

ZERLINA
Zerlina.

DON GIOVANNI
E il tuo?

MASETTO
Masetto.

DON GIOVANNI
Oh caro il mio Masetto! cara la mia Zerlina, v'esibisco la mia protezione. Leporello! cosa fai là birbone?

LEPORELLO
Anch'io, caro padrone, esibisco la mia protezione.

DON GIOVANNI
Presto va con costor, nel mio palazzo conducili sul fatto: ordina ch'abbiano cioccolatte, caffè, vini, presciutti—cerca divertir tutti. Mostra loro il giardino, la galleria, le camere; in effetto fa che resti contento il mio Masetto. Hai capito?

LEPORELLO
Ho capito. Andiam.

MASETTO
Signore!

DON GIOVANNI
Cosa c'è?

MASETTO
La Zerlina senza me non può star.

LEPORELLO
In vostro loco ci starà sua eccellenza—e saprà bene fare le vostre parti.

DON GIOVANNI
Oh la Zerlina è in man d'un cavalier. Va pur; fra poco ella meco verrà.

ZERLINA
Va; non temere: nelle mani son io d'un cavaliere.

MASETTO
E per questo—

DON GIOVANNI
Well spoken, at my service. You speak like a man who knows his position.

LEPORELLO
That's why he's getting married.

ZERLINA
Yes, my Masetto has a lovely disposition.

DON GIOVANNI
So much the better. Then we shall be good friends. What is your name?

ZERLINA
Zerlina.

DON GIOVANNI
And yours?

MASETTO
Masetto.

DON GIOVANNI
Well then, my dear Masetto, and you, my dear Zerlina, I am taking you under my protection. Leporello! What are you doing, you rascal?

LEPORELLO (*who is making love to one of the women*)
I too, my dearest master, have been taking her under my protection.

DON GIOVANNI
That will do for today. Take all these people directly to my castle, serve them refreshments and spare no efforts to keep them in good spirits; do your best to amuse them, let them stroll in the garden, show them the gallery, the armory—most of all, make it your bus'ness to keep Masetto happy, understand me?

LEPORELLO
All too clearly. Come along.

MASETTO
Your Lordship!

DON GIOVANNI
What's the matter?

MASETTO
I can't leave my Zerlina alone.

LEPORELLO
My Lord is kind enough to stay in your place. No man on earth could more ably represent you.

DON GIOVANNI
Your dear Zerlina is in the best of hands. Go on, we'll join you in no time at all.

ZERLINA
Go, and don't worry. After all, I am safe with my protector.

MASETTO
And why should I?

ZERLINA

Just because you've no right to have such doubts.

ZERLINA

E per questo non c'è da dubitar.

MASETTO

I'm still not going!

MASETTO

Ed io, sospetto!

DON GIOVANNI

Enough, why all this argument! Unless you go at once, without another word and hurry, Masetto, watch your step, or you'll be sorry!

DON GIOVANNI

Olà! Finiam le dispute; se subito senz'altro replicar, non te ne vai, Masetto, guarda ben, ti pentirai.

Aria

MASETTO

Now I see it, plain as day!
I will bow my head and go.
You command and I obey,
But don't think I like it so,
No, no, no, no, no, no, no!
You're a noble cavalier—
You have just one end in mind—
Being friendly, helpful, kind!
Your unselfish aim is clear,
Yes, very clear
(*to* ZERLINA)
How revolting, how disgusting!
You're a fool to be so trusting!
(*to* LEPORELLO)
I am coming,
(*to* ZERLINA)
You may stay here.
What a cozy situation!
You may reach a lady's station
If the don will condescend.
How disgusting and how stupid!
To believe that noble Cupid!
Oh, how can you be so stupid!
Coming, coming—you can stay here!
But I warn you, don't forget it:
Very soon you will regret it.
Go ahead and you will see!
(LEPORELLO, MASETTO, *and peasants leave*)

MASETTO

Ho capito, signor sì! signor sì!
Chino il capo e me ne vo
Giacchè piace a voi così
Altre repliche non fo,
No, no, no, no, no, no, non fo.
Cavalier voi siete già,
Dubitar non posso affè,
Me lo dice la bontà,
Che volete aver per me.
Bricconaccia! malandrina!
Fosti ognor la mia ruina!
Vengo, vengo.
Resta! resta!
È una cosa molto onesta;
Faccia il nostro cavaliere,
Cavaliere ancora te.

Bricconaccia! malandrina!
Fosti ognor la mia ruina!
Vengo, vengo.
Resta! resta!
È una cosa molto onesta;
Faccia il nostro cavaliere,
Cavaliere ancora te.

Scene 8

(DON GIOVANNI *and* ZERLINA)

Recitative

DON GIOVANNI

At last, my dear Zerlina, he has left us alone, that clumsy bumpkin. Are you satisfied with me, my little sweetheart?

DON GIOVANNI

Alfin siam liberati, Zerlinetta gentil da quel scioccone. Che ne dite, mio ben, so far pulito?

ZERLINA
Signore, è mio marito.

DON GIOVANNI
Chi! colui? Vi par ch'un'onest'uomo, un nobil cavalier, qual io mi vanto, possa soffrir che quel visetto d'oro, quel viso inzuccherato da un bifolcaccio vil sia strapazzato?

ZERLINA
Ma, signore, io gli diedi parola di sposarlo.

DON GIOVANNI
Tal parola non vale un zero; voi non siete fatta per esser paesana. Un'altra sorte vi procuran quegli occhi bricconcelli, quei labretti sì belli, quelle dituccia candide, e odorose, parmi toccar giuncata, e fiutar rose.

ZERLINA
Ah, non vorrei—

DON GIOVANNI
Che non vorreste?

ZERLINA
Alfine ingannata restar. Io so che rado colle dome voi altri cavalieri siete onesti e sinceri.

DON GIOVANNI
Eh un'impostura della gente plebea: la nobiltà ha dipinta negli occhi l'onestà. Orsù, non perdiam tempo; in questo istante io vi voglio sposar.

ZERLINA
Voi?

DON GIOVANNI
Certo io. Quel casinetto è mio: soli saremo: e là, giojello mio, ci sposeremo.

DON GIOVANNI
Là ci darem la mano,
Là mi dirai di sì!
Vedi, non è lontano
Partiam, ben mio, da qui!

ZERLINA
Vorrei e non vorrei;
Mi trema un poco il cor.
Felice, è ver sarei,
Ma può burlarmi ancor.

DON GIOVANNI
Vieni, mio bel diletto!

ZERLINA
Your Lordship, he's my bridegroom.

DON GIOVANNI
Who, that clod? How can a man of my kind, a noble cavalier, possibly stand for seeing a girl of such exquisite beauty, so precious and adorable, wasted on a rustic ignoramus?

ZERLINA
But My Lord, I have promised to marry my Masetto!

DON GIOVANNI
Such a promise is not worth keeping. You were not created to be a common peasant—a girl like you, of such exquisite, delicate perfection, made for love and affection, surely deserves the tenderest protection—dresses of silk and velvet, a bed of roses!

ZERLINA
I don't believe you!

DON GIOVANNI
You don't believe me?

ZERLINA
I think you are joking with me. I have often heard them say that you men of noble standing take advantage of women.

DON GIOVANNI
That is a slander and a mere invention! A man of breeding and rank is a nobleman at heart. And I myself can prove it. If you are willing, we'll be married at once.

ZERLINA
We?

DON GIOVANNI
Can you doubt it! There is my little castle, there is its tower, and there we shall be married, my precious flower!

Duettino

DON GIOVANNI
Give me your hand, my sweetheart,
Promise to be my wife.
There we will share together
A bright and happy life.

ZERLINA
I would, and then I waver—
It may be tempting fate.
My heart is in your favor,
My reason tells me: wait!

DON GIOVANNI
Darling, you must not say so!

ZERLINA
I cannot leave Masetto!

DON GIOVANNI
My love is so much stronger!

ZERLINA
I can't resist much longer,

DON GIOVANNI
Come, my darling,
Give me your hand, my sweetheart,
Promise to be my wife.

ZERLINA
I would, and then I waver,
I long to be your bride;

DON GIOVANNI
And share a happy life.

ZERLINA
No, I cannot decide.

DON GIOVANNI
My love is so much stronger
Darling, resist no longer.

ZERLINA
Soon I'll resist no longer
Soon I'll resist no longer!

DON GIOVANNI
Decide! My love!

ZERLINA
At last!

ZERLINA, DON GIOVANNI
The future lies before us,
New pleasures will restore us,
Our love is sweet and pure.
No sadness will remind us
Of all we leave behind us,
Our new-found joy is sure.

DON GIOVANNI
You'll come?

ZERLINA
I will! My love!

DON GIOVANNI
My love!

ZERLINA, DON GIOVANNI
My darling let us go,
Our love is sweet and pure
And always will endure!

(*as they begin to walk arm in arm toward his villa,* DONNA ELVIRA *enters*)

ZERLINA
Mi fa pietà Masetto.

DON GIOVANNI
Io cangierò tua sorte.

ZERLINA
Presto non son più forte.

DON GIOVANNI
Vieni! Vieni!
Là ci darem la mano
Là mi darai di sì.

ZERLINA
Vorrei e non vorrei
Mi trema un poco il cor.

DON GIOVANNI
Partiam, ben mio da qui.

ZERLINA
Ma può burlarmi ancor.

DON GIOVANNI
Vieni, mio bel diletto
Io cangierò tua sorte.

ZERLINA
Mi fa pietà Masetto
Presto non son più forte.

DON GIOVANNI
Andiam! andiam!

ZERLINA
Andiam!

ZERLINA, DON GIOVANNI
Andiam, andiam mio bene,
A ristorar le pene
D'un innocente amor.
Andiam, andiam, mio bene
A ristorar la pene
D'un innocente amor.

DON GIOVANNI
Andiam!

ZERLINA
Andiam! Andiam!

DON GIOVANNI
Andiam!

ZERLINA, DON GIOVANNI
Andiam, mio bene, andiam!
Le pene ristorar
D'un innocente amor!

Scene 9

(*The same*—DONNA ELVIRA.)

Recitative

DONNA ELVIRA
Fermati, scellerato! Il ciel mi fece udir le tue perfidie; io sono a tempo di salvar questa misera innocente dal tuo barbaro artiglio.

DONNA ELVIRA
Reprobate, do not touch her! It's providence that made me overhear you. I'm not too late yet to save this poor innocent from falling in your net of deception!

ZERLINA
Meschina! cosa sento!

ZERLINA
Good heavens, this is awful!

DON GIOVANNI
(Amor, consiglio!) Idol mio, non vedete ch'io voglio divertirmi.

DON GIOVANNI
(I must think fast.) Dearest heart, don't begrudge me this innocent diversion.

DONNA ELVIRA
Divertirti, è vero, divertirti? Io sò, crudele, come tu ti diverti.

DONNA ELVIRA
This diversion? I see it! A diversion! How well I know all about your diversions.

ZERLINA
Ma signor cavaliere, è ver quel ch'ella dice?

ZERLINA
But My Lord, I am puzzled, why does she say those things?

DON GIOVANNI
La povera infelice è di me innamorata, e per pietà deggio fingere amore, ch'io son per mia disgrazia uom di buon core.

DON GIOVANNI (*disregarding* DONNA ELVIRA)
Poor unfortunate lady, she adores me so madly, and from sheer pity I pretend that I love her. If only out of kindness, I do it gladly.

DONNA ELVIRA
Ah! fuggi il traditor!
Non lo lasciar più dir;
Il labbro è mentitor,
Fallace il ciglio!
Da miei tormenti impara
A creder a quel cor;
E nasca il tuo timor
Dal mio periglio,
Ah fuggi, fuggi!
Ah fuggi il traditor!

DONNA ELVIRA
Believe me, I implore—
While there is time, depart.
A thousand girls before
Have known his evil heart.
I came in time to spare you
A sad, unhappy fate,
A heart betrayed and sore,
The pain I suffered!
Ah, leave him quickly,
Ah, leave him, I implore!
Go, it is not too late!
I know his words are lies
And false the vows he swore.
(*she leaves, taking* ZERLINA *with her*)

Scene 10

(DON GIOVANNI, DON OTTAVIO, DONNA ANNA, *afterward* DONNA ELVIRA.)

DON GIOVANNI
Mi par ch'oggi il demonio si diverta d'opporsi a' miei piacevoli progressi, vanno mal tutti quanti.

DON GIOVANNI
It seems that this is my unlucky day. All my adventures take a turn against me—I don't know what to think.

DON OTTAVIO
The time for pain and tears is past and over—our object is vengeance. Oh, Don Giovanni!

DON GIOVANNI (*aside*)
This had to happen, too!

DONNA ANNA
Señor! Your coming is opportune. You're strong and fearless. You are a man who is just and gen'rous!

DON GIOVANNI
(Could it be that the devil has put her on my trail?) Can you doubt it? But why?

DONNA ANNA
It is important that we have your assistance.

DON GIOVANNI
(I feel a little easier!) I am honored by your confidence. My possessions, my strong arm, and my sword, my life, I place at your disposal with pleasure. But you, lovely Donn' Anna, your eyes are filled with tears? Who could be so unkind and dare to trouble your calm, serene existence?
(DONNA ELVIRA *comes in*)

DONNA ELVIRA
Do I find you once more? Brazen persistence!

Quartet

DONNA ELVIRA (*to* DONNA ANNA)
Heaven forbid you trust this man,
Deceit is his domain!
Basely as he betrayed before
He will betray again.

DONNA ANNA, DON OTTAVIO (*aside*)
Heavens, what great nobility,
What proud majestic grace,
What sad despair, what bitter grief
Written upon her face!

DON GIOVANNI
Poor girl, her mind is hazy!
She's absolutely crazy—
She fears that you may harm her,
I'll try my best to calm her.
Leave me alone with her.

DONNA ELVIRA
Do not believe the reprobate!
I beg you, don't desert me!

DON GIOVANNI
She lost her mind completely!

DONNA ANNA, DON OTTAVIO
Whose word should we believe?
It's very hard to tell.

DONNA ELVIRA
I beg you, do not believe this reprobate,

DON OTTAVIO
Ah! ch'ora, idolo mio, son vani i pianti! Di vendetta si parli. Oh, Don Giovanni!

DON GIOVANNI
(Mancava questo inver!)

DONNA ANNA
Amico! a tempo vi ritroviam! Avete core, avete anima generosa?

DON GIOVANNI
(Sta a vedere che il diavolo le ha detto qualche cosa?) Che domanda! perchè?

DONNA ANNA
Bisogno abbiamo della vostra amicizia.

DON GIOVANNI
(Mi torna il fiato in corpo.)
Comandate: i congiunti,
i parenti; questa
man, questo ferro i beni, il
sangue spenderò per servirvi.
Ma voi, bella Donn' Anna,
perchè così piangete? Il
crudele chi fu, che osò la
calma turbar del viver
vostro?

DONNA ELVIRA
Ah ti ritrovo ancor, perfido mostro.

Non ti fidar, o misera!
Di quel ribaldo, cor!
Me già tradì quel barbaro—
Ti vuol tradir ancor.

DONNA ANNA, DON OTTAVIO
Cieli! che aspetto nobile!
Che dolce maestà
Il suo dolor, le lagrime
M'empiono di pietà.

DON GIOVANNI
La povera ragazza
È pazza, amici miei:
Lasciatemi con lei!
Forse si calmerà.

DONNA ELVIRA
Ah, non credete al perfido!
Restate, oh Dei! restate.

DON GIOVANNI
È pazza; non badate.

DONNA ANNA, DON OTTAVIO
A chi si crederà?
A chi si crederà?

DONNA ELVIRA
Restate! Ah, non credete al perfido!

Sdegno, rabbia, dispetto, pavento, Dentro l'alma girare mi sento.	Fury, anger, disdain, and vexation Stir my heart to great agitation.
DONNA ANNA, DON OTTAVIO Certo moto d'ignoto tormento Dentro l'alma girare mi sento.	DONNA ANNA, DON OTTAVIO There is surely a good explanation For her anguish and great agitation.
DON GIOVANNI Certo moto d'ignoto tormento Dentro l'alma girare mi sento.	DON GIOVANNI I must think of a good explanation For her anguish and great agitation.
DONNA ANNA, DON OTTAVIO Che mi dice per quella infelice Cento cose che intender non sa.	DONNA ANNA, DON OTTAVIO I am anxious to know what has happened To cause her such grief and despair.
DONNA ELVIRA Che mi dice di quel traditore Cento cose che intender non sa.	DONNA ELVIRA I am anxious to tell you what happened. He himself brought me grief and despair.
DON GIOVANNI Che mi dice per quella infelice Cento cose che intender non sa.	DON GIOVANNI I am anxious to hide what has happened, And what caused her such grief and despair.
DONNA ELVIRA Che mi dice di quel traditore, quel traditore cento cose, che intender Non sa.	DONNA ELVIRA If I could only tell you what anguish And torture I suffered through this traitor, What grief and despair!
DON OTTAVIO (Io di quà non vado via, Se non so com'è l'affar.)	DON OTTAVIO (*aside*) I will never rest contented Till the truth is clear and plain.
DONNA ANNA (Non ha l'aria di pazzia Il suo tratto, il suo parlar.)	DONNA ANNA (*aside*) I don't think she is demented. All she says appears quite sane.
DON GIOVANNI (Se m'èn vado, si potria Qualche cosa sospettar.)	DON GIOVANNI (*aside*) I must stay here—if I left her, She might give my plan away.
DONNA ELVIRA Da quel ceffo si dovria La ner'alma giudicar.	DONNA ELVIRA Can't you see that he is acting In a most suspicious way?
DON OTTAVIO Dunque quella?	DON OTTAVIO So you call it—
DON GIOVANNI È pazzarella.	DON GIOVANNI Hallucination!
DONNA ANNA Dunque quegli?	DONNA ANNA You accuse him?
DONNA ELVIRA È un traditore.	DONNA ELVIRA Of fabrication.
DON GIOVANNI Infelice!	DON GIOVANNI What a pity!
DONNA ELVIRA Mentitore! Mentitore!	DONNA ELVIRA He's a liar and betrayer!
DONNA ANNA, DON OTTAVIO Incomincio a dubitar.	DON GIOVANNI (*to* ELVIRA) I begin to have my doubts!
DON GIOVANNI Zitto, zitto, che la gente Si raduna a noi d'intorno:	DONNA ANNA, DON OTTAVIO Do you want a crowd to gather? Try to master your emotion,

Be a little bit more careful,
And consider your good name!

DONNA ELVIRA

You are very much mistaken
If you think you can escape me.
I am lonely and forsaken
But they all shall know my shame!

DONNA ANNA, DON OTTAVIO

His behavior is suspicious.
His emphatic protestations
Are the clearest indications
It is he who is to blame.

DONNA ELVIRA

Though you say it is my madness,
I'll defy you.
Your iniquity and badness
To the world I shall proclaim!

DON GIOVANNI

Be a little bit more careful
And consider your position and good name.
(DONNA ELVIRA *leaves*)

Recitativo

DON GIOVANNI

Ah, such a case is tragic! I must protect the poor creature from harm. I don't want an accident to happen. Will you pardon me, beautiful Donn' Anna. Whenever you need me, you will find me at your disposal. My friends, till later!
(*exits*)

Recitative and Aria

DONNA ANNA

Don Ottavio, stay near me!

DON OTTAVIO

What has happened?

DONNA ANNA

Now's the time I depend on you!

DON OTTAVIO

Beloved, have faith and courage!

DONNA ANNA

Oh heaven! Oh heaven! He is the murderer of my poor father!

DON OTTAVIO

Impossible!

DONNA ANNA

He gave himself away. The suave inflection, the accent and the tone, bearing and manner recall to my mind that bold seducer who broke into my rooms.

DON OTTAVIO

Good God! Is it possible that he abused our friendship

Siate un poco più prudente,
Vi farete criticar.

DONNA ELVIRA

Non sperarlo, o scellerato!
Ho perduta la prudenza,
Le tue colpe ed il mio stato
Voglio a tutti palesar.

DONNA ANNA, DON OTTAVIO

Quegli accenti sì sommessi!
Quel cangiarsi di colore
Sono indizi troppo espressi
Che mi fan determinar.

DONNA ELVIRA

Ho perduta la prudenza!
Non sperarlo!
Le tue colpe ed il mio stato
Voglio a tutti palesar!

DON GIOVANNI

Siate un poco più prudente!
Vi farete, vi farete criticar!

DON GIOVANNI

Povera sventurata! i passi suoi
Voglio seguir, non voglio
Che faccia un precipizio.
Perdonate,
Bellissima Donn'Anna:
Se servirvi poss'io,
In mia casa v'aspetto. Amici, addio!

DONNA ANNA

Don Ottavio, son morta.

DON OTTAVIO

Cos'è stato?

DONNA ANNA

Per pietà soccorretemi!

DON OTTAVIO

Mio bene, fate coraggio.

DONNA ANNA

Oh, Dei! oh Dei! quegli è il carnefice del padre mio!

DON OTTAVIO

Che dite?

DONNA ANNA

Non dubitate più. Gli ultimi accenti
Che l'empio proferì, tutta la voce
Richiamar nel cor mio di quell'indegno,
Che nel mio appartamento—

DON OTTAVIO

Oh, ciel! possibile

Che sotto il sacro manto
d'amicizia—
Ma come fu? Narratemi
Lo strano avvenimento.

and our confidence—but let that be. Describe to me precisely what has happened.

DONNA ANNA
Era già alquanto
Avanzata la notte,
Quando nelle mie stanze, ove
soletta
Mi trovai per sventura, entrar
io vidi
In un mantello avvolto,
Un uom, che al primo istante
Avea preso per voi;
Ma riconobbi poi
Ch'un inganno era il mio.

DONNA ANNA
Late on that evening—it was well toward midnight, when all of a sudden, while by mischance I was alone in my chambers, a man appeared, all wrapped in a mantle; a man whom, for an instant I mistook for you. I soon was to discover how far I was mistaken.

DON OTTAVIO
Stelle! Seguite.

DON OTTAVIO
Heavens, continue!

DONNA ANNA
Tacito a me s'appressa,
E mi vuol abbracciar;
sciogliermi cerco,
Ei più mi stringe, io grido;
Non viene alcun; con una mano
cerca
D'impedire la voce,
E coll'altra m'afferra
Stretta così, che già mi credo
vinta.

DONNA ANNA
Quietly he approached me, tried to take me in his arms. As I repulsed him, he held me tighter; I screamed then, but no one heard me. With one of his hands, he tried to smother my outcries, with the other he held me so very tight, I almost lost my senses.

DON OTTAVIO
Perfido! e alfin?

DON OTTAVIO
Horrible! And then?

DONNA ANNA
Alfine il duol, l'orrore
Dell'infame attentato accrebbe
si
La lena mia; che a forza
Di svincolarmi, torcermi, e
piegarmi
Da lui mi sciolsi.

DONNA ANNA
At last the pain, the terror of this infamous outrage incited me to one great effort; by dint of tremendous struggling, finally I succeeded in gaining my freedom.

DON OTTAVIO
Ohimè! respiro!

DON OTTAVIO
Thank God! Good fortune!

DONNA ANNA
Allora
Rinforzo i stridi miei, chiamo
soccorso—
Fugge il felon, arditamente il
seguo
Fin nella strada per fermarlo; e
sono
Assalitrice d'assalita. Il padre
V'accorre, vuol conoscerlo, e
l'indegno;
Che del povero vecchio era più
forte,
Compiè il misfatto suo col
dargli morte.

DONNA ANNA
And then I renewed my frantic efforts. I cried for help. He tried to flee. I followed close behind him, hoping to stop him from escaping, and even to detain him as my pris'ner. My father appeared then, and confronted him. But the villain, who was younger and stronger than my poor father, saw his misdeeds completed and killed my father.

Aria

Or sai chi l'onore rapire a me
volse,
Chi fu il traditore, che il padre
mi tolse.
Vendetta ti chieggo, la chiede
il tuo cor.

DONNA ANNA
At last I can name him,
My fiendish betrayer,
The ruthless seducer,
My father's assailant and slayer!
I beg you for vengeance

As pledge of your love.
If ever your ardor should waver or languish,
Remember my father, who lay there so helpless in anguish!
Avenge him, I beg you,
By heaven above.
(*exit*)

Rammenta la piaga del misero seno,
Rimira di sangue coperto il terreno,
Se l'ira in te langue d'un giusto furor.

Recitative

DON OTTAVIO

I can hardly believe that a man of nobility could be so vile a felon! Somehow I shall discover all the truth of what happened. I know my duties: one to friendship, one to love. A most grave obligation: either complete acquittal, or vindication!

DON OTTAVIO

Come mai creder deggio
Di sì nero delitto
Capace un cavaliere!
Ah di scoprire il vero
Ogni mezzo si cerchi, io sento in petto
E di sposo, e d'amico
Il dover che mi parla.
Disingannarla voglio, o vendicarla.

Aria

Calmly forbearing,
Loving and tender,
Faithfully caring
I shall defend her,
Sharing her anguish,
Sorrow and pain,
Sorrow, sorrow and pain.
Her suff'rings grieve me,
Her fears and sighing;
Her tears bereave me,
My heart is dying;
When she rejoices
I live again.

Dalla sua pace la mia dipende;
Quel che a lei piace, vita mi rende,
Quel che le incresce, morte mi dà,
Morte, morte mi dà.
S'ella sospira, sospiro anch'io,
È mia quell'ira, quel pianto è mio.
E non ho bene, s'ella non l'ha.

Scene 11

(DON GIOVANNI'S *palace* LEPORELLO, *afterward* DON GIOVANNI.)

Recitative

LEPORELLO

This time I really mean it—I'll leave my crazy master once for all. Here he comes now, the devil—as unconcerned and happy as an angel!

LEPORELLO

Io deggio ad ogni patto
Per sempre abbandonar questo bel matto.
Eccolo qui: guardate
Con qual indifferenza se ne viene.

DON GIOVANNI

Well, good old Leporello, how are we doing?

DON GIOVANNI

Oh Leporello mio, va tutto bene?

LEPORELLO

Well, good old Don Giovanni, nothing doing.

LEPORELLO

Don Giovannino mio, va tutto male.

DON GIOVANNI

What do you mean by that?

DON GIOVANNI

Come? va tutto male?

LEPORELLO

As you told me, I took all those people back to your country palace.

LEPORELLO

Vado a casa
Come voi m'ordinaste
Con tutta quella gente.

DON GIOVANNI
Bravo!

LEPORELLO
A forza di chiacchere.
Di vezzi, e di bugie,
Ch'ho imparato sì bene a star con voi,
Cerco d'intrattenerli.

DON GIOVANNI
Bravo!

LEPORELLO
Dico mille cose a Masetto per placarlo
Per trargli dal pensier la gelosia,

DON GIOVANNI
Bravo! bravo in coscienza mia!

LEPORELLO
Faccio che bevano e gli uomini e le donne;
Son già mezz ubbriiachi:
Altri canta, altri scherza,
Altri seguita a ber; in sul più bello chi credete che capiti?

DON GIOVANNI
Zerlina.

LEPORELLO
Bravo!
E con lei chi viene?

DON GIOVANNI
Donna Elvira.

LEPORELLO
Bravo! e disse di voi.

DON GIOVANNI
Tutto quel mal che in bocca le venia!

LEPORELLO
Bravo! in coscienza mia!

DON GIOVANNI
E tu, cosa facesti?

LEPORELLO
Tacqui.

DON GIOVANNI
Ed ella?

LEPORELLO
Seguì a gridar.

DON GIOVANNI
E tu?

LEPORELLO
Quando mi parve,
Che già fosse sfogata, dolcemente
Fuor dell'orto la trassi, e con bell'arte
Chiusa la porta a chiave io mi cavai,
E sulla via soletta io la lasciai.

DON GIOVANNI
Bravo!

LEPORELLO
I managed to keep them there by means of lies and flattery, a technique I might add I learned from you, sir. As usual, it worked wonders.

DON GIOVANNI
Bravo!

LEPORELLO
If you could have heard what I had to tell Masetto to make the stupid clown forget his jealousy!

DON GIOVANNI
Bravo. I must give you credit!

LEPORELLO
As we expected, they all were drinking plenty. Before long, they were tipsy, some were singing, others laughing—you can see for yourself. All of a sudden, can you guess who dropped in on us?

DON GIOVANNI
Zerlina!

LEPORELLO
Bravo! Guess who else came with her?

DON GIOVANNI
Donna Elvira.

LEPORELLO
Bravo! And said about you—

DON GIOVANNI
All the bad words she could possibly think of.

LEPORELLO
Bravo! I must give you credit!

DON GIOVANNI
And meanwhile, what did you say?

LEPORELLO
Nothing.

DON GIOVANNI
And she?

LEPORELLO
Went on and on!

DON GIOVANNI
What then?

LEPORELLO
When she got tired and the storm had blown over, I just eased her out the door to the garden and locked the gate behind her with caution before she knew what happened, and left her in the street all by herself.

DON GIOVANNI

Bravo, bravo, you're a wizard! It can't go any better! What you have started, I will bring to an end. Those pretty peasant girls happened by at the right time. I'll take good care of them till it is nighttime!

Aria

Here's to an evening,
Peerless in splendor,
Love and surrender,
Laughter and song!
Comb all the highways,
Alleys and byways,
When you see women,
Bring them along.
We shall let everyone do as he pleases,
Each to his liking, free as the breezes.
Only remember: Folly is king!
Meanwhile I'll wander
Hither and yonder,
Straying at random,
Keeping a tryst, a secret tryst.
And by tomorrow
You'll have some new names,
Long-overdue names,
Gracing your list.
I shall pursue them,
Tenderly woo them,
Dark ones and fair ones,
Ladies galore!
And by tomorrow, dear Leporello,
Add to the list a dozen or more!
Let there be gaiety, ev'ryone jolly,
Fun and excitement, freedom and folly,
Pleasure for all as never before,
And by tomorrow, dear Leporello,
Add to the list a dozen or more!
(*leaves with* LEPORELLO)

DON GIOVANNI

Bravo! Bravo! arcibravo! L'affar non può andar meglio; incominciasti, Io saprò terminar. Troppo mi premono Queste contadinotte: Le voglio divertir finchè vien notte.

Finch'han dal vino
Calda la testa,
Una gran festa,
Fa preparar:
Se trovi in piazza,
Qualche ragazza,
Teco ancor quella
Cerca menar:
Senz'alcun ordine,
La danza sia,
Ch'il minuetto,
Chi la follia
Chi l'alemana,
Farai ballar;
Ed io frattanto,
Dall'altro canto,
Con questa e quella,
Vo' amoreggiar.
Ah la mia lista,
Doman mattina,
D'una decina devi aumentar.
Se trovi in piazza,
Qualche ragazza,
Teco ancor quella
Cerca menar:
Ah la mia lista
Doman mattina
D'una decina
Devi aumentar.

Scene 12

(*A garden; on one side, the palace of* DON GIOVANNI; *on the other, a pavilion.*)

Recitative

ZERLINA

Masetto, won't you hear, Masetto, listen!

MASETTO

Stay away from me!

ZERLINA

Masetto, senti un po'! Masetto, dico!

MASETTO

Non mi toccar.

ZERLINA
Perchè?

MASETTO
Perchè mi chiedi?
Perfida! il tatto sopportar dovrei
D'una mano infedele?

ZERLINA
Ah, no! taci, crudele!
Io non merto da te tal trattamento.

MASETTO
Come? ed hai l'ardimento di scusarti?
Star sola con un uom? abbandonarmi
Il dì delle mie nozze, porre in fronte
A un villano d'onore
Questa marca d'infamia! Ah, se non fosse,
Se non fosse lo scandalo, vorrei—

ZERLINA
Ma se colpa io non ho, ma se da lui
Ingannata rimasi; E poi che temi?
Tranquillati, mia vita!
Non mi toccò la punta delle dita.
Non me lo credi, ingrato?
Vien qui, sfogati, ammazzami,
Fa tutto di me quel che ti piace,
Ma poi, Masetto poi, ma poi fa pace.

ZERLINA
But why?

MASETTO
And you can ask? Shame on you! Am I supposed to be delighted after all you have done?

ZERLINA
Don't say such nasty things! I don't deserve to be treated so unkindly.

MASETTO
Is that so? You are brazen enough to make excuses? You meet another man, abandon me on the day of our wedding, bring disgrace on a decent fellow by your shameless behavior! Ah, if it wasn't for the neighborhood gossiping, I'd like to—

ZERLINA
But I've done nothing wrong. I ran away before anything happened. Is that so bad? You take it much too seriously. He did not touch the tip of my finger. You don't believe it? How naughty! Come here—punish me or kill me—you may even tear me limb from limb. But then, Masetto darling, then you'll forgive me.

ZERLINA
Batti, batti, o bel Masetto,
La tua povera Zerlina;
Starò qui come agnellina,
Le tue botte ad aspettar.
Batti, batti la tua Zerlina:
Starò qui, starò qui
Lascierò straziarmi il crine;
Lascierò cavarmi gli occhi;
E le care tue manine
Lieta poi saprò baciar.
Le tue botte ad aspettar.
Ah! lo vedo, non hai core!
Pace, pace, o vita mia!
In contento, ed allegria,
Notte e dì vogliam passar.
Sì, sì, sì, sì, sì,
Notte e dì vogliam passar.

Aria

ZERLINA
I am sorry, dear Masetto,
I behaved so very badly.
I will take a scolding gladly,
Mild and patient as a lamb.
I was in the wrong completely,
So no matter how you treat me,
I will kiss the hand that beat me,
Kiss your dear beloved hand.
I am sorry, dear Masetto,
Go ahead, I will not grumble!
Here I am, resigned and humble—
Your Zerlina, tame and meek.
Oh please, Masetto, hurry, hurry—
Beat me hard,
Then I'll turn the other cheek.
Ah, I see it, come admit it—
You are not angry any longer,
Thank you, thank you, dear Masetto,
I'm so happy you relented!
From now on, we'll live contented,
You and I forevermore!

MASETTO

I give up—and as usual, she has wrapped me round her finger! Men are putty in the hands of their women.

MASETTO

Guarda un po', come seppe
Questa strega sedurmi!
Siamo pure i deboli di testa.

Scene 13

(DON GIOVANNI, SERVANTS)

DON GIOVANNI

(from outside)

Let us begin the banquet if all is ready.

DON GIOVANNI

Sia preparato tutto a una gran festa.

ZERLINA

Oh Masetto, Masetto, listen to that, it's the voice of His Lordship.

ZERLINA

Ah, Masetto, Masetto! odi la voce
Del monsù cavaliero!

MASETTO

Well then, so what?

MASETTO

Ebben, che c'è?

ZERLINA

He'll come!

ZERLINA

Verrà.

MASETTO

He does not scare me!

MASETTO

Lascia che venga.

ZERLINA

Maybe he doesn't, but I am scared to death!

ZERLINA

Ah! se vi fosse
Un buco da fuggir—

MASETTO

And for what reason? What makes you shake and tremble so? Ah, I see it! You shrewd little vixen! You're afraid I might find out what really has happened! Was I a fool to trust you!

Maybe this time I will catch him,
I will hide and do some spying.
It's worth trying,
From the corner I can get a perfect view.

MASETTO

Di cosa temi?
Perchè diventi pallida? Ah, capisco!
Capisco, bricconcella!
Hai timor, ch'io comprenda
Com'è tra voi passata la faccenda.
Presto, presto! pria ch'ei venga
Por mi vo' da qualche lato:
V'è una nicchia, qui celato
Cheto, cheto, mi vo' star.

ZERLINA

Listen, listen, he is coming!
Ah, do not stay here, I implore you,
What would happen if he saw you?
Who can say what he would do?

ZERLINA

Senti, senti! dove vai!
Ah, non t'asconder, o Masetto!
Se ti trova, poveretto,
Tu non sai quel che può far?

MASETTO

I don't care, I'm not his flunky!

MASETTO

Faccia, dica quel che vuole.

ZERLINA

What a foolish stubborn donkey!

ZERLINA

Ah! non giovan le parole!

MASETTO

Who is he to be afraid of?

MASETTO

Parla forte e qui t'arresta.

ZERLINA

What contrary stuff you're made of!
If he only would believe me!
But today he is a bear!
He is acting like a bear!

ZERLINA

Che capriccio ha nella testa?
Quell'ingrato, quel crudele,
Oggi vuol precipitar!
Oggi vuol precipitar!

MASETTO
Capirò se m'è fedele,
E in qual modo andò l'affar.

MASETTO
I'll find out if you deceive me,
You'll be sorry for this affair!

DON GIOVANNI
Su svegliatevi da bravi!
Su coraggio, o buona gente.
Vogliam stare allegramente!
Vogliam ridere e scherzar.
Alla stanza della danza
Conducete tutti quanti;
Ed a tutti in abbondanza
Gran rinfreschi fate dar.

DON GIOVANNI
(*to the country folk*)
Friends, I bid you all be welcome.
I extend an invitation!
Come and join the celebration,
Let us have a rousing time!
Make them feel at home and happy,
Offer them the finest dishes,
Gratifying all their wishes,
Entertain them all night long.
Give them music, dance and song!

CORO
Su svegliatevi da bravi!
Su corraggio, o buona gente.
Vogliam stare allegramente!
Vogliam ridere e scherzar.
Alla stanza della danza
Conducete tutti quanti;
Ed a tutti in abbondanza
Gran rinfreschi fate dar.

CHORUS
Don Giovanni bids you welcome!
He extends an invitation
For a splendid celebration.
Ev'ryone may come along.
What a wonderful occasion!
Entertainment all night long,
Fun and laughter, dance and song!
(*they all go into the palace*)

ZERLINA
Tra quest'alberi celata,
Si può dar che non mi veda.

ZERLINA
I can hide here, if I hurry.
In this arbor, he won't see me.

DON GIOVANNI
Zerlinetta mia garbata! T'ho già vista,
T'ho già vista—non scappar!

DON GIOVANNI
Sweet Zerlina, don't you worry,
I can see you, I can see you plain as day.

ZERLINA
Ah! lasciatemi andar via!

ZERLINA
Do not hold me, I implore you!

DON GIOVANNI
No, no, resta, gioja mia.

DON GIOVANNI
No, Zerlina, I adore you!

ZERLINA
Se pietade avete in core!

ZERLINA
Let me go then, if you love me!

DON GIOVANNI
Sì, ben mio, son tutto amore
Vieni un poco, in questo loco,
Fortunata io ti vo' far.

DON GIOVANNI
Yes, you know how much I love you,
You belong to me, my darling.
This will be your happy day!
(*he discovers* MASETTO, *hiding*)

ZERLINA
Ah! s'ei vede il sposo mio,
So ben io quel che può far.

ZERLINA
If Masetto ever saw us,
He would have a lot to say!

DON GIOVANNI
Masetto!

DON GIOVANNI
(*surprised*)
Masetto?

MASETTO
Sì, Masetto!

MASETTO
(*comes forward*)
Yes, Masetto!

DON GIOVANNI
How long have you been here?
How nice that you are staying!
Zerlina just was saying,
She's lost when you're not here!
Yes, she is lost when you're not here!

DON GIOVANNI
E chiuso là, perchè?
La bella tua Zerlina
Non può, la poverina,
Più star senza di te.
Non può più star senza di te.

MASETTO
She surely is, Your Lordship!

MASETTO
Capisco, sì signore.

DON GIOVANNI
Now let us all be cheerful, very cheerful.
The music is beginning,
So let's be on our way.

DON GIOVANNI
Adesso fate core;
I suonatori udite!
Venite omai con me.

ALL THREE
Yes, yes, let us be cheerful
And do as all the others—
Enjoy ourselves today.
We all shall be happy on this day
So let's be on our way.
(*exit, arm in arm.*)

ZERLINA, DON GIOVANNI, MASETTO
Sì, sì facciamo core,
Ed a ballar cogli altri.
Venite omai con me,
Andiamo tutti tre.
Andiamo tutti tre.

Scene 14

(DONNA ANNA, DONNA ELVIRA, *and* DON OTTAVIO, *masked.*)

DONNA ELVIRA
We must proceed with caution
To reach our great objective.
To make our plan effective,
My friends, we must be shrewd as he.

DONNA ELVIRA
Bisogna aver coraggio,
O cari amici miei;
E i suoi misfatti rei scoprir,
Scoprir potremo allor.

DON OTTAVIO
Her words are wisely spoken!
We all must be courageous.
(*to* DONNA ANNA)
Allay your fears, beloved,
Take heart and trust in me.

DON OTTAVIO
L'amica dice bene—
Coraggio aver conviene.
Discaccia, o vita mia!
L'affanno ed il timor.

DONNA ANNA
Who knows what lies before us,
What danger may befall us?
I tremble with fear and terror
For you, beloved, for you and for us all!

DONNA ANNA
Il passo è periglioso,
Può nascer qualche imbroglio;
Temo pel caro sposo,
E per noi temo ancor.

Scene 15

(DON GIOVANNI, LEPORELLO; *the same.*)

LEPORELLO
(*from the window*)
Oh see the masqueraders!
They have not been invited.

LEPORELLO
Signor, guardate un poco!
Che maschere galanti!

DON GIOVANNI
Falle passar avanti,
Dì che ci fanno onor.

DON GIOVANNI (*at the window*)
Tell them we'd be delighted
If they would join our dance.

DONNA ANNA, DONNA ELVIRA, DON OTTAVIO
Al volto, ed alla voce
Si scopre il traditore.

DONNA ANNA, DONNA ELVIRA, DON OTTAVIO
He noticed our arrival,
We must keep on pretending.

LEPORELLO
Ps! ps! signore maschere!

LEPORELLO
Pst, pst! You masqueraders there!

DONNA ANNA, DONNA ELVIRA
Via rispondete.

DONNA ANNA, DONNA ELVIRA, DON OTTAVIO
What shall we tell him?

LEPORELLO
Zi! zi! signore maschere!

LEPORELLO
Pst, pst! You masqueraders there!

DON OTTAVIO
Cosa chiedete?

DON OTTAVIO
Did you address me?

LEPORELLO
Al ballo, se vi piace
V'invita il mio signor.

LEPORELLO
My master bids you welcome—
He opens wide his door.

DON OTTAVIO
Grazie di tanto onore.
Andiam, compagne belle.

DON OTTAVIO
Thank you, we shall be honored!
We'll come, with your permission.

LEPORELLO
L'amico anche su quelle
Prova farà d'amor.

LEPORELLO
A very nice addition
For Don Giovanni's score!

DONNA ANNA, DON OTTAVIO
Protegga il giusto Cielo
Il zelo del mio cor!
Protegga il giusto Cielo
Il zelo del mio cor.

DONNA ANNA, DON OTTAVIO
Oh grant us Thy protection,
Almighty God above,
And aid the cause of justice,
Unfailing in Thy love!

DONNA ELVIRA
Vendichi il giusto Cielo
Il mio tradito amor!
Vendichi, il giusto cielo
Il mio tradito amor;
Il mio tradito amor.

DONNA ELVIRA
Let me bring to justice
The one who scorned my love,
Help me deliver the one to justice,
The heartless traitor who scorned my love!
(*exit*)

Scene 16

(*A ballroom in the palace of* DON GIOVANNI. ZERLINA, DON GIOVANNI, LEPORELLO, MASETTO; *male and female peasants; servants and musicians.*)

DON GIOVANNI
Riposate, vezzose ragazze.

DON GIOVANNI
Now it's time for a little refreshment!

LEPORELLO
Rinfrescatevi, bei giovinetti.

LEPORELLO
Rest a moment and empty your glasses,

DON GIOVANNI, LEPORELLO
Tornerete a far presto le pazze,
Tornerete a scherzar e ballar!

BOTH
Later on, at your pleasure, dear lasses,
We'll continue the rollicking dance!

DON GIOVANNI
Ehi caffè!

DON GIOVANNI
More coffee!

LEPORELLO
Here is brandy!

LEPORELLO
Cioccolatte!

MASETTO
Let me warn you, Zerlina.

MASETTO
Ah, Zerlina, giudizio!

DON GIOVANNI
Bring more wine!

DON GIOVANNI
Sorbetti!

LEPORELLO
And candy!

LEPORELLO
Confetti!

MASETTO
Don't go near him, Zerlina!

MASETTO
Ah, Zerlina, giudizio!

ZERLINA, MASETTO
Things are going too nicely to suit me,
There is sure to be danger ahead

ZERLINA, MASETTO
Troppo dolce comincia la scena;
In amaro potria terminar.

DON GIOVANNI
I adore you, my darling Zerlina!

DON GIOVANNI
Sei pur vaga, brillante Zerlina.

ZERLINA
Please, My Lord!

ZERLINA
Sua bontà.

MASETTO
See her flirting and flouncing!

MASETTO
La briccona fa festa!

LEPORELLO
I adore you, Lolita and Nina!

LEPORELLO
Sei pur cara, Giannotta, Sandrina!

MASETTO
How I wish I could give her a trouncing!

MASETTO
Tocca pur, che ti cada la testa!

ZERLINA, DON GIOVANNI, LEPORELLO
My (her) Masetto is ranting and raving,
He is jealous, it's only too plain!

ZERLINA
Quel Masetto mi par stralunato.
Brutto, brutto si fa quest'affar.

DON GIOVANNI, LEPORELLO
Quel Masetto mi par stralunato.
Qui bisogna cervello adoprar.

MASETTO
See her preening and prancing!
I will settle her fancy romancing!

MASETTO
La briccona fa festa!
Tocca pur, che ti cada la testa!

ZERLINA, DON GIOVANNI, LEPORELLO
I can see from the way he's behaving,
There'll be trouble all over again
All over again!

ZERLINA, DON GIOVANNI, LEPORELLO
Quel Masetto mi par stralunato.
Qui bisogna cervello adoprar.
Brutto, brutto si fa quest' affar.

MASETTO
(*to Zerlina*)
You'll be sorry!
Ah Zerlina, you drive me insane!

MASETTO
Tocca, tocca!
Ah, briccona, mi vuoi disperar!

Scene 17

(DONNA ANNA, DONNA ELVIRA, DON OTTAVIO *in masquerade; the same.*)

LEPORELLO
Dear friends, we are delighted
To welcome you among us!

LEPORELLO
Venite pur avanti,
Vezzose mascherette.

DON GIOVANNI
È aperto a tutti quanti,
Viva la libertà.

DONNA ANNA, DONNA ELVIRA, DON OTTAVIO
Siam grati a tanti segni
Di generosità.

DON GIOVANNI
È aperto a tutti
A tutti quanti
Viva, viva la liberta!

TUTTI
Viva la libertà!

DON GIOVANNI
Ricominciate il suono!
Tu accoppia i ballerini.

LEPORELLO
Da bravi via ballate!

DONNA ELVIRA
Quella è la contadina.

DONNA ANNA
Io moro!

DON OTTAVIO
Simulate.

DON GIOVANNI, LEPORELLO
Va bene in verità.

MASETTO
Va bene, va bene
Va bene in verità.

DON GIOVANNI
A bada tien Masetto.

LEPORELLO
Non balli poveretto.
Vien qua, Masetto caro,
Facciam quel che altri fa.

DON GIOVANNI
Il tuo compagno io sono,
Zerlina, vien pur quà.

MASETTO
No, no, ballar non voglio.

LEPORELLO
Eh balla, amico mio.

MASETTO
No.

LEPORELLO
Sì, caro Masetto. Balla!

MASETTO
No no, non voglio.

DONNA ANNA
Resister non poss'io.

DON GIOVANNI
In honor of you masquers,
Let me propose a toast!

DONNA ANNA, DONNA ELVIRA, DON OTTAVIO
We're pleased to be invited
By such a gen'rous host!
We thank you!

DON GIOVANNI
A toast to freedom in all its glory!
Freedom, freedom shall never die!

ALL
Freedom shall never die!

DON GIOVANNI
Now let us have some music, (*to* LEPORELLO) and you direct the dances!
(*the dance begins*)

LEPORELLO
That's fine, you're doing nicely!

DONNA ELVIRA
That is the girl in danger!

DONNA ANNA
How dreadful!

DON OTTAVIO
Feign indiff'rence.

DON GIOVANNI, LEPORELLO
It's going well indeed!

MASETTO
I see it, I see it,
It's going well indeed!

DON GIOVANNI
You chaperone Masetto.

LEPORELLO
We'll dance a minuetto, dear Masetto.
Come on, I'll teach you how to do it,
Just follow where I lead.

DON GIOVANNI
And I will be your partner, Zerlina,
You follow where I lead.

MASETTO
No, no, I do not want to!

LEPORELLO
You'll dance, my friend, and like it!

MASETTO
No!

LEPORELLO
Yes! Don't make me coax you! Do it!

MASETTO
No, no, I will not!

DONNA ANNA
How hard to bear this calmly!

DONNA ELVIRA, DON OTTAVIO
Don't give yourself away!

LEPORELLO
You'll dance, my friend, and like it,
You'll learn to dance today!

MASETTO
Let me go, no, no! Zerlina!

DON GIOVANNI
Let us not stay, my darling!
Come, my angel!
(forces her away with him)

ZERLINA
Oh heaven, what is happening?

LEPORELLO
Oh, oh, there will be trouble!

DONNA ANNA, DONNA ELVIRA, DON OTTAVIO
Events are moving swiftly,
We must be on our guard!

ZERLINA
(off-stage)
Help me, help me, save me, save me!

DONNA ANNA, DONNA ELVIRA, DON OTTAVIO
Let us hurry to her rescue!

MASETTO
Ah Zerlina, ah Zerlina!

ZERLINA
Help me, help me!

DONNA ANNA, DONNA ELVIRA, DON OTTAVIO
We must find a way to save her from this villain!
Let us force the door and hurry to her rescue!

ZERLINA
Come and rescue me!
I can't defend myself any longer!

ALL
We are ready to defend you
We come to save you, we will defend you!

DON GIOVANNI
(re-entering with his sword drawn, to LEPORELLO, *whom he has seized)*
Here's the scoundrel who attacked you!
He shall suffer for his crime, his vicious crime!

LEPORELLO
What are you doing? You must believe me!

DON GIOVANNI
I shall kill you,

DON OTTAVIO
Do not hope you can deceive me!

DONNA ELVIRA, DON OTTAVIO
Fingete per pietà!

LEPORELLO
Eh! balla, amico mio:
Facciam quel che altri fa.

MASETTO
Lasciami. Ah no! Zerlina!

DON GIOVANNI
Vieni con me, mia vita! Vieni, vieni.

ZERLINA
Oh, Numi! son tradita!

LEPORELLO
Qui nasce una ruina!

DONNA ANNA, DONNA ELVIRA, DON OTTAVIO
L'iniquo da se stesso,
Nel laccio se ne va.

ZERLINA
Gente! Ajuto! ajuto gente!

DONNA ANNA, DONNA ELVIRA, DON OTTAVIO
Soccorriamo l'innocente.

MASETTO
Ah, Zerlina! Ah, Zerlina!

ZERLINA
Scellerato!

DONNA ANNA, DONNA ELVIRA, DON OTTAVIO
Ora grida da quel lato, da quel lato!
Ah gittiamo giù la porta, giù la porta!

ZERLINA
Scellerato!
Soccorretemi! Son morta!

TUTTI
Siam qui noi per tua difesa,
Per tua difesa, per tua difesa!

DON GIOVANNI
Ecco il birbo che t'ha offesa;
Ma da me la pena avrà!
Mori iniquo!

LEPORELLO
Ah cosa fate? Ah, cosa fate?

DON GIOVANNI
Mori, dico!

DON OTTAVIO
Nol sperate, nol sperate.

DONNA ANNA, DONNA ELVIRA, DON OTTAVIO
L'empio crede con tal frode
Di nasconder l'empietà.

DON GIOVANNI
Donna Elvira?

DONNA ELVIRA
Sì, malvagio!

DON GIOVANNI
Don Ottavio?

DON OTTAVIO
Sì, signore!

DON GIOVANNI
Ah, credete—

DONNA ANNA
Traditore!

DONNA ANNA, DONNA ELVIRA, ZERLINA, DON OTTAVIO, MASETTO
Traditore! Traditore!
Tutto, tutto già si sa!
Tutto, tutto già si sa!
Tutto, tutto già si sa!
Tutto, tutto già si sa!
Trema, trema! scellerato!
Trema, trema! scellerato!

DON GIOVANNI, LEPORELLO
È confusa la mia (sua) testa:
Non so (sa) più quel ch'io
mi (ei si) faccia.

TUTTI GLI ALTRI
Saprà tosto il mondo intero
Il misfatto orrendo e nero,
La tua fiera crudeltà.

DON GIOVANNI, LEPORELLO
È un'orribile tempesta
Minacciando, oh Dio, mi (lo)
va!

DONNA ANNA, DONNA ELVIRA, ZERLINA, DON OTTAVIO, MASETTO
Trema, trema,
O scellerato!
Odi il tuon della vendetta,
Che ti fischia intorno intorno,
Sul tuo capo in questo giorno
Il suo fulmine cadrà.
Trema, trema, o scellerato!
Odi il tuon della vendetta,
Che ti fischia intorno intorno,
Sul tuo capo in questo giorno
Il suo fulmine cadrà.

DON GIOVANNI, LEPORELLO
Ma non manca in me (lui)
coraggio.

TUTTI GLI ALTRI
Odi il tuon!

DONNA ANNA, DONNA ELVIRA, DON OTTAVIO
No, this time you won't deceive us,
We have seen through all your lies!
(*they unmask*)

DON GIOVANNI
Donna Elvira?

DONNA ELVIRA
Yes, Elvira!

DON GIOVANNI
Don Ottavio?

DON OTTAVIO
Stands before you!

DON GIOVANNI
Let me tell you—

DONNA ANNA
Don Giovanni—

DONNA ANNA, DONNA ELVIRA, ZERLINA, DON OTTAVIO, MASETTO
We despise and we abhor you!
Your repulsive, shocking crimes
Went unpunished many times.
To deny it would be vain.
You will never, you will never sin again.
Fear our vengeance, Don Giovanni!
Hear our sentence, Don Giovanni!

DON GIOVANNI, LEPORELLO
A surprising situation!
I don't know my course of action!

DONNA ANNA, DONNA ELVIRA, ZERLINA, DON OTTAVIO, MASETTO
Your depraved, inhuman actions,
Your misdeeds and malefactions
Soon the whole wide world shall know.

DON GIOVANNI, LEPORELLO
Their audacious accusation
Is an unexpected blow!

DONNA ANNA, DONNA ELVIRA, ZERLINA, DON OTTAVIO, MASETTO
Sinner! Villain!
We have come for retribution,
There is nothing that can save you.
Neither force nor wily ruses
Can prevent retaliation.
We have come for vindication
And shall strike the fatal blow!
Hear your sentence, Don Giovanni:
Now the righteous hand of heaven
Will descend to overtake you,
And while mortal men forsake you
To perdition you will go!

DON GIOVANNI, LEPORELLO
Idle words cannot alarm me (him)!

ALL OTHERS
You shall die!

DON GIOVANNI
None of you can ever harm me!

LEPORELLO
None of you can ever harm him!

ALL OTHERS
You shall die!

DON GIOVANNI, LEPORELLO
There's no force of earth or heaven,
No force of earth or heaven
I (he) will not defy, will not defy.

ALL OTHERS
Heaven shall be our defender,
Seek no mercy from on high.
We command you to surrender
Or prepare yourself to die.

DON GIOVANNI, LEPORELLO
Non mi perdo, o mi confondo.

LEPORELLO
Non si perde o si confonde.

TUTTI GLI ALTRI
Odi il tuon!

DON GIOVANNI, LEPORELLO
Se cadesse ancora il mondo,
Nulla mai temer mi (lo) fa!

TUTTI GLI ALTRI
Sul tuo capo in questo giorno
Il suo fulmine cadrà.
Sul tuo capo in questo giorno
Il suo fulmine cadrà.

ACT II

Scene 1

(DON GIOVANNI, LEPORELLO. *Scene as in Act I.* ELVIRA'S *room upstairs at the side, with window, balcony, and door.*)

Duet

DON GIOVANNI
Eh via buffone,
Eh via buffone,
Non mi seccar.

LEPORELLO
No, no, padrone,
No, no, padrone,
Non vo' restar.

DON GIOVANNI
Sentimi, amico.

LEPORELLO
Vo' andar, vi dico.

DON GIOVANNI
Ma che ti ho fatto,
Che vuoi lasciarmi?

LEPORELLO
Oh niente affatto!
Quasi ammazzarmi.

DON GIOVANNI
Va che sei matto,
Va che sei matto.
Matto, matto, fu per burlar.

LEPORELLO
Ed io non burlo.
Ed io non burlo,
Burlo, burlo, ma voglio andar.

DON GIOVANNI
Eh via, buffone, sentimi amico!
Va che sei matto,
Va che sei matto,
Va che sei matto.

LEPORELLO
No, no, padrone,
Vo' andar, vi dico.
No, no, no, no, no, no, no,
Non vo' restar, no,
Non vo' restar, sì, sì, sì, sì, sì!

DON GIOVANNI
Va che sei matto,
Va che sei matto.

LEPORELLO
Sì, sì, sì, sì, sì, sì, sì,
Sì voglio andar.

DON GIOVANNI
Eh via, buffone,
Non mi seccar.

DON GIOVANNI
What are you saying?
You are not staying?
Don't talk such rot!

LEPORELLO
That's what I'm saying,
I am not staying,
No, I am not!

DON GIOVANNI
You are misguided.

LEPORELLO
I have decided.

DON GIOVANNI
Why are you fretting?
Nothing's absurder!

LEPORELLO
Not too upsetting—
No less than murder!

DON GIOVANNI
But Leporello,
Be a good fellow!
That was only one of my jokes!

LEPORELLO
I am not after
That kind of laughter,
I am leaving you and your hoax.

DON GIOVANNI
You are too childish, listen to reason!
Did I mistreat you
Or did I cheat you?
You're very silly.

LEPORELLO
I may be silly, but I have reason!
No, no, no, no, no, no, no,
I will not stay, no,
I'm on my way, yes, yes, yes, yes, yes!

DON GIOVANNI
You are too childish,
You're very silly!

LEPORELLO
I may be very silly,
But I won't stay,

DON GIOVANNI
Come Leporello, old fellow,
Don't go away.

LEPORELLO
I will not mellow,
Don't call me fellow!

LEPORELLO
No, no, padrone,
No, no, padrone.

DON GIOVANNI
You must be joking
Don't go away.

DON GIOVANNI
Eh via, buffone,
Fu per burlar.

LEPORELLO
I'll go away, I am not joking,
I'll go away.

LEPORELLO
Non vo' restar!
Ed io non burlo, ma voglio andar.

Recitative

DON GIOVANNI
Leporello!

DON GIOVANNI
Leporello!

LEPORELLO
What now, please?

LEPORELLO
Signore?

DON GIOVANNI
Come here, let us make peace, and take this.

DON GIOVANNI
Vien qui, facciamo pace.
Prendi.

LEPORELLO
What?

LEPORELLO
Cosa?

DON GIOVANNI
Four sovereigns.

DON GIOVANNI
Quattro doppie.

LEPORELLO
Well, all right then, for this last time I'll consent to take the money, but don't make it a habit; do not think you can get around me like all your women, with money and with flattery.

LEPORELLO
Oh sentite!
Per questa volta ancora
La cerimonia accetto;
Ma non vi ci avvezzate—non credete;
Di sedurre i miei pari
Come le donne, a forza di danari.

DON GIOVANNI
Let's not talk about that. Are you now willing to do what I tell you?

DON GIOVANNI
Non parliam più di ciò. Ti basta l'animo
Di far quel ch'io ti dico?

LEPORELLO
But please, no more women!

LEPORELLO
Purchè lasciam le donne.

DON GIOVANNI
No more women! Idiot! What are you saying! To me they are far more important than the bread that I eat and the air I breathe!

DON GIOVANNI
Lasciar le donne! Pazzo!
Lasciar le donne! Sai qu'elle per me
Son necessarie più del pan che mangio,
Più dell'aria che spiro.

LEPORELLO
How is it then that you cheat every one of them?

LEPORELLO
E avete core
D'ingannarle poi tutte?

DON GIOVANNI
I love them all. If you're true to one only, you're unfair to the others. This pains my heart and offends my sense of justice. I never can play favorites. But since the women do not understand that, they call my harmless weakness deception.

DON GIOVANNI
È tutto amore,
Chi a una sola è fedele
Verso l'altre è crudele. Io, che in me sento.
Sì esteso sentimento,
Vo bene a tutte quante.
Le donne poichè calcolar non sanno,
Il mio buon natural chiamano inganno.

LEPORELLO
Non ho veduto mai
Naturale più vasto e più benigno!
Orsù cosa vorreste?

LEPORELLO
Never in my life have I known any man with a stronger weakness!

DON GIOVANNI
Odi! Vedesti tu la cameriera
Di Donn' Elvira?

DON GIOVANNI
Listen: have you seen the little chambermaid of Donn' Elvira?

LEPORELLO
Io no.

LEPORELLO
Not yet.

DON GIOVANNI
Non hai veduto
Qualche cosa di bello,
Caro il mio Leporello: ora io con lei
Vo' tentar la mia sorte; ed ho pensato,
Giacchè siam verso sera,
Per aguzzarle meglio l'appetito,
Di presentarmi a lei col tuo vestito.

DON GIOVANNI
Well, let me tell you—you have seen nothing like her, good old Leporello! I have decided to make her my next conquest, and since the darkness is rapidly descending, I am convinced I'll reach my goal much faster by borrowing your clothes for this adventure.

LEPORELLO
E perchè non poteste
Presentarvi col vostro?

LEPORELLO
Will you give me one good reason why you can't wear your own?

DON GIOVANNI
Han poco credito
Con gente di tal rango
Gli abiti signorili
Sbrigati, via!

DON GIOVANNI
I am a nobleman and I want to present myself as a man of your kind. Off with it, hurry!

LEPORELLO
Signor, per più ragioni—

LEPORELLO
My Lord, in my position.

DON GIOVANNI
Finiscila, non soffro opposizioni.

DON GIOVANNI
No arguments, I brook no opposition.
(*they exchange cloaks and hats*)

Scene 2

(DONNA ELVIRA *appears at the window. It gradually becomes dark.*)

Trio

DONNA ELVIRA
Ah taci, ingiusto core!
Non palpitarmi in seno!
È un empio, è un traditore
È colpa aver pietà.

DONNA ELVIRA
Oh wounded heart, be silent!
Be calm, do not regret him.
He's wicked, you must forget him—
Unworthy of your tears.

LEPORELLO
Zitto! di Donna Elvira.
Signor, la voce io sento.

LEPORELLO
Listen, that's Donn' Elvira!
My Lord, we must avoid her!

DON GIOVANNI
Cogliere io vo' il momento!
Tu fermati un po' là.
Elvira, idolo mio!

DON GIOVANNI
I welcome this occasion
To play a little joke.
Elvira, I adore you!

DONNA ELVIRA
Non è costui l'ingrato?

DONNA ELVIRA
Can it be Don Giovanni?

DON GIOVANNI
Yes, sweetheart, see me repentant,
Forgive me, I implore!

DONNA ELVIRA
His words arouse a feeling,
So tender and appealing,

LEPORELLO
She really would be crazy
To trust him any more.

DON GIOVANNI
Come down, my precious jewel,
My glorious treasure,
Enjoy new bliss and pleasure
With your repentant lover,
Embraced in his longing arms!

DONNA ELVIRA
No, I will not believe in you.

DON GIOVANNI
Ah, trust in me, I implore you!

DONNA ELVIRA
I abhor you!

LEPORELLO
I can't refrain from laughing,
This really is too funny,
Very funny, very, very, very funny!

DONNA ELVIRA
Shall I resist temptation
Or heed my inclination?

DON GIOVANNI, LEPORELLO
Will she resist temptation
Or heed her inclination?

DONNA ELVIRA
May God in heaven help me
To guide this heart of mine!
(*she withdraws*)

DON GIOVANNI
There never was a talent so manifold as mine!

LEPORELLO
May God in heaven help her
To see through his design.

DON GIOVANNI
A happy inspiration!
A fertile brain is mine!

Recitative

Well, what do you say now?

LEPORELLO
I say but one thing, your heart is made of stone.

DON GIOVANNI
Sì, vita mia, son io,
E chieggo carità.

DONNA ELVIRA
Numi! che strano effetto
Mi si risveglia in petto!

LEPORELLO
State a veder la pazza!
Che ancor gli crederà!

DON GIOVANNI
Discendi, o gioia bella!
Vedrai che tu sei quella,
Che adora l'alma mia,
Pentito io sono già!

DONNA ELVIRA
No! non ti credo, o barbaro.

DON GIOVANNI
Ah, credimi, o m'uccido!

DONNA ELVIRA
Non ti credo!

LEPORELLO
Se seguitate, io rido.
Se seguitate, io rido
Rido, rido!

DONNA ELVIRA
Dei! che cimento è questo?
Non so s'io vado, o resto!

DON GIOVANNI
Spero che cada presto,
Che bel colpetto è questo!

LEPORELLO
Già quel mendace labbro
Torna a sedur costei.

DONNA ELVIRA
Ah proteggete voi
La mia credulità!

DON GIOVANNI
Più fertile talento
Del mio, no, non si dà!

LEPORELLO
Deh proteggete, o Dei!
La sua credulità!

DON GIOVANNI
Più fertile talento
Del mio, no, non si dà!
Amico, che ti par!

LEPORELLO
Mi par che abbiate
Un'anima di bronzo.

DON GIOVANNI
Va là, che se' il gran gonzo! Ascolta bene;
Quando costei qui viene,
Tu corri ad abbracciarla,
Falle quattro carezze,
Fingi la voce mia; poi con bell'arte
Cerca teco condurla in altra parte.

DON GIOVANNI
Come, come, you're sentimental. Now pay attention: when Donn' Elvira gets here, give her a hearty welcome, be a passionate lover, speak to her in my voice, and then use your own judgment in the moonlight.

LEPORELLO
Ma, signore—

LEPORELLO
But I ask you—

DON GIOVANNI
Non più repliche!

DON GIOVANNI
No more arguments!

LEPORELLO
E se poi mi conosce?

LEPORELLO
If she finds out I'm not you!

DON GIOVANNI
Non ti conoscerà, se tu non vuoi.
Zitto! ell'apre—ehi, giudizio!

DON GIOVANNI
How could she find out if you are clever.
Quiet, she's coming!
Sh! Be careful!
(*he hides*)

Scene 3

(*The same.*)

DONNA ELVIRA
Eccomi a voi!

DONNA ELVIRA
Here I am, beloved!

DON GIOVANNI
(Veggiamo che farà.)

DON GIOVANNI (*aside*)
Let's see what he will do!

LEPORELLO
(Che imbroglio!)

LEPORELLO (*aside*)
What confusion!

DONNA ELVIRA
Dunque creder potrò, che pianti miei
Abbian vinto quel cor? Dunque pentito
L'amato Don Giovanni al suo dovere,
E all'amor mio ritorna?

DONNA ELVIRA
Can it really be true that I convinced you by my love and my tears? Have you repented, beloved Don Giovanni?

LEPORELLO
Sì, carina!

LEPORELLO (*imitating* DON GIOVANNI'S *voice*)
Yes, my darling.

DONNA ELVIRA
Crudele! se sapeste
Quante lagrime, e quanti
Sospir voi mi costate!

DONNA ELVIRA
Giovanni, if you knew how much unhappiness, what heartache and anguish you have cost me.

LEPORELLO
Io, vita mia?

LEPORELLO
I, did I really?

DONNA ELVIRA
Voi!

DONNA ELVIRA
Yes, dear.

LEPORELLO
Poverina, quanto mi dispiace!

LEPORELLO
Poor Elvira! I behaved so badly!

DONNA ELVIRA
Mi fuggirete più?

DONNA ELVIRA
You'll never leave again?

LEPORELLO
No dear, I promise.

DONNA ELVIRA
You'll always stay with me?

LEPORELLO
Always.

DONNA ELVIRA
I love you so!

LEPORELLO
I dote on you! (*aside*) I'm doing myself proudly.

DONNA ELVIRA
My Adonis!

LEPORELLO
My sugarplum!

DONNA ELVIRA
I am burning with passion!

LEPORELLO
And I am smoldering.

DON GIOVANNI (*aside*)
I could not do much better.

DONNA ELVIRA
You never will deceive me?

LEPORELLO
Never, never.

DONNA ELVIRA
Then swear to it.

LEPORELLO
I swear by this sweet hand which I cover with my kisses that I will always—

DON GIOVANNI (*pretends to attack someone*)
Ih eh ah ah . . . surrender!

LEPORELLO, DONNA ELVIRA
A robber!
(*they rush off*)

DON GIOVANNI
Ih eh ih eh ah ah! And now it will be very easy to persuade her. I'll serenade her.

Canzonetta

DON GIOVANNI (*accompanies himself on a mandolin*)
Beloved, hear me calling
Beneath your window.
Console my lovelorn heart
And come to me, I pray.
If you will not return
My ardent longing,
Before your very eyes
I'll end my life today.
Your lips are red as roses,
Smiling and tender,
Your sweet eyes have the splendor

LEPORELLO
No, muso bello!

DONNA ELVIRA
Sarete sempre mio?

LEPORELLO
Sempre!

DONNA ELVIRA
Carissimo!

LEPORELLO
Carissima!
(La burla mi dà gusto!)

DONNA ELVIRA
Mio tesoro!

LEPORELLO
Mia Venere!

DONNA ELVIRA
Son per voi tutta foco!

LEPORELLO
Io tutto cenere!

DON GIOVANNI
(Il birbo si riscalda.)

DONNA ELVIRA
E non m'ingannerete?

LEPORELLO
No, sicuro.

DONNA ELVIRA
Giuratelo.

LEPORELLO
Lo giuro a questa mano,
Che bacio con trasporto, e a quei bei lumi!

DON GIOVANNI
Ih, eh, ah, ih! sei morto!

DONNA ELVIRA, LEPORELLO
Oh, Numi!

DON GIOVANNI
Ih, eh, ah, ih! Par che la sorte
Mi secondi. Veggiamo;
Le finestre son queste: ora cantiamo.

Deh vieni alla finestra,
O mio tesoro;
Deh vieni a consolar
Il pianto mio.
Se neghi a me di dar qualche ristoro;
Davanti agli occhi tuoi, morir vogl'io.
Tu ch'hai la bocca dolce più il mele.
Tu che il zucchero porti in mezzo al core;
Non esser gioja mia con me crudele,

Lasciate almen veder, mio bell'amore!

Of sunlight's golden shine.
Ah do not leave me here
So sad alone to pine!
Won't you at last appear,
Oh precious love of mine!

Scene 4

(DON GIOVANNI, MASETTO, *armed peasants.*)

DON GIOVANNI
V'è gente alla finestra;
Forse è dessa. Zi, zi!

DON GIOVANNI
She's coming to the window! My darling! I'm here!

MASETTO
Non ci stanchiamo; il cor mi dice
Che trovarlo dobbiam.

MASETTO (*entering with armed companions*)
Let's not give up yet; something tells me that we will find him at last.

DON GIOVANNI
Qualcuno parla.

DON GIOVANNI (*aside*)
I hear some voices.

MASETTO
Fermatevi—mi pare
Che alcuno qui si mova.

MASETTO
Stand still, fellows. I think I saw a figure in the dark.

DON GIOVANNI
Se non fallo, è Masetto.

DON GIOVANNI
It seems to be Masetto.

MASETTO
Chi va là? Non risponde?
Animo, schioppo al muso:
Chi va là?

MASETTO
Who goes there? No one answers. Company: raise your guns.
Who goes there?

DON GIOVANNI
(Non è solo,
Ci vuol giudizio.) Amici,
(Non mi voglio scoprir.) Sei tu, Masetto?

DON GIOVANNI
There are many, I must outwit them (*imitating* LEPORELLO) Good friends; (*aside*) I must play my part well.
Is it you, Masetto?

MASETTO
Appunto quello; e tu?

MASETTO
How did you guess it? And you?

DON GIOVANNI
Non mi conosci? Il servo
Son io di Don Giovanni.

DON GIOVANNI
You do not know me? I'm your friend. My name is Leporello.

MASETTO
Leporello!
Servo di quell'indegno cavaliere?

MASETTO
Leporello! Servant of that depraved immoral master?

DON GIOVANNI
Certo, di quel briccone.

DON GIOVANNI
Yes, sir, of that wicked scoundrel!

MASETTO
Di quell'uom senza onore, ah dimmi un poco,
Dove possiam trovarlo;
Lo cerco con costor per trucidarlo.

MASETTO
That base wretched seducer! Say, can you tell me, where we can find your master? We men are determined to kill him.

DON GIOVANNI
(Bagatelle!) Bravissimo, Masetto.
Anch'io con voi m'unisco
Per fargliela a quel birbo di padrone;

DON GIOVANNI
(Nothing to it.) Bravo, my friend Masetto! I, too, would like to join you and help to teach my master a lesson. We must be smart and cleverly outguess him.

Aria

A few of you go over there
And softly stalk your prey.
The rest explore the other side,
He can't be far away,
As soon as you discover
A lady and her lover
Parading, promenading,
Persuading, serenading,
Then strike him all the faster
For that will be my master
And you have caught My Lord.
He wears a hat with feathers
And boots of shiny leather,
A cloak of silk and velvet
And at his side a sword.
Then grab him, and stab him.
Then grab him fast and stab him,
Attack and whack and crack him,
Be off and hunt the traitor,
I'll come and meet you later.
I told you how to find him.
You must hurry right behind him.
(*the peasants go off*)
But you must stay with me,
Masetto, you stay here
Alone with me.
I have some news to tell you—
A most important clue,
But it must be a secret
A secret for us two,
A great surprise for you,
I'll tell you what to do,
Exactly what to do.

Ma udite un po' qual è la mia
intenzione.
Metà di voi quà vadano
E gli altri vadan là,
E pian pianin lo cerchino
Lontan non sia di quà, no,
Lontan, lontan non sia di quà.
Se un uom e una ragazza
Passeggian per la piazza,
Se sotto a una finestra
Fare all'amor sentite,
Ferite, pur ferite,
Ferite, pur ferite
Il mio padron sarà.
In testa egli ha un cappello
Con candidi pennacchi,
Addosso un gran mantello,
E spada al fianco egli ha.
Se un uom e una ragazza
Passegian per la piazza,
Se sotto a una finestra
Far all'amor sentite,
Ferite, ferite,
Ferite, pur ferite.
Metà di voi quà vadano
E gli altri vadan là,
E pian pianin lo cerchino,
Lontan non sia di quà, no,
Lontan, lontan non sia di quà.
Andate, fate presto
Andate, fate presto,
Fate presto, fate presto.
Tu sol verrai con me,
Verrai con me.
Noi far dobbiam il resto,
E già vedrai cos'è.
Noi far dobbiam il resto
E già vedrai cos'è,
E già vedrai cos'è.

Scene 5

(DON GIOVANNI, MASETTO.)

DON GIOVANNI
Shhh! Let me make sure that no one's listening. So you insist on killing him?

MASETTO
Of course.

DON GIOVANNI
It would not be enough to beat him up and to break a few bones?

MASETTO
No, no, I want to kill him and cut him up in pieces.

DON GIOVANNI
Zitto! lascia ch'io senta, ottimamente!
Dunque dobbiami ucciderlo?

MASETTO
Sicuro.

DON GIOVANNI
E non ti basteria rompergli l'ossa
Fracassargli le spalle?

MASETTO
No, no! voglio ammazzarlo!
Vo' farlo in cento brani.

DON GIOVANNI
Hai buone arme?

MASETTO
Cospetto!
Ho pria questo moschetto;
E poi questa pistola.

DON GIOVANNI
E poi?

MASETTO
Non basta?

DON GIOVANNI
Eh, basta certo. Or prendi:
Questa per la pistola,
Questa per il moschetto.

MASETTO
Ahi! ahi! La testa mia—

DON GIOVANNI
Taci, o t'uccido.
Questa per l'ammazzarlo,
Questa per farlo in brani!
Villano, mascalzon, ceffo da cane!

DON GIOVANNI
Have you weapons?

MASETTO
Oh have I? Take a look at this musket and then at this pistol. (*hands them to* DON GIOVANNI)

DON GIOVANNI
Is that all?

MASETTO
Won't they do?

DON GIOVANNI
Yes, they will do. Now watch me:
(*beating him*)
This one is for your pistol, this one is for your musket.

MASETTO
Help, save my life, murder!

DON GIOVANNI
Hush, or I'll kill you!
(*beating him again*)
This is for planning murder, this for cutting in pieces. You miserable dog! This ought to show you!
(*he leaves*)

Scene 6

(MASETTO; *afterward* ZERLINA)

MASETTO
Ahi, ahi! La testa mia!
Ahi, ahi, le spalle! E il petto!

ZERLINA
Di sentire mi parve
La voce di Masetto.

MASETTO
Oh, Dio! Zerlina!
Zerlina mia, soccorso!

ZERLINA
Cos'è stato?

MASETTO
L'iniquo il scellerato
Mi ruppe l'ossa, e i nervi.

ZERLINA
O poveretta me! chi?

MASETTO
Leporello.
O qualche diavol che somiglia a lui.

ZERLINA
Crudel! non tel diss'io,
Che con questa tua pazza gelosia
Ti ridurresti a qualche brutto passo.
Dove ti duole?

MASETTO
Ow, ow, I hurt all over, my back, my shoulders, my stomach!

ZERLINA
I heard someone calling, it sounded like Masetto.

MASETTO
Thank God you are here; my good Zerlina, please help me.

ZERLINA
What's the matter?

MASETTO
That scoundrel, that vicious killer has battered me to pieces.

ZERLINA
Oh what an awful shame! Who?

MASETTO
Leporello, or someone else who looked like his twin brother.

ZERLINA
You see! Did I not warn you that your jealous ridiculous behavior sooner or later would get you into trouble! Where does it hurt?

MASETTO
Here.

ZERLINA
Where else?

MASETTO
Here and also here.

ZERLINA
There's nothing else that hurts you?

MASETTO
Something's wrong with this one foot and this elbow, and with this finger.

ZERLINA
Oh come, that's not so bad, no bones broken. Let us go home together. If you will promise to be a little less jealous, I'll make you well again, darling Masetto.

MASETTO
Qui.

ZERLINA
E poi?

MASETTO
Qui, e ancora qui.

ZERLINA
E poi non ti duol altro?

MASETTO
Duolmi un poco
Questo piè, questo braccio, e questa mano.

ZERLINA
Via via, non è gran mal, se il resto è sano.
Vientene meco a casa.
Purchè tu mi prometta
D'essere men geloso,
Io, io ti guarirò, caro il mio sposo.

Aria

Darling, I'll cure you;
I can assure you,
I have a remedy all of my own.
It works like magic,
Cures all diseases.
How to prepare it I know alone.
This priceless medicine comforts and eases,
And I will share it with you alone.
Are you not curious what it can be?
Feel how it palpitates,
It is right here.
Right here inside of me
Beating excitedly, it is right here.
Here is my medicine,
Wonderful medicine,
My loving heart,
Beating so rapidly,
Waiting to cure you,
It is my heart, my loving heart.

Vedrai carino,
Se sei buonino,
Che bel rimedio,
Ti voglio dar.
È naturale,
Non dà disgusto,
E lo speziale,
Non lo sa far, no.
È un certo balsamo,
Che porto addosso,
Dare tel posso,
Se il vuoi provar!
Saper vorresti
Dove mi sta?
Sentilo battere
Toccami quà!

Scene 7

(*Dark, inner court in the house of* DONNA ANNA, DONNA ELVIRA, LEPORELLO.)

LEPORELLO
I see a glow of torchlights—there are people nearby; hide in this doorway so that they will not see us.

DONNA ELVIRA
But my darling, do you mind if they see us?

LEPORELLO
Di molte faci il lume
S'avvicina, o mio ben; stiamo qui un poco.
Finchè da noi si scosta.

DONNA ELVIRA
Ma che temi,
Adorato mio sposo?

LEPORELLO
Nulla, nulla.
Certi riguardi—Io vo' veder
se il lume
È gia lontano. (Ah come
Da costei liberarmi?)
Rimanti, anima bella!

LEPORELLO
Not at all, dear, but at this moment I would prefer to remain incognito. (I must at once get rid of this woman.)
I'll soon be back, beloved.

DONNA ELVIRA
Ah, non lasciarmi!

DONNA ELVIRA
Please, don't be long.

Sextet

DONNA ELVIRA
Sola, sola, in bujo loco,
Palpitar il cor mi sento!
E m'assale un tal spavento,
Che mi sembra di morir.

DONNA ELVIRA
Once again I am deserted,
Left alone, forlorn, rejected,
In the darkness and unprotected,
I am almost dead with fear,
With a mortal, hopeless fear!

LEPORELLO
Più che cerco, men ritrovo
Questa porta sciagurata.
Piano, piano, l'ho trovata,
Ecco il tempo di fuggir.

LEPORELLO
I've been looking for that doorway.
Where the devil, where the devil can I find it?
Wait a minute, this may be it, yes, I've found it,
Here's my chance to disappear
And to get away from here.
(*he hides*)

Scene 8

(DON OTTAVIO, DONNA ANNA. *The same.*)

DON OTTAVIO
Tergi il ciglio, o vita mia!
E dà calma al tuo dolore!
L'ombra omai del genitore
Pena avrà de' tuoi martir.

DON OTTAVIO
Dry your tears, beloved Anna,
Do not let despair control you.
Time and my love will help console you,
Let your father rest in peace,
Eternal peace.

DONNA ANNA
Lascia almen alla mia pena
Questo piccolo ristoro,
Sol la morte, o mio tesoro,
Il mio pianto può finir!

DONNA ANNA
Tears are one small consolation
For my loss and tribulation.
No, beloved, never, never,
My laments will never cease.

DONNA ELVIRA
Ah, dov'è lo sposo mio?

DONNA ELVIRA
Ah, if only I could find him!

LEPORELLO
Se mi trova, son perduto.

LEPORELLO
I am lost if she should find me.

DONNA ELVIRA, LEPORELLO
Una porta là vegg'io.

DONNA ELVIRA, LEPORELLO
Over there I see a doorway.

DONNA ELVIRA
Cheto, cheto io vo' partir.

DONNA ELVIRA
Maybe I can find my way.

LEPORELLO
Cheto, cheto io vo' partir.

LEPORELLO
Maybe I can slip away.

Scene 9

(ZERLINA, MASETTO, *with torches. The same.*)

ZERLINA, MASETTO
Scoundrel, surrender,
You can't escape us!

DONNA ANNA, DON OTTAVIO
There's the offender,
Captured at last!

ALL FOUR
Give him his punishment,
Death to the traitor.

DONNA ELVIRA
I beg you, spare him,
I am to be his wife!

ALL OTHERS
It's Donna Elvira!
Now that we've caught him,
You ask us to spare him?
No, no, no, no, he'll die!

DONNA ELVIRA
Oh spare him!

ALL OTHERS
No! He'll die!

LEPORELLO
Dear friends, have mercy, please do not kill me!
I am not guilty—look at me closely—
It's all a big mistake,
It's only I,
Ah, please, for pity's sake,
Don't make me die.

ALL OTHERS
What? Leporello?
This is confounding!
You shameless fellow!
This is astounding!
It is indeed a shock to me,
How it occurred, I cannot see!

LEPORELLO
Still another complication!
Unforeseen recrimination!

OTHERS
Still another provocation!
Unforeseen dissimulation!

LEPORELLO
Through the cunning of my master,
I am heading for disaster!

ZERLINA, MASETTO
Ferma briccone! dove ten vai.

DONNA ANNA, DON OTTAVIO
Ecco il fellone! Com'era quà?

DONNA ANNA, ZERLINA, DON OTTAVIO, MASETTO
Ah! mora il perfido,
Che m'ha tradito!

DONNA ELVIRA
È mio marito!
Pietà! pietà!

DONNA ANNA, ZERLINA, DON OTTAVIO, MASETTO
È Donna Elvira
Quella ch'io vedo?
Appena il credo?
No; no, no, no! morrà!

DONNA ELVIRA
Pietà!

DONNA ANNA, ZERLINA, DON OTTAVIO, MASETTO
No, morrà!

LEPORELLO
Perdon, perdono!
Signori miei;
Quello io non sono,
Sbaglia costei.
Viver lasciatemi
Per carità!

ALTRI
Dei! Leporello!
Che inganno è questo!
Che inganno è questo!
Stupida o resto.
Che mai sarà,
Che mai sarà,
Che mai sarà,
Che mai sarà?

LEPORELLO
Mille torbidi pensieri
Mi s'aggiran per la testa.

DONNA ANNA, ZERLINA, DON OTTAVIO, MASETTO
Mille torbidi pensieri
Mi s'aggiran per la testa.

LEPORELLO
Mille torbidi pensieri
Mi s'aggiran per la testa.
Se mi salvo in tal tempesta,

È un prodigio in verità!
È un prodigio in verità.

ALTRI
Che giornata, o stella, è questa—
Che impensata novità?
Che impensata novità,
Che impensata novità,
Che impensata novità.

ZERLINA
Dunque quello sei tu che il mio Masetto poco fa crudelmente maltrattasti!

DONNA ELVIRA
Dunque tu m'ingannasti, o scellerato, spacciandoti con me da Don Giovanni!

DON OTTAVIO
Dunque tu in questi panni venisti qua per qualche tradimento!

DONNA ELVIRA
A me tocca punirlo.

ZERLINA
Anzi a me.

DON OTTAVIO
No, no, a me.

MASETTO
Accoppatelo meco tutti tre.

LEPORELLO
Ah, pietà! Signori miei
Ah, pietà di me, pietà.
Do ragione a voi, a lei,
Ma, ma il delitto mio non è.
Il padron con prepotenza
L'innocenza mi rubò
Donn'Elvira! Compatite
Voi capite come andò!
Voi capite come andò.
Di Masetto non so nulla
Non so nulla, nulla nulla
Vel dirà questa fanciulla.
E un oretta, circumcirca,
Che con lei girando vo,
Che con lei girando vo.
A voi, Signore! Non dico niente,
Certo timore, certo accidente,
Di fuori chiaro,
Di dentro oscuro
Non c'è riparo
La porta, il muro lo - il - la -
Vò da quel lato,
Poi qui celato,
L'affar si sa,
Ma s'io sapeva,
Fuggia per qua!
Fuggia per qua.

If I only can escape them,
I will never stray again,
I will never betray again!

OTHERS
What misfortune, a new disaster,
He betrayed us once again,
All endeavors were in vain.
But our vengeance will not fail,
Right and justice shall prevail!
(*exit* DONNA ANNA)

Recitative

ZERLINA (*to* LEPORELLO)
So it was you who not long ago so brutally attacked and mistreated my Masetto?

DONNA ELVIRA
And it was you who deceived me, pretending all along to be Don Giovanni?

DON OTTAVIO
Since you disguised your person it must have been for some ulterior motive.

DONNA ELVIRA
To punish him is my task.

ZERLINA
Also mine.

DON OTTAVIO
No, no, it is mine!

MASETTO
Let us all have some fun and break his spine!

Aria

LEPORELLO
Please don't kill me right away,
Hear what I have got to say,
In heaven's name, please do.
I can give you an explanation.
But, but I assure you,
I myself am not to blame.
Could I help it if my master
Made me carry out his aim,
Made me play this little game?
Donna Elvira, you can prove it,
You have seen it for yourself,
Of Masetto and a beating,
I know nothing.
I was then with Donna Elvira,
We were strolling over yonder
Just about an hour ago,
She herself can tell you so!
And Don Ottavio, you see it's this way:
There I am frightened, out in the darkness,
It was a nightmare! I did see a light there,
Then out of nowhere, I enter the door there,

I was patiently waiting,
Just meditating—
I meant no wrong,
I was just trying to get along.
(*he runs away*)

DONNA ELVIRA
Catch him, he is escaping!

DONNA ELVIRA
Ferma, perfido, ferma!

MASETTO
He vanished like a shadow!

MASETTO
Il birbo ha l'ali ai piedi.

ZERLINA
What a rascal, how he slipped through our fingers!

ZERLINA
Con qual arte
Si sottrasse l'iniquo!

DON OTTAVIO
I can't deny it, after all that has happened, I am fully convinced that Don Giovanni was the fiend who has murdered the father of Donn' Anna. Will you be kind enough to stay in her company. I'll proceed with the necessary measures to bring us vengeance, to assure her protection. So does duty demand devotion, affection!

DON OTTAVIO
Amici miei.
Dopo eccessi sì enormi,
Dubitar non possiam, che Don Giovanni
Non sia l'empio uccisore
Del padre di Donn'Anna. In questa casa
Per poche ore fermatevi: un ricorso
Vo' far a chi si deve; e in poch'istanti
Vendicarvi prometto
Così vuole dover, pietade, affetto.

Aria

Yours is my love and affection,
Beloved, beloved evermore.
Mine is your rare perfection
To treasure and adore,
To cherish, to cherish,
To treasure and adore.
I'll be your true defender,
Bringing you vindication
My sacred obligation.
I promise I shall render
Justice by sword and law.
Ours is a happier morrow,
Beloved, beloved, not to part,
And to allay your sorrow,
I shall devote my heart
Forever, forever,
My loving, faithful heart.
I shall avenge your honor,
Burning with wrath and ardor,
I shall defend your honor—
That is the vow I swore.

Il mio tesoro intanto
Andate, andate a consolar!
E del bel ciglio il pianto.
Cercate di asciugar.
Cercate, cercate,
Cercate di asciugar.
Ditele che i suoi torti
A vendicar io vado.
Che sol di stragi e morti
Nunzio vogl'io tornar.
Il mio tesoro intanto
Andate, andate a consolar!
E del bel ciglio il pianto.
Cercate di asciugar.
Cercate, cercate,
Cercate di asciugar.
Ditele che i suoi torti
A vendicar io vado.
Che sol di stragi e morti
Nunzio vogl'io tornar.

Recitative and Aria

DONNA ELVIRA
What hateful acts of dishonor
And what unspeakable, villainous transgressions
This wicked man committed!
But soon, I know it—

DONNA ELVIRA
In quali eccessi, o Numi,
In quai misfatti orribili, tremendi
E avvolto il sciagurato!
Ah no! non puote tardar l'ira del cielo,

La giustizia tardar.
Sentir già parmi la fatale saetta,
Que gli piomba sul capo!
Aperto veggio il baratro mortal!
Misera Elvira! che contrasto d'affetti
In sen ti nasce!
Perchè questi sospiri?
E quest'ambascie?

His doom will overtake him
So that justice be done.
I almost see the flash of lightning descending,
Spelling death and destruction!
I see before him the gates of hell ajar!
Wretched Elvira!
What conflicting emotions,
What doubts oppress you?
You still can be forgiving?
What qualms distress you?

Mi tradì quell'alma ingrata,
Quell'alma ingrata,
Infelice,
O Dio, mi fa,
Infelice, O Dio, mi fa,
Ma tradita,
E abbandonata,
Provo ancor per lui pietà.
Quando sento il mio tormento, il mio tormento,
Di vendetta il cor favella,
Ma se guardo il suo cimento,
Palpitando il cor mi va,
Palpitando!

He betrayed my love and honor,
Deceived and spurned me,
Dearly I loved him,
Believed in his word,
Believed in the promise he made.
Brokenhearted,
And torn by sorrow
For his soul I am afraid.
He betrayed my love and honor.
Though for all his shameful deeds I justly hate him,
Though my heart cries out for vengeance,
Yet the punishment that must await him
Wakes compassion in my heart,
My anguished heart.

Scene 10

(*A walled cemetery, in the midst of which the statue of the* COMMENDATORE *is seen.* DON GIOVANNI, *who leaps over the wall; afterward* LEPORELLO.)

DON GIOVANNI
Ah! ah! ah! questa è buona!
Or lasciala cercar. Che bella notte!
È più chiara del giorno; sembra fatta
Per gir a zonzo, a cacciar di ragazze.
È tardi? Oh
Ancor non son o due della notte. Avrei
Voglia un po' di saper com'è finito
L'affar tra Leporello e Donna Elvira;
S'egli ha avuto giudizio.

DON GIOVANNI
Hahahaha, I was lucky, now let them look for me! What a lovely moonlight, it's clearer than daylight. It seems just made for love and roaming in search of pretty girls. What time is it? Not even two o'clock in the morning. I'm eager to know what has happened in the meantime between Leporello and Elvira. If the rascal was clever . . .

LEPORELLO
Alfin vuole ch'io faccia un precipizio!

LEPORELLO (*behind the wall*)
He has made me his scapegoat once too often.

DON GIOVANNI
È desso! Oh, Leporello!

DON GIOVANNI
He's here. Hey, Leporello!

LEPORELLO
Chi mi chiama?

LEPORELLO
Who is calling?

DON GIOVANNI
Don't you know your master's voice?

LEPORELLO
I wish I'd never known it!

DON GIOVANNI
Oh, you rascal!

LEPORELLO
Oh! Is it you? I'm sorry!

DON GIOVANNI
What has happened?

LEPORELLO
Instead of you, those people almost killed me.

DON GIOVANNI
I think you should be flattered! What an honor for you.

LEPORELLO
No thanks, you keep it.

DON GIOVANNI
Come, come, don't be a fool. Wait till you hear the exciting news.

LEPORELLO
What are you doing here?

DON GIOVANNI
Come closer and I'll tell you. A few of the adventures which have happened to me since we have parted I will save until later, but the best one you must hear right away.

LEPORELLO
Again a woman?

DON GIOVANNI
What else? During the evening I encountered a young and very beautiful lady; first I addressed her. I took her by her hand, she acted timid, and when I reassured her, the darling took me—guess for whom?

LEPORELLO
For a man.

DON GIOVANNI
For Leporello!

LEPORELLO
For me?

DON GIOVANNI
For you.

LEPORELLO
How flattering!

DON GIOVANNI
Right away she became very friendly.

LEPORELLO
Goes without saying.

DON GIOVANNI
Non conosci il padron!

LEPORELLO
Così nol conoscessi!

DON GIOVANNI
Come? birbo!

LEPORELLO
Ah, siete voi? Scusate!

DON GIOVANNI
Cosa è stato?

LEPORELLO
Per cagion vostra io fui quasi accoppato.

DON GIOVANNI
Ebben, non era questo
Un onore per te?

LEPORELLO
Signor, vel dono!

DON GIOVANNI
Via, via, vien quà:
Che belle cose ti deggio dir!

LEPORELLO
Ma cosa fate qui?

DON GIOVANNI
Vien dentro, e lo saprai.
Diverse istorielle,
Che accadute mi son dacchè partisti,
Ti dirò un'altra volta; or la più bella
Ti vo' solo narrar.

LEPORELLO
Donnesca, al certo.

DON GIOVANNI
C'è dubbio! Una fanciulla,
Bella, giovin, galante,
Per la strada incontrai; le vado appresso,
La prendo per la man—fuggir mi vuole;
Dico poche parole, ella mi piglia
Sai per chi?

LEPORELLO
Non lo so.

DON GIOVANNI
Per Leporello!

LEPORELLO
Per me?

DON GIOVANNI
Per te!

LEPORELLO
Va bene!

DON GIOVANNI
Per la mano
Essa allora mi prende.

LEPORELLO
Ancora meglio!

DON GIOVANNI
M'accarezza, m'abbraccia—
'Caro il mio Leporello!
Leporello, mio caro!' Allor m'accorsi
Ch'era qualche tua bella.

DON GIOVANNI
She embraced me and kissed me: "Darlingest Leporello, Leporello my darling!" Now it was obvious, I'd met one of your sweethearts.

LEPORELLO
Oh, maledetto!

LEPORELLO
It almost seems so!

DON GIOVANNI
Dell'inganno approfitto; non so come
Mi riconosce, grida, sento gente,—
A fuggire mi metto; e pronto pronto
Per quel muretto in questo loco io monto.

DON GIOVANNI
I made use of her error till suddenly she saw my face and started screaming. I heard people so I had to take flight. I saw the churchyard and swift as an arrow I jumped that wall to safety.

LEPORELLO
E mi dite la cosa
Con tale indifferenza?

LEPORELLO
And you tell me all that without blinking an eye?

DON GIOVANNI
Perchè no?

DON GIOVANNI
And why not?

LEPORELLO
Ma se fosse costei stata mia moglie?

LEPORELLO
Suppose the lady were my wife?

DON GIOVANNI
Meglio ancora!

DON GIOVANNI (*laughs loudly*)
That would be perfect!

COMMENDATORE
Di rider finirai
Pria dell'aurora!

STATUE
Your laughter will have died ere it is morning.

DON GIOVANNI
Chi ha parlato?

DON GIOVANNI
Did you hear that?

LEPORELLO
Ah! qualche anima
Sarà dall'altro mondo,
Che vi conosce a fondo.

LEPORELLO
Ah, it must have been a ghost who knows you well, speaking to you from hell.

DON GIOVANNI
Taci, sciocco! Chi va là? chi va là?

DON GIOVANNI
Don't talk nonsense. Who goes there? Who goes there?

COMMENDATORE
Ribaldo, audace!
Lascia a' morti la pace.

STATUE
Seducer and murd'rer, leave the dead to their slumber.

LEPORELLO
Ve l'ho detto.

LEPORELLO
See, I told you!

DON GIOVANNI
Sarà qualcun di fuori,
Che si burla di noi.
Ehi! del Commendatore
Non è questa la statua! Leggi un poco quella iscrizion.

DON GIOVANNI
There must be someone hiding who is trying to fool us. Say, that must be the statue of our friend, the commendatore. Read what's written upon the tombstone.

LEPORELLO
Scusate:
Non ho imparato a leggere
A' raggi della luce.

LEPORELLO
I'm sorry, I am a little shortsighted, especially by moonlight.

DON GIOVANNI
Leggi, dico!

DON GIOVANNI
Read, I tell you!

LEPORELLO
'Dell'empio, che mi trasse al passo estremo,
'Qui attendo la vendetta.'
Udiste! io tremo!

LEPORELLO
"Here lies the fallen victim, awaiting vengeance upon his wanton slayer." You heard that? I am frightened!

DON GIOVANNI
What could be more ridiculous! Tell him that I invite him to be my guest for supper.

LEPORELLO
No, not that! Are you mad? Can't you see him? What a horrible look is in his eyes! I'm certain that he hears us and that he wants to speak!

DON GIOVANNI
Do as I say, or I shall kill you and bury you beside him.

LEPORELLO
Not so hasty, My Lord, I shall invite him.

Duet

LEPORELLO (*addressing statue*)
O worthy mister monument,
Revered and late commander—
My Lord, my knees are shaking,
Ah, master, continue I cannot.

DON GIOVANNI
Go on with it, or I promise
I'll kill you on the spot.

LEPORELLO
How can he be so spiteful!

DON GIOVANNI
This scene is most delightful!

LEPORELLO
My tongue is frozen tight!

DON GIOVANNI
He is a sorry sight!

LEPORELLO
Oh what a dreadful night!
Oh worthy mister monument,
Forgive me for my daring—
Ah, My Lord, do you see him,
He's staring, and glaring
His eyes are all alight.

DON GIOVANNI
Now I'll kill you!

LEPORELLO
No, no, no, I will do it,
(*to the statue*)
Dear sir, if you are free, sir,
My master asks, not me, sir,
Pray dine with him tonight—
(*the statue nods its head*)
Ah, ah, ah, just see that statue!
Ah, ah, ah, he looks right at you—
Good Lord, he says he's coming.

DON GIOVANNI
O vecchio buffonissimo
Digli che questa sera
L'attendo a cena meco.

LEPORELLO
Che pazzia!
Ma vi par! Oh, Dei! mirate
Che terribile occhiate
Egli ci dà! Par vivo! par che senta e che voglia parlar.

DON GIOVANNI
Orsù va là
O qui t'ammazzo! E poi ti seppellisco!

LEPORELLO
Piano, piano, signore—ora ubbidisco.

LEPORELLO
O statua gentilissima
Del gran Commendatore—
Padron, mi trema il core;
Non posso terminar.

DON GIOVANNI
Finiscila, o nel petto
Ti metto questo acciar.

LEPORELLO
Che impiccio! che capriccio!

DON GIOVANNI
Che gusto, che spassetto!

LEPORELLO
Io sentomi gelar!

DON GIOVANNI
Lo voglio far tremar.

LEPORELLO
Io sentomi gelar!
O, statua gentilissima,
Benchè de marmo siate—
Ah, padron mio! mirate
Che seguita a guardar.
Che seguita a guardar.

DON GIOVANNI
Mori, mori!

LEPORELLO
No, no, attendete!
Signor, il padron mio—
Badate ben, no io—
Vorria con voi cenar.
Ah! ah! che scena è questa!
Oh, ciel! chinò la testa!

DON GIOVANNI
Va là che sei un buffone,
Va là che sei un buffone!

LEPORELLO
Guardate, guardate!
Guardate ancor, padrone.

DON GIOVANNI
E che deggio guardar?

LEPORELLO
Colla marmorea testa
Ei fa così, così.

DON GIOVANNI
Parlate, se potete,
Verrete a cena?

COMMENDATORE
Sì!

LEPORELLO
Mover mi posso appena!
Mi manca, oh Dei, la lena!

DON GIOVANNI
Bizzarra è in ver la scena
Verrà il buon vecchio a cena!
A prepararla andiamo,
Partiamo via di quà.

LEPORELLO
Per carità partiamo:
Andiamo via di quà!

DON GIOVANNI
Andiamo via di quà!
Bizzarra è in ver la scena
Verrà il buon vecchio a cena!
A prepararla andiamo,
Partiamo via di quà.

DON GIOVANNI
Oh, come don't be so silly,
It's all imagination.

LEPORELLO
But master, just watch him,
Look now or you will miss it!

DON GIOVANNI
Whatever shall I miss?

LEPORELLO
Slowly and very clearly,
He nods his head like this.

DON GIOVANNI
Now answer, if you're able!
You'll come to supper?

STATUE
Yes.

LEPORELLO
Oh, I am fainting nearly,
That statue nodded clearly.

DON GIOVANNI
How very strange and eerie,
The statue answered and nodded clearly.
To make the preparations
We must not lose a moment.
We must go home at once.

LEPORELLO
For heaven's sake, dear master,
We must not lose a moment.
We must go home at once.

DON GIOVANNI
This is indeed mysterious,
The joke is getting serious;
To make the preparations
We must go home at once.

Scene 11

(*A room.* DONNA ANNA; DON OTTAVIO.)

Recitative

DON OTTAVIO
Calmatevi, idol mio, di quel ribaldo
Vedrem puniti in breve i gravi eccessi.
Vendicati sarem.

DONNA ANNA
Ma il padre, oh Dio!

DON OTTAVIO
Convien chinare il ciglio
Al volere del ciel. Respira, o cara,

DON OTTAVIO
Rest assured, my beloved, soon we shall see Don Giovanni duly punished for his crimes, and attain our revenge.

DONNA ANNA
My father, my father!

DON OTTAVIO
We must bear the burden the Almighty imposes. Take courage, beloved, do not dwell on your sorrow. If you

give your consent, we shall be married, and my heart, my devotion will atone for your grief.

Di tua perdita amara
Fia domani, se vuoi, dolce compenso,
Questo cor, questa mano,
Che il mio tenero amor!

DONNA ANNA
Oh God, how can you speak of marriage at this moment?

DONNA ANNA
Oh, Dei! che dite,
In sì tristi momenti?

DON OTTAVIO
Why not? You wish, then, by further delaying, to make me more unhappy! How heartless!

DON OTTAVIO
E che? vorresti
Con indugi novelli
Accrescer le mie pene?
Crudele!

Aria

DONNA ANNA
I heartless? Ah, do not say so.
Mourning my father, I cannot yet enjoy the future blessing that we both so desire! In mourning—oh heavens!
Trust my word and be patient,
And respect my emotion.
You will always possess
My true devotion!
Know, my dear, I'm yours forever!
I could never be cruel to you.
And remember, I always love you,
And my heart is warm and true.
Calm your anguish, I implore you!
Do not make me suffer tortures,
Unending tortures.
God in heaven may reward me,
Mend my heart of all its pain.
Loving pity may He accord me.
Bring me calm and joy again!

DONNA ANNA
Crudele! ah no, Mio bene!
Troppo mi spiace
Allontanarti un ben che lungamente
La nostr'alma desia: ma il mondo! oh Dio!
Non sedur la costanza
Del sensibil mio core.
Abbastanza per te mi parla amore.
Non mi dir bell'idol mio,
Che son io crudel con te;
Tu ben sai quant'io t'amai,
Tu conosci la mia fè.
Calma, calma il tuo tormento!
Se di duol non vuoi ch'io mora.
Forse un giorno il cielo ancora
Sentirà pietà di me.

DON OTTAVIO
Ah, I'll never desert her! I want to share all her anguish and her sorrow. I shall love and protect her faithfully always.
(*exit*)

DON OTTAVIO
Ah! si segua il suo passo,
Io vo' con lei dividere i martiri:
Saran meco men gravi i suoi sospiri.

Scene 12

(*A large hall, illuminated, with a table laid out.* DON GIOVANNI, LEPORELLO. *A band of musicians, several beautiful ladies sitting at the table with* DON GIOVANNI)

DON GIOVANNI
Let us have a splendid supper!
Come, my ladies, please be seated.
As my guests you shall be treated
To the finest of the fine!
Leporello, serve the supper!

DON GIOVANNI
Già la mensa è preparata.
Voi suonate, amici cari;
Già che spendo i miei danari,
Io mi voglio divertir.
Leporello, presto in tavola.

LEPORELLO Son prontissimo a servir, Son prontissimo a servir.	**LEPORELLO** I have ev'rything prepared. No expenses have been spared!
DON GIOVANNI Già che spendo i miei danari, Io mi voglio divertir. Voi suonate, amici cari! Già che spendo i miei danari, Io mi voglio divertir!	**DON GIOVANNI** Since I'm sparing no expenses, Do not save on food and wine! My dear friends, begin your playing, For it goes without my saying, I like music when I dine. (*the musicians play a piece from Martín y Soler's* Una Cosa Rara)
LEPORELLO Bravi! "Cosa rara!" *	**LEPORELLO** This is from an opera!
DON GIOVANNI Che ti par del bel concerto?	**DON GIOVANNI** Do you like that composition?
LEPORELLO È conforme, è conforme vostro merto.	**LEPORELLO** Very much—and a very good rendition!
DON GIOVANNI Ah che piatto saporito! Ah che piatto saporito! Ah che piatto saporito!	**DON GIOVANNI** My, the cook has been ambitious! What a choice of tasty dishes! I must say they are delicious!
LEPORELLO Ah, che barbaro appetito! Che bocconi da gigante. Mi par proprio di svenir.	**LEPORELLO** (*aside*) How can one man be so greedy! While I stand here, starved and needy, He is eating half a calf!
DON GIOVANNI Nel veder i miei bocconi Gli par proprio di svenir.	**DON GIOVANNI** Oh, that rascal is so greedy That he really makes me laugh.
LEPORELLO Ah che barbaro appetito! Che bocconi da gigante.	**LEPORELLO** No one ever gobbled faster Than my hungry lord and master!
DON GIOVANNI Nel veder i miei bocconi, Gli par proprio di svenir, di svenir.	**DON GIOVANNI** I will try a leg of mutton. See the envy in his eyes, in his eyes!
LEPORELLO Che bocconi da gigante!	**LEPORELLO** Was there ever such a glutton!
DON GIOVANNI Gli par proprio di svenir.	**DON GIOVANNI** He is speechless with surprise.
LEPORELLO Mi par proprio di svenir.	**LEPORELLO** I can scarcely trust my eyes!
DON GIOVANNI Piatto!	**DON GIOVANNI** Wine, please. (*the musicians play "Come un agnello" from Sarti's* I Due Litiganti)
LEPORELLO Servo; Evvivano i "Litiganti!"	**LEPORELLO** Yes, sir! Another delightful aria.

* A pun referring to the opera *Una Cosa Rara* by Vicente Martín y Soler, which, as an immediate success, left almost no room on the operatic stage for even *The Marriage of Figaro*.

DON GIOVANNI
Serve the ladies.
This Madeira is rich and mellow.

DON GIOVANNI
Versa il vino.
Eccellente marzimino!

LEPORELLO
I will eat this wing of pheasant,
Slyly, slyly, slyly, slyly, slyly,
On the sly!

LEPORELLO
Questo pezzo di fagiano,
Piano, piano, piano, piano,
piano.
Vo' inghiottir.

DON GIOVANNI
I can watch him, clumsy peasant,
From the corner of my eye.
(*the musicians play Figaro's aria from* The Marriage of Figaro)

DON GIOVANNI
Sta mangiando quel marrano!
Fingerò di non capir.

LEPORELLO
That's *The Marriage of Figaro* by Mozart!

LEPORELLO
Questa poi la conosco pur troppo!

DON GIOVANNI
Leporello!

DON GIOVANNI
Leporello!

LEPORELLO (*with his mouth full*)
Yes, my master!

LEPORELLO
Padron mio!

DON GIOVANNI
Has your speech begun to suffer some affliction?

DON GIOVANNI
Parla schietto,
Parla schietto, mascalzone.

LEPORELLO
I have trouble with my diction
When I serve and talk at once.

LEPORELLO
Non mi lascia una flussione
Le parole proferir.

DON GIOVANNI
Well then, whistle while I'm dining.

DON GIOVANNI
Mentre io mangio, fischia un poco.

LEPORELLO
Not a note!

LEPORELLO
Non so far.

DON GIOVANNI
And why?

DON GIOVANNI
Cos'è?

LEPORELLO
I'm sorry, forgive me.
But your cook is such a genius—
Extraordinary culinary genius—
That I felt the least I could do
Is to try his dishes too.

LEPORELLO
Scusate! Scusate!
Sì eccellente è il vostro cuoco,
Sì eccellente è il vostro cuoco,
Che lo volli anch'io provar—
Che lo volli anch'io provar—

DON GIOVANNI
Yes, my cook is such a genius,
That he tried his dishes too.

DON GIOVANNI
Sì eccellente è il cuoco mio,
Che lo volle anch'ei provar.

Scene 13

(DONNA ELVIRA. *The same.*)

DONNA ELVIRA (*rushes in*)
This is the last time
That I beseech you,
(*she kneels*)
Hoping to reach you
Ere it's too late.

DONNA ELVIRA
L'ultima prova
Dell'amor mio
Ancor vogl'io
Fare con te:
Più non rammento
Gl'inganni tuoi,
Pietade io sento—

Free of all anger, malice or rancor,
Mine is a mission of pure compassion.
(DON GIOVANNI *makes a sign dismissing the musicians*)

DON GIOVANNI, LEPORELLO
Cos'è? cos'è?

DON GIOVANNI, LEPORELLO
How so, how so?

DONNA ELVIRA
Da te non chiede
Quest'alma oppressa
Della sua fede
Qualche mercè.

DONNA ELVIRA
I ask no kindness, no understanding,
I'm not demanding favors from you.

DON GIOVANNI
Mi maraviglio?
Cosa volete.
Se non sorgete
Non resto in piè.

DON GIOVANNI
That is surprising; then may I ask you
Why you have come here?
But if you're kneeling, I must kneel too.
(*he kneels down beside her*)

DONNA ELVIRA
Ah, non deridere
Gli affanni miei!
Ah, non deridere.

DONNA ELVIRA
You are deriding me, mocking my sorrow!
You are deriding me!

LEPORELLO
Quasi da piangere
Mi fa costei!
Sì, da piangere
Mi fa costei.

LEPORELLO
How can he laugh at her, mocking her sorrow!
I truly pity her, poor Donn' Elvira!
(*both rise*)

DON GIOVANNI
Io ti deridere!
Cielo! perchè?
Che vuoi, mio bene?

DON GIOVANNI
I am deriding you? How can that be?
What are you asking?

DONNA ELVIRA
Che vita cangi!

DONNA ELVIRA
Reform completely!

DON GIOVANNI
Brava!

DON GIOVANNI
Bravo!

DONNA ELVIRA
Cor perfido! Cor perfido!
Cor perfido!

DONNA ELVIRA
You profligate, you reprobate, how merciless!

LEPORELLO
Cor perfido!

LEPORELLO
How merciless!

DON GIOVANNI
Lascia ch'io mangi;
E se ti piace,
Mangia con me.

DON GIOVANNI
Right now I'm dining:
Why don't you join us and dine with me?

DONNA ELVIRA
Restati, barbaro,
Nel lezzo immondo,
Esempio orrible
D'iniquità.

DONNA ELVIRA
You are incurable, nothing can save you,
Sink of iniquity, evil and vice!

LEPORELLO
Se non si muove
Del suo dolore,
Di sasso ha il core,
O cor non ha.

LEPORELLO
If such great sorrow does not impress him,
He must possess a heart of ice!

DON GIOVANNI
Vivan le femmine!
Viva il buon vino!
Sostegno e gloria
D'umanità.

DON GIOVANNI (*raises glass*)
Long live all womankind,
Wine and amusement,
Joy of humanity, worth any price!

DONNA ELVIRA
Ah!

DONNA ELVIRA
(*rushes out, screams*)
Ah!

DON GIOVANNI
The devil, what has happened?

LEPORELLO
What is it? I heard somebody screaming.

DON GIOVANNI
Go and see, go and see what is the matter.
(LEPORELLO *goes out, and returns at once, frightened*)

LEPORELLO
Ah!

DON GIOVANNI
Again that awful screaming,
Disturbance and excitement!
Leporello, what is wrong, what is wrong?

LEPORELLO
Ah, My Lord, don't leave this room
Or you meet a certain doom!
It's the statue, and no error,
Ah, dear master, I'm frozen with terror!
Hear his footsteps on the stairway,
With an echo like a drum,
Plum, plum, plum, plum!

DON GIOVANNI
What a lot of crazy nonsense!
What a fool you have become!
(*a knocking is heard*)

LEPORELLO
There, you hear him!

DON GIOVANNI
Someone's knocking! Open!

LEPORELLO
I'm frightened!

DON GIOVANNI
Go and open.

LEPORELLO
Ah!

DON GIOVANNI
Open!

LEPORELLO
Ah!

DON GIOVANNI
Coward! You chicken-hearted craven,
I shall go myself and see, I'll go and see!
(*he goes to open.*)

LEPORELLO
If I only found a haven
You would see no more of me!
(*hides himself under the table*)

DON GIOVANNI
Che grido è questo mai?

LEPORELLO
Chi grido è questo mai?

DON GIOVANNI
Va a veder che cosa è stato.

LEPORELLO
Ah!

DON GIOVANNI
Che grido indiavolato?
Che grido indiavolato?
Leporello, che cos'è?
Che cos'è?

LEPORELLO
Ah, signor, per carità
Non andate fuor di quà!
L'uom di sasso, l'uomo bianco,
Ah, padrone, io gelo, io manco!
Se vedeste che figura
Se sentiste come fa!
Ta, ta, ta, ta!

DON GIOVANNI
Non capisco niente affatto.
Tu sei matto in verità.

LEPORELLO
Ah sentite!

DON GIOVANNI
Qualcun batte:
Apri!

LEPORELLO
Io tremo!

DON GIOVANNI
Apri, dico!

LEPORELLO
Ah!

DON GIOVANNI
Apri!

LEPORELLO
Ah!

DON GIOVANNI
Matto!
Per togliermi d'intrico
Ad aprir io stesso andrò!

LEPORELLO
Non vo'più veder l'amico,
Pian pianin masconderò—

COMMENDATORE
Don Giovanni, a cenar teco
M'invitasti! e son venuto!

DON GIOVANNI
Non l'avrei giammai creduto;
Ma farò quel che potrò.
Leporello, un'altra cena
Fa che subito si porti.

LEPORELLO
Ah, padron, ah, padron, siam tutti morti!

DON GIOVANNI
Vanne, dico!

COMMENDATORE
Ferma un po'!
Non si pasce di cibo mortale
Chi si pasce di cibo celeste;
Altre cure più gravi di queste
Altra brama quaggiù mi guidò!

DON GIOVANNI
Parla dunque! che chiedi? che vuoi?

LEPORELLO
La terzana d'avere mi sembra,
E le membra fermar più non so!
La terzana d'avere mi sembra,
E le membra fermar più non so.

COMMENDATORE
Parlo, ascolta! più tempo no ho!

DON GIOVANNI
Parla, parla! ascoltando ti sto.

COMMENDATORE
Tu m'invitasti a cena,
Il tuo dover or sai!
Rispondimi: verrai
Tu a cenar meco!

LEPORELLO
Oibò! oibò! tempo non ha, scusate.

DON GIOVANNI
A torto di viltate
Tacciato mai sarò.

COMMENDATORE
Risolvi!

DON GIOVANNI
Ho già risolto.

COMMENDATORE
Verrai?

Scene 14

STATUE (*appears at the door*)
Don Giovanni, I've come to supper.
You have asked me, and I accepted.

DON GIOVANNI
That is more than I expected,
But I'll do the best I can!
Leporello, serve His Honor!
Bring the best we have to offer!

LEPORELLO
Ah, my Lord, ah my Lord, let us run or we are done for!

DON GIOVANNI
I command it!

STATUE
Stay where you are!
Those who passed through the heavenly portals
Have no need for the nurture of mortals.
Other reasons, more solemn and weighty,
Guided me on my journey tonight.

DON GIOVANNI
What's your mission? I ask you.
I'm waiting.

LEPORELLO
I am stricken with chills and the fever,
I am shaking with terror and fright!
What a gruesome and terrible nightmare,
What a horrible, horrible night!

STATUE
Harken, Giovanni, the time flies away!

DON GIOVANNI
What have you to say?

STATUE
Since you have shown the boldness
Asking me here for supper,
I ask you now to honor me
By dining at my own table.

LEPORELLO
No, no, not that! Say that you are too busy!

DON GIOVANNI
I have no fear of heaven,
Nor earth, nor hell below!

STATUE
Decide then!

DON GIOVANNI
I have decided.

STATUE
You'll come then?

LEPORELLO
For heaven's sake, say no, say no!

DON GIOVANNI
No danger can deter me,
I have no fear, I'll go.

STATUE
Give me your hand in promise.

DON GIOVANNI
Here it is!
(STATUE *grasps his hand*)
Alas!

STATUE
At last!

DON GIOVANNI
Your hand is cold as ice!

STATUE
Now is the fatal moment!
Repent or face damnation!

DON GIOVANNI
Whatever be my sentence,
Never shall I repent!

STATUE
Heaven demands repentance!

DON GIOVANNI
I have no such intention!

STATUE
Save yourself!

DON GIOVANNI
No!

STATUE
Yes!

DON GIOVANNI
No, no!

STATUE
Then all your time is spent.
(STATUE *disappears, flames shoot up, earth trembles*)

DON GIOVANNI (*in despair*)
What is this unknown agony
Grasping my spirit cruelly,
What are these fires devouring me,
These flames that sear and roar?
What fiendish force is goading me,
Tormenting and corroding me?
Oh dreadful, hopeless anguish
No mortal man can bear!

CHORUS OF SPIRITS (*invisible*)
Here in the deep inferno
You'll suffer evermore!

LEPORELLO
In frantic desperation
He goes to his damnation!

LEPORELLO
Dite di no! Dite di no!

DON GIOVANNI
Ho fermo il core in petto;
Non ho timor: verrò!

COMMENDATORE
Dammi la mano in pegno!

DON GIOVANNI
Eccola;—ohimè!

COMMENDATORE
Cos'hai!

DON GIOVANNI
Che gelo è questo mai!

COMMENDATORE
Pentiti, cangia vita.
È l'ultimo momento!

DON GIOVANNI
No, no, ch'io non mi pento,
Vanne lontan da me!

COMMENDATORE
Pentiti! scellerato!

DON GIOVANNI
No, vecchio infatuato!

COMMENDATORE
Pentiti!

DON GIOVANNI
No!

COMMENDATORE
Sì!

DON GIOVANNI
No! no!

COMMENDATORE
Ah tempo più non v'è.

DON GIOVANNI
Dal qual tremore insolito
Sento assalir gli spiriti!
Dond'escono quei vortici
Di foco pien d'orror?
Chi l'anima mi lacera,—
Chi m'agita le viscere!
Che strazio ohimè! che smania
Che inferno! che terror!

CORO
Tutto a tue colpe è poco,
Vieni c'è un mal peggior!

LEPORELLO
Che ceffo disperato!
Che gesti da dannato!

Che gridi! che lamenti
Come mi fa terror!

CORO
Vieni, vieni, vieni,
C'è un mal peggior!

DON GIOVANNI
Che inferno! che terror! Ah!

LEPORELLO
Ah!

DONNA ELVIRA, ZERLINA,
DON OTTAVIO, MASETTO
Ah, dov'è il perfido?
Dov'è l'indigno?
Tutto il mio sdegno sfogar io vo'!

DONNA ANNA
Solo mirandolo stretto in catene
Alle mie pene calma darò.

LEPORELLO
Più non sperate di ritrovarlo
Più non cercate, lontano andò, lontano andò!

ALTRI
Cos'è, favella! Cos'è favella!
Via presto, sbrigati!

LEPORELLO
Venne un colosso, venne un colosso.
Ma se non posso, ma se non posso!

ALTRI
Presto, favella, sbrigati!

LEPORELLO
Tra fumo e fuoco—
Badate un poco—
L'uomo di sasso—
Fermate il passo—
Giusto là sotto—
Diede il gran botto—
Giusto là il diavolo
Se'l trangugiò.

ALTRI
Stelle! Che sento!

LEPORELLO
Vero è l'evento!

ELVIRA
Ah, certo è l'ombra.
Che m'incontrò!

ALTRI
Ah, certo è l'ombra
Che l'incontrò.

Such dreadful, hopeless anguish
No mortal man can bear, no man can bear.

CHORUS
Suffer, suffer, suffer forevermore!

DON GIOVANNI
What anguish, what despair! Ah!
(*disappears*)

LEPORELLO
Ah!

Last Scene

DONNA ELVIRA, ZERLINA, DON OTTAVIO, MASETTO
Where is the reprobate,
Where's the offender?
He can't escape us,
He cannot flee!

DONNA ANNA
For all the suffering
He has inflicted,
He stands convicted by law's decree!

LEPORELLO
Don't try to find him, for it is useless,
Utterly hopeless!
He's gone away and won't return.

OTHERS
He's gone? Where is he?
Tell us what happened, hurry, explain to us!

LEPORELLO
All of a sudden, there stood the statue,
Thunder and lightning. It was so fright'ning . . .

OTHERS
Hurry, what happened? Out with it!

LEPORELLO
While he was dining, all of a sudden,
There stood the statue, grasping him firmly,
While flames were smoking, gasping and choking—
Thus Don Giovanni descended to hell!

OTHERS
Heavens, you mean it?

LEPORELLO
Yes, I have seen it!

ELVIRA
That was the shadow crossing my path!

OTHERS
Claiming his soul in justice and wrath!

We saw it. That was the ghostly shadow crossing her path.

DON OTTAVIO
Now that heaven has brought us vengeance,
Joyful days lie before us.
So, beloved, I who adore you,
Come to claim the love you swore.

DONNA ANNA
Dear Ottavio, let me implore you,
Only wait for one year more!

DON OTTAVIO
Now, beloved, and forever
You possess my faithful love.

DONNA ANNA
You will always possess my love, my faithful love!

DONNA ELVIRA
In a holy, peaceful cloister,
I'll forget that evil sinner!

ZERLINA, MASETTO
Come with me, my dear Masetto (Zerlina),
Let's be going home for dinner!

LEPORELLO
I'll be off to find a master who will pay me well.

ZERLINA, MASETTO, LEPORELLO
Let the wicked scoundrel dwell
In the flaming pits of hell!
While each one of us rejoices,
Let us gladly raise our voices
In the age-old honoured song:

ALL
WICKED MEN SHALL BE CONDEMNED.
HE WHO LEADS A LIFE OF EVIL
ALWAYS MEETS A DREADFUL END.

Ah, certo è l'ombra
Che l'incontrò.
Ah, certo è l'ombra
Che l'incontrò.

DON OTTAVIO
Or che tutti, o mio tesoro,
Vendicati siam dal cielo,
Porgi a me un ristoro
Non mi fa languire ancor.

DONNA ANNA
Lascia o caro, un anno ancora
Allo sfogo del mio cor.

DON OTTAVIO
Al desio di chi m'adora
Ceder deve un fido amor.

DONNA ANNA
Al desio di chi t'adora,
Ceder deve un fido amor.

DONNA ELVIRA
Io men vado in un ritiro,
A finir la vita mia!

ZERLINA, MASETTO
Noi, Masetto (Zerlina) a casa andiamo
A cenar in compagnia.

LEPORELLO
Ed io vado all' osteria
A trovar padron miglior.

ZERLINA, MASETTO, LEPORELLO
Resti dunque quel birbon
Con Proserpina e Pluton!
E noi tutti, o buona gente,
Ripetiam allegramente
L'antichissima canzon:

TUTTI
QUESTO È IL FIN DI CHI FA MAL.
E DE' PERFIDI LA MORTE
ALLA VITA È SEMPRE UGUAL.

FALSTAFF

by Giuseppe Verdi (1813–1901)

LIBRETTO BY ARRIGO BOITO.

Translated by WALTER DUCLOUX

Based on Shakespeare's *Merry Wives of Windsor* and *Henry IV.*

CHARACTERS

DR. CAIUS		*Tenor*
SIR JOHN FALSTAFF		*Baritone*
BARDOLPH	*Falstaff's henchmen*	*Tenor*
PISTOL		*Bass*
MISTRESS MEG PAGE		*Mezzo-soprano*
MISTRESS ALICE FORD		*Soprano*
ANN (NANETTA), *her daughter*		*Soprano*
DAME QUICKLY		*Mezzo-soprano*
FORD, *a wealthy burgher*		*Baritone*
FENTON, *a young gentleman in love with Ann*		*Tenor*
THE HOST OF THE GARTER INN		
TOWNSPEOPLE, SERVANTS, PAGES, MASQUERADERS AS SPRITES AND WITCHES		

Place: Windsor
Time: The reign of Henry IV
First performance: Teatro La Scala, Milan, February 9, 1893

COPYRIGHT © 1962 BY WALTER DUCLOUX

ACT I

Part 1

(*Inside the Garter Inn. A table. A large armchair. A bench. On the table the remnants of a meal, several bottles, and a goblet. An inkwell with quills, some paper, and a lit candle. A broom leaning against the wall. A main entrance up-stage, another door to the left.*

FALSTAFF *is busy heating a stick of sealing wax over the candle and sealing two letters with the help of a ring. This done, he extinguishes the candle and starts drinking, stretched out comfortably in the armchair.*

FALSTAFF, DR. CAIUS, BARDOLPH, PISTOL. *The innkeeper in the background.*)

DR. CAIUS (*entering from door at left, shouting menacingly*)
Falstaff!

FALSTAFF (*ignoring him, calls the innkeeper, who comes closer*)
Come here!

DR. CAIUS (*raising his voice even more*)
Sir John Falstaff!

BARDOLPH (*to* DR. CAIUS)
Oh! Why the shouting?

DR. CAIUS (*still shouting and approaching* FALSTAFF, *who pays no attention to him*)
You've mistreated my servants. . . !

FALSTAFF (*to the innkeeper*)
Quickly! Go! Bring me some more of this sherry!

DR. CAIUS
You have beaten my mare until she's dying,
You broke into my quarters.

FALSTAFF
But spared your keeper's crying!

DR. CAIUS
Thank you kindly! Such an ugly old creature!
Mighty Sir Mountain, if twenty times as noble and twenty times Sir Falstaff
I'd force you yet to answer me.

FALSTAFF (*lazily*)
Well then, I'll tell you loudly:
I've done the things you mention . . .

DR. CAIUS
Go on!

FALSTAFF
. . . and done them proudly.

DR. CAIUS (*screaming*)
I shall appeal to the court of the King.

FALSTAFF
Heaven may keep you! The joke will be on you, sir.
Take it from me, John Falstaff!

DR. CAJUS
Falstaff!

FALSTAFF
Olà!

DR. CAJUS
Sir John Falstaff!!

BARDOLFO
Oh! che vi piglia?!

DR. CAJUS
Hai battuto i miei servi! . . .

FALSTAFF
Oste! un'altra bottiglia
Di Xeres.

DR. CAJUS
Hai fiaccata la mia giumenta baia,
Sforzata la mia casa.

FALSTAFF
Ma non la tua massaia.

DR. CAJUS
Troppa grazia! Una vecchia cisposa. Ampio Messere,
Se foste venti volte John Falstaff Cavaliere
Vi forzerò a rispondermi.

FALSTAFF
Ecco la mia risposta:
Ho fatto ciò che hai detto.

DR. CAJUS
E poi?

FALSTAFF
L'ho fatto apposta.

DR. CAJUS
M'appellerò al Consiglio Real.

FALSTAFF
Vatti con Dio.
Sta zitto o avrai le beffe; quest'è il consiglio mio.

DR. CAJUS
Non è finita!!

FALSTAFF
Al diavolo!

DR. CAJUS
Bardolfo!

BARDOLFO
Ser Dottore.

DR. CAJUS
Tu, ier, m'hai fatto bere.

BARDOLFO
Pur troppo! e che dolore! . . .
Sto mal. D'un tuo pronostico
m'assisti. Ho l'intestino
Guasto. Malanno agli osti che
dan la calce al vino!
Vedi questa meteora?

DR. CAJUS
La vedo.

BARDOLFO
Essa si corca,
Rossa così ogni notte.

DR. CAJUS
Pronostico di forca!
M'hai fatto ber, furfante, con
lui, narrando frasche;
Poi, quando fui ben ciùschero,
m'hai vuotate le tasche.

BARDOLFO
Non io.

DR. CAJUS
Chi fu?

FALSTAFF
Pistola!

PISTOLA
Padrone.

FALSTAFF
Hai tu vuotate
Le tasche a quel Messere?

DR. CAJUS
Certo fu lui. Guardate
Come s'atteggia al niego quel
ceffo da bugiardo!
Qui c'eran due scellini del
regno d'Edoardo
E sei mezze-corone. Non ne
riman più segno.

PISTOLA
Padron, chiedo di battermi con
quest'arma di legno.
Vi smentisco!

DR. CAIUS (*turning his fury on* BARDOLPH)
And now to this one!

FALSTAFF
To hell with you!

DR. CAIUS
You rascal!

BARDOLPH
Honored Doctor!

DR. CAIUS
Last night we both were drinking.

BARDOLPH
Indeed, sir! I still am paying the bill!
(*inviting* CAIUS *to feel his pulse*)
I need your help, my dear physician.
Have I a shrunken liver? This blasted host
Must have thinned his wine with poison!
(*pointing to his own nose*)
See what shines here so brightly!

DR. CAIUS
I see it.

BARDOLPH
Fiery and red, it glows like a star in the darkness.

DR. CAIUS (*furious*)
A light by which to hang you!
You made me drunk, you rascal,
(*pointing to* PISTOL)
While he was telling stories.
Then, when my mind was deaf and numb,
You took all I had on me.

BARDOLPH
(*with dignity*) Not I!

DR. CAIUS
Who then?

FALSTAFF
(*addressing* PISTOL) You, Pistol!

PISTOL
(*approaching* FALSTAFF) My master?

FALSTAFF (*still stretching lazily in his chair*)
Have you divested this man of his belongings?

DR. CAIUS
(*advancing on* PISTOL) Yes, it was he! Behold him!
Read what his snout is telling
Although he would deny it!
(*turning his pockets inside out*)
I know that I had on me two good Edwardian shillings
And six florins of silver.
Nothing is left, so help me!

PISTOL (*solemnly brandishing the broom*)
Sir John, allow me kindly now to sweep him off the
premise!

(*to* DR. CAIUS, *with intent*)
You're a liar!

DR. CAIUS
You blockhead! Offend a man of station!

PISTOL
Stupid!

DR. CAIUS
You beggar!

PISTOL
Varlet!

DR. CAIUS
Dog!

PISTOL
Lout!

DR. CAIUS
You scarecrow!

PISTOL
Pixy!

DR. CAIUS
You feeble-minded idiot!

PISTOL
Who?

DR. CAIUS
You!

PISTOL
You mean it?

DR. CAIUS
Yes.

PISTOL (*attacking* DR. CAIUS) I'll show you!

FALSTAFF (*motioning* PISTOL *to hold back*)
Wait! Wait! You hothead! This is no place to fight.
(*to* BARDOLPH)
You, Bardolph . . . who have emptied the pockets of the doctor?

DR. CAIUS (*quickly*) I'm sure they both did!

BARDOLPH (*serenely pointing to* DR. CAIUS)
He was drinking, heavily drinking,
Till he had lost his senses.
Now he tells you a fairy tale, some fancy fable
No doubt dreamed up while under the table.

FALSTAFF (*to* DR. CAIUS)
Well now . . . this man's veracity can not in faith be doubted.
Your statements stand refuted. I bid you leave in peace.

DR. CAIUS
Hear me! If I drink once again and lower my defenses
'Twill be with men of worth and honor
Who pay their expenses!
(*exits through the door at the left*)

DR. CAJUS
Bifolco! tu parli a un gentiluomo!

PISTOLA
Gonzo!

DR. CAJUS
Pezzente!

PISTOLA
Bestia!

DR. CAJUS
Can!

PISTOLA
Vil!

DR. CAJUS
Spauracchio!

PISTOLA
Gnomo!

DR. CAJUS
Germoglio di mandràgora!

PISTOLA
Chi?

DR. CAJUS
Tu.

PISTOLA
Ripeti!

DR. CAJUS
Sì.

PISTOLA
Saette!!!

FALSTAFF
Ehi là! Pistola! Non scaricarti qui.
Bardolfo! Chi ha vuotate le tasche a quel Messere?

DR. CAJUS
Fu l'un dei due.

BARDOLFO
Costui beve, poi pel gran bere
Perde i suoi cinque sensi, poi ti narra una favola
Ch'egli ha sognato mentre dormì sotto la tavola.

FALSTAFF
L'odi? Se ti capaciti, del ver tu sei sicuro.
I fatti son negati. Vattene in pace.

DR. CAJUS
Giuro
Che se mai mi ubbriaco ancora all'osteria
Sarà fra gente onesta, sobria, civile e pia.

BARDOLFO, PISTOLA
Amen.

FALSTAFF
Cessi l'antifona. La urlate in contrattempo.
L'arte sta in questa massima: «Rubar con garbo e a tempo».
Siete dei rozzi artisti.
6 polli: 6 scellini.
30 giarre di Xeres: 2 lire, 3 tacchini . . .
Fruga nella mia borsa. 2 fagiani. Un'acciuga.

BARDOLFO
Un mark, un mark, un penny.

FALSTAFF
Fruga.

BARDOLFO
Ho frugato.

FALSTAFF
Fruga!

BARDOLFO
Qui non c'è più uno spicciolo.

FALSTAFF
Sei la mia distruzione!
Spendo ogni sette giorni dieci ghinee! Beone!
So che se andiam, la notte, di taverna in taverna,
Quel tuo naso ardentissimo mi serve da lanterna!
Ma quel risparmio d'olio tu lo consumi in vino.
Son trent'anni che abbevero quel fungo porporino!
Costi troppo.
E tu pure. Oste! un'altra bottiglia.
Mi struggete le carni! Se Falstaff s'assottiglia
Non è più lui, nessun più l'ama; in quest'addome
C'è un migliaio di lingue che annunciano il mio nome!

BARDOLPH, PISTOL (*escorting the doctor to the door, grotesquely chanting*)
Amen!

FALSTAFF
Cease your antiphonals! Your counterpoint is dreadful.
(BARDOLPH *and* PISTOL *stop singing and draw nearer to* FALSTAFF)
Theft has its laws of artistry:
To steal with charm and good timing!
Ludicrous pair of artists!
(*he starts examining the bill, which the innkeeper has brought along with the bottle of sherry*)
Six pullets: six shillings. Thirty flagons of sherry:
Two florins. Three partridges . . .
(*to* BARDOLPH, *throwing him his purse, then slowly reading on*)
See how much I have left here!
Brace of pheasants . . . an anchovy!

BARDOLPH (*taking coins out of the purse and putting them on the table*)
A shilling, a shilling, a penny.

FALSTAFF
Go on!

BARDOLPH
This is all, sir.

FALSTAFF
Nonsense!

BARDOLPH (*throwing the purse on the table*)
See . . . there is not a penny left!

FALSTAFF (*rising*)
Ah, you lout, you destroy me!
Week after week I spend ten guineas to indulge you,
You drunkard!
Night after night I ponder,
As from inn to inn we wander,
How your monstrous nose can yield the glow
To guide me here and yonder.
But what I save on lamp oil
You waste on drink and dining.
So for thirty long years I keep
Your fiery nose a-shining!
You're too costly,
(*to* PISTOL, *then to the innkeeper*)
And you also. Ho there! A flagon of sherry!
(*to* BARDOLPH *and* PISTOL)
You are threatening my substance.
A weak and slender Falstaff
Is not himself! A fearsome nightmare!
For in this paunch here you will find all the reasons
For my immortal glory.

PISTOL (*assenting*) Falstaff the Mighty!

BARDOLPH
Tremendous Falstaff!

FALSTAFF (*looking at himself and patting his paunch*)
This royal treasure, I'll make it grow!
The mind, though, no longer yield to matter!

BARDOLPH, PISTOL
Then let us think!
(*all three in a huddle*)

FALSTAFF
There lives in town a certain gentleman whose name is Ford.

BARDOLPH
Yes.

PISTOL
Yes.

FALSTAFF
A man of wealth and of distinction.

PISTOL
Most wealthy and most gen'rous.

BARDOLPH
A lord!

FALSTAFF
His wife has beauty . . .

PISTOL
. . . and holds the purse strings . . .

FALSTAFF
. . . such beauty! Oh, love!
Starlike her eyes! Swanlike her bosom!
Like blossoms her rosy lips beguiling!
Her name is Alice. One morning she saw me from her window,
And I beheld her smiling!
Then lightning struck in the deep of my heart.
Divine, her radiant eyes turned
Their brilliant and blinding light on me, on me!
(*strutting*)
On chest and shoulders,
On legs like boulders,
This paunch so proud, this manly stature,
Noble, imposing.
And then her glance, aglow with wild desire,
Would plainly tell me what I hoped to hear:
"I love you, Sir John Falstaff!"

BARDOLPH
Unquote!

FALSTAFF
Yet, hear me: There's someone . . .

BARDOLPH, PISTOL
Another?

PISTOLA
Falstaff immenso!

BARDOLFO
Enorme Falstaff!

FALSTAFF
Quest'è il mio regno.
Lo ingrandirò. Ma è tempo d'assottigliar l'ingegno.

BARDOLFO, PISTOLA
Assottigliam.

FALSTAFF
V'è noto un tal, qui del paese
Che ha nome Ford?

BARDOLFO
Sì.

PISTOLA
Sì.

FALSTAFF
Quell'uomo è un gran borghese . . .

PISTOLA
Più liberal d'un Creso.

BARDOLFO
E' un Lord!

FALSTAFF
Sua moglie è bella.

PISTOLA
E tien lo scrigno.

FALSTAFF
È quella! O amor! Sguardo di stella!
Collo di cigno! e il labbro?! un fior. Un fior che ride.
Alice è il nome, e un giorno come passar mi vide
Ne' suoi paraggi, rise. M'ardea l'estro amatorio
Nel cor. La Dea vibrava raggi di specchio ustorio
Su me, su me, sul fianco baldo, sul gran torace,
Sul maschio pie', sul fusto saldo, erto, capace;
E il suo desir in lei fulgea sì al mio congiunto
Che parea dir: «Io son di Sir John Falstaff».

BARDOLFO
Punto.

FALSTAFF
E a capo. Un'altra . . .

BARDOLFO, PISTOLA
Un'altra?

FALSTAFF
E questa ha nome: Margherita.

PISTOLA
La chiaman Meg.

FALSTAFF
È anch'essa de' miei pregi invaghita.
E anch'essa tien le chiavi . . .

FALSTAFF, BARDOLFO, PISTOLA
Dello scrigno.

FALSTAFF
Saran le mie Golconde e le mie Coste d'oro!
Guardate. Io sono ancora una piacente estate
Di San Martino. A voi, due lettere infuocate.
Tu porta questa a Meg; tentiam la sua virtù.
Già vedo che il tuo naso arde di zelo.
E tu
Porta questa ad Alice.

PISTOLA
Porto una spada al fianco.
Non sono un Messer Pandarus. Ricuso.

FALSTAFF
Saltimbanco.

BARDOLFO
Sir John, in quest'intrigo non posso accondiscendervi.
Lo vieta . . .

FALSTAFF
Chi?

BARDOLFO
L'Onore.

FALSTAFF
Ehi! paggio!
Andate a impendervi,
Ma non più a me!
Due lettere, prendi, per due signore.
Consegna tosto, corri, via, lesto, va!
L'Onore!
Ladri! Voi state ligi all'onor vostro, voi!
Cloache d'ignominia, quando, non sempre, noi
Possiam star ligi al nostro. Io stesso, sì, io, io,
Devo talor da un lato porre il timor di Dio
E, per necessità, sviar l'onore, usare
Stratagemmi ed equivoci, destreggiar, bordeggiare.
E voi, coi vostri cenci e coll'occhiata torta

FALSTAFF
. . . her name, it seems, is Mistress Page.

PISTOL
They call her Meg.

FALSTAFF
For her, too, I hold a fatal fascination,
And darling Meg is mistress . . .

ALL THREE
. . . of the purse strings!

FALSTAFF
These beauties on wings of gold
Shall take Sir John to Eldorado.
Behold me! I shall yet be the knight in shining armor
Who will redeem you!
And you shall expedite the matter:
(*handing* BARDOLPH *one of the two letters on the table*)
This letter take to Meg. Her virtue shall be tried!
(BARDOLPH *takes the letter*)
I see: Your fiery nose glows at the prospect.
(*to* PISTOL, *tending him the other letter*)
And you, you bring this one to Alice!

PISTOL (*refusing with dignity*)
No! By my sword, I shall not!
A low and shameful go-between? No, never!

FALSTAFF (*with calm contempt*) Ah, you windbag!

BARDOLPH (*stepping forth and depositing the letter on the table*)
Sir John, in this endeavor you must proceed without me.
I'm bound by . . .

FALSTAFF (*interrupting him*) . . . what?

BARDOLPH
. . . my honor.

FALSTAFF (*noticing the page,* ROBIN, *just entering the door*)
Hey, Robin!
(*turns to* BARDOLPH *and* PISTOL)
Get out and hang yourselves . . . but not on me!
(*to the page, who takes the letters and runs off*)
These letters here, take them to two young ladies.
Go, take them quickly, hurry, go!
Fly, scurry, go!
(*turning back to* BARDOLPH *and* PISTOL)
Your honor? Scoundrels!
You dare to speak to me of honor? You?
You foul and filthy mongrels . . .
When on occasion *we* may find our own in peril?
I . . . listen: I have had to hide my glances,
Asking the grace of heaven,
As in the throes of need I pawned my honor,
Sought refuge in some guile or some deception,
In a ruse or a falsehood.

And you, decrepit wretches, you stinking, vile hyenas
Who feed on carrion, you putrefied rapscallions,
You speak of honor . . . and this to me?
What honor? Speak up! Come on, you idiots, you asses!
Can your honor fill your paunch when it's empty? No!
Or can honor cure a broken ankle? Oh no!
A finger? No. A toenail? No! Or a whisker? No.
For honor is no surgeon.
What is it? Only a word!
What is it, what is it really?
Just a breeze that will vanish . . .
Fancy fiction!
A dead man, can he take pride in honor? No!
Yet he who is living? Not either.
For he who owns it has no way to defend it.
It is frail and will crumble,
Killed off by human weakness.
Therefore I do not want it, no,
Do not want it, no! No, no!
But to return to you, you you scoundrels:
I've been too lenient. I now dismiss you.
(*he grabs the broom and chases* BARDOLPH *and* PISTOL *around the room. They try to hide behind the table*)
Away! Quickly, scurry! I shall teach you how to hurry.
From the gallows you'll soon swing and sway.
Robbers, scoundrels, rascals, bandits!
If you stay you will pay. Go away! On your way!
(BARDOLPH *flees through the door at the left,* PISTOL *through the center after having received some blows.* FALSTAFF *follows* PISTOL *out the door*)

Da gattopardo e i fetidi sghignazzi avete a scorta
Il vostro Onor! Che onore?! che onor? che onor! che ciancia!
Che baia! Può l'onore riempirvi la pancia?
No. Può l'onor rimettervi uno stinco? Non può.
Nè un piede? No. Nè un dito? No. Nè un capello? No.
L'onor non è chirurgo. Che è dunque? Una parola.
Che c'è in questa parola? C'è dell'aria che vola.
Bel costrutto! L'onore lo può sentir chi è morto?
No. Vive sol coi vivi? . . . Neppure: perchè a torto
Lo gonfian le lusinghe, lo corrompe l'orgoglio,
L'ammorban le calunnie; e per me non ne voglio!
Ma, per tornare a voi, furfanti, ho atteso troppo,
E vi discaccio.
Olà! Lesti! Lesti! al galoppo!
Al galoppo! Il capestro assai bene vi sta.
Ladri! Via! Via di qua! Via di qua! Via di qua!

Part 2

(*A garden. To the left* FORD'S *house. A group of trees center-stage.*

ALICE, ANN, MEG, DAME QUICKLY, *later* FORD, FENTON, DR. CAIUS, BARDOLPH, *and* PISTOL.

MEG *and* DAME QUICKLY *enter from the right and cross toward* FORD'S *house, on whose threshold they encounter* ALICE *and* ANN *just leaving the house.*)

MEG
Oh, Alice!

MEG
Alice.

ALICE
Meg!

ALICE
Meg.

MEG
Good morning!

MEG
Nannetta.

ALICE
Escivo appunto.
Per ridere con te.
Buon dì, comare.

QUICKLY
Dio vi doni allegria.
Botton di rosa!

ALICE
Giungi in buon punto.
M'accade un fatto da trasecolar.

MEG
Anche a me.

QUICKLY
Che?

NANNETTA
Che cosa?

ALICE
Narra il tuo caso.

MEG
Narra il tuo.

ALICE
Promessa
Di non ciarlar.

MEG
Ti pare?!

QUICKLY
Oibò! Vi pare?!

ALICE
Dunque: se m'acconciassi a entrar ne' rei
Propositi del diavolo sarei
Promossa al grado di Cavalleressa!

MEG
Anch'io.

ALICE
Motteggi.

MEG
Non più parole,
Chè qui sciupiamo la luce del sole.
Ho una lettera.

ALICE
Anch'io.

NANNETTA, QUICKLY
Oh!!

ALICE
Leggi.

MEG
Leggi.
«Fulgida Alice! amor t'offro . . .» . . . Ma come?!
Che cosa dice?
Salvo che il nome
La frase è uguale.

ALICE
I'm glad you're here for I was on my way to you.
(*to* MRS. QUICKLY) Good day, Dame Quickly!

QUICKLY
Heaven grant you good fortune!
(*patting* ANN'S *cheek*) My Ann, my rosebud!

ALICE (*still speaking to* MEG) Now let me tell you:
I am amazed at something that occurred.

MEG
So am I.

QUICKLY (*having conversed with* ANN, *now approaching inquisitively*)
What?

ANN (*coming closer, too*) What was it?

ALICE (*to* MEG) Speak out and tell me!

MEG
No, I listen.

ALICE (*mysteriously*) But promise: No word of this!

MEG
Of course not!

QUICKLY
Oh no! Of course not!

ALICE
Hear then: If I were willing to make a naughty bargain
With the devil,
My sin would be rewarded with the rank of Lady!

MEG
Mine also!

ALICE
You're joking!

MEG (*drawing a letter out of her pocket*)
Why go on talking when we should call
On the sunlight to help us? I have a letter.

ALICE
I also.

ANN, QUICKLY
Oh?

ALICE
Read it! (*gives her letter to* MEG)

MEG (*exchanging her own letter with that of* ALICE)
Read it!
(*reading* ALICE'S *letter*)
"Exquisite Alice! I adore you . . ."
What is this? I can't believe it.
But for the name the words are the same.

ALICE (*her eyes on the letter in her hand, repeats the contents of* MEG'S *letter*)
"Exquisite Meg! I adore you . . ."

MEG (*reading from the letter in her hand*)
"I implore you . . ."

ALICE
Here "Meg," there "Alice"!

MEG
Letter for letter!
"Ah, do not ask me why, but say . . ."

ALICE
". . . I love you!"
I cannot see what this means.

MEG
I find it all most confusing.
(*all in the group crowd around the letters, perusing them and fingering them with great interest*)

QUICKLY
Let's not be hasty!

MEG
The same expressions!

ALICE
Alike the writing!

QUICKLY
Even the paper.

ANN
Everything matches.

ALICE, MEG (*reading jointly, each her own letter*)
"You are cheerful and charming,
I debonair and disarming:
We are a pair joined by our fortune."

ALICE
Well!

ANN
She . . . you . . . he . . .

QUICKLY
. . . a pair of three!

ALICE
". . . in love united a pair of doves so tender, the fairest lady . . ."

ALL
". . . a man of weight and splendor!"

ALICE
"Your radiant beauty on me will shed its light
As bright and smiling out of the sky
A star will shine at night."

ALL (*laughing*) Ha, ha, ha, ha.

ALICE
«Fulgida Meg! amor t'offro . . .»

MEG
«. . . amor bramo»

ALICE
Qua «Meg», là «Alice».

MEG
È tal e quale.
«Non domandar perchè ma dimmi:»

ALICE
«. . . t'amo.»
Pur non gli offersi
Cagion.

MEG
Il nostro
Caso è pur strano.

QUICKLY
Guardiam con flemma.

MEG
Gli stessi versi.

ALICE
Lo stesso inchiostro.

QUICKLY
La stessa mano.

NANNETTA
Lo stesso stemma.

ALICE, MEG
«Sei la gaia comare, il compar gaio
«Son io, e fra noi due facciamo il paio».

ALICE
Già.

NANNETTA
Lui, lei, te.

QUICKLY
Un paio in tre.

ALICE
«Facciamo il paio in un amor ridente»
«di donna bella e d'uom . . .»

TUTTE
«. . . appariscente . . .»

ALICE
«E il viso tuo su me risplenderà come una stella, come una stella sull' immensità.»

TUTTE
Ah! Ah! Ah! Ah! Ah! Ah! Ah! Ah!

ALICE
«Rispondi al tuo scudiere,
John Falstaff Cavaliere».

TUTTE
Mostro!

ALICE
Dobbiam gabbarlo.

NANNETTA
E farne chiasso.

ALICE
E metterlo in burletta.

NANNETTA
Oh! Oh! che spasso!

QUICKLY
Che allegria!

MEG
Che vendetta!

ALICE
Quell'otre! quel tino!
Quel Re delle pancie,
Ci ha ancora le ciance
Del bel vagheggino.
E l'olio gli sgocciola
Dall'adipe unticcio
E ancor ei ne snocciola
La strofa e il bisticcio!
Lasciam ch'ei le pronte
Sue ciarle ne spifferi;
Farà come i pifferi
Che sceser dal monte.
Vedrai che, se abbindolo
Quel grosso compar,
Più lesto d'un guindolo
Lo faccio girar.

QUICKLY
Un flutto in tempesta
Gittò sulla rena
Di Windsor codesta
Vorace balena.
Ma qui non ha spazio
Da farsi più pingue;
Ne fecer già strazio
Le vostre tre lingue.
Tre lingue più allegre
D'un trillo di nacchere,
Che spargon più chiacchiere
Di sei cingallegre.
Tal sempre s'esilari
Quel bel cinguettar.
Così soglion l'ilari
Comari ciarlar.
Movenza di gonna!
Se il vischio lo impegola
Lo udremo strillar,

ALICE
"Reply to your admirer!
Your servant, Sir John Falstaff."

ALL
Monster!

ALICE
We must defy him . . .

ANN
. . . and twit and taunt him . . .

ALICE
. . . We'll fool him and will chide him . . .

ANN
. . . and hit and haunt him!

QUICKLY
We will cool him . . .

MEG
. . . and deride him!

ALICE (*turning from one to the other, all huddling together*)
This monstrous decanter,
This prince of dilation,
Shall harvest vexation
From frolic and banter!
His crass notoriety
Will be his perdition,
We'll teach him sobriety
But cause no suspicion.
He'll follow us gladly
And tumble more readily
For he who courts headily
Will often court badly.
Watch out, you polygamist
Disguised as a vat:
The fate of a bigamist,
A tri—or tetragamist,
Is something to fear,
Above all when you're fat!

QUICKLY (*to* ALICE)
That gun with its thunder,
We'll dampen its powder
And laugh even louder
While calling its blunder!
But as you pursue him
And shrewdly ensnare him
Before you undo him
You'd better beware him:
He's artful and wily,
Of canny felinity,
And may trick your trinity
Unless you act slyly!
For all his fatuity
He's quick as a cat.

'Twill take ingenuity
And great assiduity
To puncture his pride
And to batter him flat.

E allor la sua fregola
Vedremo svampar.

ANN (*to* ALICE)
Oh, let me, dear Mother,
Share frolic and laughter.
This game like no other
Will ring down the rafter.
Denying our amity
We'll gaily forsake him,
And blackest calamity
Will soon overtake him.
His silly pretensions,
His shaky morality
Increase his mortality
To dreadful dimensions.
You symbol of vanity,
You lecher, you gnat,
We'll bring you to sanity,
Respect and urbanity,
Yes, all these you'll learn
As we hand you your hat!

NANNETTA
Se ordisci una burla,
Vo' anch'io la mia parte.
Conviene condurla
Con senno, con arte.
L'agguato ov'ei sdrucciola
Convien ch'ei non scerna;
Già prese una lucciola
Per una lanterna.
Che il gioco riesca
Perciò più non dubito;
Poi coglierlo subito.
Bisogna offrir l'esca
E se i scilinguagnoli
Sapremo adoprar,
Vedremo a rigagnoli
Quell'orco sudar.

MEG
Come up from the ocean
To harry and hound us
A monster has bound us
In fear and commotion.
So let's be unanimous
And plan our defenses!
This man pusillanimous
Let's bring to his senses!
Our ways must be cunning,
Discreet and believable.
Our end is achievable,
Hilarious and stunning.
Your shameless duplicity,
You scoundrel, you rat,
Will bring us felicity
And bring you publicity. . .
You'll never again
Want to bargain for that!
(*they all exit*)
(MR. FORD, DR. CAIUS, FENTON, BARDOLPH, *and* PISTOL *enter from the right while the women exit on the left.* FORD *is in the center, on his right* PISTOL, *and* BARDOLPH *on his left.* FENTON *and* CAIUS *are behind* FORD. *They all converge on* FORD, *whispering to him in great agitation*)

MEG
Quell'uom è un cannone!
Se scoppia, ci spaccia.
Colui, se l'abbraccia,
Ti schiaccia Giunone.
Ma certo si spappola
Quel mostro a tuo cenno
E corre alla trappola
E perde il suo senno.
Potenza d'un fragil
Sorriso di donna!
Scienza d'un agile

DR. CAJUS
È un ribaldo, un furbo, un ladro,
Un furfante, un turco, un vandalo;
L'altro dì mandò a soqquadro
La mia casa e fu uno scandalo.
Se un processo oggi gl'intavolo
Sconterà le sue rapine,
Ma la sua più degna fine
Sia d'andare in man del diavolo.
E quei due che avete accanto
Genti son di sua tribù,
Non son due stinchi di santo
Nè son fiori di virtù.

DR. CAIUS (*to* FORD)
He's a liar and a lecher,
All he knows is rape and robbery.
He's a lout and rake and retcher
And a paragon of snobbery.
He has broken all my crockery,
Whipped my mare until she's dying.
Devil take him, keep him frying
As reward for all his mockery.
These two rascals here beside you
They are evil through and through.
Let my friendly council guide you:
I'd beware if I were you!

BARDOLFO
Falstaff, sì, ripeto, giuro,
(Per mia bocca il ciel v'illumina)
Contro voi John Falstaff rumina
Un progetto alquanto impuro.
Son uom d'arme e quell'infame
Più non vo' che v'impozzangheri;
Non vorrei, no, escir dai gangheri
Dell'onor per un reame!
Messer Ford, l'uomo avvisato
Non è salvo che a metà.
Tocca a voi d'ordir l'agguato
Che l'agguato stornerà.

BARDOLPH (*to* FORD)
Falstaff, as I keep repeating,
Is a genius at cheating.
Master Ford, let me reiterate:
It is you he will obliterate.
I'm a soldier but no booty
Ever dulls my sensitivity
And compels me to activity
Which offends my sense of duty.
Master Ford, I know you need me:
Let my warning come in time:
It is you who now must heed me
To prevent this ugly crime!

FORD
Un ronzio di vespe e d'avidi
Calabron brontolamento,
Un rombar di nembi gravidi
D'uragani è quel ch'io sento.
Il cerèbro un ebro allucina
Turbamento di paura;
Ciò che intorno a me si buccina,
È un susurro di congiura.
Parlan quattro ed uno ascolta;
Qual dei quattro ascolterò?
Se parlaste uno alla volta
Forse allor v'intenderò.

FORD (*to himself, then to the others*)
Ah, around me all this flummery
Has begun to overcome me
Like a bumbling kind of mummery
Which will stun me and benumb me.
How I wish they would be sensible
So I'd know what each is doing!
Though they are incomprehensible
I can feel a danger brewing.
I should highly praise and cheer you
If you only were aware:
Four to speak and one to hear you . . .
This indeed is hardly fair!

PISTOLA
Sir John Falstaff già v'appresta,
Messer Ford, un gran pericolo.
Già vi pende sulla testa
Qualche cosa a perpendicolo.
Messer Ford, fui già un armigero
Di quell'uom dall'ampia cute;
Or mi pento e mi morigero
Per ragioni di salute.
La minaccia or v'è scoperta,
Or v'è noto il ciurmador.
State all'erta, all'erta, all'erta!
Qui si tratta dell'onor.

PISTOL (*to* FORD)
Every man in town will scorn you.
Falstaff has a plan perfidious
For he wishes to adorn you
With a headgear worse than hideous.
I know well I was unsavory.
Falstaff made me lose my senses.
I repent and hope my bravery
Will atone for my offenses.
There is nothing more to mention,
Now the rest is up to you:

Be on guard and pay attention
And find out what he will do!

FENTON (*to* FORD)
For his scandalous temerity
I should like to see him suffer.
And my fury and severity
Will defeat the brazen bluffer.
And my heart flies high and higher,
I can feel my senses quivering
When I think of that old liar
On his knees, all spent and shivering,
I will first appeal to reason
But if this should not do well,
Then it would amount to treason
Not to send him down to hell!

FENTON
Se volete, io non mi perito
Di ridurlo alla ragione
Colle brusche o colle buone,
E pagarlo al par del merito.
Mi dà il cuore e mi solletica
(E sarà una giostra gaia)
Di sfondar quella ventraia
Iperbolico-apoplettica.
Col consiglio o colla spada
Se lo trovo al tu per tu,
O lui va per la sua strada
O lo assegno a Belzebù.

FORD (*to* PISTOL)
Continue!

FORD
Ripeti.

PISTOL (*to* FORD)
I'll tell you shortly:
Sir Falstaff round and portly
Is yearning for some headroom.
Your till could be his treasure,
Your wife provide his pleasure
While he commands your bedroom!

PISTOLA
In due parole:
L'enorme Falstaff vuole
Entrar nel vostro tetto.
Beccarvi la consorte,
Sfondar la cassaforte
E sconquassarvi il letto.

DR. CAIUS
Dash it all!

DR. CAJUS
Caspita!

FORD
Ah, I'll die!

FORD
Quanti guai!

BARDOLPH (*to* FORD)
And a letter he penned her . . .

BARDOLFO
Già le scrisse un biglietto . . .

PISTOL
. . . through me he meant to send her.
"No!" said I.

PISTOLA
Ma quel messaggio abbietto
Ricusai.

BARDOLPH
So did I.

BARDOLFO
Ricusai.

PISTOL
So be on guard!

PISTOLA
Badate a voi!

BARDOLPH
Remember . . .

BARDOLFO
Badate!

PISTOL
For him no woman's holy,
Tall, lean, or roly-poly,
In May or in December!

PISTOLA
Falstaff le occhieggia tutte
Che siano belle o brutte,
Pulzelle o maritate.

BARDOLPH
Single . . .

BARDOLFO
Tutte!

PISTOL
Married . . .

PISTOLA
Tutte!

BARDOLPH
Maiden . . .

BARDOLFO
Tutte!

PISTOLA, BARDOLFO
Tutte!

BARDOLFO
La corona che adorna
D'Atteòn l'irte chiome
Su voi già spunta.

FORD
Come
Sarebbe a dir?

BARDOLFO
Le corna.

FORD
Brutta parola!

DR. CAJUS
Ha voglie
Voraci il Cavaliere.

FORD
Sorveglierò la moglie.
Sorveglierò il messere.
Salvar vo' i beni miei
Dagli appetiti altrui.

FENTON
(È lei.)

NANNETTA
(È lui.)

FORD
(È lei.)

ALICE
(È lui.)

DR. CAJUS
(È lei.)

MEG
(È lui.)

ALICE
(S'egli sapesse! . . .)

NANNETTA
Guai!

ALICE
Schiviamo i passi suoi.

MEG
Ford è geloso?

ALICE
Assai.

QUICKLY
Zitto.

ALICE
(Badiamo a noi).

FENTON
Pst, pst, Nannetta. Vien qua.

BOTH
Matron!

BARDOLPH
Or the crowning adornment of Actaeon's fair brow
Will be found on you, sir.

FORD
What do you mean by that?

BARDOLPH
The horns, sir!

FORD
Ghastly expression!

DR. CAIUS
The gentleman's greed shocks me indeed!

FORD
My wife and that old charmer,
That knight in rusting armor:
(*the four women re-enter from the left*)
She still belongs to me,
This much I guarantee!

FENTON (*noticing* ANN) 'Tis she!

ANN (*noticing* FENTON) 'Tis he!

FORD (*noticing* ALICE) 'Tis she!

ALICE (*noticing* FORD) 'Tis he!

DR. CAIUS (*to* FORD *pointing to* ALICE) 'Tis she!

MEG (*to* ALICE, *pointing to* FORD) 'Tis he!

ALICE (*to the others, referring to* FORD) If he should guess it . . . !

ANN
My . . . !

ALICE
We'd better now avoid him.

MEG
Why? Is he jealous?

ALICE
Insanely.

QUICKLY
Silence!

ALICE
We'd better hide!
(ALICE, MEG, *and* QUICKLY *exit to the left.* FORD, DR. CAIUS, BARDOLPH, *and* PISTOL *exit to the right.* ANN *and* FENTON *remain on-stage*)

FENTON (*from the bushes, softly calling* ANN)
Pst! Ann! My darling, come here!

ANN (*putting her forefinger to her lips to caution him*)
Quiet! 'Tis you?

FENTON
Come, kiss me!

ANN
But quickly!

FENTON
Yes, quickly!
(*rapid exchange of kisses*)

ANN
Lips, oh so burning!

FENTON
Lips red as roses!

ANN
Lips where my yearning sweetly reposes!

FENTON
Sometimes revealing pearls shining brightly,
Kissing me lightly, wounding or healing!
Kisses that haunt me . . .
(*tries to embrace her*)

ANN (*defending herself and looking around*)
Brazen offender!

FENTON
Glances so tender,
Why do you taunt me?
Kiss me . . .
(*tries to kiss her again*)

ANN
They will hear us! No . . .

FENTON
Please . . . two kisses!

ANN (*freeing herself*)
Rascal!

FENTON
Ah, how I love you!

ANN
They're near us.
(*they leave each other while the women re-enter*)

FENTON (*hiding behind the bushes*)
"Just kiss me soon, and you always will do it!"

ANN (*continuing* FENTON'S *song while approaching the women*)
"Trust in the moon, Love will always renew it!"

ALICE
Falstaff tells us a fable.

MEG
Wait till we turn the table!

ALICE
What if I wrote a letter?
(*rejoining the women in an offhand manner*)

NANNETTA
Taci.
Che vuoi?

FENTON
Due baci.

NANNETTA
In fretta.

FENTON
In fretta.

NANNETTA
Labbra di foco!

FENTON
Labbra di fiore! . . .

NANNETTA
Che il vago gioco
Sanno d'amore.

FENTON
Che spargon ciarle,
Che mostran perle,
Belle a vederle,
Dolci a baciarle!
Labbra leggiadre!

NANNETTA
Man malandrine!

FENTON
Ciglia assassine!
Pupille ladre!
T'amo!

NANNETTA
Imprudente.
No.

FENTON
Sì . . . Due baci.

NANNETTA
Basta.

FENTON
Mi piaci
Tanto!

NANNETTA
Vien gente.

FENTON
«Bocca baciata non perde ventura».

NANNETTA
«Anzi rinnova come fa la luna».

ALICE
Falstaff m'ha canzonata.

MEG
Merita un gran castigo.

ALICE
Se gli scrivessi un rigo? . . .

NANNETTA
Val meglio un'ambasciata.

ALICE
Sì.

QUICKLY
Sì.

ALICE
Da quel brigante
Tu andrai. Lo adeschi all'offa
D'un ritrovo galante
Con me.

QUICKLY
Questa è gaglioffa!

NANNETTA
Che bella burla!

ALICE
Prima
Per attirarlo a noi,
Lo lusinghiamo . . .

NANNETTA
E poi . . .

ALICE
. . . e poi
Gliele cantiamo in rima.

QUICKLY
Non merita riguardo.

ALICE
È un bove.

MEG
È un uomo senza
Fede.

ALICE
È un monte di lardo.

MEG
Non merita clemenza.

ALICE
È un ghiotton che scialacqua
Tutto il suo aver nel cuoco.

NANNETTA
Lo tufferem nell'acqua.

ALICE
Lo arrostiremo al fuoco.

NANNETTA
Che gioia!

ALICE
Che allegria!

MEG
Procaccia di far bene
La tua parte.

QUICKLY
Chi viene?

MEG
La c'è qualcun che spia.

ANN
A messenger were better.

ALICE
Yes.

QUICKLY
Yes.

ALICE (*to* QUICKLY)
The one to see him is you.
And you invite him to a tender appointment with me.

QUICKLY
This will excite him.

ANN
It will delight him.

ALICE
First we will bait a trap to lure him and secure him.

ANN
And then?

ALICE
And then . . . and then we'll let him have it!

QUICKLY
A long belated matter!

ALICE
That bulldog!

MEG
That miscreant seducer!

ALICE
That mountain of batter!

MEG
We'll show him no compassion.

ALICE
He keeps eating and drinking until his senses fail him.

ANN
We'll dunk him till he's sinking . . .

ALICE
. . . and boil and roast and scale him!

ANN
Delightful!

ALICE
This is priceless!

MEG (*to* QUICKLY)
You know your part, now play it to perfection!

QUICKLY (*noticing* FENTON *hiding nearby*)
Who is this?

MEG
Beware! There's someone spying!
(*the women, except* ANN, *rapidly exit to the right.* FENTON *comes forward as soon as they are gone*)

FENTON
Now I shall storm you.

ANN (*pretending to defy him*)
You won't embrace me. Just try it!

FENTON
Face me!
(*he tries to kiss her. She covers her face with her hand, which* FENTON *kisses. Then she raises her hand too high for him to reach it with his lips*)

ANN
I shall reform you.
In love the frail and fair defender
Will in the end be victorious
And will win surrender.

FENTON
Soon I shall bind you
And shall disarm you.

ANN
But I will charm you.

FENTON
My kiss will find you.
Careful! Your tresses
So soft and tender
Will now surrender
To my caresses.
(*he kisses her hair*)

ANN (*puts one of her tresses around his neck, as if to capture him*)
Caught is the sinner!

FENTON
Ah, heed my pleading!

ANN
Wounded and bleeding,
I am the winner.

FENTON
I yield the field, hand over my weapon, and then . . .

ANN
. . . and then?

FENTON
And then we start it all over.

ANN
Let me invite you!
I love to fight you . . . later!

FENTON
Do not flee me!

ANN
I hear them . . . they'll see me!
(*exit to the right*)

FENTON (*while withdrawing*)
"Just kiss me soon, and you always will do it!"

FENTON
Torno all'assalto.

NANNETTA
Torno alla gara.
Ferisci!

FENTON
Para!

NANNETTA
La mira è in alto.
L'amor è un agile
Torneo, sua corte
Vuol che il più fragile
Vinca il più forte.

FENTON
M'armo, e ti guardo.
T'aspetto al varco.

NANNETTA
Il labbro è l'arco.

FENTON
E il bacio è il dardo.
Bada! la freccia
Fatal già scocca
Dalla mia bocca
Sulla tua treccia.

NANNETTA
Eccoti avvinto.

FENTON
Chiedo la vita!

NANNETTA
Io son ferita,
Ma tu sei vinto.

FENTON
Pietà! Facciamo
La pace e poi . . .

NANNETTA
E poi?

FENTON
Se vuoi,
Ricominciamo.

NANNETTA
Bello è quel gioco
Che dura poco.
Basta.

FENTON
Amor mio!

NANNETTA
Vien gente. Addio!

FENTON
«Bocca baciata non perde ventura».

NANNETTA
«Anzi rinnova come fa la luna».

BARDOLFO
Udrai quanta egli sfoggia
Magniloquenza altera.
FORD
Diceste ch'egli alloggia
Dove?
PISTOLA
Alla Giarrettiera.

FORD
A lui mi annuncerete,
Ma con un falso nome;
Poscia vedrete come
Lo piglio nella rete.
Ma . . . non una parola.

BARDOLFO
In ciarle non m'ingolfo.
Io mi chiamo Bardolfo.

PISTOLA
Io mi chiamo Pistola.

FORD
Siam d'accordo.

BARDOLFO
L'arcano
Custodirem.
PISTOLA
Son sordo
E muto.
FORD
Siam d'accordo
Tutti. Qua la mano.
BARDOLFO, PISTOLA
Sì.

DR. CAJUS
Del tuo barbaro diagnostico
Forse il male è assai men barbaro.
Ti convien tentar la prova
Molestissima del ver.
Così avvien col sapor ostico
Del ginepro e del rabarbaro;
Il benessere rinnova
L'amarissimo bicchier.

PISTOLA
Voi dovete empirgli il calice,
Tratto tratto, interrogandolo,
Per tentar se vi riesca
Di trovar del nodo il bandolo.
Come all'acqua inclina il salice,
Così al vin quel Cavalier.
Scoverete la sua tresca,
Scoprirete il suo pensier.

ANN (*answering him from off-stage*)
"Trust in the moon, Love will always renew it!"
(*re-enter* FORD, DR. CAIUS, BARDOLPH, *and* PISTOL. FENTON *rejoins them presently*)
BARDOLPH (*to* FORD)
To listen to his braying makes any man a martyr.

FORD
You mentioned where he's staying . . . tell me!

PISTOL
Close by, at the Garter.

FORD
You ask him to receive me,
Hiding my name and station!
John Falstaff's castigation
Is under way, believe me!
If you're discreet and loyal . . .

BARDOLPH
Regard me as your servant!
I am Bardolph and fervent.

PISTOL
I am Pistol and trusty.

FORD
Will you promise?

BARDOLPH
Our word is as good as gold . . .

PISTOL
. . . and even better.

FORD
Are we in agreement? On your honor?

BARDOLPH, PISTOL
Yes.
(*the four women appear in the background*)

DR. CAIUS (*to* FORD)
Even when of utmost gravity
A disease is often curable.
Nature's power will surprise you
And assist you when you're ill.
In a matter of depravity
That to you seems unendurable
As a doctor I advise you:
Hold your nose and take a pill!

PISTOL (*to* FORD)
One good way to make him pliable
Is to flatter his cupidity.
You remember what I told you
Of his liking for liquidity.
For it is quite undeniable:
Wine will quickly make him fall.
In his arms he will enfold you
And at last will tell you all.

FORD (*to* PISTOL)
You will see my virtuosity
In the way I shall ensnare him,
Then the tigerish ferocity
I'll display when I shall tear him.
The old rascal will be sorry—
For my vengeance cannot fail—
When the hunter turns to quarry
And the snake will bite its tail!

FORD
Tu vedrai se bene adopera
L'arte mia con quell'infame.
E sarà prezzo dell'opera
S'io discopro le sue trame.
Se da me storno il ridicolo
Non avrem sudato invan.
S'io mi salvo dal pericolo,
L'angue morde il cerretan.

BARDOLPH (*to* FORD)
Master Ford, you must be drastic
For this case is most precarious:
With your wife a total stranger
Who will surely go too far!
Yes, I know it seems fantastic,
But that drunkard is nefarious.
You will run a fatal danger
Leaving matters as they are.

BARDOLFO
Messer Ford, un infortunio
Marital in voi s'incorpora;
Se non siete astuto e cauto
Quel Sir John vi tradirà.
Quel paffuto plenilunio
Che il color del vino imporpora
Troverebbe un pasto lauto
Nella vostra ingenuità.

FENTON (*to himself*)
Ah, these men and all this blabbering
They are planning and are scheming,
Over there the women jabbering.
How did all this clamor start?
There I see her, sweet and beautiful,
Her, whose love is mine forever,
Like a star come down from heaven.
She will always hold my heart.

FENTON
Qua borbotta un crocchio
d'uomini,
C'è nell'aria una malìa.
Là cinguetta un stuol di femine,
Spira un vento agitator.
Ma colei che in cor mi nomini,
Dolce amor, vuol esser mia!
Noi sarem come due gemine
Stelle unite in un ardor.

ALICE (*to* MEG)
Watch out, you polygamist
Disguised as a vat,
The fate of a bigamist
Is sad when you're fat!

ALICE
Vedrai che, se abbindolo
Quel grosso compar.
Più lesto d'un guindolo
Lo faccio girar.

MEG (*to* ALICE)
Your shameless duplicity,
You monster, you rat,
Will bring you publicity,
We'll wager on that!

MEG
Se il vischio lo impegola
Lo udremo strillar,
E allor la sua fregola
Vedremo svampar.

ANN (*to* ALICE)
You symbol of vanity,
You lecher, you gnat,
We'll bring you to sanity,
And hand you your hat.

NANNETTA
E se i scilinguagnoli
Sapremo adoprar,
Vedremo a rigagnoli
Quell'orco sudar.

QUICKLY
For all his fatuity
He's quick as a cat:
'Twill take ingenuity
To batter him flat.
(*all the men exit*)

QUICKLY
Tal sempre s'esilari
Quel bel cinguettar;
Così soglion l'ilari
Comari ciarlar.

ALICE
Enough of this jabbering!

ALICE
Qui più non si vagoli . . .

NANNETTA
Tu corri all'ufficio
Tuo.

ALICE
Vo' ch'egli miagoli
D'amor come un micio.
È intesa.

QUICKLY
Sì.

NANNETTA
È detta.

ALICE
Domani.

QUICKLY
Sì. Sì.

ALICE
Buon dì, Meg.

QUICKLY
Nannetta,
Buon dì.

NANNETTA
Addio.

MEG
Buon dì.

ALICE
Vedrai che quell'epa
Terribile e tronfia
Si gonfia.

ALICE, NANNETTA
Si gonfia.

ALICE, NANNETTA, MEG
Si gonfia.

ALICE, MEG, QUICKLY, NANNETTA
Si gonfia e poi crepa.

ALICE
«Ma il viso mio su lui
risplenderà . . . »

ALICE, NANNETTA
«Come una stella.»

TUTTE
«Come una stella sull'immensità».
Ah! ah! ah! ah!

ANN (*to* QUICKLY)
'Tis time now for you to go.

ALICE
He shall be howling like a cat in the moonlight.
(*to* QUICKLY)
You follow?

QUICKLY
Yes.

ANN
That's splendid.

ALICE
Tomorrow!

QUICKLY
Yes! Yes!

ALICE
Good day, Meg.

QUICKLY
My Annie, good day!

ANN
Good day.

MEG
Good day.

ALICE (*holding the others back*)
We'll see how his belly will soon be expanding,
And growing . . .

ALICE and ANN
. . . and bloating . . .

ALICE, ANN, MEG
. . . and growing . . .

ALL FOUR WOMEN
. . . and bloating until it bursts!

ALICE
"Your radiant beauty on me will shed its light . . ."

ALICE, ANN
". . . as bright and smiling . . ."

ALL
". . . out of the sky a star will shine at night!"
Ha, ha, ha, ha!
(*they all leave laughing*)

ACT II

Part 1

(*At the Garter Inn, as in Act I.*
FALSTAFF *again seated in his armchair, drinking his sherry.* BARDOLPH *and* PISTOL *near the door to the left.*)

BARDOLPH, PISTOL (*singing together and beating their chests in a gesture of contrition*)
See us sighing, weak from crying!

BARDOLFO, PISTOLA
Siam pentiti e contriti.

FALSTAFF (*barely turning toward* BARDOLPH *and* PISTOL)
Men will return to vice like mice to the larder.

FALSTAFF
L'uomo ritorna al vizio,
La gatta al lardo . . .

BARDOLPH, PISTOL
Let us return once more to serve you!

BARDOLFO, PISTOLA
E noi, torniamo al tuo servizio.

BARDOLPH (*to* FALSTAFF)
Outside the door there's someone waiting . . .
A woman who would like you to see her.

BARDOLFO
Padron, là c'è una donna che alla vostra presenza
Chiede d'essere ammessa.

FALSTAFF
I'll see her.
(BARDOLPH *exits to the left and returns at once with* DAME QUICKLY)

FALSTAFF
S'inoltri.

QUICKLY (*curtsying deeply toward* FALSTAFF, *who remains seated*)
I am honored.

QUICKLY
Reverenza!

FALSTAFF
Advance, my worthy woman!

FALSTAFF
Buon giorno, buona donna.

QUICKLY
I am honored. Sir John, with your permission
(*advancing cautiously*)
I shall, but most discreetly,
Submit a proposition.

QUICKLY
Se Vostra Grazia vuole,
Vorrei, segretamente, dirle quattro parole.

FALSTAFF
Your wish be granted.
(*to* BARDOLPH *and* PISTOL, *who have remained in the background to listen*)
Pray, leave us!
(*the two leave, showing their disappointment*)

FALSTAFF
T'accordo udienza.
Escite.

QUICKLY (*curtsies again, then draws nearer to* FALSTAFF)
I am honored. You know a Mistress Ford . . .

QUICKLY
Reverenza! Madonna
Alice Ford . . .

FALSTAFF (*rises and turns toward* QUICKLY, *displaying great interest*)
I do . . . ?

FALSTAFF
Ebben?

QUICKLY
Alas! Unhappy woman! You're a brazen seducer . . .

QUICKLY
Ahimè! Povera donna!
Siete un gran seduttore!

FALSTAFF
I know. Continue!

FALSTAFF
Lo so. Continua.

QUICKLY
The lady is raving with delirious passion for you.
Your letter fills her with love and gratitude.

QUICKLY
Alice
Sta in grande agitazione d'amor per voi; vi dice

Ch'ebbe la vostra lettera, che vi ringrazia e che
Suo marito esce sempre dalle due alle tre.

FALSTAFF
Dalle due alle tre.

QUICKLY
Vostra Grazia a quell'ora
Potrà liberamente salir dove dimora
La bella Alice. Povera donna! le angosce sue
Son crudeli! ha un marito geloso!

FALSTAFF
Dalle due
Alle tre.
Le dirai che impaziente aspetto
Quell'ora. Al mio dovere non mancherò.

QUICKLY
Ben detto.
Ma c'è un'altra ambasciata per Vostra Grazia.

FALSTAFF
Parla.

QUICKLY
La bella Meg (un angelo che innamora a guardarla)
Anch'essa vi saluta molto amorosamente;
Dice che suo marito è assai di rado assente.
Povera donna! un giglio di candore e di fe'!
Voi le stregate tutte.

FALSTAFF
Stregoneria non c'è,
Ma un certo qual mio fascino personal . . . Dimmi: l'altra
Sa di quest'altra?

QUICKLY
Oibò! La donna nasce scaltra.
Non temete.

FALSTAFF
Or ti vo' remunerar . . .

QUICKLY
Chi semina
Grazie, raccoglie amore.

FALSTAFF
Prendi, Mercurio-femina.
Saluta le due dame.

QUICKLY
M'inchino.

This I should tell you . . .
And that daily her husband is absent
From eleven to one.

FALSTAFF
From eleven to one!

QUICKLY
'Tis the time Your Grace could meet her
And free of danger venture
In her own home to greet her.
What an adventure! Unhappy woman!
For what she suffers is inhuman:
Master Ford is a demon!

FALSTAFF (*mulling over* QUICKLY'S *remarks*)
. . . from eleven to one!
(*to* QUICKLY)
Go and tell her that my heart is waiting to see her.
My duty tells me what to do!

QUICKLY
I bless you.
There is still one more message I am to bring you.

FALSTAFF
Tell me!

QUICKLY
This one from Meg—an angel whom to behold is to worship!
She, too, has asked me to assure you of her great ardor.
She has a spouse who all the time
Stays in the house to guard her. Unhappy woman!
As white as snow is her innocent heart!
No one escapes your magic.

FALSTAFF
I cast no magic spell.
And yet I wield a certain charm of my own.
Tell me: Each one keeps her own secret?

QUICKLY
Of course! No woman tells another . . . not in this case.

FALSTAFF (*searching his purse*)
You have earned a just reward.

QUICKLY
Who soweth his favors shall harvest love.

FALSTAFF (*offering her a small coin*)
Take this, you female Mercury!
(*dismissing her with a gesture*)
Be sure to greet my ladies!

QUICKLY
Your servant!
(*exits*)
(FALSTAFF *alone, later* BARDOLPH, FORD, *and* PISTOL)

FALSTAFF
She's mine! I've won her!
Go, gallant John, go, go onward to glory!
You, mighty mound of matter, once more shall render
Your gen'rous help to me.
Women are haunted by your spacious splendor,
As anyone can see.
My paunch, at last I know why I should feed you.
Thanks! I shall need you.

BARDOLPH (*entering from the left*)
Sir John, I have a message from a Master Brook
Who wants to have a word with you,
And he offers you a demijohn of Cyprus
To assure you of a pleasant morning.

FALSTAFF
And this Brook, is he here now?

BARDOLPH
Yes.

FALSTAFF
I am fond of brooks that run so freely,
Whose flow bespeaks such tasty tidings.
He's welcome!
(BARDOLPH *exits*)
Go, gallant John, onward to glory!
(FORD *enters in disguise from the left, preceded by* BARDOLPH, *who stays near the entrance and bows as* FORD *passes. The latter is followed by* PISTOL, *who carries a demijohn, which he sets on the table.* PISTOL *and* BARDOLPH *remain in the background.* FORD *is holding a bag of money*)

FORD (*after bowing low*)
Your Worship, may heaven bless you!

FALSTAFF (*returning the greeting*)
His mercy may be on you, sir!

FORD (*respectfully*)
As I am aware, my bold intrusion—
With your kindly forbearance—
Seems to be quite ill-mannered,
An insolent presumption,
As a gentleman ought to know.

FALSTAFF
You could not be more welcome!

FORD
In me you see a man who lives in wealth and bounty,
Whose every wish is granted—
A man who lends and spends and never cared, never counted.
Sir, I shall no longer bore you:
Master Brook stands before you.

FALSTAFF
Alice è mia!
Va, vecchio John, va, va per la tua via.
Questa tua vecchia carne ancora spreme
Qualche dolcezza a te.
Tutte le donne ammutinate insieme
Si dannano per me!
Buon corpo di Sir John, ch'io nutro e sazio,
Va, ti ringrazio.

BARDOLFO
Padron, di là c'è un certo Messer Mastro Fontana
Che anela di conoscervi; offre una damigiana
Di Cipro per l'asciolvere di Vostra Signoria.

FALSTAFF
Il suo nome è Fontana?

BARDOLFO
Sì.

FALSTAFF
Bene accolta sia
La fontana che spande un simile liquore!
Entri.
Va, vecchio John, per la tua via.

FORD
Signore,
V'asssista il cielo!

FALSTAFF
Assista voi pur, signore.

FORD
Io sono,
Davver, molto indiscreto, e vi chiedo perdono,
Se, senza cerimonie, qui vengo e sprovveduto
Di più lunghi preamboli.

FALSTAFF
Voi siete il benvenuto.

FORD
In me vedete un uomo ch'ha un'abbondanza grande
Degli agi della vita; un uom che spende e spande
Come più gli talenta pur di passar mattana.
Io mi chiamo Fontana!

FALSTAFF
Caro signor Fontana!
Voglio fare con voi più ampia conoscenza.

FORD
Caro Sir John, desidero parlarvi in confidenza.

BARDOLFO
(Attento!)

PISTOLA
(Zitto!)

BARDOLFO
(Guarda! Scommetto! Egli va dritto
Nel trabocchetto.)

PISTOLA
(Ford se lo intrappola . . .)

BARDOLFO
(Zitto!)

FALSTAFF
Che fate là?
V'ascolto.

FORD
Sir John, m'infonde ardire
Un ben noto proverbio popolar: si suol dire
Che l'oro apre ogni porta, che l'oro è un talismano,
Che l'oro vince tutto.

FALSTAFF
L'oro è un buon capitano
Che marcia avanti.

FORD
Ebbene. Ho un sacco di monete
Qua, che mi pesa assai. Sir John, se voi volete
Aiutarmi a portarlo . . .

FALSTAFF
Con gran piacer . . . non so,
Davver, per qual mio merito, Messer . . .

FORD
Ve lo dirò.
C'è a Windsor una dama, bella e leggiadra molto.
Si chiama Alice; è moglie d'un certo Ford.

FALSTAFF
V'ascolto.

FORD
Io l'amo e lei non m'ama; le scrivo, non risponde;
La guardo, non mi guarda; la cerco e si nasconde.
Per lei sprecai tesori, gittai doni su doni,

FALSTAFF (*shaking his hand most cordially*)
Good Master Brook, I greet you.
From the first you have made a most profound impression.

FORD
Gallant Sir John, I trust I may have faith in your discretion.

BARDOLPH (*whispering to* PISTOL, *both hiding in the background*)
Attention!

PISTOL (*softly to* BARDOLPH)
Quiet!

BARDOLPH
Watch it! How wily!
You can't deny it . . . he does it slyly!

PISTOL
Netting the butterfly!

BARDOLPH
Quiet!

FALSTAFF (*to* BARDOLPH *and* PISTOL, *who subsequently disappear*)
Are you still here?
(*to* FORD, *who remains alone with him*)
Continue!

FORD
Sir John, will you allow me to resort to a wise
And ancient saw: "When the key is of gold, no lock
Will resist it"?
To gold and all its splendor,
To gold they all surrender.

FALSTAFF
Gold will conquer the world, proudly marching onward.

FORD
Precisely! Perchance I find this bag of gold
Weighs too much for me. Sir John,
May I impose upon your kindness to help me?

FALSTAFF (*taking the bag and placing it on the table*)
Of course I shall!
But may I know why it is I whom you have chosen . . .

FORD
You may indeed.
In Windsor lives a lady, lovely, demure, and haunting.
Her name is Alice, her husband a certain Ford.

FALSTAFF
Enchanting.

FORD
I woo her . . . cannot subdue her,
Implore her . . . seem to bore her,
Beseech her . . . cannot reach her,
Pursue her . . . cannot get to her!

In desperate delusion, to show that I adore her,
In unrestrained profusion I spread my wealth before her.
Alas . . . all this was useless!
A castaway crusader, I flounder and fly around her,
And sadly serenade her!

FALSTAFF (*gaily*)
I know, I know that Love is blessed and blighted,
How Love will twit and taunt you, and like a shadow . . .

FORD
. . . it will haunt you . . .

FALSTAFF
. . . you fight it . . .

FORD
. . . and as you fight it . . .

FALSTAFF
'twill haunt you!

FORD
You know . . .

FALSTAFF
. . . quite so . . .

FORD
. . . my woe . . .

FALSTAFF
. . . I know!

FORD
To suffer and to languish I've paid my weight in gold.

FALSTAFF
The amatory anguish will torture young and old!
And not even once she seemed to be yielding?

FORD
No.

FALSTAFF
But why pour out your heart to me?

FORD
Let me explain:
You are a man of bearing, noble, well spoken, and cunning.
A man of fearless daring whose gallantry is stunning.

FALSTAFF (*humbly*)
. . . well . . .

FORD
I am serious. My gold shall serve to make you happy:
Away with it! Go, play with it! You shall spend and expend it,
You shall cherish and befriend it, you shall live in its splendor!
All I am asking is that to you she must surrender.

FALSTAFF
What do you mean?

Escogitai, tremando, il vol delle occasioni.
Ahimè! tutto fu vano! Rimasi sulle scale,
Negletto, a bocca asciutta, cantando un madrigale.

FALSTAFF
«L'amor, l'amor che non ci dà mai tregue»
«Finchè la vita strugge»
«È come l'ombra . . .»

FORD
«. . . che chi fugge . . .»

FALSTAFF
«. . . insegue . . .»

FORD
«E chi l'insegue . . .»

FALSTAFF
«. . . fugge.»

FORD
«L'amor,»

FALSTAFF
«L'amor,»

FORD
«L'amor!»

FALSTAFF
«L'amor!»

FORD
E questo madrigale l'ho appreso a prezzo dor.

FALSTAFF
Quest'è il destin fatale del misero amator.
Essa non vi die' mai luogo a lusinghe?

FORD
No.

FALSTAFF
Ma infin, perchè v'aprite a me?

FORD
Ve lo dirò:
Voi siete un gentiluomo prode, arguto, facondo,
Voi siete un uom di guerra, voi siete un uom di mondo . . .

FALSTAFF
Oh! . . .

FORD
Non vi adulo, e quello è un sacco di monete:
Spendetele! spendetele! sì, spendete e spandete
Tutto il mio patrimonio! Siate ricco e felice!
Ma, in contraccambio, chiedo che conquistiate Alice!

FALSTAFF
Strana ingiunzion!

FORD
Mi spiego: Quella crudel beltà
Sempre è vissuta in grande fede di castità.
La sua virtù importuna m'abbarbagliava gli occhi:
La bella inespugnabile dicea: «Guai se mi tocchi.»
Ma se voi l'espugnate, poi, posso anch'io sperar:
Da fallo nasce fallo e allor . . . Che ve ne par?

FALSTAFF
Prima di tutto, senza complimenti, Messere,
Accetto il sacco. E poi (fede di cavaliere,
Qua la mano!) farò le vostre brame sazie.
Voi, la moglie di Ford possederete.

FORD
Grazie!!

FALSTAFF
Io son già molto innanzi; (non c'è ragion ch'io taccia
Con voi) fra una mezz'ora sarà nelle mie braccia.

FORD
Chi? . . .

FALSTAFF
Alice. Essa mandò dianzi una . . . confidente
Per dirmi che quel tanghero di suo marito è assente
Dalle due alle tre.

FORD
Lo conoscete?

FALSTAFF
Il diavolo
Se lo porti all'inferno con Menelao suo avolo!
Quel tanghero, quel tanghero, vedrai!
Vedrai! Te lo cornifico netto! se mi frastorna
Gli sparo una girandola di botte sulle corna!
Quel Messer Ford è un bue! Un bue! Te lo corbello, vedrai!
Vedrai! Te lo cornifico netto
Quel tanghero, quel tanghero!
Ma è tardi. Aspettami qua.
Vado a farmi bello.

FORD
Quite simply:
My lovely iceberg prides herself
On being thought a paragon of chastity.
Her virtuous demeanor has made my passion keener.
Her eyes will tell the world for all to see:
"No one come near me!"
But if you, sir, should win her,
I, in due time, may, too:
One fall makes her a sinner . . . and then . . . is this not true?

FALSTAFF
Now to begin and expedite the matter
I shall accept your money. Then (here is my hand upon it.
You may trust me!) your pain and trouble shall be ended. (*shaking* FORD's *hand*)
You shall win Mistress Ford . . . she will surrender!

FORD
Splendid!

FALSTAFF
I'm well along my way, sir,
(Why should I hide my secret from you?)
This very day, sir, I swear I shall embrace her!

FORD (*surprised, half choking*)
Whom?

FALSTAFF (*calmly*)
Your lady. Someone she sent to me this morning
Has told me that the simpleton she calls a husband
Is absent from eleven to one.

FORD
Pray, do you know him?

FALSTAFF
For all I care he may simmer in hell
And choke on his own stupidity!
That simpleton, that addlehead,
The scamp, the fool, the lout, I'll cast him out,
Make him horniferous, neatly, sweetly!
Should he be mulish I'll show him how to crown his brow
And even seem more foolish!
Ford is a cow, a bullock! He's mooing and chewing and booing.
Watch out how I shall twit him!
No doubt I shall outwit him. The lout, I clout his snout!
Make him horniferous, neatly, sweetly.
That simpleton, I'll better him, that vagabond, I'll fetter him!
You wait here until I return, harnessed in grace and beauty!

(FALSTAFF *takes the bag of money and exits through the door in the back.* FORD *remains alone*)

FORD
A nightmare . . . an evil dream? A monstrous fork
Is growing out of my forehead!
A nightmare? Master Ford, Master Ford . . . awaken,
Rouse yourself, look and listen!
Your wife is straying . . . her scandalous flirtation
Will go on to adult'ry and degradation!
Planned with affection and timed to perfection!
Go and try to prevent it! And yet they'll tell me
That a man who is jealous is demented!
All over town I hear them taunt and jeer me,
Whisp'ring their insults, whistling when they're near me.
Marriage is treason infernal,
Torment eternal!
Ah, what a fool, he who trusts in a woman!
I should entrust my champagne to a Frenchman
Or ask a Dutchman to patrol my pantry,
I'd trust a scoundrel without name or gentry
But no wife and her virtue! Oh fright, oh sorrow!
I remember the words he spoke to warn me:
"The horns, sir!" Horror . . . 'tis true . . .
Maybe tomorrow . . . Ah, they're growing, they're showing!
Ah, I will take revenge! You sniper . . . swiper . . .
You Godforsaken viper!
First I'll abet them, then I shall fret them,
Beset them, and net them . . .
Abet them, then fret, beset them and get them and finally net them,
Yes, net them!
I shall avenge my honor!
Come triumph or perdition,
I thank my guiding star for my suspicion!
(FALSTAFF *returns through the door in the background, dressed up in a new vest, wearing a hat, and carrying a cane*)

FALSTAFF
Shall we proceed? I'm ready.
You'll take me on my way, sir?

FORD
I could not bear to stay, sir.
(*they start leaving. Near the door they stop, each one motioning to the other to be the first to leave*)

FALSTAFF
If you please . . .

FORD
After you . . .

FORD
È sogno? o realtà . . . Due rami enormi
Crescon sulla mia testa.
È un sogno? Mastro Ford! Mastro Ford! Dormi?
Svegliati! Su! ti desta!
Tua moglie sgarra e mette in mal'assetto
L'onor tuo, la tua casa ed il tuo letto!
L'ora è fissata, tramato l'inganno;
Sei gabbato e truffato! . . .
E poi diranno
Che un marito geloso è un insensato!
Già dietro a me nomi d'infame conio
Fischian passando; mormora lo scherno.
O matrimonio: Inferno!
Donna: Demonio!
Nella lor moglie abbian fede i babbei!
Affiderei
La mia birra a un Tedesco,
Tutto il mio desco
A un Olandese lurco,
La mia bottiglia d'acquavite a un Turco,
Non mia moglie a se stessa. O laida sorte!
Quella brutta parola in cor mi torna:
Le corna! Bue! capron! le fusa torte!
Ah! *le corna! le corna!*
Ma non mi sfuggirai! no! sozzo, reo,
Dannato epicureo!
Prima li accoppio
E poi li colgo. Io scoppio!
Vendicherò l'affronto!
Laudata sempre sia
Nel fondo del mio cor la gelosia.

FALSTAFF
Eccomi qua. Son pronto.
M'accompagnate un tratto?

FORD
Vi metto sulla via.

FALSTAFF
Prima voi.

FORD
Prima voi.

FALSTAFF
No. Sono in casa mia.
Passate.

FORD
Prego . . .

FALSTAFF
È tardi. L'appuntamento
preme.

FORD
Non fate complimenti . . .

FALSTAFF
Passate!

FORD
Prego!

FALSTAFF
Ebben; passiamo insieme.

FALSTAFF
No, no! You're my guest, remember!
I pray you!

FORD
You first!

FALSTAFF
A lady should never be kept waiting.

FORD
On this there's no debating.

FALSTAFF
I beg you . . .

FORD
Please, sir!

FALSTAFF
Well then . . . two friends united!
(*they leave together, arm in arm*)

Part 2

(*A room in* FORD'*s house. A large window in the back through which we look out into the garden. Two doors, one to the left and one to the right. A third door leading to the stairway in the background, to the right. A folded screen leaning against the wall to the left, near a large fireplace. A cupboard on the right. A small table. A chest. Along the walls an armchair and several other chairs. On the armchair a lute. Flowers on the table.*
ALICE, MEG, *later* QUICKLY *entering from the door to the right. Later* ANN.)

ALICE
Presenteremo un *bill*, per una
tassa
Al parlamento, sulla gente
grassa.

QUICKLY
Comari!

ALICE
Ebben?

MEG
Che c'è?

QUICKLY
Sarà sconfitto!

ALICE
Brava!

QUICKLY
Fra poco gli farem la festa!

ALICE, MEG
Bene!

ALICE
A bill we'll send to Parliament
Will shortly set a tax on people fat and portly.

QUICKLY (*entering*)
My ladies!

ALICE (*running toward her, as does* MEG, *while* ANN, *entering simultaneously, stays aside, obviously unhappy*)
So soon?

MEG
The news?

QUICKLY
. . . could not be better!

ALICE
Really?

QUICKLY
Our gallant knight will be unseated . . .

ALICE, MEG
Splendid!

QUICKLY
. . . Sir Falstaff utterly defeated!

ALICE
What happened? Come and tell us!

QUICKLY
Stepping inside the Garter Inn to greet him
I conveyed my respects, only to mention
That I was sent by someone else to meet him.
Sir John at once lent me his kind attention.
His welcome truly bespoke his vast dimension:
"Advance, my worthy woman". . ."I am honored."
I curtsied deeply in my most obsequious manner.
Then I proceeded to ensnare him, a willing victim.
I saw him pick and lick the candystick I gave him.
In short, Sir Falstaff's haughtiness
Is certain of your naughtiness
And sure that for his beauty
You will forget your duty.
(*to* ALICE)
So be prepared to see him at your knees this very day!

ALICE
Heavens!

QUICKLY
Surely! Now . . . from eleven to one!

MEG
From eleven to one?

ALICE (*looking at the clock*)
'Tis now eleven.
(*hurrying to the door and calling outside*)
Come here, Ned! Will!
(*to* QUICKLY)
I've cleared the deck for action.
(*calling back to the outside*)
Bring in the basket ready for the laundry!

QUICKLY
We'll drive him to distraction.

ALICE (*to* ANN)
My goodness! You are so serious. Tell me why!
You're weeping. Tell me why! Come, tell your mother!

ANN (*sobbing*)
My father . . .

ALICE
Go on!

ANN
My father . . .

QUICKLY
Piombò nel laccio a capo fitto.

ALICE
Narrami tutto, lesta.

QUICKLY
Giunta all'Albergo della Giarrettiera
Chiedo d'essere ammessa alla presenza
Del Cavalier, segreta messaggera.
Sir John si degna d'accordarmi udienza,
M'accoglie tronfio in furfantesca posa:
«Buon giorno, buona donna.»
«Reverenza.»
A lui m'inchino molto ossequïosa-
-mente, poi passo alle notizie ghiotte.
Lui beve grosso ed ogni mia massiccia
Frottola inghiotte.
Infin, per farla spiccia,
Vi crede entrambe innamorate cotte
Delle bellezze sue.
E lo vedrete presto ai vostri pie'.

ALICE
Quando?

QUICKLY
Oggi, qui, dalle due alle tre.

MEG
Dalle due alle tre.

ALICE
Son già le due.
Olà! Ned! Will!
Già tutto ho preparato.
Portate qui la cesta del bucato.

QUICKLY
Sarà un affare gaio!

ALICE
Nannetta, e tu non ridi? Che cos'hai?
Tu piangi? Che cos'hai? Dillo a tua madre.

NANNETTA
Mio padre . . .

ALICE
Ebben?

NANNETTA
Mio padre . . .

ALICE
Ebben?

NANNETTA
Mio padre . . .
Vuole ch'io mi mariti al Dottor Cajo!!

ALICE
A quel pedante?!

QUICKLY
Oibò!

MEG
A quel gonzo!

ALICE
A quel grullo!

NANNETTA
A quel bisavolo!

TUTTE
No! No!

NANNETTA
Piuttosto lapidata viva . . .

ALICE
Da una mitraglia di torsi di cavolo.

QUICKLY
Ben detto!

MEG
Brava!

ALICE
Non temer.

NANNETTA
Evviva!
Col Dottor Cajo non mi sposerò!

ALICE
Mettete là. Poi, quando avrò chiamato,
Vuoterete la cesta nel fossato.

NANNETTA
Bum!

ALICE
Taci. - Andate.

NANNETTA
Che bombardamento!

ALICE
Prepariamo la scena.
Qua una sedia.

NANNETTA
Qua il mio liuto.

ALICE
Apriamo il paravento.

ALICE
Speak up!

ANN
My father (*breaking out in tears*) told me
That I should marry Dr. Caius!

ALICE
That dodd'ring dandy?

QUICKLY
Good Lord!

MEG
That old pillbox?

ALICE
. . . scabby millfox?

ANN
. . . so thin and underweight!

ALL
No! No!

ANN
I'd rather drown or die of fever!

ALICE
. . . or be shot dead by a volley of pomegranate!

QUICKLY
No question!

MEG
Really!

ALICE
Have no fear!

ANN (*jumping with joy*)
Ah, thank you!
Dear Dr. Caius, my reply is No!
(*two servants have brought a basket filled with linen and other objects to be laundered*)

ALICE (*to the servants*)
Put it down here. As soon as I shall call you
You will empty the basket into the river.

ANN
Splash!

ALICE (*to* ANN, *then to the servants about to leave*)
Quiet! Be ready!

ANN
What a mighty tumble!

ALICE
Let's prepare the arena!
(*picks up a chair and sets it near the table*)
Here the chair.

ANN (*bringing the lute from the armchair and putting it on the table*)
Here my lute!

ALICE
The screen we'd better open.

(ANN *and* MEG *open the screen and place it between the basket and the fireplace*)
Just put it there . . . like this! A little wider!
The stage is set, the comedy has started.
Merrily pulling the curtain, we greet you,
Meet you with smiles and most gaily entreat you:
Join in the folly and frolic and banter
We'll pour on that jolly and foolish enchanter!
See how we beat him with lances of laughter,
See how we cheat him, how we defeat him,
How we delete him and tear him apart!
Yet all that is done
Will only be fun
And make all of us happy in mind and in heart.
(*to* MEG)
But now . . . You will know what to do . . . are you certain?

MEG (*to* ALICE)
You're taking your chances with mighty Sir John.

QUICKLY
I'll stay at the curtain.

ALICE (*to* QUICKLY)
. . . and watch his advances!

ANN
And I'd better go, but be sure I'll look on!

ALICE
Now let us show our husbands so imperious
That fun and folly need not disgrace a lady.
When a woman pretends to be too serious
She's likely to be shady!

QUICKLY
Quiet now! He's here.

ALICE
But where?

QUICKLY
Right near the entrance.

ANN
Hurry!

QUICKLY
He is in the doorway.

ALICE (*first motioning* ANN *to leave to the left, then to* MEG *to leave to the right*)
You go there! And you there! Your places!

ANN (*running off to the left*)
Let's hurry!

MEG (*running off to the right*)
Our places!

QUICKLY (*running off toward the rear*)
Let's hurry!

Bravissime! Così. Più aperto ancora.
Fra poco s'incomincia la commedia,
Gaie comari di Windsor! è l'ora!
L'ora d'alzar la risata sonora!
L'alta risata che scoppia, che scherza,
Che sfolgora, armata
Di dardi e di sferza!
Gaie comari! festosa brigata!
Sul lieto viso
Spunti il sorriso,
Splenda del riso—l'acuto fulgor!
Favilla incendiaria
Di gioia nell'aria,
Di gioia nel cor.
A noi! - Tu la parte
Farai che ti spetta.

MEG
Tu corri il tuo rischio
Col grosso compar.

QUICKLY
Io sto alla vedetta.

ALICE
Se sbagli ti fischio.

NANNETTA
Io resto in disparte
Sull'uscio a spiar.

ALICE
E mostreremo all'uom che l'allegria
D'oneste donne ogni onestà comporta.
Fra le femine quella è la più ria
Che fa la gattamorta.

QUICKLY
Eccolo! È lui!

ALICE
Dov'è?

QUICKLY
Poco discosto.

NANNETTA
Presto.

QUICKLY
A salir s'avvia.

ALICE
Tu di qua. Tu di là.

NANNETTA
Al posto!

MEG
Al posto!

QUICKLY
Al posto!

(ALICE *alone. Later* FALSTAFF. ALICE *sits near the table, playing some chords on the lute*)

FALSTAFF
«Alfin t'ho colto,»
«Raggiante fior,»
«T'ho colto!»
Ed or potrò morir felice.
Avrò vissuto molto
Dopo quest'ora di beato amor.

FALSTAFF (*entering rapidly. Seeing her play the lute, he starts singing*)
"I broke you, blossom so fair, so dear! I broke you!"
(*he tries to embrace* ALICE, *who stops playing and rises*)
Come, King of Death, I now ignore you:
For paradise has opened in the enchantment of supreme delight!

ALICE
O soave Sir John!

ALICE
Oh, my charming Sir John!

FALSTAFF
Mia bella Alice!
Non so far lo svenevole,
Nè lusingar, nè usar frase fiorita,
Ma dirò tosto un mio pensier colpevole.

FALSTAFF
How I adore you!
I am not made for jollity,
I cannot spin such fine, flowery phrases.
But I'll reveal to you an odd frivolity: . . .

ALICE
Cioè?

ALICE
How so?

FALSTAFF
Cioè:
Vorrei che Mastro Ford
Passasse a miglior vita . . .

FALSTAFF
I wish . . . I wish that Master Ford
Should rest beneath the daisies!

ALICE
Perchè?

ALICE
And why?

FALSTAFF
Perchè? Lo chiedi?
Saresti la mia Lady
E Falstaff il tuo Lord.

FALSTAFF
And why? You ask me?
Then you could be my lady, and I could be your lord.

ALICE
Povera Lady inver!

ALICE
I am too plain, I fear!

FALSTAFF
Degna d'un Re.
T'immagino fregiata del mio stemma,
Mostrar fra gemma e gemma
La pompa del tuo sen.
Nell'iri ardente e mobile dei rai
Dell'adamante,
Col picciol pie' nel nobile
Cerchio d'un guardinfante
Risplenderai
Più fulgida d'un ampio arcobalen.

FALSTAFF
Fit for a king!
My coat-of-arms, ennobled by your beauty,
Will shine anew when worn by you on your heaving heart!
Your eyes will steal the milky glow
Of pearls craving to grace you,
Your bosom feel the silky flow
Of gowns eager to enlace you.
The stars on high will not deny
Your throne up in the sky!

ALICE
Ogni più bel gioiel mi nuoce e spregio
Il finto idolo d'or.
Mi basta un vel legato in croce, un fregio
Al cinto e in testa un fior.

ALICE
In all this splendor you might scorn me,
A woman much too humble for you.
Oh let your tenderness adorn me!
Instead of furbelows a rose will do.
(*puts a flower into her hair*)

FALSTAFF
Sirena!

FALSTAFF (*trying to embrace her*)
Enchantress!

ALICE
Adulator!

ALICE (*taking a step away from him*)
Oh please, Sir John!

FALSTAFF
You are with me, and no one will surprise you.

ALICE
You mean . . . ?

FALSTAFF
I love you!

ALICE (*keeping her distance from him*)
Your conscience will despise you.

FALSTAFF (*following her*)
My conscience tells me of our hearts' attraction.

ALICE
Sir John!

FALSTAFF
. . . compels me to pursue my action!
Passion never needs excuses . . .

ALICE (*cutting him short*)
. . . not even when it prompts severe abuses?

FALSTAFF
Once when in Norfolk in service to the Duke—
I was a page then, vivacious and tender—
I was a swain as light as the rain,
I was slight then and slender, yes, slender!
May of my youth so full of love and rapture,
Day that in truth I wish I could recapture!
I was as swift and slick as a sparrow,
Nimble as a deer and as quick as an arrow.

ALICE
You really charm me! And yet I know you'll harm me.
I have a rival!

FALSTAFF
Whom?

ALICE
Meg . . .

FALSTAFF
Good Grace! That old, repulsive creature?

ALICE
Do not leave me, my John!

FALSTAFF
Insane with longing, I love your every feature. Always . . .
(*he pursues her again, trying to embrace her*)

ALICE (*defending herself*)
Please let me go!

FALSTAFF (*putting his arms around her waist*)
Always!

QUICKLY (*from off-stage, screaming*)
Oh, Mistress Alice!

FALSTAFF (*releasing* ALICE, *confused*)
Who is that?

FALSTAFF
Soli noi siamo
E non temiamo agguato.

ALICE
Ebben?

FALSTAFF
Io t'amo!

ALICE
Voi siete nel peccato!

FALSTAFF
Sempre l'amor l'occasione azzecca.

ALICE
Sir John!

FALSTAFF
Chi segue vocazion non pecca.
T'amo! e non è mia colpa . . .

ALICE
Se tanta avete vulnerabil polpa . . .

FALSTAFF
Quand'ero paggio
Del Duca di Norfolk ero sottile,
Ero un miraggio
Vago, leggero, gentile, gentile.
Quello era il tempo del mio verde Aprile,
Quello era il tempo del mio lieto Maggio.
Tant'era smilzo, flessibile e snello
Che avrei guizzato attraverso un anello.

ALICE
Voi mi celiate.
Io temo i vostri inganni.
Temo che amiate . . .

FALSTAFF
Chi?

ALICE
Meg.

FALSTAFF
Colei? M'è in uggia la sua faccia.

ALICE
Non traditemi, John . . .

FALSTAFF
Mi par mill'anni
D'averti fra le braccia.
T'amo . . .

ALICE
Per carità . . .

FALSTAFF
Vieni!

QUICKLY
Signora Alice!

FALSTAFF
Chi va là?

QUICKLY
Signora Alice!

ALICE
Che c'è?

QUICKLY
Mia signora!
C'è Mistress Meg e vuol parlarvi, sbuffa . . .
Strepita, s'abbaruffa . . .

FALSTAFF
Alla malora!

QUICKLY
E vuol passar e la trattengo a stento . . .

FALSTAFF
Dove m'ascondo?

ALICE
Dietro il paravento.

MEG
Alice! che spavento!
Che chiasso! Che discordia!
Non perdere un momento.
Fuggi! . . .

ALICE
Misericordia!
Che avvenne?

MEG
Il tuo consorte
Vien gridando «accorr'uomo!»
Dice . . .

ALICE
(Parla più forte.)

MEG
Che vuol scannare un uomo!

ALICE
(Non ridere.)

MEG
Ei correva
Invaso da tremendo
Furor! Maledicendo
Tutte le figlie d'Eva!

ALICE
Misericordia!

MEG
Dice
Che un tuo ganzo hai nascosto;
Lo vuole ad ogni costo
Scoprir . . .

QUICKLY
Signora Alice!
Vien Mastro Ford! Salvatevi!
È come una tempesta!
Strepita, tuona, fulmina,
Si dà dei pugni in testa,

QUICKLY (*entering, feigning excitement*)
Oh Mistress Alice!

ALICE
What now?

QUICKLY (*out of breath, stammering*)
Please forgive me! . . . 'Tis Mistress Meg.
She wants to see you . . . trembling, staggering, and rattled.

FALSTAFF
Speak of the devil!

QUICKLY
She's at the door. I could not bar her entry.

FALSTAFF
Where can I hide?

ALICE
The screen here will conceal you.
(FALSTAFF *hides behind the screen. As soon as he is out of sight,* QUICKLY *motions* MEG *to enter.* MEG *enters, pretending to be highly agitated.* QUICKLY *turns to leave again*)

MEG
Oh, dear me! What an uproar! What turmoil! What commotion!
Away from here and quickly! Hurry!

ALICE
My goodness gracious! What happened?

MEG
Your husband's voice shakes every rooftop and girder,
Howling . . .

ALICE (*under her breath, to* MEG)
Can you speak louder?

MEG
. . . that he is bent on murder.
(*almost bursting out with laughter*)

ALICE (*under her breath*)
Contain yourself!

MEG
He is on his way, insane and frantic with rage,
And even curses women in bitter fury.

ALICE
My goodness gracious!

MEG
Sure that you're concealing a lover
He promises to skin him alive.

QUICKLY (*returning in great agitation, screaming even louder than before*)
May heaven help us! 'Tis Master Ford!
Go, hide yourself! He'll tear us all asunder.
Deafening, roaring, shattering,

He's rolling in like thunder,
Violent and delirious.

ALICE (*somewhat alarmed, under her breath to* QUICKLY)
In jest or are you serious?

QUICKLY
I'm serious. In wild vexation,
A crowd of people near him,
As red as a carnation,
He's running . . . I seem to hear him!
Oh think of your salvation . . . I pray you . . .

FORD (*screaming from off-stage*)
I will spear him!

FALSTAFF (*he already has set out to flee but stops upon hearing* FORD*'s voice.* ALICE *folds the screen around him to conceal him completely*)
The devil's reputation is cause enough to fear him.

FORD (*from up-stage, shouting to those who follow him*)
Now block all the doorways and watch in the alley!
We'll see the seducer in chains on a galley!
(*after* FORD *enter* DR. CAIUS *and* FENTON, *shortly afterward* BARDOLPH *and* PISTOL)
(*to* CAIUS)
You follow his scent till you find him!
(*to* FENTON)
Explore all the passages!

BARDOLPH, PISTOL
To action!

FORD (*to* BARDOLPH *and* PISTOL, *pointing to the right*)
Cut off his escape and examine the pantry!

ALICE (*somewhat haughtily, to* FORD)
You seem to be crazy . . . but why?

FORD (*noticing the basket*)
Well, well . . . what's in the basket?

ALICE
Dirty linen.

FORD (*to* ALICE)
Yes, dirty, quite dirty!
(*to* CAIUS, *handing him a bunch of keys*)
Go, here are the keys to the cupboards and caskets.
(*to* ALICE)
Angel of virtue!!!
(*kicking the basket*)
To hell with these tatters!
(*shouting toward the rear*)
Go on, reconnoiter the garden!
(*starts pulling the wash out of the basket, strewing it all over the floor*)
The drawers . . . and blouses . . . now I'll catch you, you lout!
. . . dirty napkins, out! Out!

Scoppia in minaccie ed urla . . .

ALICE
(Dassenno oppur da burla?)

QUICKLY
Dassenno. Egli scavalca
Le siepi del giardino . . .
Lo segue una gran calca
Di gente . . . è già vicino . . .
Mentr'io vi parlo ei valca
L'ingresso . . .

FORD
Malandrino!!!

FALSTAFF
Il diavolo cavalca
Sull'arco di un violino!!

FORD
Chiudete le porte! Sbarrate le scale!
Seguitemi a caccia! Scoviamo il cignale!
Correte sull'orme, sull'usta.
Tu fruga
Negli anditi.

BARDOLFO, PISTOLA
A caccia!

FORD
Sventate la fuga!
Cercate là dentro!

ALICE
Sei tu dissennato?
Che fai?

FORD
Chi c'è dentro quel cesto?

ALICE
Il bucato.

FORD
Mi lavi!! rea moglie!
Tu, piglia le chiavi,
Rovista le casse, va.
Ben tu mi lavi!
Al diavolo i cenci!
Sprangatemi l'uscio
Del parco!
Camicie . . . gonnelle . . .
Or ti sguscio,
Briccon! - Strofinacci! Via! Via!
Cuffie rotte!
- Ti sguscio. - Lenzuola . . .
berretti da notte . . .
Non c'è . . .

Here some stockings! I'll catch you . . . and bedsheets . . . some silly old nightcaps . . . not yet! (*searching furiously*)

ALICE, MEG, QUICKLY
Che uragano!!

ALICE, MEG, QUICKLY (*looking at the scattered wash*)
Howling tempest!

FORD
Cerchiam sotto il letto,
Nel forno, nel pozzo, nel bagno, sul tetto,
In cantina . . .

FORD (*running to and fro, yelling to all and sundry*)
Go, search in the attic, the cistern, the arbor,
The kitchen, the bedroom and the cellar!
(*off to the left*)

ALICE
È farnetico!

ALICE
He's a lunatic!

QUICKLY
Cogliam tempo.

QUICKLY
Let us hurry!

ALICE
Troviamo
Modo com'egli esca.

ALICE
How can our portly friend escape him?

MEG
Nel panier.

MEG
In the basket!

ALICE
No, là dentro
Non c'entra, è troppo grosso.

ALICE
No, it never will hold him. He's far too bulky.

FALSTAFF
Vediam; sì, c'entro, c'entro.

FALSTAFF (*coming out from behind the screen*)
Let's see!
(*squeezing himself into the basket*)
Ah . . . it is . . . easy . . .

ALICE
Corro a chiamare i servi.

ALICE
I'll go to call the servants.
(*exits to the rear*)

MEG
Sir John! Voi qui? Voi?

MEG (*to* FALSTAFF, *feigning surprise*)
Sir John, you here . . . you?

FALSTAFF
T'amo!
Amo te sola . . . salvami! salvami!

FALSTAFF (*still fighting the basket*)
Angel! Only beloved!
Help me now! Rescue me!

QUICKLY
Svelto!

QUICKLY (*to* FALSTAFF, *collecting the pieces of wash*)
Hurry!

MEG
Lesto!

MEG
Head down!

FALSTAFF
Ahi! . . . Ahi! . . . Ci sto . . .
Copritemi . . .

FALSTAFF (*making a supreme effort to squeeze fully into the basket*)
Ah! Ouch! I'm in. Now cover me!

QUICKLY
Presto! colmiamo il cesto.

QUICKLY
Grumble before you tumble!
(*the women cover him with wash.* ANN *and* FENTON *enter from the left, speaking softly and cautiously*)

NANNETTA
Vien qua.

ANN
Come here!

FENTON
Che chiasso!

FENTON
I worry!

NANNETTA
Quanti schiamazzi!
Segui il mio passo.

ANN
Don't be so lazy! Come, let us hurry!

FENTON
Casa di pazzi!

FENTON
All this is crazy!

ANN
See how they're fuming, jostle and shove,
As mad with fury . . .

FENTON
. . . as we with love!

ANN (*taking him by the hand to pull him behind the screen*)
Follow me, but lightly!

FENTON
I'm here beside you.

ANN
The screen will hide you . . .

FENTON
. . . shielding us tightly.

ANN
We're safe from detection.

FENTON (*drawing her close*)
Let me caress you!

ANN
Welcome protection,
. . . Fondly we bless you!
(ANN *and* FENTON *are hiding behind the screen. Enter* FORD *and* CAIUS *from the left,* BARDOLPH *and* PISTOL *from the right, together with a group of neighbors.* QUICKLY *and* MEG *stay near the basket. Later* ALICE *returns from the rear*)

NANNETTA
Qui ognun delira
Con vario error.
Son pazzi d'ira . . .

FENTON
E noi d'amor.

NANNETTA
Seguimi. Adagio.

FENTON
Nessun m'ha scorto.

NANNETTA
Tocchiamo il porto.

FENTON
Siamo a nostr'agio.

NANNETTA
Sta zitto e attento.

FENTON
Vien sul mio petto!

NANNETTA
Il paravento
Sia benedetto!

DR. CAIUS (*yelling from the outside*)
Behead him!
(*enters*)

DR. CAJUS
Al ladro!

FORD (*still outside*) To the gallows!
(*enters*)

FORD
Al pagliardo!

DR. CAIUS
. . . and quarter him!

DR. CAJUS
Squartatelo!

FORD
The scoundrel! There?
(*on their way in,* FORD *and* CAIUS *collide with* PISTOL *and* BARDOLPH)

FORD
Al ladro!
C'è?

PISTOL
No.

PISTOLA
No.

FORD (*to* BARDOLPH)
There?

FORD
C'è?

BARDOLPH
Not here! No.

BARDOLFO
Non c'è, no.

FORD (*running about, searching the chest*)
I vow to Satan I'll find him!

FORD
Vada a soqquadro
La casa.

DR. CAIUS (*searching in the fireplace and looking up the chimney*)
Where is he? I wonder.
(PISTOL *and* BARDOLPH *exit to the left*)

DR. CAJUS
Non trovo nessuno.

FORD
Eppur giuro
Che l'uomo è qua dentro. Ne sono sicuro!
Sicuro! Sicuro!

DR. CAJUS
Sir John! Sarò gaio
Quel dì ch'io ti veda dar calci a rovaio!

FORD
Vien fuora, furfante! T'arrendi! O bombardo
Le mura!

DR. CAJUS
T'arrendi!

FORD
Vien fuora! Codardo!
Sugliardo!

BARDOLFO, PISTOLA
Nessuno!

FORD
Cercatelo ancora!
T'arrendi! Scanfardo!
Non c'è!!

DR. CAJUS
Vieni fuora!
Non c'è!
Pappalardo! Beòn! Bada a te!

FORD
Scagnardo! Falsardo! Briccon!!

FORD
C'è.

DR. CAJUS
C'è.

FORD
Se t'agguanto!

DR. CAJUS
Se ti piglio!

FORD
Se t'acciuffo!

DR. CAJUS
Se t'acceffo!

FORD
Ti sconquasso!

DR. CAJUS
T'arronciglio
Come un can!

FORD
Ti rompo il ceffo!

FORD
I swear he still is here in the house,
Yes, I know it for certain, I know it for certain.

DR. CAIUS
Sir John, I'll be dying with laughter
The day you will hang from the rafter.

FORD (*trying to break open the cupboard*)
Come out here, you ronyon, or I'll tear you to tatters!

DR. CAIUS (*looking for a key to the cupboard*)
Surrender!

FORD
Come out here, you traitor! You coward!

BARDOLPH, PISTOL (*re-entering from the left*)
There's no one!

FORD (*still busy, with* DR. CAIUS *trying to open the cupboard while* BARDOLPH *and* PISTOL *re-exit*)
You filthy rapscallion! Surrender, you demon!
(*finally opening the cupboard*) Not here?

DR. CAIUS (*opening the chest*)
Surrender! Not here?
(*runs through the room, searching*)
You debaucher, you'll wish you were dead!

FORD (*opening the drawer of the little table*)
You Satan, you lecher, you villain, you lout . . . come out!
(*during all this,* ANN *and* FENTON *have paid no heed to the turmoil around them. Their caresses come to a head in a resounding kiss, which immediately stops all activity. Everyone has heard the sound of the kiss*)

FORD (*whispering, his eyes on the screen*)
There!

DR. CAIUS
There!
(*everyone's attention now centers on the screen*)

FORD (*cautiously approaching the screen*)
When I catch you . . .

DR. CAIUS (*imitating* FORD)
When I snatch you . . .

FORD
When I grab you . . .

DR. CAIUS
When I nab you . . .

FORD
I will thrash you . . .

DR. CAIUS
I will break your every bone . . .

FORD
. . . beat up and smash you.

DR. CAIUS
. . . with a stone!

DR. CAJUS
Guai a te!

FORD
No one can save you.

FORD
Prega il tuo santo!

QUICKLY (*to* MEG)
(*near the basket*)
Our friend in the basket,
You cannot deny it,
Unless he is quiet
Turns basket to casket.
He wants to disarm us
But progress is slow.
He still may alarm us,
But harm us, oh no!

QUICKLY
Facciamo le viste
D'attendere ai panni;
Pur ch'ei non c'inganni
Con mosse impreviste.
Fin'or non s'accorse
Di nulla; egli può
Sorprenderci forse,
Confonderci no.

MEG (*to* QUICKLY)
Our cunning devices
At first lead to shambles,
Providing our gambles
With savor and spices.
We're taking our chances
As never before,
But danger enhances
Our fun even more.

MEG
Facciamogli siepe
Fra tanto scompiglio.
Ne' giuochi il periglio
È un grano di pepe.
Il rischio è un diletto
Che accresce l'ardor,
Che stimola in petto
Gli spiriti e il cor.

FALSTAFF (*poking his head out of the basket*)
I'm choking.

FALSTAFF
Affogo!

QUICKLY (*pushing him down*)
Lie low!

QUICKLY
Sta sotto.

BARDOLPH (*entering from the left*)
It is useless.

BARDOLFO
Non si trova.

PISTOL (*returning with several neighbors*)
We can't find him!

PISTOLA
Non si coglie.

FORD (*to* BARDOLPH, PISTOL, *and the others*)
Pssst . . . be quiet!
(*pointing to the screen*)
I have found him.
With my wife he's there in hiding.

FORD
Psss . . . Qua tutti.
L'ho trovato.
Là c'è Falstaff con mia moglie.

BARDOLPH
What a scandal, what an outrage!

BARDOLFO
Sozzo can vituperato!

FORD
Silence!

FORD
Zitto!

PISTOL, DR. CAIUS
Silence!

PISTOLA, DR. CAJUS
Zitto!!

FORD (*to* BARDOLPH)
You hold your thunder!
We have heard the sound of kisses.

FORD
Urlerai dopo.
Là s'è udito il suon d'un bacio.

BARDOLPH
In this case of sinful blisses
Slay the man and spare the missus!

BARDOLFO
Noi dobbiam pigliare il topo
Mentre sta rodendo il cacio.

FENTON (*to* ANN)
So sweet and tender

FENTON
Bella! ridente!

Oh! come pieghi
Verso i miei prieghi
Donnescamente!

I feel you near me,
Forever cheer me
Your radiant splendor
I stood before you,
Under your spell . . .
How I adore you . . .
You know it well!

NANNETTA
Mentre quei vecchi
Corron la giostra,
Noi di sottecchi
Corriam la nostra.
L'amor non ode
Tuon nè bufere,
Vola alle sfere
Beate e gode.

ANN (*to* FENTON)
(*behind the screen*)
They yell and chatter,
Hunting their quarry.
What does it matter,
We shall not worry.
Thunder and lightning
To us are not fright'ning
Onward we fly, like doves
On golden wings of love.

FORD
Ragioniam. Colpo non vibro
Senza un piano di battaglia.

FORD
Not so fast! Now pay attention!
We shall draw a plan of battle.

NANNETTA
Lo spiritello
D'amor, volteggia.

ANN
The stars above web a veil around us.

FENTON
Già un sogno bello
D'Imene albeggia.

FENTON
The god of love has forever bound us.

FALSTAFF
Affogo!

FALSTAFF (*in the basket*)
I'm smoking.

MEG
Or questi s'insorge.

MEG (*pushing him down*)
'Tis good for your diet.

QUICKLY
Se l'altro ti scorge
Sei morto.

QUICKLY (*bending down and addressing* FALSTAFF *in the basket*)
You're causing a riot, be quiet!

DR. CAJUS
Un uom di quel calibro
Con un soffio ci sbaraglia.

DR. CAIUS
A man of vast dimension,
He may slaughter us like cattle.

FORD
La mia tattica maestra
Le sue mosse pria registra.
Voi sarete l'ala destra,
Noi sarem l'ala sinistra.
E costor con pie' gagliardo
Sfonderanno il baluardo.

FORD
I'm a master at deception,
Let me tell you my conception:
(*to* PISTOL *and two neighbors*)
While the right wing will dislodge him
(*to* BARDOLPH *and* DR. CAIUS)
On the left you'll draw and dodge him.
(*to everyone else*)
Then the center under cover
Will exterminate our lover.

TUTTI GLI ALTRI
Bravo, bravo, Generale.

THE OTHERS
What a fine display of cunning!

DR. CAJUS
Aspettiamo un tuo segnale.

DR. CAIUS
Tell us when and we'll be running.

GLI ALTRI
Bravo.

THE OTHER MEN
Truly stunning!

MEG
How much more can we do for his comfort?

FALSTAFF
Just one single breath or in clothes I will drown!

QUICKLY
You're courting your death, so be silent! Go down!

ANN
Trying to flee you,
Sighing, delirious,
My heart mysterious
Cries out to see you.
Sweet is the torment of love!
Yes, I shall love you forever.

FENTON
Your eyes shall meet me,
Radiant, beguiling,
Like starlets smiling
Come down to greet me.
Tell me you love me!
I love you always.

FORD
Bend an ear and you can hear them!
Hear their billing and their cooing!
From this hotbed of misdoing
I'll dispatch him to the moon.

DR. CAIUS
Yes, I hear them, I perceive it
But can't believe it.
Can it really be . . .
Can a woman be so bold?

BARDOLPH
I am certain 'tis the woman
Answering her lover's call.

PISTOL
If he knew that we are near him!
In a moment I shall spear him:
I should say 'tis none too soon.

CHORUS OF NEIGHBORS
Sinful love may bring you glory
While the sinning's going well:
'Twill be quite another story
When you pay for it in hell.

MEG
We'd better defy him
And better beware.
'Tis better to fry him
Than render him rare.

QUICKLY
'Tis really a quandary:
So black is our swain,

MEG
Il ribaldo
Vorrebbe un ventaglio.

FALSTAFF
Un breve spiraglio
Non chiedo di più.

QUICKLY
Ti metto il bavaglio
Se parli. Giù!

NANNETTA
Tutto delira,
Sospiro e riso.
Sorride il viso
E il cor sospira.
Come in sua zolla
Si schiude un fior,
La sua corolla
Svolve il mio cor.

FENTON
Fra quelle ciglia
Vedo due fari
A meraviglia
Sereni e chiari.
Bocca mia dolce
Pupilla d'or.
Voce che molce
Com'arpa il cor.

FORD
Senti, accosta un po' l'orecchio!
Che patetici lamenti!!
Su quel nido d'usignuoli
Scoppierà fra poco il tuon.

DR. CAJUS
Sento, sento, sento intendo,
E vedo chiaro.
Delle femmine,
Delle femmine gl'inganni.

BARDOLFO
È la voce della donna
Che risponde al cavalier.

PISTOLA
Ma fra poco il lieto gioco
Egli canta, ma fra poco
Muterà la sua canzon.

CORO
S'egli cade più non scappa,
Nessun più lo può salvar.
Nel tuo diavolo t'incappa;
Che tu possa stramazzar!

MEG
Parliam sottovoce
Guardando il Messer
Che brontola e cuoce
Nel nostro panier.

QUICKLY
Costui s'è infardato
Di tanta viltà,

Che darlo al bucato
È averne pietà.

FORD
Zitto! A noi! Quest'è il
momento.
Zitto! Attenti! Attenti a me.

FALSTAFF
Ouff . . . Cesto molesto!

ALICE
Silenzio!

FALSTAFF
Protesto!

MEG, QUICKLY
Che bestia restìa!

FALSTAFF
Portatemi via!

DR. CAJUS
Dà il segnal.

MEG, QUICKLY
È matto furibondo

FALSTAFF
Aiuto! aiuto! aiuto!

FORD
Uno . . . Due . . . Tre . . .

DR. CAJUS
Non è lui!!

TUTTI
Sbalordimento!

FORD
Ancor nuove rivolte!
Tu va pe' fatti tuoi!
L'ho detto mille volte: Costei
non fa per voi.

BARDOLFO
È là! Ferma!

FORD
Dove?

PISTOLA
Là sulle scale.

FORD
Squartatelo!

DR. CAJUS, BARDOLFO, PISTOLA ED I COMPAGNI
A caccia!

That even a laundry
Won't clean him again.

FORD
Silence! Stand by! This is our moment.
Silence! Attention! And follow me!

FALSTAFF (*gasping for air*)
Oh! Oh, hear me crying!

ALICE (*having returned to the basket*)
Be quiet!

FALSTAFF (*emerging again*)
I'm dying!

MEG, QUICKLY
Why, how can you dare it?

FALSTAFF (*in agony*)
Ah, I cannot bear it!

DR. CAIUS (*to* FORD)
Tell us when!

MEG, QUICKLY
He must have lost his senses.

FALSTAFF
Oh, help me! Oh, help me! Oh, help me!
(*the women push him down and sit on the basket*)

FORD
One . . . two . . . three!
(*on the count of "three" the men open the screen, revealing* ANN *and* FENTON *in tender embrace. Utmost consternation on everyone's face*)

DR. CAIUS
Where is *he*?

ALL
The search has ended!

FORD (*to* ANN *furiously*)
A fine way to behold you!
(*to* FENTON)
From now on you'll obey.
How often have I told you:
Keep off my daughter's way!
(ANN *flees disconsolately.* FENTON *leaves through the rear*)

BARDOLPH (*running to the rear*)
He's there! Stop him!

FORD
Where?

PISTOL
There, in the staircase!

FORD
Take hold of him!

CAIUS, BARDOLPH, PISTOL, NEIGHBORS
We'll catch him.
(*all running off toward the rear*)

QUICKLY
I wish them good hunting!

ALICE (*calling to the rear*)
Ned! Will! Tom! And Jack!
(ANN *returns with four servants and a page*)
Come! Come here quickly!
Go and empty this basket out of the window and into the river, there, where you see the women about to launder all the dirty linen!

ANN, MEG, QUICKLY
Yes, yes, yes, yes!

ANN (*to the servants trying to lift the basket*)
It may be somewhat heavy.

ALICE (*to the page, who obeys her request*)
You go and call my master!
(*to* MEG, *while* ANN *and* QUICKLY *watch the servants lifting the basket*)
. . . so he may witness old Sir John's disaster.
Seeing his rival in this sad condition
Should cool his own suspicion
That much faster.

QUICKLY (*to the servants*)
Try it!

ALICE, MEG (*to the servants approaching the window*)
Come on now!

ANN
The bottom will fall out.

MEG, QUICKLY *and* ANN
Up!

ALICE
Upend it! That's splendid!
(*the contents of the basket tumble out the window*)

ANN, MEG
That's splendid!
(*a loud scream and gales of laughter of the women outside. At that moment* FORD *and the other men return to the room*)

ALL
What a splash!—
(ALICE *takes her husband's arm and quickly leads him to the window. Great hilarity all around*)

QUICKLY
Che caccia infernale!

ALICE
Ned! Will! Tom! Isaac! Su!
Presto! Presto!
Rovesciate quel cesto
Dalla finestra nell'acqua del fosso . . .
Là! presso alle giuncaie
Davanti al crocchio delle lavandaie.

NANNETTA, MEG, QUICKLY
Sì, sì, sì, sì!

NANNETTA
C'è dentro un pezzo grosso.

ALICE
Tu chiama mio marito;
Gli narreremo il nostro caso pazzo.
Solo al vedere il Cavalier nel guazzo,
D'ogni gelosa ubbìa sarà guarito.

QUICKLY
Pesa!

ALICE, MEG
Coraggio!

NANNETTA
Il fondo ha fatto crac!

MEG, QUICKLY, NANNETTA
Su!

ALICE
Trionfo! Che tonfo!

NANNETTA, MEG
Che tonfo!

TUTTE
Patatrac!

ACT III

Part 1

FALSTAFF
Ehi! Taverniere!
Mondo ladro. Mondo rubaldo.
Reo mondo!
Taverniere: un bicchier di vin caldo.
Io, dunque, avrò vissuto tanti anni, audace e destro
Cavaliere, per essere portato in un canestro
E gittato al canale co' pannilini biechi,
Come si fa coi gatti e i catellini ciechi.
Che se non galleggiava per me quest'epa tronfia
Certo affogavo. Brutta morte. L'acqua mi gonfia.
Mondo reo. Non c'è più virtù. Tutto declina.
Va, vecchio John, va, va per la tua via; cammina
Finchè tu muoia. Allor scomparirà la vera
Virilità dal mondo.
Che giornataccia nera!
M'aiuti il ciel! Impinguo troppo. Ho dei peli grigi.
Versiamo un po' di vino nell'acqua del Tamigi.
Buono. Ber del vin dolce e sbottonarsi al sole,
Dolce cosa! Il buon vino sperde le tetre fole
Dello sconforto, accende l'occhio e il pensier, dal labbro
Sale al cervel e quivi risveglia il picciol fabbro
Dei trilli; un negro grillo che vibra entro l'uom brillo
Trilla ogni fibra in cor, l'allegro etere al trillo
Guizza e il giocondo globo squilibra una demenza
Trillante! E il trillo invade il mondo!!! . . .

QUICKLY
Reverenza.
La bella Alice . . .

(An open square. To the right the Garter Inn with the sign inscribed "honi soit qui mal y pense." Next to the entrance a bench of stone. It is dusk.

FALSTAFF *is seated on the bench, deep in thought. Suddenly he shakes himself violently, pounds the bench with his fist, and calls for the innkeeper.)*

FALSTAFF
Ho! Is there no one?
(sinks back into meditation)
Nasty world! Villainous world! Vile world!
(the innkeeper appears)
Bring some wine here! Serve it hot to revive me!
(the innkeeper exits)
John Falstaff who led a life of adventure,
A noble knight, a gallant fighter,
At last has had to cower in a basket
To be dumped into a ditch with a load of dirty linen
As if he were a cat or some repulsive mongrel!
Unless my mighty paunch like a cork had kept me floating
I should have perished, filled with water,
Swelling and bloating. Rotten world!
All has run to seed. Virtue is crumbling.
Go, gallant John, go, go onward to glory!
Go on till you end your journey!
With you once and for all will die
The enchanted flow'r of manhood.
What an infernal nightmare! My gracious Lord!
I grow too portly, my hair is turning gray . . .
(the innkeeper brings a large goblet of hot wine and deposits it on the bench, then exits)
I trust this bracing potion
Will warm the icy ocean!
(drinks slowly, savoring every sip, then he unbuttons his vest, stretches comfortably, drinks again. His mood is changing for the better)
Splendid! To drink good wine is to enjoy the sunshine,
Warm and tender. All at once, good wine will dispel
The clouds of sorrow and worry,
Revive the heart and the eye.
Your mind will flutter and fly
While millions of bells will ring in joyous carillon.
And slyly winking a goblin keeps you drinking.
Trilling its siren song the wine thrills us all,
Cruel or tender. And a world contented,
Delirious in its folly, demented,
Shall willingly surrender!

QUICKLY *(interrupting* FALSTAFF*'s happy musings)*
I am honored. Fair Mistress Alice . . .

FALSTAFF (*rising violently*)
Go, take her to hell and remain there forever!
The Devil will adore her . . . for me she is too clever.

QUICKLY
You are mistaken . . .

FALSTAFF
I know her now, and my ears are still aching
From the screams of her husband.
My broken bones still shaking,
Tossed in a tiny basket, my body bent as if it were
A blade of Spanish steel, hilt to point and head to heel!
Madmen shrieking! Linen reeking!
I, melting like a candle
In heat that even Satan would find too hot to handle!
Then, while I'd burn like tinder
And slowly would turn to cinder,
In the end they would drown me!
Those rascals!

(ALICE, MEG, ANN, FORD, CAIUS, *and* FENTON *are seen hiding behind a building to the left. They listen intently, emerging in turn from their hiding place*)

FALSTAFF
Al diavolo te con Alice bella!
Ne ho piene le bisaccie! Ne ho piene le budella!

QUICKLY
Voi siete errato . . .

FALSTAFF
Un canchero!! Sento ancor le cornate
Di quell'irco geloso! Ho ancor l'ossa arrembate
D'esser rimasto curvo, come una buona lama
Di Bilbào, nello spazio d'un panierin di dama!
Con quel tufo! E quel caldo! Un uom della mia tempra,
Che in uno stillicidio continuo si distempra!
Poi, quando fui ben cotto, rovente, incandescente,
M'han tuffato nell'acqua. Canaglie!!!

QUICKLY
But she is blameless, completely blameless!
She could do nothing . . .

QUICKLY
Essa è innocente.
Prendete abbaglio.

FALSTAFF
Out with you!

FALSTAFF
Vattene!!

QUICKLY (*feverishly*)
The fault lay with those duffers
Whom she despises! She is in torment, crying . . .
Ah, how she suffers! Unhappy woman!
See here, she loves you!

(*she takes a letter from her pocket and hands it to* FALSTAFF, *who starts reading it*)

QUICKLY
La colpa è di quei fanti
Malaugurati! Alice piange, urla, invoca i santi.
Povera donna!! V'ama. Leggete.

ALICE (*in the background, whispering to the others*)
Reading?

ALICE
Legge.

FORD
Reading!

FORD
Legge.

ANN
His mien looks much more jolly.

NANNETTA
Vedrai che ci ricasca.

ALICE
Man never sheds his folly.

ALICE
L'uomo non si corregge.

MEG (*to* ALICE, *alerted by a sign from* QUICKLY)
Conceal yourself!

MEG
Nasconditi.

DR. CAIUS
He's reading.

DR. CAJUS
Rilegge.

FORD
He's nibbling and will swallow!

FORD
Rilegge. L'esca inghiotte.

FALSTAFF (*rereading the letter with great concentration*)
"I shall await you on the stroke of midnight in the park.

FALSTAFF
«T'aspetterò nel parco Real, a mezzanotte.»

«Tu verrai travestito da Cacciatore nero»
«Alla quercia di Herne.»

QUICKLY
Amor ama il mistero.
Per rivedervi Alice, si val d'una leggenda
Popolar. Quella quercia è un luogo da tregenda.
Il Cacciatore nero s'è impeso ad un suo ramo.
V'ha chi crede vederlo ricomparir . . .

FALSTAFF
Entriamo.
Là si discorre meglio. Narrami la tua frasca.

QUICKLY
Quando il rintocco della mezzanotte . . .
Cupo si sparge nel silente orror . . .

FORD
Ci casca.

ALICE
Quando il rintocco della mezzanotte
Cupo si sparge nel silente orror,
Sorgon gli spirti vagabondi a frotte
E vien nel parco il nero Cacciator.
Egli cammina lento, lento, lento,
Nel gran letargo della sepoltura.
S'avanza livido . . .

NANNETTA
Oh! che spavento

MEG
Già sento il brivido della paura!

ALICE
Fandonie che ai bamboli
Raccontan le nonne
Con lunghi preamboli,
Per farli dormir.

ALICE, NANNETTA, MEG
Vendetta di donne
Non deve fallir.

ALICE
S'avanza livido e il passo converge
Al tronco ove esalò l'anima prava.
Sbucan le Fate. Sulla fronte egli erge
Due corna lunghe, lunghe, lunghe . . .

You will come quite alone, in the guise of the Black Huntsman, to the Oak of Herne."

QUICKLY
Mysterious but entrancing!
Longing to see you, fearing to fail,
Alice recalled an ancient tale.
You should know the Oak of Herne is haunted.
Clad all in black, a hunter
Was found hanging from its branches.
Weird and eerie, his ghost still is seen at night.

FALSTAFF (*taking* QUICKLY *by the arm and guiding her inside the inn*)
We'll enter. Let us converse in private!
Tell me that fearsome story!

QUICKLY (*starts to tell him the legend while entering the inn*)
Oft when the chimes of twelve o'clock have sounded,
Leaving the world in dark and silent gloom . . .

FORD (*from the background*)
He's biting!

ALICE (*advancing in a huddle with the others, grotesquely and mysteriously imitating* QUICKLY'S *narration*)
Oft when the chimes of twelve o'clock have sounded,
Leaving the world in dark and silent gloom,
Demons and ghosts will hold the oak surrounded:
Back comes the hunter arising from his tomb.
He is approaching slowly, slowly, slowly,
As though entranced and walking without waking,
His bones are clattering . . .

ANN
Phantom unholy!

MEG
I feel my blood congeal . . .
And I am shaking.

ALICE (*resuming her natural tone of voice*)
A fancy-free, a fairy tale,
For children to ponder,
To set them on their merry way
And lull them to sleep!

ALICE, ANN, MEG
Our hunter will wonder . . .
Our meeting we'll keep!

ALICE (*resuming her narration*)
. . . his bones are clattering, he's reaching his station
Where long ago his life sadly had ended.
See, from his forehead, to his consternation,
Two horns keep growing, growing, growing . . .

FORD
Splendid!
May these horns bring me never-ending gladness!

ALICE (*to* FORD)
Now repent your inanity!
You and your jealous madness!

FORD
Forgive me . . . I am cured of my insanity!

ALICE
Beware lest your suspicion
Should once again discover
In the shell of a nut a secret lover
To mar your disposition!
But time is fleeting. Let's keep our wits about us!

MEG
You are right.

FENTON
. . . or the play will start without us!

ALICE
Now, Annie!

ANN
At your command!

ALICE
You'll play the part of the queen of all the fairies.
Your royal mantle shall be white
And your veil girdled by roses.

ANN
In tender song my heart sweetly reposes.

ALICE (*to* MEG)
You, dear Meg, clad in green,
Will be the wood nymph
And our dear Mistress Quickly shall be a sorceress.

ANN (*happily*)
Ah, this is priceless!
(*evening falls. The scene turns darker and darker*)

ALICE
A host of tiny tots will play
In most delightful roundelay
As ghostly pixies clad in gray
And devils who will haunt him.
Until we shall assault our lovelorn hunter
And mercilessly taunt him.

ANN, MEG, FENTON
Haunt him! Taunt him!

ALICE
Until the old offender
Is ready to surrender
And eat his humble pie.

FORD
Brava.
Quelle corna saranno la mia gioia!

ALICE
Bada! tu pur ti meriti
Qualche castigatoia!

FORD
Perdona. Riconosco i miei demeriti.

ALICE
Ma guai se ancor ti coglie
Quella mania feroce
Di cercar dentro il guscio d'una noce
L'amante di tua moglie.
Ma il tempo stringe e vuol fantasia lesta.

MEG
Affrettiam.

FENTON
Concertiam la mascherata.

ALICE
Nannetta!

NANNETTA
Eccola qua!

ALICE
Sarai la Fata
Regina delle Fate in bianca vesta
Chiusa in candido vel, cinta di rose.

NANNETTA
E canterò parole armoniose.

ALICE
Tu la verde sarai Ninfa silvana,
E la comare Quickly una befana.

NANNETTA
A meraviglia!

ALICE
Avrò con me dei putti
Che fingeran folletti
E spiritelli,
E diavoletti,
E pipistrelli,
E farfarelli.
Su Falstaff camuffato in manto e corni
Ci scaglieremo tutti

ANN, MEG, FENTON
Tutti! tutti!

ALICE
E lo tempesteremo
Finch'abbia confessata
La sua perversità.
Poi ci smaschereremo
E, pria che il ciel raggiorni,

La giuliva brigata
Se ne ritornerà.

Then, only then we'll free him
When quite contrite we see him.
Gaily laughing we'll flee him,
Bid him a fond good-by!

MEG
Vien sera. Rincasiam.

MEG
Let's leave now, it is late.

ALICE
L'appuntamento
È alla quercia di Herne.

ALICE
Are we agreed when we meet near the oak tree?

FENTON
È inteso.

FENTON
At midnight!

NANNETTA
A meraviglia!
Oh! che allegro spavento!

ANN
Wish it were sooner! How divine and romantic!

ALICE, NANNETTA, FENTON
Addio.

ALICE, ANN, FENTON
Farewell now!

MEG
Addio.

MEG
Till midnight!
(ALICE, ANN, *and* FENTON *exit toward the left,* MEG *toward the right. Just before disappearing* ALICE *calls to* MEG, *who is already out of sight. At the same time* QUICKLY, *leaving the Garter Inn, notices* FORD *and* CAIUS *in confidential conversation and stops to eavesdrop on them*)

ALICE
Provvedi le lanterne.

ALICE (*to* MEG)
Do not forget the lanterns!

FORD
Non dubitar, tu sposerai mia figlia.
Rammenti bene il suo travestimento?

FORD (*to* CAIUS)
You may be sure. Soon you will wed my daughter.
Do you remember the dress she will be wearing?

DR. CAJUS
Cinta di rose, il vel bianco e la vesta.

DR. CAIUS
Belt trimmed with roses, white her veil and her garment.

ALICE
Non ti scordar le maschere.

ALICE (*calling from off-stage left*)
You will provide the dominoes!

MEG
No, certo.
Nè tu le raganelle!

MEG (*from off-stage right*)
They're ready.
You bring the bones and rattles.

FORD
Io già disposi
La rete mia. Sul finir della festa
Verrete a me col volto ricoperto
Essa dal vel, tu da un mantel fratesco
E vi benedirò come due sposi.

FORD (*continuing his conversation with* CAIUS)
My plan is laid, its success is certain:
Well disguised by a hood you will come to me
As soon as all is over.
Ann will be there, still hidden by her veil . . . and I shall bestow my blessing on the both of you.

DR. CAJUS
Siam d'accordo.

DR. CAIUS
Fine suggestion!

QUICKLY
(Stai fresco!)
Nannetta! Ohè! Nannetta!
Nannetta! Ohè!

QUICKLY (*giving the two men a telling look, then disappearing rapidly to the right*)
No question!
(*from off-stage right*)
Oh, Ann! Pst! My Annie, pst!

NANNETTA
Che c'è? Che c'è?

ANN (*from off-stage*)
I'm here. What is it?

QUICKLY
You know the song of the Queen of the Fairies?
ANN
It never varies!
ALICE (*off-stage*)
You will be late!
QUICKLY (*from faraway*)
The sooner there, the better!

QUICKLY
Prepara la canzone della Fata.
NANNETTA
È preparata.
ALICE
Tu non tardar.
QUICKLY
Chi prima arriva, aspetta.

Part 2

(*Windsor Park. In the center, the Oak of Herne. To the rear, indications of a gully. Thick foliage. Bushes in bloom. It is night.*
In the distance the horn calls of the foresters are heard. Gradually the forest is brightened by moonlight.
FENTON, *later* ANN *disguised as Queen of the Fairies. Later* ALICE, *not disguised, carrying a hood over one arm and a mask in her hand.* QUICKLY *carrying the paraphernalia of her disguise as a witch, including a broomstick. Later* MEG, *garbed in green veils and wearing a mask.*)

FENTON
From burning lips my song of love enchanted,
Through the dark of the night so gently calling,
Shall fly beyond to where the stars are falling
Until at last my ardent plea is granted.
Out of the long and lonely night around me
A tender song, a ray of light confound me.
Oh magic song whose sounds always will bind me,
Oh, guide my loved one till at last she will find me!
Once you have brought her here, herald so tender,
You will soon have to die: You must surrender
Unto the silence of our burning kisses.
Just kiss me soon, and you always will do it!

FENTON
Dal labbro il canto estasiato vola
Pe' silenzi notturni e va lontano
E alfin ritrova un altro labbro umano
Che gli risponde colla sua parola.
Allor la nota che non è più sola
Vibra di gioia in un accordo arcano
E innamorando l'aer antelucano
Come altra voce al suo fonte rivola.
Quivi ripiglia suon, ma la sua cura
Tende sempre ad unir chi lo disuna.
Così baciai la disiata bocca!
Bocca baciata non perde ventura.

ANN (*from faraway, coming nearer*)
Trust in the moon, love will always renew it!
FENTON (*in the direction of where he heard* ANN'*s voice*)
Yes, song will die on lips that are united.

NANNETTA
Anzi rinnova come fa la luna.
FENTON
Ma il canto muor nel bacio che lo tocca.

ALICE (*stepping between* ANN *and* FENTON *and forcing him to don the black hood*)
Just a moment! Put on this robe, and hurry!
(ANN *and* ALICE *help* FENTON *to put on the robe.* QUICKLY *has appeared, wearing a huge bonnet and a gray coat. Her mask is that of an animal's snout*)

ALICE
Nossignore! Tu indossa questa cappa.

FENTON
Che vuol dir ciò?

NANNETTA
Lasciati fare.

ALICE
Allaccia.

NANNETTA
È un fraticel sgusciato dalla Trappa.

ALICE
Il tradimento che Ford ne minaccia
Tornar deve in suo scorno e in nostro aiuto.

FENTON
Spiegatevi.

ALICE
Ubbidisci presto e muto.
L'occasione come viene scappa.
Chi vestirai da finta sposa?

QUICKLY
Un gaio
Ladron nasuto
Che abborre il Dottor Cajo.

MEG
Ho nascosto i folletti lungo il fosso.
Siam pronte.

ALICE
Zitto. Viene il pezzo grosso.

NANNETTA
Via!

ALICE
Via!

MEG
Via!

QUICKLY
Via!

FALSTAFF
Una, due, tre, quattro, cinque, sei, sette botte,
Otto, nove, dieci, undici, dodici. Mezzanotte.
Questa è la quercia. Numi, proteggetemi! Giove!
Tu per amor d'Europa ti trasformasti in bove;
Portasti corna. I numi c'insegnan la modestia.
L'amore metamorfosa un uom in una bestia.
Odo un soave passo!
Alice! Amor ti chiama!
Vieni! l'amor m'infiamma!

FENTON
But what is this?

ANN
I'll tell you later.

ALICE
Don't worry!

ANN (*looking at* FENTON *in disguise*)
He looks like one escaping from a convent.

ALICE (*helping* FENTON *to don the mask*)
The wily ruse that my husband is planning,
Let us use it and turn it back upon him!

FENTON
A ruse, you say?

ALICE
Take my word! Be clever! Obey me!
The iron's hot . . . we strike it now or never.
(*to* QUICKLY) As bride-to-be whom have you chosen?

QUICKLY
That rogue with the big red nose
Who has raised the doctor's dander.

MEG (*entering from the rear, to* ALICE)
All the children are hiding in the bushes. We're ready.

ALICE (*listening*)
Silence! Hear the happy hunter!

ANN
Hurry!

ALICE
Vanish!

MEG
Vanish!

QUICKLY
Hurry!
(*the women, together with* FENTON, *exit left.* FALSTAFF, *wearing an enormous pair of antlers and a wide coat, enters warily. During his entrance the midnight chimes are heard*)

FALSTAFF
One, two, three, four, five, six, seven strokes . . .
Eight, nine, ten, eleven, twelve. It is midnight.
(*noticing the Oak of Herne*)
Here is the oak tree. Mighty powers, stay with me!
Help me, Jove, who became a bull wearing horns
For love of fair Europa. I need your council.
The gods teach us grace and resignation,
As love to humble beast will turn the glory of creation.
(ALICE *appears in the rear.* FALSTAFF *listens*)
Is this her tender footstep?
She's near me, drawn by my passion . . .
(*goes toward her*)

Near me, for me to capture!

ALICE (*approaching* FALSTAFF)
Sir John!

FALSTAFF
Show me compassion!

ALICE
Sir John!

FALSTAFF
Yield to my rapture!

ALICE
Oh blazing flame of love!

FALSTAFF (*vainly trying to embrace her*)
Hear me . . . answer my craving!

ALICE (*always avoiding his embraces*)
Sir John!

FALSTAFF
You are my doe and I am your stag, ranting and raving.
In a shower of truffles, radishes, and custard
The sky provide the supper
And love the mustard!
Alone here . . .

ALICE
Wait! There in the wood behind us is Mistress Page.

FALSTAFF
Good Fortune has combined us all on one stage!
Now both of you, cut me in two! Divide me!
Dismember me! Unto my altar you shall guide me!
I love you! I love you! I love you! . . . love you.

MEG (*off-stage*)
Oh help me!

ALICE (*pretending to be frightened*)
Good heavens, a scream!

MEG (*appearing unmasked but staying in the shadow*)
The host unholy! (*flees*)

ALICE
Alas! Let's flee them!

FALSTAFF (*terrified*)
Where to?

ALICE
I pray to God for my salvation.
(*runs off to the right*)

FALSTAFF (*hiding near the oak tree*)
I never have a chance to court damnation!

ANN (*off-stage*)
Elfins! Fairies! Pixies! Spirits all, oh hear me!
Casting his magic spell on us, the moon is smiling.
Arise now, shadows who cheer me!
(*she has appeared among the trees.* FALSTAFF, *in panic, has thrown himself to the ground, face down*)

ALICE
Sir John!

FALSTAFF
Sei la mia dama!

ALICE
Sir John!

FALSTAFF
Sei la mia dama!

ALICE
O sfavillante amor!

FALSTAFF
Vieni! Già fremo e fervo!

ALICE
Sir John!

FALSTAFF
Sono il tuo servo!
Sono il tuo cervo imbizzarrito.
Ed or
Piovan tartufi, rafani e
finocchi!!!
E sien la mia pastura!
E amor trabocchi!
Siam soli . . .

ALICE
No. Qua nella selva densa
Mi segue Meg.

FALSTAFF
È doppia l'avventura!
Venga anche lei! Squartatemi
Come un camoscio a mensa!!
Sbranatemi!!! Cupìdo
Alfin mi ricompensa
Io t'amo! t'amo!

MEG
Aiuto!!!

ALICE
Un grido!
Ahimè!

MEG
Vien la tregenda!

ALICE
Ahimè! Fuggiamo!

FALSTAFF
Dove?

ALICE
Il cielo perdoni al mio peccato!

FALSTAFF
Il diavolo non vuol ch'io sia
dannato.

NANNETTA
Ninfe! Elfi! Silfi! Doridi!
Sirene!
L'astro degli incantesimi in
cielo è sorto.
Sorgete! Ombre serene!

FALSTAFF
Sono le Fate. Chi le guarda è morto.

FALSTAFF
Unholy demons! No one lives who sees them.
(ANN now is fully visible, disguised as Queen of the Fairies. A number of girls are dressed as white and blue fairies. FALSTAFF remains on the ground, motionless)

ALICE
Inoltriam.

ALICE *(cautiously stepping forth with some of the fairies)*
Follow me!

NANNETTA
Egli è là.

ANN *(cautiously advancing from the opposite side, noticing FALSTAFF)*
There he lies.

ALICE
Steso al suol.

ALICE *(noticing FALSTAFF also and pointing him out to the others)*
. . . on the ground.

NANNETTA
Lo confonde
Il terror.

ANN
He is dying with fear.
(they all advance steathily)

LE FATE
Si nasconde.

FAIRIES
He is hiding.

ALICE
Non ridiam!

ALICE
You be still!

LE FATE
Non ridiam!

FAIRIES
Yes, we will.

NANNETTA
Tutte qui, dietro a me.
Cominciam.

ANN *(instructing the fairies with regard to their actions, places, etc., while ALICE exits rapidly to the left)*
Do you know what to do?
Watch my cue!

LE FATE
Tocca a te.

FAIRIES
We're with you.
(a group of fairies form a circle around ANN. Another, taller group gathers to the left)

LA REGINA DELLE FATE
Sul fil d'un soffio etesio
Scorrete, agili larve;
Fra i rami un baglior cesio
D'alba lunare apparve.
Danzate! e il passo blando
Misuri un blando suon,
Le magiche accoppiando
Carole alla canzon.

THE QUEEN OF THE FAIRIES
Agleam in shimm'ring silver glow
And bathed in misty lather
Over the vale and hill, below
Elves of the night foregather.
And gently, gently we sway
As we dance, beneath the moon,
Smiling at him from far away
We sing our haunting tune.

LE FATE
La selva dorme e sperde
Incenso ed ombra; e par
Nell'aer denso un verde
Asilo in fondo al mar.

CHORUS OF ELVES
The forest slumbers without the slightest motion,
A world beneath an ocean,
A paradise below the sea.

LA REGINA DELLE FATE
Erriam sotto la luna
Scegliendo fior da fiore,
Ogni corolla in core
Porta la sua fortuna.
Coi gigli e le viole
Scriviam de' nomi arcani,
Dalle fatate mani
Germoglino parole,

THE QUEEN OF THE FAIRIES
The blossoms here and yonder,
Awakened by our dances,
View us with sleepy glances,
Rubbing their eyes in wonder.
The roses tell us a story
Of love and sweet surrender,

Lilies so proud and slender
Will sing of might and glory.
Trust in their magic powers,
Trust in their friendship true!
Knowing a secret, the flowers
Always confide it to you.

Parole alluminate
Di puro argento e d'or,
Carmi e malìe. Le Fate
Hanno per cifre i fior.

CHORUS OF ELVES (*gathering flowers*)
Now slowly let us wander
There in the shadows blue
To the big oak-tree yonder
Where we pay Herne his due.
(*during this chorus, all the fairies slowly approach the oak*)

LE FATE
Moviamo ad una ad una
Sotto il lunare albor,
Verso la quercia bruna
Del nero Cacciator.

BARDOLPH (*coming from up-stage left, followed by* ALICE *in mask,* MEG *as the green wood nymph,* QUICKLY *as a witch,* DR. CAIUS *in a gray cloak, not masked,* PISTOL *disguised as a satyr,* FORD *undisguised,* FENTON *in black robe and mask. Several others wear fantastic costumes, carrying lanterns of various shapes and sizes*)
What is this?
(*holding back the others as he comes upon* FALSTAFF'S *body*)

BARDOLFO
Alto là!

PISTOL (*joining* BARDOLPH)
Who lies there?

PISTOLA
Chi va là?

FALSTAFF
Alas!

FALSTAFF
Pietà!

QUICKLY (*touching* FALSTAFF *with her broomstick*)
A human!

QUICKLY
C'è un uomo!

ALICE, MEG, ANN
A man!

ALICE, MEG, NANNETTA
C'è un uom!

THE FAIRIES
A man!

LE FATE
Un uom!

FORD (*having come close to* FALSTAFF)
His horns bespeak defiance.

FORD
Cornuto come un bue!

PISTOL
He must be born of giants.

PISTOLA
Rotondo come un pomo!

BARDOLPH
Fit to serve on a platter.

BARDOLFO
Grosso come una nave!

BARDOLPH, PISTOL (*kicking* FALSTAFF)
Up with you, arise!

BARDOLFO, PISTOLA
Alzati, olà!

FALSTAFF (*lifting his head*)
Without the help of science . . . I cannot!

FALSTAFF
Portatemi una grue!
Non posso.

FORD
A weighty matter!

FORD
È troppo grave.

QUICKLY
He's a monster.

QUICKLY
È corrotto!

FAIRIES
He's a monster.

LE FATE
È corrotto!

ALICE, ANN, MEG
What pollution!

ALICE, NANNETTA, MEG
È impuro!

LE FATE
È impuro!

BARDOLFO
Si faccia lo scongiuro!

ALICE
(Evita il tuo periglio.
Già il Dottor Cajo ti cerca.)

NANNETTA
(Troviamo
Un nascondiglio.)

QUICKLY
(Poi tornerete lesti al mio richiamo.)

BARDOLFO
Spiritelli! Folletti!
Farfarelli! Vampiri! Agili insetti
Del palude infernale! Punzecchiatelo!
Ortichеggiatelo!
Martirizzatelo
Coi grifi aguzzi!

FALSTAFF
Ahimè! tu puzzi
Come una puzzola.

FOLLETTI, DIAVOLI
Ruzzola, ruzzola, ruzzola, ruzzola!

ALICE, MEG, QUICKLY
Pizzica, pizzica,
Pizzica, stuzzica,
Spizzica, spizzica,
Pungi, spilluzzica,
Finch'egli abbài!

FALSTAFF
Ahì! Ahì! Ahì! Ahì!

FOLLETTI, DIAVOLI
Scrolliam crepitacoli,
Scarandole e nacchere!
Di schizzi e di zacchere
Quell'otre si macoli.
Meniam scorribandole,
Danziamo la tresca,
Treschiam le faràndole
Sull'ampia ventresca.
Zanzàre ed assilli,
Volate alla lizza
Coi dardi e gli spilli!
Ch'ei crepi di stizza!

ALICE, MEG, QUICKLY, FATE
Pizzica, pizzica,
Pizzica, stuzzica,
Spizzica, spizzica,
Pungi, spilluzzica

FAIRIES
What pollution!

BARDOLPH (*with gestures of a sorcerer*)
Let's plan his execution!

ALICE (*aside to* ANN *while* DR. CAIUS *is looking for someone.* FENTON *and* QUICKLY *are hiding* ANN)
Danger is near, be careful!
Our Dr. Caius is snooping.

ANN
We'd better go in hiding.

QUICKLY
But come back here the moment I shall call you!
(ANN *and* FENTON *disappear to the rear*)

BARDOLPH (*standing over* FALSTAFF'S *body, pretending to exorcise his spirit*)
Wicked servants of Satan! Ghouls and goblins and demons!
Let us determine what to do with this vermin!
Sap his sanity! Scratch at his vanity!
Hurt his humanity! Pluck him to pieces!
(*a group of boys dressed as devils, ghouls, etc., come running from the rear and pounce on* FALSTAFF. *Some of them swing rattles and make noise in other ways. Many of them carry little red lamps*)

FALSTAFF (*to* BARDOLPH)
I fear my fleece is shorn in profanity!

DEVILS, GOBLINS (*tumbling* FALSTAFF *and rolling him over*)
Bundle him busily, trundle him dizzily!
Jumble and rumble and tumble and humble him!
(*the goblins pinch and prick him*)

ALICE, MEG, QUICKLY
Pricking and kicking torment him and trick him
For all his mendacity and his audacity!
Nick-to-the-quick him until you will lick him!

FALSTAFF
Oh! Oh! Oh! Oh!

DEVILS, GOBLINS
Deflate his propensity to shocking immensity!
His splendor so billowy turn slender and willowy!
The Master of Devilry shall lend you his lances,
The faster the revelry, the better the chances
To bite him and blight him, to smite and to spite him.
So pounce on him, hit him, and trounce him and twit him
Until in the end you completely defeat him!

ALICE, MEG, QUICKLY, FAIRIES
Tackle and shackle him, tatter and shatter him,
Knock him and rock him and sock him and batter him!
Prick him and tickle him for his audacity,

Pick-like-a-pickle him for his mendacity!
Fret and beset him for all his cupidity,
Make him regret his stupendous stupidity!
Prick him and nick him and kick him and tickle him!
(FORD, CAIUS, PISTOL, *and* BARDOLPH *lift him up and force him to his knees*)

DR. CAIUS, FORD
You loon!

BARDOLPH, PISTOL
Poltroon!

DR. CAIUS, FORD
Buffoon!

BARDOLPH, PISTOL
Balloon!

DR. CAIUS, FORD
Raccoon!

BARDOLPH, PISTOL
Baboon!

DR. CAIUS, BARDOLPH, FORD, PISTOL
You laughed too soon!

FORD
Treacherous gambler!

ALICE
Lecherous ambler!

BARDOLPH
Flasket abuser!

QUICKLY
Basket misuser!

PISTOL
Wonder conniver!

MEG
Blundering diver!

DR. CAIUS
Paunchy rapscallion!

FORD
Haunchy old stallion!
(BARDOLPH *has taken* QUICKLY's *broomstick and is beating* FALSTAFF)

BARDOLPH, PISTOL
Do you repent now?

FALSTAFF
I do repent now.

THE MEN
Can we relent now?
(BARDOLPH *again beating* FALSTAFF)

FALSTAFF
I do repent now.

THE MEN
Do you consent now?

Finch'egli abbài!
Cozzalo, aizzalo
Dai pie' al cocuzzolo!
Strozzalo, strizzalo!
Gli svampi l'uzzolo!
Pizzica, pizzica, l'unghia rintuzzola!
Ruzzola, ruzzola, ruzzola, ruzzola!

DR. CAJUS, FORD
Cialtron!

BARDOLFO, PISTOLA
Poltron!

DR. CAJUS, FORD
Ghiotton!

BARDOLFO, PISTOLA
Pancion!

DR. CAJUS, FORD
Beòn!

BARDOLFO, PISTOLA
Briccon!

DR. CAJUS, BARDOLFO, FORD, PISTOLA
In ginocchion!

FORD
Pancia ritronfia!

ALICE
Guancia rigonfia!

BARDOLFO
Sconquassa-letti!

QUICKLY
Spacca-farsetti!

PISTOLA
Vuota-barili!

MEG
Sfonda-sedili!

DR. CAJUS
Sfianca-giumenti!

FORD
Triplice mento!

BARDOLFO, PISTOLA
Di' che ti penti!

FALSTAFF
Ahi! Ahi! mi pento!

TUTTI GLI UOMINI
Uom frodolento!

FALSTAFF
Ahi! Ahi! mi pento!

GLI UOMINI
Uom turbolento!

FALSTAFF Ahi! Ahi! mi pento!	FALSTAFF I do repent now.
GLI UOMINI Capron! Scroccon! Spaccon!	THE MEN You loon! Poltroon! Buffoon!
FALSTAFF Perdon!	FALSTAFF I swoon.
BARDOLFO Riforma la tua vita!	BARDOLPH (*coming close to* FALSTAFF'S *face*) You keep the Bible handy!
FALSTAFF Tu puti d'acquavita.	FALSTAFF You rascal reek of brandy.
LE DONNE Domine fallo casto!	THE WOMEN May the Almighty frighten him!
FALSTAFF Ma salvagli l'addomine.	FALSTAFF But never shrink or slighten him!
LE DONNE Domine fallo guasto!	THE WOMEN May the good Lord enlighten him!
FALSTAFF Ma salvagli l'addomine.	FALSTAFF But not reduce or tighten him!
LE DONNE Fallo punito Domine!	THE WOMEN Justice may put her bite on him.
FALSTAFF Ma salvagli l'addomine.	FALSTAFF Good Luck bestow her might on him!
LE DONNE Fallo pentito Domine!	THE WOMEN Heaven may shed its light on him!
FALSTAFF Ma salvagli l'addomine.	FALSTAFF And Venus set her sight on him!
DR. CAJUS, FORD, BARDOLFO, PISTOLA Globo d'impurità! Rispondi.	THE MEN Mountain of mortal sin . . . your answer!
FALSTAFF Ben mi sta.	FALSTAFF I agree.
DR. CAJUS, FORD, BARDOLFO, PISTOLA Monte d'obesità! Rispondi.	THE MEN Fountain of port and gin . . . your answer!
FALSTAFF Ben mi sta.	FALSTAFF I agree.
DR. CAJUS, FORD, BARDOLFO, PISTOLA Otre di malvasia! Rispondi.	THE MEN Spout of deceit and outrage . . . your answer!
FALSTAFF Così sia.	FALSTAFF If you say so . . .
BARDOLFO Re dei panciuti!	BARDOLPH Lout, let me warn you . . .
FALSTAFF Va via, tu puti.	FALSTAFF You reek of liquor . . .
BARDOLFO Re dei cornuti!	BARDOLPH I shall unhorn you!
FALSTAFF Va via, tu puti.	FALSTAFF . . . and make me sicker.

THE MEN
Watch how we beat you . . .

FALSTAFF
Let me entreat you . . .

THE MEN
How we defeat you!

FALSTAFF
Let me entreat you!

BARDOLPH (*violently*)
. . . until the Devil will finally heat you.
(*his hood slides off his head*)

FALSTAFF (*rising abruptly*)
Thunder and lightning! Satan! This is Bardolph, so help me!
(*furiously assaulting* BARDOLPH, *who retreats*)
Nose like a bunion,
Nose of a ronyon,
Bump of bibacity,
Lump of salacity!
Salamander! Blunted battle-ax! Fork of the Devil!
Miserable mongrel! Infernal viper!
You scum incarnate! You bat, you gnat, you rat!
You gallows vulture! You varlet!
I have spoken. And if I am lying
No single bone of mine shall stay unbroken!

ALL
Bravo!

FALSTAFF
Let's rest for a moment. I am tired.

QUICKLY (*aside to* BARDOLPH, *whom she then draws behind the bushes*)
Come, it is time for you to be attired.

FORD
And now, while we shall all enjoy a respite,
Sir John, tell me: Which of us wears the horns?

ALICE, MEG
Say, who! Yes, who?

ALICE (*taking off her mask*)
You seem confused and shaken.

FALSTAFF (*reaching for* FORD's *hand*)
Good Master Brook, I greet you . . .

ALICE (*interrupting him*)
I fear you are mistaken . . .
This is Ford, my good husband.

QUICKLY (*returning*)
I am honored!
So you fancied two ladies, choosing freely,
Could be so silly
And court, body and soul, their own perdition

GLI UOMINI
Furfanteria!

FALSTAFF
Ahi! Così sia.

GLI UOMINI
Gaglioferia!

FALSTAFF
Ahi! Così sia.

BARDOLFO
Ed or che il diavolo ti porti via!!!

FALSTAFF
Nitro! Catrame! Solfo!!!
Riconosco Bardolfo!
Naso vermiglio!
Naso bargiglio!
Puntùta lesina!
Vampa di resina!
Salamandra! Ignis fatuus! Vecchia alabarda! Stecca
Di sartore! Schidion d'inferno! Aringa secca!
Vampiro! Basilisco!
Manigoldo! Ladrone!
Ho detto. E se mentisco
Voglio che mi si spacchi il cinturone!!!

TUTTI
Bravo!

FALSTAFF
Un poco di pausa. Sono stanco.

QUICKLY
(Vieni. Ti coprirò col velo bianco.)

FORD
Ed or, mentre vi passa la scalmana,
Sir John, dite: Il cornuto
Chi è?

ALICE, MEG
Chi è? Chi è?

ALICE
Vi siete fatto muto?

FALSTAFF
Caro signor Fontana!

ALICE
Sbagliate nel saluto,
Questo è Ford mio marito.

QUICKLY
Cavaliero,
Voi credeste due donne così grulle,
Così citrulle,
Da darsi anima e corpo all'Avversiero,

Per un uom vecchio, sudicio
ed obeso . . .

MEG, QUICKLY
Con quella testa calva . . .

ALICE, MEG, QUICKLY
E con quel peso!!

FORD
Parlano chiaro.

FALSTAFF
Incomincio ad accorgermi
D'esser stato un somaro.

ALICE
Un cervo.

FORD
Un bue.

TUTTI
Ah! Ah!

FORD
E un mostro raro!

FALSTAFF
Ogni sorta di gente dozzinale
Mi beffa e se ne gloria;
Pur, senza me, costor con tanta
boria
Non avrebbero un bricciolo di
sale.
Son io che vi fa scaltri.
L'arguzia mia crea l'arguzia
degli altri.

LE DONNE, CORO
Ma bravo!

FORD
Per gli Dei!
Se non ridessi ti sconquasserei!
Ma basta. Ed or vo' che
m'ascoltiate.
Coronerem la mascherata bella
Cogli sponsali della
Regina delle Fate.
Già s'avanza la coppia degli
sposi.
Attenti!

FALSTAFF, CORO
Attenti!

FORD
Eccola in bianca vesta
Col velo e il serto delle rose in
testa
E il fidanzato suo ch'io le
disposi.
Circondatela, o Ninfe.

ALICE
Un'altra coppia

For some old charmer clearly out of season . . .

MEG, QUICKLY
. . . whose vanity and fat have . . .

ALICE, MEG, QUICKLY
. . . clouded his reason?

FORD
Now you know it!

FALSTAFF
I begin to perceive that likely
I shall have been made an ass.

ALICE
A roebuck

FORD
A bullock!

ALL (*laughing*)
Ha, ha, ha!

FORD
. . . a curious monster, a funny freak!

FALSTAFF (*having regained his composure*)
Thus a rabble of commonplace barbarians derides me,
Gloating in glory!
Yet, but for me, this dull and witless story
Would not even have a pinch of salt to spice it!
'Tis I, yes, I alone, noble and clever,
Whose gay adventure you will remember forever!

THE WOMEN, CHORUS
Well spoken!

FORD
Be it said
That, had I not had fun, you would be dead!
Enough now! There are more important matters:
Before this gay, enchanted night is ended
A royal wedding feast now bids fair to be attended!
(DR. CAIUS *and* BARDOLPH *disguised as Queen of the Fairies advance slowly, holding hands.* BARDOLPH'S *face is hidden by his veil while* CAIUS *wears a mask*)
See the couple approaching from the distance.
Behold them!

FALSTAFF, CHORUS
Behold them!

FORD
Ravishing, so fair and slender,
The lovely bride all garbed in silv'ry splendor!
He, manly, strong and handsome, chosen with my assistance.
Let the elfins surround them.
(BARDOLPH *and* CAIUS *arrive center-stage, surrounded by fairies*)

ALICE (*presenting* ANN *and* FENTON. ANN *is covered by a long blue veil,* FENTON *still wears his monk's robe*)

Another pair of young hearts in sweet communion
Came here, fervently hoping that you would sanction their union.

FORD
How charming! We heartily invite them.
Bring on the lights and lanterns! May heav'n unite them!
(led by ALICE*, a group of goblins come forward, carrying lanterns. The smallest one, carried by* ALICE*, holds his tiny lantern on a level with* BARDOLPH*'s face.* ANN *and* FENTON*, hand in hand, are standing slightly off center-stage.)*
Now remove your disguises! Apotheosis!
(as soon as they hear FORD*'s command,* CAIUS *and* FENTON *drop their masks.* ANN *unveils her face, and* QUICKLY *pulls the hood off* BARDOLPH*'s head. All the faces are uncovered.)*

ALL *except* FORD, DR. CAIUS
Ha, ha, ha, ha!

DR. CAIUS *(recognizing* BARDOLPH*)*
Oh terror!

FORD *(thunderstruck)*
What an error!

FALSTAFF, PISTOL, CHORUS
Apotheosis!

FORD *(noticing the other couple)*
Fenton with my daughter!

DR. CAIUS
I am married to Bardolph! Oh terror!

ALL
Ha! Ha!

THE WOMEN
Be happy! Be happy!

FORD *(still in a state of shock)*
I cannot grasp it.

ALICE
The finest web our perfidy can fashion
Will often trap the weaver!

FALSTAFF *(walking up to* FORD *and bowing, with irony)*
Ah, my good Master Ford, I pray you, tell me
Which of us is the fool!

FORD *(pointing to* DR. CAIUS*)*
He.

DR. CAIUS *(pointing to* FORD*)*
You.

FORD
No.

DR. CAIUS
Yes.

BARDOLPH *(to* FORD *and* CAIUS*)*
You.

D'amanti desiosi
Chiede d'essere ammessa agli augurosi
Connubi!

FORD
E sia. Farem la festa doppia.
Avvicinate i lumi.
Il ciel v'accoppia.
Giù le maschere e i veli.
Apoteosi!

TUTTI TRANNE FORD, DR. CAJUS
Ah! Ah! Ah! Ah!

DR. CAJUS
Spavento!

FORD
Tradimento!

FALSTAFF, PISTOLA, CORO
Apoteòsi!

FORD
Fenton con mia figlia!!!

DR. CAJUS
Ho sposato Bardolfo! Spavento!

TUTTI
Ah! Ah!

LE DONNE
Vittoria! Evviva!

FORD
Oh, meraviglia!

ALICE
L'uom cade spesso nelle reti ordite
Dalle malizie sue.

FALSTAFF
Caro buon Messer Ford, ed ora, dite:
Lo scornato chi è?

FORD
Lui.

DR. CAJUS
Tu.

FORD
No.

DR. CAJUS
Sì.

BARDOLFO
Voi.

FENTON
Lor.

DR. CAJUS
Noi.

FALSTAFF
Tutti e due.

ALICE
No. Tutti e tre.
Volgiti e mira quelle ansie leggiadre.

NANNETTA
Perdonateci, padre.

FORD
Chi schivare non può la propria noia
L'accetti di buon grado.
Facciamo il parentado
E che il ciel vi dia gioia.

TUTTI
Evviva!

FALSTAFF
Un coro e terminian la scena.

FORD
Poi con Sir Falstaff, tutti, andiamo a cena.

TUTTI
Evviva!

Tutto nel mondo è burla.
L'uom è nato burlone,
La fede in cor gli ciurla,
Gli ciurla la ragione.
Tutti gabbàti! Irride
L'un l'altro ogni mortal.
Ma ride ben chi ride
La risata final.

FENTON (*indicating both* FORD *and* CAIUS)
Both.

CAIUS (*stepping close to* FORD)
We.

FALSTAFF
There are two now!

ALICE
No!
(*pointing to* FALSTAFF, FORD, *and* CAIUS)
There are three!
(*to* FORD, *referring to* ANN *and* FENTON)
Look on the children on pins and needles!

ANN (*entreating* FORD *with hands folded*)
Dearest Father, forgive us!

FORD
When you suffer defeat, don't let it blight you:
It never shall disgrace you!
My children, I embrace you!
Let me bless and unite you!

ALL
Be happy!

FALSTAFF
A rousing tribute to the winner!

FORD
Then with Sir John I ask you all to dinner.

ALL
We thank you!

Fugue

Let us enjoy our folly!
Man is born to be jolly!
His idle pretenses, vain defenses
Trouble his senses, confound his mind.
Leaner or fatter we frolic and flatter,
Let us be merry and let us pretend:
Fun is the triumph of mind over matter
If we laugh in the end!

FAUST

by Charles Gounod (1818–93)

LIBRETTO BY JULES BARBIER AND MICHEL CARRÉ

Translated by GEORGE MEAD

Based on Goethe's tragedy *Faust,* Part One

CHARACTERS

FAUST	*Tenor*
MÉPHISTOPHÉLÈS	*Bass*
WAGNER, *a young student*	*Baritone*
VALENTIN, *a soldier, brother of Marguerite*	*Baritone*
SIEBEL, *a youth in love with Marguerite*	*Soprano*
MARGUERITE	*Soprano*
MARTHE SCHWERLEIN, *neighbor and companion of Marguerite*	*Contralto or mezzo-soprano*
SOLDIERS, STUDENTS, VILLAGERS, DANCERS, DEMONS	

Place: A village in Germany
Time: Sixteenth century
First performance: Théâtre Lyrique, Paris, March 19, 1859

ENGLISH VERSION COPYRIGHT 1954, BY GEORGE MEAD. PERFORMANCE RIGHTS RESERVED

ACT I

Scene 1—Faust's Study

(FAUST, *alone. His lamp is flickering. He is seated at a table on which parchments are lying about. Before him lies an open book. It is nearly dawn.*)

Recitative

FAUST

No! I search all in vain
Through days and nights unending,
And I ponder the midnight skies;
I call to nature and I cry to heaven,
And still no voice replies.
Here am I, old and weak and lonely.
Oh, to break the bond that binds my life
To this mortal world and its madness!
Nothing remains! Nothing remains! No! No!
(*he closes the book and rises; day begins to dawn*)
The sky is pale. Now the dawn is approaching
And one more night passes away.
(*despairingly*)
Another day! Yet one more day begins!
O Death, when will you come,
When will you come to take me?
(*picking up a flask from the table*)
What then? Death will not come for me;
Why should I not go forth to meet him?
To you, last of my days on earth!
To you, my last day on earth!
I greet you unafraid; at last I end my journey
With this drink that makes me the master,
Yes, the master of my fate!
This drink, this drink that makes me the master,
Yes, the master of my fate!
(*he pours the contents of the flask into a cup. As he raises the cup to his lips, the voices of women singing are heard outside*)

FAUST

Rien! . . . —En vain j'interroge, en mon ardente veille,
La nature et le Créateur;
Pas une voix ne glisse à mon oreille
Un mot consolateur!
J'ai langui triste et solitaire,
Sans pouvoir briser le lien
Qui m'attache encore à la terre! . . .
Je ne vois rien! — Je ne sais rien! . . .
Le ciel pâlit!—Devant l'aube nouvelle
La sombre nuit
S'évanouit! . . .
Encore un jour!—encore un jour qui luit! . . .
O mort, quand viendras-tu m'abriter sous ton aile?
Eh bien! puisque la mort me fuit,
Pourquoi n'irais-je pas vers elle? . . .
Salut! ô mon dernier matin!
J'arrive sans terreur au terme du voyage;
Et je suis, avec ce breuvage,
Le seul maître de mon destin!

CHORUS OF YOUNG WOMEN

Lazy little maiden, deep in slumber still,
Wake and see the sunlight shining on the hill!
The sweet birds are singing a gay morning song,
Murmuring through the meadows the brook flows along.
Now the blossom opens to the sun above;
See how all creation is waking to love!
See how all creation is waking to love!

CHOEUR DE JEUNES FILLES.

Paresseuse fille
Qui sommeille encor!
Déjà le jour brille
Sous son manteau d'or.
Déjà l'oiseau chante
Ses folles chansons;
L'aube caressante
Sourit aux moissons;
Le ruisseau murmure,
La fleur s'ouvre au jour,
Toute la nature
S'éveille à l'amour!

FAUST

Empty echoes of mortal pleasure,
Be still, be still! Pass on your way!

FAUST

Vains échos de la joie humaine
Passez, passez votre chemin!

O coupe des aïeux, qui tant
fois fus pleine,
Pourquoi trembles-tu dans ma
main? . . .

Away! Away!
(he raises the cup again)
Ah, well-remembered cup! You offer all I long for,
But why do you tremble in my hand?
(the voices of men on their way to work are heard outside)

CHOEUR DE LABOUREURS
Aux champs l'aurore nous
rappelle;
Le temps est beau, la terre est
belle;
Béni soit Dieu!
A peine voit-on l'hirondelle,
Qui vole et plonge d'un coup
d'aile
Dans le profondeur du ciel
bleu!

CHORUS OF MEN
We must awaken with the swallow;
The sun is calling us to follow.
We must awaken with the swallow
Soaring through the blue of the sky.
The earth is fair and full of beauty;
The harvest calls us to our duty.
The earth is fair and full of beauty.
Praise be to God on high!

JEUNES FILLES, LABOUREURS
Béni soit Dieu!

CHORUS OF MEN AND WOMEN
Praise be to God—to God on high!

FAUST
Dieu!

FAUST
God! God! God!
(he sinks into his chair)
Duet

FAUST
Mais ce Dieu, que peut-il pour
moi!
Me rendra-t-il l'amour,
l'espérance et la foi?
Maudites soyez-vous, ô
voluptés humaines!
Maudites soient les chaînes
Qui me font ramper ici-bas!
Maudit soit tout ce qui nous
leurre,
Vain espoir qui passe avec
l'heure,
Rêves d'amour ou de combats!
Maudit soit le bonheur,
maudites la science,
La prière et la foi!
Maudite sois-tu, patience!
A moi, Satan! à moi!

FAUST
But this God, what is He to me?
(rising)
Will He give back my youth, my desire and my joy?
(in a rage)
I curse this mortal life, and every human passion,
I curse the mortal chains
That bind me to my life here on earth!
And I curse every vain illusion,
All desires that pass in a moment,
Visions of love, glory and fame!
And I curse every joy! I curse all human learning,
Every hope, every prayer!
Come to me now, mighty Satan!
I call to you! I call!

MÉPHISTOPHÉLÈS
Me voici! . . . D'où vient ta
surprise?
Ne suis-je pas mis à ta guise?
L'épée au côté, la plume au
chapeau,
L'escarcelle pleine, un riche
manteau
Sur l'épaule;—en somme
Un vrai gentilhomme!
Eh bien! que me veux-tu,
docteur!
Parle, voyons! . . . —Te fais-je
peur?

MÉPHISTOPHÉLÈS *(appearing suddenly)*
I am here! Why should it surprise you?
Or is it my clothes that displease you?
My sword at my side, a plume in my cap,
I have gold in my pocket, a gentleman's cloak
On my shoulder. Behold me!
A man of the world!
And so, my friend, what would you like?
But wait! Tell me, are you afraid?

FAUST
Non.

FAUST
No.

MÉPHISTOPHÉLÈS
Doutes-tu ma puissance? . . .

MÉPHISTOPHÉLÈS
Do you doubt my power to help you?

FAUST
I wonder. . .

MÉPHISTOPHÉLÈS
Tell me how I may prove it.

FAUST
Go away!

MÉPHISTOPHÉLÈS
So! My friend, that's no way to greet me!
It is not right when Satan calls
That he should be made to feel unwelcome.
When I've come from far away,
Just to be with you today,
All you have to say is "Go away!"

FAUST
What can you do for me?

MÉPHISTOPHÉLÈS
All! All! But first I must know
What you desire. Is it gold?

FAUST
Why would I be asking for gold?

MÉPHISTOPHÉLÈS
Good! I think, that I know the answer.
You seek for glory?

FAUST
More than that!

MÉPHISTOPHÉLÈS
Is it power?

FAUST
No. I have one desire which contains them all.
I long to be young again!
I long for the days
Of beauty and gladness,
The moment of madness
When life is ablaze.
I long to be yearning,
Yearning with desire,
Once more to be burning
With love and its fire!
Oh give me the rapture,
The joy and the pain!
Oh let me recapture
My youth once again!
Oh let me recapture
My youth once again!

MÉPHISTOPHÉLÈS
Why not? Why not?
It's I who can give you all you ask for.
It's I who can give you your heart's desire.

FAUST
So! And what must I give in return?

FAUST
Peut-être!

MÉPHISTOPHÉLÈS
Mets-la donc à l'épreuve! . . .

FAUST
Va-t'en!

MÉPHISTOPHÉLÈS
Fi!—c'est là ta reconnaissance!
Apprends de moi qu'avec Satan
L'on en doit user d'autre sorte,
Et qu'il n'était pas besoin
De l'appeler de si loin
Pour le mettre ensuite à la
porte!

FAUST
Et que peux-tu pour moi?

MÉPHISTOPHÉLÈS
Tout.—Mais dis-moi d'abord
Ce que tu veux;—est-ce de l'or?

FAUST
Que ferais-je de la richesse?

MÉPHISTOPHÉLÈS
Bien! je vois où le bât te blesse!
Tu veux la gloire?

FAUST
Plus encore!

MÉPHISTOPHÉLÈS
La puissance!

FAUST
Non! je veux un trésor
Qui les contient tous! . . . je
veux la jeunesse!
A moi les plaisirs,
Les jeunes maîtresses!
A moi leurs caresses!
A moi leurs désirs!
A moi l'énergie
Des instincts puissants,
Et la folle orgie
Du cœur et des sens!
Ardente jeunesse,
A moi tes désirs!
A moi ton ivresse!
A moi tes plaisirs! . . .

MÉPHISTOPHÉLÈS
Fort bien! je puis contenter ton
caprice
Je puis contenter ton caprice.

FAUST
Et que te donnerai-je en retour?

MÉPHISTOPHÉLÈS
Presque rien:
Ici, je suis à ton service,
Mais là-bas tu seras au mien.

MÉPHISTOPHÉLÈS
Nothing much, nothing much.
On earth I'll be your humble servant,
But in hell, you shall be mine.

FAUST
Là-bas? . . .

FAUST
In hell?

MÉPHISTOPHÉLÈS
Là-bas.
Allons, signe.—Eh quoi! ta main tremble!
Que faut-il pour te décider?
La jeunesse t'appelle; ôse la regarder! . . .

MÉPHISTOPHÉLÈS
In hell!
(*he holds out a parchment*)
Come on, sign it.
My friend, you are trembling.
Very well. Here is something more.
It is youth that is calling.
See what you have in store!
(*he makes a sign; a vision appears showing* MARGUERITE *at her spinning wheel*)

FAUST
O merveille! . . .

FAUST
Ah, how lovely!

MÉPHISTOPHÉLÈS
Eh bien! que t'ensemble?

MÉPHISTOPHÉLÈS
What now? Does she please you?
(*he offers the parchment*)

FAUST
Donne! . . .

FAUST
Give it here!
(*he signs*)

MÉPHISTOPHÉLÈS
Allons donc!
Et maintenant,
Maître, c'est moi qui te convie
A vider cette coupe où fume en bouillonnant
Non plus la mort, non plus le poison;—mais la vie!

MÉPHISTOPHÉLÈS
Yes indeed!
(*he picks up the cup from the table*)
Now I am yours, Master,
And so I'll fill this cup with my own precious potion.
It bubbles to the brim, but not with death.
Do not be afraid! It is life itself!
(FAUST *takes the cup and addresses the vision of* MARGUERITE)

FAUST
A toi, fantôme adorable et charmant! . . .

FAUST
To you, to you,
The desire of my heart!

MÉPHISTOPHÉLÈS
Viens!

MÉPHISTOPHÉLÈS
Come!

FAUST
Je la reverrai?

FAUST
I'll see her again?

MÉPHISTOPHÉLÈS
Sans doute.

MÉPHISTOPHÉLÈS
I promise.

FAUST
Quand?

FAUST
When?

MÉPHISTOPHÉLÈS
Aujourd'hui.

MÉPHISTOPHÉLÈS
Today.

FAUST
C'est bien!

FAUST
Today!

MÉPHISTOPHÉLÈS
En route! En route!

MÉPHISTOPHÉLÈS
Come on, then! Come on, then!

FAUST, MÉPHISTOPHÉLÈS
And now for the days
Of beauty and gladness,
The moment of madness
When life is ablaze!
And now for the yearning,
Yearning with desire,
Once more to be burning
With love and its fire!
And now for the rapture,
The joy and the pain.

FAUST
And now to recapture
My youth once again,
And now to recapture
My youth once again!

MÉPHISTOPHÉLÈS
And now to recapture
Youth once again,
And now to recapture
Your youth once again!

FAUST, MÉPHISTOPHÉLÈS
And now for the joy,
And now for the pain,
Oh now to be happy
And young once again!
(*they rush off; the curtain falls*)

FAUST, MÉPHISTOPHÉLÈS
A moi (toi) les plaisirs,
Les jeunes maîtresses!
A moi (toi) leurs caresses,
A moi (toi) leurs désirs!
A moi (toi) l'énergie
Des instincts puissants,
E la folle orgie
Du cœur et des sens!

FAUST
Ardente jeunesse,
A moi tes désirs,
A moi ton ivresse,
A moi tes plaisirs.

MÉPHISTOPHÉLÈS
A toi la jeunesse,
A toi ses désirs,
A toi son ivresse,
A toi ses plaisirs.

FAUST, MÉPHISTOPHÉLÈS
A moi (toi) ton (son) ivresse,
A moi (toi) tes (ses) plaisirs!
A moi (toi) ton (son) ivresse,
A moi (toi) tes (ses) plaisirs,
A moi (toi) ton (son) ivresse,
A moi (toi), a moi (toi) tes (ses) plaisirs!

ACT II

Scene 1

The Kermesse

(*At one of the city gates, at the left an inn, with a sign showing the wine god Bacchus.*)

Chorus

WAGNER, STUDENTS, BURGHERS, SOLDIERS, YOUNG WOMEN, OLDER WOMEN

ETUDIANTS
Vin ou bière,
Bière ou vin,
Que mon verre
Soit plein!
Sans vergogne,
Coup sur coup,
Un ivrogne
Boit tout!

STUDENTS
Beer or brandy,
Brandy or beer,
We're not particular,
Bring it here!
We've no prejudice,
Glass for glass,
We'll drink anything you pass!

WAGNER, ETUDIANTS
Jeune adepte
De tonneau
N'en excepte
Que l'eau!
Que ta gloire,
Tes amours,
Soient de boire
Toujours!

WAGNER, STUDENTS
Learned scholars
Of the wine keg,
Drinking water is a sin!
Drink to glory,
Drink to love,
Get your glass
And let's begin!

SOLDATS
Filles ou forteresses,
C'est tout un, morbleu!
Vieux burgs, jeunes maîtresses
Sont pour nous un jeu!
Celui qui sait s'y prendre
Sans trop de façon,
Les oblige à se rendre
En payant rançon!

SOLDIERS
Battles, big or small ones,
They are all the same!
Ladies, short or tall ones,
They are all fair game!
We have learned how to take them
That's not hard to do.
We have learned how to make them
Pay a ransom, too!

BOURGEOIS
Aux jours de dimanche et de fête,
J'aime à parler guerre et combats;
Tandis que les peuples là-bas
Se cassent la tête.
Je vais m'asseoir sur les coteaux
Qui sont voisins de la rivière,
Et je vois passer les bateaux
En vidant mon verre!

BURGHERS
All I ask is time on a Sunday,
Time for a joke, time for a talk,
Time to take a leisurely walk,
Leaving my work till Monday.
Time for a rest, time for a glass,
Dozing a little if I choose to,
Time to watch the young people pass,
Raising the devil as I used to!

(SOLDIERS *and* BURGHERS *go back; a group of* YOUNG GIRLS *enters*)

LES JEUNES FILLES
Voyez ces hardis compères
Qui viennent là-bas;
Ne soyons pas trop sévères,
Retardons le pas.

YOUNG GIRLS
See that jolly crowd of students
Coming down the street.
Let us walk a little slower,
Maybe we will meet!

(*they go right; another group of* STUDENTS *enters*)

YOUNG STUDENTS
See the way those girls are smiling!
What a saucy air!
Set a guard upon your hearts now,
Brothers, have a care!

DEUXIEME CHOEUR D'ETUDIANTS
Voyez ces mines gaillardes
Et ces airs vainqueurs!
Amis, soyons sur nos gardes,
Tenons bien nos cœurs!

OLDER WOMEN (*observing the* STUDENTS *and the* YOUNG GIRLS)
See those brazen hussies beckon,
See the men pursue!
We are just as worth pursuing,
If they only knew!
You want to please them,
That's not the way.
How could you please them,
I couldn't say.

CHOEUR DE MATRONES
Voyez après ces donzelles
Courir ces messieurs!
Nous sommes aussi bien
qu'elles,
Si non beaucoup mieux!
Vous voulez leur plaire
Nous le savons bien!

STUDENTS
Drink and be gay,
Drink and be gay today!
Beer or brandy, brandy or beer,
We're not particular, bring it here!

ETUDIANTS
Vin ou bière,
Bière ou vin,
Que mon verre
Soit plein!

SOLDIERS
Here's to the soldier, and to the fray!
We march away, we march away!
We know how to seize them
We know how to please them,
We know how to please any girl that's near.

SOLDATS
Vive la guerre! Vive la guerre!
Métier divin! Métier divin!
Pas de beauté fière!
Nous savons leur plaire
En un tour de main!

BURGHERS
Come on, I say! Come on, I say!
We'll have a drink and I will pay.
We'll have a drink and I will pay.
So fill your glass with brandy or beer!

BOURGEOIS
Allons, voisin! Allons, voisin!
Vidons, vidons un verre de vin!
Vidons un verre
De ce bon vin!

YOUNG STUDENTS
What this will come to is hard to say.
Now she's growing angry, pretty little dear!

JEUNES ETUDIANTS
De cette affaire
Voyons la fin!
Voyez leur colère,
Voyez leur maintien!

YOUNG WOMEN
We'd like to please them, they look away.
Why pretend you're angry?
What have we to fear?

JEUNES FILLES
On voudrait plaire,
Mais c'est en vain!
De votre colère
Nous ne craignons rien!

Scene 2

Recitative and Cavatina

VALENTIN
O blessed remembrance
From the sister I love!

VALENTIN
O sainte médaille,
Qui me viens de ma sœur,
Au jour de la bataille,

Pour écarter la mort, reste là
sur mon cœur!

WAGNER
Ah! voici Valentin qui nous
cherche sans doute!

VALENTIN
Un dernier coup, messieurs, et
mettons-nous en route!

WAGNER
Qu'as-tu donc? . . . quels
regrets attristent nos
adieux?

VALENTIN
Comme vous, pour longtemps,
je vais quitter ces lieux;
J'y laisse Marguerite, et pour
veiller sur elle,
Ma mère n'est plus là!

SIEBEL
Plus d'un ami fidèle
Saura te remplacer a ses côtés!

VALENTIN
Merci!

SIEBEL
Sur moi tu peux compter!

ETUDIANTS
Compte sur nous aussi!

VALENTIN
Avant de quitter ces lieux,
Sol natal de mes aïeux,
A toi, Seigneur et Roi des cieux,
Ma soeur je confie.
Daigne de tout danger
Toujours, toujours la protéger,
Cette soeur si chérie,
Daigne de tout danger la
protéger,
Daigne la protéger de tout
danger.
Délivré d'une triste pensée,
J'irai chercher la gloire au sein
des ennemis,
Le premier, le plus brave au
fort de la mêlée,
J'irai combattre pour mon pays.
Et si, vers lui, Dieu me
rappelle,
Je veillerai sur toi fidèle,
O Marguerite!
Avant de quitter ces lieux,
Sol natal de mes aïeux,
A toi, Seigneur et Roi des cieux,
Ma soeur je confie!
O Roi des cieux,
Jette les yeux,
Protège Marguerite, Roi des
cieux!

When I go into battle,
O sacred little charm,
You shall keep me from harm!

WAGNER
Ah! I see that the captain has come to join us.

VALENTIN
Just one drink more, my friends, then I fear we must
leave you.

WAGNER
What is wrong? Are you sad because we have to go?

VALENTIN
I am sad when I think how long I'll be away from my
sister Marguerite,
For since our mother died, my sister needs me near.

SIEBEL
I promise to protect her
I swear that I'll be here to take your place!

VALENTIN
My thanks!
(*gives him his hand*)

SIEBEL
My friend, rely on me.

STUDENTS
You may rely on us.

VALENTIN
As I leave the home I love,
Hear me now, O God above,
As I leave my sister here,
Ah, Lord, be Thou ever near!
Oh may Thy mighty arm
Guard her from every threat of harm!
She is young and very dear to me.
Lord, may Thy mighty arm
Protect my home from every threat
Of danger and of harm.
When the trumpet shall call me to battle,
I pray that my sword be keen and bright!
O Lord, let my arm be the bravest in the fight,
In the strength of God and the right.
What if at last death may call me,
If I may know that she is safe with Thee!
O Marguerite!
As I leave the home I love,
Hear me now, O God above!
As I leave my sister here,
Ah, Lord, be ever near.
O Lord of heaven,
Give strength to my arm,
And keep Marguerite safe from harm!

WAGNER

Cheer up, my lads! It's no time to be thinking!
This is the time for a man to be drinking!
Let's drink, let's drink
And I shall sing a song,
And all of you shall follow along.

STUDENTS

Let's drink, and he will sing a song,
And all of us will follow along!

WAGNER (*getting up on a table*)

A rat!
What a sneaking little,
Dirty little rat!
He sat
In a cellar full of wine
Beneath a vat.
A cat . . .

WAGNER

Allons, amis! point de vaines alarmes!
A ce bon vin ne mêlons pas de larmes!
Buvons, trinquons, et qu'un joyeux refrain
Nous mette en train!

ETUDIANTS

Buvons, trinquons, et qu'un joyeux refrain
Nous mette en train!

WAGNER

Un rat plus poltron que brave,
Et plus laid que beau,
Logeait au fond d'une cave,
Sous un vicux tonneau;
Un chat . . .

Scene 3

(MÉPHISTOPHÉLÈS *suddenly appears among the students; he interrupts* WAGNER)

MÉPHISTOPHÉLÈS

My friend!

WAGNER

Huh!

MÉPHISTOPHÉLÈS

May I join the party?
You'll find that I am hale and hearty,
And when this lad has finished singing of his rat,
I have a repertoire of songs better than that!

WAGNER

Sing us *one*, if you must.
I yield my place before you.

MÉPHISTOPHÉLÈS

I will give you my best,
I would not wish to bore you.

MÉPHISTOPHÉLÈS

Pardon!

WAGNER

Hein?

MÉPHISTOPHÉLÈS

Parmi vous, de grâce
Permettez-moi de prendre place!
Que votre ami d'abord achève sa chanson!
Moi, je vous en promets plusieurs de ma façon!

WAGNER

Une seule suffit, pourvu qu'elle soit bonne!

MÉPHISTOPHÉLÈS

Je ferai de mon mieux pour n'ennuyer personne!

The Calf of Gold.

MÉPHISTOPHÉLÈS

Sing a song to the Calf of Gold!
All the world must bow before him,
All the people must adore him,
Rich and poor and young and old.
His dominion is eternal,
Kings obey his firm command.

Le veau d'or est toujours debout;
On encense
Sa puissance
D'un bout du monde à l'autre bout!
Pour fêter l'infâme idole,
Rois et peuples confondus,

Au bruit sombre des écus
Dansent une ronde folle
Autour de son piédestal! . . .
Et Satan conduit le bal,
Conduit le bal!

Wise and foolish join the band,
Striking up the dance infernal,
Rich man, poor man, young and old,
Dancing round his throne of gold!
And the dream of one and all
Is power and pelf,
And the leader of the ball
Is Satan himself!

ETUDIANTS
Et Satan conduit le bal,
Conduit le bal!

STUDENTS
And the leader of the ball
Is Satan himself!

MÉPHISTOPHÉLÈS
Le veau d'or est vainqueur des dieux;
Dans sa gloire
Dérisoire
Le monstre abject insulte aux cieux!
Il contemple, ô rage étrange!
A ses pieds le genre humain
Se ruant, le fer en main,
Dans le sang et dans la fange
Où brille l'ardent métal! . . .
Et Satan conduit le bal,
Conduit le bal!

MÉPHISTOPHÉLÈS
He is lord of the gods of old,
And the proudest of immortals
Come at last within the portals
Of the temple made of gold.
All the fools and all the sages,
Men of pleasure, men of toil,
Run to share the golden spoil
With the beast of all the ages!
(*refrain*)
Rich man, poor man, young and old,
Dancing round his throne of gold!
And the dream of one and all
Is power and pelf,
And the leader of the ball
Is Satan himself!

TOUS
Et Satan conduit le bal,
Conduit le bal!

ALL
And the leader of the ball
Is Satan himself!

Scene and Chorus

CHOEUR
Merci de ta chanson!

STUDENTS
We thank you for your song!

VALENTIN
Singulier personnage!

VALENTIN
What a curious fellow!
(WAGNER *offers a cup to* MÉPHISTOPHÉLÈS)

WAGNER
Nous ferez-vous l'honneur de trinquer avec nous?

WAGNER
And now sir, if you please, may we buy you a drink?

MÉPHISTOPHÉLÈS
Volontiers! . . .
Ah! voici qui m'attriste pour vous!
Vous voyez cette ligne?

MÉPHISTOPHÉLÈS
That you may!
(*he takes* WAGNER'*s hand and reads his palm*)
Ah, what's this that I see in your hand?
Do you see that line?

WAGNER
Eh bien?

WAGNER
Of course.

MÉPHISTOPHÉLÈS
Fâcheux présage!
Vous vous ferez tuer en montant à l'assaut!

MÉPHISTOPHÉLÈS
A fatal sign!
It seems that you will die
When the battle begins.

SIEBEL
And what about me?

MÉPHISTOPHÉLÈS
I know enough about you to read here in your hand
What the fates have decreed,
And that any flower you may touch
Shall wither and perish.

SIEBEL
Ah!

MÉPHISTOPHÉLÈS
No more bouquets for Marguerite!

VALENTIN
My sister! Be careful how you speak!

MÉPHISTOPHÉLÈS (*to* VALENTIN)
O my captain, I warn you
You're going to meet your death through a man I know.
(*takes the cup from* WAGNER)
I drink to your health!
(*he throws the wine from the cup*)
Peuh! What a terrible wine! May I not offer a little wine of my own?
(*he jumps on a table under the inn's sign of Bacchus and strikes on a small cask that Bacchus is holding*)
Come on, Bacchus my lad! Some wine here!
(*wine flows from the cask*)
Everyone come!
Whatever wine you like you shall obtain.
And will you join me in a toast
That no one can refuse? Our Marguerite!

VALENTIN
Enough!
I'll stop your dirty mouth
Though I die in the trying!
(*the wine bursts into flame*)

WAGNER
Come on!

STUDENTS
Come on!
(*they draw their swords*)

MÉPHISTOPHÉLÈS (*mockingly*)
Why do you shake, O my brave cavaliers?
(*he draws a circle around himself with his sword.* VALENTIN *comes on to attack him. His sword breaks*)

VALENTIN
My sword! It is broken!
This is some enchantment!
(VALENTIN *and the rest advance on* MÉPHISTOPHÉLÈS, *holding toward him the cross-shaped guards of their swords.* MÉPHISTOPHÉLÈS *backs away*)

SIEBEL
Vous êtes donc sorcier?

MÉPHISTOPHÉLÈS
Tout juste autant qu'il faut
Pour lire dans ta main que le ciel te condamne
A ne plus toucher une fleur
Sans qu'elle se fane!

SIEBEL
Moi!

MÉPHISTOPHÉLÈS
Plus de bouquets à Marguerite! . . .

VALENTIN
Ma sœur! . . .
Qui vous a dit son nom?

MÉPHISTOPHÉLÈS
Prenez garde, mon brave!
Vous vous ferez tuer par quelqu'un que je sais!
A votre santé! . . .
Peuh! que ton vin est mauvais! . . .
Permettez-moi de vous en offrir de ma cave!
Holà! seigneur Bacchus! à boire! . . .
Approchez-vous!
Chacun sera servi selon ses goûts!
A la santé que tout à l'heure
Vous portiez, mes amis, à Marguerite!

VALENTIN
Assez! . . .
Si je ne te fais taire à l'instant, que je meure!

WAGNER
Holà! . . .

ETUDIANTS
Holà!

MÉPHISTOPHÉLÈS
Pourquoi trembler, vous qui me menacez?

VALENTIN
Mon fer, ô surprise!
Dans les airs se brise! . . .

VALENTIN, WAGNER, SIEBEL, ETUDIANTS, SOLDATS
De l'enfer qui vient émousser
Nos armes!
Nous ne pouvons pas repousser
Les charmes!
Mais puisque tu brises le fer,
Regarde! . . .
C'est une croix qui, de l'enfer,
Nous garde!

VALENTIN, WAGNER, SIEBEL STUDENTS, SOLDIERS
When the powers of hell are allied against us,
We cannot depend on our worldly armor.
Still, though you may break every sword,
Behold this!
It is the cross that shall protect and guard us,
It is the cross that shall protect and guard us!
(*they go out*)

Scene 4

MÉPHISTOPHÉLÈS
Nous nous retrouverons, mes amis!—Serviteur!

MÉPHISTOPHÉLÈS
I'll see you soon again, so till then,
Fare you well!

FAUST
Qu'as-tu donc?

FAUST (*as he enters*)
What is wrong?

MÉPHISTOPHÉLÈS
Rien!—A nous deux, cher docteur!
Qu'attendez-vous de moi? par où commencerai-je?

MÉPHISTOPHÉLÈS
Bah! Tell me now,
Tell me now what sort of life you like
And where shall we begin it?

FAUST
Où se cache la belle enfant
Que ton art m'a fait voir?—Est-ce un vain sortilège?

FAUST
I must find her, that lovely maid
Who appeared in my dream.
Was it all merely magic?

MÉPHISTOPHÉLÈS
Non pas! mais contre nous sa vertu la protège;
Et le ciel même la défend!

MÉPHISTOPHÉLÈS
Oh no. But all the powers of heaven are against us,
Virtue and innocence are on her side.

FAUST
Qu'importe? je le veux! viens! conduis-moi vers elle!
Ou je me sépare de toi!

FAUST
What of it, so she's mine! Come, show me where I'll find her,
Otherwise I leave you at once!

MÉPHISTOPHÉLÈS
Il suffit! . . . je tiens trop à mon nouvel emploi
Pour vous laisser douter un instant de mon zèle!
Attendons! . . . Ici même, à ce signal joyeux,
La belle et chaste enfant va paraître à vos yeux!

MÉPHISTOPHÉLÈS
Very well. I enjoy my newfound work so well
I would not have you say that I'm lacking in zeal!
You shall see!
Never fear, if you will wait right here,
That most enchanting maid very soon will appear!

Scene 5

(*Students and girls enter arm in arm, followed by musicians. The burghers and townspeople are behind them.*)

Waltz and Chorus

CHOEUR
Ainsi que la brise légère
Soulève en épais tourbillons
La poussière des sillons,

STUDENTS, YOUNG GIRLS
As the wind that whirls in the meadow,
May gather from over the plain

Swirls of dust and drifting grain,
Swirls of dust and drifting grain.
As the wind that whirls in the meadow
May gather from over the plain
Swirls of dust and drifting grain,
Swirls of dust and drifting grain,
So the waltz sweeps up the dancer,
Even earth-bound feet must answer
To the music's gay refrain,
To the music's gay refrain!
So the waltz sweeps up the dancer,
Even earth-bound feet must answer
To the music's gay refrain,
To the music's gay refrain.
(*the musicians get up on the tables, and the waltz begins*)

La poussière des sillons,
Ainsi que la brise légère
Soulève en épais tourbillons
La poussière des sillons,
La poussière des sillons.
Que la valse nous entraîne!
Faites retentir la plaine
De l'éclat de nos chansons,
De l'éclat de nos chansons!
Que la valse nous entraîne!
Faites retentir la plaine
De l'éclat de nos chansons,
De l'éclat de nos chansons!

MÉPHISTOPHÉLÈS (*to* FAUST)
See these lovely young ladies.
May I suggest that you offer one of these girls your arm?

MÉPHISTOPHÉLÈS
Vois ces filles
Gentilles!
Ne veux-tu pas
Aux plus belles
D'entre elles
Offrir ton bras?

FAUST
No! I've nothing to do with them,
Just leave me alone with my dreaming!

FAUST
Non! fais trêve
A ce ton moqueur!
Et laisse mon cœur
A son rêve! . . .

SIEBEL
Soon she will pass, and I shall see Marguerite.

SIEBEL
C'est par ici que doit passer
Marguerite!

A FEW GIRLS (*to* SIEBEL)
And must a young lady invite a young man to dance?

QUELQUES JEUNES FILLES
Faut-il qu'une fille à danser
Vous invite?

SIEBEL
No, No! I do not wish to dance!

SIEBEL
Non! . . . non! je ne veux pas valser! . . .

CHORUS (*the waltz continues*)
As the wind that whirls in the meadow
May gather from over the plain
Swirls of dust and drifting grain,
Swirls of dust and drifting grain,
So the waltz sweeps up the dancer,
Even earth-bound feet must answer
To the music's gay refrain,
To the music's gay refrain!
(MARGUERITE *enters and crosses the scene*)

CHOEUR
Ainsi que la brise légère
Soulève en épais tourbillons
La poussière des sillons,
La poussière des sillons.
Que la valse nous entraîne!
Faites retentir la plaine
De l'éclat de nos chansons!
De l'éclat de nos chansons!

FAUST
It is she, my vision!

FAUST
Ah! . . . la voici . . . c'est elle! . . .

MÉPHISTOPHÉLÈS
Come on! Don't be afraid!
(SIEBEL *approaches* MARGUERITE)

MÉPHISTOPHÉLÈS
Eh bien, aborde-là!

SIEBEL
Marguerite!
(MÉPHISTOPHÉLÈS *bars the way*)

SIEBEL
Marguerite! . . .

MÉPHISTOPHÉLÈS
Plaît-il! . . .

SIEBEL
Maudit homme! encor là! . . .

MÉPHISTOPHÉLÈS
Eh quoi! mon ami! vous voilà! . . .
Ah, vraiment, mon ami!

FAUST
Ne permettrez-vous pas, ma belle demoiselle,
Qu'on vous offre le bras pour faire le chemin?

MARGUERITE
Non, monsieur! je ne suis demoiselle, ni belle,
Et je n'ai pas besoin qu'on me donne la main.

FAUST
Pas le ciel! que de grâce . . . et quelle modestie! . . .
O belle enfant, je t'aime! . . .

SIEBEL
Elle est partie!

MÉPHISTOPHÉLÈS
Eh bien?

FAUST
On me repousse! . . .

MÉPHISTOPHÉLÈS
Allons! à tes amours
Je vois qu'il faut prêter secours! . . .

QUELQUES JEUNES FILLES
Qu'est-ce donc! . . .

DEUXIEME GROUPE DE JEUNES FILLES
Marguerite,
Qui de ce beau seigneur refuse la conduite! . . .

ETUDIANTS
Valsons encor!

JEUNES FILLES
Valsons toujours!

MÉPHISTOPHÉLÈS
What now?

SIEBEL
Oh, it's you. Go away!

MÉPHISTOPHÉLÈS
So you are still here!
Must you go? Ha ha! Too bad!
Must you go? Fare thee well.
(SIEBEL *recoils from* MÉPHISTOPHÉLÈS, *who chases him around the scene behind the dancers*)
(FAUST *approaches* MARGUERITE)

FAUST
Pray, do not think me bold, my fair and gentle maiden.
Will you not take my arm to keep you safe from harm?

MARGUERITE
No, My Lord. I am not such a fair or gentle maiden.
Pray forgive me, and leave me,
And I shall find my way without your guiding arm.

FAUST (*gazing after her*)
By the gods! She is lovely. So modest and so charming!
Beautiful maid,
I love you, I love you forever!

SIEBEL (*coming back*)
She did not see me.

MÉPHISTOPHÉLÈS (*to* FAUST)
What luck?

FAUST
She's gone! She would not have me.

MÉPHISTOPHÉLÈS (*laughing*)
Oho! I know the cure!
It is time that you learned the techniques of amour!
(*he goes off with* FAUST *in the direction taken by* MARGUERITE)

SOME YOUNG GIRLS (*who have observed the scene between* FAUST *and* MARGUERITE)
What is this?

OTHER YOUNG GIRLS
Marguerite would not allow a handsome noble to escort her.

STUDENTS
Let's dance, let's dance,
Let's dance, let's dance once more!

ALL
Let's dance, let's dance,
Let's dance, let's dance once more!
(*the waltz is repeated*)

ACT III

Scene 1

Marguerite's Garden

(*A wall at back, with a little door. A bower at left, a pavilion at right with a window toward the audience. Trees and shrubs, etc.*)

(SIEBEL *enters, and stops by a clump of roses and lilies.*)

Intermezzo and Song

SIEBEL

Let these flowers convey
What I would say!
Let their beauty remind her
How much fairer I find her,
Let each petal declare
The love I bear!
Lovely blossoms convey
What I would say!
When she holds you before her,
Tell her how I adore her,
That no flower can be
As fair as she!
(*he picks a flower*)
It's withered!
(*throws it away*)
It's just as that stranger foretold
When he read my hand.
(*he picks another flower, which also withers*)
If my hand touches any flower,
It withers and dies!
What if I dip my hand in holy water?
(*he dips his fingers in a little font attached to the wall*)
It's here that Marguerite
Comes to pray every evening.
I'll try again.
Here's a flower
(*he picks two or three*)
Will it be withered? No!
The spell passes away!
Let these flowers convey
What I would say!
Let their beauty remind her
How much fairer I find her,
Let each petal declare
The love I bear.
Lovely blossoms, convey
What I would say!
When she holds you before her,
Tell her how I adore her,

SIEBEL

Faites-lui mes aveux,
Portez mes vœux,
Fleurs écloses près d'elle,
Dites-lui qu'elle est belle . . .
Que mon cœur nuit et jour
Languit d'amour!
Révélez à son âme
Le secret de ma flamme!
Qu'il s'exhale avec vous
Parfums plus doux! . . .

Fanée! . . . hélas!
Ce sorcier que Dieu damne
M'a porté malheur!
Je ne puis sans qu'elle se fane
Toucher une fleur! . . .
Si je trempais mes doigts dans l'eau bénite? . . .
C'est là que chaque soir vient prier Marguerite!
Voyons maintenant! voyons vite! . . .

Elles se fanent? . . . Non! . . .
Satan, je ris de toi . . .
C'est en vous que j'ai toi;
Parlez pour moi!
Qu'elle puisse connaître
L'ardeur qu'elle a fait naître,
Et dont mon cœur troublé
N'a point parlé!
Si l'amour l'effarouche,
Que la fleur sur sa bouche
Sache au moins déposer
Un doux baiser! . . .

That no flower can be
As fair as she.
Lovely blossoms, tell her this:
That I send, I send a kiss!

Scene 2

FAUST
C'est ici?

MÉPHISTOPHÉLÈS
Suivez-moi!

FAUST
Que regardes-tu là?

MÉPHISTOPHÉLÈS
Siebel, votre rival.

FAUST
Siebel!

MÉPHISTOPHÉLÈS
Chut! . . . le voilà!

SIEBEL
Mon bouquet n'est-il pas charmant?

MÉPHISTOPHÉLÈS
Charmant!

SIEBEL
Victoire!
Je lui raconterai demain toute l'histoire;
Et, si l'on veut savoir le secret de mon cœur,
Un baiser lui dira le reste!

MÉPHISTOPHÉLÈS
Séducteur!

(MÉPHISTOPHÉLÈS *and* FAUST *enter cautiously.*)

FAUST
Is it here?

MÉPHISTOPHÉLÈS
Follow me.

FAUST (*seeing* SIEBEL *across the scene*)
Is that someone you know?

MÉPHISTOPHÉLÈS
Siebel. He is your rival.

FAUST
Siebel!

MÉPHISTOPHÉLÈS
Hush! Here he comes.
(*they conceal themselves*)

SIEBEL (*with a bouquet*)
Was there ever a flower so sweet?

MÉPHISTOPHÉLÈS (*aside*)
So sweet!

SIEBEL
I'll tell her how I defied
The evil spell of that wicked stranger,
And then I shall reveal all the love in my heart!
One kiss, then she will know I love her!

MÉPHISTOPHÉLÈS (*aside*)
What a man!
(SIEBEL *fastens the bouquet to the pavilion door and exits*)

Scene 3

MÉPHISTOPHÉLÈS
Attendez-moi là, cher docteur!
Pour tenir compagnie aux fleurs de votre élève,
Je vais vous chercher un trésor
Plus merveilleux, plus riche encor
Que tous ceux qu'elle voit en rêve!

FAUST
Laisse-moi!

MÉPHISTOPHÉLÈS
You wait for me here for a while.
We must bring her a gift, a nice expensive present,
To make her forget his bouquet.
Something so fine, so rich and rare
That her young heart will be enchanted.

FAUST
Then go!

MÉPHISTOPHÉLÈS
I obey. Wait here till I return.
(*he goes*)

MÉPHISTOPHÉLÈS
J'obéis! . . . daignez m'attendre ici.

Scene 4

(FAUST *alone*)

Cavatina

FAUST
Ah, what is this long-forgotten yearning?
It is love and its rapture returning!
O Marguerita! Take my heart for your own!
To you, the home of my beloved,
To you I bring my heart's devotion,
Here in the beauty of her presence,
The shrine of an angel from heaven!
What hidden treasures in this humble place!
What happy dreams, what wealth of joy and grace!
What hidden treasures lie within this place,
What happy dreams, what wealth of joy and grace!
Kind creation, ah, here you bloomed in full perfection!
This garden was the glade where the sun
Sent his brightness to shine from her eyes.
Here, through the hours of darkness,
Heaven sent its radiant starlight
To crown a mortal maid,
To form her like an angel
Sent down from the skies.
To you here, to you!
To you the home of my beloved,
To you I bring my heart's devotion,
Here in the beauty of her presence.
The shrine of an angel from heaven!
To you, the home of my beloved,
Here in the beauty of her presence,
The shrine of an angel sent from heaven!

FAUST
Quel trouble inconnu me pénètre!
Je sens l'amour s'emparer de mon être.
O Marguerite! à tes pieds me voici!
Salut! demeure chaste et pure, où se devine
La présence d'une âme innocente et divine! . . .
Que de richesse en cette pauvreté!
En ce réduit, que de félicité! . . .

O nature, c'est là que tu la fis si belle!
C'est là que cette enfant a dormi sous ton aile,
A grandi sous tes yeux.
Là que, de ton haleine enveloppant son âme,
Tu fis avec amour épanouir la femme
En cet ange des cieux!
C'est là, oui, c'est là!
Salut! demeure chaste et pure, où se devine
La présence d'une âme innocente et divine! . . .
Salut! demeure chaste et pure, où se devine
La présence d'une âme innocente et divine! . . .

Scene 5

(MÉPHISTOPHÉLÈS *returns, carrying a jewel case*)

MÉPHISTOPHÉLÈS
Wake up, sir, she is here!
If she ignores our gift and takes the flowers,
What's the use of my satanic powers!
(*he opens the case and shows the jewels*)

MÉPHISTOPHÉLÈS
Alerte! la voilà! . . . Si le bouquet l'emporte
Sur l'écrin, je consens à perdre mon pouvoir!

FAUST
Fuyons! . . . je veux ne jamais la revoir!

MÉPHISTOPHÉLÈS
Quel scrupule vous prend! . . .
Sur le seuil de la porte,
Voici l'écrin placé! . . . venez! . . . j'ai bon espoir!

FAUST
Oh come! I cannot approach such a maid!

MÉPHISTOPHÉLÈS
Put your conscience to sleep!
(he puts the jewel case at the door of the pavilion)
When she comes to the garden
Our gift will catch her eye, and soon you'll be repaid!
*(*MÉPHISTOPHÉLÈS *leads* FAUST *away, and they hide in the garden.* MARGUERITE *enters through the little door, and comes silently to the front)*

Scene 6

The King of Thule

MARGUERITE
Je voudrais bien savoir quel était ce jeune homme,
Si c'est un grand seigneur, et comment il se nomme?
"Il était un roi de Thulé,
Qui, jusqu' à la tombe fidèle,
Eut, en souvenir de sa belle,
Une coupe en or ciselé! . . ."
Il avait bonne grâce, à ce qu'il m'a semblé.
"Nul trésor n'avait plus de charmes!
Dans les grands jours il s'en servait,
Et chaque fois qu'il y buvait,
Ses yeux se remplissaient de larmes! . . ."
"Quand il sentit venir la mort,
Etendu sur sa froide couche,
Pour la porter jusqu'à sa bouche
Sa main fit un suprême effort! . . ."
Je ne savais que dire, et j'ai rougi d'abord.
"Et puis, en l'honneur de sa dame,
Il but un dernière fois;
La coupe trembla dans ses doigts.
Et doucement il rendit l'âme!"
Les grands seigneurs ont seuls des airs si résolus,
Avec cette douceur.
Allons! n'y pensons plus!
Cher Valentin, si Dieu m'écoute,
Je te reverrai! . . . me voilà
Toute seule! . . .

MARGUERITE
I wish I knew the name of that young handsome stranger.
I wonder who he was . . . how he came to address me!
(she sits down at her spinning wheel in the pavilion and as she spins she sings an old ballad)
"Once there lived a king of Thule
Faithful all his life to his lady,
Ever guarding the golden cup
Of his loved one, long long away."
(she interrupts herself)
He behaved like a noble, but still he was so kind . . .
(resuming the song)
"More than crown and more than his treasure
This precious goblet was to him,
And when he filled it to the brim,
His tears would overflow its measure."
(she rises and moves away from the spinning wheel)
"Then, when he knew his days were past,
On his cold, narrow deathbed lying,
He took the cup as he lay dying,
For the drink that would be his last."
(interrupting herself)
I knew that I was blushing. I could not say a word!
(resuming)
"One drink to his long-lost beloved,
One drink to his fair young bride!
Then he laid her goblet aside,
And so the faithful king lay down and died!"
Only a lord could speak with such a lordly air and yet with so much grace.
(she goes back toward the pavilion.)
Ah well! No more of that!
I'm so alone, I wish my brother could be here with me.
I am lonely without him.

(*she sees* SIEBEL'*s bouquet*)
A bouquet!
(*she takes it up*)
It was Siebel who brought it!
Poor faithful child!
(*she sees the jewel case*)
But what is this?
What is this pretty jewel case doing here? It can't be for me.
Do I dare? Here is the key for it.
I'd like to try.
I am trembling! But why?
It could not be so wrong just to see what is in it.
(*she opens the jewel case and drops the bouquet*)
Oh, heaven! What lovely jewels!
Are there truly such jewels in the world, or am I dreaming?
Whoever could believe there could be such treasure?
(*she puts the jewel case on a seat, then kneels in order to examine them*)
If I dared, if I dared,
I would see how it feels
To wear these golden earrings.
(*she takes out the earrings*)
Ah! But here, underneath,
I see a little mirror, made of gold.
Why not pretend I am a lady?
Why not, only for a moment?
(*she puts on the earrings, rises and looks at herself in the mirror*)

Un bouquet!
C'est de Siebel sans doute!
Pauvre garçon!

Que vois-je là?
D'où ce riche coffret peut-il venir? Je n'ose
Y toucher et pourtant . . . —
Voici la clef, je crois! . . .
Si je l'ouvrais! . . . ma main tremble! . . . Pourquoi!
Je ne fais, en l'ouvrant, rien de mal, je suppose! . . .

O Dieu! que de bijoux! . . . est-ce un rêve charmant
Qui m'éblouit, ou si je veille!—
Mes yeux n'ont jamais vu de richesse pareille! . . .
Si j'osais seulement
Me parer un moment
De ces pendants d'oreille!
Ah! Voici tout justement,
Au fond de la cassette,
Un miroir! . . . comment
N'être pas coquette?
N'être pas coquette?

Jewel Song

Ah, I see
Beauty that is smiling back to me.
Ah, I see
Beauty that is smiling back to me.
Is it true?
Marguerite, is it you?
Can it be? Answer me!
Tell me, tell me am I dreaming?
No, no! What can this mean?
No! How could you be Marguerite?
You are more like a queen.
You're as fair as a queen!
What can this mean?
What can this mean?
You are dressed like a queen!
Hail to Queen Marguerite!
Ah, could he look at me,
Dressed as I want to be!
Now if I could be near him,
Now I would wait to hear him.

Ah! je ris de me voir
Si belle en ce miroir! . . .
Ah! je ris de me voir
Si belle en ce miroir! . . .
Est-ce toi,
Marguerite? Est-ce toi?
Réponds-moi, réponds-moi,
Réponds, réponds, réponds vite!
Non! non! ce n'est plus toi!
Non, non, ce n'est plus ton visage;
C'est la fille d'un roi,
C'est la fille d'un roi,
Ce n'est plus toi,
Ce n'est plus toi,
C'est la fille d'un roi,
Qu'on salue au passage!
Ah! S'il était ici!
S'il me voyait ainsi!
Comme une demoiselle
Il me trouverait belle.
Ah! Comme une demoiselle
Il me trouverait belle!
Comme une demoiselle
Il me trouverait belle.
Achevons la metamorphose.
Il me tarde encor d'essayer

Le bracelet et le collier!
Dieu! c'est comme une main
Qui sur mon bras se pose! Ah! ah!

Ah! And one so high above me
Might begin to love me!
Now if I could be near him,
Now I would wait to hear him.
If my lord could only behold me,
See me with the gold and the gems
And with the bracelet on my arm!
(*she puts on the necklace and the bracelets and rises*)
Ah, it is like a hand
Laid on my arm to hold me!

Ah! je ris de me voir
Si belle en ce miroir
Ah! je ris de me voir
Si belle en ce miroir!
Est-ce toi,
Marguerite, Est-ce toi?
Réponds-moi, réponds-moi,
Réponds, réponds, réponds vite!
Ah! S'il était ici!
S'il me voyait ainsi!
Comme une demoiselle
Il me trouverait belle!
Ah comme une demoiselle
Il me trouverait belle!
Comme une demoiselle
Il me trouverait belle!
Marguerite ce n'est plus toi,
Ce n'est plus ton visage!
Non! c'est la fille d'un roi
Qu'on salue au passage!

Ah, I see
Beauty that is smiling back to me!
Ah, I see
Beauty that is smiling back to me!
Is it true?
Marguerite, is it you?
Can it be? Answer me!
Tell me, tell me am I dreaming?
Ah, could he look at me,
Dressed as I want to be!
Now, if I could be near him,
Now I would wait to hear him!
Ah! And one so high above me
Might begin to love me!
Now, if I could be near him
Now I would wait to hear him!
Marguerite, what can this mean?
Whose is the image before you?
Ah! You're as fair as a queen
And your king would adore you!

Scene 7

(MARTHE *enters*)

Quartet

MARTHE
Que vois-je, Seigneur Dieu! . . . comme vous voilà belle,
Mon ange! . . .—D'où vous vient ce riche écrin?

MARGUERITE
Hélas!
On l'aura par mégarde apporté!

MARTHE
Que non pas!
Ces bijoux sont à vous, ma chère demoiselle!
Oui! c'est là le cadeau d'un seigneur amoureux!
Mon cher époux jadis était moins généreux!

MARTHE
I declare! How lovely!
How beautiful you look, Marguerite!
How on earth did you get these?

MARGUERITE
Oh dear!
I'm afraid they were sent by mistake.

MARTHE
Not at all!
I am sure they're for you, my pretty little lady.
Yes my dear, your admirer must be very rich.
(*she sighs*)
I never had such gifts from that husband of mine!

Scene 8

(MÉPHISTOPHÉLÈS *and* FAUST *enter.*)

MÉPHISTOPHÉLÈS
Is Madame Marthe Schwerlein at home?

MARTHE
Who is calling?

MÉPHISTOPHÉLÈS
I hope you will excuse this unexpected call
(*aside to* FAUST)
You can see that the jewels are just to her taste.
(*to* MARTHE)
Are you Madame Schwerlein?

MARTHE
I am.

MÉPHISTOPHÉLÈS
I must bring you painful tidings
And news that will sadden your heart.
Your absent husband is dead,
And sends you his blessings.

MARTHE
Lord in heaven!

MARGUERITE
What is that?

MÉPHISTOPHÉLÈS
Nothing!
(*as* MÉPHISTOPHÉLÈS *looks at her,* MARGUERITE *lowers her eyes, and hastens to take off the jewels and put them back in the case*)

MARTHE
Ah, what shall I do?
Ah, this news is so sudden!

MARGUERITE (*aside*)
All my heart seems to tremble
with the joy of its beating!

FAUST (*aside*)
The fever dies away in the joy of this meeting.

MÉPHISTOPHÉLÈS (*to* MARTHE)
Ah yes, your husband
Is dead and sends his greeting.

MARTHE (*to* MÉPHISTOPHÉLÈS)
You're certain he sent nothing more?

MÉPHISTOPHÉLÈS
No. That being the case, why not, this very day, this very hour,
Go out and find another husband?

FAUST (*to* MARGUERITE)
Why remove your beautiful jewels?

MÉPHISTOPHÉLÈS
Dame Marthe Schwerlein, s'il vous plait?

MARTHE
Qui m'appelle?

MÉPHISTOPHÉLÈS
Pardon d'oser ainsi nous présenter chez vous!
Vous voyez qu'elle a fait bel accueil aux bijoux?
Dame Marthe Schwerlein?

MARTHE
Me voici!

MÉPHISTOPHÉLÈS
La nouvelle
Que j'apporte n'est pas pour vous mettre en gaité:—
Votre mari, madame, est mort et vous salue!

MARTHE
Ah! . . . grand Dieu! . . .

MARGUERITE
Qu'est ce donc?

MÉPHISTOPHÉLÈS
Rien! . . .

MARTHE
O calamité!
O nouvelle imprévue! . . .

MARGUERITE
Malgré moi mon cœur tremble et tressaille à sa vue!

FAUST
La fièvre de mes sens se dissipe à sa vue!

MÉPHISTOPHÉLÈS
Votre mari, madame, est mort et vous salue!

MARTHE
Ne m'apportez-vous rien de lui?

MÉPHISTOPHÉLÈS
Rien! . . . et, pour le punir, il faut dès aujourd'hui
Chercher quelqu'un qui le remplace!

FAUST
Pourquoi donc quitter ces bijoux?

MARGUERITE
Ces bijoux ne sont pas à moi!
. . . Laissez, de grâce!

MÉPHISTOPHÉLÈS
Que ne serait heureux
d'échanger avec vous
La bague d'hyménée?

MARTHE
Ah, bah!
Plait-il?

MÉPHISTOPHÉLÈS
Hélas! cruelle destinée! . . .

FAUST
Prenez mon bras un moment!

MARGUERITE
Laissez! . . . Je vous en conjure! . . .

MÉPHISTOPHÉLÈS
Votre bras! . . .

MARTHE
Il est charmant!

MÉPHISTOPHÉLÈS
La voisine est un peu mûre!
La voisine est un peu mûre!

MARGUERITE
Je vous en conjure.

MARTHE
Quelle noble allure.

FAUST
Âme douce et pure.

MÉPHISTOPHÉLÈS
Elle est un peu mûre.

MARTHE
Ainsi vous voyagez toujours?

MÉPHISTOPHÉLÈS
Dure nécessité, madame!
Sans amis, sans parents! . . .
sans femme.

MARTHE
Cela sied encore aux beaux jours!
Mais plus tard, combien il est triste
De vieillir seul, en égoïste!

MÉPHISTOPHÉLÈS
J'ai frémi souvent, j'en conviens,
Devant cette horrible pensée!

MARTHE
Avant que l'heure en soit passée!
Digne seigneur, songez-y bien!

MARGUERITE
But they do not belong to me.
Ah no! I must not wear them.

MÉPHISTOPHÉLÈS (*to* MARTHE)
Who would not thrill with joy if he dreamed
He might place his ring upon your finger?

MARTHE (*aside*)
Ah, bah!
(*to* MÉPHISTOPHÉLÈS)
You were saying . . . ?

MÉPHISTOPHÉLÈS (*sighing*)
Alas, that fate can be so cruel!

FAUST (*to* MARGUERITE)
May I not give you my arm?

MARGUERITE (*drawing away*)
Oh no, oh no! I entreat you!

MÉPHISTOPHÉLÈS (*offering his arm to* MARTHE)
My arm . . .

MARTHE
How very kind!

MÉPHISTOPHÉLÈS (*aside*)
She is just a trifle faded,
But she's easily persuaded!
(MARGUERITE *takes* FAUST'S *arm and they move away together from* MÉPHISTOPHÉLÈS *and* MARTHE)

MARGUERITE
Please, you must excuse me!

MARTHE (*with* MÉPHISTOPHÉLÈS)
See how he pursues me!

FAUST (*to* MARGUERITE)
Ah, do not refuse me!

MÉPHISTOPHÉLÈS
See how she pursues me!

MARTHE (*to* MÉPHISTOPHÉLÈS)
You say you travel all the time?

MÉPHISTOPHÉLÈS
I must. I haven't any choice about it,
I haven't any choice.
Not a friend, nor a home, nor loved ones!

MARTHE
That's all right as long as you're young.
Later on, ah then . . . what thought is so hateful
As growing old with none to love you,
No one to befriend you!

MÉPHISTOPHÉLÈS
I have trembled many a time
At that same appalling idea!

MARTHE
Then while you still have time for thinking,
You would be wise to think of that.

Now while you still have time for thinking,
Make up your mind.
Oh, think it over while you can.

MÉPHISTOPHÉLÈS
Yes, yes indeed!

MARTHE
Make up your mind!

MÉPHISTOPHÉLÈS
Yes, yes indeed! Indeed I will!
(*they walk away together.* FAUST *and* MARGUERITE *re-enter from the garden*)

FAUST (*to* MARGUERITE)
My dear, you're alone then?

MARGUERITE
My brother's a soldier,
And I've lost my mother.
Then . . . bitterest sorrow of all . . .
Then my dear little sister died.
Poor angel! Poor angel! I loved her very dearly.
I cared for nobody but her.
I lived for nobody but her.
How I prayed for her! How I sorrowed!
But when our hearts are overburdened,
It is death that must bring release!
Ah! When our hearts are overburdened,
It is death that must bring release!
In the morning when she woke,
There she would lie, calling me to come.
Her only love was Marguerite.
And today, if I could but see her,
I would bear it all once again!

FAUST
If this child, by the grace of heaven,
Was as gentle and pure as you,
She was an angel, an angel! Yes, that I know.

MARGUERITE
That is not true.

FAUST
Yes, you're an angel.

MARGUERITE
That is not so.
How can that be so?
Inwardly, I know,
You must laugh to hear me!
I know it is wrong,
Wrong for you to stay.
It is wrong, I fear me,
Very wrong, I fear me.
It's wrong, yet I'm longing
To keep you near me!

MÉPHISTOPHÉLÈS
J'y songerai!

MARTHE
Songez-y bien!

MÉPHISTOPHÉLÈS
J'y songerai, j'y songerai!

FAUST
Eh quoi! toujours seule? . . .

MARGUERITE
Mon frère
Est soldat; j'ai perdu ma mère;
Puis ce fut un autre malheur,
Je perdis ma petite sœur!
Pauvre ange! . . . Elle m'était bien chère! . . .
C'était mon unique souci;
Que de soins, hélas! . . . que de peines!
C'est quand nos âmes en sont pleines
Que la mort nous les prend ainsi! . . .
Sitôt qu'elle s'éveillait, vite
Il fallait que je fusse là! . . .
Elle n'aimait que Marguerite!
Pour la voir, la pauvre petite,
Je reprendrais bien tout cela! . . .

FAUST
Si le ciel, avec un sourire,
L'avait faite semblable à toi,
C'était un ange! . . . Oui, je le crois! . . .

MARGUERITE
Vous moquez-vous! . . .

FAUST
Non! je t'admire!

MARGUERITE
Je ne vous crois pas
Et de moi tout bas
Vous riez sans doute! . . .
J'ai tort de rester
Pour vous écouter! . . .
Et pourtant j'écoute! . . .

MARTHE
Vous n'entendez pas,
Ou de moi tout bas
Vous riez sans doute!
Avant d'écouter,
Pourquoi vous hâter
De vous mettre en route?

MARTHE (*to* MÉPHISTOPHÉLÈS)
I don't think you heard.
You are very rude,
Laughing up your sleeve now.
Do you have to go?
When you laugh I know
You don't care to hear me.
It won't take you long
To hear what I say.
Must you run away?
Won't you stay and hear me?

FAUST
Non, non, je t'admire.
Laisse-moi ton bras! . . .
Dieu ne m'a-t-il pas
Conduit sur ta route? . . .
Pourquoi redouter,
Hélas! d'écouter? . . .
Mon cœur parle; écoute? . . .

FAUST (*to* MARGUERITE)
Yes, yes, you're an angel!
Ah, do you not know?
Heaven led me to you,
And how can you fear me?
But why is it wrong, my dear,
If you say I may stay?
Ah, why won't you say I may stay?
My heart begs you to hear me!

MÉPHISTOPHÉLÈS
Ne m'accusez pas,
Si je dois, hélas!
Me remettre en route.
Faut-il attester
Qu'on voudrait rester
Quand on vous écoute?

MÉPHISTOPHÉLÈS (*to* MARTHE)
Every single word!
Do not think me rude if I
Should say that I must leave now.
Now it's time to go.
Now, alas, alas, I must
Be on my way, I fear me!
You've got to believe what I say:
I would rather stay here
Where you are near me.

MARGUERITE
Retirez-vous! . . . voici la nuit.

MARGUERITE
It's growing late, and you must go.

FAUST
Chère âme!

FAUST (*puts his arm around her*)
My darling!

MARGUERITE
Laissez-moi!

MARGUERITE
You must go.
(*she slips from him and goes out*)

FAUST
Quoi! méchante! . . . on me fuit!

FAUST
Ah, beloved, must we part?
(*he goes after her*)

MÉPHISTOPHÉLÈS
L'entretien devient trop tendre!
Esquivons-nous!

MÉPHISTOPHÉLÈS
What a tender conversation! We must be off!
(*he hides behind a tree*)

MARTHE
Comment m'y prendre?
Eh bien! il est parti! . . .
Seigneur! . . .

MARTHE
How can I hold him! Oh dear! He's gone away!
My Lord! But My Lord!
(*exits, looking for* MÉPHISTOPHÉLÈS)

MÉPHISTOPHÉLÈS
Oui! Cours après moi! . . .
Ouf! cette vieille impitoyable
De force ou de gré, je crois,

MÉPHISTOPHÉLÈS
The hunt is on! Ouf!
That relentless old pursuer

Is so hell-bent on marrying
She would even wed the devil!

Allait épouser le diable!

FAUST (*outside*)
Marguerite! Marguerite!

FAUST
Marguerite! Marguerite!

MARTHE (*outside*)
Ah, My Lord! Ah, My Lord!

MARTHE
Cher seigneur! Cher seigneur.

MÉPHISTOPHÉLÈS
Au revoir.

MÉPHISTOPHÉLÈS
Serviteur!

Scene 9

MÉPHISTOPHÉLÈS (*alone*)
It was high time! Here comes the loving couple
To walk under the trees in the darkness.
All's well!
Let us leave them alone to the night and to love!
O Night, spread out your wings above them!
O Love, take from their hearts every thought of remorse!
And now let all the flowers of night blossom under my hand!
Let their forbidden perfume
Overwhelm the innocent heart of Marguerite!
(*he disappears in the shadows*)

MÉPHISTOPHÉLÈS
Il était temps! sous le feuillage sombre
Voici nos amoureux que reviennent! . . .
C'est bien!
Gardons nous de troubler un si doux entretien!
O nuit, étends sur eux ton ombre!
Amour, ferme leur âme aux remords importuns!
Et vous, fleurs aux subtils parfums,
Epanouissez-vous sous cette main maudite!
Achevez de troubler le cœur de Marguerite! . . .

Scene 10

(FAUST *and* MARGUERITE *in the garden*)

Duet

MARGUERITE
Now you must go. Adieu!

MARGUERITE
Il se fait tard! adieu!

FAUST
Ah, must I leave you now, so soon!
Give me your hand, let me hold it in mine.
Stay, my dear, stay and hear
What my heart has to tell you!
How I feel the enchantment of your lovely eyes!
Now the pale evening star
Peers through the darkening skies,
Striving to surpass your beauty,
And failing, must worship from afar!

FAUST
Quoi! je t'implore en vain!
Attends! laisse ma main s'oublier dans la tienne!
Laisse-moi, laisse-moi contempler ton visage
Sous la pâle clarté
Dont l'astre de la nuit, comme dans un nuage,
Caresse ta beauté! . . .

MARGUERITE
Oh, the wonder! Oh, the joy of the night's deep enchantment!
You and I here together from the world apart!
In the spell of this night I hear and understand
All the meaning of the music,

MARGUERITE
O silence! ô bonheur! ineffable mystère!
Enivrante langueur!
J'écoute! . . . Et je comprends cette voix solitaire
Qui chante dans mon cœur!
Laissez un peu, de grâce! . . .

FAUST
Qu'est-ce donc?

MARGUERITE
Un simple jeu!
Laissez un peu!

FAUST
Que dit ta bouche à voix
basse! . . .

MARGUERITE
Il m'aime!—Il ne m'aime pas!—
Il m'aime!—pas!—Il m'aime!—
pas!—Il m'aime!

FAUST
Oui! . . . crois en cette fleur
éclose sous tes pas! . . .
Qu'elle soit pour ton cœur
l'oracle du ciel même! . . .
Il t'aime! . . . comprends-tu
ce mot sublime et doux? . . .
Aimer! porter en nous
Une ardeur toujours nouvelle!
. . .
Nous enivrer sans fin d'une joie
éternelle!

MARGUERITE, FAUST
Eternelle! . . . Eternelle! . . .

FAUST
O nuit d'amour . . . ciel
radieux! . . .
O douces flammes! . . .
Le bonheur silencieux
Verse les cieux
Dans nos deux âmes! . . .

MARGUERITE
Je veux t'aimer et te chérir!
Parle encore!
Je t'appartiens! . . . je
t'adore! . . .
Pour toi je veux mourir! . . .

FAUST
Marguerite! Marguerite!

MARGUERITE
Ah! partez! Ah! partez!

FAUST
Cruelle!

MARGUERITE
Je chancelle!

The music that sings within my heart.
(*taking her hand away from his*)
Now turn away one moment.
(*she picks a daisy*)

FAUST
What is this?

MARGUERITE
A little game. Just wait and you shall see.
(*she plucks the daisy's petals*)

FAUST
What is this game that you are playing?

MARGUERITE
He loves me, he loves me not.
He loves me . . . not! He loves me . . . not!
He loves me!

FAUST
Yes, believe in your flower,
It tells you what is true.
Let it be to your heart a messenger from heaven!
I love you! Do you know the meaning of that word?
To love! To feel the flame of desire beyond denying,
Knowing the sweet delight of a joy never-dying!

MARGUERITE, FAUST
Love undying! Love undying!

FAUST
O star of love serene and bright,
Shine down and hold us
In the sweet spell of the night.
Love's tender light,
Forevermore enfold us!

MARGUERITE
Take all my love,
I lay my heart here before you,
I only live to adore you,
To live or die with you.
Darling! I adore you!
Ah, I implore you
To let me live or die,
To live or die with you!

FAUST
Marguerite! Marguerite!
(*she tears herself away from his embrace*)

MARGUERITE
You must go! You must go!

FAUST
I beg you!

MARGUERITE
You must leave me.

FAUST
How can I leave you now?

MARGUERITE
Oh my dear!

FAUST
I beg you!

MARGUERITE
Oh my dear, leave me now!

FAUST
I cannot leave you now!

MARGUERITE
Leave me now! Go now, go now, ah, I implore you,
Go now, I beg you, my love, my life!
Ah, do not break the heart of Marguerite!

FAUST
Ah, let me stay, Marguerite, my love, my life!
(she kneels before him imploringly)
O sweet and tender maid,
Pure as an angel,
Your gentle virtue
Has triumphed over my desire.
I obey. But tomorrow . . .

MARGUERITE
Yes, tomorrow, yes, tomorrow,
And all the days . . .

FAUST
Before I leave you,
Repeat the word I long to hear.
Do you love me?

MARGUERITE
Adieu!
(she enters the pavilion. As she goes she blows a kiss to FAUST*)*

FAUST
O joy surpassing heaven! Ah, farewell!
(he starts for the garden door. MÉPHISTOPHÉLÈS *bars his way)*

FAUST
Me séparer de toi!

MARGUERITE
Laissez-moi!

FAUST
Cruelle!

MARGUERITE
Laissez-moi! Laissez-moi!

FAUST
Me séparer de toi!

MARGUERITE
Laissez-moi! partez, partez, ah, partez vite . . .
Partez, je tremble, hélas! . . . j'ai peur!
Ne brisez pas le cœur de Marguerite!

FAUST
Vois ma douleur, Marguerite! Vois ma douleur!
Divine pureté!
Chaste innocence,
Dont la puissance
Triomphe de ma volonté!
J'obéis! mais demain . . .

MARGUERITE
Oui, demain! . . . dès l'aurore!

FAUST
Un mot encore! . . .
Répète-moi ce doux aveu!
Tu m'aimes!

MARGUERITE
Adieu! . . .

FAUST
Félicité du ciel . . . Ah . . . fuyons . . .

Scene 11

MÉPHISTOPHÉLÈS
What a lover!

FAUST
Did you overhear?

MÉPHISTOPHÉLÈS
Just by chance.
Oh, Doctor dear, it seems to me
That you need to go back to school again!

MÉPHISTOPHÉLÈS
Tête folle! . . .

FAUST
Tu nous écoutais?

MÉPHISTOPHÉLÈS
Par bonheur.
Vous auriez grand besoin, docteur,
Qu'on vous renvoyât à l'école.

FAUST
Laisse-moi.

MÉPHISTOPHÉLÈS
Daignez seulement
Ecouter un moment
Ce qu'elle va conter aux étoiles, cher maître.
Tenez; elle ouvre sa fenêtre.

FAUST
Let me be!

MÉPHISTOPHÉLÈS
I think we should stay here and listen a while.
She may confide her thoughts to the stars, dear Master!
Look there! She opens her window!
(MARGUERITE *opens the window of the pavilion and gazes out*)

Scene 12

MARGUERITE
Il m'aime; . . . quel trouble en mon cœur,
L'oiseau chante! . . . le vent murmure! . . .
Toutes les voix de la nature
Semblent me répéter en chœur:
Il t'aime! . . . —Ah! qu'il est doux de vivre! . . .
Le ciel me sourit; . . . l'air m'enivre! . . .

Est-ce de plaisir et d'amour
Que la feuille tremble et palpite? . . .
Demain? . . . —Ah! presse ton retour,
Cher bien-aimé! . . .
viens! . . .

MARGUERITE
He loves me! He loves me! O wonderful world!
Birds are singing,
The winds are sighing.
All the sweet voices of nature
Join the chorus of joy!
He loves me! He loves me! Ah, it is good to be alive!
The stars smiling down, the scent of flowers, the scent of flowers!
Can it be the power of love
That is causing the leaves to tremble?
Tomorrow, tomorrow! Ah, must I wait so long,
Love of my life! Come! Come!
(FAUST *rushes to the window*)

FAUST
Marguerite! . . .

MÉPHISTOPHÉLÈS
Ho! ho!

FAUST
Marguerite!

MÉPHISTOPHÉLÈS
Ho!
(MARGUERITE *gives herself to* FAUST'S *embrace.* MÉPHISTOPHÉLÈS *laughs loudly and cynically as he leaves the garden. The curtain falls*)

ACT IV

Scene 1

(MARGUERITE *at her spinning wheel.*)

MARGUERITE
They've left me all alone, all the friends whom I laughed with in days gone by. But now . . .

YOUNG GIRLS (*outside*)
The gallant stranger ran away,
He's running still.
(*they laugh*)

MARGUERITE
Ah, they were hiding! Oh, how cruel!
Yet I must confess that I used to speak with scorn
Of the sins of girls I've known.
Now comes the day
When the world has no pity for my own.
And now it is I who must weep!
When I sinned, heaven knows I had no thought of evil.
I let my foolish heart persuade me, I gave all the world away for love!

He will not return,
He will not return!
I tremble and cry
While the days go by
And still no reply!
He will not return.

Oh, where can he be?
Here at my window
I wait and I yearn
For my love's return.
Alas! Oh where can he be?
He will not return.

I dare not complain,
Concealing my pain
And hiding my tears,
My hopes and my fears.
If my love could learn
What has become of me!
Oh, where can he be?
He will not return.

Ah, to see him!
How long must I await
His step on the street,

MARGUERITE
Elles ne sont plus là . . . je riais avec elles
Autrefois . . . maintenant . . .

SOPRANES
Le galant étranger s'enfuit
Et court encor! Ah! ah!

MARGUERITE
Elles se cachaient! ah! cruelles!
Je ne trouvais pas d'outrage assez fort, jadis,
Pour les péchés des autres!
Un jour vient
Où l'on est sans pitié pour les nôtres!
Je ne suis que honte à mon tour!
Et pourtant Dieu le sait, je n'étais pas infâme.
Tout ce qui t'entraîna, mon âme,
N'était que tendresse et qu'amour!

Il ne revient pas,
Il ne revient pas!
J'ai peur, je frissonne;
Je languis, hélas!
En vain l'heure sonne;
Il ne revient pas!

Où donc peut-il être?
Seule a ma fenêtre,
Je plonge là-bas
Mon regard, hélas, hélas!
Où donc peut-il être?
Il ne revient pas.

Je n'ose me plaindre,
Il faut me contraindre!
Je pleure tout bas,
Je pleure tout bas.
S'il pouvait connaître
Ma douleur! hélas!
Où donc peut-il être?
Il ne revient pas!

Oh! le voir,
Entrendre le bruit de ses pas.
Mon cœur est si las,
Si las de l'attendre!

Il ne revient pas,
Il ne revient pas!

Mon seigneur, mon seigneur,
Mon maître!
S'il allait paraître,
S'il allait paraître,
Quelle joie!
Hélas! hélas!
Où donc peut-il être!
Il ne revient pas!

SIEBEL
Marguerite!

MARGUERITE
Siebel! . . .

SIEBEL
Encor des pleurs.

MARGUERITE
Hélas!
Vous seul ne me maudissez pas.

SIEBEL
Je ne suis qu'un enfant, mais j'ai le cœur d'un homme
Et je vous vengerai de son lâche abandon!
Je le tuerai!

MARGUERITE
Qui donc?

SIEBEL
Faut-il que je le nomme?
L'ingrat qui vous trahit! . . .

MARGUERITE
Non! . . . taisez-vous! . . .

SIEBEL
Pardon!
Vous l'aimez encore?

MARGUERITE
Oui! . . . toujours! toujours!
Mais ce n'est pas à vous de plaindre mon ennui,
J'ai tort, Siebel, de vous parler de lui.

SIEBEL
Si le bonheur à sourire t'invite,
Joyeux alors, je sens un doux émoi;
Si la douleur t'accable, Marguerite,
O Marguerite, je pleure alors,
Je pleure comme toi!

Comme deux fleurs sur une même tige,
Notre destin suivant le même cours,
De tes chagrins en frère je m'afflige,
O Marguerite, comme une sœur,
Je t'aimerai toujours!

His hand at the gate!
He will not return,
He will not return.

Ah, my lord, my master!
If I could but see him,
Ah, what joy for me!
Alas! Oh where can he be?
He will not return.
(*enter* SIEBEL)

SIEBEL
Marguerite!

MARGUERITE
Siebel!

SIEBEL
You're weeping still!

MARGUERITE
Alas! You only do not come to jeer.

SIEBEL
I am still very young, but I'm a man at heart, and that scoundrel shall pay for the wrong he has done. I'll have his life!

MARGUERITE
Ah, no!

SIEBEL
I need not ask who betrayed you. I need not speak his name.

MARGUERITE
No, say no more!

SIEBEL
Why not? Do you love him still?

MARGUERITE
Yes, forever! Forever! But I must not complain to you about my woes.
It's wrong, Siebel, to speak of him to you.

SIEBEL (*takes her hand*)
When all your life was filled with laughter and gladness,
I was your friend and I was happy too.
Now that your days are burdened down with sadness,
Oh Marguerite, my heart must weep with you.

We are like flowers that bloomed in summer weather,
We have been happy when the skies were blue.
Now in your sorrow we still shall be together,
Oh Marguerite, now and forevermore, my heart is true!

MARGUERITE (*thanking* SIEBEL)
You are my only friend,
God bless you for your kindness!
Those who look down on me
With cruel blindness
Cannot deny me room
In the church which is my home.
I'll pray to God above
For my child and my love.

MARGUERITE
Soyez béni, Siebel! votre amitié m'est douce!
Ceux dont la main cruelle me repousse,
N'ont pas fermé pour moi la porte du saint lieu;
J'y vais pour mon enfant . . . et pour lui prier Dieu!

Scene 2

(*In the Church*)

(MARGUERITE, *then* MÉPHISTOPHÉLÈS)

(*Some women enter the church.* MARGUERITE *enters after them and kneels.*)

MARGUERITE
O Lord, let me unburden my soul at Thine altar.
Hear me as I kneel here in prayer.

MARGUERITE
Seigneur, daignez permettre à votre humble servante
De s'agenouiller devant vous!

MÉPHISTOPHÉLÈS
No! Do not dare to pray! No! Do not dare to pray!
Oh my spirits of evil! Demons of hell!
Come to my call!

MÉPHISTOPHÉLÈS
Non! . . . tu ne prieras pas! . . . Frappez-la d'épouvante!
Esprits du mal, accourez tous!

CHORUS OF DEMONS
Marguerite!

VOIX DE DEMONS INVISIBLES
Marguerite!

MARGUERITE
Who is calling?

MARGUERITE
Qui m'appelle?

CHORUS OF DEMONS
Marguerite!

VOIX
Marguerite!

MARGUERITE
Who is calling? O God! O God! Gracious Lord,
Is this my torment for what I have done?
(*a tomb opens.* MÉPHISTOPHÉLÈS *leans from it toward* MARGUERITE)

MARGUERITE
Je chancelle!
Je meurs!—Dieu bon! Dieu clément!
Est-ce déjà l'heure du châtiment?

MÉPHISTOPHÉLÈS
Now remember the time when the angels of heaven
Smiled on all of your days,
When you came here to church with a soul filled with virtue
And a heart filled with praise!
When your voice was uplifted in prayer at the altar,
And heaven was your guide!
When your lips knew only a mother's kiss,
And God was at your side!
Now hear the voice of hell as the spirits assemble
In their fiendish delight!
Now you shall know remorse and despair never-ending
In the eternal night!

MÉPHISTOPHÉLÈS
Souviens-toi du passé, quand sous l'aile des anges,
Abritant ton bonheur,
Tu venais dans son temple, enchantant ses louanges,
Adorer le Seigneur!
Lorsque tu bégayais une chaste prière
D'une timide voix,
Et portais dans ton cœur les baisers de ta mère,
Et Dieu tout à la fois!
Écoute ces clameurs! c'est l'enfer qui t'appelle! . . .
C'est l'enfer qui te suit!
C'est l'éternel remords et l'angoisse éternelle
Dans l'éternelle nuit!

MARGUERITE
Dieu! quelle est cette voix qui me parle dans l'ombre?
Dieu tout puissant!
Quel voile sombre
Sur moi descend! . . .

CHOEUR RELIGIEUX
Quand du Seigneur le jour luira,
Sa croix au ciel resplendira,
Et l'univers s'écroulera . . .

MARGUERITE
Hélas! . . . ce chant pieux est plus terrible encore! . . .

MÉPHISTOPHÉLÈS
Non!
Pour toi Dieu n'a plus de pardon!
Pour toi le ciel n'a plus d'aurore!

CHOEUR RELIGIEUX
Que dirai-je alors au Seigneur?
Où trouverai-je un protecteur,
Quand l'innocent n'est pas sans peur!

MARGUERITE
Ah! ce chant m'ètouffe et m'oppresse!
Je suis dans un cercle de fer!

MÉPHISTOPHÉLÈS
Adieu les nuits d'amour et les jours pleins d'ivresse!
A toi malheur! A toi l'enfer!

MARGUERITE, CHOEUR RELIGIEUX
Seigneur, accueillez la prière
Des cœurs malheureux!
Qu'un rayon de votre lumière
Descende sur eux!

MÉPHISTOPHÉLÈS
Marguerite!
Sois maudite! A toi l'enfer!

MARGUERITE
Ah!

MARGUERITE
Lord! What voice do I hear coming out of the darkness!
Father in heaven,
What is this horror that falls on me?

CHURCH CHOIR
When that last dread day is breaking,
When the sinful world is quaking,
When the earth and sky pass away.

MARGUERITE
Alas, alas! That blessed chant is more than I can bear!

MÉPHISTOPHÉLÈS
No! Your God will not pardon you now! Your God has banished you from heaven.

CHURCH CHOIR
How may I deserve salvation,
When the just fear condemnation,
What shall I, a poor sinner, say?

MARGUERITE
They sing of my condemnation,
It pierces my heart like a sword!

MÉPHISTOPHÉLÈS
Farewell to nights of love, days of bliss, hours of rapture!
All that is gone! Now you are mine!

MARGUERITE, CHURCH CHOIR
O Lord, O Lord, hear the prayer of Thy servant
In sorrow and pain!
Send the light of Thy blessed presence
Upon her again!

MÉPHISTOPHÉLÈS
Marguerite! Damned forever! Now you are mine!

MARGUERITE
Ah!
(*he disappears*)

Scene 3

(*On the street*)

VALENTIN, CHOEUR
Déposons les armes,
Déposons les armes,
Dans nos foyers enfin
Nous voici revenus,
Nos mères en larmes,
Nos mères et nos sœurs
Ne nous attendront plus.
Déposons les armes,
Nos mères en larmes,
Nos mères et nos sœurs
Ne nous attendront plus,

VALENTIN, SOLDIERS
Lay your swords away, lads,
Here's the happy day, lads!
Now we are home again,
We are home from the war!
Our mothers are waiting,
Oh, let us dry their tears,
And drive away their fears!
Ah, this is the day, lads!

And we're here to stay, lads!
Your mothers and sweethearts
Need to fear no more.
So lay your arms away,
For we are home from the war!
Now to tell the story,
Now to gain the glory!

Nos mères et nos sœurs
Ne nous attendront plus.
Déposons les armes,
Déposons les armes!

VALENTIN (*seeing* SIEBEL)
My friend. Siebel!

VALENTIN
Eh! parbleu! c'est Siebel!

SIEBEL (*embarrassed*)
Yes, it's I . . . but . . .

SIEBEL
Cher Valentin . . .

VALENTIN
Come here, lad! Come to my arms! And Marguerite?

VALENTIN
Viens vite!
Viens dans mes bras.
Et Marguerite?

SIEBEL
She went to the church, I believe . . .

SIEBEL
Elle est à l'église, je crois.

VALENTIN
Praying for me, no doubt, praying to God for me! My dear sister! How excited she will be when I tell her my adventures in the war!

VALENTIN
Oui, priant Dieu pour moi . . .
Chère sœur, tremblante et craintive,
Comme elle va prêter une oreille attentive
Au récit de nos combats!

SOLDIERS
Yes, we enjoy getting the glory
When they all gather round
To hear what we have done,
Young and old, wanting the story
Of war, and how we won.

CHOEUR
Oui, c'est plaisir dans les familles
De conter aux enfants qui frémissent tout bas,
Aux vieillards, aux jeunes filles,
La guerre et ses combats.

The Soldiers' Chorus

Here's to the men who have gone before,
Heroes of many an ancient war!
Here's to the courage that they impart,
And may it live on,
And may it live on,
In every heart!
For the land of our birth
We have fought again.
We have proven the worth
Of her fighting men,
That the bountiful earth
Which the father won
May have at her call,
Whatever befall,
The sword of the son!
Here's to the men who have gone before,
Heroes of many an ancient war!
Here's to the courage that they impart
And may it live on in every heart!
Home once again!
The fight is won,

Gloire immortelle
De nos aïeux,
Sois-nous fidèle,
Mourons comme eux!
Et sous ton aile,
Soldats vainqueurs,
Dirige nos pas, dirige nos pas, enflamme nos cœurs!
Pour toi, mère patrie,
Affrontant le sort,
Tes fils, l'âme aguerie
Ont bravé la mort.
Ta voix sainte nous crie:
En avant, soldats!
Le fer à la main, le fer à la main courez aux combats!
Gloire immortelle
De nos aïeux,
Sois-nous fidèle,
Mourons comme eux!
Et sous ton aile,
Soldats vainqueurs,
Dirige nos pas, enflamme nos cœurs!
Vers nos foyers
Hâtons le pas,
On nous attend, la paix est faite,

Plus de soupirs! ne tardons pas,
Vers nos foyers hâtons le pas.
Notre pays nous tend les bras,
L'amour nous rit, l'amour nous fête,
Et plus d'un cœur frémit tous bas, frémit tout bas
Au souvenir au souvenir de nos combats.
L'amour nous fête,
Et plus d'un cœur frémit, frémit tout bas, frémit tout bas
Au souvenir de nos combats
Hâtons le pas,
Ne tardons pas,
Hâtons le pas,
Ne tardons pas.
Gloire immortelle
De nos aïeux,
Sois-nous fidèle,
Mourons comme eux!
Et sous ton aile,
Soldats vainqueurs,
Dirige nos pas, enflamme nos cœurs!

Our duty's done,
The war is ended.
Ah, what delight
To hear the laughter of the girls we love so well!
Now here tonight,
We'll know the comfort of the homes we have defended.
The bravest heart will quake with fear,
To hear the tale we have to tell.
The war is past,
We're home at last,
Here's to the men who have gone before,
Heroes of many an ancient war!
Here's to the courage that they impart,
And may it live on in every heart!

Scene 4

Recitative

VALENTIN
Allons, Siebel! entrons dans la maison!
Le verre en main, tu me feras raison!

SIEBEL
Non! n'entre pas!

VALENTIN
Pourquoi? . . . —tu détournes la tête?
Ton regard fuit le mien? . . . —Siebel, explique-toi!

SIEBEL
Eh bien!—non, je ne puis!

VALENTIN
Que veux-tu dire?

SIEBEL
Arrête!
Sois clément, Valentin!

VALENTIN
Laisse-moi! laisse-moi!

SIEBEL
Pardonne-lui!
Mon Dieu, protégez-la.
Mon Dieu, protégez-la.

VALENTIN
Come on, Siebel. Let's go into the house
Where you and I may have a glass of wine.

SIEBEL
No, do not go!

VALENTIN
Why not? You are turning away!
You're avoiding my eyes!
Siebel! Tell me what's wrong!

SIEBEL
My friend . . . No—I cannot.

VALENTIN
What are you saying?
(*he starts toward the house*)

SIEBEL
I beg you, won't you try to be kind?
(*he tries to hold* VALENTIN *back*)

VALENTIN
Let me go, let me go!
(*he enters the house*)

SIEBEL
Try to forgive!
O God, make him forgive her!
O God, she needs your aid!
(SIEBEL *goes away.* FAUST *and* MÉPHISTOPHÉLÈS *enter.* MÉPHISTOPHÉLÈS *carries a guitar*)

Scene 5

(FAUST *goes toward* MARGUERITE's *house, then stops*)

MÉPHISTOPHÉLÈS
Why do you keep her waiting?
Go in there right away!

FAUST
Don't speak to me! I fear
That I can only bring to her shame and despair.

MÉPHISTOPHÉLÈS
Tell me why you return when once you had left her?
I know a place where we are sure to be more welcome!
There's a revel tonight!

FAUST
Marguerite!

MÉPHISTOPHÉLÈS
Why should I give my advice
When it is love that moves you?
She does not answer when you call her,
But maybe she will come if I sing her a song.
(FAUST, *deep in thought, moves away.* MÉPHISTOPHÉLÈS *accompanies himself on the guitar as he sings toward* MARGUERITE's *window*)

MÉPHISTOPHÉLÈS
Qu'attendez-vous encore?
Entrons dans la maison.

FAUST
Tais-toi, maudit! . . . j'ai peur
De rapporter ici la honte et le malheur.

MÉPHISTOPHÉLÈS
A quoi bon la revoir, après l'avoir quitté?
Notre présence ailleurs serait bien mieux fêtée!
Le sabbat nous attend!

FAUST
Marguerite!

MÉPHISTOPHÉLÈS
Je vois
Que mes avis sont vains et que l'amour l'emporte!
Mais, pour vous faire ouvrir la porte,
Vous avez grand besoin du secours de ma voix!

Serenade

"Don't pretend that you are sleeping
On your downy cot,
For I know you're not!
Now your lovely eyes are peeping
Through the window slot
On this very spot!"
So a lover sings politely,
So he comes to greet you nightly
With a serenade.
Don't you smile at him too brightly,
If you're still a maid!
Bar your doors and windows tightly
If you're still a maid.

"Vous qui faites l'endormie,
N'entendez-vous pas,
O Catherine, ma mie,
Ma voix et mes pas . . . ?"
Ainsi ton galant t'appelle,
Et ton cœur l'en croit!
N'ouvre ta porte, ma belle,
Que le bague au doigt!

"Why do you behave so badly
On a night like this?
Don't you know I love you madly,
Can't I have a kiss,
Just a little kiss?"
Thus a lover comes a-wooing,

"Catherine que j'adore,
Pourquoi refuser
A l'amant qui vous implore
Un si doux baiser? . . ."
Ainsi ton galant supplie,
Et ton cœur l'en croit!
Ne donne un baiser, ma mie,
Que la bague au doigt!

Lady, watch what you are doing,
When you hear him sing.
Don't let him come any closer,
Till you wear his ring.
Tell him no, no, no, no, no sir!
Till you wear his ring!
(MÉPHISTOPHÉLÈS *laughs devilishly*)

Scene 6

(VALENTIN *rushes from the house*)

Trio: The Duel

VALENTIN
Que voulez-vous, messieurs?

VALENTIN
What do you want with me?

MÉPHISTOPHÉLÈS
Pardon! mon camarade,
Mais ce n'est pas pour vous
qu'était la sérénade!

MÉPHISTOPHÉLÈS
Oh sir, won't you forgive me?
Alas, my little serenade was never meant for you, sir.

VALENTIN
Ma sœur l'écouterait mieux que
moi, je le sais!

VALENTIN
My sister heard it better than I, that I know!

FAUST
Sa sœur!

FAUST
His sister!
(VALENTIN *draws his sword and breaks* MÉPHISTOPHÉLÈS' *guitar*)

MÉPHISTOPHÉLÈS
Quelle mouche vous pique?
Vous n'aimez donc pas la
musique?

MÉPHISTOPHÉLÈS
Maybe something upset you? Maybe you do not like music?

VALENTIN
Assez d'outrage! . . .
assez! . . .
A qui de vous dois-je demander
compte
De mon malheur et de ma
honte? . . .
Qui de vous deux doit tomber
sous mes coups? . . .

VALENTIN
No more of that, sir! No more!
Which of you two shall answer for this outrage?
For all my shame, all my dishonor!
Which of you two is to die by my sword?

MÉPHISTOPHÉLÈS
Vous le voulez? . . .—Allons,
docteur, à vous! . . .

MÉPHISTOPHÉLÈS
You want to fight? My friend, all right! The fight is on!

FAUST
Terrible et frémissant,
Il glace mon courage!
Dois-je verser le sang
Du frère que j'outrage? . . .

FAUST (*aside*)
He hates me, and well he might,
But now I have to meet him.
Ah, must it be my fate
That I'm the one to slay him?

VALENTIN
Redouble, ô Dieu puissant,
Ma force et mon courage!
Permets que dans son sang
Je lave mon outrage!

VALENTIN
I call on Thee, O Lord,
Ah, help me to defeat him!
For all the wrong he's done,
My sword shall repay him.
Mighty Lord, mighty Lord!
I shall repay him!

MÉPHISTOPHÉLÈS
What a fool, what a fool!
His rage shall help me beat him!
What a fool! Poor, foolish man,
My mighty arm shall slay him!

MÉPHISTOPHÉLÈS
De son air menaçant,
De son aveugle rage,
Je ris! . . . mon bras puissant
Va détourner l'orage! . . .

VALENTIN
This charm that kept my life from harm,
Blessed by the prayers of Marguerite;
I cannot call on you for aid!
Her sin has defiled you!
I cannot call on you for aid!
(*he throws the sacred medal away*)

VALENTIN
Et toi qui préservas mes jours,
Toi qui me viens de Marguerite,
Je ne veux plus de ton secours,
Médaille maudite! . . .

MÉPHISTOPHÉLÈS (*aside*)
That was a sad mistake!

MÉPHISTOPHÉLÈS
Tu t'en repentiras!

VALENTIN
On guard, sir! Now let's begin!

VALENTIN
En garde! . . . et défends-toi! . . .

MÉPHISTOPHÉLÈS (*to* FAUST)
You stay close to me!
You be ready to thrust, nothing else.
I will parry.
(*they fight.* VALENTIN *falls*)

MÉPHISTOPHÉLÈS
Serrez-vous contre moi! . . .
Et poussez seulement, cher docteur! . . . moi, je pare.

MÉPHISTOPHÉLÈS
And so this is the end of our brave, noble hero!
And now we must be off. Come on, sir!
(*he drags* FAUST *away. They leave the scene*)

MÉPHISTOPHÉLÈS
Voici notre héros étendu sur le sable! . . .
Au large maintenant! au large! . . .

Scene 7

(MARTHE *enters, and townsfolk carrying torches*)

The Death of Valentin

MARTHE, TOWNSFOLK
Over here, come and see over here!
They were fighting a duel.
The stranger struck him down!
Come and see, come and see!
Do you think he is dead?
Someone said he was moving.
Come right away,
Let's see what we can do.
(VALENTIN *raises himself with an effort*)

MARTHE, BOURGEOIS
Par ici! . . .
Par ici, mes amis! on se bat dans la rue! . . .—
L'un d'eux est tombé là!—
Regardez . . . le voici! . . .
Il n'est pas encore mort! . . .—
on dirait qu'il remue! . . .—
Vite, approchez! . . . il faut le secourir!

VALENTIN
Ah, no, ah no!
Let there be no weeping and mourning!
I've looked upon the face of death
So many times that I am not afraid!
(MARGUERITE *enters with* SIEBEL)

VALENTIN
Merci!
De vos plaintes, faites-moi grace! . . .
J'ai vu, morbleu! la mort en face
Trop souvent pour en avoir peur! . . .

MARGUERITE
Valentin! . . . Valentin! . . .

MARGUERITE
Oh, my brother! Oh, my brother!
(she pushes through the crowd and kneels beside VALENTIN*)*

VALENTIN
Marguerite! ma sœur! . . .
Que me veux-tu? . . . va-t'en!

VALENTIN
Marguerite! It's you. Why are you here? Now go!
(he pushes her away)

MARGUERITE
O Dieu!

MARGUERITE
O God!

VALENTIN
Je meurs par elle!
J'ai sottement
Cherché querelle
À son amant.

VALENTIN
I die for her sake.
I was a fool
To start a quarrel
With her lover.

LA FOULE
Son amant!

TOWNSFOLK
With her lover!

SIEBEL
Grâce! Grâce!

SIEBEL *(to* VALENTIN*)*
Forgive her! Forgive her!

MARGUERITE
Douleur cruelle! Ô châtiment!
Ô châtiment!

MARGUERITE
Dear God, he's dying! God help me now! God help me now!

SIEBEL
Grâce pour elle! grâce! grâce!
Soyez clément!

SIEBEL
Ah, he is dying. Pardon! Pardon! Forgive her now!

LA FOULE
Il meurt frappé par son amant!

TOWNSFOLK
For her he's dying! Her lover struck him down!

VALENTIN
Ecoute-moi bien, Marguerite! . . .
Ce qui doit arriver arrive à l'heure dite!
La mort nous frappe quand il faut,
Et chacun obéit aux volontés d'en haut! . . .
—Toi! . . . te voilà dans la mauvaise voie!
Tes blanches mains ne travailleront plus!
Tu renieras, pour vivre dans la joie,
Tous les devoirs et toutes les vertus!
Va! la honte t'accable
Le remords suit tes pas!
Mais enfin l'heure sonne!
Meurs! et si Dieu te pardonne,
Soit maudite ici-bas.

VALENTIN
Now hear what I say, Marguerite!
Every man in his time must face his mortal hour,
And no man knows when it will be.
He can only obey when it is heaven's will.
You! You have chosen a life of evil!
Your pretty hands will have nothing to do,
So you will spend your life looking for pleasure,
Casting aside all that is good and true!
Go! Your shame will go with you,
And the pangs of remorse
Till the day when you die!
Die, and though God may forgive you,
Yet as long as you live,
Though God may forgive you,
Though God may forgive you,
You shall bear my curse till you die!

LA FOULE
O terreur, ô blasphème
A ton heure suprême, infortuné,
Songe, hélas, a toi-même,
Pardonne, si tu veux être un jour pardonné!

TOWNSFOLK
Blessed saints! This is blasphemy!
Such a sin when he's dying!
O foolish man, soon you will die.
If you hope for salvation, forgive her,
If you hope for salvation on high!

VALENTIN
Marguerite! Sois maudite!

VALENTIN
Marguerite, now I curse you!

Evil in life, lonely in death!
I . . . I die because of you,
But I die like a soldier!

La mort t'attend sur ton grabat!
Moi je meurs de ta main
Et je tombe en soldat!

TOWNSFOLK

O Lord, receive his soul,
And forgive all his sins!
(the curtain falls) *

LA FOULE

Que le Seigneur ait son âme
Et pardonne au pêcheur.

* In Gounod's original score he supplied another scene at this point—often omitted in production, and omitted here. In this scene, mostly ballet, Faust and Méphistophélès come to watch the revels of Walpurgis Night.

Act V

Scene 1

Trio: The Prison Scene

(*The prison.* MARGUERITE *asleep.* FAUST *and* MÉPHISTOPHÉLÈS *enter.*)

FAUST
Va t'en!

FAUST
Go now!

MÉPHISTOPHÉLÈS
Le jour va luire.—On dresse l'échafaud!
Décide sans retard Marguerite à te suivre.
Le geôlier dort.—Voici les clefs.—Il faut
Que ta main d'homme la délivre.

MÉPHISTOPHÉLÈS
The day is dawning, the scaffold is prepared.
Persuade your Marguerite that we've come to save her.
The jailer sleeps . . . Here are the keys.
A mortal hand is needed to release her.

FAUST
Laisse-nous!

FAUST
Won't you go?

MÉPHISTOPHÉLÈS
Hâtez-toi.—Moi, je veille au dehors.

MÉPHISTOPHÉLÈS
Don't delay. I will watch at the door.

FAUST
Mon cœur est pénétré d'épouvante!—O torture
O source de regrets et d'éternels remords!
C'est elle!—La voici, la douce créature
Jetée au fond d'une prison
Comme une vile criminelle!
Le désespoir égara sa raison!
Son pauvre enfant, ô Dieu! tué par elle!
Marguerite! Marguerite!

FAUST
This place fills me with fear and remorse! Ah, to see her!
How can I bear the anguish that is in my heart!
My darling, here she lies, my lovely Marguerite,
Alone within this wretched cell,
Like some depraved and evil creature.
Sorrow and grief have beclouded her mind.
In her despair . . . dear God . . . in her despair she slew her newborn baby!
Marguerite! Marguerite!

MARGUERITE
Ah! c'est la voix du bien-aimé!
A son appel mon cœur s'est ranimé.

MARGUERITE (*waking*)
Ah, it's the voice of my beloved.
(*she sits up*)
My lonely heart revives, hearing him speak.

FAUST
Marguerite!

FAUST
Marguerite!

MARGUERITE
Au milieu de vos éclats de rire,
Démons qui m'entourez, j'ai reconnu sa voix!

MARGUERITE
O you demons that have come to plague me,
In spite of your laughter,
Now I can hear his voice!

FAUST
Marguerite!

FAUST
Marguerite!

MARGUERITE
Sa main, sa douce main m'attire!
Je suis libre! Il est là! je l'entends! je la vois.
Oui, c'est toi, je t'aime,
Les fers, la mort même
Ne me font plus peur!
Tu m'as retrouvée,
Me voilà sauvée!
C'est toi, je suis sur ton cœur!

MARGUERITE
His hand! Now it is here to touch me!
I am free now! He is here! I am free!
I can see him and hear him once more.
Yes, you're here; I love you!
And death, even death shall never make us part.
Evil all around me,
But now you have found me.
You have come to save me!
Ah, love, take me to your heart!

FAUST
Yes, it's I; I love you.
Though demons of hell would keep us two apart.
Evil all around you,
But now I have found you.
I have come to save you,
I have come to save you!
My love, come, come to my heart!
(FAUST *attempts to take her away; she gently avoids his arms*)

FAUST
Oui, c'est moi, je t'aime,
Malgré l'effort même
Du démon moqueur,
Je t'ai retrouvée,
Te voilà sauvée,
C'est moi, viens sur mon cœur!

MARGUERITE
Ah, yes! Here is the street
Where first you saw me,
That day when first we met.
Where your dear hand,
Your dear hand came to touch my own.
"Pray do not think me bold, my fair and gentle maiden.
Will you not take my arm to keep you safe from harm?"
"No, My Lord, I am not such a fair or gentle maiden.
Pray forgive me and leave me,
And I shall find my way without your guiding arm."

MARGUERITE
Attends! . . . voici la rue
Où tu m'as vue
Pour la première fois! . . .
Où votre main osa presque effleurer mes doigts!
"—Ne permettrez-vous pas, ma belle demoiselle,
Qu'on vous offre le bras pour faire le chemin?"
"—Non, monsieur, je ne suis demoiselle ni belle,
Et je n'ai pas besoin qu'on me donne la main!"

FAUST
Yes, how well I recall . . . You must come. Time is passing.

FAUST
Oui, mon cœur se souvient!—
Mais fuyons! l'heure passe!

MARGUERITE
And the garden where you and I
Walked amid the blooms of the roses,
And where you came, hid from the world,
Among the shadows of the evening!

MARGUERITE
Et voici le jardin charmant,
Perfumé de myrte et de rose,
Où chaque soir discrètement
Tu pénétrais à la nuit close.

FAUST
Come, come, Marguerite!

FAUST
Viens, viens, Marguerite!

MARGUERITE
No!

MARGUERITE
Non!

FAUST
Come, come away!

FAUST
Viens, viens, fuyons!

MARGUERITE
No! No! We are happy here.

MARGUERITE
Non, non! reste encore.

FAUST
O God! She does not understand!

FAUST
O ciel, elle ne m'entende pas!

Scene 2

MÉPHISTOPHÉLÈS
Come on there! Come on there! Or you're sure to be lost!
Do not blame it on me if you cannot escape.

MÉPHISTOPHÉLÈS
Alerte! alerte! ou vous êtes perdus!
Si vous tardez encor, je ne m'en mêle plus!

MARGUERITE
It is he! It is he! He is there in the shadows!

MARGUERITE
Le démon! le démon!—Le

vois-tu? . . . là . . .
dans l'ombre
Fixant sur nous son œil de feu!
Que nous veut-il?—Chasse-le du saint lieu!

Now I can see his evil eye!
What does he want? Make him go while I pray!

MÉPHISTOPHÉLÈS
Quittons ce lieu sombre,
La jour est levé
De leur pied sonore
J'entends nos chevaux frapper le pavé.
Viens! sauvons-la. Peut-être il en est temps encore!

MÉPHISTOPHÉLÈS
The morning is breaking, the sky is aglow!
Hear the horses tramping and stamping below!
Persuade her to go!
(*trying to drag* FAUST *away*)
Come, it is time! We still may have a chance to save her!

MARGUERITE
Mon Dieu, protégez-moi! Mon Dieu, je vous implore!

MARGUERITE
O God, come to my aid, protect me I implore you!

FAUST
Viens! Fuyons! Peut-être il en est temps encore!

FAUST
Come! O come! There still may be a chance to save her.
(MARGUERITE *falls to her knees*)

MARGUERITE
Anges purs, anges radieux!
Portez mon âme au sein des cieux!
Dieu juste, à toi je m'abandonne!
Dieu bon, je suis à toi!—pardonne!
Anges purs, anges radieux,
Portez mon âme au sein des cieux!

MARGUERITE
Angel hosts, shining in the sky
Lift up my soul to God on high!
O Father, let my sin be forgiven,
O Lord, take me with Thee to heaven!
Angel hosts shining in the sky,
Lift up my soul to God on high!

FAUST
Viens, suis-moi! je le veux!

FAUST
Come, it's I! Come away!

MARGUERITE
Anges purs, anges radieux!
Portez mon âme au sein des cieux!
Dieu juste, à toi je m'abandonne!
Dieu bon, je suis à toi—pardonne!
Anges purs, anges radieux!
Portez mon âme au sein des cieux!

MARGUERITE
Angel hosts, shining in the sky
Lift up my soul to God on high!
O Father, let my sin be forgiven,
O Lord, take me with Thee to heaven!
Angel hosts shining in the sky,
Lift up my soul to God on high!

FAUST
Viens! suis moi! viens! suis moi!
Viens! viens! quittons ces lieux!
Déjà le jour envahit les cieux!

FAUST
Come, it's I! Come away!
Come, come, let us fly!
Night is gone and the day is nigh!

MÉPHISTOPHÉLÈS
Hâtons-nous! L'heure sonne!
Déjà le jour envahit, envahit les cieux!
Hâtons-nous, hâtons-nous,
de quitter ces lieux.

MÉPHISTOPHÉLÈS
Come away! It is morning!
Night is gone, night is gone and the day is nigh!
Come away, come away,
It is time to fly.

FAUST
Marguerite!

FAUST
Marguerite!

MARGUERITE
Pourquoi ce regard menaçant?

MARGUERITE
But why are your eyes full of evil?

FAUST
Marguerite!

FAUST
Marguerite!

MARGUERITE
And why are your hands stained with blood?
Go! Go away from me!

MÉPHISTOPHÉLÈS (*to* MARGUERITE)
Your soul is damned!

Apotheosis

CHORUS OF ANGELS
Forgiven!
Christ is risen again!
Christ rises victorious!
Peace and good will to those,
Those who follow the Master.
Christ rises victorious!
Christ rises victorious!
Christ is risen again!

(*the prison walls open. The soul of* MARGUERITE *is transported to heaven.* FAUST *in despair gazes after her and falls to his knees in prayer.* MÉPHISTOPHÉLÈS *turns away before the glory of the archangel's sword*)

MARGUERITE
Pourquoi ces mains rouges de sang?
Va! . . . tu me fais horreur!

MÉPHISTOPHÉLÈS
Jugée!

CHOEUR DES ANGES
Sauvée! Christ est ressuscité!
Christ vient de renaître!
Paix et félicité
Aux disciples du Maître!
Christ vient de renaître.
Christ vient de renaître.
Christ est ressuscité!

MADAMA BUTTERFLY

by Giacomo Puccini (1858–1924)

LIBRETTO BY LUIGI ILLICA AND GIUSEPPE GIACOSA

Translated by RUTH and THOMAS MARTIN.

Based on John Luther Long's story and David Belasco's play *Madam Butterfly*.

CHARACTERS

GORO, a nakodo, *or marriage broker*	*Tenor*
B. F. PINKERTON, *lieutenant, United States Navy*	*Tenor*
SUZUKI, *maid to Cio-cio-san*	*Mezzo-soprano*
SHARPLESS, *American Consul at Nagasaki*	*Baritone*
MADAMA BUTTERFLY (*Cio-cio-san*)	*Soprano*
THE COUSIN	*Soprano*
MOTHER OF CIO-CIO-SAN	*Mezzo-soprano*
YAKUSIDÉ, *uncle of Cio-cio-san*	*Baritone*
IMPERIAL COMMISSIONER	*Bass*
CIVIL REGISTRAR	*Baritone*
THE BONZE, *a Buddhist priest, also an uncle of Cio-cio-san*	*Bass*
PRINCE YAMADORI, *a suitor of Cio-cio-san*	*Baritone*
KATE PINKERTON, *wife of Lieutenant Pinkerton*	*Mezzo-soprano*
SORROW, *Cio-cio-san's child*	
RELATIVES AND COMPANIONS OF CIO-CIO-SAN, SERVANTS	

Place: Nagasaki, Japan
Time: Nineteenth century
First performance: La Scala, Milan, February 17, 1904

COPYRIGHT 1954 BY G. RICORDI & CO., NEW YORK BY PERMISSION OF G. RICORDI & CO.

ACT I

Hill near Nagasaki. A Japanese house, terrace and garden. Below, in the background, the bay, the harbor and the town of Nagasaki. GORO *is showing* PINKERTON *over the house.* PINKERTON *passes from one surprise to another.*

PINKERTON
All the doors and partitions . . .

GORO (*enjoying his surprise*)
You can easily change them
And quickly rearrange them,
So without any trouble,
You have varied effects and dispositions.

PINKERTON (*looking around*)
The newly married pair sleep where?

GORO (*pointing in two directions*)
Here, or there!—depending . . .

PINKERTON
Surpises never ending!
The parlor?

GORO (*showing the terrace*)
I'll show you.

PINKERTON (*amazed*)
In the open?

GORO (*making a partition slide out*)
A simple motion . . .

PINKERTON
It's novel! . . . and easy!
Another—

GORO
Sliding wall!

PINKERTON
Frail as a paper parasol!

GORO
Solid as any fortress,
Convenient for expansion.

PINKERTON
What a practical mansion!

GORO (*claps his hands twice loudly; enter two men and a woman, who go down on their hands and knees in front of* PINKERTON)
This is your bride's companion,
Dependable and steady.
She has served her already.
The servant—and then the cook . . .
They're confused by the signal honor.

PINKERTON
Who are they?

GORO (*introducing them*)
Miss Floating Cloud in Heaven—

PINKERTON
E soffitto . . . e pareti . . .

GORO
Vanno e vengono a prova
a norma che vi giova
nello stesso locale
alternar nuovi aspetti ai consueti.

PINKERTON
Il nido nuzial
dov'è?

GORO
Qui, o là! . . . secondo . . .

PINKERTON
Anch'esso a doppio fondo!
La sala?

GORO
Ecco!

PINKERTON
All'aperto? . . .

GORO
Un fianco scorre . . .

PINKERTON
Capisco! Un altro . . .

GORO
Scivola!

PINKERTON
E la dimora frivola . . .

GORO
Salda come una torre
da terra, fino al tetto.

PINKERTON
È una casa a soffietto.

GORO
Questa è la cameriera
che della vostra sposa
fu già serva amorosa.
Il cuoco—il servitor. Sono confusi
del grande onore.

PINKERTON
I nomi?

GORO
Miss *Nuvola leggiera.*

Raggio di sol nascente. Esala aromi.

SUZUKI
Sorride Vostro Onore?
Il riso è frutto e fiore.
Disse il savio Ocunama:
dei crucci la trama
smaglia il sorriso. Schiude alla perla il guscio,
apre all'uom l'uscio
del Paradiso.
Profumo degli Dei . . .
Fontana della vita . . .
Disse il savio Ocunama:
dei crucci la trama smaglia il sorriso.

PINKERTON
A chiacchiere costei
mi par cosmopolita.
Che guardi?

GORO
Se non giunge ancor la sposa.

PINKERTON
Tutto è pronto?

GORO
Ogni cosa.

PINKERTON
Gran perla di sensale!

GORO
Qui verran: l'Ufficiale
del registro, i parenti, il vostro console,
la fidanzata. Qui si firma l'atto
e il matrimonio è fatto.

PINKERTON
E son molti i parenti?

GORO
La suocera, la nonna, lo zio Bonzo
(che non ci degnerà di sua presenza)
e cugini, e le cugine . . .
Mettiam fra gli ascendenti
ed i collaterali, un due dozzine.
Quanto alla discendenza . . .
provvederanno assai
Vostra Grazia e la bella Butterfly.

PINKERTON
Gran perla di sensale!

Ray of the Sun at Dawning—
Perfume of Roses.

SUZUKI (*grown bolder*)
Your Excellence is smiling?
"A smile is like a flower," said the sage Ocunama:
"Smiles unfold the wonder of heaven's portals.
A smile can destroy
All woe by its power.
Rivaling pearls in spendor,
The blessing of the gods and the spark of life of mortals."
Said the sage Ocunama;
"A smile can destroy all woe by its power."
(GORO, *perceiving that* PINKERTON *begins to be bored at* SUZUKI'S *loquacity, claps his hands twice. The three rise and quickly disappear into the house*)

PINKERTON
No matter where her home,
A woman likes to chatter.
(*to* GORO *who has gone to the back to look out*)
You're looking?

GORO
For the bride and her companions.

PINKERTON
Your arrangements?

GORO
All completed.

PINKERTON
A most efficient fellow!

GORO (*thanks with a deep bow*)
Now the guests . . . First of all the town recorder,
The relations, the bride to be, of course—
And then your consul.
Then a simple ritual,
And the marriage is official.
Are there many relations?

PINKERTON

GORO
Her mother and an uncle who's the Bonze—
(But he will never grace us with his presence)—
Then the male and female cousins—
With kind felicitations,
The in-laws and their kindred—about two dozens.
As to your own descendants—
(*with obsequious presumption*)
I know there will be many,
Thanks to you, sir, and Madame Butterfly.

PINKERTON
A most efficient follow!
(*the voice of the consul* SHARPLESS, *who is climbing the hill, is heard*)

THE VOICE OF SHARPLESS (*rather far off*)
I'm climbing courageously—puffing outrageously!

GORO (*who has run to the back, announces*)
His grace, the consul.

SHARPLESS (*enters, quite out of breath.* GORO *bows low before him*)
Ah! those pebblestones
Left me exhausted!

PINKERTON (*goes to meet the consul; they shake hands*)
I bid you welcome!

GORO
I bid you welcome!

PINKERTON
Hurry, Goro,
Bring us refreshments.
(GORO *hurries into the house*)

SHARPLESS (*looking about*)
Airy!

PINKERTON (*showing him the view*)
But lovely!

SHARPLESS (*looking at the sea and the town below*)
Nagasaki—the ocean—the harbor—

PINKERTON (*pointing to the house*)
Nothing to say
Of my little chalet!

SHARPLESS
Yours?

PINKERTON
Yes, I have bought it
For nine hundred and ninety-nine years only,
But ev'ry month, at my option,
I can void the transaction,
This Japan is fantastic—
The contracts and the houses
Are elastic.

SHARPLESS
A clever man can make his profit.
(GORO *comes bustling out of the house, followed by the two servants. They bring glasses, bottles, and two wicker lounges, place the glasses and bottles on a small table, and return to the house*)

PINKERTON (*inviting him to be seated*)
Surely.
Afar and yonder,
Americans will wander,
Follow their lucky star,
Scornful of danger.
They anchor anywhere
They find alluring—

LA VOCE DI SHARPLESS
E suda e arrampica!
sbuffa, inciampica!

GORO
—il console sale.

SHARPLESS
Ah! . . . quei ciottoli
m'hanno sfiaccato!

PINKERTON
Bene arrivato.

GORO
Bene arrivato.

PINKERTON
Presto Goro
qualche ristoro.

SHARPLESS
Alto.

PINKERTON
Ma bello!

SHARPLESS
Nagasaki, il mare!
il porto . . .

PINKERTON
E una casetta
che obbedisce a bacchetta.

SHARPLESS
Vostra?

PINKERTON
La comperai
per novecento novantanove
anni,
con facoltà, ogni mese,
di rescindere i patti.
Sono in questo paese
elastici del par, case e contratti.

SHARPLESS
E l'uomo esperto ne profitta.

PINKERTON
Certo
Dovunque al mondo il Yankee
vagabondo
si gode e traffica
sprezzando i rischi.
Affonda l'ancora alla ventura . . .
Milk-Punch o Wisky?
finchè una raffica
scompigli nave, ormeggi,
alberatura.

La vita ei non appaga
se non fa suo tesor
i fiori d'ogni plaga,
d'ogni bella gli amor.

SHARPLESS
È un facile vangelo
che fa la vita vaga
ma che intristisce il cuor.

PINKERTON
Vinto si tuffa la sorte
riacciuffa.
Il suo talento
fa in ogni dove.
Così mi sposo all'uso
giapponese
per novecento
novantanove anni,
Salvo a prosciogliermi
ogni mese.

SHARPLESS
È un facile vangelo.

PINKERTON
"America forever!"

SHARPLESS
"America forever."
Ed è bella
la sposa?

GORO
Una ghirlanda
di fiori freschi, Una stella
dai raggi d'oro.
E per nulla; sol cento
yen.
Se Vostra Grazia mi comanda
ce n'ho un assortimento.

PINKERTON
Va, conducila Goro.

SHARPLESS
Quale smania vi prende!
Sareste addirittura
cotto?

PINKERTON
Non so! Dipende.
dal grado di cottura!
Amore o grillo
dir non saprei Certo costei
m'ha coll'ingenue arti
invescato.
Lieve qual tenue vetro soffiato
alla statura al portamento
sembra figura da paravento.

(*breaking off to offer* SHARPLESS *a drink*)
Another whiskey?
(*resuming*)
Till one big hurricane or sweeping wave
Will tear them from their mooring.
They live in fullest measure
On a far foreign shore
Until they reap its treasure . . .

SHARPLESS
That's a light and carefree gospel!
It may offer you pleasure,
But hurt your spirit more.

PINKERTON (*continuing*)
No one can rival their will for survival,
Always successful, nothing is beyond them.
This country's law is worthy of adoption:
I wed for nine hundred ninety-nine years only.
But I reserve the right to drop the option.

SHARPLESS
A light and carefree gospel.

PINKERTON (*raising his glass*)
"America forever!"

SHARPLESS
"America forever"
Is your bride very pretty?

GORO (*who has overheard, approaches the terrace officiously*)
Fair as a garland
Of fragrant flowers!
Golden sunlight's own radiant daughter.
And for only a hundred yen!
And if Your Honor so desires,
I have a fine selection.
(*the consul laughingly declines*)

PINKERTON (*very impatiently*)
Quick, go out and escort her.
(GORO *runs to the back and disappears down the hill*)

SHARPLESS
How you're longing to see her!
That's what I call infatuation!

PINKERTON (*rises impatiently.* SHARPLESS *rises also*)
Maybe! Depends what you call infatuation!
It may be love or a whim that is fleeting.
My heart is beating,
Madly ensnared with her charm that excites me.
Artless and tender, her candor delights me,
Fragile and slender, with a serene air
Such as you see a carved figurine wear.

Suddenly free of her shiny surrounding,
Fluttering on with a grace that's astounding,
My lovely Butterfly moves or reposes,
Softly as zephyrs touching the roses.
Driven by strong desire, I must pursue her,
Unmindful of the harm that I may do her.

Ma dal suo lucido fondo di lacca
come con subito moto si stacca,
qual farfalletta svolazza e posa
con tal grazietta silenzioza
che di rincorrerla furor m'assale
se pure infrangerne dovessi l'ale.

SHARPLESS (*seriously and kindly*)
She came to pay a visit
To the consulate one day last week.
I did not see her, but I heard her speak;
Her mysterious charming voice was a joy to hear.
Surely only the voice of love is so sincere!
It would indeed be shameful
To break such delicate wings
And bring despair to a poor trusting heart.
A voice so charming,
And so disarming,
Never should know a moment grieved and sad.

SHARPLESS
Ier l'altro, il Consolato
sen' venne a visitar!
Io non la vidi, ma l'udii parlar.
Di sua voce il mistero
l'anima mi colpì.
Certo quando è sincero
l'amor parla così.
Sarebbe gran peccato
le lievi ali strappar
e desolar forse un credulo cuor.
Quella divina
mite vocina
non dovrebbe dar note di dolor.

PINKERTON
Sharpless, my friend, don't worry,
And try to understand.
Men of your age are beyond romantic love.
What's so alarming—
Whom am I harming?
I'll guide those wings to love,
Is that so bad?
(*offers him another drink*)
Whiskey?

PINKERTON
Console mio garbato,
quetatevi! Si sa,
la vostra età è di flebile umor.
Non c'è gran male
s'io vo' quell'ale
drizzar ai dolci voli dell'amor!
Wiskey?

SHARPLESS
All right, then, another.
(PINKERTON *fills up his own glass as well*)
Here's to your dear ones
At home and so distant.

SHARPLESS
Un altro bicchiere.
Bevo alla vostra famiglia lontana.

PINKERTON (*raising his glass*)
And to that not so distant day,
When I shall marry—once and for all time—
One chosen American girl.

PINKERTON
E al giorno in cui mi sposerò
con vere nozze,
a una vera sposa americana.

GORO (*reappears running breathlessly up the hill*)
Listen! They're coming—
A lively swarm of bees!
Already you can hear the female chatter,
As clear as wind in the trees.
(*the confused and lively hubbub of many voices is heard from the path.* PINKERTON *and* SHARPLESS *retire to the back of the garden, watching the path on the hill*)

GORO
Ecco! Son giunte al sommo del pendìo.
Già del femmineo sciame
qual di vento in fogliame
s'ode il brusìo.

BUTTERFLY'S VOICE
Another moment more . . . Be patient.

VOCE DI BUTTERFLY
Ancora un passo or via.
—Aspetta.—

OTHER VOICES
Ah! Sky and ocean, near and far.

ALTRE VOCI
Ah, Quanto cielo! quantomar!

Come sei tarda.
Ecco la vetta.—
—Guarda, guarda,
quanti fior!

Why don't you hurry?
We're at the summit.
See the lovely, lovely view!

VOCE DI BUTTERFLY
Spira sul mare o sulla terra
un primaveril soffio
giocondo.

BUTTERFLY'S VOICE
Above the smiling land and ocean
The air of springtime seems to hover!

SHARPLESS
O allegro cinguettar di gioventù!

SHARPLESS
Oh happy carefree heart of joyous youth!

VOCE DI BUTTERFLY
Io sono la fanciulla
più lieta del Giappone, anzi del
mondo.
Amiche, io son venuta
al richiamo d'amor
d'amor venni alle soglie
ove s'accoglie
il bene di chi vive e di chi
muor.

BUTTERFLY'S VOICE
I know I am the happiest girl in all Japan
Or the world over.
Companions, love has summoned,
And I heeded the call—the call to dawning glory,
Proudly bestowing the precious gifts
That life and death mean for all.
I am happy, I am content
With my fortune, and more—
I have answered Love's call—
And I stand with faith unbounded—
Before Love's door.

LE AMICHE
Gioia a te sia
dolce amica, ma pria
di varcar la soglia che t'attira
volgiti e mira
le cose che ti son sì care.
Quanto cielo! Quanti fiori!
Quanto mar!

HER GIRL FRIENDS
Dearest friend, we wish you joy
For your future,
But pause as you depart
To all your heart's desiring,
And turn admiring.
Marvel at the beauty overflowing
Near and far.
Dearest friend, may your new life
Be bright and joyous,
But as you depart, remember
All that you once held so dear
And turn, admiring.

BUTTERFLY
Siam giunte.

BUTTERFLY
We're here now.

(she sees the three men standing together and recognizes PINKERTON. *She promptly closes her sunshade and introduces* PINKERTON *to her friends)*

B. F. Pinkerton. Giù.

B. F. Pinkerton. Bow.

LE AMICHE
Giù.

THE GIRL FRIENDS *(close their sunshades and go to their knees)*
Bow!

(then they all rise and ceremoniously approach PINKERTON*)*

BUTTERFLY
Gran ventura

BUTTERFLY
We are honored—

LE AMICHE
Riverenza.

THE GIRL FRIENDS
We are honored—

PINKERTON
È un po' dura
la scalata?

PINKERTON *(smiling)*
Was the climb a little tiring?

BUTTERFLY
Any bride who waits aspiring,
Finds the waiting far more tiring.

PINKERTON (*gently, but a trifle sarcastically*)
That's a rare and gracious tribute.

BUTTERFLY (*ingenuously*)
I could pay you many more.

PINKERTON (*good-humoredly*)
Priceless treasures!

BUTTERFLY (*anxious to show off her stock of compliments*)
Would you like
To hear me say them . . .

PINKERTON (*gently*)
Thank you—no.

SHARPLESS
(*after scanning the group of maidens with curiosity, approaches* BUTTERFLY, *who listens to him attentively*)
Miss Butterfly—how charming!
It fits you exactly. Are you from Nagasaki?

BUTTERFLY
Yes, I am, and my people
At one time were wealthy.
(*to her friends*)
Is it true?

HER GIRL FRIENDS (*assenting with alacrity*)
It is true!

BUTTERFLY
There's no one who admits that his family was poor . . .
Ev'ry homeless beggar will proclaim his descent
From noble parents.
However, we were really wealthy.
But a hurricane in fury can fell the strongest oak tree . . .
We turned to geisha dancing, to earn our living.
(*to her friends*)
Did we?

THE FRIENDS (*corroborating*)
Surely!

BUTTERFLY
I do not hide it,
It's not shameful.
(*seeing that* SHARPLESS *smiles*)
You're laughing? But why? Fate so decided!

PINKERTON (*has listened with interest and turns to* SHARPLESS)
(She's so sweet and adorable, she completely enchants me.)

SHARPLESS (*interested in* BUTTERFLY'S *prattle, continues to question her*)
Have you brothers and sisters?

BUTTERFLY
A una sposa
costumata
più penosa
l' impaziena.

PINKERTON
Molto raro
complimento.

BUTTERFLY
Dei più belli
ancor ne so.

PINKERTON
Dei gioielli!

BUTTERFLY
Se vi è caro
sul momento . . .

PINKERTON
Grazie—no.

SHARPLESS
Miss Butterfly. Bel nome,
vi sta a meraviglia.
Siete di Nagasaki?

BUTTERFLY
Signor sì. Di famiglia
assai prospera un tempo.
Verità?

LE AMICHE
Verità!

BUTTERFLY
Nessuno si confessa mai nato in povertà
non c'è vagabondo che a sentirlo non sia
di gran prosapia. Eppure
conobbi la ricchezza. Ma il turbine rovescia
le quercie più robuste—e abbiam fatto la ghescia
per sostentarci. Vero?

LE AMICHE
Vero!

BUTTERFLY
Non lo nascondo
nè m'adonto.
Ridete? Perchè? . . . Cose del mondo.

PINKERTON
(Con quel fare di bambola
quando parla m'infiamma.)

SHARPLESS
E ci avete sorelle?

BUTTERFLY
No signore. Ho la mamma.

GORO
Una nobile dama.

BUTTERFLY
Ma senza farle torto
povera molto anch'essa.

SHARPLESS
E vostro padre?

BUTTERFLY
Morto.

SHARPLESS
Quant'anni avete?

BUTTERFLY
Indovinate.

PINKERTON
Dieci.

BUTTERFLY
Crescete.

SHARPLESS
Venti.

BUTTERFLY
Calate.
Quindici, netti, netti;
sono vecchia diggià.

SHARPLESS
Quindici anni!

PINKERTON
Quindici anni!

SHARPLESS
L'età dei giuochi . . .

PINKERTON
E dei confetti.

GORO
L'imperial Commissario,
l'Ufficiale
del registro—i congiunti.

PINKERTON
Fate presto.
Che burletta! La sfilata
della nova parentela
Tolta in prestito, a mesata.

ALCUNI PARENTI
Dov'è? dove'è?

BUTTERFLY
Eccolo là!

PINKERTON
Certo dietro a quella vela

BUTTERFLY
No, Your Honor. Just my mother.

GORO (*importantly*)
She's a lady of station.

BUTTERFLY
Truly, it must be said, though,
She lives in great privation.

SHARPLESS
And your father?

BUTTERFLY (*stops short in surprise, then answers very shortly*)
Dead!

SHARPLESS (*to* BUTTERFLY)
And how old are you?—

BUTTERFLY (*with almost childish coquetry*)
I'll let you guess it!

SHARPLESS
Ten, say.

BUTTERFLY
Too little.

SHARPLESS
Twenty.

BUTTERFLY
Too high now. Fifteen I am exactly;
I am well on in years.

SHARPLESS
Only fifteen!

PINKERTON
Only fifteen!

SHARPLESS
A tender age . . .

PINKERTON
But how delightful!
(GORO *perceives more people climbing the hill; he goes to look, then runs to announce the new arrivals to* PINKERTON *and* SHARPLESS)

GORO (*importantly*)
The Imperial Commissioner—
The Municipal Recorder—the relations.

PINKERTON (*to* GORO)
Get it over.
What a comedy, this parading
Of my Nipponese relations,
Rented out by monthly trading.
(GORO *runs into the house*)

SOME OF THE RELATIONS (*with great curiosity, to* BUTTERFLY)
He's where?

BUTTERFLY (*pointing to* PINKERTON)
Right over there!

PINKERTON
Just at present I'm deciding

If beneath those peacock feathers
My new mother'n-law is hiding.
And that doubtful-looking groper
Is her uncle who's a toper.

FIRST COUSIN
He's not so fine—if you ask me—

BUTTERFLY (*offended*)
No man could be
Finer than he—
Too good for you!

BUTTERFLY'S MOTHER
He looks divine!

THE UNCLE
He's wealthy too!

FIRST COUSIN
But he was offered first to me!

BUTTERFLY (*contemptuously*)
That's what you think!

SOME MALE AND FEMALE FRIENDS
You will agree, if that is true,
Then that's why she looks down on you.

SOME OTHER GIRL FRIENDS
She's losing her good looks of course—

MALE AND FEMALE COUSINS
They will divorce.

OTHERS
I hope they do.

GORO
For heaven's sake,
Not so much noise.

THE UNCLE
Is there no wine? I'd like to know!

THE MOTHER AND THE AUNT
Let's look around.

SOME FRIENDS
They're serving some
That looks like tea, a lot like tea.

FRIENDS AND RELATIONS
He's not so fine if you ask me,
He's not so fine
But he was offered first to me,
But I said no.
They will divorce, you wait and see!

OTHERS
He looks divine and you have found
The man for you. He looks divine
And wealthy too. If you ask me,
He is a dream.
They will divorce, you wait and see!

Di ventaglio pavonazzo
La mia suocera si cela.
E quel coso da strapazzo
E lo zio briaco e pazzo.

LA CUGINA
Bello non è
in verità.

BUTTERFLY
Bello è così
che non si può
sognar di più.

LA MADRE DI BUTTERFLY
Mi pare un re!

LO ZIO
Vale un Perù.

LA CUGINA
Goro l'offrì
pur anche a me.

BUTTERFLY
Sì, giusto tu!

ALCUNI AMICI ED ALCUNE AMICHE
Ecco, perchè
prescelta fu,
vuol far con te
la soprappiù.

ALTRE AMICHE
La sua beltà
gia disfiorì.

CUGINI E CUGINE
Divorzierà.

ALTRI
Spero di sì.

GORO
Per carità
tacete un po' . . .

LO ZIO
Vino ce n'è?

LA MADRE E LA ZIA
Guardiamo un po'.

ALCUNE AMICHE
Ne vidi già.
color di thè,
e chermisì!

AMICHE E PARENTI
Bello non è in verità,
Bello non è.
Goro l'offirì pur anco a me
ma s'ebbe un no.
Divorzierà, spero di sì.

ALTRI
Bello è così che non si può
Sognar di più! Mi pare un re
Vale un Perù! In verita
è così bel.
Divorzierà, spero di sì.

GORO
Per carità, tacete un po', sh! sh!

SHARPLESS
O amico fortunato!
O fortunato Pinkerton,
Che in sorte v'è toccato
Un fior pur or sbocciato!
Non più bella è d'assai
Fanciulla io vidi mai
Di questa Butterfly.
E se a voi sembran scede
Il patto e sua fede,
Badate! Ella ci crede.

PINKERTON
Sì è vero, è un fiore, un fiore!
L'esotico suo odore
M'ha il cervello sconvolto.
E in fede mia l'ho colto!

BUTTERFLY
Mamma, vien qua.
Badate a me:
attenti, orsù,
uno—due—tre
e tutti giù.

PINKERTON
Vieni, amor mio!
Vi piace la casetta?

BUTTERFLY
Signor B. F. Pinkerton, perdono . . .
lo vorrei . . . pochi oggetti
da donna . . .

PINKERTON
Dove sono?

BUTTERFLY
Sono qui—vi dispiace?

PINKERTON
O perchè mai,
mia bella Butterfly!?

BUTTERFLY
Fazzoletti.—La pipa.—Una cintura.—
Un piccolo fermaglio.—
Uno specchio.—Un ventaglio.

GORO
For goodness' sake, not so much noise! Sh! Sh!

SHARPLESS
Kind fate has smiled upon you!
Good fortune rules your destiny.
Its kindly favor won you
This rare and precious flower.
So enchanting a maiden
Has never met my eye
As your Miss Butterfly.
If you think she is merely a pastime
You err severely
Remember! She loves sincerely.

PINKERTON
This fairest of all flowers!
Her fragrance overpowers
And bewilders my feeling.
Yes, she of all the flowers,
Is most divinely appealing.

BUTTERFLY
Mamma, come here!
(to the others)
Listen to me:
Let us all bow—
One—two—three—
Do it right now.
(they all bow low before PINKERTON, *then they rise and disperse in the garden.* GORO *shows some of the relatives into the house.)*

PINKERTON *(takes* BUTTERFLY *by the arm and leads her towards the house)*
My sweet beloved!
You like our little cottage?

BUTTERFLY
My Lord, B. F. Pinkerton . . . forgive me—
(shows her hands and arms, which are encumbered by stuffed-out sleeves; pointing to her sleeves)
Ev'ry woman—has a few treasured keepsakes . . .

PINKERTON
And where are they?

BUTTERFLY *(pointing to her sleeves)*
Right in here . . . you're offended?

PINKERTON *(rather astonished, smiles—then quickly and gallantly reassures her)*
Good heavens, why, my lovely Butterfly!

BUTTERFLY *(empties her sleeves, placing their contents one by one on a stool)*
Satin ribbons—a clay pipe—this pretty bar pin—
A little fan of iv'ry—and a mirror
Some embroid'ry—

PINKERTON
What's the other thing?

BUTTERFLY
A tiny jar of carmine.

PINKERTON
Oho!

BUTTERFLY
You're angry?
(*throws it away*)
There!
(*draws out a long and narrow sheath*)

PINKERTON
And this one?

BUTTERFLY (*very gravely*)
That is something sacred.

PINKERTON
And won't you let me see it?

BUTTERFLY (*beseeching and grave*)
Too many people!
Please forgive me.
(*she lays down the sheath very reverently*)

GORO (*has meanwhile approached and whispers to* PINKERTON)
It's a dagger the Mikado sent her father . . .
And suggested—
(*imitating the action of suicide by hara-kiri*)

PINKERTON (*softly to* GORO)
And her father?

GORO
Did as requested.
(*he withdraws, mingling with the guests*)

BUTTERFLY (*takes some images from her sleeves and shows them to* PINKERTON)
The Ottokè.

PINKERTON (*takes one and examines it curiously*)
Little puppets?—The explanation?

BUTTERFLY
The spirits of my forebears.

PINKERTON
Ah! My veneration.
(*he puts down the image near the others, then rises*)

BUTTERFLY (*leads* PINKERTON *to one side and says to him in respectfully confiding tones:*)
Yesterday in the morning,
All in secret I visited the mission.
Now a new life is dawning—
I shall begin it with my new religion.
But the Bonze doesn't know,
Neither do my people.
Wherever Fate will lead me,

PINKERTON
Quel barattolo?

BUTTERFLY
Un vaso di tintura.

PINKERTON
Ohibò!

BUTTERFLY
Vi spiace? . . .
Via!

PINKERTON
E quello?

BUTTERFLY
Cosa sacra e mia.

PINKERTON
E non si può vedere?

BUTTERFLY
C'è troppa gente.
Perdonate.

GORO
È un presente
del Mikado a suo padre . . .
coll'invito . . .

PINKERTON
E . . . suo padre?

GORO
Ha obbedito.

BUTTERFLY
Gli Ottokè.

PINKERTON
Quei pupazzi? . . . Avete detto?

BUTTERFLY
Son l'anime degli avi.

PINKERTON
Ah! . . . il mio rispetto.

BUTTERFLY
Ieri sono salita
tutta sola in secreto alla Missione.
Colla nuova mia vita
posso adottare nuova religione.
Lo zio Bonzo nol sa,
nè i miei lo sanno. Io seguo il mio destino
e piena d'umiltà
al Dio del signor Pinkerton m'inchino.

È mio destino.
Nella stessa chiesetta in ginocchio
con voi pregherò lo stesso Dio.
E per farvi contento
potrò forse obliar la gente mia.
Amore mio!

I follow willingly.
I know my husband's kindly God will heed me.
My fate will lead me.
In the same little chapel we shall worship and pray,
To the same kind God above.
And to make you quite happy,
I might even forget my home and people . . .
My only love! . . .

GORO
Tutti zitti!

GORO (*re-entering with* SHARPLESS *and the* COMMISSIONER)
All be quiet!
(*the chattering ceases; they all leave off eating and drinking and come forward in a circle, listening with much interest;* PINKERTON *and* BUTTERFLY *stand in the center*)

IL COMMISSARIO IMPERIALE
È concesso al nominato
Benjamin Franklin Pinkerton,
Luogotenente nella cannoniera
Lincoln, marina degli Stati Uniti
America del Nord:
ed alla damigella Butterfly
del quartiere di Omura-Nagasaki,
d'unirsi in matrimonio, per dritto
il primo, della propria volontà,
. . . ed ella per consenso dei parenti
qui testimonî all'atto.

THE IMPERIAL COMMISSIONER (*reads*)
It is granted to the herein named
Benjamin Franklin Pinkerton,
A first lieutenant stationed on the gunboat *Lincoln,*
Of the navy of the United States of North America;
And to the herewith mentioned Butterfly,
Who was born in Omura Nagasaki,
To join in legal marriage,
The first named party by the grace of his free will,
The latter by permission of her kindred,
Witnessing while contracted.
(*hands the deed for signature*)

GORO
Lo sposo.
Poi la sposa.
E tutto è fatto.

GORO (*with much unction*)
The bridegroom;
(PINKERTON *signs*)
Then the bride.
(BUTTERFLY *signs*)
The deed's enacted.

LE AMICHE
Madama Butterfly!

THE GIRL FRIENDS (*surround* BUTTERFLY, *congratulating her*)
Dear Madame Butterfly.

BUTTERFLY
Madama B. F. Pinkerton.

BUTTERFLY (*corrects them*)
Now Madame B. F. Pinkerton.
(*the* CIVIL REGISTRAR *withdraws the bond and informs the* COMMISSIONER *that the ceremony is over*)

IL COMMISSARIO IMPERIALE
Augurî molti.

THE COMMISSIONER (*taking leave of* PINKERTON)
Sincerest wishes.

PINKERTON
I miei ringraziamenti.

PINKERTON
I thank you very much, sir.

IL COMMISSARIO IMPERIALE
Il signor Consol scende?

THE COMMISSIONER (*to the Consul*)
I guess Your Honor is leaving?

SHARPLESS
L'accompagno.
Ci vedrem domani.

SHARPLESS
I'll go with you.
(*shaking hands with* PINKERTON)
We shall meet tomorrow!

PINKERTON
A meraviglia.

PINKERTON
That will be splendid!

REGISTRAR
May you have sons!

PINKERTON
I'll do my best.

SHARPLESS
(*significantly*)
Remember!
(*he leaves*)
(PINKERTON *accompanies the three as far as the path which leads down to the town and waves his hand to them as they vanish from sight.* BUTTERFLY *has withdrawn close to her mother.* PINKERTON *returns and is naturally anxious to get rid of the wedding guests*)

PINKERTON
(And now to dispatch the fam'ly!)
(*the servants bring bottles of Saki and distribute glasses among the guests*)
A little wine and liquor will do it quicker.
(*raising his own glass*)
Good Luck! . . .

ALL (*toasting*)
O Kami! O Kami!

PINKERTON
A toast to the happy bride and bridegroom.

ALL
O Kami! O Kami!
(*the toasts are interrupted by strange cries from the hill; all of a sudden a weird figure appears in the background, at the sight of whom all are thunderstruck. It is the* BONZE, *who comes forward in a towering rage and, catching sight of* BUTTERFLY, *stretches out threatening hands toward her, crying:*)

THE BONZE
Cio-cio-san! Cio-cio-san!
You have disgraced us!

ALL (*huddling together in a corner in terror*)
Heaven help us!

GORO (*annoyed at the* BONZE's *intrusion*)
Confound that fool's intrusion!
Why must he come to spoil the day
By spreading confusion?

THE BONZE (*to* BUTTERFLY, *who stands isolated from the rest*)
What did you do at the Mission?

PINKERTON (*annoyed*)
This fanatic, who is it?

THE BONZE
Why did you make that visit?

ALL
What was it, Cio-cio-san?

UFFICIALE
Posterità

PINKERTON
Mi proverò.

SHARPLESS
Giudizio.

PINKERTON
(Ed eccoci in famiglia.)
Sbrighiamoci al più presto—in modo onesto.

TUTTI
O Kami! O Kami!

PINKERTON
Beviamo ai novissimi legami.

TUTTI
O Kami! O Kami!

IL BONZO
Cio-cio-san! . . . Cio-cio-san! . . .
Abbominazione!

TUTTI
Lo zio Bonzo!

GORO
Un corno al guastafeste!
Chi ci leva d'intorno
le persone moleste?! . . .

IL BONZO
Che hai
tu fatto alla Missione?

PINKERTON
Che mi strilla quel matto?

IL BONZO
Rispondi, che hai tu fatto?

TUTTI
Rispondi Cio-cio-san!

IL BONZO
Come, hai tu gli occhi asciutti?
Son dunque questi i frutti?
Ci ha rinnegato tutti!

TUTTI
Hou! Cio-cio-san!

IL BONZO
Rinnegato, vi dico,
il culto antico.

TUTTI
Hou! Cio-cio-san!

IL BONZO
Kami, sarundasico!
All'anima tua guasta
qual supplizio sovrastra!

PINKERTON
Ehi, dico: basta, basta!

IL BONZO
Venite tutti—Andiamo!
Ci hai rinnegato e noi . . .
Ti rinneghiamo!

TUTTI
Ti rinneghiamo!

PINKERTON
Sbarazzate all'istante. In casa mia
niente baccano e niente bonzeria.

TUTTI
Hou! Cio-cio-san!
Kami sarundasico
Ti vinneghiamo!
Hou! Cio-cio-san!

PINKERTON
Bimba, bimba, non piangere
per gracchiar di ranocchi.

BUTTERFLY
Urlano ancor!

THE BONZE
Answer, did you dare defy us,
Abandon and deny us?
(*shouting*)
She has renounced her people!

ALL
Hou! Cio-cio-san!
(BUTTERFLY, *overcome with shame, hides her face in her hands*)

THE BONZE (*shouting into her face*)
She foreswears and outrages
Our cult of ages!

ALL
Hou! Cio-cio-san!

THE BONZE
Kami, sarundasico!
Your soul be damned to languish
In unbearable anguish!

PINKERTON (*authoritatively*)
Be silent, I command it!

THE BONZE
No one must stay here!
Come with me!
Because you have renounced us,
We now renounce you!

ALL
We now renounce you!

PINKERTON (*authoritatively*)
I won't stand for this nonsense!
I'll have no stupid riot in my house,
I order you to leave!

ALL (*while leaving*)
Hou! Cio-cio-san!
Kami sarundasico!
We all renounce you!
Hou! Cio-cio-san!
(*all the guests, including the* BONZE, *depart in great haste, going down the hillside and continuing to hurl threats and imprecations at* BUTTERFLY. *By degrees the voices die away in the distance.* BUTTERFLY, *who has been standing motionless and mute with her face buried in her hands, bursts into childish tears. Evening begins gradually, then night sets in, serene and starlit*)

PINKERTON (*goes up to* BUTTERFLY *and gently draws her hands from her face*)
Dearest, do not shed tears for them,
For their ranting and snarling.

BUTTERFLY (*still hears the yells of her relations and holds her ears*)
Hear how they scream!

PINKERTON (*cheering her*)
No matter what they do,
Not all the Bonzes of Japan
Deserve even one small tear
From your sweet eyes, beloved.

BUTTERFLY (*smiling with childlike pleasure*)
You're sure? Then I won't cry.
I shall forget their curse, so harsh and hateful.
I am ever so grateful—
Your consoling words are balm to my heart.
(*stoops to kiss* PINKERTON's *hand*)

PINKERTON (*surprised at her action, gently stops her*)
My hand?—But why?

BUTTERFLY
I've heard that in your land
With the very finest people,
It is a sign of great respect and honor.

SUZUKI
(*murmuring inside the house*)
Izaghi and Izanami,
Sarundasico and Kami . . .

PINKERTON (*hears a subdued murmuring*)
Who's murmuring up there?

BUTTERFLY
It's Suzuki; she's offering
Her pray'r for the night . . .

PINKERTON (*drawing her close to him*)
Darkness is falling—

BUTTERFLY
And calmness is reigning—

PINKERTON
My own beloved—

BUTTERFLY
All alone and outcast—cursed forever!
Yet, so happy!

PINKERTON (*has clapped his hands and the servants have hastened in*)
You, servants—close the doors.

BUTTERFLY
Yes, we are all alone now—
The world is dreaming . . .

PINKERTON (*laughing*)
No raving Bonze is screaming—

BUTTERFLY (*to* SUZUKI, *who has come in with the servants and is awaiting orders*)
Suzuki, bring the white robe.
(SUZUKI *rummages in a lacquer trunk*)

SUZUKI (*after having given* BUTTERFLY *her night attire and a small box with toiletries, bows low to* PINKERTON)

PINKERTON
Tutta la tua tribù
e i Bonzi tutti del Giappon non valgono
il pianto di quegli occhi
cari e belli.

BUTTERFLY
Davver? Non piango più.
E quasi del ripudio non mi duole
per le vostre parole
che mi suonan così dolci nel cuor.

PINKERTON
Che fai? . . . la man?

BUTTERFLY
M'han detto
che laggiù fra la gente costumata
è questo il segno del maggior rispetto.

SUZUKI
E Izaghi ed Izanami
Sarundasico e Kami

PINKERTON
Chi brontola lassù?

BUTTERFLY
È Suzuki che fa la sua preghiera
seral.

PINKERTON
Viene la sera . . .

BUTTERFLY
e l'ombra e la quiete.

PINKERTON
E sei qui sola.

BUTTERFLY
Sola e rinnegata!
Rinnegata e felice!

PINKERTON
A voi—chiudete.

BUTTERFLY
Sì, sì, noi tutti soli . . .
E fuori il mondo.

PINKERTON
E il Bonzo furibondo.

BUTTERFLY
Suzuki, le mie vesti.

SUZUKI
Buona notte.

Good night, sir!
(BUTTERFLY *retires to a corner and, assisted by* SUZUKI, *carefully performs her toilet for the night, exchanging her wedding garment for one of pure white.* SUZUKI *goes out*).

BUTTERFLY
Quest'obi pomposa
di scioglier mi tarda
si vesta la sposa
di puro candor.
Tra motti sommessi
sorride e mi guarda.
Celarmi potessi!
ne ho tanto rossor!
E ancor l'irata
voce mi maledice . . .
Butterfly . . . rinnegata,
Rinnegata . . . e felice.

BUTTERFLY
This obi is far too ornate and imposing . . .
A bride's sacred robe must be white as the snow.
He smiles and observes me, his glances caressing.
How can I escape them? I'm blushing, I know!
Again, I hear that furious curse pursue me . . .
"Butterfly . . . We renounce you."
—Yet, I'm happy.

PINKERTON
Con moti di scojattolo
i nodi allenta e scioglie! . . .
Pensar che quel giocattolo
è mia moglie. Mia moglie:
Ma tal grazia dispiega,
ch'io mi struggo per la febbre
d'un subito desìo.
Bimba dagli occhi pieni di malìa
ora sei tutta mia.
Sei tutta vestita di giglio.
Mi piace la treccia tua bruna
fra candidi veli . . .

PINKERTON (*lolling on the wicker lounge, takes a cigarette and watches* BUTTERFLY, *who is busy adorning herself*)
She's graceful as a kitten,
So full of charm and life!
To think that precious child,
Is now my wife! My wife!
So enchanting a vision
That my heart is beating madly
With sudden glowing fever.
(*goes up to* BUTTERFLY, *raises her gently, and goes out on the terrace with her*)
Dear little flower, blossoming so sweetly . . .
Now you are mine completely . . .
The aura of lilies surrounds you,
Your hair shining dark in profusion
From under the veiling . . .

BUTTERFLY
Somiglio
la Dea della luna,
la piccola Dea della luna che scende
la notte dal ponte del ciel . . .

BUTTERFLY (*goes down from the terrace*)
I feel like the goddess of moonlight,
Arrayed in a starry illusion,
Descending each night by her skybridge of dreams.

PINKERTON
E affascina i cuori . . .

PINKERTON (*following her*)
Enflaming our senses.

BUTTERFLY
E li prende,
li avvolge in un bianco mantel.
E via se li reca
negli alti reami.

BUTTERFLY
Gently bending—
She enfolds ev'ry heart in her rays . . .
And bears them to the regions in heaven above us.

PINKERTON
Ma intanto finor non m'hai detto,
ancor non m'hai detto che m'ami,
Le sa quella Dea le parole
che appagan gli ardenti desir?

PINKERTON
You still have not told me you love me . . .
Those words so inspiring to lovers . . .
Your goddess, will she know the token,
The words that no love can deny?

BUTTERFLY
Le sa. Forse dirle non vuole
per tema d'averne a morir!

BUTTERFLY
She knows, but she leaves them unspoken
For fear she will say them and die.

PINKERTON
Foolish delusion, that love should destroy her!
Love is living, freely giving,
Its joys overflowing,
Warm as the spark
In your dark eyes, lovingly glowing.

BUTTERFLY
You are the sunlight, the god of day . . .
Humbly I shall adore you,
I knew what love meant the moment I saw you,
My own beloved . . .
You are strong and manly,
Your laughter is generous and telling
And what you say is so new and compelling.
I am so happy—I am so happy!
Just like me a little, and only let me please you
The way a child may please you,
That is all I could hope for.
My people never measures contentment by splendor,
But by the small and tender,
Quiet little pleasures whose worth is far more boundless
Than the sky, or the ocean's abysses.

PINKERTON
Give me you hands, I'll cover them with kisses!
(*bursts out very tenderly*)
My Butterfly!—How very well they named you,
Tender, fragile creature!—

BUTTERFLY (*at these words her face clouds over and she draws away her hands*)
There across the ocean, when butterflies are caught,
I've often heard it is the custom to impale them—
Then on cardboard to nail them!

PINKERTON (*gently taking her hands again and smiling*)
That's true, I can't deny,
But shall I tell you why?—
So they can't fly away!
(*embracing her*)
And I have caught you, and so I want to hold you.
Be mine now!

BUTTERFLY
Now and forever.
(*throwing herself in his arms*)

PINKERTON
Come, beloved.
Come, be done with all anguish,
Enchaining, enclosing.
(*pointing to the starlit sky*)
The dark night is reigning!
All the world is reposing!

PINKERTON
Stolta paura, l'amor non uccide
ma dà vita, e sorride
per gioie celestiali

come ora fa nei tuoi lunghi
occhi ovali.

BUTTERFLY
Adesso voi
siete per me l'occhio del firmamento.
E mi piaceste dal primo momento
che vi ho veduto. Siete
alto, forte. Ridete
con modi si palesi!
E dite cose che mai non intesi.
Or son contenta.
Vogliatemi bene,
un bene piccolino,
un bene da bambino
quale a me si conviene.
Noi siamo gente avvezza
alle piccole cose
umili e silenziose,
ad una tenerezza
sfiorante e pur profonda
come il ciel, come l'onda
del mare.

PINKERTON
Dammi ch'io baci le tue mani
care.
Mia Butterfly! . . . come t'han
ben nomata
tenue farfalla . . .

BUTTERFLY
Dicon ch'oltre mare
se cade in man dell'uom, ogni
farfalla
da uno spillo è trafitta
ed in tavola infitta!

PINKERTON
Un po' di vero c'è.
E tu lo sai perchè?
Perchè non fugga più.
Io t'ho ghermita . . .
Ti serro palpitante.
Sei mia.

BUTTERFLY
Sì, per la vita.

PINKERTON
Vieni, vieni.
Via dall'anima in pena
l'angoscia paurosa.
È notte serena!
Guarda: dorme ogni cosa!

BUTTERFLY
Ah! Dolce notte! Quante stelle!
Non le vidi mai sì belle!
Trema, brilla, ogni favilla
col baglior d'una pupilla.
Oh! quanti occhi fisi, attenti
d'ogni parte a riguardar!
Pei firmamenti,
via pei lidi, via pel mare.
Ah! quanti occhi fissi, attenti!
Quanti sguardi,
Ride il ciel!
Ah! Dolce notte!
Tutto estatico d'amor
ride il ciel!
PINKERTON
Vieni, vieni!
Vien, sei mia!
Via l'angoscia del tuo cor!
Ti serro palpitante.
Sei mia.
Ah! vieni guarda:
Dorme ogni cosa!
Ti serro palpitante, ah, vien!
Guarda; dorme ogni cosa.
Ah vien! Ah vieni!
Ah vien, sei mia!

BUTTERFLY
Ah, hour of beauty! Soft and tender,
Night of starry, shining splendor!
Sparkling, streaming–
The stars are gleaming
While the world below is dreaming.
A thousand million glances there to guard us,
All the stars in heaven's expanses,
Bathed in glory high above us!
Ah! Golden moment!
Hold the world's enraptured love in your spell.
PINKERTON (*with passionate longing*)
Hasten, hasten!
Come beloved!
Cast your anguish, from your heart!
Rejoicing in surrender.
Beloved, be mine!
The night has fallen,
Calmness is reigning.
I hold you to my heart, my love.
All the world is reposing
Ah come, ah my beloved!
Ah! Be mine, my beloved!

ACT II

Inside BUTTERFLY's *little house* SUZUKI, *coiled up in front of the image of Buddha, is praying; from time to time she rings the prayer bell.* BUTTERFLY *is standing rigid and motionless near the screen.*

SUZUKI (*praying*)
Izaghi and Izanami,
Sarundasico and Kami.
(*breaking off*)
My mind is wand'ring!
(*rings the prayer bell to invoke the attention of the gods*)
And you, Ten-Sjoo-daj!
(*looking at* BUTTERFLY)
Grant us that Butterfly
May weep no more, no more, no more!

SUZUKI
E Izaghi ed Izanami
Sarundasico e Kami . . .
Oh! la mia testa!
E tu
Ten-Sjoo-daj!
Fate che Butterfly
non pianga più, mai più, mai più.

BUTTERFLY (*to* SUZUKI)
Dull and obese gods
Are your own Japanese gods.
The God of my new country
Is far more kindly,
Glad to answer the people
Who adore him.
He'd grant what I implore him
If he knew where to find me.
(*remains pensive, then she turns to* SUZUKI, *who has risen to her feet and has drawn back the partition leading to the garden*)
Suzuki, what money is remaining?

BUTTERFLY
Pigri ed obesi
son gli Dei Giapponesi.
L'americano Iddio son persuasa
ben più presto risponde e chi l'implori.
Ma temo ch'egli ignori
che noi stiam qui di casa.
Suzuki, è lungi la miseria?

SUZUKI (*opens a small cabinet and, taking a few coins from it, shows them to* BUTTERFLY)
This is all we possess now.

SUZUKI
Questo è
l'ultimo fondo.

BUTTERFLY
Is it?—Oh! We are spendthrifts!

BUTTERFLY
Questo? Oh! Troppe spese!

SUZUKI (*replaces the money in the cabinet, which she closes, saying with a sigh*)
Unless he comes, and quickly,
We'll have nothing to live on.

SUZUKI
S'egli non torna e presto,
siamo male in arnese.

BUTTERFLY (*with decision*)
He will though!

BUTTERFLY
Ma torna.

SUZUKI (*shaking her head*)
Who can tell!

SUZUKI
Tornerà!

BUTTERFLY (*vexed, to* SUZUKI)
Why did he order that ev'ry month
The Consul pay the rent then? You tell me, why?
Why did he make so sure then
To fit the doors with latches and secure them,
If he was not returning by and by?

BUTTERFLY
Perchè dispone
che il Console provveda alla pigione,
rispondi, su!
Perchè con tante cure
la casa riforni di serrature,
s'ei non volesse ritornar mai più?

SUZUKI
I don't know.

SUZUKI
Non lo so.

BUTTERFLY
Non lo sai?
Io te lo dico. Per tener ben fuorì
le zanzare, i parenti ed i dolori
e dentro, con gelosa
custodia, la sua sposa
che son io: Butterfly.

SUZUKI
Mai non s'è udito
di straniero marito
che sia tornato al suo nido.

BUTTERFLY
Taci, o t'uccido.
Quell'ultima mattina:
tornerete signor?—gli domandai.
Egli, col cuore grosso,
per celarmi la pena
sorridendo rispose:
—O Butterfly
piccina mogliettina,
tornerò colle rose
alla stagion serena
quando fa la nidiata il pettirosso.
Tornerà.

SUZUKI
Speriam.

BUTTERFLY
Dillo con me:
Tornerà.

SUZUKI
Tornerà . . .

BUTTERFLY
Piangi? Perchè?
Ah la fede ti manca!

Senti
Un bel dì, vedremo
levarsi un fil di fumo sull'-estremo
confin del mare.
E poi la nave appare
E poi la nave bianca.
Entra nel porto, romba il suo saluto.
Vedi? È venuto!
Io non gli scendo incontro, Io no.
Mi metto là sul ciglio del colle e aspetto, e aspetto

BUTTERFLY (*surprised at such ignorance*)
You don't know?
(*with proud confidence*)
Then I will tell you. So we might keep out
The swarming gnats and relations, as well as sorrow.
And inside, would be waiting
His faithful wife forever—
His wife and his beloved, Butterfly.

SUZUKI (*still far from convinced*)
But, who has ever heard
Of foreigner husbands
Returning once they've departed!

BUTTERFLY (*furious*)
Ah! Stop it! Or I'll kill you.
(*still trying to persuade* SUZUKI)
The morning he departed,
When I asked him, "My Lord will you return?"
Hiding his grief he told me,
And assured me with reason
As he smiled, and consoled me—
(*imitating* PINKERTON)
"Dear Butterfly, my precious little darling,
I'll return with the roses
In that idyllic season
When the robins are starting
To do their nesting."
(*calm and convinced*)
He'll return.

SUZUKI (*still incredulous*)
I hope—

BUTTERFLY (*insisting*)
Say it with me:
He'll return!

SUZUKI (*repeats, to please her*)
He'll return.
(*then she bursts out weeping*)

BUTTERFLY (*surprised*)
You're crying? But why?
It is faith you are lacking!
(*she then continues, full of faith, and smiling*)
Listen.
One fine day we'll notice
A tiny smoke-cloud nearing
On the sea in the far horizon—
And then his ship appearing.
Now the mighty warship
Slowly comes to harbor.
Cannons roar a welcome.
See there! How I knew it!
I shall not go to meet him. Oh, no!
I'll wait until much later to greet him,

Awaiting, awaiting his coming, uncounted hours,
Among the flowers.—
A man emerges from the crowded city,
A tiny dot ascending,
And slowly looming clearer.
Is it he? And at his journey's ending,
Can it be?
He will call, "Butterfly!" as he comes nearer;
I, then, without replying,
Will hide awhile in silence;
Perhaps to tease him, but more
To keep from dying of rejoicing.
And then in agitation, he will call, he will call:
"My precious little darling,
My lovely silver goddess!"
Those loving names I always will remember—
(to SUZUKI*)*
All I say will come true,—You must believe me!
Love cannot be mistaken—
My faith remains forever unshaken!
(dismisses SUZUKI, *who goes out of door on left.* BUTTERFLY *looks after her, sadly;* GORO *and* SHARPLESS *appear in the garden;* GORO *looks into the room, sees* BUTTERFLY, *and says to* SHARPLESS*)*

gran tempo e non mi pesa,
la lunga attesa.
E uscito dalla folla cittadina
un uomo, un picciol punto
s'avvia per la collina.
Chi sarà? chi sarà?
E come sarà giunto
che dirà? che dirà?
Chiamerà Butterfly dalla lontana
Io senza far risposta
me ne starò nascosta
un po' per celia, e un po' per non morire
al primo incontro, ed egli alquanto in pena
chiamerà, chiamerà:
"Piccina mogliettina
olezzo di verbena"
i nomi che mi dava al suo venire.
Tutto questo avverrà, te lo prometto
Tienti la tua paura, io con sicura
fede l'aspetto.

GORO
There, you may enter.
(brings SHARPLESS *in, then goes outside again at once and peeps in from the garden every now and then)*

GORO
C'è.—Entrate.

SHARPLESS *(knocks cautiously at the door on the right)*
May I come in—
(catches sight of BUTTERFLY, *who has risen on hearing him enter)*
Madame Butterfly!

SHARPLESS
Chiedo scusa . . .
Madama Butterfly . . .

BUTTERFLY *(corrects him, without turning round)*
I'm Madame Pinkerton—Come in!
(she turns round, recognizes the Consul, and claps her hands for joy)
Your Honor, the Consul here. Oh!
Here to visit me!
*(*SUZUKI *enters eagerly and prepares a small table with smoking materials, some cushions, and a stool)*

BUTTERFLY
Madama Pinkerton
Prego.
Oh! il mio signor Console!
Signor Console!

SHARPLESS *(surprised)*
You do remember?

SHARPLESS
Mi ravvisate?

BUTTERFLY *(doing the honors of the house)*
You are welcome;
This is an American household.

BUTTERFLY
Benvenuto in casa
americana.

SHARPLESS
Thank you!

SHARPLESS
Grazie.

BUTTERFLY *(invites the Consul to be seated near the table;* SHARPLESS *drops awkwardly onto a cushion.* BUTTERFLY

BUTTERFLY
Avi, antenati
tutti bene?

sits down on the other side and slyly smiles behind her fan at his discomfort, then with much grace!)

Parents and relations,
Well and happy?

SHARPLESS
Ma spero.

SHARPLESS (*thanks her, smiling*)
I hope so—

BUTTERFLY
Fumate?

BUTTERFLY (*signs to* SUZUKI, *who prepares the pipe*)
A pipe, sir?

SHARPLESS
Grazie.
Ho qui . . .

SHARPLESS
Thank you!
(*he is anxious to explain the object of his visit and draws a letter from his pocket*)
I came . . .

BUTTERFLY
Signore—io vedo
il cielo azzurro.

BUTTERFLY (*interrupting him*)
Your Lordship,
How glad I am to see you!
(*after having taken a draw at the pipe, she offers it to the Consul*)

SHARPLESS
Grazie . . .
Ho . . .

SHARPLESS (*refusing*)
Thank you.
(*trying again to resume the thread of his talk*)
Well . . .

BUTTERFLY
Preferite
forse le sigarette
Americane?

BUTTERFLY (*lays down the pipe on the table and says very importantly*)
Would Your Honor rather try
An imported American cigarette?
(*offers him some*)

SHARPLESS
Grazie.
Ho da mostrarvi . . .

SHARPLESS (*taking one*)
Thank you!
(*rises and tries to resume*)
I'd like to show you—

BUTTERFLY
A voi.

BUTTERFLY (*hands him a lighted match*)
A light?

SHARPLESS
Mi scrisse
Mr. Benjamin Franklin
Pinkerton . . .

SHARPLESS (*lights his cigarette, but then puts it down at once and, showing her the letter, sits down on the stool*)
A letter from Benjamin Franklin Pinkerton.

BUTTERFLY
Davvero!
È in salute?

BUTTERFLY (*with intense earnestness*)
Oh! Really?
And how is he?

SHARPLESS
Perfetta.

SHARPLESS
Just splendid.

BUTTERFLY
Io son la donna
più lieta del Giappone.
Potrei farvi
una domanda?

BUTTERFLY (*jumping up very joyfully*)
In all Japan—
There's no woman quite so happy!
Would you answer me one question?
(SUZUKI *is busy preparing tea*)

SHARPLESS
Certo.

SHARPLESS
Gladly.

BUTTERFLY (*sits down again*)
When do robins begin, in America,
To do their nesting?

BUTTERFLY
Quando fanno
il lor nido in America
i pettirossi?

SHARPLESS (*amazed*)
Do their nesting?

SHARPLESS
Come dite?

BUTTERFLY
Yes.
Not so often as here?

BUTTERFLY
Sì,
prima o dopo di qui?

SHARPLESS
Well . . . but why?
(GORO *comes up from the garden onto the terrace and listens unseen by* BUTTERFLY)

SHARPLESS
Ma . . . perchè? . . .

BUTTERFLY
My beloved husband promised
He would return here in the lovely season
When all the robins were starting their nesting.
Here they have done so three times already,
But it could be that over there,
They do not nest so often.
(GORO *bursts out laughing*)
Who's laughing?
(*sees* GORO)
Oh! only Goro.
(*softly to* SHARPLESS)
A nasty fellow!

BUTTERFLY
Mio marito m' ha promesso
di ritornar nella stagion beata
che il pettirosso rifà la nidiata.
Qui l' ha rifatta ben tre volte,
ma può darsi che di là
usi nidiar men spesso.
Chi ride?
Oh, c'è il nakodo,
Un uom cattivo.

GORO (*bowing obsequiously*)
Thank you!

GORO
Godo . . .

BUTTERFLY
Quiet.
(*to* SHARPLESS)
He has dared—No, first I beg you answer
This important question.

BUTTERFLY
Zitto.
Egli osò . . . No, prima rispondete
alla domanda mia.

SHARPLESS (*embarrassed*)
I am sorry, my apology.
I never studied ornithology.

SHARPLESS
Mi rincresce ma ignoro . . .
Non ho studiato ornitologia.

BUTTERFLY (*trying to understand*)
Orni . . . ?

BUTTERFLY
Orni . . .

SHARPLESS
. . . thology.

SHARPLESS
. . . tologia.

BUTTERFLY
Then you can't tell me either?

BUTTERFLY
Non lo sapete insomma.

SHARPLESS
No.
(*tries to return to his point*)
We were saying . . .

SHARPLESS
No.
Dicevamo . . .

BUTTERFLY (*interrupts him, pursuing her thoughts*)
As, yes, Goro!
As soon as B. F. Pinkerton departed,
That Goro came and started,
To plague me with proposals
In the hope I'd consider some alliance—

BUTTERFLY
Ah, sì—Goro,
appena B. F. Pinkerton fu in mare
mi venne ad assediare
con ciarle e con presenti
per ridarmi ora questo,
or quel marito.

Or promette tesori
per uno scimunito . . .

Like the match he suggests
With one fool among his clients—

GORO
Il ricco Yamadori.
Ella è povera in canna. I suoi
parenti
l'han tutti rinnegata.

GORO (*to justify himself, tries to explain to* SHARPLESS)
The wealthy Yamadori.
In her wretched condition—
She can't afford to reject this proposition.
(*beyond the terrace the* PRINCE YAMADORI *is seen, followed by two servants carrying flowers*)

BUTTERFLY
Eccolo. Attenti.

BUTTERFLY (*sees* YAMADORI, *and points him out to* SHARPLESS *with a smile*)
Here he is. You'll see him.
(YAMADORI *enters with much pomp, bows gracefully to* BUTTERFLY, *then salutes the Consul. The two servants deliver their flowers to* SUZUKI *and retire to the back.* GORO, *full of servility, brings a stool for* YAMADORI, *between* SHARPLESS *and* BUTTERFLY, *and is very much in evidence throughout the interview.* SHARPLESS *and* YAMADORI *sit down; to* YAMADORI)

Yamadori ancor le pene
dell'amor, non v'han deluso?
Vi tagliate ancor le vene
se il mio bacio vi ricuso?

Yamadori—Once more
Your unrequited love can't disabuse you?
As you said before,
You'll swear to end your life
If I refuse you?

YAMADORI
Tra le cose più moleste
è l' inutil sospirar.

YAMADORI (*to* SHARPLESS)
Sadly sighing, longing vainly,
Those are things I loathe to do.

BUTTERFLY
Tante mogli omai toglieste,
vi doveste abituar.

BUTTERFLY (*with graceful raillery*)
You've had many wives already . . .
That should not be hard for you.

YAMADORI
L'ho sposate tutte quante
e il divorzio mi francò.

YAMADORI
I had many wives; however
I won freedom by divorce.

BUTTERFLY
Obbligata.

BUTTERFLY
Very flatt'ring!

YAMADORI
A voi però
giurerei fede costante.

YAMADORI
To you, of course,
I will swear my faith forever.

SHARPLESS
(Il messaggio, ho gran paura,
a trasmetter non riesco.)

SHARPLESS (*sighing, replaces the letter in his pocket*)
(In delivering my message—
I'm not getting any further.)

GORO
Ville, servi, oro, ad Omura
un palazzo principesco.

GORO (*pointing out* YAMADORI *to* SHARPLESS, *with emphasis*)
Houses, servants, money,
A magnificent palace in Omura!

BUTTERFLY
Già legata è la mia fede.

BUTTERFLY (*seriously*)
But I am already married—

GORO, YAMADORI
Maritata ancor si crede.

GORO and YAMADORI (*to* SHARPLESS)
She still thinks that she is married—

BUTTERFLY
Non mi credo: sono, sono.

BUTTERFLY (*emphatically*)
I don't think so, but I know so.

GORO
Ma la legge . . .

GORO
But the laws says . . .

BUTTERFLY (*interrupting him*)
It's not in force!

GORO (*continues*)
When a wife has been abandoned,
It is equal to divorce.

BUTTERFLY
That may be Japanese law,
But not the one I honor.

GORO
Which one?

BUTTERFLY (*with emphasis*)
United States law.

SHARPLESS
(Oh, what a pity!)

BUTTERFLY (*strenuously, and growing excited*)
A man who has a mind to,
Turns his wife out of doors
When he's inclined to.
Here, that's divorce, they tell me.
But in America, that could never be.
(*to* SHARPLESS)
Could it?

SHARPLESS (*embarrassed*)
Hardly . . . although . . .

BUTTERFLY (*interrupts him, turning to* YAMADORI *and* GORO *in triumph*)
There a good magistrate,
Just and impartial,
Says to the husband:
"You have enough of her?
"Why would that be?"
"My wife is lazy,
She drives me crazy!"
Comes the decision:
"Ah, you're a scoundrel,
"You go to prison!"
(*to put an end to the subject, she orders* SUZUKI)
Suzuki, tea.

YAMADORI (*softly, to* SHARPLESS, *while* BUTTERFLY *makes tea*)
You heard her?

SHARPLESS
I am saddened by so much blindness
To the truth.

GORO (*whispers to* YAMADORI *and* SHARPLESS)
Pinkerton's vessel soon will enter the harbor—

YAMADORI (*in despair*)
The moment that she sees him—

SHARPLESS (*whispers to both*)
He does not want to see her—
I came expressly to explain what happened—

BUTTERFLY
Io non la so.

GORO
. . . per la moglie, l'abbandono
al divorzio equiparò.

BUTTERFLY
La legge giapponese . . .
non gia del mio paese.

GORO
Quale?

BUTTERFLY
Gli Stati Uniti.

SHARPLESS
(Oh, l' infelice!)

BUTTERFLY
Si sa che aprir la porta
e la moglie cacciar per la più corta
qui divorziar si dice.
Ma in America questo non si può.
Vero?

SHARPLESS
Vero . . . Però . . .

BUTTERFLY
Là un bravo giudice
serio, impettito
dice al marito:
"Lei vuol andarsene?
"Sentiam perchè?"
"Sono seccato
"del coniugato!"
E il magistrato:
"Ah, mascalzone,
"presto in prigione!"
Suzuki, il thè.

YAMADORI
Udiste?

SHARPLESS
Mi rattrista una si piena
cecità.

GORO
Segnalata è già la nave
di Pinkerton.

YAMADORI
Quand'essa lo riveda . . .

SHARPLESS
Egli non vuol mostrarsi. Io venni appunto
per levarla d'inganno.

(seeing that BUTTERFLY *is approaching him with tea, he cuts short his sentence)*

BUTTERFLY
Vostra Grazia permette . . .
Che persone moleste!

BUTTERFLY *(charmingly, offering* SHARPLESS *a cup of tea)*
Will Your Honor permit me—
(opens her fan, and behind it points to the two others, laughing)
What bothersome persons! . . .
(offers tea to YAMADORI, *who refuses)*

YAMADORI
Addio. Vi lascio il cuor pien di cordoglio:
ma spero ancor.

YAMADORI *(rises with a sigh and bows to* BUTTERFLY *with hand on heart)*
I leave you. You have my heart,
Heavy, but hopeful, as I depart.

BUTTERFLY
Padrone.

BUTTERFLY
Your privilege.

YAMADORI
Ah! se voleste . . .

YAMADORI *(is leaving but returns to* BUTTERFLY*)*
If you were willing . . .

BUTTERFLY
Il guaio è che non voglio . . .

BUTTERFLY
Too bad I am not willing.
*(*YAMADORI, *after having bowed to* SHARPLESS, *goes off sighing, followed by his servants.* BUTTERFLY *signs to* SUZUKI *to remove the tea.* SUZUKI *obeys, then retires to the back of the room.* GORO *promptly follows* YAMADORI*)*

SHARPLESS
Ora a noi. Sedete qui.
Legger con me volete
questa lettera?

SHARPLESS *(assumes a grave and serious aspect; with great respect, however, and some emotion, he invites* BUTTERFLY *to be seated, and once more draws the letter from his pocket)*
We're alone—Sit here with me.
*(*BUTTERFLY *merrily seats herself near* SHARPLESS, *who shows her the letter)*
And if you like, you'll read this letter through with me?

BUTTERFLY
Date.
Sulla bocca, sul cuore . . .
Siete l'uomo migliore
del mondo.—Incominciate.

BUTTERFLY
May I?
(takes the letter, kisses it, then places it on her heart)
Let me kiss it, caress it . . .
(gives it back to SHARPLESS, *saying,)*
No one ever was kinder than you are.
Now, won't you read it.

SHARPLESS
"*Amico cercherete*
quel bel fior di fanciulla . . ."

SHARPLESS *(reads)*
"Dear friend, I beg you go and see
"That sweet little flower—"

BUTTERFLY
Dice proprio così?

BUTTERFLY *(interrupting him joyfully)*
Did he say it like that?

SHARPLESS
Sì, così dice
ma se ad ogni momento . . .

SHARPLESS
Yes, to the letter,
But if at ev'ry moment . . .

BUTTERFLY
Taccio, taccio—più nulla.

BUTTERFLY *(calming down again)*
I'll be quiet—I promise.

SHARPLESS
"*Da quel tempo felice*
tre anni son passati."

SHARPLESS *(resumes)*
"Since those fair days together,
Three years have now gone by—"

BUTTERFLY (*unable to contain herself*)
He has counted them also!

SHARPLESS (*continues*)
"And maybe Butterfly
Forgot me long ago."

BUTTERFLY (*surprised*)
I could forget him?
(*turning to* SUZUKI)
Suzuki, you should know.
(*repeats as though scandalized at the words of the letter*)
"Forgot me long ago!"
(SUZUKI *nods her head affirmatively, then goes into room on left*)

SHARPLESS (*to himself*)
Dear heaven!
(*continues reading*)
"If she thinks of me still—
If she's waiting . . ."

BUTTERFLY (*deeply moved*)
Oh, what heart-warming phrases!
(*takes the letter and kisses it*)
Oh, blessed letter!

SHARPLESS (*takes the letter back and boldly resumes reading, though his voice is trembling with emotion*)
"In order to prepare her,
I think it would be better
If you were to tell her gently—"

BUTTERFLY (*anxiously, but radiant*)
He's coming—

SHARPLESS
"The shock might—"

BUTTERFLY (*jumping for joy and clapping her hands*)
Really? When? When?

SHARPLESS (*resignedly folds up the letter and replaces it it in his pocket*)
(The devil!
I can spare her no longer—)
(*shaking his head in vexation*)
(I'll have to tell the truth to her.)
(*rises, and looking straight into* BUTTERFLY'S *eyes, very seriously*)
Now tell me, Madame Butterfly,
What would you do
If he should never come back to you?

BUTTERFLY (*motionless, like one who has received a deathblow, bows her head and says with childlike submissiveness*)
Two courses would remain—
Again to entertain the people with my songs—
Or else—better—to die.

BUTTERFLY
Anche lui li ha contati.

SHARPLESS
*"E forse Butterfly
non mi rammenta più."*

BUTTERFLY
Non lo rammento?
Suzuki, dillo tu.
"Non mi rammenta più!"

SHARPLESS
(Pazienza!)
*"Se mi vuol
bene ancor, se m'aspetta . . ."*

BUTTERFLY
Oh le dolci parole!
Tu, benedetta!

SHARPLESS
*"A voi mi raccomando
perchè vogliate con
circospezione
prepararla . . ."*

BUTTERFLY
Ritorna . . .

SHARPLESS
"al colpo . . ."

BUTTERFLY
Quando?
Presto! presto!

SHARPLESS
(Benone.
Qui troncarla conviene . . .
Quel diavolo d'un Pinkerton!)
Ebbene,
che fareste Madama Butterfly
s'ei non dovesse ritornar più
mai?

BUTTERFLY
Due cose potrei far:
tornar a divertir
la gente col cantar
oppur, meglio, morire.

SHARPLESS Di strapparvi assai mi costa dai miraggi ingannatori. Accogliete la proposta di quel ricco Yamadori.	SHARPLESS (*is deeply moved, and walks up and down excitedly—then he turns to* BUTTERFLY, *takes her hands in his, and says with fatherly tenderness*) To destroy all your illusions Makes me feel extremely sorry. But I beg you, take the offer Of that wealthy Yamadori.
BUTTERFLY Voi, signor, mi dite questo!	BUTTERFLY (*withdrawing her hands from his*) You, even you, Of all people . . .
SHARPLESS Santo Dio, come si fa?	SHARPLESS (*embarrassed*) Oh, dear God, what can I do?
BUTTERFLY Qui, Suzuki, presto presto che Sua Grazia se ne va.	BUTTERFLY (*claps her hands—*SUZUKI *hastens in*) Quick, Suzuki, hurry, hurry— Show His Honor to the door.
SHARPLESS Mi scacciate?	SHARPLESS You dismiss me? (*is on the point of leaving, but* BUTTERFLY *runs to him, sobbing, and holds him back*)
BUTTERFLY Ve ne prego, già l'insistere non vale.	BUTTERFLY Please forgive me— But your words upset me greatly. (*dismisses* SUZUKI, *who goes into the garden*)
SHARPLESS Fui brutale, non lo nego.	SHARPLESS (*making excuses*) I was cruel, I don't deny it.
BUTTERFLY Oh, mi fate tanto male, tanto male, tanto, tanto!	BUTTERFLY (*sadly, laying her hand on her heart*) Oh, it hurt my heart so deeply, You have hurt my heart so deeply! (BUTTERFLY *totters;* SHARPLESS *is about to support her, but she quickly rallies*)
Niente, niente! Ho creduto morir. Ma passa presto come passan le nuvole sul mare . . . Ah! . . . m'ha scordata?	Nothing, nothing! I was sure I would die— But soon it passed away— As gently as clouds above the ocean. Ah! He forgot me? (*runs into the room on the left, and comes back in triumph, carrying her baby on her shoulder, and shows him to* SHARPLESS, *full of pride*)
E questo? . . . e questo? . . . e questo egli potrà pure scordare? . . .	The baby—the baby— Could he forget this little darling? (*puts the child down on the ground and holds him close to her*)
SHARPLESS Egli è suo?	SHARPLESS (*deeply touched*) It is his?
BUTTERFLY Chi vide mai a bimbo del Giappon occhi azzurrini? E il labbro? E i ricciolini d'oro schietto?	BUTTERFLY (*pointing to his features one by one*) What Japanese child has eyes like his, As light as tiny bluebells? Or features, and curly hair So fair and pretty?

SHARPLESS (*more and more moved*)
It is obvious.
And does his father know?

BUTTERFLY
No, my husband was far away then,
In his own native country.
(*caressing the child*)
You know now, so you will write him
He's the father of a son no child can rival!
And he will speed the day of his arrival,
Proud and happy to embrace him!
(*seats the child on the cushion and kisses him fondly*)
Do you know, my darling,
What His Honor has been thinking?
(*points to* SHARPLESS)
With my child in my arms I ought to wander
Throughout the city,
Through biting wind and blinding rain,
Begging for food, the bitter crumbs of pity,
The trembling hand of supplication
Extended time and time again!
Imploring, "Have mercy, have mercy—
"And hear a mother's song—
"A plaintive song her grief-stricken lips impart—
"May pity move your heart!"
And Butterfly, beneath the star of evil,
Now will dance for you!
And as she did before,
The geisha sings once more!
The joyous song will soon die away
To end a brokenhearted sigh!
No, I'd rather die!—
I shall not live if living means dishonor!
Horror! Horror!
It's best by far—to end a life
That grievous shame would mar!
Ah! Never!
(*she strains the child to her heart and, crouching down on the ground, hugs him passionately*)

SHARPLESS (*cannot restrain his tears*)
(Poor little heart!)
(*conquering his emotion, he says*)
I must be going—Will you forgive me?
(BUTTERFLY *rises to her feet and with a charming gesture gives* SHARPLESS *her hand; he shakes it cordially with both of his*)

BUTTERFLY (*to the child*)
Your hand—Just as I taught you.

SHARPLESS (*takes the child in his arms*)
You golden-headed baby!
(*kisses him*)

SHARPLESS
È palese.
E Pinkerton lo sa?

BUTTERFLY
No. No. È nato quand'egli stava in quel suo gran paese.
Ma voi gli scriverete che l'aspetta
un figlio senza pari!
e mi saprete dir s' ei non s'affretta
per le terre e pei mari!
Sai cos' ebbe cuore
di pensare quel signore?
Che tua madre dovrà
prenderti in braccio ed alla pioggia e al vento
andar per la città
a guadagnarti il pane e il vestimento.
Ed alle impietosite
genti, la man tremante stenderà!
gridando: "Udite, udite,
la triste mia canzon. A un infelice
madre la carità, muovetevi a pietà!"
E Butterfly, orribile destino,
danzerà per te!
E come fece già
La Ghesha canterà!
E la canzon giuliva e lieta
in un singhiozzo finirà!
Ah, no! no! questo mai!
questo mestier che al disonore porta!
Morta! Morta!
Mai più danzar!
Piuttosto la mia vita vo'troncar!
Ah! morta!

SHARPLESS
(Quanta pietà!)
Io scendo al piano.
Mi perdonate?

BUTTERFLY
A te, dagli la mano.

SHARPLESS
I bei capelli biondi!

Caro: come ti chiamano?

Tell me what is your name, my dear?

BUTTERFLY
Rispondi:
Oggi il mio nome è: *Dolore.*
Però
dite al babbo, scrivendogli,
che il giorno
del suo ritorno
Gioia, mi chiamerò.

BUTTERFLY
You tell him:
Now at this hour it is "Sorrow." But soon
When my daddy comes back to me,
The day of his returning,
"Joy" will be my name.

SHARPLESS
Tuo padre lo saprà, te lo prometto.

SHARPLESS
Your father will be told, that I can promise.
(puts down the child, bows to BUTTERFLY, *and goes out quickly by door on the right)*

SUZUKI
Vespa! Rospo maledetto!

SUZUKI *(shouting outside)*
Vermin, evil-minded demon!
(she then comes in, roughly dragging in GORO, *who tries in vain to escape)*

BUTTERFLY
Che fu?

BUTTERFLY
What's wrong?

SUZUKI
Ci ronza intorno
il vampiro! e ogni giorno
ai quattro venti
spargendo va
che niuno sa
chi padre al bimbo sia!

SUZUKI
This fiendish vandal, lying devil,
Is spreading scandal in ev'ry quarter!
His story goes—that no one knows
Who is the baby's father!
(she releases GORO, *who tries to justify himself)*

GORO
Dicevo solo
che là in America
quando un figliolo è nato
maledetto trarrà sempre
reietto la vita fra le genti!

GORO
I merely mentioned
That there in America
The child of someone,
Deserted and neglected,
Must live in shame and mis'ry,
Forsaken and rejected!
*(*BUTTERFLY, *enraged, runs to the shrine, and takes down the sword that was used for the hara-kiri—condemned suicide—of her father, crying)*

BUTTERFLY
Ah! tu menti! menti!
Dillo ancora e t'uccido! . . .

BUTTERFLY
Ah! You're lying, lying!
(seizes GORO, *who falls down, and threatens to kill him;* GORO *utters desperate howls)*
One more word and I'll kill you!

SUZUKI
No!

SUZUKI *(thrusts herself between them)*
No!
(horrified at such a scene, she takes the baby and carries him into the room on the left)

BUTTERFLY
Va via!

BUTTERFLY *(seized with disgust, pushes him away with her foot)*
Get out!
*(*GORO *makes his escape;* BUTTERFLY *rouses herself and goes to put away the dagger and, her thoughts turning to her child, she exclaims)*

Vedrai, piccolo amor,
mia pena e mio conforto,
mio piccolo amor.
Ah! vedrai che il tuo vendicator

Dear love I so adore,—
My only joy and solace,
Dear love I adore.

Ah! He'll avenge you,
So you'll be proud once more—
And take us far from sorrow,
Away to his own country—
So far away, so far!
(*a cannon shot*)

SUZUKI (*enters breathlessly*)
The cannon from the harbor!
(*runs toward the terrace*—BUTTERFLY *follows her*)
It seems to be a warship . . .

BUTTERFLY (*breathless with excitement*)
White, white—and it's flying
The Star-Spangled Banner—
Now it stops and is dropping anchor!
(*takes a telescope from the table and runs on to the terrace; all trembling with excitement, she directs the telescope toward the harbor and says to* SUZUKI)
Help me hold the glass so I can see the name—
The name—I see it, there it is: "Abraham Lincoln."
(*gives the telescope to* SUZUKI *and goes down from the terrace in the greatest state of excitement*)
They all were lying, all were lying!
But I knew it always—because I love him!
(*to* SUZUKI)
Were you not foolish ever to doubt him?
I knew it! I knew it!
Just at the moment ev'ry one told me
All hope had vanished—
My love has prevailed, and my faith,
Yes, my faith prevailed unvanquished,
For he still loves me!
(*in greatest excitement and joy, she goes onto the terrace, saying*)
Let the cherry blossoms rain in showers,
Let me drown in their balm
Let their perfume and their soft silken petals
Cool my forehead.
(*sobbing for tenderness*)

SUZUKI (*soothing her*)
My lady, you must be calm—
You're weeping!

BUTTERFLY
No, I'm laughing, laughing!
Will we have to wait very long? I wonder?
An hour?

SUZUKI
At least . . .

BUTTERFLY (*thoughtfully*)
Or maybe two then.
Flowers—Flowers—As many flow'rs
As there are stars when night has fallen.

ci porterà lontano, lontan,
nella sua terra, lontan ci porterà.

SUZUKI
Il cannone del porto!
Una nave da guerra.

BUTTERFLY
Bianca . . . bianca . . . il vessillo americano
delle stelle . . . Or governa
per ancorare.
Reggimi la mano
ch'io ne discerna il nome,
il nome, il nome.
Eccolo: ABRAMO LINCOLN!
Tutti han mentito!
tutti! tutti! sol io
lo sapevo sol io—che l'amo.
Vedi lo scimunito
tuo dubbio?
È giunto! è giunto!
proprio nel punto
che ognun diceva: piangi e dispera,
Trionfa il mio amor, il mio amor;
la fè trionfa intera.
Ei torna e m'ama!
Scuoti quella fronda
di ciliegio e m'innonda di fior.
Io uò tuffar nella pioggia odorosa
l'arsa fronte.

SUZUKI
Signora, quetatevi:
quel pianto . . .

BUTTERFLY
No: rido, rido!
Quanto lo dovremo aspettar?
Che pensi? Un' ora?

SUZUKI
Di più.

BUTTERFLY
Due ore forse.
Tutto tutto sia pien di fior,
come la notte è di faville.
Va pei fior.

SUZUKI
Tutti i fior? . . .

BUTTERFLY
Tutti i fior, tutti, tutti
Pesco, viola, gelsomin,
quanto di cespo, o d' erba, o
d' albero fiori.

SUZUKI
Uno squallor d' inverno sarà
tutto il giardin.

BUTTERFLY
Tutta la primavera voglio che
olezzi qui.

SUZUKI
A voi signora.

BUTTERFLY
Cogline ancora.

SUZUKI
Soventi a questa siepe veniste a
riguardare
lungi, piangendo nella deserta
immensità.

BUTTERFLY
Giunse l'atteso, nulla più
chiedo al mare;
diedi pianto alla zolla, essa i
suoi fior mi dà.

SUZUKI
Spoglio è l'orto.

BUTTERFLY
Spoglio è l'orto?
Vien, m' aiuta.

SUZUKI
Rose al varco
della soglia.

BUTTERFLY
Tutta la primavera
voglio che olezzi qui.

SUZUKI
Tutta la primavera
tutta tutta.
Gigli? Viole?

BUTTERFLY
Intorno, intorno spandi.

SUZUKI
Seminiamo intorno april.

(*signs to* SUZUKI *to go into the garden*)
Bring them all!

SUZUKI (*from the terrace*)
Bring them all?

BUTTERFLY
Bring them all . . . many, many
Iris, lilies, sprays of green,
Ev'ry kind of leaf and blossom,
Buds from ev'ry tree.

SUZUKI
Barren as winter's wasteland,
The whole garden will be.
(*goes into the garden*)

BUTTERFLY
I want the whole of springtime's glory
For him to see.

SUZUKI (*appears on the terrace and holds out a large bunch of flowers and foliage to* BUTTERFLY)
I've brought so many.

BUTTERFLY (*taking the bunch*)
Gather some more—
(BUTTERFLY *distributes the flowers about the room, while* SUZUKI *goes back to the garden*)

SUZUKI (*from the garden*)
So often you have waited and gazed across the ocean,
Longing and yearning, scanning the blue immensity.

BUTTERFLY
Now his returning answers my heart's devotion;
I bathed the earth with my teardrops,
She gave me all her flow'rs!

SUZUKI (*reappears on the terrace with another load of flowers*)
None are left now—

BUTTERFLY (*taking the flowers*)
None are left now? Come and help me.
(*they scatter flowers everywhere*)

SUZUKI
Scatter roses on the threshold.

BUTTERFLY
Gather the heart of springtime
Blooming in fragrance here.

SUZUKI
Sunshine and springtime ev'rywhere,
There for his eyes to see.
Lilies, Violets?

BUTTERFLY
The golden glow of springtime—

SUZUKI
Like a lovely day in May—

BUTTERFLY

Like a lovely day in May.
Garland his chair with leaves entwining,
Scented rosy wreaths designing,
Lilies, violets freshly shining
With the golden glow of May!

BUTTERFLY and SUZUKI

The balm of tender flowers,
(lightly swaying their bodies to a dance measure, they scatter flowers everywhere)
Jasmine and budding roses,
In softly falling showers,
Gently unfold the spring!
(BUTTERFLY, assisted by SUZUKI, fetches out her toilet requirements)

BUTTERFLY *(to SUZUKI)*

Now help adorn me, too—
No, first bring me the baby.
(SUZUKI goes into the room on the left and brings the child, whom she seats near BUTTERFLY, who meanwhile looks at herself in a small hand mirror and says sadly)
How time has changed me!
Longing and grieving have saddened my smile . . .
My eyes too long a while
Have been gazing in distance.
Maybe you'll give my face a touch of color . . .
And some for you, my darling,
Lest all the waiting through the passing hours,
Rob your cheeks of their flowers.
(takes a brush and puts rouge on the cheeks of the baby)

SUZUKI

You must stay quiet while I am arranging your hair—

BUTTERFLY *(pursuing her thoughts)*

And my relations! What will they say now?
They were so pleased to see my damnation!
And Yamadori in all his glory!
My triumph will pain them, I shame them,
I scorn and disdain them!

SUZUKI *(has finished BUTTERFLY's toilet)*

I'm ready.

BUTTERFLY

The obi I wore at my wedding—
(SUZUKI goes to a small coffer and brings out the obi and the white garment, returns with two garments, and gives one with the obi to BUTTERFLY)

BUTTERFLY *(puts down the child)*

Now I shall wear it. So he may see me
Just as I was my wedding night.

BUTTERFLY

Seminiamo intorno april.
Il suo sedil s' inghirlandi,
di convolvi s' inghirlandi.
Gigli e viole intorno spandi,
Seminiamo intorno april.

BUTTERFLY, SUZUKI

Gettiamo a mani piene
mammole e tuberose,
corolle di verbene
petali d' ogni fior!

BUTTERFLY

Or vienmi ad adornar . . .
No. Pria, portami il bimbo.
Non son più quella!
Troppi sospiri la bocca mandò,
e l'occhio riguardò
nel lontan troppo fisso.
Dammi sul viso
un tocco di carmino . . .
ed anche a te piccino
perchè la veglia non ti faccia
vôte
per pallore le gote.

SUZUKI

Non vi movete che v'ho a
ravviare i capelli.

BUTTERFLY

Che ne diranno!
E lo zio Bonzo?
già del mio danno
tutti contenti!
E Yamadori
coi suoi languori!
Beffati, scornati,
spennati gl' ingrati!

SUZUKI

È fatto.

BUTTERFLY

L' obi che vestii da sposa.

BUTTERFLY

Qua ch'io lo vesta.
Vo' che mi veda indosso
il vel del primo dì.

E un papavero rosso
nei capelli . . .
Così

In my hair I will wear a scarlet poppy,
(SUZUKI, *who has finished dressing the baby, fetches the flower and places it in* BUTTERFLY'S *hair. The latter looks at herself in the glass, and is pleased with the effect*)
That's right.
(*she then signs to* SUZUKI *to lower the shosi*)

Nello *shosi* or farem tre forellini
per riguardar,
e starem zitti come topolini
ad aspettar.

In the shosi we'll make three little holes
So that we can see . . .
Like little mice we'll wait for him
As quietly as can be.
(*she carries the child close to the shosi, in which she makes three holes, one high up for herself, one lower down for* SUZUKI, *and a third one lower still for the baby, whom she seats on a cushion, showing him how to look out of his hole.* SUZUKI *crouches down and also gazes out through her hole.* BUTTERFLY *stands in front of the top hole and gazes through it. After some time* SUZUKI *and the child fall asleep. Meanwhile night has fallen, and the rays of the moon shed their light from without the shosi.* BUTTERFLY *remains motionless, rigid as a statue. From the harbor, voices are heard humming the melody of the letter.*)

ACT III

The weary night of watching passes. The clanging of chains and anchors and the distant voices of sailors rise from the harbor at the foot of the hill. At the rising of the curtain it is already dawn; BUTTERFLY, *still motionless, is gazing out into the distance.*

VOICES OF SAILORS (*from the bay*)
Oh, eh, oh eh!

SUZUKI (*awakening with a start*)
It's morning!
(*rises and taps* BUTTERFLY *lightly on the shoulder*)
Cio-cio-san!

BUTTERFLY (*starts, and says confidently*)
He'll come, I know he'll come.
(*sees that the child has fallen asleep, and takes him in her arms*)

SUZUKI
Go in and take a rest, you are exhausted . . .
And I will call you when he arrives.

BUTTERFLY (*singing softly as she goes up the staircase*)
Sleep, child of sorrow,
Sleep, my darling boy;
Maybe tomorrow,
Our grief will change to joy;
For there above,
God reigns in love,
Sleep, child of sorrow!
(*goes into the room above*)

SUZUKI (*watches her go and says with deep pity*)
Poor little Butterfly . . .
(SUZUKI *kneels before the image of Buddha, then goes to open the shosi;* PINKERTON *and* SHARPLESS *knock gently at the door*)

SUZUKI
Who could that be?
(*goes to open the door, and stands greatly surprised*)
Oh!

SHARPLESS (*signing her not to make a noise*)
Ssh! Quiet! Quiet!
(PINKERTON *and* SHARPLESS *enter cautiously on tiptoe*)

PINKERTON (*anxiously, to* SUZUKI)
Quiet! Don't call her yet.

SUZUKI
She was dreadfully tired!
She waited for your coming
The whole night long with the baby.

PINKERTON
How did she know?

SUZUKI
The last three years no ship entered the port

VOCI DI MARINA
Oh eh! oh eh!

SUZUKI
Già il sole!
Cio-cio-san!

BUTTERFLY
Verrà.
Verrà, vedrai.

SUZUKI
Salite a riposare affranta
siete! Al suo venire
vi chiamerò

BUTTERFLY
Dormi amor mio
dormi sul mio cor.
Tu sei con Dio
ed io col mio dolor.
A te i rai
degli astri d' or:
Bimbo mio dormi.

SUZUKI
Povera Butterfly!

SUZUKI
Chi sia?
Oh! . . .

SHARPLESS
Zitta! zitta!

PINKERTON
Zitta. Non la destar.

SUZUKI
Era stanca si tanto! Vi stette
ad aspettare
tutta la notte col bimbo.

PINKERTON
Come sapea? . . .

SUZUKI
Non giunge

da tre anni una nave nel porto,
che da lunge
Butterfly non ne scruti il color,
la bandiera.

That she has not observed from here,
To determine the flag and the colors.

SHARPLESS
Ve lo dissi? . . .

SHARPLESS (*to* PINKERTON)
See, I told you!

SUZUKI
La chiamo . . .

SUZUKI (*going*) I'll call her . . .

PINKERTON
No, non ancora.

PINKERTON (*stopping her*)
No, not just now.

SUZUKI
Lo vedete,
ier sera,
la stanza volle sparger di fiori.

SUZUKI
Look around you,
Last night she adorned the room
With blossoms and flowers.

SHARPLESS
Ve lo dissi?

SHARPLESS (*deeply touched*)
See, I told you!

PINKERTON
Che pena!

PINKERTON (*distressed*)
Dear heaven!

SUZUKI
Chi c' è là fuori nel giardino?
Una donna! ! . . .

SUZUKI (*distressed—hears sounds from the garden*)
Who is that waiting in the garden?
It's a lady!

PINKERTON
Zitta!

PINKERTON (*leading her forward again*)
Quiet!

SUZUKI
Chi è? chi è?

SUZUKI (*excitedly*)
Who is she? Who is she?

SHARPLESS
Meglio dirle ogni cosa.

SHARPLESS
It is better to tell her . . .

PINKERTON
È venuta con me.

PINKERTON (*in confusion*)
She has come here with me.

SHARPLESS
È sua moglie.

SHARPLESS (*deliberately*)
She's his wife!

SUZUKI
Anime sante degli avi!
alla piccina
s'è spento il sol!
s'è spento il sol.

SUZUKI (*stupefied, raises her arms to heaven, then falls on her knees with her face to the ground*)
Heavenly spirits, have mercy!
All poor Butterfly's hope is gone,
Her hope is gone.

SHARPLESS
Scegliemmo quest'ora mattutina
per ritrovarti sola, Suzuki, e
alla gran prova
un aiuto, un sostegno cercar
con te.

SHARPLESS (*calming her, and raising her from the ground*)
We came here so early in the morning
To speak to you alone first, Suzuki,
So we may ask your support and assistance
In all this woe.

SUZUKI
Che giova?

SUZUKI (*in despair*)
It's hopeless!
(SHARPLESS *takes her aside and tries with entreaties to get her consent, while* PINKERTON, *getting more and more agitated, wanders about the room, noting every detail*)

SHARPLESS
Io so che alle sue pene
non ci sono conforti!
Ma del bimbo conviene
assicurar le sorti!
La pietosa
che entrar non osa

SHARPLESS (*to* SUZUKI)
I know we're hoping vainly
To console such a sorrow!
But our one aim is mainly
To secure the child's tomorrow!

Full of pity, that kindly lady,
Will give him love and a mother's care.

SUZUKI
Such a message! And you want me
To tell that to a mother?

SHARPLESS (*persisting*)
Do us this favor,
Go out and speak to her for just a moment,
And then bring her inside;
And if she met with Butterfly, does it matter?
Better even if she were to learn the bitter truth
Once she has seen her.

SUZUKI
How to tell her!
(SHARPLESS *pushes her into the garden, where she joins* MRS. PINKERTON)

PINKERTON
Oh, how bitter these flowers'
Forlorn perfume,
Faded blossoms once as fair
As the love that was ours in this very room.
The touch of death fills the air!
(*sees his own likeness and takes it up*)
Here is my picture.
(*puts it down*)
Three years ago we parted,
Three years have gone already,
And she has marked their going,
Forever counting the steady flowing
Of days and hours!
(*overcome by emotion, he turns to* SHARPLESS)
I cannot bear to stay,
Sharpless, I cannot remain here!

SHARPLESS
Remember how I warned you?

PINKERTON
See to her needs, provide some resources,
How cruel my remorse is!

SHARPLESS
Remember what I told you?
Then I foresaw it clearly:
"Remember, she loves sincerely!"
My prophecy came true.
Deaf to friendly pleading,
Deaf to warning and unheeding,
Faithfully persevering,
She trusted you.

PINKERTON
Yes, now I understand it,
My grave and fatal error!

materna cura
del bimbo avrà.

SUZUKI
Oh me trista!
E volete ch'io chieda
a una madre . . .

SHARPLESS
Suvvia,
parla con quella pia
e conducila qui—s'anche la veda
Butterfly, non importa.
Anzi, meglio se accorta
del vero si facesse alla sua vista.
Vien, Suzuki, vien!

SUZUKI
Oh me trista!

PINKERTON
Oh! l'amara fragranza
di questi fior
velenosa al cor mi va.
Immutata è la stanza
dei nostri amor . . .
ma un gel di morte vi sta.
Il mio ritratto!—
Tre ani son passati—e noverati
n'ha i giorni e l'ore
nell'immobile fede . . .
Non posso rimaner. Sharpless
v'aspetto
per via.

SHARPLESS
Non ve l'avevo detto?

PINKERTON
Datele voi qualche soccorso . . .
Mi struggo dal rimorso.

SHARPLESS
Vel dissi? vi ricorda?
quando la man vi diede:
"Badate, ella ci crede"
e fui profeta allor!
Sorda ai consigli, sorda
ai dubbii vilipesa
nell'ostinata attesa
raccolse il cor.

PINKERTON
Sì. Tutto in un istante
io vedo il fallo mio e sento

che di questo tormento
tregua mai non avrò. No!

My guilt will always haunt and torment me—
Peace will never return, no!

SHARPLESS
Andate—il triste vero
da sola apprenderà.

SHARPLESS
Then leave us;
She'll hear the sorrowful truth
When you are gone . . .

PINKERTON
Addio fiorito asil
di letizia e d'amor.
Sempre il mite suo sembiante
con strazio atroce vedrò.

PINKERTON
Farewell, my beloved dream,
Sweet remembrance evermore . . .
Telling of joyous love in springtime—
Happiness I turned to woe . . .

SHARPLESS
Ma or quel cor sincero presago
è già . . .
Vel dissi . . . vi ricorda?
e fui profeta allor.

SHARPLESS
Already dark forebodings possess her heart!
I told you, you remember?
I said it all before.

PINKERTON
Non reggo al tuo squallor!
Fuggo, fuggo—son vil.

PINKERTON
My guilty heart is sore!
Farewell then, I must flee!
(PINKERTON *wrings the Consul's hands, goes out quickly as* KATE *and* SUZUKI *come in from the garden*)

KATE
Glielo dirai?

KATE
And you will tell her?

SUZUKI
Prometto.

SUZUKI
I promise.

KATE
E le darai consiglio
di affidarmi? . . .

KATE
Assure her from my heart
That she can trust me.

SUZUKI
Prometto.

SUZUKI
I promise.

KATE
Lo terrò come un figlio.

KATE
I shall treat him as my son.

SUZUKI
Vi credo. Ma bisogna ch'io le
sia sola accanto . . .
Nella grande ora—sola!
Piangerà tanto tanto!

SUZUKI
I trust you! But let no one besides myself be with her
In her darkest moment . . . No one!
For her heart will be breaking!

BUTTERFLY
Suzuki, dove sei
Suzuki! . . .

BUTTERFLY (*calling from the room above*)
Suzuki, Suzuki, do you hear me?
Where are you?

SUZUKI
Son qui . . . pregavo e ri-
mettevo a posto . . .
No . . . no . . . non scen-
dete . . .

SUZUKI (*signs to the others to keep quiet, then answers*)
I'm here. I'm praying, and putting things in order—
(BUTTERFLY *comes down.* SUZUKI *rushes toward the staircase to prevent her from coming*)
No, no, do not come down yet.

BUTTERFLY
È qui . . . dov'è nascosto?
Ecco il Console . . . e . . .
dove? dove? . . .
Non c'è.
Quella donna,
Che vuol da me.
Niuno parla!
Perchè piangete?

BUTTERFLY (*comes down quickly, freeing herself from* SUZUKI, *who tries in vain to hold her back; then she paces the room in a state of great excitement but happiness*)
He's here—where is he hiding?
(*sees* SHARPLESS)
There's the Consul—Where is he?—Tell me?
(*looks behind the screens*)

He's not here!
(turns and sees MRS. PINKERTON*)*
That lady?
What does she want?—No one answers!—
Why are you crying?
No, I don't want to hear it—ever—
For I might die at the moment I hear it.
You, Suzuki, so good and so faithful,
Don't cry for me! For I know that you love me,
Say yes or no, just softly,
He's alive?

SUZUKI
Yes.

BUTTERFLY
But he won't return—
They have told you!
(angered at SUZUKI'S *silence)*
Viper! Answer what I have asked you.

SUZUKI
He won't.

BUTTERFLY
He did arrive, though?

SUZUKI
Yes.

BUTTERFLY *(looks at* KATE *as though compelled)*
Ah! That lady makes me terribly frightened!

SHARPLESS
She's the innocent cause
Of all your grief and misfortune. Please forgive her.

BUTTERFLY
Ah! She's his wife!
All is over for me—
All is ended!

SHARPLESS
Have courage.

BUTTERFLY
They'll take ev'rything from me!
They'll take my baby?

SHARPLESS
Only so he may have a brighter future.

BUTTERFLY
To ask a mother to leave her son—forever.
So be it—I must do as he says!

KATE *(gently)*
Then you can forgive me, Butterfly?

BUTTERFLY *(solemnly)*
Under the arches of heaven
There's no woman as happy as you are.
Stay so forever,
Never feel sorry for me.

No: non ditemi nulla . . .
nulla—forse potrei
cader morta sull'attimo.
Tu Suzuki che sei
tanto buona—
non piangere! e
mi vuoi tanto bene
un Sì un No—di'piano
Vive?

SUZUKI
Sì.

BUTTERFLY
Ma non viene più.
Te l'han detto! . . .
Vespa! Voglio che tu risponda.

SUZUKI
Mai più.

BUTTERFLY
Ma è giunto ieri?

SUZUKI
Sì.

BUTTERFLY
Ah! Quella donna
mi fa tanta paura! tanta paura!

SHARPLESS
È la causa innocente d' ogni
vostra sciagura
Perdonatele.

BUTTERFLY
Ah! è sua moglie!
Tutto è morto per me!
Tutto è finito!

SHARPLESS
Coraggio!

BUTTERFLY
Voglion prendermi tutto!
il figlio mio.

SHARPLESS
Fatelo pel suo bene il sacrifizio.

BUTTERFLY
Ah! triste madre!
Abbandonar mio figlio
E sia! A lui devo obbedir!

KATE
Potete perdonarmi, Butterfly?

BUTTERFLY
Sotto il gran ponte del cielo
non v' è
donna di voi più felice.
Siatelo sempre,
non v'attristate per me.

KATE
Povera piccina!

KATE (*going away, says to* SHARPLESS)
Poor little creature!

SHARPLESS
È un' immensa pietà!

SHARPLESS (*deeply moved*)
It is utter despair!

KATE
E il figlio lo darà?

KATE (*whispers to* SHARPLESS)
And may he have his son?

BUTTERFLY
A lui lo potrò dare
se lo verrà a cercare.
Fra mezz' ora salite la collina.

BUTTERFLY (*who has heard*)
I'll give him to his father,
If he will come to take him.
Within half an hour you may return.
(SUZUKI *escorts* KATE *and* SHARPLESS, *who go out by the door on the right;* BUTTERFLY *is on the point of collapsing;* SUZUKI *hastens to support her*)

SUZUKI
Come una mosca prigioniera
l' ali batte il piccolo cuor!

SUZUKI (*laying her hand on* BUTTERFLY'*s heart*)
Hear how her little heart is beating,
Like a bird all trembling with fright.

BUTTERFLY
Troppo luce è di fuor,
e troppa primavera.
Chiudi.
Il bimbo ove sia?

BUTTERFLY (*gradually recovers; seeing that it is now broad daylight she disengages herself from* SUZUKI *and says*)
All the room is too bright,
Too full of joy and springtime!
Make it darker.
(*pointing to the curtains;* SUZUKI *closes doors and curtains—the room is almost in total darkness*)
Where is the baby?

SUZUKI
Giuoca. Lo chiamo?

SUZUKI
Playing. Shall I call him?

BUTTERFLY
Lascialo giuocar.
Va.—Fagli compagnia.

BUTTERFLY
Leave him there to play!
(*dismissing her*)
You go and keep him company

SUZUKI
Resto con voi.

SUZUKI
I'll stay with you.
(*throws herself weeping at* BUTTERFLY'*s feet*)

BUTTERFLY
Va—va. Te lo comando.

BUTTERFLY (*resolutely—clapping her hands*)
Go—go—I must command you!
(*makes the weeping* SUZUKI *rise and pushes her outside the exit on the left. Then* BUTTERFLY *goes in front of the image of Buddha, bows before it, and remains motionless, lost in sad thought; she goes to the shrine and takes from it a large white veil, which she throws across the screen; she takes the dagger, which, in a waxen sheath, is leaning against the wall near the image of Buddha, and piously kisses the blade, holding it with both hands by the point and by the handle; then she reads the words inscribed on the blade*)

"Con onor muore
Chi non può serbar vita con
onore."

"He shall die with honor
Who no longer can live his life with honor."
(*she points the dagger at her throat; the door on the left opens and shows* SUZUKI'*s arm pushing in the child to his mother; the child runs to her with outstretched*

hands. BUTTERFLY *lets fall the dagger, darts toward the child and hugs and kisses him almost to suffocation)*

You, you, my dearest treasure!
My joy beyond all measure,
Bloom of roses and lilies,
You shall never know—I die for you,
Your adoring mother, poor Butterfly,
So you'll live happily—beyond the ocean,
Spared of the bitter knowledge
When you grow older,
Of your mother's devotion.
My son sent down from heaven,
Most fair of God's own creatures,
Rest your eyes on my features,
That a trace of their semblance
Linger on in your remembrance!
Look again, beloved angel!
Forever we say good-by!
Go—play—play.

Tu, tu, piccolo Iddio!
Amore, amore mio,
fior di giglio e di rosa.
Non saperlo mai
per te, per tuoi puri
occhi, muor Butterfly
perché tu possa andar
di là dal mare
senza che ti rimorda ai dì
maturi,
il materno abbandono.
O a me, sceso dal trono
dell' alto Paradiso,
guarda ben fiso, fiso
di tua madre la faccia! . . .
che te'n resti una traccia,
guarda ben!
Addio! piccolo amor!
Va. Gioca, gioca.

(BUTTERFLY *takes the child, sets him on a stool with his face turned to the left, puts the American flag and a doll in his hands, and motions him to play with them, while she gently bandages his eyes. Then she seizes a dagger and, her eyes still fixed on the child, goes behind the screen. The knife is heard falling to the ground, and the large white veil disappears, as though drawn by an invisible hand.* BUTTERFLY *emerges from behind the screen, the large white veil is around her neck. Tottering, she gropes her way toward the child and, smiling feebly, has just enough strength to embrace him before she falls to the ground beside him. At this moment* PINKERTON'S *voice is heard outside, on the right, calling repeatedly:*

Butterfly! Butterfly!

then the door on the right is violently burst open, PINKERTON *and* SHARPLESS *rush into the room and up to* BUTTERFLY, *who, with a feeble gesture, points to the child and dies.* PINKERTON *falls on his knees, while* SHARPLESS *takes the child and kisses him, sobbing)*

PINKERTON
Butterfly! Butterfly!

THE MAGIC FLUTE

(Die Zauberflöte)

by Wolfgang Amadeus Mozart (1756–1791)

LIBRETTO BY
EMMANUEL SCHIKANEDER AND
JOHANN GEORG METZLER (GIESECKE)

Translated by RUTH and THOMAS MARTIN.

Based on Liebeskind's oriental story *Lulu, oder Die Zauberflöte.*

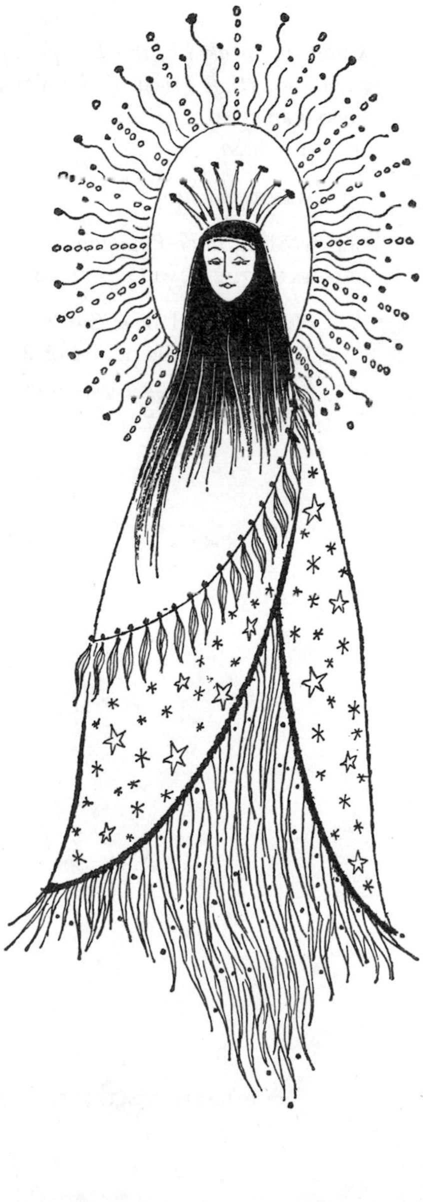

CHARACTERS

TAMINO, *an Egyptian prince*	*Tenor*
THREE LADIES, *attendants of the Queen of Night*	*Two sopranos* *Mezzo-soprano*
PAPAGENO, *a birdcatcher*	*Baritone*
THE QUEEN OF NIGHT	*Soprano*
MONOSTATOS, *a Moorish slave in the palace of Sarastro*	*Tenor*
PAMINA, *daughter of the Queen of Night*	*Soprano*
THREE SPIRITS	*Soprano* *Mezzo-soprano* *Contralto*
A PRIEST, *Speaker of the Temple of Isis*	*Baritone*
SARASTRO, *High Priest of the Temple of Isis*	*Bass*
FIRST PRIEST	*Tenor*
SECOND PRIEST	*Baritone*
TWO MEN IN ARMOR	*Tenor* *Baritone*
OLD WOMAN, *later Papagena*	*Soprano*
PRIESTS OF THE TEMPLE, ATTENDANTS, SLAVES	

Place: In and near the Temple of Isis in Egypt
Time: About the period of Rameses I
First performance: Theater auf der Wieden, Vienna, September 30, 1791

COPYRIGHT, 1941, 1951, 1952 BY G. SCHIRMER, INC.

ACT I

Introduction

(*Rough, rocky landscape.* TAMINO *runs in, richly dressed, with a bow but without arrows, pursued by a serpent.*)

TAMINO
Oh help me, protect me, my powers forsake me!
The treacherous serpent will soon overtake me.
Ah, heavens, have mercy! I see it draw near!
(*the serpent becomes visible*)
Oh rescue me, protect me, save me, rescue me!
(*he sinks, unconscious, to the ground. Three ladies hurry in, with silver javelins*)

TAMINO
Zu Hilfe! zu Hilfe! Sonst bin ich verloren, der listigen Schlange zum Opfer erkoren!
Barmherzige Götter! Schon nahet sie sich!
Ach, rettet mich! Ach, schützet mich!

THREE LADIES
Die, vicious snake, before our might!
(*they kill the serpent*)
Rejoice! Rejoice!
The deed is done and won the fight!
We saved this youth from certain death!

3 DAMEN
Stirb, Ungeheu'r, durch uns're Macht!
Triumph! Triumph! Sie ist vollbracht,
Die Heldentat! Er ist befreit
Durch unsres Armes Tapferkeit.

FIRST LADY (*watching* TAMINO)
What beauty in this gentle face!

1. DAME
Ein holder Jüngling, sanft und schön!

SECOND LADY
I never saw more lovely grace!

2. DAME
So schön als ich noch nie gesehn!

THIRD LADY
Yes, yes, indeed, for art to trace!

3. DAME
Ja, ja, gewiss zum malen schön!

THREE LADIES
If I should yield to love's sweet voice
This youth indeed would be my choice.
But now I think we ought to hurry
To tell the Queen this startling story.
Perhaps this youth will help restore
The peace she felt in days of yore.

ALLE DREI
Würd' ich mein Herz der Liebe weihn,
So müsst' es dieser Jüngling sein.
Lasst uns zu unsrer Fürstin eilen,
Ihr diese Nachricht zu erteilen.
Vielleicht dass dieser schöne Mann
Die vor'ge Ruh ihr geben kann.

FIRST LADY
You both go on your way,
And I would like to stay.

1. DAME
So geht und sagt es ihr,
Ich bleib indessen hier.

SECOND LADY
No, no, you go ahead,
And let me stay instead!

2. DAME
Nein, nein, geht ihr nur hin,
Ich wache hier für ihn.

THIRD LADY
No, that would never do.
I'll guard him here for you!

3. DAME
Nein, nein, das kann nicht sein;
Ich schütze ihn allein.

FIRST LADY
I'll watch him here alone!

1. DAME
Ich bleib indessen hier!

SECOND LADY
I want to stay with him!

2. DAME
Ich wache hier für ihn!

THIRD LADY
I'll guard him quite alone!

3. DAME
Ich schütze ihn allein!

FIRST LADY
I'll watch him!

1. DAME
Ich bleibe!

2. DAME
Ich wache!

3. DAME
Ich schütze!

ALLE 3
Ich! Ich! Ich!
Ich sollte fort? Ei, ei! Wie fein!
Sie wären gern bei ihm allein.
Nein, nein, das kann nicht sein.
Was wollte ich darum nicht geben,
Könnt' ich mit diesem Jüngling leben!
Hätt ich ihn doch so ganz allein!
Doch keine geht, es kann nicht sein.
Am besten ist es nun ich geh'—
Du Jüngling, schön und liebevoll,
Du trauter Jüngling, lebe wohl,
Bis ich dich wieder seh'.

SECOND LADY
I'll stay here!

THIRD LADY
I'll guard him!

THREE LADIES
I! I! I!
(*aside*) I am to go?
Well, well, how sly!
Each one would stay with him alone.
No, no! No, no! it can't be done!
With glowing love my heart is burning,
And stronger grows this ardent yearning.
Oh could I only call him mine!
But duty calls! We cannot stay,
Together we must go away!
Fair youth, in peaceful slumber dwell.
We leave you here and say farewell
Until we meet again!
(*exit*)

TAMINO
Wo bin ich? Ist's Phantasie, dass ich noch lebe, oder hat eine höhere Macht mich gerettet? Wie?—Die bösartige Schlange liegt tot zu meinen Füssen?

Was hör ich? Wo bin ich?
Welch unbekannter Ort?
Ha, eine männliche Figur nähert sich dem Tal.

TAMINO (*regains consciousness, looks around, frightened*)
Where am I? Is it fantasy that I am still alive? Or did some higher power save me?
(*rises and looks around*)
That vicious snake dead at my feet?
(*the sound of a Panpipe is heard*)
What do I hear? Where am I? What a strange place! I see a queer figure approaching.
(*withdraws, observing.* PAPAGENO, *dressed in a suit of feathers, hurries by, carrying a large birdcage on his back and a Panpipe in his hands*)

Song

I

PAPAGENO
Der Vogelfänger bin ich ja,
Stets lustig, heisa, hopsasa!
Ich Vogelfänger bin bekannt
Bei Alt und Jung im ganzen Land.
Weiss mit dem Locken umzugehn
Und mich aufs Pfeifen zu versteh'n.
Drum kann ich froh und lustig sein,
Denn alle Vögel sind ja mein.

PAPAGENO
I am a man of widespread fame,
And Papageno is my name.
To tell you all in simple words:
I make my living catching birds.
The moment they attract my eye
I spread my net and in they fly.
I whistle on my pipe of Pan,
In short I am a happy man.

II

Der Vogelfänger bin ich ja,
Stets lustig, heisa, hopsasa!
Ich Vogelfänger bin bekannt
Bei Alt und Jung im ganzen Land.

Although I am a happy man,
I also have a future plan.
I dearly love my feathered friends,
But that's not where my int'rest ends.
To tell the truth I'd like to find

A pretty girl of my own kind.
In fact, I'd like to fill my net
With all the pretty girls I met.

III

Once all the girls were in my net,
I'd keep the fairest for my pet,
My sweetheart and my bride-to-be,
To love and cherish tenderly.
I'd bring her cake and sugar plums,
And be content to eat the crumbs.
She'd share my little nest with me,
A happier pair could never be.
(he whistles on his pipe and turns to leave)

TAMINO *(steps in his way)*
Hey, there!

PAPAGENO
Who's there?

TAMINO
Tell me who you are, my jolly friend.

PAPAGENO
Who I am?
(to himself)
Silly question!
(to TAMINO*)*
A man, like you. Suppose I asked who you were?

TAMINO
Then I would tell you that I am of noble blood.

PAPAGENO
That's above me. You must explain yourself more clearly if you want me to understand you.

TAMINO
My father is a king, who rules over many lands and peoples. That is why they call me "Prince."

PAPAGENO
Lands? Peoples? Prince? Tell me, are there any lands and peoples beyond these mountains?

TAMINO
Thousands and thousands!

PAPAGENO
Perhaps I could do a little speculating there with my birds.

TAMINO
What is this land called? Who rules it?

Ein Netz für Mädchen möchte ich,
Ich fing sie dutzendweis für mich;
Dann sperrte ich sie bei mir ein,
Und alle Mädchen wären mein.

Wenn alle Mädchen wären mein,
So tauschte ich brav Zucker ein,
Die, welche mir am liebsten wär',
Der gäb ich gleich den Zucker her.
Und küsste sie mich zärtlich dann,
Wär' sie mein Weib und ich ihr Mann.
Sie schlief an meiner Seite ein,
Ich wiegte wie ein Kind sie ein.

TAMINO
Heda!

PAPAGENO
Was da?

TAMINO
Sag mir, du lustiger Freund, wer du bist.

PAPAGENO
Wer ich bin? Dumme Frage! Ein Mensch, wie du. Wenn ich dich nun fragte, wer du bist?

TAMINO
So würde ich dir antworten, dass ich aus fürstlichem Geblüt bin.

PAPAGENO
Das ist mir zu hoch.—Musst dich deutlicher erklären, wenn ich dich verstehen soll!

TAMINO
Mein Vater ist Fürst, der über viele Länder und Menschen herrscht; darum nennt man mich Prinz.

PAPAGENO
Länder?—Menschen?—Prinz?—Sag du mir zuvor: gibt's ausser diesen Bergen auch noch Länder und Menschen?

TAMINO
Viele Tausende!

PAPAGENO
Da liess' sich eine Spekulation mit meinen Vögeln machen.

TAMINO
Wie nennt man eigentlich diese Gegend? Wer beherrscht sie?

PAPAGENO
Das kann ich dir ebensowenig beantworten, als ich weiss, wie ich auf die Welt gekommen bin.

PAPAGENO
I can't answer you that any more than I can tell you how I happened to come into this world.

TAMINO
Wie? Du wüsstest nicht, wo du geboren, oder wer deine Eltern waren?

TAMINO (*laughing*)
What? Do you mean to tell me that you do not know where you were born, or who your parents were?

PAPAGENO
Kein Wort!—Ich weiss nur so viel, dass nicht weit von hier meine Strohhütte steht, die mich vor Regen und Kälte schützt.

PAPAGENO
Not a word! I only know that not far from here is my straw hut, which protects me from the cold and rain.

TAMINO
Aber wie lebst du?

TAMINO
But by what do you live?

PAPAGENO
Von Essen und Trinken, wie alle Menschen.

PAPAGENO
By eating and drinking, just as everyone else does.

TAMINO
Wodurch erhältst du das?

TAMINO
How do you get it?

PAPAGENO
Durch Tausch.—Ich fange für die sternflammende Königin und ihre Jungfrauen verschiedene Vögel; dafür erhalt ich täglich Speise und Trank von ihr.

PAPAGENO
By exchange. I catch all kinds of birds for the star-flaming Queen and her ladies. In return, I receive food and drink every day from them.

TAMINO
Sternflammende Königin?—Sag mir, guter Freund, warst du schon so glücklich, diese Göttin der Nacht zu sehen?

TAMINO (*to himself*)
Star-flaming Queen?
(*to* PAPAGENO)
Tell me, good friend, were you ever fortunate enough to see this Goddess of the Night?

PAPAGENO
Sehen?—Die sternflammende Königin sehen?—Welcher Sterbliche kann sich rühmen, sie je gesehn zu haben? Wie er mich so starr anblickt! Bald fang ich an, mich vor ihm zu fürchten. Warum siehst du so verdächtig und schelmisch nach mir?

PAPAGENO
See her? See the star-flaming Queen? What mortal can boast of ever having seen her?
(*to himself*)
The way he stares at me! Pretty soon I shall begin to be afraid of him.
(*to* TAMINO)
Why do you look at me with such a suspicious stare?

TAMINO
Weil—weil ich zweifle, ob du ein Mensch bist.—

TAMINO
Well, I—I was wondering whether you are a human being or not.

PAPAGENO
Wie war das?

PAPAGENO
What was that?

TAMINO
Nach deinen Federn, die dich bedecken, halt ich dich—

TAMINO
Considering those feathers covering you, you look rather——
(*approaches him*)

PAPAGENO
Doch für keinen Vogel?—Bleib zurück, sag ich, und traue mir nicht; denn ich habe Riesenkraft. Wenn er sich nicht bald von mir schrecken lässt, so lauf ich davon.

PAPAGENO
Not like a bird, by any means? Stay away from me, I tell you, and don't trust me, because I have the strength of a giant.
(*to himself*)

If he doesn't begin to be afraid of me soon, I shall have to run for it.

TAMINO

Strength of a giant?

(looks at the serpent)

Then perhaps it was you who saved me, and fought this poisonous snake?

PAPAGENO

Snake?

(trembling, draws back a few steps)

Is it dead or alive?

TAMINO

But, tell me, friend, how in the world did you ever fight this monster? You have no weapons!

PAPAGENO *(who has mastered himself again)*

I don't need weapons. With me, a good squeeze of the hand is more than weapons.

TAMINO

Then you choked it?

PAPAGENO

Choked it.

(to himself)

Never in my life was I so strong as I am today.

(the THREE LADIES *appear, veiled)*

THREE LADIES *(in a menacing tone)*

Papageno!

PAPAGENO

Ah, that's for me!

(to TAMINO*)*

Turn around, friend!

TAMINO

Who are these ladies?

PAPAGENO

Who they actually are, I do not know myself. I only know this much: each day they take in my birds, and give me wine, sugar bread, and sweet figs in return.

TAMINO

I suppose they are very beautiful?

PAPAGENO

I dont think so, for if they were, they would not have to cover up their faces.

THREE LADIES *(coming nearer, menacingly)*

Papageno!

PAPAGENO *(aside to* TAMINO*)*

Wait a minute. Now they are after me.

(aloud)

You asked me whether these ladies are beautiful, and I

TAMINO

Riesenkraft? Also warst du wohl gar mein Erretter, der diese giftige Schlange bekämpfte?

PAPAGENO

Schlange! Ist sie tot oder lebendig?

TAMINO

Freund, wie hast du dieses Ungeheuer bekämpft?—Du bist ohne Waffen.

PAPAGENO

Brauch keine!—Bei mir ist ein starker Druck mit der Hand mehr als Waffen.

TAMINO

Du hast sie also erdrosselt?

PAPAGENO

Erdrosselt! Bin in meinem Leben nicht so stark gewesen, als heute.

DIE DREI DAMEN

Papageno!

PAPAGENO

Aha, das geht mich an!—Sieh dich um, Freund!

TAMINO

Wer sind diese Damen?

PAPAGENO

Wer sie eigentlich sind, weiss ich selbst nicht. Ich weiss nur soviel, dass sie mir täglich meine Vögel abnehmen, und mir dafür Wein, Zuckerbrot und süsse Feigen bringen.

TAMINO

Sie sind vermutlich sehr schön?

PAPAGENO

Ich denke nicht!—Denn wenn sie schön wären, würden sie ihre Gesichter nicht bedecken.

DIE DREI DAMEN

Papageno!

PAPAGENO

Sei still! Sie drohen mir schon. —Du fragst, ob sie schön sind, und ich kann dir darauf nichts antworten, als dass ich in meinem Leben nichts Reizenderes sah.—Jetzt werden sie bald wieder gut werden.—

DIE DREI DAMEN
Papageno!

PAPAGENO
Was muss ich denn heute verbrochen haben, dass sie so aufgebracht wider mich sind? —Hier, meine Schönen, übergeb ich meine Vögel.

1. DAME
Dafür schickt dir unsere Fürstin heute zum ersten Mal statt Wein, reines, klares Wasser.

2. DAME
Und mir befahl sie, dass ich, statt Zuckerbrot, diesen Stein dir überbringen soll. Ich wünsche, dass er dir wohlbekommen möge.

PAPAGENO
Was? Steine soll ich fressen?

3. DAME
Und statt der süssen Feigen, hab ich die Ehre, dir dies goldene Schloss vor den Mund zu schlagen.

1. DAME
Du willst vermutlich wissen, warum die Fürstin dich heute so wunderbar bestraft?

2. DAME
Damit du künftig nie mehr Fremde belügst.

3. DAME
Und dass du nie dich der Heldentaten rühmest, die And're vollzogen.

1. DAME
Sag an, hast du diese Schlange bekämpft?

2. DAME
Wer denn also?

3. DAME
Wir waren's, Jüngling, die dich befreiten.—Hier, dies Gemälde schickt dir die grosse Fürstin: es ist das Bildnis ihrer Tochter. Findest du, sagte sie, dass diese Züge dir nicht gleichgültig sind, dann ist Glück, Ehr und Ruhm dein Los!—Auf Wiedersehen.

can only say that never in my life have I seen anyone more charming.
(*aside*)
Now I guess that will put them in a good humor again.

THREE LADIES (*still nearer, and more menacingly*)
Pa-pa-ge-no!

PAPAGENO (*aside*)
Heavens, what can I have done today to have made them so angry?
(*he hands them the cage. Aloud*)
Here, lovely ladies, I have brought you my birds.

FIRST LADY (*gives him a jug of water*)
This time, in return, the Queen sends you, instead of wine, pure, clear water.

SECOND LADY
And she ordered me, instead of sugar bread, to give you this stone.
(*gives him the stone*)
Here's good health to you!

PAPAGENO
What, I shall eat stones?

THIRD LADY
And instead of sweet figs, I have the honor of locking up your mouth with this golden padlock.
(*does so.* PAPAGENO *shows his pain through gestures*)

FIRST LADY
I imagine you would like to know why the Queen punishes you in such a strange way?
(PAPAGENO *nods yes*)

SECOND LADY
So that in the future you will never again tell lies to strangers!

THIRD LADY
And that you will never boast of heroic deeds achieved by others.

FIRST LADY
Tell us, did *you* kill this serpent?
(PAPAGENO *shakes his head*)

SECOND LADY
Who did, then?
(PAPAGENO *shrugs his shoulders*)

THIRD LADY
Prince, it was we who saved you. The great Queen sends you this portrait of her daughter.
(*hands it to him*)
If you find that these features are not indifferent to you, she says, then happiness, honor, and glory will be your destiny. Farewell.
(*exit*)

SECOND LADY

Adieu, Monsieur Papageno!

(exit)

FIRST LADY

Don't drink too fast!

(exit laughing. Exit PAPAGENO, *who has continued to pantomime.* TAMINO *has not taken his eyes off the picture since he received it)*

Aria

TAMINO

O image angel-like and fair!
No mortal can with thee compare!
I feel it, how this godly sight
Pervades my heart with new delight.
I cannot name this strange desire
Which burns my heart with glowing fire.
Can this emotion love reveal?
Ah yes! 'Tis love alone I feel.
'Tis love, 'tis love. Love alone!
Oh, how to see her I am yearning!
Oh, how to free her I am burning!
I would then, would then, fond and true——
What would I do?
Upon this heart would I press her,
Within these loving arms caress her.
Forever then she would be mine!

(he starts to leave. The THREE LADIES *approach him)*

FIRST LADY

Prepare yourself with courage and steadfastness, noble Prince, for the Queen——

SECOND LADY

bade me to tell you——

THIRD LADY

that the path to your future happiness now lies open to you.

FIRST LADY

She has heard every word you said. She has——

SECOND LADY

—read every expression of your features——

THIRD LADY

—decided to make you completely happy. "Oh, if this youth," said she, "is as zealous and brave as he is kindhearted, then my daughter will certainly be saved!"

TAMINO

Come, maidens, lead me. She shall be saved! I swear it by my love and by my heart.

2. DAME

Adieu, Monsieur Papageno!

1. DAME

Fein nicht zu hastig getrunken!

TAMINO

Dies Bildnis ist bezaubernd schön,
Wie noch kein Auge je gesehn!
Ich fühl' es, wie dies Götterbild
Mein Herz mit neuer Regung füllt.
Dies Etwas kann ich zwar nicht nennen
Doch fühl' ich's hier wie Feuer brennen.
Soll die Empfindung Liebe sein?
Ja, ja, die Liebe ist's allein.
O wenn ich sie nur finden könnte!
O wenn sie doch schon vor mir stände!
Ich würde, würde, warm und rein,
Was würde ich? Ich würde sie voll Entzücken
An diesen heissen Busen drücken
Und ewig wäre sie dann mein.

1. DAME

Rüste dich mit Mut und Standhaftigkeit, schöner Jüngling!—Die Fürstin—

2. DAME

hat mir aufgetragen, dir zu sagen—

3. DAME

dass der Weg zu deinem künftigen Glücke nunmehr gebahnt sei.

1. DAME

Sie hat jedes deiner Worte gehört;—sie hat—

2. DAME

jeden Zug in deinem Gesichte gelesen,—

3. DAME

hat beschlossen, dich ganz glücklich zu machen.—Hat dieser Jüngling, sprach sie, auch so viel Mut und Tapferkeit, als er zärtlich ist, o, so ist meine Tochter ganz gewiss gerettet.

TAMINO

Kommt, Mädchen, führt mich! —Sie sei gerettet!—Das schwöre ich bei meiner

Liebe, bei meinem Herzen!
Ihr Götter, was ist das?

DIE DREI DAMEN
Fasse dich!

1. DAME
Es verkündet die Ankunft unserer Königin.

DIE DREI DAMEN
Sie kommt!—

Sie kommt!—

Sie kommt!

KÖNIGIN DER NACHT
O zitt're nicht, mein lieber Sohn!
Du bist unschuldig, weise, fromm.
Ein Jüngling, so wie du, vermag am besten,
Dies tiefbetrübte Mutterherz zu trösten.
Zum Leiden bin ich auserkoren,
Denn meine Tochter fehlet mir;
Durch sie ging all mein Glück verloren,
Ein Bösewicht entfloh mit ihr.
Noch seh' ich ihr Zittern
Mit bangem Erschüttern,
Ihr ängstliches Beben,
Ihr schüchternes Streben.
Ich musste sie mir rauben sehen;
"Ach helft!" war alles, was sie sprach.
Allein vergebens war ihr Flehen,
Denn meine Hilfe war zu schwach.
Du wirst sie zu befreien gehen,
Du wirst der Tochter Retter sein;
Und werd' ich dich als Sieger sehen,
So sei sie dann auf ewig dein.

TAMINO
Ist's denn auch Wirklichkeit, was ich sah?—O ihr guten Götter, täuscht mich nicht.

PAPAGENO
Hm hm hm hm hm hm hm hm!

(short, loud thunder)
Ye Gods! What is that?
(it becomes dark)

THREE LADIES
Take heart!

FIRST LADY
That betokens the arrival of our queen.
(thunder)

THREE LADIES
She comes!
(thunder)
She comes!
(thunder)
She comes!
(thunder. The mountains part; against a starry heaven the QUEEN OF THE NIGHT'S *throne is revealed)*

Recitative and Aria

QUEEN OF THE NIGHT *(steps forward with* TAMINO*)*
Oh, tremble not, my son, arise,
For you are guiltless, noble, wise.
A gentle youth like you could, like no other,
Console the deepest sorrow of a mother.
In lonely grief I am forsaken,
For my poor child no more I see.
With her my happiness was taken;
An evil fiend tore her from me.
How helpless she cowered,
Her strength overpowered!
What sad consternation!
What vain desperation!
With nameless woe my heart was bleeding.
"Ah help, ah help!" was all I heard her speak.
However, futile was her pleading,
For all my effort was too weak.
You, you, you shall free her from bonds of slavery!
You shall release this child of mine!
And to reward thee for thy bravery,
Forever then she shall be thine!
(she steps back. Thunder. The mountains close; it becomes light. Rocky landscape as before)

TAMINO *(after a pause)*
Was it reality I saw? O good gods, do not deceive me!
(he starts to leave, but PAPAGENO *steps in his path)*

Quintet

PAPAGENO *(points sadly to the padlock on his mouth)*
Hm! hm! hm! hm! hm! hm! hm! hm!

TAMINO
The poor young lad must surely suffer,
He tries to talk, but all in vain!

PAPAGENO
Hm! hm! hm! hm! hm! hm! hm! hm!

TAMINO
I can no help or comfort offer.
I wish I could relieve your pain.
(*enter the* THREE LADIES)

FIRST LADY
The Queen forgives you graciously.
(*removes his padlock*)
From punishment you shall be free.

PAPAGENO
Oh, what a joy again to chatter!

SECOND LADY
Be truthful, and you will fare better!

PAPAGENO
No lie shall ever come from me.

THREE LADIES
This padlock shall your warning be!
If one could seal the lips of liars
With such a padlock fast and tight,
Then hatred, slander's poisoned briers,
Would yield to brotherhood and right.

FIRST LADY (*gives* TAMINO *a golden flute*)
O Prince, upon our queen's command,
We lay this treasure in your hand.
This magic flute will power lend you.
Its tones in danger will defend you.

THREE LADIES
Whene'er this power is asserted,
All human passions are converted;
The saddest man to smile will learn;
The coldest heart with love will burn.
More than gold and treasures
A magic flute like this is worth;
By its spell would human woe
Change to happiness and mirth.

PAPAGENO
To withdraw now, fairest beauties,
May I take the liberty?

THREE LADIES
No, to new and urgent duties
Our queen has ordered you:

TAMINO
Der Arme kann von Strafe
sagen,
Denn seine Sprache ist dahin.

PAPAGENO
Hm hm hm hm hm hm hm hm!

TAMINO
Ich kann nichts tun, als dich
beklagen,
Weil ich zu schwach zu helfen
bin.

1. DAME
Die Königin begnadigt dich,
Erlässt die Strafe dir durch
mich.

PAPAGENO
Nun plaudert Papageno wieder.

2. DAME
Ja, plaud're. Lüge nur nicht
wieder.

PAPAGENO
Ich lüge nimmer mehr, nein,
nein!

DIE DREI DAMEN
Dies Schloss soll deine Warnung
sein.
Bekämen doch die Lügner alle
Ein solches Schloss vor ihren
Mund:
Statt Hass, Verleumdung,
schwarzer Galle,
Bestünde Lieb' und Bruder-
bund.

1. DAME
O Prinz, nimm dies Geschenk
von mir!
Dies sendet uns're Fürstin dir.
Die Zauberflöte wird dich
schützen,
Im grössten Unglück unter-
stützen.

DIE DREI DAMEN
Hiermit kannst du allmächtig
handeln,
Der Menschen Leidenschaft
verwandeln:
Der Traurige wird freudig sein,
Den Hagestolz nimmt Liebe
ein.
O so eine Flöte ist mehr als
Gold und Kronen wert,
Denn durch sie wird Men-
schenglück und Zufrieden-
heit vermehrt.

PAPAGENO
Nun, ihr schönen Frauenzim-
mer,
Darf ich, so empfehl ich mich.

DIE DREI DAMEN
Dich empfehlen kannst du
immer,

Doch bestimmt die Fürstin dich,
Mit dem Prinzen ohn' Verweilen
Nach Sarastros Burg zu eilen.

PAPAGENO
Nein, dafür bedank ich mich!
Von euch selbsten hörte ich,
Dass er wie ein Tigertier.
Sicher liess' ohn' alle Gnaden
Mich Sarastro rupfen, braten,
Setzte mich den Hunden für.

DIE DREI DAMEN
Dich schützt der Prinz, trau ihm allein.
Dafür sollst du sein Diener sein.

PAPAGENO
Dass doch der Prinz beim Teufel wäre!
Mein Leben ist mir lieb;
Am Ende schleicht, bei meiner Ehre,
Er von mir wie ein Dieb.

1. DAME
Hier, nimm dies Kleinod, es ist dein.

PAPAGENO
Ei, ei! Was mag darinnen sein?

DIE DREI DAMEN
Darinnen hörst du Glöckchen tönen.

PAPAGENO
Werd ich sie auch wohl spielen können?

DIE DREI DAMEN
O ganz gewiss, ja, ja, gewiss!

ALLE
Silberglöckchen, Zauberflöten
Sind zu eurem Schutz vonnöten
Lebet wohl! Wir wollen geh'n.
Lebet wohl, auf Wiederseh'n!

TAMINO
Doch, schöne Damen, saget an—

PAPAGENO, TAMINO
Wie man die Burg wohl finden kann?

DIE DREI DAMEN
Drei Knäbchen, jung, schön, hold und weise,
Umschweben euch auf eurer Reise;
Sie werden eure Führer sein,
Folgt ihrem Rate ganz allein.

TAMINO, PAPAGENO
Drei Knäbchen, jung, schön, hold und weise,
Umschweben uns auf unsrer Reise.

To Sarastro's temple yonder
With the Prince you are to wander.

PAPAGENO
No, my ladies, thank you, no!
You yourselves have told me so:
That he's savage as a boar,
Surely would Sarastro roast me,
Fry and toast me, fry and toast me,
Nothing less and nothing more!

THREE LADIES
The Prince will shield you, have no fear;
You will be safe while he is near.

PAPAGENO (*aside*)
Oh, would the devil only get him!
My life I rate too high.
He'll steal away, upon my honor,
Like a thief on the sly!

FIRST LADY (*hands* PAPAGENO *a little box containing bells*)
This precious case is meant for you.

PAPAGENO
Well! Well! And may I see it too?

THREE LADIES
Herein are bells of silver swaying.

PAPAGENO
But shall I learn to set them playing?

THREE LADIES
Oh yes indeed! Oh yes indeed!

ALL
Flute and bell tones' magic power
Shall be yours (ours) in danger's hour.
Fare you well, we'll meet again.
(*the* THREE LADIES *turn to go*)

TAMINO
But, fairest ladies, tell us pray:

PAPAGENO AND TAMINO
Who will as guide show us the way?
(*the* THREE LADIES *return*)

THREE LADIES
Three spirits young and wise will guide you,
And on your journey stay beside you.
Rely on them where they may lead.
Only their counsel shall you heed.

TAMINO, PAPAGENO
Three spirits young and wise will guide us,
And on our journey stay beside us.

THREE LADIES
Rely on them where they may lead.
Only their counsel shall you heed.

DIE DREI DAMEN
Sie werden eure Führer sein,
Folgt ihrem Rate ganz allein.

ALL
So fare you well, we go our way,
May fortune be with us (you) today!
So fare you well!

(All leave. Change of scene.)
(Elaborate Egyptian room. Two slaves bring embroidered pillows and a beautiful Turkish table, they spread out rugs, then the THIRD SLAVE *appears)* *

ALLE
So lebet wohl, wir wollen geh'n.
Lebt wohl, lebt wohl, auf Wiederseh'n!

THIRD SLAVE
Ha! ha! ha!

3. SKLAVE
Hahaha!

FIRST SLAVE
Sh! sh!

1. SKLAVE
Pst! Pst!

SECOND SLAVE
What is the meaning of that laughter?

2. SKLAVE
Was soll denn das Lachen?

THIRD SLAVE
Our torturer, the ever-spying Moor, will surely be hanged or put on the rack tomorrow. Pamina! Ha! ha!

3. SKLAVE
Unser Peiniger, der alles belauschende Mohr wird morgen sicherlich gehangen oder gespiesst.—Pamina!—Hahaha!

FIRST SLAVE
Well?

1. SKLAVE
Nun?

THIRD SLAVE
The beautiful maiden—ha! ha! ha!

3. SKLAVE
Das reizende Mädchen!—Hahaha!

SECOND SLAVE
Well?

2. SKLAVE
Nun?

THIRD SLAVE
Has run away.

3. SKLAVE
Ist entsprungen.

FIRST AND SECOND SLAVES
Run away?

1. UND 2. SKLAVE
Entsprungen?

FIRST SLAVE
And she escaped?

1. SKLAVE
Und sie entkam?

THIRD SLAVE
Without doubt! At least it is my sincere wish.

3. SKLAVE
Unfehlbar!—Wenigstens ist's mein wahrer Wunsch.

FIRST SLAVE
Oh, thank you, good gods! You have heard my plea!

1. SKLAVE
O, Dank euch, ihr guten Götter! Ihr habt meine Bitte erhört.

THIRD SLAVE
Did I not always tell you that there would come a day for us when we will be avenged, and the black Monostatos will be punished?

3. SKLAVE
Sagt' ich euch nich immer, es wird doch ein Tag für uns scheinen, wo wir gerochen, und der schwarze Monostatos bestraft werden wird?

SECOND SLAVE
What does the Moor say to all this?

2. SKLAVE
Was spricht nun der Mohr zu der Geschichte?

FIRST SLAVE
He knows about it, does he not?

1. SKLAVE
Er weiss doch davon?

THIRD SLAVE
Naturally! She escaped before his very eyes! As some brothers told me, who were working in the garden and

3. SKLAVE
Natürlich! Sie entlief vor seinen Augen.—Wie mir einige Brüder erzählten, die im

* This scene is frequently omitted or very much shortened in performance.

Garten arbeiteten und von weitem sahen und hörten, so ist der Mohr nicht mehr zu retten; auch wenn Pamina von Sarastros Gefolge wieder eingebracht würde.

who listened and watched from the distance, the Moor no longer can be saved, even if Pamina should be brought back again by Sarastro's suite.

1. UND 2. SKLAVE
Wieso?

FIRST, SECOND SLAVES
How so?

3. SKLAVE
Du kennst ja den üppigen Wanst und seine Weise; das Mädchen aber war klüger, als ich dachte.—In dem Augenblicke, als er zu siegen glaubte, rief sie Sarastros Namen: das erschütterte den Mohren; er blieb stumm und unbeweglich stehen.—Indes lief Pamina nach dem Kanal und schiffte von selbst in einer Gondel dem Palmen—wäldchen zu.

THIRD SLAVE
You know the old thick-paunch and his ways. The maiden was more clever, however, than I thought. At the moment when he believed he had won, she called Sarastro's name. That terrified the Moor. He stood silent and motionless. Meanwhile Pamina ran to the canal and floated, driven by the stream, in a gondola toward the palm grove.

1. SKLAVE
O, wie wird das schüchterne Reh mit Todesangst dem Palast ihrer zärtlichen Mutter zueilen!

FIRST SLAVE
Oh, how the shy deer will hurry, frightened to death, to the palace of her mother!

MONOSTATOS
He, Sklaven!

MONOSTATOS (*off-stage*)
Ho, slaves!

1. SKLAVE
Monostatos' Stimme!

FIRST SLAVE
Monostatos' voice!

MONOSTATOS
He Sklaven! Schafft Fesseln herbei!

MONOSTATOS
Ho, slaves! Bring chains!

DIE DREI SKLAVEN
Fesseln??

THREE SLAVES
Chains?

1. SKLAVE
Doch nicht für Pamina? O ihr Götter! Da seht, Brüder, das Mädchen ist gefangen.

FIRST SLAVE (*runs to the side door*)
Not for Pamina! Oh, heavens! Look there, brothers! The maiden has been caught!

2. UND 3. SKLAVE
Pamina?—Schrecklicher Anblick!

SECOND AND THIRD SLAVES
Pamina? Horrible sight!

1. SKLAVE
Seht, wie der unbarmherzige Teufel sie bei ihren zarten Händchen fasst—das halt ich nicht aus.

FIRST SLAVE
See how the relentless devil grasps her by her tender hands—I cannot bear it!
(*exit, at the other side*)

2. SKLAVE
Ich noch weniger.

SECOND SLAVE
Even less can I.
(*exit by the same way*)

3. SKLAVE
So was sehen zu müssen ist Höllenmarter!

THIRD SLAVE
To have to see such a thing is the torture of hell!
(*exit*)

Trio

MONOSTATOS
Du feines Täubchen, nur herein!

MONOSTATOS
My dainty lambkin, enter please!

PAMINA
O welche Marter, welche Pein!

PAMINA
Oh will my tortures never cease?

MONOSTATOS
Your life is at my mercy!

PAMINA
But death cannot dismay me.
Yet for my mother's grief I mourn.
Her heart will break, by anguish torn.

MONOSTATOS (*to the slaves standing in the background, who approach quickly*)
Bring chains, ye slaves, and fetter her!
I'll force you to obey me.

PAMINA
I beg you rather slay me,
If naught can stir your evil heart!
(*she sinks unconscious on a sofa*)

MONOSTATOS
Get out, get out! Leave me alone with her!
(*exit slaves*)

PAPAGENO (*outside, at the window.* MONOSTATOS *does not notice him*)
Where am I now?
I'll have a glance.
Aha! There are some people.
All right, I'll take a chance.
(*enters the room*)
Dear maiden, young and fair,
Much whiter than a pigeon——
(PAPAGENO *and* MONOSTATOS *see each other and are frightened of one another*)

PAPAGENO, MONOSTATOS
Hoo, that is the devil certainly!
Have pity! Be merciful! Hoo! Hoo! Hoo! Hoo!
(*exit*)

PAMINA (*speaks as in a dream*)
Mother! Mother! Mother!
(*she recovers, looks around*)
What, my heart still beats? Am I still alive? Do I wake to new troubles? Oh, that is hard, very hard! This is more bitter to me than death!
(PAPAGENO *enters again*)

PAPAGENO
Wasn't I a fool to be frightened? There are black birds in the world, so why not black people? Ah, see there! Here is the lovely maiden. You, daughter of the Queen of the Night——

PAMINA (*rises*)
Queen of the Night? Who are you?

PAPAGENO
A messenger of the star-flaming Queen.

MONOSTATOS
Verloren ist dein Leben!

PAMINA
Der Tod macht mich nicht beben,
Nur meine Mutter dauert mich;
Sie stirbt vor Gram ganz sicherlich.

MONOSTATOS
He, Sklaven, legt ihr Fesseln an!
Mein Hass soll dich verderben.

PAMINA
Lass mich lieber sterben
Weil nichts, Barbar, dich rühren kann.

MONOSTATOS
Nun fort! Lasst mich bei ihr allein.

PAPAGENO
Wo bin ich wohl? Wo mag ich sein?
Aha! da find ich Leute.
Gewagt, ich geh hinein.
Schön Madchen, jung und fein,
Viel weisser noch als Kreide.

BEIDE
Hu! das ist der Teufel sicherlich;
Hab' Mitleid! Verschone mich!
Hu, hu, hu!

PAMINA
Mutter—Mutter—Mutter! Wie?
—Noch schlägt dies Herz?—
Zu neuen Qualen erwacht?—
O, das ist hart, sehr hart!—
Mir bitterer, als der Tod.

PAPAGENO
Bin ich nicht ein Narr, dass ich mich schrecken liess?—Es gibt ja schwarze Vögel in der Welt, warum denn nicht auch schwarze Menschen?—Ah, sieh da! Hier ist das schöne Mädchen noch.—Du Tochter der nächtlichen Königin—

PAMINA
Nächtliche Königin?—Wer bist du?

PAPAGENO
Ein Abgesandter der sternflammenden Königin.

PAMINA
Meiner Mutter?—O Wonne!—Dein Name?

PAPAGENO
Papageno.

PAMINA
Papageno?—Papageno—ich erinnere mich, den Namen oft gehört zu haben, dich selbst aber sah ich nie.

PAPAGENO
Ich dich ebensowenig.

PAMINA
Du kennst also meine gute, zärtliche Mutter?

PAPAGENO
Wenn du die Tochter der nächtlichen Königin bist—ja!

PAMINA
O, ich bin es.

PAPAGENO
Das will ich gleich erkennen. Die Augen schwarz—richtig, schwarz.—Die Lippen rot—richtig, rot.—Blonde Haare—blonde Haare.—Alles trifft ein, bis auf Hände und Füsse. Nach dem Gemälde zu schliessen, sollst du weder Hände noch Füsse haben; denn hier sind keine angezeigt.

PAMINA
Erlaube mir—Ja, ich bin's!—Wie kam es in deine Hände?

PAPAGENO
Ich muss dir das umständlicher erzählen.—Ich kam heute früh, wie gewöhnlich, zu deiner Mutter Palast mit meiner Lieferung—

PAMINA
Lieferung?

PAPAGENO
Ja, ich liefere deiner Mutter und ihren Jungfrauen schon seit vielen Jahren alle die schönen Vögel in den Palast.—Eben als ich im Begriff war, meine Vögel abzugeben, sah ich einen Menschen vor mir, der sich Prinz nennen lässt.—Dieser Prinz hat deine Mutter so eingenommen, dass sie ihm dein Bildnis schenkte und ihm befahl, dich zu befreien.—Sein Entschluss war so schnell, als seine Liebe zu dir.

PAMINA
Liebe? Er liebt mich also? O, sage mir das noch einmal, ich höre das Wort Liebe gar zu gern.

PAMINA (*joyfully*)
My mother? Oh joy! Your name?

PAPAGENO
Papageno.

PAMINA
Papageno? Papageno—I remember having heard your name often, but you yourself I never saw.

PAPAGENO
Nor I you.

PAMINA
Then you know my good, loving mother?

PAPAGENO
If you are the daughter of the Queen of the Night—yes.

PAMINA
Yes, I am.

PAPAGENO
I'll soon find out.
(*he looks at the portrait that previously had been given to the Prince and that* PAPAGENO *now wears around his neck on a ribbon*)
Eyes black—right—black. Lips red—right—red. Blond hair—blond hair. Everything is correct, except the hands and feet, because judging from this picture, you haven't any hands and feet, for none are painted here.

PAMINA
Let me see. Yes, it is my portrait, but how did it come into your hands?

PAPAGENO
To tell you that will be a longer story. I went, early this morning, as usual, to your mother's palace to make my delivery.

PAMINA
Delivery?

PAPAGENO
Yes, for years I have delivered all the finest birds I could catch to your mother and her ladies, at the palace. Just as I was about to hand over the birds, I saw someone standing in front of me who called himself "Prince." This prince so impressed your mother that she gave him your portrait, and ordered him to set you free. His decision was just as quick as his love for you.

PAMINA (*joyfully*)
Love? He loves me, then? Oh, say that again! It feels so good to hear the word "love"!

PAPAGENO

That I believe, for you are a girl. But where was I then?

PAMINA

You said "love."

PAPAGENO

Right, love. That's what I call memory! Come, your eyes will be bright when you see the handsome youth.

PAMINA

Well then, let us go.

(*they start to go;* PAMINA *turns around*)

But suppose this is only a trap? Suppose you are but an evil genius of Sarastro?

(*she looks at him doubtfully*)

PAPAGENO

I? An evil genius? What are you thinking of? I am no genius at all.

PAMINA

Friend, forgive me if I have offended you. You have a tender heart.

PAPAGENO

Ah, certainly I have a tender heart! But what good does it do me? Sometimes I feel like ripping out all my feathers when I think that Papageno hasn't found a Papagena yet.

PAMINA

Poor man! Then you have no wife?

PAPAGENO

Not even a girl, let alone a wife! And people like us have their gay hours, too, when they would like to have some fun.

PAMINA

Have patience, friend. The gods will take care of you. They will send you a wife, before you even think.

PAPAGENO

If they would only send her soon!

Duet

PAMINA

The man who feels sweet love's emotion
Will always have a kindly heart.

PAPAGENO

Each maid must share his deep devotion,
And from this duty never part.

PAPAGENO

Das glaube ich dir, du bist ja ein Mädchen.—Wo blieb ich denn?

PAMINA

Bei der Liebe.

PAPAGENO

Richtig, bei der Liebe! Das nenn ich ein Gedächtnis haben! Komm, du wirst Augen machen, wenn du den schönen Jüngling erblickst.

PAMINA

Wohl denn, es sei gewagt! Aber wenn dies ein Fallstrick wäre —wenn dieser nun ein böser Geist von Sarastros Gefolge wäre?—

PAPAGENO

Ich ein böser Geist?—Wo denkst du hin.—Ich bin der beste Geist von der Welt.

PAMINA

Vergib, vergib, wenn ich dich beleidigte! Du hast ein gefühlvolles Herz.

PAPAGENO

Ach, freilich habe ich ein gefühlvolles Herz! Aber was nützt mir das alles?—Ich möchte mir oft alle meine Federn ausrupfen, wenn ich bedenke, dass Papageno noch keine Papagena hat.

PAMINA

Armer Mann! Du hast also noch kein Weib?

PAPAGENO

Noch nicht einmal ein Mädchen, viel weniger ein Weib! —Und unsereiner hat doch auch bisweilen seine lustigen Stunden, wo man gern gesellschaftliche Unterhaltung haben möchte.—

PAMINA

Geduld, Freund! Der Himmel wird auch für dich sorgen; er wird dir eine Freundin schicken, ehe du dir's vermutest.

PAPAGENO

Wenn er sie nur bald schickte!

PAMINA

Bei Männern, welche Liebe
fühlen,
Fehlt auch ein gutes Herze
nicht.

PAPAGENO

Die süssen Triebe mitzufühlen.
Ist dann der Weiber erste
Pflicht.

BEIDE
Wir wollen uns der Liebe freu'n,
Wir leben durch die Lieb' allein.

PAMINA
Die Lieb' versüsset jede Plage,
Ihr opfert jede Kreatur.

PAPAGENO
Sie würzet uns're Lebenstage.
Sie wirkt im Kreise der Natur.

BEIDE
Ihr hoher Zweck zeigt deutlich an,
Nichts edlers sei, als Weib und Mann.
Mann und Weib, und Weib und Mann
Reichen an die Gottheit an.

PAMINA, PAPAGENO
Let joyous love for grief atone;
We live by love, by love alone.

PAMINA
To love's sweet might yields every creature.
It offers everlasting joy.

PAPAGENO
Its blessings are the gift of nature,
Which no one ever can destroy.

PAMINA, PAPAGENO
Its noble aim shows clear in life:
No greater good than man and wife.
Wife and man, and man and wife,
Reach the height of godly life.
(exit. Change of scene. A grove, in the middle of which stand three temples. THREE SPIRITS *lead in* TAMINO*)*

Finale

3 KNABEN
Zum Ziele führt dich diese Bahn,
Doch musst du, Jüngling, männlich siegen.
Drum höre uns're Lehre an:
Sei standhaft, duldsam und verschwiegen.

TAMINO
Ihr holden Kleinen, sagt mir an,
Ob ich Pamina retten kann?

3 KNABEN
Dies kund zu tun, steht uns nicht an;
Sei standhaft, duldsam und verschwiegen.
Bedenke dies; kurz, sei ein Mann,
Dann, Jüngling, wirst du männlich siegen.

TAMINO
Die Weisheitslehre dieser Knaben
Sei ewig mir ins Herz gegraben.
Wo bin ich nun? Was wird mit mir?
Ist dies der Sitz der Götter hier?
Es zeigen die Pforten, es zeigen die Säulen,
Dass Klugheit und Arbeit und Künste hier weilen;
Wo Tätigkeit thronet und Müssiggang weicht,
Erhält seine Herrschaft das Laster nicht leicht.
Ich wage mich mutig zur Pforte hinein,
Die Absicht ist edel und lauter und rein.

THREE SPIRITS
Your journey's end you soon will reach;
Yet win you must by manly daring;
But harken to these words we teach:
Be silent, steadfast, and forbearing.

TAMINO *(has hung his flute around his neck)*
Ye kindly spirits, tell me, please,
May I Pamina soon release?

THREE SPIRITS
To answer this is not allowed;
Be silent, steadfast, and forbearing!
Have courage, Prince, brave be and proud.
Then you will win by manly daring.
(exit)

TAMINO
These words of wisdom truly spoken
Be in my heart engraved as token.
Where am I now? What will betide?
Do here the mighty gods abide?
These arches and portals, mysterious dwelling,
Of reason, and labor, and arts are foretelling;
Where man is achieving and idleness banned.
There vice and dishonesty never may stand.
Without hesitation I'll enter the shrine!
My purpose is blameless and noble and fine.
You, mean offender, fear my scorn!
Pamina's rescue have I sworn!
(goes to portal at right)

Erzitt're, feiger Bösewicht!
Pamina retten ist mir Pflicht.

A VOICE (*from within*)
Go back!

PRIESTER
Zurück!

TAMINO
Go back! Go back!
Then I'll try here my luck.
(*goes to portal at left*)

TAMINO
Zurück! So wag ich hier mein Glück.

A VOICE (*from within*)
Go back!

PRIESTER
Zurück!

TAMINO
Again the call "go back"?
(*goes to the portal at center*)
Another door there is near.
Perhaps I'll gain an entrance here.
(*while he is approaching the center portal, it opens and an old priest appears*)

TAMINO
Auch hier ruft man zurück.
Da seh' ich noch eine Tür!
Vielleicht find ich den Eingang hier.

PRIEST
Who nears this holy temple door?
What are you, stranger, seeking for?

PRIESTER
Wo willst du, kühner Fremdling hin?
Was sucht du hier im Heiligtum?

TAMINO
'Tis love and virtue that I seek.

TAMINO
Der Lieb' und Tugend Eigentum.

PRIEST
These words a lofty mind bespeak.
And yet how do you hope to earn them?
Not love nor virtue do you heed;
With death and vengeance you are burning.

PRIESTER
Die Worte sind von hohem Sinn!
Allein wie willst du diese finden?
Dich leitet Lieb' und Tugend nicht,
Weil Tod und Rache dich entzünden.

TAMINO
Yes, vengeance for a villain's deed!

TAMINO
Nur Rache für den Bösewicht.

PRIEST
My son, you are ensnared in error.

PRIESTER
Den wirst du wohl bei uns nicht finden.

TAMINO (*quickly*)
Is this Sarastro's realm of terror?

TAMINO
Sarastro herrscht in diesen Gründen?

PRIEST
It's true! Sarastro is our lord.

PRIESTER
Ja, ja! Sarastro herrschet hier.

TAMINO (*quickly*)
But not in wisdom's temple, too?

TAMINO
Doch in dem Weisheitstempel nicht?

PRIEST (*slowly*)
He rules in wisdom's temple, too.

PRIESTER
Er herrscht im Weisheitstempel hier.

TAMINO
Then all is false as false can be!
(*wishes to go*)

TAMINO
So ist denn alles Heuchelei!

PRIEST
You mean to leave us then?

PRIESTER
Willst du schon wieder geh'n?

TAMINO
Yes, I will leave, glad and free,
Never return again.

TAMINO
Ja, ich will geh'n, froh und frei,
Nie euren Tempel seh'n.

PRIESTER
Erklär dich näher mir,
Dich täuschet ein Betrug.

TAMINO
Sarastro wohnet hier,
Das ist mir schon genug.

PRIESTER
Wenn du dein Leben liebst,
So rede, bleibe da!
Sarastro hassest du?

TAMINO
Ich hass ihn ewig, ja!

PRIESTER
So gib mir deine Gründe an.

TAMINO
Er ist ein Unmensch, ein Tyrann!

PRIESTER
Ist das, was du gesagt, erwiesen?

TAMINO
Durch ein unglücklich Weib bewiesen,
Das Gram und Jammer niederdrückt.

PRIESTER
Ein Weib hat also dich berückt?
Ein Weib tut wenig, plaudert viel.
Du, Jüngling, glaubst dem Zungenspiel?
O legte doch Sarastro dir
Die Absicht seiner Handlung für!

TAMINO
Die Absicht ist nur allzu klar!
Riss nicht der Räuber ohn' Erbarmen
Paminen aus der Mutter Armen?

PRIESTER
Ja, Jüngling, was du sagst, ist wahr.

TAMINO
Wo ist sie, die er uns geraubt?
Man opferte vielleicht sie schon?

PRIESTER
Dir dies zu sagen, teurer Sohn,
Ist jetzt und mir noch nicht erlaubt.

TAMINO
Erklär dies Rätsel, täusch mich nicht!

PRIESTER
Die Zunge bindet Eid und Pflicht.

TAMINO
Wann also wird die Decke schwinden?

PRIESTER
Sobald dich führt der Freundschaft Hand

PRIEST
Do not act hastily.
You have been told a lie.

TAMINO
Sarastro is your lord,
And that will do for me!

PRIEST
If you don't want to die, give answer; do not go!
You hate Sarastro so?

TAMINO
Now and forevermore!

PRIEST
So let me know the reason then.

TAMINO
He is a tyrant, foe of men!

PRIEST
Have you for such a charge foundation?

TAMINO
A woman, bowed by tribulation,
Who suffers anguished pain and grief.

PRIEST
A woman do you grant belief?
Few deeds, much chatter, artless youth,
Is this not woman's way forsooth?
O may you hear Sarastro say
What purpose in his action lay!

TAMINO
His purpose I can clearly read!
Was it not he, and no one other,
Who tore Pamina from her mother?

PRIEST
What you have said is true indeed.

TAMINO
Where is she whom he stole away?
Has she to death already gone?

PRIEST
No further word, beloved son,
Am I as yet allowed to say.

TAMINO
To solve this myst'ry, help me now!

PRIEST
My lips are sealed by solemn vow.

TAMINO
When will this veil of dark be lifted?

PRIEST
As soon as friendship's guiding hand

Will lead you to the holy band.
(*exit*)

TAMINO
When, endless night, will you be riven?
When will the light to me be given?

CHORUS (*from within*)
Soon, soon, stranger, or no more.

TAMINO
Soon, soon, soon, stranger, or no more?
Mysterious voices, answer me:
Does then Pamina live?

CHORUS (*from within*)
Pamina, Pamina, yes, she lives.

TAMINO (*joyfully*)
She lives? She lives? Oh, blessed words of cheer!
Oh, could I show you my emotion,
My gratitude and my devotion!
With every tone let me your praise be singing,
As from here,
(*pointing to his heart*)
here it springs!
(*plays the flute*)
How strong your tone with magic spell,
Dear flute, is binding.
By your tone, dear flute, each being
But happiness and joy is finding.
(*plays*)
But Pamina does not come.
(*plays*)
Pamina,
(*plays*)
Pamina hear me, hear me, pray!
(*plays*)
In vain! in vain!
(*plays*)
Where?
(*plays*)
Where? Where shall I discover you?
(*plays;* PAPAGENO *replies on his pipe*)
Ah, that is Papageno's sound.
(*plays;* PAPAGENO *replies*)
Oh, might he have Pamina found,
Oh, might she come with him to me!
Oh, might the tone bring her to me!
(*exit.* PAPAGENO *and* PAMINA *hurry in*)

PAPAGENO, PAMINA
Nothing ventured, nothing won!
To escape them let us run.
Let us to Tamino speed,
Or they will catch us soon indeed.

Ins Heiligtum zum ew'gen Band.

TAMINO
O ew'ge Nacht! Wann wirst du schwinden?
Wann wird das Licht mein Auge finden?

CHOR
Bald, Jüngling, oder nie!

TAMINO
Bald, sagt ihr, oder nie?
Ihr Unsichtbaren, saget mir,
Lebt denn Pamina noch?

CHOR
Pamina lebet noch.

TAMINO
Sie lebt? Ich danke euch dafür.
O wenn ich doch im Stande wäre,
Allmächtige, zu eurer Ehre,
Mit jedem Tone meinen Dank
Zu schildern, wie er hier, entsprang.
Wie stark ist nicht dein Zauberton,
Weil, holde Flöte, durch dein Spielen
Selbst wilde Tiere Freude fühlen.
Doch nur Pamina bleibt davon.
Pamina, höre, höre mich!
Umsonst! Wo? Ach, wo find' ich dich?
Ha, das ist Papagenos Ton!
Vielleicht sah er Pamina schon,
Vielleicht eilt sie mit ihm zu mir!
Vielleicht führt mich der Ton zu ihr.

PAPAGENO, PAMINA
Schnelle Füsse, rascher Mut
Schützt vor Feindes List und Wut.
Fänden wir Tamino doch,
Sonst erwischen sie uns noch!

PAMINA
Holder Jüngling!

PAMINA (*calls*)
Oh Tamino!

PAPAGENO
Stille, stille, ich kann's besser!

PAPAGENO
Quiet, quiet, let me show you how to call him.
(*he whistles.* TAMINO *replies*)

PAPAGENO, PAMINA
Welche Freude ist wohl grösser?
Freund Tamino hört uns schon!
Hieher kam der Flötenton.
Welch ein Glück, wenn ich ihn finde!
Nur geschwinde, nur geschwinde!

PAPAGENO, PAMINA
Then no harm did yet befall him!
What a joy to hear his tone;
It was he, yes he alone!
Now no more we have to worry!
Let us hurry, scurry, hurry!
(*they try to hurry away.* MONOSTATOS *steps in their path, mocking them*)

MONOSTATOS
Nur geschwinde, nur geschwinde!
Ha, hab' ich euch noch erwischt!
Nur herbei mit Stahl und Eisen!
Wart, ich will euch Mores weisen.
Den Monostatos berücken!
Nur herbei mit Band und Stricken.
He, ihr Sklaven, kommt herbei!

MONOSTATOS
Let us hurry, scurry, hurry!
Ha! Just in the nick of time!
I will cast you both in irons!
I shall throw you to the lions!
So you thought that you could fool me!
(*calling up-stage*)
I shall rule by force and cruelty!
Ho, you slaves, bring chains and rope!
(*the slaves come in with fetters*)

PAPAGENO, PAMINA
Ach, nun ist's mit uns vorbei!

PAPAGENO, PAMINA
Now there is no more to hope!

PAPAGENO
Wer viel wagt, gewinnt oft viel!
Komm, du schönes Glockenspiel,
Lass die Glöckchen klingen, klingen,
Dass die Ohren ihnen singen!

PAPAGENO
Now it's time to work the spell.
Come, my lovely magic bell,
Let your melody be ringing.
Save us by your magic singing!
(PAPAGENO *plays on his bells. The slaves dance spellbound and withdraw while singing*)

MONOSTATOS, SKLAVEN
Das klinget so herrlich, das klinget so schön!
Larala la la larala la la larala!
Nie hab' ich so etwas gehört und geseh'n!
Larala la la larala la la larala!

MONOSTATOS, SLAVES
This jingles so softly, this jingles so clear!
La la ra, la la la la ra, la la la ra.
How gently it touches my heart and my ear,
La la ra, la la la la ra, la la la la ra.

PAPAGENO, PAMINA
Könnte jeder brave Mann
Solche Glöckchen finden!
Seine Feinde würden dann
Ohne Mühe schwinden,
Und er lebte ohne sie
In der besten Harmonie.
Nur der Freundschaft Harmonie
Mildert die Beschwerden;
Ohne diese Sympathie
Ist kein Glück auf Erden.

PAPAGENO, PAMINA
If to every honest man
Bells like these were given,
All his foes would swiftly then
Far away be driven;
He would live contentedly,
In the sweetest harmony.
Only friendship's harmony
Lessens pain and grieving;
Without friendly sympathy,
Joy this earth is leaving.
(*A strong march with trumpets and drums is heard*)

CHORUS (*from within*)
We praise thee, Sarastro, the king of wisdom!

PAPAGENO
What noise are they making?
I'm trembling, I'm shaking.

PAMINA
O friend we both are lost, I fear;
The trumpets mean Sarastro's near!

PAPAGENO
I wish I were a mouse,
To hiding I would hurtle!
Or could I, like a turtle,
Creep in my little house!
But say, what answer shall we give him?

PAMINA
Be truthful, we shall not deceive him!
(SARASTRO *and his suite appear*)

CHORUS
We praise thee, Sarastro, with great exultation!
We hail thee, Sarastro, in deep admiration!
Forever thy wisdom may govern our mind!
Then lead us, Sarastro, perfection to find!

PAMINA (*kneels*)
Sire! My offense is all too plain
I tried escape from your domain.
Alas! The guilt falls not on me.
The cruel Moor wants me to love him;
Therefore, My Lord, I tried to flee.

SARASTRO
Arise, console yourself, Pamina!
The name of your devoted lover
I need not ask you to impart,
I read the secret of your heart.
Through me you will not have to suffer,
But yet I will not set you free.

PAMINA
Not for myself I make this plea,
But my poor mother——

SARASTRO
—stands within my might;
What would become of truth and right
If I had left you with your mother?

PAMINA
So sweet a name there is no other,
For she is . . . for she is . . .

CHOR
Es lebe Sarastro! Sarastro lebe!

PAPAGENO
Was soll das bedeuten? Ich zittre, ich bebe!

PAMINA
O Freund, nun ist's um uns getan,
Dies kündigt den Sarastro an!

PAPAGENO
O wär ich eine Maus,
Wie wollt' ich mich verstecken!
Wär' ich so klein wie Schnecken,
So kröch ich in mein Haus!
Mein Kind, was werden wir nun sprechen?

PAMINA
Die Wahrheit, wär sie auch Verbrechen.

CHOR
Es lebe Sarastro! Sarastro soll leben!
Er ist es, dem wir uns mit Freuden ergeben!
Stets mög' er des Lebens als Weiser sich freun,
Er ist unser Abgott, dem alle sich weihn.

PAMINA
Herr, ich bin zwar Verbrecherin,
Ich wollte deiner Macht entfliehn!
Allein, die Schuld ist nicht an mir;
Der böse Mohr verlangte Liebe;
Darum, o Herr, entfloh ich dir.

SARASTRO
Steh auf, erheitre dich, o Liebe!
Denn ohne erst in dich zu dringen,
Weiss ich von deinem Herzen mehr:
Du liebest einen Andern sehr.
Zur Liebe will ich dich nicht zwingen,
Doch geb ich dir die Freiheit nicht.

PAMINA
Mich rufet ja die Kindespflicht,
Denn meine Mutter—

SARASTRO
Steht in meiner Macht.
Du würdest um dein Glück gebracht,
Wenn ich dich ihren Händen liesse.

PAMINA
Mir klingt der Muttername süsse!
Sie ist es—

SARASTRO
Und ein stolzes Weib.
Ein Mann muss eure Herzen leiten,
Denn ohne ihn pflegt jedes Weib
Aus ihrem Wirkungskreis zu schreiten.

MONOSTATOS
Nun stolzer Jüngling, nur hieher!
Hier ist Sarastro, unser Herr.

PAMINA
Er ist's!

TAMINO
Sie ist's!

PAMINA, TAMINO
Es ist kein Traum!
Es schling mein Arm sich um ihn (sie) her
Und wenn es auch mein Ende wär!

CHOR
Was soll das heissen?

MONOSTATOS
Welch eine Dreistigkeit!
Gleich auseinander! Das geht zu weit!
Dein Sklave liegt zu deinen Füssen:
Lass den verwegnen Frevler büssen!
Bedenk, wie frech der Knabe ist!
Durch dieses seltnen Vogels List
Wollt' er Pamina dir entführen.
Allein ich wusst ihn auszuspüren.
Du kennst mich! Meine Wachsamkeit—

SARASTRO
Verdient, dass man ihr Lorbeer streut!
He, gebt dem Ehrenmann sogleich—

MONOSTATOS
Schon deine Gnade macht mich reich.

SARASTRO
Nur sieben und siebenzig Sohlenstreich!

MONOSTATOS
Ach Herr, den Lohn verhofft ich nicht!

SARASTRO
Nicht Dank, es ist ja meine Pflicht!

CHOR
Es lebe Sarastro, der göttliche Weise! Er lohnet und strafet in ähnlichem Kreise.

SARASTRO
She is all too proud!
By man your course must be decided,
For by herself a woman
Steps beyond her sphere and is misguided.
(*enter* MONOSTATOS *and* TAMINO)

MONOSTATOS
My proud young friend, come here right now!
Before Sarastro you will bow.

PAMINA
'Tis he!

TAMINO
'Tis she!

PAMINA, TAMINO
It is no dream!
My arms will hold him (her) tight embraced
Although with death I may be faced.
(*they embrace*)

CHORUS
This is outrageous!

MONOSTATOS
Ha! What impertinence!
Asunder, wretches! What new offense!
(*he separates them and kneels before* SARASTRO)
Your slave lies here in supplication:
This traitor must make expiation!
Can you imagine what he dared?
(*pointing to* PAPAGENO)
With this rare bird he was prepared
To snatch Pamina from your power,
But I appeared in time to cow her.
You know me, and my eagle eye——

SARASTRO
Deserves reward, I can't deny!
As your reward you shall receive——

MONOSTATOS
Your grace already makes me rich.

SARASTRO
Just seventy-seven blows with the switch!

MONOSTATOS (*kneels*)
Ah, sire! That's how you thank your faithful Moor!
(*is led away by the slaves*)

SARASTRO
My friend you're welcome, I am sure!

CHORUS
May long live Sarastro, his wisdom prevailing!
He praises and chastens in justice unfailing.

SARASTRO

To enter in our temple doors, these strangers may not be denied.
So place the veils upon their heads; they must at first be purified.
(*two* PRIESTS *bring veils and cover the heads of* TAMINO *and* PAPAGENO)

SARASTRO

Führt diese beiden Fremdlinge
In unsern Prüfungstempel ein;
Bedecket ihre Häupter dann,
Sie müssen erst gereinigt sein.

CHORUS

Let virtue and integrity
Throughout our life the mentors be.
Then doomed are evil, sin and vice,
And earth becomes a paradise.
(SARASTRO *gives* PAMINA *his hand and goes with her to the center portal.* TAMINO *and* PAPAGENO, *guided by the* TWO PRIESTS, *turn to the temple*)

CHOR

Wenn Tugend und Gerechtigkeit
Der Grossen Pfad mit Ruhm bestreut,
Dann ist die Erd' ein Himmelreich,
Und Sterbliche den Göttern gleich.

ACT II

March of the Priests

(*Forest of palm trees. The priests circle the stage in a festive procession, and take their places. At the end,* SARASTRO *appears, advancing to a position in their midst. Three blasts on the horns are sounded by the priests.*)

SARASTRO
Ihr, in dem Weisheitstempel eingeweihten Diener der grossen Götter Osiris und Isis!—Mit reiner Seele erklär ich euch, dass unsere heutige Versammlung eine der wichtigsten unserer Zeit ist.—Tamino, ein Königssohn, wandelt an der nördlichen Pforte unseres Tempels, und seufzt mit tugendvollem Herzen nach einem Gegenstand, den wir alle mit Mühe und Fleiss erringen müssen.—Diesen Tugendhaften zu bewachen, ihm freundschaftlich die Hand zu bieten, sei heute eine unserer wichtigsten Pflichten.

SARASTRO
Consecrated servants of the great gods Osiris and Isis in the Temple of Wisdom, with pure heart I declare that today's assembly is one of the most important of our time. Tamino, a prince, waits at the northern portal of our temple, longing with a virtuous soul for the enlightenment toward which all of us have been striving with energy and zeal. To watch over this high-minded youth, and to extend to him the hand of friendship, will be one of our foremost duties this day.

ERSTER PRIESTER
Er besitzt Tugend?

FIRST PRIEST
He is virtuous?

SARASTRO
Tugend!

SARASTRO
Virtuous.

ZWEITER PRIESTER
Auch Verschwiegenheit?

SECOND PRIEST
Can he keep silent?

SARASTRO
Verschwiegenheit!

SARASTRO
He can.

DRITTER PRIESTER
Ist wohltätig?

THIRD PRIEST
Is he benevolent?

SARASTRO
Wohltätig!—Haltet ihr ihn für würdig, so folgt meinem Beispiele.

Gerührt über die Einigkeit eurer Herzen, dankt Sarastro euch im Namen der Menschheit.—Pamina, das sanfte, tugendhafte Mädchen, haben die Götter dem holden Jünglinge bestimmt; dies ist der Grund, warum ich sie der stolzen Mutter entriss.—Das Weib dünkt sich gross su sein, hofft durch Blendwerk und Aberglauben das Volk zu berükken und unsern festen Tempelbau zu zerstören. Allein, das soll sie nicht! Tamino, der holde Jüngling selbst, soll ihn mit uns befestigen und als Eingeweihter der

SARASTRO
Benevolent. If you consider him worthy, follow my example.
(*they blow three times on their horns*)
Moved by the unanimity of your hearts, Sarastro thanks you in the name of all mankind. Pamina, the gentle, virtuous maiden, has been designated by the gods for this noble youth; therefore I have torn her from the side of her proud mother. This woman considers herself great, and hopes through delusion and superstition to beguile the populace and to destroy the firm foundations of our temples. However, in that she shall not succeed. Tamino himself shall become one of us, and aid us to strengthen the power of virtue and wisdom.
(*the three blasts on the horns are repeated*)

SPEAKER

Great Sarastro, we admire your wise discourse. However, will Tamino be able to contend against the hard ordeals that await him? He is a prince.

SARASTRO

More than that—he is a man.

SPEAKER

What if now, in his early youth, he pales in death?

SARASTRO

Then he would experience the celestial joys of Osiris and Isis sooner than we.

(*the three blasts on the horns are repeated*)

Let Tamino and his companion be led into the court of the temple

(*to the* SPEAKER, *who kneels before him*)

and you, friend, fulfill your holy office and teach to both what duty to humanity is; teach them to perceive the might of the gods.

(*exit* SPEAKER *and* SECOND PRIEST)

Aria and Chorus of the Priests

O Isis and Osiris, favor
This noble pair with wisdom's light!
Grant them your aid in their endeavor,
Lead them to find the path of right!

CHORUS

Lead them to find the path of right!

SARASTRO

Let them be strong against temptation;
But if they fail in their probation,
Do not their virtue meed deny.
Take them to your abode on high.

CHORUS

Take them to your abode on high.

(*Change of scene*)

(*Court of the temple. It is night.* TAMINO *and* PAPAGENO *are led in by the* SPEAKER *and the* SECOND PRIEST. *The priests remove their veils and depart with them*)

TAMINO

What a horrible night! Papageno, are you still with me?

PAPAGENO

Most certainly I am!

TAMINO

Where do you think we are now?

Tugend Lohn, dem Laster aber Strafe sein.

SPRECHER

Grosser Sarastro, deine weisheitsvollen Reden erkennen und bewundern wir; allein, wird Tamino auch die harten Prüfungen, so seiner warten, bekämpfen?—Er ist Prinz.

SARASTRO

Noch mehr—er ist Mensch!

SPRECHER

Wenn er nun aber in seiner frühen Jugend leblos erblasste?

SARASTRO

Dann ist er Osiris und Isis gegeben, und wird der Götter Freuden früher fühlen, als wir. Man führe Tamino mit seinem Reisegefährten in den Vorhof des Tempels ein. Und du, Freund, vollziehe dein heiliges Amt und lehre sie die Macht der Götter erkennen!

O Isis und Osiris, schenket
Der Weisheit Geist dem neuen Paar!
Die ihr der Wand'rer Schritte lenket,
Stärkt mit Geduld sie in Gefahr.

CHOR

Stärkt mit Geduld sie in Gefahr.

SARASTRO

Lasst sie der Prüfung Früchte sehen;
Doch sollten sie zu Grabe gehen,
So lohnt der Tugend kühnen Lauf,
Nehmt sie in euren Wohnsitz auf.

CHOR

Nehmt sie in euren Wohnsitz auf.

TAMINO

Eine schreckliche Nacht!—Papageno, bist du noch bei mir?

PAPAGENO

Ei, freilich!

TAMINO

Wo denkst du, dass wir uns nun befinden?

PAPAGENO
Wo? Ja, wenn's nicht finster wäre, wollt ich dir's schon sagen—aber so—O weh!—

TAMINO
Was ist's?

PAPAGENO
Mir wird nicht wohl bei der Sache!

TAMINO
Du hast Furcht, wie ich höre.

PAPAGENO
Furcht eben nicht, nur eiskalt läuft's mir über den Rücken. O weh!

TAMINO
Was soll's?

PAPAGENO
Ich glaube, ich bekomme ein kleines Fieber.

TAMINO
Pfui, Papageno! Sei ein Mann!

PAPAGENO
Ich wollt, ich wär ein Mädchen! O! o! o! Das ist mein letzter Augenblick!

SPRECHER
Ihr Fremdlinge, was sucht oder fordert ihr von uns? Was treibt euch an, in unsere Mauern zu dringen?

TAMINO
Freundschaft und Liebe.

SPRECHER
Bist du bereit, es mit deinem Leben zu erkämpfen?

TAMINO
Ja!

SPRECHER
Auch wenn Tod dein Los wäre?

TAMINO
Ja!

SPRECHER
Prinz, noch ist's Zeit zu weichen—einen Schritt weiter, und es ist zu spät.

TAMINO
Weisheitslehre sei mein Sieg; Pamina, das holde Mädchen, mein Lohn.

SPRECHER
Du unterziehst dich jeder Prüfung?

PAPAGENO
Where we are? Well, if it were not so dark, I might be able to tell you; but this way——
(*thunder*)
Help! Help!

TAMINO
What is wrong?

PAPAGENO
I don't feel quite at ease in this affair.

TAMINO
You are afraid, I can see.

PAPAGENO
Not afraid, really—I just have ice-cold shivers up and down my spine.
(*loud thunder*)
Oh, heavens!

TAMINO
What is it?

PAPAGENO
I think I am getting a slight fever.

TAMINO
Shame on you, Papageno, be a man!

PAPAGENO
I wish I were a girl!
(*very loud thunder*)
Oh! Oh! My hour has come!
(SPEAKER *and* SECOND PRIEST *appear with torches*)

SPEAKER
Strangers, what do you seek from us? What prompts you to intrude upon our sanctuary?

TAMINO
Friendship and love.

SPEAKER
Are you prepared to fight for these virtues at risk of your very life?

TAMINO
I am.

SPEAKER
Even if death were your lot?

TAMINO
Yes.

SPEAKER
Prince, there is still time to turn back. One step more and it will be too late!

TAMINO
Wisdom will gain my victory; Pamina, the lovely maiden, will be my reward!

SPEAKER
Are you willing to undergo every one of the trials?

TAMINO
Every one.

SPEAKER
Give me your hand.
(*they clasp hands*)

SECOND PRIEST (*to* PAPAGENO)
Will you, too, fight for the love of wisdom?

PAPAGENO
Fighting is not exactly in my line. To be truthful, I don't demand any wisdom, either. I'm just a child of nature, who is satisfied with sleep, food, and drink. And if I once could catch a pretty little wife——

SECOND PRIEST
That you shall never do unless you undergo our trials.

PAPAGENO
Of what do these trials consist?

SECOND PRIEST
You must subject yourself to all our laws, and not even fear death.

PAPAGENO
I'll remain single.

SECOND PRIEST
But if Sarastro has already chosen a bride for you who resembles you in color and dress perfectly?

PAPAGENO
Resembles me? Is she young?

SECOND PRIEST
Young and beautiful!

PAPAGENO
And her name is?

SECOND PRIEST
Papagena.

PAPAGENO
Pa–pa——?

SECOND PRIEST
Papagena!

PAPAGENO
Papagena! I really would like to see her out of sheer curiosity.

SECOND PRIEST
See her you may——

PAPAGENO
But after I see her, then will I have to die?
(SECOND PRIEST *shrugs his shoulders*)
Yes? I'll remain single.

TAMINO
Jeder!

SPRECHER
Reiche mir deine Hand!–So!

2. PRIESTER
Willst auch du dir Weisheitsliebe erkämpfen?

PAPAGENO
Kämpfen ist meine Sache nicht. –Ich verlange auch im Grunde gar keine Weisheit. Ich bin so ein Naturmensch, der sich mit Schlaf, Speise und Trank begnügt;–und wenn es ja sein könnte, dass ich mir einmal ein schönes Weibchen fange–

2. PRIESTER
Die wirst du nie erhalten, wenn du dich nicht unseren Prüfungen unterziehst.

PAPAGENO
Worin besteht diese Prüfung?

2. PRIESTER
Dich allen unseren Gesetzen zu unterwerfen, selbst den Tod nicht zu scheuen.

PAPAGENO
Ich bleibe ledig!

2. PRIESTER
Wenn nun aber Sarastro dir ein Mädchen aufbewahrt hätte, das an Farbe und Kleidung dir ganz gleich wäre?

PAPAGENO
Mir gleich? Ist sie jung?

2. PRIESTER
Jung und schön!

PAPAGENO
Und heisst?

2. PRIESTER
Papagena.

PAPAGENO
Wie? Pa–?

2. PRIESTER
Papagena!

PAPAGENO
Papagena?–Die möcht ich aus blosser Neugierde sehen.

2. PRIESTER
Sehen kannst du sie!–

PAPAGENO
Aber wenn ich sie gesehen habe, hernach muss ich sterben? Ja? Ich bleibe ledig!

2. PRIESTER
Sehen kannst du sie, aber bis zur verlaufnen Zeit kein Wort mit ihr sprechen. Wird dein Geist so viel Standhaftigkeit besitzen, deine Zunge in Schranken zu halten?

PAPAGENO
O ja!

2. PRIESTER
Deine Hand! Du sollst sie sehen.

SPRECHER
Auch dir, Prinz, legen die Götter ein heilsames Stillschweigen auf; ohne dieses seid ihr beide verloren.–Du wirst Pamina sehen, aber nicht sie sprechen dürfen; dies ist der Anfang eurer Prüfungszeit.

SPRECHER, PRIESTER
Bewahret euch vor Weibertücken:
Dies ist des Bundes erste Pflicht.
Manch weiser Mann liess sich berücken,
Er fehlte und versah sich's nicht.
Verlassen sah er sich am Ende,
Vergolten seine Treu mit Hohn.
Vergebens rang er seine Hände,
Tod und Verzweiflung war sein Lohn.

PAPAGENO
He, Lichter her! Lichter her!—Das ist doch wunderlich, so oft einen die Herren verlassen, sieht man mit offenen Augen nichts.

TAMINO
Ertrag es mit Geduld, und denke, es ist der Götter Wille.

DIE DREI DAMEN
Wie, wie, wie?
Ihr an diesem Schreckensort?
Nie, nie, nie
Kommt ihr glücklich wieder fort!
Tamino, dir ist Tod geschworen!
Du, Papageno, bist verloren!

PAPAGENO
Nein, nein, das wär zu viel!

TAMINO
Papageno, schweige still!
Willst du dein Gelübde brechen,

SECOND PRIEST
You may see her, but as yet you must not speak a single word to her. Will your mind have sufficient strength to control your tongue?

PAPAGENO
Oh yes!

SECOND PRIEST
Your hand! You shall see her!
(*they clasp hands*)

SPEAKER (*to* TAMINO)
On you, too, Prince, the gods impose a reverent silence. If you fail in this, you both are lost. You will see Pamina, but you must not speak to her. This is the beginning of your probation time.

Duet

SPEAKER, SECOND PRIEST
Beware of woman's crafty scheming:
This is the Order's first command!
Many a man, of wiles not dreaming,
Was tempted and could not withstand.
But then he saw he was mistaken,
The truth he came to know too late.
At last he found himself forsaken.
Death and damnation were his fate.
(*both priests leave. It becomes dark*)

PAPAGENO
Hey! Lights! Lights! It is really strange: each time these gentlemen leave us, you cannot see your hand in front of your face!

TAMINO
Bear it with patience—remember, it is the will of the gods!
(*enter the* THREE LADIES, *with torches*)

Quintet

THREE LADIES
You, in this place of night and gloom?
Flee, or you meet a certain doom!
Tamino, sworn is your damnation!
For Papageno, no salvation!

PAPAGENO
This is more than I can bear!

TAMINO
Papageno, have a care!
You are bound in your probation

To be brave against temptation!

PAPAGENO
You heard yourself—this is our end!

TAMINO
Keep your promise and be still!

PAPAGENO
Always still, and always still!

THREE LADIES
The Queen has secretly come here.
In yonder temple she is near.

PAPAGENO
What's that? The Queen herself is here?

TAMINO
Quiet, quiet! hush, be still!
Thus your solemn oath forswearing
Is indeed a foolish daring.

THREE LADIES
Tamino, gone are love and glory
If so the Queen you will betray!
From lip to lip there goes a story
That you will die this very day.

TAMINO (*aside*)
A wise man hears but does not mind
The common talk of lower kind.

THREE LADIES
Who joins their order, we have heard,
Will be condemned to go to hell!

PAPAGENO
This is outrageous, on my word!
Tell me, Tamino, is it so?

TAMINO
Such gossip women oft repeat.
'Tis but a hypocrite's deceit.

PAPAGENO
But did the Queen not say it too?

TAMINO
She talks just as all women do.
Believe my word and hold your tongue.
Act like a man! Be brave and strong!

THREE LADIES
Tamino, why so cold and callous?
(TAMINO *indicates by gestures that he dares not speak*)
And Papageno too? Pray, tell us.

PAPAGENO (*aside to the* THREE LADIES)
I would with pleasure, but——

TAMINO
Hush!

Nichts mit Weibern hier zu sprechen?

PAPAGENO
Du hörst ja wir sind beide hin.

TAMINO
Stille, sag ich, schweige still!

PAPAGENO
Immer still und immer still!

DIE DREI DAMEN
Ganz nah' ist euch die Königin.
Sie drang im Tempel heimlich ein.

PAPAGENO
Wie? Was? Sie soll im Tempel sein?

TAMINO
Stille, sag ich, schweige still!
Wirst du immer so vermessen
Deiner Eidespflicht vergessen?

DIE DREI DAMEN
Tamino, hör, du bist verloren!
Gedenke an die Königin.
Man zischelt viel sich in die Ohren
Von dieser Priester falschem Sinn.

TAMINO
Ein Weiser prüft und achtet nicht,
Was der gemeine Pöbel spricht.

DIE DREI DAMEN
Man sagt, wer ihrem Bunde schwört,
Der fährt zu Höll mit Haut und Haar.

PAPAGENO
Das wär' beim Teufel unerhört!
Sag an, Tamino, ist das wahr?

TAMINO
Geschwätz von Weibern nachgesagt,
Von Heuchlern aber ausgedacht.

PAPAGENO
Doch sagt es auch die Königin.

TAMINO
Sie ist ein Weib, hat Weibersinn.
Sei still, mein Wort sei dir genug:
Denk deiner Pflicht und handle klug.

DIE DREI DAMEN
Warum bist du mit uns so spröde?
Auch Papageno schweigt, so rede!

PAPAGENO
Ich möchte gerne—woll—

TAMINO
Still!

PAPAGENO
Ihr seht, dass ich nicht soll—

TAMINO
Still!

PAPAGENO, TAMINO
Dass ich (du) nicht kann (kannst) das Plaudern lassen
Ist wahrlich eine Schand für mich! (dich!)

DIE DREI DAMEN
Wir müssen uns mit Scham verlassen:
Es plaudert keiner sicherlich.

ALLE
Wir (Sie) müssen sie (uns) mit Scham verlassen:
Es plaudert keiner sicherlich.
Von festem Geiste ist ein Mann,
Er denket, was er sprechen kann.

PRIESTER
Entweiht ist die heilige Schwelle,
Hinab mit den Weiben zu Hölle!

DIE DREI DAMEN
O weh, o weh!

PAPAGENO
O weh, o weh, o weh!

SPRECHER
Heil dir, Jüngling! Dein standhaft männliches Betragen hat gesiegt. Wir wollen also mit reinem Herzen unsere Wanderschaft weiter fortsetzen. So! Nun komm!

2. PRIESTER
Was seh ich! Freund, stehe auf! Wie ist dir?

PAPAGENO
Ich lieg in einer Ohnmacht!

2. PRIESTER
Auf! Sammle dich und sei ein Mann!

PAPAGENO
Aber sagt mir nur, meine Herren, warum muss ich denn alle diese Qualen und Schrecken empfinden?— Wenn mir ja die Götter eine Papagena bestimmten, warum denn mit so viel Gefahren sie erringen?

2. PRIESTER
Diese neugierige Frage mag deine Vernunft dir beantworten. Komm! Meine Pflicht heischt, dich weiterzuführen.

PAPAGENO
You see, my mouth is shut!

TAMINO
Hush!

PAPAGENO, TAMINO
That I (you) cannot resist temptation
Is really a disgrace for me (to see.)

THREE LADIES
We must withdraw in resignation;
No one will talk, I clearly see.

THREE LADIES, PAPAGENO, TAMINO
We (they) must withdraw in resignation;
No one will talk, I (they) clearly see.
A man is firm and strong of will;
He stands aloof, reserved, and still.

CHORUS (*from within*)
These women profane our station.
Condemn them to death and damnation!
(*the stage darkens, thunder and lightning*)

THREE LADIES
Alas! Alas!
(*they rush out, horrified.* PAPAGENO *falls to the ground*)

PAPAGENO
Alas! alas! alas!
(SPEAKER *and* PRIEST *enter, carrying veils and torches*)

SPEAKER
Hail to thee, Prince! Thy steadfast, manly bearing has gained a victory! Thus we wish, with purest heart, to continue our travels.
(*covers* TAMINO's *head with a veil*)
Come, then!
(*exit* SPEAKER *and* TAMINO)

SECOND PRIEST
What do I see? Friend, arise! What has befallen you?

PAPAGENO
I am lying in a faint!

SECOND PRIEST
Arise! Collect yourself, and be a man!

PAPAGENO (*rises*)
But tell me, sir, why must I become acquainted with all these torments and horrors? If the gods really have selected a Papagena for me, why do I have to exert myself so hard to win her?

SECOND PRIEST
Let your reason answer that inquisitive question. Come, my duty demands that I lead you onward.
(*covers* PAPAGENO's *head with a veil*)

PAPAGENO

With such eternal wandering, one really feels like giving up love forever.

(*exit* SECOND PRIEST *and* PAPAGENO)

(*Change of scene. Garden.* PAMINA *asleep under the rosebushes. Moonlight*)

PAPAGENO

Bei so einer ewigen Wanderschaft möcht einem wohl die Liebe auf immer vergehen.

MONOSTATOS

Ha, here I find the prudish beauty! What man could remain cold and unmoved before such a vision! The fire which burns within me will surely consume me. (*he looks around*)

If I knew—that I was all alone and unobserved—one little kiss, I should think, could be excused.

MONOSTATOS

Ha, da find ich ja die spröde Schöne! Welcher Mensch würde bei so einem Anblick kalt und unempfindlich bleiben? Das Feuer, das in mir glimmt, wird mich noch verzehren! Wenn ich wüsste—dass ich so ganz allein und unbelauscht wäre—Ein Küsschen, dächte ich, liesse sich entschuldigen.

Aria

All the world is full of lovers,
Man and maiden, bird and bee.
Why am I not like the others?
No one ever looks at me!
Why should I not be a match for
Some delightful demoiselle?
If I have to die a bachelor,
I prefer to live in hell!
This is just the right occasion,
It's too good a chance to miss!
I don't need to use persuasion,
All I do is steal a kiss!
I'm alone—well then, so be it!
Just one tender warm embrace!
Moon, if you don't want to see it,
Turn away your jealous face.

(*creeps softly up to* PAMINA. *The* QUEEN *appears suddenly, with thunder and lightning*)

Alles fühlt der Liebe Freuden,
Schnäbelt, tändelt, herzt und küsst;
Und ich sollt die Liebe meiden,
Weil ein Schwarzer hässlich ist!
Ist mir denn kein Herz gegeben?
Bin ich nicht von Fleisch und Blut?
Immer ohne Weibchen leben
Wäre wahrlich Höllenglut!
Drum so will ich, weil ich lebe,
Schnäbeln, küssen, zärtlich sein!
Lieber guter Mond vergebe:
Eine Weisse nahm mich ein.
Weiss ist schön, ich muss sie küssen!
Mond, verstecke dich dazu!
Sollt' es dich zu sehr verdriessen,
O so mach' die Augen zu!

QUEEN (*to* MONOSTATOS)

Away with you!

KÖNIGIN

Zurück!

PAMINA (*awakens*)

O Gods!

PAMINA

Ihr Götter!

MONOSTATOS (*startled, jumps back*)

What's this?—The Queen of the Night!

MONOSTATOS

O weh!—Die Göttin der Nacht.

PAMINA

Mother! Mother! My Mother!

(*falls into her arms*)

PAMINA

Mutter! Mutter! meine Mutter!

MONOSTATOS (*aside*)

Mother! Hm! I'll have to watch this from a distance.

MONOSTATOS

Mutter? Hm, das muss man von weitem belauschen.

QUEEN

You may thank the power by which you were torn from me, that I still call myself your mother. Do you see

KÖNIGIN

Verdank es der Gewalt, mit der man dich mir entriss, dass ich noch deine Mutter mich nenne.—Siehst du hier diesen Stahl?—Er ist für Sarastro geschliffen.—Du wirst ihn töten.

PAMINA
Aber, liebste Mutter!—

KÖNIGIN
Kein Wort!

Der Hölle Rache kocht in meinem Herzen,
Tod und Verzweiflung flammet um mich her!
Fühlt nicht durch dich Sarastro Todesschmerzen,
So bist du meine Tochter nimmermehr!
Verstossen sei auf ewig,
Verlassen sei auf ewig,
Zertrümmert sei'n auf ewig
Alle Bande der Natur,
Wenn nicht durch dich Sarastro wird erblassen!
Hört, Rachegötter, hört der Mutter Schwur!

PAMINA
Morden soll ich?—Götter, das kann ich nicht! Götter, was soll ich tun?

MONOSTATOS
Dich mir anvertrauen.

PAMINA
Ha!

MONOSTATOS
Warum zitterst du? Vor meiner schwarzen Farbe, oder vor dem ausgedachten Mord?

PAMINA
Du weisst also?—

MONOSTATOS
Alles.—Du hast also nur einen Weg, dich und deine Mutter zu retten.

PAMINA
Der wäre?

MONOSTATOS
Mich zu lieben.

PAMINA
Götter!

MONOSTATOS
Nun, Mädchen! Ja oder nein!

PAMINA
Nein!

this dagger? It has been sharpened for Sarastro. You will kill him——

PAMINA
But dearest Mother——

QUEEN
Not a word!

Aria

The wrath of hell within my breast I cherish;
Death, desperation prompt the oath I swore.
If by your hand Sarastro does not perish,
Then as my child I shall know you nevermore.
Abandoned be forever,
Forsaken be forever,
And shattered be forever
All the force of nature's tie
If not through you Sarastro's life be taken!
Hark! Gods of vengeance, hear a mother's cry!
(*she disappears; thunder*)

PAMINA (*dagger in hand*)
I shall murder? Gods! I cannot, I cannot do that! What shall I do?
(MONOSTATOS *comes to her side quickly, stealthily, and with joy*)

MONOSTATOS
Confide yourself to me.
(*takes the dagger away from her*)

PAMINA (*frightened*)
Ah!

MONOSTATOS
Why do you tremble? Because I am black, or because of the murder that is planned?

PAMINA (*timidly*)
You know, then?

MONOSTATOS
Everything. There is only one way for you to save yourself and your mother.

PAMINA
And that is?

MONOSTATOS
To love me!

PAMINA (*trembling, aside*)
O Gods!

MONOSTATOS
Well, maiden, yes or no?

PAMINA (*firmly*)
No!

MONOSTATOS (*angrily*)
No?
(SARASTRO *comes up to them.* MONOSTATOS *raises the dagger*)
Then die!
(SARASTRO *holds* MONOSTATOS *back*)
Lord, I am innocent!
(*falls upon his knees*)

MONOSTATOS
Nein? So fahre denn hin! Herr, ich bin unschuldig.

SARASTRO
I know that your soul is just as black as your face. Go!

SARASTRO
Ich weiss, dass deine Seele ebenso schwarz als dein Gesicht ist.—Geh!

MONOSTATOS (*while leaving*)
Now I shall look up the mother, because the daughter is not meant for me.

MONOSTATOS
Jetzt such ich die Mutter auf, weil die Tochter mir nicht beschieden ist.

PAMINA
Sire, do not punish my mother. The sorrow over having lost me——

PAMINA
Herr, strafe meine Mutter nicht! Der Schmerz über meine Abwesenheit—

SARASTRO
I know everything. However, you shall see how I take revenge upon your mother.

SARASTRO
Ich weiss alles. Du sollst sehen, wie ich mich an deiner Mutter räche.

Aria

Within these holy portals,
Revenge remains unknown,
And to all erring mortals
Their way by love is shown.
And guided forth by friendship's hand,
They journey to a better land.
Within this holy dwelling,
In brother-love one lives.
Of hatred is no telling,
For man his foe forgives.
Who by this law is led aright,
Will ever share the gods' delight.
(*he leads* PAMINA *gently off*)
(*Change of scene. A short hallway.* TAMINO *and* PAPAGENO, *without the veils, are led in by the* TWO PRIESTS)

In diesen heil'gen Hallen
Kennt man die Rache nicht,
Und ist ein Mensch gefallen,
Führt Liebe ihn zur Pflicht.
Dann wandelt er an Freundes Hand
Vergnügt und froh ins bess're Land.
In diesen heil'gen Mauern,
Wo Mensch den Menschen liebt,
Kann kein Verräter lauern,
Weil man dem Feind vergibt.
Wen solche Lehren nicht erfreun
Verdienet nicht ein Mensch zu sein.

SPEAKER
Once more you are both left by yourselves. As soon as you hear the trumpet call, start on your way in this direction.
Prince, farewell. (*points to the right*)
Once more, do not forget the word: silence.
(*exit*)

SPRECHER
Hier seid ihr euch beide allein überlassen.—Sobald die Posaune tönt, dann nehmt ihr euren Weg dahin.—Prinz, lebt wohl! Noch einmal, vergesst das Wort nicht: Schweigen.

SECOND PRIEST
Papageno, anyone who breaks his silence in this place is punished by the gods with thunder and lightning. Farewell.
(*exit.* TAMINO *sits on a bench*)

ZWEITER PRIESTER
Papageno, wer an diesem Ort sein Stillschweigen bricht, den strafen die Götter durch Donner und Blitz. Leb wohl!

PAPAGENO Tamino!	PAPAGENO (*after a pause*) Tamino!
TAMINO St!	TAMINO Sh!
PAPAGENO Das ist ein lustiges Leben!—Wär ich lieber in meiner Strohhütte, oder im Wald, so hört ich doch manchmal einen Vogel pfeifen.	PAPAGENO This is a jolly life! If only I were in my straw hut or in the woods, at least I would hear a bird sing once in a while.
TAMINO St!	TAMINO (*reprimanding*) Sh!
PAPAGENO Mit mir selbst werd ich wohl sprechen dürfen; und auch wir zwei können zusammen sprechen, wir sind ja Männer.	PAPAGENO Well, I should think at least I am allowed to talk to myself! And also, we two can talk to each other, because we are men.
TAMINO St!	TAMINO (*reprimanding*) Sh!
PAPAGENO La la la—la la la!—Nicht einmal einen Tropfen Wasser bekommt man bei diesen Leuten, viel weniger sonst was. Ist das für mich?	PAPAGENO (*sings*) La la la—la la la. Not even a single drop of water does one get from these people, let alone anything else. (*an old, ugly* WOMAN *appears, a big cup in her hands.* PAPAGENO *looks at her for a long time*) Is that for me?
WEIB Ja, mein Engel!	WOMAN Yes, my angel!
PAPAGENO Nicht mehr und nicht weniger als Wasser.—Sag du mir, du unbekannte Schöne, werden alle fremden Gäste auf diese Art bewirtet?	PAPAGENO (*looks at her again, drinks*) No more, no less than water. Tell me, you unknown beauty, are all foreign guests treated in this fashion?
WEIB Freilich, mein Engel!	WOMAN Surely, my angel.
PAPAGENO So, so!—Auf diese Art werden die Fremden auch nicht gar zu häufig kommen.—	PAPAGENO Is that so? In that case, the foreigners don't come too frequently, I guess.
WEIB Sehr wenig.	WOMAN Very seldom.
PAPAGENO Kann mir's denken.—Geh, Alte, setze dich her zu mir, mir ist die Zeit verdammt lange.—Sag mir, wie alt bist du denn?	PAPAGENO That's what I thought. Come, Grandma, sit down here with me. I feel frightfully bored here. (*the* WOMAN *sits down at his side*) You tell me, how old are you?
WEIB Wie alt?	WOMAN How old?
PAPAGENO Ja!	PAPAGENO Yes.
WEIB Achtzehn Jahr und zwei Minuten.	WOMAN Eighteen years and two minutes.
PAPAGENO Achtzig Jahr und zwei Minuten?	PAPAGENO Eighty years and two minutes?

WOMAN
Eighteen years and two minutes.

PAPAGENO
Ha ha ha! Well, you young angel! Tell me, do you have a sweetheart?

WOMAN
Naturally.

PAPAGENO
And is he as young as you are?

WOMAN
Not quite, he is ten years older.

PAPAGENO
Ten years older than you? That must be quite a fiery love! What is the name of your sweetheart?

WOMAN
Papageno.

PAPAGENO (*falls from his seat*)
Papageno? Where is he then, this Papageno?

WOMAN
He is sitting right here, my angel.

PAPAGENO
There he *was* sitting.
So I am your sweetheart?

WOMAN
Yes, my angel.

PAPAGENO
Tell me, what is your name?

WOMAN
My name is——
(*loud thunder.* WOMAN *quickly hobbles away*)

PAPAGENO
Oh, oh!
(TAMINO *rises, shakes a warning finger at him*)
From now on I won't speak another word!
(*the* THREE SPIRITS *bring flute and bells*)

Trio

THREE SPIRITS
Here in Sarastro's hallowed border
We bid you welcome once again,
And by Sarastro's will and order
You may your flute and bells regain.
(*a table, with food and drink, rises from out of the ground*)
No more shall you privation suffer;
May what we bring for all amend.
When for the third time aid we proffer,
Hardship and trouble are at end.
Tamino, hear: triumph you will.

WEIB
Achtzehn Jahr und zwei Minuten.

PAPAGENO
Ha ha ha!—Ei, du junger Engel! Hast du auch einen Geliebten?

WEIB
Ei, freilich!

PAPAGENO
Ist er auch so jung wie du?

WEIB
Nicht ganz, er ist um zehn Jahre älter.

PAPAGENO
Um zehn Jahre ist er älter als du?—Das muss eine Liebe sein!—Wie nennt sich denn dein Liebhaber?

WEIB
Papageno!

PAPAGENO
Papageno?—Wo ist er denn, dieser Papageno?

WEIB
Da sitzt er, mein Engel!

PAPAGENO
Ich wär dein Geliebter?

WEIB
Ja, mein Engel!

PAPAGENO
Sag mir, wie heisst du denn?

WEIB
Ich heisse—

PAPAGENO
O weh! Nun sprech ich kein Wort mehr!

3 KNABEN
Seid uns zum zweiten Mal willkommen,
Ihr Männer, in Sarastros Reich.
Er schickt, was man euch abgenommen,
Die Flöte und die Glöckchen euch.
Wollt ihr die Speisen nicht verschmähen,
So esset, trinket froh davon.
Wenn wir zum dritten Mal uns sehen,
Ist Freude eures Mutes Lohn.
Tamino, Mut! Nah ist das Ziel.
Du, Papageno, schweige still!

You, Papageno, pray be still!
(*they hand* TAMINO *the flute and* PAPAGENO *the glockenspiel, and withdraw*)

PAPAGENO
Tamino, wollen wir nicht speisen? Blase du nur fort auf deiner Flöte, ich will meine Brocken blasen.—Herr Sarastro führt eine gute Küche.—Auf die Art, ja, da will ich schon schweigen, wenn ich immer solche gute Bissen bekommen.—Nun, ich will sehen, ob auch der Keller so gut bestellt ist. Ha! das ist Götterwein!

PAPAGENO
Tamino, shall we have something to eat?
(TAMINO *plays on his flute.* PAPAGENO *eats*)
You just keep on playing your flute, and I will play a game for myself! Mr. Sarastro certainly has a good cook. This way I would not mind keeping quiet, if I am always treated to such good food. Now I will see if his cellar is a good as his kitchen.
(*drinks*)
Ha, this is wine fit for the gods!
(*the flute is silent*)

PAMINA
Du hier?—Gütige Götter! Dank euch! Ich hörte deine Flöte —und so lief ich pfeilschnell dem Tone nach.—Aber du bist traurig?—Sprichst nicht eine Silbe mit deiner Pamina? Liebst du mich nicht mehr? Papageno, sage du mir, sag, was ist meinem Freund? Wie? Auch du? O, das ist mehr als Tod! Liebster, einziger Tamino!

PAMINA (*entering joyfully*)
You here? Kindly gods! I thank you. I heard the sound of your flute and I followed the tone swift as an arrow. But you are sad? You speak no word to your Pamina?
(TAMINO *sighs and motions her away*)
Do you love me no more?
(TAMINO *sighs again*)
Papageno, you tell me what troubles my friend?
(PAPAGENO *has his mouth full and motions her away:* Hm, hm, hm!)
You too? Oh, this is worse than death!
(*pause*)
My dearest Tamino!

Aria

Ach, ich fühl's, es ist verschwunden,
Ewig hin der Liebe Glück!
Nimmer kommt ihr, Wonnestunden,
Meinem Herzen mehr zurück.
Sieh, Tamino, diese Tränen,
Fliessen, Trauter, dir allein!
Fühlst du nicht der Liebe Sehnen,
So wird Ruhe im Tode sein.

Ah, I feel, to grief and sadness
Ever turned is love's delight.
Gone forever joy and gladness,
In my heart reigns mournful night.
See, Tamino, see my anguish,
See my tears for you, my own.
If for love you do not languish,
Peace I find then in death alone.
(*exit slowly*)

PAPAGENO
Nicht wahr, Tamino, ich kann auch schweigen, wenn's sein muss.—Der Herr Koch und der Herr Kellermeister sollen leben! Geh du nur voraus, ich komm schon nach. Der Stärkere bleibt da! Jetzt will ich mir's erst recht wohl sein lassen. Ich ging jetzt nicht fort, und wenn Herr Sarastro seine sechs Löwen an mich spannte. O Barmherzigkeit, ihr gütigen Götter! Tamino rette mich! Die Herren Löwen machen eine Mahlzeit

PAPAGENO (*eats eagerly*)
Isn't it true, Tamino, that I, too, can keep silent if need be?
(*drinks*)
Long live the chef and the wine steward!
(*three blasts of the trumpet.* TAMINO *motions* PAPAGENO *to go with him*)
You just go ahead, I'll come right after you.
(TAMINO *tries to lead him away by force*)
The strongest one stays here.
(*exit* TAMINO)
Now I'll begin to have a good time. I would not leave

now, even if Mr. Sarastro sent his six lions after me.
(the lions appear)
Have mercy! Ye good gods! Tamino, save me! These lions will make a meal of me!
(TAMINO returns, blows his flute, and the lions retire)
I'm coming, I'm coming. Call me a rascal if I don't do everything you tell me.
(three blasts of the trumpet)
That is for us. We are coming! But hear, Tamino, whatever will become of us?
(TAMINO points skyward)
I should ask the gods?
(TAMINO nods)
Yes, they really could tell us more than we know.
(three trumpet blasts. TAMINO drags PAPAGENO away by force)
Don't hurry so much, we shall be there in time to be roasted!
(exit)
(Change of scene. The interior of a pyramid. The priests enter, led by SARASTRO)

aus mir. Ich gehe schon! Heiss du mich einen Schelmen, wenn ich dir nicht in allem folge. Das geht uns an.—Wir kommen schon.—Aber hör einmal, Tamino, was wird denn noch alles mit uns werden? Die Götter soll ich fragen? Ja, die könnten uns freilich mehr sagen, als wir wissen! Eile nur nicht so, wir kommen noch immer zeitig genug, um uns braten zu lassen.

Chorus of the Priests

CHORUS OF PRIESTS
O Isis and Osiris! Sacred wonder!
The gloomy night by light is rent asunder.
The noble youth, through suffering recreated,
Shall be to holy office consecrated.
His heart is bold, and pure his mind;
Soon will the gods be satisfied.
(TAMINO is led in)

CHOR
O Isis und Osiris, welche Wonne!
Die düst're Nacht verscheucht der Glanz der Sonne.
Bald fühlt der edle Jüngling neues Leben,
Bald ist er unserm Dienste ganz ergeben.
Sein Geist ist kühn, sein Herz ist rein,
Bald wird er unser würdig sein.

SARASTRO
Prince, thus far your actions have been manly and patient. Now you have still two dangerous trials to undertake. If your heart still beats as warmly for Pamina, and if in time to come you wish to rule as a wise monarch, then may the gods lead you further. Your hand. Have Pamina brought here.
(TWO PRIESTS bring her in, veiled)

SARASTRO
Prinz, dein Betragen war bis hieher männlich und gelassen; nun hast du noch zwei gefährliche Wege zu wandern. Schlägt dein Herz noch ebenso warm für Pamina, und wünschest du einst als ein weiser Fürst zu regieren, so mögen die Götter dich ferner begleiten.—Deine Hand.—Man bringe Pamina!

PAMINA
Where am I? Where is Tamino?

PAMINA
Wo bin ich?—Saget, wo ist mein Jüngling?

SARASTRO
He awaits you, to bid you a last farewell.

SARASTRO
Er wartet deiner, um dir das letzte Lebewohl zu sagen.

PAMINA
A last farewell?

PAMINA
Das letzte Lebewohl?—

SARASTRO
Here.

SARASTRO
Hier!

PAMINA
Tamino!

TAMINO
Zurück!

PAMINA (*joyfully*)
Tamino!

TAMINO (*motions her to stay away*)
Away!

Trio

PAMINA
Soll ich dich, Teurer, nicht mehr sehn?
SARASTRO
Ihr werdet froh euch wiedersehn.
PAMINA
Dein warten tödliche Gefahren.
TAMINO
Die Götter mögen mich bewahren.
PAMINA
Dein warten tödliche Gefahren.
TAMINO, SARASTRO
Die Götter mögen mich (ihn) bewahren.
PAMINA
Du wirst dem Tode nicht entgehen,
Mir flüstert dieses Ahnung ein.
TAMINO, SARASTRO
Der Götter Wille mag geschehen,
Ihr Wink soll mir (ihm) Gesetze sein.
PAMINA
O liebest du, wie ich dich liebe,
Du würdest nicht so ruhig sein.
TAMINO, SARASTRO
Glaub mir, ich fühle (er fühlet) gleiche Triebe,
Werd (Wird) ewig dein Getreuer sein.
SARASTRO
Die Stunde schlägt, nun müsst ihr scheiden.
PAMINA, TAMINO
Wie bitter sind der Trennung Leiden!
SARASTRO
Tamino muss nun wieder fort.
TAMINO
Pamina.
PAMINA
Tamino.
PAMINA, TAMINO
Lebe wohl!
SARASTRO
Nun eile fort,
Dich ruft dein Wort.

PAMINA
So must we two forever part?
SARASTRO
To meet again with joyous heart.
PAMINA
Your path is dark with death and terror.
TAMINO
The gods preserve my steps from error.
PAMINA
Your path is dark with death and terror.
TAMINO, SARASTRO
The gods preserve my (his) steps from error.
PAMINA
Within my soul a voice is sighing:
A certain death awaits you here.
TAMINO, SARASTRO
To heaven's will is no denying
What fate decrees, we all must bear.
PAMINA
If you did love as I do love you,
Your grief were equal to my own,
You would not have so stern a tone.
TAMINO, SARASTRO
This (his) heart does warmly glow, believe me,
My (his) faithful heart is yours alone.
SARASTRO
The hour has come, the time of parting!
PAMINA, TAMINO
Oh, bitter, bitter pain of parting.
SARASTRO
Tamino now must go away.
TAMINO
Pamina.
PAMINA
Tamino.
PAMINA, TAMINO
Fare you well!
SARASTRO
Now hasten forth,
To prove your worth.

PAMINA, TAMINO

Oh, golden calmness, end this grieving.

SARASTRO

The time has come, you must be gone!
But not forever, but not forever!

PAMINA, TAMINO

Fare you well! Fare you well!

(PAMINA *is led away by* TWO PRIESTS. SARASTRO *withdraws with* TAMINO; *the* PRIESTS *follow. It becomes dark*)

PAPAGENO (*off-stage*)

Tamino! Tamino! Are you leaving me all alone?

(*enters, feeling his way*)

If I only knew where I was! Tamino! Tamino! As long as I live I shall never leave your side again. Just this once don't desert your poor fellow traveler!

(*he comes to the door through which* TAMINO *has left*)

A VOICE (*from outside*)

Halt!

(*thunder; flames burst from the door*)

PAPAGENO

Merciful gods, where shall I turn? If I only knew where I came in!

(*comes to the door where he had entered*)

VOICE (*from outside*)

Halt!

(*thunder; flames burst from the door*)

PAPAGENO

Now I can go neither forward nor backward.

(*cries*)

Perhaps I will have to starve here! Serves me right! Why did I come with him?

SPEAKER (*with a torch*)

Wretched man! You deserve to wander forever in the dark abysses of the earth! But the clement gods exempt you from this punishment. However, you shall never experience the heavenly pleasures of the ordained.

PAPAGENO

I don't care a fig about the ordained. Anyway, there are more people like me in the world. At the moment, to me the greatest pleasure would be a glass of wine.

SPEAKER

Other than this you have no further wish in the world?

PAPAGENO

Not so far.

SPEAKER

You shall be served with it.

PAMINA, TAMINO

Ach, gold'ne Ruhe, kehre wieder!

SARASTRO

Nun eile fort.
Dich ruft dein Wort.
Die Stunde schlägt, wir seh'n uns wieder.

PAMINA, TAMINO

Lebe wohl! Lebe wohl!

PAPAGENO

Tamino! Tamino! Willst du mich denn gänzlich verlassen? Wenn ich nur wenigstens wüsste, wo ich wäre.—Tamino!—Tamino!—So lang ich lebe, bleib ich nicht mehr von dir!—Nur diesmal verlass mich armen Reisegefährten nicht!

EINE STIMME

Zurück!

PAPAGENO

Barmherzige Götter!—Wo wend ich mich hin? Wenn ich nur wüsste, wo ich hereinkam!

DIE STIMME

Zurück!

PAPAGENO

Nun kann ich weder vorwärts noch zurück! Muss vielleicht am Ende gar verhungern!—Schon recht!—Warum bin ich mitgereist.

SPRECHER

Mensch! Du hättest verdient, auf immer in finsteren Klüften der Erde zu wandern—die gütigen Götter aber entlassen dich der Strafe.—Dafür aber wirst du das himmlische Vergnügen der Eingeweihten nie fühlen.

PAPAGENO

Je nun, es gibt noch mehr Leute meinesgleichen!—Mir wäre jetzt ein gutes Glas Wein das grösste Vergnügen.

SPRECHER

Sonst hast du keinen Wunsch in dieser Welt?

PAPAGENO

Bis jetzt nicht.

SPRECHER

Man wird dich damit bedienen!

(exit. A big cup filled with wine appears at once)

PAPAGENO
Juchhe! da ist er schon!—Herrlich!—Himmlisch!—Göttlich! —Ha! ich bin jetzt so vergnügt, dass ich bis zur Sonne fliegen wollte, wenn ich Flügel hätte!—Ha!—Mir wird ganz wunderlich ums Herz! —Ich wünschte—ja, was denn?

PAPAGENO
Hurrah! There it is already!
(drinks)
Marvelous! Heavenly! Divine! Ha! I am so delighted now that I should like to fly to the sun, if I had wings. Ha! Something strange is happening in my heart! I want—I wish—but what?
(plays the glockenspiel)

Aria

Ein Mädchen oder Weibchen
Wünscht Papageno sich!
O so ein sanftes Täubchen
Wär Seligkeit für mich.
Dann schmeckte mir Trinken und Essen,
Dann könnt' ich mit Fürsten mich messen,
Des Lebens als Weiser mich freun
Und wie im Elysium sein.

I'd give my finest feather
To find a pretty wife,
Two turtledoves together,
We'd share a happy life.
And happily then ever after
We'd frolic in gladness and laughter!
And all of my dreams would come true!
Our life would be heaven for two!

II

Ein Mädchen oder Weibchen
Wünscht Papageno sich!
O so ein sanftes Täubchen
Wär Seligkeit für mich.
Ach kann ich denn keiner von allen
Den reizenden Mädchen gefallen?
Helf eine mir nur aus der Not,
Sonst gräm ich mich wahrlich zu Tod.

I'd give my finest feather
To find a pretty wife,
Two turtledoves together,
We'd share a happy life.
I'm sure there are girls all around me
But none of them seems to have found me.
With no one to love me or care,
I'll certainly die of despair.

III

Ein Mädchen oder Weibchen
Wünscht Papageno sich!
O so ein sanftes Täubchen
Wär Seligkeit für mich.
Wird keine mir Liebe gewähren,
So muss mich die Flamme verzehren;
Doch küsst mich ein weiblicher Mund,
So bin ich schon wieder gesund.

I'd give my finest feather
To find a pretty wife,
Two turtledoves together,
We'd share a happy life.
With no one to give me affection,
I'm buried in hopeless dejection!
But all that I need is a kiss
To put me in heavenly bliss.
(the old WOMAN *enters, hobbling and supporting herself on her stick)*

WEIB
Da bin ich schon, mein Engel!

WOMAN
Here I am, my angel!

PAPAGENO
Du hast dich meiner erbarmt?

PAPAGENO
So you took pity on me, then?

WEIB
Ja, mein Engel!

WOMAN
Yes, my angel.

PAPAGENO
Das ist ein Glück!

PAPAGENO
What wonderful luck I have!

WOMAN

And if you promise to be true to me forever, then you will see how tenderly your little wife will love you.

PAPAGENO

Oh, what a tender goose you are!

WOMAN

Oh, how I shall embrace you, caress you, press you to my heart!

PAPAGENO

Even press me to your heart?

WOMAN

Come, give me your hand as a pledge of our union.

PAPAGENO

Not so fast, dear angel! Such a marriage needs some considerations, after all.

WOMAN

Papageno, I advise you, don't hesitate! Your hand, or you shall be imprisoned here forever.

PAPAGENO

Imprisoned?

WOMAN

Bread and water shall be your daily diet. You must live without friends or sweetheart and renounce the world forever.

PAPAGENO

Renounce the world forever? Drink water? No! In that case I'll taken an old one rather than none at all. Well, here you have my hand with the assurance that I shall always be true to you

(aside)

until I find someone prettier.

WOMAN

You swear that?

PAPAGENO

Yes, I swear it.

(WOMAN *changes into a maiden, dressed like* PAPAGENO)

Pa-Pa-Papagena!

(he wishes to embrace her)

SPEAKER *(enters and takes her by the hand)*

Begone, young woman! He is not yet worthy of you. *(he drags her out.* PAPAGENO *wants to follow)*

Back, I say, or woe unto you!

PAPAGENO

Before I withdraw, the earth shall swallow me up!

(he sinks into the earth)

Oh, Gods above!

WEIB

Und wenn du mir versprichst, mir ewig treu zu bleiben, dann sollst du sehen, wie zärtlich dein Weibchen dich lieben wird.

PAPAGENO

Ei, du zärtliches Närrchen!

WEIB

O, wie will ich dich umarmen, dich liebkosen, dich an mein Herz drücken!

PAPAGENO

Auch ans Herz drücken?

WEIB

Komm, reich mir zum Pfand unseres Bundes deine Hand!

PAPAGENO

Nur nicht so hastig, lieber Engel! So ein Bündnis braucht doch auch seine Überlegung.

WEIB

Papageno, ich rate dir, zaudre nicht!—Deine Hand, oder du bist auf immer hier eingekerkert.

PAPAGENO

Eingekerkert?

WEIB

Wasser und Brot wird deine tägliche Kost sein.—Ohne Freund, ohne Freundin musst du leben, und der Welt auf immer entsagen.

PAPAGENO

Wasser trinken?—der Welt entsagen? Nein, da will ich doch lieber eine Alte nehmen, als gar keine.—Nun, da hast du meine Hand mit der Versicherung, dass ich dir immer getreu bleibe, so lang' ich keine Schönere sehe.

WEIB

Das schwörst du?

PAPAGENO

Ja, das schwör ich! Pa-Pa-Papagena!—

SPRECHER

Fort mit dir, junges Weib! Er ist deiner noch nicht würdig! Zurück! sag ich.

PAPAGENO

Eh ich mich zurückziehe, soll die Erde mich verschlingen. O ihr Götter!

3 KNABEN
Bald prangt, den Morgen zu verkünden,
Die Sonn' auf goldner Bahn.
Bald soll der Aberglaube schwinden,
Bald siegt der weise Mann.
O holde Ruhe, steig hernieder,
Kehr in der Menschen Herzen wieder;
Dann ist die Erd' ein Himmelreich,
Und Sterbliche den Göttern gleich.

1. KNABE
Doch seht, Verzweiflung quält Paminen!

2. UND 3. KNABE
Wo ist sie denn?

1. KNABE
Sie ist von Sinnen!

3 KNABEN
Sie quält verschmähter Liebe Leiden.
Lasst uns der Armen Trost bereiten.
Fürwahr, ihr Schicksal geht uns nah.
O wäre nur ihr Jüngling da!
Sie kommt, lasst uns bei Seite gehn,
Damit wir, was sie mache, sehn.

PAMINA
Du also bist mein Bräutigam!
Durch dich vollend ich meinen Gram!

3 KNABEN
Welch dunkle Worte sprach sie da?
Die Arme ist dem Wahnsinn nah.

PAMINA
Geduld, mein Trauter, ich bin dein!
Bald werden wir vermählet sein!

3 KNABEN
Wahnsinn tobt ihr im Gehirne,
Selbstmord steht auf ihrer Stirne.
Holdes Mädchen, sieh uns an!

PAMINA
Sterben will ich, weil der Mann
Den ich nimmermehr kann hassen,
Sein Traute kann verlassen.
Dies gab meine Mutter mir.

(*jumps out of the trap, calls after the* SPEAKER)
Sir, how dare you meddle in my family affairs?
(*change of scene. Palm garden*)

Finale

THREE SPIRITS
Soon speeds the morning light proclaiming
The sunshine's golden way.
This youth, the pow'rs of dark defaming,
Shall see the light of day.
O calmness from above descending,
Reprieve all men from grief unending.
Then doomed are evil, sin, and vice,
And earth becomes a paradise.

FIRST SPIRIT
But see, Pamina's torn by sadness!

SECOND, THIRD SPIRITS
Where is she then?

FIRST SPIRIT
She strays in madness.

THREE SPIRITS
Condemned by love to desperation;
Come, let us bring her consolation.
In truth, her life to us is dear!
Oh, were her lover only here!
She comes, let's stand aside and wait.
We must prevent her tragic fate.
(*they withdraw.* PAMINA *rushes in with a dagger in her hand*)

PAMINA (*to the dagger*)
So only you remain to me?
My heart from pain through you I free.

THREE SPIRITS (*aside*)
What darksome words we overhear?
Poor maiden, she is mad, I fear.

PAMINA
O death, receive me as your bride,
With you I will in peace abide.

THREE SPIRITS
Madness at her heart is tearing.
Thus to death she goes despairing.
(*to* PAMINA)
Lovely maiden, hear us now.

PAMINA
End my being—'tis the vow
That despairing I have taken;
By my love I am forsaken!

(pointing to the dagger)
This my mother gave to me!

THREE SPIRITS
Heaven's law will chasten thee!

PAMINA
Rather by this blade I perish,
Than a loveless life to cherish.
Mother, Mother. Your curse is my bane
And through you I suffer pain.

THREE SPIRITS
Maiden, will you come with us?

PAMINA
No! I drain the cup of woe!
Faithless lover, I must go!
See, Pamina dies through thee!
(tries to stab herself)
Deadly weapon, set me free!
(the THREE SPIRITS *snatch the dagger from her)*

THREE SPIRITS
Ah, unhappy maid, have done!
Of your prince let me remind you;
He would die should thus he find you.
For 'tis you he loves alone.

PAMINA
Oh, he was not then unfeeling,
But his love within concealing,
As he turned his face away?
Why in silence did he stay?

THREE SPIRITS
This to tell thee is forbidden,
But no longer be it hidden
That his heart is thine alone.
He is faithful, he is wise,
Even death for thee defies.
Come, Tamino waits for thee!

PAMINA
Guide me on, my love to see!

THREE SPIRITS, AND PAMINA
Two hearts which love has bound together
The storms of life will firmly weather.
No foe will threaten them with wrath;
The gods will smile upon their path.
(they leave with PAMINA
Scene: Rocky caves. At left, glowing fire; at right, a waterfall. Twilight. Two men in armor guard the entrance gate to the caves)

TWO MEN IN ARMOR
Man, wandering on his road, must bear the tribulation
Of fire and water, earth and air's probation.

3 KNABEN
Selbstmord strafet Gott an dir!

PAMINA
Lieber durch dies Eisen sterben,
Als durch Liebesgram verderben.
Mutter, durch dich leide ich,
Und dein Fluch verfolget mich.

3 KNABEN
Mädchen, willst du mit uns gehn?

PAMINA
Ha, des Jammers Mass ist voll!
Falscher Jüngling, lebe wohl!
Sieh, Pamina stirbt durch dich,
Dieses Eisen töte mich!

3 KNABEN
Ha! Unglückliche, halt ein!
Sollte dies dein Jüngling sehen,
Würde er vor Gram vergehen;
Denn er liebet dich allein.

PAMINA
Was? Er fühlte Gegenliebe,
Und verbarg mir seine Triebe,
Wandte sein Gesicht von mir?
Warum sprach er nicht mit mir?

3 KNABEN
Dieses müssen wir verschweigen,
Doch wir wollen dir ihn zeigen,
Und du wirst mit Staunen sehen,
Dass er dir sein Herz geweiht,
Und den Tod für dich nicht scheut.
Komm, wir wollen zu ihm gehn.

PAMINA
Führt mich hin, ich möcht' ihn sehn.

ALLE 4
Zwei Herzen, die vor Liebe brennen,
Kann Menschenohnmacht niemals trennen.
Verloren ist der Feinde Müh,
Die Götter selbsten schützen sie.

2 GEHARNISCHTE MÄNNER
Der, welcher wandert diese Strasse voll Beschwerden,
Wird rein durch Feuer, Wasser, Luft und Erden:

Wenn er des Todes Schrecken überwinden kann,
Schwingt er sich aus der Erde himmelan:
Erleuchtet wird er dann im Stande sein,
Sich den Mysterien der Isis ganz zu weih'n.

If he prevails against the lures of evil's might,
He soon will know the joys of heaven's light.
Enlightened, he will now himself prepare,
The holy mysteries of Isis all to share.
(TAMINO *is led in by the* TWO PRIESTS)

TAMINO
Mich schreckt kein Tod als Mann zu handeln,
Den Weg der Tugend fortzuwandeln.
Schliesst mir die Schreckenspforten auf!
Ich wage froh den kühnen Lauf.

TAMINO
By fear of death I am not shaken.
The path of virtue I have taken.
Unlock the fatal doors to me;
My course will firm and gallant be.

PAMINA
Tamino, halt! Ich muss dich sehn!

PAMINA (*off-stage*)
Tamino, wait! Ah, wait for me!

TAMINO
Was hör ich? Paminens Stimme?

TAMINO
What is this? Pamina calling.

2 GEHARN. MÄNNER
Ja, ja, das ist Paminens Stimme.

MEN IN ARMOR
Ah yes, that is Pamina calling.

TAMINO, 2 GEHARN. MÄNNER
Wohl mir (dir), nun kann sie mit mir (dir) geh'n,
Nun trennet uns (euch) kein Schicksal mehr,
Wenn auch der Tod beschieden wär!

TAMINO, MEN IN ARMOR
Rejoice! Together we (you) may fare.
No force on earth our (your) lives shall rend,
Even though death may be our (your) end.

TAMINO
Ist mir erlaubt, mit ihr zu sprechen?

TAMINO
Am I allowed to break my silence?

2 GEHARN. MÄNNER
Dir ist erlaubt, mit ihr zu sprechen.

MEN IN ARMOR
You are allowed to break your silence.
(*exit the* TWO PRIESTS)

TAMINO, 2 GEHARN. MÄNNER
Welch Glück, wenn wir uns (euch) wiederseh'n,
Froh Hand in Hand in Tempel geh'n!
Ein Weib, das Nacht und Tod nicht scheut,
Ist würdig und wird eingeweiht.

TAMINO, AND MEN IN ARMOR
What joy when next we meet again,
And hand in hand the temple gain!
A woman who has death disdained
Is worthy and will be ordained.
(*the* TWO PRIESTS *enter with* PAMINA)

PAMINA
Tamino mein! O welch ein Glück!

PAMINA (*embracing* TAMINO)
Tamino mine! Oh, happy fate!

TAMINO
Pamina mein! O welch ein Glück!—
Hier sind die Schreckenspforten,
Die Not und Tod mir dräu'n.

TAMINO
Pamina mine! Oh, happy fate!
(*points toward the rocky caves*)
Beyond those gates unfolding
Both death and menace hide.

PAMINA
Ich werde aller Orten
An deiner Seite sein;
Ich selbsten führe dich,
Die Liebe leitet mich.
Sie mag den Weg mit Rosen streu'n
Weil Rosen stets bei Dornen sein.

PAMINA
Your every act upholding,
I shall not leave your side.
In me your trust confide,
For Love my way will guide.
(*she takes him by the hand*)
Our path with roses it adorns,

For roses always grow with thorns.
Take now the magic flute and play;
Its golden tones protect our way.
'Twas shaped at midnight's witching hour
By my father, with his magic power,
From branch of oak tree, strong and old,
While storming thunder wildly rolled.
Now take the magic flute and play;
Its tones will guide our fearsome way.

Spiel du die Zauberflöte an;
Sie schütze uns auf unsrer Bahn.
Es schnitt in einer Zauberstunde
Mein Vater sie aus tiefstem Grunde
Der tausendjähr'gen Eiche aus,
Bei Blitz und Donner, Sturm und Braus.
Nun komm und spiel die Flöte an,
Sie leite uns auf grauser Bahn.

PAMINA, TAMINO, AND TWO MEN IN ARMOR
We (you) wander by sweet music's might
With gladness through the vale of night.
(TAMINO *and* PAMINA *pass through the fiery cave, she with her hand on* TAMINO*'s shoulder, while he plays his flute*)

ALLE 4
Wir wandeln (Ihr wandelt) durch des Todes Macht
Froh durch des Todes düstre Nacht.

PAMINA, TAMINO (*embracing*)
The fire's flames we have transcended,
The danger we have firm withstood;
And still by magic tones defended,
We penetrate the water's flood.
(*they turn to the water cave*)

PAMINA, TAMINO
Wir wandelten durch Feuergluten,
Bekämpften mutig die Gefahr.
Dein Ton sei Schutz in Wasserfluten,
So wie er es im Feuer war.

PAMINA, TAMINO
O gods, what ecstasy divine!
On us the smiles of Isis shine!

PAMINA, TAMINO
Ihr Götter, welch ein Augenblick!
Gewähret ist uns Isis Glück!

CHORUS (*off-stage*)
Rejoice! The victory is gained!
The journey's end you have attained!
On you the smiles of Isis shine!
Come enter in the temple's shrine!
(SARASTRO *leads* TAMINO *and* PAMINA *into the temple.*)
(*Change of scene. Garden. Enter* PAPAGENO, *girded with a rope. He whistles on his pipe*)

CHOR
Triumph, Triumph, du edles Paar!
Besieget hast du die Gefahr;
Der Isis Weihe ist nun dein.
Kommt, tretet in den Tempel ein!

PAPAGENO
Papagena, Papagena, Papagena!
(*whistles*)
Dearest! Sweetest! Papagena!
'Tis hopeless! Ah! How she has failed me!
Since I was born bad luck has trailed me!
By chattering I lost my maid,
And for this crime I am repaid.
Since I have tasted of that wine,
Since I have seen my lovely bride,
All I can do is fume and fret!
I am upset, I can't forget.
Papagena! Pretty darling!
Papagena, lovely starling!
No more hope, there's no forgiving!
Sick and tired am I of living.
Since my love was all in vain,
I shall die to end my pain.

PAPAGENO
Papagena! Papagena! Papagena!
Weibchen! Täubchen, meine Schöne!
Vergebens! Ach, sie ist verloren.
Ich bin zum Unglück schon geboren.
Ich plauderte, und das war schlecht,
Und drum geschieht es mir schon recht.
Seit ich gekostet diesen Wein,
Seit ich das schöne Weibchen sah,
So brennt's im Herzenskämmerlein,
So zwickt es hier, so zwickt es da.
Papagena, Herzensweibchen!
Papagena, liebes Täubchen!
's ist umsonst, es ist vergebens!
Müde bin ich meines Lebens!
Sterben macht der Lieb ein End,

Wenn's im Herzen noch so brennt.
Diesen Baum da will ich zieren,
Mir an ihm den Hals zuschnüren,
Weil das Leben mir missfällt;
Gute Nacht, du schwarze Welt!
Weil du böse an mir handelst,
Mir kein schönes Kind zubandelst,
So ist's aus, so sterbe ich;
Schöne Mädchen, denkt an mich!
Will sich eine um mich Armen,
Eh' ich hänge, noch erbarmen,
Wohl, so lass ich's diesmal sein.
Rufet nur; ja oder nein!
Keine hört mich; alles stille.
Also ist es euer Wille?
Papageno, frisch hinauf!
Ende deinen Lebenslauf!
Nun, ich warte noch, es sei,
Bis man zählet eins, zwei, drei
Eins! Zwei! Drei!
Nun wohlan, es bleibt dabei,
Weil mich nichts zurücke hält,
Gute Nacht, du falsche Welt!

(*takes the rope in his hands*)
Yonder tree shall be my gallows.
There I'll hang to end my sorrows.
Thus to life I make rebuff.
World, good night, I have enough!
For I was too harshly treated,
All my hopes have been defeated.
Very soon I'll cease to be.
Lovely maidens, think of me!
Will not someone show compassion
Ere I hang in such a fashion?
Well, this once I let it go.
Just reply: say yes or no.
(*looks around*)
No one answers, all is quiet, here I stand deserted!
Then my end can't be averted.
Papageno, go ahead,
Tie the noose and you are dead!
(*looks around*)
Well, once more I'll try, let's see,
Till I count from one to three.
(*whistles and speaks very slowly*)
One, two, two and a half, two and three quarters, three.
(*sings*)
No one came, my lot is cast;
So this moment is my last.
Not a hand will mine restrain.
Fare you well, you world of pain!
(*starts to hang himself; the* THREE SPIRITS *enter swiftly*)

3 KNABEN
Halt ein! Halt ein! Halt ein!
O Papageno! und sei klug,
Man lebt nur einmal, dies sei dir genug!

THREE SPIRITS
Hold back! Hold back! Hold back!
O Papageno, hear our plea:
You live but once, and that enough should be.

PAPAGENO
Ihr habt gut reden, habt gut scherzen;
Doch brennt es euch wie mich im Herzen,
Ihr würdet auch nach Mädchen gehn.

PAPAGENO
My little friends, you are mistaken;
For if like me you were forsaken,
You, too, your luck with girls would try.

3 KNABEN
So lasse deine Glöckchen klingen;
Dies wird dein Weibchen zu dir bringen.

THREE SPIRITS
Then take your magic bells and play them.
Your little sweetheart will obey them.

PAPAGENO
Ich Narr vergass der Zauberdinge.
Erklinge, Glockenspiel, erklinge!
Ich muss mein liebes Mädchen seh'n!
Klinget, Glöckchen, klinget!
Schafft mein Mädchen her!
Klinget, Glöckchen, klinget!
Bringt mein Weibchen her.

PAPAGENO
How very foolishly I acted,
I truly must have been distracted.
Play out, my silver bells, keep ringing,
And bring my maiden to my side.
(*plays the glockenspiel*)
Silver bells, keep ringing, bring my maiden here.
(*the* THREE SPIRITS *bring* PAPAGENA)

THREE SPIRITS
Now, Papageno, turn around.
(exit)

3 KNABEN
Nun, Papageno, sieh dich um.

PAPAGENO, PAPAGENA
Pa-pa-pa-pa-pa-pa-pa-ge-na(o)!

PAPAGENO, PAPAGENA
Pa—pa—pa—pa—pa—pa—Papagena(o)!

PAPAGENO
Now you will be mine forever.

PAPAGENO
Bist du mir nun ganz gegeben?

PAPAGENA
Now I will be thine forever.

PAPAGENA
Nun bin ich dir ganz gegeben.

PAPAGENO
Come and be my little starling.

PAPAGENO
Nun, so sei mein liebes Weibchen!

PAPAGENA
I will be your heart's own darling!

PAPAGENA
Nun, so sei mein Herzenstäubchen!

BOTH
What a joy for us is near
When the gods, their bounty showing,
And their grace on us bestowing,
Will send us tiny children dear.

BEIDE
Welche Freude wird das sein,
Wenn die Götter uns bedenken,
Unsrer Liebe Kinder schenken,
So liebe, kleine Kinderlein!

PAPAGENO
First we will have a Papageno.

PAPAGENO
Erst einen kleinen Papageno.

PAPAGENA
Then we will have a Papagena.

PAPAGENA
Dann eine kleine Papagena.

PAPAGENO
Then comes another Papageno.

PAPAGENO
Dann wieder einen Papageno.

PAPAGENA
Then comes another Papagena

PAPAGENA
Dann wieder eine Papagena.

BOTH
It is the greatest joy of any
When many, many
Pa-pa-pa-pa-pa-pa-pa-page-nos (as)
Upon their parents blessing bring.
(they run off)
*(Change of scene:
Rocky landscape. Night. Enter* MONOSTATOS, *the* QUEEN, *and the* THREE LADIES, *with burning torches)*

BEIDE
Es ist das höchste der Gefühle,
Wenn viele, viele, viele, viele
Papageno, Papagena
Der Eltern Segen werden sein.

MONOSTATOS
Now stilly, stilly, stilly, stilly,
As we approach the temple door.

MONOSTATOS
Nur stille, stille, stille, stille!
Bald dringen wir im Tempel ein.

QUEEN, THREE LADIES
Now stilly, stilly, stilly, stilly.
As we approach the temple door.

KÖNIGIN UND DAMEN
Nur stille, stille, stille, stille!
Bald dringen wir im Tempel ein.

MONOSTATOS
My lady, keep your word, fulfill it:
Your child must wed the faithful Moor.

MONOSTATOS
Doch, Fürstin, halte Wort! Erfülle—
Dein Kind muss meine Gattin sein.

QUEEN
I keep my word, I firmly wish it!
My child shall wed the faithful Moor.

KÖNIGIN
Ich halte Wort; es ist mein Wille,
Mein Kind soll deine Gattin sein.

3 DAMEN
Ihr Kind soll deine Gattin sein.

THREE LADIES
Her child shall wed the faithful Moor.
(thunder and sound of water)

MONOSTATOS
Doch still, ich höre schrecklich rauschen
Wie Donnerton und Wasserfall.

MONOSTATOS
Be still, I hear a fearful roaring,
Like thunder's rage and waterfall.

KÖNIGIN UND DAMEN
Ja, fürchterlich ist dieses Rauschen,
Wie fernen Donners Widerhall.

QUEEN, THREE LADIES
Yes, dreadfully resounds the roaring,
Like distant thunder's sullen call.

MONOSTATOS
Nun sind sie in des Tempels Hallen.

MONOSTATOS
Within these halls they now assemble.

ALLE 5
Dort wollen wir sie überfallen,
Die Frömmler tilgen von der Erd
Mit Feuersglut und mächt'gem Schwert.

QUEEN, THREE LADIES, AND MONOSTATOS
We will assail them in their temple.
We shall destroy this canting horde
By savage blow and flaming sword.

DAMEN UND MONOSTATOS
Dir, grosse Königin der Nacht,
Sei uns'rer Rache Opfer gebracht.

THREE LADIES, MONOSTATOS *(kneeling)*
Thou great and mighty Queen of Night,
Their lives are thine by law and right.
(thunder, lightning, storm)

KÖNIGIN DER NACHT, 3 DAMEN, UND MONOSTATOS
Zerschmettert, zernichtet ist unsere Macht,
Wir alle gestürzet in ewige Nacht!

QUEEN, THREE LADIES, MONOSTATOS
Demolished, extinguished, defeated our might,
We plunge to destruction and infinite night.
(they sink into the earth.)
(Change of scene without curtain. Temple of the Sun. SARASTRO *stands on an eminence. Before him stand* TAMINO *and* PAMINO*)*

SARASTRO
Die Strahlen der Sonne vertreiben die Nacht,
Vernichten der Heuchler erschlichene Macht.

SARASTRO
The sun's radiant glory has vanquished the night,
The powers of darkness have yielded to light.

CHOR
Heil sei euch Geweihten! Ihr dranget durch Nacht.
Dank sei dir, Osiris, dank dir, Isis, gebracht!
Es siegte die Stärke, und krönet zum Lohn
Die Schönheit und Weisheit mit ewiger Kron.

CHORUS
Hail to thee, great Isis!
Hail to thee, Osiris!
You guided their ways.
Praise, praise, praise to thee, Osiris!
Thanks, thanks to Isis we raise!
Thus courage has triumphed, and virtue will rise,
The laurels of wisdom receiving as prize.

THE MARRIAGE OF FIGARO

(Le Nozze di Figaro)

by Wolfgang Amadeus Mozart (1756–91)

LIBRETTO BY LORENZO DA PONTE

Translated by RUTH and THOMAS MARTIN

Based on the comedy of the same name by Pierre Augustin Caron de Beaumarchais.

CHARACTERS

COUNT ALMAVIVA	*Baritone*
COUNTESS ALMAVIVA	*Soprano*
FIGARO, *Almaviva's valet*	*Bass*
SUSANNA, *the Countess's maid and fiancée of Figaro*	*Soprano*
CHERUBINO, *page to the Count*	*Soprano*
BARBARINA, *the gardener's daughter*	*Soprano*
DR. BARTOLO	*Bass*
MARCELLINA, *Bartolo's housekeeper*	*Mezzo-Soprano*
DON BASILIO, *a music teacher*	*Tenor*
DON CURZIO, *a lawyer*	*Tenor*
ANTONIO, *a gardener*	*Bass*

Time: Early Eighteenth Century
Place: Home of Count Almaviva, near Seville, Spain
First performance: Vienna, May 1, 1786

COPYRIGHT, 1947, 1948, 1951, BY G. SCHIRMER, INC.

ACT I

(An incompletely furnished room, with an armchair in the middle. FIGARO *has a ruler in his hand;* SUSANNA *is seated at a mirror, trying on a small, flowered hat.)*

Duet

FIGARO *(measuring)*
Seven . . . fourteen . . . twenty . . .
Thirty . . . thirty-seven . . . and forty-three . . .

SUSANNA *(looking at herself in the mirror)*
I must say, it's to my liking,
Just the very thing for me.
Won't you look, my darling Figaro.
Turn around, turn around.
Isn't this a lovely bonnet?

FIGARO
Seven . . . fourteen . . . twenty . . .
thirty . . . thirty-seven . . . and forty-three . . .

SUSANNA *(continuing to look in the mirror)*
Tell me frankly, my dear Figaro,
Do you like me in this bonnet?
Don't you love the trimming on it?

FIGARO
Yes, my sweet, the way you've done it,
It's a pretty sight to see,
And it suits you to a T.

SUSANNA
Just look at it!

FIGARO
Yes, my sweetheart. It's very charming!

SUSANNA
I must say, it's to my liking,
Very smart and very striking,
Just the very thing for me.

FIGARO
Very smart and very striking,
And it suits you to a T.

BOTH
I (you) have made it myself (yourself) for the wedding,
As your (my) bride I am (you are) planning to wear it.
I'm so happy, I hardly can bear it!
What a wonderful day that will be!

FIGARO
Susanna, my Susanna!

SUSANNA
My darling, my beloved!

BOTH
What a wonderful day that will be!

RECITATIVE

SUSANNA
Will you tell me, my precious, what on earth you are doing?

FIGARO
Cinque—dieci—venti—trenta—
Trentasei—quarantatre—

SUSANNA
Ora sì ch'io son contenta,
Sembra fatto in ver per me.
Guarda un po', mio caro Figaro,
Guarda adesso il mio cappello.

FIGARO
Cinque—dieci—venti—trenta—
trentasei—quarantatre

SUSANNA
Guarda un po', mio caro Figaro,
Guarda adesso il mio cappello,
Il mio cappello, il mio cappello.

FIGARO
Sì, mio core or è più bello,
Sembra fatto in ver per te.

SUSANNA
Guarda un po'.

FIGARO
Sì, mio core or è più bello.

SUSANNA
Ora sì ch'io son contenta,
Ora sì ch'io son contenta,
Sembra fatto in ver per me.

FIGARO
Sì, mio core or è più bello.
Sembra fatto in ver per te.

SUSANNA, FIGARO
Ah! il mattino alle nozze vicino,
Quant' è dolce al mio (tuo) tenero sposo
Questo bel cappellino vezzoso,
Che Susanna ella stessa si fe'!

FIGARO
Susanna, ella stessa.

SUSANNA
Susanna, ella stessa.

SUSANNA, FIGARO
Che Susanna ella stessa si fe'!

SUSANNA
Cosa stai misurando,
Caro il mio Figaretto?

FIGARO
Io guardo se quel letto.
Che ci destina il Conte,
Farà buona figura in questo loco.

FIGARO
I was just making sure that the space I have been measuring is sufficient for the bed the Count will give us.

SUSANNA
In questa stanza?

SUSANNA
You mean we'll sleep here?

FIGARO
Certo! a noi la cede
Generoso il padrone.

FIGARO
Surely! The Count was kind enough to make this our bedroom.

SUSANNA
Io per me te la dono.

SUSANNA
You can have it, for my part!

FIGARO
E la ragione?

FIGARO
Why, don't you like it?

SUSANNA
La ragione l'ho qui.

SUSANNA
I should say that I don't.

FIGARO
Perchè non puoi far, che passi un po' qui!

FIGARO
Then why not speak out and say what is wrong?

SUSANNA
Perchè non voglio; sei tu mio servo, o no?

SUSANNA
I just don't want to. Must you know all I'm thinking?

FIGARO
Ma non capisco,
Perchè tanto ti spiace
La più comoda stanza del palazzo.

FIGARO
But I can't fathom why you find it so distasteful that we're getting the best room in the castle.

SUSANNA
Perch' io son la Susanna, e tu sei pazzo.

SUSANNA
Because I am Susanna, and you are stupid.

FIGARO
Grazie!—non tanti elogi!
Guarda un poco
Se potriasi star meglio in altro loco.

FIGARO
Thank you, I like your frankness. Look around, then, and perhaps you can find us better quarters.

Se a caso Madama
La notte ti chiama:
Din—din—in due passi
Da quella puoi gir.
Vien poi l' occasione,
Che vuolmi il padrone:
Don—don—in tre salti
Lo vado a servir.

Duet

Some night if your mistress should ring for assistance,
Ding ding ding ding—
In a wink you could answer the call.
Suppose I am needed to wait on my master,
Dong dong dong dong—
I could be there in no time at all.

SUSANNA
Così se il mattino
Il caro Contino
Din—din—din e ti manda
Tre miglia lontan,
Don—don—a mia porta
Il diavol lo porta,
Ed ecco in tre salti . . .

SUSANNA
Suppose your dear master
Should send you on an errand,
Our dearest, our generous master,
Ding ding ding ding—
On an errand some three miles away,
Dong dong, dong dong—
In no time he would stand in my doorway.
Before I could stop him. . .

FIGARO
Susanna, pian pian!
Susanna, pian pian!

FIGARO
Susanna, hold on, Susanna, no more.

SUSANNA
Ed ecco in tre salti . . .

SUSANNA
While you are on an errand . . .

FIGARO
No more.

SUSANNA
And further . . .

FIGARO
Let's hear it.

SUSANNA
I'll tell you the story, the whole of the story,
But cast all suspicions and doubts from your mind.

FIGARO
I must hear the story, the whole of the story,
For doubts and suspicions still torture my mind.

RECITATIVE

SUSANNA
All right, then, but listen calmly.

FIGARO (*worriedly*)
Tell me, what is your story?

SUSANNA
Our noble master, tired of pursuing foreign beauties as partners for romances, has decided his castle will provide better chances. It's not his own dear wife, though, I can tell you, who has captured his fancy.

FIGARO
Well then, who is it?

SUSANNA
I give you three guesses!

FIGARO (*surprised*)
Not you?

SUSANNA
You're right the first time, and he is hoping that having us so near him will go far to advance his little project.

FIGARO
Perfect! We're making headway.

SUSANNA
That's why he seems so kind, therefore so thoughtful in respect to the bridal couple's comfort.

FIGARO
Just think of that! Such overwhelming kindness!

SUSANNA
But listen, now comes the best part: Don Basilio, who teaches me singing, acts as his mouthpiece, and during ev'ry lesson he keeps harping forever on the subject.

FIGARO
Who, Basilio? How revolting!

SUSANNA
Did you imagine the Count promised me a dowry on the strength of your good looks?

FIGARO
I was inclined to think so!

FIGARO
Pian pian!

SUSANNA
Ascolta—

FIGARO
Fa presto!

SUSANNA
Se udir brami il resto,
Discaccia i sospetti
Che torto mi fan.

FIGARO
Udir bramo il resto,
I dubbi, i sospetti
Gelare mi fan.

SUSANNA
Or bene, ascolta, e taci.

FIGARO
Parla, che c' è di nuovo?

SUSANNA
Il signor Conte,
Stanco d' andar cacciando
Le straniere bellezze forestiere,
Vuolo ancor nel castello
Ritentar la sua sorte;
Nè già di sua consorte, bada bene, appetito gli viene.

FIGARO
E di chi dunque?

SUSANNA
Della tua Susannetta.

FIGARO
Di te?

SUSANNA
Di me medesma, ed ha speranza ch'al nobil suo progetto utilissima sia tal vicinanza.

FIGARO
Bravo! Tiriamo avanti!

SUSANNA
Queste le grazie son; questa la cura ch' egli prende di te, della tua sposa.

FIGARO
O guarda un po', che carità pelosa!

SUSANNA
Chetati, or viene il meglio; Don Basilio, mia maestro di canto, e suo factotum, nel darmi la lezione, mi ripete ogni di questa canzone.

FIGARO
Chi! Basilio! oh, birbante!

SUSANNA
E tu credevi,
Che fosse la mia dote
Merto del tuo bel muso?

FIGARO
Me n'era lusingato!

SUSANNA
Ei la destina per ottener da me
certe mezz'ore . . . che il
diritto feudale . . .

FIGARO
Come! ne' feudi suoi non l'ha
il Conte abolito?

SUSANNA
Ebben, ora è pentito e par che
tenti riscattarlo da me.

FIGARO
Bravo! mi piace! che caro si-
gnor Conte!
Ci vogliam divertir; trovato
avete . . .
Chi suona?—la Contessa.

SUSANNA
Addio, Fi-Fi-Figaro bello.

FIGARO
Coraggio, mio tesoro.

SUSANNA
E tu cervello!

FIGARO
Bravo, signor padrone! Ora in-
comincio
A capir il mistero, e a veder
schietto
Tutto il vostro progetto; A
Londra, è vero?
Voi ministro, io corriero; e la
Susanna,
Secreta ambasciatrice!—
Non sarà—non sarà, Figaro il
dice!

Se vuol ballare, signor Contino,
Il chitarrino le suonerò.
Se vuol venire nella mia scuola,
La capriola le insegnerò.
Saprò, ma piano—meglio ogni
arcano
Dissimulando scoprir potrò.
L' arte schermendo, l' arte
adoprando,
Di quà pungendo, di là
scherzando,
Tutte le machine rovescierò.
Se vuol ballare
Signor Contino.
Il chitarrino le suonerò.

SUSANNA
He wants to bribe me to grant him his feudal right as lord and master on the night of our wedding.

FIGARO
What? Did he not abolish that right when he got married?

SUSANNA
He did, but now he's sorry and he would like to restore it for me.

FIGARO
Would he? Who wouldn't? A truly noble gesture. How amusing indeed! But I will show him.
(*a bell is heard*)
Who's ringing? It's the Countess.

SUSANNA
I'll have to answer.
Fi-Fi-Figaro, darling!

FIGARO
Good-by, my love, be cheerful!

SUSANNA
And you, be careful.
(*exit*)

FIGARO (*striding forcefully up and down the room and rubbing his hands*)
Splendid, my dearest master! Now I'm beginning to unscramble this puzzle and see your purpose in its proper dimensions. We're off to London. You as envoy, I as courier, and my Susanna . . . ambassadress in secret!
That shall never be so . . . Figaro has spoken!

CAVATINA

Should my dear master want some diversion,
I'll play the music on my guitar,
Should he, for instance, wish to go dancing,
He'll face the music, I'll lead the band.
And then I'll take my cue, without ado,
And slyly, very, very, very, very, very slyly,
Using discretion, I shall uncover his secret plan.
Subtly outwitting, innocent seeming,
Cleverly hitting, planning and scheming,
I'll get the best of the hypocrite yet,
I'll beat him yet!
Subtly outwitting, innocent seeming
Cleverly hitting, planning and scheming,
Teach him a lesson he'll never forget.
This time I shall upset his plan.
Should my dear master want some diversion,
I'll play the music on my guitar.

RECITATIVE

(*enter* BARTOLO *and* MARCELLINA)

BARTOLO
Why did you have to wait till the morning of their wedding to appoint me as your lawyer?

MARCELLINA (*holding a contract in her hand*)
I am well able, even at the last moment, to separate a couple engaged to be married. All I need is a pretext. And as for Figaro, he has made me commitments for some money I lent him. Therefore, our strategy is only too clear. If we succeed in making Susanna reject the Count's advances, then, for the sake of vengeance, he will favor our project and Figaro will thus become my husband.

BARTOLO (*takes the contract from* MARCELLINA)
Splendid! I'll do all I can, sparing no efforts to accomplish your object.
(*to himself*)
How I would love to arrange a match for my old servant Marcellina with the rogue who foiled my marriage to Rosina.
(*exit* MARCELLINA)

ARIA

Taking vengeance, yes, taking vengeance!
That's the peak of exultation
For a man of rank and station.
Bearing shame without opposition,
Taking insults with submission,
That's behaving in basest form,
That's behaving just like a worm,
A frightened worm.
Do it my way, take the sly way,
Spread confusion, and distraction.
Give them action, give them action!
I will show you how to function,
Using strategy and unction,
Show no pity, no compunction,
And before they know what hit them
You will outwit them!
Take my word, it can be done,
And the case can still be won.
Always proceeding with utmost legality
I shall discover a fine technicality,
I shall equivocate, argue, and litigate
Until a loophole I can produce.
I have ability, mental agility,
Legal facility and versatility,
With my experience and infallibility
Any opponent surely will lose.

BARTOLO
Ed aspettaste il giorno
Fissato per le nozze
A parlarmi di questo?

MARCELLINA
Io non mi perdo,
Dottor mio, di coraggio.
Per romper de' sponsali
Più avanzati di questo
Bastò spesso un pretesto; ed egli ha meco,
Oltre questo contratto,
Certi impegni . . . so io . . . basta . . . conviene
La Susanna atterrir, convien con arte
Impuntigliarla a rifiutare il Conte.
Egli, per vendicarsi,
Prenderà il mio partito,
E Figaro così fia mia marito.

BARTOLO
Bene, io tutto farò: senza riserva
Tutto a me palesate. (Avrei pur gusto
Di dare in moglie la mia serva antica
A chi mi fece un dì rapir l'amica.)

La vendetta—oh! la vendetta
È un piacer serbato ai saggi
L' obbliar l' onte, gli oltraggi
È bassezza, è ognor viltà
Coll'astuzia, coll'arguzia,
Col giudizio, col criterio
Si potrebbe—il fatto è serio!
Ma credete si farà.
Se tutto il codice dovessi volgere,
Se tutto l' indice dovessi leggere,
Con un equivoco, con un sinonimo
Qualche garbuglio si troverà.
Tutta Siviglia conosce Bartolo,
Il birbo Figaro vinto sarà.

MARCELLINA
Tutto ancor non ho perso,
Mi resta la speranza;
Ma Susanna s' avanza—io vo' provarmi—. . .
Fingiam di non vederla.
E quella buona perla
La vorrebbe sposar.

SUSANNA
(Di me favella.)

MARCELLINA
Ma da Figaro, alfine,
Non può meglio sperarsi; l'argent fait tout!

SUSANNA
(Che lingua! manco male
Ch' ognun sa quanto vale!)

MARCELLINA
Brava! questo è giudizio!
Con quegli occhi modesti,
Con quell' aria pietosa!
E poi . . .

SUSANNA
Meglio è partir.

MARCELLINA
Che cara sposa!

Via resti servita, madama brillante.

SUSANNA
Non sono sì ardita, madama piccante.

MARCELLINA
No, prima a lei tocca.

SUSANNA
No, no, tocca a lei.

MARCELLINA
No, prima a lei tocca.

SUSANNA
No, no, tocca a lei.

MARCELLINA
Io so i dover miei, non fo inciviltà.
Io so i dover miei,
non fo inciviltà.

Oh, what confusion I shall produce!
All of the city knows Dr. Bartolo—
As for that Figaro,
I'll cook his goose.
(exit)

RECITATIVE

(MARCELLINA *enters, then* SUSANNA, *with a nightcap, a ribbon, and a dressing gown*)

MARCELLINA
With such expert assistance I'm confident of winning. If it isn't Susanna!
(to herself)
I shall pretend that I don't even see her.
(aloud)
And that's the little gem he has chosen for a wife!

SUSANNA *(aside, remaining in the background)*
She speaks of me.

MARCELLINA
After all, from a Figaro, one can't really expect much, but, "money talks."

SUSANNA *(to herself)*
Old spinster! It's too bad that she could not find a husband.

MARCELLINA
Really! I can't imagine what he sees in this female. She's all skin and bones. I wish——
(both are about to leave but meet at the door)

SUZANNA *(with false sweetness)*
How do you do?

MARCELLINA *(with false sweetness)*
How nice to see you!

DUET

MARCELLINA *(curtsying)*
To greet you, my lady, I'm honored supremely.

SUSANNA *(curtsying)*
By your recognition I'm flattered extremely.

MARCELLINA *(curtsying)*
Please enter before me!

SUSANNA *(curtsying)*
No, no, you go first!

MARCELLINA *(curtsying)*
I beg you, ignore me!

SUSANNA *(curtsying)*
No, no, you go first.

MARCELLINA *(curtsying)*
I know my position,
Bow to tradition,
Fine and patrician,
With all due respect.

SUSANNA (*curtsying*)
Your noble position,
Fine and patrician,
Inspires respect.

MARCELLINA (*curtsying*)
I know my position,
Bow to tradition,
And my ambition is being correct.
The bride of the hour!

SUSANNA (*curtsying*)
A lady of station!

MARCELLINA (*curtsying*)
The Count's little flower!

SUSANNA (*curtsying*)
The pride of the nation!

MARCELLINA (*to herself*)
Her attitude! Her poses!

SUSANNA
Dignified! Mature!

MARCELLINA (*infuriated*)
I swear I shall fly at her
In one, in one minute more.

SUSANNA (*mockingly*)
Decrepit old battle-ax, I'll settle your score.

MARCELLINA (*curtsying*)
I praise your deportment without reservation!

SUSANNA (*curtsying*)
And I, your experience and broad reputation.

MARCELLINA (*curtsying*)
So young and so pretty!

SUSANNA (*curtsying*)
The belle of the city!

MARCELLINA (*curtsying*)
What distance between us!

SUSANNA (*curtsying*)
The true Spanish Venus!

MARCELLINA
So innocent! So simple!

SUSANNA (*infuriated*)
Durable! So old!

MARCELLINA
How dare she make fun of me,
It is a disgrace!

SUSANNA (*mockingly*)
So old, so old, so old!
Decrepit old battle-ax,
I'll laugh right in her face!
(*exit* MARCELLINA *angrily*)

SUSANNA
Io so i dover miei,
So i dover miei
Non fo inciviltà.

MARCELLINA
Io so i dover miei,
So i dover miei,
So i dover miei,
Non fo inciviltà.
La sposa novella.

SUSANNA
La dama d'onore!

MARCELLINA
Del Conte la bella!

SUSANNA
Di Spagna l'amore!

MARCELLINA
I meriti! Il posto!

SUSANNA
L'abito! L'età!

MARCELLINA
Per Bacco! precipito,
Se ancor resto quà!

SUSANNA
Sibilla decrepita
Da rider mi fa!

MARCELLINA
Via resti servita, madama brillante.

SUSANNA
Non sono sì ardita, madama piccante.

MARCELLINA
Sa sposa novella!

SUSANNA
La dama d'onore!

MARCELLINA
Del conte la bella!

SUSANNA
Di Spagna l'amore!

MARCELLINA
I meriti! il posto!

SUSANNA
L'abito! l'età!

MARCELLINA
Per Bacco! precipito,
Se ancor resto quà!

SUSANNA
L'età, l'età, l'età!
Sibilla decrepita,
Da rider, da rider mi fa!

Va là, vecchia pedante, dottoressa arrogante, perchè hai letti due libri, e
seccata madama in gioventù.

CHERUBINO
Susannetta, sei tu?

SUSANNA
Son io, cosa volete?

CHERUBINO
Ah! cor mio, che accidente!

SUSANNA
Cor vostro? cosa avvenne?

CHERUBINO
Il Conte ieri,
Perchè trovommi sol con Barbarina
Il congedo mi diede:
E se la Contessina,
La mia bella comare,
Grazia non m' intercede, io vado via,
Io non ti vedo più, Susanna mia.

SUSANNA
Non vedete più me? Bravo!
Ma dunque
Non più per la Contessa
Segretamente il vostro cor sospira?

CHERUBINO
Ah, che troppo rispetto ella m'inspira!
Felice te, che puoi vederla quando vuoi, che la vesti il mattino, che la sera la spogli, che le metti gli spilloni, i merletti . . . ah! se in tuo loco . . .
Cos' hai lì? dimmi un poco.

SUSANNA
Ah! il vago nastro, e la notturna cuffia
Di comare sì bella!

CHERUBINO
Deh dammelo, sorella—
Dammelo per pietà.

SUSANNA
Presto quel nastro.

CHERUBINO
O caro, o bello, o fortunato nastro!
Io non te'l renderò che colla vita!

SUSANNA
Cos' è quest' insolenza?

CHERUBINO
Eh via, sta cheta.
In ricompensa poi
Questa mia canzonetta io ti vò dare.

RECITATIVE

Conceited old spinster! Do you think you can snub me just because, in the old days, you taught my mistress her ABC's?

CHERUBINO (*entering in haste*)
Ah, Susanna, it's you!

SUSANNA
Come here, what's the matter?

CHERUBINO
Ah, he caught me! What misfortune!

SUSANNA
He caught you? Who has caught you?

CHERUBINO
Yesterday the Count found me visiting alone with Barbarina, and for that he dismissed me. And if my dearest Countess, my kind benefactress, cannot obtain my pardon,
(*anxiously*)
I have to leave and won't see you again, my dear Susanna.

SUSANNA
You won't see me again? How dreadful! But I always thought it was the Countess who was the object of your secret affection.

CHERUBINO
Ah, my lady is much too high above me! Oh, lucky you! You may always see her when you want to; you dress her each morning, you undress her each evening, you may fasten all her pins, tie her ribbons . . .
(*with a sigh*)
Were I in your place . . . What is that? Let me see it.

SUSANNA (*imitating* CHERUBINO)
Ah, that is one of her favorite ribbons and belongs to her nightcap.

CHERUBINO (*snatching the ribbon from her*)
Oh give it to me, Susanna, please, you must let me see.

SUSANNA (*trying to get it back*)
What are you doing?

CHERUBINO (*circling the chair*)
O sweetest, O loveliest, O most divine of ribbons!
(*covering the ribbon with kisses*)
Not for the whole wide world will I return it.

SUSANNA (*following him, but then stopping, as though exhausted*)
How dare you take that ribbon?

CHERUBINO
Don't get excited! I'll give you my new love song in exchange. That will make the bargain even.

SUSANNA
What shall I do with love songs?

CHERUBINO
Sing it to the Countess, sing it to yourself, sing it to Barbarina, to Marcellina,
(*in an ecstasy of joy*)
sing it to all the ladies in the castle!

SUSANNA
You must have lost your mind, poor Cherubino!

SUSANNA
E che ne debbo fare?

CHERUBINO
Leggila alla padrona,
Leggila tu medesma,
Leggila a Barbarina, a Marcellina,
Leggila ad ogni donna del palazzo.

SUSANNA
Povero Cherubin, siete voi pazzo?

ARIA

CHERUBINO
I can't give you a good explanation
For this new and confusing sensation.
Ev'ry lady I see makes me tremble,
Makes me tremble with pleasure and pain.
When of love there is merely a mention,
I am spellbound and rapt with attention.
I weave romances and daydreams together,
Filled with longing I cannot explain.
If I knew what it is I'd confess it,
But I am at a loss to express it,
Yet I know that it always excites me,
That it thrills me again and again.
Love is my inspiration,
Only consideration.
In rivers, woods and flowers,
I feel its magic streaming,
Awake, asleep and dreaming.
In gentle winds and showers,
I hear its mellow tone.
Love is my conversation,
Theme without variation,
I tell my love song
To glens and mountains,
To rivers and fountains,
To moon and stars in heaven.
The gentle breezes echo my ev'ry word and tone.
And if no one will listen . . .
Then I will talk alone of love,
Talk to myself alone.

CHERUBINO
Non so più cosa son, cosa faccio,
Or di foco, ora sono di ghiaccio;
Ogni donna cangiar di colore,
Ogni donna mi fa palpitar.
Solo ai nomi d'amor, di diletto,
Mi si turba, mi s' altera il petto,
E a parlare mi sforza d' amore
Un desio ch'io non posso spiegar.
Parlo d'amor vegliando,
Parlo d' amor sognando,
All' acqua, all' ombra, ai monti,
Ai fiori, all' erbe, ai fonti,
All' eco, all' aria, ai venti,
Che il suon de' vani accenti
Portano via con se.
E se non ho chi m' oda,
Parlo d'amor con me.

RECITATIVE

(*as* CHERUBINO *is leaving, he sees the* COUNT *in the distance, turns around in fright, and hides himself behind the armchair*)
Wait, I hear footsteps.

SUSANNA (*trying to screen* CHERUBINO)
It's the Count!
Hide quickly or you are lost!

COUNT (*entering*)
Susanna, you seem nervous, so confused and excited.

Ah, son perduto!

SUSANNA
Che timor!
Il Conte! Misera me!

IL CONTE
Susanna, tu mi sembri
Agitata e confusa.

SUSANNA
Signor—io chiedo scusa,
Ma se mai qui sorpresa
Per carità, partite!

IL CONTE
Un momento e ti lascio:
Odi.

SUSANNA
Non odo nulla.

IL CONTE
Due parole: tu sai,
Che ambasciatore a Londra
Il Re mi dichiarò; di condur meco
Figaro destinai.

SUSANNA
Signor—se osassi—

IL CONTE
Parla parla, mia cara; e con quel dritto,
Ch' oggi prendi su me, finchè tu vivi,
Chiedi, imponi, prescrivi—

SUSANNA
Lasciatemi, signor, dritti non prendo, non ne vò, non ne intendo.
Oh, me infelice!

IL CONTE
Ah no Susanna, io ti vò far felice! Tu ben sai quanto io t'amo; a te Basilio tutto già disse. Or senti, se per pochi momenti meco in giardin sull' imbrunir del giorno, ah per questo favore io pagherei.

BASILIO
E uscito poco fa.

IL CONTE
Chi parla?

SUSANNA
O Dei!

IL CONTE
Esci, ed alcun non entri.

SUSANNA
Ch' io vi lasci quì solo?

BASILIO
Da madama sarà; vado a cercarlo.

IL CONTE
Quì dietro mi porrò.

SUSANNA
Non vi celate.

IL CONTE
Taci, e cerca ch' ei parta.

SUSANNA
Ohimè! che fate!

SUSANNA
My Lord, you must excuse me, but if someone should come in now . . . I beg of you, don't stay here.

COUNT (*seats himself in the armchair and takes* SUSANNA'S *hand*)
It will take but a minute. Listen.

SUSANNA (*pulling her hand back*)
I will not listen.

COUNT
Just two words. You know the king has appointed me ambassador to London, and I arranged for Figaro to go with me.

SUSANNA (*timidly*)
If I dared ask you——

COUNT (*rising*)
Ask me, ask me, my darling, and with that right you exert over me,
(*tenderly, and trying to take her hand again*)
now and always, ask me, compel me, command me.

SUSANNA (*angrily*)
I do not wish that right, I ask no privilege, I don't want to exert it. I'm so unhappy.

COUNT
No, no, Susanna, I want you to be happy. You must know how much I love you. I'm sure Basilio told you already! Now listen, if you only consent to meet me tonight in the garden of the castle, I will amply repay you for this favor.

BASILIO (*off-stage*)
He left not long ago.

COUNT
Basilio!

SUSANNA
Good heavens!

COUNT
Hurry, don't let him enter.

SUSANNA (*very agitated*)
I should leave you alone here?

BASILIO (*off-stage*)
He can't be very far, perhaps with the Countess.

COUNT (*pointing to the chair*)
I'll step behind this chair.

SUSANNA
No, that's too risky.

COUNT
Quiet, get rid of him quickly.

SUSANNA
Oh, Lord, how awful!
(*the* COUNT *tries to hide behind the armchair;* SUSANNA

stands between him and CHERUBINO; *the* COUNT *draws her gently away. Meanwhile the page passes in front of the chair, and crouches in it.* SUSANNA *covers him with the dressing gown)*

BASILIO (*enters*)
Susanna, heaven bless you! Do you by chance know where the Count is?

BASILIO
Susanna, il ciel vi salvi; avreste a caso
Veduto il Conte?

SUSANNA
And what on earth should the Count do here? Go now, I'm busy.

SUSANNA
E cosa
Deve far meco il Conte? Animo, uscite.

BASILIO
Just a minute, it seems that Figaro wants to see him.

BASILIO
Aspettate, sentite
Figaro di lui cerca.

SUSANNA
The Count, the one man who hates him more than you do?

SUSANNA
(O cielo!) ei cerca
Chi, dopo voi, più l' odia.

COUNT (*aside*)
Let's see how he will serve me.

IL CONTE
(Vediam come mi serve.)

BASILIO
That is not so. There is no such conclusion, that if one loves the wife, one must hate the husband. In fact, my master loves you.

BASILIO
Io non ho mai
Nella moral sentito,
Ch' uno ch' ama la moglie odi il marito, per dir che il Conte v'ama.

SUSANNA
Get out of here this minute with your hints and suggestions.
(*resentfully*)
I have no interest in your lectures on morals, in your master, in his love.

SUSANNA
Sortite, vil ministro dell'altrui sfrenatezza; io non ho d'uopo della vostra morale, del Conte, del suo amor.

BASILIO
Don't take it that way, I don't mean to offend you. I was just thinking that you would prefer the type of lover which most women admire, a lord who is liberal and prudent, to a young pipsqueak, a pageboy.

BASILIO
Non c'è alcun male. Ha ciascun i suoi gusti,
Io mi credea che preferir doveste per amante come fan tutte quante, un signor liberal, prudente, e saggio, a un giovinastro, a un paggio.

SUSANNA (*anxiously*)
Not Cherubino?

SUSANNA
A Cherubino?

BASILIO
Yes, Cherubino, Cherubin the Cupid, who earlier this morning was prowling near your door, trying to enter.

BASILIO
A Cherubino, Cherubin d'amore, ch'oggi sul far del giorno passegiava quì intorno per entrar.

SUSANNA (*forcefully*)
You're a villain who tells malicious falsehoods!

SUSANNA
Uom maligno, un' impostura è questa.

BASILIO
To have eyes in one's head, is that malicious? For instance, this love song . . . tell me, just between us, I can be trusted, and will breathe it to no one . . . is it for you or the Countess?

BASILIO
È un maligno con voi, chi ha gli occhi in testa?
E quella canzonetta
Ditemi in confidenza, io sono amico,
Ed altrui nulla dico,
È per voi? per madama?

SUSANNA (*in consternation, to herself*)
Who the devil could have told him?

SUSANNA
(Chi diavol gliel' ha detto?)

BASILIO
Apropos, my dear girl, you should train him much better.

BASILIO
A proposito, figlia,
Instruitelo meglio.

Egli la guarda a tavola sì spesso,
E con tale immodestia,
Che s' il Conte s' accorge, e sul tal punto,
Sapete, egli è una bestia.

SUSANNA
Scellerato! e perchè andate voi
Tai menzogne spargendo?

BASILIO
Io! che ingiustizia!
Quel che compro io vendo;
A quel che tutti dicono
Io non ci aggiungo un pelo.

IL CONTE
Come! che dicon tutti?

BASILIO
(O bello!)

SUSANNA
O cielo!

IL CONTE
Cosa sento? tosto andate
E scacciate il seduttor.

BASILIO
In mal punto son quì giunto!
Perdonate, o mio signor.

SUSANNA
Che ruina! me meschina!
Son' oppressa dal dolor!

IL CONTE
Tosto andate, andate,
e scacciate il seduttor.

SUSANNA
Che ruina! me meschina!
Me meschina!
Son' oppressa dal dolor!

IL CONTE, BASILIO
Ah! già svien la poverina!
Come, oh Dio! le batte il cor!
Come, oh Dio! le batte il cor!

BASILIO
Pian pianin su questo seggio . . .

SUSANNA
Dove sono? Cosa veggio?
Che insolenza! andate fuor!

When he serves at table, he gazes at the Countess with such obvious longing that if the Count should take notice you can imagine, in that case, what's bound to happen.

SUSANNA
Oh, you liar! Have you nothing more to do than to spread vicious gossip?

BASILIO
I? You're mistaken. I just sell what I purchase, I echo what they all say, not adding in the slightest.

COUNT (*steps forward*)
Really! What are they saying?

BASILIO (*to himself*)
Delightful!

SUSANNA
Ah, heavens!

TRIO

COUNT (*to* BASILIO)
That's the limit!
Go this minute,
Find the culprit and throw him out.

BASILIO
How ill-chosen was my story,
Just a rumor, without a doubt.

SUSANNA
We'll be ruined by the scandal
If this gossip gets about!

COUNT
Don't delay any longer,
Go and throw the scoundrel out.

SUSANNA
This is awful! What will happen?
Heaven help us!
(*half fainting*)
I am feeling very faint.

COUNT, BASILIO
(*both support her*)
Ah, poor girl her strength is failing!
We must help her, revive her fast,
Or, good Lord, she might not last.

BASILIO (*approaching the armchair to sit down in it*)
Let us put her in this armchair.

SUSANNA
Ah, where am I?
Am I dreaming?
(*recovering*)
You insult me,
(*repulsing them both*)
Go away, leave me alone.

COUNT, BASILIO
We are only here to help you,
I assure you, we meant no harm.

BASILIO (*to the* COUNT)
What I told you
Was a rumor, mere suspicion,
With no foundation.

SUSANNA
He is vicious and malicious;
It's a lie, it is not true.

COUNT
Order him to leave the city.

SUSANNA, BASILIO
What a pity!

COUNT (*ironically*)
What a pity!
I have caught him once before!

SUSANNA
Caught him?

BASILIO
How?

SUSANNA
How?

BASILIO
Did you?

SUSANNA, BASILIO
Really? Where?

COUNT
At Barbarina's.
Yesterday I went to see Antonio.
I knocked, Barbarina opened and looked extremely nervous. I began to grow suspicious and examined every corner.
When I gently drew the cover
From the table, I found beneath it . . .
(*showing how he found the page, he lifts the dressing gown from the chair and discovers* CHERUBINO; *astonished*)
Cherubino!
Ha! What does this mean?

SUSANNA (*agitated*)
Ah, this is awful!

BASILIO (*laughing sardonically*)
Ah! This is priceless!

COUNT
Now at last my eyes are open!

SUSANNA
Nothing worse than this could happen!

COUNT
Now I see how matters stand!

IL CONTE, BASILIO
Siamo qui per aiutarvi,
È sicuro il vostro onor.

BASILIO
Ah! del paggio quel che ho detto,
Era solo un mio sospetto.

SUSANNA
È un' insidia, una perfidia.
Non credete all' impostor.

IL CONTE
Parta, parta il damerino.

SUSANNA, BASILIO
Poverino! poverino!

IL CONTE
Poverino! poverino!
Ma da me sorpreso ancor.

SUSANNA
Come?

BASILIO
Che?

SUSANNA
Che?

BASILIO
Come?

SUSANNA, BASILIO
Come? Che?

IL CONTE
Da tua cugina.
L' uscio ier trovai rinchiuso
Picchio; m' apre Barbarina
Paurosa fuor dell' uso,
Io dal muso insospettito
Guardo, cerco in ogni sito.
Ed alzando pian pianino
Il tappeto al tavolino,
Vedo il paggio—
Ah! cosa veggio?

SUSANNA
Ah, crude stelle!

BASILIO
Ah, meglio ancora!

IL CONTE
Onestissima signora!

SUSANNA
Accader non può di peggio!

IL CONTE
Or capisco come va!

SUSANNA
Giusti Dei! che mai sarà!
Che mai sarà!
Giusti Dei! che mai sarà!
BASILIO
Così fan tutte le belle,
Non c'è alcuna novità.

IL CONTE
Onestissima signora,
Or capisco come va!

Basilio, in traccia tosto
Di Figaro volate; io vo' che veda.

SUSANNA
Ed io che senta; andate.
IL CONTE
Restate: che baldanza! E quale scusa
Se la colpa è evidente?
SUSANNA
Non ha d' uopo di scusa un' innocente.
IL CONTE
Ma costui quando venne?
SUSANNA
Egli era meco, quando voi quì giungeste e mi chiedea d'impegnar la padrona a intercedergli grazia. Il vostro arrivo in scompiglio lo pose, ed allor in quel loco si nascose.
IL CONTE
Ma s'io stesso m'assisi, quando in camera entrai!
CHERUBINO
Ed allora di dietro io mi celai.
IL CONTE
E quando io là mi posi?
CHERUBINO
Allor io pian mi volsi, e quì m'ascosi.
IL CONTE
O cielo! dunque ha sentito
Quello ch'io ti diceal
CHERUBINO
Feci per non sentir quanto potea.
IL CONTE
O perfidia!
BASILIO
Frenatevi, vien gente.
IL CONTE
E voi restate quì, picciol serpente!

SUSANNA
This affair is out of hand. How will this end?
No one knows how this will end.
BASILIO
That's the way all women do it,
They will never show their hand.
COUNT
Now at last my eyes are open,
Now I see how matters stand.

RECITATIVE

Basilio, go right away and tell Figaro I want him.
(*pointing to* CHERUBINO, *who does not move from the spot*)
He has to see this.
SUSANNA (*animatedly*)
Yes, and hear this. Hurry.
COUNT
No, wait. Are you brazen? How dare you face him, if your guilt is so obvious?
SUSANNA
I have nothing to hide, for I am blameless.
COUNT
What about Cherubino?
SUSANNA
He was with me when we heard you approaching. He came to beg me to plead for my lady's gracious intercession. And your arrival completely upset him, so he hid in that chair in desperation.
COUNT
But I sat in that armchair when I entered the room.
CHERUBINO (*timidly*)
At that time I was hiding behind it.
COUNT
But when I stepped behind it?
CHERUBINO
Then I slipped into the seat, under this cover.
COUNT (*to* SUSANNA)
Confound it! Then he has heard the whole of our conversation.
CHERUBINO
I tried my very best not to listen.
COUNT
Oh, you rascal!
BASILIO
Someone's coming, be careful!
COUNT (*pulling* CHERUBINO *out of the armchair*)
And you stand up at once, you little serpent.
(*enter* FIGARO, *carrying a white veil in his hand, and*

peasants, dressed in white, who strew flowers from small baskets before the COUNT)

CHORUS

Strew in his praises
Roses and daisies,
Let us all honor him,
Master and lord.
He has respected,
Nobly protected
Maidenly honor,
Virtue's reward.
He is sagacious,
Friendly and gracious
In his benevolence,
Loved and adored,
Our noble lord.

CORO

Giovani liete, fiori spargete
Davanti il nobile nostro Signor;
Il suo gran core vi serba intatto
D'un più bel fiore l'almo candor.

RECITATIVE AND CHORUS

COUNT (*surprised, to* FIGARO)

What's the meaning of this nonsense?

IL CONTE

Cos'è questa commedia?

FIGARO (*aside to* SUSANNA)

The fun is beginning! You bear me out, Susanna.

FIGARO

(Eccoci in danza: secondami, cor mio.)

SUSANNA (*aside*)

I am discouraged.

SUSANNA

(Non ci ho speranza.)

FIGARO

My Lord, we beg your pardon, do not reject this token of our loyal affection. You abolished a custom, so repulsive to all who love sincerely.

FIGARO

Signor, non isdegnate questo del nostro affetto meritato tributo; or che aboliste un diritto sì ingrato a chi ben ama.

COUNT

That custom has been annulled, why do you worry?

IL CONTE

Quel dritto or non v'è più, cosa si brama?

FIGARO

We are the first ones to reap the fruits of the new decree. We have already set the time for our wedding, and call upon you to place this symbol of virtue on the head of my bride, chaste and spotless, thanks to your noble deed, your gen'rous action.

FIGARO

Della vostra saggezza il primo frutto oggi noi coglierem: le nostre nozze si son già stabilite, or a voi tocca costei che un vostro dono illibata serbò, coprir di questo simbolo d'onestà, candida vesta.

COUNT (*aside*)

What devilish cunning! But I will play along.
(*aloud*)
I'm truly grateful for your keen understanding; but I merit no credit, neither tribute nor praises for changing laws which were unjust and immoral. I am bound to uphold the rights of nature.

IL CONTE

(Diabolica astuzia! ma fingere convien.) Son grato, amici, ad un senso si onesto! ma non merto per questo, nè tributi, nè lodi, è un dritto ingiusto ne' miei feudi abolendo, a natura, al dover lor dritti io rendo.

ALL

Three cheers for our generous master!

TUTTI

Evviva! evviva! evviva!

SUSANNA (*sarcastically*)

He is great!

SUSANNA

Che virtù!

FIGARO

He is noble!

FIGARO

Che giustizia!

IL CONTE
A voi prometto compier la cerimonia, chiedo sol breve indugio; io voglio in faccia de' miei più fidi, e con più ricca pompa rendervi appien felici.
(Marcellina si trovi.) Andate amici.

COUNT (*to* FIGARO *and* SUSANNA)
You have my promise to celebrate this marriage. Give me a little time though. I need it to gather my faithful subjects; then, with fitting pomp and circumstance I shall unite you.
(*aside*)
I will send for Marcellina.
(*aloud*)
Farewell, till later.
(*the peasants strew the rest of the flowers*)

CORO
Giovani liete, fiori spargete
Davanti il nobile nostro signor;
Il suo gran core vi serba intatto
D'un più bel fiore l'almo candor.

CHORUS
Strew in his praises
Roses and daisies,
Let us all honor him,
Master and lord.
He has respected,
Nobly protected
Maidenly honor,
Virtue's reward.
He is sagacious,
Friendly and gracious
In his benevolence,
Loved and adored,
Our noble lord.
(*exit*)

RECITATIVE

FIGARO
Evviva!

FIGARO
Let's cheer him!

SUSANNA
Evviva!

SUSANNA
Let's cheer him!

BASILIO
Evviva!

BASILIO
Let's cheer him!

FIGARO
E voi non applaudite?

FIGARO (*to* CHERUBINO)
Why don't you join the cheering?

SUSANNA
È afflitto poveretto,
Perchè il padron lo scaccia dal castello.

SUSANNA
Poor fellow, he's dejected because the Count has banned him from the castle.

FIGARO
Ah! in un giorno sì bello!

FIGARO
What? On this festive occasion?

SUSANNA
In un giorno di nozze.

SUSANNA
On the day of our wedding?

FIGARO
Quando ognuno v'amira!

FIGARO
When the whole world admires you!

CHERUBINO
Perdono, mio signor!

CHERUBINO (*kneeling*)
Forgive me, noble lord.

IL CONTE
Nol meritate.

COUNT
You don't deserve it.

SUSANNA
Egli è ancora fanciullo.

SUSANNA
He is only a child.

IL CONTE
Men di quel che tu credi.

COUNT
Don't belittle his talents.

CHERUBINO
I may be little, but I hear like a grownup.

COUNT (*raising* CHERUBINO *from his knees*)
Enough. I will forgive you. And I will do even more. I need a captain in my regiment stationed at Seville. The post is yours, depart at once.
(*the* COUNT *prepares to leave;* SUSANNA *and* FIGARO *detain him*)
Good-by.

SUSANNA, FIGARO
Please let him stay today.

COUNT
No, you have heard me.

CHERUBINO (*sighing with great feeling*)
I'm prepared to obey Your Lordship's order.

COUNT
For the very last time, kiss Susanna good-by. (CHERUBINO *embraces* SUSANNA, *who is still confused; aside*)
That was a stroke of genius!

FIGARO
Well, mister captain,
(*exit* COUNT *and* BASILIO)
best of luck on your journey.
(*softly, to* CHERUBINO)
Despite his order, stay till tomorrow.
(*with feigned joy*)
Good-by, now, dear little Cherubino! What a glorious future lies before you!

ARIA

(*to* CHERUBINO)
From now on, my adventurous lover,
No romantic philand'ring excursions.
Such diversions are done with and over,
Cherubino, my young cavalier.
Such diversions are done with and over,
Cherubino, my young cavalier.
You had better forget all your fin'ry,
Feathered caps which you wore to perfection,
Powdered ringlets and creamlike complexion
In the army will soon disappear,
In the army will soon disappear.
You had better forget all your fin'ry
Feathered caps, powdered ringlets, creamlike complexion!
From now on, my adventurous lover,
No romantic philand'ring excursions.
Such diversions are done with and over,
Cherubino, my young cavalier.
Such diversions are done with and over,
Cherubino, my young cavalier.
Off with soldiers coarsely swearing,

CHERUBINO
È ver mancai; ma dal mio labbro alfine.

IL CONTE
Ben, ben, io vi perdono;
Anzi farò di più; vacante è un posto
D'uffizial nel reggimento mio;
Io sceglo voi; partite tosto, addio.

SUSANNA, FIGARO
Ah! fin domani sol.

IL CONTE
No, parta tosto.

CHERUBINO
A ubbidirvi, signor, son già disposto.

IL CONTE
Via per l'ultima volta
La Susanna abbracciate.
(Inaspettato è il colpo.)

FIGARO
Ehi, capitano,
A me pure la mano. (Io vuò parlarti, pria che tu parta;) addio, picciolo Cherubino;
Come cangia in un punto il tuo destino!

Non più andrai, farfallone amoroso,
Notte e giorno d'intorno girando,
Delle belle turbando il riposo,
Narcisetto, Adoncino d'amor
Delle belle turbando il riposo,
Narcisetto, Adoncino d'amor.
Non più avrai, questi bei pennacchini,
Quel cappello leggiero e galante,
Quella chioma, quell'aria brillante.
Quel vermiglio donnesco color.
Quel vermiglio donnesco color.
Non più avrai quei pennacchini,
Quel cappello, quella chioma, quell'aria brillante!
Non più andrai, farfallone amoroso,
Notte e giorno d'intorno girando,
Delle belle turbando il riposo,
Narcisetto, Adoncino d'amor.
Delle belle turbando il riposo,
Narcisetto, Adoncino d'amor.
Fra guerrieri, poffar Bacco!

Gran mustacchi, stretto sacco,
Schioppo in spalla, sciabla al fianco,
Collo dritto, muso franco;
O un gran casco, o un gran turbante,
Molto onor, poco contante.
Poco contante, poco contante.
Ed invece del fandango
Una marcia per il fango.
Per montagne, per valloni
Colle nevi, e i sollioni,
Al concerto di tromboni
Di bombarde, e di cannoni,
Che le palle in tutti i tuoni
All'orecchio fan fischiar.
Non più avrai quei pennacchini,
Non più avrai quel cappello,
Non più avrai quella chioma,
Non più avrai quell'aria brillante!
Non più andrai, farfallone amoroso,
Notte e giorno d'intorno girando,
Delle belle turbando il riposo,
Narcisetto, Adoncino d'amor.
Delle belle turbando il riposo,
Narcisetto, Adoncino d'amor.
Cherubino, alla vittoria,
Alla gloria militar.

Long mustaches proudly wearing!
With a rifle and a saber
In the army you will labor,
Trumpets clashing, and helmets flashing,
Lots of fame, but not much money,
But not much money, but not much money.
And instead of minuetting,
Through the mud you'll stagger sweating.
Up the stony mountains wheezing,
Sometimes broiling, sometimes freezing,
To the tune of trumpets wailing,
While the cannonballs are hailing
And the rifle bullets sailing,
Whistling by your pretty ear.
You had best forget your fin'ry which you wore to perfection,
And forget feathered caps, powdered curls and creamlike complexion.
From now on, my adventurous lover,
No romantic, philandering excursions.
Such diversions are done with and over,
Cherubino, my young cavalier.
Cherubino, on to glory,
On to vict'ry and to fame,
Cherubino, on to glory,
On to glory and to fame.
(*exit in military style*)

ACT II

(*a luxurious room, with an alcove and three doors*)

Cavatina

COUNTESS

Pour, O Love,
Sweet consolation
On my lonely, my broken heart.
Give me back his lost affection,
Or, I beg you, let me die.
Bring me comfort in my suff'ring,
Hear my brokenhearted sigh.
Give me back my lord and husband,
Or, I beg you, let me die.

Recitative

Come, Susanna, sit down here and finish the story.

SUSANNA (*entering*)

That's all there is to it.

COUNTESS

And you say that he loves you?

SUSANNA

Oh no, my master doesn't pay such a compliment to a girl of my station; he thinks he can buy me with money.

COUNTESS

So he loves me no longer?

SUSANNA

How is it, then, that he's jealous of you?

COUNTESS

It is the same way with all modern husbands, by nature unfaithful, by character capricious, and conceited enough to be jealous. But if Figaro loves you, he might be able . . .

FIGARO (*enters singing*)

La, la, la, la, la, la, la, la . . .

SUSANNA

There he is!
(*to* FIGARO)
Come, my darling, my lady is waiting.

FIGARO (*with casual gaiety*)

No need to worry, there's no reason whatever. The matter's very simple: my noble lord takes a fancy to my Susanna, so he decides in secret that he'll restore a custom he has lately abolished. The thing is very possible and very natural.

COUNTESS

Very possible?

SUSANNA

Very natural?

LA CONTESSA

Porgi, amor, qualche ristoro
Al mia duolo, a' miei sospir!
O mi rendi il mio tesoro,
O mi lascia, almen morir!
Porgi, amor, qualche ristoro
Al mia duolo, a' miei sospir!
O mi rendi il mio tesoro,
O mi lascia, almen morir!

Vieni, cara Susanna,
Finiscimi l'istoria.

SUSANNA

È già finita.

LA CONTESSA

Dunque volle sedurti?

SUSANNA

Oh il signor Conte non fa tai complimenti colle donne mie pari; egli venne a contratto di danari.

LA CONTESSA

Ah! il crudel più non m'ama.

SUSANNA

E come poi è geloso di voi?

LA CONTESSA

Come lo sono i moderni mariti, per sistema infedeli, per genio capricciosi, e per orgoglio poi tutti gelosi. Ma se Figaro t'ama, ei sol potria . . .

FIGARO

La lalalalalalala . . .

SUSANNA

Eccolo, vieni, amico, madama impaziente.

FIGARO

A voi non tocca stare in pena per questo.
Alfin di che si tratta? Al signor Conte piace la sposa mia; indi secretamente ricuperar vorria il diritto feudale; possibile è la cosa e naturale.

LA CONTESSA

Possibil?

SUSANNA

Natural?

FIGARO
Naturalissima, e se Susanna vuol, possibilissima.

SUSANNA
Finiscila una volta.

FIGARO
Ho già finito, quindi prese il partito, di sceglier me corriero, e la Susanna consigliera segreta d'ambasciata; a perch'ella ostinata ognor rifiuta il diploma d'onor, ch'ei le destina, minaccia di protegger Marcellina, questo e tutto l'affare.

SUSANNA
Ed hai coraggio di trattar scherzando un negozio si serio?

FIGARO
Non vi basta
Che scherzando io ci pensi?
Ecco il progetto:
Per Basilio un biglietto
Io gli fo capitar che l'avvertisca
Di certo appuntamento,
Che per l'ora del ballo
A un amante voi deste.

LA CONTESSA
O ciel! che sento?
Ad un uom si geloso?

FIGARO
Ancora meglio; così potrem più presto imbarazzarlo, confonderlo, imbrogliarlo, rovesciargli i progetti, empierlo di sospetti, e porgli in testa, che la moderna festa ch'ei di fare a me tenta, altri a lui faccia, onde quà perda il tempo, ivi la traccia, cosi quasi ex abrupto, e senza ch'abbia fatto per frastonarci alcun disegno vien l'ora delle nozze, in faccia a lei non fia, ch'osi d'opporsi ai voti miei.

SUSANNA
È ver, ma in di lui vece, s'opporrà Marcellina.

FIGARO
Aspetta, al Conte
Farai subito dir, che verso sera
Attendati in giardino;
Il picciol Cherubino,
Per mio consiglio, non ancor partito,
Da femmina vestito
Faremo che in sua vece ivi sen vada;
Questa è l'unica strada
Onde Monsù sorpreso de Madama
Sia costretto a far poi quel che si brama.

FIGARO
It is most natural, and, if Susanna wants it, is most possible.

SUSANNA
When will you ever finish?

FIGARO
I have already. That is why he decided he needs me as his courier and that Susanna should become his ambassadress in secret; and because she has stubbornly refused to accept the assignment, he's offended and threatens to take sides with Marcellina. That's the gist of the story.

SUSANNA
How can you treat such a serious business as a matter of joking?

FIGARO
Aren't you happy that I don't take it seriously? Here is my project: through Basilio I'll send a little note to the Count to inform him about an appointment
(*to the* COUNTESS)
that the Countess supposedly made with a lover.

COUNTESS
Good Lord! How risky! With a husband so jealous!

FIGARO
So much the better. Because we can more readily attack him, and baffle him, disconcert him, get him wholly bewildered, inflame him with suspicion, and make him grasp that what he does to others they will do unto him, and even with int'rest! While he is losing time as well as his bearings, our wedding hour will come before he ever finds an opportunity to hinder us from getting married,
(*indicating the* COUNTESS)
or has a chance to make any effective opposition.

SUSANNA
That's true, but in his stead Marcellina will oppose us.

FIGARO
I know it, so therefore, you give the Count a hint that late this evening you'll meet him in the garden, and little Cherubino (on my advice he has not yet departed) dressed up as a woman, will keep the rendezvous in place of Susanna. That's the only solution whereby His Lordship, surprised by my lady, can be forced to accede to all her dictates.

COUNTESS
How is that?

SUSANNA
Good enough.

COUNTESS
All things considered . . .

SUSANNA
If he thinks it will work . . . But is there time left?

FIGARO
The Count has gone hunting and won't come back here for at least sev'ral hours. I'll go now and
(*about to go*)
send you Cherubino immediately. You have ample time to get him ready.

COUNTESS
And then?

FIGARO
And then?
Should my dear master want some diversion,
I'll play the music on my guitar.
(*exit* FIGARO)

RECITATIVE

COUNTESS
How it grieves me, Susanna, to think that Cherubino heard all the nonsense my wayward husband told you. Ah, you don't know yet . . . but for what earthly reason didn't he see me in person? Where did you put his love song?

SUSANNA
Here it is. As soon as he comes we'll have him sing it. Listen, who is it? Our hero!
(*Enter* CHERUBINO)
Come in, come in, most worthy major gen'ral!

CHERUBINO
Please do not call me by such a fatal title, for it reminds me that soon I must leave her, my dearest kindest lady . . .

SUSANNA
Who is so pretty!

CHERUBINO (*sighing*)
So sweet! So lovely!

SUSANNA (*mocking him*)
So sweet! So lovely! You little hypocrite! Now quickly sing that lovesong which you gave me this morning so the Countess may hear it.

COUNTESS
Who wrote the song?

LA CONTESSA
Che ti par?

SUSANNA
Non c'è mal.

LA CONTESSA
Nel nostro caso . . .

SUSANNA
Quand'egli è persuaso . . .
E dove è il tempo?

FIGARO
Ito è il Conte alla caccia, e per qualch'ora
Non sarà di ritorno. Io vado, e tosto
Cherubino vi mando. Lascio a voi
La cura di vestirlo.

LA CONTESSA
E poi?

FIGARO
E poi
Se vuol ballare,
Signor Contino,
Il chitarrino
Le suonerò.

LA CONTESSA
Quanto duolmi, Susanna,
Che questo giovinotto abbia del Conte
Le stravaganze udito!—ah! tu non sai
Ma per qual causa mai
Da me stessa ei non venne?
Dov'è la canzonetta?

SUSANNA
Eccola. Appunto
Facciam che ce la canti.
Zitto! vien gente, è desso.
Avanti, avanti,
Signor uffiziale!

CHERUBINO
Ah! non chiamarmi
Con nome sì fatale; ei mi rammenta
Che abbandonar deggio comare tanto buona!

SUSANNA
E tanto bella!

CHERUBINO
Ah! sì, certo.

SUSANNA
Ah sì, certo! Ah sì, certo! Ipocritone!
Via presto la canzone,
Che stamane a me deste,
A madama cantate.

LA CONTESSA
Chi n'è l'autor?

SUSANNA
Guardate, egli ha due brace
Di rossor sulla faccia.

LA CONTESSA
Prendi la mia chitarra, e l'accompagna.

CHERUBINO
Io sono sì tremante,
Ma se madama vuole . . .

SUSANNA
Lo vuole, si, lo vuol, manco parole.

CHERUBINO
Voi che sapete
che cosa è amor,
Donne vedete
s'io l'ho nel cor.
Quello ch'io provo
vi ridirò,
È per me nuovo
capir nol so.
Sento un affetto
pien di desir
Ch'ora è diletto
ch'ora è martir.
Gelo, e poi sento
l'alma avvampar,
E in un momento
torno a gelar.
Ricerco un bene
fuori di me,
Non so ch'il tiene
non so cos'è.
Sospiro, e gemo
senza voler.
Palpito e tremo
senza saper.
Non trovo pace
notte nè dì;
Eppur mi piace
languir così.

LA CONTESSA
Bravo! che bella voce! Io non sapea
Che cantaste sì bene.

SUSANNA
Oh! in verità
Egli fa tutto ben quello che fa.
Presto, a noi, bel soldato;
Figaro v'informò . . .

CHERUBINO
Tutto mi disse.

SUSANNA
Lasciatemi veder—andrà benissimo;
Siam d'uguale statura. Giù quel manto.

LA CONTESSA
Che fai?

SUSANNA (*pointing to* CHERUBINO)
Who wrote it? Look at his face and see him blush like a schoolgirl.

COUNTESS
Take my guitar, Susanna, and accompany.

CHERUBINO
Today I'm not in voice, but if Madame desires . . .

SUSANNA
She surely does. Come on, no more preambles.

ARIA

(SUSANNA *plays on the guitar*)

CHERUBINO
You know the answer, you hold the key.
Love's tender secret, share it with me,
Ladies, I beg you, share it with me.
This new sensation I undergo,
It is so diff'rent from all I know.
Filled with excitement, walking on air,
First I am happy, soon I despair.
Now I am chilly, next time aflame,
Not for a moment am I the same.
I am pursuing some sunny ray,
But it eludes me, try as I may.
I can't stop sighing, hard as I try,
And then I tremble, not knowing why.
From this dilemma I find no peace,
And yet I want it never to cease.
You know the answer, you hold the key
Love's tender secret, share it with me,
Ladies, I beg you, share it with me,
Ladies, I beg you, share it with me.

RECITATIVE

COUNTESS
Bravo, your voice is lovely. I did not know you were such an expert singer.

SUSANNA
To tell the truth, all he does he always does well. Now come here, handsome soldier. Figaro told you all?

CHERUBINO
Every detail.

SUSANNA
Then let me see your height.
(*measuring herself with* CHERUBINO)
It will go splendidly . . . you are just about my size. Take your coat off.
(*takes off his cloak*)

COUNTESS
Be careful!

SUSANNA
No need to worry.

COUNTESS
If somebody should enter?

SUSANNA
Let him, what harm are we doing?
(*locking the door*)
But I must lock the door. What shall we do so his hair will not show?

COUNTESS
Get him a bonnet out of my wardrobe dresser, hurry!
(SUSANNA *goes into the small room to get a bonnet.* CHERUBINO *approaches the* COUNTESS *and shows her the commission, which he carries in his pocket. She takes it, opens it, and notices that the seal is missing*)
What have you got there?

CHERUBINO
My commission.

COUNTESS
They didn't waste a moment.

CHERUBINO
I got it from Basilio.

COUNTESS (*returns the commission to him*)
In their hurry they even forgot the seal.

SUSANNA (*returning with a cap in her hand*)
The seal on what?

COUNTESS
On his commission.

SUSANNA
How could they be so careless? Here is the bonnet.

COUNTESS
There you are. That's perfect! How disastrous for us if the Count came home now!

ARIA

SUSANNA
Come here and kneel in front of me,
(*she takes* CHERUBINO *and makes him kneel a slight distance from the* COUNTESS, *who has seated herself*)
And let me try my skill.
Don't wiggle, don't wiggle!
For heaven's sake, stand still,
Be patient and stand still.
(*she combs his hair, first from one side, then takes him by the chin and turns him as she combs the other side*)
Now slowly turn your head around.
Bravo, that's very nice.
(*while* SUSANNA *is dressing his hair,* CHERUBINO *regards the* COUNTESS *tenderly*)
Now turn your face the other way,
And look me in the eye!

SUSANNA
Niente paura.

LA CONTESSA
E se qualcuno entrasse?

SUSANNA
Entri, che mal facciamo?
La porta chiuderò; ma come poi
Acconciargli i cappelli?

LA CONTESSA
Una mia cuffia prendi nel gabinetto,
Presto—che carta è quella?

CHERUBINO
La patente.

LA CONTESSA
Che sollecita gente!

CHERUBINO
L'ebbi or or da Basilio.

LA CONTESSA
Dalla fretta obbliato hanno il sigillo.

SUSANNA
Il sigillo di che?

LA CONTESSA
Della patente.

SUSANNA
Cospetto, che premura!
Ecco la cuffia.

LA CONTESSA
Spicciati: va bene;
Miserabili noi, se il Conte viene!

SUSANNA
Venite, inginocchiatevi,
Restate fermo lì.
Restate, restate
Restate fermo lì.
Restate fermo lì.
Pian piano or via giratevi;
Bravo! va ben così!
La faccia ora volgetemi,
Olà! quegli occhi a me.
Drittissimo, drittissimo,
Guardatemi, guardatemi,
Madama quì non è.
La faccia ora volgetemi,
Olà! quegli occhi a me,
Drittissimo, guardatemi!
Madama, madama quì non è
Madama quì non è.
Restate fermo
Or via giratevi
Guardatemi, bravo!

Più alto quel colletto;
Quel ciglio un po' più basso,
Le mani sotto il petto
Vedremo poscia il passo
Quando sarete in piè.
Mirate il bricconcello,
Mirate quanto è bello!
Che furba guardatura,
Che vezzo, che figura!
Mirate il bricconcello,
Mirate quanto è bello,
Che furba guardatura,
Che vezzo, che figura!
Se l'amano le femmine,
Han certo il lor perchè,
Se l'amano, han certo il lor perchè.

(continues to dress his hair; she places the bonnet on him)
Hold still and let me try.
Look straight at me, not ev'rywhere.
The Countess is not sitting there,
So wait till by and by.
If you would keep your mind on this
We'd get it over soon.
The more you play, the more delay.
At this rate we'll take all afternoon.
Can't you be quiet?
Don't be so fidgety!
Behave yourself! That's it!
The motions slightly slower,
The skirt a little lower,
The glance a trifle shyer,
The motions slightly slower,
Now you must walk around.
We'll give you some suggestions
While you are passing by.
(aside to the COUNTESS*)*
Just see our prima donna!
He plays his part with honor.
The clever little shammer
Is full of charm and glamor.
No powder or cosmetic would better his complexion.
His glance is so poetic, his figure is perfection!
If women fall in love with him, they know the reason why,
Oh, certainly, they know the reason why.
Yes, yes, I see it clearly,
The reason why.

RECITATIVE

LA CONTESSA
Quante buffonerie!

SUSANNA
Ma se ne sono io medesma gelosa!
Ehi, serpentello, volete tralasciar d'esser sì bello?

LA CONTESSA
Finiam le ragazzate; or quelle maniche oltre il gomito gli alza, onde più agiatamente l'abito gli si adatti.

SUSANNA
Ecco!

LA CONTESSA
Più indietro, così. Che nastro è quello?

SUSANNA
E quel ch'esso involommi.

COUNTESS
My, you are worse than children!

SUSANNA
He looks so sweet I could almost be jealous!
(takes CHERUBINO *by the chin)*
You little rascal, where do you get the right to look so pretty?

COUNTESS
I wish you'd stop this nonsense. I think you'd better roll up his sleeves past his elbows. Then, when we put his dress on, it will not fit so tightly.

SUSANNA *(doing so)*
This way.

COUNTESS
Up farther, like this.
(discovers a ribbon wrapped about his arm)
What is that ribbon?

SUSANNA
The one he stole this morning.

COUNTESS
Why is it bloodstained?

CHERUBINO
Oh, really, I can't imagine. Just before, when I stumbled on the gravel, I guess I scraped my elbow, and I bandaged the wound with this ribbon.

SUSANNA
Let's see it. That's not bad! Good gracious! His arm is much whiter than my own, just like a woman's!

COUNTESS
You still keep up this nonsense? Go and look in my closet, and get a piece of adhesive plaster. Quick, it's in the dresser. As for that ribbon, you know, I like the color, I would hate to part with it.
(SUSANNA *dashes off; the* COUNTESS *contemplates her ribbon;* CHERUBINO, *kneeling, observes her attentively*)

SUSANNA (*gives the plaster and the scissors to the* COUNTESS)
I found it, but don't we need a bandage?

COUNTESS
Another ribbon! Bring it along when you come back.
(SUSANNA *leaves through the door at the back, taking with her* CHERUBINO'S *cloak*)

CHERUBINO
Ah, the old one would have healed it much quicker!

COUNTESS
And why? This one is better.

CHERUBINO
But any ribbon which touched the skin, or bound the hair of someone, somebody——

COUNTESS (*interrupting him*)
—who's a stranger will heal your cuts and bruises, don't you think so? It seems to have some pow'rs I never heard of.

CHERUBINO
My lady's joking, and I must go away.

COUNTESS
My poor boy! What misfortune!

CHERUBINO
How I am suff'ring!

COUNTESS (*much moved*)
You're crying!

CHERUBINO
O Lord, why don't you let me die now? Close to my death, I might get up the courage to confess how I really . . .

COUNTESS (*drying his eyes with her handkerchief*)
Cherubino, you are a little baby.
(*a knock is heard at the door*)
Who's knocking at my door?

LA CONTESSA
E questo sangue?

CHERUBINO
Quel sangue . . . io non so come, poco pria sdrucciolando . . . in un sasso . . . la pelle io mi sgraffiai . . . e la piaga col nastro io mi fasciai.

SUSANNA
Mostrate: non è mal; cospetto! ha il braccio più candido del mio! qualche ragazza . . .

LA CONTESSA
E segui a far la pazza? Va nel mio gabinetto, e prendi un poco d'inglese taffetà, ch'è sullo scrigno. In quanto al nastro . . . in ver . . . per il colore mi spiacea di privarmene.

SUSANNA
Tenete, e da legargli il braccio?

LA CONTESSA
Un altro nastro prendi insiem col mio vestito.

CHERUBINO
Ah, più presto m'avria quello guarito!

LA CONTESSA
Perchè? questo è migliore . . .

CHERUBINO
Allor che un nastro . . . legò la chioma . . . ovver toccò la pelle . . . d'ogetto . . .

LA CONTESSA
Forestiero, è buon per le ferite, non è vero? Guardate qualità ch'io non sapea!

CHERUBINO
Madama scherza, ed io frattanto parto!

LA CONTESSA
Poverin! Che sventura!

CHERUBINO
Oh me infelice!

LA CONTESSA
Or piange . . .

CHERUBINO
Oh ciel! Perchè morir non lice! Forse vicino all'ultimo momento . . . questa bocca oseria!

LA CONTESSA
Siate saggio, cos'è questa follia? Chi picchia alla mia porta?

IL CONTE
Perchè chiusa?

LA CONTESSA
Il mio sposo!
O Dei! son morta!
Voi quì senza mantello!
In questo stato—un ricevuto foglio,
La sua gran gelosia!

IL CONTE
Cosa indugiate?

LA CONTESSA
Son sola—ah sì, son sola.

IL CONTE
E a chi parlate?

LA CONTESSA
A voi . . . certo a voi stesso.

CHERUBINO
Dopo quel ch' è successo,
Il suo furore . . . non trovo altro consiglio.

LA CONTESSA
Ah! mi difenda il cielo in tal periglio!

IL CONTE
Che novità? Non fu mai vostra usanza
Di rinchiudervi in stanza.

LA CONTESSA
È ver, ma io . . .
Io stava quì mettendo . . .

IL CONTE
Via mettendo . . .

LA CONTESSA
Certe robe, era meco la Susanna,
Che in sua camera è andata.

IL CONTE
Ad ogni modo
Voi non siete tranquilla.
Guardate questo foglio.

LA CONTESSA
(Numi! è il foglio,
Che Figaro gli scrisse.)

IL CONTE
Cos' è codesto strepito?
In gabinetto
Qualche cosa è caduta.

LA CONTESSA
Io non intesi niente.

IL CONTE
Convien che abbiate gran pensieri in mente.

LA CONTESSA
Di che?

IL CONTE
Là v' è qualcuno.

COUNT (*outside*)
Why locked in?

COUNTESS
It's my husband! Good heavens! I'm ruined . . . with you here without your jacket . . . in this condition . . . he has received a letter . . . he's so terribly jealous!

COUNT (*more loudly*)
Why this delay?

COUNTESS (*confused*)
I'm alone. Yes, yes, I'm coming . . .

COUNT
To whom were you speaking?

COUNTESS
To you . . . surely to you only.

CHERUBINO
After all that has happened, his awful temper, I cannot let him find me!
(*runs into the small room and shuts the door*)

COUNTESS
May God above protect me in this danger!
(*takes the key and runs to admit the* COUNT)

COUNT (*enters, in a hunting costume*)
This is something new! It was never your custom to lock yourself in.

COUNTESS
That's true, but this time, I only was arranging . . .

COUNT
Arranging . . .

COUNTESS
Some of my dresses, and Susanna was with me; she has gone into her own room . . .

COUNT
At any rate, it seems that something upset you. Can you explain this letter?

COUNTESS (*aside*)
Heavens! The letter that Figaro has written!
(CHERUBINO, *in the small room, noisily knocks over a small table and chair*)

COUNT
What was that awful noise in there? A piece of furniture fell down in your boudoir.

COUNTESS
Strange, I did not hear it.

COUNT
In that event, you must be hard of hearing.

COUNTESS
Who, I?

COUNT
Somebody's in there!

COUNTESS
Who could possibly be there?

COUNT
I'm asking you that. I only just came in here.

COUNTESS
Of course, Susanna. How could I . . .

COUNT
Just before, you were saying she went to her room.

COUNTESS
Maybe to her room or that one, I was not watching.

COUNT
Then tell me, how does it happen you are so embarrassed?

COUNTESS (*with a forced laugh*)
For what possible reason?

COUNT
I can't explain it, but you do seem embarrassed.

COUNTESS
Is it not you, rather, who should be embarrassed about Susanna?

COUNT
That's not the issue! If it's Susanna, then I must see her.

TRIO

(SUSANNA *enters through the door she used on leaving, and halts on seeing the* COUNT *at the door of the small room*)

COUNT
Susanna, what's the matter?
Come out now, do you hear?

COUNTESS
Impossible, she cannot,
Right now she can't appear.

SUSANNA (*aside*)
What's all this angry chatter?
The page no longer here?

COUNT
What reason can prevent her? Speak!

COUNTESS
She's modest, she's modest!
That is why.
A wedding dress was sent her,
She has to try it on.

COUNT (*to himself*)
I grasp the situation,
Her lover hides inside.

COUNTESS
Your shameful accusation
Severely wounds my pride.
Your impudent accusation
Is baseless and unwise.

LA CONTESSA
Chi volete che sia?

IL CONTE
Lo chiedo a voi;
Io vengo in questo punto.

LA CONTESSA
Ah! sì . . . Susanna . . . appunto . . .

IL CONTE
Che passò, mi diceste alla sua stanza?

LA CONTESSA
Alla sua stanza, o quì, non vidi bene.

IL CONTE
Susanna, e d'onde viene,
Che siete sì turbata?

LA CONTESSA
Per la mia cameriera?

IL CONTE
Io non so nulla;
Ma turbata senz' altro.

LA CONTESSA
Ah questa serva
Più che non turba me, turba voi stesso

IL CONTE
È vero, è vero, e lo vedrete adesso.

IL CONTE
Susanna, or via sortite,
Sortite, così vo'!

LA CONTESSA
Fermatevi! sentite!
Sortire ella non può.

SUSANNA
(Cos' è codesta lite—
Il paggio dove andò?)

IL CONTE
E chi vietarlo or osa? Chi?

LA CONTESSA
Lo vieta l' onestà.
Un abito di sposa
Provando ella si stà.

IL CONTE
(Chiarissima è la cosa,
L' amante qui sarà!)

LA CONTESSA
(Bruttissima è la cosa,
Chi sa cosa sarà!)
(Bruttissima è la cosa,
Chi sa cosa sarà!)

SUSANNA
(Capisco qualche cosa,
Veggiamo come va!)
(Capisco qualche cosa,
Veggiamo come va.)

IL CONTE
(Chiarissima è la cosa,
L'amante quì sarà.)
Susanna, or via sortite,
Sortite, io così vo'!

LA CONTESSA
Fermatevi! sentite,
Sortire ella non può.

IL CONTE
Dunque parlate almeno,
Susanne se quì siete!

LA CONTESSA
Nemmen, nemmen, nemmeno,
Io v'ordino, tacete.

IL CONTE
Consorte mia, giudizio!
Giudizio, Giudizio!

SUSANNA
O ciel, un precipizio,
Un scandalo, un disordine
Quì certo certo nascerà.

LA CONTESSA
Consorte mio, giudizio!
Un scandalo, un disordine,
Schiviam per carità!

SUSANNA
O ciel! un precipizio,
Un scandalo, un disordine
Quì certo certo nascerà.

IL CONTE, LA CONTESSA, SUSANNA
Un scandalo, un disordine,
Schiviam per carità!

IL CONTE
Dunque, voi non aprite?

LA CONTESSA
E perchè deggio
Le mie camere aprir?

IL CONTE
Ebben, lasciate,
L' aprirem senza chiave. Ehi, gente!

LA CONTESSA
Come?
Porreste a repentaglio
D'una dama l' onore?

SUSANNA (*aside*)
A ticklish situation,
It cannot be denied.
A ticklish situation,
He took us by surprise.

COUNT
Disgraceful situation!
I took them by surprise.
Susanna, what is the matter?
Come out now! Haven't you heard?

COUNTESS
Impossible! She cannot!
Right now she can't appear.

COUNT
Well, if I may not see you,
Susanna, let me hear you,

COUNTESS
You will not hear her talking.
Expressly, I forbid it!
(SUSANNA *hides in the alcove*)

COUNT
My Lady, please consider,
Be careful, I warn you.

SUSANNA
Oh heavens! This is dreadful!
A scandal, a catastrophe
Will surely come to pass.

COUNTESS
Your Lordship, think it over,
No scandal or catastrophe
Must ever come to pass.

SUSANNA
Good Lord, what a disaster,
A scandal, a catastrophe
Will surely come to pass.

COUNT, COUNTESS, SUSANNA
Your Lordship (My Lady), think it over,
A scandal, a catastrophe
Will surely come to pass.

RECITATIVE

COUNT
Are you going to open?

COUNTESS
And for what reason should I open my room?

COUNT
All right, don't open. I'll get in just the same. Ho, servants!

COUNTESS
How dare you! Can it be your intention to disgrace me in public?

COUNT

Of course not, why should I? Without noise or disturbance, nor arousing a scandal before our servants, I'll go myself, then, to get all that is needed. You will wait for me here. But before leaving, so that all doubts are excluded, I shall make sure and lock all the doors.

(*locks the door to* SUSANNA's *room*)

IL CONTE

È vero, io sbaglio, posso senza rumore, senza scandalo alcun di nostra gente, andar io stesso a prender l'occorrente. Attendete pur quì . . . ma perchè in tutto sia il mio dubbio distrutto, anco le porte io primo chiuderò.

COUNTESS (*aside*)

This is worse yet.

LA CONTESSA

(Che imprudenza!)

COUNT

No, on second thought, be kind enough to come with me.

(*with feigned gaiety*)

My Lady, may I escort you? Here is my arm.

IL CONTE

Voi la condiscendenza
Di venir meco avrete;
Madama, eccovi il braccio; andiamo!

COUNTESS (*shuddering*)

So be it.

LA CONTESSA

Andiamo!

COUNT (*indicating the small room*)

Susanna won't mind waiting till we are back here.

(*exit*)

IL CONTE

Susanna starà quì finchè torniamo.

Duet

(SUSANNA *runs out of the alcove*)

SUSANNA (*at the door of the small room*)

Unlock the door and hurry!
It's I, it is Susanna!
Come out now, and quickly,
Come out this very minute,
You must get out of here!

SUSANNA

Aprite, presto aprite,
Aprite, è la Susanna
Sortite via, sortite,
Andate via di quà.

CHERUBINO (*coming out of the small room, confused and breathless*)

Oh, Lord, what a calamity,
How can I get away?

CHERUBINO

Ahimè! che scena orribile!
Che gran fatalità!

SUSANNA

You can't, I fear.

SUSANNA

Di là, di là!

CHERUBINO

I've got to get away!

CHERUBINO

Che gran fatalità!

SUSANNA

He locked the door from outside.
In heaven's name, what can we do?

SUSANNA

Le porte son serrate,
Che mai sarà, che mai sarà!

CHERUBINO

To stay is out of question.

CHERUBINO

Qui perdersi non giova.

SUSANNA

Then make a good suggestion.

SUSANNA

V' uccide se vi trova.

CHERUBINO (*going toward the window that looks out on the garden, as though he were going to jump out*)

Let's see about the window,
It is above the garden.

CHERUBINO

Veggiamo un po' qui fuori,
Dà proprio nel giardino.

SUSANNA (*holding him back*)

Don't do it, Cherubino,
Don't do it, don't jump, it is too high!

SUSANNA

Fermate, Cherubino.
Fermate, per pietà.

CHERUBINO (*trying to free himself from her*)

It's suicide, I know it!

CHERUBINO

Qui perdersi non giova.

SUSANNA
Fermate, Cherubino.

SUSANNA
Don't do it, Cherubino.

CHERUBINO
M'uccide se mi trova.

CHERUBINO
It really does not matter!

SUSANNA
Tropp' alto per un salto,
Fermate per pietà!

SUSANNA
It's much too high for jumping,
You never will get by.

CHERUBINO
Lasciami, pria di nuocerle,
Nel foco volerei.
Abbraccio te per lei;
Addio così si fa.

CHERUBINO
No other way is left for me.
(*releasing himself from her*)
I would never cause my lady any shame.
Embrace her in my name!
Good-by now, and here I go.

SUSANNA
Ei va a perire, o Dei!
Fermate per pietà!

SUSANNA
He really means to do it!
For heaven's sake, stay here,
Don't do it, don't do it!
(CHERUBINO *jumps out.* SUSANNA *screams, sits down for a moment, and then goes to the balcony*)

Recitative

Oh! guarda il demonietto, come fugge!
È già un miglio lontano
Ma non perdiamci invano;
Entriam in gabinetto;
Venga poi lo smargiasso,
Io quì l'aspetto.

Look at the little devil! How he can run! He's already a mile away. But it is up to me now to deal with our lord and master. Come ahead, Mister Tyrant, I shall be ready.
(*she enters the small room and locks the door behind her. The* COUNTESS *and the* COUNT *enter. The* COUNT *brings a hammer and a crowbar. After entering he examines all the doors*)

IL CONTE
Tutto è come il lasciai, volete dunque
Aprir voi stessa, o deggio?

COUNT
Ev'rything's as we left it. Will you yourself unlock the door now, or shall I?
(*preparing to force open the door*)

LA CONTESSA
Ahimè! fermate,
E ascoltatemi un poco;
Mi credete capace
Di mancar al dover?

COUNTESS
Just wait one moment. I entreat you to listen.
(*the* COUNT *tosses the hammer and crowbar onto a chair*)
Do you think I could fail you in my duty as your wife?

IL CONTE
Come vi piace,
Entro quel gabinetto;
Chi v'è chiuso vedrò.

COUNT
That is the question. Meanwhile I am proceeding to find out who is there.

LA CONTESSA
Si, lo vedrete,
Ma uditemi tranquillo.

COUNTESS (*timidly and trembling*)
Yes, there is someone, but listen to me calmly.

IL CONTE
Non è dunque Susanna?

COUNT (*incensed*)
So it's not Susanna?

LA CONTESSA
No, ma invece è un oggetto, che ragion di sospetto, non vi deve lasciar; per questa sera, una burla innocente, di far si disponeva, ed io vi giuro che l'onor, l'onestà . . .

COUNTESS
No, but somebody else who can give you no reason for suspicion or doubt. We were rehearsing, just a harmless diversion, a frolic for this evening, and I assure you that my honor, your good faith . . .

COUNT
Who is it? Say it,
(with increasing anger)
I'll strike him dead!

COUNTESS
Please listen? Ah! I'm afraid!

COUNT
Speak freely.

COUNTESS
It's just a child.

COUNT
Just a child?

COUNTESS
Yes, Cherubino.

COUNT *(aside)*
Why must I find that pageboy trailing my footsteps like a shadow?
(aloud)
What? Has he not left? He defied me. Now I begin to see daylight in this confusion. This is the cunning plot of which the letter warned me.

FINALE

(with violence, at the door of the small room)
Out you come. Don't waste a moment, wretched, disobedient page!

COUNTESS *(pulling him back from the small room)*
Dearest husband, what excitement!
I am frightened by your rage.

COUNT
And you still would dare oppose me?

COUNTESS
You must listen!

COUNT
I am waiting!

COUNTESS
Let me tell you.

COUNT
I am waiting. The answer, what is it?

COUNTESS
As a joke you have to take it,
No bad intention,
(trembling and alarmed)
And the costume, in which you find him,
Open collar, shoulders naked . . .

COUNT
Open collar! Shoulders naked! Do continue!

COUNTESS
To disguise him as a woman . . .

COUNT *(goes toward the small room, then turns around)*
How indecent, how outrageous!
For his boldness he shall pay!

IL CONTE
Chi è dunque? dite . . .
l'ucciderò.

LA CONTESSA
Sentite, (ah non ho cor!)

IL CONTE
Parlate.

LA CONTESSA
È un fanciullo.

IL CONTE
Un fanciul?

LA CONTESSA
Sì, Cherubino.

IL CONTE
(E mi farà il destino
Ritrovar questo paggio in ogni loco?)
Com? Non è partito?
Scellerati!
Ecco i dubbi spiegati; ecco l'imbroglio,
Ecco il raggiro, onde m'avverte il foglio.

Esci ormai, garzon malnato;
Sciagurato, non tardar!

LA CONTESSA
Ah! signore, quel furore,
Per lui fammi il cor tremar!

IL CONTE
E d'opporvi ancor osate?

LA CONTESSA
No, sentite!

IL CONTE
Via parlate.

LA CONTESSA
No, sortite.

IL CONTE
Via parlate, parlate, parlate!

LA CONTESSA
Giuro al ciel ch'ogni sospetto
E lo stato, in che il trovate,
Sciolto il collo, nudo il petto.

IL CONTE
Sciolto il collo, nudo il petto!
Seguitate!

LA CONTESSA
Per vestir femminee spoglie . . .

IL CONTE
Ah! comprendo, indegna moglie,
Mi vo' tosto vendicar.

LA CONTESSA
Mi fa torto quel trasporto,
M'oltraggiate a dubitar.

IL CONTE
Quà la chiave.

LA CONTESSA
Egli è innocente!
Voi sapete.

IL CONTE
Non so niente.
Va lontan dagli occhi miei!
Un'infida, un'empia sei,
E mi cerchi d'infamar.

LA CONTESSA
Vado, sì, ma . . .

IL CONTE
Non ascolto.

LA CONTESSA
Ma . . .

IL CONTE
Non ascolto.

LA CONTESSA
Non son rea!

IL CONTE
Vel leggo in volto!
Mora, mora!

LA CONTESSA
Ah! la cieca gelosia
Qualche eccesso gli fa far.

IL CONTE
Mora mora, e più non sia,
Ria cagion del mio penar.
Ah, comprendo!

LA CONTESSA
Mia fa torto,
Quel trasporto!

IL CONTE
Susanna!

LA CONTESSA
Susanna!

SUSANNA
Signore!
Cos'è quel stupore?
Il brando prendete,
Il paggio uccidete,
Quel paggio malnato
Vedetelo quà.

COUNTESS (*forcefully*)
You offend me most severely
By accusing me this way.

COUNT
Let me enter!
(*turning back*)

COUNTESS
He is not guilty.
(*gives him the key*)
You know better.

COUNT
I know nothing!
Go away at once and leave me,
You're unfaithful and deceived me.
You have covered me with shame.

COUNTESS
I leave you, yes . . . but . . .

COUNT
I won't listen.

COUNTESS
But . . .

COUNT
I won't listen.

COUNTESS
I am blameless.

COUNT
I don't believe you!
I shall kill him.

COUNTESS
Ah, his ear is deaf to reason,
Jealous rage has made him blind.

COUNT
He must die for his treason!
Nothing less can ease my mind!
Now I know you!

COUNTESS
What suspicion! What injustice!

COUNT (*opens the door*)
Susanna!
(SUSANNA *gravely issues from the doorway and remains there*)

COUNTESS (*astonished*)
Susanna!

SUSANNA
Your Lordship! You seem so bewildered!
(*ironically*)
The wicked offender has come to surrender.
Your treacherous rival is standing right here.

COUNT (*aside*)
They fooled me!
This thing is confusing my brain!

COUNTESS (*aside*)
I can't understand it.
Susanna, explain!

SUSANNA (*aside*)
How all this has happened
They cannot explain.

COUNT
However . . .

SUSANNA
You mean, sir, he still might be there?
Why don't you go look, then,
He still might be there.

COUNT
All right, then, he still might be there.
(*the* COUNT *goes into the small room*)

COUNTESS
Susanna, I'm weary, I'm breathless with terror.

SUSANNA (*quickly indicates to the* COUNTESS *the window from which* CHERUBINO *leaped*)
Don't worry, be cheerful, the page is not there.

COUNT (*comes out of the small room in confusion*)
How badly mistaken,
Completely mistaken!
I scarcely believe it . . .
If I did offend you,
I beg your forgiveness.
I'm sure you will give it.
But such cruel escapades
Are quite out of place.

COUNTESS (*with her handkerchief at her mouth to conceal her agitation*), SUSANNA
Your foolish behavior
Can merit no grace.

COUNT
I love you!

COUNTESS (*gradually recovering from her confusion*)
Don't say it!

COUNT
I swear it!

COUNTESS
You're lying!
(*forcefully and angrily*)
I'm wicked, unfaithful,
And always deceive you.

COUNT
Please help me, Susanna,
Her anger to calm.

IL CONTE
Che scola! la testa,
Girando mi va!

LA CONTESSA
Che storia è mai questa!
Susanna v'è là!

SUSANNA
Confusa han la testa,
Non san come va.

IL CONTE
Sei sola?

SUSANNA
Guardate!
Quì ascoso sarà.
Guardate, guardate!
Quì ascoso sarà!

IL CONTE
Guardiamo, guardiamo,
Quì ascoso sarà.

LA CONTESSA
Susanna, son morta,
Il fiato mi manca.

SUSANNA
Più lieta, più franca;
In salvo è di già.

IL CONTE
Che sbaglio mai presi!
Appena lo credo!
Se a torto v'offesi
Perdono vi chiedo,
Ma far burla simile
È poi crudeltà.

LA CONTESSA, SUSANNA
Le vostre follie
Non mertan pietà.

IL CONTE
Io v'amo.

LA CONTESSA
Nol dite!

IL CONTE
Vel giuro!

LA CONTESSA
Mentite!
Son l'empia, l'infida,
Che ognora v'inganna.

IL CONTE
Quell'ira, Susanna,
M'aita a calmar!

SUSANNA
Così si condanna
Chi può sospettar.

LA CONTESSA
Ah! dunque la fede
D'un'anima amante
Si fiera mercede
Doveva sperar!

IL CONTE
Quell'ira, Susanna,
M'aita a calmar.

SUSANNA
Così si condanna
Chi può sospettar.
Signora!

IL CONTE
Rosina!

LA CONTESSA
Crudele!
Più quella non sono!
Ma il misero oggetto
Del vostro abbandono,
Che avete diletto
Di far disperar.

SUSANNA
Confuso, pentito,
È troppo punito;
Abbiate pietà!

IL CONTE
Confuso, pentito
Son troppo punito
Abbiate pietà.

LA CONTESSA
Soffrir si gran torto
Quest'alma non sa!

IL CONTE
Ma il paggio rinchiuso?

LA CONTESSA
Fu sol per provarvi.

IL CONTE
Ma i tremiti, i palpiti?

LA CONTESSA
Fu sol per burlarvi.

IL CONTE
Ma un foglio sì barbaro?

LA CONTESSA, SUSANNA
Di Figaro è il foglio,
E a voi, per Basilio.

IL CONTE
Ah! perfidi! io voglio . . .

SUSANNA
Your jealous suspicion has done all this harm.

COUNTESS (*resentfully*)
My love, always faithful,
So true and unswerving,
Is surely deserving of better reward.

COUNT
Oh, help me, Susanna,
Her anger to calm.

SUSANNA
Your jealous suspicion has done all this harm.
(*beseechingly*)
My lady!

COUNT (*beseechingly*)
Rosina!

COUNTESS (*to the* COUNT)
You traitor!
Those days are forgotten!
I once was contented,
Adored by my lover,
But now I'm tormented
And scorned by my lord.

SUSANNA
Dejected, repentant,
He begs for your pardon.
Don't harbor resentment,
Be kind and forgive.

COUNT
Dejected, repentant,
I beg your forgiveness.
Ah, don't harbor resentment,
Have mercy, forgive.

COUNTESS
You traitor,
I'll never forgive you as long as I live.

COUNT
But what of the page, then?

COUNTESS
To test and provoke you.

COUNT
Your fright and embarrassment?

COUNTESS
Was just to mislead you.

COUNT
But what does the letter mean?

COUNTESS, SUSANNA
By Figaro written and sent through Basilio.

COUNT
What infamy, how dare they . . .

COUNTESS, SUSANNA
If you want forgiveness,
You, too, must forgive.

LA CONTESSA, SUSANNA
Perdono non merta
Chi agli altri nol da.

COUNT (*tenderly*)
If all have consented,
The quarrel is ended.
Rosina, I beg of you,
This time to forgive.

IL CONTE
Ebben, se vi piace,
Commune è la pace,
Rosina inflessibile
Con me non sarà.

COUNTESS
I feel it, Susanna, I weaken already.
Why is it that women can never be firm?

LA CONTESSA
Oh! quanto Susanna,
Son dolce di core!
Di donne al furore,
Chi più crederà!

SUSANNA
When men are in question,
However you treat them,
You never defeat them,
As hard as you scheme.

SUSANNA
Cogli uomin, signora,
Girate, volgete,
Vedrete, che ognora
Si cade poi là.

COUNT (*tenderly*)
You pardon me?

IL CONTE
Guardatemi!

COUNTESS
I cannot.

LA CONTESSA
Ingrato!

COUNT (*covering her hand with kisses*)
I treated you unjustly,
I am sorry.

IL CONTE
Ho torto; e mi pento.

SUSANNA, COUNTESS, COUNT
He means (I mean) it sincerely,
He hopes (I hope) from now on his (my) mistake to redeem.

SUSANNA, LA CONTESSA, IL CONTE
Da questo momento,
Quest'alma a conoscerla (mi, vi)
Apprender potrà.

FIGARO (*enters*)
Dear master, just listen,
The music is sounding,
The trumpets are blaring,
The fiddles are playing,
The echoes are ringing,
The people are singing,
(*taking* SUSANNA *by the arm and about to leave*)
The wedding procession is ready to start.

FIGARO
Signore, di fuori
Son già i suonatori;
Le trombe sentite,
I pifferi udite;
Tra canti, tra balli
De' vostri vassalli
Corriamo, voliamo
Le nozze a compir.

COUNT (*detaining him*)
There's time, so don't hurry.

IL CONTE
Pian piano, men fretta.

FIGARO
The crowd is impatient.

FIGARO
La turba m'aspetta.

COUNT
There's time, so don't hurry, just one explanation before we depart.

IL CONTE
Un dubbio toglietemi
In pria di partir.

COUNTESS, SUSANNA, FIGARO
A new complication with which to contend.
A bad situation, but how will it end?

LA CONTESSA, SUSANNA, FIGARO
La cosa è scabrosa,
Com' ha da finir?

COUNT
I know that this ruse will accomplish my end.
With this complication they cannot contend.
Kindly tell me, Mister Figaro,

IL CONTE
Con arte le carte
Convien quì scoprir.
Conoscete, signor Figaro,
Questo foglio chi vergò?

(*shows him the letter*)
Did you ever see this note?

FIGARO
Nol conosco. Nol conosco.

FIGARO (*pretending to examine it*)
Never saw it, never saw it.

IL CONTE, LA CONTESSA, SUSANNA
Nol conosco?

COUNT, COUNTESS, SUSANNA
Never saw it?

FIGARO
No.

FIGARO
No.

SUSANNA
E nol desti a Don Basilio?

SUSANNA
Didn't give it to Basilio?

LA CONTESSA
Per recarlo.

COUNTESS
To deliver . . .

IL CONTE
Tu c'intendi?

COUNT
What about it?

FIGARO
Oibò! Oibò!

FIGARO
Oh no, oh no!

SUSANNA
E non sai del damerino?

SUSANNA
You don't know about a lover . . .

LA CONTESSA
Che stasera nel giardino.

COUNTESS
Who this evening in the garden . . .

IL CONTE
Già caspisci?

COUNT
You remember?

FIGARO
Io non lo sò!

FIGARO
Why, not at all.

IL CONTE
Cerchi invan difesa e scusa,
Il tuo ceffo già t'accusa,
Vedo ben, che vuoi mentir.

COUNT
Stop evading and denying,
I can see that you are lying.
It is written on your face.

FIGARO
Mente il ceffo, io già non mento.

FIGARO
Well, my face may lie but I don't.

LA CONTESSA, SUSANNA
Il talento aguzzi invano
Palesato abbiam l'arcano,
Non v'è nulla da ridir.

COUNTESS, SUSANNA
What's the use of all the ruses?
We can see through your excuses,
And the truth you can't deny.

IL CONTE
Che rispondi?

COUNT
What's your answer?

FIGARO
Niente, niente.

FIGARO
Nothing, nothing.

IL CONTE
Dunque accordi?

COUNT
You admit it?

FIGARO
Non accordo.

FIGARO
No, I will not.

LA CONTESSA, SUSANNA
Eh! via chetati, balordo,
La burletta ha da finir.

COUNTESS, SUSANNA
There's no point in telling stories,
You have carried things too far.

FIGARO
Per finirla lietamente
E all'usanza teatrale,
Un'azion matrimoniale
Le faremo ora seguir.

FIGARO
In theatrical tradition,
Let us have a happy ending,
(*taking* SUSANNA *by the arm*)

With a wedding celebration
When the final curtain falls.

COUNTESS, SUSANNA, FIGARO
Won't you give us (them) your permission,
Say the word we (they) long to hear?
Let us (the) two at last be married,
Say the word we (they) long to hear.

COUNT (*aside*)
Marcellina, Marcellina,
You are late in getting here.

ANTONIO (*enters excitedly with a pot of geraniums*)
Ah, My Lord, My Lord!

COUNT (*anxiously*)
What has happened?

ANTONIO (*enraged*)
Who has dared, who has done this to me?

THE OTHERS
What's the matter with you,
What has happened?

ANTONIO
I won't have it!

THE OTHERS
What have you to say?

ANTONIO
I won't have it.

THE OTHERS
What have you to say?

ANTONIO
From the window that looks on the garden
Ev'ry day they throw down many objects.
But today, it is really the limit,
They have thrown a whole man to the ground.

COUNT (*with vivacity*)
From the window?

ANTONIO (*showing the pot*)
Just look at the geraniums.

COUNT
Into the garden?

ANTONIO
Yes.

COUNTESS, SUSANNA (*softly to* FIGARO)
Figaro, help us!

COUNT
Do you mean it?

COUNTESS, SUSANNA, FIGARO (*aside*)
Our plan will be ruined!
(*aloud*)
Is this drunkard quite out of his mind?

COUNT (*to* ANTONIO, *fiercely*)
And this man, what became of him later?

LA CONTESSA, SUSANNA, FIGARO
Deh! signor, nol contrastate,
Consolate i miei (lor) desir!

IL CONTE
(Marcellina, Marcellina,
Quanto tardi a comparir!)

ANTONIO
Ah! signor, signor!

IL CONTE
Cosa è stato?

ANTONIO
Che insolenza! ch'il fece? chi fu?

LA CONTESSA, SUSANNA, IL CONTE, FIGARO
Cosa dici? cos' hai? cosa è nato?

ANTONIO
Ascoltate.

GLI ALTRI
Via parla, di' su.

ANTONIO
Ascoltate.

GLI ALTRI
Via parla, di' su.

ANTONIO
Dal balcone che guarda in giardino,
Mille cose ogni dì gettar veggio,
E poc'anzi può darsi di peggio,
Vidi un uom, signor mio, gettar giù.

IL CONTE
Dal balcone?

ANTONIO
Vedete i garofani.

IL CONTE
In giardino?

ANTONIO
Sì!

LA CONTESSA, SUSANNA
Figaro all'erta.

IL CONTE
Cosa sento?

LA CONTESSA, SUSANNA, FIGARO
Costui ci sconcerta!
Quel briaco che viene a far quì?

IL CONTE
Dunque un uom . . . ma dov'è gito?

ANTONIO
Ratto, ratto il birbone è fugito,
E ad un tratto di vista m'uscì.

SUSANNA
Sai che il paggio?

FIGARO
So tutto, lo vidi.
Ah! ah! ah! ah!

IL CONTE
Taci là!

FIGARO
Ah! ah! ah! ah!

ANTONIO
Cosa ridi?

FIGARO
Ah! ah! ah! ah!

IL CONTE
Taci là, taci là, taci là!

FIGARO
Tu sei cotto dal sorger del dì.

IL CONTE
Or ripetimi; un uom dal balcone?

ANTONIO
Dal balcone.

IL CONTE
In giardino?

ANTONIO
In giardino.

LA CONTESSA, SUSANNA, FIGARO
Ma, signore, se in lui parla il vino!

IL CONTE
Segui pure: nè in volto il vedesti?

ANTONIO
No, nol vidi.

LA CONTESSA, SUSANNA
Olà, Figaro ascolta!

FIGARO
Via, piangone, sta zitto una volta,
Per tre soldi far tanto tumulto!
Giacchè il fatto non può stare occulto,
Sono io stesso saltato di lì.

IL CONTE, ANTONIO
Chi? voi stesso?

FIGARO
Che stupor!

LA CONTESSA, SUSANNA
Che testa! che ingegno!

ANTONIO
He went by like a shot from a cannon,
In a flash he had left me behind.

SUSANNA (*softly, to* FIGARO)
Cherubino . . .

FIGARO (*softly, to* SUSANNA)
I know it, I saw him.
(*aloud*)
Ha, ha, ha, ha!

COUNT
Quiet there!

FIGARO
Ha, ha, ha, ha!

ANTONIO
What's so funny?

FIGARO
Ha, ha, ha, ha!

COUNT
Hold your tongue, all of you, hold your tongue!

FIGARO
Are you tipsy from morning till night?

COUNT
Now repeat what you just said to me! He fell from the window?

ANTONIO
From the window.

COUNT
On the flowers?

ANTONIO
On the flowers.

COUNTESS, SUSANNA, FIGARO
But, Your Lordship, he's drunk, can't you see?

COUNT
Just continue! Tell your story!
You saw what he looked like?

ANTONIO
No, I did not.

COUNTESS, SUSANNA, (*softly, to* FIGARO)
Look out, Figaro, help us, Figaro, help us!

FIGARO (*to* ANTONIO)
Will you ever be finished complaining?
Such a fuss over nothing whatever.
(*pointing contemptuously to the geraniums*)
If the truth can no longer be hidden,
I myself was the man whom you saw.

COUNT, ANTONIO
You! And why?

FIGARO
What surprise!

COUNTESS, SUSANNA (*aside*)
How brilliant! How clever!

ANTONIO
You? And why?

COUNT
I cannot believe it!

ANTONIO
In that case you have grown very quickly.

COUNT
That sounds unlikely.

ANTONIO
After jumping you looked very small.

FIGARO
When one jumps one becomes very small.

ANTONIO
You don't say so!

COUNTESS, SUSANNA (*aside*)
Who believes all this nonsense?

COUNT (*to* ANTONIO)
Come, describe him.

ANTONIO
He looked like a youngster.

COUNT (*violently*)
Cherubin?

COUNTESS, SUSANNA (*aside*)
I can't bear it. I can't bear it.

FIGARO
Cherubino, Cherubino!
(*ironically*)
Who returned from Seville on horseback,
For it's there he was sent by the Count.

ANTONIO (*with stupid simplicity*)
No, no, no! He was not on horseback,
He jumped out the window on foot.

COUNT
Don't be foolish. Let's get to the point.

COUNTESS, SUSANNA (*aside*)
Heavens knows what will come out of this.

COUNT (*to* FIGARO, *fiercely*)
It was you?

FIGARO (*innocently*)
That is true.

FIGARO
But what for?

FIGARO
I was scared.

COUNT
You were scared?

FIGARO (*indicating the maid's room*)
I had come here and was waiting to see my Susanna,
When I heard angry voices from outside.
You were raging; I thought of my letter;

ANTONIO
Chi? voi stesso?

IL CONTE
Già creder nol posso!

ANTONIO
Come mai diventasti sì grosso!

IL CONTE
Già creder nol posso!

ANTONIO
Dopo il salto non fosti così.

FIGARO
A chi salta succede così.

ANTONIO
Chi'l direbbe?

LA CONTESSA, SUSANNA
Ed insiste quel pazzo!

IL CONTE
Tu che dici?

ANTONIO
A me parve il ragazzo.

IL CONTE
Cherubin?

LA CONTESSA, SUSANNA
Maledetto! Maledetto!

FIGARO
Esso appunto
Da Siviglia a cavallo quì giunto
Da Siviglia, ov'ei forse sarà!

ANTONIO
Questo no, questo no, che il cavallo
Io non vidi saltare di là.

IL CONTE
Che pazienza! Finiam questo ballo.

LA CONTESSA, SUSANNA
Come mai, giusto ciel, finirà!

IL CONTE
Dunque tu?

FIGARO
Saltai giù.

IL CONTE
Ma perchè?

FIGARO
Il timor.

IL CONTE
Che timor?

FIGARO
Là rinchiuso;
Aspettando quel caro visetto
Tippe, tappe, un susurro fuor d'uso

Voi gridaste, lo scritto biglietto,
Saltai giù dal terrore confuso,
E stravolto m'ho un nervo del pié.

ANTONIO
Vostre dunque saran queste carte,
Che perdeste?

IL CONTE
Olà, porgile a me!

FIGARO
Sono in trappola!

LA CONTESSA, SUSANNA
Figaro all'erta!

IL CONTE
Dite un pò questo foglio cos'è?

FIGARO
Tosto, tosto, n'ho tante, aspettate.

ANTONIO
Sarà forse il sommario dei debiti.

FIGARO
No, la lista degli osti.

IL CONTE
Parlate!
E tu lascialo.

LA CONTESSA, SUSANNA, FIGARO
Lascialo (mi), e parti.

ANTONIO
Parto si, ma se torno a trovarti.

FIGARO
Vanne, vanne, non temo di te.

LA CONTESSA, SUSANNA, FIGARO
Lascialo (mi), e parti.

IL CONTE
Dunque?

LA CONTESSA
O ciel! la patente del paggio.

SUSANNA
Giusti Dei! la patente!

IL CONTE
Corragio!

FIGARO
Oh che testa! quest'è la patente
Che poc'anzi il fanciullo mi diè.

Scared to death, I jumped down from the window
(pretends that his foot hurts him)
And I twisted my foot when I fell.

ANTONIO
Then these papers
(handing FIGARO *some folded papers)*
I found in the garden must be yours?

COUNT
Oho!
(takes them from him)
Give them to me.

FIGARO *(softly, to the* COUNTESS *and* SUSANNA*)*
Now I'm in for it.

COUNTESS, SUSANNA *(softly, to* FIGARO*)*
Figaro, help us, Figaro, help us!

COUNT *(opens the paper and immediately folds it again)*
Do you know what this paper may be?

FIGARO *(taking some papers out of his pocket)*
Yes, I know it, I know it,
Just a moment.

ANTONIO
Well, perhaps it's a list of his creditors.

FIGARO
No, I don't buy on credit.

COUNT *(to* FIGARO*)*
Speak up now.
(to ANTONIO*)*
And you, let him be.

COUNTESS, SUSANNA, FIGARO
Off with you, Antonio.

ANTONIO
I will go, but the next time I see you . . .
(exit)

FIGARO
Go away, I'm not frightened of you.

COUNTESS, SUSANNA, FIGARO
Off with you, good riddance.

COUNT *(reopens the paper and folds it again quickly; to* FIGARO*)*
Well now?

COUNTESS *(to* SUSANNA*)*
Good heavens, the page's commission!

SUSANNA *(to* FIGARO*)*
That is right, his commission!

COUNT *(ironically, to* FIGARO*)*
Speak freely.

FIGARO *(pretending to recollect)*
Oh how stupid, now I know it.
That is the commission
Which the boy had entrusted to me.

COUNT
For what reason?
FIGARO (*confused*)
It needed . . .
COUNT
It needed . . .
COUNTESS (*to* SUSANNA, *softly*)
Needed sealing.
SUSANNA (*to* FIGARO, *softly*)
Needed sealing.
COUNT
I'm waiting . . .
FIGARO (*pretending to ponder*)
It's the custom . . .
COUNT
Well, what is the custom?
FIGARO
It's the custom to seal a commission.
COUNT (*aside, notices that the seal is missing, tears up the paper, and angrily throws it away*)
Oh, that rascal is driving me crazy.
This affair is a myst'ry to me.
COUNTESS, SUSANNA (*aside*)
If I ever escape from this shipwreck,
Nevermore will I venture to sea.
FIGARO (*aside*)
Let him threaten as much as he pleases,
He will not get the better of me.
(*enter* MARCELLINA, BASILIO, *and* BARTOLO)
MARCELLINA, BASILIO, BARTOLO
Lord, our case demands a hearing.
That is why we came today.
COUNT (*aside*)
They have come here for retribution.
Things begin now to go my way.
COUNTESS, SUSANNA, FIGARO (*aside*)
They have come to give us trouble,
We must lead their plans astray.
FIGARO
Bent on asinine obstruction,
Those three fools are here today.
COUNT
Let's not make a rash deduction,
First each one must have his say.
MARCELLINA
This man gave his solemn promise
That in time we would be married;
I insist upon this bargain
Being promptly carried out.
COUNTESS, SUSANNA, FIGARO
Bargain? Bargain?

IL CONTE
Perchè fare?

FIGARO
Vi manca . . .

IL CONTE
Vi manca?

LA CONTESSA
Il suggello.

SUSANNA
Il suggello.

IL CONTE
Rispondi!

FIGARO
È l'usanza . . .

IL CONTE
Su via, ti confondi?

FIGARO
È l'usanza di porvi il suggello.

IL CONTE
Questo birbo mi toglie il cervello!
Tutto, tutto è un mistero per me!

LA CONTESSA, SUSANNA
Se mi salvo da questa tempesta,
Più non havvi naufragio per me!

FIGARO
Sbuffa invano, e la terra calpesta,
Poverino! ne sa men di me.

MARCELLINA, BASILIO, BARTOLO
Voi, signor, che giusto siete,
Ci dovete or ascoltar.

IL CONTE
(Son venuti a vendicarmi,
Io mi sento a consolar!)

LA CONTESSA, SUSANNA, FIGARO
(Son venuti a sconcertarmi,
Qual rimedio ritrovar!)

FIGARO
Son tre stolidi, tre pazzi,
Cosa mai vengono a far?

IL CONTE
Pian pianin, senza schiamazzi
Dica ognun quel che gli par.

MARCELLINA
Un impegno nuziale
Ha costui con me contratto,
E pretendo ch'il contratto
Deva meco effettuar.

LA CONTESSA, SUSANNA, FIGARO
Come? come?

IL CONTE
Olà! silenzio!
Io son quì per giudicar.

COUNT
No more, let nobody dare interrupt me,
It is I who judge this case.

BARTOLO
Io da lei scelto avvocato
Vengo a far le sue difese,
Le legittimi pretese
Io vi vengo a palesar.

BARTOLO
With this lady's wish compliant
I am here as her attorney,
And I warrant that my client
Has a strictly legal case.

LA CONTESSA, SUSANNA, FIGARO
È un birbante, è un birbante.

COUNTESS, SUSANNA, FIGARO
He's a scoundrel, he's a scoundrel!

IL CONTE
Olà! silenzio, silenzio, silenzio.
Io son quì per giudicar.

COUNT
Enough! Be silent! Let's hear Don Basilio.
It is I who judge this case.

BASILIO
Io com'uom al mondo cognito
Vengo quì per testimonio,
Del promesso matrimonio
Con prestanza di danar.

BASILIO
I, as man of prime celebrity,
Give my word and testimonial
That their plans were matrimonial,
With a bonus in advance.

LA CONTESSA, SUSANNA
Son tre matti, son tre matti!

COUNTESS, SUSANNA
Ev'ry one of them is crazy.

IL CONTE
Olà! silenzio, lo vedremo,
Il contratto leggeremo,
Tutto in ordin deve andar.

COUNT
Hold on! According to proper proceeding,
We must first give the contract a reading,
We must follow the legal course.

LA CONTESSA, SUSANNA, FIGARO
Son confusa(o) son stordita(o).

COUNTESS, SUSANNA, FIGARO
What a course events have taken!

MARCELLINA, BARTOLO, IL CONTE, BASILIO
Che bel colpo! che bel caso!

MARCELLINA, BARTOLO, COUNT, BASILIO
What a perfect case of trapping.

LA CONTESSA, SUSANNA, FIGARO
Disperata(o), sbalordita(o).

COUNTESS, SUSANNA, FIGARO
We are beaten, badly shaken.

MARCELLINA, BARTOLO, IL CONTE, BASILIO
È cresciuto a tutti il naso!

MARCELLINA, BARTOLO, COUNT, BASILIO
This time we have caught them napping.

LA CONTESSA, SUSANNA, FIGARO
Certo un diavol del inferno
Quì li ha fatti capitar!

COUNTESS, SUSANNA, FIGARO
Surely some infernal power
Must have brought them here today.

IL CONTE, MARCELLINA, BARTOLO, BASILIO
Qualche nume a noi propizio
Quì ci ha fatti capitar!

COUNT, MARCELLINA, BARTOLO, BASILIO
Some propitious, kindly power
Must have brought us here today,
On this day!

ACT III

(A richly decorated hall prepared for a wedding festivity, with two thrones.)

Recitative

COUNT *(walking up and down)*
What a hopeless confusion! An anonymous letter, the maid in waiting shut in her mistress's boudoir, her mistress embarrassed, one man who jumps out of the window to the garden, somebody else who claims that he has done it. I don't know what to think. It might have been even one of the domestics, they are the kind who would take such a chance. As for the Countess . . . any doubt would be insult; she has too much respect for herself and for my honor. My honor! What has human weakness done to my honor!

IL CONTE
Che imbarazzo è mai questo!
Un foglio anonimo,
La cameriera in gabinetto chiusa,
La padrona confusa—un uom che salta
Dal balcone in giardino,
Un altro appresso,
Che dice esser quel desso,
Non sò cosa pensar!
Potrebbe forse qualcun de' miei vassalli . . . a simil razza è commune l'ardir, ma la Contessa—ah, che un dubbio l'offende! Ella rispetta troppo se stessa, e l'honor mio, l'onore . . . dove, diamin, l'ha posto umano errore!

COUNTESS *(entering with* SUSANNA *and keeping in the background, unseen by the* COUNT*)*
Come, don't be downcast. Tell him he may meet you in the garden.

LA CONTESSA
Via! fatti core, digli che ti attenda in giardino.

COUNT
I'll make sure that Cherubino arrived at Seville. I've sent Basilio expressly for that purpose.

IL CONTE
Saprò se Cherubino era giunto a Siviglia, a tale oggetto ho mandato Basilio.

SUSANNA
Good heavens, and Figaro?

SUSANNA
O cielo! e Figaro?

COUNTESS
He must not know about it. Instead of you, I'll await him myself.

LA CONTESSA
A lui non dei dir nulla, invece tua, voglio andarci io medesma.

COUNT
Before this evening he ought to be back.

IL CONTE
Avanti sera dovrebbe ritornar.

SUSANNA
My Lady, I'm frightened!

SUSANNA
O Dio! non oso!

COUNTESS
Remember that my fate is in your hands now.
(she retires)

LA CONTESSA
Pensa ch'è in tua mano il mio riposo.

COUNT
And Susanna? Who knows, maybe she has already betrayed my secret. If she has done so, Figaro must marry Marcellina.

IL CONTE
E Susanna? Chi sà, ch'ella tradito abbia il segreto mio, oh, se ha parlato, gli fo sposar la vecchia.

SUSANNA *(aside)*
Marcellina!
(aloud)
My Lord!

SUSANNA
(Marcellina!)
Signor?

COUNT *(gravely)*
What do you wish?

IL CONTE
Cosa bramate?

SUSANNA
You seem in bad humor.

SUSANNA
Mi par che siate in collera.

IL CONTE
Volete qualche cosa?

SUSANNA
Signor, la vostra sposa
Ha i soliti vapori,
E vi chiede il vasetto degli odori.

IL CONTE
Prendete.

SUSANNA
Or vel riporto.

IL CONTE
Ah no, potete
Riternerlo per voi.

SUSANNA
Per me? Questi non son mali
Da donne triviali.

IL CONTE
Un'amante che perde il caro sposo,
Sul punto d'otternerlo.

SUSANNA
Pagando Marcellina colla dote
Che voi mi prometteste.

IL CONTE
Ch'io vi promisi! Quando?

SUSANNA
Credea d'averlo inteso.

IL CONTE
Sì, se voluto aveste
Intendermi voi stessa.

SUSANNA
È mio dovere,
E quel di sua Eccellenza è il mio volere.

IL CONTE
Crudel! perchè finora
Farmi languir così?
Perchè, crudel!
Farmi languir così?

SUSANNA
Signor, la donna ognora
Tempo ha di dir di sì.

IL CONTE
Dunque, in giardin varrai?

SUSANNA
Se piace a voi, verrò.

IL CONTE
E non mi mancherai?

SUSANNA
No, non vi mancherò.

IL CONTE
Verrai?

SUSANNA
Sì.

COUNT
What is it that you want?

SUSANNA
My Lord, just now the Countess is suff'ring from a headache and sent me to get your flask of smelling salts.

COUNT
Take it.

SUSANNA
I'll soon return it.

COUNT
No, no, don't bother, you may need it yourself.

SUSANNA
Myself? People of my kind do not suffer from headaches.

COUNT
But a bride about to lose her bridegroom on the day of her wedding?

SUSANNA
I'll pay off Marcellina with the dowry that you promised to give me.

COUNT
I made that promise? Did I?

SUSANNA
That's how I understood you.

COUNT
Yes, yes, if you had only wished to understand me.

SUSANNA
It is my duty, and what Your Lordship wishes is my desire.

DUET

COUNT
But why, why make me suffer,
Longing for your reply?
But why, but why?
Will you not tell me why?

SUSANNA
In time we women grant you
What we at first deny.

COUNT
Then we shall meet this evening?

SUSANNA
If so you wish, My Lord.

COUNT
You will not fail to be there?

SUSANNA
No, no, you have my word.

COUNT
You promise?

SUSANNA
Yes.

COUNT
Won't disappoint me?

SUSANNA
No.

COUNT
This very evening?

SUSANNA
You have my word,
I will not fail my word.

COUNT
The sweet promise you gave me
Raises my hope so high.

SUSANNA (*aside*)
All those who know what love is,
Forgive me for this lie.

COUNT
You'll meet me in the garden?

SUSANNA
If that's your wish, I might.

COUNT
You will not disappoint me?

SUSANNA
I shall be there tonight.

COUNT
You promise?

SUSANNA
Yes.

COUNT
Won't disappoint me?

SUSANNA
No.

COUNT
I have your promise?

SUSANNA
No.

COUNT
No?

SUSANNA
Yes, I shall be there tonight.

COUNT
Won't disappoint me?

SUSANNA
No.

COUNT
And you will be there?

SUSANNA
Yes.

COUNT
Won't disappoint me?

SUSANNA
Yes.

IL CONTE
Non mancherai?

SUSANNA
No.

IL CONTE
Non mancherai?

SUSANNA
Non mancherò.
No, non vi mancherò.

IL CONTE
Mi sento dal contento
Pieno di gioia il cor.

SUSANNA
Scusatemi se mento
Voi che intendete amor!

IL CONTE
Dunque in giardin verrai?

SUSANNA
Se piace a voi, verrò.

IL CONTE
E non mi mancherai?

SUSANNA
No, non vi mancherò.

IL CONTE
Verrai?

SUSANNA
Sì!

IL CONTE
Non mancherai?

SUSANNA
No!

IL CONTE
Dunque verrai?

SUSANNA
No.

IL CONTE
No?

SUSANNA
Sì, se piace a voi verrò.

IL CONTE
Non mancherai?

SUSANNA
No.

IL CONTE
Dunque verrai?

SUSANNA
Sì.

IL CONTE
Non mancherai?

SUSANNA
Sì!

IL CONTE
Sì?

SUSANNA
No, no, non vi mancherò.

IL CONTE
Mi sento dal contento . . .
Pieno di gioia il cor.

IL CONTE
E perchè fosti meco stamattina sì austera?

SUSANNA
Col paggio ch'ivi c'era.

IL CONTE
Ed a Basilio, che per me ti parlò?

SUSANNA
Ma qual bisogno abbiam noi che un Basilio . . .

IL CONTE
È vero, è vero, e mi prometti poi . . . se tu manchi, o cor mio . . .
Ma la Contessa attenderà il vasetto.

SUSANNA
Eh, fu un pretesto,
Parlato io non avrei senza di questo.

IL CONTE
Carissima!

SUSANNA
Vien gente.

IL CONTE
(È mia senz'altro!)

SUSANNA
Forbitevi la bocca signor scaltro.

FIGARO
Ehi, Susanna, ove vai?

SUSANNA
Taci; senz'avvocato
Hai già vinta la causa.

FIGARO
Cos'è nato?

IL CONTE
Hai già vinta la causa! Cosa sento?
In qual laccio cadea! Perfidi! Io voglio, io voglio
In tal modo punirvi, a piacer mio
La sentenza sarà. Ma s'ei pagasse
La vecchia pretendente?
Pagarla? in qual maniera? E poi v'è Antonio,

COUNT
Yes?

SUSANNA
No, I shall be there tonight.

COUNT
The sweet promise you gave me,
Raises my hope so high.

RECITATIVE

COUNT
But why in the world were you so cross to me this morning?

SUSANNA
I knew the page was listening.

COUNT
And to Basilio, who was speaking for me?

SUSANNA
I do not see why we need a Basilio . . .

COUNT
Of course, dear, how clever! And I may have your word you will not disappoint me? But the Countess, she is waiting for her smelling salts.

SUSANNA
She really isn't. I had to make some pretext to address you.

COUNT (*taking her hand*)
Adorable!

SUSANNA (*drawing it away*)
They're coming!

COUNT (*aside*)
She has surrendered.

SUSANNA (*aside*)
Don't count your chickens before they're hatched.

FIGARO (*enters; aside to* SUSANNA)
Say, Susanna, what's up?

SUSANNA (*aside, to* FIGARO)
Plenty! Without a lawyer we have won the decision. (*exit*)

FIGARO (*follows her*)
What has happened?

RECITATIVE AND ARIA

COUNT
You have won the decision?
What the devil!
Are they trying to fool me?
Hypocrites!
I'll cure them.
I'll see that both the traitors are punished.
I'll base the verdict on my pleasure alone.
If he succeeded in paying Marcellina!

How can he? He has no money!
Besides, Antonio won't permit his beloved niece, Susanna,
To marry such a nobody as Figaro.
I will flatter the ego
Of that conceited drunkard.
It will further my purpose.
It can't go better!
Shall I look on desiring,
And see my servant happy?
Shall I see him acquiring
Favors for which I yearn?
Shall I, in helpless fashion,
Allow a hateful marriage,
While I restrain a passion
Which she does not return?
Shall I not lift a finger
To conquer her affection,
Look on without objection,
Aloof and unconcerned?
Ah, no! I won't!
Ah, no, I will not give you
So great a satisfaction.
You shall not dare to spite me,
Oppose me and torment me.
You'll have no chance to laugh at me,
While I am cast aside.
Only the thought of vengeance
Offers me consolation.
Triumphant vindication
Shall satisfy my pride,
My deeply wounded pride.
Ah, I will never give you
So great a satisfaction
You shall not dare to spite me,
Oppose me and torment me,
You'll have no chance to laugh at me,
While I am cast aside.
Only the thought of vengeance
Offers me consolation.
Triumphant vindication
Shall satisfy my pride,
My deeply wounded pride,
And fill my heart with joy.
(*prepares to leave, but meets* DON CURZIO *who enters with* MARCELLINA, FIGARO, *and* BARTOLO)

Che all'incognito Figaro ricusa
Di dare una nipote in matrimonio.
Coltivando l'orgoglio
Di questo mentecatto,
Tutto giova a un raggiro:
Il colpo è fatto.
Vedrò, mentr'io sospiro,
Felice un servo mio?
E un ben che invan desio,
Ei posseder dovrà!
Vedrò per man d'amore
Unita a un vile oggetto
Chi in me destò un affetto,
Che per me poi non ha!
Che per me poi non ha!
Vedrò, mentr'io sospiro,
Felice un servo mio?
Vedrò che un ben ch'io desio,
Ei posseder dovrà?
Vedrò, per man d'amore,
Unita a un vile oggetto,
Chi in me destò un affetto,
Che per me poi non ha,
Che per me poi non ha,
Vedrò? Vedrò? Vedrò? Vedrò?
Ah no! lasciarti in pace
Non vo' questo contento:
Tu non nascesti, audace,
Tu non nascesti, audace,
Per dare a me tormento,
E forse ancor per ridere, per ridere
Di mia infelicità!
Già la speranza sola
Delle vendette mie
Quest'anima consola,
E giubilar mi fa!
E giubilar, e giubilar mi fa.
Ah, che lasciarti in pace.
Non vo'questo contento,
Tu non nascesti, audace,
Per dare a me tormento,
E forse ancor per ridere, per ridere
Di mia infelicità.
Già la speranza sola
Del vendette mie,
Quest'anima consola,
E giubilar mi fa.

Recitative

CURZIO (*stammering*)
The ca-case has b-been d-decided. He must marry her or pay her, th-that is the v-verdict.

MARCELLINA
What a wedding!

DON CURZIO
È decisa la lite;
O pagarla, o sposarla.
Ora ammutite.

MARCELLINA
Io respiro.

FIGARO
Ed io moro.

FIGARO
What a funeral!

MARCELLINA
(Alfin sposa io sarò d'un uom
che adoro.)

MARCELLINA (*aside*)
At last I'll be the wife of the man I worship!

FIGARO
Eccellenza! m'appello . . .

FIGARO
I appeal this, Your Lordship.

IL CONTE
È giusta la sentenza;
O pagar, o sposar, bravo Don
Curzio!

COUNT
The sentence is a just one, either marry or pay. Good work, Don Curzio.

DON CURZIO
Bontà di sua Eccellenza.

CURZIO
You-f-f-flatter me, Your L-lordship.

BARTOLO
Che superba sentenza!

BARTOLO
What a glorious sentence!

FIGARO
In che superba?

FIGARO
In what way glorious?

BARTOLO
Siam tutti vendicati.

BARTOLO
Full justice has been rendered.

FIGARO
Io non la sposerò.

FIGARO
But I will not give in.

BARTOLO
La sposerai.

BARTOLO
Oh yes, you will!

DON CURZIO
O pagarla, o sposarla, lei t'ha
prestati due mille pezzi duri.

CURZIO
Either m-marry or p-pay her; did she not l-lend you two thousand silver pieces?

FIGARO
Son gentiluomo, e senza
L' assenso de' miei nobili
parenti . . .

FIGARO
I am a nobleman and cannot be married without my parents' consent.

IL CONTE
Dove sono? chi sono?

COUNT
And these parents, where are they?

FIGARO
Lasciate ancor cercarli;
Dopo dieci anni io spero di
trovarli.

FIGARO
I still am on the lookout. In about ten years I am sure I will have found them.

BARTOLO
Qualche bambin trovato?

BARTOLO
So you are a foundling?

FIGARO
No, perduto, dottor, anzi
rubato.

FIGARO
No, a lostling. It seems that I was kidnaped.

IL CONTE
Come?

COUNT
Kidnaped?

MARCELLINA
Cosa?

MARCELLINA
Kidnaped?

BARTOLO
La prova?

BARTOLO
Then prove it!

DON CURZIO
Il testimonio?

CURZIO
Where is your evidence?

FIGARO
L'oro, le gemme, e i ricamati
panni,
Che ne' più teneri anni
Mi ritrovaro addosso i
masnadieri,
Sono gl' indizi veri

FIGARO
That I can offer! The gold and precious jewels that my abductors found near me, the fine embroidered linen I was wearing are the confirmation of my noble extraction. Still more conclusive, there is a symbol branded on my arm.

Di mia nascità illustre: e sopra tutto,
Questo al mio braccio impresso geroglifico.

MARCELLINA
A spatula printed on your right arm?

FIGARO
How did you know that?

MARCELLINA
Great heavens, it's he, then!

FIGARO
Of course, it's I, then.

CURZIO
Who?

COUNT
Who?

BARTOLO
Who?

MARCELLINA
Rafaello!

BARTOLO
You say that robbers stole you?

FIGARO
From near a castle.

BARTOLO
Here is your mother.

FIGARO
My wet nurse?

BARTOLO
No, your mother.

COUNT, CURZIO
His mother?

FIGARO
You don't mean it?

MARCELLINA
And here's your father!

SEXTET

MARCELLINA
(*embracing* FIGARO)
Now at last I may embrace you,
For I am your loving mother.

FIGARO (*to* BARTOLO)
Father dear, why not do likewise?
Do not make me blush with shame!

BARTOLO (*embracing* FIGARO)
It's my duty to inform you
Of the justice of your claim.

CURZIO
He the father, and she his mother!
Then this match is null and void.

MARCELLINA
Una spatola impressa al braccio destro.

FIGARO
E a voi ch'il disse?

MARCELLINA
O Dio! È desso.

FIGARO
È ver, son io.

DON CURZIO
Chi?

IL CONTE
Chi?

BARTOLO
Chi?

MARCELLINA
Rafaello!

BARTOLO
E i ladri ti rapir?

FIGARO
Presso un castello.

BARTOLO
Ecco tua madre.

FIGARO
Balia?

BARTOLO
No, tua madre.

IL CONTE, DON CURZIO
Sua madre!

FIGARO
Cosa sento?

MARCELLINA
Ecco tuo padre.

MARCELLINA
Riconosci in questo amplesso
Una madre, amato figlio.

FIGARO
Padre mio, fate lo stesso,
Non mi fate più arrossir.

BARTOLO
Resistenza la coscienza
Far non lascia al tuo desir.

DON CURZIO
Ei suo padre? ella sua madre?
L'imeneo non può seguir.

IL CONTE
Son smarrito, son stordito!
Meglio è assai di quà partir!

COUNT
Worse misfortune could not happen!
All my hopes have been destroyed.
(*about to go*)

MARCELLINA
Figlio amato!

MARCELLINA
I'm your mother!

BARTOLO
Figlio amato!

BARTOLO
I'm your father!

FIGARO
Parenti amati!

FIGARO
Beloved parents!

MARCELLINA
Figlio amato!

MARCELLINA
He's your father!

BARTOLO
Figlio amato!

BARTOLO
She's your mother!

FIGARO
Parenti amati!

FIGARO
Beloved parents!
(*enter* SUSANNA *with a purse in her hand*)

SUSANNA
Alto alto, signor Conte,
Mille doppie son quì pronte,
A pagar vengo per Figaro,
Ed a porlo in libertà.

SUSANNA (*detaining the* COUNT)
Wait a minute, not so hasty!
I have brought along the money.
It's the ransom for my Figaro,
So that I can buy him free.

IL CONTE, DON CURZIO
Non sappiam com' è la cosa,
Osservate un poco là.

COUNT, CURZIO
There has been a great sensation.
Take a look and you will see.

MARCELLINA, BARTOLO
Figlio amato!

MARCELLINA, BARTOLO
Come, embrace me!

FIGARO
Parenti amati!

FIGARO
I love you dearly!

SUSANNA
Già d'accordo colla sposa!
Giusti Dei! che infedeltà!
Lascia, iniquo!

SUSANNA (*turns and sees* FIGARO *embracing* MARCELLINA)
So he marries Marcellina!
Lord in heav'n,
To be so false, so false to me!
Don't come near me!
(*about to go*)

FIGARO
No, t'arresta.
No, t'arresta.
Senti, o cara, senti, senti.

FIGARO (*detaining* SUSANNA)
Wait a moment!
You're mistaken!
Listen, my darling, listen, listen!

SUSANNA
Senti questa.

SUSANNA (*tears herself away and boxes* FIGARO*'s ears*)
I am list'ning!

MARCELLINA, BARTOLO
È un effetto di buon core,
Tutto amore è quel che fa,
Tutto amore è quel che fa.

MARCELLINA, BARTOLO
This peculiar fit of fury
Shows you truly how she loves you.
Women often act that way.

SUSANNA
Fremo! smanio dal furore
Una vecchia me la fa!
Fremo! smanio dal furore,
Fremo, smanio dal furore,
Una vecchia smania me la fa.

SUSANNA
I'm beside myself with fury,
Being tricked in such a way;
Tricked and cheated by a spinster
In a most dishonest fashion,
In a most distasteful way.

COUNT
I'm beside myself with fury,
Things have not turned out my way.

CURZIO
Anger and quarrels, jealous rages, fits of fury
Are the order of the day.

MARCELLINA (*runs to embrace* SUSANNA)
No longer be angry, my dear little daughter,
From this moment onward
I'm mother to you.
For I am his mother
And mother to you.

SUSANNA (*to* BARTOLO)
His mother?

BARTOLO
His mother!

SUSANNA (*to the* COUNT)
His mother?

COUNT
His mother!

SUSANNA (*to* DON CURZIO)
His mother?

CURZIO
His mother!

SUSANNA (*to* MARCELLINA)
His mother?

MARCELLINA
His mother!

ALL
His mother!

SUSANNA (*to* FIGARO)
Your mother?

FIGARO
And this is my father,
He says so himself.

SUSANNA (*to* BARTOLO)
His father?

BARTOLO
His father!

SUSANNA (*to the* COUNT)
His father?

COUNT
His father!

SUSANNA (*to* DON CURZIO)
His father?

CURZIO
His father!

SUSANNA (*to* MARCELLINA)
His father?

MARCELLINA
His father!

IL CONTE
Fremo! smanio dal furore
Il destino me la fa!

DON CURZIO
Freme e smania dal furore,
Il destino glie la fa!

MARCELLINA
Lo sdegno calmate
Mia cara figliuola.
Sua madre abbracciate,
Che or vostra sarà.
Sua madre abbraciate,
Che or vostra sarà.

SUSANNA
Sua madre?

BARTOLO
Sua madre.

SUSANNA
Sua madre?

IL CONTE
Sua madre.

SUSANNA
Sua madre?

DON CURZIO
Sua madre.

SUSANNA
Sua madre?

MARCELLINA
Sua madre.

TUTTI
Sua madre!

SUSANNA
Tua madre?

FIGARO
E quello è mio padre,
Che a te lo dirà.

SUSANNA
Suo padre?

BARTOLO
Suo padre!

SUSANNA
Suo padre?

IL CONTE
Suo padre!

SUSANNA
Suo padre?

DON CURZIO
Suo padre!

SUSANNA
Suo padre?

MARCELLINA
Suo padre!

TUTTI
Suo padre!

SUSANNA
Tuo padre?

FIGARO
E quella è mia madre,
Che a te lo dirà.

SUSANNA, MARCELLINA, FIGARO, BARTOLO
Al dolce contento di questo momento
Quest'anima appena resister or sà.

IL CONTE, DON CURZIO
Al fiero tormento—di questo momento
Quest'anima appena resister or sà.
Al fiero tormento
Di questo momento
Quest'anima appena resister or sà.
Al fiero tormento di questo momento
Quest'anima appena resister or sà.

MARCELLINA
Eccovi, o caro amico, il dolce frutto dell'antico amor nostro.

BARTOLO
Or non parliamo di fatti sì rimoti, egli è mio figlio, mia consorte voi siete, e le nozze farem quando volete.

MARCELLINA
Oggi, e doppie saranno.
Prendi, questo è il biglietto
Del denar che a me devi, ed è tua dote.

SUSANNA
Prendi ancor questa borsa.

BARTOLO
E questa ancora.

FIGARO
Bravi! gettate pur, ch'io piglio ognora.

SUSANNA
Voliamo ad informar d' ogni avventura Madama e nostro zio.
Chi al par di me contenta?

FIGARO
Io.

BARTOLO
Io.

ALL
His father!

SUSANNA (*to* FIGARO)
Your father?

FIGARO (*to* SUSANNA)
And this is my mother.
She'll tell you I'm right.
(*all four rush to embrace each other.*)

SUSANNA, MARCELLINA, FIGARO, BARTOLO
In one blessed moment
Our fears have been thwarted.
A happier future at last is in sight.

COUNT, CURZIO
In one cursed moment
My (his) plans have been thwarted.
It fills me (him) with envy
And bitter resentment
To see them all so happy with sudden delight.
In one cursed moment
My (his) plans have been thwarted.
Not even the hope of revenge is in sight.
(*exit the* COUNT *and* DON CURZIO)

RECITATIVE

MARCELLINA
There he is, dearest Doctor, the blooming flower of our onetime romance.

BARTOLO
Let's not warm up such overaged proceedings. He is my offspring, you indeed are his mother, so our marriage shall be whenever you want it.

MARCELLINA
Today! It shall be a double wedding. Take this,
(*gives the note to* FIGARO)
it is the note for the money you owe me. Take it as dowry.

SUSANNA (*throws a purse to the ground*)
Take this purse in addition.

BARTOLO (*does the same*)
And also this one.

FIGARO
Thank you! Just keep right on, I'm getting wealthy.

SUSANNA
Now let us go and tell all that has happened to the Countess and Uncle Antonio. Who is as glad as I am? Who is as glad as I am?

FIGARO
I am!

BARTOLO
I am!

MARCELLINA
I am!

ALL
The Count is wild with fury, but we don't care a bit!
(*all, exit, embracing*)

RECITATIVE

(*enter* BARBARINA *and* CHERUBINO)

BARBARINA
Come on, come on, dear page, you will have fun if you come along to my house. You will see all the pretty girls of the castle, but none of them is as beautiful as you are.

CHERUBINO
But, if the Count should find me, heaven forbid! You know, he believes I have left for Seville.

BARBARINA
Since when does that disturb you? And if he found you, it would not be the first time. Listen, you must let us dress you like a girl. Then we all will present a nice bouquet of flowers to the Countess. Just leave it all to me, your Barbarina.
(*exit*)

RECITATIVE AND ARIA

(*the* COUNTESS *enters*)

COUNTESS
And Susanna is late . . . .
I am anxious to find out
How His Lordship accepted the proposal.
I must admit that our project is bold.
And with a husband so impulsive and so jealous!
But what's the harm?
I only want to meet him in a dress of Susanna's while she wears mine,
By the favor of darkness.
Ah, heaven! To what shameful state of existence
Have I descended through the fault of my husband,
Who, after treating me with scorn unexampled
And with disdain,
With jealous rages betrayed me,
First beloved, then offended,
At last deserted,
Forced me to plead now for my maid's assistance!
Are they over, those cherished moments,
Hours together so sweetly shared?
Are they broken, those fervent pledges
His deceitful lips declared?
If a bitter fate inclined me
Such unhappiness to know,
Why do memories remind me
Of those joys of long ago?

MARCELLINA
Io.

SUSANNA, MARCELLINA, FIGARO, BARTOLO
E schiatti il signor Conte al gusto mio!

BARBARINA
Andiam, andiam, bel paggio; in casa mia tutte ritroverai
Le più belle ragazze del castello.
Di tutte sarai tu certo il più bello.

CHERUBINO
Ah! se il Conte mi trova,
Misero me! Tu sai
Che partito ei mi crede per Siviglia.

BARBARINA
O ve' che maraviglia
E se ti trova, non sarà cosa nuova.
Odi: vogliamo vestirti come noi;
Tutte insiem andrem poi
A presentar de' fiori a Madamina;
Fidati, Cherubin, di Barbarina.

LA CONTESSA
E Susanna non vien! Sono ansiosa
Di saper come il Conte
Accolse la proposta; alquanto ardito
Il progetto mi par, ad uno sposo
Sì vivace e geloso!
Ma che mal c'è? Cangiando i miei vestiti
Con quelli di Susanna, e i suoi co' miei
Al favor della notte . . . O cielo! a qual
Umil stato fatale io son ridotta
Da un consorte crudel, che dopo avermi
Con un misto inaudito
D'infedeltà, di gelosia, di sdegno
Prima amata, indi offesa, e alfin tradita,
Fammi or cercar da una mia serva aita!
Dove sono i bei momenti
Di dolcezza e di piacer?
Dove andaro i giuramenti
Di quel labbro menzogner?
Perchè mai, se in pianti e in pene
Per me tutto si cangiò
La memoria di quel bene
Dal mio sen non trapassò!

Dove sono i bei momenti
Di dolcezza e di piacer?
Dove andaro i giuramenti
Di quel labbro menzogner?
Ah! se almen la mia costanza
Nel languire amando ognor.
Mi portasse una speranza
Di cangiar l'ingrato cor!

Are they over, those cherished moments,
Hours together so sweetly shared?
Are they broken, those fervent pledges
His deceitful lips declared?
If at last my heart's devotion
Could achieve but one reward,
And revive the dead emotion
Of my false and heartless lord!
(*exit*)

RECITATIVE

(*enter the* COUNT *and* ANTONIO *with a hat in his hand*)

ANTONIO
Io vi dico, signor, che
Cherubino
È ancora nel castello,
E vedete per prova il suo cappello.

ANTONIO
There's no doubt, My Lord, that Cherubino is still here in the castle, and I brought his hat with me to prove it.

IL CONTE
Ma come se a quest'ora
Esser giunto a Siviglia egli dovria?

COUNT
But how can that be? By this time he is due at Seville.

ANTONIO
Scusate, oggi Siviglia è a casa mia.
Là vestissi da donna, e là lasciati
Ha gli altri abiti suoi.

ANTONIO
Today, sir, if you'll excuse me, Seville is my house. There they dressed him in girls' clothes and there he also has left his new uniform.

IL CONTE
Perfidi!

COUNT
Reprobates!

ANTONIO
Andiam, e li vedrete voi.

ANTONIO
Please come, and I'll be glad to show you.
(*exit*)
(*enter the* COUNTESS *and* SUSANNA)

LA CONTESSA
Cosa mi narri? E che ne disse il Conte?

COUNTESS
Isn't that marvelous? What was the Count's reaction?

SUSANNA
Gli si leggeva in fronte
Il dispetto e la rabbia.

SUSANNA
Oh, he was so furious that he hardly could bear it.

LA CONTESSA
Piano che meglio or lo porremo in gabbia!
Dov'è l'appuntamento
Che tu gli proponesti?

COUNTESS
Was he! So much the better for our intentions. And where is the appointment which you proposed to give him?

SUSANNA
In giardino.

SUSANNA
In the garden.

LA CONTESSA
Fissiamigli un loco.
Scrivi.

COUNTESS
Be more specific. Write to him.

SUSANNA
Ch'io scriva? ma signora. . . .

SUSANNA
But is that not too daring?

LA CONTESSA
Eh, scrivi dico, e tutto
Io prendo su me stessa.
Canzonetta sull'aria.

COUNTESS
Do as I tell you.
(SUSANNA *sits down and writes*)
Let all the blame fall on my shoulders.
(*dictating*)
Write a message "To Romeo."

Duet

SUSANNA (*writing*)
"To Romeo."

COUNTESS (*dictating*)
"When the breeze is gently blowing,

SUSANNA
gently blowing . . .

COUNTESS
And the evening shadows fall,

SUSANNA
and the evening shadows fall . . .

COUNTESS
In the grove where pines are growing,

SUSANNA (*inquiringly*)
pines are growing? . . .

COUNTESS
In the grove where pines are growing."

SUSANNA (*writing*)
In the grove where pines are growing."

COUNTESS
And the rest he will recall.

SUSANNA
Yes, the rest he will recall.

COUNTESS
Let us read it together.
(*they read the letter together*)

COUNTESS, SUSANNA
"When the breeze is gently blowing,
"And the evening shadows fall,
"In the grove where pines are growing,
"And the rest he will recall."

SUSANNA (*folds the letter*)
The note is ready, and how shall we seal it?

COUNTESS (*draws a pin and gives it to her*)
This way. Let's take a pin. We will use that to seal it. And further, write on the back of the letter: "Return the pin, please."

SUSANNA
That's an idea. It makes it sound mysterious.

COUNTESS
Hurry and hide it! I hear somebody coming.
(SUSANNA *puts the note in her bosom*)

Chorus

(*enter* CHERUBINO, *dressed as a country girl; and* BARBARINA, *with several other country girls, dressed in the same way, carrying nosegays*)

GIRLS
Mistress dear, accept these flowers,
Daisies, roses bright with dew,
Freshly cut in morning hours

SUSANNA
Sull'aria.

LA CONTESSA
Che soave zefiretto,

SUSANNA
Zefiretto . . .

LA CONTESSA
Questa sera spirerà,

SUSANNA
Questa sera spirerà . . .

LA CONTESSA
Sotto i pini del boschetto.

SUSANNA
Sotto i pini?

LA CONTESSA
Sotto i pini del boschetto.

SUSANNA
Sotto i pini del boschetto.

LA CONTESSA
Ei già il resto capirà.

SUSANNA
Certo, certo il capirà.

LA CONTESSA
Canzonetta sull'aria.

LA CONTESSA, SUSANNA
Che soave zefiretto
Questa sera spirerà.
Sotto i pini del boschetto.
Ei già il resto capirà.

SUSANNA
Piegato è il foglio; or come si sigilla?

LA CONTESSA
Ecco, prendi una spilla,
Servirà di sigillo. Attendi, scrivi,
Sul riverso del foglio:
Rimandate il sigillo.

SUSANNA
È più bizzarro
Di quel della patente.

LA CONTESSA
Presto, nascondi, io sento venir gente.

CORO
Ricevete, o padroncina,
Queste rose, e questi fior,
Che abbiam colti stamattina
Per mostrarvi il nostro amor.

Siamo tante contadine,
E siam tutte poverine,
Ma quel poco che rechiamo
Ve lo diamo di buon cuor.

Just to show our love for you.
Though we're poor and simple peasants,
Please accept these humble presents
As a token of affection
From our hearts so loyal and true.

RECITATIVE

BARBARINA
Queste sono. Madama,
Le ragazze del loco,
Che il poco ch'han vi vengono ad offrire,
E vi chiedon perdon del loro ardire.

BARBARINA
There they are, My Lady, all the girls of the village who bring to you the best they have to offer, and they hope you'll forgive them their presumption.

LA CONTESSA
O bravel vi ringrazio,

COUNTESS
How lovely! I am grateful.

SUSANNA
Come sono vezzose.

SUSANNA
They're so pretty and charming.

LA CONTESSA
E chi è, narratemi, quell'amabil fanciulla ch'ha l'aria si modesta?

COUNTESS
And who is, I ask you, that delightful young girl there? She looks so shy and modest.

BARBARINA
Ell'è una mia cugina e per le nozze è venuta ier sera.

BARBARINA
That one? She is my cousin. She came last night to be here for the wedding.

LA CONTESSA
Onoriamo la bella forestiera, venite quì, datemi i vostri fiori.
Come arrossì! Susanna, non ti pare
Che somigli ad alcuno?

COUNTESS
Let us honor our guest on her arrival. Come here to me. (*takes* CHERUBINO'S *flowers and kisses him on the forehead*)
May I accept your flowers? Look at her blush! Susanna, do you not notice a resemblance to someone?

SUSANNA
Al naturale!

SUSANNA
Yes, it is striking.
(ANTONIO *enters stealthily, pulls off* CHERUBINO'S *bonnet, and puts his officer's cap on him*)

ANTONIO
Eh! cospettaccio, è questi l'uffiziale.

ANTONIO
What do you know! If that's not Cherubino!

LA CONTESSA
Oh stelle!

COUNTESS
Good heavens!

SUSANNA
(Malandrinio!)

SUSANNA (*aside*)
What a devil!

IL CONTE
Ebben, madama?

COUNT
What now, My Lady!

LA CONTESSA
Io sono, o signor mio, irritata e sorpresa al par di voi.

COUNTESS
This time, my dear husband, I'm annoyed and astonished as much as you are.

IL CONTE
Ma stamane?

COUNT
But this morning?

LA CONTESSA
Stamane per l'odierna festa volevan travestirlo al modo stesso, che l'han vestito adesso.

COUNTESS
This morning we were getting ready for tonight's celebration and we dressed him exactly as you see him.

IL CONTE
E perchè non partisti?

COUNT
And why have you not left?

CHERUBINO (*tearing his cap off his head*)
My Lord . . .

COUNT
I'll have you punished for insubordination.

BARBARINA
Dearest master, dearest master, ev'ry time when you kissed me, do you remember, you always told me: "Barbarina, if you love me, there's no wish I won't grant you."

COUNT
So, did I say that?

BARBARINA
Surely. Now, dearest master, let me marry Cherubino, and in return I'll love you like my kitten.

COUNTESS (*to the* COUNT)
My Lord, it's up to you now.

ANTONIO
Well said, my daughter. One can see you had an expert teacher.

COUNT (*aside*)
I'd like to know what nemesis, what demon, converts each situation to my undoing?
(FIGARO *enters*)

FIGARO
My Lord, if you detain these girls here very much longer, good-by party, good-by dancing!

COUNT
What's that? You're planning to dance with your twisted foot?

FIGARO (*pretends to straighten his leg, then tries to dance. He calls all the girls, starts to go; the* COUNT *calls him back*)
It doesn't hurt at all now. Come on, girls, let's be going.

COUNTESS (*to* SUSANNA)
Now how will he get out of this predicament?

SUSANNA (*to the* COUNTESS)
Oh, don't be concerned about him.

COUNT
It's very lucky the flower bed was a soft one.

FIGARO
Very lucky. No more delaying, let's go now.
(*starts to go*)

ANTONIO (*holds him back*)
And meanwhile, on horseback, Cherubino was galloping to Seville!

FIGARO
Maybe galloping, maybe trotting, what's the difference? You girls, we must be off now.
(*starts to go*)

CHERUBINO
Signor.

IL CONTE
Saprò punire la tua disubbidienza.

BARBARINA
Eccellenza! Eccellenza! voi mi dite sì spesso qual volta m'abbraciate, e mi baciate: "Barbarina, se m'ami, ti darò quel che brami."

IL CONTE
Io dissi questo?

BARBARINA
Voi, or datemi, padrone, in sposo
Cherubino, e v'amerò, com'amo il mio gattino.

LA CONTESSA
Ebbene, or tocca a voi.

ANTONIO
Brava, figliuola! Hai buon maestro, che ti fa la scola.

IL CONTE
(Non sò, qual uom, qual demone, qual Dio, rivolga tutto quanto a torto mio.)

FIGARO
Signor, se trattenete
Tutte queste ragazze,
Addio festa, addio danza.

IL CONTE
E che? vorresti
Ballar col piè stravolto?

FIGARO
Eh, non mi duol più molto.
Andiam, belle fanciulle.

LA CONTESSA
Come si caverà dall'imbarazzo?

SUSANNA
Lasciate fare a lui.

IL CONTE
Per buona sorte,
I vasi eran di creta.

FIGARO
Senza fallo!
Andiamo, dunque, andiamo.

ANTONIO
Ed intanto a cavallo
Di galoppo a Siviglia andava il paggio.

FIGARO
Di galoppo o di passo, buon viaggio.
Venite o belle giovani.

IL CONTE
E a te la sua patente era in tasca rimasta.

FIGARO
Certamente! (Che razza di domande.)

ANTONIO
Via non gli far più moti, ei non t'intende. Ed ecco chi pretende che sia un bugiardo il mio signor nipote.

FIGARO
Cherubino!

ANTONIO
Or ci sei.

FIGARO
Che diamin canta?

IL CONTE
Non canta, no, ma dice, ch'egli saltò stamane in sui garofani.

FIGARO
Ei lo dice! Sarà . . . se ho saltato io, si può dare ch'anch'esso abbia fatto lo stesso.

IL CONTE
Anch'esso?

FIGARO
Perchè no? Io non impugno mai quel che non sò.

Ecco la marcia, andiamo!
Ai vostri posti, o belle;
Susanna, dammi il braccio!

SUSANNA
Eccolo.

IL CONTE
Temerari!

CONTESSA
Io son di ghiaccio!

IL CONTE
Contessa!

LA CONTESSA
Or non parliamo,
Ecco quì le due nozze,
Riceverle dobbiamo; alfin si tratta
D'una vostra protetta.
Seggiamo!

COUNT (*conducts him back to the center of the stage*)
But you had his commission still in your pocket.

FIGARO
Why, of course, sir!
(*aside*)
He kills me with his questions!

ANTONIO (*to* SUSANNA, *who is making signs to* FIGARO)
Don't make him any signals, he cannot see them.
(*he leads* CHERUBINO *forward and presents him to* FIGARO)
Here's someone who maintains that my brilliant nephew is a champion liar.

FIGARO
Cherubino!

ANTONIO
That's the one.

FIGARO (*to the* COUNT)
What is his story?

COUNT
He told the truth. He said that he was the one who jumped on the geraniums.

FIGARO
Did he say so? Could be . . . just because I jumped, there's no possible reason why he could not do likewise.

COUNT
He also?

FIGARO
And why not? One sheep will blindly follow the other's lead.
(*the Spanish march is heard in the distance*)

FINALE

There's the procession, let's join it.
Go to your places, dear ladies, take your places!
Susanna, be my partner!
(*takes* SUSANNA'S *arm*)

SUSANNA
Willingly!
(*all exit except the* COUNT *and* COUNTESS. *The march is heard more clearly*)

COUNT
How dare they!

COUNTESS
Ah, were it over!

COUNT
My Lady!

COUNTESS
Let's not discuss it!
Both the couples are coming,
We must receive them well.
At least in one bride

You have shown special interest.
Be seated.

COUNT
With pleasure;
(*aside*)
and plan a fitting vengeance.
(*the* COUNT *and* COUNTESS *seat themselves on the thrones. Enter* FIGARO, SUSANNA, MARCELLINA, BARBARINA, BARTOLO, ANTONIO, *hunters with guns, court attendants and country people. Two girls bring the little bridal hat with white plumes, two others a white veil, two others gloves and a nosegay. They are followed by* FIGARO *with* MARCELLINA. *Two other girls carry a similar hat for* SUSANNA, *etc. They are followed by* BARTOLO *with* SUSANNA. BARTOLO *leads* SUSANNA *to the* COUNT, *and she kneels to receive from him the hat, etc.* FIGARO *leads* MARCELLINA *to the* COUNTESS *for the same purpose*)

IL CONTE
Seggiamo; (e meditiam vendetta!)

2 GIRLS
Oh, come, faithful lovers, in happy accord,
And gratefully join us in praise of our lord.
The right of his forebears he kindly ignored,
Revoking a custom his subjects abhorred.
Oh, come, lift your voices in praise of our lord.
A practice he ended
Which shamed and offended,
And leaves chaste and spotless
The one you adored.
Come all, lift your voices in praise of our lord.

DUE DONNE
Amanti costanti, seguaci d'onor,
Cantate, lodate, sì saggio signor,
Amanti costanti, seguaci d'onor,
Cantate, lodate, sì saggio signor.
Cantate, lodate, sì saggio signor.
A un dritto cedendo,
Che oltraggia, che offende,
Ei caste vi rende, ai vostri amator,
A un dritto cedendo,
Che oltraggia, che offende
Ei caste vi rende, ai vostri amator.

ALL
With hearts ever grateful
We sing to our lord,
And may heaven's blessing
His wisdom reward.
(SUSANNA, *kneeling, plucks the* COUNT'S *sleeve, shows him the note, then reaches to her head, and while the* COUNT *pretends to adjust her bonnet, she gives him the note. He quickly hides it, and she rises and curtsies.* FIGARO *comes to receive* SUSANNA *and they dance. A little later* MARCELLINA *rises.* BARTOLO *receives her from the* COUNTESS)

TUTTI
Cantiamo, lodiamo, sì saggio signor.
Cantiamo, lodiamo, sì saggio signor.

COUNT (*takes out the note and pricks his finger with the pin as he opens it; he shakes his finger, squeezes it, sucks it, and throws the pin to the ground*)
I wonder why these careless females must fasten all they handle with pins and needles!
Ha, ha, I get the point now!

IL CONTE
È già solita usanza;
Le donne ficcan gli aghi in ogni loco,
Ah! ah! capisco il gioco!

FIGARO (*sees it all and says to* SUSANNA)
Just a note of affection
Which some lady has given him in passing.

FIGARO
Un biglietto amoroso
Che gli diè nel passar qualche galante,

Ed era sigillato d'una spilla
Ond'ei si punse il dito;
Il Narcisso or lo cerca: oh, che stordito!

She must have used a pin to seal the letter, see.
And now he stuck his finger.
(*the* COUNT *reads the note, kisses it, looks for the pin, finds it, and sticks it in his lapel*)
Now he is trying to find it.
Oh, is he stupid!

IL CONTE
Andate amici, e sia per questa sera
Disposto l'apparato nuziale,
Colla più ricca pompa; io vo' che sia
Magnifica la festa; e canti, e fuochi,
E gran cena, e gran ballo; e ognuno impari
Com'io tratto color che a me son cari.

COUNT
Dear friends and subjects,
I'll see you all this evening.
Tonight we'll celebrate the double wedding
With the greatest of splendor,
For this must be a magnificent occasion,
With music and fireworks,
And a banquet, also dancing,
So I may show you
How much love and good will
I feel I owe you.

CORO
Amanti costanti, seguaci d'onor,
Cantate, lodate, si saggio signor.
A un dritto cedendo,
Ch' oltraggia, ch' offende,
Ei caste vi rende, ai vostri amator.
Ei caste vi rende, ai vostri amator.
Cantiamo, lodiamo sì saggio signor,
Cantiamo, lodiamo sì saggio signor.

CHORUS
Oh, come, faithful lovers, in happy accord,
And gratefully join us in praise of our lord.
A practice he ended
Which shamed and offended,
And leaves chaste and spotless
The one you adored.
Come all, lift your voices in praise of our lord.
With hearts ever grateful
We sing to our lord,
And may heaven's blessing
His wisdom reward.

ACT IV

(A small room. Enter BARBARINA. *She looks for something on the floor.)*

Cavatina

BARBARINA
I have lost it,
Heaven help me,
I have lost the little pin.
How on earth could that have been?
I can't find it, I can't find it,
This is awful, simply awful!
Oh, what trouble I am in!
I keep looking, but cannot find it.
This is dreadful, I am desperate!
This is my unlucky day!
Cousin Susanna, and the Count . . .
What will they say, what will they say?

BARBARINA
L'ho perduta, me meschina!
Ah! chi sa dove sarà?
Non la trovo, non la trovo,
L'ho perduta! meschinella!
Ah! chi sa dove sarà?
Non la trovo, ah non la trovo!
Meschinella! L'ho perduta!
Ah, chi sa dove sarà!
Ei, mia cugina, e il padron,
Cosa dirà? Cosa dirà?

Recitative

*(*FIGARO *enters with* MARCELLINA*)*

FIGARO
Barbarina, what is it?

FIGARO
Barbarina, cos' hai?

BARBARINA
I have lost it, dear Cousin.

BARBARINA
L'ho perduta, cugino.

FIGARO
Lost it?

FIGARO
Cosa?

MARCELLINA
Lost it?

MARCELLINA
Cosa?

BARBARINA
The pin that His Lordship gave me to take back to Susanna.

BARBARINA
La spilla,
Che a me diede il padrone
Per recar a Susanna.

FIGARO
To Susanna, a pin?
(angrily)
I am awfully happy that you show so much talent . . . in performing assignments you are given.

FIGARO
A Susanna la spilla?
E così, tenerella, il mestiero già sai . . . di far tutto si ben quel che tu fai?

BARBARINA
What's wrong? Why do you growl at me?

BARBARINA
Cos'è? vai meco in collera?

FIGARO
Can't you see I am joking?
(searches the floor for a moment, then draws a pin from MARCELLINA*'s dress or bonnet and gives it to* BARBARINA*)*
Now listen: this is the pin the Count has given you to return to Susanna; it had served as a seal upon a letter. See, I know all about it.

FIGARO
E non vedi ch'io scherzo? osserva: questa è la spilla che il Conte da recare ti diede alla Susanna, e servia di sigillo a un bigliettino; vedi s'io sono instrutto.

BARBARINA
If you know more than I, why do you ask me?

BARBARINA
E perchè il chiedi a me quando sai tutto?

FIGARO
I just wanted to hear how my dear master has worded his instructions.

FIGARO
Avea gusto d'udir come il padrone ti diè la commissione.

BARBARINA
Che miracoli! "Tieni, fanciulla, reca questa spilla a la bella Susanna, e dille: questo è il sigillo de' pini!"

FIGARO
Ah! ah! de' pini.

BARBARINA
È ver ch'ei mi soggiunse; "guarda che alcun non veda." Ma tu già tacerai.

FIGARO
Sicuramente.

BARBARINA
A te già niente preme.

FIGARO
Oh niente, niente.

BARBARINA
Addio, mio bel cugino; vo da Susanna, e poi da Cherubino.

FIGARO
Madre!

MARCELLINA
Figlio!

FIGARO
Son morto.

MARCELLINA
Calmati, figlio mio!

FIGARO
Son morto, dico.

MARCELLINA
Flemma, flemma, e poi flemma: il fatto è serio, e pensarci convien. Ma guarda un poco, che ancor non sai di chi si prenda gioco.

FIGARO
Ah quella spilla, o madre, è quella stessa che poc'anzi ei raccolse.

MARCELLINA
È ver, ma questo al più ti porge un dritto di stare in guardia e vivere in sospetto; ma non sai se in effetto—

FIGARO
All'erta dunque! il loco del congresso so dov'è stabilito.

MARCELLINA
Dove vai, figlio mio?

FIGARO
A vendicar tutt'i mariti, addio.

MARCELLINA
Presto avvertiam Susanna. Io la credo innocente. Quella

BARBARINA
Oh, is that it? "Please, Barbarina, take this little pin here, bring it back to Susanna and tell her: 'Here is the seal to the pine grove.' "

FIGARO
Ah, ha, the pine grove!

BARBARINA
It's true, though, that he added: "Don't let a soul observe you." But you don't really count.

FIGARO
Why of course not.

BARBARINA
It's none of your business.

FIGARO
Indeed not, it isn't!

BARBARINA
It's high time that I hurried to see Susanna, and later, Cherubino.
(*dances off*)

FIGARO (*as if crushed*)
Mother!

MARCELLINA
Yes, dear.

FIGARO
This kills me!

MARCELLINA
Don't get excited, Son.

FIGARO
This is outrageous!

MARCELLINA
Not so hasty, think it over.
It is a problem; we must give it some thought. You must make sure that you're not the target of some new deception.

FIGARO
But, dearest Mother, I tell you, that is the pin for which the Count was looking.

MARCELLINA
If so, that makes it all the more important to act with caution and foster your least suspicion. After all, you do not know yet.

FIGARO
But soon I will. I know the spot exactly they have set for their meeting.

MARCELLINA
My dear son, where are you going?

FIGARO
To take revenge for cheated husbands, so help me!
(*he leaves, furious*)

MARCELLINA
Quickly, I'll warn Susanna, I believe she is guiltless. She

looks honest and surely true to Figaro . . . and if by chance I should be mistaken . . . now that I am her mother and no longer her rival, as a woman I am bound to become a defender of the whole female sex; for all men are ungrateful and should be punished.

faccia! quell'aria di modestia . . . è caso ancora ch'ella non fosse . . . ah, quando il cor non ciurma personale interesse, ogni donna è portata a la difesa del suo povero sesso, da quest'uomini ingrati a torto oppresso.

ARIA

The birds and beasts are able
To live in loving pairs.
The horses in ev'ry stable
Will never fight their mares.
A goose will find her gander
A friendly good companion,
Never will he philander
Or wander very far.
The rooster loves each feather
Of his beloved hen,
The lion and his chosen lioness
Are happy in their den.
The most ferocious creatures
Have some redeeming features.
But when it comes to mankind
That's something else again.
We members of the female sex
Are victims of the men we love.
For all his faults and shameless ways
The woman always pays.
We tolerate their jealousy,
We offer them fidelity,
We love with lavish generosity.
They pay us back with misery
And break our tender hearts.

Il capro e la capretta
Son sempre in amistà,
L'agnello all'agnelletta
La guerra mai non fa.
Le più feroci belve
Per selve e per campagne
Lascian le lor compagne
In pace e libertà.
Il capro e la capretta
Son sempre in amistà,
L'agnello all'agnelletta
La guerra mai non fa.
Le più feroci belve
Per selve e per campagne
Lascian le lor compagne
In pace e libertà.
Sol noi povere femmine,
Che tanto amiam quest'uomini,
Trattate siam dai perfidi
Ognor con crudeltà.
Sol noi povere femmine,
Che tanto amiam quest'uomini,
Trattate siam dai perfidi
Ognor con crudeltà.

RECITATIVE

(*change of scene. A thickly grown garden with two parallel pavilions*)

BARBARINA (*alone, holding some fruit and cookies*)

He said the left pavilion, it must be here.
I see it, yes, this one. I only hope he'll get here. Good Lord, what stingy people!
The most I could make them give me was an apple and a tomato. "For whom are those provisions?"
"Just for a certain person." "That's what I thought."
The misers! The Count can't stand him, but I, I love him dearly. A kiss is what it cost me . . . it does not matter. I'll get it back very soon.
(*frightened, she enters the pavilion on the left*)
Good gracious!
(*enter* FIGARO *in a cloak, and carrying a lantern, then* BASILIO, BARTOLO, *a group of workmen*)

BARBARINA

Nel padiglione a manca, ei così disse, è questo, è questo. E poi se non venisse? Oh, ve', che brava gente! A stento darmi un arancio, una pera, e una ciambella, "Per chi, madamigella?" "Oh per qualcun, signori." "Già lo sappiam," ebbene! il padron l'odia; ed io gli voglio bene, però costommi un bacio, e cosa importa, forse qualcun me'l renderà. Son morta!

FIGARO

It's Barbarina! Who is there?

FIGARO

È Barbarina! Chi va là?

BASILIO
Son quelli che invitasti a venir.

BARTOLO
Che brutto ceffo! sembri un cospirator?
Che diamin sono quegli infausti apparati?

FIGARO
Lo vedrete tra poco. In questo stesso loco celebrerem la festa della mia sposa onesta e del feudal signor.

BASILIO
(Ah buono, buono, capisco come egli è, accordati si son senza di me.)

FIGARO
Voi da questi contorni non vi scostate, intanto io vado a dar certi ordini, e torno in pochi istanti, a un fischio mio correte tutti quanti.

BASILIO
Hai diavoli nel corpo!

BARTOLO
Ma che guadagni?

BASILIO
Nulla; Susanna piace al Conte; ella d'accordo gli diè un appuntamento ch'a Figaro non piace.

BARTOLO
E che? dunque dovria soffrirlo in pace?

BASILIO
Quel che soffrono tanti ei soffrir non potrebbe? E poi sentite che guadagno può far? Nel mondo, amico, l'accozzarla con grandi, fu pericolo ognora, dan novanta per cento e han vinto ancora.

In quegl'anni, in cui val poco
La mal pratica ragion,
Ebbi anch'io lo stesso foco,
Fui quel pazzo, ch'or non son,
Ma col tempo e coi perigli,
Donna Flemma capitò;
E i capricci ed i puntigli
Dalla testa mi cavò.
Presso un picciolo abituro,
Seco lei mi trasse un giorno,
E togliendo giù dal muro
Del pacifico soggiorno
Una pelle di somaro.
Prendi, disse, o figlio caro,
Poi disparve, e mi lasciò,
Mentre ancor tacito guardo quel dono,
Il ciel s'annuvola
Rimbomba il tuono,

BASILIO
Remember, you have asked us to come.

BARTOLO
You look so savage, ready to cut our throats.
What is the point of these infernal preparations?

FIGARO
Very soon you shall know it. You are about to witness the unannounced revival of an old Spanish custom by the Count and my bride.

BASILIO (*aside*)
Oh, charming, charming! I see the light of day.
They arranged this affair without my help.

FIGARO
Stand where no one can see you and watch what happens. I'll give a few last-minute orders, but I'll return here shortly, and when I whistle, rush forward and surprise them.
(*all exit except* BARTOLO *and* BASILIO)

BASILIO
He's acting like a madman.

BARTOLO
Can you explain it?

BASILIO
Gladly. The Count loves Susanna; she is pleased to accord him an appointment, and Figaro is displeased.

BARTOLO
Well? And? Is he supposed to take it calmly?

BASILIO
Why should he be exempted from what so many have suffered? And then, I ask you, what on earth could he gain? One learns one's lesson. In this life, dearest Doctor, one must be realistic. You can't eat your cake and also have it.

ARIA

Youth is headstrong, overbearing,
Too impulsive, as a rule.
I myself was young and daring,
I was just as big a fool.
But the passing years have brought me
Sense enough to swallow pride;
And experience at last has taught me
Not to swim against the tide.
Once, while I was on a journey,
I met Father Time in person.
In his hand he held an object
Which he offered me as present.
'Twas the hide of a donkey.
"Son," he said, "take this and wear it,
You won't regret it."

Then he disappeared in air,
Left me speechless standing there.
While I was lost in amazement and wonder,
A dreadful storm arose.
Thunder was crashing,
And like a waterfall the rain was splashing,
And lightning flashing.
I had no shelter, coat, or umbrella.
Only the donkey hide lay there nearby.
I slipped it over me,
It kept me dry.
The sun came out again and I proceeded.
A horrid animal came out of nowhere,
Its mouth wide open, about to eat me.
I stood there, petrified.
What could I do?
My life was doomed, that much I knew.
All of a sudden the beast turned and bolted,
Smelling the donkey hide, it was revolted.
I smelled so horrible, it lost its appetite
And ran away.
Take this advice, my friend,
And learn this lesson:
Malice and calumny, injustice, dishonor,
Will never penetrate a donkey's hide.

Mista alla grandine scroscia la piova.
Ecco le membra coprir mi giova
Col manto d'asino che mi donò.
Finisce il turbine, io fo due passi.
Che fiera orribile dianzi a me fassi;
Già, già mi tocca, l'ingorda bocca,
Già di difendermi speme non ho,
Ma il fiuto ignobile del mio vestito,
Tolse alla belva sì l'appetito,
Che disprezzandomi si rinselvò.
Così conoscere mi fè la sorte,
Ch'onte, pericoli, vergogna, e morte,
Col cuoio d'asino fuggir si può.

(BASILIO *and* BARTOLO *leave*)

RECITATIVE AND ARIA

(FIGARO *enters*)

FIGARO

It won't be long now, they should arrive at any moment.
Someone is coming . . . Susanna?
No, it's not, the darkness deceived me.
On the night of my wedding
I am already playing the role of jealous husband. Imagine!
At the moment of the wedding procession,
When the Count read her message,
I was laughing!
I was laughing at myself, and did not know it!
Oh Susanna, Susanna, what despair you have caused me!
Who could have thought you faithless,
You were always so honest,
So naïve and so winning!
Ah, to put faith in Woman, in Woman!
Foolish beginning!
Oh, fellow man, be smarter!
Don't be a blinded martyr.
Wake up and look at womenfolk
And see them as they are,
And see them as they really are.
Though you may call them angels,

FIGARO

Tutto è disposto: l'ora
Dovrebbe esser vicina; io sento gente . . .
È dessa! non è alcun; buia è la notte,
Ed io comincio omai
A far il scimunito
Mestiere di marito!
Ingrata! nel momento
Della mia cerimonia
Ei godeva leggendo, e nel vederlo,
Io rideva di me senza saperlo!
O Susanna! Susanna!
Quanta pena mi costi!
Con quell'ingenua faccia,
Con quegli occhi innocenti,
Chi creduto l'avria!
Ah! che il fidarsi a donna è ognor follia!
Aprite un po' quegl'occhi,
Uomini incauti, e sciocchi,
Guardate queste femmine,
Guardate cosa son.
Guardate, guardate cosa son!
Queste chiamate Dee
Dagli ingannati sensi,
A cui tributa incensi
La debole ragion, la debole ragion

La debole ragion.
Son streghe, che incantano per farci penar;
Sirene che cantano per farci affogar;
Civette che allettano per trarci, le piume,
Comete che brillano per toglierci il lume;
Son rose spinose,
Son volpi vezzose!
Son orse benigne,
Colombe maligne:
Maestre d'inganni, amiche d'affanni,
Che fingono, mentono,
Amore non senton,
Non senton pietà,
Non senton pietà,
no, no, no, no!
Il resto nol dico.
Già ognuno lo sa.

And like a slave adore them,
Your love will merely bore them,
But you will bear the scar.
Like witches with sorcery, they charm and decoy.
Like sirens with treachery, they sing and destroy.
They flatter their vanity and cater to fashion,
They cause us unhappiness and show no compassion.
Like roses with briars,
Like soft-spoken liars,
Appearing delightful,
Yet vicious and spiteful.
Their dealings are double,
They get us in trouble.
Deceitful and jealous,
To love they are callous,
Their heart is of stone,
Yes, made of stone!
The rest I need hardly to tell you,
All that is sufficiently known.
(*retires*)

RECITATIVE

(*enter the* COUNTESS, SUSANNA, *disguised, and* MARCELLINA)

SUSANNA
Signora, ella mi disse,
Che Figaro verravvi.

SUSANNA
My Lady, I heard from Marcellina that Figaro will be here.

MARCELLINA
Anzi è venuto,
Abbassa un po' la voce.

MARCELLINA
He's here already, so better speak more softly.

SUSANNA
Dunque un ci ascolta, e l'altro
Dee venir a cercarmi:
Incominciam.

SUSANNA
One man in ambush, the other should be here any moment. The fun begins!

MARCELLINA
Io voglio quì celarmi.

MARCELLINA (*enters the pavilion where* BARBARINA *is;* FIGARO *in the background*)
I will leave you alone here.

SUSANNA
Madama, voi tremate; avreste freddo?

SUSANNA
My Lady, you are trembling. Are you cold?

LA CONTESSA
Parmi umida, la notte: io mi ritiro.

COUNTESS
The night is damp and chilly. I'll go inside now.

FIGARO
(Eccoci de la crisi al grande istante!)

FIGARO (*aside*)
We are arriving at the crucial moment.

SUSANNA
Io sotto queste piante, (se madama il permette), resto al prendere il fresco una mezz'ora.

SUSANNA
I'll stay a little longer, if My Lady will permit me. It is early and the night air is refreshing.

FIGARO
Il fresco! il fresco!

FIGARO
Refreshing! Refreshing!

LA CONTESSA
Restaci in buon'ora.

COUNTESS (*hides herself*)
You have my permission.

SUSANNA (*aside*)

I know the rogue is spying. It will give me much pleasure to reimburse him in full for his suspicions.

RECITATIVE AND ARIA

This at last is the moment,
So divine and so cherished,
I longingly awaited.
Soon he will come here,
With loving arms embrace me,
And no worry or fear shall mar our rapture.
Close to the heart of Nature's friendly powers,
Delicate, fragrant flowers,
The pine trees, the sky surround us.
Aiding the lovers,
Night casts her veil around us.
Beloved, don't delay, the night is falling.
Hasten where love's delight is sweetly calling.
Until the stars grow pale and night is waning,
While the world is still and calm is reigning.
The brooklet rustles on, the breeze is blowing,
And the timorous heart with hope is glowing,
The flowers all with shining dew are gleaming,
While the world is long asleep and dreaming.
Come, my beloved, the starry sky above you,
Come, my beloved, with all my heart I love you.

RECITATIVE

FIGARO

Shame on her! Behind my back she plans to deceive me!
It's like a dreadful nightmare!

CHERUBINO (*enters*)

La, la, la, la, la, la, la.

COUNTESS

It's Cherubino.

CHERUBINO

Here are the pavilions. Barbarina must be in the left one.
I recognized my lady.

COUNTESS

I can't avoid him!

CHERUBINO

But no. I was mistaken; by her dress I can tell it is Susanna.

COUNTESS

If my husband comes now, heaven protect me!

FINALE

CHERUBINO

On my tiptoes I'll go nearer,
Here's the chance to have some fun.

SUSANNA

(Il birbo è in sentinella,
Divertiamci anche noi,
Diamogli la mercè de'dubbi suoi.)

SUSANNA

Giunse alfin il momento,
Che godrò senza affanno
In braccio all'idol mio:
Timide cure, uscite dal mio petto,
A turbar non venite il mio diletto.
Oh! come par che all'amoroso foco
L'amenità del loco,
La terra, e il ciel risponda,
Come la notte i furti miei seconda!
Deh! vieni, non tardar, o gioia bella,
Vieni ove amore per goder t'appella;
Finchè non splende in ciel notturna face,
Finchè l'aria è ancor bruna, e il mondo tace.
Quì mormora il ruscel, quì scherza l'aura,
Che col dolce susurro il cor ristaura;
Quì ridono i fioretti, e l'erba è fresca
Ai piaceri d'amor quì tutto adesca.
Vieni, ben mio, tra queste piante ascose,
Ti vo' la fronte incoronar di rose.

FIGARO

Perfida! e in quella forma
Meco mentia! non so s'io veglio o dormo!

CHERUBINO

La, la, la, la,
la, la, la.

LA CONTESSA

Il picciol paggio.

CHERUBINO

Io sento gente, entriamo
Ove entrò Barbarina.
Oh! vedo quì una donna.

LA CONTESSA

Ahimè meschina!

CHERUBINO

M'inganno! a quel cappello,
Che nell'ombra vegg'io, parmi Susanna.

LA CONTESSA

E se il Conte ora vien, sorte tiranna!

CHERUBINO

Pian pianin le andrò più presso;
Tempo perso non sarà.

LA CONTESSA
Ah! se il Conte arriva adesso.
Qualche imbroglio accaderà.

CHERUBINO
Susannetta?
Non risponde?
Colla mano il volto asconde
Or la burlo, or la burlo in verità,
Or la burlo in verità.

LA CONTESSA
Arditello! sfacciatello,
Ite presto via di quà.

CHERUBINO
Smorfiosa, maliziosa,
Io già so perchè sei quà.
Smorfiosa, maliziosa.
Io già so perchè sei quà.

LA CONTESSA
Arditello! sfacciatello!
Ite presto via di quà!
Sfacciatello! ite presto via di quà!
Arditello! sfacciatello!
Ite presto via di quà!

IL CONTE
Ecco quì la mia Susanna!

SUSANNA, FIGARO
Ecco quì l'uccellatore!

CHERUBINO
Non far meco la tiranna!

SUSANNA, IL CONTE, FIGARO
Ah, nel sen mi batte il core!

LA CONTESSA
Via, partite o chiamo gente!

CHERUBINO
Dammi un bacio, o non fai niente.

SUSANNA, IL CONTE, FIGARO
Alla voce è quegli il paggio.

LA CONTESSA
Anche un bacio! che corragio!

CHERUBINO
E perchè far io non posso,
Quel che il Conte ognor farà?

3 ALTRI
Temerario! Temerario!

CHERUBINO
Oh! ve'che smorfie! Oh! ve'che smorfie!
Oh! ve'che smorfie! che smorfie!
Sai ch'io fui dietro il sofà.

COUNTESS
Oh, good Lord, it's Cherubino,
Now the trouble has begun.

CHERUBINO (*to the* COUNTESS)
Come, Susanna! Won't you answer?
She pretends she does not see me,
But I'll show her that I know her little game,
Posing as a noble dame.
(*takes her hand and caresses it*)

COUNTESS (*tries to free herself; disguising her voice*)
Shameless meddler, don't come near me,
Take yourself away from here.

CHERUBINO
Susanna, stop pretending,
I know well why you are here.
You needn't be condescending . . .
You await your cavalier,
And you hope he'll soon be here!
That's the reason you are here.

COUNTESS
Who allowed you to molest me?
Go at once away from here!
Shameless meddler! Go at once away from here!
Who allowed you to molest me?
Go at once away from here!

COUNT (*in the distance*)
Here you are, my sweet Susanna!

SUSANNA, FIGARO (*in the distance*)
Here's our roving Don Giovanni.

CHERUBINO
Don't act prudish and affected!

SUSANNA, COUNT, FIGARO
Ah, this shock came unexpected!

COUNTESS
Go, or I must call assistance!

CHERUBINO (*keeping her hand in his*)
Let me kiss you, don't be so silly.

OTHERS
I am sure it's Cherubino.

COUNTESS
I should kiss you, what presumption!

CHERUBINO
Why am I not once permitted
What the Count does ev'ry day?

OTHERS (*aside*)
How offensive, how insulting!

CHERUBINO
Is it not time to stop pretending?
This very morning, remember,
When I hid behind the chair?

SUSANNA
What effront'ry!

COUNTESS
What presumption!

COUNT, FIGARO
His behavior is outrageous!

ALL EXCEPT CHERUBINO (*aside*)
If this rascal keeps insisting,
He will lead our plans astray.

CHERUBINO (*tries to kiss the* COUNTESS)
To begin with . . .
(*the* COUNT *comes between the* COUNTESS *and* CHERUBINO *and receives the kiss*)

COUNTESS
Good Lord, my husband!

CHERUBINO (*joins* BARBARINA *in the pavilion*)
Good Lord, my master!

FIGARO (*drawing near the* COUNT)
I must see what's going on.

COUNT (*intending to give a box on the ear to* CHERUBINO, *he gives it to* FIGARO)
Just to cool youthful ardor,
Take this little gift from me!

FIGARO
This is pretty meager payment
For the int'rest I have shown!

SUSANNA (*laughing*)
He is getting the proper treatment,
He received the proper treatment
For the envy he has shown!

COUNT, COUNTESS (*laughing*)
That is just the proper treatment
For the boldness he has shown.
He received the proper treatment
For the boldness he has shown.

SUSANNA
Serves him right for being curious,
Always spying on his own!
Maybe next time he'll know better,
And leave well enough alone.

COUNT, COUNTESS
He has made me simply furious
With his high and mighty tone,
Maybe next time he'll know better
And leave well enough alone.

FIGARO
All I got for being curious,
Is a bruised and aching bone, ah,
The next time I shall know better
And leave well enough alone.

SUSANNA
Temerario!

CONTESSA
Temerario!

CONTE, FIGARO
Temerario! Temerario!

TUTTI (ma non Cherubino)
(Se il ribaldo ancor sta saldo,
La faccenda guasterà.)

CHERUBINO
Prendi intanto!

LA CONTESSA
O cielo! il Conte!

CHERUBINO
O cielo! il Conte

FIGARO
Vo' veder cosa fan là.

IL CONTE
Perchè voi non ripetete,
Ricevete questo quà.

FIGARO
Ah! Ci ho fatto un bel guadagno,
Colla mia curiosità.

SUSANNA
Ah! Ci ha fatto un bel guadagno.
Colla sua curiosità.

CONTE, CONTESSA
Ah! Ci ha fatto un bel guadagno,
Colla sua temerità.
Ah, ci ha fatto un bel guadagno,
Colla sua temerità.

SUSANNA
Ah! ci ha fatto un bel guadagno,
Colla sua curiosità!
Ah! ci ha fatto un bel guadagno,
Colla sua curiosità!

CONTE, CONTESSA
Ah! ci ha fatto un bel guadagno,
Colla sua curiosità!
Ah! ci ha fatto un bel guadagno,
Colla sua curiosità.

FIGARO
Ah! ci ho fatto un bel guadagno,
Colla mia curiosità, ah!
Ah! ci ho fatto un bel guadagno.
Colla mia curiosità!

(FIGARO *retires*)

IL CONTE
Partito è alfin l'audace,
Accostati, ben mio!

COUNT (*to the* COUNTESS)
At last no one disturbs us.
Come over here, my dearest.

LA CONTESSA
Giacchè cosi vi piace,
Eccomi quì, signor!

COUNTESS (*feigning* SUSANNA'S *voice*)
Your word is my commandment,
Here I am, My Lord.

FIGARO
Che compiacente femmina!
Che sposa di buon cor!

FIGARO
How willing and obedient!
She's always in accord.

IL CONTE
Porgimi la manina.

COUNT
Give me your hand, my darling.

LA CONTESSA
Io ve la do.

COUNTESS
Here is my hand.

IL CONTE
Carina!

COUNT
I love you!

FIGARO
Carina?

FIGARO
He loves her!

IL CONTE
Che dita tenerelle!
Che delicata pelle!
Mi pizzica, mi stuzzica,
M'empie d'un nuovo ardor!

COUNT
What soft and lovely fingers!
Their tender touch still lingers,
It moves my heart to ecstasy,
Rapture and joy combined.

SUSANNA, LA CONTESSA, FIGARO
La cieca prevenzione
Delude la ragione,
Inganna i sensi ognor.

SUSANNA, COUNTESS, FIGARO
Such wild infatuation
Is mere hallucination,
It blinds the human mind, the feeble human mind.

IL CONTE
Oltre la dote, o cara!
Ricevi anco un brillante
Che a te porge un'amante
In pegno del suo amor.

COUNT
Darling, besides your dowry,
Accept this little present,
A diamond ring as token
Of my undying love.
(*gives the* COUNTESS *a ring*)

LA CONTESSA
Tutto Susanna piglia
Dal suo benefattor.

COUNTESS
Gladly Susanna welcomes
Her benefactor's gift.

SUSANNA, IL CONTE, FIGARO
Va tutto a maraviglia,
Ma il meglio manca ancor.

SUSANNA, COUNT, FIGARO
Our (My) plan is fast proceeding,
The best is yet to come.

LA CONTESSA
Signor, d'accese fiaccole,
Io veggio il balenar.

COUNTESS (*to the* COUNT)
My lord, I see the glow of flaming torches in the night.

IL CONTE
Entriam, mia bella Venere,
Andiamoci a celar!

COUNT
Well, then, let us avoid them all
And hurry out of sight.

SUSANNA, FIGARO
Mariti scimuniti,
Venite ad imparar!

SUSANNA, FIGARO
Come on, you foolish husbands,
It's time you saw the light!

LA CONTESSA
Al buio signor mio?

COUNTESS
You mean there in the dark?

COUNT
What else would suit us better?
I do not want to read to you in there, Susanna dear.

COUNTESS, SUSANNA
Our plan is working splendidly,
Now comes the best of all.

FIGARO
She follows very willingly.
There is no doubt at all.
(crosses the stage)

COUNT *(in a feigned voice)*
Who goes there?

FIGARO *(in a rage)*
Lots of people!

COUNTESS
It's Figaro! I'll hide.
(goes into the right pavilion)

COUNT
You go ahead, then; I'll meet you soon.
(disappears among the bushes)

FIGARO
Now all is still and calm again.
The lovers meet in secrecy,
But I shall guide their destiny,
Biding my time judiciously,
To catch them both at once.

SUSANNA *(in a feigned voice)*
Ho, Figaro! Be quiet!

FIGARO *(aside)*
Ah, that must be the Countess.
(aloud)
Your coming here is timely.
Observe in what a manner
Your husband and my Susanna
Arranged a secret meeting.
Just wait and you will see.

SUSANNA *(forgetting to change her voice)*
Be careful and speak softly.
I swear I will not leave here
Till I have had revenge!

FIGARO *(aside)*
Susanna!
(aloud)
You want vengeance?

SUSANNA
Yes.

FIGARO
Vengeance? May I be at your service?

SUSANNA *(aside)*
The traitor thinks he's fooling me,
But he is very wrong.

IL CONTE
È quello che vogl'io,
Tu sai, che là per leggere,
Io non desio entrar.

LA CONTESSA, SUSANNA
I furbi sono in trappola,
Comincia ben l'affar.

FIGARO
La perfida lo seguita,
È vano il dubitar.

IL CONTE
Chi passa?

FIGARO
Passa gente.

LA CONTESSA
È Figaro! men vo!

IL CONTE
Andate, andate! io poi verrò.

FIGARO
Tutto è tranquillo e placido;
Entrò la bella Venere,
Col vago Marte prendere
Nuovo Vulcan del secolo
In rete la potrò.

SUSANNA
Ehi? Figaro, tacete!

FIGARO
(Oh! questa è la Contessa.)
A tempo quì giungete,
Vedrete là voi stessa
Il Conte, e la mia sposa;
Di propria man la cosa
Toccar io vi farò.

SUSANNA
Parlate un po' più basso:
Di quà non muovo il passo,
Ma vendicar mi vo'.

FIGARO
(Susanna!) Vendicarsi?

SUSANNA
Sì.

FIGARO
Come potria farsi?

SUSANNA
(L'iniquo io vo' sorprendere,
Poi so quel che farò.)

FIGARO
(La volpe vuol sorprendermi,
E secondarla vo'.)
Ah se madama il vuole!

SUSANNA
(Su via, manco parole!)

FIGARO
Ah, madama!

SUSANNA
(Su via, manco parole.)

FIGARO
Eccomi a' vostri piedi,
Ho pieno il cor di foco,
Esaminate il loco,
Pensate al traditor!

SUSANNA
(Come la man mi pizzica!)

FIGARO
(Come il polmon mi s'altera!)

SUSANNA
(Che smania! che furor!)

FIGARO
(Che smania che calor.)

SUSANNA
(Che smania, che furor, che smania,
Che smania, che furor.)

FIGARO
(Che smania, che calor, che smania,
Che calor, o che calor.)

SUSANNA
E senz' alcun affetto?

FIGARO
Suppliscavi il rispetto!
Non perdiam tempo invano:
Datemi un po' la mano,
Datemi un po'—

SUSANNA
Servitevi, signor!

FIGARO
Che schiaffo!

SUSANNA
E questo! e questo,
E ancora questo, e questo,
E poi quest' altro.

FIGARO
Non batter così presto!

FIGARO (*aside*)
The vixen thinks she's fooling me,
So I will play along.
(*slyly joining the game*)
Countess, I am delirious!

SUSANNA (*aside*)
What's this, can he be serious?

FIGARO
Ah, My Lady!

SUSANNA (*aside*)
Indeed, he must be serious.

FIGARO
I'm on my knees before you,
You know that I adore you.
Remember what you told me,
You're here to take revenge!

SUSANNA (*aside*)
I hardly can restrain myself!

FIGARO (*aside*)
What a delightful comedy!

SUSANNA (*aside*)
My blood begins to boil!

FIGARO (*aside*)
Her blood begins to boil!

SUSANNA (*aside*)
I hardly can restrain my temper.
Now he has gone too far!

FIGARO (*aside*)
She hardly can restrain her temper,
And I fear I've gone too far!

SUSANNA (*disguising her voice slightly*)
Suppose you are rejected?

FIGARO
That would be unexpected.
We can't lose time debating.
(*rubbing his hands*)
Grant me some sign of favor . . .
Give me your hand.

SUSANNA (*resumes her natural voice, and boxes his ears*)
Right here where it belongs!

FIGARO
You slapped me!

SUSANNA
Take this one, and this one,
(*continues to box his ears*)
And still another, and this one,
And still another!

FIGARO
Don't hit so hard, I beg you!

SUSANNA
And take this, you scheming traitor,
Take this one and still another one!

FIGARO
Oh, precious welcome punishment
From her beloved hand!

SUSANNA
I'll teach you to behave yourself,
And mind your own affairs!

FIGARO
I am a happy man!

SUSANNA
I warn you not to let it happen again.
You got what you deserve as punishment,
You false and wicked man!

FIGARO (*kneels*)
My apology, darling, I owe you.
From your voice it was easy to know you,
From your sweet little voice I adore.

SUSANNA (*surprised and laughing*)
From my voice?

FIGARO
How could I mistake it?

SUSANNA, FIGARO
Darling, darling, I love and adore you,
Dearest love, let us quarrel no more.

COUNT (*enters*)
Where she is I cannot discover.

SUSANNA, FIGARO
That's the voice of the frustrated lover.

COUNT (*turns toward the pavilion in which the* COUNTESS *has hidden and opens it*)
Ho, Susanna! Can't you hear me? Where are you?

SUSANNA
Splendid, splendid, he still does not know her.

FIGARO
Who?

SUSANNA
My lady.

FIGARO
The Countess?

SUSANNA
The Countess!

SUSANNA, FIGARO
Now to bring the burlesque to an ending,
We must even the score with the Count.

FIGARO (*falls at* SUSANNA'*s feet*)
Ah, My Lady, I love you so madly!

SUSANNA
E questo, signor scaltro,
E poi quest' altro ancor.

FIGARO
O schiaffi graziosissimi,
O mio felice amor.

SUSANNA
Impara, impara o perfido!
A fare il seduttor.

FIGARO
O mio felice amor!

SUSANNA
Impara, impara a fare il seduttor.
Impara, impara, impara, o perfido,
A fare il seduttor!

FIGARO
Pace, pace, mio dolce tesoro!
Io conobbi la voce che adoro,
E che impressa ognor serbo nel cor.

SUSANNA
La mia voce?

FIGARO
La voce che adoro.

SUSANNA, FIGARO
Pace, pace, mio dolce tesoro,
Pace, pace, mio tenero amor.

IL CONTE
Non la trovo, e girai tutto il bosco.

SUSANNA, FIGARO
Questi è il Conte, alla voce il conosco.

IL CONTE
Ehi? Susanna? Sei sorda? Sei muta?

SUSANNA
Bella! bella! non l'ha conosciuta!

FIGARO
Chi?

SUSANNA
Madama.

FIGARO
Madama?

SUSANNA
Madama!

SUSANNA, FIGARO
La commedia, idol mio, terminiamo,
Consoliamo il bizzarro amator.

FIGARO
Sì, Madama, voi siete il ben mio.

IL CONTE
La mia sposa? Ah, senz'arme son io!

FIGARO
Un ristoro al mio cor concedete?

SUSANNA
Io son quì, faccio quel che volete.

IL CONTE
Ah! ribaldi!

SUSANNA, FIGARO
Ah! corriamo, mio bene,
E le pene compensi il piacer.

IL CONTE
Gente, gente! all'armi!

FIGARO
Il padrone!

IL CONTE
Gente, aiuto! aiuto, aiuto!

FIGARO
Son perduto!

BASILIO, DON CURZIO, ANTONIO, BARTOLO
Cos'avvenne?

IL CONTE
Il scellerato
M'ha tradito, m'ha infamato,
E con chi, state a veder!

BARTOLO, BASILIO, ANTONIO, DON CURZIO
Son stordito, sbalordito!
Non mi par che ciò sia ver.

FIGARO
Son storditi sbalorditi!
Oh che scena! che piacer!

IL CONTE
Invan resistete; uscite Madama,
Il premio or avrete di vostra onestà.
Il paggio!

ANTONIO
Mia figlia!

FIGARO
Mia madre!

BASILIO, BARTOLO, ANTONIO, DON CURZIO
Madama!

IL CONTE
Scoperta è la trama, la perfida è quà.

COUNT
It's the Countess! Ah, and I have no weapons!

FIGARO
Won't you favor my loving proposal?

SUSANNA
I am ready and at your disposal.

COUNT
Ah, betrayers, betrayers!

SUSANNA, FIGARO
Let us hurry away and be happy,
Let us bury our troubles in joy.
(SUSANNA *enters the pavilion on the left*)

COUNT
Hurry, hurry, come with weapons!

FIGARO (*pretending great fear*)
That's my master.
(*enter* BARTOLO, BASILIO, DON CURZIO, ANTONIO, *servants with torches*)

COUNT
Guards and servants, come and help me!

FIGARO
I'm outnumbered!

BASILIO, CURZIO, ANTONIO, BARTOLO
What has happened?

COUNT
This wretched scoundrel has betrayed me,
Acted basely, and with whom you soon shall see.

BASILIO, CURZIO, ANTONIO, BARTOLO
I am speechless and bewildered!
Can it be that this is true?

FIGARO
They are speechless and bewildered.
They cannot believe it's true.

COUNT
There's no use resisting, insisting on hiding.
Come out now, my Countess, and get your reward!
(*the* COUNT *reaches into the left pavilion and pulls out a resisting* CHERUBINO, *then* BARBARINA, MARCELLINA, *and* SUSANNA)
Cherubino!

ANTONIO
My daughter!

FIGARO
My mother!

BASILIO, CURZIO, ANTONIO, BARTOLO
My Lady!

COUNT
Your plot is discovered, most faithless of wives,
So false to her lord!

SUSANNA (*kneels before the* COUNT, *holding her handkerchief before her face*)
Forgive me, forgive me!

COUNT
No, never, never!

FIGARO (*kneels*)
Forgive her, forgive her!

COUNT
There's no chance whatever!

ALL OTHERS (*kneeling*)
Forgive her!

COUNT
No!

ALL OTHERS
Forgive her!

COUNT (*more forceful*)
No, no, no, no, no, no!

COUNTESS (*comes out of the other pavilion and is about to kneel when the* COUNT *prevents her*)
I know you'll forgive them,
For my sake at least!

BASILIO, CURZIO, COUNT, ANTONIO
I cannot conceive it, I scarcely believe it,
I hardly can credit my eyes!
What's this I see?

COUNT (*supplicatingly*)
My Lady, forgive me,
Beloved, forgive me!

COUNTESS
How could I refuse it,
My heart speaks for you.

ALL
We are all contented and happy again.
All day long we were tormented,
Angry, foolish, and excited,
But at last we are united
By the magic force of love.
Lovers and couples,
With laughter and singing,
Let the wedding bells chime in with joyous ringing!
And to joyous strains of music,
Sing and dance till break of day.
Let's make merry,
And to joyous strains of music,
Sing and dance till break of day!

SUSANNA
Perdono! perdono!

IL CONTE
No, no, non sperarlo!

FIGARO
Perdono! Perdono!

IL CONTE
No, no! non vo' darlo!

TUTTI
Perdono!

IL CONTE
No!

TUTTI
Perdono!

IL CONTE
No, no, no, no, no, no!

LA CONTESSA
Almeno per loro perdono
otterrò.

BASILIO, CURZIO, CONTE, ANTONIO
O cielo! che veggio! delirio!
vaneggio!
Che creder, che creder non so!
Non so, non so!

IL CONTE
Contessa, perdono!
Perdono, perdono!

LA CONTESSA
Più docile io sono,
E dico di sì.

TUTTI
Ah! tutti contenti saremo così.
Questo giorno di tormenti,
Di capricci e di follia,
In contenti, e in allegria
Solo amor può terminar.
Sposi, amici! al ballo, al gioco
Alle mine date foco.
Ed al suon di lieta marcia
Corriam tutti a festeggiar.
Corriam tutti,
Corriam tutti, corriam tutti
Corriam tutti a festeggiar.

OTELLO

by Giuseppe Verdi (1813–1901)

LIBRETTO BY ARRIGO BOITO

Translated by WALTER DUCLOUX.

Based on Shakespeare's tragedy *Othello, the Moor of Venice.*

CHARACTERS

MONTANO, *Otello's predecessor as governor of Cyprus*	*Bass*
CASSIO, *Otello's lieutenant*	*Tenor*
IAGO, *Otello's ensign*	*Baritone*
RODERIGO, *a Venetian gentleman*	*Tenor*
OTELLO, *a noble Moor in the service of Venice*	*Tenor*
DESDEMONA, *Otello's wife*	*Soprano*
EMILIA, *Iago's wife and Desdemona's companion*	*Mezzo-soprano*
LODOVICO, *Ambassador of Venice*	*Bass*
A HERALD	*Bass*

PEOPLE OF CYPRUS, VENETIAN SOLDIERS AND SAILORS, INNKEEPER, SERVANTS, VENETIAN LADIES AND GENTLEMEN

Place: A seaport in Cyprus
Time: Late fifteenth century
First performance: La Scala, Milan, February 5, 1887

COPYRIGHT © 1962 BY WALTER DUCLOUX
BY PERMISSION OF G. RICORDI & CO.

ACT I

(*Outside the castle. A tavern with an arbor. A view of the harbor. It is evening. A violent storm, lightning and thunder.*)

Scene 1

(IAGO, RODERIGO, CASSIO, MONTANO, *later* OTELLO. *Cypriots and Venetian soldiers.*)

CHORUS TENORS
See the sail there!

CHORUS BASSES
Yes, I see it.

CHORUS TENORS
. . . and the banner?

CHORUS BASSES
Can you see it?

MONTANO
'Tis a lion in white.

CASSIO
What a frightful disaster!

CHORUS TENORS
Hear the trumpet!

CHORUS BASSES
They are sinking.

CHORUS MEN
Hear the roar of their gun!

CASSIO
'Tis the ship of Otello.

MONTANO
It is gone now. All is over.

CASSIO
. . . and again it rises skyward.

CHORUS TENORS
Deep in mist we can see it no more.

CHORUS MEN
Here in lightning emerges its prow.
Roaring, howling, crashing fury of a world in agony!

CHORUS TENORS
Crashing breakers . . .

CHORUS BASSES
. . . roaring thunder . . .

CHORUS TENORS
. . . battle of the elements . . .

CHORUS BASSES
. . . and in blind, demented anger
Satan throws his thunderbolts
As he fights with savage fury heaven's starry light.

CHORUS MEN
Through the foam and froth and fire

ALCUNI DEL CORO
Una vela!

ALTRI DEL CORO
Una vela!

IL PRIMO GRUPPO
Un vessillo!

IL SECONDO GRUPPO
Un vessillo!

MONTANO
È l'alato Leon!

CASSIO
Or la folgor lo svela.

ALCUNI
Uno squillo!

ALTRI
Uno squillo!

TUTTI
Ha tuonato il cannon!

CASSIO
È la nave del Duce.

MONTANO
Or s'affonda.
Or s'inciela . . .

CASSIO
Erge il rostro dall'onda.

METÀ DEL CORO
Nelle nubi si cela e nel mar.
E alla luce dei lampi ne appar.

TUTTI
Lampi! tuoni! gorghi! turbi
tempestosi e fulmini!
Treman l'onde, treman l'aure,
treman basi e culmini.
Fende l'etra un torvo e cieco—
spirto di vertigine,
Iddio scuote il cielo bieco,—
come un tetro vel.
Tutto è fumo! tutto è fuoco!
l'orrida caligine
Si fa incendio, poi si spegne
più funesta, spasima
L'universo, accorre a valchi—
l'aquilon fantasima,
I titanici orcalchi—squillano nel
ciel.

Wild, infernal ghosts appear, come up from hell
To scourge the world which lies in terror.
Is this the Day of Judgment?
Is this the day on which the world will crumble,
When with clarion calls from heaven
All will come to end?

(a large group of women have assembled among the men. Everyone shows signs of great anxiety, and as the storm reaches its height, many raise their arms in supplication)

TUTTI
Dio, fulgor della bufera!
Dio, sorriso della duna!
Salva l'arca e la bandiera
Della veneta fortuna!
Tu, che reggi gli astri e il Fato!
Tu, che imperi al mondo e al ciel!
Fa che in fondo al mar placato
Posi l'àncora fedel.

ENTIRE CHORUS
Lord, in lightning and in thunder
See us here as we implore Thee:
Do not rend the world asunder
As Thy children pray before Thee!
Let Thine angels stand beside him,
Safely lead the ship to shore!
Let Thy boundless mercy guide him
As Thou always didst before!

JAGO
È infranto l'artimon!

IAGO
The mast has crashed on deck.

RODERIGO
Il rostro piomba
Su quello scoglio!

RODERIGO
The ship is lost and nothing can save it.

CORO
Aita! Aita!

CHORUS
Almighty, oh help him!

JAGO
(L'alvo
Frenetico del mar sia la sua tomba!)

IAGO *(aside)*
And so Otello will go down and all is ended.

CORO
È salvo! è salvo!

CHORUS
They're safe now. Oh wonder!

VOCI INTERNE
Gittate i palischermi!
Mano alle funi! Fermi!

VOICES OFF-STAGE
Oh hurry to the rescue! All hands are needed. Quickly!

PRIMA PARTE DEL CORO
Forza ai remi!

CHORUS TENORS
Come, let's help them!

SECONDA PARTE
Alla riva! . . .

CHORUS BASSES
Yes, let's help them!

VOCI INTERNE
All'approdo! allo sbarco!

VOICES OFF-STAGE
To the harbor, come, hurry!
They've landed.

CORO
Evviva! Evviva!

ENTIRE CHORUS
Thank heaven!

(OTELLO, followed by sailors and soldiers, appears on the balustrade)

OTELLO
Esultate! L'orgoglio musulmano
Sepolto è in mar, nostra e del ciel è gloria!
Dopo l'armi lo vinse l'uragano.

OTELLO
Rise in glory! At last the Moslem found his deserved reward:
Deep in the ocean's darkness lies his pride,
Drowned in blood now and forever.

CORO
Evviva Otello! Vittoria! Vittoria!!

CHORUS
Long live Otello! Otello!

(OTELLO *enters the castle, followed by* CASSIO, MONTANO, *and the soldiers*)
We honor our leader, our savior, Otello.
Defeated, deleted, disgraced and debased
On the deep of the ocean floor!
The crashing of thunder, the howling of tempests,
The roaring of breakers will sing them to sleep
In the abyss so terrible, so frightful and horrible
Deep under the sea.
At last the storm is over.

IAGO (*aside to* RODERIGO)
Roderigo, speak out, what is it?

RODERIGO
Let me perish!

IAGO
Fool who wants to perish for the love of woman!

RODERIGO
There is no way . . .
(*people are moving to and fro, carrying weapons, bundles, etc. Some of them are busy piling up wood for a fire. Gradually the crowd gathers around them*)

IAGO
Be wise, have patience, await the propitious moment!
For Desdemona's beauty, the secret cause of all your
Sleepless torment, will not always be ravished by
Embraces and brutal kisses of that savage monster.
Gallant Roderigo, you know how much my soul suffers at your sorrow.
Let me find a way to alleviate your heart!
For woman's love and her sacred vow are frail indeed
When faced with the cunning brain of a man like Iago.
Soon you will hold the lady as your mistress!
Now listen: Though I feign to be loyal I hate Otello.
(CASSIO *enters and joins a group of soldiers*)
One reason for my hatred . . . there it is! (*indicating* CASSIO)
Listen: This overbearing little captain
Took from me what is mine: my rank,
A rank for which I risked my life
In a hundred brutal encounters.
This is Otello's justice.
I stay the humble footman of my Moorish master, oh glory!
(*billows of smoke start to rise from the pile of wood*)
But mark my word, for what I say is this:
Were I Otello I should hate to suffer
So close to me a man whose name is Iago!
That's why I tell you . . .
(IAGO *leads* RODERIGO *toward the rear. The woodpile*

Vittoria! Sterminio!
Dispersi, distrutti,
Sepolti nell'orrido
Tumulto piombâr.
Avranno per *requie*
La sferza dei flutti,
La ridda dei turbini,
L'abisso del mar.
Si calma la bufera.

JAGO
(Roderigo,
Ebben, che pensi?)

RODERIGO
D'affogarmi . . .

JAGO
Stolto
È chi s'affoga per amor di donna.

RODERIGO
Vincer nol so.

JAGO
Suvvia, fa senno, aspetta
L'opra del tempo. A Desdemona bella,
Che nel segreto dei tuoi sogni adori,
Presto in uggia verranno i foschi baci
Di quel selvaggio dalle gonfie labbra.
Buon Roderigo, amico tuo sincero
Mi ti professo, nè in più forte ambascia
Soccorrerti potrei. Se un fragil voto
Di femmina non è tropp'arduo nodo
Pel genio mio nè per l'inferno, giuro
Che quella donna sarà tua. M'ascolta:
Benchè finga d'amarlo, odio quel Moro . . .
. . . È una cagion dell'ira, eccola, guarda.
Quell'azzimato capitano usurpa
Il grado mio, il grado mio che in cento
Ben pugnate battaglie ho meritato;
Tal fu il voler d'Otello, ed io rimango
Di sua Moresca signoria l'alfiere!
Ma, com'è ver che tu Roderigo sei,

Così è pur vero che se il Moro io fossi
Vedermi non vorrei d'attorno un Jago.
Se tu m'ascolti . . .

is burning brightly. The soldiers gather around the tables in the tavern. Waiters are decorating the arbor with multicolored lamps, pouring wine, rushing to and fro)

CORO

Fuoco di gioia! - l'ilare vampa
Fuga la notte - col suo splendor,
Guizza, sfavilla, - crepita, avvampa,
Fulgido incendio - che invade il cor.
Dal raggio attratti - vaghi sembianti
Movono intorno - mutando stuol.
E son fanciulle - dai lieti canti,
E son farfalle - dall'igneo vol.
Arde la palma - col sicomoro,
Canta la sposa - col suo fedel;
Sull'aurea fiamma, - sul lieto coro
Soffia l'ardente - spiro del ciel.
Fuoco di gioia - rapido brilla!
Rapido passa - fuoco d'amor!
Splende, s'oscura, - palpita, oscilla,
L'ultimo guizzo - lampeggia e muor.

CHORUS

Flame of our triumph, flick'ring and dancing,
Turning the night into radiance of day,
Sizzle and crackle, merrily prancing,
Filling our hearts with your splendor so gay.
Vaguely arising out of the darkness,
Hov'ring around us visions so fair,
Could they be maidens so nimbly fleeting,
Could they be goblins dancing on air?
Blazing so brightly, burning so sprightly,
Sing of my passion, sing of my love,
You that caress me, kissing me lightly,
Oh take me with you to heaven above!
See now the glimmer rapidly sinking!
Love's tender spark will be lost in the skies.
Quickly now failing, quivering and blinking,
Only a sparklet lights up and dies.

(the fire gradually dies out. The storm has ceased. IAGO, RODERIGO, *and* CASSIO *are seen in the company of several soldiers, around a table where wine is being served)*

JAGO

Roderigo, beviam! qua la tazza, Capitano.

CASSIO

Non bevo più.

JAGO

Ingoia
Questo sorso.

CASSIO

No.

JAGO

Guarda! oggi impazza
Tutta Cipro! è una notte di gioia,
Dunque . . .

CASSIO

Cessa. Già m'arde il cervello
Per un nappo vuotato.

JAGO

Sì, ancora
Bever devi. Alle nozze d'Otello
E Desdemona!

TUTTI

Evviva!

CASSIO

Essa infiora
Questo lido.

JAGO

(Lo ascolta.)

IAGO

Now, Roderigo, let's drink! Will you join us, Captain Cassio?

CASSIO

I drink no more.

IAGO *(offering more wine to* CASSIO*)*

Tonight you can't refuse it.

CASSIO *(withdrawing his goblet)*

No.

IAGO

Captain, 'tis a night we shall remember,
And all Cyprus is feasting. Therefore . . .

CASSIO

Leave me! For already now my eyes behold you but vaguely.

IAGO

Yet tonight you shall not rue it.
To Otello's beloved, to Desdemona!

EVERYONE *(lifting their goblets in a toast)*

The lady!

CASSIO *(taking a sip from his goblet)*

She's the blossom of this island . . .

IAGO *(aside to* RODERIGO*)*

You hear him?

CASSIO
. . . whose soft and radiant smile
Warms the heart of her people.

RODERIGO
Yet she's modest and virtuous.

CASSIO
You, Iago, sing a song to exalt her!

IAGO (*aside to* RODERIGO)
You hear him?
(*aloud to* CASSIO)
I am not good at poetry.

CASSIO
'Tis true, no song could ever do her justice.

IAGO (*aside to* RODERIGO)
Be careful of this Cassio!

RODERIGO (*aside to* IAGO)
Why careful?

IAGO
His poetic raves give away what he feels.
Hot and loquacious is his youthful entrancement.
A notorious seducer, he'd know how to cheat you. Watch him!

RODERIGO
Good Lord!

IAGO
There is one way to trick him: Make him drunk!
(*to the waiters*)
Hey, you rascals, bring wine!
(IAGO *fills three goblets:* CASSIO'S, RODERIGO'S, *and his own. Then he addresses* CASSIO *while more and more soldiers turn to them and watch them*)
Come here, my dear old friend,
Twinkle and sparkle!
Drown in your crimson blood
Life's every pain!

CASSIO (*to* IAGO, *goblet in hand*)
Drown in your noble flood
What makes us waver!
Bring sadness and care to end,
Let freedom reign!

IAGO (*to everyone*)
For every sorrow has found a cure,
Yes, a cure so sure! So drink it away!

CHORUS
For every sorrow has found a cure,
Yes, a cure so sure. So keep on drinking! Drink it away!

CASSIO
Col vago
Suo raggiar chiama i cori a raccolta.

RODERIGO
Pur modesta essa è tanto.

CASSIO
Tu, Jago,
Canterai le sue lodi!

JAGO
(Lo ascolta.)
Io non sono che un critico.

CASSIO
Ed ella
D'ogni lode è più bella.

JAGO
(Ti guarda
Da quel Cassio.)

RODERIGO
(Che temi?)

JAGO
Ei favella
Già con troppo bollor, la gagliarda
Giovinezza lo sprona; è un astuto
Seduttor che t'ingombra il cammino.
Bada . . .

RODERIGO
Ebben?

JAGO
S'ei s'inebria è perduto!
Fallo ber.
Qua, ragazzi, del vino!
Inaffia l'ugola!
Trinca, tracanna!
Prima che svampino
Canto e bicchier!

CASSIO
Questa del pampino
Verace manna
Di vaghe annugola
Nebbie il pensier.

JAGO
Chi all'esca ha morso
Del ditirambo
Spavaldo e strambo
Beva con me.

CORO
Chi all'esca ha morso
Del ditirambo
Spavaldo e strambo
Beve con te.

JAGO
(Un altro sorso
E brillo egli è.)
RODERIGO
(Un altro sorso
E brillo egli è.)
JAGO
Il mondo palpita
Quand'io son brillo!
Sfido l'ironico
Nume e il destin!

CASSIO
Come un armonico
Lïuto oscillo;
La gioia scalpita
Sul mio cammin!

JAGO
Chi all'esca ha morso
Del ditirambo
Spavaldo e strambo
Beva con me!
TUTTI
Chi all'esca ha morso
Del ditirambo
Spavaldo e strambo
Beve con te.

JAGO
(Un altro sorso
E brillo egli è.)
RODERIGO
(Un altro sorso
E brillo egli è.)
JAGO
Fuggan dal vivido
Nappo i codardi
Che in cor nascondono frodi.
Chi all'escaha mor . . .
Del ditiramb . . . bevi con me.
CASSIO
In fondo all'anima
Ciascun mi guardi!
Non temo il ver . . .
Non temo il ver . . . bevo . . .
Del calice
Gli orli s'imporporino! . . .

JAGO
(Egli è briaco fradicio. Ti scuoti.
Lo trascina a contesa; è pronto all'ira,
T'offenderà . . . ne seguirà tumulto!
Pensa che puoi così del lieto Otello!
Turbar la prima vigilia d'amor!)
RODERIGO
(Ed è ciò che mi spinge.)

MONTANO
Capitano,
V'attende la fazione ai baluardi.

IAGO (*aside to* RODERIGO)
Watch him and see his mind go blank!
RODERIGO (*aside to* IAGO)
Yes, I can see his mind go blank.
IAGO (*aloud*)
Let's praise the god of wine,
Sing him hosannah!
Let wine alone be god!
Live for today!
CASSIO (*drinking copiously*)
Vainly I try to keep my lips away
From the cup of joy divine,
So light and gay.
IAGO (*to everyone*)
For every sorrow has found a cure,
Yes, a cure so sure. So drink it away!

CHORUS
For every sorrow has found a cure,
Yes, a cure so sure. Keep on drinking!
Drink it away!
IAGO (*aside to* RODERIGO)
Watch him and see his mind go blank!
RODERIGO
Yes, I can see his mind go blank.
IAGO (*to everyone*)
Drinking reveals our innermost scheming.
Beware if your heart has secrets.
Go on! Keep on! Drinking away. Let's drink!

CASSIO (*raising his glass*)
Let everyone know what I am dreaming,
Never I fear the light of day.
Come on, let's drink . . . oh flood of joy . . .
Drinking . . . come on . . . keep drinking, friends!
(*reeling*)
IAGO (*aside to* RODERIGO)
Now is the time to work on him.
Go closer to him and provoke him.
Go, make him furious! He will offend you . . .
There will be a scandal.
Think of how sweet a wedding night
Otello will spend while mutiny threatens the palace!

RODERIGO (*resolutely*)
You're right. I must do it.
(MONTANO *enters and addresses* CASSIO)
MONTANO
Captain Cassio, the time has come for you to go on duty.

CASSIO (*unsteadily*)
Let's go then!

MONTANO
Great heavens!

IAGO (*to* MONTANO)
'Tis the way our dear Cassio
Likes to begin his night watch.

MONTANO
I'll tell Otello.

CASSIO
Come on, we must be going!

RODERIGO, then OTHERS
Ha, ha!

CASSIO
Who's laughing?

RODERIGO (*provoking him*)
How could you notice?

CASSIO (*attacking* RODERIGO)
Watch what you are saying, you idiot!

RODERIGO (*defending himself*)
I loathe you, you drunkard.

CASSIO
You scoundrel, you'll live to regret this.

MONTANO (*trying to separate the two, addressing* CASSIO)
Good friends, what has happened? Let go, I beseech you!

CASSIO (*to* MONTANO)
Keep out of this fight
Or your brain will be splattered!

MONTANO
You're drunk, come to reason!

CASSIO
I'll show you.
(CASSIO *draws his sword,* MONTANO *does likewise. They fight. The crowd retreats before them*)

IAGO (*aside to* RODERIGO, *hastily*)
Roderigo, go down to the harbor
And spread it around: A riot! A riot! Go!
Shout it all over the town,
And the bells, have them ring in the tower!
(RODERIGO *runs off.* IAGO *turns to the two men fighting*)
My comrades, enough of this foolish commotion!

CHORUS WOMEN (*while fleeing the scene*)
Away!

IAGO
See, the valiant Montano is bleeding! Oh terrible fury!

WOMEN
Away!

IAGO
Stop it!

CASSIO
Andiamo!

MONTANO
Che vedo?

JAGO
Ogni notte in tal guisa
Cassio preludia al sonno.

MONTANO
Otello il sappia.

CASSIO
Andiamo ai baluardi . . .

RODERIGO POI TUTTI
Ah! Ah!

CASSIO
Chi ride?

RODERIGO
Rido d'un ebro . . .

CASSIO
Bada alle tue spalle!
Furfante!

RODERIGO
Briaco ribaldo!

CASSIO
Marrano!
Nessun più ti salva

MONTANO
Frenate la mano,
Signor, ve ne prego.

CASSIO
Ti spacco il cerèbro
Se qui t'interponi.

MONTANO
Parole d'un ebro . . .

CASSIO
D'un ebro?!

JAGO
(Va al porto, con quanta più possa
Ti resta, gridando: sommossa! sommossa!
Va! spargi il tumulto, l'orror. Le campane
Risuonino a stormo.)
Fratelli! l'immane
Conflitto cessate!

MOLTE DONNE DEL CORO
Fuggiam!

JAGO
Ciel! già gronda
Di sangue Montano! Tenzon furibonda!

ALTRE DONNE
Fuggiam!

JAGO
Tregua!

TUTTI
Tregua!

DONNE
S'uccidono!

UOMINI
Pace!

JAGO
Nessun più raffrena quel nembo pugnace!
Si gridi l'allarme! Satana gl'invade!!

VOCI
All'armi!!

TUTTI
Soccorso!!

CHORUS
Stop it!

WOMEN (*in flight*)
'Tis desperate.

MEN (*to the two fighters*)
Hear us!

IAGO (*to the onlookers*)
Can no one prevent this preposterous slaughter?
Go, run for assistance!
The bells set a-ringing!

VOICES OFF-STAGE
Oh help us! Come quickly!

CHORUS
Oh help us!

Scene 2

OTELLO, IAGO, CASSIO, MONTANO. *People and soldiers. later* DESDEMONA. OTELLO *enters, followed by torch-bearers.)*

OTELLO
Abbasso le spade!
Olà! che avvien? son io fra i Saraceni?
O la turchesca rabbia è in voi trasfusa
Da sbranarvi l'un l'altro? . . . Onesto Jago,
Per quell'amor che tu mi porti, parla.

OTELLO
Ho, down with your weapons!
(*the fight stops.* MONTANO *leans on a soldier. The clouds are gradually lifting.*)
You two, speak out! Am I amongst barbarians
Or are you Turks in senseless, savage fury,
With your fangs in each other?
My trusted Iago, on your devotion I command you: Tell me!

JAGO
Non so . . . qui tutti eran cortesi amici,
Dianzi, e giocondi . . . ma ad un tratto, come
Se un pianeta maligno avesse a quelli
Smagato il senno, sguainando l'arme
S'avventano furenti . . . avess'io prima
Stroncati i pie' che qui m'addusser!

IAGO
I'm stunned. One moment, happy and gay companions,
Both were together. All at once, as though some madness
Had overcome them, some fatal illness brought on by Satan,
They drew their weapons and locked in brutal combat.
I should have rather both my feet cut off
Than be a witness.

OTELLO
Cassio,
Come obliasti te stesso a tal segno? . . .

OTELLO
Cassio, how could you so disgrace your position?

CASSIO
Grazia . . . perdon . . . parlar non so . . .

CASSIO
Pardon . . . forgive me . . . I can . . . not speak.

OTELLO
Montano . . .

OTELLO
Montano . . .

MONTANO
Son ferito . . .

MONTANO (*supported by a soldier*)
I am wounded.

OTELLO
You, wounded? By heaven, my blood begins to boil.
Ah, but my anger ebbs into nothingness before my angel!
(DESDEMONA *enters.* OTELLO *approaches her.*)
Here, see the lovely Desdemona, aroused from her dreams
By you and your commotion.
Cassio, you're no longer my captain.
(CASSIO *drops his sword.* IAGO *picks it up and hands it to an officer*)

OTELLO
Ferito! . . . pel cielo
Già il sangue mio ribolle. Ah! l'ira volge
L'angelo nostro tutelare in fuga!
Che? . . . la mia dolce Desdemona anch'essa
Per voi distolta da' suoi sogni? - Cassio,
Non sei più capitano.

IAGO (*aside*)
At last I triumph.

JAGO
(Oh! mio trionfo!)

OTELLO
Iago, there's unrest still around. So go now.
Restore the peace and bid the town be quiet!
(IAGO *exits*)
Dress the wounds of Montano!
(MONTANO *is led off into the castle.*)
(*to all the others, with great authority*)
Let everyone go to rest at last.
I alone shall stay here till I know
That peace reigns again all around me.
(*everyone leaves except* OTELLO *and* DESDEMONA)

OTELLO
Jago, tu va nella città sgomenta
Con quella squadra a ricompor la pace.
Si soccorra Montano.
Al proprio tetto
Ritorni ognun.
Io da qui non mi parto
Se pria non vedo deserti gli spalti.

Scene 3

(OTELLO *and* DESDEMONA)

OTELLO
Fragrant in silent splendor,
Without the faintest sound
Night in her arms so tender
Brings peace to every heart and calm surrender.
Thunder and war may rend the world asunder
And yet, our love, oh wonder!
Will be in glory crowned.

OTELLO
Già nella notte densa
S'estingue ogni clamor.
Già il mio cor fremebondo
S'ammansa in quest'amplesso e si rinsensa.
Tuoni la guerra e s'inabissi il mondo
Se dopo l'ira immensa
Vien quest'immenso amor!

DESDEMONA
Oh, my warrior so proud! Mem'ries of sorrow,
Of despair and of sadness slowly give way
To rising hope of a radiant life tomorrow.
Ah, it is sweet to whisper in your slumber:
Do you remember?
When first we met I often heard you speaking
Of wondrous adventures, war, and stormy seas.
My heart in rapture silently was seeking
A way to tell you: My love will never cease.

DESDEMONA
Mio superbo guerrier! quanti tormenti,
Quanti mesti sospiri e quanta speme
Ci condusse ai soavi abbracciamenti!
Oh! com'è dolce il mormorare insieme:
Te ne rammenti!
Quando narravi l'esule tua vita
E i fieri eventi e i lunghi tuoi dolor,
Ed io t'udia coll'anima rapita
In quei spaventi e coll'estasi in cor.

OTELLO
I told you of my destiny, of battles

OTELLO
Pingea dell'armi il fremito, la pugna

E il vol gagliardo alla breccia mortal,
L'assalto, orribil edera, coll'ugna
Al baluardo e il sibilante stral.

DESDEMONA
Poi mi guidavi ai fulgidi deserti,
All'arse arene, al tuo materno suol;
Narravi allor gli spasimi sofferti
E le catene e dello schiavo il duol.

OTELLO
Ingentilìa di lagrime la storia
Il tuo bel viso e il labbro di sospir;
Scendean sulle mie tenebre la gloria,
Il paradiso e gli astri a benedir.

DESDEMONA
Ed io vedea fra le tue tempie oscure
Splender del genio l'eterea beltà.

OTELLO
E tu m'amavi per le mie sventure
Ed io t'amavo per la tua pietà.

DESDEMONA
Ed io t'amavo per le tue sventure
E tu m'amavi per la mia pietà.

OTELLO
Venga la morte! e mi colga nell'estasi
Di quest'amplesso
Il momento supremo!
Tale è il gaudio dell'anima che temo,
Temo che più non mi sarà concesso
Quest'attimo divino
Nell'ignoto avvenir del mio destino.

DESDEMONA
Disperda il ciel gli affanni
E Amor non muti col mutar degli anni.

OTELLO
A questa tua preghiera
Amen risponda la celeste schiera.

DESDEMONA
Amen risponda.

OTELLO
Ah! la gioia m'innonda
Sì fieramente . . . che ansante mi giacio
Un bacio . . .

DESDEMONA
Otello! . . .

Where valiant warriors laugh at death they defy,
Of slaughter and final victory, of soldiers marching onward
To conquer or to die.

DESDEMONA
Then you would guide me far across the ocean,
There, where the sun will forever kiss the sand,
Where in despair, for want of cooling potion,
Men die forgotten far in a distant land.

OTELLO
Your heart was torn in sorrow, and the tears
Of bitter weeping like pearls would fill your eyes.
Like diamonds they would fall on me, like brilliant rays
From heaven, out of the starlit skies.

DESDEMONA
And I would notice in your mien so tender
Burning a fire that shone so deep and true.

OTELLO
Truly you loved me for my life's dark splendor.
For your compassion I did worship you.

DESDEMONA
Truly I loved you for your life's dark splendor
And my compassion made you love me, too.

OTELLO
Were I to die now! No delight up in paradise
Is so divine as this hour of enchantment.
(*the sky has cleared now. The stars start shining brightly, and moonlight is gradually flooding the scene*)
Yet, so great is my joy, so full my heart
That fate can no longer hold an earthly promise.
In darkness lies enshrouded
What the Lord will bestow upon Otello.

DESDEMONA
I vowed before the altar:
Our love shall ever grow and never falter.

OTELLO
The angels sing beside you:
Amen! they're chanting, smiling as they guide you.

DESDEMONA
Amen! they're chanting.

OTELLO (*leaning against the parapet*)
Ah! My heart is in turmoil, beating in frenzy . . .
I cannot endure it! To kiss you . . .

DESDEMONA
Otello!

OTELLO

. . . to kiss you . . . once more to kiss you.

(*rising, with a look at the starlit sky*)

See, the stars soon will kiss the silv'ry ocean!

DESDEMONA

Late is the night.

OTELLO

Come! Venus shall guide us!

(*embracing each other, they slowly walk toward the castle*)

DESDEMONA

Otello!

OTELLO

Un bacio . . . ancora un bacio.
Già la pleiade ardente in mar discende.

DESDEMONA

Tarda è la notte.

OTELLO

Vien . . . Venere splende.

DESDEMONA

Otello!

ACT II

(A hall on the ground floor of the castle. Two colonnades, one on each side, through which we look out into the garden.)

Scene 1

(IAGO *inside the hall.* CASSIO *across from him, at a bay window.*)

JAGO
Non ti crucciar. Se credi a me, tra poco
Farai ritorno ai folleggianti amori
Di Monna Bianca, altiero capitano,
Coll'elsa d'oro e col balteo fregiato.

IAGO
There is no doubt. I am quite sure in less than a week you will kiss her again, your sweet little love, Bianca; and, even more important, you will be Captain of the Guard of Honor.

CASSIO
Non lusingarmi . . .

CASSIO
You must be joking.

JAGO
Attendi a ciò ch'io dico.
Tu dêi saper che Desdemona è il Duce
Del nostro Duce, sol per essa ei vive.
Pregala tu, quell'anima cortese
Per te interceda e il tuo perdono è certo.

IAGO
Now hear what I shall tell you:
As you must know, Desdemona is mistress of our master,
Her wish is his command. Go, speak to her,
Arouse her noble soul and her woman's compassion,
And she will speak to him.

CASSIO
Ma come favellarle?

CASSIO
But how can I approach her?

JAGO
È suo costume
Girsene a meriggiar fra quelle fronde
Colla consorte mia. Quivi l'aspetta.
Or t'è aperta la via di salvazione;
Vanne.

IAGO
Daily at noontime, there, underneath the trees
She and my wife enjoy resting in the shadows.
There you shall meet her, and all your
Sorrow shall be relieved at once. Go on!
(CASSIO *exits*)

Scene 2

(IAGO *alone, following* CASSIO *with his eyes*)

JAGO
Vanne; la tua meta già vedo.
Ti spinge il tuo dimone,
E il tuo dimon son io.
E me trascina il mio, nel quale io credo
Inesorato Iddio.
– Credo in un Dio crudel che m'ha creato
Simile a sè, e che nell'ira io nomo.
– Dalla viltà d'un germe o d'un atòmo
Vile son nato.
—Son scellerato
Perchè son uomo;

IAGO
Go on! Well I know what will follow,
For you are but a puppet, a babbling tool of mischief.
Your fiendish guide am I,
And I myself am but a servant of Evil.
(*leaving the colonnade and paying no longer any attention to* CASSIO, *who has gone out of sight*)
Yes, I believe that I was made the image of someone on high,
Someone himself a monster.
Foul is the seed I come from,
Filthy and rotten is all that's in me.

He is eternal and is infernal,
And I must go my evil path with him.
Yes, this is Iago's creed:
Firmly I do believe that I am but an obedient tool
Of my demon's will.
My vile intent must never cease nor weaken
Till it has reached its goal.
They speak of justice and do not know
That all these noble words are but lies,
A figment of delusion: fairness, friendship, honor . . .
All is nonsense and rot!
Here is my faith:
We are but fools of fortune, of blind and senseless fortune,
Our life's a stupid farce.
Death in the end will pull the final curtain.
And then? And then there's nothing!
'Tis all a monstrous lie!

E sento il fango originario in me.
— Sì! quest'è la mia fe'!
— Credo con fermo cuor, siccome crede
La vedovella al tempio,
Che il mal ch'io penso e che da me procede
Per mio destino adempio.
— Credo che il giusto è un istrïon beffardo
E nel viso e nel cuor,
Che tutto è in lui bugiardo:
Lagrima, bacio, sguardo,
Sacrificio ed onor.
— E credo l'uom gioco d'iniqua sorte
Dal germe della culla
Al verme dell'avel.
— Vien dopo tanta irrisïon la Morte.
— E poi? - La Morte è il Nulla.
È vecchia fola il Ciel.

(*in the garden* DESDEMONA *and* EMILIA *are seen entering from the left.* IAGO *quickly moves to the colonnade in order to observe them and* CASSIO, *who is waiting for them*)
(*to* CASSIO)
Here she is! Cassio, go on!
This is the moment . . . but hurry!
Here's Desdemona.
(CASSIO *approaches the ladies, greeting them courteously*)
(*to himself*)
He's near her . . . and he greets her.
Now she steps closer. Now I must fetch Otello.
My demon down in hell, oh lend me your assistance!
What a friendly encounter!
Her lovely face is close to his and she is smiling.
One single ray of such a charming smile will do
To warp the great Otello's heart forever. To work!
(*walks rapidly toward the right, but stops suddenly*)
Already I perceive good fortune: Here he is!
(*sarcastically*)
My master, I serve you.
(*he stands motionless at the window and observes* CASSIO *and* DESDEMONA)

Eccola . . . - Cassio . . . a te.
. . . Questo è il momento.
Ti scuoti . . . vien Desdemona.
S'è mosso; la saluta
E s'avvicina.
Or qui si tragga Otello! . . . aiuta, aiuta
Satana il mio cimento! . . .
Già conversano insieme . . . ed essa inclina,
Sorridendo, il bel viso.
Mi basta un lampo sol di quel sorriso
Per trascinare Otello alla ruina.
Andiam . . .
Ma il caso in mio favor s'adopra.
Eccolo . . . al posto, all'opra.

Scene 3

(IAGO *and* OTELLO)
(OTELLO *enters.* IAGO *mutters to himself, pretending to be unaware of* OTELLO*'s presence.*)

JAGO
Ciò m'accora . . .

OTELLO
Che parli?

JAGO
Nulla . . . voi qui? una vana
Voce m'uscì dal labbro . . .

OTELLO
Colui che s'allontana
Dalla mia sposa, è Cassio?

JAGO
Cassio? no . . . quei si scosse
Come un reo nel vedervi.

OTELLO
Credo che Cassio ei fosse.

JAGO
Mio signore . . .

OTELLO
Che brami? . . .

JAGO
Cassio, nei primi dì
Del vostro amor, Desdemona
non conosceva?

OTELLO
Sì.
Perchè fai tale inchiesta?

JAGO
Il mio pensiero è vago
D'ubbìe, non di malizia.

OTELLO
Di' il tuo pensiero, Jago.

JAGO
Vi confidaste a Cassio?

OTELLO
Spesso un mio dono o un cenno
Portava alla mia sposa.

JAGO
Dassenno?

OTELLO
Sì, dassenno.
Nol credi onesto?

JAGO
Onesto?

OTELLO
Che ascondi nel tuo cuore?

JAGO
Che ascondo in cor, signore?

OTELLO
«Che ascondo in cor, signore?»
Pel cielo! tu sei l'eco dei detti
miei; nel chiostro
Dell'anima ricetti qualche
terribil mostro.
Sì, ben t'udii poc'anzi mor-
morar: *ciò m'accora.*
Ma di che t'accoravi? nomini
Cassio e allora

IAGO
Makes one wonder!

OTELLO
What is it?

IAGO
Nothing. You here? Just a chance remark without rhyme or reason . . .

OTELLO
Who was it who just left my noble lady? Was it Cassio?

IAGO
Cassio? No. Why should Cassio sneak away when he sees you?

OTELLO
I still believe 'twas Cassio.

IAGO
Sir, forgive me . . .

OTELLO
What is it?

IAGO
Cassio . . . do you remember if he knew Desdemona
Ere you had loved her?

OTELLO
Yes . . . but I don't understand you.

IAGO
'Tis just an idle thought of this moment . . .
Nothing important.

OTELLO
Why did you ask this question?

IAGO
. . . and did you trust in Cassio?

OTELLO
He was the go-between in the early days of our courtship.

IAGO
You're certain?

OTELLO
Yes, I am certain. Is he dishonest?

IAGO
Dishonest?

OTELLO
Why did you ask that question?

IAGO
Forgive me my suggestion!

OTELLO
'Forgive me my suggestion!'
May heaven know the purpose of your mocking me!
Your heart in its deep and somber vault
Entombs a terrible, frightful secret.
Yes, I remember what you said in whisp'ring:
'Makes one wonder.' Tell me then, what made you wonder?

You spoke of Cassio and then I saw your brow get furrowed.
Speak out then, if you are loyal!

Tu corrughi la fronte. Suvvia, parla se m'ami.

IAGO
Do not doubt that I am loyal!

JAGO
Voi sapete ch'io v'amo.

OTELLO
This is why I command you: Tell me all that you're thinking!
Let me read in your soul, reveal me your innermost heart,
Your darkest, most dreadful suspicion!

OTELLO
Dunque senza velami
T'esprimi e senza ambagi. T'esca fuor dalla gola
Il tuo più rio pensiero colla più ria parola!

IAGO
Even with all my devotion, all my love for Otello,
This I cannot.

JAGO
S'anco teneste in mano tutta l'anima mia
Nol sapreste.

OTELLO
Ha!

OTELLO
Ah!

IAGO
(*sidling up close to* OTELLO, *whispering to him*)
Allow me to warn you of a demon:
It is the demon Jealousy . . .
Jealousy, drinking the blood of its wretched victim,
Sinking its poisonous fang till it has killed its prey.

JAGO
Temete, signor, la gelosia!
È un'idra fosca, livida, cieca, col suo veleno
Sè stessa attosca, vivida piaga le squarcia il seno.

OTELLO
Oh Lord in heaven!
No! I shall not be a prey to suspicion.
Ere I doubt I shall verify. After that I want proof.
And when I have it—for this is the essence of justice—
Away at once with jealousy and love together!

OTELLO
Miseria mia!! No, il vano sospettar nulla giova.
Pria del dubbio l'indagine, dopo il dubbio la prova,
Dopo la prova (Otello ha sue leggi supreme),
Amore e gelosia vadan dispersi insieme!

IAGO (*with a degree of insolence*)
A noble word, My Lord, which breaks the silence of my lips.
I do not speak of proof yet . . .
But, my noble lord and master, be on guard now.
Too often are free and trusting natures like yours
Abused by falsehood and deception. Watch her closely!
Observe her well with Cassio. One unguarded word,
One gesture perhaps will prove her guiltless . . .
Or confirm your suspicion. Here she is. Watch her closely!
(DESDEMONA *reappears in the garden, surrounded by women, children, Cypriot fishermen who in turn offer her flowers and gifts. Some of them accompany their song on the guitar or other instruments*)

JAGO
Un tal proposto spezza di mie labbra il suggello.
Non parlo ancor di prova; pur, generoso Otello,
Vigilate; soventi le oneste e ben create
Coscienze non sospettano la frode: vigilate.
Scrutate le parole di Desdemona, un detto
Può ricondur la fede, può affermare il sospetto . . .
Eccola; vigilate . . .

CHORUS (*in the garden*)
Pure and radiant out of the sky,
Like sunshine smiling, shines on us your heavenly eye,
Oh, so beguiling.
Fair as roses in the lovely time of spring,
Your smile has called us here
To praise you and to sing.

CORO
Dove guardi splendono
Raggi, avvampan cuori;
Dove passi scendono
Nuvole di fiori.
Qui fra gigli e rose
Come a un casto altare
Padri, bimbi, spose
Vengono a cantar.

CHILDREN (*strewing lilies before* DESDEMONA)
We bring you lilies so fair and white.

FANCIULLI
T'offriamo il giglio,
Soave stel

Che in man degli angeli
Fu assunto in ciel,
Che abbella il fulgido
Manto e la gonna
Della Madonna
E il santo vel.

The angels on high have brought them down last night.
Our Lady has kissed them
And gently did bless them.
You now caress them and bathe in their light.

DONNE E MARINAI
Mentre all'aura vola
Lieta la canzon,
L'agile mandòla
Ne accompagna il suon.

WOMEN AND FISHERMEN
Gently strum the mandolin
And sing a song of praise
While the zephyr's lazy breezes
Spin in sunshine's golden rays.

MARINAI
A te le porpore,
Le perle e gli ostri,
Nella voragine
Côlti del mar.
Vogliam Desdemona
Coi doni nostri
Come un'immagine
Sacra adornar.

FISHERMEN (*offering* DESDEMONA *jewelry made of coral and pearls*)
Oh smile upon our offering
From ocean's secret treasure!
Proudly we are proffering
Our homage from the sea.
Let us crown Desdemona
In gay delight and pleasure,
Like the Virgin whom we all
Revere on bended knee.

FANCIULLI, DONNE
Mentre all'aura vola
Lieta la canzon,
L'agile mandòla
Ne accompagna il suon.

CHILDREN AND WOMEN
Gently strum the mandolin
And sing a song of praise
While the zephyr's lazy breezes
Spin in sunshine's golden rays.

LE DONNE
A te la florida
Messe dai grembi
Spargiam, spargiam al suolo,
A nembi, a nembi
Spargiamo al suol.
L'april circonda
La sposa bionda
D'un'etra rorida
Che vibra al sol.

WOMEN (*casting garlands and flowers before* DESDEMONA)
For you, for you these garlands fair,
Tokens of beauty!
Oh let them crown your golden hair
Which like the sunlight irradiates your face.
On your creation showers her brightest flowers.
Oh praise her in tribute to her eternal grace!

DESDEMONA
Splende il cielo, danza
L'aura, olezza il fior.
Gioia, amor, speranza
Cantan nel mio cor.

DESDEMONA
Boughs of blossoms, balmy breezes, songs so fair,
Joy and love lift up my heart in hopeful prayer.

CORO
Vivi felice! Addio. Qui regna Amor.

CHORUS
May you be blessed forever more!
(*during the entire scene* OTELLO *and* IAGO *have observed* DESDEMONA)

OTELLO
. . . Quel canto mi conquide.
S'ella m'inganna, il ciei sè stesso irride!

OTELLO (*deeply moved*)
Their tender song relieves me.
If she is guilty the Lord himself deceives me.

JAGO
(Beltà ed amor in dolce inno concordi!
I vostri infrangerò soavi accordi.)

IAGO (*aside*)
See love and beauty in harmony befriended.
Through me their sweet tune will be ended.

Scene 4

(DESDEMONA *kisses the brow of several children while some of the women kiss the hem of her dress. After she has handed a purse to the fishermen the chorus leaves.* DESDEMONA, *followed by* EMILIA, *advances into the hall and approaches* OTELLO)

DESDEMONA
My Lord and husband, I have spoken with someone
Who has felt your displeasure . . .

OTELLO
Pray continue!

DESDEMONA
Cassio.

OTELLO
Then 'twas he who spoke to you a little while this morning?

DESDEMONA
None other. In deep distress he sought my pity.
He seemed so humble, so sincerely grieving
That I beg you for him: Have mercy, Otello!
You must forgive him.

OTELLO
I cannot.

DESDEMONA
Why, My Lord, do you refuse me? Ah, forgive him!

OTELLO
I heard you.

DESDEMONA
In your voice there is a harshness, a strange annoyance
As though of pain or illness.

OTELLO
Here on my forehead.
(DESDEMONA *folds her handkerchief as if to bandage* OTELLO's *forehead*)

DESDEMONA
Soon the wicked pain will be no more.
'Twill be well again if you will let me soothe
Your burning temples.

OTELLO (*tearing the kerchief from her hand and throwing it to the ground*)
I've no need of your help.

DESDEMONA
Ah, you are angry, My Lord.

OTELLO
Now leave me! Ah, leave me!

DESDEMONA
D'un uomo che geme sotto il tuo disdegno
La preghiera ti porto.

OTELLO
Chi è costui?

DESDEMONA
Cassio.

OTELLO
Era lui
Che ti parlava sotto quelle fronde?

DESDEMONA
Lui stesso, e il suo dolor che in me s'infonde
Tant'è verace che di grazia è degno.
Intercedo per lui, per lui ti prego.
Tu gli perdona.

OTELLO
Non ora.

DESDEMONA
Non oppormi il tuo diniego.
Gli perdona.

OTELLO
Non ora.

DESDEMONA
Perchè torbida suona
La tua voce? Qual pena t'addolora?

OTELLO
M'ardon le tempie . . .

DESDEMONA
Quell'ardor molesto
Svanirà, se con questo
Morbido lino la mia man ti fascia.

OTELLO
Non ho d'uopo di ciò.

DESDEMONA
Tu sei crucciato,
Signor.

OTELLO
Mi lascia! mi lascia!

(EMILIA *picks up the handkerchief*)

DESDEMONA
Se inconscia, contro te, sposo,
ho peccato,
Dammi la dolce e lieta
Parola del perdono.
La tua fanciulla io sono
Umile e mansueta;
Ma il labbro tuo sospira,
Hai l'occhio fiso al suol.
Guardami in volto e mira
Come favella amore.
Vien, ch'io t'allieti il core,
Ch'io ti lenisca il duol.

DESDEMONA
If, not knowing, oh my lord, I have aggrieved you
Do not deny your ear to my plea and grant me pardon!
See me before you, guiltless, eager to serve my master!
Your silence speaks of sadness, your face is turned from me.
See in my eyes the token of vows of love unbroken!
Oh let me cheer your sadness, oh let me ease your pain!

JAGO
(Quel vel mi porgi
Ch'or hai raccolto.)

IAGO (*to* EMILIA, *whispering*)
Give me the kerchief in your possession!

EMILIA
Qual frode scorgi?
Ti leggo in volto.

EMILIA (*to* IAGO)
What are you planning? I do not trust you.

JAGO
T'opponi a vôto
Quand'io comando.

IAGO
Why this reluctance when I command you?

EMILIA
Il tuo nefando
Livor m'è noto.

EMILIA
Too well I know how your brain is working.

JAGO
Sospetto insano!

IAGO
You must be dreaming.

EMILIA
Guardia fedel
È questa mano.

EMILIA
I will not soil this hand with treason.

JAGO
Dammi quel vel!
Su te l'irosa
Mia man s'aggrava!

IAGO
Do as I say!
Obey me or else you will live to rue it.

EMILIA
Son la tua sposa,
Non la tua schiava.

EMILIA
I am your wife and not your servant.

OTELLO
(Forse perchè gli inganni
D'arguto amor non tendo,
Forse perchè discendo
Nella valle degli anni,
Forse perchè ho sul viso
Quest'atro tenebror,
Ella è perduta e irriso
Io sono e il cor m'infrango
E ruinar nel fango
Vedo il mio sogno d'ôr.)

OTELLO (*to himself*)
Maybe I have no ear for the art of conversation,
Maybe the passing years have made me bitter and grim,
Maybe my dark complexion has deepened my distrust.
She has defamed me, forever shamed me!
Nothing but sorrow will remain tomorrow.
My golden dream is ended until the hour I die.

JAGO
La schiava impura
Tu sei di Jago.

IAGO
You are the creature and slave of Iago.

EMILIA
Ho il cor presago
D'una sventura.

EMILIA
A dark foreboding bids me refuse you.

JAGO
Nè mi paventi?

IAGO
Do not provoke me . . .

EMILIA
Uomo crudel!
Che tenti?

EMILIA
Pitiless man . . . I tremble . . .

JAGO
A me quel vel!
(Già la mia brama
Conquido, ed ora
Su questa trama
Jago lavora!

IAGO
For me that handkerchief!
(IAGO *suddenly tears the kerchief out of* EMILIA'S *hand*)
(*to himself*) This precious banner will lead my master to his disaster!

EMILA (*to herself*)
Father in heaven, merciful God,
Look upon your daughter praying in anguish!

OTELLO
Go, leave me! Leave me to myself!

IAGO (*to* EMILIA, *who is about to leave*)
Not one word of this, I warn you!
(DESDEMONA *and* EMILIA *leave.* IAGO *starts to leave also, but reconsiders and stays near the door*)

EMILIA
(Vinser gli artigli
Truci e codardi.
Dio dai perigli
Sempre ci guardi.)

OTELLO
Escite! Solo vo' restar.

JAGO
(Ti giova
Tacer. Intendi?)

Scene 5

(OTELLO. IAGO *in the background*)

OTELLO (*sinking upon a chair*)
Desdemona faithless!

IAGO (*looking at the kerchief, then placing it carefully into his doublet*)
This tender web will furnish me the rope
With which to trap that innocent wench. Now let me play it
Into the hands of Cassio.

OTELLO
. . . monstrous idea . . . !

IAGO (*observing* OTELLO)
Begin your work, my poison!

OTELLO
Betraying me . . . shaming me . . . ?

IAGO (*darkly*)
Howl and thunder!

OTELLO
A nightmare! A nightmare!

IAGO (*having stepped closer to* OTELLO, *good-naturedly*)
Do not give it much thought!

OTELLO
You demon! Stop it! You have rent me asunder!
My heart . . . Far worse than any crime itself
Is to suspect, yet not know it.
What could I know of her infernal passion, concealed and secret?
Never held my heart the slightest suspicion.
Free and happy, unknowing, blissful the days went by,
When so divine her splendid beauty was mine,
Trembling in passion. In the glow of her kisses
How could I taste the lips of Cassio?
'Tis over . . . forever!
And now, forever farewell, gallant desire!
Farewell, you great and noble thoughts of fame!
Farewell, glory of war, of fight and fire,

OTELLO
Desdemona rea!

JAGO
(Con questi fili tramerò la prova
Del peccato d'amor. Nella dimora
Di Cassio ciò s'asconda.)

OTELLO
Atroce idea!

JAGO
(Il mio velen lavora.)

OTELLO
Rea contro me! contro me!!!

JAGO
(Soffri e ruggi!)

OTELLO
Atroce!!! . . . atroce!!! . . .

JAGO
Non pensateci più.

OTELLO
Tu?! Indietro! Fuggi!!
M'hai legato alla croce! . . .
Ahimè! . . . Più orrendo d'ogni orrenda ingiuria
Dell'ingiuria è il sospetto.
Nell'ore arcane della sua lussuria
(E a me furate!) m'agitava il petto
Forse un presagio? Ero baldo, giulivo . . .
Nulla sapevo ancor; io non sentivo
Sul suo corpo divin che m'innamora
E sui labbri mendaci
Gli ardenti baci
Di Cassio! Ed ora! . . . ed ora . . .

Ora e per sempre addio, sante memorie,
Addio, sublimi incanti del pensier!
Addio, schiere fulgenti, addio, vittorie,
Dardi volanti e volanti corsier!
Addio, vessillo trionfale e pio,
E diane squillanti in sul mattin!
Clamori e canti di battaglia, addio! . . .
Della gloria d'Otello è questo il fin.

Valiant companions, ever proud of your name!
Farewell, my faithful steed, you who bore me so nobly,
My beloved ships I bid you farewell!
Farewell, you trumpets and the cannon's roaring thunder!
In this final farewell Otello's day has turned to night.

JAGO
Pace, signor.

IAGO
Quiet, My Lord!

OTELLO
Sciagurato! mi trova
Una prova secura
Che Desdemona è impura . . .
Non sfuggir! non sfuggir! nulla ti giova!
Vo' una secura, una visibil prova!
O sulla tua testa
S'accenda e precipiti il fulmine
Del mio spaventoso furor che si desta!

OTELLO
Ha, you villain! By sowing the seeds of suspicion
You are risking your own perdition. Give me proof!
Give me proof! Nothing can save you.
Give me the proof so mine own eyes can see it!
Or . . . mind what I tell you . . .
If you cannot show that what I fear and doubt is true
Then the fury of hell will destroy you!
(OTELLO *takes hold of* IAGO's *throat and throws him to the ground*)

JAGO
Divina grazia, difendimi! Il cielo
Vi protegga. Non son più vostro alfiere.
Voglio che il mondo testimon mi sia
Che l'onestà è periglio.

IAGO
The grace of heaven protect me!
(*getting up*)
May God protect Your Lordship!
I resign my commission.
Witness, oh world, that it is safe no longer
To be sincere and loyal!
(*pretends to leave*)

OTELLO
No . . . rimani.
Forse onesto tu sei.

OTELLO
No . . . remain here! You are honest . . . perhaps . . .

JAGO
Meglio varrebbe
Ch'io fossi un ciurmador.

IAGO (*still about to leave*)
I should be happy to seek an honest trade.

OTELLO
Per l'universo!
Credo leale Desdemona e credo
Che non lo sia; te credo onesto e credo
Disleale . . . La prova io voglio! voglio
La certezza!!

OTELLO
Heaven may help me!
Still I have faith in Desdemona . . . however . . . she may betray me!
You I think loyal . . . however . . . you may not be!
I must be certain. Proof is what I want.

JAGO
Signor, frenate l'ansie.
E qual certezza v'abbisogna? Avvinti
Vederli forse?

IAGO (*returning to* OTELLO)
My Lord, you are impatient.
What proof will you accept as certain?
In Cassio's embrace to see her?

OTELLO
Ah! Morte e dannazione!!

OTELLO
Death and damnation!

JAGO
Ardua impresa sarebbe; e qual certezza
Sognate voi se quell'immondo fatto

IAGO
. . . they are not so obliging!
But in what way can you gain your proof, unless the secret lovers

Kindly reveal themselves?
And yet I tell you: I think I can convince you,
Giving you proof of such unquestioned assurance
That your doubts will yield at once and you will know the truth.
For instance:
(*whispering in* OTELLO's *ear*)
Long after midnight, Cassio was sleeping
While I lay near him,
When in his slumber softly he whispered,
Yet I could hear him;
His lips were parted, smiling in rapture;
Sighing in ecstasy he lay a-dreaming.
Then I could hear it as he was saying:
"Desdemona, darling, let our sweet love be secret!
Let us be careful! Night alone shall know of our love
And our passion!"
But now his vision seemed to forsake him.
He tried to hold it, tenderly scold it,
Cried, brokenhearted, as it departed:
"Oh threefold cursed fortune that gave you to the Moor!"
And after that the dream was over
And nothing more was said.

Sempre vi sfuggirà? . . . Ma pur se guida
È la ragione al vero, una sì forte
Congettura riserbo che per poco
Alla certezza vi conduce.
Udite:
Era la notte, Cassio dormìa, gli stavo accanto.
Con interrotte voci tradìa l'intimo incanto.
Le labbra lente, lente, movea, nell'abbandono
Del sogno ardente; e allor dicea, con flebil suono:
Desdemona soave! Il nostro amor s'asconda.
Cauti vegliamo! L'estasi del ciel tutto m'innonda.
Seguia più vago l'incubo blando; con molle angoscia,
L'interna imago quasi baciando, ei disse poscia:
Il rio destino impreco che al Moro ti donò.
E allora il sogno in cieco letargo si mutò.

OTELLO
Oh gracious Lord in heaven!

OTELLO
Oh! mostruosa colpa!

IAGO
'Twas but a dream, remember!

JAGO
Io non narrai
Che un sogno.

OTELLO
A dream which is a revelation!

OTELLO
Un sogno che rivela un fatto.

IAGO
A dream, airy and vague, may lead us on to firmer matter.

JAGO
Un sogno che può dar forma di prova
Ad altro indizio.

OTELLO
How so?

OTELLO
E qual?

IAGO
Do you remember in Desdemona's hand a silken kerchief
Beset with flowers, yet thin as mist on roses?

JAGO
Talor vedeste
In mano di Desdemona un tessuto
Trapunto a fior e più sottil d'un velo?

OTELLO
It was a symbol of our courtship and my first gift of love.

OTELLO
È il fazzoletto ch'io le diedi, pegno
Primo d'amor.

IAGO
That selfsame kerchief, lately—I am quite sure—
Was in the hands of Cassio.

JAGO
Quel fazzoletto ieri
(Certo ne son) lo vidi in man di Cassio.

OTELLO
Ah! Why did God not give him forty thousand lives?
One is all too weak to still my fury.
Iago, my heart is frozen, and now at last I see
My fate before me:
Gone are my love, my pity, my compassion.

OTELLO
Ah! mille vite gli donasse Iddio!
Una è povera preda al furor mio!!
Jago, ho il cuore di gelo.
Lungi da me le pïetose larve!
Tutto il mio vano amor esalo al cielo;

Guardami, ei sparve.
Nelle sue spire d'angue
L'idra m'avvince! Ah! sangue!
sangue! sangue!!
Sì, pel ciel marmoreo giuro!
Per le attorte folgori!
Per la Morte e per l'oscuro mar
sterminator!
D'ira e d'impeto tremendo
presto fia che sfolgori
Questa man ch'io levo e stendo!

Free am I, a demon!
Dragon of hate, embrace me! Lend me your terror!
Vengeance! Vengeance! Vengeance!
(*kneels*)
You, immense expanse of heaven, you, eternal lights above,
You, immortal sea around us, deep silent and dark:
Hear my vow on my sacred honor:
Vengeance be my last resolve,
And this hand, it shall achieve it!
(*lifts his hand; he tries to rise, but* IAGO *holds him down and kneels beside him*)

JAGO
Non v'alzate ancor!
Testimon è il Sol ch'io miro,
che m'irradia e inanima,
L'ampia terra e il vasto spiro
del Creator inter,
Che ad Otello io sacro ardenti,
core, braccio ed anima
S'anco ad opere cruenti s'armi il
suo voler!

IAGO
Do not yet arise!
Splendid sun that shines above us,
Splendor of my breath and life,
Let your rays like eyes behold the justice of my cause!
Be my witness, you, Creation,
Give me strength of heart and will,
As in sacred vindication I my vow fulfill!

OTELLO, JAGO
Sì, pel ciel marmoreo giuro! per
le attorte folgori!
Per la morte e per l'oscuro mar
sterminator!
D'ira e d'impeto tremendo
presto fia che sfolgori
Questa man ch'io levo e stendo.
Dio vendicator!

OTELLO, IAGO (*both kneeling and raising their right hand*)
You, immense expanse of heaven,
You, eternal lights above,
You, immortal sea around me,
Deep, silent and dark,
Hear my vow on my sacred honor:
Vengeance be my last resolve,
And my hand, it will achieve it!
So help me, O God!

ACT III

(The main hall in the castle; to the right a wide portico, leading to a smaller hall; to the rear an alcove.)

Scene 1

(OTELLO, IAGO, a HERALD)

HERALD *(from the portico, to* OTELLO, *who, like* IAGO, *is in the hall)*
My Lord, the commander of the harbor has just announced the arrival of the galley which brings to Cyprus the Venetian delegation.

OTELLO
Go, bid them welcome!
(he dismisses the HERALD; *to* IAGO*)*
Continue!

IAGO
I spoke to Cassio. He must be on his way and will speak without restraint.
(pointing to the alcove)
You go in hiding whence you can see us both.
Observe him closely, his features and gestures!
But be patient, Master, or the proof will escape you!
Here comes Desdemona! Be on your guard now! I leave you!
(he starts to leave, then stops and returns to OTELLO*)*
Remember the kerchief!

OTELLO
Go! Oh, that kerchief I would gladly forget!
*(*IAGO *exits)*

ARALDO
La vedetta del porto ha segnalato
La veneta galea che a Cipro adduce
Gli Ambasciatori.

OTELLO
Bene sta.
Continua.

JAGO
Qui trarrò Cassio e con astute inchieste
Lo adescherò a ciarlar. Voi là nascosto
Scrutate i modi suoi, le sue parole,
I lazzi, i gesti. Pazïente siate
O la prova vi sfugge. Ecco Desdemona.
Finger conviene . . . io vado.
Il fazzoletto . . .

OTELLO
Va! volentieri obliato l'avrei.

Scene 2

(OTELLO, DESDEMONA *entering from the left)*

DESDEMONA *(from the threshold)*
God bless my lord and master in whom my heart reposes!

OTELLO *(on his way to meeting* DESDEMONA, *taking her hand)*
Thank you, My Lady! Let me hold your hand as fair as roses!
Glowing in soft caresses it soothes every care.

DESDEMONA
Never it felt the stresses of age and of despair.

OTELLO
And yet it may become a tool of mischief and perdition.
It can destroy the trusting fool who does not know suspicion!

DESDEMONA
Dio ti giocondi, o sposo dell'alma mia sovrano.

OTELLO
Grazie, madonna, datemi la vostra eburnea mano.
Caldo mador ne irrora la morbida beltà.

DESDEMONA
Essa ancor l'orme ignora del duolo e dell'età.

OTELLO
Eppur qui annida il demone gentil del mal consiglio,
Che il vago avorio allumina del piccioletto artiglio.

Mollemente alla prece s'atteggia e al pio fervore . . .	So to heaven raise this hand in devotion's sincere endeavor!
DESDEMONA	DESDEMONA
Eppur con questa mano io v'ho donato il core. Ma riparlar vi debbo di Cassio.	And yet this hand so slender gave you my heart forever. But once again I plead with you for Cassio.
OTELLO	OTELLO
Ancor l'ambascia Del mio morbo m'assale; tu la fronte mi fascia.	I feel the symptoms of my illness recurring. Will you lend me your kerchief?
DESDEMONA	DESDEMONA
A te.	I will. (*produces a handkerchief*)
OTELLO	OTELLO
No; il fazzoletto voglio ch'io ti donai.	No! I only want the handkerchief which I gave you.
DESDEMONA	DESDEMONA
Non l'ho meco.	I have left it . . .
OTELLO	OTELLO
Desdemona, guai se lo perdi! guai! Una possente maga ne ordìa lo stame arcano; Ivi è riposta l'alta malìa d'un talismano. Bada! smarrirlo, oppur donarlo, è ria sventura!	Desdemona! Woe should you lose it! Hear me: Once a magician spun in its texture an incantation Dooming the one who'd lose or abuse it to dark damnation. Therefore be careful! If you have lost it you will regret it.
DESDEMONA	DESDEMONA
Il vero parli?	Are you in earnest?
OTELLO	OTELLO
Il vero parlo.	I speak in earnest.
DESDEMONA	DESDEMONA
Mi fai paura! . . .	Oh, God in heaven!
OTELLO	OTELLO
Che?! l'hai perduto forse?	What? Tell me . . . have you lost it?
DESDEMONA	DESDEMONA
No . . .	No . . .
OTELLO	OTELLO
Lo cerca.	Go, fetch it!
DESDEMONA	DESDEMONA
Fra poco . . . Lo cercherò . . .	Oh hear me! It is not lost.
OTELLO	OTELLO
No, tosto!	Go, fetch it!
DESDEMONA	DESDEMONA
Tu di me ti fai gioco. Storni così l'inchiesta di Cassio; astuzia è questa Del tuo pensier.	I am sure you are jesting, Hoping to silence my pleading for Cassio. Yes, this is why you have frightened me.
OTELLO	OTELLO
Pel cielo! l'anima mia si desta! Il fazzoletto . . .	Great heavens! I feel my blood starts boiling. Fetch me that kerchief!
DESDEMONA	DESDEMONA
È Cassio l'amico tuo diletto.	But Cassio's your friend so true and loyal!
OTELLO	OTELLO
Il fazzoletto!!	Fetch me that kerchief!

DESDEMONA
For Cassio I'm pleading for mercy.

DESDEMONA
A Cassio perdona . . .

OTELLO
Fetch me that kerchief!

OTELLO
Il fazzoletto!!

DESDEMONA
Great God! In your expression there's wild and fearsome fury.

DESDEMONA
Gran Dio! nella tua voce v'è un grido di minaccia!

OTELLO
Lift up your eyes!

OTELLO
Alza quegli occhi!

DESDEMONA
What is in your mind?
(*he takes hold of her chin and forces her to look at him*)

DESDEMONA
Atroce idea!

OTELLO
Look in my face! Tell me: Who are you?

OTELLO
Guardami in faccia!
Dimmi chi sei!

DESDEMONA
Otello's devoted wife.

DESDEMONA
La sposa fedel d'Otello.

OTELLO
Swear it! Swear to this falsehood!

OTELLO
Giura!
Giura e ti danna . . .

DESDEMONA
Otello believes me faithful.

DESDEMONA
Otello fedel mi crede.

OTELLO
I think you are lying.

OTELLO
Impura
Ti credo.

DESDEMONA
Great God, oh help me!

DESDEMONA
Iddio m'aiuti!

OTELLO
Courting your own damnation, swear by your virtue!

OTELLO
Corri alla tua condanna,
Di' che sei casta.

DESDEMONA
I do . . . I swear!

DESDEMONA
Casta . . . io son . . .

OTELLO
Heaven shall damn you!

OTELLO
Giura e ti danna!!!

DESDEMONA
My brow turns pale with terror.
You seem to speak of treason.
I hear the sounds of madness,
So frightening, yet without reason.
Behold me: My eyes, not words, shall now implore you!
My heart lies open before you.
I cry to heaven in anguished desolation,
My eyes bedewed and blind,
Let your tears tell my lord for me,
Eyes that have never lied before,
Tears that I never cried before,
Bear witness to my plea: Oh, tell him I am true!

DESDEMONA
Esterrefatta fisso lo sguardo tuo tremendo,
In te parla una Furia, la sento e non l'intendo.
Mi guarda! il volto e l'anima ti svelo; il core infranto
Mi scruta . . . io prego il cielo per te con questo pianto.
Per te con queste stille cocenti aspergo il suol.
Guarda le prime lagrime che da me spreme il duol.

OTELLO
If your demon should see you now
He'd take you for an angel and would renounce you.

OTELLO
S'or ti scorge il tuo démone, un angelo ti crede
E non t'afferra.

DESDEMONA
God up above knows I am blameless.

DESDEMONA
Vede l'Eterno la mia fede!

OTELLO
No! La vede l'inferno.

DESDEMONA
La tua giustizia impetro,
Sposo mio!

OTELLO
Ah! Desdemona! - Indietro! indietro! indietro!

DESDEMONA
Tu pur piangi?! . . . e gemendo freni del cor lo schianto
E son io l'innocente cagion di tanto pianto! . . .
Qual è il mio fallo?

OTELLO
E il chiedi? . . . Il più nero delitto
Sovra il candido giglio della tua fronte è scritto.

DESDEMONA
Ahimè!

OTELLO
Che? non sei forse una vil cortigiana?

DESDEMONA
Ciel! No . . . no . . . pel battesmo della fede cristiana! . . .

OTELLO
Che?

DESDEMONA
Ah! non son ciò che esprime quella parola orrenda.

OTELLO
Datemi ancor l'eburnea mano, vo' fare ammenda.
Vi credea (perdonate se il mio pensiero è fello)
Quella vil cortigiana che è la sposa d'Otello.

OTELLO
No, 'tis Satan who knows it!

DESDEMONA
'Tis justice I demand of you, Otello.

OTELLO
Ah! Desdemona, step back there! Go from me! Go from me!

DESDEMONA
You are weeping, and your heart is tortured
In silent horror.
Ah, 'tis I am the innocent cause of all your sorrow.
How have I wronged you?

OTELLO
You ask me? 'Tis a crime foul and sordid.
On your forehead forever its stains will remain recorded.

DESDEMONA
Alas!

OTELLO
Ha! 'Tis the crime that is called prostitution!

DESDEMONA
God! No, no! In the name of all that's sacred, I swear it!

OTELLO
What?

DESDEMONA
Ah, I am chaste and guiltless of such a monstrous outrage!
(OTELLO *abruptly changes from violent fury to biting sarcasm. He courteously takes* DESDEMONA'S *hand and guides her to the door through which she had entered*)

OTELLO
Your gentle hand once more, My Lady!
I shall do penance! O forgive me
That I hinted that one so sweet and mellow
Could indeed be a strumpet . . . like the wife of Otello!
(*with the last words,* OTELLO, *twisting her arm, has pushed her through the door. He returns center-stage in a state of complete dejection*)

Scene 3

(OTELLO)

OTELLO
Dio! mi potevi scagliar tutti i mali
Della miseria, - della vergogna,
Far de' miei baldi trofei trionfali

OTELLO
God, Thou canst try me with all the bereavements
If Thy displeasure I have brought on me.
Take all my vict'ries and all my achievements,
All that I treasure, turn it upon me,

And I shall carry with patience the crown
Of bitter dejection, without objection
And shall abide in Thy will without a frown.
Why, My Lord, but why have they all been reviling,
Rending apart what's noble and tender?
Why must it die, what so sunlit, so smiling
Brought to my heart its heavenly splendor?
You, pious Angel, you Angel of Grace,
Your reign has ended:
Under his mask of terror let Satan be raising his face!

Una maceria, - una menzogna . . .
E avrei portato la croce crudel
D'angoscie e d'onte
Con calma fronte
E rassegnato al volere del ciel.
Ma, o pianto, o duol! m'han rapito il miraggio
Dov'io, giulivo, - l'anima acqueto.
Spento è quel sol, quel sorriso, quel raggio
Che mi fa vivo, - che mi fa lieto!
Tu alfin, Clemenza, pio genio immortal
Dal roseo riso,
Copri il tuo viso
Santo coll'orrida larva infernal!

Scene 4

(OTELLO, *later* IAGO)

OTELLO
Death and damnation! I shall get his confession
And then I'll kill her! Confession! Confession!
Now the evidence!
(IAGO *appears, pointing to the door*)

IAGO
Cassio is here!

OTELLO
Here? Heaven, I praise thee!
O Lord, why must I bear this?

IAGO
Be patient! Go in hiding!
(IAGO *quickly leads* OTELLO *to the rear, then turns to meet* CASSIO, *who is entering somewhat hesitantly*)

OTELLO
Ah! Dannazione!
Pria confessi il delitto e poscia muoia!
Confession! Confession! . . .
La prova! . . .

JAGO
Cassio è là!

OTELLO
Là?! Cielo! gioia!!
Orror! - i Supplizi immondi!!

JAGO
Ti frena! Ti nascondi.

Scene 5

(OTELLO, *in hiding,* IAGO, CASSIO)

IAGO
Come now! No one can hear us. How are you, my noble captain?

CASSIO
You have mentioned the cause why I am sad and distressed.

IAGO
Your rank? Have no fear for you know how well you are represented.

CASSIO
I was quite certain here to find Desdemona.

OTELLO (*aside*)
He spoke her name!

JAGO
Vieni; l'aula è deserta.
T'inoltra, o Capitano.

CASSIO
Questo nome d'onor suona ancor vano
Per me.

JAGO
Fa cor, la tua causa è in tal mano
Che la vittoria è certa.

CASSIO
Io qui credea di ritrovar Desdemona.

OTELLO
(Ei la nomò.)

CASSIO
Vorrei parlarle ancora,
Per saper se la mia grazia è profferta.

CASSIO
I should much like to ask her if her husband
To her plea has consented.

JAGO
L'attendi; e intanto, giacchè non si stanca
Mai la tua lingua nelle folle gaie,
Narrami un po' di lei che t'innamora.

IAGO (*gaily*)
Await her!
(*he pulls* CASSIO *toward the front column of the colonnade, farther away from* OTELLO)
But meanwhile I know that your tongue is eager
To tell me all your gay adventures.
Come, let me hear: How is your heart's beloved?

CASSIO
Di chi?

CASSIO
Which one?

JAGO
Di Bianca.

IAGO
Why . . . Bianca!

OTELLO
(Sorride!)

OTELLO (*aside*)
He's laughing.

CASSIO
Baie! . . .

CASSIO
Nonsense!

JAGO
Essa t'avvince
Coi vaghi rai.

IAGO
I have observed you from the beginning.

CASSIO
Rider mi fai.

CASSIO
I can't help grinning.

JAGO
Ride chi vince.

IAGO
Grinning means winning!

CASSIO
In tal disfide, - per verità,
Vince chi ride. - Ah! Ah!

CASSIO (*laughing*)
You are observant, this I declare . . .
Winning means grinning! Ha, ha!

JAGO
Ah! Ah!

IAGO
Ha, ha!

OTELLO
(L'empio trionfa, il suo scherno m'uccide;
Dio, frena l'ansia che in core mi sta!)

OTELLO (*aside*)
This hellish laughter like a dagger impales me,
Fury assails me and darkest despair.

CASSIO
Son già di baci
Sazio e di lai.

CASSIO
And yet, to kiss her has become tedious.

JAGO
Rider mi fai.

IAGO
Why, how insidious!

CASSIO
O amor' fugaci!

CASSIO
I shall not miss her.

JAGO
Vagheggi il regno - d'altra beltà.
Colgo nel segno?

IAGO
Another beauty, luscious and fair?
Say, did I guess it?

CASSIO
Ah! Ah!

CASSIO
Ha, ha!

JAGO
Ah! Ah!

IAGO
Ha, ha!

OTELLO
(L'empio m'irride, - il suo scherno m'uccide;
Dio, frena l'ansia che in core mi sta!)

OTELLO (*aside*)
Oh, how this laughter like a dagger impales me.
Fury assails me and darkest despair.

CASSIO
Yes, you did guess it. I must confess it. Listen . . .

IAGO
Let us be careful! Now tell me . . .
(draws CASSIO *even farther away from* OTELLO*)*

CASSIO
Iago, the house where I live, remember . . .
(his words become unintelligible)

OTELLO *(advancing cautiously from his hiding place in order to hear their conversation)*
Now he will tell him the manner, the hideout, the moment!

CASSIO
No one did see her . . .
(his words are lost again)

OTELLO *(aside)*
I could not understand him . . .
Still I must hear what they say. . . .
This I have come to!

CASSIO
. . . a flowered kerchief . . .

IAGO
How curious! Surprising!

OTELLO *(aside)*
I should go nearer, Iago keeps advising.
(he hides behind a column)

IAGO
No one did see her? Nonsense!

CASSIO
I'm serious. How to behold her I have been yearning!

IAGO *(after a quick side glance at* OTELLO, *to himself)*
His ears are burning!
(to CASSIO*)* Where is it?

CASSIO *(drawing* DESDEMONA'S *handkerchief from his doublet)*
See here!

IAGO *(taking the handkerchief out of* CASSIO'S *hand)*
Fit for a princess!
(after another side glance at OTELLO*)*
(aside)
Otello winces. Soon he will stand his despair no longer!
(jokingly, to CASSIO*)*
My worthy Cassio, let me salute you!
Angels themselves could not withstand your charm.

CASSIO
Nel segno hai côlto.
Sì, lo confesso.
M'odi . . .

JAGO
Sommesso
Parla. T'ascolto.

CASSIO
Jago, t'è nota
La mia dimora . . .
. . . .
. . . .

OTELLO
(Or gli racconta il modo,
Il luogo e l'ora . . .)

CASSIO
. . . .
Da mano ignota . . .
. . . .
. . . .

OTELLO
(Le parole non odo . . .
Lasso! e udir le vorrei! Dove son giunto!)

CASSIO
. . . .
Un vel trapunto . . .
. . . .

JAGO
È strano! È strano!

OTELLO
(D'avvicinarmi Jago mi fa cenno.)

JAGO
Da ignota mano?
Baie!

CASSIO
Da senno.
Quanto mi tarda
Saper chi sia . . .

JAGO
(Otello spia.)
L'hai teco?

CASSIO
Guarda.

JAGO
Qual meraviglia!
(Otello origlia.
Ei s'avvicina
Con mosse accorte.)
Bel cavaliere, nel vostro ostello
Perdono gli angeli l'aureola e il vel.

OTELLO
(E' quello! è quello!
Ruina e Morte!)

JAGO
(Origlia Otello.)

OTELLO
(Tutto è spento! Amore e duol.
L'alma mia nessun più
smuova.
Tradimento, la tua prova
Spaventosa mostri al Sol.)

JAGO
Quest'è una ragna
Dove il tuo cuor
Casca, si lagna,
S'impiglia e muor.
Troppo l'ammiri,
Troppo la guardi;
Bada ai deliri
Vani e bugiardi.
Quest'è una ragna
Dove il tuo cuor
Casca, si lagna,
S'impiglia e muor.

CASSIO
Miracolo vago
Dell'aspo e dell'ago
Che in raggi tramuta
Le fila d'un vel,
Più bianco, più lieve
Che fiocco di neve,
Che nube tessuta
Dall'aure del ciel.

JAGO
Bada!
Quest'è il segnale che annuncia
l'approdo
Della trireme veneziana.
Ascolta.
Tutto il castel co' suoi squilli
risponde.
Se qui non vuoi con Otello
scontrarti,
Fuggi.

CASSIO
Addio.

JAGO
Va.

OTELLO (*hidden by the column, tries to take a good look at the handkerchief, which* IAGO *holds behind his back for* OTELLO *to see*)
The kerchief . . . I see it! The world has ended.

IAGO (*to himself*)
Look here, Otello!

OTELLO (*aside*)
All is over, both love and pain,
And my heart has turned to stone.
Her betrayal, it is proven clear as day.

IAGO (*to* CASSIO, *referring to the handkerchief*)
Prettily spinning, pretending to play
Spiders are winning and killing their prey,
Letting it quiver and flitter and fly
Till at last it will shiver and flicker and die.

CASSIO (*having retaken the handkerchief from* IAGO *and looking at it*)
I know not who brought you,
I know not who wrought you,
Of sunrays she spun you
And stars from her eyes.
You're softer and lighter,
You shimmer much brighter
Than clouds white and shiny
That float through the skies.
(*a trumpet flourish off-stage, later a shot from a cannon.* OTELLO *returns to his hiding place*)

IAGO
Listen! This is the signal announcing that the delegates from Venice are ashore now. Be careful! All over town they are sounding the trumpets.
It would be bad if Otello should see you both.

CASSIO
Till later!

IAGO
Go!
(CASSIO *exits*)

Scene 6

(IAGO, OTELLO)

OTELLO (*coming forward toward* IAGO)
How shall I kill my wife?

IAGO
So you have heard his brazen laughter?

OTELLO
Yes.

IAGO
. . . and saw the kerchief?

OTELLO
Yes, I saw it.

CHORUS (*off-stage, in the distance*)
Be welcome! Go and meet them!
To the harbor!

OTELLO
She stands convicted.
Bring a phial of poison for tonight

CHORUS (*a little nearer*)
May God bless the Lion of San Marco!

IAGO
With poison? No! Far better 'tis to choke her . . .
There in her bed, yes, there where she lay in sin.

OTELLO
I must admire your sense of justice.

IAGO
And Cassio shall be in Iago's care.

OTELLO
Iago, henceforth you shall be my aide and a captain.

IAGO
My Lord, I'm humbly grateful.
Here are our guests from Venice . . . you receive them!
But, to avoid suspicion,
Desdemona should be with you to greet them.

OTELLO
Yes, go and call her!
(IAGO *off to the left.* OTELLO *walks to the rear to re-receive the delegation from Venice*)

OTELLO
Come la ucciderò?

JAGO
Vedeste ben com'egli ha riso?

OTELLO
Vidi.

JAGO
E il fazzoletto?

OTELLO
Tutto vidi.

VOCI
Evviva!
Alla riva!
Allo sbarco!

OTELLO
È condannata.
Fa ch'io m'abbia un velen per questa notte.

VOCI
Evviva! Evviva il Leon di San Marco!

JAGO
Il tosco no, val meglio soffocarla,
Là nel suo letto, là, dove ha peccato.

OTELLO
Questa giustizia tua mi piace.

JAGO
A Cassio
Jago provvederà.

OTELLO
Jago, fin d'ora
Mio Capitano t'eleggo.

JAGO
Mio Duce,
Grazie vi rendo.
Ecco gli Ambasciatori.
Li accogliete. Ma ad evitar sospetti,
Desdemona si mostri a quei Messeri.

OTELLO
Sì, qui l'adduci.

Scene 7

(OTELLO, LODOVICO, RODERIGO, *the* HERALD. *Dignitaries of the Republic of Venice. Ladies and gentlemen. Soldiers, officers. Later* IAGO, DESDEMONA, *and* EMILIA *entering from the left.*)

LODOVICO
Il Doge ed il Senato
Salutano l'eroe trionfatore
Di Cipro. Io reco nelle vostre mani
Il messaggio dogale.

LODOVICO (*holding a document*)
The Government of Venice takes pride in paying homage
To the hero of Cyprus.
I'm honored now to place their message in the hands of Otello.

OTELLO
Io bacio il segno
Della Sovrana Maestà.

OTELLO (*accepting the scroll and kissing the seal*)
I kiss the symbol of its proud majesty and might.
(*he breaks open the seal*)

LODOVICO
Madonna,
V'abbia il cielo in sua guardia.

LODOVICO (*approaching* DESDEMONA)
The Lord may grant my lady His mercy!

DESDEMONA
E il ciel v'ascolti.

DESDEMONA
Your prayers be answered!

EMILIA
(Come sei mesta!)

EMILIA (*aside to* DESDEMONA)
You seem to suffer.

DESDEMONA
(Emilia! una gran nube
Turba il senno d'Otello e il mio destino.)

DESDEMONA (*aside to* EMILIA)
Emilia, a heavy cloud has cast its shadow o'er Otello,
Dark and foreboding.

JAGO
Messere, son lieto di vedervi.

IAGO (*to* LODOVICO)
Be welcome! I'm happy to salute you.
(DESDEMONA, IAGO, *and* LODOVICO *are conversing*)

LODOVICO
Jago,
Quali nuove? . . . ma in mezzo a voi non trovo
Cassio.

LODOVICO
Greetings, my good Iago.
Where is your friend and comrade, Cassio?

JAGO
Con lui crucciato è Otello.

IAGO
Otello has disowned him.

DESDEMONA
Credo
Che in grazia tornerà.

DESDEMONA
. . . but soon he will regain his grace.

OTELLO
Ne siete certa?

OTELLO (*while reading the scroll, under his breath to* DESDEMONA)
Are you so certain?

DESDEMONA
Che dite?

DESDEMONA
What is it?

LODOVICO
Ei legge, non vi parla.

LODOVICO
He's reading and said nothing.

JAGO
Forse
Che in grazia tornerà.

IAGO
Perhaps he will regain his grace!

DESDEMONA
Jago, lo spero;
Sai se un verace affetto io porti a Cassio . . .

DESDEMONA
Iago, I hope so.
You know the friendship which I always felt for Cassio.

OTELLO
Frenate dunque le labbra loquaci . . .

OTELLO (*still reading, but feverish with excitement, whispering to* DESDEMONA)
Hold back your tongue so unseemly loquacious!

DESDEMONA
Perdonate, signor . . .

DESDEMONA (*referring to* CASSIO)
Oh, forgive him, My Lord!

OTELLO
Demonio, taci!!

OTELLO (*suddenly turning on* DESDEMONA)
You wench, be silent!

LODOVICO
Ferma!

LODOVICO (*holding back* OTELLO)
Stop it!

THE OTHERS
Oh horror! Oh horror!

CORO
Orrore! Orrore!

LODOVICO
My mind dare not believe what my eyes have had to witness.

LODOVICO
La mente mia non osa
Pensar ch'io vidi il vero.

OTELLO (*to the* HERALD, *with strong emphasis*)
Call in Cassio!

OTELLO
A me Cassio!

IAGO (*aside to* OTELLO)
Why call him?

JAGO
(Che tenti?)

OTELLO (*aside to* IAGO)
Watch her when first he enters!

OTELLO
(Guardala mentr'ei giunge.)

CHORUS
Unhappy lady!

CORO
Ah! triste sposa!

LODOVICO (*taking* IAGO *aside, to him*)
Is this truly the hero, great as a warrior
And revered as a leader?

LODOVICO
Quest'è dunque l'eroe? quest'è il guerriero
Dai sublimi ardimenti?

IAGO (*shrugging his shoulders, to* LODOVICO)
He is what he is.

JAGO
È quel ch'egli è.

LODOVICO
Come, let me share your thinking!

LODOVICO
Palesa il tuo pensiero.

IAGO
This matter I prefer to treat discreetly.

JAGO
Meglio è tener su ciò la lingua muta.

Scene 8

OTELLO (*keeping his eyes on the door till* CASSIO *enters*)
Here he comes!
(*to* IAGO)
Watch out! Observe his every motion!
(*to everyone*)
You nobles, my orders . . .
(*to* DESDEMONA)
What a splendid actress!
(*to everyone*)
. . . do recall me to Venice.

OTELLO
(Eccolo! È lui!
Nell'animo lo scruta.)
Messeri! Il Doge . . .
- (ben tu fingi il pianto)
Mi richiama a Venezia.

RODERIGO
What consternation!

RODERIGO
(Infida sorte!)

OTELLO (*to everyone*)
As new commander has been appointed
A man who served beside me here on Cyprus: Cassio.

OTELLO
E in Cipro elegge
Mio successor colui che stava accanto
Al mio vessillo, Cassio.

IAGO (*furious and surprised*)
Hell and damnation!

JAGO
(Inferno e morte!)

OTELLO (*continuing and pointing to the document*)
I'll abide by the order from my sovereign.

OTELLO
La parola Ducale è nostra legge.

CASSIO (*bowing to* OTELLO)
I shall obey.

CASSIO
Obbedirò.

OTELLO (*quickly to* IAGO, *pointing to* CASSIO)
Watch him! The villain seems disappointed.

OTELLO
(Vedi? non par che esulti
L'infame?)

JAGO
(No.)

OTELLO
La ciurma e la coorte
(Continua i tuoi singulti . . .)
E la navi e il castello
Lascio in poter del nuovo Duce.

LODOVICO
Otello
Per pietà la conforta o il cor le infrangi.

OTELLO
Noi salperem domani.
A terra! . . . e piangi! . . .

DESDEMONA
A terra! . . . sì . . . nel livido
Fango . . . percossa . . . io giacio . . .
Piango . . . m'agghiaccia il brivido
Dell'anima che muor.
E un dì sul mio sorriso
Fioria la speme e il bacio
Ed or . . . l'angoscia in viso
E l'agonia nel cor.
Quel Sol sereno e vivido
Che allieta il cielo e il mare
Non può asciugar le amare
Stille del mio dolor.

EMILIA
Quell' innocente un fremito
D'odio non ha nè un gesto,
Trattiene in petto il gemito
Con doloroso fren.
La lagrima si frange
Muta sul volto mesto:
No, chi per lei non piange
Non ha pietade in sen.

RODERIGO
Per me s'oscura il mondo,
S'annuvola il destin;
L'angiol soave e biondo
Scompar dal mio cammin.

CASSIO
L'ora è fatal! un fulmine
Sul mio cammin l'addita.
Già di mia sorte il culmine
S'offre all'inerte man.
L'ebbra fortuna incalza
La fuga della vita.

IAGO
Yes.

OTELLO (*to everyone*)
The garrison and sailors . . .
(*to* DESDEMONA)
Go on! Keep up your whining!
(*to everyone*)
. . . all the fleet and the fortress
I leave in charge of my successor.

LODOVICO (*pointing to* DESDEMONA)
Otello, I beseech you, be kind to her! She's failing.

OTELLO (*to* LODOVICO *and* DESDEMONA)
We shall depart tomorrow.
(*suddenly taking hold of* DESDEMONA, *in wild fury*)
Go down and keep wailing!
(*during* OTELLO's *outburst the scroll has dropped to the floor.* IAGO *takes it and reads it unobserved.* DESDEMONA *has fallen to the ground.* EMILIA *and* LODOVICO *come to her aid. Everyone is petrified by* OTELLO's *fury*)

DESDEMONA
In sorrow, faint, and mortally wounded, in anguish I tremble.
Dying, I feel an icy hand gripping my heart and mind.
My dream of love has ended, of smiles and sweet caresses.
The night that has descended made his heart go blind.
The sun, so high above the world
In all its radiant splendor,
No solace can it tender to my broken heart,
No solace for my grief I shall ever find.

EMILIA
Silent and still, so woebegone,
Broken, her heart is sighing.
Never her lips so whitely drawn
Sounded of hate a tone.
Of tears a bitter river
Softly her eyes are crying.
He who will not forgive her
Must have a heart of stone.

RODERIGO
Shrouded in deepest sorrow
Cries in despair my heart,
For with my love tomorrow
Will all my hopes depart.

CASSIO
Out of the dark a flash so bright
Turns my disgrace to splendor.
Startled, I see how starless night
Yields to a radiant day.

Fate writes a wondrous story:
We helplessly surrender,
Ride on a wave to glory
Then sink again away.

Questa che al ciel m'innalza
È un'onda d'uragan.

LODOVICO
How could in blind vexation
Heartlessly he revile her?
Weeping in desperation
She lifts to God her face.
Why all his strange behavior?
How could he so defile her?
I pray that God, our Savior
May grant them both His grace.

LODOVICO
Egli la man funerea
Scuote anelando d'ira,
Essa la faccia eterea
Volge piangendo al ciel.
Nel contemplar quel pianto
La carità sospira,
E un tenero compianto
Stempra del core il gel.

CHORUS (*in various groups, discussing the event*)

LADIES
Oh Lord!

MEN
What happened?

LADIES
Lord, see us fearful, trembling and tearful.
Thou up on high hast made him blind.

MEN
Terror has gripped my anxious mind.
How could this monster strike and revile her?
The Lord in unrelenting fury has made him blind.

LADIES
Ah, cruel sight!

MEN
Oh shame, oh horror, he must be raving,
His evil look will stare us down!
He curses heaven with evil glances.
Even the sun must fear his frown.

LADIES
She stands in sadness, so pale and lonely,
Her tears are falling from burning eyes.
So weep in heaven the host of angels
When unrepenting a sinner dies.

IL CORO

DONNE
Pietà!

CAVALIERI
Mistero!

DONNE
Ansia mortale, bieca,
Ne ingombra, anime assorte in
lungo orror.

CAVALIERI
Quell'uomo nero è sepolcrale, e
cieca
Un'ombra è in lui di morte e di
terror.

DONNE
Vista crudel!

CAVALIERI
Strazia coll'ugna l'orrido
Petto! Gli sguardi figge immoti
al suol.
Poi sfida il ciel coll'atre pugna,
l'ispido
Aspetto ergendo ai dardi alti
del Sol.

DONNE
Ei la colpì! quel viso santo,
pallido,
Blando, si china e tace e piange
e muor.
Piangon così nel ciel lor pianto
gli angeli
Quando perduto giace il
peccator.

IAGO (*approaching* OTELLO, *who leans against an armchair*)
Let me advise you!

JAGO
Una parola.

OTELLO
Speak out!

OTELLO
E che?

IAGO
Strike quickly! Now is the time to plan your vengeance.
Do not delay it!

JAGO
T'affretta! Rapido
Slancia la tua vendetta! Il
tempo vola.

OTELLO
Well spoken.

OTELLO
Ben parli.

IAGO
Your wrath alone is useless. Act on it!

JAGO
E' l'ira inutil ciancia. Scuotiti!

All'opra ergi tua mira! All'opra sola!
Io penso a Cassio. Ei le sue trame espia.
L'infame anima ria l'averno inghiotte!

OTELLO
Chi gliela svelle?

JAGO
Io.

OTELLO
Tu?

JAGO
Giurai.

OTELLO
Tal sia.

JAGO
Tu avrai le sue novelle in questa notte . . .
I sogni tuoi saranno in mar domani
E tu sull'aspra terra!

RODERIGO
Ahi, triste!

JAGO
Ahi, stolto
Stolto! Se vuoi, tu puoi sperar; gli umani,
Orsù! cimenti afferra, e m'odi.

RODERIGO
T'ascolto.

JAGO
Col primo albor salpa il vascello. Or Cassio
È il Duce. Eppur se avvien che a questi accada
Sventura . . . allor qui resta Otello.

RODERIGO
Lugubre
Luce d'atro balen!

JAGO
Mano alla spada!
A notte folta io la sua traccia vigilo.
E il varco e l'ora scruto, il resto a te.
Sarò tua scolta. A caccia! a caccia! Cingiti
L'arco!

RODERIGO
Sì! t'ho venduto onore e fe'.

JAGO
Corri al miraggio! il fragile tuo senno
Ha già confuso un sogno menzogner.
Segui l'astuto ed agile mio cenno,

Don't waste a single moment in idle fury!
I'll handle Cassio: Soon he will cheat no longer.
In hell he shall pay for his corruption.

OTELLO
Who will dispatch him?

IAGO
I!

OTELLO
You?

IAGO
I swear!

OTELLO
He's yours.

IAGO
Tonight you shall have news that he has ended . . .
(*leaving* OTELLO *and approaching* RODERIGO; *with irony, to* RODERIGO)
Your sweetheart will be on the sea tomorrow
While you are left without her!

RODERIGO
I'm suff'ring.

IAGO
You idiot! Idiot! But it is up to you:
You can prevent them both from leaving. I'll tell you . . .

RODERIGO
I listen.

IAGO
The new commander will be Cassio, but not tonight yet.
So, if perchance he should be seriously injured
Otello would remain here.
(*touching his sword*)

RODERIGO
Small is your comfort in my despair.

IAGO
Don't be a coward!
Leave it to me to be on guard and follow him!
I set the trap—you catch him and do the rest!
I stalk the quarry and you do the hunting!
Sharpen your arrows!

RODERIGO
Yes, I have sold my soul to you.

IAGO (*to himself*)
Caught in my cobweb! Go then, you fool!
Delusion will now propel him along his path of crime.
Demon of lies and spirit of confusion,
Guide him along on the path I show him!

For I'm his will sublime
Until the end of time!

RODERIGO (*to himself*)
I have decided. Without a qualm and fearless,
I shall accomplish what destiny commands.
Dauntless and confident I place my trust in chance!
Love be my guide, a love so pure and peerless
That through darkness and death shines her glance.

Amante illuso, io seguo il mio pensier.

RODERIGO
Il dado è tratto! Impavido t'attendo
Ultima sorte, occulto mio destin.
Mi sprona amor, ma un avido, tremendo
Astro di morte infesta il mio cammin.

OTELLO (*turning on the crowd in a terrifying way*)
Ah, leave me!

OTELLO
Fuggite!

EVERYONE
God!

TUTTI
Ciel!

OTELLO (*attacking the crowd*)
Flee from Otello's fury!

OTELLO
Tutti fuggite Otello!

IAGO (*to the others*)
An old and strange disease
Has deprived him of his reason.

JAGO
Lo assale una malia
Che d'ogni senso il priva.

OTELLO
They who remain will be arraigned as rebels!

OTELLO
Chi non si scosta è contro me rubello.

LODOVICO (*trying to induce* DESDEMONA *to go with him*)
Come with me!

LODOVICO
Mi segui . . .

VOICES FROM OFF-STAGE
Otello!

VOCI
Evviva!

DESDEMONA (*tearing herself away from* LODOVICO *and rushing to* OTELLO)
My husband!

DESDEMONA
Mio sposo!

OTELLO (*to* DESDEMONA)
May the Almighty forever damn you!

OTELLO
Anima mia,
Ti maledico!

EVERYONE
Oh God!
(DESDEMONA *leaves, supported by* EMILIA *and* LODOVICO)

TUTTI
Orror! . . .

Scene 9

(OTELLO *and* IAGO *alone*)

OTELLO (*more and more shattered*)
But I must stay behind. Vengeance! . . . Ah . . .
I never forget it . . . Makes one wonder . . .
(*reeling, in spasms*)
In Cassio's arms to see her . . .
and then the kerchief . . . and then the kerchief . . .
the cursed kerchief . . . ah . . . ah . . . ah . . .
(*he faints*)

OTELLO
Fuggirmi io sol non so! . . . Sangue! Ah! l'abbietto
Pensiero! . . . ciò m'accora!
Vederli insieme avvinti . . . il fazzoletto! . . .
Ah!

IAGO (*aside*)
My poison proves effective.

JAGO
(Il mio velen lavora).

VOICES FROM OFF-STAGE
Hail, Otello!

FANFARE E VOCI
Viva Otello!

JAGO
L'eco della vittoria
Porge sua laude estrema.
Chi può vietar che questa fronte prema
Col mio tallone?

FANFARE E VOCI
Evviva Otello! Gloria
Al Leon di Venezia!

JAGO
Ecco il Leone! . . .

IAGO (*listening to the shouting and the fanfares, then contemplating the prostrate* OTELLO)
There! They're sounding your glory,
Paying their brassy tribute!
And on his brow I now could place my heel without
Harm or hindrance!

FANFARES AND VOICES OFF-STAGE
Oh glory! Long live Otello!
Hail to the Lion of Venice!

IAGO (*drawing himself up and pointing with a horrifying gesture of triumph to the motionless body of* OTELLO)
Here lies your lion!

ACT IV

DESDEMONA's *bedroom. A bed, a prayer bench, a table, several chairs and mirrors. A burning lamp is suspended in front of a statue of the Virgin above the prayer bench. A door to the right. It is night. A lamp is burning on the table.*)

Scene 1

(DESDEMONA, EMILIA)

EMILIA

He looked more gentle?

DESDEMONA

So it seemed. He told me to go to rest and to wait for him.
Emilia, let me ask you: Before you go to sleep
Replace these sheets with those that lay there at my wedding!
Listen: If God will have me die before you
Let me be shrouded in one of these linens!

EMILIA

My lady, what a notion!

DESDEMONA

My heart is sad and heavy.
(*sitting down mechanically in front of the mirror*)
My mother long, long ago had a maiden as fair as
She was faithful. Her name was Barbara.
She was in love, the man she loved was false.
I heard her sing a song . . . 'twas called "The Willow-Song."
(*to* EMILIA)
With my hair come and help me!
That song, this evening strangely it fills my heart
With its strain so sad and haunting:
"Softly her tears were falling, and she sat lonely.
Her heart was sinking.
Oh willow! Willow! Willow!
Sadly the birds were calling,
The trees were winking.
Willow! Willow! Willow!
Keep singing, keep singing,
Because tomorrow your bloom will crown my sorrow."
(*to* EMILIA)
Come, finish it! I'm waiting for Otello.
"Brook with your gentle murmur, kiss my golden hair
Among the kindly flowers,
And drink the tears of sadness and despair
Of love's enchanted hours!
Willow! Willow! Willow!
Keep singing, keep singing!

EMILIA

Era più calmo?

DESDEMONA

Mi parea. M'ingiunse
Di coricarmi e d'attenderlo. Emilia,
Te ne prego, distendi sul mio letto
La mia candida veste nuziale.
Senti. Se pria di te morir dovessi,
Mi seppellisci con un di quei veli.

EMILIA

Scacciate queste idee.

DESDEMONA

Son mesta tanto.
Mia madre aveva una povera ancella
Innamorata e bella;
Era il suo nome
Barbara. Amava
Un uom che poi l'abbandonò; cantava.
Una canzone: *la canzon del Salice.*
Mi disciogli le chiome;
Io questa sera ho la memoria piena
Di quella cantilena:
*«Piangea cantando
Nell'erma landa,
Piangea la mesta.
O Salce! Salce! Salce!
Sedea chinando
Sul sen la testa!
O Salce! Salce! Salce!
Cantiamo, cantiamo! il Salce funebre
Sarà la mia ghirlanda.»*
Affrettati; fra poco giunge Otello.
*«Scorreano i rivi fra le zolle in fior,
Gemea quel core affranto,
E dalle ciglia le sgorgava il cor
L'amara onda del pianto.
O Salce! Salce! Salce!
Cantiamo, cantiamo! il Salce funebre
Sarà la mia ghirlanda.»
«Scendean gli augelli a vol dai rami cupi*

Verso quel dolce canto.
E gli occhi suoi piangean tanto, tanto,
Da impietosir le rupi.»
Riponi quest'anello.
Povera Barbara! Solea la storia
Con questo semplice suono finir:
«*Egli era nato—per la sua gloria,*
Io per amar . . . . . .»
Ascolta. Odo un lamento.
Taci. Chi batte a quella porta? . . .

For by tomorrow your bloom will crown my sorrow.
Sweet birds come flying from their shady dwelling,
Moved by her song so tender.
In silent stones is pity's power welling.
They hark in grief and wonder."
(*to* EMILIA, *taking a ring off her finger*)
Be sure to guard this closely!
Unhappy Barbara!
She used to end her sad little song with a sentence like this:
"For he was destined to live in glory,
And I, to love him . . ."
(*interrupting herself*)
Listen! Someone is sighing.
(EMILIA *takes a few steps*)
Listen! I think someone is knocking.

EMILIA
È il vento.

EMILIA
The night wind!

DESDEMONA
«*Io per amarlo e per morir. Cantiamo, cantiamo!*
Salce! Salce! Salce!»
Emilia, addio. Come m'ardon le ciglia!
È presagio di pianto. Buona notte.
Ah, Emilia, Emilia, addio, Emilia, addio!

DESDEMONA
". . . and I, to love him and to die!
Keep singing, keep singing!
Willow! Willow! Willow!"
Farewell, Emilia! How my eyes are burning!
I shall surely be weeping. Good night.
(*she embraces* EMILIA, *who exits. Then suddenly breaks out:*)
Ah, Emilia, farewell, farewell, Emilia!

Scene 2

(DESDEMONA *alone*)

DESDEMONA
Ave Maria, piena di grazia, eletta
Fra le spose e le vergine sei tu;
Sia benedetto il frutto, o benedetta,
Di tue materne viscere, Gesù.
Prega per chi adorando a te si prostra,
Prega pel peccator, per l'innocente
E pel debole oppresso e pel possente,
Misero anch'esso, tua pietà dimostra.
Prega per chi sotto l'oltraggio piega
La fronte e sotto la malvagia sorte;
Per noi tu prega
Sempre e nell'ora della nostra morte.
Ave Maria . . . .
. . . .

DESDEMONA (*kneeling at the prayer bench*)
Hail to Thee, Mary, full of grace. The Lord is with Thee.
Blessed art Thou amongst women, and blessed is the fruit,
Oh Thou most blessed, the fruit of Thy womb,
Our Lord, Jesus.
Ah, pray for her who lies in prayer before Thee,
Take her into Thy grace! Pray for the guiltless!
Give Thine aid to the oppressed and to the mighty.
He, too, will need it. Pray for all who pray to Thee!
Pray, pray for the sinner who can no more bear his burden,
Lost in deepest night and darkness!
Ah, pray for us in heaven, now and forever!
Grant us Thy mercy that we may die forgiven,
Mother of God, Mother of God, oh pray!
(DESDEMONA *remains kneeling, leaning her forehead against the prayer bench. Only the first and last words of the prayer are heard*)

Hail to Thee, Mary . . .
. . . that we may die forgiven!
Mother of God! Amen.
(*she rises, crossing herself, and prepares to go to sleep*)

. . . .
. . . . nell'ora della morte.
Amen.

Scene 3

(DESDEMONA, OTELLO)

(OTELLO *enters through a secret door, deposits a scimitar on the table, stops before the lit lamp, undecided whether to extinguish it. He looks at* DESDEMONA, *then extinguishes the lamp. The only source of light in the room is the lamp over the prayer bench.* OTELLO, *suddenly seized by fury, approaches the bed but stops. He contemplates the sleeping* DESDEMONA *for a long time, then kisses her three times. With the last kiss,* DESDEMONA *awakens*)

DESDEMONA
Who's there?
(*rising*)
Otello?

OTELLO
Yes. Say, have you prayed tonight,
Tell me, Desdemona!

DESDEMONA
I have.

OTELLO
Can you remember a crime for which you omitted
To ask the mercy of God? Do it now without waiting!

DESDEMONA
My lord!

OTELLO
Well, do it! In killing you I want your soul to be saved.

DESDEMONA
You want to kill me?

OTELLO
Yes.

DESDEMONA
Oh God, have mercy on me!

OTELLO
Amen.

DESDEMONA
Otello, have mercy on your wife!

OTELLO
All your crimes remember!

DESDEMONA
All my crime is my love!

DESDEMONA
. . . Chi è là? . . .
Otello?

OTELLO
Sì. Diceste questa sera
Le vostre preci?

DESDEMONA
Orai.

OTELLO
Se vi sovviene
Di qualche colpa commessa che attenda
Grazia dal ciel, imploratela tosto.

DESDEMONA
Perchè?

OTELLO
T'affretta. Uccidere non voglio
L'anima tua.

DESDEMONA
D'uccider parli?

OTELLO
Sì.

DESDEMONA
Pietà di me, mio Dio.

OTELLO
Amen.

DESDEMONA
E abbiate
Pietà voi pure.

OTELLO
Pensa ai tuoi peccati.

DESDEMONA
Mio peccato è l'amor.

OTELLO
Perciò tu muori.

DESDEMONA
E perchè t'amo m'uccidi? . . .

OTELLO
Ami Cassio.

DESDEMONA
No! sull'anima mia!!

OTELLO
Quel fazzoletto
Ch'io ti donai gli desti.

DESDEMONA
Non è vero!

OTELLO
Nella sua man lo vidi.

DESDEMONA
Io rea non sono!

OTELLO
Confessa!

DESDEMONA
Giuro!

OTELLO
Bada allo spergiuro . . .
Pensa che sei sul letto di morte.

DESDEMONA
Non per morir.

OTELLO
Per morir tosto.

DESDEMONA
Aita!
Cassio non amo . . . ch'ei qui venga . . . ei parli.

OTELLO
Muto è per sempre.

DESDEMONA
Cielo! Morto?

OTELLO
Morto.

DESDEMONA
Son perduta! . . . ei tradito!

OTELLO
E pianger l'osi?

DESDEMONA
Otello . . . non uccidermi . . .

OTELLO
Tu invano
Ti difendi.

DESDEMONA
Ch'io viva ancor . . .

OTELLO
Giù, cadi,
Prostituta! . . .

DESDEMONA
Pietà!

OTELLO
And love shall fell you!

DESDEMONA
Because I love you, you kill me?

OTELLO
You love Cassio.

DESDEMONA
No! So help me God!

OTELLO
That handkerchief I gave you, you gave to Cassio.

DESDEMONA
'Tis a falsehood.

OTELLO
In his own hand I saw it.

DESDEMONA
But I am guiltless.

OTELLO
Confess now!

DESDEMONA
I swear it!

OTELLO
So you swear it falsely . . .
Ah, be aware that you're lying on your deathbed!

DESDEMONA
. . . but not to die!

OTELLO
To die at once!

DESDEMONA
Oh help me . . . I don't love Cassio!
Go and call him and ask him!

OTELLO
He speaks no longer.

DESDEMONA
Heaven! Murdered?

OTELLO
Punished.

DESDEMONA
He, betrayed! I, forsaken!

OTELLO
And you bewail him?

DESDEMONA
Expel me, do not murder me!

OTELLO
Too late is all your pleading.

DESDEMONA
Oh spare my life . . .

OTELLO
You die, you whore, you dirty strumpet!

DESDEMONA
Have pity!

OTELLO
No!

DESDEMONA
Just let me live till morning!

OTELLO
No!

DESDEMONA
. . . an hour . . .

OTELLO
No!

DESDEMONA
. . . but one moment!

OTELLO
No!

DESDEMONA
. . . while I say my prayer . . .

OTELLO
Too late!
(he chokes her; DESDEMONA *screams. There is knocking on the door)*
(looking at the motionless body of DESDEMONA*)*
Calm and still as the tomb.

EMILIA *(from outside)*
Open! Open!

OTELLO *(reeling about)*
Who's there? Who's knocking?

EMILIA *(still outside)*
My lord, I beg you: I must speak to you at once. Do open!

OTELLO *(opening the door)*
Emilia? What is it?

EMILIA *(entering)*
A frightful murder: Cassio murdered Roderigo.

OTELLO
And Cassio?

EMILIA
Lives!

OTELLO
Cassio living!!

DESDEMONA *(from her bed)*
I'm dying guiltless . . . I have been killed unjustly . . .

EMILIA *(running to the bed)*
What cry is this? Great God!

DESDEMONA
Ah, I am guiltless . . .

EMILIA
Oh heaven! Who did this deed?

DESDEMONA
Oh . . . no one . . . I cannot . . . pray to my Lord . . . unto His mercy . . .

OTELLO
Muori!!

DESDEMONA
Ch'io viva
Questa notte . . .

OTELLO
No.

DESDEMONA
Un'ora.

OTELLO
No.

DESDEMONA
Un istante.

OTELLO
No.

DESDEMONA
Sol ch'io dica un'Ave.

OTELLO
È tardi . . .
Calma come la tomba.

EMILIA
Aprite! Aprite!

OTELLO
Chi è là! Chi batte?

EMILIA
Signor mio . . . ven prego,
Lasciate ch'io vi parli . . .
Aprite!

OTELLO
Emilia.
Che avvenne?

EMILIA
Un gran delitto! Cassio uccise
Roderigo.

OTELLO
E Cassio?

EMILIA
Vive.

OTELLO
Cassio vive!!

DESDEMONA
Ingiustamente . . . uccisa ingiustamente . . .

EMILIA
Chi geme là? . . . Orror!

DESDEMONA
Muoio innocente . . .

EMILIA
Gran Dio! . . . Chi fu?

DESDEMONA
Nessuno . . . io stessa . . . al mio
Signor mi raccomanda . . .

Muoio innocente . . .
Addio . . .

I die here guiltless . . . I'm dying . . .
(DESDEMONA *dies*)

OTELLO
O mentitrice! io l'uccisi.

OTELLO
She dies a liar: I have killed her.

EMILIA
Assassino!

EMILIA
Vile assassin!

OTELLO
Fu di Cassio la druda. A Jago il chiedi.

OTELLO
She betrayed me with Cassio. Your husband told me.

EMILIA
A Jago?!

EMILIA
My husband?

OTELLO
A Jago.

OTELLO
Yes, Iago!

EMILIA
Stolto!! e tu il credesti? . . .

EMILIA
Fool! You did believe him?

OTELLO
Negarlo ardisci?!

OTELLO (*threatening* EMILIA)
You dare deny it?

EMILIA
Non ti temo.

EMILIA
Yes, I dare it.

OTELLO
Bada!

OTELLO
You wench!
(*he grabs hold of her*)

EMILIA
Olà! Soccorso! Aiuto! Otello uccise
Desdemona!

EMILIA
Oh God! Oh help me!
(*she frees herself and runs screaming to the door*)
Otello killed the fair Desdemona!

Scene 4

(OTELLO, EMILIA, LODOVICO, CASSIO, IAGO, *later* MONTANO *with some soldiers*)

JAGO, CASSIO, LODOVICO
Quai grida!
Orrore! Orror!

ALL EXCEPT OTELLO AND EMILIA
Oh horror! Oh horror! Alas!

EMILIA
Jago, smentisci quel vile assassino.
Hai tu creduto Desdemona infida?
Parla!

EMILIA
Iago, you tell this assassin the truth:
You did believe in our lady's betrayal? Answer!

JAGO
Tal la credea.

IAGO
So I believed.

OTELLO
Quel fazzoletto
Che un dì le diedi, a Cassio essa donava.

OTELLO
The flowered kerchief which first I gave her . . .
'Twas Cassio to whom she gave it!

EMILIA
O potenza divina!

EMILIA
All you heavenly powers!

JAGO
Taci.

IAGO (*to* EMILIA, *aside*)
Quiet!

EMILIA
No.
Tutto rivelo!

EMILIA
No! I shall reveal it!

IAGO
Silence!

EMILIA
No! That handkerchief he tore away from me
And forced me not to tell her.

CASSIO
And I did never know how it came to me.

MONTANO (*entering and pointing to* IAGO)
Roderigo revealed me ere he died
All the dark plots of this villain.

OTELLO (*to* IAGO)
Ah . . . refute the charge!

IAGO (*fleeing*)
No!

LODOVICO
Stop him!

MONTANO
Arrest him!

CASSIO AND LODOVICO
Stop the murderer!
(*several men pursue* IAGO)

OTELLO (*runs to the table to seize the scimitar*)
Oh God, hast Thou no lightning left?

LODOVICO
Give me your sword!

OTELLO
Don't dare it!
No one fear me and my powerless weapon!
All now is over. This is the end.
Oh glory! Otello was.
(*he drops the sword, then slowly moves close to the bed to gaze at* DESDEMONA)
And you, you are so pale, my love,
So tired, so silent, so beautiful.
Star-crossed beloved so tender,
Born in a world of evil.
Cold now, pure as a child, like an angel
You go to heaven . . .
Desdemona! Desdemona!
Ah, dearest, dead beloved!
(*he furtively draws a dagger from his doublet*)
I'll go with you!
(*stabs himself*)

CASSIO
Ah, hold him!

LODOVICO AND MONTANO
Ah, Otello!

JAGO
Taci.

EMILIA
No! Costui
Dalla mia man quel fazzoletto svelse
A viva forza.

CASSIO
E nella mia dimora
Trovai quel vel.

MONTANO
Roderigo morente
Mi svelò di quest'uom l'arti nefande.

OTELLO
Ah! discolpati!!

JAGO
No.

LODOVICO
Ferma.

MONTANO
S'insegua.

CASSIO, LODOVICO
Afferratelo!

OTELLO
E il ciel non ha più fulmini?! . . .

LODOVICO
La spada a me!

OTELLO
Tant'osi! Niun mi tema
S'anco armato mi vede. Ecco la fine
Del mio cammin . . . Oh! Gloria! Otello fu.
E tu . . . come sei pallida! e stanca, e muta, e bella,
Pia creatura nata sotto maligna stella.
Fredda come la casta tua vita, e in cielo assorta.
Desdemona! Desdemona! . . . Ah! . . . morta! . . . morta! . . . morta! . . .
Ho un'arma ancor!

CASSIO
Ah! Ferma!

LODOVICO, MONTANO
Sciagurato!

OTELLO

Pria d'ucciderti . . . sposa . . .
ti baciai.
Or morendo . . . nell'ombra
. . . in cui mi giacio . . .
Un bacio . . . un bacio ancora . . . un altro bacio . . .

OTELLO

When I entered here I kissed you ere I killed you.
Now I'm dying, and night enshrouds my senses . . .
to kiss you . . . once more to kiss you . . .
once more to kiss you . . .

(OTELLO *dies*)

I PAGLIACCI

by Ruggiero Leoncavallo (1858–1919)

LIBRETTO BY THE COMPOSER

Translated by GEORGE MEAD

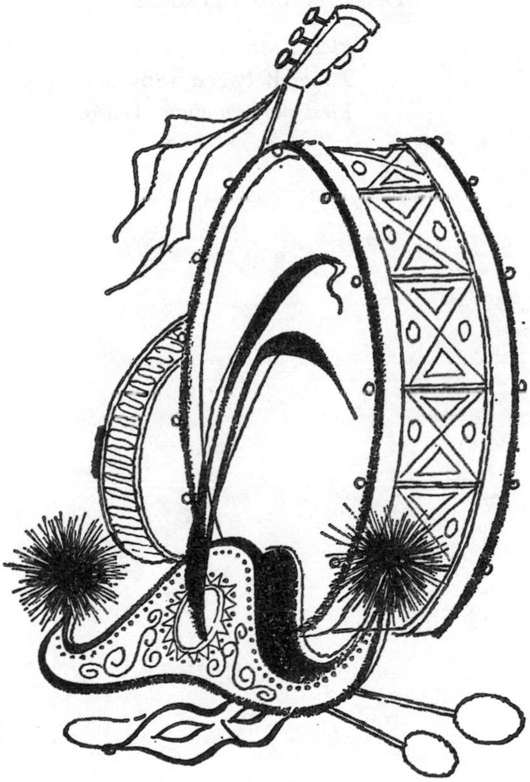

CHARACTERS

CANIO, *head of a troupe of strolling players ("Pagliaccio," First Clown, in the play)*	*Tenor*
NEDDA, *his wife ("Columbine" in the play)*	*Soprano*
TONIO, *an actor ("Taddeo," Second Clown, in the play)*	*Baritone*
PEPPE, *or* BEPPE, *an actor ("Harlequin" in the play)*	*Tenor*
SILVIO, *a villager, lover of Nedda*	*Baritone*
PEASANTS AND VILLAGERS	

Place: Montalto, province of Calabria, Italy
Time: Between 1865 and 1870
First performance: Teatro dal Verme, Milan, May 21, 1892

ENGLISH VERSION COPYRIGHT 1959, BY GEORGE MEAD. PERFORMANCE RIGHTS RESERVED

PROLOGUE

(TONIO, *dressed as Taddeo, the Clown of the traditional Commedia, comes in front of the curtain.*)

TONIO

My friends! My friends! Dear ladies and gentlemen! You'll pardon me for appearing alone here. I am the Prologue. The author of the play wished to revive the old masks and costumes. He wished to bring to life again the old conventions, and therefore I stand before you. Not with the words they used to say: "Do not be afraid if we sigh and suffer! If we weep for you, it is only a play, do not alarm yourselves!" No, no! The author desires his play to portray for you life as all of us know it, and that the artist must be first of all a man. All that he writes is for man's understanding, and he writes with the truth in him.

A dream of tender memories sang in his inmost soul early one morning. He wrote every word with tears of compassion, and his sobs beat the tempo of that surging song. Therefore, love will appear as human love that we see all around us, and hate will be shown with its sad fulfillment, sorrow's tears and grief's despair, flashes of rage and anger, and sneering laughter!

I pray you, remember that the foolish garb which we must wear should not deceive you. It's the souls of us you must consider, for we are men like you, the same lonely mortals. Flesh and blood, we breathe all together the life-giving air of this sad world of ours.

That's the dream of the author. Now you will see how he has portrayed it.

(*calling toward the wings*)

Let's go! Time to be starting!

(*exit* TONIO, *the curtain rises*)

TONIO

Si può? Si può? . . . Signore! Signori! . . . Scusatemi se da sol mi presento.—Io sono il Prologo. Poichè in iscena ancor le antiche maschere mette l'autore, in parte ei vuol riprendere le vecchie usanze, e a voi di nuovo inviami. Ma non per dirvi come pria: "Le lacrime che noi versiam son false: Degli spasimi e de' nostri martir non allarmatevi!" No, no. L'autore ha cercato invece pingervi uno squarcio di vita. Egli ha per massima sol che l'artista è un uomo e che per gli uomini scrivere ei deve.—Ed al vero ispiravasi.

Un nido di memorie in fondo a l'anima cantava un giorno, ed ei con vere lacrime scrisse, e i singhiozzi il tempo gli battevano! Dunque, vedrete amar sì come s'amano gli esseri umani; vedrete de l'odio i tristi frutti. Del dolor gli spasimi, urli di rabbia, udrete, e risa ciniche!

E voi, piuttosto che le nostre povere gabbane d'istrioni, le nostr'anime considerate, poichè siam uomini di carne e d'ossa, e che di quest'orfano mondo al pari di voi spiriamo l'aere!

Il concetto vi dissi.—Or ascoltate com'egli è svolto. Andiamo. Incominciate!

ACT I

Scene 1

(*A crossroads at the entrance to a village in Calabria. At right, a traveling theater. As the curtain rises there are sounds of an out-of-tune trumpet alternating with loud bass-drum beats. Villagers in holiday clothes come in laughing, whistling, and shouting.* TONIO *the clown looks up the road on the left, then, exasperated by the staring crowd, he lies down in front of the theater.*

The time is the Feast of the Assumption in August. It is three o'clock on a sunny afternoon.)

(*Chorus of men and women,* NEDDA, CANIO, TONIO, *and* PEPPE.)

CORO DI UOMINI E DONNE
Son quà!
Ritornano . . .
Pagliaccio è là.
Tutti lo seguono,
Grandi e ragazzi,
Ai motti, ai lazzi.
Applaude ognun.
Ed egli serio
Saluta e passa,
E torna a battere
Sulla gran cassa.
Già fra le strida i monelli.
In aria gittano
I lor cappelli diggià.
Fra strida e sibili diggià.

CHORUS
They're here!
They're here again . . .
Pagliaccio's here.
The people follow them,
The old and young folks,
They all have gathered
To see the fun.
He's very serious!
See how politely
He bows as he passes!
Now he is beating the drum again.
The boys are cheering now,
They throw their caps in the air!

RAGAZZI
Ehi, sferza l'asino, bravo Arlecchino!

BOYS (*from behind*)
Hey you, Harlequin, wake up the donkey!

CANIO
Itene al diavolo!

CANIO (*from behind*)
Go to the devil!

PEPPE
To, birichino!

PEPPE (*from behind*)
Hey! Hey! Get along!
(*a group of boys enters running from the left*)

CORO
Indietro, arrivano . . .
Ecco il carretto . . .
Che diavolerio!
Dio benedetto!

CHORUS
And there's the wagon . . .
Get back there . . . they're here again!
Oh, what a devil of a noise!
O blessed Lord in heaven!
(PEPPE, *dressed as Harlequin, enters leading a donkey that is drawing a gaily decorated cart.* NEDDA, *dressed as a gypsy, is lying in the cart, and behind her is* CANIO, *dressed as Pagliaccio, with a trumpet in one hand and drumsticks in the other. The bass drum stands in the cart behind* NEDDA. *The villagers gaily surround the cart*)

CORO
Evviva! il principe
Se' dei pagliacci!
I guai discacci tu

CHORUS
Here's to the best of all, our friend Pagliaccio,
Here's to the man

Who brings us fun and laughter!
You drive our sorrows all away,
Hurray!

Co 'l lieto umore.
Evviva!

CANIO
Thank you!

CANIO
Grazie . . .

CHORUS
Bravo!

CORO
Bravo!

CANIO
My friends!

CANIO
Vorrei . . .

CHORUS
When does the show begin?

CORO
E lo spettacolo?

CANIO (*banging the drum to subdue the crowd*)
Ladies and gentlemen!

CANIO
Signori miei!

CHORUS (*putting their hands over their ears*)
Hey! You'll deafen us . . . ! It's time we stopped . . .

CORO
Uh! ci assorda! . . . finiscila!

CANIO (*taking off his cap with a sweeping, comic gesture*)
Now may I say a word?

CANIO
Mi accordan di parlar?

THE CROWD (*laughing*)
All right, let's give in to him!
Be quiet, and let him speak!

LA FOLLA
Oh! con lui si dee cedere,
Tacere ed ascoltar.

CANIO
Tonight you will see
A most wonderful play,
Prepared and produced
By your humble servant.
You'll see poor Pagliaccio
And how he was betrayed,
You'll see his revenge
And the traps that he laid.
And Tonio the Clown
All trembling and shaking,
And plotting and scheming,
And going astray.
So, ladies and gentlemen,
We hope for your presence
Tonight at eleven,
Tonight at eleven!

CANIO
Un grande spettacolo
A ventitrè ore
Prepara il vostr'umile
E buon servitore.
Vedrete le smanie
Del bravo Pagliaccio;
E com'ei si vendica
E tende un bel laccio.
Vedrete di Tonio
Tremar la carcassa,
E quale matassa
D'intrighi ordirà.
Venite, onorateci,
Signori e Signore.
A ventitrè ore!
A ventitrè ore!

THE CROWD
We'll come if you promise us
That we will enjoy it,
Tonight at eleven,
Tonight at eleven!

LA FOLLA
Verremo, e tu serbaci
Il tuo buon umore.
A ventitrè ore!
A ventitrè ore!

(TONIO *comes to help* NEDDA *down from the cart, but* CANIO, *who is already on the ground, gives him a box on the ear.*)

CANIO
Get away!

CANIO
Via da lì.

(*he takes* NEDDA *by the arms and lifts her down from the cart*)

WOMEN (*laughing at* TONIO)
That for you, you handsome lover!

LE DONNE
Prendi questo, bel galante!

I RAGAZZI
Con salute!

TONIO
La pagherai! . . . brigante.

UN CONTADINO
Di', con noi vuo' tu bevere
Un buon bicchiere sulla crocevia?

CANIO
Con piacere.

PEPPE
Aspettatemi . . .
Anch'io ci sto!

CANIO
Di' Tonio, vieni via?

TONIO
Io netto il somarello.
Precedetemi.

UN CONTADINO
Bada, Pagliaccio, ei solo vuol restare
Per far la corte a Nedda.

CANIO
Eh! Eh! vi pare?
Un tal gioco, credetemi, è meglio non giocarlo
Con me, miei cari; e a Tonio . . . e un poco a tutti or parlo.
Il teatro e la vita non son la stessa cosa;
E se lassù Pagliaccio sorprende la sua sposa
Col bel galante in camera, fa un comico sermone,
Poi si calma od arrendesi ai colpi di bastone! . . .
Ed il pubblico applaude, ridendo allegramente.
Ma se Nedda sul serio sorprendessi . . . altramente
Finirebbe la storia, com'è ver che vi parlo . . .
Un tal gioco, credetemi, è meglio non giocarlo.

NEDDA
Confusa io son! . . .

ALCUNI CONTADINI
Sul serio pigli dunque la cosa?

BOYS (*making fun of him*)
What a man!
(TONIO *shakes his fist at the boys, who run away.* TONIO *goes off, grumbling*)

TONIO (*aside*)
I'll make him pay for this, the blackguard!
(PEPPE *leads off the donkey and cart behind the theater*)

A VILLAGER
Say, would you like to come with us down to the inn
To drink a glass together. Come, what say?

CANIO
Yes, with pleasure!
(PEPPE *reappears, and throws down his whip in front of the theater*)

PEPPE
Count me in on that! I want one too.
(*he enters the theater to change his clothes*)

CANIO (*calling toward the theater*)
Hey, Tonio! Are you coming?

TONIO (*behind*)
I have to rub down the donkey.
Do not wait for me.

VILLAGER (*to* CANIO, *laughing*)
Watch him, Pagliaccio, he wants to stay behind here
So he can make love to Nedda!

CANIO (*smiling, but with a slight frown*)
Eh! Eh! Are you joking?
(*half in earnest, half ironically*)
Jokes like that, believe me, had better not be played
On me, good people. I say this to Tonio, and to you, my friends,
For the stage, there, is one thing, but life is quite another.
They are not the same thing at all!
Our play will show Pagliaccio, his lady, and her lover,
And when they make a fool of him, you'll see him boiling over!
Not for long, though. He subsides when his betrayer starts to beat him.
How the audience will laugh and applaud when they mistreat him!
But if Nedda in real life should betray me, then the story
Would have a different ending. And it would not be pretending!
Jokes like that, believe me . . . it's better not to play them!

NEDDA (*aside*)
What does he know?

OTHER VILLAGERS
Pagliaccio, can you really be serious?

CANIO (*slightly moved*)
Me! Be serious! Excuse me!
I love my wife most dearly!
(*he kisses* NEDDA *on the forehead. Sound of bagpipes off-stage. People run left and look off*)

CANIO
Io? . . . Vi pare! . . . Scusatemi . . .
Adoro la mia sposa!

BOYS
Here come the bagpipes! Here come the bagpipes!

I RAGAZZI
I zampognari! . . . I zampognari! . . .

MEN
All of our friends are going to church now.

GLI UOMINI
Verso la chiesa vanno i compari.

THE OLD FOLKS
All of the people are going to vespers,
All the young lovers are going together.

I VECCHI
Essi accompagnano la comitiva
Che a coppie al vespero sen va giuliva.

WOMEN
Come! The church bell is ringing
The call of the Lord.

LE DONNE
Andiam.—La campana
Ci appella al signore.

CANIO
Be sure to be here with us
Tonight at eleven.

CANIO
Ma poi . . . ricordatevi,
A ventitrè ore.

(*the bagpipe players enter from the left in holiday dress. A group of villagers follows. Villagers on-stage greet them. The crowd breaks up into couples and small groups. At the end of the chorus below they go off singing, down the road behind the theater*)

CHORUS
Ding! Dong! goes the vesper bell.
You lasses and lads,
Let's go to church all arm in arm!
Ding! Dong! Now the sun is setting
Golden and fair.
The mothers are watching
Their daughters with care.
Ding! Dong! All the world is shining
With love and joy.
But the old folks keep watchful eyes
On each girl and boy.

CORO
Din, don,—suona vespero,
Ragazze e garzon!
A coppie al tempio
Ci affretiam—din, don,
Din, don, diggià i culmini
Il sol vuol baciar
Le mamme ci adocchiano,
Attenti, compar.
Din, don.—Tutto irradiasi
Di luce, d'amor;
Ma i vecchi sorvegliano,
Gli arditi amador.

(*during the chorus* CANIO *enters the theater, and then returns, having changed from his stage costume into street clothes. With a smile, he nods good-by to* NEDDA, *then goes off with* PEPPE *and several villagers.* NEDDA *remains*)

Scene 2

NEDDA (*musing*)
What a piercing look he gave me!
I looked away, for my eyes might have betrayed all the thoughts my heart is concealing.
Oh, what if he should catch me! How cruel he would be!

NEDDA
Qual fiamma avea nel guardo!
Gli occhi abbassai per tema ch'ei leggesse
Il mio pensier segreto.
Oh! s'ei mi sorprendesse . . .

Brutale come egli è . . . Ma basti, orvia.
Son questi sogni paurosi e fole!
O che bel sole
Di mezz'agosto! Io son piena di vita, e, tutta illanguidita
Per arcano desio, non so che bramo!

Oh! che volo d'augelli, e quante strida! . . .
Che chiedon? dove van? chissà . . . La mamma
Mia, che la buona ventura annunziava,
Comprendeva il lor canto e a me bambina così cantava:
Hui! stridono lassù, liberamente,
Lanciati a vol come frecce, gli augel.
Disfidano le nubi e 'l sol cocente,
E vanno, e vanno per le vie del ciel.
Lasciateli vagar per l'atmosfera
Questi assetati d'azzurro e splendor:
Seguono anch'essi un sogno, una chimera,
E vanno, e vanno fra le nubi d'or.
Che incalzi il vento e latri la tempesta,
Con l'ali aperte san tutto sfidar;
La pioggia, i lampi, nulla mai li arresta,
E vanno, e vanno, sugli abissi e i mar.
Vanno laggiù verso un paese strano,
Che sognan forse e che cercano invan.
Ma i boëmi del ciel seguon l'arcano
Poter che li sospinge . . . e van . . . e van!

NEDDA
Sei là? credea che te ne fossi andato.

TONIO
È colpa del tuo canto. Affascinato
Io mi beava!

NEDDA
Oh! quanta poesia! . . .

TONIO
Non rider, Nedda . . .

NEDDA
Va, va all'osteria.

TONIO
So ben che difforme, contorto son io,
Che desto soltanto lo scherno e l'orror.

Enough of that! No more now. I've had enough of all these dreadful dreams.
Now all the world is aglow with summer,
With the joy of living,
And I am filled with longing,
With a strange, sweet desire beyond my knowing.
(*looking at the sky*)
Oh, you brave little birds, what are you seeking?
My dear old mother, who knew all the secrets of the woodland,
Knew the meaning of your song.
When I was a child,
I would hear her singing:
Hui! Hear them call and cry, wheeling and gliding,
Off on the wing, as swift as an arrow in flight.
They sail up to the clouds where the sun is riding,
Forever climbing to the heavenly height.
May life never confine them, free may they wander,
Searching the clouds for the heaven they know is there!
How, like my heart, they pursue a vision of rapture,
Forever climbing in the golden air.
Storms may beset them, the lightning flash may blind them,
Winds may delay them, the thunder may roar,
They never falter, they never waver
As on they journey over sea and shore.
Onward they fly! Who knows where they are going,
Flying and dreaming of lands beyond the sky?
Wandering gypsies of heaven, never, never knowing
The power driving them onward, they fly! They fly!
(*during the song* TONIO *comes from behind the theater and leans against a tree, listening. As* NEDDA *moves to go off, she sees him*)

NEDDA (*suddenly annoyed*)
You here! I thought you had gone to the tavern.

TONIO (*coming forward*)
I stayed because you were singing.
It was a blessing sent from heaven!

NEDDA (*laughing with scorn*)
Haha! Isn't that poetic!

TONIO
Nedda, don't laugh!

NEDDA
Go! Go to the tavern!

TONIO
I know that my body is ugly and broken,
That people avoid me as one set apart,

But I have my dreams and desires unspoken within my poor heart!
And when you pass by me, my hope of salvation
As I pass my days here in sorrow and strife,
How can you deny me my heart's adoration?
For you are my love, the love of my life!
I want to come close to you . . . and tell you . . .

Eppure ha 'l pensiero un sogno, un desio, e un palpito il cor!
Allor che sdegnosa mi passi d'accanto
Non sai tu che pianto mi spreme il dolor!
Perchè, mio malgrado, subito ho l'incanto,
M'ha vinto l'amor!
Oh! lasciami, lasciami
Or dirti . . .

NEDDA (*interrupting and scoffing at him*)
You love me!
The time to declare your love
Is later tonight,
When you're playing the fool
Up there on the stage!
But now is no time for love.
We'll take care of you later!

NEDDA
Che m'ami?
Hai tempo a ridirmelo
Stassera, se brami!
Facendo le smorfie
Colà, sulla scena.
Per ora tal pena
Ti puoi risparmiar!

TONIO
No, it's now that I must speak to you,
It's now that you must hear me!
I love you, Nedda, I long for you,
I long to make you my own!

TONIO
No, è qui che voglio dirtelo—
E tu m'ascolterai—
Che t'amo e ti desidero,
E che tu mia sarai!

NEDDA (*with studied insolence*)
What! Maybe, Master Tonio,
Your back needs to be scratched,
Maybe your ears need to be pulled
To bring your fever down!

NEDDA
Eh! dite, mastro Tonio!
La schiena oggi vi prude, o una tirata
D'orecchi è necessaria
Al vostro ardor?

TONIO
You mock me! You devil!
By the holy cross, Nedda,
Those words will cost you dear!

TONIO
Ti beffi? sciagurata!
Per la croce di Dio, bada che puoi
Pagarla cara! . . .

NEDDA
You threaten me?
Maybe I should call for Canio!

NEDDA
Minacci? . . . Vuoi
Che vada a chiamar Canio?

TONIO
But not before I kiss you . . .

TONIO
Non prima ch'io ti baci!

NEDDA (*drawing back*)
Stop!

NEDDA
Bada!

TONIO
You're mine and I shall have you!
(*moving toward her*)
(*moving backward toward the theater, she sees the whip left by* PEPPE, *picks it up, and strikes* TONIO *in the face*)

TONIO
Oh, tosto sarai mia! . . .

NEDDA
You dog!

NEDDA
Miserabile! . . .

TONIO (*screaming and drawing back*)
By the Blessed Virgin of the Assumption, Nedda,
I swear . . . you shall pay for this!
(*he goes off, threatening*)

TONIO
Ah! Per la Vergin pia di mezz'agosto
Nedda, lo giuro . . . me la pagherai! . . .

NEDDA
Aspide! va.—Ti sei svelato ormai
Tonio lo scemo!—Hai l'animo
Siccome il corpo tuo difforme
. . . lurido! . . .

NEDDA (*motionless, watching him*)
Beast! Go! At last you have revealed yourself . . . Tonio, the Beast!
The soul of you is like your crooked body . . .
Deformed . . . evil . . .

Scene 3

SILVIO
Nedda!

SILVIO (*he leans over the wall at right, and calls in a low voice*)
Nedda!

NEDDA
Silvio! a quest'ora . . . che imprudenza.

NEDDA (*hurrying toward him*)
Silvio! at such a time! How unwise!

SILVIO
Ah bah! sapea ch'io non
Rischiavo nulla.
Canio e Peppe da lunge a la taverna
Ho scorto! . . . Ma prudente
Per la macchia a me nota qui ne venni.

SILVIO (*he jumps lightly over the wall and comes smiling toward* NEDDA)
Bah! But really I was not risking much.
Canio and Peppe are safe inside the tavern.
I watched them go in together.
So I came here unobserved by the pathway that we know.

NEDDA
E ancora un poco in Tonio t'imbattevi.

NEDDA
You took a chance, though. You nearly met with Tonio.

SILVIO
Oh! Tonio il gobbo!

SILVIO (*laughing*)
Hah! Tonio the Fool!

NEDDA
Il gobbo è da temersi.
M'ama . . . Ora qui mel disse! . . . e nel bestial
Delirio suo, baci chiedendo, ardia
Correr su me . . .

NEDDA
A fool, and yet I fear him.
He loves me . . . just now he told me
And in a burst of wild desire he tried to kiss me
And to take me in his arms!

SILVIO
Per Dio!

SILVIO
By God!

NEDDA
Ma con la frusta
Del cane immondo la foga calmai.

NEDDA
I took this whip . . . I calmed him down,
The sly, sneaking scoundrel!

SILVIO
E fra quest'ansie in eterno vivrai?
Decidi il mio destin,
Nedda, Nedda rimani!
Tu il sai; la festa ha fin
E parte ognun domani.
E quando tu di qui sarai partita
Che addiverrà di me . . . della mia vita? . . .

SILVIO
Is all your life, dear, to be filled with such pain?
Nedda! What is to be my fate?
Nedda! Joy or sorrow?
The fair will end tonight,
You will be gone by tomorrow.
What will be left for me when you have gone?
What is my life to be when I am here alone?

NEDDA
Silvio!

NEDDA (*deeply moved*)
Silvio!

SILVIO
Nedda, Nedda, rispondimi.
Se è ver che Canio non amasti mai,
Se è vero che t'è in odio

SILVIO
Nedda, Nedda, oh answer me,
If it is true you have no love for Canio,
If you hope to be happy,

Hope to be free from this wretched existence,
If your love for me is not just for a day,
Let us leave here tonight, Nedda! Come, come away!

NEDDA
Don't tempt me so! Would you add to all my sadness?
Darling Silvio, be still! What you ask of me is madness.
My love is only for you, I give you all my heart.
Be kind to me, and true when we are far apart.
Don't tempt me so! Maybe it's best that I go away.
Fate has kept us apart. There's nothing more to say.
And yet, my love is yours, my love is yours forever,
And your love shall sustain my poor heart now and ever.
(TONIO *appears at back, left*)

SILVIO
No! You do not love me!

TONIO (*aside*)
I've caught you, I've caught you!

NEDDA
I love you, love you!

SILVIO
And tomorrow you would leave me!
(*lovingly, trying to persuade her*)
Why did you give me all you have given
If you can leave me, leave me like this?
Letting me dream that I was in heaven,
Knowing the rapture of your sweet kiss!
Can you forget our moments together,
Can you forget the joy we have known?
I shall remember, I shall remember
Each moment forever, Nedda, my own!

NEDDA (*overcome and yielding*)
Could I forget? Ah, how could I ever,
When I can see all the love that shines in your eyes!
Ah, if I were your own, all your own forever,
All my life would be heaven, sunlight and cloudless skies.
Always beside you, waking and sleeping,
Soul and body forever in your keeping!

BOTH
Let me forget all the world and its sorrow in your dear eyes!
One kiss and all is forgotten in your dear eyes!

SILVIO (*taking her in his arms*)
You'll come?

Il ramingar e 'l mestier che tu fai,
Se l'immenso amor tuo una fola non è,
Questa notte partiam! . . . fuggi, fuggi con me.

NEDDA
Non mi tentar! . . . Vuoi tu perder la vita mia?
Taci Silvio, non più . . .—È delirio . . . è follìa! . . .
Io mi confido a te—a te cui diedi il cor
Non abusar di me—del mio febbrile amor! . . .
Non mi tentar! . . . E poi . . . —Chissà! meglio è partir:
Sta il destin contro noi.—È vano il nostro dir.
Eppure da l' mio cor—strapparti non poss'io,
Vivrò sol de l'amor—ch'hai destato al cor mio.

SILVIO
No, più non m'ami!

TONIO
T'ho colta, sgualdrina!

NEDDA
Sì, t'amo! t'amo!

SILVIO
E parti domattina? . . .
E allor perchè, di', tu m'hai stregato
Se vuoi lasciarmi senza pietà?
Quel bacio tuo perchè me l'hai dato
Fra spasmi ardenti di voluttà?
Se tu scordasti l'ore fugaci
Io non lo posso, e voglio ancor
Que' spasmi ardenti, que' caldi baci
Che tanta febbre m'han messo in cor!

NEDDA
Nulla scordai—sconvolta e turbata
M'ha questo amor che ne 'l guardo ti sfavilla.
Viver voglio a te avvinta, affascinata
Una vita d'amor calma a tranquilla.
A te mi dono; su me solo impera.
Ed io ti prendo e m'abbandono intera.

NEDDA, SILVIO
Tutto scordiam, tutto scordiam.
Negli occhi mi guarda (ti guardo)
Baciami (ti bacio), tutto scordiamo!

SILVIO
Verrai? . . .

NEDDA
Sì—Baciami! . . .

NEDDA
Yes! Kiss me!

NEDDA, SILVIO
Sì, mi (ti) guarda(o) e mi (ti) bacio! T'amo . . . t'amo!

BOTH
Yes! Oh, kiss me once more! I love you, love you!

Scene 4

(*While* NEDDA *and* SILVIO *move toward the wall, talking,* CANIO *and* TONIO *enter stealthily from the short path.*)

TONIO
Cammina adagio e li sorprenderai.

TONIO (*holding* CANIO *back*)
Now just step softly. We'll take them by surprise.
(CANIO *advances cautiously, still held back by* TONIO. *They cannot see* SILVIO, *who is getting over the wall*)

SILVIO
Ad alta notte laggiù mi terrò.
Cauta discendi e mi ritroverai.

SILVIO (*halfway over the wall*)
I'll come at midnight. I'll meet you down there . . . I will be waiting.
Take care that no one sees you!
(SILVIO *disappears,* CANIO *approaches the corner of the theater*)

NEDDA
A stanotte—e per sempre tua sarò!

NEDDA (*to* SILVIO *as he goes*)
Till tonight . . . and forever I shall be yours!

CANIO
Oh! . . .

CANIO (*who has heard what* NEDDA *said*)
Ah!

NEDDA
Fuggi!

NEDDA (*she turns at* CANIO*'s shout, then calls in the direction where* SILVIO *went over the wall*)
Go!
(CANIO *rushes toward the wall.* NEDDA *bars his way. They struggle, he pushes her aside and leaps over the wall and disappears.* TONIO *remains at left watching* NEDDA. NEDDA *is at the wall trying to see what is happening on the other side*)

NEDDA
Aiutalo . . . Signor! . . .

NEDDA
May God protect him now!

TONIO
Ah! . . . ah!

TONIO (*laughing cynically*)
Ah! Ah!

LA VOCE DI CANIO
Vile! t'ascondi!

CANIO (*outside*)
Scoundrel! Where are you!

NEDDA
Bravo! Bravo il mio Tonio!

NEDDA (*turns at the sound of* TONIO*'s laugh and looks at him with disgust*)
Bravo, bravo, my Tonio!

TONIO
Fo quel che posso!

TONIO
I did all I could.

NEDDA
È quello che pensavo!

NEDDA
It's just what I expected.

TONIO
Ma di far assai meglio non dispero.

TONIO
But I hope very soon to do even better.

NEDDA
Mi fai schifo e ribrezzo.

NEDDA
You low, evil beast!

TONIO
You can't imagine how happy I feel!
(CANIO *comes back over the wall. He looks pale, and is wiping the perspiration from his forehead with a dark-colored handkerchief*)

CANIO (*trying to hold in his anger*)
They have made a fool of me!
He's gone! How well he must have known that secret path!
But no matter . . . because you're going to tell me . . .
Tell me his name!

NEDDA (*turning, confused*)
Me!

CANIO (*in a fury*)
You, by God in heaven!
(*drawing a stiletto from his belt*)
If perhaps you are wondering why I haven't used my knife,
It's because I hate to stain it with your false, faithless blood.
You have betrayed me! Who is your lover?
Who is your lover? Tell me!

NEDDA
I'll never tell you. I swear I'll never tell you!

CANIO (*shouting*)
His name . . .! You tell me! I command you to tell me!

NEDDA
No! I'll never tell!

CANIO (*rushing on her furiously, raising the dagger*)
Ah! By the Virgin!
(PEPPE *entering left and hearing* NEDDA'S *answer, snatches the dagger from* CANIO *and throws it away among the trees*)

PEPPE
Master! For the love of heaven!
The church service is over. Soon they will be here to see the show.
Come on! Come, control yourself!

CANIO (*struggling*)
Peppe, let go of me! His name! His name!

PEPPE
Tonio, help me to hold him!
(TONIO *takes* CANIO *by the hand*)
Let's go! Here come the people!
(*to* CANIO)
Speak to her later!
(*to* NEDDA)
It's best for you to leave us now.
Get ready for the show.
Remember . . . Canio, though he's rough, he's good.

TONIO
Oh, non sai come
Lieto ne son!

CANIO
Derisione e scherno!
Nulla! Ei ben lo conosce quel sentier.
Fa lo stesso; poichè del drudo il nome
Or mi dirai.

NEDDA
Chi? . . .

CANIO
Tu, pel padre eterno! . . .
E se in questo momento qui scannata
Non t'ho già, gli è perchè pria di lordarla
Nel tuo fetido sangue, o svergognata,
Codesta lama, io vo' il suo nome.—Parla.

NEDDA
Vano è l'insulto.—È muto il labbro mio.

CANIO
Il nome, il nome, non tardare, o donna!

NEDDA
No, nol dirò giammai . . .

CANIO
Per la madonna! . . .

PEPPE
Padron! che fate! . . . Per l'amor di Dio . . .
La gente esce di chiesa e a lo spettacolo
Qui muove . . . andiamo via calmatevi!

CANIO
Lasciami Peppe—il nome, il nome!

PEPPE
Tonio, vieni a tenerlo.
Andiamo; arriva il pubblico.
Vi spiegherete.—E voi di lì tiratevi,
Andatevi a vestir. Sapete, Canio
È violento, ma buon . . .

CANIO
Infamia! infamia!

TONIO
Calmatevi padrone.—È meglio fingere;
Il ganzo tornerà.—Di me fidatevi.
Io la sorveglio—Ora facciam la recita.
Chissà ch'egli non venga a lo spettacolo
E si tradisca! Or via.—Bisogna fingere
Per riuscir . . .

PEPPE
Andiamo, via, vestitevi,
Padrone.—E tu batti la cassa, Tonio.

CANIO
Recitar! . . . mentre preso dal delirio
Non so più quel che dico e quel che faccio!
Eppur . . . è d'uopo . . . sforzati!
Bah, sei tu forse un uom? Tu se' Pagliaccio!
Vesti la giubba e la faccia infarina.
La gente paga e rider vuole quà.
E se Arlecchin t'invola Colombina,
Ridi, Pagliaccio . . . e ognun applaudirà!
Tramuta in lazzi lo spasmo ed il pianto;
In una smorfia il singhiozzo e 'l dolor . . .
Ridi, Pagliaccio, sul tuo amore infranto!
Ridi del duol che t'avvelena il cor!

CANIO (*holding his head in his hands*)
She betrayed me! Betrayed me!

TONIO (*softly to* CANIO, *pushing him toward the front of the stage*)
Control yourself, my master! You must pretend a while.
Her lover will return. You can be sure of that.
(CANIO *makes a fierce gesture, but* TONIO, *keeping hold of his arm, pushes him forward*)
I will be watching her. Let us prepare the stage now.
Who knows? Maybe he'll come to see the play tonight . . .
And betray himself. Come on! We'll set a trap for him.
All will be well.

PEPPE (*re-entering, to* CANIO)
Let's go now! Go dress yourself, my master,
And you beat your drum now, Tonio!
(TONIO *and* PEPPE *go into the theater.* CANIO, *torn with emotion, makes his way slowly toward the curtain of the theater*)

CANIO
To play a part . . . with my mind verging on madness!
I don't know what I'm doing . . . nor what I'm saying.
And yet Pagliaccio must go on!
Bah . . . ! Are you not a man? You're just Pagliaccio!
On with your costume and the grease paint and powder,
The crowd will pay you to make them laugh once more.
When Harlequin and Columbine betray you,
Laugh then, Pagliaccio . . . and then the crowd will roar!
You must amuse them with sobbing and sighing,
And show them all how the artist plays his part . . .
Laugh then, Pagliaccio, for the love that is dying,
Laugh through the pain that is destroying your heart!
(*he passes under the curtain of the stage theater, while the curtain slowly falls*)

ACT II

Scene 1

(TONIO *appears with a big drum and takes up a position in the left angle of the theater. People come from different directions for the performance.* PEPPE *places benches for the women.*)

CHORUS (*as they arrive*)
If we expect to get a seat
We'll have to hurry,
It's about time
For the show to begin.
Let's find our places
Down toward the front!

CORO
Presto, affrettiamoci
Svelto, compare,
Chè lo spettacolo
Dee cominciare.
Cerchiam di metterci
Ben sul davanti.

TONIO (*beating the drum*)
Come on there!
It's time to start now!

TONIO
Si dà principio;
Avanti! avanti!

CHORUS
The early birds are scurrying
To find their places.
Good Lord, what a crowd!
Sit here, you girls,
And show your pretty faces!
See how they hurry!

CORO
Veh, come corrono
Le bricconcelle!
Accomodatevi
Comari belle.
O Dio, che correre
Per giunger tosto!

TONIO
Please take your places,
Come, take your places here, this way!

TONIO
Si dà principio
Pigliate posto!

WOMEN (*sitting down, pushing each other*)
Who are you pushing!
It's hot! It's awful!
Hey, Peppe, come and help us
Find a place!

LE DONNE
Ma non pigiatevi,
Fa caldo tanto!
Su; Peppe aiutaci.
V'è posto accanto!

(NEDDA *enters dressed as Columbine, with a plate to receive money.* PEPPE *tries to find places for the women.* TONIO *goes back into the theater carrying the drum*)

A PART OF THE CHORUS (*to* PEPPE)
Why don't they start the play?
It's getting late now!
What's all the big delay?
Why must we wait now?

UNA PARTE DEL CORO
Suvvia, spicciatevi,
Incominciate.
Perchè tardate?
Siam tutti là.

ANOTHER PART OF THE CHORUS
They're tearing their hair out,
They're shouting for help!
Come on, sit down there,
And stop your noise!

UN'ALTRA PARTE DEL CORO
Veh, s'accapigliano! . . .
Chiamano aiuto! . . .
Ma via, sedetevi
Senza gridar.

SILVIO (*quietly to* NEDDA)
Nedda!

SILVIO
Nedda!

NEDDA
Be careful!
He did not see you!

NEDDA
Sii cauto!
Non t'ha veduto.

SILVIO
Verrò ad attenderti.
Non obliar! . . .

SILVIO
Then I shall wait for you.
Do not forget!

PEPPE
Che furia, diavolo!
Prima pagate.
Nedda, incassate.

PEPPE
Be quiet, damn it all!
Nedda, be careful,
Be sure they pay you!

CORO
Di qua—di qua!

CHORUS (*all trying to pay at once*)
Let's go, let's go!
(NEDDA *leaves* SILVIO *and goes to collect money for the seats, then she goes into the theater with* PEPPE)

CORO
Suvvia questa commedia
Incominciate.
Perchè tardar?
Perchè indugiar?
Facciamo strepito,
Facciam rumore!
Diggià suonar
Ventitrè ore
Allo spettacolo
Ognun anela! . . .
S'alza la tela!
Silenzio.—Olà!

FULL CHORUS
Let's go, it's time
To start now!
So why delay,
We've paid our money!
Come on, come on
And show us something funny!
It's time to start,
Everyone's here.
Start the show
Or there'll be a riot!
(*a bell rings loud and long*)
There goes the curtain!
Be quiet, be quiet!
(*by this time some of the women are seated on benches facing the theater, some are standing with the men on a rise in the ground under the tree, while others stand at left.* SILVIO *is in this group*)

Scene 2

The Play

(NEDDA (*Columbine*), PEPPE (*Harlequin*), CANIO (*Pagliaccio*), TONIO (*Taddeo*), *and* SILVIO)
(*The curtain of the theater rises. Scene: a small room with two side doors, a window at the back, a table and two chairs at right.* NEDDA, *dressed as Columbine, walks anxiously back and forth.*)

COLOMBINA
Pagliaccio, mio marito,
A tarda notte sol ritornerà.
E quello scimunito
Di Taddeo perchè mai non è ancor quà!

COLUMBINE
My husband Pagliaccio
Won't be returning till very late tonight.
That little fool Taddeo ought to be here!
Why on earth has he not come?
(*a guitar is off-stage.* COLUMBINE *runs to the window making gestures of love and impatience*)

LA VOCE DI ARLECCHINO
O Colombina, il tenero

VOICE OF HARLEQUIN
O Columbine, your faithful

Harlequin is near,
Open and hear!
Hear how I sigh
Because I'm dying for you to appear!
Show me your lovely face
And let me know my fate!
Why hesitate?
Oh don't you miss me?
Oh won't you kiss me? My love will kill me if I have to wait.
Open your window, Columbine,
And let me in!
Your Harlequin
Sighs on your doorstep,
Dies here on your step . . . So why not let me in!

COLUMBINE (*returning anxiously to the front*)
It's time for me to give the signal.
My darling is waiting,
My Harlequin is waiting there.
(*she sits down with her back to the door at the right. Through this door comes* TONIO, *dressed as Taddeo, with a basket on his left arm. He stops and gazes at* NEDDA *with an exaggerated melodramatic air*)

TADDEO
Behold her!
(*he lifts up his hands and the basket toward heaven*)
Is she not lovely!
(*the audience laughs*)
If I could speak of my heart's devotion,
All the stones would be trembling with emotion!
Husband's away now,
So why delay now?
We're all alone,
Now I shall make her my own!
Why not? I'll try it.
(*gives a long, exaggerated sigh*)
Ah . . . !
(*the audience laughs*)

COLUMBINE (*turning*)
Is that you, stupid?

TADDEO (*without moving*)
Yes, that's me!

COLUMBINE
Has Pagliaccio gone away?

TADDEO (*as before*)
He's gone away.

COLUMBINE
Why stand there like a statue?
Did you buy the chicken?

TADDEO
Behold it, O Goddess of Beauty!

Fido Arlecchin
È a te vicin!
Di te chiamando,
E sospirando—aspetta il poverin! . . .
La tua faccetta mostrami,
Ch'io vo' baciar
Senza tardar
La tua boccuccia.
Amor mi cruccia—e mi sta a tormentar!
O Colombina, schiudimi
Il finestrin,
Che a te vicin
Di te chiamando
E sospirando è il povero Arlecchin!
A te vicin è Arlecchin!

COLOMBINA
Di fare il segno convenuto appressa
L'istante, ed Arlecchino aspetta! . . .

TADDEO
È dessa!
Dei, com'è bella!
Se a la rubella
Io disvelassi
L'amor mio che commuove fino i sassi!
Lungi è lo sposo.
Perchè non oso?
Soli noi siamo
E senza alcun sospetto! Orsù. Proviamo!
Oh! . . .

COLOMBINA
Sei tu, bestia?

TADDEO
Quell'io sono, sì!

COLOMBINA
E Pagliaccio è partito?

TADDEO
Egli partì!

COLOMBINA
Che fai così impalato?
Il pollo hai tu comprato?

TADDEO
Eccolo, vergin divina!

Ed anzi eccoci entrambi ai piedi tuoi.
Poichè, l'ora è suonata, o Colombina,
Di svelarti il mio cor. Di', udirmi vuoi?
Dal dì . . .

(*he throws himself on his knees before* COLUMBINE, *offering her the basket*)
The chicken and I, who adore you . . . we kneel before you.
For the moment is here, O Lady Dear,
When I open my heart! Ah, do you not hear?
From the day . . .
(COLUMBINE *goes to the window and makes a signal, then turns to* TADDEO)

COLOMBINA
Quanto spendesti dal trattore?

COLUMBINE (*snatching the basket*)
How much did you squander at the tavern?

TADDEO
Una e cinquanta. Da quel dì il mio core . . .

TADDEO
Only one fifty! From the day when I met you . . .

COLOMBINA
Non seccarmi Taddeo!

COLUMBINE (*near the table*)
Don't you bother me now!
(HARLEQUIN *enters by the window and places on the floor the bottle he is carrying. He goes toward* TADDEO, *who pretends not to see him*)

TADDEO
So che sei pura
E casta al par di neve! E ben che dura
Ti mostri, ad obliarti non riesco!

TADDEO (*meaningfully*)
I know how pure you are, how well I know . . .
As pure as the driven snow!
Why be so cruel, why so unkind?
Lady, I cannot get you out of my mind.

ARLECCHINO
Va a pigliar fresco! . . .

HARLEQUIN (*taking* TADDEO *by the ear and kicking him*)
Go take the air!
(*audience laughs*)

TADDEO
Numi! s'aman! m'arrendo ai detti tuoi.
Vi benedico! . . . là . . . veglio su voi!

TADDEO (*moving back comically to the door*)
She loves him, he loves her! My claim is good no more.
Bless you, my children! Now I'll watch outside the door.
(*he goes out. The audience laughs and applauds*)

COLOMBINA
Arlecchin!

COLUMBINE
Harlequin!

ARLECCHINO
Colombina! Alfin s'arrenda
Ai nostri prieghi amor!

HARLEQUIN (*with exaggerated manner*)
Oh my Columbine! At last, at last!
Love has answered all our prayers.

COLOMBINA
Facciam merenda!
Guarda, amor mio, che splendida
Cenetta preparai!

COLUMBINE
Let's have our supper!
(*she points to the table where she has placed the chicken, knives, forks, etc.*)
Behold, my love, the luscious feast
That I have been preparing!

ARLECCHINO
Guarda, amor mio, che nettare
Divino t'apportai!

HARLEQUIN (*pointing to the wine he has placed on the table*)
Behold, my love, the wondrous wine
That we two shall be sharing!

COLOMBINA, ARLECCHINO
L'amor ama gli effluvii
Del vin, de la cucina!

BOTH
Affection thrives on wining,
And love does well on dining.

ARLECCHINO
Mia ghiotta Colombina!

HARLEQUIN
My hungry little Columbine!

COLUMBINE
My thirsty little Harlequin!
(they sit at the table, helping each other)

HARLEQUIN *(taking a phial from his tunic)*
Here is something to put him to sleep.
Give it to Pagliaccio just before his bedtime,
And then we'll run away.

COLUMBINE
Yes, give it here!

TADDEO *(entering the scene by the door on the right, with exaggerated trembling)*
Watch out there!
Pagliaccio is here! He's very angry, he's looking for a weapon!
He knows everything! It's time for me to hide!
(he rushes through the door at left, the audience laughs)

COLUMBINE *(to* HARLEQUIN*)*
Go now!

HARLEQUIN *(going out through the window)*
Put the drug in Pagliaccio's cup tonight!
*(*CANIO*, dressed as Pagliaccio, appears at the door at right)*

COLUMBINE *(at the window, to* HARLEQUIN*)*
Till tonight . . . and forever I shall be yours!

CANIO *(puts his hand over his heart and murmurs aside)*
Those are the words that she said to her lover!
(he advances to play his part)
Lord, help me!
Who was that other man?

NEDDA
What nonsense! Are you drunk?

CANIO
Drunk?
(looking at her meaningfully)
Since an hour ago!

NEDDA *(returning to the play)*
You're home quite early.

CANIO *(pointedly)*
In time, though!
My little wife, my sweet wife! Am I *too* early?
(resuming the play)
Ah, I thought you were alone here.
(he points to the table)
There are places for two!

NEDDA (COLUMBINE)
For me and for Taddeo.
He's afraid. He's hiding in the closet.
(she goes to door, left)
Come out! Speak!

COLOMBINA
Amabile beone!

ARLECCHINO
Prendi questo narcotico,
Dallo a Pagliaccio pria che s'addormenti,
E poi fuggiamo insiem.

COLOMBINA
Sì, porgi.

TADDEO
Attenti! . . .
Pagliaccio è là tutto stravolto . . . ed armi
Cerca! Ei sa tutto. Io corro a barricarmi!

COLOMBINA
Via!

ARLECCHINO
Versa il filtro ne la tazza sua.

COLOMBINA
A stanotte.—E per sempre sarò tua!

CANIO
Nome di Dio! . . . quelle stesse parole! . . .
Coraggio!
Un uomo era con te.

NEDDA
Che folle!
Sei briaco?

CANIO
Briaco! sì . . . da un'ora! . . .

NEDDA
Tornasti presto.

CANIO
Ma in tempo!
T'accora? dolce sposina!
Ah! sola io ti credea
E due posti son là.

NEDDA
Con me sedea
Taddeo che là si chiuse per paura.
Orsù, parla! . . .

TONIO
Credetela. Essa è pura! . . .
E abborre dal mentir quel labbro pio!

CANIO
Per la morte!
Smettiamo. Ho dritto anch'io
D'agir come ogn'altr'uomo. Il nome suo.

NEDDA
Di chi?

CANIO
Vo' il nome de l'amante tuo,
Del drudo infame a cui ti desti in braccio,
O turpe donna!

NEDDA
Pagliaccio! Pagliaccio!

CANIO
No, Pagliaccio non son; se il viso è pallido
È di vergogna, e smania di vendetta!
L'uom riprende i suoi dritti, e il cor che sanguina
Vuol sangue a lavar l'onta, o maledetta! . . .
No, Pagliaccio non son! . . . Son quei che stolido
Ti raccolse orfanella in su la via
Quasi morta di fame, e un nome offriati
Ed un amor ch'era febbre e follìa! . . .

GRUPPI DI DONNE A PARTE
Comare, mi fa piangere!
Par vera questa scena!

UN GRUPPO DI UOMINI
Zitti laggiù.—Che diamine!

SILVIO
Io mi ritengo appena!

CANIO
Sperai, tanto il delirio accecato m'aveva,
Se non amor, pietà . . . mercè!
Ed ogni sacrifizio
Al cor, lieto, imponeva,
E fidente credeva,
Più che in Dio stesso, in te!
Ma il vizio alberga sol ne l'alma tua negletta;
Tu viscere non hai . . . sol legge è 'l senso a te . . .
Va, non merti il mio duol, o meretrice abbietta,
Vo' ne lo sprezzo mio schiacciarti sotto il piè! . . .

LA FOLLA
Bravo! . . .

TONIO (*pretending to be afraid, pointedly*)
Believe her, sir, believe her, sir! She is pure as snow!
How could she tell a lie with those lovely lips!
(*the audience laughs*)

CANIO (*angry at the audience*)
Lord in heaven!
(*to* NEDDA)
I have my rights like any decent man.
Tell me the name!

NEDDA (*laughing and keeping the play going*)
Of whom?

CANIO
Of the man who is your lover,
Of the man whose arms have just embraced you!
How could you do it!

NEDDA (*keeping to the play*)
Pagliaccio! Pagliaccio!

CANIO
No! Pagliaccio no more! My face is white, it's true,
But from dishonor, from shame and indignation!
Now the fool sees his folly, the bleeding heart cries out for blood!
My curse be on you, and all damnation!
No! Pagliaccio no more! For now the man appears,
The fool who befriended you in sadness.
You were hungry and lonely. I gave my name to you,
I gave you love that was folly and madness!
(*falls on a chair, overcome*)

WOMEN (*to each other*)
Good heaven! He has made me cry!
He makes it seem so true!

SOME OF THE MEN
Quiet down there! What's the trouble here?

SILVIO (*aside*)
I cannot stand this much longer!

CANIO (*recovering himself and becoming gradually more excited*)
Alas! Love made me hope for devotion and kindness,
To have your faith, if not your love.
I labored and I sacrificed, but all in blindness,
I believed in your virtue more than in God above!
And now this is the way you have at last repaid me,
You think everything you desire is yours to take.
You're beneath all contempt, you cheated and betrayed me,
And now I cast you down, I crush you like a snake!

THE CROWD (*enthusiastically*)
Bravo . . . !

NEDDA (*coldly and seriously*)
If you think that I'm so bad,
Why not send me away?

NEDDA
Ebben se mi giudichi
Di te indegna, mi scaccia in questo istante.

CANIO (*laughs*)
Ah! Ah! You'd have me sending you away so you can hurry to your lover! How clever!
No, by God! You stay right here!
You stay until you tell me! What's his name . . . !

CANIO
Ah! ah! di meglio chiedere
Non dèi che correr tosto al caro amante.
Sei furba!—No, per Dio, tu resterai
E 'l nome del tuo ganzo mi dirai.

NEDDA (*with a forced smile, trying to resume the play*)
I s'pose it must look bad to you,
But still you need not fear, sir.
Taddeo here will vouch for me,
He will make it clear, sir.
The man who came to visit me
Before you blundered in,
Believe me . . . He was only that harmless fellow, Harlequin.
(*stops laughing as she sees how* CANIO *is taking this*)

NEDDA
Suvvia, così terribile
Davver non ti credeo!
Qui nulla v'ha di tragico.
Vieni a dirgli, o Taddeo,
Che l'uom seduto or dianzi a me vicino
Era . . . il pauroso ed innocuo Arlecchino!

CANIO (*violent and furious*)
Ah, you defy me! You still don't understand!
I am your husband! Now tell me or I shall kill you!
What's his name?

CANIO
Ah! tu mi sfidi! E ancor non l'hai capita
Ch'io non ti cedo? Il nome, o la tua vita! Il nome!

NEDDA (*bursting out*)
Ah . . . ! No, by all that's holy, whatever you may call me . . . !
Say that I'm evil, but don't call me a coward;
Though you may despise me, my love for him is stronger!
I'll never tell . . . No, no . . . never . . . though you kill me!

NEDDA
Ah! No, per mia madre!
Indegna esser poss'io,
Quello che vuoi, ma vil non son, per Dio!
Di quel tuo sdegno è l'amor mio più forte . . .
Non parlerò. No . . . A costo de la morte! . . . No!

VOICES IN THE CROWD
Are they in earnest? Can they be serious? Quiet down there!
(PEPPE *tries to pass through the door on left, but* TONIO *holds him back*)

VOCI TRA LA FOLLA
Fanno davvero? Seria è la cosa e oscura!
Zitti laggiù!

PEPPE
We've got to stop him . . . Tonio!

PEPPE
Bisogna uscire, Tonio.

TONIO
Quiet, Peppe!

TONIO
Taci sciocco! . . .

PEPPE
I'm afraid!

PEPPE
Ho paura!

SILVIO (*aside*)
It's more than I can bear.
What a strange sort of drama!

SILVIO
Io non resisto più! . . .
Oh la strana commedia!

CANIO (*yelling, takes knife from table*)
His name! His name!

CANIO
Il nome! Il nome!

NEDDA (*defiantly*)
No!

NEDDA
No!

SILVIO (*drawing his dagger*)
God in heaven!
He means it!

SILVIO
Santo diavolo! . . .
Fa davvero . . .

(the women draw back frightened, overturning the benches, thus preventing the men from coming forward, SILVIO *struggles to get clear of the crowd. Meanwhile* CANIO *has seized* NEDDA *and stabbed her from behind as she tries to escape to the crowd)*

CANIO A te! A te! Di morte negli spasimi Lo dirai!	CANIO Take that, and that! Maybe now that you're dying you will speak!
LA FOLLA E PEPPE Ferma! Ferma!	THE CROWD AND PEPPE Stop him, stop him!
NEDDA Soccorso . . . Silvio!	NEDDA Oh, help me, Silvio! *(dies)*
SILVIO Nedda!	SILVIO *(who has nearly reached her)* Nedda! *(on hearing* SILVIO's *voice* CANIO *savagely turns around. He leaps at* SILVIO *and stabs him)*
CANIO Ah! sei tu? Ben venga!	CANIO Ah! Is it you? It's done! *(*SILVIO *falls dead)*
GLI UOMINI DEL CORO Arresta!	MEN Hold him!
LE DONNE Gesummaria! . . .	WOMEN Mother of God! *(some of the people throw themselves at* CANIO *to disarm and hold him. He stands stupefied and lets the knife fall)*
CANIO La commedia è finita! . . .	CANIO The comedy is finished.

PARSIFAL

by Richard Wagner (1813–83)

LIBRETTO BY THE COMPOSER

Translated by STEWART ROBB.

Based on Wolfram von Eschenbach's poem *Parzifal*, a 14th century book of Welsh tales known as the *Mabinogion*, and Chrétien de Troyes's *Perceval, ou, Le Conte del Graal.*

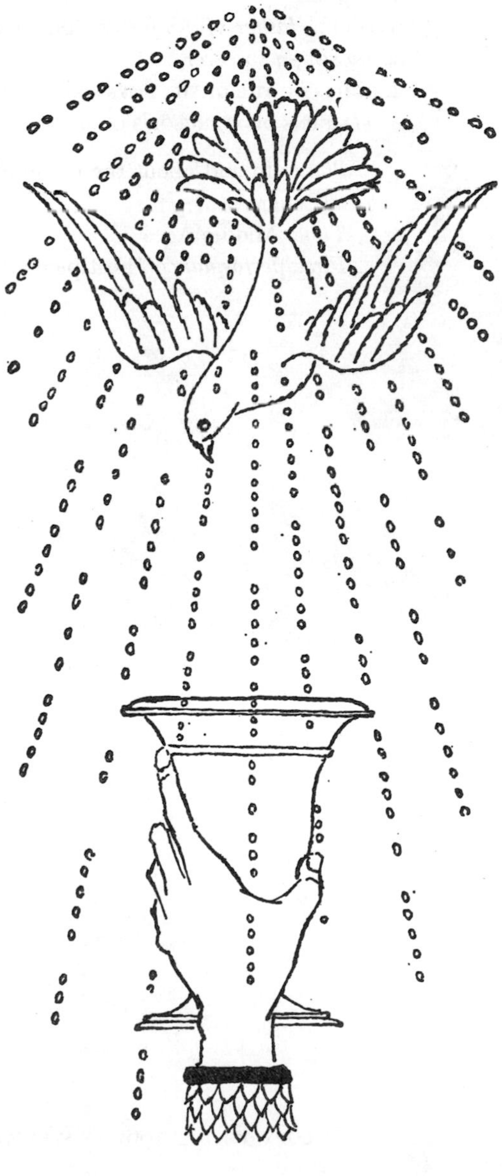

CHARACTERS

GURNEMANZ, *an elderly knight of the Grail*	*Bass*
FOUR SQUIRES	*Sopranos* / *Tenors*
FIRST KNIGHT	*Tenor*
SECOND KNIGHT	*Bass*
KUNDRY, *part sorceress, part mortal woman*	*Soprano*
AMFORTAS, *King of the knights of the Holy Grail*	*Baritone*
PARSIFAL	*Tenor*
TITUREL, *father of Amfortas, former King of Monsalvat*	*Bass*
KLINGSOR, *a sorcerer*	*Bass*
KNIGHTS OF THE GRAIL, BOYS AND YOUTHS, FLOWER MAIDENS OF KLINGSOR'S GARDEN	

Place: In and about the castle of Monsalvat in the Spanish Pyrenees

Time: Middle Ages

First performance: Festspielhaus, Bayreuth, July 26, 1882

COPYRIGHT © 1962 BY STEWART ROBB

ACT I

(The domain of the Grail. A shadowy forest, impressive, but not gloomy. A glade in the middle. A road leading to the Grail's castle rises left. In the background can be glimpsed a low-lying forest lake. Daybreak. Two young squires are lying asleep under a tree. GURNEMANZ, *an old but vigorous man, also under the tree, has just awakened, for the solemn morning reveille of trombones is heard at rise of curtain.)*

GURNEMANZ *(shaking the youngsters)*

Hey! Ho! Woodkeepers there!
Sleepkeepers more likely!
Awake at least with the morning!
(the two squires spring up)
There is the call. Give thanks to God
that you are privileged to hear it!
(he sinks to his knees with the squires and they offer up a silent morning prayer, then they rise slowly)
Now up, young fellows; see to the bath!
Time now to wait there for your master.
(he looks off, left)
The sickbed bearing him is near:
I see the heralds coming now.
(two heralds appear)
Hail there! How fares the King today?
He seeks his healing bath quite early.
The balsam which Gawain
with skill and boldness won for him—
I trust it helped to ease his pain?

SECOND KNIGHT

You only trust, you who know the truth?
Amfortas' pains soon returned,
and keener than before.
Sleepless, from sheer exhaustion,
he urged us get the bath prepared.

GURNEMANZ *(drooping his head sorrowfully)*

Fools are we, to hope to ease his torment,
where only healing eases!
For every simple, every potion,
seek and hunt throughout the world.
There's but one healing,
but one Healer!

SECOND KNIGHT

Then give his name!

GURNEMANZ

Look to the bath!

SECOND SQUIRE

See there! The woman riding wild!

FIRST SQUIRE

Hey!
The mane of her devil's mare is flying!

GURNEMANZ

He! Ho! Waldhüter ihr!
Schlafhüter mitsammen!
So wacht doch mindest am Morgen!
Hört ihr den Ruf? Nun danket Gott,
dass ihr berufen ihn zu hören!
Jetzt auf, ihr Knaben; seht nach dem Bad;
Zeit ist's, des Königs dort zu harren:
dem Siechbett, das ihn trägt, voraus
seh' ich die Boten vor uns nah'n.
Heil euch! Wie geht's Amfortas heut'?
Wohl früh verlangt er nach dem Bade: das Heilkraut, das Gawan
mit List und Kühnheit ihm gewann,
ich wähne, dass es Lind'rung schuf?

DER ZWEITE RITTER

Das wähn'st du, der doch Alles weiss?
Ihm kehrten sehrender nur
die Schmerzen bald zurück:
schlaflos von starkem Bresten
befahl er eifrig uns das Bad.

GURNEMANZ

Thoren wir, auf Lind'rung da zu hoffen, wo einzig Heilung lindert!
Nach allen Kräutern, allen Tränken forscht und jagt weit durch die Welt: ihm hilft nur Eines—nur der Eine.

ZWEITER RITTER

So nenn' uns den?

GURNEMANZ

Sorgt für das Bad.

DER ZWEITE KNAPPE

Seht dort die wilde Reiterin!

ERSTER KNAPPE

Hei!
Wie fliegen der Teufelsmähre die Mähnen!

ZWEITER RITTER
Ha! Kundry dort.

ERSTER RITTER
Die bringt wohl wicht'ge Kunde?

ZWEITER KNAPPE
Die Mähre taumelt.

ERSTER KNAPPE
Flog sie durch die Luft?

ZWEITER KNAPPE
Jetzt kriecht sie am Boden.

ERSTER KNAPPE
Mit den Mähnen fegt sie das Moos.

ZWEITER RITTER
Da schwang sich die Wilde herab.

KUNDRY
Hier nimm du!—Balsam!

GURNEMANZ
Woher brachtest du dies?

KUNDRY
Von weiter her, als du denken kannst: Hilft der Balsam nicht, Arabien birgt
nichts mehr dann zu seinem Heil.—
Frag' nicht weiter!—Ich bin müde.

GURNEMANZ
Er naht: sie bringen ihn getragen.—
O weh'! Wie trag' ich's im Gemüthe,
in seiner Mannheit stolzer Blüthe
des siegreichsten Geschlechtes Herrn
als seines Siechthums Knecht zu seh'n!
Behutsam! Hört, der König stöhnt.

AMFORTAS
So recht!—Habt Dank!—Ein wenig Rast.—
Nach wilder Schmerzensnacht
nun Wälder-Morgenpracht; im heil'gen See
wohl labt mich auch die Welle:
es staunt das Weh',

SECOND KNIGHT
Ha! Kundry there?

FIRST KNIGHT
No doubt with weighty tidings.

SECOND SQUIRE
The mare is reeling.

FIRST SQUIRE
Did she fly through air?

SECOND SQUIRE
She's skimming along the ground.

FIRST SQUIRE
And her mane is sweeping the moss.
(*all look eagerly off left*)

SECOND SQUIRE
The wild woman flings from her horse.
(KUNDRY *rushes in, almost reeling; wild garb fastened high; girdle of snakeskin hanging; long, black hair flowing in loose locks; dark brownish-red complexion, piercing black eyes, sometimes wild and blazing, but usually fixed and glassy. She hurries over to* GURNEMANZ *and presses upon him a small crystal flask*)

KUNDRY
Take this!—Balsam!

GURNEMANZ
But where did you get it?

KUNDRY
From farther off than your thoughts can dream.
Should the balsam fail,
all Araby
then holds nothing to help his cure.
Ask no further!—I am weary!
(*she throws herself on the ground. A train of squires and knights appears, bearing and attending a litter*)

GURNEMANZ
He comes. They bear him on the litter.
Oh woe! What sorrow pulls my heartstrings
to see this king in bloom of manhood,
once ruler of a conq'ring race,
admitting sickness liege and lord!
(*to the squires*)
Be careful! Hear, the master groans.
(*the squires set down the litter*)

AMFORTAS (*raising himself a little*)
Right!—So!—My thanks!—A little rest!
My night of pain has fled,
my morning joy has come!
The sacred lake's
cool waves will also help me,

will stint my woe.
The night of pain will lighten!
Gawain!

SECOND KNIGHT
Sire! Gawain left again;
for when his healing herb,
obtained through toilsome effort
did but betray your hopes,
he sallied forth again upon the venture.

AMFORTAS
Without leave? May he then repent it—
to keep so ill the Grail's command!
Oh woe to him, so rashly valiant,
if he should fall in Klingsor's toils!
Let no one break my peace with problems.
I wait for him, the promised Saviour,
"through pity, knowing,"
was't not thus?

GURNEMANZ
You said that it was thus.

AMFORTAS
"The holy fool"—
I think Death is that saviour,
did I but dare to name him!

GURNEMANZ (*handing* AMFORTAS *the flask*)
Take of this: and see if it will help you.

AMFORTAS
Whence came this curious-looking flask?

GURNEMANZ
Brought for your cure from Araby's distant land.

AMFORTAS
And who obtained it?

GURNEMANZ (*pointing*)
Right there the wild one lies.
Up, Kundry! Come!
(KUNDRY *refuses, and remains on the ground*)

AMFORTAS
You, Kundry?
Am I again to thank you,
you timid, restless soul?
Well then!
I'll take the balsam brought for me,
to show my thanks for such devotion.

KUNDRY (*stirring uneasily on the ground*)
No thanks!—Ha, ha! How will that help one?
No thanks! Go, go! Your bath!
(AMFORTAS *gives the sign, and the procession disap-*

die Schmerzensnacht wird
helle.—
Gawan!

ZWEITER RITTER
Herr, Gawan weilte nicht
Da seines Heilkrauts Kraft,
wie schwer er's auch errungen,
doch deine Hoffnung trog,
hat er auf neue Sucht sich
fortgeschwungen.

AMFORTAS
Ohn' Urlaub?—Möge das er
sühnen,
dass schlecht er Gralsgebote
hält!
O wehe ihm, dem trotzig
Kühnen,
wenn er in Klingsors Schlingen
fällt!
So breche Keiner mir den
Frieden:
ich harre dess', der mir
beschieden.
„Durch Mitleid wissend"—
war's nicht so?

GURNEMANZ
Uns sagtest du es so.

AMFORTAS
„der reine Thor"——:
mich dünkt, ihn zu erkennen:—
dürft' ich den Tod ihn nennen!

GURNEMANZ
Doch zuvor: versuch' es
noch mit diesem!

AMFORTAS
Woher dies heimliche Gefäss?

GURNEMANZ
Dir ward es aus Arabia
hergeführt.

AMFORTAS
Und wer gewann es?

GURNEMANZ
Da liegt's, das wilde Weib.—
Auf, Kundry! komm!

AMFORTAS
Du, Kundry!
Muss ich dir nochmals danken,
du rastlos scheue Magd?—
Wohl denn!
Den Balsam nun versuch' ich
noch;
es sei aus Dank für deine Treu'!

KUNDRY
Nicht Dank!—Ha ha! Was wird
es helfen?
Nicht Dank! Fort, fort! Zum
Bad!

pears toward the valley. KUNDRY *remains crouching on the ground. Squires pass to and fro)*

DRITTER KNAPPE
He! Du da!—
Was liegst du dort wie ein wildes Thier?

KUNDRY
Sind die Thiere hier nicht heilig?

DRITTER KNAPPE
Ja! doch ob heilig du,
das wissen wir grad' noch nicht.

VIERTER KNAPPE
Mit ihrem Zaubersafte, wähn' ich,
wird sie den Meister vollends verderben.

GURNEMANZ
Hm!—Schuf sie euch Schaden je?—Wann Alles rathlos steht
wie kämpfenden Brüdern in fernste Länder
Kunde sei zu entsenden,
und kaum ihr nur wisst, wohin?—
Wer, ehe ihr euch nur besinnt,
stürmt und fliegt da hin und zurück,
der Botschaft pflegend mit Treu' und Glück?
Ihr nährt sie nicht, sie naht euch nie, nichts hat sie mit euch gemein;
doch wann's in Gefahr der Hilfe gilt,
der Eifer führt sie schier durch die Luft,
die nie euch dann zum Danke ruft.
Ich wähne, ist dies Schaden,
so thät' er euch gut gerathen?

DRITTER KNAPPE
Doch hasst sie uns.—
Sieh'nur, wie hämisch sie dort nach uns blickt!

VIERTER KNAPPE
Eine Heidin ist's, ein Zauberweib.

GURNEMANZ
Ja, eine Verwünschte mag sie sein:
hier lebt sie heut',—
vielleicht erneut,
zu büssen Schuld aus früh'rem Leben,
die dorten ihr noch nicht vergeben.
Uebt sie nun Buss' in solchen Thaten,
die uns Ritterschaft zum Heil gerathen,
gut thut sie dann ganz sicherlich,
dienet uns, und hilft auch sich.

THIRD SQUIRE
Hey you there!
Why lie you there like a brutish beast?

KUNDRY
Are the beasts here then not holy?

THIRD SQUIRE
Yes! But that you are so
is something we still don't know.

FOURTH SQUIRE
And with her magic brew, perhaps,
she could cut off the life of our master.

GURNEMANZ
Hm! Has she done harm to you?
When we are all perplexed
how best to send tidings to far-off countries,
where our brothers are fighting,
we hardly know where, what then?
Who comes to your aid while you think,
flies away, and straightway is back,
a message bearer both tried and true?
She asks no food, and keeps away—
nothing's in common with you.
Yet when you need help, with danger near,
afire with duty she flies through the air.
She never even asks your thanks.
If this is what is harmful,
the harmful is what is helpful!

THIRD SQUIRE
She hates us though.
Just see the baleful glance she casts at us!

FOURTH SQUIRE
She's a heathen, sure; a sorceress!

GURNEMANZ
Yes, possibly burdened with a curse.
Here let her live.
She seems renewed,
repenting sin long since committed,
which at that time was not forgiven.
See, she atones in deeds of goodness
that both help and heal our noble knighthood.
Good are her deeds, and right, certainly:
good for us, and good for her.

THIRD SQUIRE
But is it not she we should blame,
she who has caused our want and woe?

GURNEMANZ
Yes, many times she ventures far away,
and when she goes our woe begins.
I knew her long ago,
but Titurel knew her still longer,
who found—that time he built the castle—
her sleeping in the underbrush,
benumbed, lifeless—as dead.
And thus again I found her lately,
just when that trouble came on us
which yonder wizard over the mountain
so shamefully did bring to pass.
(*to* KUNDRY)
Hey, you! Hear me, and speak:
Where were you wandering about,
that time our lord had lost the spear?
(KUNDRY *maintains a gloomy silence*)
Why did you not help us then?

KUNDRY
I never help.

FOURTH SQUIRE
She says't herself.

THIRD SQUIRE
If she's so true, so brave and bold,
then send her in quest of the missing spear!

GURNEMANZ
That's something diff'rent. That is not allowed.
(*with deep emotion*)
Oh, wounding, wonderful and sanctified spear!
I saw you brandished by unsanctified hand!
(*becoming lost in remembrance*)
Protected with it, Amfortas, all too valiant,
what power then could keep you
from laying low the wizard?
Our valiant king, while near the wall, is seized.
A gorgeous, fearsome witch holds him in thrall,
and her embraces make him drunken.
He lets the spear fall idly.
A frightful cry! I hurry there:
to see a laughing Klingsor leave.
The holy spear is gone with him.
I fought to help our king escape to safety;
but on his body now a wound was burning:
a wound so bad that it will never close!

DRITTER KNAPPE
Dann ist's wohl auch jen' ihre Schuld,
was uns so manche Noth gebracht?

GURNEMANZ
Ja, wann sie oft uns lange ferne blieb,
dann brach ein Unglück wohl herein.
Und lang' schon kenn' ich sie:
noch länger kennt sie Titurel:
der fand, als er die Burg dort baute,
sie schlafend hier im Waldgestrüpp',
erstarrt, leblos, wie todt.
So fand ich selbst sie letztlich wieder,
als uns das Unheil kaum, gescheh'n,
das jener Böse dort über'm Berge
So schmählich über uns gebracht.—
He! Du!—Hör' mich, und sag':
wo schweiftest damals du umher,
als unser Herr den Speer verlor?—
Warum halfst du uns damals nicht?

KUNDRY
Ich helfe nie.

VIERTER KNAPPE
Sie sagt's da selbst.

DRITTER KNAPPE
Ist sie so treu und kühn in Wehr,
so sende sie nach dem verlor' nen Speer!

GURNEMANZ
Das ist ein And'res:—
jedem ist's verwehrt.—
Oh, wunden-wundervoller
heiliger Speer!
Dich sah ich schwingen
von unheiligster Hand!—
Mit ihm bewehrt, Amfortas, Allzukühner,
wer mochte dir es wehren
den Zaub'rer zu beheeren!——
Schon nah' dem Schloss, wird uns der Held entrückt:
ein furchtbar schönes Weib hat ihn entzückt:
in seinen Armen liegt er trunken,
der Speer ist ihm entsunken;—
ein Todesschrei!—ich stürm' herbei;—
von dannen Klingsor lachend schwand,
den heil'gen Speer hat er entwandt.

Des Königs Flucht gab kämpfend ich Geleite;
doch eine Wunde brannt' ihm in der Seite:
die Wunde ist's, die nie sich schliessen will.

(*the first and second squires return from the lake*)

DRITTER KNAPPE
So kanntest du Klingsor?

THIRD SQUIRE
So then you knew Klingsor?

GURNEMANZ
Wie geht's dem König?

GURNEMANZ (*to the returning squires*)
How fares our master?

ERSTER KNAPPE
Ihn frischt das Bad.

FIRST SQUIRE
The bath was good.

ZWEITER KNAPPE
Dem Balsam wich der Schmerz.

SECOND SQUIRE
The balsam eased his woe.

GURNEMANZ
Die Wunde ist's, die nie sich schliessen will!—

GURNEMANZ
A wound so bad that it will never close!
(*the third and fourth squires seat themselves at* GURNEMANZ'S *feet; the other two join them under the great tree*)

DRITTER KNAPPE
Doch, Väterchen, sag' und lehr' uns fein:
du kanntest Klingsor,—wie mag das sein?

THIRD SQUIRE
Now fatherkin, speak and let us hear:
you knew the wizard, how could that be?

GURNEMANZ
Titurel, der fromme Held,
der kannt' ihn wohl.
Denn ihm, da wilder Feinde List und Macht
des reinen Glaubens Reich bedrohten,
ihm neigten sich in heilig ernster Nacht
dereinst des Heilands sel'ge Boten:
daraus er trank beim letzten Liebesmahle,
das Weihgefäss, die heilig edle Schale,
darein am Kreuz sein göttlich Blut auch floss,
zugleich den Lanzenspeer, der dies vergoss,—
der Zeugengüter höchstes Wundergut,—
das gaben sie in unsres Königs Hut.
Dem Heilthum baute er das Heiligthum.
Die seinem Dienst ihr zugesindet
auf Pfaden, die kein Sünder findet,
ihr wisst, das nur dem Reinen vergönnt ist sich zu einen
den Brüdern, die zu höchsten Rettungswerken
des Grales heil'ge Wunderkräfte stärken:
d'rum blieb es dem, nach dem ihr fragt, verwehrt,
Klingsor'n, so hart ihn Müh' auch drob beschwert.

GURNEMANZ
Titurel, the pious king,
knew Klingsor well.
There came a mighty heathen horde to threat
our realm of Christian faith—our stronghold;
but help arrived one sacred, solemn night.
Down came our Saviour's heavenly heralds:
the cup once used at that last holy supper,
that noble cup, that consecrated vessel,
wherein was caught His blood from off the cross;
thereto the holy lance which shed that blood.
These precious proofs of Love's great healing power
were given by angels to our ruler's care.
He gave these holy things a holy place.
And you, who serve by holy orders,
who took the path no sinner knows of,
you know the pure alone
are allowed to join the Brothers
in service, those devoted to the works
of salvation through the Grail's great power.
So, for the mage of whom you ask, he failed
outright, although he strove to enter in.
And then he settled in a lonely valley,
and all around was rankest heathen land.
What his sin was did never reach my knowledge.
His aim was penance though, yes, holy actions.
Yet lacking strength to slay the sins that were within him,
he laid rough hands upon himself
in hope that thus he'd gain the Grail.
But full of scorn our master spurned him forth.

For that was Klingsor seized with furious rage,
which made him turn his loathesome deed
to practice of wicked magic art,
which now he does.
The desert Klingsor made a pleasure garden
where flourish dev'lish lovely women.
There does he lie in waiting for the Grail knights,
with wicked lust and hellish torments.
Those whom he snares follow his banner.
Already he has ruined many.
Then Titurel, his body worn and waning,
empowered his son to take the kingdom.
Amfortas took no time to rest,
but tried to choke this wizard woe.
You know then what the sequel was:
the spear is now in Klingsor's hand,
which he can use to wound our holy knighthood.
Then he thinks to seize the holy chalice.

Jenseits im Thale war er eingesiedelt;
darüber hin liegt üpp'ges Heidenland:
unkund blieb mir, was dorten er gesündigt;
doch büssen wollt' er nun, ja heilig werden.
Ohnmächtig, in sich selbst die Sünde zu ertödten,
an sich legt er die Frevlerhand, die nun, dem Grale zugewandt,
verachtungsvoll dess' Hüter von sich stiess.
Darob die Wuth nun Klingsor'n unterwies,
wie seines schmählichen Opfers That
ihm gäbe zu bösem Zauber Rath;
den fand er jetzt:—
die Wüste schuf er sich zum Wonnegarten
d'rinn wachsen teuflisch holde Frauen;
dort will des Grales Ritter er erwarten
zu böser Lust und Höllengrauen:
wen er verlockt, hat er erworben;
schon Viele hat er uns verdorben.—
Da Titurel, in hohen Alters Mühen,
dem Sohne nun die Herrschaft hier verliehen,
Amfortas liess es da nicht ruh'n
der Zauberplag' Einhalt zu thun.
Das wisst ihr, wie es da sich fand:
der Speer ist nun in Klingsors Hand;
kann er selbst Heilige mit dem verwunden,
den Gral auch wähnt er fest schon uns entwunden.

FOURTH SQUIRE
So first of all we must get back the spear.

VIERTER KNAPPE
Vor Allem nun: der Speer kehr' uns zurück!

THIRD SQUIRE
Whoso could, would win both fame and joy.

DRITTER KNAPPE
Ha! wer ihn brächt', ihm wär's zu Ruhm und Glück!

GURNEMANZ
Before the orphaned holy place
Amfortas knelt in ardent prayer,
imploring God a sign in answer.
A blessed shimm'ring flowed from out the chalice;
a holy, dreamlike face now clearly spoke to him
through bright-appearing, wondrous demonstration:
"Through pity, knowing—the holy fool.
Wait for him,

GURNEMANZ
Vor dem verwaisten Heiligthum
in brünst'gem Beten lag Amfortas,
ein Rettungszeichen bang erflehend:
ein sel'ger Schimmer da entfloss dem Grale;
ein heilig' Traumgesicht
nun deutlich zu ihm spricht
durch hell erschauter Wortezeichen Male:—

„Durch Mitleid wissend
der reine Thor,
harre sein',
den ich erkor."

DIE VIER KNAPPEN
„Durch Mitleid wissend, der reine Thor . . ."

RITTER UND KNAPPEN
Weh'! Wehe!—Hoho!
Auf!—Wer ist der Frevler?

GURNEMANZ
Was giebt's?

VIERTER KNAPPE
Dort!

DRITTER KNAPPE
Hier!

ZWEITER KNAPPE
Ein Schwan!

VIERTER KNAPPE
Ein wilder Schwan!

DRITTER KNAPPE
Er ist verwundet.

ANDERE KNAPPEN
Ha! Wehe! Wehe!

GURNEMANZ
Wer schoss den Schwan?

ERSTER RITTER
Der König grüsst' ihn als gutes Zeichen.
als über dem See dort kreiste der Schwan:
da flog ein Pfeil.—

NEUE KNAPPEN
Der war's! Der schoss! Dies der Bogen!—

ZWEITER RITTER
Hier der Pfeil, den seinen gleich.

GURNEMANZ
Bist du's, der diesen Schwan erlegte?

PARSIFAL
Gewiss! Im Fluge treff' ich was fliegt.

GURNEMANZ
Du thatest das? Und bangt es dich nicht vor der That?

DIE KNAPPEN
Strafe den Frevler!

GURNEMANZ
Unerhörtes Werk!

whom I ordained."

THE FOUR SQUIRES
"Through pity, knowing—the holy fool."
(from the lake come cries and exclamations of the knights and squires. GURNEMANZ *and the four squires start up in alarm)*

KNIGHTS AND SQUIRES *(off-stage)*
Woe! Woe! Ho-ho!
Up! Who is the miscreant?
(a wild swan flutters feebly from over the lake. The squires and knights enter following it)

GURNEMANZ
What's up?

FOURTH SQUIRE
There!

THIRD SQUIRE
Here!

SECOND SQUIRE
A swan!

FOURTH SQUIRE
A forest swan!

THIRD SQUIRE
See! He is wounded!

ALL
Ha! Shameful! Shameful!

GURNEMANZ
Who shot the swan?
(the swan, after painful flight, sinks helplessly to earth. The second knight draws an arrow from its breast)

FIRST KNIGHT
Our master hailed it as a happy omen,
to see the swan circle the lake.
A shaft then flew! . . .
(knights and squires bring PARSIFAL *in)*

SQUIRES AND KNIGHTS
'Twas he! . . . who shot! See the bow here!

SECOND KNIGHT
Here's the shaft—just like the rest!

GURNEMANZ
It's you who dealt the swan its deathblow?

PARSIFAL
Yes, I! In flight I hit all that flies.

GURNEMANZ
You slew the swan! And feel no horror for your deed?

ALL
Punish the culprit!

GURNEMANZ
Execrable deed!

You could do murder? Here in sacred forest,
whose silent peace enwrapped you round,
whose woodland beasts approached you without fear,
greeted you friendly and tame?
From the branches what warbled the birds to you?
What harm did the faithful swan?
In seeking his mate he flew aloft
to circle with her over the lake,
thus nobly consecrating the bath.
This gave you no awe? Is all you want
a wild, puerile shot from your bow?
He had our love. What is he to you?
Here, just look! See where you hit!
There hardens his blood! Look!—Wings hanging lifeless!
His snowy plumage flecked with the stains!
No light in his eye! Notice the look?
(PARSIFAL *has listened to* GURNEMANZ *with increasing emotion. He now breaks his bow to pieces and flings the arrows from him*)
Are you now conscious of your misdeed?
(PARSIFAL *draws his hand across his eyes*)
Speak, boy—are you aware of grievous guilt?
Just how could you do this deed?

Du konntest morden? Hier im heil'gen Walde,
dess' stiller Frieden dich umfing!
Des Haines Thiere nahten dir nicht zahm?
Grüssten dich freundlich und fromm?
Aus den Zweigen, was sangen die Vöglein dir?
Was that dir der treue Schwan?
Sein Weibchen zu suchen flog der auf,
mit ihm zu kreisen über dem See;
den so er herrlich weih'te zum heilenden Bad:
dem stauntest du nicht, dich lockt' es nur
zu wild kindischem Bogengeschoss?—
Er war uns hold: was ist er nun dir?
Hier—schau' her!—hier traf'st du ihn:
da starrt noch das Blut, matt hängen die Flügel;
das Schneegefieder dunkel befleckt,—
gebrochen das Aug', siehst du den Blick?
Wirst deiner Sündenthat du inne?—
Sag', Knab'! Erkennst du deine grosse Schuld?
Wie konntest du sie begeh'n?

PARSIFAL
I did not know this.

PARSIFAL
Das weiss ich nicht.

GURNEMANZ
Where are you from?

GURNEMANZ
Wo bist du her?

PARSIFAL
I do not know.

PARSIFAL
Das weiss ich nicht.

GURNEMANZ
Who is your father?

GURNEMANZ
Wer ist dein Vater?

PARSIFAL
I do not know.

PARSIFAL
Das weiss ich nicht.

GURNEMANZ
Who sent you to these environs?

GURNEMANZ
Wer sandte dich dieses Weg's?

PARSIFAL
I do not know.

PARSIFAL
Das weiss ich nicht.

GURNEMANZ
Then what's your name?

GURNEMANZ
Dein Name dann?

PARSIFAL
I once had many, but now I know not what they are.

PARSIFAL
Ich hatte viele,
doch weiss ich ihrer keinen mehr.

GURNEMANZ
You do not know at all?
(*aside*)
I never knew one dumb as you—save Kundry there!

GURNEMANZ
Das weisst du Alles nicht?
So dumm wie den
erfand bisher ich Kundry nur.—
Jetzt geht!

Versäumt den König im Bade
nicht!—Helft!

(to the squires, who have assembled in still greater numbers)
Now go! Do not neglect our king at bath! Off!
(the squires place the dead swan reverently on a bier of green boughs and bear it away toward the lake. Finally only GURNELMANZ, PARSIFAL, *and—apart—*KUNDRY, *remain.* GURNEMANZ *turns to* PARSIFAL*)*

Nun sag'! Nichts weisst du, was
ich dich frage:
jetzt melde, was du weisst!
denn etwas musst du doch
wissen.

Now speak! Since you know nothing I asked you,
just tell what you know—for surely you must know something.

PARSIFAL
Ich hab' eine Mutter; Herzeleide sie heisst:
im Wald und auf wilder Aue
waren wir heim.

PARSIFAL
Yes! I have a mother,
Heart of Sorrow her name.
I know that a wild and trackless moor was our home.

GURNEMANZ
Wer gab dir den Bogen?

GURNEMANZ
Who gave you your weapon?

PARSIFAL
Den schuf ich mir selbst,
vom Forst die rauhen Adler zu
scheuchen.

PARSIFAL
I made it myself, to scare the savage eagles from the forest.

GURNEMANZ
Doch adelig scheinst du selbst
und hochgeboren:
warum nicht liess deine Mutter
bessere Waffen dich lehren?

GURNEMANZ
Yet you seem eagle too, and born most nobly.
Why did your mother not let you handle
a weapon more manly?
*(*PARSIFAL *is silent)*

KUNDRY
Den Vaterlosen gebar die
Mutter,
als im Kampf erschlagen
Gamuret;
vor gleichem frühen Heldentod
den Sohn zu wahren, waffen-
fremd
in Oeden erzog sie ihn zum
Thoren—die Thörin!

KUNDRY
His father Gamuret died in battle,
so he only knows a mother's care.
To save him from like hero's death,
she raised him cloistered in the wild,
a fool now, and ignorant of weapons.
(she laughs)
More fool she!

PARSIFAL
Ja! Und einst am Waldessaume
vorbei,
auf schönen Thieren sitzend,
kamen glänzende Männer:
ihnen wollt' ich gleichen;
sie lachten und jagten davon.
Nun lief ich nach, doch konnte
sie nicht erreichen;
durch Wildnisse kam ich, berg-
auf, thalab;
oft ward es Nacht; dann wieder
Tag:
mein Bogen musste mir frommen
gegen Wild und grosse Männer.

PARSIFAL *(who has listened with keen attention)*
Yes! One day I saw some glittering men
that rode along the forest's edge
on beautiful horses.
I desired to be like them.
They laughed, and they galloped away.
I ran quite fast, but never could overtake them.
I traveled on, through woods, up hill, down dale.
Oft came the night, then day again.
My weapon had to protect me
from strong men and savage creatures . . .

KUNDRY
Ja, Schächer und Riesen traf
seine Kraft:
den freislichen Knaben lernten
sie fürchten.

KUNDRY
Yes! Robbers and giants sampled its strength.
The valorous stripling taught them to fear him.

PARSIFAL
Wer fürchtet mich? Sag'!

PARSIFAL *(surprised)*
Who had this fear? Who?

KUNDRY

The wicked!

PARSIFAL

Then those who threatened—were they then bad?

(GURNEMANZ *laughs*)

Who is good?

GURNEMANZ (*seriously*)

Your dear mother, whom you deserted,
and who now pines and grieves for you.

KUNDRY

Her grief is done, for his mother is dead.

PARSIFAL (*in fearful horror*)

Dead? My mother? Says who?

KUNDRY

Once riding by I saw her dying.
And, fool, she sent you her greeting.

(PARSIFAL *springs enraged at* KUNDRY *and seizes her by the throat.* GURNEMANZ *holds him back*)

GURNEMANZ

You rascally youngster! Always with force!

(*after* GURNEMANZ *has released* KUNDRY, PARSIFAL *stands awhile as if petrified*)

Now, what has she done? She spoke the truth.
For though she sees much, she never lies.

PARSIFAL (*falling into violent trembling*)

I am fainting!

(KUNDRY, *on perceiving* PARSIFAL's *condition, hastens to a brook, brings water in a horn, and sprinkles* PARSIFAL *with it, giving him some to drink*)

GURNEMANZ

That's right! So, as the Grail inspires us!
The evil ends, when repaid with the good.

KUNDRY (*gloomily*)

Good do I never.

(*she turns sadly away and while* GURNEMANZ *is attending to* PARSIFAL *with fatherly care, she crawls, unperceived, toward a thicket*)

It's rest I long for.
Just rest, ah! Ah! This tiredness!
Sleep now! Oh, would that none might wake me!
No! No sleep now! Terror grips me!

(*she trembles violently; her arms drop powerlessly*)

Vain to resist! The time has come!
Sleep now! Sleep now! I must!

(*she sinks down behind the thicket*)

GURNEMANZ

The king has had his bath and comes.
The sun's at highest.
Now let me lead the way to our pious supper,

KUNDRY

Die Bösen.

PARSIFAL

Die mich bedrohten, waren sie bös'?
Wer ist gut?

GURNEMANZ

Deine Mutter, der du entlaufen,
und die um dich sich nun härmt und grämt.

KUNDRY

Zu End' ihr Gram: seine Mutter ist todt.

PARSIFAL

Todt?—Meine Mutter?—Wer sagt's?

KUNDRY

Ich ritt vorbei, und sah sie sterben:
dich Thoren hiess sie mich grüssen.
Verrückter Knabe! Wieder Gewalt?
Was that dir das Weib? Es sagte wahr.
Denn nie lügt Kundry, doch sah

GURNEMANZ

sie viel.

PARSIFAL

Ich—verschmachte!—

GURNEMANZ

So recht! So nach des Grales Gnade:
das Böse bannt, wer's mit Gutem vergilt.

KUNDRY

Nie thu' ich Gutes;—nur Ruhe will ich.
Nur Ruhe! Ruhe, ach, der Müden!—
Schlafen!—Oh, dass mich keiner wecke!
Nein! Nicht schlafen!—Grausen fasst mich!
Machtlose Wehr! Die Zeit ist da.
Schlafen—schlafen—: ich muss.

GURNEMANZ

Vom Bade kehrt der König
hoch steht die Sonne:
nun lass' mich zum frommen heim; hoch steht die Sonne:

Mahl dich geleiten;
denn,—bist du rein,
wird nun der Gral dich tränken
und speisen.

for if you're pure,
the Holy Grail will quench you and feed you.
(GURNEMANZ *gently lays* PARSIFAL'S *arm on his own neck, and supporting him, leads him slowly along. The scene begins to change*)

PARSIFAL
Wer ist der Gral?

PARSIFAL
Who is the Grail?

GURNEMANZ
Das sagt sich nicht:
doch bist du selbst zu ihm erkoren,
bleibt dir die Kunde unverloren.—
Und sieh'!—
Mich dünkt, dass ich dich recht erkannt:
kein Weg führt zu ihm durch das Land,
und Niemand könnte ihn beschreiten,
den er nicht selber möcht' geleiten.

GURNEMANZ
I may not tell.
But if you're chosen for its service,
you'll know the truth that brings you knowledge.
And see!
I think that I do know you now.
No way leads to it through the land,
and no one could so guide his footsteps,
unless the Grail itself did show him.

PARSIFAL
Ich schreite kaum,—
doch wähn' ich mich schon weit.

PARSIFAL
I hardly walk,
yet seem t'have gone quite far.

GURNEMANZ
Du siehst, mein Sohn,
zum Raum wird hier die Zeit.

GURNEMANZ
You see, my son,
that here time turns to space.
(*as* PARSIFAL *and* GURNEMANZ *appear to walk, the scene changes more and more visibly. The forest disappears and a doorway appears in rocky walls concealing the two. The two enter the vast hall of the Grail castle. We see a pillared hall with a high dome in the center over the refectory. Enter the knights of the Grail, who take their places at the tables*)

Jetzt achte wohl; und lass' mich seh'n,
bist du ein Thor und rein,
welch Wissen dir auch mag beschieden sein.—

Now heed me well and let me see,
—if you're a fool, and pure—
what knowledge will be granted you by grace.

DIE GRALSRITTER
Zum letzten Liebesmahle
gerüstet Tag für Tag,
gleich ob zum letzten Male
es heut' ihn letzen mag,
wer guter That sich freut,
ihm sei das Mahl erneut;
der Labung darf er nah'n,
di hehrste Gab' empfah'n.

THE GRAIL KNIGHTS
This sacred meal is daily.
Each time is as the last.
Our God sustains us truly
In this divine repast.
(*a second train of squires crosses the hall*)
Who joys in deeds of love
New food gains from Above.
Who dares approach the Grail,
Will through its light prevail.
(*the assembled knights place themselves at the tables. Voices of younger men, coming from the mid-height of the hall, are heard. Through the opposite door* AMFORTAS *is brought in on a litter by squires and serving brethren. Before him march the four squires bearing the draped shrine. The procession wends to the center*

of the background, where a raised couch stands. On this AMFORTAS *is placed. Before it is a longish stone table on which the boys set down the Grail*)

BOYS' VOICES

As once our dear Master
In love for mankind
His blood in anguish offered,
So in happy rapture,
With love in turn for my Saviour
My blood's now proffered.
The Christ, whose blood for us did pay,
Now lives in us and heals today.

JÜNGERE MÄNNERSTIMMEN

Den sündigen Welten
mit tausend Schmerzen
wie einst sein Blut geflossen,
dem Erlösungshelden
mit freudigem Herzen
sie nun mein Blut vergossen.
Den Leib, den er zur Sühn' uns bot,
er lebt in uns durch seinen Tod.

BOYS' VOICES

Our God is Love,
And sends the dove,
Harmonious peace revealing;
Take of the wine,
Perception divine,
And bread that brings you healing.

(*when all have taken their seats and there is a pause, from the distance, behind* AMFORTAS' *couch, is heard* TITUREL'S *voice*)

KNABENSTIMMEN

Der Glaube lebt;
Die Taube schwebt,
des Heilands holder Bote:
der für euch fliesst,
des Wein's geniesst,
und nehmt vom Lebensbrode!

TITUREL'S VOICE

My son Amfortas, do you still serve?
Shall I again look to the Grail to heal me?
(*long pause*)
Must I die then, unguided by my Saviour?

TITUREL

Mein Sohn Amfortas! Bist du am Amt?
Soll ich den Gral heut' noch erschau'n und leben?
Muss ich sterben, vom Retter ungeleitet?

AMFORTAS (*half raising himself, in a despairing outburst*)

Torment! Torment! Endless pain!
Oh Father, once more perform
what the Holy Grail requires.
Carry on, and let me perish!

AMFORTAS

Wehe! Wehe mir der Qual!—
Mein Vater, oh! noch einmal
verrichte du das Amt!
Lebe! Leb' und lass' mich sterben!

TITUREL'S VOICE

I live entombed through our Redeemer's grace,
too feeble now to ever serve Him.
Make your atonement for your guilt.
Uncover the Grail!

TITUREL

Im Grabe leb' ich durch des Heilands Huld;
zu schwach doch bin ich, ihm zu dienen:
du büss' im Dienste deine Schuld!—
Enthüllet den Gral!

AMFORTAS (*restraining the boys*)

No! Let it stay concealed.
Oh, that no one, no one here should know my pain,
caused by the sacred sight that gives you joy.
What is the spear wound and its torment
compared to the pain, the hellish hurt
of being condemned to serve the Grail?
Dolorous duty on me has fallen.
I—only sinner in the knighthood,
must tend this highest holy relic
and call down its blessing upon the pure ones!
Infliction! Punishment unequaled

AMFORTAS

Nein! Lasst ihn unenthüllt!—Oh!—
Dass Keiner, Keiner diese Qual ermisst,
die mir der Anblick weckt, der euch entzückt!—
Was ist die Wunde, ihrer Schmerzen Wuth,
gegen die Noth, die Höllenpein,
des höchstein Heiligthums zu sein!—
Wehvolles Erbe, dem ich verfallen,
ich, einziger Sünder unter Allen,

des höchstein Heiligthums zu pflegen,
auf Reine herabzuflehen seinen Segen!—
Oh, Strafe! Strafe ohne Gleichen
des—ach—gekränkten Gnadenreichen!—
Nach Ihm, nach Seinem Weihegrusse
muss sehnlich mich's verlangen;
aus tiefster Seele Heilesbusse
zu Ihm muss ich gelangen:—
die Stundte nakt:
der Lichtstrahl senkt sich auf das heilige Werk;
die Hülle sinkt:
des Weihgefässes göttlicher Gehalt
erglüht mit leuchtender Gewalt;—
durchzückt von seligsten Genusses Schmerz,
des heiligsten Blutes Quell
fühl' ich sich giessen in mein Herz:
des eig'nen sündigen Blutes Gewell'
in wahnsinniger Flucht
muss mir zurück dann fliessen,
in die Welt der Sündenzucht
mit wilder Scheu sich ergiessen:—
von Neuem sprengt er das Thor,
daraus es nun strömt hervor,
hier durch die Wunde, der Seinen gleich,
geschlagen von desselben Speeres Streich,
der dort dem Erlöser die Wunde stach,
aus der mit blutigen Thränen
der Göttliche weint' ob der Menschheit Schmach
in Mitleids heiligem Sehnen,—
und aus der nun mir, an heiligster Stelle,
dem Pfleger göttlichster Güter,
des Erlösungsbalsams Hüter,
das heisse Sündenblut entquillt,
ewig erneut aus des Sehnens Quelle,
das, ach! keine Büssung je mir stillt!
Erbarmen! Erbarmen!
Du Allebarmer, ach! Erbarman!
Nimm mir mein Erbe,
schliesse die Wunde,
dass heilig ich sterbe,
rein Dir gesunde!

KNABEN UND JÜNGLINGE
„Durch Mitleid wissend,
der reine Thor:
harre sein',
den ich erkor."

from—ah!—the troubled Fount of Mercy!
For Him and for His benediction,
my eager heart is yearning.
My inmost soul desires atonement from God,
our only Saviour.
The hour draws near.
The light streams down upon the sanctified work.
The covering falls.
The vessel's holy contents glow again
with healing power upon us all.
I feel a rapturous and rending pain
that comes from our Saviour's blood,
which pours itself into my heart.
The furious tide of my own sinning blood
deliriously rushes back in surging torrents,
for it seeks this world of lust
to pour itself out headlong.
Again it forces the door,
again it emerges forth,
here through this lance wound—like unto His,
inflicted by the stab of that same spear,
which gave our Redeemer the holy wound,
and bloodstained tears of anguish
the Son of Man shed for all mankind's shame,
with tender, pitiful yearning.
And now too from me, in holiest office,
the guard of godliest relics
and of healing balm from heaven,
my fev'rish, sinful blood flows forth,
ever renewed from that sensual fountain
which—ah!—no repentance ever stills.
Have mercy! Have mercy!
God of Mercy, show me mercy!
Free me from service,
save me and heal me,
that I may die holy,
pure—with salvation!
(*he sinks back as if unconscious*)

BOYS, YOUNG MEN FROM THE HEIGHT
"Made wise through pity,
the holy fool.
Wait for him,
the one I chose."

THE KNIGHTS
Such were the words predicted.
Wait and believe. Perform your office still.

DIE RITTER
So ward es dir verkündet,
Harre getrost;
des Amtes walte heut'!

TITUREL'S VOICE
Uncover the Grail!
(AMFORTAS raises himself slowly and painfully. The boys remove the covering from the golden shrine, take out an antique crystal cup, from which they also remove a covering, and set it before AMFORTAS)
The blessing!

TITUREL
Enthüllet den Gral!
Der Segen!

BOYS' VOICES *(from above)*
"Take my body and eat.
Take my blood and drink.
This is my loving order."
(while AMFORTAS bows himself before the Cup in prayer, an increasing gloom spreads in the hall, culminating in complete darkness)
"Take my blood and drink,
Take my body and eat.
Do this in thought of me."
(a blinding ray of light shoots down from above upon the Cup, which then glows with an increasing purple luster, shedding a soft radiance on all around. AMFORTAS, with brightened mien, raises the Grail aloft and waves it gently about, blessing the bread and wine. All kneel)

KNABEN
„Nehmet hin meinen Leib,
nehmet hin mein Blut,
um uns'rer Liebe Willen!"

„Nehmet hin mein Blut,
nehmet hin meinen Leib,
auf dass ihr mein gedenkt!"

TITUREL'S VOICE
Oh! Rapture from heaven,
how joyful today is the Word!
(AMFORTAS sets down the Grail again, which now, while the deep gloom wanes, grows paler. The boys cover it as before, and return it to the shrine, which they also veil. The former daylight returns. The four boys apportion, during the following, bread and wine from two baskets and two pitchers)

TITUREL
Oh! Heilige Wonne!
Wie hell grüsst uns heute der Herr!

BOYS
Wine and bread to substance changing,
This the Grail's dear Lord's arranging,
Through the power of Love divine,
Into bread that is His flesh,
Into blood of that true Vine.

KNABENSTIMMEN
Wein und Brod des letzten Mahles
wandelt' einst der Herr des Grales,
durch des Mitleids Liebesmacht,
in das Blut, das er vergoss,
in den Leib, den dar er bracht'.

YOUNG MEN
Blood and flesh, as His creation,
Show His love, our true Salvation.
God is Spirit, God is Love,
God inspires with Wine from Heaven,
God is manna from Above.

JÜNGLINGSSTIMMEN
Blut und Leib der heil'gen Gabe
wandelt heut' zu eurer Labe
sel'ger Tröstung Liebesgeist
in den Wein, der euch nun floss,
in das Brod, das heut' ihr speis't.

DIE RITTER, ERSTE HÄLFTE
Nehmet vom Brod,
wandelt es kühn
zu Leibes Kraft und Stärke;
treu bis zum Tod,
fest in Müh'n,
zu wirken des Heilands Werke.

DIE RITTER, ZWEITE HÄLFTE
Nehmet vom Wein,
Wandelt ihn neu
zu Lebens feurigem Blute.

ALLE RITTER
Froh im Verein,
brudergetreu
zu kämpfen mit seligem Muthe.
Selig im Glauben und Liebe!

JÜNGLINGE
Selig in Liebe!

KNABEN
Selig im Glauben!

GURNEMANZ
Was stehst du noch da?
Weisst du, was du sah'st?

Du bist doch eben nur ein
Thor!
Dort hinaus, deinem Wege zu!
Doch räth dir Gurnemanz,
lass' du hier künftig die
Schwäne in Ruh',
und suche dir Gänser die Gans!

THE KNIGHTS
FIRST HALF
Take of the bread,
Quickening power,
For with it strength is given.
True to the death,
Now is the hour
To follow the will of heaven.

THE KNIGHTS, SECOND HALF
Take of the wine,
Change it anew,
To blood of zealous defiance.

ALL KNIGHTS
Right is divine,
Brotherhood true,
So battle with holy reliance!

YOUNG MEN
Love is our Saviour.

BOYS
Faith is our fortress.

(the knights rise and advance from opposite sides solemnly to embrace one another. During the meal, of which he has not partaken, AMFORTAS *gradually relapses from his state of exaltation; he droops his head and presses his hand to the wound. The boys approach him, their actions denoting the wound has burst out afresh. They tend him and assist him to his litter. Then, while all prepare to leave, they bear off* AMFORTAS *and the shrine in the order in which they came. The knights and squires fall in, and slowly quit the hall in solemn procession. The procession with* AMFORTAS *disappears. Waning daylight returns. Squires again march quickly through the hall. They disappear and the doors are closed.* PARSIFAL, *on hearing* AMFORTAS' *last cry of agony, clutches his heart and remains in that position for some time)*

GURNEMANZ *(ill-humoredly shaking* PARSIFAL *by the arm)*
You stand like a stock.
Just what have you seen?
*(*PARSIFAL, *still clutching his heart, shakes his head slightly)*
(very angrily)
You are then nothing but a fool!
Leave the place! Away with you!
(he opens a narrow side door)
Yet hark to Gurnemanz:
Hereafter do not go after our swans.
Just seek—foolish gander—a goose!
(he pushes PARSIFAL *out and slams the door after him. As he himself turns to follow the knights an alto voice is heard)*

ALTO (*from above*)
"Made wise through pity,
the holy fool."

CHORUS
Blessed and steadfast.

ALTO
„Durch Mitleid wissend,
der reine Tor."

CHOR
Selig im Glauben!

ACT II

(KLINGSOR's *magic castle, inner dungeon of a tower open at the top. Stone stairs lead to the edge of the battlements. Darkness in lower part of scene. Instruments of magic and necromancy.* KLINGSOR *is seated before a metal mirror.*)

KLINGSOR
Die Zeit ist da,—
Schon lockt mein Zauberschloss den Thoren,
den, kindisch jauchzend, fern ich nahen seh'.—
Im Todesschlafe hält der Fluch sie fest,
der ich den Krampf zu lösen weiss.—
Auf denn! Ans Werk!
Herauf! Herauf! Zu mir!
Dein Meister ruft dich Namenlose:
Ur-Teufelin! Höllen-Rose!
Herodias warst du, und was noch?
Gundryggia dort, Kundry hier:
Hieher! Hieher denn, Kundry!
Zu deinem Meister, herauf!
Erwachst du? Ha!
Meinem Banne wieder
verfallen heut' zur rechten Zeit.
Sag', wo triebst du dich wieder umher?
Pfui! Dort, bei dem Ritter-Gesipp',
wo wie ein Vieh du dich halten lässt?
Gefällt's dir bei mir nicht besser?
Als ihren Meister du mir gefangen—
ha ha!—den reinen Hüter des Grales,—
was jagte dich da wieder fort?

KLINGSOR
The time has come.
The boy now nears with childish outcries.
My magic castle lures the lad this way.
A deathly slumber still binds fast my slave,
so let me end her cramping curse.
Up then! To work!
(*he steps down, kindles incense, which immediately fills the background with a bluish light, then seats himself before the magical apparatus and with mystical gestures calls down into the abyss*)
Get up! Get up! Come here!
Your master calls you, nameless creature,
First sorceress! Rose of Hades!
Herodias one time, and what else?
Gundrygia there, Kundry here!
Come here! Come here then, Kundry!
Your master calls: arise!
(KUNDRY's *figure rises up through the bluish light. She appears asleep, then gives signs of awakening. She utters a fearful cry*)
You're wak'ning? Ha!
You have fallen again to my spell today—in time of need.
(KUNDRY *utters a loud lament that diminishes to a whimper*)
Say, where have you been roaming again?
Pfui! There, by that rabble of knights,
where you are looked upon as a beast!
With me don't you fare much better?
You lured their master into my power
—ha ha!—the virgin guard of the chalice,
so what was it drove you away?

KUNDRY
Ach!—Ach!
Tiefe Nacht—
Wahnsinn!—Oh!—Wuth!—
Oh! Jammer!—
Schlaf—Schlaf—
tiefer Schlaf!—Tod!

KUNDRY (*hoarsely, and in broken sounds as if seeking to regain speech*)
Ah!—Ah!
Gloomy night—
Madness!—Oh!—Rage!—
Oh! Anguish—
Sleep—sleep—
Deepest sleep!—Death!

KLINGSOR
Da weckte dich ein And'rer? He?

KLINGSOR
Then did another wake you? Hey?

KUNDRY
Ja!—Mein Fluch!—
Oh!—Sehnen—Sehnen!—

KUNDRY (*as before*)
Yes!—My curse!
Oh!—Longing—longing!

KLINGSOR
Ha ha! there—for the virgin knighthood?

KUNDRY
There—I—served them.

KLINGSOR
Yes, yes! You thought to make repayment for harm you had done to the band?
But they cannot help;
all are corrupted—
if I just ask their price.
The firmest will fall,
yielding to your embraces,
and then be quelled by the spear,
which from their lord himself I purloined.
(*looking sharply at* KUNDRY)
Our most dangerous foe is due on this day:
one armed with folly's shield.

KUNDRY
I—will not. No! No!

KLINGSOR
You will well, for you must.

KUNDRY
You cannot compel me.

KLINGSOR
But I can seize you.

KUNDRY
You?

KLINGSOR
Your master.

KUNDRY
And by what power?

KLINGSOR
Ha! The power of a man
who's immune to your charms.

KUNDRY
Ha! ha! Are you chaste?

KLINGSOR
And why ask that, accursed witch?—
Horrible lack!
So laughs the devil now
because I strove for holiness once!
Horrible lack!
Irrepressible longing pain!
Terrible pricking lust from hell
—which once I quelled to quiet of death—
laughs and mocks me aloud
through you, the devil's bride!
Have a care!
Well did he pay for scorn and derision
—that proud one—strong in holiness,

KLINGSOR
Ha ha!—dort nach den keuschen Rittern!

KUNDRY
Da—da—dient' ich.

KLINGSOR
Ja, ja!—den Schaden zu vergüten,
den du ihnen böslich gebracht?
Sie helfen dir nicht:
feil sind sie Alle,
biet' ich den rechten Preis;
der festeste fällt,
sinkt er dir in die Arme:
und so verfällt er dem Speer,
den ihrem Meister selbst ich entwandt.—
Den Gefährlichsten gilt's nun heut' zu besteh'n:
ihn schirmt der Thorheit Schild.

KUNDRY
Ich—will nicht!—Oh!—Oh!

KLINGSOR
Wohl willst du, denn du musst.

KUNDRY
Du—kannst mich—nicht—halten.

KLINGSOR
Aber dich fassen.

KUNDRY
Du?

KLINGSOR
Dein Meister.

KUNDRY
Aus welcher Macht?

KLINGSOR
Ha! Weil einzig an mir
deine Macht—nichts vermag.

KUNDRY
Ha! ha!—Bist du keusch?

KLINGSOR
Was fräg'st du das, verfluchtes Weib?—
Furchtbare Noth!—
So lacht nun der Teufel mein',
dass ich einst nach dem Heiligen rang!
Furchtbare Noth!
Ungebändigten Sehnens Pein!
Schrecklichster Triebe Höllendrang,
den ich zu Todesschweigen mir zwang,—
lacht und höhnt er nun laut
durch dich, des Teufels Braut?—
Hüte dich!
Hohn und Verachtung büsste schon Einer:
der Stolze, stark in Heiligkeit,

der einst mich von sich stiess,
sein Stamm verfiel mir,
unerlöst
soll der Heiligen Hüter mir
schmachten;
und bald—so wähn' ich—
hüt' ich mir selbst den Gral.
— —
Ha! Ha!
Gefiel er dir wohl, Amfortas,
der Held,
den ich dir zur Wonne gesellt?

KUNDRY
Oh!—Jammer!—Jammer!
Schwach auch Er! Schwach—
Alle!
Meinem Fluche mit mir
Alle verfallen!—
Oh, ewiger Schlaf,
einziges Heil,
wie,—wie dich gewinnen?

KLINGSOR
Ha! Wer dir trotzte, löste dich
frei:
versuch's mit dem Knaben, der
nah't!

KUNDRY
Ich—will nicht!

KLINGSOR
Jetzt schon erklimmt er die
Burg.

KUNDRY
Oh Wehe! Wehe!
Erwachte ich darum?
Muss ich?—Muss?

KLINGSOR
Ha!—Er ist schön, der Knabe!

KUNDRY
Oh!—Oh!—Wehe mir!—

KLINGSOR
Ho! Ho!—Ihr Wächter! Ritter!
Helden!—Auf!—Feinde nah'!
Hei!—Wie zur Mauer sie stür-
men,
die bethörten Eigenholde,
zum Schutz ihres schönen
Geteufels!—
So!—Muthig! Muthig!—
Haha!—Der fürchtet sich
nicht:—
dem Helden Ferris entwand er
die Waffe;
die führt er nun freislich wider
den Schwarm.—
Wie übel den Tölpeln der Eifer
gedeiht!
Dem schlug er den Arm,—
Jenem den Schenkel.
Haha!—Sie weichen,—sie
fliehen:
seine Wunde trägt Jeder nach
heim!—
Wie das ich euch gönne!—

who spurned me from him once.
His stock is blasted.
Unredeemed
shall the holy custodian suffer;
and soon, I fancy,
I shall be lord of the Grail—
Haha!
And did you not like Amfortas, the brave,
he whom I gave you for your joy?

KUNDRY
Oh! Torment! Torment!
Weak—he too! All weaklings!
For the curse I bear
brings all to their ruin—
Oh, sleep without end,
only release,
how, how may I win you?

KLINGSOR
Ha! He who braves you, saves you as well:
so try out the lad, who draws near!

KUNDRY
I—will not!

KLINGSOR (*who has mounted to the tower wall*)
So soon! He's climbing the wall.

KUNDRY
O sorrow! Sorrow!
Was this why you woke me?
Must I?—This?

KLINGSOR (*looking below*)
Ha! Quite a handsome youngster!

KUNDRY
Oh!—Oh!—Woe is me!

KLINGSOR (*blowing a horn*)
Ho! You watchmen! Ho! Warriors!
Heroes! Up! Foes are near!
Hey! How they rush to the ramparts,
the besotted vassals,
meaning to guard their beautiful devils!
So! Courage! Courage!
Ha-ha! He's quite without fear:
he took the sword from the valorous Ferris,
and with it he cuts his way through the swarm.
(KUNDRY *gives a gloomy, hysterical laugh*)
The louts lack the ardor to cope with his zeal!
This—struck in the arm, that one—his thigh cut!
Ha-ha! They waver! They're fleeing!
Each campaigner runs home with his hurts!
You're welcome to all that!
Would that this crew,
this troublesome gang,

only might strangle each other!
Ha! How proudly he stands on the ramparts.
His count'nance is laughing and rosy,
he's gazing amazed
at the garden deserted so soon!
Hey, Kundry!
(*he turns around.* KUNDRY *has disappeared; the bluish light has gone out, and deep darkness lies below.*)
How? Started work?
Ha-ha! I know the magic well,
which always will fetch you
whenever I wish!
(*he looks toward the garden*)
You there! innocent sprout:
though your mission was foretold,
you're young and dumb,
and therefore fit for a fall:
your pur'ty once departed,
my power will make you serve me!
(*he and the tower sink quickly, and at the same time the magic garden emerges, with tropical vegetation and luxurious flowers. In the background is the battlemented castle, in elaborate Arabic style.* PARSIFAL *is standing on the wall, looking down on the garden in amazement. Then from garden and palace beautiful maidens rush out, clad in filmy veils, which seem to have been donned hastily, as if their wearers had been suddenly wakened from sleep.*)

MAIDENS (*coming from the garden*)
Here was the tumult,
weapons, horrid outcries!

MAIDENS (*coming from the castle*)
Sorrow! Vengeance! Up!
Who is the culprit?

ONE GROUP
My beloved is wounded.

ANOTHER
O, where is my sweetheart?

ANOTHER
When I woke, he had left me.
Where has he fled to?

OTHERS
Inside the castle?
They're bleeding! Horrors!
Who is the foe?
There! See him!
See, my Ferris' sword is in his hand!
I saw, he just stormed the walls.
I heard, too, the master's horn.
My knight ran this way;
they all of them rushed this way;

Möge denn so
das ganze Rittergezücht
unter sich selber sich würgen!—
Ha! Wie stolz er nun steht auf der Zinne!
Wie lachen ihm die Rosen der Wangen,
da kindisch erstaunt
in den einsamen Garten er blickt!—
He! Kundry!
Wie? Schon am Werk?—
Haha! Den Zauber kannt' ich wohl,
der immer dich wieder zum
Dienst mir gesellt.—
Du dort, kindischer Spross!
Was—auch
Weissagung dir wies,—
zu jung and dumm
fielst du in meine Gewalt:—
die Reinheit dir entrissen,
bleibst mir du zugewiesen!

MÄDCHEN
Hier war das Tosen,
Waffen, wilde Rüfe!

MÄDCHEN
Wehe! Rache! Auf!
Wo ist der Frevler?

EINZELNE
Mein Geliebter verwundet.

ANDERE
Wo ist der Meine?

ANDERE
Ich erwachte allein,
wohin entfloh er?

IMMER ANDERE
Drinnen im Saale!—
Sie bluten! Wehe!
Wer ist der Feind?—
Da steht er! Seht!—
Meines Ferris Schwert?—
Ich sah's, er stürmte die Burg.—
Ich hörte des Meisters Horn.
Mein Held lief herzu.
Sie Alle kamen, doch Jeden
empfing er mit blutiger Wehr.
Der Kühne! Der Feindliche!
Alle sie flohen ihm.—

Du dort! Du dort!
Was schufst du uns solche Noth?
Verwünscht, verwünscht sollst du sein!

DIE MÄDCHEN
Ha! Kühner! Wagst du zu nahen?
Was schlugst du uns're Geliebten?

PARSIFAL
Ihr schönen Kinder, musst' ich sie nicht schlagen?
Zu euch Holden ja wehrten sie mir den Weg.

MÄDCHEN
Zu uns wolltest du?
Sah'st du uns schon?

PARSIFAL
Noch nie sah ich solch' zieres Geschlecht,
nenn' ich euch schön, dünkt euch das recht?

DIE MÄDCHEN
So willst du uns wohl nicht schlagen?

PARSIFAL
Das möcht' ich nicht.

MÄDCHEN
Doch Schaden
schufst du uns grossen und vielen;
du schlugest uns're Gespielen!
Wer spielt nun mit uns?

PARSIFAL
Das thu' ich gern.

DIE MÄDCHEN
Bist du uns hold, so bleib' nicht fern;
und willst du uns nicht schelten,
wir werden dir's entgelten:
Wir spielen nicht um Gold,
wir spielen um Minnes Sold:
Willst du auf Trost uns sinnen,
sollst den du uns abgewinnen.

DIE GESCHMÜCKTEN MÄDCHEN
Lasset den Knaben!—Er gehöret mir.—
Nein!—Nein!—Mir!—Mir!

DIE ANDERN MÄDCHEN
Ah, die Schlimmen!—Sie schmückten sich heimlich.

yet each was beat back by his might.
That bold one! That enemy!
All of them fled from him.
You there! You there!
Why have you caused us this woe!
Accursed, accursed may you be!

(PARSIFAL *leaps toward the garden. The maidens start back.*)

MAIDENS
Dare you come near us?
Why have you injured our lovers?

PARSIFAL
You lovely children, should I not have struck them?
They tried, fair maidens, to bar my way from your bower.

MAIDENS
Were we what you sought?
Are we so fair?

PARSIFAL
Indeed, I've never witnessed such grace.
Am I not right, calling you fair?

MAIDENS
You have no thought, then, to harm us?

PARSIFAL
How could I have!

MAIDENS
You've done us
inj'ries, many inj'ries.
You badly injured our playmates!
Who'll play with us now?

PARSIFAL
I will—with joy!

MAIDENS
Be nice to us, and don't go far.
And if you do not chide us,
you'll gather love beside us.
We do not play for gold,
we play to let love unfold.
Would you like to console us,
then try to catch us and hold us!

(*some, who had stepped out, return now in floral dresses, looking very much like flowers, and rush toward* PARSIFAL.)

DECKED-OUT MAIDENS
Let go the youngster!—He belongs to me.
No!—No!—Me!—Me!

OTHER MAIDENS
Ah, how tricky!—They went and changed raiment!

MAIDENS
Come! Come!
Gallant youngster,
I'll be your lover,
and then you'll discover
love each rapturous hour!

PARSIFAL (*standing among them*)
How sweetly you smell!
Are you then flowers?

MAIDENS
Our garden's pride
and pleasant aroma!
Our lord plucked us in springtime!
We flourish here
in sunlight of summer,
thus blooming for our newcomer.
Now be our sweetheart true,
begrudge not the flowers their due!
Sweetly must you love us and cherish,
or else we will wither and perish.

FIRST MAIDEN
Oh take me, love, to your heart!

SECOND MAIDEN
Your brow needs a cool blessing!

THIRD MAIDEN
Your cheeks were meant for caressing!

FOURTH MAIDEN
Your mouth asks me for kisses!

FIFTH MAIDEN
No! No! No! I am the fairest!

SIXTH MAIDEN
No! My smell is sweeter!

PARSIFAL (*gently putting off their advances*)
You wild, lovely cluster of flowers,
if I join your frolic I must have more room here!

MAIDENS
Why do you chide?

PARSIFAL
Because you quarrel.

MAIDENS
We quarrel but for you.

PARSIFAL
Then stop it.

FIRST MAIDEN
Let him alone! See, he wants me!

SECOND MAIDEN
No, me!

DIE MÄDCHEN
Komm'! Komm'!
Holder Knabe,
lass mich dir blühen!
Dir zu wonniger Labe
gilt mein minniges Mühen.

PARSIFAL
Wie duftet ihr hold!
Seid ihr denn Blumen?

DIE MÄDCHEN
Des Gartens Zier
und duftende Geister,
im Lenz pflückt uns der Meister!
Wir wachsen hier
in Sommer und Sonne,
für dich erblühend in Wonne.
Nun sei uns freund und hold!
Nicht karge den Blumen den Sold:
Kannst du uns nicht lieben und minnen,
wir welken und sterben dahinnen.

ERSTES MÄDCHEN
An dienen Busen nimm mich!

ZWEITES MÄDCHEN
Die Stirn lass' mich dir kühlen!

DRITTES
Lass mich die Wange dir fühlen!

VIERTES
Den Mund lass' mich dir küssen!

FÜNFTES
Nein, mich! Die Schönste bin ich.

SECHSTES
Nein! Ich dufte süsser.

PARSIFAL
Ihr wild holdes Blumengedränge,
Soll ich mit euch spielen, entlasst mich der Enge!

MÄDCHEN
Was zankest du?

PARSIFAL
Weil ihr euch streitet.

MÄDCHEN
Wir streiten nur um dich.

PARSIFAL
Das meidet!

ERSTES MÄDCHEN
Du lass' von ihm! Sieh', er will mich.

ZWEITES MÄDCHEN
Nein, mich!

DRITTES
Mich lieber!

VIERTES
Nein, mich!

ERSTES MÄDCHEN
Du wehrest mir?

ZWEITES
Du scheuchest mich fort?

MÄDCHEN
Bist du feige vor Frauen?
Magst nicht dich getrauen?
Wie schlimm bist du, Zager und Kalter!
Die Blumen lässt du umbuhlen den Falter?
Wie ist er zag! Wie ist er kalt!
Auf! Weichet dem Thoren!
Wir geben ihn verloren.

ANDERE MÄDCHEN
Doch sei er uns erkoren.
Nein, uns!—Nein, mir!—
Auch mir!—Hier, hier!—

PARSIFAL
Lass't ab! Ihr fangt mich nicht!

KUNDRY
Parisfal—Weile!

PARSIFAL
Parsifal . . . ?
So nannte träumend mich einst die Mutter.—

KUNDRY
Hier weile, Parsifal!—
Dich grüsset Wonne und Heil zumal.— —
Ihr kindischen Buhlen, weichet von ihm:
früh welkende Blumen,
nicht euch ward er zum Spiel bestellt!
Geht heim, pfleget der Wunden:
einsam erharrt euch mancher Held.

DIE MÄDCHEN
Dich zu lassen, dich zu meiden,—
O weh'! O weh' der Pein!
Von Allen möchten gern wir scheiden,
mit dir allein zu sein.—
Leb' wohl! Leb' wohl!
Du Holder! Du Stolzer!
Du—Thor!

THIRD MAIDEN
Me rather!

FOURTH MAIDEN
No, me!

FIRST MAIDEN
Avoiding me?

SECOND MAIDEN
You turn me away?

MAIDENS
Why of women so chary,
so fearful and wary?
How timid you are, and how prudish!
You'd have the butterflies wooed by the flowers?
How faint he is! How cold he is!
A blockhead, so let's leave him!
He's lost, so why receive him?

OTHERS
Why then let us retrieve him!
No, us!—No, me!—
And me!—And me!—

PARSIFAL
Let be! I'll not be caught!
(*he is about to flee when he hears* KUNDRY'S *voice and stands stone-still. The maidens make an outcry*)

KUNDRY (*gradually coming into sight*)
Parsifal! Tarry!

PARSIFAL
Parsifal . . . ?
The name my mother once called me while dreaming.

KUNDRY
Here tarry, Parsifal.
Now look for bliss and delight at once.
(*to the maids*)
You frivolous wantons, leave him alone.
Fast-withering flowers,
who said he was to serve for your sport?
Go home, tend to your wounded!
Many neglected wait for your care.

MAIDENS (*as they tremblingly and reluctantly leave* PARSIFAL)
Must we leave you, must we part so?
Oh woe! Oh woe for the pain!
We'd gladly part from all companions
to be alone with you.
Farewell! Farewell!
Most gracious! Most valiant!
Most—fool!
(*they disappear into the castle, laughing.* PARSIFAL *looks timidly in the direction from which he heard the voice. The branches of the arbor separate and a young*

woman of surpassing beauty is seen: KUNDRY, *quite different from before. She is lying on a flowery couch in diaphanous drapery of somewhat Arabian fashion)*

PARSIFAL

Have I been in a dream just now?
Did you call me—who am nameless?

PARSIFAL

Dies Alles—hab' ich nun geträumt?
Riefest du mich Namenlosen?

KUNDRY

I called you, foolish pure one,
"Fal-parsi,"
Thus, pure and foolish: "Parsifal."
The name was uttered in far Araby's land,
by Gamuret, your father, to that son
who still was locked within his mother;
and with this utt'rance death did take him.
I've waited for you just to give this news.
What drew you here, if not the wish to know?

KUNDRY

Dich nannt' ich, thör'ger Reiner,
„Fal parsi",—
Dich, reinen Thoren: „Parsifal".
So rief, da in arab'schem Land er verschied,
dein Vater Gamuret dem Sohne zu,
den er, im Mutterschoss verschlossen,
mit diesem Namen sterbend grüsste.
Dir ihn zu künden, harrt' ich deiner hier:
was zog dich her, wenn nicht der Kunde Wunsch?

PARSIFAL

I've not seen, nor even dreamed, what now
I see, and what with terror fills my heart!
And did you too bloom in this flower garden?

PARSIFAL

Nie sah' ich, nie träumte mir, was jetzt
ich schau', und was mit Bangen mich erfüllt.—
Entblühtest du auch diesem Blumenhaine?

KUNDRY

No, Parsifal, you foolish virgin!
Far, far, the land I hale from.
I only tarried to be here when you came.
And through this journey I have seen a lot.
I saw the child upon its mother's breast,
its cooing cries still linger in my ear.
Though filled with sorrow
she laughed through the tears of that sorrow,
to hear the joy of her eyes
make cries of lovely laughter!
She gently made a mossy cradle;
it fell asleep from her caresses.
The anxious mother
protected its rest with sleepless vigil,
and in the morning
a mother's dewy tears awaked it.
Her face was tearful, sorrow's picture.
The cause: your father's love and death.
She uttered ardent, holy prayers,
to save you from a fate like his.
Her dear desire was all to keep you sheltered,
far from all arms, and mankind's warring madness.
She loved you, watched you, and still sorrowed:
all news of evil was kept from your knowledge.
Do you not still hear her anguished cry,

KUNDRY

Nein, Parsifal, du thör'ger Reiner!
Fern—fern—ist meine Heimath:—
Dass du mich fändest, verweilte ich nur hier.
Von weither kam ich, wo ich viel ersah'.
Ich sah das Kind an seiner Mutter Brust,
sein erstes Lallen lacht mir noch im Ohr;
das Leid im Herzen,
wie lachte da auch Herzeleide,
als ihren Schmerzen
zujauchzte ihrer Augen Weide!
Gebettet sanft auf weichen Moosen,
den hold geschläfert sie mit Kosen,
dem, bang in Sorgen,
den Schlaf bewacht der Mutter Sehnen,
ihn weckt' am Morgen
der heisse Thau der Mutter-thränen.
Nur Weinen war sie, Schmerz-gebahren
um deines Vaters Lieb' und Tod;
vor gleicher Noth dich zu bewahren,
galt ihr als höchster Pflicht Gebot.

Den Waffen fern, der Männer Kampf und Wüthen,
wollte sie still dich bergen und behüten.
Nur Sorgen war sie, ach! und Bangen:
nie sollte Kunde zu dir hergelangen.
Hör'st du nicht noch ihrer Klage Ruf,
wann fern und spät du geweilt?
Hei! Was ihr das Lust und Lachen schuf,
wann suchend sie dann dich ereilt!
Wann dann ihr Arm dich wüthend umschlang,
ward dir es wohl gar beim Küssen bang?—
Ihr Wehe doch du nicht vernahmst,
nicht ihrer Schmerzen Toben,
als endlich du nicht wieder kamst,
und deine Spur verstoben.
Sie harrte Nächt' und Tage,
bis ihr verstummt die Klage,
der Gram ihr zehrte den Schmerz,
um stillen Tod sie warb:
ihr brach das Leid das Herz,
und—Herzeleide—starb.

when you tarried far from home?
Hey! How she rejoiced and laughed that time
when she found you after her search,
and clutched her arms around you, relieved,
what fear did you have of kisses then?
Yet you could not perceive her sorrow,
nor know that frenzied anguish.
And then at last you went for all time,
and left no trace behind you.
She waited for you daily,
until her woe was silenced,
till all was dull and dead.
She prayed for death to come,
then sorrow broke her heart,
and—Heart of Sorrow—died.

PARSIFAL

Wehe! Wehe! Was that ich? Wo war ich?
Mutter! Süsse, holde Mutter!
Dein Sohn, dein Sohn musste dich morden
O Thor! Blöder, taumelnder Thor!
Wo irrtest du hin, ihrer vergessend?
Deiner, deiner vergessend,
traute, theuerste Mutter?

Sorrow! Sorrow! My misdeed? Where was I?
Mother! Sweetest, dearest Mother!
Your son it was, your son that slew you!
Oh fool! Blind and blundering fool!
Forgetful of you! Wandering wildly!
Forgetful, blindly forgetful!
Sweetest, dearest of mothers!

KUNDRY

War dir fremd noch der Schmerz,
des Trostes Süsse
labte nie auch dein Herz:
das Wehe, das dich reut,
die Noth nun büsse
im Trost, den Liebe dir beut!

Had you not harbored pain,
sweet consolation
could not visit your heart.
The woe that rends your soul
shall now give place to a joy
that springs from my love.

PARSIFAL

Die Mutter, die Mutter konnt' ich vergessen!
Ha! Was Alles vergass ich wohl noch?
Wess' war ich je noch eingedenk?
Nur dumpfe Thorheit lebt in mir!

My mother, my mother! Could I forget her?
Ha! Why is it I always forget?
Why don't I remember at all?
Just stupid folly lives in me!

KUNDRY (*encircling his neck with her arm*)

Bekenntniss
wird Schuld und Reue enden,
Erkenntniss

Confession
makes guilt for errors vanish.

Admission
to self will folly banish.
Just learn to love in fashion
that Gamuret once loved,
when Heart of Sorrow's passion
his passion hotly moved.
And she who gave you
body and senses
must keep both death and folly far.
She sends by me
her final blessing and farewell:
she gives you love's—first kiss!
(*bending completely over him, she plants a long kiss upon his lips.* PARSIFAL *starts up in terror, pressing his hand against his heart*)

in Sinn die Thorheit wenden.
Die Liebe lerne kennen,
die Gamuret umschloss,
als Herzeleid's Entbrennen
ihn sengend überfloss.
Die Leib und Leben
einst dir gegeben,
der Tod und Thorheit weichen muss,
sie beut'
dir heut'—
als Muttersegens letzten Gruss
der Liebe—ersten Kuss.

PARSIFAL

Amfortas!
The spear wound! The spear wound!
The pain burns in my bosom!
Oh sorrow! Sorrow!
Terrible torture!
A cry of anguish wells from my heart!
Wretched one!
Woeful suff'rer!
The wound has started bleeding!
I feel it bleed within.
Here, here!
No! No! Not the wound I thought it.
Let that outpour in streams if it will!
Here! Here! The brand in my heart!
The longing, the terrible longing,
that grips my senses in error's thrall!
Oh, love that torments!
How all within me thrills, and quakes
and throbs in sinful longing!
(*while* KUNDRY *stares in mingled fear and wonderment* PARSIFAL *appears to have fallen into a trance*)
My glance is fixed fast on the healing cup,
the holy blood glows red.
Redemption's rapture, pure and mild,
sends healing power through creation.
But here, within me will the pain not lessen.
I hear the voice of our Redeemer,
ah, lamenting, lamenting
for the polluted sanctuary.
"Redeem me! Rescue me
from hands that guilt has tainted!"
So calls the voice from heaven,
fearful, loud, piercing my being.
And I, the fool, the craven,
to wild and childish actions hurry on!

PARSIFAL

Amfortas!— —
Die Wunde!—Die Wunde!
Sie brennt in meinem Herzen.—
Oh, Klage! Klage!
Furchtbare Klage!
Aus tiefstem Inner'n schreit sie mir auf.
Oh! Oh!—
Elender!
Jammervollster!—
Die Wunde sah' ich bluten:
nun blutet sie mir selbst—
hier—hier!
Nein, nein! Nicht ist es die Wunde:
fliesse ihr Blut in Strömen dahin!
Hier! Hier im Herzen der Brand!
Das Sehnen, das furchtbare Sehnen,
das alle Sinne mir fasst und zwingt!
Oh!—Qual der Liebe!—
Wie Alles schauert, bebt und zuckt
in sündigem Verlangen! . . .
Es starrt der Blick dumpf auf das Heilsgefäss:
das heilige Blut erglüht;—
Erlösungswone, göttlich mild,
durchzittert weithin alle Seelen;
nur hier, im Herzen, will die Qual nicht weichen.
Des Heilands Klage da vernehm' ich,
die Klage, ach! die Klage
um das entweihte Heiligthum:—
„Erlöse, rette mich
aus schuldbefleckten Händen!"
So—rief die Gottesklage
furchtbar laut mir in die Seele.
Und ich? Der Thor, der Feige?
Zu wilden Knabenthaten floh' ich hin!

Erlöser! Heiland! Herr der Huld!
Wie büss' ich Sünder solche Schuld?

KUNDRY
Gelobter Held! Entflieh' dem Wahn!
Blick' auf! Sei hold der Huldin Nah'n!

PARSIFAL
Ja! Diese Stimme! So rief sie ihm;—
und diesen Blick, deutlich erkenn' ich ihn,—
auch diesen, der ihm so friedlos lachte.
Die Lippe,—ja—so zuckte sie ihm;—
so neigte sich der Nacken,—
so hob sich kühn das Haupt;—
so flatterten lachend die Locken,—
so schlang um den Hals sich der Arm—
so schmeichelte weich die Wange—!
Mit aller Schmerzen Qual im Bund,
das Heil der Seele
entküsste ihm ihr Mund!—
Ha!—dieser Kuss!—
Verderberin! Weiche von mir!
Ewig—ewig—von mir!

KUNDRY
Grausamer!—Ha!—
Fühlst du im Herzen,
nur Anderer Schmerzen,
so fühle jetzt auch die meinen!
Bist du Erlöser,
was bannt dich, Böser,
nicht mir auch zum Heil dich zu einen?
Seit Ewigkeiten—harre ich deiner,
des Heilands, ach! so spät,
den einst ich kühn verschmäht.—
Oh!—
Kenntest du den Fluch,
der mich durch Schlaf und Wachen,
durch Tod und Leben,
Pein und Lachen,
zu neuem Leiden neu gestählt,
endlos durch das Dasein quält!—
Ich sah—Ihn—Ihn—
und—lachte . . .
da traf mich sein Blick.—
Nun such' ich ihn von Welt zu Welt
ihm wieder zu begegnen:
in höchster Noth—
wähn' ich sein Auge schon nah',
den Blick schon auf mir ruh'n:—

Redeemer! Saviour! Lord of Grace!
How may a sinner blot such guilt?

KUNDRY (*now passionately admiring, timidly approaches* PARSIFAL)
O valiant knight! Cast off this spell!
Look up! And love the one who loves!

PARSIFAL (*staring blindly up at* KUNDRY *while she leans over him and caresses him*)
Ha! So she called him.
This was the voice, and this the look,—
clearly I know it well.
And this too, this was the smile she gave him.
The lips, too—yes, they quivered like that.
The neck was bent this manner,
the head was proudly raised.
Thus, laughing, she dangled her tresses,
and so put her arm round his neck.
His cheeks too she touched so gently,
and in league with mortal pain and error,
she kissed away the salvation of his soul!
Ha!—That dread kiss!
(*he pushes* KUNDRY *away*)
You sorceress! Out of my sight!
Leave me—forever—be gone!

KUNDRY
Dreadful one!
If you feel pain
in your heart for others,
then let me too share this pity!
If you're the Saviour,
what keeps you, bad one,
from granting the solace I ask for?
Through endless ages
I've waited your coming,
an advent, ah!—so late!—
of one I rashly spurned.
Oh, could you know the curse,
which through me, sleeping, waking,
in death or living,
pain and laughter,
—which meets new strength to front new foes—
gives my being endless woe!
I saw Him—Him—
and—mocked Him—
I felt then—His look:
I seek Him now from world to world.
Again I hope to meet Him.
I feel His eye near, in the time of my need.
His glance rests on me now.

Yet from me—comes again this cursed laughter!
A sinner sinks in my embraces!
Just laughter moves me, for tears cannot;
just shouting, raging,
fuming, raving,
cloud upon cloud from error's night,
from which, repentant, scarce I've waked.
In mortal shame I waited sadly
the one that I rejected madly.
So let me weep upon your bosom,
and give me solace, an hour's a-tone-ment,
and though I'm spurned by God and man,
my soul will be redeemed, and at peace.

da kehrt mir das verfluchte Lachen wieder,—
ein Sünder sinkt mir in die Arme!
Da lach' ich—lache,—
kann nicht weinen:
nur schreien, wüthen,
toben, rasen
in stets erneu'ter Wahnsinns Nacht,
aus der ich büssend kaum erwacht.—
Den ich ersehnt in Todesschmachten,
den ich erkannt, den blöd Verlachten,
lasts mich an seinem Busen weinen,
nur eine Stunde mich dir vereinen,
und, ob mich Gott und Welt verstösst,
in dir entsündigt sein und erlöst!

PARSIFAL
A full damnation
both of us would share
for such a-tone-ment,
if I forgot my mission
within your arms' embraces!
Yet I was sent to heal you too,
if you put off your wrong desire.
The solace which will end your sorrow
does not arise from error's source;
and never will you gain your healing
until you stop the source of sin.
Far otherwise, far diff'rent, ah,
for me to see that grievous sight—
the Brothers there, in direful need,
with their bodies wasting, lost in anguish.
But who has such unclouded sight
to know the truth that makes man free?
Oh, wretched, where is counsel gone?
Oh, dreadful night of error,
to seek with zeal the source of good,
though it's perdition's chains you pine for!

PARSIFAL
In Ewigkeit
wärst du verdammt mit mir
für eine Stunde
Vergessens meiner Sendung
in deines Arms Umfangen!—
Auch dir bin ich zum Heil gesandt,
bleibst du dem Sehnen abgewandt.
Die Labung, die dein Leiden endet,
beut nicht der Quell, aus dem es fliesst:
das Heil wird nimmer dir gespendet,
wenn jener Quell sich dir nich schliesst.
Ein Andrer ist's,—ein Andres, ach!
nach dem ich jammernd schmachten sah,
die Brüder dort in grausen Nöthen
den Leib sich quälen und ertödten.
Doch wer erkennt ihn klar und hell,
des einz'gen Heiles wahren Quell?
Oh, Elend! Aller Rettung Flucht!
Oh, Weltenwahns Umnachten:
in höchsten Heiles heisser Sucht
nach der Verdammniss Quell zu schmachten!

KUNDRY (*in wild ecstasy*)
So was it my kiss
that gave this all-seeing vision?
Then let my loving embraces
give you the Godhood you look for!
The world's redemption, is this your charge?

KUNDRY
So war es mein Kuss,
der welthellsichtig dich machte?
Mein volles Liebes-Umfangen
lässt dich dann Gottheit erlangen.

Die Welt erlöse, ist dies dein Amt:
schuf dich zum Gott die Stunde,
für sie lasse mich ewig verdammt,
nie heile mir die Wunde.

It's God who made this moment,
for it let me perish evermore,
my wound unhealed forever!

PARSIFAL

Erlösung, Frevlerin, biet' ich auch dir.

Redemption, wanton one, take of it now.

KUNDRY

Lass' mich dich Göttlichen lieben,
Erlösung gabst du dann auch mir.

Let me, divine one, then love you.
Salvation such as that I want.

PARSIFAL

Lieb' und Erlösung soll dir lohnen,—zeigest du
zu Amfortas mir den Weg.

Love and redemption I can offer
If the way to Amfortas is revealed.

KUNDRY

Nie—sollst du ihn finden!
Den Verfall'nen, lass' ihn verderben,—
den Unseligen,
Schmachlüsternen,
den ich verlachte—lachte—lachte!
Haha! Ihn traf ja der eig'ne Speer!

No! Never shall you find him!
Leave that lost one, and let him perish,
so unholy, vile, lecherous,
fit but for laughter, laughter, laughter, ha-ha!
He fell by the spear that he owned!

PARSIFAL

Wer durft' ihn verwunden mit heil'ger Wehr?

Who dared, though, to wound him with that holy spear?

KUNDRY

Er—Er—,
der einst mein Lachen bestraft:
sein Fluch—ha!—mir giebt er Kraft;
gegen dich selbst ruf' ich die Wehr,
giebst du dem Sünder des Mitleids Ehr'!—
Ha! Wahnsinn!—
Mitleid! Mitleid mit mir!
Nur eine Stunde mein,—
nur eine Stunde dein—:
und des Weges—
sollst du geleitet sein!

He—He!
Who gave me reason to laugh.
His curse, ha, it gives me strength.
(*threateningly*)
Against you too I turn the spear,
since you show pity where none is due!
Ha! Madness! Pity? Pity for me?
(*suddenly softening*)
Were you just one hour mine!
Were I just one hour yours!
And then, after, I would reveal the path.

PARSIFAL

Vergeh', unseliges Weib!

Away, iniquitous wretch!
(*she tries to embrace him, but he repulses her violently. She becomes furious and makes an outcry*)

KUNDRY

Hilfe! Hilfe! Herbei!
Haltet den Frechen! Herbei!
Wehrt ihm die Wege!
Wehrt ihm die Pfade!—
Und flöh'st du von hier, und fändest
all Wege der Welt,
den Weg, den du suchst,
dess' Pfade sollst du nicht finden!
Denn Pfad und Wege,
die mir dich entführen,
so—verwünsch' ich sie dir:

Help me! This way! Oh, help!
Stop the marauder! Come here!
Guard all the ways there.
Bar every roadway!
And though you flee from here,
and seek through all the ways of the world,
one road which you seek,
one road you shall find—never:
that path and highway which leads you
from my presence.

Thus, I curse them for you!
Wander! Wander! Back you will come!
(KLINGSOR *has stepped out on the castle wall and aimed the lance at* PARSIFAL)
Here is the guide that you need!

Irre! Irre,—
mir so vertraut—
dich weih' ich ihm zum Geleit'!

KLINGSOR

Halt there!
This weapon serves to bar your way!
The holy fool shall now meet his master's spear.
(*he hurls the lance, but it stops suspended in air over* PARSIFAL'S *head.* PARSIFAL *seizes it and holds it over his head*)

KLINGSOR

Halt da! dich bann' ich mit der rechten Wehr:
den Thoren stell' mir seines Meisters Speer!

PARSIFAL

With this blest sign I banish all your magic.
As the spear that has wounded
shall be used for healing,
so let this destruction
fall on illusory pomp.
(*he makes the sign of the cross. The castle is swallowed up, the garden becomes a wilderness, and* KUNDRY, *shrieking, sinks to the ground.* PARSIFAL *hurries away but turns again to* KUNDRY, *when he reaches the top of the ruined wall*)
You know
where you can find me once again.
(*as he leaves,* KUNDRY *raises her head and stares after him.*)

PARSIFAL

Mit diesem Zeichen bann' ich deinen Zauber:
Wie die Wunde er schliesse,
die mit ihm du schlugest,—
in Trauer und Trümmer
stürze die trügende Pracht!
Du weisst—
wo einzig du mich wieder-sieh'st?

ACT III

(*A pleasant landscape in the domain of the Grail. A flowery meadow whose foreground is occupied by the edge of a forest that stretches out over a rocky ascent toward the right. Near the edge of the woods is a spring opposite to which, a little farther back, can be seen the simple hut of a hermit, built against a rock. It is very early morning.*

GURNEMANZ, *greatly aged, clad as a hermit in the tunic of a knight of the Grail, steps out of the hut and listens.*)

GURNEMANZ
Von dorther kam das Stöhnen.–
So jammervoll klagt kein Wild,
und gewiss gar nicht am heiligsten Morgen heut'.–
Mich dünkt, ich kenne diesen Klageruf.
Ha! Sie–wieder da?
Das winterlich rauhe Gedörn'
hielt sie verdeckt: wie lang' schon?–
Auf!–Kundry!–Auf!
Der Winter floh, und Lenz ist da!
Erwach', erwache dem Lenz!–
kalt–und starr!–
Diesmal hielt' ich sie wohl für todt;–
doch war's ihr Stöhnen, was ich vernahm?

Du tolles Weib!
Hast du kein Wort für mich?
Ist dies der Dank,
dass dem Todesschlafe
noch einmal ich dich entweckt?

KUNDRY
Dienen . . . dienen!–

GURNEMANZ
Das wird dich wenig müh'n!
Auf Botschaft sendet sich's nicht mehr:
Kräuter und Wurzeln

GURNEMANZ
From over there the moans came.
No beast would make sounds like that
–and the least upon this holiest day on earth.
(KUNDRY'S *voice is heard in low groans*)
I think I know that sad, complaining cry.
(*he walks toward a thicket of thorns. He pulls the dense bushes forcibly apart, then stops suddenly*)
Ha! She here again?
Discourteous, wintery thorns kept her concealed.
How long now?
Up! Kundry! Up!
The winter's fled, and spring has come!
(*he draws* KUNDRY, *stiff and lifeless, from the bushes and carries her to a grassy mound nearby*)
Awaken, awake to the spring!
Cold–and stiff!
This time really I thought her dead:
Yet was it not her groans that I heard?
(*he rubs her hands and temples. Finally she opens her eyes, then shrieks. How different she is! She is clad in the coarse garb of a penitent, as in the first act, but her complexion is paler. She has lost her wildness. She stares long at* GURNEMANZ, *then she arises, arranges her clothing and hair, and appears ready to serve the Knights*)
You harebrained wench,
have you no word for me?
Is this the thanks
that I get
for breaking
your deathlike sleep once again?

KUNDRY (*slowly bows her head, then cries brokenly and hoarsely*)
Service! Service!

GURNEMANZ (*shaking his head*)
There's little toil for you:
We have no errands any more.
Herbs and simples

everyone finds for himself.
The beasts of the forest showed how.
(KUNDRY *enters the hut, to* GURNEMANZ's *surprise*)
How changed her step from what it was.
Did the holy day bring the change?
O day of grace without an equal!
Thank God, I was allowed
to banish the wretch's
deathlike sleep, for her salvation.
(*she comes out of the hut, carrying a pitcher, which she takes to the spring. Looking toward the forest, she sees something and calls* GURNEMANZ's *attention to the fact.*)
Who comes here toward the holy spring?
(*She disappears into the hut again to work. At the same moment* PARSIFAL *enters*)
Those somber, warlike trappings?
I see it's not a Brother.
(*head bowed low,* PARSIFAL *advances dreamily, hesitatingly, then seats himself on the grassy mound by the spring. He is in black armor, with closed visor. He sets down his spear.* GURNEMANZ, *having gazed long at* PARSIFAL *in astonishment, now approaches him*)
Greetings, Sir Guest!
Did you get lost, and shall I direct you?
(PARSIFAL *merely shakes his head*)
You offer no greeting to me?
(PARSIFAL *bows his head*)
Hey! What?
If you are bound by a solemn vow of silence,
I have a duty too: that I should tell you what is meet.
The present place is holy ground.
No man comes here with arms of war,
with visored helmet, shield and spear.
And least today!
Do you not know what holy day this is?
(PARSIFAL *shakes his head*)
Well! From where have you come?
Among what pagans have you lived, not to know
that this is the ever-holiest Good Friday morn?
(PARSIFAL *sinks his head still lower*)
Off with your weapons!
Injure not the Lord, who on this day shed His blood,
and not resisting evil, redeemed most sinful man!
(*after a further moment of silence* PARSIFAL *rises, thrusts his spear into the ground, lays shield and sword beside it, raises his visor, takes the helmet from his head, and places it beside the other weapons. He kneels in silent prayer before the spear.* GURNEMANZ *watches him with wonder and emotion. Then he beckons to* KUNDRY, *who has just returned from the hut*)

findet ein Jeder sich selbst,
wir lernen's im Walde vom Thier.
Wie anders schreitet sie als sonst!
Wirkte das der heilige Tag?
Oh! Tag der Gnade ohne Gleichen!
Gewiss zu ihrem Heile
durft' ich der Armen heut'
den Todesschlaf verscheuchen.
Wer nahet dort dem heiligen Quell?
Im düst'ren Waffenschmucke,
das ist der Brüder keiner.
Heil dir, mein Gast!
Bist du verirrt, und soll ich dich weisen?
Entbietest du mir keinen Gruss?
Hei!—Was?—
Wenn dein Gelübde
dich bindet mir zu schweigen,
so mahnt das meine mich,
dass ich dir sage, was sich ziemt.—
Hier bist du an geweihtem Ort:
da zieht man nich mit Waffen her,
geschloss'nen Helmes, Schild und Speer.
Und heute gar! Weisst du denn nicht,
welch' heil'ger Tag heut' ist?
Ja! Woher komm'st du denn?
Bei welchen Heiden weiltest du,
zu wissen nicht, dass heute
der allerheiligste Char Freitag sei?
Schnell ab die Waffen!
Kränke nicht den Herrn, der heute,
bar jeder Wehr, sein heilig Blut
der sündigen Welt zur Sühne bot!

Erkennst du ihn? . . .
Der ist's, der einst den Schwan erlegt.
Gewiss 's ist Er!
Der Thor, den ich zürnend von uns wies?
Ha! Welche Pfade fand er?
Der Speer,–ich kenne ihn.
Oh!–Heiligster Tag,
zu dem ich heut' erwachen sollt'!–

PARSIFAL
Heil mir, dass ich dich wieder finde!

GURNEMANZ
So kennst auch du mich noch?
Erkennst wich wieder,
den Gram und Noth so tief gebeugt?
Wie kamst du heut'? Woher?

PARSIFAL
Der Irrniss und der Leiden Pfade kam ich;
soll ich mich denen jetzt entwunden wähnen,
da dieses Waldes Rauschen
wieder ich vernehme,
dich guten Alten neu begrüsse?
Oder–irr' ich wieder?
Verwandelt dünkt mich Alles.

GURNEMANZ
So sag', zu wem den Weg du suchtest.

PARSIFAL
Zu ihm, dess' tiefe Klagen
ich thörig staunend einst vernahm,
dem nun ich Heil zu bringen
mich auserlesen wähnen darf.
Doch–ach!–
den Weg des Heiles nie zu finden,
in pfadlosen Irren
jagt' ein wilder Fluch mich umher:
zahllose Nöthe,
Kämpfe und Streite
zwangen mich ab vom Pfade,
wähnt' ich ihn recht schon erkannt.
Da musste Verzweiflung mich fassen,
das Heilthum heil mir zu bergen,
um das zu hüten, das zu wahren
ich Wunden jeder Wehr mir gewann.
Denn nicht ihn selber
durft' ich führen im Streite;
unentweiht
führt' ich ihn mir zur Seite,
den ich nun heim geleite,

(*softly*)
D'you know this man?
It's he who once laid low our swan!
(KUNDRY *nods*)
Indeed, it's he, the fool, whom I roughly turned away.
Ha! Yet he found the pathway?
I know that spear of his.
Oh, holiest day, to which my soul awakes with joy!
(PARSIFAL *rises slowly, looks calmly about, recognizes* GURNEMANZ, *and extends his hand to him in kindly greeting*)

PARSIFAL
Thank God that I again have found you.

GURNEMANZ
Then do you know me still,
the patient Brother, whose frame is bent from grief and care?
How came you here, and whence?

PARSIFAL
My errors and the path of sorrow brought me.
Yet let me fancy my trials are over,
since I can hear the sweetly sounding forest murmurs.
And is it you, good sage, who greet me,
or else–further error?
For all things here seem diff'rent.

GURNEMANZ
Now say just who it is you look for.

PARSIFAL
For him I heard lamenting,
and listened awe-struck, like a fool!
I think perhaps that I have been sent
to heal him of his woes.
But ah, I never found the path of healing.
I wandered in error, so enforced by a clinging curse.
Numberless troubles, battles and conflicts,
forced me to leave the pathway,
just when I thought myself right.
Then did a desperation seize me
to keep the spear in concealment
and thus protect it from all hazard.
I gathered wounds from every fray
because in conflict never once did I wear it.
Unprofaned at my side now I bear it,
so home and knights may share it.
You see it shimm'ring, pure and clear:
the Grail's most holy spear!

der dort dir schimmert heil und hehr,—
des Grales heil'gen Speer.

GURNEMANZ

O glorious healing grace!
O wonder! Holy, lofty wonder!
Dear lord,
if 'twas a curse that kept you from the proper path,
be sure that curse is ended.
Here are you in the Grail's domain,
the noble band awaits you still.
Ah, they have need of healing, the healing that you bring!
Since that sojourn, when you tarried here,
the mourning which you witnessed then,
the sorrow, greatly has increased.
Amfortas, fighting with his suff'ring,
racked with pain of soul and body,
at last in raging defiance craved for death.
Beseechings, nor outcries of his knighthood
could move him any more to serve the chalice,
and long it rested, hidden in the shrine.
Its guardian, sinful but repentant,
because he could not die while looking on the Grail,
would force his own quietus,
and end his life and all his pains together.
Our holy manna thus is quite denied.
We're nourished now with common viands
and so our valor all has passed away.
No message ever comes,
nor call to holy warfare from far countries.
Pale and wretched, now,
our knights do mope,
they're lacking both a lord and heart!
I've sought seclusion
here within these woods,
and wait that death in silence,
which has already called my lord at arms:
for Titurel, my holy lord,
at last no more enjoyed the holy vessel
and died, a man, and mortal!

GURNEMANZ

O Gnade! Höchtes Heil!
O Wunder! Heilig hehrstes Wunder!—
O Herr! War es ein Fluch,
der dich vom rechten Pfad vertrieb,
so glaub', er ist gewichen.
Hier bist du; dies des Grals Gebiet,
dein harret seine Ritterschaft.
Ach, sie bedarf des Heiles,
des Heiles, das du bringst!—
Seit jenem Tage, den du hier geweilt,
die Trauer, so da kund dir ward,
das Bangen wuchs zur höchsten Noth.
Amfortas, gegen seiner Wunde,
seiner Seele Qual sich wehrend,
begehrt' in wildem Trotze nun den Tod;
kein Fleh'n, kein Elend seiner Ritter
bewog ihn mehr des heil'gen Amt's zu walten.
Im Schrein verschlossen bleibt seit lang' der Gral:
so hofft sein sündenreu'ger Hüter,
da er nicht sterben kann,
wann je er ihn erschaut,
sein Ende zu erzwingen,
und mit dem Leben seine Qual zu enden.
Die heil'ge Speisung bleibt uns nun versagt,
gemeine Ätzung muss uns nähren;
darob versiegte unsrer Helden Kraft:
nie kommt uns Botschaft mehr,
noch Ruf zu heil'gen Kämpfen aus der Ferne;
bleich und elend wankt umher
die muth- und führerlose Ritterschaft,
Hier in der Waldeck' barg ich einsam mich,
des Todes still gewärtig,
dem schon mein alter Waffenherr verfiel,
denn Titurel, mein heil'ger Held,
den nun des Grales Anblick nicht mehr labte,
er starb,—ein Mensch wie Alle!

PARSIFAL (*springing up in intense grief*)

And I am he, the cause of all this woe!
Ha! What transgressions, what outrageous guilt
must this mad, foolish head
be evermore bemoaning!

PARSIFAL

Und ich—ich bin's,
der all' dies Elend schuf!
Ha! Welcher Sünden,
welcher Frevel Schuld
muss dieses Thoren Haupt

seit Ewigkeit belasten,
da keine Busse, keine Sühne
der Blindheit mich entwindet,
zur Rettung selbst ich auserkoren,
in Irrniss wild verloren
der Rettung letzter Pfad verschwindet!

Since no repentance, no atonement
can wash away my blindness!
To point the pathway I was chosen,
but now I'm lost in error,
and so myself I need that pathway.
(*he is about to fall in a faint.* GURNEMANZ *sustains him and seats him on the mound.* KUNDRY *hastens to bring a basin of water to revive him. She returns*)

GURNEMANZ
Nicht so!—
Die heil'ge Quelle selbst
erquicke uns'res Pilgers Bad.
Mir ahnt, ein hohes Werk
hat er noch heut' zu wirken,
zu walten eines heil'gen Amtes:
so sei er fleckenrein,
und langer Irrfahrt Staub
soll jetzt von ihm gewaschen sein.

GURNEMANZ
Not yet!
But let the holy spring itself refresh the pilgrim's bath.
I sense a mighty work remains to do this morning,
to mind the Grail in holy service.
He must be free from stain, so let the trav'ler's dust
that spots him fast be washed away.
(*the two gently turn* PARSIFAL *toward the spring. During what follows* KUNDRY *loosens his greaves;* GURNEMANZ *removes his breastplate*)

PARSIFAL
Werd' heut' ich zu Amfortas noch geleitet?

PARSIFAL
Do you mean to lead me now to Amfortas?

GURNEMANZ
Gewisslich, uns'rer harrt die hehre Burg:
die Todtenfeier meines lieben Herrn,
sie ruft mich selbst dahin.
Den Gral noch einmal uns da zu enthüllen,
des lang versäumten Amtes
noch einmal heut' zu walten—
zur Heiligung des hehren Vaters,
der seines Sohnes Schuld erlag,
die der nun also büssen will,—
gelobt' Amfortas uns.

GURNEMANZ
Most surely! For the noble court awaits.
The funeral service of my dearest lord
now summons me within.
For us the Grail must be once more uncovered,
whose long-neglected service once more must be attended,
to sanctify that noble father,
who by his son's great guilt was slain,
for which the son would now atone.
Amfortas made this vow.
(KUNDRY, *with humble zeal, bathes* PARSIFAL'S *feet; he gazes on her with silent wonderment*)

PARSIFAL
Du wuschest mir die Füsse:—
nun netze mir das Haupt der Freund.

PARSIFAL (*turning to* GURNEMANZ)
You've washed my feet with water, so sprinkle now my head, my friend.
(GURNEMANZ *takes water and does so*)

GURNEMANZ
Gesegnet sei, du Reiner, durch das Reine,
So weiche jeder Schuld
Bekümmerniss von dir!

GURNEMANZ
May you be blessed, O pure one,
through your pur'ty!
Forevermore may you be free from guilt and care!
(*while* GURNEMANZ *is performing this ceremony* KUNDRY *takes a gold flask from her bosom and pours some of the contents over* PARSIFAL'S *feet, drying them with her hair, which she has hastily unbound.* PARSIFAL *gently takes the flask from* KUNDRY *and passes it to* GURNEMANZ)

PARSIFAL
Du salbtest mir die Füsse,
das Haupt nun salbe Titurels Genoss',

PARSIFAL
You laved my feet, and thank you.
(*to* GURNEMANZ)

Anoint my head, O friend of Titurel,
that so as king I may be greeted!
(GURNEMANZ *pours the remainder of the contents of the flask on* PARSIFAL'*s head and places his hands on it in blessing*)

dass heute noch als König er
mich grüsse.

GURNEMANZ
Thus was it all predicted!
My blessing on your head:
I greet you as our master!
O pure one!
Patient and pitying one, healing and knowing one!
As the Redeemer suffered, you have suffered.
Remove the last of burdens from his head!
(PARSIFAL *has quietly taken some water from the spring in his hands, and now he bends over* KUNDRY, *who is kneeling before him and pours it over her head*)

GURNEMANZ
So ward es uns verhiessen,
so segne ich dein Haupt,
als König dich zu grüssen.
Du—Reiner,—
mitleidsvoll Duldender,
heilthatvoll Wissender!
Wie des Erlösten Leiden du
gelitten,
die letzte Last entnimm nun
seinem Haupt.

PARSIFAL
I thus perform my first of tasks:
be now baptized,
believe in the Redeemer!
(KUNDRY *sinks her head to the ground and appears to weep passionately.* PARSIFAL *turns about and with gentle ecstasy gazes upon woods and meadows now bathed in the light of morning*)
How beautiful the meadows seem today!
Well I recall the wondrous flowers
which once did try to twine themselves around me.
Yet they did not compare with these.
The grasses, blossoms and flowers
are fragrant in their innocence,
and speak to me with loving trust.

PARSIFAL
Mein erstes Amt verricht' ich
so:—
die Taufe nimm,
und glaub' an den Erlöser!
Wie dünkt mich doch die Aue
heut' so schön!—
Wohl traf ich Wunderblumen
an,
die bis zum Haupte süchtig
mich umrankten;
doch sah' ich nie so mild und
zart
die Halme, Blüthen und
Blumen,
noch duftete All' so kindisch
hold
und sprach so lieblich traut zu
mir.

GURNEMANZ
That is Good Friday's magic, lord!

GURNEMANZ
Das ist Char Freitags Zauber,
Herr!

PARSIFAL
O sorrow, that day of greatest grief,
When all that's living, all that breathes and blossoms, living once again,
should only weep and sorrow!

PARSIFAL
O weh', des höchsten Schmer-
zentags!
Da sollte, wähn' ich, was da
blüht
was athmet, lebt und wieder
lebt,
nur trauern, ach! und weinen?

GURNEMANZ
You see, it is not so.
The tears of sorrow wept by sinners
today have sprinkled field and plain with holy dew,
which thereby consecrates them.
Today all living things rejoice
to see the signs of God's dear grace,
and with their thoughts they praise Him.
The cross is lofty, so they cannot view it.
But still their gaze can reach to man redeemed,
who feels himself set free from sin and sorrow,

GURNEMANZ
Du siehst, das ist nicht so.
Des Sünders Reuethränen sind
es,
die heut' mit heil'gem Thau
beträufet Flur und Au':
der liess sie so gedeihen.
Nun freut sich alle Kreatur,
auf des Erlösers holder Spur,
will ihr Gebet ihm weihen.
Ihn selbst am Kreuze kann sie
nicht erschauen:
da blickt sie zum erlösten
Menschen auf;

der fühlt sich frei von Sünden-
last und Grauen,
durch Gottes Liebesopfer rein
und heil:
das merkt nun Halm und Blume
auf den Auen,
dass heut' des Menschen Fuss
sie nicht zertritt,
doch wohl, wie Gott mit himm-
lischer Geduld
sich sein erbarmt und für ihn
litt,
der Mensch auch heut' in
frommer Huld
sie schont mit sanftem Schritt.
Das dankt dann alle Kreatur,
was all' da blüht und bald
erstirbt,
da die entsündigte Natur
heut' ihren Unschuldstag
erwirbt.

by Love's great power made both pure and whole.
The grass knows well, and flower of the meadow,
today the foot of man can do no harm;
for just as God reveals to man
His gentle, loving care, and for him died,
so man this day reflects His love and walks with gentle stride.
All creatures now show gratitude,
—which bloom a spell and then pass hence,—
that smiling Nature is renewed
in this sweet day of innocence.

(KUNDRY *has again slowly lifted her head and now looks with moist eyes in serious, quiet appeal*)

PARSIFAL

Ich sah sie welken, die mir
lachten:
ob heut' sie nach Erlösung
schmachten?—
Auch deine Thräne wird zum
Segensthaue:
du weinest—sieh'! es lacht die
Aue.

PARSIFAL

One time they jeered me, and now they wither.
Do they, too, seek redemption hither?
With blessed dew your gentle eyes are filling.
You're crying. Look, the fields are smiling!

(*he kisses her gently on the forehead, a distant pealing of bells is heard*)

GURNEMANZ

Mittag.—
Die Stund' ist da:—
gestatte, Herr, dass dich dein
Knecht geleite!—

GURNEMANZ

Midday: the time has come.
Give leave, My Lord, for your servant to lead you.

(GURNEMANZ *brings out his mantle as knight of the Grail, and with* KUNDRY'S *help places it upon* PARSIFAL, *who, solemnly taking up his lance, slowly follows* GURNEMANZ *with* KUNDRY. *The scene gradually changes to a landscape like that of the first act. After a time the three are lost to sight as the forest changes into a vaulted, rocky passage. The sound of bells continually increases in the rocky passage.*

Finally the scene opens into the great hall of the Grail Temple as in the first act, save that the refection tables are missing. From one side approach knights of the Grail bearing Titurel in his coffin; from the other a similar train escorting Amfortas on his litter, preceded by the Grail.)

ERSTER ZUG

Geleiten wir im bergenden
Schrein,
den Gral zum heiligen Amte,
wen berget ihr im düst'ren
Schrein
und führt ihn trauernd daher?

FIRST PROCESSION

We slowly bear in sheltering shrine
the Grail to holiest service.
What lies within your gloomy shrine?
What's brought with sorrowing steps?

(*the two processions march past each other*)

ZWEITER ZUG

Es birgt den Helden der
Trauerschrein,
er birgt die heilige Kraft;
der Gott selbst einst zur Pflege
sich gab:
Titurel führen wir her.

SECOND PROCESSION

The hero lies in the fun'ral shrine.
It hides the heavenly power
which God Himself once gave to His charge.
Titurel lies in this bier.

FIRST PROCESSION
What happened to him, who with loving care
God Himself protected?

SECOND PROCESSION
He bowed to belief of conquering age
when the sight of the Grail was denied him.

FIRST PROCESSION
Who was it withheld the grace of the Grail?

SECOND PROCESSION
The one you are bearing, both guardian and sinner.

FIRST PROCESSION
We must bear him today, just one time longer.
This last time only let him carry the office.
Ah, the final time! Sorrow!
Guardian of the Grail, the final time let him carry the office.

SECOND PROCESSION
Sorrow, O guardian of the Grail.
Ah, this final time. Now let the rite be performed.
This final time let him carry the office.

AMFORTAS (*wearily raising himself a little*)
Yes, sorrow! Sorrow! Sorrow through me.
Yes, all your sorrows are mine.
Gladly would I take my death from you,
for sin like mine, that is little.
(*the coffin is opened. At sight of* TITUREL *all lament.* AMFORTAS *raises himself high on his couch and turns to* TITUREL'S *corpse*)
My father! Highest blest among all heroes!
The purest,
obeyed once even by angels!
For whom I would give my life!
To you I brought death!
Oh, you who now in heavenly rapture do gaze upon our Lord,
implore Him for me, that His holiest blood
(if but once more now His blessing
may quicken all the brothers,
renewing life within them)
may fin'lly bring me to death!
Death—only, only mercy!
These terrible tortures, their sting, this poison!
Oh let it end! Crush life from my heart!
O Father, I call you!
Ask for help. Plead for me:
"Redeemer, grant to my son relief!"
(*the knights press nearer to* AMFORTAS)

ERSTER ZUG
Wer hat ihn gefällt, der in Gottes Hut
Gott selbst einst beschirmte?

ZWEITER ZUG
Ihn fällte des Alters tödtende Last,
da den Gral er nicht mehr erschaute.

ERSTER ZUG
Wer wehrt' ihm des Grales Huld zu erschauen?

ZWEITER ZUG
Den dort ihr geleitet, der sündige Hüter.

ERSTER ZUG
Wir geleiten ihn heut', denn heut' noch einmal
—zum letzten Male:—
will des Amtes er walten.

ZWEITER ZUG
Wehe! Wehe! Du Hüter des Grals!
Zum letzten Male
sei deines Amtes gemahnt!

AMFORTAS
Ja, Wehe! Wehe! Weh' über mich!—
So ruf' ich willig mit euch:
Williger nähm' ich von euch den Tod, der Sünde mildeste Sühne!

Mein Vater!
Hochgesegneter der Helden!
Du Reinster, dem einst die Engel sich neigten!
Der einzig ich sterben wollte,
dir—gab ich den Tod!
Oh! der du jetzt in göttlichem Glanz
den Erlöser selbst erschau'st,
erflehe von ihm, dass sein heiliges Blut,
wenn noch einmal jetzt sein Segen
die Brüder soll erquicken,
wie ihnen neues Leben,
mir endlich spende—den Tod!
Tod!—Sterben!
Einzige Gnade!
Die schreckliche Wunde, das Gift ersterbe,
das es zernagt, erstarre das Herz!
Mein Vater! Dich ruf' ich,
rufe du ihm es zu:
"Erlöser, gieb meinem Sohne Ruh'!"

ERSTER ZUG
Walte des Amtes!
Du musst! Du musst! Du musst!

FIRST PROCESSION
Serve now your office!
You must! You must! You must!

ZWEITER ZUG
Enthüllet den Gral!
Dich mahnet dein Vater:
Du musst! Du musst!

SECOND PROCESSION
Uncover the Grail!
Your father commands you:
You must! you must!
(AMFORTAS *springs up in raging despair and rushes into the midst of his knights*)

AMFORTAS
Nein!—Nicht mehr!—Ha!—
Schon fühl' ich den Tod mich umnachten,—
und noch einmal sollt' ich ins Leben zurück?
Wahnsinnige!
Wer will mich zwingen zu leben?
Könnt ihr doch Tod nur mir geben!
Hier bin ich,—die off'ne Wunde hier!
Das mich vergiftet, hier fliesst mein Blut.
Heraus die Waffen! Taucht eure Schwerter
tief—tief bis ans Heft!
Auf! Ihr Helden,
Tödtet den Sünder mit seiner Qual,
von selbst dann leuchtet euch wohl der Gral!

AMFORTAS
No more! Ha!
Death comes, for I feel him approaching!
And yet you would summon me back to life?
Insanity!
Who would enforce me to live now,
when death is all I am seeking?
(*he tears open his garment*)
Here am I! My open wound is here!
Here is the poison! Here flows my blood!
Out with your weapons!
Bury your swords here, deep, deep—to the hilt!
Up! You heroes!
Slay both at once: sinner and his sin.
Perhaps the Grail will shine then for you!
(*the knights have all fallen back in fear, leaving* AMFORTAS *standing alone in horrible ecstasy.* PARSIFAL, *accompanied by* GURNEMANZ *and* KUNDRY, has appeared *unnoticed. He now steps forward and with the point of the lance touches the side of* AMFORTAS)

PARSIFAL
Nur eine Waffe taugt:—
die Wunde schliesst
der Speer nur, der sie schlug.

PARSIFAL
One weapon only serves:
only the spear which gave the wound heals the wound.
(*the features of* AMFORTAS *light up as with sacred rapture. He staggers and is supported by* GURNEMANZ)

PARSIFAL
Sei heil, entsündigt und gesühnt!
Denn ich verwalte nun dein Amt.
Gesegnet sei dein Leiden,
das Mitleids höchste Kraft
und reinsten Wissens Macht
dem zagen Thoren gab.
Den heil'gen Speer—
ich bring' ihn euch zurück.—
Oh! Welchen Wunders höchstes Glück!—
Der deine Wunde durfte schliessen,
ihm seh' ich heil'ges Blut entfliessen
in Sehnsucht nach dem verwandten Quelle,
der dort fliesst in des Grales Welle!
Nicht soll der mehr verschlossen
enthüllt den Gral! Öffnet den Schrein!
sein:

Be whole, forgiven, and absolved!
For I must now perform your charge!
And blessed be your suff'ring,
which gave the power of love
and strength of purity to him—
the timid fool!
(PARSIFAL *walks solemnly toward the center, holding the spear aloft before him*)
The sacred spear—I bring it back to you!
(*all gaze in the highest exaltation upon the spear, while* PARSIFAL, *looking upon the point, continues in a tone of exaltation*)
Oh! Wondrous joy beyond compare!
The spear that touched the wound and healed it
is flowing now with blood most holy
which seeks to rejoin its kindred fountain
that wells within the holy vessel.

Nevermore let the cup be hid!
Uncover the Grail! Open the shrine!

(PARSIFAL ascends the altar steps, takes the Grail from the shrine, which has been opened by the esquires, and kneels before it in silent prayer. The Grail gradually glows with a soft light. The darkness increases from below, and the illumination from above)

CHORUS

Highest healing's wonder!
Salvation to the Saviour!

(a ray of light falls: the Grail's glow is at its brightest. A white dove descends from the dome and hovers over PARSIFAL's head. KUNDRY, eyes uplifted to PARSIFAL, slowly sinks lifeless to the ground before him. *AMFORTAS and GURNEMANZ kneel in homage before PARSIFAL, who waves the Grail in blessing over the worshiping Templars)*

ALLE

Höchsten Heiles Wunder!
Erlösung dem Erlöser!

PELLÉAS ET MÉLISANDE

by Claude Achille Debussy (1862–1918)

LIBRETTO BY MAURICE MAETERLINCK

Translated by BORIS GOLDOVSKY after HENRY GRAFTON CHAPMAN.

Adapted from Maeterlinck's play of the same name.

CHARACTERS

MÉLISANDE	*Soprano*
GOLAUD, *grandson of King Arkel*	*Baritone*
GENEVIÈVE, *daughter of Arkel, mother of Golaud and Pelléas*	*Contralto*
ARKEL, *King of Allemonde*	*Bass*
PELLÉAS, *Golaud's half brother*	*Tenor*
YNIOLD, *Golaud's young son*	*Mezzo-soprano*
PHYSICIAN	*Bass*

WOMEN SERVANTS, AN UNSEEN CHORUS OF SAILORS, AN UNSEEN SHEPHERD, THREE OLD MEN

Place: The mythical kingdom of Allemonde
Time: Legendary
First performance: Opéra-Comique, Paris, April 30, 1902

COPYRIGHT © 1962 BY BORIS GOLDOVSKY
PERMISSION GRANTED BY G. SCHIRMER, INC., AS AGENT FOR DURAND & FILS, PARIS

ACT I

Scene 1: A Forest

(As the curtain rises MÉLISANDE *is discovered at the edge of a well. Enter* GOLAUD.*)*

GOLAUD

Will I never find my way out of this forest? Heav'n knows how long this beast has led me on. Yet I was certain my arrow had found its mark, and here there are traces of blood. But now, it's gone, it is nowhere in sight. I followed until I got lost in the forest and my hounds will never find me again. I must try and find my way back. Someone's crying . . . oh! oh! What have we there beside the well? I believe it's a girl who is crying near the water.

(he coughs)

She does not seem to hear me, nor can I yet see her face . . .

(he approaches MÉLISANDE *and touches her shoulder)*

Why do you weep?

*(*MÉLISANDE *trembles, starts, and is about to run away)*

Don't be afraid. There's no reason to be frightened. Tell me what has made you cry, all alone here?

GOLAUD

Je ne pourrai plus sortir de cette forêt.—Dieu sait jusqu'où cette bête m'a mené. Je croyais cependant l'avoir blessée à mort; et voici des traces de sang. Mais maintenant, je l' ai perdue de vue; je crois que je me suis perdu moi-même—et mes chiens ne me retrouvent plus—je vais revenir sur mes pas . . .— J'entends pleurer . . . Oh! oh! qu'y a-t-il là au bord de l'eau? . . . Une petite fille qui pleure au bord de l'eau? Elle ne m'entend pas. Je ne vois pas son visage. Pourquoi pleures-tu? N'ayez pas peur. Vous n'avez rien à craindre. Pourquoi pleurez-vous ici toute seule?

MÉLISANDE

Do not touch me, do not touch me . . .

MÉLISANDE

Ne me touchez pas! ne me touchez pas!

GOLAUD

Don't be afraid. I will do you no harm . . . Oh! You are so lovely!

GOLAUD

N'ayez pas peur . . . Je ne vous ferai pas . . . Oh! vous êtes belle!

MÉLISANDE

Do not touch me! Do not touch me or I will throw myself in!

MÉLISANDE

Ne me touchez pas! ne me touchez pas! ou je me jette à l'eau! . . .

GOLAUD

There, there, I will not touch you. See here, I will stay where I am, at a distance. Don't be afraid. Has anyone tried to hurt you?

GOLAUD

Je ne vous touche pas . . . Voyez, je resterai ici, contre l'arbre. N'ayez pas peur. Quelqu'un vous a-t-il fait du mal?

MÉLISANDE

Oh! Yes! Yes! Yes!

(she sobs)

MÉLISANDE

Oh! oui! oui, oui! . . .

GOLAUD

Who is it who has tried to hurt you?

GOLAUD

Qui est-ce qui vous a fait du mal?

MÉLISANDE

All of them! All!

MÉLISANDE

Tous! tous!

GOLAUD

And how have they hurt you?

GOLAUD

Quel mal vous a-t-on fait?

MÉLISANDE

No, no, I will not tell you! No, I cannot tell you!

MÉLISANDE

Je ne veux pas le dire; Je ne peux pas le dire! . . .

GOLAUD

Come, come, you must not weep like this. Where are you from?

GOLAUD

Voyons; ne pleurez pas ainsi. D'où venez-vous?

MÉLISANDE
Je me suis enfuie! . . . enfuie . . . enfuie!

GOLAUD
Oui; mais d'où vous êtes-vous enfuie?

MÉLISANDE
Je suis perdue! . . . perdue ici . . . Je ne suis pas d'ici . . . Je ne suis pas née là . . .

GOLAUD
D'où êtes-vous? Où êtes-vous née?

MÉLISANDE
Oh! oh! loin d'ici . . . loin . . . loin . . .

GOLAUD
Qu'est-ce qui brille ainsi au fond de l'eau?

MÉLISANDE
Où donc?—Ah! c'est la couronne qu'il m'a donnée. Elle est tombée en pleurant.

GOLAUD
Une couronne?—Qui est-ce qui vous a donné une couronne? —Je vais essayer de la prendre . . .

MÉLISANDE
Non, non; je n'en veux plus! je n'en veux plus! Je préfère mourir tout de suite . . .

GOLAUD
Je pourrais la retirer facilement. L'eau n'est pas très profonde.

MÉLISANDE
Je n'en veux plus! Si vous la retirez, je me jette à sa place! . . .

GOLAUD
Non, non; je la laisserai là: on pourrait la prendre sans peine cependant. Elle semble très belle.—Y a-t-il longtemps que vous avez fui?

MÉLISANDE
Oui, oui . . . Qui êtes-vous?

GOLAUD
Je suis le prince Golaud—le petit-fils d' Arkël, le vieux roi d'Allemonde . . .

MÉLISANDE
Oh! vous avez déjà les cheveux gris . . .

GOLAUD
Oui; quelques-uns, ici, près des tempes . . .

MÉLISANDE
Et la barbe aussi . . . Pourquoi me regardez-vous ainsi?

GOLAUD
Je regarde vos yeux.—Vous ne fermez jamais les yeux?

MÉLISANDE
I ran away! I left them, I left them.

GOLAUD
But who are the people you have left?

MÉLISANDE
I am lost here! I'm lost here! Oh! Oh! Everything's lost . . . I don't belong here, I came from far away!

GOLAUD
Where did you come from? Where is your birthplace?

MÉLISANDE
Oh! Oh! far from here . . . far . . . far . . .

GOLAUD
There's something shining there beneath the water . . .

MÉLISANDE
Oh, where? Ah! It is the crown, the crown that he gave me! It fell in the water while I wept!

GOLAUD
It fell in the water? Who was it may I ask who gave you the crown? I'll try to see if I can reach it . . .

MÉLISANDE
No, no, I do not want it! I do not want it! I had much rather die . . . yes, die this very moment!

GOLAUD
It would be very easy to retrieve it . . . it's not very deep here.

MÉLISANDE
Leave it alone! If you try to reach it, I will never forgive you.

GOLAUD
Oh well, I shall let it alone; it seems such a pity to leave it down there . . . it looks very lovely. Was it long ago that you ran away?

MÉLISANDE
Yes, yes . . . but who are you?

GOLAUD
I am the Prince Golaud, the grandson of King Arkel, in the land of Allemonde.

MÉLISANDE
Oh! Why, your hair has begun to turn gray!

GOLAUD
Yes, just a little. Right here, at my temples . . .

MÉLISANDE
And your beard as well. But why do you stare at me so?

GOLAUD
I was watching your eyes; do you ever close your eyes?

MÉLISANDE
Yes, yes, I close them at night . . .

GOLAUD
Why do you look at me in such amazement?

MÉLISANDE
You seem to be a giant!

GOLAUD
I am a man just like all others . . .

MÉLISANDE
What brought you here to the forest?

GOLAUD
I really cannot tell you. I was hunting in the woods. I was following a boar, and so I went out of my way. You seem so very young . . . how old may you be?

MÉLISANDE
I feel a sudden chill!

GOLAUD
Would you like to come with me?

MÉLISANDE
No, no, I shall stay here.

GOLAUD
But you can't remain here all alone in the forest, all alone in the wilderness, all night long . . . Tell me, what is your name?

MÉLISANDE
Mélisande . . .

GOLAUD
You cannot stay here all alone, Mélisande. Please come with me!

MÉLISANDE
I shall stay here.

GOLAUD
You'll be afraid all alone here, there is no telling what may happen . . . the whole night long, you'll be frightened. I cannot permit it, Mélisande, come child, give me your hand . . .

MÉLISANDE
Oh! Don't touch me, I beg you!

GOLAUD
Don't be afraid . . . I'll not touch you again . . . but let me take you away! The night will be so dark and so cold . . . we'll go together.

MÉLISANDE
Where shall we go?

GOLAUD
I do not know! For I also am lost . . .
(*They go out*)

MÉLISANDE
Si, si; je les ferme la nuit . . .

GOLAUD
Pourquoi avez-vous l'air si étonné?

MÉLISANDE
Vous êtes un géant!

GOLAUD
Je suis un homme comme les autres . . .

MÉLISANDE
Pourquoi êtes-vous venu ici?

GOLAUD
Je n'en sais rien moi-même. Je chassais dans la forêt. Je poursuivais un sanglier. Je me suis trompé de chemin.– Vous avez l'air très jeune. Quel âge avez-vous?

MÉLISANDE
Ja commence à avoir froid . . .

GOLAUD
Voulez-vous venir aveo moi?

MÉLISANDE
Non, non; je reste ici . . .

GOLAUD
Vous ne pouvez pas rester seule. Vous ne pouvez pas rester ici toute la nuit . . . Comment vous nommcz-vous?

MÉLISANDE
Mélisande.

GOLAUD
Vous ne pouvez pas rester ici, Mélisande. Venez avec moi . . .

MÉLISANDE
Je reste ici . . .

GOLAUD
Vous aurez peur, toute seule. On ne sait pas ce qu'il y a ici . . . Toute la nuit . . . toute seule . . . Ce n'est pas possible. Mélisande, venez, donnez-moi la main . . .

MÉLISANDE
Oh! ne me touchez pas! . . .

GOLAUD
Ne criez pas . . . Je ne vous toucherai plus. Mais venez avec moi. La nuit sera très noire et très froide. Venez avec moi . . .

MÉLISANDE
Où allez-vous?

GOLAUD
Je ne sais pas . . . Je suis perdu aussi . . .

Scene 2: A room in the castle

GENEVIÈVE

Voici ce qu'il a écrit à son frère Pelléas: «Un soir, je l'ai trouvée tout en pleurs au bord d'une fontaine, dans la forêt où je m'étais perdu. Je ne sais ni son âge, ni qui elle est, ni d'où elle vient, et je n'ose pas l'interroger, car elle doit avoir eu une grande épouvante, et quand on lui demande ce qui lui est arrivé, elle pleure tout à coup comme un enfant et sanglote si profondément qu'on a peur. Il y a maintenant six mois que je l'ai épousée et je n'en sais pas plus qu'au jour de notre rencontre. En attendant, mon cher Pelléas, toi que j'aime plus qu'un frère, bien que nous ne soyons pas nés du même père; en attendant, prépare mon retour . . . Je sais que ma mère me pardonnera volontiers. Mais j'ai peur d' Arkël, malgré toute sa bonté, car j'ai déçu, par ce mariage étrange, tous ses projets politiques, et je crains que la beauté de Mélisande n'excuse pas à ses yeux, si sages, ma folie. S'il consent néanmoins à l'accueillir comme il accueillerait sa propre fille, le troisième soir qui suivra cette lettre, allume une lampe au sommet de la tour qui regarde la mer. Je l'apercevrai du pont de notre navire; si non j'irai plus loin et ne reviendrai plus . . .» Qu'en dites-vous?

GENEVIÈVE

Let me read what he writes to his brother Pelléas . . . "One evening, I found her sitting in tears by the side of a fountain, deep in the woods where I also was lost. I don't know her age, nor who she is, nor where she belongs, and I do not dare to ask questions. It is quite clear she has been frightened by someone. But if one asks her to tell what had happened she starts trembling like a child, and her tears are so moving that one can scarcely endure it. It is now, as you know, six months since I made her my wife. Yet I know just as little as I knew the day that I found her. And now I must ask you my dear Pelléas, whom I love more than a brother, though we are not the sons of the same father, have all in readiness for my return . . . I know that my mother will only too gladly forgive me, but I'm afraid of Arkel, in spite of his great kindness. But should he consent to receive her as though she were his daughter, then on the third day after receiving this letter, place a lamp in the window of the tower that looks over the sea. From the deck of my ship I will watch for the signal, and if I don't see it, I shall go on and will never return." . . . What do you say?

ARKËL

Je n'en dis rien. Cela peut nous paraître étrange, parce que nous ne voyons jamais que l'envers des destinées . . . Il avait toujours suivi mes conseils jusqu'ici; j'avais cru le rendre heureux en l'envoyant demander la main de la princesse Ursule . . . Il ne pouvait pas rester seul, et depuis la mort de sa femme il était triste d'être seul; et ce mariage allait mettre fin à de longues guerres et à de vieilles haines . . . Il ne l'a pas voulu ainsi. Qu'il en soit

ARKEL

I've little to say. All this, perhaps, may seem unusual. That is because we never see but the surface of life, our own destiny included. He had followed my advice all his life till now. It was my intention to help him when I sent him to ask for the hand of Princess Ursula. He could not continue alone. Indeed, since the death of his wife, he's been much too quiet and depressed. I hoped this marriage would bring to an end all these tedious wars, all these feuds of long standing. And yet he decided against it . . . Let it be according to his wish. I've not the slightest desire to govern the lives of my children. They know better than I what they want. I believe our fate is preordained, and no one ever can change it.

comme il l'a voulu: je ne me suis jamais mis en travers d'une destinée; et il sait mieux que moi son avenir. Il n'arrive peut-être pas d'évènements inutiles . . .

GENEVIÈVE

He's always been so prudent and wise, so steady and thoughtful. And since the death of his wife, he's given all his thoughts to his son, his little Yniold. And now he's forgotten them both. What shall we tell him? (*enter* PELLÉAS)

GENEVIÈVE

Il a toujours été si prudent, si grave et si ferme . . . Depuis la mort de sa femme il ne vivait plus que pour son fils, le petit Yniold. Il a tout oublié . . .—Qu'allons-nous faire? . . .

ARKEL

Has someone entered the room?

ARKËL

Qui est-ce qui entre là?

GENEVIÈVE

Yes, it's Pelléas. I think he has been crying!

GENEVIÈVE

C'est Pelléas. Il a pleuré.

ARKEL

Is it you, Pelléas? Come a little closer, I cannot see you there in the darkness.

ARKËL

Est-ce toi, Pelléas?—Viens un peu plus près, que je te voie dans la lumière . . .

PELLÉAS

Grandfather, I received at the same time as the letter from my brother, another letter; it is a message from Marcellus, my friend. He's very ill and he has called me. He knows exactly the day and the hour he's going to die, so he writes and begs me to reach his bedside before it's too late. But then I must leave without delaying . . .

PELLÉAS

Grand-père, j'ai reçu, en même temps que la lettre de mon frère, une autre lettre; une lettre de mon ami Marcellus . . . Il va mourir et il m'appelle.

Il dit qu'il sait exactement le jour où la mort doit venir . . . Il me dit que je puis arriver avant elle si je veux, mais qu'il n'y a plus de temps à perdre.

ARKEL

I would advise you to wait . . . your friend might recover. Besides, we don't know as yet how your brother's return may affect us. And, what's more, you must remember your father lying sick in his chamber, nearer death perhaps than your friend. Will you be able to choose between your father and your friend? (*he goes out*)

ARKËL

Il faudrait attendre quelque temps cependant . . . Nous ne savons pas ce que le retour de ton frère nous prépare. Et d'ailleurs ton père n'est-il pas ici, au-dessus de nous, plus malade peut-être que ton ami? . . . Pourras-tu choisir entre le père et l'ami? . . .

GENEVIÈVE

Place the lamp in the tower before it gets dark, Pelléas. (*they go out separately*)

GENEVIÈVE

Aie soin d'allumer la lampe dès ce soir, Pelléas . . .

Scene 3: Before the castle

(*enter Geneviève and Mélisande*)

MÉLISANDE

It is so dark here in the gardens. The trees are immense . . . I have never seen trees such as these!

MÉLISANDE

Il fait sombre dans les jardins. Et quelles forêts, quelles forêts autour des palais! . . .

GENEVIÈVE

Yes, I was very much surprised at first when I came here. They astonish everyone who sees them. There

GENEVIÈVE

Oui; cela m'étonnait aussi quand je suis arrivée ici, et cela étonne tout le monde. Il y a des endroits où l'on ne voit jamais le soleil. Mais l'on s'y fait si vite . . . Il y a longtemps, il y a longtemps . . . Il y a près de quarante ans que je vis ici . . . Regardez de l'autre côté, vous aurez la clarté de la mer . . .

MÉLISANDE
J'entends du bruit au-dessous de nous . . .

GENEVIÈVE
Oui; c'est quelqu'un qui monte vers nous . . . Ah! c'est Pelléas . . . Il semble encore fatigué de vous avoir attendue si longtemps . . .

MÉLISANDE
Il ne nous a pas vues.

GENEVIÈVE
Je crois qu'il nous a vues, mais il ne sait ce qu'il doit faire . . . Pelléas, Pelléas, est-ce toi?

PELLÉAS
Oui! . . . Je venais du côté de la mer . . .

GENEVIÈVE
Nous aussi; nous cherchions la clarté. Ici, il fait un peu plus clair qu'ailleurs! et cependant la mer est sombre.

PELLÉAS
Nous aurons une tempête cette nuit: il y en a toutes les nuits depuis quelque temps . . . et cependant elle est si calme ce soir . . . On s'embarquerait sans le savoir et l'on ne reviendrait plus.

MÉLISANDE
Quelque chose sort du port . . .

PELLÉAS
Il faut que ce soit un grand navire . . . Les lumières sont très hautes, nous le verrons tout à l'heure quand il entrera dans la bande de clarté . . .

GENEVIÈVE
Je ne sais si nous pourrons le voir . . . il y a encore une brume sur la mer . . .

PELLÉAS
On dirait que la brume s'élève lentement . . .

MÉLISANDE
Oui; j'aperçois, là-bas, une petite lumière que je n'avais pas vue . . .

PELLÉAS
C'est un phare; il y en a d'autres que nous ne voyons pas encore.

are places, they say, where the sunshine can never be seen. But you will get used to it. It's a very long time since I arrived here. Yes, it is nearly forty years that I've lived in this place. Over there when the weather is clear, one can watch the most colorful sunsets.

MÉLISANDE
What was that noise I heard down below?

GENEVIÈVE
Oh . . . it is someone climbing up here. Yes . . . it's Pelléas . . . he must have grown impatient and tired having to wait for us there all this time.

MÉLISANDE
But he has not yet seen us.

GENEVIÈVE
Oh yes, he must have seen us, but he wonders what he should do . . . Pelléas, Pelléas . . . is it you?
(*enter* PELLÉAS)

PELLÉAS
Yes! I was eager to look at the sea . . .

GENEVIÈVE
So were we. It's so warm in the gardens. Up here one gets the breeze from the harbor. Yet even so, the sea looks gloomy.

PELLÉAS
I believe we'll have a storm again tonight. Have we not had one every night for several days? And yet at sunset the sea looks calm and serene. One now could set sail without a thought—never again to return.
(*chorus of sailors in distance: "Heave ho! Yo heave ho!"*)

MÉLISANDE
A ship must be leaving the harbor!

PELLÉAS
It looks like a fairly large vessel, for her lights are very high. We shall see her much clearer when she comes to sail through that strip of light.

GENEVIÈVE
I'm not certain we'll be able to see her. There's quite a heavy mist that is hanging o'er the sea.

PELLÉAS
I believe that the mist is slowly lifting up.

MÉLISANDE
Oh, I think I can see the tiniest little light shining there in the darkness.

PELLÉAS
It's a beacon. There are other beacons, but in the mist we cannot see them.

MÉLISANDE

Look, now the ship is coming into the open. I can see her quite clearly.

PELLÉAS

Oh, how swiftly she is sailing . . .

MÉLISANDE

It is the ship that brought us here. Her sails are very large . . . it is by her sails that I know her.

PELLÉAS

It will be rough upon the water tonight.

MÉLISANDE

Why set sail on a night such as this? Now she's almost out of sight. Who knows perhaps she will be shipwrecked!

PELLÉAS

It grows dark very quickly!

GENEVIÈVE

It is late, we must return. I shall go first. Please show the way to Mélisande. I'm afraid I've been neglecting my grandchild, our little Yniold.
(*she goes out*)

PELLÉAS

Nothing can be seen on the sea.

MÉLISANDE

I can see some other lights.

PELLÉAS

Yes, those are the other beacons. Hear the rush of the sea? The wind is rising. We'll go down by this path. May I hold you by the hand?

MÉLISANDE

But look! I must keep these flow'rs in my hands!

PELLÉAS

I will hold you up by your arm. The path is very steep and it's growing quite dark now. I shall be leaving tomorrow.

MÉLISANDE

Oh! . . . Are you sure you must leave?
(*they go out*)

MÉLISANDE

Le navire est dans la lumière . . . Il est déjà bien loin . . .

PELLÉAS

Il s'éloigne à toutes voiles . . .

MÉLISANDE

C'est le navire qui m'a menée ici. Il a de grandes voiles . . . Je le reconnais à ses voiles . . .

PELLÉAS

Il aura mauvaise mer cette nuit . . .

MÉLISANDE

Pourquoi s'en va-t-il cette nuit? . . . On ne le voit presque plus . . . Il fera peut-être naufrage . . .

PELLÉAS

La nuit tombe très vite . . .

GENEVIÈVE

Il est temps de rentrer. Pelléas, montre la route à Mélisande. Il faut que j'aille voir, un instant, le petit Yniold.

PELLÉAS

On ne voit plus rien sur la mer . . .

MÉLISANDE

Je vois d'autres lumières.

PELLÉAS

Ce sont les autres phares . . . Entendez-vous la mer? . . . C'est le vent qui s'élève . . . Descendons par ici. Voulez-vous me donner la main?

MÉLISANDE

Voyez, voyez, j'ai les mains pleines de fleurs.

PELLÉAS

Je vous soutiendrai par le bras, le chemin est escarpé et il y fait très sombre . . . Je pars peut-être demain . . .

MÉLISANDE

Oh! . . . pourquoi partez-vous?

ACT II

Scene 1: A well in the park

PELLÉAS
Vous ne savez pas où je vous ai menée?—Je viens souvent m'asseoir ici, vers midi, lorsqu'il fait trop chaud dans les jardins. On étouffe, aujourd'hui, même à l'ombre des arbres.

MÉLISANDE
Oh! l'eau est claire . . .

PELLÉAS
Elle est fraîche comme l'hiver. C'est une vieille fontaine abandonnée. Il paraît que c'était une fontaine miraculeuse,—elle ouvrait les yeux des aveugles.—On l'appelle encore la «fontaine des aveugles.»

MÉLISANDE
Elle n'ouvre plus les yeux des aveugles?

PELLÉAS
Depuis que le roi est presque aveugle lui-même, on n'y vient plus . . .

MÉLISANDE
Comme on est seul ici . . . On n'entend rien.

PELLÉAS
Il y a toujours un silence extraordinaire . . . On entendrait dormir l'eau . . . Voulez-vous vous asseoir au bord du bassin de marbre? Il y a un tilleul où le soleil n'entre jamais . . .

MÉLISANDE
Je vais me coucher sur le marbre.—Je voudrais voir le fond de l'eau . . .

PELLÉAS
On ne l'a jamais vu.—Elle est peut-être aussi profonde que la mer.

MÉLISANDE
Si quelque chose brillait au fond, on le verrait peut-être . . .

PELLÉAS
Ne vous penchez pas ainsi . . .

MÉLISANDE
Je voudrais toucher l'eau . . .

PELLÉAS
Prenez garde de glisser . . . Je vais vous tenir la main . . .

MÉLISANDE
Non, non, je voudrais y plonger mes deux mains . . . on dirait que mes mains sont malades aujourd'hui . . .

(*enter* PELLÉAS *and* MÉLISANDE)

PELLÉAS
Do you know this place where I have brought you? Often I come here all alone about noon when the gardens have become too warm. Yes, it's stifling today even here in the shadows.

MÉLISANDE
Oh! What limpid water!

PELLÉAS
Yes, it's always cool and refreshing. It's an ancient well that for years has been abandoned. At one time, so it seems, this well had miraculous powers; it could heal the eyes of the sightless. It's called to this day the Fountain of the Blind Men.

MÉLISANDE
Does it cure no longer the eyes of the sightless?

PELLÉAS
No, now that the King himself is almost a blind man, they come here no more . . .

MÉLISANDE
Oh! How quiet it is . . . there's not a sound.

PELLÉAS
Everything is filled with a deep and wonderful silence . . . one can hear the water sleep. Won't you sit down a while beside this basin of marble? Here the trees cast a shadow through which the sunlight never passes . . .

MÉLISANDE
I'm going to lie down on the marble, to see the bottom of the well . . .

PELLÉAS
It has never been seen . . . and I imagine it must be as deep as the sea.

MÉLISANDE
If something bright were shining below, perhaps one then could see it.

PELLÉAS
Do not lean so far . . .

MÉLISANDE
I am trying to reach . . .

PELLÉAS
Please be careful not to slip . . . perhaps if I held your hand . . .

MÉLISANDE
No, no, I should like to dip in both my hands . . . don't you think that my hands look pale and fragile today?

PELLÉAS
Oh! Oh! Please be careful . . . oh, be careful! Mélisande! Mélisande! Oh! Your hair has fallen . . .

MÉLISANDE
There is no use, I'm not able to reach it!

PELLÉAS
Look, your hair has slipped into the water.

MÉLISANDE
Yes, it falls below my knees. It reaches to my ankles . . .

PELLÉAS
Was it not beside an ancient well that he first saw you?

MÉLISANDE
Yes . . .

PELLÉAS
What did he say?

MÉLISANDE
Nothing . . . I can't remember what he said . . .

PELLÉAS
Did he try to come near you?

MÉLISANDE
Yes, he wanted to embrace me . . .

PELLÉAS
You didn't want him to do it?

MÉLISANDE
No . . .

PELLÉAS
Tell me what made you refuse?

MÉLISANDE
Oh! Oh! There is something at the bottom of the well!

PELLÉAS
Please be careful! Oh, be careful! You're going to fall . . . What is that in your hand?

MÉLISANDE
It is the ring he gave to me.

PELLÉAS
Do not toss it about like a toy above such deep water . . .

MÉLISANDE
You need not be afraid!

PELLÉAS
How it shines in the sun! Please do not toss it so high in the air!

MÉLISANDE
Oh!

PELLÉAS
It's fallen down!

MÉLISANDE
It has dropped in the well!

PELLÉAS
Oh! oh! prenez garde! prenez garde! Mélisande! . . . Mélisande! . . .—Oh! votre chevelure! . . .

MÉLISANDE
Je ne peux pas, je ne peux pas l'atteindre.

PELLÉAS
Vos cheveux ont plongé dans l'eau . . .

MÉLISANDE
Oui, ils sont plus longs que mes bras . . . Ils sont plus longs que moi . . .

PELLÉAS
C'est au bord d'une fontaine aussi, qu'il vous a trouvée?

MÉLISANDE
Oui . . .

PELLÉAS
Que vous a-t-il dit?

MÉLISANDE
Rien;—je ne me rappelle plus . . .

PELLÉAS
Était-il tout près de vous?

MÉLISANDE
Oui; il voulait m'embrasser . . .

PELLÉAS
Et vous ne vouliez pas?

MÉLISANDE
Non.

PELLÉAS
Pourquoi ne vouliez-vous pas?

MÉLISANDE
Oh! oh! j'ai vu passer quelque chose au fond de l'eau . . .

PELLÉAS
Prenez garde! prenez garde!—Vous allez tomber!—Avec quoi jouez-vous?

MÉLISANDE
Avec l'anneau qu'il m'a donné . . .

PELLÉAS
Ne jouez pas ainsi, au-dessus d'une eau si profonde . . .

MÉLISANDE
Mes mains ne tremblent pas.

PELLÉAS
Comme il brille au soleil!—Ne le jetez pas si haut vers le ciel . . .

MÉLISANDE
Oh! . . .

PELLÉAS
Il est tombé!

MÉLISANDE
Il est tombé dans l'eau! . . .

PELLÉAS
Où est-il? où est-il?

MÉLISANDE
Je ne le vois pas descendre . . .

PELLÉAS
Je crois la voir briller . . .

MÉLISANDE
Ma bague?

PELLÉAS
Oui, oui, . . . là-bas . . .

MÉLISANDE
Oh! oh! elle est si loin de nous! . . . non, non, ce n'est pas elle . . . ce n'est plus elle . . . Elle est perdue . . . perdue . . . Il n'y a plus qu'un grand cercle sur l'eau . . . Qu'allons-nous faire maintenant? . . .

PELLÉAS
Il ne faut pas s'inquiéter ainsi pour une bague. Ce n'est rien . . . nous la retrouverons peut-être. Ou bien nous en retrouverons une autre.

MÉLISANDE
Non, non; nous ne la retrouverons plus, nous n'en trouverons pas d'autres non plus . . . Je croyais l'avoir dans les mains cependant . . . J'avais déjà fermé les mains, et elle est tombée malgré tout . . . Je l'ai jetée trop haut, du côté du soleil . . .

PELLÉAS
Venez, nous reviendrons un autre jour . . . venez, il est temps. On irait à notre rencontre . . . Midi sonnait au moment où l'anneau est tombé . . .

MÉLISANDE
Qu'allons-nous dire à Golaud s'il demande où il est?

PELLÉAS
La vérité, la vérité, la vérité . . .

GOLAUD
Ah! ah! tout va bien, cela ne sera rien. Mais je ne puis m'expliquer comment cela s'est passé. Je chassais tran-

PELLÉAS
Tell me where! Tell me where!

MÉLISANDE
I do not see where it's sinking!

PELLÉAS
I think I can see it!

MÉLISANDE
Where is it?

PELLÉAS
Down there, you see?

MÉLISANDE
Oh! Oh! It's such a long way down! . . . No, no, it's not the ring . . . it's lost forever! The ring is lost . . . forever . . . only a circle of water remains . . . what shall we do about it now?

PELLÉAS
There's no need of being so distressed over a trinket. It is nothing . . . Perhaps the ring will be recovered! Or else, no doubt we can find you another.

MÉLISANDE
No, no, we'll never find the ring again, nor will another one ever be found. I thought I held it in my hands quite securely. I had already closed my hands, and yet it slipped out and fell down. I tossed it up too high into the rays of the sun.

PELLÉAS
We must go . . . we will return some other day. It is time, we must go. Or they'll be coming out to look for us . . . Noon was striking at the moment the ring disappeared.

MÉLISANDE
What shall we say to Golaud if he asks where it is?

PELLÉAS
Tell him the truth, tell him the truth . . .
(*they go out*)

Scene 2: A room in the castle

(GOLAUD *is seen lying on his bed;* MÉLISANDE *is at the bedside.*)

GOLAUD
Ha! Ha! All goes well. 'Twas nothing after all. But what I cannot explain is the way it all took place. I was hunting quite calmly in the forest. Suddenly my horse

reared up without reason, without warning. Can it be that he saw something strange and unusual? I had just been counting the bells that struck the noonday hour. Then, on the last stroke, he suddenly took fright and ran as if blinded straight into a tree trunk. I hardly know what took place after that. I must have fallen, the horse must have fallen on me. And I felt as though the whole forest had fallen on top of me. I felt sure that my heart had been torn in two. But my heart is not injured, and it seems no harm was done.

quillement dans la forêt. Mon cheval s'est emporté tout à coup, sans raison. A-t-il vu quelque chose d'extraordinaire? . . . Je venais d'entendre sonner les douze coups de midi. Au douzième coup, il s'effraie subitement, et court, comme un aveugle fou, contre un arbre. Je ne sais plus ce qui est arrivé. Je suis tombé, et lui doit être tombé sur moi. Je croyais avoir toute la forêt sur la poitrine; je croyais que mon cœur était déchiré. Mais mon cœur est solide. Il paraît que ce n'est rien . . .

MÉLISANDE
Would you like a little water?

MÉLISANDE
Voulez-vous boire un peu d'eau?

GOLAUD
No thanks. I am not thirsty.

GOLAUD
Merci; je n'ai pas soif.

MÉLISANDE
Would you like me to change your pillow . . . there is a little drop of blood on this one.

MÉLISANDE
Voulez-vous un autre oreiller? . . . Il y a une petite tache de sang sur celui-ci.

GOLAUD
No . . . it's not worth the trouble.

GOLAUD
Non, non; ce n'est pas la peine.

MÉLISANDE
Are you quite sure? But aren't you still in pain?

MÉLISANDE
Est-ce bien sûr? . . . Vous ne souffrez pas trop?

GOLAUD
No, no . . . you must not worry. I am made of iron and steel.

GOLAUD
Non, non, j'en ai vu bien d'autres. Je suis fait au fer et au sang . . .

MÉLISANDE
Now, close your eyes and try to go to sleep. I will stay here through the night.

MÉLISANDE
Fermez les yeux et tâchez de dormir. Je resterai ici toute la nuit . . .

GOLAUD
No, no. I will not have you worry yourself in that way. There's nothing more I need; now I shall sleep like a child . . . What is wrong, Mélisande? Why what's made you weep all at once?

GOLAUD
Non, non; je ne veux pas que tu te fatigues ainsi. Je n'ai besoin de rien; je dormirai comme un enfant . . . Qu'y a-t-il, Mélisande? Pourquoi pleures-tu tout à coup? . . .

MÉLISANDE
Because . . . I am ill in this place.

MÉLISANDE
Je suis . . . Je suis malade ici . . .

GOLAUD
You say you're ill here? In what way, tell me how, Mélisande?

GOLAUD
Tu es malade? . . . Qu'as-tu donc, qu'as-tu donc, Mélisande? . . .

MÉLISANDE
I do not know . . . I am ill in this house. I have thought it best to tell you today. My Lord, I am not happy in this place.

MÉLISANDE
Je ne sais pas . . . Je suis malade ici . . . Je préfère vous le dire aujourd'hui; seigneur, je ne suis pas heureuse ici . . .

GOLAUD
You must tell me what happened . . . has someone done you wrong? Or did someone give you offense?

GOLAUD
Qu'est-il donc arrivé? . . . Quelqu'un t'a fait du mal? . . . Quelqu'un t'aurait-il offensée?

MÉLISANDE
Non, non; personne ne m'a fait le moindre mal . . . Ce n'est pas cela . . .

GOLAUD
Mais tu dois me cacher quelque chose? . . . Dis-moi toute la vérité, Mélisande . . . Est-ce le roi? . . . Est-ce ma mère? . . . Est-ce Pelléas? . . .

MÉLISANDE
Non, non; ce n'est pas Pelléas. Ce n'est personne . . . Vous ne pouvez pas me comprendre . . . C'est quelque chose qui est plus fort que moi . . .

GOLAUD
Voyons; sois raisonnable, Mélisande.—Que veux-tu que je fasse?—Tu n'es plus une enfant.—Est-ce moi que tu voudrais quitter?

MÉLISANDE
Oh! non; ce n'est pas cela . . . Je voudrais m'en aller avec vous . . . C'est ici, que je ne peux plus vivre . . . Je sens que je ne vivrais plus longtemps . . .

GOLAUD
Mais il faut une raison cependant. On va te croire folle. On va croire à des rêves d'enfant.—Voyons, est-ce Pelléas, peut-être?—Je crois qu'il ne te parle pas souvent . . .

MÉLISANDE
Si, si; il me parle parfois. Il ne m'aime pas, je crois; je l'ai vu dans ses yeux . . . Mais il me parle quand il me rencontre . . .

GOLAUD
Il ne faut pas lui en vouloir. Il a toujours été ainsi. Il est un peu étrange. Il changera, tu verras; il est jeune . . .

MÉLISANDE
Mais ce n'est pas cela . . . ce n'est pas cela . . .

GOLAUD
Qu'est-ce donc?—Ne peux-tu pas te faire à la vie qu'on mène ici? Fait-il trop triste ici?—Il est vrai que ce château est très vieux et très sombre . . . Il est très froid et tres profond. Et tous ceux qui l'habitent sont déjà vieux. Et la campagne peut sembler bien triste aussi, avec toutes ses forêts, toutes ses vieilles forêts sans lumière. Mais on peut égayer tout cela si l'on veut. Et puis, la joie, la joie,

MÉLISANDE
No . . . no . . . no one has done the slightest harm. No, that is not it.

GOLAUD
Is there something that you are concealing? Tell me frankly, tell me the truth, Mélisande . . . is it the King? Is it my mother? Is it Pelléas?

MÉLISANDE
No, no, it is not Pelléas. It is no one. I don't know how to explain it. But it is something that's stronger than myself . . .

GOLAUD
Come, come; be reasonable, Mélisande. Tell me how I can help you. You're no longer a child. Is it from me you would like to escape?

MÉLISANDE
Oh! No, no, that is not it . . . I should like to go away with you. It is here I can't live any longer. I feel that I shall die very soon.

GOLAUD
There must be some reason nevertheless. People will think you foolish. They will think it's the dream of a child. Let's see, is it Pelléas, I wonder? I believe he prefers not to speak to you.

MÉLISANDE
Oh, he will speak to me sometimes. But he does not like me, I think; I can tell by his eyes. But he speaks when he happens to meet me.

GOLAUD
You must not take offense at that. For that has always been his way. He behaves rather strangely. He will soon change, you will see; he is young still . . .

MÉLISANDE
It is not that at all . . . no, it is not that . . .

GOLAUD
Well, then what? Can you not yet get used to the life we're leading here? Do you find it too sad? To be sure, the castle is very old and very gloomy . . . It's very cold and very deep. And the people who live here are mostly quite old. Even the landscape may seem sad and forlorn with the forest all around and those dark and ancient woods bereft of sunshine. But one still might enliven all this if one would. We know that sunshine and joy cannot be had every day; but tell me more about it, no matter what, and whatever you wish shall be done.

on n'en a pas tous les jours; il faut prendre les choses comme elles sont. Mais dis-moi quelque chose; n'importe quoi; je ferai tout ce que tu voudras . . .

MÉLISANDE
Yes, it's true . . . one hardly ever sees the sky. Till today, I had not seen it at all.

MÉLISANDE
Oui, c'est vrai . . . on ne voit jamais le ciel clair . . . Je l'ai vu pour la première fois ce matin . . .

GOLAUD
Oh, is it this then that made you weep, my little Mélisande? Is it nothing but that? You weep because you cannot see the sky? Come, come, you're surely too old to weep about that . . . besides, the summer will soon be here . . . you will see the sky ev'ry day. And then another year . . . come, come, let me have your hand; there now, give me both your little hands . . . Oh! These two little hands that I could so easily crush as though they were flowers . . . Wait—where is the ring, the ring that I gave you?

GOLAUD
C'est donc cela qui te fait pleurer, ma pauvre Mélisande?—Ce n'est donc que cela?—Tu pleures de ne pas voir le ciel?—Voyons, tu n'es plus à l'âge où l'on peut pleurer pour ces choses . . . Et puis l'été n'est-il pas là? Tu vas voir le ciel tous les jours.—Et puis l'année prochaine . . . Voyons, donne-moi ta main; donne-moi tes deux petites mains. Oh! ces petites mains que je pourrais écraser comme des fleurs . . .—Tiens, où est l'anneau que je t'avais donné?

MÉLISANDE
The ring?

MÉLISANDE
L'anneau?

GOLAUD
Yes, the token of our marriage. Come, where is it?

GOLAUD
Oui; la bague de nos noces, où est-elle?

MÉLISANDE
I think . . . I think it fell off.

MÉLISANDE
Je crois . . . Je crois qu'elle est tombée . . .

GOLAUD
Fell off? Well then, where has it fallen? You mean that you have lost it?

GOLAUD
Tombée?—Où est-elle tombée . . .—Tu ne l'as pas perdue?

MÉLISANDE
No—I must have dropped it . . . I am quite sure that I dropped it . . . but I know where it is . . .

MÉLISANDE
Non, elle est tombée . . . elle doit être tombée . . . mais je sais où elle est . . .

GOLAUD
Where is it?

GOLAUD
Où est-elle?

MÉLISANDE
You know the place . . . you know the place . . . where there's a cave by the sea?

MÉLISANDE
Vous savez bien . . . vous savez bien . . . la grotte au bord de la mer?

GOLAUD
Yes.

GOLAUD
Oui.

MÉLISANDE
You see, 'twas there . . . that's where it must have been . . . yes, yes, of course I remember. This morning when I went down to gather some shells for little Yniold . . . there are some lovely ones there . . . it was there the ring slipped off . . . then the tide started rising, so I had to leave before I was able to find it.

MÉLISANDE
Eh bien, c'est là . . . Il faut que ce soit là . . . Oui, oui; je me rappelle. . . J'y suis allée ce matin, ramasser des coquillages pour le petit Yniold . . . Il y en a de très beaux . . . Elle a glissé de mon doigt . . . puis la mer est entrée; et j'ai dû sortir avant de l'avoir retrouvée.

GOLAUD
Es-tu sûre que ce soit là?

MÉLISANDE
Oui, oui; tout à fait sûre . . . Je l'ai sentie glisser . . .

GOLAUD
Il faut aller la chercher tout de suite.

MÉLISANDE
Maintenant?—tout de suite?—dans l'obscurité?

GOLAUD
Maintenant, tout de suite, dans l'obscurité. J'aimerais mieux avoir perdu tout ce que j'ai plutôt que d'avoir perdu cette bague. Tu ne sais pas ce que c'est. Tu ne sais pas d'où elle vient. La mer sera très haute cette nuit. La mer viendra la prendre avant toi . . . dépêche-toi.

MÉLISANDE
Je n'ose pas . . . Je n'ose pas aller seule . . .

GOLAUD
Vas-y, vas-y avec n'importe qui. Mais il faut y aller tout de suite, entends-tu?—Dépêche-toi; demande à Pelléas d'y aller avec toi.

MÉLISANDE
Pelléas?—Avec Pelléas?—Mais Pelléas ne voudra pas . . .

GOLAUD
Pelléas fera tout ce que tu lui demandes. Je connais Pelléas mieux que toi. Vas-y, hâte-toi. Je ne dormirai pas avant d'avoir la bague.

MÉLISANDE
Oh! oh! Je ne suis pas heureuse! . . . Je ne suis pas heureuse!

GOLAUD
Are you certain it is there?

MÉLISANDE
Yes, yes, I am certain . . . yes, I felt it slip off.

GOLAUD
You will have to go and fetch it at once then.

MÉLISANDE
Go there now? Now, this moment? Alone in the dark?

GOLAUD
Go there now. Go at once, even in the darkness . . . I had far rather lose all else that I possess than to discover you'd lost that ring. You do not know what it is. You do not know from whence it came. Tonight, the tide will rise very high. The sea will come and get to it first . . . you must make haste.

MÉLISANDE
I am afraid. I don't dare to go alone there . . .

GOLAUD
Go, go, it matters not with whom you go. But you will have to go there this instant, do you hear? Do not delay. Ask Pelléas if he will not go with you.

MÉLISANDE
Pelléas? Go with Pelléas? But Pelléas will refuse . . .

GOLAUD
Pelléas will do whatever you ask him. I know him better than you. But go, don't delay. I shall not sleep until the ring has been recovered.

MÉLISANDE
Oh; Oh! I am very unhappy, I am very unhappy.
(*she goes out weeping*)

Scene 3: Before a grotto

(*enter* PELLÉAS *and* MÉLISANDE)

PELLÉAS
Oui; c'est ici, nous y sommes. Il fait si noir que l'entrée de la grotte ne se distingue pas du reste de la nuit . . . Il n'y a pas d'étoiles de ce côté. Attendons que la lune ait déchiré ce grand nuage; elle éclairera toute la grotte et alors nous pourrons y entrer sans danger. Il y a des endroits dangereux et le sentier est très étroit, entre deux lacs dont on n'a pas

PELLÉAS
Yes, here is the place, we have reached it. It is so dark the entrance to the grotto can scarcely be distinguished against the sky. The night is dark and gloomy . . . there's not a star. Let us wait till the moon breaks out through the clouds. It will throw some light into the cave, and I think that it will be safe to go in. There are dangerous places inside . . . I remember a path between two pools of which the bottom has never been found. It never occurred to me but we ought to have brought a lantern. Still I imagine the light of the moon

will suffice. Have you ever found your way to the grotto?

MÉLISANDE

No . . .

PELLÉAS

You should see it . . . you ought to be able to describe the place where you lost the ring, in case he should ask you. It's very large and impressive . . . it is full of blue and purple shadows. If a tiny candle is lighted inside, the roof of the grotto lights up as if it were studded with stars. Let me hold your hand. You need not tremble . . . There's not the slightest danger . . . we'll not venture any further . . . until the moon casts its light and illumines the sky. Is it the roar of the grotto you are afraid of? Can you hear the sea outside beyond us? It seems to grumble and lament as if in pain.

(*the moon throws a flood of light into the entrance of the grotto and shows three white-haired paupers sleeping huddled together, leaning against a boulder*)

Oh! Now here is the light!

MÉLISANDE

Ah!

PELLÉAS

What has happened?

MÉLISANDE

Who are they? Who are they?

PELLÉAS

Oh! I wonder why they're here . . .

MÉLISANDE

I want to leave, please let us go!

PELLÉAS

Those are three old beggars who have fallen asleep . . . There has been a dreadful famine all over the land. Still, I don't understand what brought them to this grotto.

MÉLISANDE

Please let us leave! I beg you! Please let us go!

PELLÉAS

Oh, be careful, do not speak quite so loud . . . we must not wake them up . . . they are tired and they're sleeping so soundly . . . let's go.

MÉLISANDE

Let me go . . . I prefer to walk alone . . .

PELLÉAS

We shall return some other day.

(*they go out*)

encore trouvé le fond. Je n'ai pas songé à emporter une torche ou une lanterne, mais je pense que la clarté du ciel nous suffira.—Vous n'avez jamais pénétré dans cette grotte?

MÉLISANDE

Non . . .

PELLÉAS

Entrons-y . . . Il faut pouvoir décrire l'endroit où vous avez perdu la bague, s'il vous interroge . . . Elle est très grande et très belle. Elle est pleine de ténèbres bleues. Quand on y allume une petite lampe, on dirait que la voûte est couverte d'étoiles, comme le ciel. Donnez-moi la main, ne tremblez pas, ne tremblez pas ainsi. Il n'y a pas de danger: nous nous arrêterons au moment que nous n'apercevrons plus la clarté de la mer . . . Est-ce le bruit de la grotte qui vous effraie? Entendez-vous la mer derrière nous?—Elle ne semble pas heureuse cette nuit . . . Ah! voici la clarté!

MÉLISANDE

Ah!

PELLÉAS

Qu'y a-t-il?

MÉLISANDE

Il y a . . . Il y a . . .

PELLÉAS

Oui, oui; je les ai vus aussi . . .

MÉLISANDE

Allons-nous-en! . . . Allons-nous-en! . . .

PELLÉAS

Ce sont trois vieux pauvres qui se sont endormis . . . Il y a une famine dans le pays . . . Pourquoi sont-ils venus dormir ici?

MÉLISANDE

Allons-nous-en! . . . Venez . . . Allons-nous-en! . . .

PELLÉAS

Prenez garde, ne parlez pas si fort . . . Ne les éveillons pas . . . Ils dorment encore profondément . . . Venez.

MÉLISANDE

Laissez-moi; je préfère marcher seule . . .

PELLÉAS

Nous reviendrons un autre jour . . .

MÉLISANDE
Mes longs cheveux descendent jusqu'au seuil de la tour!
Mes cheveux vous attendent tout le long de la tour!
Et tout le long du jour!
Et tout le long du jour!
Saint Daniel et Saint Michel,
Saint Michel et Saint Raphaël,
Je suis née un dimanche!
Un dimanche à midi!

PELLÉAS
Holà! Holà! ho!

MÉLISANDE
Qui est là?

PELLÉAS
Moi, moi, et moi! . . . Que fais-tu là à la fenêtre en chantant comme un oiseau qui n'est pas d'ici?

MÉLISANDE
J'arrange mes cheveux pour la nuit . . .

PELLÉAS
C'est là ce que je vois sur le mur! . . . Je croyais que c'était un rayon de lumière . . .

MÉLISANDE
J'ai ouvert la fenêtre. Il fait trop chaud dans la tour, il fait beau cette nuit.

PELLÉAS
Il y a d'innombrables étoiles; je n'en ai jamais autant vu que ce soir; . . . mais la lune est encore sur la mer . . . Ne reste pas dans l'ombre, Mélisande, penche-toi un peu, que je voie tes cheveux dénoués.

MÉLISANDE
Je suis affreuse ainsi.

PELLÉAS
Oh! Mélisande! . . . oh! tu es belle! . . . tu es belle ainsi! . . . penche-toi! penche-toi! . . . laisse-moi venir plus près de toi . . .

MÉLISANDE
Je ne puis pas venir plus près de toi . . . je me penche tant que je peux . . .

PELLÉAS
Je ne puis pas monter plus haut . . . donne-moi du moins ta main ce soir . . . avant que je m'en aille . . . Je pars demain . . .

ACT III

Scene 1: One of the towers of the castle

(*A watchman's path passes under one of the windows of the tower.*)

MÉLISANDE (*at the window combing her unbound hair*)
My long, long hair is reaching to the foot of the towers; my hair is waiting for you down the tower all the way, it is waiting all day, yes, waiting night and day. St. Arlene and St. Christine, St. Christine and St. Josephine . . . I was born on a Sunday, on a Sunday at noon.

(PELLÉAS *enters by the path*)

PELLÉAS
Hello! Hello, ho!

MÉLISANDE
Who is there?

PELLÉAS
It's I, yes, it's I! What are you doing at the window singing like a bird that comes from afar?

MÉLISANDE
I am arranging my hair for the night . . .

PELLÉAS
Is that what I see there on the wall? I thought you had a light in the tower . . .

MÉLISANDE
I have opened the window; it was too warm here in the tower. It is lovely tonight . . .

PELLÉAS
The stars are shining so brightly . . . I've never seen so many stars all at once. But the moon is still hidden in the sea . . . You must not remain in the shadow, Mélisande, lean out of the window, let me look at your lovely hair.

MÉLISANDE
But I look so ugly.

PELLÉAS
Oh! Oh! Mélisande, oh, you are lovely! You're lovelier than the stars. Please come closer, Mélisande. Oh, do not stay so far away . . .

MÉLISANDE
You see, this is as near as I can come . . . I am leaning as far as I can . . .

PELLÉAS
And I can't reach any higher . . . oh, let me touch your hand just once, I beg you, before I go away . . . I'm leaving tomorrow . . .

MÉLISANDE
No—no, no!

PELLÉAS
Yes, yes, I must, tomorrow I shall be gone! Let me have your hand, your hand, let me cover your hand with my kisses . . .

MÉLISANDE
I will not let you touch my hand if you go . . .

PELLÉAS
Let me, let me kiss it . . .

MÉLISANDE
Then you promise to stay?

PELLÉAS
I shall wait, I shall wait . . .

MÉLISANDE
I can see a rose down there in the darkness . . .

PELLÉAS
Where's that? I can see but the limbs of the willow reaching over the wall.

MÉLISANDE
Far away, far away, there in the garden down there, among the shadows . . .

PELLÉAS
But that is not a rosebud . . . I will look at it later. First, you must give me your hand, Mélisande! First give me your hand . . .

MÉLISANDE
Here it is, here it is . . . I cannot lean any farther . . .

PELLÉAS
Come closer, I cannot reach your hand with my lips!

MÉLISANDE
But I cannot lean out any farther . . . it's all I can do not to fall . . . Oh! Oh! All my hair has fallen from the tower . . .

PELLÉAS
Oh! Oh! What is this? It's your hair, your hair descended from the tower! All your beautiful tresses, Mélisande, all your beautiful locks floating down from the tower . . . it is here in my hands, I can touch and caress it. It is here near my lips, I shall never release it again . . . I shall embrace it and keep it forever.

MÉLISANDE
Let me go! Let me go! I am afraid I shall fall!

PELLÉAS
No, no, no! Oh, I've never seen hair like yours, Mélisande, Mélisande! Look, look, look, your hair fell down from

MÉLISANDE
Non, non, non . . .

PELLÉAS
Si, si; je pars, je partirai demain . . . donne-moi ta main, ta main, ta petite main sur mes lèvres . . .

MÉLISANDE
Je ne te donne pas ma main si tu pars . . .

PELLÉAS
Donne, donne, donne . . .

MÉLISANDE
Tu ne partiras pas? . . .

PELLÉAS
J'attendrai, j'attendrai.

MÉLISANDE
Je vois une rose dans les ténèbres . . .

PELLÉAS
Où donc? . . . Je ne vois que les branches du saule qui dépassent le mur . . .

MÉLISANDE
Plus bas, plus bas, dans le jardin; là-bas, dans le vert sombre.

PELLÉAS
Ce n'est pas une rose . . . J'irai voir tout à l'heure, mais donne-moi ta main d'abord; d'abord ta main . . .

MÉLISANDE
Voilà, voilà; . . . je ne puis me pencher davantage . . .

PELLÉAS
Mes lèvres ne peuvent pas atteindre ta main . . .

MÉLISANDE
Je ne puis pas me pencher davantage . . . Je suis sur le point de tomber . . .— Oh! oh! mes cheveux descendent de la tour! . . .

PELLÉAS
Oh! oh! qu'est-ce que c'est? . . . Tes cheveux, tes cheveux descendent vers moi! . . . Toute ta chevelure, Mélisande, toute ta chevelure est tombée de la tour! . . . Je les tiens dans les mains, je les tiens dans ma bouche . . . Je les tiens dans les bras, je les mets autour de mon cou . . . Je n'ouvrirai plus les mains cette nuit . . .

MÉLISANDE
Laisse-moi! laisse-moi! . . . Tu vas me faire tomber! . . .

PELLÉAS
Non, non, non; . . . je n'ai jamais vu de cheveux comme les tiens, Mélisande! . . .

Vois, vois, vois, ils viennent de si haut et ils m'inondent jusqu'au cœur . . . Ils m'inondent encore jusqu'aux genoux . . . Et ils sont doux, ils sont doux comme s'ils tombaient du ciel! . . . Je ne vois plus le ciel à travers tes cheveux. Tu vois, tu vois, mes mains ne peuvent plus les tenir . . . Il y en a jusque sur les branches du saule . . . Ils vivent comme des oiseaux dans mes mains . . . et ils m'aiment, ils m'aiment mille fois mieux que toi! . . .

heaven and it's weaving a web around my heart . . . I am captured within this golden net, and it is soft, as soft as the petals of a rose . . . all the stars are gone, I cannot see the sky. Just look, oh look, I can hardly hold it in my hands . . . some of it floats on the breeze and caresses the foliage . . . it lives, it flutters and breathes like a bird in my hands. And it loves me . . . it yields to my caresses . . .

MÉLISANDE

Laisse-moi, laisse-moi . . . quelqu'un pourrait venir . . .

MÉLISANDE

Let me go, let me go! If someone were to come . . .

PELLÉAS

Non, non, non; je ne te délivre pas cette nuit . . . Tu es ma prisonnière cette nuit; toute la nuit, toute la nuit . . .

PELLÉAS

No, no, no, I shall not give you your freedom tonight . . . I shall keep you my own throughout the night, throughout the night, throughout the night . . .

MÉLISANDE

Pelléas! Pelléas! . . .

MÉLISANDE

Pelléas . . . Pelléas!

PELLÉAS

Tu ne t'en iras plus . . . Je les noue, je les noue aux branches du saule, tes cheveux. Je ne souffre plus au milieu de tes cheveux. Tu entends mes baisers le long de tes cheveux? Ils montent le long de tes cheveux. Il faut que chacun t'en apporte. Tu vois, tu vois, je puis ouvrir les mains . . . Tu vois, j'ai les mains libres et tu ne peux m'abandonner . . .

PELLÉAS

It is mine, it is mine . . . I'll never release it. You will never escape . . . no, you will not escape! Behold me . . . behold me. My lips caress your hair. I'm carried to heaven when I grasp it to my heart. Can you sense, can you feel the passion of my kisses . . . Can you feel them ascending to your lips? You are mine, I will never release you, just look, oh look! I'm holding you no longer . . . My hands are free and still you cannot escape . . .

(*some doves come out of the tower and fly in the darkness*)

MÉLISANDE

Oh! oh! tu m'as fait mal . . . Qu'y a-t-il, Pelléas?—Qu'est-ce qui vole autour de moi?

MÉLISANDE

Oh! Oh! You have hurt me . . . What was that, Pelléas? What is flying all around me?

PELLÉAS

Ce sont les colombes qui sortent de la tour . . . Je les ai effrayées; elles s'envolent.

PELLÉAS

Those are the doves that are coming from the tower . . . we have scared them away, they look so frightened . . .

MÉLISANDE

Ce sont mes colombes, Pelléas.—Allons-nous-en, laisse-moi; elles ne reviendraient plus . . .

MÉLISANDE

Oh, those are my doves, Pelléas, we have frightened my doves; now they will never return . . .

PELLÉAS

Pourquoi ne reviendraient-elles plus?

PELLÉAS

What makes you think they won't return?

MÉLISANDE

Elles se perdront dans l'obscurité laisse-moi . . . Laisse-moi relever la tête . . . J'entends un bruit de pas . . . Laisse-moi!—C'est Golaud! . . . Je crois que c'est Golaud! . . . Il nous a entendus . . .

MÉLISANDE

They will get lost out there in the darkness . . . let me go! Let me lift my head, I beg you! I hear the sound of steps . . . let me go! It's Golaud! I think it is Golaud! I believe he has heard us.

PELLÉAS

Be still! Be still! Your hair is caught in the branches . . . it got tangled among them here in the darkness. Be still! Be still! It is dark . . .

PELLÉAS

Attends! Attends! . . . Tes cheveux sont autour des branches . . . Ils se sont accrochés dans l'obscurité. Attends, attends! . . . Il fait noir . . .

(GOLAUD *enters by the path*)

GOLAUD

What is the meaning of this?

GOLAUD

Que faites-vous ici?

PELLÉAS

The meaning of this? I . . .

PELLÉAS

Ce que je fais ici? . . . Je . . .

GOLAUD

You're acting like two children . . . Mélisande, do not lean so far out of the window, you might fall down. Don't you know it is late? It is nearly midnight! Stop playing like this out here in the dark. You're acting like two children . . . like children . . . just like children!

(*he goes out with* PELLÉAS)

GOLAUD

Vous êtes des enfants . . . Mélisande, ne te penche pas ainsi à la fenêtre, tu vas tomber . . . Vous ne savez pas qu'il est tard?—Il est près de minuit.—Ne jouez pas ainsi dans l'obscurité.—Vous êtes des enfants . . . Quels enfants! Quels enfants! . . .

Scene 2: The vaults of the castle

(*enter* GOLAUD *and* PELLÉAS)

GOLAUD

Now be careful; come with me over here. Have you ever before come down to these vaults?

GOLAUD

Prenez garde: par ici, par ici.—Vous n'avez jamais pénétré dans ces souterrains?

PELLÉAS

Yes, once I did, only once; but that was long ago . . .

PELLÉAS

Si, une fois, dans le temps; mais il y a longtemps.

GOLAUD

See there, the stagnating water I told you about. Can you smell the odor of death? Now let us go by the pathway down there a little farther. It will rise up and strike you in the face . . . now stoop down, don't be afraid . . . I will hold you . . . let me have . . . no, no, not your hand, your hand could slip . . . your arm. Can you see the chasm, Pelléas? Pelléas?

GOLAUD

Eh bien, voici l'eau stagnante dont je vous parlais . . . Sentez-vous l'odeur de mort qui monte?—Allons jusqu'au bout de ce rocher qui surplombe et penchez-vous un peu. Elle viendra vous frapper au visage. Penchez-vous; n'ayez pas peur . . . je vous tiendrai . . . donnez-moi . . . non, non, pas la main . . . elle pourrait glisser . . . le bras . . . Voyez-vous le gouffre? . . . Pelléas? Pelléas? . . .

PELLÉAS

Yes, I think I can see the very bottom! What is this light that is flick'ring about?

(*he stands up, turns, and looks at* GOLAUD)

You . . .

PELLÉAS

Oui, je crois que je vois le fond du gouffre . . . Est-ce la lumière qui tremble ainsi? . . . Vous . . .

GOLAUD

Yes, it was the lantern . . . you see . . . I waved about so to throw the light on the walls . . .

GOLAUD

Oui; c'est la lanterne . . . Voyez, je l'agitais pour éclairer les parois.

PELLÉAS
J'étouffe ici . . . sortons.

GOLAUD
Oui, sortons . . .

PELLÉAS
I'm stifling here . . . let us leave!

GOLAUD
Yes, let's go . . .
(*they go out in silence*)

Scene 3: A terrace at the entrance of the vaults

(*enter* GOLAUD *and* PELLÉAS)

PELLÉAS
Ah! je respire enfin! J'ai cru un instant que j'allais me trouver mal dans ces énormes grottes; j'ai été sur le point de tomber . . . Il y a là un air humide et lourd comme une rosée de plomb, et des ténèbres épaisses comme une pâte empoisonnée. Et maintenant tout l'air de toute la mer! . . . Il y a un vent frais, voyez; frais comme une feuille qui vient de s'ouvrir, sur les petites lames vertes. Tiens! On vient d'arroser les fleurs au pied de la terrasse et l'odeur de la verdure et des roses mouillées monte jusqu'ici . . . Il doit être près de midi, elles sont déjà dans l'ombre de la tour. Il est midi; j'entends sonner les cloches et les enfants descendent sur la plage pour se baigner.
Tiens, voilà notre mère et Mélisande à une fenêtre de la tour.

GOLAUD
Oui, elles se sont réfugiées du côté de l'ombre. A propos de Mélisande, j'ai entendu ce qui s'est passé et ce qui s'est dit hier au soir. Je le sais bien, ce sont là jeux d'enfant; mais il ne faut pas que cela se répète. Elle est très délicate et il faut qu'on la ménage, d'autant plus qu'elle sera peut-être bientôt mère et la moindre émotion pourrait amener un malheur. Ce n'est pas la première fois que je remarque qu'il pourrait y avoir quelque chose entre vous. Vous êtes plus âgé qu'elle; il suffira de vous l'avoir dit . . . Évitez-la autant que possible; mais sans affectation d'ailleurs; sans affectation.

PELLÉAS
Ah! . . . I can breathe again . . . I thought for a while I was going to be ill in those enormous caverns; for a moment I thought I would faint. The very air seemed as heavy and dank as a thick oppressive cloud, and there was a darkness so deep it seemed to hang in poisoned clusters, but now, out here, one breathes the air of the sea! Oh, how fresh is the breeze! How sweet, how joyous! Like a petal that starts to unfold on the delicate stem of a flower . . . Look! They must have been watering the flowers along the terrace for the perfumed smell of lilies and roses is felt even over here . . . it must now be nearly noon . . . for the shadows are creeping close to the tower . . . of course, it's noon, the bells are ringing and I see the children going to the shore to bathe in the sea . . . look, Mélisande and our mother are sitting together at a window of the tower.

GOLAUD
Yes . . . they must have fled from the heat into the cooling shadows . . . With regard to Mélisande, I am aware of what took place and what was spoken last night. Of course I know it was an innocent game, but nevertheless it must not be repeated. Her health is very delicate and she needs to be treated with care, since she may very soon become a mother, and the slightest of shocks might lead to a serious misfortune . . . This is not the first time I have noticed that there might exist something between her and you . . . You are older than she is. What I've told you should be enough. You will avoid her as much as possible, but not too pointedly of course, not too pointedly . . .
(*they go out*)

Scene 4: Before the castle

(*enter* GOLAUD *and* YNIOLD)

GOLAUD

Come, suppose we sit down here a while, Yniold; come sit on my knee. From here we can see whatever happens in the forest. You have not sat on my knee for ever so long. You are neglecting your father! You always play with Mother Mélisande. Look! Why here we are sitting just under the windows of your little mother. And perhaps she's kneeling at her evening prayers, just at this moment. Tell me though, Yniold, she spends much time with your uncle Pelléas, does she not?

GOLAUD

Viens, nous allons nous asseoir ici, Yniold; viens sur mes genoux: nous verrons d'ici ce qui se passe dans la forêt. Je ne te vois plus du tout depuis quelque temps. Tu m'abandonnes aussi tu es toujours chez petite-mère . . . Tiens, nous sommes tout juste assis sous les fenêtres de petite-mère.—Elle fait peut-être sa prière du soir en ce moment . . . Mais dis-moi, Yniold, elle est souvent avec ton oncle Pelléas, n'est-ce pas?

YNIOLD

Yes, yes, she does, dearest Father, whenever you're not there.

YNIOLD

Oui, oui; toujours, petit-père; quand vous n'êtes pas là.

GOLAUD

Ah! Look, I believe someone's crossing the garden with a lantern. But I've been told that they don't love each other . . . it seems they quarrel when they are together . . . eh? Is it true?

GOLAUD

Ah! Tiens, quelqu'un passe avec une lanterne dans le jardin.—Mais on m'a dit qu'ils ne s'aimaient pas . . . Il paraît qu'ils se querellent souvent . . . non? Est-ce vrai?

YNIOLD

Yes, yes, it's true.

YNIOLD

Oui, c'est vrai.

GOLAUD

Yes? Ah, ah! Do you know what it is that they fight about?

GOLAUD

Oui?—Ah! ah!—Mais à propos de quoi se querellent-ils?

YNIOLD

It's all about the doorway . . .

YNIOLD

A propos de la porte.

GOLAUD

What's that? What is that about the doorway? What do you mean by saying that?

GOLAUD

Comment? à propos de la porte?—Qu'est-ce que tu racontes là?—Mais voyons, explique-toi; pourquoi se querellent-ils à propos de la porte?

YNIOLD

Why, because it must not remain open.

YNIOLD

Parce qu'elle ne peut pas être ouverte.

GOLAUD

Who does not wish that the door stay open? Is that the reason that they quarrel?

GOLAUD

Qui ne veut pas qu'elle soit ouverte?—Voyons, pourquoi se querellent-ils?

YNIOLD

I don't quite know, dearest Father; it's all about the light or something . . .

YNIOLD

Je ne sais pas, petit-père, à propos de la lumière.

GOLAUD

It is not about the light that I am asking; I am speaking of the doorway. Do not ever put your hand in your mouth, child . . . Yniold!

GOLAUD

Je ne te parle pas de la lumière: je te parle de la porte . . . Ne mets pas ainsi la main dans la bouche . . . voyons . . .

YNIOLD
Petit-père! petit-père! . . . Je ne le ferai plus . . .

GOLAUD
Voyons; pourquoi pleures-tu? Qu'est-il arrivé?

YNIOLD
Oh! oh! petit-père, vous m'avez fait mal . . .

GOLAUD
Je t'ai fait mal?—Où t'ai-je fait mal? C'est sans le vouloir . . .

YNIOLD
Ici, à mon petit bras . . .

GOLAUD
C'est sans le vouloir; voyons, ne pleure plus, je te donnerai quelque chose demain . . .

YNIOLD
Quoi, petit-père?

GOLAUD
Un carquois et des flèches; mais dis-moi ce que tu sais de la porte.

YNIOLD
De grandes flèches?

GOLAUD
Oui, de très grandes flèches.—Mais pourquoi ne veulent-ils pas que la porte soit ouverte? —Voyons, réponds-moi à la fin!—non, non; n'ouvre pas la bouche pour pleurer. Je ne suis pas fâché. De quoi parlent-ils quand ils sont ensemble?

YNIOLD
Pelléas et petite-mère?

GOLAUD
Oui; de quoi parlent-ils?

YNIOLD
De moi; toujours de moi.

GOLAUD
Et que disent-ils de toi?

YNIOLD
Ils disent que je serai très grand.

GOLAUD
Ah! misère de ma vie! . . . je suis ici comme un aveugle qui cherche son trésor au fond de l'océan! . . . Je suis ici comme un nouveau-né perdu dans la forêt, et vous . . . Mais voyons, Yniold, j'étais distrait; nous allons causer sérieusement. Pelléas et petite-mère ne parlent-ils jamais de moi quand je ne suis pas là? . . .

YNIOLD
Dearest Father! Dearest Father! I will not do it again!

GOLAUD
Come, come! There's surely no reason to cry! What's happened to you?

YNIOLD
Oh! Oh! Dearest Father, you've hurt my arm!

GOLAUD
I did not mean to . . . show me where it hurts. I did not mean to hurt you . . .

YNIOLD
You see, right here on my shoulder . . .

GOLAUD
I did not mean to hurt you, Yniold, you must not cry . . . if you are good I promise to give you a present.

YNIOLD
What, dearest Father?

GOLAUD
I'll give you a quiver of arrows. But now tell me what you know of the doorway.

YNIOLD
A quiver of arrows?

GOLAUD
Yes, with very long arrows . . . Tell me why they don't seem to wish that the door should be open? See here, you must answer my questions. Now, now, do not start to cry again, Yniold. Don't think that I'm displeased. Of what do they talk when they are together?

YNIOLD
Pelléas and my little mother?

GOLAUD
Yes; of what do they talk?

YNIOLD
Of me; they speak of me.

GOLAUD
And what is it that they say?

YNIOLD
How tall I'll be someday when I'm grown up.

GOLAUD
Oh! Oh fury and damnation! . . . I am confused, like a blind man who's searching for a treasure at the bottom of the ocean . . . I grope for light like a newborn child left in the wilderness . . . while they . . . but come, come Yniold, what were we saying? We must keep our mind on what we were saying . . . Pelléas and Mother Mélisande, do they often talk of me when I am not with them?

YNIOLD
Yes, yes, dearest Father.

YNIOLD
Si, si, petit-père.

GOLAUD
Ah! And what is it they are saying?

GOLAUD
Ah! . . . Et que disent-ils de moi?

YNIOLD
They tell me that I will grow up to be just as tall as you.

YNIOLD
Ils disent que je deviendrai aussi grand que vous.

GOLAUD
You're with them all the time?

GOLAUD
Tu es toujours près d'eux?

YNIOLD
Yes, yes, of course, little Father.

YNIOLD
Oui; oui; toujours, petit-père.

GOLAUD
Do they not tell you sometimes to run away and play?

GOLAUD
Ils ne te disent jamais d'aller jouer ailleurs?

YNIOLD
No, dearest Father, they're afraid to have me go away.

YNIOLD
Non, petit-père; ils ont peur quand je ne suis pas là.

GOLAUD
They're afraid . . . ? How can you tell they're afraid?

GOLAUD
Ils ont peur? . . . à quoi vois-tu qu'ils ont peur?

YNIOLD
I see them tremble in the darkness . . .

YNIOLD
Ils pleuront toujours dans l'obscurité.

GOLAUD
Ah ha!

GOLAUD
Ah! ah! . . .

YNIOLD
That makes me also feel so sad!

YNIOLD
Cela fait pleurer aussi . . .

GOLAUD
Yes, yes?

GOLAUD
Oui, oui . . .

YNIOLD
I see her crying, dearest Father!

YNIOLD
Elle est pâle, petit-père.

GOLAUD
Ah! Ah! Give me patience, oh Lord, give me patience . . .

GOLAUD
Ah! ah! . . . patience, mon Dieu, patience . . .

YNIOLD
What, dearest Father?

YNIOLD
Quoi, petit-père?

GOLAUD
Nothing, child, it was nothing . . . I saw a wolf passing by in the forest . . . Do they kiss from time to time? Eh?

GOLAUD
Rien, rien, mon enfant.—J'ai vu passer un loup dans la forêt.—Ils s'embrassent quelque fois?—Non?

YNIOLD
I don't think so, dearest Father. No, no . . . Oh! Yes, dearest Father, yes, once they did . . . once they did when it rained . . .

YNIOLD
Ils s'embrassent, petit-père?—Non, non.—Ah! si, petit-père, si; une fois . . . une fois qu'il pleuvait . . .

GOLAUD
You are sure you have seen it? . . . Tell me how, yes how, in what way did they kiss?

GOLAUD
Ils se sont embrassés?—Mais comment, comment se sont-ils embrassés?—

YNIOLD
Why, like this, dearest Father, just like this . . . (*laughing, he gives him a kiss on the mouth*)
Oh! oh! How it tickles, dearest Father! . . . You have scratched me with your whiskers! Look, oh, look dearest Father . . . did you notice, your hair is turning gray . . . so gray, so gray.

YNIOLD
Comme ça, petit-père, comme ça! . . . Ah! ah! votre barbe, petit-père! . . . Elle pique! elle pique! Elle devient toute grise, petit-père, et vos cheveux aussi; tout gris, tout gris . . . Ah! ah! petite-mère a allumé sa

lampe. Il fait clair, petit-père; il fait clair.

GOLAUD
Oui; il commence à faire clair . . .

YNIOLD
Allons-y aussi, petit-père . . .

GOLAUD
Où veux-tu aller?

YNIOLD
Où il fait clair, petit-père.

GOLAUD
Non, non, mon enfant: restons encore un peu dans l'ombre . . . on ne sait pas, on ne sait pas encore . . . Je crois que Pelléas est fou . . .

YNIOLD
Non, petit-père, il n'est pas fou, mais il est très bon.

GOLAUD
Veux-tu voir petite-mère?

YNIOLD
Oui, oui; je veux la voir!

GOLAUD
Ne fais pas de bruit; je vais te hisser jusqu'à la fenêtre. Elle est trop haute pour moi, bien que je sois si grand . . . Ne fais pas le moindre bruit; petite-mère aurait terriblement peur . . . La vois-tu?—Est-elle dans la chambre?

YNIOLD
Oui . . . Oh! il fait clair!

GOLAUD
Elle est seule?

YNIOLD
Oui . . . non, non; mon oncle Pelléas y est aussi.

GOLAUD
Il! . . .

YNIOLD
Ah! ah! petit-père! vous m'avez fait mal! . . .

GOLAUD
Ce n'est rien; tais-toi; je ne le ferai plus; regarde, regarde, Yniold! . . . J'ai trébuché; parle plus bas. Que font-ils?—

YNIOLD
Ils ne font rien, petit-père.

GOLAUD
Sont-ils près l'un de l'autre? Est-ce qu'ils parlent?

(*the window under which they are sitting is lighted up, and the light falls upon them*)
Oh! Look! Mother Mélisande must be there in the tower. There's a light, dearest Father, there's a light . . .

GOLAUD
Yes, I see a little light.

YNIOLD
Let us go inside, dearest Father, let us go in too.

GOLAUD
Where is it you want to go?

YNIOLD
Up there where it's light, dearest Father.

GOLAUD
No, no, Yniold. Let's stay a while here in the shadow. One can't be certain, one does not know as yet . . . I think Pelléas must be mad.

YNIOLD
No, dearest Father, he is not mad, he is very kind.

GOLAUD
Would you like to see your mother?

YNIOLD
Yes, yes, I'd like to see her.

GOLAUD
Then be very quiet, I will lift you up as high as the window. It is too high for me, though I am pretty tall. (*he lifts up the child*)
Do not make the slightest noise. We must be careful, we must not frighten little Mother . . . Can you see her? Is she in the room?

YNIOLD
Yes . . . oh, there's so much light!

GOLAUD
Is she alone there?

YNIOLD
Yes . . . no, no! My uncle Pelléas is also in the room.

GOLAUD
He . . .

YNIOLD
Oh! Oh! Dearest Father, you have hurt me again!

GOLAUD
Never mind; Yniold, be quiet . . . I will be careful . . . Keep looking, keep looking, Yniold! Don't be afraid! Speak very softly . . . what are they doing?

YNIOLD
Nothing at all, dearest Father.

GOLAUD
Are they close to each other? Are they speaking?

YNIOLD
No, dearest Father, they are very quiet.

GOLAUD
But what are they doing?

YNIOLD
They are gazing at the fire.

GOLAUD
He and she?

YNIOLD
Yes, dearest Father.

GOLAUD
And they do not speak?

YNIOLD
No, dearest Father. Their eyes remain wide open.

GOLAUD
Aren't they coming nearer each other?

YNIOLD
No, dearest Father, and their eyes remain wide open . . . I'm afraid, so afraid!

GOLAUD
Of what are you afraid? Keep looking! Keep looking!

YNIOLD
Dearest Father, put me down, I beg you . . .

GOLAUD
Keep looking!

YNIOLD
Oh! I'm going to scream, dearest Father! Put me down, I beg you! You must let me down now!

GOLAUD
Come, we'll go and see now what has taken place! (*they go out*)

YNIOLD
Non, petit-père; ils ne parlent pas.

GOLAUD
Mais que font-ils?

YNIOLD
Ils regardent la lumière.

GOLAUD
Tous les deux?

YNIOLD
Oui, petit-père.

GOLAUD
Ils de disent rien?

YNIOLD
Non, petit-père; ils ne ferment pas les yeux.

GOLAUD
Ils ne s'approchent pas l'un de l'autre?

YNIOLD
Non, petit-père; ils ne bougent pas, ils ne ferment jamais les yeux . . . J'ai terriblement peur . . .

GOLAUD
De quoi donc as-tu peur? Regarde! Regarde!

YNIOLD
Petit-père, laissez-moi descendre!

GOLAUD
Regarde!

YNIOLD
Oh! je vais crier, petit-père! Laissez-moi descendre! laissez-moi descendre!

GOLAUD
Viens! nous allons voir ce qui est arrivé.

ACT IV

Scene 1: A room in the castle

(PELLÉAS *and* MÉLISANDE *enter and meet.*)

PELLÉAS
Où vas-tu? Il faut que je te parle ce soir. Te verrai-je?

MÉLISANDE
Oui.

PELLÉAS
Je sors de la chambre de mon père. Il va mieux. Le médecin nous a dit qu'il était sauvé. Il m'a reconnu. Il m'a pris la main, et il m'a dit de cet air étrange qu'il a depuis qu'il est malade: «Est-ce toi, Pelléas? Tiens, je ne l'avais jamais remarqué, mais tu as le visage grave et amical de ceux qui ne vivront pas longtemps. Il faut voyager; il faut voyager . . .» C'est étrange; je vais lui obéir . . . Ma mère l'écoutait et pleurait de joie. Tu ne t'en es pas aperçue? Toute la maison semble déjà revivre, on entend respirer, on entend marcher . . . Écoute, j'entends parler derrière cette porte. Vite, vite, réponds vite, où te verrai-je?

MÉLISANDE
Où veux-tu?

PELLÉAS
Dans le parc: près de la fontaine des aveugles? Veux-tu? Viendras-tu?

MÉLISANDE
Oui.

PELLÉAS
Ce sera le dernier soir. Je vais voyager comme mon père l'a dit. Tu ne me verras plus . . .

MÉLISANDE
Ne dis pas cela, Pelléas . . . Je te verrai toujours; je te regarderai toujours . . .

PELLÉAS
Tu auras beau regarder . . . je serai si loin que tu ne pourras plus me voir.

MÉLISANDE
Qu'est-il arrivé, Pelléas? Je ne comprends plus ce que tu dis . . .

PELLÉAS
Va-t-en, va-t-en, séparons-nous. J'entends parler derrière cette porte.

PELLÉAS
Mélisande . . . I have something important to tell you . . . may I see you?

MÉLISANDE
Yes.

PELLÉAS
Listen . . . I have just seen my father, he's much better . . . and the physician assures us his life is saved . . . he knew me at once. First he took my hands and then he spoke with that faraway look he's had ever since he has been ailing: "Is it you, Pelléas? Strange, I have not noticed it before . . . nevertheless, you have the gentle look of one who won't live very long . . . you must leave this place, you must go away!" He is right! And I must obey him . . . my mother heard him speak and wept tears of joy. And you must have noticed it also . . . the very air is alive with excitement. Everyone's talking and smiling and coming to life! . . . One moment! I hear someone moving there behind this door. . . . Tell me quickly, Mélisande, where can you see me?

MÉLISANDE
Where would you like to?

PELLÉAS
In the park beside the Fountain of the Blind Men? You'll come, you'll be there?

MÉLISANDE
Yes.

PELLÉAS
Tonight will be the very last time . . . I'm going to leave, just as my father has told me. You will see me no more.

MÉLISANDE
That is not so, Pelléas . . . for I shall always see you. Yes, I shall be looking at you always . . .

PELLÉAS
It will be useless to look, for I'll be so far, you'll never be able to see me . . .

MÉLISANDE
What is the matter, Pelléas? I can hardly understand what you are saying?

PELLÉAS
Now go . . . they must not hear us. There's someone listening behind this doorway . . .
(PELLÉAS *leaves*)

Scene 2

(*enter* ARKEL)

ARKEL

Now that the father of Pelléas has been saved, and the fearful disease, that sturdy old minister of death, has gone from the castle, some measure of joy and a gleam of the sun may at last find entrance to our house. And it was time. For ever since you came here, we have lived in the darkness, moving in whispers round an invalid's chamber. My poor child, I've been sorry for you, Mélisande . . . I've watched you often, seemingly carefree and never complaining, and yet with that strange and hurt expression of one who awaits a disaster and pines away at the thought of it . . . I cannot explain how I felt . . . but I've been sorry to see you suffer, for you're much too young and too lovely to move day and night in the shadow of death and despair . . . but now at last all this will be changed. At my age—and this, perhaps is the greatest lesson the years have taught me, at my age—I have learned to trust in the ultimate wisdom of life and of destiny, and I've always found that someone who's young and lovely creates around him feelings of youthful excitement, joy and delight. You will now be the one whose gentle innocent charm will open the door for sunshine and joy . . . Mélisande, what makes you stand like that without speaking or raising your eyes? Let me look at you closely . . . I have kissed you but one single time . . . the day when you arrived. And yet, believe me, an old man feels the need now and then to touch with his lips the brow of a maid or the cheek of a child, to keep on trusting in the freshness of life and drive away for a moment the menaces of death. Are my lips so old that you fear them? Oh, I've been concerned about you all these months . . .

ARKËL

Maintenant que le père de Pelléas est sauvé, et que la maladie, la vieille servante de la mort, a quitté le château, un peu de joie et un peu de soleil vont enfin rentrer dans la maison . . . Il était temps!—Car depuis ta venue, on n'a vécu ici qu'en chuchotant autour d'une chambre fermée . . . Et vraiment, j'avais pitié de toi, Mélisande . . . Je t'observais, tu étais là, insouciante peut-être, mais avec l'air étrange et égaré de quelqu'un qui attendrait toujours un grand malheur, au soleil, dans un beau jardin . . . Je ne puis pas expliquer . . . Mais j'étais triste de te voir ainsi; car tu es trop jeune et trop belle pour vivre déjà, jour et nuit, sous l'haleine de la mort . . . Mais à présent tout cela va changer. A mon âge,—et c'est peut-être là le fruit le plus sûr de ma vie,—à mon âge, j'ai acquis je ne sais quelle foi à la fidélité des événements, et j'ai toujours vu que tout être jeune et beau, créait autour de lui des événements jeunes, beaux et heureux . . . Et c'est toi, maintenant, qui vas ouvrir la porte à l'ère nouvelle que j'entrevois . . . Viens ici; pourquoi restes-tu là sans répondre et sans lever les yeux?—Je ne t'ai embrassée qu'une seule fois jusqu'ici, le jour de ta venue; et cependant, les vieillards ont besoin de toucher quelquefois de leurs lèvres, le front d'une femme ou la joue d'un enfant, pour croire encore à la fraîcheur de la vie et éloigner un moment les menaces de la mort. As-tu peur de mes vieilles lèvres? Comme j'avais pitié de toi ces mois-ci! . . .

MÉLISANDE

But Grandfather, I have not been unhappy . . .

MÉLISANDE

Grand-père, je n'étais pas malheureuse . . .

ARKËL
Laisse-moi te regarder ainsi, de tout près, un moment . . . on a tant besoin de beauté aux côtés de la mort . . .

GOLAUD
Pelléas part ce soir.

ARKËL
Tu as du sang sur le front.—Qu'as-tu fait?

GOLAUD
Rien, rien . . . j'ai passé au travers d'une haie d'épines.

MÉLISANDE
Baissez un peu la tête, seigneur . . . Je vais essuyer votre front . . .

GOLAUD
Je ne veux pas que tu me touches, entends-tu? Va-t'en, va-t'en!—Je ne te parle pas.—Où est mon épée?—Je venais chercher mon épée . . .

MÉLISANDE
Ici; sur le prie-Dieu.

GOLAUD
Apporte-la.—On vient encore de trouver un paysan mort de faim, le long de la mer. On dirait qu'ils tiennent tous à mourir sous nos yeux.—Eh bien, mon épée?—Pourquoi tremblez-vous ainsi?—Je ne vais pas vous tuer. Je voulais simplement examiner la lame. Je n'emploie pas l'épée à ces usages. Pourquoi m'examinez-vous comme un pauvre?—Je ne viens pas vous demander l'aumône. Vous espérez voir quelque chose dans mes yeux, sans que je voie quelque chose dans les vôtres?—Croyez-vous que je sache quelque chose?—Voyez-vous ces grands yeux?—On dirait qu'ils sont fiers d'être riches . . .

ARKËL
Je n'y vois qu'une grande innocence . . .

GOLAUD
Une grande innocence! . . . Ils sont plus grands que l'innocence! . . . Ils sont plus purs que les yeux d'un agneau . . . Ils donneraient à Dieu des leçons d'innocence! Une grande innocence! Écoutez: j'en suis si près que je sens la fraîcheur de leurs cils quand ils clignent; et cependant, je suis moins loin

ARKEL
Let me take a good look at you . . . come quite close . . . let me look . . . even near the gates of death, a craving for beauty governs our hearts. . . .
(*enter* GOLAUD)

GOLAUD
Pelléas must leave at once . . .

ARKEL
You have some blood on your forehead . . . why is that?

GOLAUD
It's nothing . . . nothing. I was trying to pass through a hedgerow of thorns . . .

MÉLISANDE
Bend your head just a little, My Lord . . . let me wipe the blood from your forehead . . .

GOLAUD
I do not want you to touch me, do you hear? Begone! I did not speak to you. Where is my sword? I have come to look for my sword . . .

MÉLISANDE
It is there in the corner.

GOLAUD
Bring it here.
(*to* ARKEL)
Another peasant was found lying by the sea, starved to death, yes, starved to death. They insist, it seems, on dying under our windows.
(*to* MÉLISANDE)
Well then, where's my sword? What makes you tremble like that? I am not going to kill you. I want to see if the blade might need sharp'ning. I would not use a sword to kill a woman. Don't look at me as if I were a beggar . . . I have not come to ask a favor. Are you hoping to see something written in my eyes, without revealing what yours might have to tell me? Are you afraid I'll discover your secret? Do you see those wide eyes . . . It is as though they are proud of their treasures . . .

ARKEL
I can see a great innocence only . . .

GOLAUD
A great innocence only! There is far more there than innocence . . . They are as pure as the eyes of a lamb. Why God has made them a model of innocent virtue. A great innocence only! Just look . . . I am so close I can trace every line in the shadow of her lashes, but nevertheless, I could sooner solve the riddle of the universe than the secret of those eyes! . . . A great innocence only! More than innocence surely! One

would think that one sees the reflection of all of the angels of heaven. I know them well, those eyes! I have seen them at work! Keep them shut! Keep them shut! Or I'll see that you close them forever! I cannot understand why you're acting so frightened. What I say is perfectly simple . . . I'm not given to idle suspicions. . . . If I had something else on my mind, I would not hide it for a moment. Ah! Ha! Do not try to escape! Come here! Give me your hand! Ah! You're running a fever . . . go away! Your flesh disgusts me, I tell you! Go away! Do not imagine I'd let you run away.
(*he seizes her by the hair*)
You shall stay with me to the end. Down you go! On your knees! Ah! Oh! Your lovely hair may after all be good for something! First up and then downward . . . to the left, then to the right side . . . Absalom! Absalom! First up and then downward, to the left side, to the right side . . . there, you see? There, you see? See how I laugh like an old man . . . Ha! ha! ha!

des grands secrets de l'autre monde que du plus petit secret de ces yeux! . . . Une grande innocence! . . . Plus que de l'innocence! On dirait que les anges du ciel y célèbrent sans cesse un baptême! . . . Je les connais ces yeux! Je les ai vus à l'œuvre! Fermez-les! fermez-les! ou je vais les fermer pour longtemps! . . .—Ne mettez pas ainsi la main à la gorge; je dis une chose très simple . . . Je n'ai pas d'arrière-pensée . . . Si j'avais une arrière-pensée, pourquoi ne la diraisje pas? Ah! ah!—ne tâchez pas de fuir!—Ici!—Donnez-moi cette main!—Ah! vos mains sont trop chaudes . . . Allez-vous-en! Votre chair me dégoûte! . . .—Il ne s'agit plus de fuir à présent!—Vous allez me suivre à genoux!—A genoux!—A genoux devant moi!—Ah! ah! vos longs cheveux servent enfin à quelque chose! . . . A droite en puis à gauche!—A gauche et puis à droite!—Absalon! Absalon!—En avant! en arrière! Jusqu'à terre! jusqu'à terre! . . . Vous voyez, vous voyez; je ris déjà comme un viellard . . . Ah! ah! ah!

ARKEL
Golaud!

ARKËL
Golaud! . . .

GOLAUD
You may do just as you please, do you see! All this has not the least importance for me . . . I'm much too old; besides I am not playing the spy. I shall leave it to chance. And then, oh! Then! Even then just because it's the custom. Even then just because it's the custom . . .
(GOLAUD *goes out*)

GOLAUD
Vous ferez comme il vous plaira, voyez-vous.—Je n'attache aucune importance à cela.—Je suis trop vieux; et puis, je ne suis pas un espion. J'attendrai le hasard; et alors . . . Oh! alors! . . . simplement parce que c'est l'usage; simplement parce que c'est l'usage . . .

ARKEL
I can hardly believe it . . . he's out of his mind.

ARKËL
Qu'a-t-il donc?—Il est ivre?

MÉLISANDE
No . . . no . . . but he loves me no more. I am very unhappy . . .

MÉLISANDE
Non, non; mais il ne m'aime plus . . . Je ne suis pas heureuse! . . .

ARKEL
If I were God, I'd show more pity for the hearts of men . . .

ARKËL
Si j'étais Dieu, j'aurais pitié du cœur des hommes . . .

Scene 3: A fountain in the park

(*The child* YNIOLD *is discovered trying to move a large boulder.*)

YNIOLD

Oh! Cette pierre est lourde . . . elle est plus lourde que moi. —Elle est plus lourde que tout le monde.—Elle est plus lourde que tout.

Je vois ma balle d'or entre le rocher et cette méchante pierre, et je ne puis pas y atteindre . . . Mon petit bras n'est pas assez long—et cette pierre ne veut pas être soulevée . . . On dirait qu'elle a des racines dans la terre . . .

Oh! oh! J'entends pleurer les moutons.—Tiens! Il n'y a plus de soleil!—Ils arrivent les petits moutons; ils arrivent . . . Il y en a! . . . Il y en a! . . . Ils ont eu peur du noir . . . Ils se serrent. Ils se serrent! Ils pleurent . . . et ils vont vite! . . . Il y en a qui voudraient prendre à droite . . . Ils voudraient tous aller à droite. Ils ne peuvent pas! . . . Le berger leur jette de la terre! . . . Ah! ah! . . . Ils vont passer par ici . . . Je vais les voir de près.—Comme il y en a! . . .—Maintenant, ils se taisent tous. Berger? Pourquoi ne parlent-ils plus?

LE BERG

Parce que ce n'est pas le chemin de l'étable!—

YNIOLD

Où vont-ils? Berger? Berger? Où vont-ils? . . . Il ne m'entend plus. Ils sont déjà trop loin . . . Ils ne font plus de bruit.—Ce n'est pas le chemin de l'étable . . . Où vont-ils dormir cette nuit? . . . Oh! oh! il fait trop noir . . . Je vais dire quelque chose à quelqu'un!

YNIOLD

Oh, what a heavy boulder . . . it is much heavier than I. It must weigh more than the whole creation. Nothing weighs more than this rock. My pretty toy has fallen in between the rock and the nasty big boulder, and I am not able to reach it. No, my arm is not long enough, and this great boulder is stubborn and will not be lifted. It is just as if it were rooted here forever.

(*distant bleating of sheep is heard*)

Oh, oh! I hear the weeping of sheep . . . Oh, there's no sunshine any more. All the little sheep are coming here; they are coming . . . there are so many, there are so many! They're scared of the dark . . . How they're pushing! How they're crowding! They are crying, they're in a hurry! There are some that are pushing to the right side . . . and now they want to go the other way . . . but they can't do that . . . Now the shepherd pelts them with pebbles . . . Oh, oh! Now they are coming over here . . . I'll see them from close by. There are so many! All of a sudden they're keeping so still! Shepherd! Why don't they talk any more?

SHEPHERD (*unseen*)

That's because they are not on their way to the stable . . .

YNIOLD

Where are they going? Shepherd? Shepherd? Where are they going? He cannot hear me. They've gone too far away . . . They're making no more noise. They were on their way to the stable . . . Then where will they sleep tonight? Oh, oh! It is so dark . . . I must tell this to someone who can help me . . .

(*he goes out*)

Scene 4

(*Enter* PELLÉAS)

PELLÉAS

This is the last time, the very last time. Now all must be ended. I've been playing like a child with fire, the existence of which I did not suspect. I have played as if in a dream with all the snares of destiny around me . . . What is it that wakes me up all at once? I'll escape with a cry of joy and of dismay. Just as a blind man might escape from a burning dwelling . . . I shall tell her the truth . . . But it's late and she is not here. It would be better if I left without seeing her. I must remember to observe her eyes. There is a look in her eyes that I must recapture. At times I could swear a century had passed since I have seen her. What is that strange and magical light within her eyes. There's nothing left for me if I leave her like that. A memory is nothing; like trying to carry water in a broken container. But tonight I will look at her, I will gaze deep into her heart . . . and I will tell her all the things that I never dared tell her.

(*enter* MÉLISANDE)

PELLÉAS

C'est le dernier soir . . . le dernier soir . . . Il faut que tout finisse . . . J'ai joué comme un enfant autour d'une chose que je ne soupçonnais pas . . . J'ai joué en rêve autour des pièges de la destinée . . . Qui est-ce qui m'a réveillé tout à coup? Je vais fuir en criant de joie et de douleur comme un aveugle qui fuirait l'incendie de sa maison . . . Je vais lui dire que je vais fuir . . . Il est tard; elle ne vient pas . . . Je ferais mieux de m'en aller sans la revoir . . . Il faut que je la regarde bien cette fois-ci . . . Il y a des choses que je ne me rappelle plus . . . on dirait, par moments, qu'il y a plus de cent ans que je ne l'ai vue . . . Et je n'ai pas encore regardé son regard . . . Il ne me reste rien si je m'en vais ainsi. Et tous ces souvenirs . . . c'est comme si j'emportais un peu d'eau dans un sac de mousseline . . . Il faut que je la voie une dernière fois, jusqu'au fond de son cœur . . . Il faut que je lui dise tout ce que je n'ai pas dit . . .

MÉLISANDE

Pelléas!

MÉLISANDE

Pelléas!

PELLÉAS

Mélisande! Is it you, Mélisande?

PELLÉAS

Mélisande!—Est-ce toi, Mélisande?

MÉLISANDE

Yes.

MÉLISANDE

Oui.

PELLÉAS

Come closer. You might be seen standing there in the moonlight. Come over here, there are so many things I must ask you . . . come here where the shadows will protect us.

PELLÉAS

Viens ici: ne reste pas au bord du clair de lune.—Viens ici. Nous avons tant de choses à nous dire . . . Viens ici dans l'ombre du tilleul.

MÉLISANDE

Let me stay in the light . . .

MÉLISANDE

Laissez-moi dans la clarté . . .

PELLÉAS

They could easily see us from the windows of the tower. Come here, in here we'll be perfectly safe . . . be careful; suppose we were seen!

PELLÉAS

On pourrait nous voir des fenêtres de la tour. Viens ici; ici, nous n'avons rien à craindre.—Prends garde; on pourrait nous voir . . .

MÉLISANDE
Je veux qu'on me voie . . .

PELLÉAS
Qu'as-tu donc?—Tu as pu sortir sans qu'on s'en soit aperçu?

MÉLISANDE
Oui; votre frère dormait . . .

PELLÉAS
Il est tard.—Dans une heure on fermera les portes. Il faut prendre garde. Pourquoi es-tu venue si tard?

MÉLISANDE
Votre frère avait un mauvais rêve. Et puis ma robe s'est accrochée aux clous de la porte. Voyez, elle est déchirée. J'ai perdu tout ce temps et j'ai couru . . .

PELLÉAS
Ma pauvre Mélisande! . . . J'aurais presque peur de te toucher . . . Tu es encore hors d'haleine comme un oiseau pourchassé . . . C'est pour moi, pour moi que tu fais tout cela? . . . J'entends battre ton cœur comme si c'était le mien . . . Viens ici . . . plus près, plus près de moi . . .

MÉLISANDE
Pourquoi riez-vous?

PELLÉAS
Je ne ris pas;—ou bien je ris de joie, sans le savoir . . . Il y aurait plutôt de quoi pleurer . . .

MÉLISANDE
Nous sommes venus ici il y a bien longtemps . . . Je me rappelle.

PELLÉAS
Oui . . . Il y a de longs mois. —Alors, je ne savais pas . . . Sais-tu pourquoi je t'ai demandé de venir ce soir?

MÉLISANDE
Non.

PELLÉAS
C'est peut-être la dernière fois que je te vois . . . Il faut que je m'en aille pour toujours . . .

MÉLISANDE
Pourquoi dis-tu toujours que tu t'en vas? . . .

PELLÉAS
Je dois te dire ce que tu sais déjà?—Tu ne sais pas ce que je vais te dire?

MÉLISANDE
I don't mind if they see us!

PELLÉAS
What has happened . . . did you manage to leave the place without being seen?

MÉLISANDE
Yes, your brother fell asleep . . .

PELLÉAS
It's so late . . . in an hour the gates will be locked. We must be careful . . . but tell me why you came so late.

MÉLISANDE
It was because your brother was quite restless. As I was leaving, one of my sleeves got caught in the doorway . . . Look here, you see, it is torn . . . it was getting so late I had to run . . .

PELLÉAS
My poor Mélisande! You are trembling like a little child. Yes, you are still out of breath, just like a frightened bird. And you ran because you wanted to see me? I can hear your heart beat just as if it were my own . . . Let me hold you. Come closer still . . .

MÉLISANDE
But why do you laugh?

PELLÉAS
I did not laugh, or else I laughed from sheer joy, just like a child. Perhaps my laughter should really turn into tears . . .

MÉLISANDE
This is the fountain where we met one day . . . I remember . . .

PELLÉAS
Yes, that was so long ago . . . but then I was not aware . . . Do you know why I have asked you to come here tonight?

MÉLISANDE
No.

PELLÉAS
Don't you know that this is the very last time we'll be together . . . that I am going away forever.

MÉLISANDE
Why must you always speak of that?

PELLÉAS
And must I tell you what you already know? Don't you know what I'm going to tell you?

MÉLISANDE

I don't know, Pelléas . . . how should I know?

PELLÉAS

Surely you must know the reason why I have to leave you . . . surely you know that it is because . . . (*he kisses her suddenly*) I love you.

MÉLISANDE

I love you also . . .

PELLÉAS

What did you say, Mélisande! I could hardly hear what you said . . . All has vanished . . . the moon and the stars stand still . . . When you said it, your voice seemed to come from far away . . . and I was hardly able to hear you . . . You love me? You love me also? How long have you known it?

MÉLISANDE

I've always known it, from the very first day . . .

PELLÉAS

One would think that your voice had come over the sea in a cloud . . . I don't think I have ever heard it till now. It's as though drops of rain fell on my heart! You said it so quietly . . . like an angel answering questions. I can hardly believe it, Mélisande . . . But why should you love me? And why do you love me? Is it true, what you have said? You would not deceive me . . . you would not pretend in order to console me?

MÉLISANDE

No, I always tell the truth, except to your brother . . .

PELLÉAS

Oh! How you utter these words! Your voice, your voice! It sounds as fresh and as clear as a spring! It caresses my ears like gentle music and it falls like fresh water on my lips . . . let me hold, let me hold your hands. Oh, your hands are so tiny. Oh! Who could have dreamed you were so very lovely. I have never known a loveliness to compare with yours. All my life, all my life, I searched in heaven and earth, looked and looked in vain, trying to discover such loveliness as I desired . . . and now today . . . today I found it here in your eyes. I don't believe there has ever been on earth a woman as lovely. What happened . . . it's almost as if your heart stopped beating . . .

MÉLISANDE

Mais non, mais non; je ne sais rien . . .

PELLÉAS

Tu ne sais pas pourquoi il faut que je m'éloigne . . . Tu ne sais pas que c'est parce que . . . je t'aime . . .

MÉLISANDE

Je t'aime aussi . . .

PELLÉAS

Oh! Qu'as-tu dit, Mélisande! Je ne l'ai presque pas entendu! . . . On a brisé la glace avec des fers rougis! . . . Tu dis cela d'une voix qui vient du bout du monde! . . . Je ne t'ai presque pas entendu . . . Tu m'aimes?—Tu m'aimes aussi? . . . Depuis quand m'aimes-tu?

MÉLISANDE

Depuis toujours . . . Depuis que je t'ai vu . . .

PELLÉAS

Oh! comme tu dis cela! . . . On dirait que ta voix a passé sur la mer au printemps! . . . je ne l'ai jamais entendue jusqu'ici . . . on dirait qu'il a plu sur mon cœur! Tu dis cela si franchement! . . . Comme un ange qu'on interroge! . . . Je ne puis pas le croire, Mélisande! . . . Pourquoi m'aimerais-tu?—Mais pourquoi m'aimes-tu?—Est-ce vrai ce que tu dis?—Tu ne me trompes pas?—Tu ne mens pas un peu, pour me faire sourire? . . .

MÉLISANDE

Non; je ne mens jamais; je ne mens qu'à ton frère . . .

PELLÉAS

Oh! comme tu dis cela! . . . Ta voix! ta voix . . . Elle est plus fraîche et plus franche que l'eau! . . . On dirait de l'eau pure sur mes lèvres! . . . On dirait de l'eau pure sur mes mains . . . Donne-moi, donne-moi tes mains . . . Oh! tes mains sont petites! . . . Je ne savais pas que tu étais si belle! . . . Je n'avais jamais rien vu d'aussi beau, avant toi . . . J'étais inquiet, je cherchais partout dans la maison . . . je cherchais partout dans la campagne . . . Et je ne trouvais pas la beauté . . . Et maintenant je t'ai trouvée! . . . Je t'ai trouvée! . . . Je ne crois pas qu'il y ait sur la terre une femme plus belle! . . . Où es-tu?—Je ne t'entends plus respirer . . .

MÉLISANDE

C'est que je te regarde . . .

PELLÉAS

Pourquoi me regardes-tu si gravement!—Nous sommes déjà dans l'ombre.—Il fait trop noir sous cet arbre. Viens dans la lumière. Nous ne pouvons pas voir combien nous sommes heureux. Viens, viens; il nous reste si peu de temps . . .

MÉLISANDE

Non, non; restons ici . . . Je suis plus près de toi dans l'obscurité . . .

PELLÉAS

Où sont tes yeux?—Tu ne vas pas me fuir?—Tu ne songes pas à moi en ce moment.

MÉLISANDE

Mais si, je ne songe qu'à toi . . .

PELLÉAS

Tu regardais ailleurs . . .

MÉLISANDE

Je te voyais ailleurs . . .

PELLÉAS

Tu es distraite . . . Qu'as-tu donc?—Tu ne me sembles pas heureuse . . .

MÉLISANDE

Si, si; je suis heureuse, mais je suis triste . . .

PELLÉAS

Quel est ce bruit?—On ferme les portes! . . .

MÉLISANDE

Oui, on a fermé les portes . . .

PELLÉAS

Nous ne pouvons plus entrer!—Entends-tu les verrous!—Écoute! écoute! . . . les grandes chaînes! . . . Il est trop tard, il est trop tard! . . .

MÉLISANDE

Tant mieux! tant mieux!

PELLÉAS

Tu? . . . Voilà, voilà! . . . Ce n'est plus nous qui le voulons! . . . Tout est perdu, tout est sauvé! tout est sauvé ce soir!—Viens! viens . . . Mon cœur bat comme un fou jusqu'au fond de ma gorge . . . Écoute! mon cœur est sur le point de m'étrangler . . . Viens! viens! . . . Ah! qu'il fait beau dans les ténèbres! . . .

MÉLISANDE

Our hearts are beating together . . .

PELLÉAS

Why do you look at me so sadly? The shadows are closing upon us . . . it's grown so dark by the fountain. Come into the moonlight. Here, in the darkness our happiness can hardly be seen. Come, come, we have only a few minutes left.

MÉLISANDE

No, no, let's stay where we are. Here in the dark of night I belong to you.

PELLÉAS

Where are your eyes? Where are your lovely eyes? What are you thinking of at this moment?

MÉLISANDE

Of you, of you alone.

PELLÉAS

You gazed far away . . .

MÉLISANDE

I saw you far away . . .

PELLÉAS

What is the matter, Mélisande! I don't believe you are happy . . .

MÉLISANDE

Yes, yes, I'm very happy, but I am sad . . .

PELLÉAS

What is that noise? They're closing the gateway.

MÉLISANDE

Yes, I heard them shut the gateway . . .

PELLÉAS

We will not be able to get back! Can you hear the chains? Can you hear them? Just listen . . . The gate has been bolted. Now it's too late, we cannot return . . .

MÉLISANDE

I'm glad, so glad . . .

PELLÉAS

Oh . . . of course, of course, we're in the hands of destiny. If all is lost, then we are free, yes, we are free forever. Come, come, my heart is beating madly. I know it will choke me . . .

(*he takes her in his arms*)

Can you hear it? My heart is nearly bursting in my breast. Come . . . Ah, it's so lovely here in the darkness!

MÉLISANDE
Who is standing there, standing and watching?

PELLÉAS
No one is watching.

MÉLISANDE
I heard a noise there.

PELLÉAS
It is only your heart that beats in the darkness.

MÉLISANDE
I heard a rustling of the leaves.

PELLÉAS
It's the wind beginning to moan. It had calmed down a while and now it starts again.

MÉLISANDE
I see our shadows down there in the light.

PELLÉAS
They seem to love each other in the moonlight. Ah! Our shadows love each other also. Can you see them, Mélisande?

MÉLISANDE
Ah! He's hiding behind a tree.

PELLÉAS
Who?

MÉLISANDE
Golaud!

PELLÉAS
Golaud? Where? I cannot see him . . .

MÉLISANDE
There, right there in our shadow.

PELLÉAS
Yes, now I see him. We must not turn round too suddenly.

MÉLISANDE
He has brought his sword . . .

PELLÉAS
And mine is not with me . . .

MÉLISANDE
He has seen us . . . He must have seen us kiss . . .

PELLÉAS
He does not know that we also see him. Do not move; do not turn your head . . . be perfectly still . . . He stands there watching. But you can still escape him . . . go on, run away . . . keep running over there . . . I will delay him, I will hold him back . . .

MÉLISANDE
No.

MÉLISANDE
Il y a quelqu'un derrière nous! . . .

PELLÉAS
Je ne vois personne . . .

MÉLISANDE
J'ai entendu du bruit . . .

PELLÉAS
Je n'entends que ton cœur dans l'obscurité . . .

MÉLISANDE
J'ai entendu craquer les feuilles mortes . . .

PELLÉAS
C'est le vent qui s'est tû tout à coup . . . Il est tombé pendant que nous nous embrassions . . .

MÉLISANDE
Comme nos ombres sont grandes ce soir! . . .

PELLÉAS
Elles s'enlacent jusqu'au fond du jardin . . . Oh! qu'elles s'embrassent loin de nous! . . . Regarde! Regarde! . . .

MÉLISANDE
A-a-h!—Il est derrière un arbre!

PELLÉAS
Qui?

MÉLISANDE
Golaud!

PELLÉAS
Golaud?—où donc?—je ne vois rien . . .

MÉLISANDE
Là . . . au bout de nos ombres . . .

PELLÉAS
Oui, oui; je l'ai vu . . . Ne nous retournons pas brusquement . . .

MÉLISANDE
Il a son épée . . .

PELLÉAS
Je n'ai pas la mienne . . .

MÉLISANDE
Il a vu que nous nous embrassions . . .

PELLÉAS
Il ne sait pas que nous l'avons vu . . . Ne bouge pas; ne tourne pas la tête . . . Il se précipiterait . . . Il nous observe . . . Il est encore immobile . . . Va-t'en, va-t'en tout de suite par ici . . . Je l'attendrai . . . Je l'arrêterai . . .

MÉLISANDE
Non!

PELLÉAS Va-t'en!	PELLÉAS Go on . . .
MÉLISANDE Non! . . .	MÉLISANDE No!
PELLÉAS Il a tout vu! . . . Il nous tuera! . . .	PELLÉAS Oh, he has seen us . . . he'll kill us both!
MÉLISANDE Tant mieux!	MÉLISANDE Let him!
PELLÉAS Il vient!	PELLÉAS Dearest . . .
MÉLISANDE Tant mieux!	MÉLISANDE I'm yours . . .
PELLÉAS Ta bouche! Ta bouche!	PELLÉAS Embrace me . . . embrace me . . .
MÉLISANDE Oui! . . . Oui! . . . Oui! . . .	MÉLISANDE Yes! Yes! Yes! (*they embrace desperately*)
PELLÉAS Oh! oh! Toutes les étoiles tombent! . . .	PELLÉAS Oh! Oh! All the stars of heav'n are falling!
MÉLISANDE Sur moi aussi! sur moi aussi! . . .	MÉLISANDE The stars are falling . . . I see them too!
PELLÉAS Encore! . . . encore! . . . donne!	PELLÉAS Beloved . . . embrace me . . . take me . . .
MÉLISANDE Toute!	MÉLISANDE Take me . . .
PELLÉAS Donne! donne!	PELLÉAS Take me . . . take me . . .
MÉLISANDE Toute! toute!	MÉLISANDE Hold me . . . hold me . . . (GOLAUD *rushes at them, sword in hand, and strikes down* PELLÉAS, *who falls at the edge of the fountain.* MÉLISANDE *flees in terror*)
MÉLISANDE Oh! oh! Je n'ai pas de courage! . . . Je n'ai pas de courage! . . .	MÉLISANDE Oh! Oh! I'm afraid he will kill me . . . I'm afraid he will kill me . . . Ah! (GOLAUD *follows her through the woods in silence*)

ACT V

A room in the castle

(ARKEL, GOLAUD, *and the* PHYSICIAN *are discovered in the corner of the room;* MÉLISANDE *lies on the bed.*)

PHYSICIAN

Please believe me, that that tiny little wound was not the thing that caused it. It wouldn't have injured even a bird. So it is not you who are to blame, my gracious Lord, do not distress yourself, I beg you. Besides, one never can tell . . . we still may be able to save her.

ARKEL

No, no; there's an air of resignation, an air of acceptance around here . . . it is not a good omen . . . Observe the way in which she sleeps! Gently, like a child . . . one would think that her soul was resting while she slept . . .

GOLAUD

I have killed for no reason. It is surely enough to make the stones cry for pity. They had kissed, to be sure, but they kissed like little children, they were brother and sister . . . and I, all of a sudden, 'twas in spite of myself, don't you see, 'twas in spite of myself . . .

PHYSICIAN

Just a moment . . . I think I saw her stirring . . .

MÉLISANDE

Won't you open the window? Please open the window . . .

ARKEL

Is this the window that you mean, Mélisande?

MÉLISANDE

No, no, the great big window, I'd like to see . . .

ARKEL

Wouldn't the air from the sea be much too cold and damp?

PHYSICIAN

Obey her, obey her!

MÉLISANDE

I thank you. Can that be the sun that is setting?

ARKEL

Yes; it is the sun that is setting on the sea; it is late. How do you feel tonight, Mélisande?

MÉLISANDE

Well . . . well . . . why do you ask me how I feel? I

LE MÉDECIN

Ce n'est pas de cette petite blessure qu'elle peut mourir; un oiseau n'en serait pas mort . . . ce n'est donc pas vous qui l'avez tuée, mon bon seigneur; ne vous désolez pas ainsi . . . Et puis, il n'est pas dit que nous ne la sauverons pas . . .

ARKËL

Non, non; il me semble que nous nous taisons trop, malgré nous, dans sa chambre . . . Ce n'est pas un bon signe . . . Regardez comme elle dort . . . lentement, lentement . . . on dirait que son âme a froid pour toujours . . .

GOLAUD

J'ai tué sans raison! Est-ce que ce n'est pas à faire pleurer les pierres! . . . Ils s'étaient embrassés comme des petits enfants . . . Ils étaient frère et sœur . . . Et moi, moi tout de suite! . . . Je l'ai fait malgré moi, voyez-vous . . . Je l'ai fait malgré moi . . .

LE MÉDECIN

Attention; je crois qu'elle s'éveille . . .

MÉLISANDE

Ouvrez la fenêtre . . . ouvrez la fenêtre . . .

ARKËL

Veux-tu que j'ouvre celle-ci, Mélisande?

MÉLISANDE

Non, non; la grande fenêtre . . . c'est pour voir . . .

ARKËL

Est-ce que l'air de la mer n'est pas trop froid ce soir?

LE MÉDECIN

Faites, faites . . .

MÉLISANDE

Merci . . . Est-ce le soleil qui se couche?

ARKËL

Oui; c'est le soleil qui se couche sur la mer; il est tard. —Comment te trouves-tu, Mélisande?

MÉLISANDE

Bien, bien.—Pourquoi demandez-vous cela? Je n'ai jamais été mieux portante.—Il me semble cependant que je sais quelque chose . . .

ARKËL

Que dis-tu?—Je ne te comprends pas . . .

MÉLISANDE

Je ne comprends pas non plus tout ce que je dis, voyez-vous . . . Je ne sais pas ce que je dis . . . Je ne sais pas ce que je sais . . . Je ne dis plus ce que je veux . . .

ARKËL

Mais si, mais si . . . Je suis tout heureux de t'entendre parler ainsi; tu as eu un peu de délire ces jours-ci, et l'on ne te comprenait plus . . . Mais maintenant, tout cela est bien loin . . .

MÉLISANDE

Je ne sais pas . . . Êtes-vous tout seul dans la chambre, grand-père?

ARKËL

Non; il y a encore le médecin qui t'a guérie . . .

MÉLISANDE

Ah . . .

ARKËL

Et puis il y a encore quelqu'un . . .

MÉLISANDE

Qui est-ce?

ARKËL

C'est . . . il ne faut pas t'effrayer . . . Il ne te veut pas le moindre mal, sois-en sûre . . . Si tu as peur, il s'en ira . . . Il est très malheureux . . .

MÉLISANDE

Qui est-ce?

ARKËL

C'est . . . c'est ton mari . . . c'est Golaud . . .

MÉLISANDE

Golaud est ici? Pourquoi ne vient-il pas près de moi?

GOLAUD

Mélisande . . . Mélisande . . .

MÉLISANDE

Est-ce vous, Golaud? Je ne vous reconnaissais presque plus . . . C'est que j'ai le soleil du soir dans les yeux . . . Pourquoi regardez-vous les murs? Vous avez maigri et vieilli . . . Y a-t-il longtemps que nous ne nous sommes vus?

GOLAUD

Voulez-vous vous éloigner un

have never felt better. There are certain little things I begin to discover.

ARKEL

What is that? I don't understand.

MÉLISANDE

Neither do I understand each word that I say, don't you see? I do not know what I have said . . . I do not know what I know . . . I cannot tell just what it means.

ARKEL

Oh yes, you can . . . I'm truly delighted you're able to say so much . . . you've been somewhat feverish of late, and it was hard to understand you . . . but now, at last, all this is past and gone.

MÉLISANDE

Perhaps you're right. Are you alone in the room, Grandfather?

ARKEL

No . . . there is the doctor who has cared for you.

MÉLISANDE

Ah!

ARKEL

Then, there's someone else as well . . .

MÉLISANDE

Who is it?

ARKEL

It is . . . you must not be alarmed. He has no desire to hurt you, that is certain. If you're afraid, he'll go away . . . He is very unhappy.

MÉLISANDE

Who is it?

ARKEL

Well, it is your husband, it's Golaud . . .

MÉLISANDE

Golaud is in here? Why doesn't he speak to me then?

GOLAUD (*dragging himself to the bed*)

Mélisande . . . Mélisande . . .

MÉLISANDE

Is that you, Golaud? I cannot see you very clearly . . . It's the ev'ning sun that shines in my eyes. But why don't you look at me? You have grown so thin and so old . . . it must be a long time since we last saw each other.

GOLAUD (*to* ARKEL *and the* PHYSICIAN)

Please let us alone for a while. . . I'm sorry, dear

friends . . . But I shall leave the door wide open. It will not be very long. I have something that I want to ask her . . . otherwise I could never die in peace. Will you go? I shall let you return in a moment. Do not refuse me, I beg you. I'm a most unhappy man.
(ARKEL *and the* PHYSICIAN *go out*)
Mélisande, are you as sorry for me as I am for you? Mélisande, can you ever forgive me, Mélisande?

instant, mes pauvres amis . . . Je laisserai la porte grande ouverte . . . Un instant seulement . . . Je voudrais lui dire quelque chose; sans cela je ne pourrais pas mourir . . . Voulez-vous?—Vous pouvez revenir tout de suite . . . Ne me refusez pas cela . . . Je suis un malheureux . . .—Mélisande, as-tu pitié de moi, comme j'ai pitié de toi? . . . Mélisande? . . . Me pardonnes-tu, Mélisande? . . .

MÉLISANDE

Yes, yes, I have forgiven you. What was there to forgive?

MÉLISANDE

Oui, oui, je te pardonne . . . Que faut-il pardonner?

GOLAUD

I did you so much wrong, Mélisande. I can never undo all the wrong I have done . . . But now I see, I can see it all so clearly right now . . . from the very first. It all has been my fault, all that has happen'd to us. Yes, all that will happen as well. If I only could tell you, you would see; as I see it now, it is clear, oh so clear! But I loved you so! I loved you so! But as it is, someone soon will die . . . I'm the one who will die. And I'm anxious to know . . . I should like to ask you now . . . You will not take offense? You must speak the absolute truth to a man who's going to die . . . And he must know the absolute truth. For if not, he could never rest in peace. Now will you swear to tell the absolute truth?

GOLAUD

Je t'ai fait tant de mal, Mélisande . . . Je ne puis pas te dire le mal que je t'ai fait . . . Mais je le vois, je le vois si clairement aujourd'hui . . . depuis le premier jour . . . Et tout est de ma faute, tout ce qui est arrivé, tout ce qui va arriver . . . Si je pouvais le dire, tu varrais comme je le vois . . . Je vois tout, je vois tout . . . Mais je t'aimais tant . . . Je t'aimais tant . . . Mais maintenant, quelqu'un va mourir . . . C'est moi qui vais mourir . . . Et je voudrais savoir . . . Je voudrais te demander . . . Tu ne m'en voudras pas? . . . Il faut dire la vérité à quelqu'un qui va mourir . . . Il faut qu'il sache la vérité, sans cela il ne pourrait pas dormir . . . Me jures-tu de dire la vérité?

MÉLISANDE

Yes . . .

MÉLISANDE

Oui.

GOLAUD

Did you love Pelléas?

GOLAUD

As-tu aimé Pelléas?

MÉLISANDE

Why yes; of course I loved him. Is he here?

MÉLISANDE

Mais oui; je l'ai aimé. Où est-il?

GOLAUD

You do not understand . . . don't you want to understand me? Mélisande, Mélisande. Well then, it's this. I now am asking if you loved him with a love that's forbidden . . . Were you, tell me, were you ever guilty? Speak, speak . . . were you?

GOLAUD

Tu ne me comprends pas?—Tu ne veux pas me comprendre? —Il me semble . . . Il me semble . . . Eh bien, voici: Je te demande si tu l'as aimé d'un amour défendu? . . . As-tu . . . avez-vous été coupables? Dis, dis, oui, oui, oui?

MÉLISANDE

No, no, we were not guilty, I assure you! Why are you asking me all this?

MÉLISANDE

Non, non; nous n'avons pas été coupables.—Pourquoi demandez-vous cela?

GOLAUD
Mélisande! . . . dis-moi la vérité pour l'amour de Dieu!

MÉLISANDE
Pourquoi n'ai-je pas dit la vérité?

GOLAUD
Ne mens plus ainsi, au moment de mourir!

MÉLISANDE
Qui est-ce qui va mourir?—Est-ce moi?

GOLAUD
Toi, toi! et moi, moi aussi, après toi! . . . Et il nous faut la vérité . . . Il nous faut enfin la vérité, entends-tu! . . . Dis-moi tout! Dis-moi tout! Je te pardonne tout! . . .

MÉLISANDE
Pourquoi vais-je mourir?—Je ne le savais pas . . .

GOLAUD
Tu le sais maintenant! . . . Il est temps! Il est temps! . . . Vite! vite! . . . La vérité! la vérité! . . .

MÉLISANDE
La vérité . . . la vérité . . .

GOLAUD
Où es-tu?—Mélisande!—Où es-tu?—Ce n'est pas naturel! Mélisande! Où es-tu?—Oui, oui; vous pouvez rentrer . . . Je ne sais rien; c'est inutile . . . Elle est déjà trop loin de nous . . . Je ne saurai jamais! . . . Je vais mourir ici comme un aveugle! . . .

ARKËL
Qu'avez-vous fait? Vous allez la tuer.

GOLAUD
Je l'ai déjà tuée . . .

ARKËL
Mélisande . . .

MÉLISANDE
Est-ce vous, grand-père?

ARKËL
Oui, ma fille . . . Que veux-tu que je fasse?

MÉLISANDE
Est-il vrai que l'hiver commence?

ARKËL
Pourquoi demandes-tu cela?

MÉLISANDE
Parce qu'il fait froid et qu'il n'y a plus de feuilles . . .

ARKËL
Tu as froid?—Veux-tu qu'on ferme les fenêtres?

GOLAUD
Mélisande! I beg you tell the truth for the love of God!

MÉLISANDE
But why should what I told you not be the truth?

GOLAUD
Lie no more like this, at the moment of death!

MÉLISANDE
Who is it that is to die? Is it I?

GOLAUD
You, you, and I, I as well, after you! And I must know the very truth. Now at last I've got to have the truth, do you hear? Tell me all! Tell me all! I will forgive you all!

MÉLISANDE
Am I really going to die? I did not know I was.

GOLAUD
Now you know it at last . . . It was time! Hurry! Hurry! Tell me the truth! The very truth!

MÉLISANDE
The very truth . . . yes . . . the very truth . . .

GOLAUD
Are you there? Mélisande! Are you there? Don't you hear my voice . . . Mélisande! Don't you hear me? (*catching sight of* ARKEL *and the* PHYSICIAN *at the door*)
Yes, yes, you may come in . . . I've learned no more. It was useless . . . her spirit is no longer here. And I will never know! I shall go to my grave in the darkness.

ARKEL
What have you done? You will kill her, Golaud.

GOLAUD
I already have killed her . . .

ARKEL
Mélisande!

MÉLISANDE
Is it you, Grandfather?

ARKEL
Yes, my daughter . . . what can I do to help you?

MÉLISANDE
Is it true that the winter's coming?

ARKEL
What makes you think about the winter?

MÉLISANDE
Because it's cold and there are not any leaves left . . .

ARKEL
Are you cold? Then we'd better shut the window . . .

MÉLISANDE

No . . . do not shut it till the sun has gone down in the sea. It goes down very slowly, that means that the winter is coming.

ARKEL

Well, don't you like the winter?

MÉLISANDE

Oh, no! I'm afraid of the cold . . . I'm afraid of the frost.

ARKEL

You're better now?

MÉLISANDE

Yes, yes, I'm no longer dejected . . .

ARKEL

Would you like to see your child?

MÉLISANDE

What child?

ARKEL

Why your baby, your own little daughter . . .

MÉLISANDE

Where is she?

ARKEL

She's here . . .

MÉLISANDE

Why how strange . . . it seems I cannot raise my arms to embrace her . . .

ARKEL

You're still quite weak, Mélisande . . . she's a lovely baby, don't you think so?

MÉLISANDE

But she does not smile; she's very little . . . she will also weep, poor child, what a pity!

(*the serving-women of the castle gradually come into the room and take their places in silence along the walls, where they wait*)

GOLAUD

What is this? Who gave permission to have all these women in here?

PHYSICIAN

I wonder who told them . . .

ARKEL

Who called them here at this hour?

PHYSICIAN

It was not I . . .

GOLAUD

What has brought you to this room? You were not called by anyone here. What business have you in here? But what is the matter, can't you answer?

(*the serving-women make no reply*)

MÉLISANDE

Non, non . . . jusqu'à ce que le soleil soit au fond de la mer.—Il descend lentement, alors c'est l'hiver qui commence?

ARKËL

Oui.—Tu n'aimes pas l'hiver?

MÉLISANDE

Oh! non. J'ai peur du froid.—Ah! J'ai peur des grands froids . . .

ARKËL

Te sens-tu mieux?

MÉLISANDE

Oui, oui; je n'ai plus toutes ces inquiétudes . . .

ARKËL

Veux-tu voir ton enfant?

MÉLISANDE

Quel enfant?

ARKËL

Ton enfant, ta petite fille . . .

MÉLISANDE

Où est-elle?

ARKËL

Ici . . .

MÉLISANDE

C'est étrange . . . je ne puis pas lever les bras pour la prendre . . .

ARKËL

C'est que tu es encore très faible . . . Je la tiendrai moi-même; regarde . . .

MÉLISANDE

Elle ne rit pas . . . Elle est petite . . . Elle va pleurer aussi . . . J'ai pitié d'elle . . .

GOLAUD

Qu'y a-t-il?—Qu'est-ce que toutes ces femmes viennent faire ici?

LE MÉDECIN

Ce sont les servantes . . .

ARKËL

Qui est-ce qui les a appelées?

LE MÉDECIN

Ce n'est pas moi . . .

GOLAUD

Porquoi venez-vous ici?—Personne ne vous a demandées . . . Que venez-vous faire ici?—mais qu'est-ce que c'est donc! Répondez! . . .

ARKËL
Ne parlez pas trop fort . . . Elle va dormir; elle a fermé les yeux . . .

GOLAUD
Ce n'est pas? . . .

LE MÉDECIN
Non, non; voyez, elle respire . . .

ARKËL
Ses yeux sont pleins de larmes. —Maintenant c'est son âme qui pleure . . . Pourquoi étend-elle ainsi les bras? Que veut-elle?

LE MÉDECIN
C'est vers l'enfant sans doute. C'est la lutte da la mère contre la mort . . .

GOLAUD
En ce moment?—En ce moment?—Il faut le dire, dites! dites!

LE MÉDECIN
Peut-être . . .

GOLAUD
Tout de suite? . . . Oh! Oh! Il faut que je lui dise . . .— Mélisande! Mélisande! . . . Laissez-moi seul! laissez-moi seul avec elle! . . .

ARKËL
Non, non; n'approchez pas . . . Ne la troublez pas . . . Ne lui parlez plus . . . Vous ne savez pas ce que c'est que l'âme . . .

GOLAUD
Ce n'est pas ma faute, ce n'est pas ma faute!

ARKËL
Attention . . . Attention . . . Il faut parler à voix basse.— Il ne faut plus l'inquiéter . . . L'âme humaine est très silencieuse . . . L'âme humaine aime à s'en aller seule . . . Elle souffre si timidement . . . Mais la tristesse, Golaud . . . mais la tristesse de tout ce que l'on voit! . . . Oh! oh! oh! . . .
Qu'y a-t-il?

LE MÉDECIN
Elles ont raison . . .

ARKËL
Je n'ai rien vu.—Êtes-vous sûr? . . .

LE MÉDECIN
Oui, oui.

ARKËL
Je n'ai rien entendu . . . Si vite, si vite . . . Tout à coup . . . Elle s'en va sans rien dire . . .

ARKEL
Please speak a little softer, she is going to sleep . . . she has closed her eyes . . .

GOLAUD
Can it be?

PHYSICIAN
No, no, she's breathing ever so gently . . .

ARKEL
Her eyes are full of tears. It's her soul that is weeping in sorrow . . . What is she doing with her arms? What does she want?

PHYSICIAN
She's calling for the child, I think . . . she is trying to help and protect it . . .

GOLAUD
At such a time? At such a time? You have to tell me, tell me! Tell me!

PHYSICIAN
It may be . . .

GOLAUD
In a moment . . . oh! Oh! I have something to tell her . . . Mélisande! Mélisande! Leave me with her! Leave us alone for a moment . . .

ARKEL
No, no, she's much too tired, you must not disturb her, she is resting now. You can tell her later, and she will forgive you.

GOLAUD
I didn't mean to do it . . . I did not mean to do it . . .

ARKEL
Not so loud, not so loud, please try to speak in a whisper if you can . . . we must try to be quiet. The human soul was created in silence . . . It likes to leave us in silence and quiet . . . See how timidly she waits for death. Oh what a pity, Golaud . . . It is a pity, and yet we have no choice . . . Oh! Oh!
(*at this point all the serving-women fall on their knees*)
What has happened?

PHYSICIAN (*approaching the bed and touching the body*)
Yes, it is so.

ARKEL
I could see nothing. Are you quite sure?

PHYSICIAN
Yes, yes.

ARKEL
I heard nothing at all . . . So quickly, so quickly . . . she has departed in silence . . .
(GOLAUD *sobs*)

I think you should leave, Golaud. Let her rest here in quiet and silence . . . You must not cry, it is dreadful, but it is not your fault. She was truly a quiet little creature; such a timid one, and silent too . . . yes, such a lonely, sad, mysterious being, as indeed we all are. There she lies, just as if she would be the elder sister of her own child . . . But come . . . we may not allow the child to remain here in this darkened chamber . . . it must have sunshine, it must take the place of its mother. It's her turn, the poor little darling . . .

Ne restez pas ici, Golaud . . . Il lui faut le silence, maintenant . . . Venez, venez . . . C'est terrible, mais ce n'est pas votre faute . . . C'était un petit être si tranquille, si timide et si silencieux . . . C'était un pauvre petit être mystérieux, comme tout le monde . . . Elle est là, comme si elle était la grande sœur de son enfant . . .—Venez; il ne faut pas que l'enfant reste ici dans cette chambre . . . Il faut qu'il vive, maintenant, à sa place . . . C'est au tour de la pauvre petite . . .

RIGOLETTO

by Giuseppe Verdi (1813–1901)

LIBRETTO BY
FRANCESCO MARIA PIAVE

Translated by RUTH and THOMAS MARTIN

Based on Victor Hugo's drama *Le Roi s'amuse*

CHARACTERS

THE DUKE OF MANTUA	*Tenor*
BORSA, *a courtier*	*Tenor*
THE COUNTESS CEPRANO	*Mezzo-soprano*
RIGOLETTO, *the Duke's jester, a hunchback*	*Baritone*
COUNT CEPRANO, *a nobleman*	*Bass*
MARULLO, *a courtier*	*Baritone*
COUNT MONTERONE, *a nobleman*	*Baritone*
SPARAFUCILE, *a professional assassin*	*Bass*
GILDA, *daughter of Rigoletto*	*Soprano*
GIOVANNA, *Gilda's nurse*	*Mezzo-soprano*
A PAGE	*Soprano*
A HERALD	*Baritone*
MADDALENA, *sister of Sparafucile*	*Contralto*
COURTIERS, LADIES AND GENTLEMEN OF THE COURT, SERVANTS	

Place: Mantua, Italy
Time: Sixteenth century
First performance: Teatro La Fenice, Venice, March 11, 1851

COPYRIGHT © 1957 BY RUTH AND THOMAS MARTIN

ACT I

(A magnificent hall in the ducal palace. Doors in the rear leading to other halls, also splendidly illuminated. Noblemen and ladies walk by in the halls in the rear, pages come and go. Dancing is seen in the rear.)

DUKE *(enters from another hall, conversing with* BORSA*)*
This very night I will finish my adventure
With that young girl I followed through the city!

BORSA
Is this the girl you noticed Sunday morning?

DUKE
Ev'ry Sunday for three months now.

BORSA
Where will you find her?

DUKE
She lives not far from here.
Ev'ry night a stranger comes to see her.

BORSA
And does she know the name of her admirer?

DUKE
Of course not!
(a group of ladies and cavaliers crosses the stage)

BORSA
Beauties galore! Enchanting!

DUKE
But none can equal the Countess of Ceprano!

BORSA
Don't let her husband hear that!

DUKE
And why should I care?

BORSA
He is jealous and spiteful.

DUKE
Then this conquest would be
Twice as delightful!

Aria

Charming women,
Whatever their name and rank,
I always pursue them
With equal abandon.
At my pleasure
I wander at random
To find adventure
Wherever I turn.
I delight in the thrill of their beauty;
Only they make my life exciting.
If today one should beckon inviting,
Then tomorrow for another
My passion may burn!

DUCA
Della mia bella incognita borghese
Toccare il fin dell'avventura io voglio.

BORSA
Di quella giovin che vedete al tempio?

DUCA
Da tre mesi ogni festa.

BORSA
La sua dimora?

DUCA
In un remoto calle;
Misterioso un uom v'entra ogni notte.

BORSA
E sa colei chi sia
L'amante suo?

DUCA
Lo ignora.

BORSA
Quante beltà! Mirate.

DUCA
Le vince tutte di Cepran la sposa.

BORSA
Non v'oda il Conte, o Duca!

DUCA
A me che importa?

BORSA
Dirlo ad altra ei potria.

DUCA
Nè sventura per me certo saria . . .

Questa o quella per me pari sono
A quant'altre d'intorno mi vedo;
Del mio core l'impero non cedo
Meglio ad una che ad altra beltà.
La costoro avvenenza è qual dono
Di che il fato ne infiora la vita;
S'oggi questa mi torna gradita
Forse un'altra doman lo sarà.
La costanza, tiranna del core,
Detestiamo qual morbo crudele.
Sol chi vuole si serbi fedele;
Non v'ha amor se non v'è libertà.
De' mariti il geloso furore,

Degli amanti le smanie derido;
Anco d'Argo i cent'occhi disfido
Se mi punge una qualche beltà.

To be faithful
Is not my intention,
I detest this unwelcome,
Tyrannic convention.
To such slavery
I'll never surrender,
For love is poor indeed
If your freedom is lost.
Jealous husbands and ill-tempered lovers
Only move me to scorn and derision.
I defy them with undaunted decision;
I must conquer wife and sweetheart,
Never minding the cost.

(*the minuet is danced. The* DUKE *addresses the* COUNTESS CEPRANO)

DUCA
Partite? Crudele!

DUKE
You're leaving? Dear Countess!

CONTESSA CEPRANO
Seguire lo sposo
M'è forza a Ceprano.

COUNTESS
My duty commands me to stay with Ceprano.

DUCA
Ma dee luminoso
In corte tal astro qual sole brillare
Per voi qui ciascuno dovrà palpitare
Per voi già possente la fiamma d'amore
Inebria, conquide, distrugge il mio core.

DUKE
Your beauty is so radiant,
Surpassing all others,
Alluring and glorious!
You reign like a goddess
In splendor victorious.
My own heart is flaming,
Desiring, imploring;
Behold me, tormented,
Admiring, adoring!

CONTESSA CEPRANO
Calmatevi!

COUNTESS
You flatter me.

DUCA
La fiamma d'amore
inebria, conquide,
distrugge il mio core!

DUKE
Desiring, imploring,
Behold me, tormented,
Admiring, adoring.

CONTESSA CEPRANO
Calmatevi, calmatevi.

COUNTESS
Your Lordship, you embarrass me!

DUCA
Per voi già possente la fiamma d'amore
Inebria, conquide, distrugge il mio core!

DUKE
My own heart is flaming
Desiring, imploring;
Behold me, tormented,
Admiring, adoring!

(*he gives his arm to the* COUNTESS *and leaves with her.* COUNT CEPRANO *makes a gesture of annoyance and follows them*)

RIGOLETTO
In testa che avete,
Signor di Ceprano?
Ei sbuffa, vedete?

RIGOLETTO (*who has observed the scene, calls after him, mockingly*)
Great honor has come to the house of Ceprano!
(*to the* COURTIERS)
He's fuming! You saw it!

COURTIERS
Delightful!
The Duke is pursuing his pleasure.

RIGOLETTO
Is that so unusual?
When has he been diff'rent?
Our Duke is enjoying himself to the fullest,
Carousing in mirth on his lighthearted path.
And now he is wooing the Countess Ceprano,
And meanwhile her husband is seething with wrath!
(*he leaves to the left; the perigordino is danced*)

MARULLO (*enters excitedly from center rear*)
Sensation! Sensation!

COURTIERS
What happened? Let's hear it!

MARULLO
I want you to guess it!

COURTIERS
How can we? You tell us!

MARULLO
Ha, ha! Rigoletto!

COURTIERS
Well, what?

MARULLO
It's too fantastic!

COURTIERS
The ugly old braggart?
Has somebody tricked him?

MARULLO
It's even more drastic!
The fool now is keeping . . .

COURTIERS
Continue!

MARULLO
A mistress!

COURTIERS
A mistress! It can't be!

MARULLO
The hunchback is playing the role of a Romeo!

COURTIERS
The hunchback? A Romeo?
I cannot believe it!

DUKE (*re-enters, followed by* RIGOLETTO)
The Count of Ceprano's becoming a bore!
His wife is an angel I madly adore.

RIGOLETTO
Make love to her!

DUKE
With pleasure, but when?

CORO
Che festa!
Il Duca qui pur si diverte! . . .

RIGOLETTO
Così non è sempre? Che nuove scoperte!
Il giuoco ed il vino, le feste, la danza,
Battaglia, conviti, ben tutto gli sta.
Or della Contessa l'assedio egli avanza.
E intanto il marito fremendo ne va.

MARULLO
Gran nuova! Gran nuova!

CORO
Che avvenne? Parlate!

MARULLO
Stupir ne dovrete!

CORO
Narrate, narrate!

MARULLO
Ah! ah! Rigoletto . . .

CORO
Ebben?

MARULLO
Caso enorme!

CORO
Perduto ha la gobba? Non è più difforme?

MARULLO
Più strana è la cosa! Il pazzo possiede . . .

CORO
Infine?

MARULLO
Un'amante.

CORO
Un'amante! Chi il crede?

MARULLO
Il gobbo in Cupido or s'è trasformato.

CORO
Quel mostro Cupido? Cupido beato!

DUCA
Ah, più di Ceprano importuno non v'è!
La cara sua sposa è un angiol per me!

RIGOLETTO
Rapitela.

DUCA
È detto; ma il farlo?

RIGOLETTO Stasera.	RIGOLETTO This evening.
DUCA Non pensi tu al Conte?	DUKE And what of Ceprano?
RIGOLETTO Non c'è la prigione?	RIGOLETTO We'll put him in prison!
DUCA Ah, no.	DUKE We can't.
RIGOLETTO Ebben . . . s'esilia.	RIGOLETTO Well then . . . we'll ban him.
DUCA Nemmeno, buffone.	DUKE We can't do that either.
RIGOLETTO Allora la testa?	RIGOLETTO In that case . . . why don't we behead him?
CEPRANO (Oh l'anima nera!)	CEPRANO (*who has overheard the conversation, aside*) You meanest of scoundrels!
DUCA Che di', questa testa?	DUKE (*patting* CEPRANO's *shoulder*) Remember, I like him.
RIGOLETTO È ben naturale. Che far di tal testa? A cosa ella vale?	RIGOLETTO Why can't we behead him? One head is a trifle! There are plenty of others!
CEPRANO Marrano!	CEPRANO (*furiously, brandishing his sword*) You villain!
DUCA Fermate!	DUKE (*to* CEPRANO) He's joking!
RIGOLETTO Da rider mi fa.	RIGOLETTO Ridiculous dunce!
CORO In furia è montato!	COURTIERS Ceprano is furious!
DUCA Buffone, vien qua.	DUKE Now stop it at once!
BORSA In furia è montato.	BORSA Let's see what will happen!
MARULLO In furia è montato.	MARULLO Ceprano is furious!
CORO In furia è montato.	COURTIERS This time it is serious!
DUCA Ah, sempre tu spingi lo scherzo all'estremo.	DUKE (*to* RIGOLETTO) You'd better be careful or else you'll be sorry!
RIGOLETTO Che coglier mi puote? Di loro non temo.	RIGOLETTO What harm could befall me? I've no need to worry!
DUCA Quell'ira che sfidi colpir ti potrà.	DUKE Beware lest your daring may once cause your fall!
RIGOLETTO Del Duca il protetto nessun toccherà.	RIGOLETTO The Duke's gracious favor makes up for them all.
CEPRANO Vendetta del pazzo! Contr'esso un rancore Di noi chi non ha? Vendetta!	CEPRANO (*to the other* COURTIERS) I call you to vengeance! There's no one among us who bears him no grudge! Agreed then?

COURTIERS
You'll lead us?
CEPRANO
This evening I'll see you, well armed, in my house!
Agreed, then?
COURTIERS
Yes, agreed!
CEPRANO, COURTIERS
The fool must be punished!
Revenge is in order!
His sharp evil tongue has offended us all.
We'll take revenge!
Yes, rely on us all.
On to vengeance!
DUKE, RIGOLETTO
Let's have music, let's have dancing!
ALL
Let's have music, let's have dancing!
Nothing shall disturb our pleasure,
Let's enjoy in fullest measure
Charming women, wine and play!
MONTERONE (*from behind scenes*)
I want to talk to him!
DUKE
No!
MONTERONE (*entering, in a commanding tone*)
It must be!
COURTIERS
Monterone!
MONTERONE
Yes, it is I . . .
My voice like warning thunder
Shall ev'rywhere pursue you!
RIGOLETTO (*aping* MONTERONE'S *voice*)
I want to talk to him!
(*the* DUKE *makes a sign of assent*)
(RIGOLETTO, *with mockery, ridiculing* MONTERONE)
You have conspired brazenly against us,
However, we have bestowed on you
Our gracious pardon.
Yet you stand here before us
And choose to bore us
With endless speeches
About your daughter's honor.
MONTERONE
A new injustice!
Another insult and defamation
You heaped upon me, my name and station;
But I shall clamor for retribution
For my own daughter's offended honor.
And if you sentence me to execution,

CORO
Ma come?
CEPRANO
In armi chi ha core
Doman sia da me,
A notte.
TUTTI
Sì. Sarà.
CEPRANO, CORTIGIANI
Vendetta del pazzo!
Contr'esso un rancore
Pei tristi suoi modi di noi chi non ha?
Vendetta!
Sì! è detto sarà.
Sì, vendetta!
DUCA, RIGOLETTO
Tutto è gioia, tutto è festa!
TUTTI
Tutto è gioia, tutto è festa!
Tutto invitaci a goder!
Oh, guardate, non par questa
Or la reggia del piacer?
MONTERONE
Ch'io gli parli.
DUCA
No.
MONTERONE
Il voglio.
TUTTI
Monterone!
MONTERONE
Sì, Monteron! la voce mia qual tuono
Vi scuoterà dovunque!
RIGOLETTO
Ch'io gli parli.
Voi congiuraste contro noi, signore,
E noi, clementi invero, perdonammo.
Qual vi piglia or delirio a tutte l'ore
Di vostra figlia a reclamar l'onore?
MONTERONE
Novello insulto! Ah sì, a turbare, ah sì, a turbare,
Sarò vostr'orgie, verrò a gridare
Fino a che vegga restarsi inulto
Di mia famiglia l'atroce insulto;
E se al carnefice pur mi darete,
Spettro terribile mi rivedrete,

Portante in mano il teschio mio,
Vendetta a chiedere al mondo,
a Dio.

DUCA
Non più, arrestatelo.

RIGOLETTO
È matto.

BORSA, MARULLO, CEPRANO
Quai detti!

MONTERONE
Ah, siate entrambi voi maledetti.

TUTTI
Ah!

MONTERONE
Slanciare il cane a leon morente
È vile, o Duca,
e tu, serpente,
Tu che d'un padre ridi al
dolore,
Sii maledetto.

RIGOLETTO
Che sento! Orrore!

TUTTI
O tu che la festa audace hai
turbato,
Da un genio d'inferno qui fosti
guidato.

RIGOLETTO
Orrore!

TUTTI
È vano ogni detto, di qua
t'allontana,
Va, trema, o vegliardo, dell'ira
sovrana.
Tu l'hai provocata, piu speme
non v'e,
Un'ora fatale fu questa per te.

RIGOLETTO
Che orrore! Orrore!

I shall continue my persecution.
As ghastly vision I'll come to haunt you.
And cry anathema before the world,
Before the world and God Almighty!

DUKE
Enough, arrest him!

RIGOLETTO
He's raving!

BORSA, MARULLO, CEPRANO
How dare he!

MONTERONE (*to the* DUKE *and* RIGOLETTO)
May both of you forever be cursed!

COURTIERS
Ah!

MONTERONE
To hurl your dogs against the dying lion,
Oh Duke, is shameful;
(*to* RIGOLETTO)
And you, his henchman,
You who deride the grief of a father,
My curse upon you!

RIGOLETTO (*terror-stricken, to himself*)
Oh heaven, he cursed me!

DUKE, COURTIERS
You foolish intruder and spreader of terror,
This time you've committed your last fatal error.

RIGOLETTO (*aside*)
Horror!

DUKE, COURTIERS
Away with your curses and vile accusation,
Beware of the Duke and his just indignation.
For you there is nothing but sorrow in store,
In prison's seclusion you'll try him no more!

RIGOLETTO
He has cursed me,
Dreadful fate, oh dreadful fate!
(MONTERONE *is led away by two guards. All others follow the* DUKE *into another room*)

CHANGE OF SCENE

(*The end of a dead-end street. At left a house of modest appearance with a small courtyard, surrounded by a wall. In the courtyard a large tree and a marble seat. In the wall a door that leads to the street. Above the wall a terrace supported by arches. The door on the second floor goes to that terrace, which is reached by a staircase from the front. At the opposite side of the street is the palace of* CEPRANO. *It is night.*)

Duet

RIGOLETTO (*appears, wrapped in his cloak*)
How heavy weighs his curse on me!

SPARAFUCILE (*who had followed him from a distance, carrying a long sword under his cloak*)
One word.

RIGOLETTO
Go, I've no money.

SPARAFUCILE
I ask none.
An expert swordsman presents himself to you.

RIGOLETTO
A bandit?

SPARAFUCILE
A man who'll rid you of a rival for a pittance.
(*mysteriously*)
You do have rivals . . .

RIGOLETTO
Have I?

SPARAFUCILE
The one you love is in there.

RIGOLETTO (*to himself, worried*)
Who told him?
(*aloud*)
And for a nobleman, how much would you require?

SPARAFUCILE
That would be somewhat higher!

RIGOLETTO
And how would you be paid?

SPARAFUCILE
Half of the sum before the deed,
The other when it's done.

RIGOLETTO (*to himself*)
A demon!
(*aloud*)
How can you safely ply such a dang'rous trade?

SPARAFUCILE
Sometimes in lonely thoroughfares,
Or better in my own house,
Waiting at night in ambush,
I stab my victims, they fall . . .

RIGOLETTO (*to himself*)
A savage!
(*to* SPARAFUCILE)
And in your dwelling?

SPARAFUCILE
That's easier.
My sister's charm procures them,
She is wily, clever, seductive!
She slyly lures them,
That's all . . .

RIGOLETTO
(Quel vecchio maledivami!)

SPARAFUCILE
Signor?

RIGOLETTO
Va', non ho niente.

SPARAFUCILE
Nè il chiesi . . . a voi presente
Un uom di spada sta.

RIGOLETTO
Un ladro?

SPARAFUCILE
Un uom che libera
Per poco da un rivale,
E voi ne avete . . .

RIGOLETTO
Quale?

SPARAFUCILE
La vostra donna è là.

RIGOLETTO
(Che sento!) E quanto spendere
Per un signor dovrei?

SPARAFUCILE
Prezzo maggior vorrei.

RIGOLETTO
Com'usasi pagar?

SPARAFUCILE
Una metà s'anticipa,
Il resto si dà poi.

RIGOLETTO
(Demonio!) E come puoi
Tanto securo oprar?

SPARAFUCILE
Soglio in cittade uccidere,
Oppure nel mio tetto.
L'uomo di sera aspetto;
Una stoccata . . . e muor.

RIGOLETTO
(Demonio!)
E come in casa?

SPARAFUCILE
È facile:
M'aiuta mia sorella.
Per le vie danza, è bella.
Chi voglio attira . . . e allor . . .

RIGOLETTO
Comprendo.

SPARAFUCILE
Senza strepito . . .

RIGOLETTO
Comprendo . . .

SPARAFUCILE
È questo il mio strumento,
Vi serve?

RIGOLETTO
No . . . al momento.

SPARAFUCILE
Peggio per voi . . .

RIGOLETTO
Chi sa?

SPARAFUCILE
Sparafucil mi nomino.

RIGOLETTO
Straniero?

SPARAFUCILE
Borgognone.

RIGOLETTO
E dove all'occasione?

SPARAFUCILE
Qui sempre a sera.

RIGOLETTO
Va.

SPARAFUCILE
Sparafucil! Sparafucil!

RIGOLETTO
Va, va, va, va.

Pari siamo! Io la lingua,
egli ha il pugnale;
L'uomo son io che ride, ei quel
che spegne!
Quel vecchio maledivami . . .
O uomini! O natura!
Vil scellerato mi faceste
voi! . . .
O rabbia! Esser difforme!
O rabbia! Esser buffone . . .
Non dover, non poter altro che
ridere!
Il retaggio d'ogni uom m'è
tolto; il pianto.
Questo padrone mio,
Giovin, giocondo, sì possente,
bello,
Sonnecchiando mi dice:
Fa' ch'io rida, buffone!
Forzarmi deggio e farlo!
Oh dannazione!

RIGOLETTO
I follow . . .

SPARAFUCILE
Very quietly . . .

RIGOLETTO
I follow . . .

SPARAFUCILE (*drawing out his dagger*)
This dagger fells the traitor.
Agreed, then?

RIGOLETTO
No, maybe later . . .

SPARAFUCILE (*hiding the dagger again*)
Very unwise . . .

RIGOLETTO
Who knows?

SPARAFUCILE
Sparafucile awaits your call . . .

RIGOLETTO
You're foreign?

SPARAFUCILE
A Burgundian.

RIGOLETTO
Supposing I want to find you?

SPARAFUCILE
Here any evening.

RIGOLETTO
Go!

SPARAFUCILE
Sparafucile, Sparafucile.
(*he disappears in the dark night*)

RIGOLETTO
Go, go, go, go!
(*alone, looking after* SPARAFUCILE)

Aria

We are equal!
I, the jester, and he the murd'rer!
I stab with cold derision,
He with the dagger.
How heavy weighs that curse on me!
Oh mankind, oh creation!
You are the reason I am vile and vicious!
Oh torture, being a cripple!
Oh torture, wearing a foolscap!
Night and day I must laugh,
Shamming hilarity!
I'm denied man's relief in sorrow,
Consoling tears!
There is my noble master,
Youthful and carefree,
Always happy, handsome,
Who commands when he pleases:

"Come, my fool, and amuse me!"
And I must always do so!
Loathsome profession!
I detest you, you debased and scornful courtiers!
How I gloat when I can hurt you!
If I am a villain,
Only to you I owe it!
But in my home I am another!
How heavy weighs that curse on me!
It pursues me, it preys upon my mind!
Why do I hear it?
Could it forebode misfortune?
Ah no, I don't fear it!

(he enters his courtyard. GILDA *comes from the house and throws herself into his arms)*

Odio a voi, cortigiani schernitori!
Quanta in mordervi ho gioia!
Se iniquo son, per cagion vostra è solo . . .
Ma in altr'uomo qui mi cangio! . . .
Quel vecchio maledivami! Tal pensiero
Perchè conturba ognor la mente mia?
Mi coglierà sventura? . . . Ah no, è follia!

Duet

Gilda!

Figlia!

GILDA

My father!

Mio padre!

RIGOLETTO

When you're beside me,
You bring a joy too often denied me!

A te d'appresso.
Trova sol gioia il core oppresso.

GILDA

Always and always!

Oh, quanto amore!

RIGOLETTO

I love you dearly!

Mia vita sei!

GILDA

I know you love me!

Oh, quanto amore!

RIGOLETTO

You bring me sunshine when you are near me!

Senza te in terra qual bene avrei?

GILDA

Always and always I shall love you!

Oh, quanto amore,
Padre mio!

RIGOLETTO

Always I love you!
(he sighs)

O figlia mia!

GILDA

But you are troubled!
I cannot bear it!
Oh tell me, I beg you,
Please, Father, tell me!
If there's a secret clouding your spirit,
Who but your daughter rather should share it?

Voi sospirate! Che v'ange tanto?
Lo dite a questa povera figlia.
Se v'ha mistero, per lei sia franto,
Ch'ella conosca la sua famiglia . . .

RIGOLETTO

I will not say!

Tu non ne hai . . .

GILDA

Tell me, who are you?

Qual nome avete?

RIGOLETTO

What does it matter?

A te che importa?

GILDA

If then your own life must be a secret . . .

Se non volete
Di voi parlarmi . . .

RIGOLETTO
Non uscir mai.

GILDA
Non vo che al tempio.

RIGOLETTO
Oh, ben tu fai.

GILDA
Se non di voi, almen chi sia
Fate ch'io sappia la madre mia.

RIGOLETTO
Ah! Deh, non parlare al misero
Del suo peduto bene.
Ella sentia, quell'angelo,
Pietà delle mie pene.
Solo, difforme, povero,
Per compassion mi amò.
Ah! Moria, moria . . . le zolle coprano
Lievi quel capo amato.
Sola or tu resti al misero,
O Dio, sii ringraziato!

GILDA
Oh! Quanto dolor! Che spremere
Sì amaro pianto può?

RIGOLETTO
Tu sola, sola resti al misero,
Sola, ah sì, tu sola resti al misero.

GILDA
Padre, non più, calmatevi,
Mi lacera tal vista.
Non più, vi calmate.
Non più, mio padre, ah vi calmate,
Padre, mi lacera padre, mi lacera tal vista.

RIGOLETTO
Sola tu resti al misero,
Dio sii ringraziato!

GILDA
Il nome vostro ditemi,
Il duol che sì v'attrista.

RIGOLETTO
A che nomarmi? È inutile!
Padre ti sono, e basti.
Me forse al mondo temono,
D'alcuno ho forse gli asti,
Altri mi maledicono . . .

GILDA
Patria, parenti, amici
Voi dunque non avete?

RIGOLETTO (*interrupting her*)
Have you been out?

GILDA
To church on Sunday . . .

RIGOLETTO
Then all is well.

GILDA
You guard this secret
Yet there's another;
Will you not tell me about my mother?

RIGOLETTO
Ah! Do not recall those memories,
Mem'ries of vanished happiness . . .
Gentle and good, she pitied me
And blessed my life with kindness.
Lonely, a cripple, destitute
Still I possessed her love! Ah!
She died . . . she died . . .
May God be merciful
And let her rest be peaceful.
You're all I have now,
All I have left to comfort me.
Dear God, receive my grateful prayer.

GILDA
Oh, what cruel fate you have endured,
What words could ever express such bitter woe!

RIGOLETTO
And you alone are all that's left me,
You only are left me now to comfort me.

GILDA
I beg you, Father, say no more!
I cannot bear to see you grieve.
Say no more, I entreat you;
My dearest Father, you must be calm now,
I cannot bear, dearest father,
To see you grieve and suffer!

RIGOLETTO
Only you are left me now,
Dear God, receive my grateful prayer!

GILDA
I beg you, tell your name to me,
What sorrow makes you suffer.

RIGOLETTO
Why should I tell you?
Enough of it! Know me as father only.
There may be men who envy me,
And some perhaps who fear me.
Others have placed a curse on me.

GILDA
Have you, O Father, no homeland,
No kin, no friends to cherish?

RIGOLETTO
Homeland and kindred to cherish!
Homeland and kindred, my daughter,
Unite within your person,
You are all I own.

RIGOLETTO
Patria! parenti!
amici!
Culto, famiglia, la patria,
Il mio universo è in te!

GILDA
To make you happy,
Gladly I'd live for this blessing,
This blessing alone.

GILDA
Ah, se può lieto rendervi,
Gioia è la vita a me!

(in a different tone)
Since we have come here
I've been so lonely,
As my companion Giovanna only.
If you allow me—I might go out . . .

Già da tre lune son qui venuta
Nè la cittade ho ancor veduta;
Se il concedete, farlo or
potrei . . .

RIGOLETTO *(suddenly getting excited and worried)*
No, no! Be truthful, have you left the house?

RIGOLETTO
Mai! mai! Uscita,
dimmi, unqua sei?

GILDA
No!

GILDA
No.

RIGOLETTO
Don't!

RIGOLETTO
Guai!

GILDA *(aside)*
Ah, I feel guilty!

GILDA
(Ah! che dissi!)

RIGOLETTO
Don't ever do it!
(to himself)
If they should find her,
They would abduct her!
Ah, what delight those villains would take
In disgracing me and my daughter!
Hateful thought!

RIGOLETTO
Ben te ne guarda!
(Potrien seguirla, rapirla an-
cora!
Qui d'un buffone si disonora
La figlia, e se ne ride . . .
Orror!)

(calls toward the house)
Ho, there!

Olà!

GIOVANNA *(coming from the house)*
My lord!

GIOVANNA
Signor?

RIGOLETTO
Did someone observe me coming?
Tell me the truth!

RIGOLETTO
Venendo, mi vede alcuno?
Bada, di'il vero.

GIOVANNA
Oh no, I'm certain.

GIOVANNA
Ah, no nessuno.

RIGOLETTO
That's good . . .
The door to the other entrance is always bolted?

RIGOLETTO
Sta ben . . . la porta che dà
al bastione
È sempre chiusa?

GIOVANNA
It always is.

GIOVANNA
Ognor si sta.

RIGOLETTO
Tell me the truth!

RIGOLETTO
Bada, di'il ver.

GIOVANNA
Oh yes, my lord, indeed, it is!

GIOVANNA
Ognor si sta, ognor si sta.

RIGOLETTO *(to* GIOVANNA*)*
Ah, guard her always, I implore you

RIGOLETTO
Ah, veglia, o donna, questo
fiore

Che a te puro confidai;
Veglia attenta, e non sia mai
Che s'offuschi il suo candor.
Tu dei venti dal furore,
Ch'altri fiori hanno piegato,
Lo difendi, e immacolato
Lo ridona al genitor.

Guard this pure and tender flower,
Guard her well each waking hour,
So that no harm will reach this door.
From the perils of existence
You must shield her with affection;
Keep her safe in your protection
For her father evermore.

GILDA
Quanto affetto! quali cure!
Che temete, padre mio?
Lassù in cielo, presso Dio
Veglia un angiol protettor.
Da noi stogiie le sventure
Di mia madre il priego santo:
Non fia mai disvelto o franto
Questo a voi diletto fior.

GILDA
What affection,
Anxious worry, dearest Father!
Why these cares and apprehensions?
There in heaven, near to God,
A guardian angel prays for me.
My beloved mother's prayer
Will avert all grief and sorrow,
Keep your tender precious flower
Free from harm for evermore.

RIGOLETTO
Ah! veglia, o donna, questo fiore
Che a te puro confi . . .
Alcun v'è fuori . . .

RIGOLETTO (*to* GIOVANNA)
Ah—guard her always, I implore you,
Guard this pure and tender . . .
Someone is out there . . .

GILDA
Cielo!
Sempre novel sospetto!

GILDA
Heavens, why is he so suspicious?
(RIGOLETTO *opens the door of the courtyard, and while he is outside and looking into the street, the* DUKE *slips into the courtyard and hides behind the tree; he throws a purse to* GIOVANNA *to make her keep silent*)

RIGOLETTO
Alla chiesa vi seguiva mai nessuno?

RIGOLETTO (*re-entering, to* GIOVANNA)
Are you certain no one followed her from church?

GIOVANNA
Mai.

GIOVANNA
Yes.

DUCA
(Rigoletto!)

DUKE (*aside, softly*)
Rigoletto!

RIGOLETTO
Se talor qui picchian,
Guardatevi d'aprire.

RIGOLETTO
Never, never open, no matter who may come here!

GIOVANNA
Nemmeno al Duca?

GIOVANNA
With no exception?

RIGOLETTO
Non che ad altri a lui! . . .
Mia figlia, addio.

RIGOLETTO (*very emphatic*)
There is no exception!
(*tenderly, to* GILDA)
Farewell, my daughter!

DUCA
(Sua figlia!)

DUKE (*as before*)
His daughter!

RIGOLETTO
Ah! veglia, o donna, questo fiore
Che a te puro confidai;
Veglia attenta, e non sia mai
Che s'offuschi il suo candor.
Tu dei venti dal furore,
Ch'altri fiori hanno piegato,

RIGOLETTO (*to* GIOVANNA)
Ah, guard her always, I implore you,
Guard this pure and tender flower,
Guard her well each waking hour,
So that no harm will reach this door.
From the perils of existence

You must shield her with affection
Keep her safe in your protection
For her father evermore.

Lo difendi, e immacolato
Lo ridona al genitor.

GILDA
What deep affection,
Anxious worry, dearest father!
Why these cares and apprehensions?
There in heaven, near to God,
A guardian angel prays for me.
In heav'n above, with tender love
A guardian angel prays for me.

GILDA
Quanto affetto! . . . quali cure!
Che temete, padre mio?
Lassù in cielo presso Dio,
Veglia un angiol protettor,
Lassù in cielo, presso Dio,
Veglia un angiol protettor.

RIGOLETTO
Protect her, Giovanna,
Protect her with watchful tender love.
Giovanna, guard her well.
Gilda, my daughter, God speed you!

RIGOLETTO
Ah! veglia, o donna,
Ah, veglia, o donna, questo fior!
Veglia, o donna, questo fiore!
Figlia, mia figlia, addio!

GILDA
In heaven, near to God,
A guardian angel prays for me
With tender love.
Father, my father,
God speed you.

GILDA
Lassù in cielo veglia un angiol protettor . . .
Padre, mio padre, addio!

(*they embrace.* RIGOLETTO *leaves, locking the door behind him*)

Scene and Duet

GILDA
Giovanna, I feel so guilty . . .

GILDA
Giovanna, ho dei rimorsi . . .

GIOVANNA
But why on earth?

GIOVANNA
E perchè mai?

GILDA
One handsome stranger followed me on Sunday.

GILDA
Tacqui che un giovin me seguiva al tempio.

GIOVANNA
Why should you tell him?
This handsome stranger,
I'm sure you don't dislike him?

GIOVANNA
Perchè ciò dirgli? L' odïate dunque
Cotesto giovin, voi?

GILDA
No, no, his loving glances
Said he adored me . . .

GILDA
No, no, chè troppo è bello e spira amore . . .

GIOVANNA
He appears to be gen'rous
And very lordly.

GIOVANNA
E magnanimo sembra e gran signore.

GILDA (*dreamily*)
My lover need not be
A prince or nobleman;
His love means more to me
If in sincerity
He's poor and humble.
Softly and secretly
My heart is calling,
Fervently yearning to say that I love . . .

GILDA
Signor nè principe io lo vorrei;
Sento che povero più l'amerei.
Sognando o vigile sempre lo chiamo,
E l'alma in estasi gli dice: t'a . . .

DUCA
T'amo!
T'amo; ripetilo sì caro accento;
Un puro schiudimi ciel di contento!

GILDA
Giovanna, Giovanna! Ahi, misera! Non v'è più alcuno
Che qui rispondami! . . .—Oh Dio! . . . nessuno?

DUCA
Son io coll'anima, che ti rispondo!
Ah, due che s'amano, son tutto un mondo!

GILDA
Chi mai, chi giungere vi fece a me?

DUCA
S'angelo o demone, che importa a te?
Io t'amo . . .

GILDA
Usciteme.

DUCA
Uscire! Adesso!
Ora che accendene un fuoco istesso!
Ah, inseparabile d'amore il Dio
Stringeva, o vergine, tuo fato al mio!
È il sol dell'anima, la vita è amore,
Sua voce è il palpito del nostro core.
E fama e gloria, potenza e trono,
Umane, fragili qui cose sono,
Una pur avvene sola, divina:
È amor che agl'angeli più ne avvicina!
Adunque amiamoci, donna celeste;
D'invidia agl'uomini sarò per te.

GILDA
Ah, de' miei vergini sogni son queste
Le voci tenere sì care a me!

DUCA
Amiamoci, amiamoci.

LE DUE
A me (per te) ah!
Care a me (per te) ah!
Sì care a me! (ah sì, per te!)

DUKE (*steps forward suddenly, makes a sign to* GIOVANNA *to leave, and, kneeling before* GILDA, *completes her sentence*)
Love you!
Say it once more to me
Now we're together!
My love for you will be flaming forever!

GILDA (*terrified*)
Giovanna, Giovanna!
Oh answer me!
Why have you left me alone,
Deserted here?
Oh heaven, I'm frightened!

DUKE
Beloved, your faith in me
Shall be requited!
Two loving hearts
Are their own world united.

GILDA
It is a mystery how you came here!

DUKE
What does it matter now,
What do you fear? I love you!

GILDA
Oh, leave me now!

DUKE
Leave you! What folly!
Now when the ecstasy of love inflames me!
Our guiding stars decree that we are fated
To share one destiny that love created!
Love is the sunlight and spark of creation,
Its power dominates our hearts' pulsation.
Honors and glory and wealth in profusion
Are human weaknesses and vain illusion.
One thing alone there is, worth while possessing:
It's love, it's love alone
That gives our lives celestial blessing!
If you belong to me in love united,
That will be paradise,
Heaven on earth,
That will be paradise,
Enjoyed on earth!

GILDA
My secret longing at last came true,
Ah, my hopes and fantasies,
The dream of love!

DUKE
So dear to me, a dream come true!

BOTH
Love's dream, ah!
Paradise, ah—enjoyed on earth!

DUKE
You love me—say it once again . . .

GILDA
I love you!

DUKE
How you enchant me!

GILDA
Now may I hear your name at last?
This favor you will grant me?

CEPRANO (*who has approached the house from outside, with* BORSA)
The house is here . . .

BORSA
That's right.
(*they disappear again*)

DUKE (*to* GILDA)
Of course you may . . .
(*he thinks for a moment*)
Gualtier Maldè—
I am a student—and penniless.

GIOVANNA (*enters excitedly*)
I hear somebody coming . . .

GILDA (*terrified*)
Maybe my father—

DUKE (*aside*)
The devil take the insolent intruder
Who dares disturb me!

GILDA (*to* GIOVANNA)
You'd better let him leave by the side door,
And hurry . . .

DUKE
You love me, you say?

GILDA
And you?

DUKE
For now and always and . . .

GILDA
No more, no more, I beg you,
It's late, please go now.

DUKE
Farewell then, beloved,

GILDA
My joy and happiness.

BOTH
My heart will always be yours alone!
Farewell, beloved, good-by, my love!
My heart and soul belong to you alone
Forevermore!
My dearest, farewell now,
Farewell, my love.

DUCA
Che m'ami, deh! ripetimi!

GILDA
L'udiste.

DUCA
Oh, me felice!

GILDA
Il nome vostro ditemi . . .
Saperlo non mi lice?

CEPRANO
Il loco è qui . . .

BORSA
Sta ben . . .

DUCA
Mi nomino. . . .
Gualtier Maldè . . .
Studente sono . . . e povero.

GIOVANNA
Rumor di passi è fuori.

GILDA
Forse mio padre . . .

DUCA
(Ah, cogliere
Potessi il traditore
Che sì mi sturba!)

GILDA
Adducilo
Di qua al bastione . . . or ite . . .

DUCA
Di': m'amerai tu?

GILDA
E voi?

DUCA
L'intera vita . . . poi . . .

GILDA
Non più . . . non più . . . partite.
Non più, partite.

DUCA
Addio, addio speranza ed anima.

GILDA
Addio, addio speranza ed anima.

LE DUE
Sol tu sarai, sarai per me.
Addio, addio, addio, addio, vivrà immutabile
L'affetto mio per te.
Addio!

(*the* DUKE *leaves quickly, escorted by* GIOVANNA)

Aria

GILDA
Gualtier Maldè! nome di
lui sì amato,
Ti scolpisci nel core
innamorato!

Caro nome che il mio cor
Festi primo palpitar,
Le delizie dell'amor
Mi dêi sempre rammentar!
Col pensier il mio desir
A te sempre volerà,
E fin l'ultimo sospir,
Caro nome, tuo sarà.
Col pensier il mio desir
A te sempre volerà,
E fin l'ultimo mio sospir,
Caro nome, tuo sarà!
Col pensier il mio desir
A te sempre volerà,
A te volerà, fin l'ultimo sospir
Caro nome, tuo sarà,
Caro nome, tuo sarà,
Il mio desir a te ognora volerà,
Fin l'ultimo sospiro tuo sarà!
Gualtier Maldè! Gualtier
Maldè!
Caro nome che il mio cor
Festi primo palpitar,
E fin l'ultimo sospir,
Caro nome, tuo sarà.
Gualtier Maldè! Gualtier
Maldè!

GILDA (*alone*)
Gualtier Maldè!
Name of my dear beloved!
Deeply graven in my heart
Be it forever!
Treasured mem'ry of his name,
Name of him that I adore!
May its bright and glowing flame
Light my soul forevermore!
Ev'ry word he said so dear
I shall keep with tender care
As a precious souvenir
Of the glorious love we share!
Ev'ry word he said so dear
I shall keep with tender care
I shall keep as a precious souvenir
Treasured mem'ry of his name,
Name of him that I adore,
All my heart belongs to you alone
And my love forevermore . . .
(*she mounts the stairs to the terrace, slowly, carrying a light; meanwhile the stage is beginning to fill up with* COURTIERS, *armed and masked*)
Gualtier Maldè, Gualtier Maldè!
Treasured mem'ry of his name,
Name of him that I adore!
May its bright and glowing flame
Light my soul forevermore!
Gualtier Maldè! Gualtier Maldè!

BORSA
È là . . .

BORSA (*softly to the* COURTIERS)
She's there.

CEPRANO
Miratela.

CEPRANO
How fair she is!

CORO
Oh, quanto è bella!

COURTIERS
No beauty rarer!

MARULLO
Par fata od angiol.

MARULLO
No queen is fairer!

CORO
L'amante è quella
di Rigoletto.
Oh, quanto è bella!

COURTIERS
She is the mistress of Rigoletto—
A pearl so priceless!
(GILDA, *with the final note of her aria, has disappeared in the house*)

RIGOLETTO
(Riedo! perchè?)

RIGOLETTO (*reappearing, in a state of anxiety*)
Why did I return?

BORSA
Silenzio! all'opra,
badate a me.

BORSA (*to the* COURTIERS)
Attention! Let's hurry,
We must prepare.

RIGOLETTO (*to himself*)
Ah, fateful curse, I cannot forget it!
(*encountering* BORSA, *aloud*)
Who goes there?

BORSA (*softly to the* COURTIERS)
Be careful, it's Rigoletto!

CEPRANO
So much the better,
Now we can slay him!

BORSA
No, for tomorrow
We'll laugh and flay him.

MARULLO
It's time for action . . .

RIGOLETTO
Whose voice is that?

MARULLO
Eh! Rigoletto—say—

RIGOLETTO (*in a terrible voice*)
Who goes there?

MARULLO
Why such a fury! I'm—

RIGOLETTO
Who?

MARULLO
Marullo.

RIGOLETTO (*gentler*)
It is so dark here,
I could not see you.

MARULLO
We'll fool Ceprano,
And when we've tricked him
We steal his countess,
A lovely victim.

RIGOLETTO (*to himself, relieved*)
I breathe more freely!
(*aloud*)
How will we do it?

MARULLO (*softly to* CEPRANO)
I need your door key!
(*to* RIGOLETTO)
There's nothing to it.
In clever planning
None can outwit us.
(*showing* RIGOLETTO *the key he has gotten from* CEPRANO)
His key will admit us.

RIGOLETTO (*feeling the key*)
Ceprano's emblem!
(*to himself*)

RIGOLETTO
(Ah, da quel vecchio fui maledetto!!)
Chi va là?

BORSA
Tacete . . . c'è Rigoletto.

CEPRANO
Vittoria doppia! L'uccideremo.

BORSA
No, che domani più rideremo.

MARULLO
Or tutto aggiusto . . .

RIGOLETTO
Chi parla qua?

MARULLO
Ehi! Rigoletto—Di—

RIGOLETTO
Chi va là?

MARULLO
Eh, non mangiarci!
Son . . .

RIGOLETTO
Chi?

MARULLO
Marullo.

RIGOLETTO
In tanto buio lo sguardo è nullo.

MARULLO
Qui ne condusse ridevol cosa,
Torre a Ceprano vogliam la sposa.

RIGOLETTO
(Ahimè! respiro!) Ma come entrare?

MARULLO
(La vostra chiave?)
Non dubitare.
Non dee mancarci lo stratagemma,
Ecco la chiave . . .

RIGOLETTO
Sento il suo stemma.
(Ah, terror vano fu dunque il mio!)

N'è là il palazzo, con voi
son io.

MARULLO
Siam mascherati.

RIGOLETTO
Ch'io pur mi mascheri!
A me una larva.

MARULLO
Sì, pronta è già.
Terrai la scala . . .

RIGOLETTO
Fitta è la tenebra.

MARULLO
La benda cieco e sordo il fa.

CORO
Zitti, zitti, moviamo a vendetta;
Ne sia colto or che men
l'aspetta.
Derisore sì audace e costante
A sua volta schernito sarà!
Cheti, cheti, rubiamgli l'amante
E la Corte doman riderà.
Cheti, cheti, cheti, cheti!
Cheti, cheti, rubiamgli l'amante
E la Corte doman riderà.
Derisore sì audace,
Sì audace e costante,
Derisore sì audace,
A sua volta schernito sarà!
Derisore sì audace,
Sì audace e costante,
Derisore sì audace,
A sua volta schernito sarà!
Zitti, zitti, zitti, zitti,
Cheti, cheti, cheti, cheti!
Attenti, attenti all'opra!

GILDA
Soccorso, padre mio!

CORO
Vittoria!

No need to worry, they bear no malice.
(*aloud*)
I'll gladly join you, this is his palace.

MARULLO
We all have masks on.

RIGOLETTO
Have you an extra mask
That you will lend me?

MARULLO
Yes, here it is.
You hold the ladder.
(*puts a mask on him and at the same time blindfolds him with a handkerchief, and places him holding a ladder against the wall*)

RIGOLETTO
How dense the darkness is . . .

MARULLO (*softly to the* COURTIERS)
The blindfold closes his eyes and ears.
(*while the following chorus is sung, some* COURTIERS *climb up to the terrace, break open the door of the first story and descend, opening the street entrance to the others*)

COURTIERS
Swiftly moving to finish our mission,
Make no sound to arouse suspicion.
He who always so boldly derides us
Shall for once be the one we will mock.
While he helps us, we steal his beloved
And tomorrow the whole court will laugh.
Careful, careful, let us hurry!
While he helps us we steal his beloved
And the palace with laughter will rock.
He who always so derides us,
Who so boldly mocks and scorns us,
Shall at last become the victim
Of our clever revenge in his own turn.
Though in malice he outstrides us,
Though he threatens and he warns us,
We shall carry out our vengeance
And his rightful reward he then shall earn.
Quiet, quiet, we are ready,
Hold the ladder steady, steady,
It's time to carry out our plan.
(*some of the* COURTIERS *have entered the house. They carry* GILDA *out. While crossing the stage she loses a scarf*)

GILDA (*from a distance*)
Oh help me, Father, help me!

COURTIERS (*from a distance*)
Victory!

GILDA
Oh, help me!

RIGOLETTO (*still holding the ladder, blindfolded*)
Why does it take so long?
It must be over.
(*puts his hand to his eyes*)
This is a blindfold!
(*he violently tears off the mask and the blindfold and, recognizing* GILDA'*s scarf, he sees the broken door, enters the house, drags the stunned* GIOVANNA *out. Frantic with despair, he finally cries out:*)
Ah—ah—ah—!
The curse of Monterone!

GILDA
Aita!

RIGOLETTO
Non han finito ancor!
Qual derisione!
Sono bendato!
Ah! la maledizione!!

ACT II

(Large hall in the ducal palace. There are two side doors, and a large one in the center that closes. At the sides hang the portraits (full-length) of the Duke and his wife. There is a big armchair near a table, covered with a velvet cloth, and other furniture.)

Aria

DUCA
Ella mi fu rapita!
E quando, o ciel? Ne' brevi istanti,
Prima che il mio presagio interno
Sull'orma corsa ancora mi spingesse!
Schiuso era l'uscio! E la magion deserta!
E dove ora sarà quell'angiol caro?
Colei che prima potè in questo core
Destar la fiamma di costanti affetti?
Colei sì pura, al cui modesto sguardo
Quasi spinto a virtù talor mi credo!
Ella mi fu rapita!
E chi l'ardiva? Ma ne avrò vendetta!
Lo chiede il pianto della mia diletta.
Parmi veder le lagrime
Scorrenti da quel ciglio,
Quando fra il dubbio e l'ansia
Del subito periglio.
Dell'amor nostro memore
Il suo Gualtier chiamò.
Ned ei potea soccorrerti,
Cara fanciulla amata;
Ei che vorria coll'anima
Farti quaggiù beata;
Ei che le sfere agl'angeli
Per te non invidiò.

DUKE *(enters in great agitation)*
Treacherous villains stole her!
I came too late!
When I had left her,
I had a sudden premonition
She was in danger,
And hastened to protect her.
Futile intention!
I found the house deserted!
And where can she be now?
My dear beloved?
My lovely angel,
The only one who moved me to real devotion
And constant affection!
She was so pure, her gentle glance so modest,
I became a better man, the more I loved her.
Now she has been abducted!
Who dared to do this?
Let them beware, for I shall take my vengeance!
So I have promised
Ah, my dear beloved!
Torn from him who adores you,
Despairing, weeping in terror,
Dearest, you must have suffered
Alone in sudden peril.
I seem to hear you calling me,
Your own Gualtier Maldè!
Nowhere I found a trace of you.
Gone was my dear beloved,
Gone all my joy and happiness,
Fled in that hour I lost you.
You are my dream of paradise,
You are my world and all.
Dearest beloved, how I am hoping,
Longing for the day
When you return to me,
My one, my only love, ah,
You are my world and all!

CORO
Duca, duca?

COURTIERS *(entering animatedly)*
Highness, hear this!

DUCA
Ebben?

DUKE
What's new?

COURTIERS
We just have snared the mistress of Rigoletto!

DUKE
Really? From where?

COURTIERS
From his own house.

DUKE
Ha, ha! Tell me, let me hear!
How you did it, let me hear!

COURTIERS
Last night in secret we all collected
And near Ceprano's house we searched around;
In one old mansion, as we expected,
A lovely girl we shortly found.
It was the mistress of Rigoletto,
Whom we beheld there with our own eyes,
We had decided to take her with us,
When he came by to our surprise.
And when we told him we were intending
To steal Ceprano's wife, the fool believed;
He held the ladder, not comprehending,
And with a blindfold he was deceived.
And then we rapidly achieved our errand,
We seized the girl and carried her away.
When he discovered that he was tricked,
One can imagine his dismay, his great dismay!

DUKE (*aside*)
Heavens, they found her, my dear beloved!

COURTIERS
It served him right,
It was a most successful night!
(*the* DUKE *rushes off in great haste;* RIGOLETTO, *entering from the center, simulating indifference*)

MARULLO (*with sincere expression*)
Poor Rigoletto!

RIGOLETTO
La ra, la ra, la ra, la ra, la ra!

COURTIERS (*softly, among themselves*)
He's there, let's watch him.
(*to* RIGOLETTO)
And how is our Rigoletto?

RIGOLETTO (*to himself*)
They all did this together!

CEPRANO
Any news yet, buffoon?

RIGOLETTO (*imitating* CEPRANO)
Any news yet, buffoon?
That you are duller on this morning than usual!

COURTIERS
Ha ha ha!

CORO
L'amante
Fu rapita a Rigoletto.

DUCA
Come? e donde?

CORO
Dal suo tetto.

DUCA
Ah! ah! dite, come fu?
Dite, dite, come fu?

CORO
Scorrendo uniti remota via,
Brev'ora dopo caduto il dì,
Come previsto ben s'era in pria,
Rara beltà ci si scoprì.
Era l'amante di Rigoletto,
Che vista appena si dileguò.
Già di rapirla s'avea il progetto,
Quando il buffon vêr noi spuntò;
Che di Ceprano noi la contessa
Rapir volessimo, stolto, credè;
La scala, quindi, all'uopo messa,
Bendato ei stesso ferma tenè.
Salimmo e rapidi la giovinetta
A noi riusciva quindi asportar.
Quand'ei s'accorse della vendetta
Restò scornato ad imprecar.

DUCA
(Cielo! È dessa la mia diletta!)

CORO
Ad imprecar,
Restò scornato ad imprecar!

MARULLO
Povero Rigoletto!

RIGOLETTO
La ra, la ra, la ra, la ra, la ra!

CORO
Ei vien! Silenzio.
Oh buon giorno, Rigoletto.

RIGOLETTO
(Han tutti fatto il colpo!)

CEPRANO
Ch'hai di nuovo, buffon?

RIGOLETTO
Ch'hai di nuovo, buffon?
Che dell'usato
Più noioso voi siete.

CORO
Ah! ah! ah!

RIGOLETTO
La ra, la ra, la ra, la ra, la ra.
(Ove l'avran nascosta? . . .)

CORO
(Guardate com'è inquieto!)

RIGOLETTO
Son felice
Che nulla a voi nuocesse
L'aria di questa notte.

MARULLO
Questa notte!

RIGOLETTO
Sì . . . Oh, fu il bel colpo!

MARULLO
S'ho dormito sempre!

RIGOLETTO
Ah, voi dormiste! . . . Avrò dunque sognato!
La ra, la ra, la ra, la ra, la ra!

CORO
(Ve' come tutto osserva!)

RIGOLETTO
(Non è il suo.)
Dorme il Duca tuttor?

CORO
Sì, dorme ancora.

PAGGIO
Al suo sposo parlar vuol la duchessa.

CEPRANO
Dorme.

PAGGIO
Qui or or con voi non era?

BORSA
È a caccia.

PAGGIO
Senza paggi! senz'armi!

CORO
E non capisci
Che per ora vedere non può alcuno?

RIGOLETTO
Ah, ella è qui dunque!
Ella è col Duca!

CORO
Chi?

RIGOLETTO (*moving about on the stage, looking around anxiously*)
La ra, la ra, la ra, la ra, la ra!
(*to himself*)
Where did they hide my darling?

COURTIERS (*among themselves*)
He's searching for his sweetheart!

RIGOLETTO
I am glad that you are not ill this morning.
Last night was very chilly.

MARULLO
Very chilly?

RIGOLETTO
Oh, our prank was funny!

MARULLO (*pretending*)
That I was sleeping soundly?

RIGOLETTO
You were sleeping soundly?
Then I must have been dreaming.
(*he moves away, singing softly, sees a handkerchief, and snatches it up*)
La rà la rà, la rà, la rà la rà . . .

COURTIERS
Look, look, he picked up a kerchief!

RIGOLETTO (*aside*)
It's not hers.
(*throwing the handkerchief away, aloud*)
Is the Duke still asleep?

COURTIERS
Yes, he is sleeping.
(*a page enters*)

PAGE
Will the Duke grant an audience to the Duchess?

CEPRANO
He's sleeping.

PAGE
That's not true, because I saw him.

BORSA
He went hunting.

PAGE
Unescorted? At this hour?

COURTIERS
Are you so stupid that you don't understand
Why he can't see you?

RIGOLETTO (*who has stood listening most attentively to the conversation, rushes suddenly toward them*)
Ah, she is in there!
She's in his bedroom!

COURTIERS
Who?

RIGOLETTO (*furiously*)
The girl that you abducted last night from my dwelling.
But I will be relentless,
Give her back!

COURTIERS
If you're looking for your mistress,
Go and find her elsewhere!

RIGOLETTO (*with terrifying intensity*)
I want my daughter!

COURTIERS (*taken aback*)
Ah, his daughter!

RIGOLETTO
Yes, she's my daughter . . .
Disappointing triumph!
Yes? I see you laugh no longer!
(*rushes toward the door, but the* COURTIERS *block his way*)
She is there! Let me see her,
No one shall wrong her!
(*with utmost hatred*)
Fawning courtiers, degraded and lowly,
For what profit have you sold my treasure?
Wanton scoundrels, your gold is your measure!
But my daughter no ransom could buy!
Give her back now, or I swear by what's holy,
My revenge shall be bloody and frightful!
There's no power so strong and so rightful
That a father would not dare defy!
Let me in there, you assassins,
I want her, my daughter, my daughter—
You fiendish assassins!
(RIGOLETTO *struggles with the courtiers, then moves forward, exhausted*)
Ah, you've banded all together,
Against me, heartless, ev'ry one!
(*in tears*)
Ah, will nothing move you . . .
Marullo, I implore you,
See my tears as I plead here before you.
Tell me where they have hidden my daughter,
Marullo, I beg you, won't you say
Where they're hiding my daughter?
In there? Won't you tell me?
No answer? Woe me!
Noble lords, I implore you, have mercy!
I entreat you, have pity on a father!
Give her back, for to you she means nothing,
While to me she is dearer
Than all the gold on earth.
Have pity, my lords,

RIGOLETTO
La giovin che stanotte
Al mio tetto rapiste.
Ma la saprò riprender!
Ella è là . . .

CORO
Se l'amante perdesti, la ricerca altrove.

RIGOLETTO
Io vo' mia figlia!

CORO
La sua figlia!

RIGOLETTO
Sì, la mia figlia . . . d'una tal vittoria
Che? . . . Adesso non ridete?
Ella è là! la vogl'io . . . la renderete.
Cortigiani, vil razza dannata,
Per qual prezzo vendeste il mio bene?
A voi nulla per l'oro sconviene,
Ma mia figlia è impagabil tesor.
La rendete . . . o, se pur disarmata,
Questa man per voi fora cruenta;
Nulla in terra più l'uomo paventa,
Se dei figli difende l'onor.
Quella porta, assassini,
Assassini, m'aprite, la porta,
La porta, assassini, m'aprite!
Ah! Voi tutti a me contro venite!
Tutti contro me!
Ah! Ebben, piango!
Marullo, signore,
Tu ch'hai l'alma gentil come il core,
Dimmi tu dove l'hanno nascosta?
Marullo . . . signore, dimmi tu
Dove l'hanno nascosta?
È là? Non è vero?
Tu taci! Ohimè!
Miei signori, perdono,
pietate
Al vegliardo, la figlia ridate
Ridonarla a voi nulla ora costa,
Tutto, tutto al mondo
È tal figlia per me.
Signori, perdon,
Perdono, pietà;
Ridate a me la figlia;
Tutto al mondo è tal figlia per me;
Ridate a me la figlia.
Tutto al mondo ell'è per me!
Pietà, pietà, signori,
Pietà signori,
Pietà.

Restore her to me,
A father begs for pity,
She is my treasure, my one and all.
My lords, let me implore you,
Give me my daughter once more.

Scene and Duet

GILDA
Mio padre!

GILDA (*entering from the room at left, throwing herself into her father's arms*)
My father!

RIGOLETTO
Dio! Mia Gilda!
Signori, in essa è tutta
La mia famiglia . . . Non temer più nulla,
Angelo mio, fu scherzo, non è vero?
Io, che pur piansi, or rido . . . E tu, a che piangi?

RIGOLETTO
Gilda, my Gilda!
(*to the* COURTIERS)
Behold her, my daughter,
My treasure, my one possession!
(*to* GILDA)
Now that I found you,
My darling, fear nothing.
(*to the* COURTIERS)
Admit it, you were joking—
Tears are forgotten for laughter . . .
(*to* GILDA)
But you, you are trembling?

GILDA
Ah, l'onta, padre mio.

GILDA
For shame and degradation . . .

RIGOLETTO
Cielo! Che dici?

RIGOLETTO
Heavens, it can't be!

GILDA
Arrossir voglio innanzi a voi soltanto.

GILDA
Let no one witness my deep humiliation!

RIGOLETTO
Ite di qua voi tutti!
Se il duca vostro d'appressarsi osasse,
Che non entri, gli dite, e ch'io ci sono.

RIGOLETTO (*turning upon the* COURTIERS *in an imperious manner*)
Leave us alone, you traitors,
And if the Duke himself should dare to return here,
You shall not let him enter,
For I forbid it!

TUTTI
(Coi fanciulli e co' dementi
Spesso giova il simular;
Partiam pur, ma quel ch'ei tenti
Non lasciamo d'osservar.)

COURTIERS (*among themselves*)
When a man has lost his reason
Better let him have his way.
It is wiser to appease him,
And pretend that we obey.
(*they leave*)

RIGOLETTO
Parla, siam soli.

RIGOLETTO (*turns tenderly to* GILDA)
Tell me . . . they're gone now . . .

GILDA
(Ciel! dammi coraggio!)
Tutte le feste al tempio
Mentre pregava Iddio,
Bello e fatale un giovane
Offriasi al guardo mio.
Se i labbri nostri tacquero
Dagl'occhi il cor parlò.
Furtivo fra le tenebre
Sol ieri a me giungeva;
Sono studente, povero,
Commosso, mi diceva,

GILDA (*to herself*)
God, give me courage!
It was in church each Sunday,
While I was humbly praying,
I saw a young man glance at me,
His inner thoughts betraying.
Though our lips were silent,
Yet our eyes began to speak of love.
Yesterday just at eventide,

Suddenly he was near me.
That he was poor he said to me,
And I believed sincerely.
Then with growing ardor
He swore his glowing love.
And then—he left—
So my heart awoke to love
Complete and all pervading.
Suddenly all those men appeared;
By ruthless force invading,
They seized me and abducted me,
And brought me this cruel ordeal.

E con ardente palpito
Amor mi protestò.
Partì partì, il mio core aprivasi
A speme più gradita,
Quando improvvisi apparvero
Color che m'han rapita,
E a forza qui m'addussero
Nell'ansia più crudel.

RIGOLETTO (*to himself*)
Ah, mine be the shame of infamy,
That was my fervent prayer
So that her life be blameless
And heaven protect and spare her.
All men who face eternity
Have one hope for salvation,
But nothing is left me,
No consolation,
My altar is destroyed, ah!
(*turning to* GILDA)
Gilda, Gilda! My daughter!
Let me console you!

RIGOLETTO
(Ah, solo per me l'infamia
A te chiedeva, o Dio
Ch'ella potesse ascendere
Quanto caduto er'io
Ah, presso del patibolo
Bisogna ben l'altare!
Ma tutto ora scompare,
L'altar si rovesciò!)
Piangi, piangi, fanciulla
Fanciulla piangi.

GILDA
Father!

GILDA
Padre!

RIGOLETTO
Never, never before you knew such grief!

RIGOLETTO
Scorrer, scorrer fa il pianto sul mio cor.

GILDA
Father, how kind you are
To console me in my grief!

GILDA
Padre, in voi parla un angel
Consolator.

RIGOLETTO
Daughter!

RIGOLETTO
Piangi.

GILDA
Your words are tender and loving.

GILDA
Padre, in voi parla un angel.

RIGOLETTO
Fate has been cruel
Though you are blameless.

RIGOLETTO
Piangi, fanciulla,
Fanciulla, piangi.

GILDA
Father, how you console me,
And ease my heart!

GILDA
Padre, voi parla un angel
consolator.

RIGOLETTO
Poor child, dearest angel,
Shed tears and ease your grieving heart!

RIGOLETTO
Piangi, piangi, piangi,
Scorrer fa il pianto sul mio cor.

GILDA
Father, how you console me and ease my heart,
My broken heart!
Father, protect me, console me,
And love me forevermore.

GILDA
Padre, in voi parla un angel
Consolator.
Padre, in voi
Un angel, un angel consolator.

RIGOLETTO
Scorrer fa il pianto,
Mia figlia, sul mio cor.

Compiuto pur quanto a fare mi resta,
Lasciare potremo quest'aura funesta.

GILDA
Sì

RIGOLETTO
(E tutto un sol giorno cangiare potè!)

USCIERE
Schiudete! ire al carcere Monteron dee.

MONTERONE
Poichè fosti invano da me maledetto,
Nè un fulmine o un ferro colpiva il tuo petto,
Felice pur anco, o Duca, vivrai.

RIGOLETTO
No, vecchio, t'inganni! un vindice avrai.
Sì, vendetta, tremenda vendetta
Di quest'anima è solo desio . . .
Di punirti già l'ora s'affretta,
Che fatale per te tuonerà.
Come fulmin scagliato da Dio
Te colpire il buffone saprà.

GILDA
O mio padre, qual gioia feroce
Balenarvi negl'occhi vegg'io!

RIGOLETTO
Vendetta!

GILDA
Perdonate . . . a noi pure una voce
Di perdono dal cielo verrà.

RIGOLETTO
Vendetta!

GILDA
(Mi tradiva, pur l'amo; gran Dio,
Per l'ingrato ti chiedo pietà!)

RIGOLETTO
Colpire te il buffone, te colpire saprà.

GILDA
A noi pure il perdono dal ciel verrà.

RIGOLETTO
Tears ease your sorrow,
May heaven be with you, forevermore.
I've only one aim now,
One goal and endeavor;
When that is accomplished,
We'll leave here forever!

GILDA
Yes.

RIGOLETTO (*to himself*)
And all this misfortune in one single day!
(COUNT MONTERONE *is led across the stage between guards*)

USHER
Make way there,
We are leading Monterone to the dungeon.

MONTERONE (*standing still before the portrait of the* DUKE)
O Duke,
Since my curse had no power to blight you,
Since no lightning from heaven descended to smite you,
Live happy forever in pleasure and vice!
(*he is led away*)

RIGOLETTO
No, you are mistaken,
An avenger will rise!
Feel the might of my dreadful vendetta!
Sealing your doom is my only desire.
Deeds so evil are wrought by a debtor
Damned by God to the flames and to ruin.
Though the power that dooms you is higher,
Fall by the hand of the scornful buffoon.

GILDA
Father, Father, although unspoken,
Savage joy fills your heart with longing!

RIGOLETTO
Vendetta!

GILDA
Please forgive him, and by that token
We'll be forgiven by heaven above.

RIGOLETTO
Vendetta!

GILDA
Though he wronged me
I love him in wronging!
God forgive him because of my love!

RIGOLETTO
You'll perish by the vengeance of your scornful buffoon!

GILDA
We shall be forgiven by heaven above!
(*they leave together, in great agitation, through the center door*)

ACT III

(*Near the shore of the river Mincio. At left is a house with two stories, half decayed. The front, toward the spectator, is open, so that one sees the inside of a tavern on the ground floor, and a dilapidated room on the second floor. In the wall facing the street there is a door. The wall is full of holes, that one can see easily from outside what happens in the tavern. The remainder of the stage represents a deserted part of the Mincio. It is night.* GILDA *and* RIGOLETTO *are in the street,* SPARAFUCILE *inside the tavern, sitting by a table, polishing his leather belt, unaware of what is said outside.*)

Scene and Aria

RIGOLETTO
You love him?

GILDA
Always.

RIGOLETTO
But I've given you time to forget him.

GILDA
I love him.

RIGOLETTO
Poor tortured heart of woman!
Depraved seducer!
But you'll be avenged, my Gilda.

GILDA
Forgive him, Father.

RIGOLETTO
If I could prove for certain that he betrayed you,
Even then you'd love him?

GILDA
Perhaps . . . but he adores me.

RIGOLETTO
Does he?

GILDA
Yes.

RIGOLETTO
Well then, I'll have to show you.
(*he leads her to one of the chinks in the wall, through which she looks; the* DUKE *in the uniform of a cavalry officer, enters the tavern*)

GILDA
I see a man there!

RIGOLETTO
Just wait a little.

GILDA
Ah, Father, spare me!

DUKE (*to* SPARAFUCILE)
Some wine here, and quickly!

RIGOLETTO
E l'ami?

GILDA
Sempre.

RIGOLETTO
Pure
tempo a guarirne t'ho lasciato.

GILDA
Io l'amo.

RIGOLETTO
Povero cor di donna! Ah, il vile infame!
Ma avrai vendetta, o Gilda.

GILDA
Pietà, mio padre.

RIGOLETTO
E se tu certa fossi
Ch'ei ti tradisse, l'ameresti ancora?

GILDA
Nol sò, ma pur m'adora.

RIGOLETTO
Egli?

GILDA
Sì.

RIGOLETTO
Ebben, osserva dunque.

GILDA
Un uomo vedo.

RIGOLETTO
Per poco attendi.

GILDA
Ah, padre mio!

DUCA
Due cose,
e tosto!

SPARAFUCILE
Quali?

DUCA
Una stanza e del vino.

RIGOLETTO
(Son questi i suoi costumi!)

SPARAFUCILE
Oh, il bel zerbino!

DUCA
La donna è mobile
Qual piuma al vento,
Muta d'accento
E di pensiero.
Sempre un amabile
Leggiadro viso,
In pianto o in riso,
È menzognero.
La donna è mobil
Qual piuma al vento,
Muta d'accento
E di pensier.
È sempre misero
Chi a lei s'affida,
Chi le confida,
Mal cauto il core!
Pur mai non sentesi
Felice appieno
Chi su quel seno
Non liba amore!
La donna è mobil
Qual piuma al vento,
Muta d'accento
E di pensier.

SPARAFUCILE
È là il vostr'uomo. Viver dee o morire?

RIGOLETTO
Più tardi tornerò l'opra a compire.

SPARAFUCILE
Surely.

DUKE
Go and send me Maddalena!

RIGOLETTO
The game is just beginning.

SPARAFUCILE
A splendid fellow!
(*he goes inside the house*)

DUKE
Woman's fidelity
Turns like the weather,
Sways like a feather
Tossed in the breezes.
Fond of variety,
She is beguiling,
Frowning or smiling,
Just as she pleases.
She is capricious,
Turns like the weather,
Sways like a feather,
Never the same.
Blind in simplicity
Men's hearts are captured,
Wholly enraptured,
Deaf to all warning.
Yet fullest happiness
No man has tasted
Whose life is wasted
Loveless and mourning!
Woman will waver,
Turn like the weather,
Sway like a feather,
Never the same.

(SPARAFUCILE *reappears with a bottle of wine and two glasses. Then he knocks with the hilt of his long sword against the ceiling. At this signal a young girl enters. She wears gypsy attire. The* DUKE *wants to embrace her, but she escapes him. Meanwhile* SPARAFUCILE *has gone out on the street and talks to* RIGOLETTO, *who reappears at the outside of the tavern*)

SPARAFUCILE (*coming into the street*)
I have your man here.
Give your orders, I obey you.

RIGOLETTO
Detain him for a while
And then I'll pay you.

Quartet

(GILDA *and* RIGOLETTO *are outside the house,* MADDALENA *and the* DUKE *inside, on the ground floor*)

DUKE
One day I saw you smile at me,
I looked at you enraptured.
Your beauty so excited me
My heart was bound and captured.
As no one else before you
Sincerely I adore you.

DUCA
Un dì, se ben rammentomi,
O bella, t'incontrai!
Mi piacque di te chiedere
E intesi che qui stai.
Or sappi che d'allora
Sol te quest'alma adora.

GILDA
The traitor!

GILDA
Iniquo!

MADDALENA
Ha ha! No one else before me!
You're telling me a story.
A libertine, believe me,
Could never once deceive me.

MADDALENA
Ah! ah! e vent'altre ap-
presso
Le scorda forse adesso?
Ha un'aria il signorino
Da vero libertino . . .

DUKE
Yes, I'm very bad . . .

DUCA
Sì, un mostro son . . .

GILDA
Ah, dearest father!

GILDA
Ah, padre mio!

MADDALENA
Enough of that, it's silly.

MADDALENA
Lasciatemi,
stordito.

DUKE
Come, don't be naughty!

DUCA
Ih, che fracasso!

MADDALENA
Be good now.

MADDALENA
Stia saggio.

DUKE
Don't act so prudishly,
Why suddenly be haughty?
Cast all your foolish qualms away.
My darling, you must surrender.
(*takes her hand*)
Your hand is white as ivory!

DUCA
E tu sii docile,
Non farmi tanto chiasso.
Ogni saggezza chiudesi
Nel gaudio e nell'amore.
La bella mano candida!

MADDALENA
You're mocking me, pretender!

MADDALENA
Scherzate voi, signore.

DUKE
No, no!

DUCA
No, no.

MADDALENA
I'm ugly.

MADDALENA
Son brutta.

DUKE
I long for you.

DUCA
Abbracciami.

GILDA
Betrayer!

GILDA
Iniquo!

MADDALENA
Liar!

MADDALENA
Ebro!

DUKE
—with glowing passion!

DUCA
D'amor ardente.

MADDALENA
It seems to be your fashion
To jest your way through life!

MADDALENA
Signor, l'indifferente,
Vi piace canzonar?

DUKE
I want you for my wife!

DUCA
No, no, ti vo' sposar!

MADDALENA
Ne voglio la parola!

DUCA
Amabile figliuola!

RIGOLETTO
E non ti basta ancor?

GILDA
Iniquo traditor!

DUCA
Bella figlia dell'amore,
Schiavo son de' vezzi tuoi;
Con un detto sol tu puoi
Le mie pene consolar.
Vieni e senti del mio core
Il frequente palpitar.

MADDALENA
Ah! ah! Rido ben di core,
Chè tai baie costan poco.

GILDA
Ah, così parlar d'amore
A me pur l'infame ho udito!

MADDALENA
Quanto valga il vostro gioco,
Mel credete, so apprezzar.

RIGOLETTO
Taci, il piangere non vale,
No, non val, no, no, non val.

DUCA
Con un detto, sol tu puoi
Le mie pene consolar!

GILDA
Infelice cor tradito,
Per angoscia non scoppiar,
No, no, non scoppiar.

MADDALENA
Sono avvezza, bel signore,
Ad un simile scherzare,
Mio bel signor!

GILDA
Infelice cor tradito,
Ah, no, non scoppiar!
Infelice core, cor tradito
Per angoscia non scoppiare,
Infelice cor tradito, per angoscia
non scoppiare.
Infelice cor tradito,
Per angoscia non scoppiar,
No, no, non scoppiar.

MADDALENA
Your promise binds forever!

DUKE
You're lovable and clever!

RIGOLETTO (*to* GILDA)
You want to hear still more?

GILDA
My heart can bear no more!

DUKE
Maddalena I adore you
You enslave me and enchant me;
Only this one favor you must grant me
Come and love me, be my radiant guiding star.
I implore you, don't refuse me
Be my radiant guiding star!

MADDALENA
Talk is cheap, there's no denying,
But your compliments amuse me.

GILDA
Ah, I know his lips are lying,
Ah, to think I once believed him!

MADDALENA
Pretty speeches don't confuse me,
I know well how false they are.

RIGOLETTO
Quiet, your crying now is useless,
Never mind him,
No, the time for tears has past.

DUKE
Don't be heartless, I implore you,
Be my radiant guiding star!

GILDA
How sincerely did I love him
And he now betrays me so,
Ah, he scorned my love!

MADDALENA
Many times I heard that story,
To believe it would be madness,
It's far too old.

Quartet

GILDA
I believed him, now he betrays me!
Ah, it breaks my heart!
All my trust and my devotion
He has scorned and now I am betrayed,
For all my love and my devotion,
He repaid me with deception.
How I loved him and adored him
And by him I am betrayed, ah—
And he, he broke my heart.

MADDALENA
Talk is cheap, there's no denying
But your compliments amuse me;
Pretty speeches don't confuse me
I know well how false they are.
Many times I heard that story
To believe it would be madness,
Ha ha ha ha! Ridiculous!

MADDALENA
Ah, ah, rido ben di core
Chè tai baie costan poco,
Quanto valga il vostro gioco,
Mel credete, so apprezzar.
Sono avvezza, bel signore,
Ad un simile scherzare.
Ha, ha, ha, ha, rido di cor!

DUKE
Ah! Maddalena I adore you,
I read a promise in your glance.
I entreat you, don't refuse me,
Make me happy and be mine,
Ah, my darling!

DUCA
Ah! con un detto sol tu puoi
Le mie pene consolar!
Vieni e senti del mio core
Il frequente palpitar.
Ah, sì, vieni!

RIGOLETTO
He was lying, I have proved it,
But I give you my assurance
That his crime shall be avenged.
All my power and endurance
I'll employ on grim revenge,
I am prepared to strike a fatal blow.

RIGOLETTO
Ch'ei mentiva sei sicura.
Taci, e mia sarà la cura
La vendetta d'affrettar.
Sì, pronta fia, sarà fatale;
Io saprollo fulminar.

Listen: you must go home now.
Take some money, then on horseback
You will travel,
Disguised as a man, to Verona;
Tomorrow I will join you.

M'odi, ritorna a casa,
Oro prendi, un destriero,
Una veste viril che t'apprestai,
E per Verona parti.
Sarovvi io pur doman.

GILDA
Please come with me!

GILDA
Or venite . . .

RIGOLETTO
Impossible!

RIGOLETTO
Impossibil.

GILDA
I'm frightened!

GILDA
Tremo.

RIGOLETTO
Go.

RIGOLETTO
Va.

(GILDA *leaves. The* DUKE *and* MADDALENA *continue to talk, laugh and drink.* RIGOLETTO *is joined by* SPARAFUCILE, *receiving some money from him*)

RIGOLETTO
We agreed on twenty scudi?
Here you have ten.
The rest when it is over.
Will he remain here?

RIGOLETTO
Venti scudi hai tu detto? Eccone dieci,
E dopo l'opra il resto.
Ei qui rimane?

SPARAFUCILE
Yes.

SPARAFUCILE
Sì.

RIGOLETTO
On the stroke of midnight I shall return.

RIGOLETTO
Alla mezzanotte
ritornerò.

SPARAFUCILE
Don't bother.
I don't need you to throw him in the river.

SPARAFUCILE
Non cale;
A gettarlo nel fiume basto io solo.

RIGOLETTO
No, no; il vo' far io stesso.

RIGOLETTO
No, no, I myself must do that.

SPARAFUCILE
Sia! il suo nome?

SPARAFUCILE
All right then. What's his name?

RIGOLETTO
Vuoi saper anco il mio?
Egli è *Delitto, Punizion* son io.

RIGOLETTO
Shall I tell you mine also?
His name is "Guilt,"
Mine is "Just retribution."
(*he leaves. A flash of lightning is seen*)

SPARAFUCILE
La tempesta è vicina!
Più scura fia la notte.

SPARAFUCILE (*to himself returning to the house*)
Soon a storm will be raging,
And there will be no moonlight.

DUCA
Maddalena?

DUKE (*inside the house, to* MADDALENA)
Maddalena . . .
(*is about to embrace her*)

MADDALENA
Aspettate . . . mio fratello viene.

MADDALENA
Wait till later,
My brother is returning.
(*from here on frequent lightning and thunder, the storm is increasing in force*)

DUCA
Che importa?

DUKE
Why should I?

MADDALENA
Tuona!

MADDALENA
It's thund'ring.

SPARAFUCILE
E pioverà tra poco.

SPARAFUCILE (*entering*)
And soon it will be raining.

DUCA
Tanto meglio.
tu dormirai
In scuderia all'inferno,
ove vorrai.

DUKE
Even better! Now you can go,
Sleep where you want to,
For all I care, go to the devil.

SPARAFUCILE
Grazie.

SPARAFUCILE (*good-humored*)
I thank you!

MADDALENA
Ah no! partite.

MADDALENA (*softly to the* DUKE)
No, you must leave.

DUCA
Con tal tempo?

DUKE
In this weather?

SPARAFUCILE
Son venti scudi d'oro.
Ben felice
D'offrirvi la mia stanza. Se a voi piace,
Tosto a vederla andiamo.

SPARAFUCILE (*aside, to* MADDALENA)
He'll earn us twenty scudos.
(*aloud to the* DUKE)
I'll be happy to offer you my own room,
If you allow me, I will let you see it.

DUCA
Ebben, sono con te! presto, vediamo.

DUKE
Well then, I'll go with you,
Quickly, so be it.
(*he whispers something to* MADDALENA, *then follows* SPARAFUCILE *to the upper story*)

MADDALENA
(Povero giovin! grazïoso tanto!
Dio! qual notte è questa!)

MADDALENA
Poor trusting stranger!
He is so handsome.
(*lightning and thunder*)
Heavens, the storm is frightful!

DUKE (*in the attic*)
This is the peak of luxury!
Really charming!
I will stay here.

SPARAFUCILE
Good night, may God protect you!
(*he descends to the ground floor*)

DUKE
I shall sleep for a while,
I'm feeling tired.
(*he stretches out on the bed, and while singing, he gradually falls asleep*)
Woman's fidelity
Turns like the weather,
Sways like a feather,
Tossed in the breezes . . .
Beguiling . . . capricious . . .
Sways like a feather,
Never the same,
She'll never be the . . .
(*he is asleep*)

MADDALENA (*in the room below*)
I like that young stranger,
He's handsome and gentle.

SPARAFUCILE
For twenty gold scudos I'm not sentimental.

MADDALENA
Just twenty? That's nothing!
A very low fee.

SPARAFUCILE
My dagger, go get it . . .
Go, bring it to me.

Scene, Trio, and Storm

GILDA (*appearing outside, in man's clothes, with boots and spurs*)
I reason no longer,
My heart is commanding,
Forgive me, dear father!
(*thunder*)
Oh night filled with horror!
And how will it end?

MADDALENA
My brother—
(*she brings the dagger to* SPARAFUCILE)

GILDA
Who spoke there?

SPARAFUCILE (*he rummages in a drawer of the cupboard*)
The devil with you!

DUCA
Si dorme all'aria aperta? bene, bene!
Buona notte.

SPARAFUCILE
Signor, vi guardi Iddio.

DUCA
Breve sonno dormiam; stanco son io.
La donna è mobile,
Qual piuma al vento,
Muta d'accento,
E di pensiero.
La donna è mobil,
Muta d'accento,
E di pensier,
D'accento e di pen . . .

MADDALENA
È amabile invero cotal giovinotto.

SPARAFUCILE
Oh sì, venti scudi ne dà di prodotto . . .

MADDALENA
Sol venti! son pochi!
valeva di più.

SPARAFUCILE
La spada, s'ei dorme, va, portami giù.

GILDA
Ah, più non ragiono!
Amor mi trascina! Mio padre, perdono.
Qual notte d'orrore! Gran Dio, che accadrà?

MADDALENA
Fratello?

GILDA
Chi parla?

SPARAFUCILE
Al diavol ten va.

MADDALENA
Somiglia un Apollo quel giovine . . . io l'amo
Ei m'ama, riposi, nè più l'uccidiamo.

GILDA
Oh cielo!

SPARAFUCILE
Rattoppa quel sacco!

MADDALENA
Perchè?

SPARAFUCILE
Entr'esso il tuo Apollo, sgozzato da me,
Gettar dovrò al fiume.

GILDA
L'inferno qui vedo!

MADDALENA
Eppure il danaro salvarti scommetto
Serbandolo in vita.

SPARAFUCILE
Difficile il credo.

MADDALENA
M'ascolta: anzi facil ti svelo un progetto.
De' scudi già dieci dal gobbo ne avesti;
Venire cogl'altri più tardi il vedrai,
Uccidilo, e venti allora ne avrai:

GILDA
Che sento! mio padre!

MADDALENA
Così tutto il prezzo goder si potrà.

SPARAFUCILE
Uccider quel gobbo! Che diavol dicesti!
Un ladro son forse? Son forse un bandito?
Qual altro cliente da me fu tradito?
Mi paga quest'uomo, fedele m'avrà.

MADDALENA
Ah, grazia per esso!

SPARAFUCILE
E d'uopo ch'ei muoia.

MADDALENA
Fuggire il fo adesso.

GILDA
Oh, buona figliuola!

SPARAFUCILE
Gli scudi perdiamo.

MADDALENA
Not even Adonis is handsomer,
I love him, he loves me,
For my sake, O Brother,
Don't kill him!

GILDA
Good heavens!

SPARAFUCILE
This sack must be mended.

MADDALENA
And why?

SPARAFUCILE
To cover your friend in his watery grave,
Below in the river.

GILDA
Unholy betrayers!

MADDALENA
Suppose we could spare him
Without any danger,
And still get your money?

SPARAFUCILE
And how would you do that?

MADDALENA
Just listen:
I'll explain how to do it, my brother:
One half of your fee you have gotten already;
At midnight the hunchback will bring you the other.
Let him die as victim instead of the stranger—

GILDA
Great heavens, my father!

MADDALENA
This way all the money is ours just the same.

SPARAFUCILE
To murder the hunchback?
What are you suggesting!
For what do you take me?
A thief or a robber?
Since when have I ever
Betrayed any client?
He'll pay for my service—
I'll stand by my word.

MADDALENA
I beg you to spare him!

SPARAFUCILE
No, no, I must kill him!

MADDALENA (*wants to go upstairs*)
I'm going to warn him!

GILDA
Thank God for her pity!

SPARAFUCILE (*holding her back*)
We're losing the money.

MADDALENA
I know!

SPARAFUCILE
I must kill him!

MADDALENA
I beg you, my brother,
I beg you to spare him!

SPARAFUCILE (*with sudden determination*)
If someone should come here
Ere midnight has sounded
Let him be the victim,
Your man may go free.

MADDALENA
The night is too stormy,
That hope is unfounded,
In such weather what chance could there be?

GILDA
There's one way to save him,
May God give me courage!
Oh heaven forgive me,
Have mercy on me!
(*the storm is at its peak, continuous thunder and lightning; a clock strikes*)

SPARAFUCILE
One half hour more . . .

MADDALENA
Be patient my brother—

GILDA
Ah, she's trying to save him
And I do not help her!
Although he has broken
The vow he has sworn me,
I'm willing to die
If his life can be spared.
(*she knocks at the door*)

MADDALENA
Who's knocking?

SPARAFUCILE
The wind . . .

MADDALENA
I'm sure someone's knocking.

SPARAFUCILE
That's strange! Who's there?

GILDA (*from outside*)
A poor homeless beggar;
I'm asking for shelter for the night only.

MADDALENA
We'll give him his shelter!

SPARAFUCILE
In just a few moments.
(*he goes to the cupboard*)

MADDALENA
È ver!

SPARAFUCILE
Lascia fare.

MADDALENA
Salvarlo dobbiamo, salvarlo dobbiamo!

SPARAFUCILE
Se pria ch'abbia il mezzo la notte toccato
Alcuno qui giunga, per esso morrà.

MADDALENA
È buia la notte, il ciel troppo irato,
Nessuno a quest'ora da qui passerà.

GILDA
Oh, qual tentazione!
Morir per l'ingrato!
Morire! È mio padre!
O cielo, pietà!

SPARAFUCILE
Ancor c'è mezz'ora.

MADDALENA
Attendi fratello . . .

GILDA
Che! Piange tal donna!
Nè a lui darò aita!
Ah, s'egli al mio amore divenne rubello,
Io vo' per la sua gettar la mia vita.

MADDALENA
Si picchia?

SPARAFUCILE
Fu il vento.

MADDALENA
Si picchia, ti dico.

SPARAFUCILE
È strano! Chi è?

GILDA
Pietà d'un mendico;
Asil per la notte a lui concedete.

MADDALENA
Fia lunga tal notte!

SPARAFUCILE
Alquanto attendete.

MADDALENA
Su spicciati, presto, fa l'opra compita:
Anelo una vita con altra salvar.

MADDALENA
You gave me your promise,
Why wait any longer?
The life of this beggar
Is all that you need!

SPARAFUCILE
Ebbene, son pronto; quell'uscio dischiudi;
Più ch'altro gli scudi, mi preme salvar.

SPARAFUCILE
So be it, I'm ready.
His life won't concern me,
As long as he'll earn me
The gold for the deed.

GILDA
Ah! presso alla morte, sì giovane sono!
Oh ciel, per quegl'empi ti chieggo perdono!
Perdona tu, o padre, a quest'infelice!
Sia l'uomo felice ch'or vado a salvar;
Perdona, perdona, o padre!

GILDA
As death lies before me,
I pray for the living.
Oh God save these sinners,
Be kind and forgiving.
Forgive me, my father,
That I must leave you;
My life I am giving
So he may live.

MADDALENA
Spicciati!

MADDALENA
Hurry!

SPARAFUCILE
Apri!

SPARAFUCILE
Open!

MADDALENA
Entrate!

MADDALENA
Be welcome!

GILDA
Dio! loro perdonate!

GILDA (*entering*)
God, grant them your pardon!

MADDALENA, SPARAFUCILE
Entrate!

MADDALENA, SPARAFUCILE
Be welcome!
(SPARAFUCILE *posts himself behind the door with his dagger.* MADDALENA *opens the door,* SPARAFUCILE *stabs* GILDA. *The storm is raging on. The house remains dark. Gradually the storm abates*)

Scene and Final Duet

RIGOLETTO
Della vendetta alfin giunge l'istante!
Da trenta dì l'aspetto
Di vivo sangue
A lagrime piangendo,
Sotto la larva del buffon.
Quest'uscio e chiuso!
Ah, non è tempo ancor! . . .
S'attenda.
Qual notte di mistero!
Una tempesta in cielo!
In terra un omicidio!
Oh, come invero qui grande mi sento! . . .
Mezzanotte!

RIGOLETTO (*returns, wrapped in a cloak*)
This is the moment,
The supreme hour of vengeance!
Full thirty days I've waited,
With searing anguish
And tears of desperation,
Under the jester's grinning mask.
(*he goes to* SPARAFUCILE'*s house*)
The entrance is bolted.
The time has not yet come.
I'll wait here.
Oh night of looming myst'ry!
Tempests arise in heaven
And here on earth a murder.
Oh how I savor the rapture of greatness!
(*it sounds midnight*)
It is midnight.

(*he knocks at the door*)

SPARAFUCILE
Who's there?

RIGOLETTO
Your client.

SPARAFUCILE
One moment.
(*he goes back and returns, dragging a sack out*)
Here's the body of your victim.

RIGOLETTO (*joyfully*)
Let's see him! A lantern!

SPARAFUCILE (*hastily*)
A lantern? No. The money!
Hurry, let's throw him in the river.

RIGOLETTO (*gives him a purse*)
No, I don't need you.

SPARAFUCILE
Do as you please.
Here the water is shallow,
But further on, it gets much deeper.
Hurry, be careful no one sees you.
Pleasant journey.
(*he re-enters the house*)

RIGOLETTO (*gloating*)
There he is! Lifeless, at last!
I'd like to see him!
But why should I?
I am certain! I feel his spurs here!
Now let the world observe me!
Here stands a jester,
There lies a mighty ruler!
See me stamp on my master!
No other! In glory!
I have avenged you,
My dear beloved daughter!
A sack will be his coffin,
His graveyard the flowing water!
The water! The water!
(*he is about to drag the sack to the river, when he hears the voice of the* DUKE, *who crosses the stage in the rear; while disappearing in the distance*)

DUKE
Woman's fidelity
Turns like the weather,
Sways like a feather
Tossed in the breezes.

RIGOLETTO
That voice!

DUKE (*behind scenes*)
Fond of variety,
She is beguiling,

SPARAFUCILE
Chi è là?

RIGOLETTO
Son io.

SPARAFUCILE
Sostate.
È qua spento il vostr'uomo!

RIGOLETTO
Oh gioia! Un lume!

SPARAFUCILE
Un lume? No, il danaro.
Lesti all'onda il gettiam.

RIGOLETTO
No, basto io solo.

SPARAFUCILE
Come vi piace. Qui men atto è il sito.
Più avanti è più profondo il gorgo. Presto,
Che alcun non vi sorprenda. Buona notte.

RIGOLETTO
Egli è là! Morto! Oh sì!
Vorrei vederlo!
Ma che importa?
È ben desso! Ecco i suoi sproni.
Ora mi guarda, o mondo!
Quest'è un buffone,
Ed un potente è questo!
Ei sta sotto i miei piedi!
È desso! Oh gioia!
È giunta alfine la tua vendetta, o duolo!
Sia l'onda a lui sepolcro,
Un sacco il suo lenzuolo!
All'onda! all'onda!

DUCA
La donna è mobile,
Qual piuma al vento,
Muta d'accento,
E di pensiero.

RIGOLETTO
Qual voce!

DUCA
Sempre un amabile
Leggiadro viso,

In pianto o in riso,
È menzognero.

Frowning or smiling,
Just as she pleases.

RIGOLETTO
Illusion notturna è questa!

RIGOLETTO
It's a dream, a foolish nightmare!

DUCA
La donna è mobil
Qual piuma al vento . . .

DUKE
She is capricious,
Turns like the weather—

RIGOLETTO
No, no!

RIGOLETTO
No, no.

DUCA
Muta d'accento
E di pensier . . .

DUKE
Sways like a feather,
Never the same.

RIGOLETTO
No . . . egli è desso!
Maledizione!
Olà! dimon, bandito!

RIGOLETTO (*terrified*)
No, it's his voice!
(*he shouts toward the house*)
Hell and damnation!
Ho there, you fiend, you demon!

DUCA
E di pensier . . .

DUKE (*his voice fading in the distance*)
Never the same—

RIGOLETTO
Chi è mai, chi è qui in sua vece?
Io tremo . . . È umano corpo!
Mia figlia! . . . Dio! mia figlia!
Ah no . . . è impossibil!
Per Verona è in via!
Fu vision . . .
È dessa! O mia Gilda!
Fanciulla, a me rispondi!
L'assassino mi svela . . .
Olà? Nessuno? Nessun!
Mia figlia? mia Gilda, oh mia figlia!

RIGOLETTO (*frightened*)
Then who can be my victim?
I tremble . . . A human being . . .
(*he cuts the sack, lightning illuminates the scene*)
My daughter, God, my daughter!
Ah no, it can't be!
She has gone to Verona!
Do I dream?
(*more lightning*)
My Gilda! Oh my Gilda!
My darling, speak to your father!
Tell me how this has happened!
(*he knocks desperately at the house*)
Ho there! No answer! They're gone!
My daughter? My Gilda? Oh my daughter!

GILDA
Chi mi chiama?

GILDA (*in a faint voice*)
Who is calling?

RIGOLETTO
Ella parla! . . . Si muove!
È viva! . . . Oh Dio!
Ah, mio ben solo in terra
Mi guarda mi conosci

RIGOLETTO
She is speaking! She hears me!
She sees me! Oh God, ah—
Beloved, my treasure,
My darling—say you know me . . .

GILDA
Ah, padre mio!

GILDA
Ah, my dear father!

RIGOLETTO
Qual mistero! che fu? dimmi, Sei tu ferita?

RIGOLETTO
Tragic myst'ry! Oh God!
How did it happen? Tell me . . .

GILDA
L'acciar qui mi piagò . . .

GILDA
The dagger . . . here . . . here through my heart . . .

RIGOLETTO
Chi t'ha colpita?

RIGOLETTO (*in desperation*)
Who dared to strike you?

GILDA (*with effort, feebly*)
Alone I am guilty . . .
I deceived you.
I adored him . . . Now I die for my lover!

RIGOLETTO (*to himself*)
God Almighty, my own innocent daughter
Bore the wrath and the force of my vengeance!
(*to* GILDA)
I implore you to hear me, my daughter . . .
Only speak to me, speak to your father!

GILDA
Ah, do not ask me! Forgive me!
Forgive, I beg of you, forgive him!
Give your blessing to your daughter,
Oh my father . . .
Soon I will be with my mother in heaven.
There near God I'll be praying for you.

RIGOLETTO
Do not die, I implore you, don't leave me,
My only child, do not leave me alone,
All alone here on earth!

GILDA
Soon I will be with my mother in heaven,
There near God I'll be praying for you.

RIGOLETTO
Without you I have no one left on this earth.
Do not die, I implore you, my child!

GILDA
No more . . . Forgive . . . forgive him . . .
My father . . . forgive me . . .
There I will pray . . . pray for you . . .
I'll pray for . . .
(*she dies*)

RIGOLETTO
Gilda! My Gilda! My daughter!
(*he throws himself upon the body of his daughter in utter despair*)
Ah! The curse of Monterone!

GILDA
V'ho ingannato . . . colpevole fui . . .
L'amai troppo . . . ora muoio per lui.

RIGOLETTO
(Dio tremendo! ella stessa fu colta
Dallo stral di mia giusta vendetta! . . .)
Angiol caro, mi guarda, m'ascolta
Parla, parlami, figlia diletta.

GILDA
Ah, ch'io taccia! a me . . . a lui perdonate . . .
Benedite alla figlia, o mio padre . . .
Lassù in cielo, vicina alla madre . . .
In eterno per voi pregherò.

RIGOLETTO
Non morir mio tesoro pietade.
Mia colomba lasciarmi non dêi
No, lasciarmi non dêi . . .

GILDA
Lassù in cielo, vicina alla madre
In eterno per voi pregherò.

RIGOLETTO
Se t'involi, qui sol, qui sol rimarrei . . .
Non morire, o qui teco morrò!

GILDA
Non più . . . A lui . . . perdonate . . .
Mio padre . . . addio!
Lassù in ciel, lassù in ciel . . .
Pregherò per voi, preghe . . .

RIGOLETTO
Gilda! mia Gilda! È morta!
Ah! la maledizione!

SIEGFRIED

by Richard Wagner (1813–1883)

LIBRETTO BY THE COMPOSER

Translated by STEWART ROBB

Wagner's vast music drama tetralogy, *Der Ring des Nibelungen* (The Ring of the Nibelung), is a powerful parable on the futility of any attempt to rule the world by force. If the gold of the Rhine is forged into a ring, its owner, renouncing love, can gain power over the world, it is said; but Alberich, ruler of the Nibelungs (gnomes), who has stolen the gold from its guardian Rhine maids, curses the ring when forced to give it up to the wily gods, and thereafter it brings disaster to all its owners, innocent and guilty alike; and in the end, with the destruction of the old order, the stolen ring has to go right back to the Rhine maids, to whom it belongs. *Siegfried* is the third drama of Wagner's tetralogy.

CHARACTERS

MIME	*Tenor*
SIEGFRIED	*Tenor*
WANDERER (*the god Wotan in disguise*)	*Bass-Baritone*
ALBERICH	*Baritone*
FAFNER (*the dragon*)	*Bass*
WOOD BIRD	*Soprano*
ERDA, *the earth-goddess*	*Contralto*
BRUNNHILDA	*Soprano*

Place: A legendary forest in Germany
Time: Antiquity
First performance: Festspielhaus, Bayreuth, August 16, 1876

COPYRIGHT © 1960 BY STEWART ROBB

ACT I

FIRST SCENE

A Forest

(In the foreground is a portion of a rocky cave. Left, against the wall stands a large smith's forge, naturally formed of stones, the bellows alone being artificial. The rough chimney leads up through the top of the cave. A very large anvil and other smith's appliances are evident.)

MIME *(sitting at the anvil, hammering, with increasing lack of heart, at a sword. At last, despairful, he stops)*

Wearisome torment!
Meaningless toil!
I never forged
a mightier sword:
though a giant gripped it,
still it would hold.
But insolent Siegfried,
the boy it was made for,
just whacks and snaps it in two,
as though 'twere only a toy!

(throws the sword angrily on the anvil, sets his arms akimbo, and gazes meditatively on the ground)

I know a sword
that he could not shatter:
Needful's fragments
would laugh at his strength
if I could put the pieces together.
But all my skill
cannot forge the sword!
If I could weld the weapon,
I'd be paid in full for my pains!
Fafner, my dragon foe,
lodges within these woods.
He is watching the Nibelung's hoard.
His terrible bulk
guards the gold well.
Siegfried's vigorous strength
may bring about Fafner's end.
The Nibelung's ring
would then be my own.
I know one sword for the deed.
There is a blade that will serve,
if Siegfried grips it in hand.
And I cannot forge it—
Needful the sword!

(picks up the sword again and resumes hammering, in deepest dejection)

Wearisome torment!
Meaningless toil!

MIME

Zwangvolle Plage!
Müh' ohne Zweck!
Das beste Schwert,
das je ich geschweisst,
in der Riesen Fäusten
hielte es fest:
doch dem ich's geschmiedet,
der schmähliche Knabe,
er knickt und schmeisst es entzwei,
als schüf' ich Kinderge-schmeid!—
Es giebt ein Schwert,
das er nicht zerschwänge:
Nothungs Trümmer
zertrotzt' er mir nicht,
könnt' ich die starken
Stücken schweissen,
die meine Kunst
nicht zu kitten weiss.
Könnt' ich's dem Kühnen schmieden,
meiner Schmach erlangt' ich da Lohn!—
Fafner, der wilde Wurm,
lagert im finst'ren Wald;
mit des furchtbaren Leibes Wucht
der Niblungen Hort
hütet er dort.
Siegfrieds kindischer Kraft
erläge wohl Fafner's Leib:
des Niblungen Ring
erränge ich mir.
Ein Schwert nur taugt zu der That;
nur Nothung nützt meinem Neid,
wenn Siegfried sehrend ihn schwingt:—
und nicht kann ich's schweissen,
Nothung das Schwert!—
Zwangvolle Plage!
Müh' ohne Zweck!
Das beste Schwert,
das je ich geschweisst,
nie taugt es je
zu der einz'gen That!
Ich tapp're und hämm're nur,
weil der Knab' es heischt:
er knickt und schmeisst es entzwei,
und schmählt doch, schmied' ich ihm nicht!

I never forged
a mightier sword.
But still its strength
is too weak for the deed!
I tinker and hammer
only because he demands.
He whacks and snaps it in two,
and scolds me, if I don't work!
(*lets the hammer fall*)

SIEGFRIED
Hoiho! Hoiho!
Hau' ein! Hau' ein!
Friss ihn! Friss ihn!
den Fratzenschmied!
Ha, ha, ha, ha, ha, ha, ha, ha,
ha, ha, ha, ha, ha, ha, ha, ha.

SIEGFRIED (*outside*)
Hoi-ho!
(*enters, in a rough forester's dress, with a silver horn hanging by a chain, and boisterously leading a large bear by a bast rope. In wanton merriment he drives the bear toward* MIME)
Hoi-ho!
come on! come on!
Tear him! tear him, the booby smith!
(MIME *drops the sword in terror and flees behind the forge*)
Ha ha ha ha ha ha ha ha ha ha ha ha ha ha ha ha!
(SIEGFRIED *drives the bear everywhere after him*)

MIME
Fort mit dem Thier!
Was taugt mir der Bär?

MIME
Take him away!
I don't want a bear!

SIEGFRIED
Zu zwei komm' ich,
dich besser zu zwicken:
Brauner, frag' nach dem Schwert!

SIEGFRIED
I come double,
the better to pinch you!
Bruin, ask for the sword!

MIME
He! lass' das Wild!
Dort liegt die Waffe:
fertig fegt' ich sie heut'.

MIME
Hey! Put him out!
There lies the weapon.
See, I forged it today.

SIEGFRIED
So fährst du heute noch heil!
Lauf', Brauner:
dich brauch' ich nicht mehr!

SIEGFRIED
Why, for today then, you're free!
(*looses the bear from the rope and gives him a stroke on the back with it*)
Run, Bruin,
I need you no more.
(*the bear runs back to the woods;* MIME *comes trembling from behind the forge*)

MIME
Wohl leid' ich's gern,
erleg'st du Bären:
was bringst du lebend
die Braunen heim?

MIME
I've no objection
when you kill them,
but why d'you bring me
your bears alive?

SIEGFRIED
Nach bess'rem Gesellen sucht' ich,
als daheim mir einer sitzt;
im tiefen Walde mein Horn
liess ich da hallend tönen:

SIEGFRIED (*sitting down to recover from his laughter*)
For want of a better comrade
than the one who sits at home,
I blew my horn in the deep woods,

and waited for an answer,
in the hope that perhaps I would find
a faithful friend,
I asked for one with my horn.
Then a bear broke through the woods,
who growled as he came to me;
and I liked him better than you.
But I'll find better than that!
Then I tied him fast
with rope I had made,
to urge you, old wretch, for the weapon.

ob sich froh mir gesellte
ein guter Freund?
das frug ich mit dem Getön'.
Aus dem Busche kam ein Bär,
der hörte mir brummend zu;
er gefiel mir besser als du,
doch bess're wohl fänd' ich
noch:
mit dem zähen Baste
zäumt' ich ihn da,
dich, Schelm, nach dem
Schwerte zu fragen.

(MIME *picks up the sword and extends it to* SIEGFRIED)

MIME

I made the weapon sharp,
and its edge will gladden your heart.

Ich schuf die Waffe scharf,
ihrer Schneide wirst du dich
freu'n.

(*he holds the sword timidly in his hand;* SIEGFRIED *grabs it from him*)

SIEGFRIED

What good are its cutting edges
if the steel's not hard and true?
(*tests the sword*)
Hey! what a useless toy is this!
You call this paltry pin a sword?
(*strikes it on the anvil and the pieces fly in all directions.* MIME *shrinks with fear*)
And now take the pieces,
blustering bungler!
Would that the blade
had broken your brain pan!
Why should I let you
cheat any longer,
prating of giants
and wonderful battles,
of deeds of daring,
and dauntless defense?
You'd fashion me weapons,
swords for battle,
praising your art,
proclaiming it good;
yet if I handle
what you have hammered,
a single handgrip
ruins the trash!
If he were not
so mangy a wretch,
I would pound him to bits
upon his own forge,
the ancient, imbecile imp!
my troubles might then have an end!
(*in a rage casts himself on a stone bench.* MIME *cautiously remains out of his way*)

Was frommt seine helle
Schneide,
ist der Stahl nicht hart und fest!
Hei! was ist das
für müss'ger Tand!
Den schwachen Stift
nennst du ein Schwert?
Da hast du die Stücke,
schändlicher Stümper:
hätt' ich am Schädel
dir sie zerschlagen!—
Soll mich der Prahler
länger noch prellen?
Schwatzt mir von Riesen
und rüstigen Kämpfen,
von kühnen Thaten
und tüchtiger Wehr;
will Waffen mir schmieden,
Schwerte schaffen;
rühmt seine Kunst,
als könnt' er 'was Rechtes:
nehm' ich zur Hand nun
was er gehämmert,
mit einem Griff
zergreif' ich den Quark!—
Wär' mir nicht schier
zu schäbig der Wicht,
ich zerschmiedet' ihn selbst
mit seinem Geschmeid,
den alten albernen Alb!
Des Aergers dann hätt' ich ein
End'!

MIME
Nun tob'st du wieder wie toll:
dein Undank, traun! ist arg.
Mach' ich dem bösen Buben
nicht alles gleich zu best,
was ich Gutes ihm schuf,
vergisst er gar zu schnell!
Willst du denn nie gedenken
was ich dich lehrt' vom Danke?
Dem sollst du willig gehorchen,
der je sich wohl dir erwies.
Das willst du wieder nicht hören!—
Doch speisen magst du wohl?
Vom Spiesse bring' ich den Braten:
versuchtest du gern den Sud?
Für dich sott' ich ihn gar.

SIEGFRIED
Braten briet' ich mir selbst:
deinen Sudel sauf' allein!

MIME
Das ist nun der Liebe
schlimmer Lohn!
Das der Sorgen
schmählicher Sold!—
Als zullendes Kind
zog ich dich auf,
wärmte mit Kleiden
den kleinen Wurm:
Speise und Trank
trug ich dir zu,
hütete dich
wie die eig'ne Haut.
Und wie du erwuchsest,
wartet' ich dein;
dein Lager schuf ich,
dass leicht du schlief'st.
Dir schmiedet' ich Tand
und ein tönend Horn;
dich zu erfreu'n
müht' ich mich froh:
mit klugem Rathe
rieth ich dir klug,
mit lichtem Wissen
lehrt' ich dich Witz.
Sitz' ich daheim
in Fleiss und Schweiss,
nach Herzenslust
schweifst du umher:
für dich nur in Plage,
in Pein nur für dich
verzehr' ich mich alter,
armer Zwerg!
Und aller Lasten
ist das nun der Lohn,

MIME
You rave as though you were mad!
Such gross ingratitude!
If what I try to make
is not done with perfect art,
the graceless, booby boy
forgets to give me thanks!
You always should be grateful.
Remember what I taught you.
You should be willing to listen
to one who loves you so much.
(SIEGFRIED *angrily turns his face to the wall, his back to* MIME)
I see you don't want to hear me!
(*stands perplexed, then goes to the hearth*)
Yet still you'd like some food!
I'll bring the meat that I roasted.
Or would you prefer the soup?
I fixed both just for you.
(*brings the food to* SIEGFRIED, *who, without turning around, strikes the bowl and meat from his hand*)

SIEGFRIED
Roasts I roast for myself.
Go and swill your slop alone!

MIME (*in a wailing voice*)
What a slim reward
for all my love!
What a shameful pay
for my pains!
A whimpering child
came to my care.
You were that babe,
and I brought you up well,
gave you warm clothes,
nourishment too,
treated you
just as I did myself.
And as you grew up
I waited on you.
I made you
a pleasant and restful bed.
I tinkered your toys
and a sounding horn;
toiling for you
gave me great joy.
My cunning counsels
sharpened your wits.
My shining wisdom
made you quite bright.
Here in my home
I toil and sweat,

while you roam
wherever you like.
I fret and I worry,
and only for you.
I wear myself out,
a poor old dwarf!
And all I get
for my worry is this:
that the petulant boy
gives me scorn and hate.

dass der hastige Knabe
mich quält und hasst!

(he sobs. SIEGFRIED *again studies* MIME'S *face.* MIME *meets his look and tries to hide the fear in his own)*

SIEGFRIED

Mime, I have learned plenty:
you taught me much that I know.
But what you would most like to teach me
is something I cannot learn:
how to endure your sight.
When you bring food and drink to me here,
I feel as though I would gag.
When you prepare
a bed for my rest,
I find it harder to sleep.
When you would teach me
how to be wise,
then I would be a fool.
What do I need
but to look at you,
to know you are evil
in all that you do.
I see you stand,
slither and slide,
crawling and slinking,
with your eyelids blinking.
I could take you
by the throat and choke you!
You loathsome wretch,
I could kill you outright!
That's how I love you, my Mime.
If you are clever,
then tell me something,
that long I have sought in vain:
in the woods roaming,
seeking to shun you,
what is it that makes me come back?
For I like the beasts
more dearly than you:
trees and birds,
and the fish in the brook,
truly I like them
much better than you.

SIEGFRIED

Vieles lehrtest du, Mime,
und manches lernt' ich von dir;
doch was du am liebsten mich lehrtest,
zu lernen gelang mir nie:—
wie ich dich leiden könnt'.—
Trägst du mir Speise
und Trank herbei—
der Ekel speis't mich allein;
schaffst du ein leichtes
Lager zum Schlaf—
der Schlummer wird mir da schwer;
willst du mich weisen
witzig zu sein—
gern bleib' ich taub und dumm.
Seh' ich dir erst
mit den Augen zu,
zu übel erkenn' ich
was alles du thu'st:
seh' ich dich steh'n,
gangeln und geh'n,
knicken und nicken,
mit den Augen zwicken:
beim Genick möcht' ich
den Nicker packen,
den Garaus geben
dem garst'gen Zwicker!—
So lernt' ich, Mime, dich leiden.
Bist du nun weise,
so hilf mir wissen,
worüber umsonst ich sann:—
in den Wald lauf' ich,
dich zu verlassen,—
wie kommt das, kehr' ich zurück?
Alle Thiere sind
mir theurer als du:
Baum und Vogel,
die Fische im Bach,
lieber mag ich sie
leiden als dich:—
wie kommt das nun, kehr' ich zurück?
Bist du klug, so thu' mir's kund.

What is it then, that makes me come back?
If you're wise, then tell me this.

MIME
Mein Kind, das lehrt dich kennen,
Wie lieb ich am Herzen dir lieg'.

MIME (*attempts to approach him winningly*)
My child, that teaches you
that I lie very close to your heart.

SIEGFRIED
Ich kann dich ja nicht leiden,—
Vergiss das nicht so leicht!

SIEGFRIED
I cannot even stand you,
and just remember that!
(MIME *goes back and sits a distance away, opposite* SIEGFRIED)

MIME
Dess' ist deine Wildheit schuld,
die du, Böser, bändigen sollst.—
Jammernd verlangen Junge
nach ihrer Alten Nest;
Liebe ist das Verlangen:
so lechzest du auch nach mir,
so lieb'st du auch deinen Mime—
so musst du ihn lieben!
Was dem Vögelein ist der Vogel,
wenn er im Nest es nährt,
eh' das flügge mag fliegen:
das ist dir kindischem Spross
der kundig sorgende Mime—
das muss er dir sein.

MIME
Your wildness is guilty there.
You should tame it, naughty boy!
Young ones are always crying,
wanting their parents' nest;
love awakens the longing,
and thus do you long for me.
Just so do you love your Mime.
And you have to love him!
As the mother bird loves the birdling,
when it is in the nest,
and before it can flutter,
so, my child, Mime loves—
your wise, considerate Mime—
he loves you like that!

SIEGFRIED
Ei, Mime, bist du so witzig,
so lass' mich eines noch wissen!—
Es sangen die Vöglein
so selig im Lenz,
das eine lockte das and're:
du sagtest selbst—
da ich's wissen wollt'—
das wären Männchen und Weibchen.
Sie kosten so lieblich,
und liessen sich nicht;
sie bauten ein Nest
und brüteten drin:
da flatterte junges
Geflügel auf,
und beide pflegten der Brut.—
So ruhten im Busch
auch Rehe gepaart,
selbst wilde Füchse und Wölfe:
Nahrung brachte
zum Nest das Männchen,
das Weibchen säugte die Welpen.
Da lernt' ich wohl
was Liebe sei;
der Mutter entwandt' ich
die Welpen nie.—
Wo hast du nun, Mime,
dein minniges Weibchen,
dass ich es Mutter nenne?

SIEGFRIED
Hey, Mime, if you're so clever,
then tell me this in your wisdom!
The birdlings were singing
so sweetly in spring,
and each was calling the other.
You said yourself,
when I wished to know,
that they were wives with their husbands.
They chirped and they chattered,
and never did part;
they builded a nest,
and brooded therein;
and after a time
little fledglings were seen,
and both took care of the brood.
And thus in the bush
lay roe deer in pairs,
and savage wolves and foxes.
Food was brought
to the lair by the father.
The mother suckled the litter.
And there I really learned of love.
And never since then
have I stolen their whelps.

Where have you now, Mime,
your sweet little wifey,
so I may call her mother?

MIME (*angrily*)
Don't be a fool!
Ah, you are dumb!
D'you think you're a bird or a fox?

SIEGFRIED
A whimpering child
came to your care,
I was that babe,
and you cared for me well.
But tell me,
where did you find the poor mite?
You didn't do badly
without a wife.

MIME (*greatly embarrassed*)
Just believe
whatever I tell you:
I am your father
and mother combined.

SIEGFRIED
You lie, contemptible gawk!
For that young ones are like their parents,
I know, for I've seen for myself.
I came to the crystal brook.
There were animals there
and trees reflected.
Thus, were mirrored,
just as they are,
most brightly, the sun and the clouds.
And there in that pool
I saw my form;
it looked to me
quite different from yours.
A glittering fish
is as much like a toad;
and fish can't have toads for their fathers!

MIME (*much vexed*)
What a display
of nonsense is this!

SIEGFRIED
See here, I find
I know at last
what I've sought so often in vain:
when I flee from you
and run to the forest,
do you know why I return?
Because you haven't yet told me
what father and mother are mine.

MIME
Was ist dir, Thor?
Ach, bist du dumm!
Bist doch weder Vogel noch Fuchs?

SIEGFRIED
Das zullende Kind
zogest du auf,
wärmtest mit Kleiden
den kleinen Wurm:—
wie kam dir aber
der kindische Wurm?
Du machtest wohl gar
ohne Mutter mich?

MIME
Glauben sollst du,
was ich dir sage:
ich bin dir Vater
und Mutter zugleich.

SIEGFRIED
Da lügst du, garstiger Gauch!—
Wie die Jungen den Alten gleichen,
das hab' ich mir glücklich erseh'n.
Nun kam ich zum klaren Bach:
da erspäht' ich die Bäum'
und Thier' im Spiegel;
Sonn' und Wolken,
wie sie nur sind,
im Glitzer erschienen sie gleich.
Da sah ich denn auch
mein eigen Bild;
ganz anders als du
dünkt' ich mir da:
so glich wohl der Kröte
ein glänzender Fisch;
doch kroch nie ein Fisch aus der Kröte.

MIME
Gräulichen Unsinn
kramst du da aus!

SIEGFRIED
Siehst du, nun fällt
auch selbst mir ein,
was zuvor ich umsonst besann:
wenn zum Wald ich laufe,
dich zu verlassen,
wie das kommt, kehr' ich doch heim?
Von dir noch muss ich erfahren,
wer Vater und Mutter mir sei!

MIME
Was Vater! Was Mutter!
Müssige Frage!

SIEGFRIED
So muss ich dich fassen,
um 'was zu wissen:
gutwillig
erfahr' ich doch nichts!
So musst' ich Alles
ab dir trotzen:
kaum das Reden
hätt' ich errathen,
entwand ich's nicht
mit Gewalt dem Schuft!
Heraus damit,
räudiger Kerl!
Wer ist mir Vater und Mutter?

MIME
Ans Leben geh'st du mir schier!—
Nun lass'! was zu wissen dich geizt,
erfahr' es, ganz wie ich's weiss.—
O undankbares,
arges Kind!
jetzt hör', wofür du mich hasst!
Nicht bin ich Vater
noch Vetter dir,—
und dennoch verdankst du mir dich!
Ganz fremd bist du mir,
deinem einz'gen Freund;
aus Erbarmen allein
barg ich dich hier:
nun hab' ich lieblichen Lohn!
Was verhofft' ich Thor mir auch Dank?
Einst lag wimmernd ein Weib
da draussen im wilden Wald:
zur Höhle half ich ihr her,
am warmen Herd sie zu hüten.
Ein Kind trug sie im Schosse;
traurig gebar sie's hier;
sie wand sich hin und her,
ich half so gut ich konnt':
stark war die Noth, sie starb—
doch Siegfried, der genas.

SIEGFRIED
So starb meine Mutter an mir?

MIME
Meinem Schutz übergab sie dich:
ich schenkt' ihn gern dem Kind.
Was hat sich Mime gemüht!

MIME
What father? What mother?
Meaningless question!

SIEGFRIED (*gripping* MIME *by the throat*)
Why then I must choke you,
till you can tell me:
good manners are wasted on you!
So I shall have
to make you answer.
If I had not
forced you to teach me,
I would not even
know how to speak!
So out with it,
scabby old fool!
Who are my father and mother?

MIME (*after making signs with his head and hands, is released by* SIEGFRIED)
You almost choked me to death!
Let go, and I'll say what you want.
I'll tell you all that I know.
Oh, unthankful
and wicked child!
Now hear and learn why you hate me!
I am no father
or kin of yours;
and yet you should thank me for life!
You owe all to me,
your one only friend;
just my pity alone
lets you stay here.
A lovely payment I get!
I'm a wishful thinker,
a fool!
A poor woman lay weeping,
out in the fearful woods:
I helped her here to this cave,
and let her stay by my hearthside.
A child lived in her body;
(Sad is the story now.)
The boy was born in woe.
I helped as best I could.
Great was her pain! she died—
but Siegfried saw the day.

SIEGFRIED
She died so that Siegfried might live?

MIME
She delivered you to my care:
I gladly took the child.
What love I lavished on you!
What kindness and care I bestowed!

A whimpering child
came to my care.

SIEGFRIED
I think you have said that before!
Now say just why I'm called Siegfried?

MIME
Because your dear mother
asked it to be so;
and with that name
you grew strong and fair.
For you were that child
and I brought you up well.

SIEGFRIED
Now tell me the name of my mother.

MIME
I hardly know her name!
Gave you warm clothes,
nourishment too——

SIEGFRIED
Her name has not yet been told me!

MIME
I don't think I know. But wait!
Sieglinda—there, now I have it!
In grief she gave you to me.
I treated you just as I did myself——

SIEGFRIED
Then tell me, who was my father?

MIME
I never saw his face.

SIEGFRIED
But my mother spoke of my father?

MIME
He fell in battle,
was all that she said;
she left you, fatherless,
here in my care.
And as you grew up,
I waited on you,
and made you
a pleasant and restful bed——

SIEGFRIED
Always the same old
starling song!
If I may but believe you,
if you are speaking truly,
then let me see some proof!

MIME
What proof then shall I show you?

was gab sich der Gute für
Noth!
„Als zullendes Kind
zog ich dich auf" . . .

SIEGFRIED
Mich dünkt, dess' gedachtest
du schon?
Jetzt sag': woher heiss' ich
Siegfried?

MIME
So hiess mich die Mutter
möcht' ich dich heissen:
als Siegfried würdest
du stark und schön.—
„Ich wärmte mit Kleiden
den kleinen Wurm" . . .

SIEGFRIED
Nun melde, wie hiess meine
Mutter?

MIME
Das weiss ich wahrlich kaum!—
„Speise und Trank
trug ich dir zu". . .

SIEGFRIED
Den Namen sollst du mir
nennen!

MIME
Entfiel er mir wohl? doch halt!
Sieglinde mochte sie heissen,
die dich in Sorge mir gab.—
„Ich hütete dich
wie die eig'ne Haut" . . .

SIEGFRIED
Dann frag' ich, wie hiess mein
Vater?

MIME
Den hab' ich nie geseh'n.

SIEGFRIED
Doch die Mutter nannte den
Namen?

MIME
Erschlagen sei er,
das sagte sie nur;
dich Vaterlosen
befahl sie mir da:—
„und wie du erwuchsest,
wartet' ich dein',
dein Lager schuf ich,
dass leicht du schlief'st". . .

SIEGFRIED
Still mit dem alten
Staarenlied!—
Soll ich der Kunde glauben,
hast du mir nichts gelogen,
so lass mich nun Zeichen seh'n!

MIME
Was soll dir's noch bezeugen?

SIEGFRIED
Dir glaub' ich nicht mit dem Ohr',
dir glaub' ich nur mit dem Aug':
welch' Zeichen zeugt für dich?

MIME
Das gab mir deine Mutter:
für Mühe, Kost und Pflege
liess sie's als schwachen Lohn.
Sieh' her, ein zerbroch'nes Schwert!
Dein Vater, sagte sie, führt' es,
als im letzten Kampf er erlag.

SIEGFRIED
Und diese Stücke
sollst du mir schmieden:
dann schwing' ich mein rechtes Schwert!
Eile dich, Mime,
mühe dich rasch;
kannst du 'was Recht's,
nun zeig' deine Kunst!
Täusche mich nicht
mit schlechtem Tand:
den Trümmern allein
trau' ich 'was zu.
Find' ich dich faul,
füg'st du sie schlecht,
flick'st du mit Flausen
den festen Stahl,—
dir Feigem fahr' ich zu Leib,
das Fegen lernst du von mir!
Denn heute noch, schwör' ich,
will ich das Schwert;
die Waffe gewinn' ich noch heut'.

MIME
Was willst du noch heut' mit dem Schwert?

SIEGFRIED
Aus dem Wald fort
in die Welt zieh'n:
nimmer kehr' ich zurück.
Wie ich froh bin,
dass ich frei ward,
nichts mich bindet und zwingt!
Mein Vater bist du nicht;
in der Ferne bin ich heim:
dein Herd ist nicht mein Haus,
meine Decke nicht dein Dach.
Wie der Fisch froh
in der Fluth schwimmt,
wie der Fink frei
sich davon schwingt:
flieg' ich von hier,
fluthe davon,
wie der Wind über'n Wald
weh' ich dahin—

SIEGFRIED
My ears can give you no trust,
I trust you but with my eyes;
what witness can you show?

MIME (*after some thought he brings the two pieces of a broken sword*)
This once your mother gave me.
For lodging, food, and service,
this was my slender pay.
See here, just a broken sword!
She said your father had borne this
in the fight in which he was slain.

SIEGFRIED (*enthusiastically*)
And you shall weld
these pieces together:
I'll swing then my rightful sword!
Up! hurry up, Mime!
Waste no more time!
What can you do?
Now show me your skill!
Fool me no more
with worthless trash!
The faith that I have
lies in this sword!
If there's a flaw
seen in your work,
if you can't fashion
this trusty steel,
then, coward, look to your skin,
for I shall polish it well!
This day, I swear
I shall handle the sword.
This weapon today shall be mine!

MIME
But why do you want it today?

SIEGFRIED
I shall wander
from this forest, nevermore to return!
I am free
and I am happy.
Nothing binds me to you,
for I am not your son.
I shall find a home afar!
Your hearth is not my house,
nor your roof my shelter now!
As the fish
sports in the water,
as the finch
wings through the heavens,
so too shall I

fly far away,
like the wind when it whistles
through the woods.
So, Mime, I leave you for good.
(*runs into the forest*)

dich, Mime, nie wieder zu seh'n!

MIME

Hey there! Hey there! Siegfried! Come back!
Hey! Siegfried! Siegfried! Hey!
(*for a while he looks in the direction of* SIEGFRIED, *stunned, then he returns to his smithy, and seats himself behind the anvil*)
He storms away!
And here I sit!
Old cares are gone;
now I have new ones.
I'm baffled, caught and nailed down!
Now what shall I do?
How keep him in tow?
How lead this young madman
to Fafner's lair?
And how forge the fragments
of obstinate steel?
There's no furnace fire
able to fuse them,
nor can dwarf-held hammer
conquer their hardness.
The Nibelung's hate,
toil and sweat,
cannot make Needful new!
All I have done—is in vain!
(*he sobs*)

MIME

Halte! halte! wohin?
He! Siegfried!
Siegfried! He!
Da stürmt er hin!—
Nun sitz' ich da:
zur alten Noth
hab' ich die neue!
vernagelt bin ich nun ganz!—
Wie helf' ich mir jetzt?
Wie halt' ich ihn fest?
Wie führ' ich den Huien
zu Fafners Nest?
Wie füg' ich die Stücke
des tückischen Stahl's?
Keines Ofens Gluth
glüht mir die ächten!
keines Zwergen Hammer
zwingt mir die harten:
des Niblungen Neid,
Noth und Schweiss
nietet mir Nothung nicht,
schweisst mir das Schwert nicht zu ganz!—

SECOND SCENE

(WANDERER *[Wotan] steps out of the woods to the back entrance of the cave. He is wearing a long dark blue cloak and bearing a spear as a staff. On his head is a round, drooping broad-brimmed hat.*)
Hail there, cunning smith!
A way-weary guest looks for shelter
at your hearth!

WANDERER

Heil dir, weiser Schmied!
Dem wegmüden Gast
gönne hold
des Hauses Herd!

MIME

What's this?
Who are you
that come to this wild
and that seek me in woodland wastes?

MIME

Wer ist's, der im wilden
Wald mich sucht?
Wer verfolgt mich im öden Forst?

WANDERER

"Wanderer"—so I am called,
much travel I've seen.

WANDERER

Wand'rer heisst mich die Welt:
weit wandert' ich schon,

auf der Erde Rücken
rührt' ich mich viel.

MIME
So rühre dich fort
und raste nicht hier,
heisst dich Wand'rer die Welt.

WANDERER
Gastlich ruht' ich bei Guten,
Gaben gönnten mir viele:
denn Unheil fürchtet,
wer unhold ist.

MIME
Unheil wohnte
immer bei mir:
willst du dem Armen es
mehren?

WANDERER
Viel erforscht' ich,
erkannte viel:
Wichtiges konnt' ich
manchem künden,
manchem wehren
was ihn mühte,
nagende Herzensnoth.

MIME
Spürtest du klug
und erspähtest du viel,
hier brauch' ich nicht Spürer
noch Späher.
Einsam will ich
und einzeln sein,
Lungerern lass' ich den Lauf.

WANDERER
Mancher wähnte
weise zu sein,
nur was ihm noth that,
wusst' er nicht;
was ihm frommte,
liess ich erfragen:
lohnend lehrt' ihn mein Wort.

MIME
Müss'ges Wissen
wahren manche:
ich weiss mir grade genug;
mir genügt mein Witz,
ich will nicht mehr:
dir Weisem weis' ich den Weg!

WANDERER
Hier sitz' ich am Herd,
und setze mein Haupt
der Wissenswette zum Pfand:
mein Kopf ist dein,
du hast ihn erkies't,

I have wandered far and wide
on this earth.

MIME
Then wander some more.
Just be on your way
if you wander the world!

WANDERER
Good men always receive me;
many even offer gifts.
Unhandsome is
as unhandsome does.

MIME
Ill-luck always
lived in my home.
Why do you want to increase it?

WANDERER (*constantly and slowly stepping nearer*)
Much I've sought for
and much I've learned.
I have made men
wise and knowing,
saving many
from their sorrows,
healing their wounded hearts.

MIME
Wisdom is yours,
you have found a great deal,
but here I don't need any teacher.
I am lonely,
and lone would be,
loiterers cannot stay here.

WANDERER
Many fancy
wisdom is theirs,
yet most of all lack
what they most need.
When they ask me,
seeking for knowledge,
then I teach them my lore.

MIME (*more and more anxious as he sees the* WANDERER *approach*)
Many cherish
worthless wisdom,
but I have knowledge enough
and my wits are good,
I want no more!
So, wise one, be on your way!

WANDERER (*sitting down at the hearth*)
I'll sit by the hearth,
and wager my head.
We'll have a battle of wits.
My head is yours,

you take it at will,
as pledge when you ask,
if you learn
knowledge you cannot find good.

erfrägst du dir nicht
was dir frommt,
lös' ich's mit Lehren nicht ein.

MIME (*who has been staring at the* WANDERER *open-mouthed, now shrinks back, aside*)
How shall I get out of this trap?
I'll ask him something quite tricky.
(*aloud*)
Your head wagered
for my hearth.
Be wise and careful to keep it!
Thrice I freely
ask what I will!

MIME
Wie werd' ich den Lauernden los?
Verfänglich muss ich ihn fragen.—
Dein Haupt pfänd' ich
für den Herd:
nun sorg', es sinnig zu lösen!
Drei der Fragen
stell' ich mir frei.

WANDERER
Three times must I hit it.

WANDERER
Dreimal muss ich's treffen.

MIME (*sets himself to meditation*)
You've roamed a great deal
on the world's broad surface,
you've wandered much on the earth.
So show me your skill.
What is the race
dwelling beneath earth's surface?

MIME
Du rührtest dich viel
auf der Erde Rücken,
die Welt durchwandert'st du weit:
nun sage mir schlau,
welches Geschlecht
tagt in der Erde Tiefe?

WANDERER
Why the dusky Nibelungs
people the rocky caverns:
Nibelhome is their land.
Black elves, those Nibelungs.
Black Alberich
mastered their might by a spell!
By a magic ring
a powerful charm
tamed this industrious folk;
wondrous treasures,
shimmering bright,
fell then to him.
With these could the world be his kingdom.
Now ask me your second point.

WANDERER
In der Erde Tiefe
tagen die Nibelungen:
Nibelheim ist ihr Land.
Schwarzalben sind sie;
Schwarz-Alberich
hütet' als Herrscher sie einst.
Eines Zauberringes
zwingende Kraft
zähmt' ihm das fleissige Volk.
Reicher Schätze
schimmernden Hort
häuften sie ihm:
der sollte die Welt ihm gewinnen.—
Zum zweiten was frägst du Zwerg?

MIME (*sinks in continually deeper meditation*)
Yes, Wanderer,
much you know
of the central caves of earth.
Now answer me straight,
what is the race
dwelling upon earth's surface?

MIME
Viel, Wanderer,
weisst du mir
aus der Erde Nabelnest:—
nun sage mir schlicht,
welches Geschlecht
ruht auf der Erde Rücken?

WANDERER
Well, the race of giants
live on the surface of earth:
Gianthome is their land.
Fasolt and Fafner,
the rowdy rulers,

WANDERER
Auf der Erde Rücken
wuchtet der Riesen Geschlecht:
Riesenheim ist ihr Land.
Fasolt und Fafner,
der Rauhen Fürsten,
neideten Nibelungs Macht;
den gewaltigen Hort

gewannen sie sich,
errangen mit ihm den Ring:
um den entbrannte
den Brüdern Streit;
der Fasolt fällte,
als wilder Wurm
hütet nun Fafner den Hort.—
Die dritte Frage nun droht.

envied the Nibelungs' might;
and they won for themselves
the powerful hoard;
and thus the ring fell to them.
The hoard brought hate,
and the brothers fought.
Grim death took Fasolt,
in dragon's shape
Fafner now watches the hoard.
One question more is to come.

MIME
Viel, Wand'rer,
weisst du mir
von der Erde rauhem Rücken;
nun sage mir wahr,
welches Geschlecht
wohnt auf wolkigen Höh'n?

MIME (*absorbed in thought*)
Yes, Wanderer,
much you know
of the earth and all its regions.
Now give me the truth!
Tell me what race
dwells on cloud-covered heights?

WANDERER
Auf wolkigen Höh'n
wohnen die Götter:
Walhall heisst ihr Saal.
Lichtalben sind sie;
Licht-Alberich,
Wotan, waltet der Schaar.
Aus der Welt-Esche
weihlichstem Aste
schuf er sich einen Schaft:
dorrt der Stamm,
nie verdirbt doch der Speer:
mit seiner Spitze
sperrt Wotan die Welt.
Heil'ger Verträge
Treue-Runen
schnitt in den Schaft er ein.
Den Haft der Welt
hält in der Hand,
wer den Speer führt,
den Wotans Faust umspannt.
Ihm neigte sich
der Niblungen Heer;
der Riesen Gezücht
zähmte sein Rath:
ewig gehorchen sie alle
des Speeres starkem Herrn.
Nun rede, weiser Zwerg:
wusst' ich der Fragen Rath?
behalte mein Haupt ich frei?

WANDERER
The gods hold the heights,
dwelling in glory.
Valhall is their home.
These gods are light elves;
Light-Alberich,
Wotan, rules them as king.
From the world ash's
mystical branches
once he fashioned a spear.
Ash trees fade,
but the shaft cannot fail;
and with its spear point
Wotan rules the world.
Deep in the shaft
he cut his runes,
telling of truth to pacts.
To own the spear
gripped by the god
is to hold sway
like Wotan, over all:
the Nibelung host
must bow to the spear.
The giants as well
call him their lord.
All must obey as their master
the one who holds the spear.
(*strikes the spear, as if by accident, on the ground. A light thunderclap is heard, which quite unsettles* MIME)
Now tell me, cunning dwarf,
have I disclosed the truth?
and please may I keep my head?
(MIME, *after having attentively watched the* WANDERER

with the spear, falls into a state of terror, confusedly seeks for his tools and looks nervously aside)

MIME
Keep it—you're free,
safe from my sword!
So, Wanderer, be on your way!

WANDERER
You should really have asked
something worth knowing,
for I had wagered my head.
Since you know nothing
that you should,
you therefore must wager your own.
You were quite
rude to your guest;
my head stood
as a pledge to you,
to win a place at your hearth.
Now duty's pledge
binds you to me.
Answer me thrice
or forfeit your life.
Be resolute, Mime, and bold!

MIME (*finally composing himself*)
I left home
many years ago,
long have parted
from my mother earth.
I feel Wotan's eye upon me,
he spies right into this cave,
his gaze withers
my mother wit.
But now it is wise to be wise,
Wanderer, ask what you will!
Perhaps fortune will help me
to ransom my dwarfish head!

WANDERER (*again leisurely seating himself*)
Now, honorable dwarf,
first of the questions.
Tell me, what is the race
that Wotan treats so harshly,
and yet loves most dearly of all?

MIME (*more cheerful now*)
Little know I
of heroes' kindred,
but just the same I shall be free.
The Volsungen are
the chosen race
that Wotan cared for
and loved so dearly,
though he was harsh to them:

MIME
Fragen und Haupt
hast du gelöst:
nun, Wand'rer, geh' deines Weg's!

WANDERER
Was zu wissen dir frommt
solltest du fragen;
Kunde verbürgte mein Kopf:—
dass du nun nicht weisst
was dir nützt,
dess' fass' ich jetzt deines als Pfand.
Gastlich nicht
galt mir dein Gruss:
mein Haupt gab ich
in deine Hand,
um mich des Herdes zu freu'n.
Nach Wettens Pflicht
pfänd' ich nun dich,
lösest du drei
der Fragen nicht leicht:
drum frische dir, Mime, den Muth!

MIME
Lang' schon mied ich
mein Heimathland,
lang' schon schied ich
aus der Mutter Schoss;
mir leuchtete Wotans Auge,
zur Höhle lugt' es herein:
vor ihm magert
mein Mutterwitz.
Doch frommt mir's, nun weise zu sein.
Wand'rer, frage denn zu!
Vielleicht glückt mir's gezwungen
zu lösen des Zwergen Haupt.

WANDERER
Nun, ehrlicher Zwerg,
sag' mir zum ersten:
welches ist das Geschlecht,
dem Wotan schlimm sich zeigt,
und das doch das liebste ihm lebt?

MIME
Wenig hört' ich
von Heldensippen:
der Frage doch mach' ich mich frei.
Die Wälsungen sind
das Wunschgeschlecht,
das Wotan zeugte
und zärtlich liebt,
zeigt er auch Ungunst ihm.
Siegmund und Sieglind'
stammten von Wälse,

ein wild verzweifeltes
Zwillingspaar:
Siegfried zeugten sie selbst,
den stärksten Wälsungenspross.
Behalt' ich, Wanderer,
zum ersten mein Haupt?

Siegmund and Sieglinda,
offspring of Volsa,
a wild and desperate
twin-born pair.
Siegfried sprang from their loins,
the strongest Volsung of all.
Now have I, Wanderer,
this once saved my head?

WANDERER
Wie doch genau
das Geschlecht du mir nennst:
schlau eracht' ich dich Argen!
Der ersten Frage
ward'st du frei:
zum zweiten nun sag' mir,
Zwerg:—
Ein weiser Niblung
wahret Siegfried:
Fafnern soll er ihm fällen,
dass er den Ring erränge,
des Hortes Herrscher zu sein.
Welches Schwert
muss nun Siegfried schwingen,
taug' es zu Fafners Tod?

WANDERER (*pleasantly*)
Yes, you have
answered me well, I confess!
Rogues like you are quite skillful.
You answered well
the first point put.
A second comes now, my friend!
A cunning Nibelung
harbors Siegfried,
Fafner's destined destroyer—
for the boy is to slay him,
to let the dwarf gain the gold.
Name the sword
that Siegfried must handle,
if he's to slay the foe?

MIME
Nothung heisst
ein neidliches Schwert;
in einer Esche Stamm
stiess es Wotan:
dem sollt' es geziemen,
der aus dem Stamm' es zög'.
Der stärksten Helden
keiner bestand's:
Siegmund, der Kühne,
konnt's allein;
fechtend führt' er's im Streit,
bis an Wotan's Speer es zersprang.
Nun verwahrt die Stücke
ein weiser Schmied;
denn er weiss, dass allein
mit dem Wotansschwert
ein kühnes, dummes Kind,
Siegfried, den Wurm versehrt.
Behalt' ich Zwerg
auch zweitens mein Haupt?

MIME (*feeling much better, now joyfully rubs his hands*)
Needful is
the coveted sword,
and Wotan thrust it deep
in an ash tree.
Just one could possess it,
he who could pull it out.
The strongest heroes
tried it in vain;
Siegmund succeeded,
he alone.
Then he bore it to war,
till on Wotan's spear it was split.
Now a cunning smith
has preserved the parts,
for he knows it is only
with Wotan's sword,
a valiant, foolish boy,
Siegfried, shall slay his foe.
(*much pleased*)
Now may I keep
my headpiece a while?

WANDERER
Ha, ha, ha, ha, ha, ha, ha, ha
Der witzigste bist du
unter den Weisen:
wer käm' dir an Klugheit gleich?
Doch bist du so klug,
den kindischen Helden
für Zwergenszwecke zu nützen:

WANDERER
Ha ha ha ha, ha ha ha ha!
One wittier I have
never encountered;
for where can your like be found?
But if by your ruse,

the valorous stripling
fulfills your dwarfish intentions,
there's a third and final
threat to come!
Tell me, you cunning weapon smith,
who shall from the mighty pieces
fashion the sword called Needful?

MIME (*starts up in extreme terror*)
The pieces! the sword!
O woe! I'm dizzy!
How shall I start?
What follows now?
Accursed steel!
Why was it I stole you!
A sword that has pierced me
with want and woe!
Still it remains
too hard for my hammer.
Rivet, solder,
fail in the test!
The cleverest smith's
lacking in skill!
(*as though out of his senses, flings his tools about, and breaks out in despair*)
Who can forge the sword
if I cannot?
How shall I give you an answer?

WANDERER
Thrice your questions were put me,
thrice the challenge was met.
You sought for knowledge
far afield,
yet failed to ask what you ought.
What would help
was right at hand.
Now when I guess it,
you are upset.
Your witty head
is the prize I have won!
Now, Fafner's dauntless destroyer,
hear, and learn your doom:
"He who has never
harbored fear,
he shall forge the sword."
(MIME *stares at him. He turns to depart*)
Guard well your head.
Henceforth take care:
I leave it forfeit to him
who has never harbored fear!
(*he turns away with a smile and disappears into the*

mit der dritten Frage
droh' ich nun!—
sag' mir, du weiser
Waffenschmied,
wer wird aus den starken
Stücken
Nothung, das Schwert, wohl
schweissen?

MIME
Die Stücke! Das Schwert!
O weh! mir schwindelt!—
Was fang' ich an?
Was fällt mir ein?
Verfluchter Stahl,
dass ich dich gestohlen!
Er hat mich vernagelt
in Pein und Noth;
mir bleibt er hart,
ich kann ihn nicht hämmern:
Niet' und Löthe
lässt mich im Stich!
Der weiseste Schmied
weiss sich nicht Rath:
wer schweisst nun das Schwert,
schaff' ich es nicht?
Das Wunder, wie soll ich's
wissen?

WANDERER
Dreimal solltest du fragen,
dreimal stand ich dir frei:
nach eitlen Fernen
forschtest du;
doch was zunächst sich dir
fand,
was dir nützt, fiel dir nicht ein.
Nun ich's errathe,
wirst du verrückt:
gewonnen hab' ich
das witzige Haupt.
Jetzt, Fafners kühner Be-
zwinger,
hör', verfallener Zwerg:—
nur wer das Fürchten
nie erfuhr,
schmiedet Nothung neu.
Dein weises Haupt
wahre von heut':
verfallen—lass ich's dem,
der das Fürchten nicht gelernt.

forest. MIME *sinks down into his seat, as if overwhelmed)*

THIRD SCENE

MIME
Verfluchtes Licht!
Was flammt dort die Luft?
Was flackert und lackert,
was flimmert und schwirrt,
was schwebt dort und webt
und wabert umher?
Da glimmert's und glitzt's
in der Sonne Gluth:
was säuselt und summt
und saust nun gar?
Es brummt und braust
und prasselt hierher!
Dort bricht's durch den Wald,
will auf mich zu!
Ein grässlicher Rachen
reisst sich mir auf!
Der Wurm will mich fangen!
Fafner! Fafner!

MIME *(staring into the sunlit forest, gradually gives way to violent trembling)*
Accursed light!
What makes the air flame?
What flickers and flashes,
what quivers and whirs,
what floats there and soars,
and flickers around?
It glimmers and gleams
in the sunlight's glow!
What rustles and hums
and whistles so loud?
It growls and roars
and crackles this way!
It breaks through the wood,
making for me!
(rises up in terror)
Its horrible jaws
open up wide:
The dragon will seize me!
Fafner! Fafner!
(sinks down shrieking behind the anvil as SIEGFRIED *breaks through the thicket)*

SIEGFRIED
Heda! Fauler!
bist du nun fertig?
Schnell! wie steht's mit dem Schwert?
Wo steckt der Schmied?
Stahl er sich fort?
Hehe! Mime! du Memme!
Wo bist du? wo birgst du dich?

SIEGFRIED
Hey, there! you slowpoke!
Are you now ready?
(enters the cave)
How much have you done?
(pauses in surprise)
Where is the smith?
Where has he hid?
Hey-hey! Mime, you 'fraid-cat!
Where are you? Reveal yourself!

MIME
Bist du es, Kind?
Kommst du allein?

MIME *(weakly, from behind the anvil)*
Is it you, child!
Come you alone?

SIEGFRIED
Hinter dem Ambos?—
Sag', was schufest du dort?
schärftest du mir das Schwert?

SIEGFRIED *(laughing)*
Under the anvil?
Say, a nice place to work!
Were you sharpening the sword?

MIME
Das Schwert? das Schwert?
wie möcht' ich's schweissen?—
„Nur wer das Fürchten
nicht erfuhr,

MIME *(coming forward greatly disturbed and confused)*
The sword? The sword?
How could I forget it?
"He who has never

harbored fear,
he shall forge the sword."
I had more sense
than to try such work!

SIEGFRIED (*vehemently*)
Will you now tell me?
or must I teach you?

MIME
I do not know what to say!
I've lost my head,
lost it by wager,
for henceforth 'tis forfeit to him
"who has never harbored fear."

SIEGFRIED
Ha! so you flout me?
thinking to flee?

MIME (*gradually taking hold of himself*)
I'd flee the man
who harbors fear!
Fear was the teaching I failed in;
I dumbly forgot
the one good thing.
Love was the lesson
that I gave you;
but alas, the lesson failed!
Now how can I make you feel fear?

SIEGFRIED (*seizes him*)
Hey! must I help you?
What's done for today?

MIME
While sunk in my thoughts,
considering your welfare,
something important I thought of.

SIEGFRIED (*laughing*)
You mean you were sunk
under the anvil.
However, get on with your tale.

MIME (*recovering himself more and more*)
I learned the meaning of fear,
so I could teach you, blockhead.

SIEGFRIED
Well, tell me about it.

MIME
You've never felt fear,
and yet you would leave
these woods for the world?
What good is the trustiest sword,
if you are lacking in fear?

SIEGFRIED (*impatiently*)
Now you give me stupid advice!

schmiedet Nothung neu."—
Zu weise ward ich
für solches Werk!

SIEGFRIED
Wirst du mir reden?
Soll ich dir rathen?

MIME
Wo nehm' ich redlichen Rath?—
Mein weises Haupt
hab' ich verwettet:
verfallen, verlor ich's an den,
„der das Fürchten nicht
gelernt."—

SIEGFRIED
Sind mir das Flausen?
Willst du mir flieh'n?

MIME
Wohl flöh' ich dem,
der's Fürchten kennt;
doch das liess ich dem Kinde zu
lehren!
Ich Dummer vergass
was einzig gut:
Liebe zu mir
sollt' er lernen;—
das gelang nun leider faul!
Wie bring' ich das Fürchten
ihm bei?

SIEGFRIED
He! Muss ich helfen?
Was fegtest du heut'?

MIME
Für dich nur besorgt,
versank ich in Sinnen,
wie ich dich Wichtiges wiese.

SIEGFRIED
Bis unter den Sitz
warst du versunken:
was Wichtiges fandest du da?

MIME
Das Fürchten lernt' ich für
dich,
dass ich's dich Dummen lehre.

SIEGFRIED
Was ist's mit dem Fürchten?

MIME
Erfuhrst du's noch nie,
und willst aus dem Wald
fort in die Welt?
Was frommte das festeste
Schwert,
blieb dir das Fürchten fern?

SIEGFRIED
Faulen Rath
erfindest du wohl?

MIME
Deiner Mutter Rath
redet aus mir:
was ich gelobt'
muss ich nun lösen,
in die listige Welt
dich nicht zu lassen,
eh' du nicht das Fürchten gelernt.

MIME (*approaching* SIEGFRIED *with increasing confidence*)
But your mother's words
sound from my lips;
such was my promise,
so I must keep it:
not to let you fare forth
away from this forest,
until you're acquainted with fear.

SIEGFRIED
Ist's eine Kunst,
was kenn' ich sie nicht?—
Heraus! Was ist's mit dem Fürchten?

SIEGFRIED (*vehemently*)
If it's an art,
why was I not taught?
Come on! Now tell me what fear is!

MIME
Fühltest du nie
im finster'n Wald,
bei Dämmerschein
am dunklen Ort,
wenn fern es säuselt,
summs't und saus't,
wildes Brummen
näher braus't,
wirres Flackern
um dich flimmert,
schwellend Schwirren
zu Leib' dir schwebt,—
fühltest du dann nicht grieselnd
Grausen die Glieder dir fah'n?
Glühender Schauer
schüttelt die Glieder,
in der Brust bebend und bang
berstet hämmernd das Herz?—
Fühltest du das noch nicht,
das Fürchten blieb dir dann fremd.

MIME
Have you not felt
in dusky woods,
when twilight falls,
in gloomy glens,
when comes a whisper,
hum and hiss,
when savage sounds approach,
flick'ring flashes
hover round you,
growing growlings
to make you shake—
(*trembling*)
have you not felt then
grisly horrors take hold of your body,
terrible shudders
set you a-tremble?
Then your heart throbbing within
bursts with terror and fright!
If this is still unknown,
then fear is strange to your heart.

SIEGFRIED
Sonderlich seltsam
muss das sein!
Hart und fest,
fühl' ich, steht mir das Herz.
Das Grieseln und Grausen,
Glühen und Schauern,
Hitzen und Schwindeln,
Hämmern und Beben—
gern begehr' ich das Bangen,
sehnend verlangt mich's der Lust.—
Doch wie bringst du,
Mime, mir's bei?
Wie wär'st du, Memme, mir Meister?

SIEGFRIED (*meditating*)
Curious, surely,
that must be.
Hard and fast
beats my heart in my breast.
The shiv'ring and shaking,
the glowing and quaking,
burning and fainting,
throbbing and trembling,
these are much to my liking.
Great is my longing for fear!
But how can you teach it to me?
How could you, coward, instruct me?

MIME
Folge mir nur,
ich führe dich wohl;
sinnend fand ich's aus.
Ich weiss einen schlimmen Wurm,

MIME
Merely obey,
I know the way well;
I have figured it out.
I know of a dragon foe,

who kills and eats his fill.
Fafner surely can teach you.
Follow me to where he lives.

SIEGFRIED
And where is his lair?

MIME
Hate-cavern,
that is its name;
due east, at end of the wood.

SIEGFRIED
Then not too far from the world?

MIME
From Hate-cave the world is not far.

SIEGFRIED
Then that is where you must lead me:
fear shall be taught me,
then forth to the world!
Be quick! Forge me the sword!
In the world fain would I swing it.

MIME
The sword? Alack!

SIEGFRIED
Quick to the smithy!
Show me your work!

MIME
Accursed steel!
The job is too much for my skill;
no dwarfish power
avails with the magic spell.
There is one for the work,
he who has never felt fear.

SIEGFRIED
Pleasant tricks
the idler would play me.
Only a bungler,
that's all you are!
You think you can trick me with lies!
Bring me the pieces!
Off with the bungler!
(*stepping to the hearth*)
My father's steel
yields but to me.
Let me fashion the sword.
(*flinging* MIME's *tools about, he sets impetuously to work*)

MIME
If you had labored
to learn your craft,
you now would know what to do;

der würgt' und schlang schon viel:
Fafner lehrt dich das Fürchten,
folgst du mir zu seinem Nest.

SIEGFRIED
Wo liegt er im Nest?

MIME
Neidhöhle
wird es genannt:
im Ost, am Ende des Wald's.

SIEGFRIED
Dann wär's nicht weit von der Welt?

MIME
Bei Neidhöhle liegt sie ganz nah'!

SIEGFRIED
Dahin denn sollst du mich führen:
lernt' ich das Fürchten,
dann fort in die Welt!
Drum schnell schaffe das Schwert,
in der Welt will ich es schwingen.

MIME
Das Schwert? O Noth!

SIEGFRIED
Rasch in die Schmiede!
Weis' was du schuf'st.

MIME
Verfluchter Stahl:
Zu flicken versteh' ich ihn nicht!
Den zähen Zauber
bezwingt keines Zwergen Kraft.
Wer das Fürchten nicht kennt,
der fänd' wohl eher die Kunst.

SIEGFRIED
Feine Finten
weiss mir der Faule;
das er ein Stümper
sollt' er gesteh'n:
nun lügt er sich listig heraus.—
Her mit den Stücken!
Fort mit dem Stümper!
Des Vaters Stahl
fügt sich wohl mir:
ich selbst schweisse das Schwert!

MIME
Hättest du fleissig
die Kunst gepflegt,
jetzt käm' dir's wahrlich zu gut;
doch lässig warst du
stets in der Lehre:

was willst du nun Rechtes rüsten?

but you were always
lazy at work:
you see what good this has done you!

SIEGFRIED
Was der Meister nicht kann,
vermöcht' es der Knabe,
hätt' er ihm immer gehorcht?
Jetzt mach' dich fort,
misch' dich nicht drein:
sonst fällst du mir mit ins Feuer!

SIEGFRIED
Where the master has failed
could pupil do better,
even if he had obeyed?
Just go away.
Make yourself scarce,
or else I will forge you also!
(makes a large pile of charcoal on the hearth and blows the fire, while he secures the pieces of sword in a vise and files away)

MIME
Was machst du da?
Nimm doch die Löthe:
den Brei braut' ich schon längst.

MIME *(who has sat down a little away, watches* SIEGFRIED *at work)*
Now what is all this?
There is the solder.
The brew waits for your skill.

SIEGFRIED
Fort mit dem Brei!
ich brauch' ihn nicht:
mit Bappe back' ich kein Schwert!

SIEGFRIED
Out with the brew,
I need it not!
I use no pap for my sword!

MIME
Du zerfeil'st die Feile,
zerreib'st die Raspel:
wie willst du den Stahl zerstampfen?

MIME
But the file is wearing,
the rasp is ruined!
You're fretting the steel to splinters.

SIEGFRIED
Zersponnen muss ich
in Spähne ihn seh'n:
was entzwei ist, zwing' ich mir so.

SIEGFRIED
It must be splintered
and ground into shreds:
what is broken
then can be patched.
(goes on filing energetically)

MIME
Hier hilft kein Kluger,
das seh' ich klar:
hier hilft dem Dummen
die Dummheit selbst!
Wie er sich müht
und mächtig regt:
ihm schwindet der Stahl,
doch wird ihm nicht schwül!—
Nun ward ich so alt,
wie Höhl' und Wald,
und hab' nicht so 'was geseh'n!
Mit dem Schwert gelingt's,
das lern' ich wohl:
furchtlos fegt er's zu ganz,—
der Wand'rer wusst' es gut!—
Wie berg' ich nun
mein banges Haupt?
Dem kühnen Knaben verfiel's,
lehrt' ihn nicht Fafner die Furcht.—
Doch weh' mir Armen!
Wie würgt' er den Wurm,
erführ' er das Fürchten von ihm?

MIME *(aside)*
No craftsman helps here,
I see that well.
What helps the booby is folly alone.
How the boy toils,
and moves with might!
The steel is in shreds,
and yet he's not tired!
*(*SIEGFRIED *has fanned the hearth fire into a very bright glow)*
Although I'm as old
as cave and wood,
I've never seen such a sight!
(while SIEGFRIED *continues his impetuous filing,* MIME *seats himself farther off)*
He will forge the sword,
I know that well.
Lacking fear he will win.
The Wand'rer knew it well.

So how to hide
my hapless head?
It goes to Siegfried unless
Fafner acquaints him with fear.
(springing up and bending low with growing restlessness)
My plight is woeful!
If Siegfried learns fear,
then how can he conquer the foe?
And I will still lack the ring.
Accursed dilemma!
What shall I do?
Who can give good advice,
so the valorous boy can be tamed?
(SIEGFRIED has now filed the pieces down and put them in a crucible, which he sets on the fire)

Wie erräng' ich mir den Ring?
Verfluchte Klemme!
Da klebt' ich fest,
fänd' ich nicht klugen Rath,
wie den Furchtlosen selbst ich bezwäng'.

SIEGFRIED
Hey Mime! Be quick!
and name the sword
that I have shredded to pieces.

SIEGFRIED
He, Mime, geschwind:
wie heisst das Schwert,
das ich in Spähne zersponnen?

MIME
Needful, that is
the name of the sword:
for your mother told me the tale.

MIME
Nothung nennt sich
das neidliche Schwert:
deine Mutter gab mir die Mär.

SIEGFRIED *(during the following song he blows the fire with the bellows)*
Needful! Needful!
conquering sword!
What mighty blow could break you?
I filed the beautiful blade
to shreds,
and now I'll fry all the filings.
Ho-ho! Ho-ho!
Ho-hei! Ho-hei! Ho-ho!
Bellows blow!
Brighten the glow!
Once I felled
a mighty ash
which grew in the forest glen.
I burned the tree
until it was coal;
now it lies heaped high on the hearth.
Ho-ho! Ho-ho!
Ho-hei! Ho-hei! Ho-ho!
Bellows blow!
Brighten the glow!
The charcoal pieces—
how fierce they burn!
How bright and fair they glow!
They shoot through the air
in showering sparks,

SIEGFRIED
Nothung! Nothung!
neidliches Schwert!
was musstest du zerspringen?
Zu Spreu nun schuf ich
die scharfe Pracht,
im Tigel brat' ich die Spähne!
Hoho! hoho!
hahei! hahei!
Blase, Balg!
blase die Gluth!—
Wild im Walde
wuchs ein Baum,
den hab' ich im Forst gefällt:
die braune Esche
brannt' ich zu Kohl',
auf dem Herd nun liegt sie gehäuft!
Hoho! hoho!
hahei! hahei! hoho!
Blase, Balg!
blase die Gluth!—
Des Baumes Kohle,
wie brennt sie kühn,
wie glüht sie hell und hehr!
In springenden Funken
sprüht sie auf,
hohei, hoho, hohei!
zerschmilzt mir des Stahles Spreu.
Hoho! hoho!
hahei! hahei!
Blase, Balg!
blase die Gluth!

ho-hei, ho-ho, ho-hei!
Now melt me my filings of steel.
Ho-ho! ho-ho! ho-ho!
Ho-hei! Ho-hei! Ho-ho!
Bellows blow!
Brighten the glow!

MIME
Er schmiedet das Schwert,
und Fafner fällt er:
das seh' ich nun sicher voraus.
Hort und Ring
erringt er im Harst:—
wie erwerb' ich mir den Gewinn?
Mit Witz und List
erlang' ich Beides,
und berge heil mein Haupt.

MIME (*still by himself, sitting at a distance*)
He'll finish the sword
and finish Fafner;
that's easy enough to foresee.
Hoard and ring
will fall to his hands.
So just how shall I win the prize?
(*a sudden thought comes to him*)
By hook or crook
I'll win both prizes
and save my head besides.

SIEGFRIED
Hoho! Hoho!
Hoho, hohei! Hohei!

SIEGFRIED (*again at the bellows*)
Ho-ho! Ho-ho!
Ho-ho, ho-hei! Ho-hei!

MIME
Rang er sich müd' mit dem Wurm,
von der Müh' erlab' ihn ein Trank
aus würz'gen Säften,
die ich gesammelt,
brau' ich den Trank für ihn;
wenig Tropfen nur
braucht er zu trinken,
sinnlos sinkt er in Schlaf:
mit der eig'nen Waffe,
die er sich gewonnen,
räum' ich ihn leicht aus dem Weg,
erlange mir Ring und Hort.

MIME
After his fight he'll be tired;
a drink should be to his taste.
I've spicy simples,
recently gathered;
these I will brew for him.
All he needs is a drop
of this potion—
senseless then he will lie.
With the very weapon
that now he is forging,
he shall be cleared from my way,
then hoard and the ring are mine.

SIEGFRIED
Nothung! Nothung!
neidliches Schwert!
schon schmilzt deines Stahles Spreu:
im eig'nen Schweisse
schwimmst du nun.

SIEGFRIED
Needful! Needful!
Sword that I need!
At last all your filings melt,
and now you swim
amid your sweat.

MIME
Hei! Weiser Wand'rer,
dünkt' ich dich dumm?
Wie gefällt dir nun
mein feiner Witz?
Fand ich mir wohl
Rath und Ruh'?

MIME (*rubs his hands with delight*)
Hey, clever Wanderer!
Was I so dumb?
Don't you think I have
a pretty wit?
Is not this
the simplest way?

SIEGFRIED
Bald schwing' ich dich als mein Schwert!
In das Wasser floss
ein Feuerfluss:
grimmiger Zorn
zischt' ihm da auf;

SIEGFRIED (*pours the glowing contents of the crucible into a mold and holds it on high*)
I'll soon be swinging my sword!
(*plunges the mold into the pail of water. Steam and hissing ensue*)

In the water flowed
a flood of fire;
furious hate
hissed from its waves!
But though it flowed hot
in the watery flood,
now does it rest.
There, see how it lies,
proud in its lordly strength.
Blood will drip soon,
bathing the blade.
(thrusts the steel into the fire and works the bellows violently. MIME *springs up, happy; he brings several vessels, shakes from them spices and herbs into a cooking pot)*
Now sweat once again,
and then I can forge you!
Needful, sword that I need!
(during his work he observes MIME, *who is carefully placing the pot on the fire)*
Hey, stupid!
What's that mess on the fire?
While I burn steel
what is it you brew?

MIME
A smith has come to shame:
a boy can now teach him skill;
for the poor old man has lost his art,
and so becomes a cook.
Burn all your iron to broth,
while I prepare you
soup with nice eggs.
(goes on cooking)

SIEGFRIED
Mime, the artist,
takes up cooking,
because he's tired of his forge.
I have shattered
all his swords into pieces.
I refuse to eat what he cooks!
(during the following SIEGFRIED *draws the mold from the fire, breaks it open, and lays the glowing steel on the anvil)*
He'd teach me the meaning
of fear and danger!
I don't want him for a teacher,
for the best he can do
is take up my time.
He's only a foolish old bungler!
Ho-ho! Ho-ho! Ho-hei!
Hammering blows make you strong and hard!

frierend zähmt' ihn der Frost.
Wie sehrend er floss,
in des Wassers Fluth
fliesst er nicht mehr;
starr ward er und steif,
herrisch der harte Stahl:
heisses Blut doch
fliesst ihm bald!—
Nun schwitze noch einmal,
dass ich dich schweisse,
Nothung, neidliches Schwert!
Was schafft der Tölpel
dort mit dem Topf?
Brenn' ich hier Stahl,
brau'st du dort Sudel?

MIME
Zu Schanden kam ein Schmied,
den Lehrer sein Knabe lehrt;
mit der Kunst ist's beim Alten aus,
als Koch dient er dem Kinde:
brennt er das Eisen zu Brei,
aus Eiern brau't
der Alte ihm Sud.

SIEGFRIED
Mime, der Künstler,
lernt nun Kochen;
das Schmieden schmeckt ihm nicht mehr:
seine Schwerter alle
hab' ich zerschmissen;
was er kocht, ich kost' es ihm nicht.
Das Fürchten zu lernen
will er mich führen;
ein Ferner soll es mich lehren:
was am besten er kann,
mir bringt er's nicht bei;
als Stümper besteht er in Allem!
Hoho! hoho! hahei!
Schmiede, mein Hammer,
ein hartes Schwert!
Hoho! hahei!
hoho! hahei!
Einst färbte Blut
dein falbes Blau;
sein rothes Rieseln
röthete dich;

kalt lachtest du da,
das warme lecktest du kühl!
Heiaho! Haha! Haheiaha!
Nun hat die Gluth
dich roth geglüht;
deine weiche Härte
dem Hammer weicht:
zornig sprüh'st du mir Funken,
das ich dich Spröden gezähmt!
Heiaho! heiaho!
heiaho! ho! ho!
Hoho! hahei! hahei! hahei!

Ho-ho! Ha-hei! Hoho! Ha-hei!
Hot blood once stained
your steely blue;
its ruddy trickling
reddened your blade.
Cold then was your laugh;
you licked the blade till it cooled.
Hei-a-ho! Ha-ha! Ha-hei-a-ha!
The fiery flame
now makes you glow,
while my hammer pounds
on your pliant steel.
Now you're tame you are angry,
and spray me fiercely with sparks.
Hei-a-ho! Hei-a-ho!
Hei-a-ho-ho-ho-ho-ho!
Ha-hei! Hahei! Ha-hei!

MIME

Er schafft sich ein scharfes Schwert,
Fafner zu fällen,
der Zwerge Feind:
ich braut' ein Truggetränk,
Siegfried zu fangen,
dem Fafner fiel.
Gelingen muss mir die List;
lachen muss mir der Lohn!

MIME

He's making a sharp-edged sword,
that's to kill Fafner
the Nibelungs' foe.
I've brewed a poisoned drink;
Siegfried will take it
when Fafner falls.
My wits must gain me the prize.
Fortune smiles on the wise.

SIEGFRIED

Hoho! hoho! hoho! hahei!
Schmiede, mein Hammer,
ein hartes Schwert!
Hoho! hahei!
hoho! hahei!
Der frohen Funken,
wie freu' ich mich!
Es ziert den Kühnen
des Zornes Kraft:
lustig lach'st du mich an,
stellst du auch grimm dich und gram!
Heiaho! haha! heiaha!
Durch Gluth und Hammer
glückt es mir!
Mit starken Schlägen
streckt' ich dich:
nun schwinde die rothe Scham;
werde kalt und hart wie du kannst.
Heiaho! heiaho!
heiaho! ho! ho! ho! ho! Heiah!

SIEGFRIED

Ho-ho! Ho-ho! Ho-ho! Ho-hei!
Hammering blows
make you strong and hard!
Ho-ho! Ha-hei!
Ho-ho! Ha-hei!
The merry sparks
make me laugh with joy!
The brave look fairer
when fired by wrath.
Lo! you're laughing at me,
yet you look grisly and grim!
Hei-a-ho, ha-ha, ha-hei-a-ha!
The heat and hammer
serve me well.
I beat you out
with sturdy strokes.
Now banish your ruddy shame,
and be as cold and hard as you can.
Hei-a-ho! Hei-a-ho!
Hei-a-ho-ho-ho-ho-ho! Hei-ah!
(*swings the blade and plunges it into the pail of water, then laughs aloud at the hissing*)

MIME

Den der Bruder schuf,

MIME

Once my brother

made a shimmering ring,
infusing a spell
of magical might.
Its shining gold
can give pow'r to men,
pow'r more than is dreamed of!
This pow'r is mine!
Alberich, you
whom once I served,
shall in your turn
be servant to me,
and down I'll descend,
Nibelungs' leader,
and all his host
shall call me lord.
The contemptible dwarf
shall now be obeyed!
For they love the gold,
gods and heroes both.
The world shall henceforth
bow to my nod,
and at my anger
tremble with fear.

den schimmernden Reif,
in den er gezaubert
zwingende Kraft,
das helle Gold,
das zum Herrscher macht—
ich hab' ihn gewonnen!
ich walte sein'!—
Alberich selbst,
der einst mich band,
zu Zwergenfrohne
zwing' ich ihn nun:
als Niblungenfürst
fahr' ich danieder;
gehorchen soll mir
alles Heer!—
Der verachtete Zwerg,
was wird er geehrt!
Zu dem Hort hin drängt sich
Gott und Held:
vor meinem Nicken
neigt sich die Welt,
vor meinem Zorne
zittert sie hin!—

SIEGFRIED
Needful! Needful!
Conquering sword!
You rest again, fast in your hilt!

SIEGFRIED
Nothung! Nothung!
neidliches Schwert!
jetzt haftest du wieder im Heft.

MIME
Why then my toil
is finished and done.

MIME
Dann wahrlich müht sich
Mime nicht mehr.

SIEGFRIED
You were in two,
but now you are one.
No blow shall evermore destroy you.

SIEGFRIED
Warst du entzwei
ich zwang dich ganz,
kein Schlag soll nun dich
zerschlagen.

MIME
Let others win for me
endless wealth.

MIME
Ihm schaffen And're
den ew'gen Schatz.

SIEGFRIED
The dying father
destroyed the steel,
the living son
forged it anew.
The blade gives a ringing laugh,
and its keenness cuts with a will!

SIEGFRIED
Dem sterbenden Vater
zersprang der Stahl,
der lebende Sohn
schuf ihn neu:
nun lacht ihm sein heller
Schein,
seine Schärfe schneidet ihm
hart.

MIME
Mime, the valiant,
Mime, is master,
Prince of Nibelungs,
lord of the world!

MIME
Mime, der Kühne,
Mime ist König,
Fürst der Alben,
Walter des Alls!

SIEGFRIED
Needful! Needful!

SIEGFRIED
Nothung! Nothung!

neu und verjüngt!
zum Leben weckt' ich dich
wieder.
Todt lagst du
in Trümmern dort,
jetzt leuchtest du trotzig und
hehr.

MIME
Hei Mime! wie glückte mir das!

SIEGFRIED
Zeige den Schächern
nun deinen Schein!

MIME
Wer glaubte wohl das von dir!

SIEGFRIED
Schlage den Falschen,
fälle den Schelm!—
Schau, Mime, du Schmied:
so schneidet Siegfrieds Schwert!

Conquering sword!
Again I've waked you to life.
Once you lay
in lifeless bits,
but now you shine
proud in your strength.

MIME
Hey, Mime, how lucky you are!

SIEGFRIED
Just let the villains
see how you shine!

MIME
Could any have dreamed of this?

SIEGFRIED
Slash at the rascal,
cut down the rogue!
See, Mime, you smith,
see how my sword can cleave!

(*strikes the anvil, which splits asunder with a mighty noise.* MIME, *who has jumped joyfully on a stool, falls terrified to the ground.* SIEGFRIED, *exultant, holds the sword aloft*)

ACT II

FIRST SCENE

(Night, in a deep forest. In the far background the entrance to a cave. To the left a fissured cliff is seen through the trees. The dwarf ALBERICH *is lying by the rocky cliff, brooding gloomily.)*

ALBERICH

Within this wood
I watch at Fafner's cave;
I prick my ear,
peering through the gloom.
Fateful day,
have you arrived?
Are you the dawn
on the heels of night?
(in the wood, from the right, a storm arises; a bluish light shines)
What is the gleam glimmering there?
Nearby shimmers
a shining light;
it runs like a fiery steed,
breaks through the wood,
rushing this way!
Is it the dragon slayer?
Is Fafner's doom so near?
The light goes out,
The glow hides from my sight.
Night is master.
(the WANDERER *enters from the wood and stops, facing* ALBERICH*)*
Who comes here, shining through shadows?

WANDERER

I come
to your Hate-cave by night.
Who confronts me within the dark?
(the moonlight breaks forth and lights up the WANDERER'S *figure)*

ALBERICH

So you dare to come here?
What would you then?
Out of the way!
Go elsewhere, shameless thief!

WANDERER *(quietly)*

Black Alberich!
Is it you
guarding old Fafner's house?

ALBERICH

What are you seeking?
More evil deeds?
Wander away!

ALBERICH

In Wald und Nacht
vor Neidhöhl' halt' ich Wacht;
es lauscht mein Ohr,
mühvoll lugt mein Aug'—
Banger Tag,
bebst du schon auf?
Dämmerst du dort
durch das Dunkel her?
Welcher Glanz glittert dort auf?
Näher schimmert
ein heller Schein;
es rennt wie ein leuchtendes Ross,
bricht durch den Wald
brausend daher.
Naht schon des Wurmes Würger?
Ist's schon der Fafner fällt?
Das Licht erlischt—
Der Glanz barg sich dem Blick:
Nacht ist's wieder.—
Wer naht dort schimmernd im Schatten?

DER WANDERER

Zur Neidhöhle
fuhr ich bei Nacht:
Wen gewahr' ich im Dunkel dort?

ALBERICH

Du selbst lässt dich hier seh'n?
Was willst du hier?
Fort, aus dem Weg!
von dannen, schamloser Dieb!

WANDERER

Schwarz-Alberich,
schweifst du hier?
Hütest du Fafners Haus?

ALBERICH

Jagst du auf neue
Neidthat umher?
Weile nicht hier!
Weiche von hinnen!

Genug deines Truges
tränkte die Stätte mit Noth.
Drum, du Frecher,
lass' sie jetzt frei!

Take yourself elsewhere!
You've drenched the place
with evil deception enough!
Therefore, bounder,
take yourself off!

WANDERER

Zu schauen kam ich, nicht zu schaffen;
wer wehrte mir Wand'rers Fahrt?

I came as watcher, not as plotter.
Who hinders the Wanderer's way?

ALBERICH

Du Rath wüthender Ränke!
wär' ich dir zu lieb
doch noch dumm wie damals,
als du mich Blöden bandest!
Wie leicht gerieth es
den Ring mir nochmals zu rauben!
Hab' Acht: deine Kunst
kenne ich wohl;
doch wo du schwach bist,
blieb mir auch nicht verschwiegen.
Mit meinen Schätzen
zahltest du Schulden;
mein Ring lohnte
der Riesen Müh',
die deine Burg dir gebaut;
was mit den Trotzigen
einst du vertragen,
dess' Runen wahrt noch heut'
deines Speeres herrischer Schaft.
Nicht du darfst,
was als Zoll du gezahlt,
den Riesen wieder entreissen:
du selbst zerspalltest
deines Speeres Schaft:
in deiner Hand
der herrische Stab,
der starke zerstiebte wie Spreu.

You vile, villainous trickster!
Were I still the fool
that I was for your sake,
the time I let you bind me,
the ring would not
be my own much longer, I warrant!
Take care; for I know
all of your tricks!
I see your weakness—
that is clear to my vision.
You paid as debtor
using my treasure;
my ring paid for
the giants' toil;
your castle grew by their work.
What you did promise once to the bullies,
in words engraved in runes
on the lordly shaft of your spear,
you dare not
contradict by your might,
by seizing wages they worked for;
or else you yourself
would cause your spear to split;
within your hand
your wonderful staff,
so mighty, would shiver to bits.

WANDERER

Durch Vertrages Treue-Runen
band er dich
Bösen mir nicht:
dich beugt' er mir durch seine Kraft;
zum Krieg' d'rum wahr' ich ihn wohl.

But its runes of truth to treaties,
wretch, did not
bind you to me.
Instead it bends your will to mine:
I guard it well in the war.

ALBERICH

Wie stolz du dräu'st
in trotziger Stärke,
und wie dir's im Busen noch bangt!
Verfallen dem Tod
durch meinen Fluch
ist Fafner, des Hortes Hüter:
wer wird ihn beerben?
Wird der neidliche Hort
dem Niblung wieder gehören?
Das sehrt dich mit ew'ger Sorge!

You proudly boast
of marvelous power,
yet there is fear in your heart!
My curse has foredoomed
to death
the guard of the golden treasure.
Then—whom will it fall to?
Will the coveted hoard

belong again to the Nibelung?
That gnaws you with endless worry!
For just let it come
again to my hand,
not like the stupid giants
will I employ its power:
then tremble, you ageless
helper of heroes!
I will conquer
Valhall with Hella's host!
The world then shall be mine!

WANDERER
I know well
what you mean,
but care not at all;
whoever wins it,
let him be lord.

ALBERICH
You tell me darkly
what already is known!
On heroes' children
pin all your pride,
those dears who have bloomed from your blood!
Have you not fostered a youngling
to pick the fruit you hope for
but dare not pluck yourself?

WANDERER
Don't taunt me:
quarrel with Mime;
he brings you danger and woe.
He is coming here with a boy.
The lad will lay Fafner low.
I'm not known to him,
the Nibelung makes him his tool.
So let me say, my friend,
freely do what you will!
(ALBERICH *makes a violent move of curiosity*)
Mark my words well!
Be on your guard!
He does not know of the ring,
but Mime soon will explain.

ALBERICH
Will the hoard stay untouched by you?

WANDERER
Those I favor
work out their own salvation.
He stands or he falls,
his own right lord;
heroes, though, help to my purpose.

Denn fass' ich ihn wieder
einst in der Faust,
anders als dumme Riesen
üb' ich des Ringes Kraft:
dann zitt're der Helden
heiliger Hüter!
Wallhalls Höhen
stürm' ich mit Hellas Heer:
der Welt walte dann ich!

WANDERER
Deinen Sinn kenn' ich;
Doch sorgt er mich nicht:
des Ringes waltet
wer ihn gewinnt.

ALBERICH
Wie dunkel sprichst du,
was ich deutlich doch weiss!
An Heldensöhne
hält sich dein Trotz,
die traut deinem Blute entblüht.
Pflegtest du wohl eines Knaben,
der klug die Frucht dir pflücke,
die du nicht brechen darfst?

WANDERER
Mit mir nicht,
had're mit Mime:
dein Bruder bringt dir Gefahr;
einen Knaben führt er daher,
der Fafner ihm fällen soll.
Nichts weiss der von mir;
der Niblung nützt ihn für sich.
Drum sag' ich dir, Gesell:
thue frei, wie's dir frommt!
Höre mich wohl,
sei auf der Hut:
nicht kennt der Knabe den Ring,
doch Mime kundet ihn aus.

ALBERICH
Deine Hand hieltest du vom Hort?

WANDERER
Wen ich liebe
lass' ich für sich gewähren:
er steh' oder fall',
sein Herr ist er:
Helden nur können mir frommen.

ALBERICH
Mit Mime räng' ich
allein um den Ring?

ALBERICH
Is none but Mime
my rival in this?

WANDERER
Ausser dir begehrt er
einzig das Gut.

WANDERER
Only he, besides you,
covets the gold.

ALBERICH
Und doch gewänn' ich ihn
nicht?

ALBERICH
And so shall I make it my own?

WANDERER
Ein Helde naht
den Hort zu befrei'n;
zwei Niblungen geizen das
Gold:
Fafner fällt,
der den Ring bewacht:—
wer ihn rafft, hat ihn gewonnen.—
Willst du noch mehr?
Dort liegt der Wurm:
warnst du ihn vor dem Tod,
willig wohl liess' er den Tand.—
Ich selber weck' ihn dir auf.—
Fafner! Fafner!
erwache, Wurm!

WANDERER
A hero nears
to rescue the hoard;
two Nibelungs covet the gold.
Fafner falls,
he who guards the ring.
After that, finders are keepers.
Would you know more?
There lies the foe.
If you warn him of death,
maybe he'll give you the toy.
So now I'll wake him for you.
Fafner! Fafner!
O Fafner, wake!

ALBERICH
Was beginnt der Wilde!
Gönnt er mir's wirklich?

ALBERICH (*astonished*)
What's the madman doing?
Mine is it really?

FAFNERS STIMME
Wer stört mir den Schlaf?

FAFNER'S VOICE
Who stirs me from sleep?

WANDERER
Gekommen ist einer,
Noth dir zu künden:
er lohnt dir's mit dem Leben,
lohnst du das Leben ihm
mit dem Horte, den du hütest.

WANDERER (*facing cave*)
A friend has arrived,
to warn you of danger—
if you will make return
of the treasure you are guarding.
(*bends his ear toward the cave, listening.*)

FAFNERS STIMME
Was will er?

FAFNER'S VOICE
What would he?

ALBERICH
Wache, Fafner!
wache, du Wurm!
Ein starker Helde naht,
dich, Heiliger, will er besteh'n.

ALBERICH (*has stepped toward the* WANDERER *and calls into the cave*)
Waken, Fafner!
Dragon, awake!
A mighty hero nears!
He means to send you to heaven!

FAFNERS STIMME
Mich hungert sein'.

FAFNER'S VOICE
My stomach hears.

WANDERER
Kühn ist des Kindes Kraft,
scharf schneidet sein Schwert.

WANDERER
Bold is the boy, and strong,
keen-cutting his sword.

ALBERICH
Den gold'nen Ring
geizt er allein:
lass' mir den Ring zum Lohn,
so wend' ich den Streit;

ALBERICH
He craves the ring,
nothing but that.
Leave it to me as pay:

no fight will take place.
Your hoard will be safe,
and long you'll live in peace.

du wahrest den Hort,
und ruhig leb'st du lang'!

FAFNER'S VOICE
I have, and I hold!
Let me slumber!

FAFNERS STIMME
Ich lieg' und besitze:—
lasst mich schlafen!

WANDERER (*laughs aloud, then turns again to* ALBERICH)
Well, Alberich, that trick failed.
Yet call me rogue no more!
I give you counsel,
listen to this:
all things go their wonted way,
think not fate can be altered.
I leave you alone here,
hold yourself firm!
Contend with Mime, your brother;
for his kind, I think, suits you better.
(*turning to go*)
The other things
you'll quickly find out!
(*vanishes into the wood. A storm arises, a bright glow breaks out, then both quickly cease.* ALBERICH'S *eyes follow the* WANDERER)

WANDERER
Nun, Alberich, das schlug fehl!
Doch schilt mich nicht mehr Schelm!
Diess Eine, rath' ich,
achte noch wohl:
Alles ist nach seiner Art:
an ihr wirst du nichts ändern.
Ich lass' dir die Stätte:
stelle dich fest!
versuch's mit Mime, dem Bruder:
der Art ja versiehst du dich besser.
Was anders ist,
das lerne nun auch!

ALBERICH
He's riding away.
His steed is fast.
He leaves me in care and shame.
Yet laugh away,
you light-spirited,
luxurious
gang of eternals!
One day
I shall see you all die!
The wise one keeps
a patient watch,
while the gold brightly gleams.
Hatred dogs you, beware!
(*slips into the cleft. The stage remains empty. Morning twilight*)

ALBERICH
Da reitet er hin
auf lichtem Ross:
mir lässt er Sorg' und Spott!
Doch lacht nur zu,
ihr leichtsinniges,
lustgieriges
Göttergelichter:
euch seh' ich
noch alle vergeh'n!
So lang' das Gold
am Lichte glänzt,
hält ein Wissender Wacht!—
trügen wird euch sein Trotz.

SECOND SCENE

(*As day breaks* SIEGFRIED *and* MIME *enter.* SIEGFRIED *is bearing a sword hung in a girdle of rope.* MIME *carefully examines the place.*)

MIME
We go no farther!
Stay right here!

MIME
Zur Stelle sind wir!
bleib' hier steh'n!

SIEGFRIED
Hier soll ich das Fürchten lernen?—
Fern hast du mich geleitet;
eine volle Nacht im Walde
selbander wanderten wir:
nun sollst du, Mime,
fortan mich meiden!
Lern' ich hier nicht
was ich lernen muss,
allein zieh' ich dann weiter:
dich werd' ich endlich da los!

MIME
Glaub' mir, Lieber!
lernst du heute
hier das Fürchten nicht:
an and'rem Ort,
zu and'rer Zeit
schwerlich erfährst du's je.—
Siehst du dort
den dunklen Höhlenschlund?
Darin wohnt
ein gräulich wilder Wurm:
unmassen grimmig
ist er und gross;
ein schrecklicher Rachen
reisst sich ihm auf;
mit Haut und Haar
auf einen Happ
verschlingt der Schlimme dich wohl.

SIEGFRIED
Gut ist's, den Schlund ihm zu schliessen;
drum biet' ich mich nicht dem Gebiss.

MIME
Giftig giesst sich
ein Geifer ihm aus:
wen mit des Speichels
Schweiss er bespei't,
dem schwinden Fleisch und Gebein.

SIEGFRIED
Dass des Geifers Gift mich nicht sehre,
weich' ich zur Seite dem Wurm.

MIME
Ein Schlangenschweif
schlägt sich ihm auf:
wen er damit umschlingt
und fest umschliesst,
dem brechen die Glieder wie Glas.

SIEGFRIED
Vor des Schweifes Schwang mich zu wahren

SIEGFRIED (*sits down under a lime tree and looks around him*)
Here then shall I learn the lesson?
Far have your footsteps led me.
We have wandered through this forest
a livelong, wearisome night,
Mime, I want you
to leave me!
Either I learn
what I ought to here,
or else I shall go elsewhere—
then I'll be finally free!

MIME
Truly, dear one,
if today
and here you seek in vain,
no other place,
no other time,
ever will serve as well.
See it there,
the gloomy cavern mouth?
Therein dwells
a fearful dragon foe;
terribly cruel
is he, and huge;
his horrible jaws
can open up wide,
and with a gulp
the wicked brute will gladly swallow you whole.

SIEGFRIED
Good then, to close up his gullet;
he'll not take a bite out of me.

MIME
Venom pours
from his slavering mouth;
if but a drop
should spatter on you,
your flesh and your bones would wilt.

SIEGFRIED
I will step aside as I fight him,
letting no poison come near.

MIME
His serpent tail
lashes about,
and should it seize you fast
and squeeze you tight,
your limbs would be broken like glass!

SIEGFRIED
I will guard myself from this twister,

keeping the monster in sight.
But answer me this:
has the brute a heart?

MIME
A terrible, cruel heart.

SIEGFRIED
And does it lie
in the normal place,
as in men or in beasts?

MIME
Of course, young one,
exactly like theirs—
and now do you feel any fear?

SIEGFRIED (*suddenly sitting up*)
Needful, pierce
the proud heart of the brute!
Is this like the fear you speak of?
Hey! You dotard!
Where's your cunning?
Can you not
teach me any more?
Go on your way then farther:
I cannot learn my fear here.

MIME
Wait just a bit!
You think I utter
nothing but empty sound;
have patience, hear and
see for yourself,
and then you will faint in your fear.
When your vision swims,
and footing grows weak,
your heart will pound
your breast in fear;
then thank the one who has led you,
and think how great is my love.

SIEGFRIED
Your love is not welcome!
Did I not say,
out of my sight for good!
Leave me alone,
I want no more talk about love,
that I can stomach no more!
That sickening nodding,
and eyelids blinking
I'm sick and tired
of such a sight!
When shall I be free from the fool?

MIME
I leave you now,
I'll lie down at the spring.

halt' ich den Argen im Aug'.—
Doch heisse mich das:
hat der Wurm ein Herz?

MIME
Ein grimmiges, hartes Herz.

SIEGFRIED
Das sitzt ihm doch
wo es Jedem schlägt,
trag' es Mann oder Thier?

MIME
Gewiss, Knabe,
da führt's auch der Wurm:
nun kommt dir das Fürchten
wohl an?

SIEGFRIED
Nothung stoss' ich
dem Stolzen ans Herz:
soll das etwa Fürchten heissen?
He, du Alter!
Ist das alles,
was deine List
mich lehren kann?
Fahr' deines Weg's dann
weiter;
das Fürchten lern' ich hier
nicht.

MIME
Wart' es nur ab!
Was ich dir sagte,
dünke dich tauber Schall:
ihn selber musst du
hören und seh'n,
die Sinne vergeh'n dir dann
schon!
Wenn dein Blick verschwimmt,
der Boden dir schwankt,
im Busen bang
dein Herz erbebt:
dann dankst du mir, der dich
führte,
gedenkst, wie Mime dich liebt.

SIEGFRIED
Du sollst mich nicht lieben!
Sagt' ich dir's nicht?
Fort aus den Augen mir;
lass' mich allein:
sonst halt' ich's hier länger
nicht aus,
fängst du von Liebe gar an!
Das eklige Nicken
und Augenzwicken,
wann endlich soll ich's
nicht mehr seh'n?
Wann werd' ich den Albernen
los?

MIME
Ich lasse dich schon:
am Quell dort lag'r' ich mich.
Steh' du nur hier;

steigt die Sonne zur Höh',
merk' auf den Wurm,
aus der Höhle wälzt er sich her:
hier vorbei
biegt er dann,
am Brunnen sich zu tränken.

Stay in this place;
then, when the sun has come up,
look for your foe.
You will see him slither this way,
heading here
from the cave.
He seeks this stream when thirsty.

SIEGFRIED
Mime, weilst du am Quell,
dahin lass' ich den Wurm wohl geh'n:
Nothung stoss' ich
ihm erst in die Nieren,
wenn er dich selbst dort
mit 'weggesoffen!
Darum, hör' meinen Rath:
raste nicht dort am Quell,
kehre dich 'weg,
so weit du kannst,
und komm' nie mehr zu mir!

SIEGFRIED (*laughing*)
Mime, wait at the spring,
and there I'll let him safely go.
First I'll wait
till I see he is drinking,
then with my sword
I will stab his kidneys.
So now hear my advice:
do not rest near the spring;
go somewhere else,
much farther off,
and stay away for good!

MIME
Nach freislichem Streit
dich zu erfrischen,
wirst du mir wohl nicht wehren?
Rufe mich auch,
darbst du des Rathes—
oder wenn dir das Fürchten gefällt.
Fafner und Siegfried—
Siegfried und Fafner—
o brächten beide sich um!

MIME
The terrible fight
may quite exhaust you,
then you may find me helpful.
(SIEGFRIED *turns away violently*)
Call for your friend
if you crave counsel,
or if fear comes to beat at your heart.
(SIEGFRIED *rises and drives* MIME *away with furious gestures*)
Fafner and Siegfried,
Siegfried and Fafner,
Oh! slay each other, you two!
(*disappears in the woods.* SIEGFRIED *stretches out comfortably under the lime tree and watches the departing* MIME)

SIEGFRIED
Dass der mein Vater nicht ist,
wie fühl' ich mich drob so froh!
Nun erst gefällt mir
der frische Wald;
nun erst lacht mir
der lustige Tag,
da der Garstige von mir schied,
und ich gar nicht ihn wiederseh'!
Wie sah wohl mein Vater aus?—
Ha!—gewiss wie ich selbst:
denn wär' wo von Mime ein Sohn,
müsst' er nicht ganz
Mime gleichen?
G'rade so garstig,
griesig und grau,
klein und krumm,
höck'rig und hinkend,

SIEGFRIED
My heart is throbbing with joy!
I know I am not his son!
Never before
was the wood so fresh;
never day
had so lovely a laugh,
since the rascally wretch has gone,
never more to confront my sight.
(*falls into silent meditation*)
How did my father look?
Ha! indeed, like myself!
For would not the son of a dwarf
look like a dwarf,
just like Mime?
Even as loathsome,

grizzled and gray,
small and wry,
humpbacked and hobbling,
with ears that are hanging,
eyes that are bleary?
Off with the imp!
I hope he's gone for good!
(leans farther back and looks up through the branches. Deep silence, forest murmurs)
I wish I knew
what my mother was like!
But thoughts cannot
show me her picture!
(very tenderly)
Her eyes must have shone,
shimmering bright,
like the eyes of a roe deer,
only more lovely!
(very softly)
She bore me when in anguish,
but why did she die through me?
Must then all human mothers
die when their children
come to the world?
Sad the world would be, faith!
Ah, might the son
only see his mother!
Lovely—mother,
who lived on earth!
(sighs softly and leans still farther back. Deep silence, growing forest murmurs. At length SIEGFRIED'S *attention is caught by the song of the wood bird. He listens with growing interest to the sounds coming from the branches above him)*
You gracious birdling,
your song is so strange!
Say, is this forest your home?
I hear, but cannot interpret!
It said something to me,
perhaps, of my dearest mother!
A quarrelsome dwarf
said to me once
he knew what the birds
were saying in song,
and men might find the meaning.
How could that really be?
Hey, I will try
after him;
on the reed echo his singing:
though lacking the meaning,
getting the mel'dy.

mit hängenden Ohren,
triefigen Augen——
fort mit dem Alb!
Ich mag ihn nicht mehr seh'n.
Aber—wie sah
meine Mutter wohl aus?
Das—kann ich
nun gar nich mir denken!—
Der Rehhindin gleich
glänzten gewiss
ihr' hell schimmernde Augen,—
nur noch viel schöner!——
Da bang sie mich geboren,
warum aber starb sie da?
Sterben die Menschenmütter
an ihren Söhnen
alle dahin?
Traurig wäre das, traun!——
Ach! möcht' ich Sohn
meine Mutter seh'n!——
Meine—Mutter—
ein Menschenweib!—

Du holdes Vöglein!
dich hört' ich noch nie:
bist du im Wald hier daheim?—
Verstünd' ich sein süsses
Stammeln
Gewiss sagt' er mir 'was,—
vielleicht von der lieben
Mutter?—
Ein zankender Zwerg
hat mir erzählt,
der Vöglein Stammeln
gut zu versteh'n,
dazu könnte man kommen;
wie das wohl möglich wär'?
Hei! ich versuch's,
sing' ihm nach:
auf dem Rohr tön' ich ihm
ähnlich!
Entrath' ich der Worte,
achte der Weise,
sing' ich so seine Sprache,

versteh' ich wohl auch, was er spricht.

If I sing in his language,
perhaps I shall learn what he says.

(runs to the nearby spring, cuts off a reed with his sword, and quickly makes a pipe of it. He listens again)

He stops, and waits,
so now I will start!

(blows into the pipe, stops, and cuts the pipe again. He blows again, shakes his head, and again cuts the pipe. He tries it, gets angry, presses the pipe with his hand, and tries again, then he stops and smiles)

Das tönt nicht recht;
auf dem Rohre taugt
die wonnige Weise nicht.—
Vöglein, mich dünkt,
ich bleibe dumm:
von dir lernt sich's nicht leicht!
Nun schäm' ich mich gar
vor dem schelmischen Lauscher:
er lugt und kann nichts erlauschen.—
Heida! so höre
nun auf mein Horn;
auf dem dummen Rohre
geräth mir nichts.
Einer Waldweise,
wie ich sie kann,
der lustigen sollst du lauschen.
Nach liebem Gesellen
lockt' ich mit ihr:
nichts Bess'res kam noch
als Wolf und Bär.
Nun will ich seh'n,
wen jetzt sie mir lockt:
ob das mir ein lieber Gesell?

The sound is false,
for my reed will not avail
for the beautiful tune.
Birdling, I think
my ear is dull;
'tis hard learning from you!

(hears the bird again and looks up)

The listening rascal
has made me feel shamefast!
He peers—and yet cannot get it!
Heida! just listen
now to my horn.

(flings the pipe away)

I am quite unskilled
with the stupid pipe.
I am better
at sounding a horn,
and here is a tune I can blow you;
I often have blown it,
calling for friends,
though none responded
but wolf and bear.
Now let me see
who comes when I call:
a trusty companion or friend.

(takes the silver hunting horn and blows, then looks expectantly at the bird. There is a movement in the background: FAFNER, *in the form of a huge dragon, has risen from his lair, breaks through the underbrush, and the front part of his body becomes visible. He utters a loud sound as if yawning.* SIEGFRIED *looks at him in astonishment)*

Haha! Da hätte mein Lied
mir 'was Liebes erblasen!
du wär'st mir ein saub'rer Gesell!

Ha ha! I see that my song
has attracted a beauty!
What a lovely comrade to have!

FAFNER

Was ist da?

What is there?

SIEGFRIED

Ei, bist du ein Thier,
das zum Sprechen taugt,
wohl liess' sich von dir 'was lernen?

Ei, are you a beast
that can speak to me?
Perhaps you can teach me something.

Here's a stripling
who knows no fear:
How would you like to teach me?

FAFNER
Are you overbold?

SIEGFRIED
Bold or overbold—
I know not!
But yet, teach me what fear is,
or you will forfeit your life.

FAFNER (*with a sound like a laugh*)
I was thirsty,
now too I find food!
(*opens his jaws and shows his teeth*)

SIEGFRIED
Those are beautiful grinders,
pleasing to see;
wonderful teeth
for an ugly brute!
I really should close up the crater;
your jaws are open too wide.

FAFNER
They're not much good
for empty talk;
yet I can eat you
with their aid.
(*lashes his tail menacingly*)

SIEGFRIED
Hoho! you ugly,
horrible brute!
I have no mind
to fill your stomach.
Better, I think, to slay you
at once, without more delay.

FAFNER (*roaring*)
Pruh! Come,
insolent child!

SIEGFRIED
Take care, roarer;
The boaster comes!
(*draws his sword, springs toward* FAFNER *and waits defiant.* FAFNER *drags himself farther up on the knoll and spits from his nostrils at* SIEGFRIED, *who avoids the slaver, springs nearer, and stands to one side.* FAFNER *tries to flail him with his tail.* SIEGFRIED *leaps over him and wounds him in the tail.* FAFNER *roars, and rears up, so offering his breast to the stroke.* SIEGFRIED *sinks his sword up to the hilt into his heart.* FAFNER *sinks as* SIEGFRIED *lets go his sword and springs aside*)
Lie there, merciless brute!
Needful lies in your vitals!

Hier kennt einer
das Fürchten nicht:
kann er's von dir erfahren?

FAFNER
Hast du Uebermuth?

SIEGFRIED
Muth und Uebermuth—
was weiss ich!
Doch dir fahr' ich zu Leibe,
lehrst du das Fürchten mich nicht!

FAFNER
Trinken wollt' ich:
nun treff' ich auch Frass!

SIEGFRIED
Eine zierliche Fresse
zeigst du mir da:
lachende Zähne
im Leckermaul!
Gut wär's, den Schlund dir zu schliessen;
dein Rachen reckt sich zu weit!

FAFNER
Zu tauben Reden
taugt er schlecht:
dich zu verschlingen
frommt der Schlund.

SIEGFRIED
Hoho! du grausam
grimmiger Kerl,
von dir verdaut sein
dünkt mich übel:
räthlich und fromm doch scheint's,
du verrecktest hier ohne Frist.

FAFNER
Pruh! komm'!
prahlendes Kind.

SIEGFRIED
Sieh' dich vor, Brüller:
der Prahler kommt!

Da lieg', neidischer Kerl!
Nothung trägst du im Herzen.

FAFNER
Wer bist du, kühner Knabe,
der das Herz mir traf?
Wer reizte des Kindes Muth
zu der mordlichen That?
Dein Hirn brütete nicht,
was du vollbracht.

SIEGFRIED
Viel weiss ich noch nicht,
noch nicht auch wer ich bin:
mit dir mordlich zu ringen
reiztest du selbst meinen Muth.

FAFNER
Du helläugiger Knabe,
unkund deiner selbst:
wen du gemordet
meld' ich dir.
Die einst der Welt gewaltet,
der Riesen ragend' Geschlecht,
Fasolt und Fafner,
die Brüder fielen nun beide.
Um verfluchtes Gold,
von Göttern vergabt,
traf ich Fasolt zu todt:
der nun als Wurm
den Hort bewachte,
Fafner, den letzten Riesen,
fällte ein rosiger Held.—
Blicke nun hell,
blühender Knabe;
des Hortes Herrn
umringt Verrath:
der dich Blinden reizte zur That,
beräth nun des Blühenden Tod.
Merk', wie's endet;—
acht' auf mich!

SIEGFRIED
Woher ich stamme,
rathe mir noch;
weise ja scheinst du
Wilder im Sterben;
rath' es nach meinem Namen:
Siegfried bin ich genannt.

FAFNER
Siegfried. . . . !

SIEGFRIED
Zur Kunde taugt kein Todter.—
So leite mich denn
mein lebendes Schwert!

FAFNER (*weaker voice*)
Who are you, valiant stripling,
that have pierced my heart?
Who prompted your boyish will
to the murderous deed?
I know you did not plan
what you fulfilled.

SIEGFRIED
Not much do I know,
not even who I am;
but you roused me to anger;
you were the cause of this strife.

FAFNER
You bold, bright-eyed youngling,
unknown to yourself;
whom you have murdered,
hear from me.
The mighty giants of earth,
Fasolt and Fafner,
the brothers—both are now fallen;
for the cursed gold
bestowed by the gods,
made me murder my kin.
In dragon shape
I kept the treasure
Fafner, the last of the giants,
slain by a valorous boy!
Watch yourself well,
blossoming hero!
He who urged you blindly to this,
designs now your blossoming death!
Mark the ending!
Think of me!
(*dying tone*)

SIEGFRIED
Who was my father,
answer me now;
show me your wisdom,
wild one, in dying.
Maybe my name can help you,
Siegfried, so am I called.

FAFNER
Siegfried——
(*raises himself and dies*)

SIEGFRIED
The dead can tell no story.
So lead me henceforth,
my quickening sword!
(FAFNER *has rolled to one side in dying.* SIEGFRIED *draws the sword from his breast, and in doing so his hand gets sprinkled with the blood: he quickly pulls it*

back, and involuntarily carries his fingers to his mouth to suck the blood from them. As he looks meditatively before him his attention is suddenly attracted by the bird's song)

Like fire—burns my blood!
Really, it seems
as though I could hear the birds speak.
Is this effect
produced by the blood?
A strange and wondrous bird—
hark, what does he sing?

Wie Feuer brennt das Blut!
Ist mir doch fast—
als sprächen die Vöglein zu mir:
Nützte mir das
des Blutes Genuss?—
Das selt'ne Vöglein hier—
horch! was singt es mir?

WOOD BIRD *(from the branches of the lime tree above* SIEGFRIED*)*

Hei! Siegfried now owns
all the Nibelung's hoard;
Oh, let him but find it
within the cave!
Let him but master the Tarnhelm,
'twill serve him for glorious deeds;
but if he could master the ring,
it would make him the lord of the world!

STIMME EINES WALDVOGELS

Hei! Siegfried gehört
nun der Niblungen Hort:
o fänd' in der Höhle
den Hort er jetzt!
Wollt' er den Tarnhelm gewinnen,
der taugt' ihm zu wonniger That:
doch möcht' er den Ring sich errathen,
der macht' ihn zum Walter der Welt!

SIEGFRIED *(softly and with emotion)*

Thanks, dearest birdling,
for your advice!
I gladly will act!

(turns and descends into the cave, where he disappears)

SIEGFRIED

Dank, liebes Vöglein,
für deinen Rath:
gern folg' ich dem Ruf.

THIRD SCENE

(MIME *slinks on, timidly looking about to assure himself that* FAFNER *is dead. At the same moment* ALBERICH *appears from the cleft at the opposite side; he watches* MIME *narrowly. As the latter turns toward the cave he darts forward and bars his way.)*

ALBERICH

Whereto, slinking,
slippery wretch,
villainous knave?

ALBERICH

Wohin schleich'st du,
eilig und schlau,
schlimmer Gesell?

MIME

Accursed brother,
who wanted you!
What brings you here?

MIME

Verfluchter Bruder,
dich braucht' ich hier!
Was bringt dich her?

ALBERICH

Greed is it, rogue,
and for my gold?
You covet my goods?

ALBERICH

Geizt es dich, Schelm,
nach meinem Gold?
Verlangst du mein Gut?

MIME

Off with the nuisance!

MIME

Fort von der Stelle!

Die Stätte ist mein:
was stöberst du hier?

ALBERICH
Stör' ich dich wohl
im stillen Geschäft,
wenn du hier stiehlst?

MIME
Was ich erschwang
mit schwerer Müh',
soll mir nicht schwinden.

ALBERICH
Hast du dem Rhein
das Gold zum Ringe geraubt?
Erzeugtest du gar
den zähen Zauber im Reif?

MIME
Wer schuf den Tarnhelm,
der die Gestalten tauscht?
Der sein bedurfte,
erdachtest du ihn wohl?

ALBERICH
Was hättest du Stümper
je wohl zu stampfen
verstanden?
Der Zauberring
zwang mir den Zwerg erst zur
Kunst.

MIME
Wo hast du den Ring?
Dir Zagem entrissen ihn Riesen!
Was du verlorst,
meine List erlangt' es für mich.

ALBERICH
Mit des Knaben That
will der Knicker noch knausern?
Dir gehört sie gar nicht.
Der Helle ist selbst ihr Herr!

MIME
Ich zog ihn auf:
für die Zucht zahlt er mir nun:
für Müh' und Last
erlauert' ich lang' meinen
Lohn.

ALBERICH
Für des Knaben Zucht
will der knick'rige
schäbige Knecht
keck und kühn
gar wohl König nun sein?
Dem räudigsten Hund
wäre der Ring
gerath'ner als dir:
nimmer erringst
du Rüpel den Herrscherreif!

The place here is mine:
so what do you want?

ALBERICH
Have I then
interrupted the thief,
right in the act?

MIME
What I achieved
through heavy toil,
shall not escape me.

ALBERICH
Was it then you
who stole the gold from the Rhine?
And who gave the ring
its wondrous, magical might?

MIME
Who made the Tarnhelm,
that changes the shapes of men?
I know you craved to,
but did you do it too?

ALBERICH
What could you, you bungler,
ever have known how to fashion?
The magic ring
taught me that wonderful art.

MIME
Where have you the ring?
You coward, the giants have seized it.
Now I will gain
by my cunning what you have lost.

ALBERICH
Must you hoard with greed
what the stripling has won you?
But the boy is lord
of the radiant hoard, not you.

MIME
I brought him up;
and he now pays for my pains
in toil and care.
My wait has been long for my wage.

ALBERICH
For the youngling's care
will the beggarly,
scabby old knave
act so briskly brave,
think himself king?
I'd rather the ring
went to a
mangy dog than to you!
Lout that you are,
you'll never possess the ring!

MIME (*scratches his head*)
Well, keep it then,
and guard it well,
your shining ring;
be its lord,
but still call me your brother!
And for the Tarnhelm,
magical toy,
take it in trade;
then both are paid,
sharing the booty this way.

MIME
Behalt' ihn denn:
hüte ihn wohl,
den hellen Reif!
Sei du Herr:
doch mich heisse auch Bruder!
Um meines Tarnhelms
lustigen Tand
tausch' ich ihn dir:
uns beiden taugt's,
theilen die Beute wir so.

ALBERICH (*with mocking laughter*)
Share it with you?
And the Tarnhelm too?
How sly you are!
Then I'd never
sleep secure from your cunning!

ALBERICH
Theilen mit dir?
und den Tarnhelm gar?
Wie schlau du bist!
Sicher schlief' ich
niemals vor deinen Schlingen!

MIME (*beyond himself*)
You'll not share it
nor exchange it?
Nothing at all?
What do you mean—
Nothing for your poor brother?

MIME
Selbst nicht tauschen?
Auch nicht theilen?
Leer soll ich geh'n,
ganz ohne Lohn?
Gar nichts willst du mir lassen?

ALBERICH
Nothing, Brother!
Mine is the treasure,
you shall not touch it.

ALBERICH
Nichts von allem,
nicht einen Nagel
sollst du mir nehmen!

MIME (*furious*)
Neither ring nor Tarnhelm
shall I allow you!
You shan't have a thing!
I shall call for valiant Siegfried
to help with his trusty sword;
the dauntless boy
will pay you, brother of mine!
(SIEGFRIED *is visible in the background*)

MIME
Weder Ring noch Tarnhelm
soll dir denn taugen!
nicht theil' ich nun mehr.
Gegen dich ruf' ich
Siegfried zu Rath
und des Recken Schwert:
der rasche Held,
der richte, Brüderchen, dich!

ALBERICH
Turn yourself round!
He is coming now from the cave!

ALBERICH
Kehre dich um:
aus der Höhle kommt er schon her.—

MIME
Surely by now
he's taken the toys.
(SIEGFRIED, *with* TARNHELM *and ring, has come slowly and meditatively from the cave. He regards his booty thoughtfully*)

MIME
Kindischen Tand
erkor er gewiss.—

ALBERICH
He has the Tarnhelm.

ALBERICH
Den Tarnhelm hat er!—

MIME
Also the ring.

MIME
Doch auch den Ring!—

ALBERICH
Accurs'd! the ring?

ALBERICH
Verflucht!—den Ring!—

MIME
Lass' ihn den Ring dir doch geben!—
ich will ihn mir schon gewinnen.—

ALBERICH
Und doch seinem Herrn
soll er allein noch gehören!

SIEGFRIED
Was ihr mir nützet
weiss ich nicht:
doch nahm ich euch
aus des Horts gehäuftem Gold,
weil guter Rath mir es rieth.
So taug' eu're Zier
als des Tages Zeuge:
mich mahne der Tand,
dass ich kämpfend Fafner erlegt,
doch das Fürchten noch nicht gelernt!

STIMME DES WALDVOGELS
Hei! Siegfried gehört
nun der Helm und Ring!
O traut' er Mime
dem Treulosen nicht!
Hörte Siegfried nur scharf
auf des Schelmen Heuchlergered':
wie sein Herz es meint
kann er Mime versteh'n;
so nützt ihm des Blutes Genuss.

MIME
Er sinnt und erwägt
der Beute Werth:—
weilte wohl hier
ein weiser Wand'rer,
schweifte umher,
beschwatzte das Kind
mit listiger Runen Rath?
Zwiefach schlau
sei nun der Zwerg:
die listigste Schlinge
leg' ich jetzt aus,
dass ich mit traulichem
Truggerede
bethöre das trotzige Kind!

MIME (*laughing maliciously*)
Maybe he'll give you the circlet!
and then I'll win it from you.
(*with these words* MIME *slips away into the woods*)

ALBERICH
The boy is its lord,
Siegfried alone is its master.
(*disappears into the cleft*)

SIEGFRIED
What shall I do
with the prize;
I picked you out
from the hoard of heaped up gold,
because I heard that I should.
At least you will serve
as this day's reminder,
to witness in truth
that I finished Fafner in fight—
though still learning nothing of fear.
(*puts the Tarnhelm in his girdle and the ring on his finger. Silence. His attention is again drawn to the bird, and he listens to it with bated breath*)

WOOD BIRD
Hei! Siegfried is owner
of the helm and the ring!
Oh, let him not trust
in the villainous dwarf!
Let the stripling beware
of the rascal's treacherous tongue!
Now the boy can read
Mime's innermost mind.
The blood that he tasted is charmed.
(SIEGFRIED'*s gestures indicate that he has understood everything. He sees* MIME *coming and remains without moving, leaning on his sword, observing and self-contained*)

MIME (*creeps forward and observes* SIEGFRIED)
He broods and weighs
the booty's worth:
Maybe the Wanderer
used his wits
and came to this place
to wheedle the boy,
with cunning, crafty runes.
I must be
doubly on guard.
My cunning meshes
now must be laid,
so I with sugary,
truthless talk
may bamboozle the swaggering lad.

(*advances nearer to* SIEGFRIED *and welcomes him with flattering gestures*)
Why! Welcome, Siegfried!
Say, my bold one,
what is the meaning of fear?

Willkommen, Siegfried!
Sag', du Kühner,
hast du das Fürchten gelernt?

SIEGFRIED
No teacher yet have I found.

SIEGFRIED
Den Lehrer fand ich noch nicht.

MIME
But the dragon foe,
tell, have you destroyed him?
He was quite a playmate, no doubt?

MIME
Doch den Schlagwurm,
du hast ihn erschlagen?
Das war doch ein schlimmer Gesell?

SIEGFRIED
Though quite a terrible foe,
his death grieves me at heart
when far wickeder rogues
remain alive and unpunished.
The one who led me here
I hate still more than the foe!

SIEGFRIED
So grimm und tückisch er war,
sein Tod grämt mich doch schier,
da viel üblere Schächer
unerschlagen noch leben!
Der mich ihn morden hiess,
den hass' ich mehr als den Wurm!

MIME (*very friendly*)
Now gently! I come
to bid you good-by:
for soon shall death
close your eyes in endless sleep.
You've done what I wanted,
finished your chore;
now all that I need
is merely to win the booty.
I think that task will be simple,
you are really easy to fool.

MIME
Nur sachte! nicht lange
sieh'st du mich mehr:
zu ew'gem Schlaf
schliess' ich die Augen dir bald.
Wozu ich dich brauchte,
das hast du vollbracht;
jetzt will ich nur noch
die Beute dir abgewinnen:—
mich dünkt, das soll mir gelingen,
zu bethören bist du ja leicht!

SIEGFRIED
You think then to do me mischief?

SIEGFRIED
So sinnst du auf meinen Schaden?

MIME (*astonished, tenderly*)
Now did I say that?
Siegfried, hear me, my baby!
Hate is in my heart:
you were always my loathing!
You nuisance, I wasted
no love upon you;
I toiled for the gold alone,
the treasure hid in Fafner's cave.
(*as though he were promising him pleasant things*)
Either give it
right now to my care,
Siegfried, my son,
or see for yourself,
(*with friendly humor*)
you'll lose your life in a hurry!

MIME
Wie sagt' ich das?—
Siegfried, hör' doch, mein Sohn!
Dich und deine Art
hasst' ich immer von Herzen;
aus Liebe erzog ich
dich Lästigen nicht;
dem Horte in Fafners Hut,
dem Golde galt meine Müh'.
Giebst du mir das
nun gutwillig nicht,—
Siegfried, mein Sohn,
das siehst du wohl selbst—
dein Leben musst du mir lassen!

SIEGFRIED
That you do hate me,

SIEGFRIED
Dass du mich hassest,
hör' ich gern:

doch auch mein Leben muss
ich dir lassen?

MIME
Das sag' ich doch nicht?
Du verstehst mich falsch!
Sieh', du bist müde
von harter Müh';
brünstig brennt dir der Leib:
dich zu erquicken
mit queckem Trank
säumt' ich Sorgender nicht.
Als dein Schwert du dir
branntest,
braut' ich den Sud:
trinkst du nun den,
gewinn' ich dein trautes
Schwert,
und mit ihm Helm und Hort.
Hi hi hi hi hi!

SIEGFRIED
So willst du mein Schwert
und was ich erschwungen,
Ring und Beute mir rauben?

MIME
Was du doch falsch mich
versteh'st!
Stamml' ich und fas'le wohl
gar?
Die grösste Mühe
geb' ich mir:
mein heimliches Sinnen
heuchelnd zu bergen,
und du dummer Bube
deutest alles doch falsch!
Oeffne die Ohren,
und vernimm genau:
höre, was Mime meint!—
Hier nimm! trinke dir Labung!
mein Trank labte dich oft:
that'st du wohl unwirsch,
stelltest dich arg:
was ich dir bot—
erbos't auch—nahmst du's doch
immer.

SIEGFRIED
Einen guten Trank
hätt' ich gern:
wie hast du diesen gebraut?

MIME
Hei! so trink' nur:
trau' meiner Kunst!
In Nacht und Nebel
sinken die Sinne dir bald:
ohne Wach' und Wissen,
stracks streck'st du die Glieder.
Liegst du nun da,

gives me joy:
yet must my life as well then be forfeit?

MIME (*crossly*)
Now did I say that?
You don't hear me aright!
(*feels for his bottle*)
See, you are weary,
from heavy toil.
Fever burns hot in your blood;
so, to refresh you,
with quickening drink
Mime wasted no time;
while you welded your sword,
I brewed you this broth;
now, if you drink,
your sword then will fall to me,
and with it helm and hoard!
Hi hi hi hi hi!

SIEGFRIED
You plot for my sword
and all I have fought for—
ring, and helmet, and booty?

MIME (*violently*)
Why is your hearing so bad!
Tell me, do I but dote?
I subtly take
the greatest of pains
to keep my thoughts secret,
cunningly hidden,
and you, stupid booby,
twist my words all awry!
Open your ears, child,
and attend to me!
Listen to Mime's words!
(*again very friendly, with evident pains*)
Here, take, and drink for refreshment!
My drinks always were good:
when you were fretful,
peevish and cross,
they quenched your thirst.
You always took what I offered.

SIEGFRIED (*without stirring*)
Now a tasty drink
would be fine.
But how has this one been brewed?

MIME (*jesting merrily, as if describing a pleasant intoxication*)
Hey, just drink it,
trust to my skill,
and soon your thoughts
will sink into darkness and night!

It will stretch your body stiff,
making it senseless.
There as you lie,
no trouble for me
to pilfer the booty:
but if you should awake,
I would nowhere
find myself safe,
though the ring were my own.
Then, with the sword
that you made so sharp,
(*with a gesture of exuberant joy*)
off will I hack
your head, my child.
Then peace will be mine, also the ring!
Hi-hi-hi-hi-hi-hi-hi-hi-hi-hi-hi!

leicht könnt' ich
die Beute nehmen und bergen:
doch erwachtest du je,
nirgends wär' ich
sicher vor dir,
hätt' ich selbst auch den Ring.
Drum mit dem Schwert,
das so scharf du schuf'st,
hau' ich dem Kind
den Kopf erst ab:
denn hab' ich mir Ruh' und den Ring!
Hi-hi-hi-hi-hi-hi-hi-hi-hi-hi-hi!

SIEGFRIED
So while I sleep you would slay me?

SIEGFRIED
Im Schlafe willst du mich morden?

MIME (*very angrily*)
Now really! Did I say that?
(*takes pains to express the tenderest tones*)
I wish, my child,
but to have your head!
(*in tone of heartfelt solicitude for* SIEGFRIED'*s health*)
For, even without
my rooted hate,
which grew from your scorn
at my shameful labor,
and cries aloud for vengeance,
I would clear you from my pathway!
Faltering would not suit me!
(*again jestingly*)
How else could I come by the booty,
which Alberich covets as well?
(*pours the draught into the drinking horn and offers it to* SIEGFRIED *with importunate gestures*)
Now, my Volsung!
Wolf son, eh?
Drink, and choke to your death!
This drink will be your last!
Hi-hi-hi-hi-hi!
(SIEGFRIED *threatens him with the sword*)

MIME
Was möcht' ich? sagt' ich denn das?
Ich will dir, Kind,
nur den Kopf abhau'n!
Denn hasste ich dich
auch nicht so hell,
und hätt' ich des Schimpfs
und der schändlichen Müh'
auch nicht so viel zu rächen:
aus dem Weg dich zu räumen
darf ich nicht rasten.
Wie käm' ich sonst anders zur Beute,
da Alberich auch nach ihr lugt?—
Nun, mein Wälsung!
Wolfssohn du!
Sauf' und würg' dich zu Tod:
nie thu'st du mehr einen Schluck!
Hi hi hi hi hi!

SIEGFRIED
Taste of my sword,
sickening babbler!
(*as if seized by violent loathing he thrusts his sword into* MIME. *The dwarf falls dead*)

SIEGFRIED
Schmeck' du mein Schwert,
ekliger Schwätzer!

ALBERICH'S VOICE (*heard from the cleft in mocking laughter*)
Ha-ha-ha-ha-ha-ha-ha-ha-ha-ha-ha-ha-ha!

ALBERICHS STIMME
Ha-ha-ha-ha-ha-ha-ha-ha-ha-ha-ha-ha-ha!

SIEGFRIED
Neides Zoll
zahlt Nothung:
Dazu durft' ich ihn schmieden.
In der Höhle hier
lieg' auf dem Hort!
Mit zäher List
erzieltest du ihn:
jetzt magst du des Wonnigen
walten!—
Einen guten Wächter
geb' ich dir auch,
dass er vor Dieben dich deckt.

SIEGFRIED (*as he looks at* MIME *on the ground he returns his sword to its belt*)
Needful pays
hate's wages:
that is why it was fashioned.
(*picks up* MIME*'s body and carries it to the knoll in front of the cave, then throws it into the cave*)
In the cavern here
lie on the hoard!
You sought the gold
with resolute craft;
now may you have joy of your treasure!
You may keep this trusty
guardian too,
thus you're protected from thieves.
(*with mighty efforts pushes the body of the dragon in front of the entrance to the cave so as to stop it up completely*)

Da lieg' auch du,
dunkler Wurm!
Den gleissenden Hort
hüte zugleich
mit dem beuterührigen Feind:
so fandet Ihr beide nun Ruh'!

Now lie there too,
dragon foe!
Take care of the hoard,
share in its watch
with your booty-coveting mate:
and so I leave you both in peace.
(*looks thoughtfully into the cave, and then turns, as though tired, passes his hand over his brow*)

Heiss ward mir
von der harten Last!—
Brausend jagt sich
mein brünstiges Blut;
die Hand brennt mir am
Haupt.——
Hoch steht schon die Sonne:
aus lichtem Blau
blickt ihr Aug'
auf den Scheitel steil mir
herab.—
Linde Kühlung
erkies' ich mir unter der Linde!

Hot am I
from the heavy toil.
Rushing flows
my fev'rish blood!
My hand burns on my head.
High is the sun already;
the shining eye
lights up heaven
and beats right down on my head.
By the lime tree
I'll find refreshment and shelter.
(*stretches out again under the lime tree. Great silence. Then woodland murmurs*)

Noch einmal, liebes Vöglein,
da wir so lang'
lästig gestört,
lauscht' ich gern deinem Sang:
auf dem Zweige seh' ich
wohlig dich wiegen;
zwitschernd umschwirren
dich Brüder und Schwestern,
umschweben dich lustig und
lieb!
Doch ich—bin so allein,
hab' nicht Bruder noch
Schwester:
meine Mutter schwand,
mein Vater fiel:
nie sah sie der Sohn!—

Still once more, dearest birdling,
whom we have
disturbed with our noise,
I would love to hear your singing.
You are rocking with the branches
so gaily; chirping and chattering.
Brothers and sisters,
fly round you in gladness and love!
Yet I—am so alone,
lacking brother and sister.
My dear mother died,
my father fell—

unknown by their son.
My one only friend
was a villainous dwarf;
love did never grow from nearness;
treacherous tricks
were planned by this plotter,
and so I was forced to slay him.

Mein einz'ger Gesell
war ein garst'ger Zwerg;
Güte zwang
nie uns zu Liebe;
listige Schlingen
warf mir der Schlaue:—
nun musst' ich ihn gar
erschlagen!—

(*again looks up at the branches*)
Generous birdling,
just tell me this now:
could you find
a loving friend for me?
Can you give me helpful counsel?
I often have called,
and yet no one has come.
You, my faithful,
surely could find one:
you always counsel me well.
(*softly*)
Now sing! I'll listen to your song.

Freundliches Vöglein,
dich frag' ich nun:
gönntest du mir
wohl ein gut Gesell?
willst du das Rechte mir
rathen?
Ich lockte so oft,
und erloost' es mir nie.
Du, mein Trauter,
träf'st es wohl besser!
So recht ja riethest du schon:
nun sing'! ich lausche dem
Sang.

WOOD BIRD
Hei! Siegfried has struck down
the wicked dwarf!
Now, soon he may take
a wonderful wife.
She sleeps surrounded by fire,
high on a mountain of rock:
who steps through the flames
wakens the bride,
Brunnhilda then may be his.
(SIEGFRIED *starts up impetuously*)

STIMME DES WALDVOGELS
Hei! Siegfried erschlug
nun den schlimmen Zwerg!
Jetzt wüsst' ich ihm noch
das herrlichste Weib.
Auf hohem Felsen sie schläft,
ein Feuer umbrennt ihren Saal:
durchschritt' er die Brunst,
erweckt' er die Braut,
Brünnhilde wäre dann sein!

SIEGFRIED
O gracious song!
Sweetest of strains!
I feel its thought
burn in my breast!
It stirs me strongly,
kindling my heart!
What courses so fast
through heart and senses?
Sing it to me, gentle friend!

SIEGFRIED
O holder Sang!
süssester Hauch!
Wie brennt sein Sinn
mir zehrend die Brust!
Wie zückt er heftig
zündend mein Herz!
Was jagt mir so jach
durch Herz und Sinne?
Sing' es mir, süsser Freund!

WOOD BIRD
Happy but sad
I sing of love;
joyful from woe,
weaving my song:
through longing alone can one hear.

DER WALDVOGEL
Lustig im Leid
sing' ich von Liebe;
wonnig und weh'
web' ich mein Lied:
nur Sehnende kennen den Sinn!

SIEGFRIED
Joy takes me,
now that I wander
forth from the wood to the rock!

SIEGFRIED
Fort jagt mich's
jauchzend von hinnen,
fort aus dem Wald auf den
Fels!

Noch einmal sage mir,
holder Sänger:
werd' ich das Feuer
durchbrechen?
Kann ich erwecken die Braut?

Yet once more answer me,
gracious singer:
Shall I then break through the fire?
Can I awaken the bride?
(listens again)

DER WALDVOGEL
Die Braut gewinnt,
Brünnhild' erweckt
ein Feiger nie:
nur wer das Fürchten nicht
kennt!

WOOD BIRD
Who wins the bride,
Brunnhild the fair,
no coward he:
there is one lacking in fear!

SIEGFRIED
Der dumme Knab',
der das Fürchten nicht kennt,
mein Vöglein, das bin ja ich!
Noch heut' gab ich
vergebens mir Müh',
das Fürchten von Fafner zu
lernen.
Nun brennt mich die Lust,
es von Brünnhild' zu wissen:
wie find' ich zum Felsen den
Weg?

SIEGFRIED
The stupid boy
who has never known fear,
my birdling, why that is I!
I toiled this day
to learn fear, but in vain.
My foe was unable to teach me:
I'm burning with joy
now to learn it from Brunnhilda.
What way shall I take to the rock?
(the BIRD *flutters up, circles over* SIEGFRIED, *and flies hesitatingly before him)*

So wird mir der Weg gewiesen:
wohin du flatterst
folg' ich dem Flug!

So I see the path is shown me:
My ready footsteps
follow your flight!
(runs after the BIRD, *who for a time teases him by leading him in different directions, then it takes a definite direction and* SIEGFRIED *follows)*

ACT III

FIRST SCENE

(*Night, a wild spot at the foot of a steeply rising rocky mountain. Storm, lightning, and violent thunder, which soon ceases, while the lightning continues to flash among the clouds. Here the* WANDERER *enters. He walks deliberately toward the mouth of a cavernous opening in a rock in the foreground and stands there, leaning on his sword.*)

WANDERER

Waken, Vala!
Vala, awake!
Awake from sleep;
wake from the cavern of night!
Arise as I call!
Arise! arise!
From vaults of the earth,
from shadowy caverns arise!
Erda! Erda!
Ancient of days!
From tenebrous darkness
soar to the light!
I sing to wake you
from dreams of wisdom;
so wake from your visions;
wake at my call!
All-knowing one!
Wisdom's mother!
Erda! Erda!
Ancient of days!
Waken, awaken, you Vala! Awaken!
(*the cavern begins to glow with a bluish light. Very gradually* ERDA *rises from below, appearing as if covered with hoar-frost, while her hair and garments shimmer*)

WANDERER

Wache! Wache!
Wala erwache!
Aus langem Schlafe
weck' ich dich Schlummernde wach.
Ich rufe dich auf:
herauf! herauf!
Aus nebliger Gruft,
aus nächtigem Grunde herauf!
Erda! Erda!
Ewiges Weib!
Aus heimischer Tiefe
tauche zur Höh'!
Dein Wecklied sing' ich,
dass du erwachst;
aus sinnendem Schlafe
sing' ich dich auf.
Allwissende!
Urweltweise!
Erda! Erda!
Ewiges Weib!
Wache, du Wala! erwache!

ERDA

Strong is the song!
Mighty magic stirs me!
I am aroused
from knowledge in dreams.
Who dares to rob my rest?

ERDA

Stark ruft das Lied;
kräftig reizt der Zauber;
ich bin erwacht
aus wissendem Schlaf:
wer scheucht den Schlummer mir?

WANDERER

Your wakener is here;
my songs have power
to waken surely
the dreamer locked in sleep.
I roam the planet,
wandering much,
questing for knowledge;
prime wisdom comes if we seek it.

WANDERER

Der Weckrufer bin ich,
und Weisen üb' ich,
dass weithin wache,
was fester Schlaf umschliesst.
Die Welt durchzog ich,
wanderte viel,
Kunde zu werben,
urweisen Rath zu gewinnen.
Kundiger giebt es
keine als dich:
bekannt ist dir,

was die Tiefe birgt,
was Berg und Thal,
Luft und Wasser durchwebt.
Wo Wesen sind,
weht dein Athem:
wo Hirne sinnen,
haftet dein Sinn:
alles, sagt man,
sei dir bekannt.
Dass ich nun Kunde gewänne,
weckt' ich dich aus dem Schlaf.

There is no being
wiser than you;
you know what lies
in the depths of earth,
what hill and dale,
air and water surround.
Where life is found,
there lives your spirit.
Where minds are thinking,
your mind thinks too.
Boundless knowledge
lives in your soul.
So I have come here for counsel,
driving sleep from your eyes!

ERDA

Mein Schlaf ist Träumen,
Mein Träumen Sinnen,
mein Sinnen Walten des Wissens.
Doch wenn ich schlafe,
wachen Nornen:
sie weben das Seil,
und spinnen fromm, was ich weiss:—
was frägst du nicht die Nornen?

ERDA

My sleep is dreaming,
my dreaming thinking,
my thinking power of knowing.
Yet while I sleep
the Norns are wakeful:
they weave the rope,
and truly spin what I know;
so why not ask the sisters?

WANDERER

Im Zwange der Welt
weben die Nornen:
sie können nichts wenden noch wandeln:
doch deiner Weisheit
dankt' ich den Rath wohl,
wie zu hemmen ein rollendes Rad?

WANDERER

They weave as they must:
nothing can turn them.
The world by fate holds them in thralldom.
And so I ask you,
mother of wisdom,
how to hinder a rolling wheel.

ERDA

Männerthaten
umdämmern mir den Muth:
mich Wissende selbst
bezwang ein Waltender einst.
Ein Wunschmädchen
gebar ich Wotan:
der Helden Wal
hiess er für ihn sie küren.
Kühn ist sie
und weise auch:
was weck'st du mich,
und fräg'st um Kunde
nicht Erdas und Wotans Kind?

ERDA

Deeds of men
cast a shadow on my soul;
my wisdom itself
once felt a conqueror's force.
A wish-maiden
I bore to Wotan:
she brought to Valhall
the heroes he asked for.
Bold is she
and wise as well.
Why waken me
and ask no counsel from
Erda's and Wotan's child?

WANDERER

Die Walküre mein'st du,
Brünnhild', die Maid,
Sie trotzte dem Stürmebezwinger:
wo am stärksten er selbst sich bezwang:
was den Lenker der Schlacht
zu thun verlangte,

WANDERER

You mean then the Valkyr,
Brunnhilda, the maid?
She flouted the master of tempests,
when he was showing most self-control:
what the guider of strife
desired with longing,

yet what he refrained from
in spite of himself,
that did the maid,
proud in her confidence,
try herself to accomplish,
right in the thick of the fray.
War-father
punished the maid;
cast a sleeping spell on her eyes;
she is resting on the rock.
The only one to waken the child
will be the man who wins her as bride.
What could I learn from the maid?

ERDA

My waking
makes me confused.
Wild and strange
seems the world!
The Valkyrie,
the Vala child,
paid, by fetters of sleep,
while her all-knowing mother slept!
Why should pride's teacher
punish pride?
Why should he who urged her
scowl at the deed,
he who guards the right,
and upholds all pledges,
strike at the right,
rule by falsehood?
Let my wisdom seek slumber!

WANDERER

You, Mother, shall not go free,
for a mighty magic is mine.
All-knowing,
since you did thrust
a thorn of sorrow
in Wotan's resolute heart,
you filled his spirit,
telling of shameful,
direful destruction,
and bound his being with fear.
Are you the world's
wisest of women?
Answer me then
how the god may master his woe!

ERDA

You are—not
what you have said!
Wild spirit, why have you come here
to trouble the Vala's sleep?

doch dem er wehrte
—zuwider sich selbst—
allzu vertraut
wagte die Trotzige,
das für sich zu vollbringen,
Brünnhild' in brennender
Schlacht.
Streitvater
strafte die Maid;
in ihr Auge drückt' er Schlaf;
auf dem Felsen schläft sie fest:
erwachen wird
die Weibliche nur,
um einen Mann zu minnen als
Weib.
Frommten mir Fragen an sie?

ERDA

Wirr wird mir's
seit ich erwacht:
wild und kraus
kreis't die Welt!
Die Walküre,
Der Wala Kind,
büsst' in Banden des Schlaf's,
als die wissende Mutter schlief.
Der den Trotz lehrte,
straft den Trotz?
Der die That entzündet,
zürnt um die That?
Der das Recht wahrt,
der die Eide hütet—
wehret dem Recht?
herrscht durch Meineid?—
Lass' mich wieder hinab:
Schlaf verschliesse mein
Wissen!

WANDERER

Dich, Mutter, lass' ich nicht
zieh'n,
da des Zaubers ich mächtig
bin.—
Urwissend
stachest du einst
der Sorge Stachel
in Wotans wagendes Herz;
mit Furcht vor schmachvoll
feindlichem Ende
füll't ihn dein Wissen,
dass Bangen band seinen Muth.
Bist du der Welt
weisestes Weib,
sage mir nun:
wie besiegt die Sorge der Gott?

ERDA

Du bist—nicht
was du dich nenn'st!
Was kam'st du, störrischer
Wilder,
zu stören der Wala Schlaf?

WANDERER
Du bist—nicht
was du dich wähn'st!
Urmütter-Weisheit
geht zu Ende:
dein Wissen verweht
vor meinem Willen.
Weisst du, was Wotan will?
Dir, Unweisen,
ruf' ich's ins Ohr,
dass du sorglos ewig nun
schläf'st.—
Um der Götter Ende
grämt mich die Angst nicht,
seit mein Wunsch es will!
Was in Zwiespalts wildem
Schmerze
verzweifelnd einst ich beschloss,
froh und freudig
führ' ich frei es nun aus:
weiht' ich in wüthendem Ekel
des Niblungen Neid schon die
Welt
dem wonnigsten Wälsung
weis' ich mein Erbe nun an.
Der von mir erkoren,
doch nie mich gekannt,
ein kühnster Knabe,
meines Rathes bar,
errang des Nibelungen Ring:
ledig des Neides,
liebesfroh,
erlahmt an dem Edlen
Alberichs Fluch;
denn fremd bleibt ihm die
Furcht.
Die du mir gebarst,
Brünnhilde,
sie weckt hold sich der Held:
wachend wirkt
dein wissendes Kind
erlösende Weltenthat.—
Drum schlaf' nun du,
schliesse dein Auge;
träumend erschau' mein Ende!
Was Jene auch wirken—
dem ewig Jungen
weicht in Wonne der Gott.—
Hinab denn, Erda!
Urmütter-Furcht!
Ur-Sorge!
Zu ewigem Schlaf
hinab! hinab!—

WANDERER
You are not
what you believe.
Prime-wisdom marches
to its downfall;
your knowledge depends
upon my wishes.
Tell me what Wotan wills.
(*long silence*)
Unwise one,
I cry in your ear,
forever may you sleep in peace!
The eternals' downfall
gives me no anguish,
since I willed it so.
What I resolved in painful sorrow,
with wild despair in my heart,
glad and joyful
now I freely bring on.
Though in my scorn I devoted
the world to the Nibelungs' greed,
the noblest of Volsungs
now may inherit from me.
One who never knew me,
yet chosen by me,
a valorous stripling,
without my teaching,
has won the Nibelungs' ring.
Free from hate,
happy in loving,
the boy is not harmed
by Alberich's curse.
He knows nothing of fear.
She you bore to me,
Brunnhilda,
will be waked by him:
then your wisdom's child
shall perform a deed
to redeem the world.
So finish your sleep,
shut fast your eyelids:
dream and behold my downfall.
Whatever these young ones
may bring to pass,
to that I joyfully yield.
So down then, Erda!
Prime mother fear!
First sorrow!
Go down, go down
to endless sleep!

(ERDA, *who, with closed eyes, has already begun to*

sink, now entirely disappears. The cavern is again quite dark. Dawn illumines the stage; the storm is over)

SECOND SCENE

(*The* WANDERER *has come to the cave and is leaning with his back against the rocks.*)

WANDERER
I see that Siegfried comes.
(SIEGFRIED's *wood bird flutters in, suddenly stops, flutters about in alarm, and then disappears quickly.* SIEGFRIED *enters and stops*)

SIEGFRIED
My birdling flew from my sight!
With fluttering flight
and sweetest song
blithely he showed me the way,
and now he's flown far away!
So I must
find out the rock by myself.
My birdling showed me the way,
that way shall be my path.
(*starts to go*)

WANDERER
Whereto, fellow?
What do you seek?

SIEGFRIED (*stopping and turning*)
Did someone speak?
Perhaps he knows the way.
There's a mountain guarded
by raging fire, and I seek it.
There sleeps a maid
whom I must awake.

WANDERER
Who told you though
to seek the mountain?
Who caused you to long for the woman?

SIEGFRIED
I heard a singing
wood birdling
who gave me welcome counsel.

WANDERER
A wood bird chatters idly;
no man can hear the words.
So how could you tell
what tale he sang you?

SIEGFRIED
The magic was worked

WANDERER
Dort seh' ich Siegfried nah'n.—

SIEGFRIED
Mein Vöglein schwebte mir
fort;—
mit flatterndem Flug
und süssem Sang
wies es mir wonnig den Weg:
nun schwand es fern mir davon.
Am besten find' ich
selbst nun den Berg:
wohin mein Führer mich wies,
dahin wandr' ich jetzt fort.

WANDERER
Wohin, Knabe,
heisst dich dein Weg?

SIEGFRIED
Da redet's ja,
wohl räth das mir den Weg.—
Einen Felsen such' ich,
von Feuer ist der umwabert:
dort schläft ein Weib,
das ich wecken will.

WANDERER
Wer sagt' es dir,
den Fels zu suchen,
wer nach der Frau dich zu
sehnen?

SIEGFRIED
Mich wies es ein singend
Waldvöglein:
das gab mir gute Kunde.

WANDERER
Ein Vöglein schwatzt wohl
manches;
kein Mensch doch kann's
versteh'n:
wie mochtest du Sinn
dem Sange entnehmen?

SIEGFRIED
Das wirkte das Blut

eines wilden Wurms,
der mir vor Neidhöhl' erblasste:
kaum netzt' es zündend
die Zunge mir,
da verstand ich der Vöglein
Gestimm'.

by a dragon's blood,
destroyed at Hate-cave before me.
His burning blood
scarce had wet my tongue,
when I fathomed the song of the bird.

WANDERER
Erschlugst den Riesen du,
wer reizte dich,
den starken Wurm zu besteh'n?

WANDERER
Who urged you on to fight
the giant foe,
the mighty dragon you slew?

SIEGFRIED
Mich führte Mime,
ein falscher Zwerg;
das Fürchten wollt' er mich
lehren:
zum Schwertschlag aber,
der ihn erschlug,
reizte der Wurm mich selbst;
seinen Rachen riss er mir auf.

SIEGFRIED
Old Mime urged me,
a wily dwarf,
who tried to teach me what fear is;
but what did urge me
most was the beast;
he was the cause himself,
with his ugly, threatening jaws.

WANDERER
Wer schuf das Schwert
so scharf und hart,
dass der stärkste Feind ihm fiel?

WANDERER
Who made the sword
so sharp and hard
that it slew the fiercest foe?

SIEGFRIED
Das schweisst' ich mir selbst,
da's der Schmied nicht konnte:
schwertlos noch wär' ich wohl
sonst.

SIEGFRIED
I forged it myself,
for the goblin could not:
else would I still lack a sword.

WANDERER
Doch wer schuf
die starken Stücke,
daraus das Schwert du geschweisst?

WANDERER
Yet who made
the mighty pieces
with which you made the needed sword?

SIEGFRIED
Was weiss ich davon!
Ich weiss allein,
dass die Stücke nichts mir
nützten,
schuf ich das Schwert mir nicht
neu.

SIEGFRIED
I really can't tell.
I only know
that unless the pieces were put together
the sword would not serve.

WANDERER
Das—mein' ich wohl auch!

WANDERER (*with a good-humored laugh*)
That surely is true!
(*looks at* SIEGFRIED *with pleasure*)

SIEGFRIED
Was lachst du mich aus?
Alter Frager,
hör' einmal auf;
lass' mich nicht lange mehr
schwatzen!
Kannst du den Weg
mir weisen, so rede:
vermagst du's nicht,
so halte dein Maul!

SIEGFRIED (*surprised*)
Now why do you laugh?
Busybody,
hear once for all,
keep me no longer here prating.
If you can help
direct me, then do so;
if not, old man,
then close your jaw!

WANDERER
Geduld, du Knabe!
Dünk' ich dich alt,
so sollst du mir Achtung bieten.

WANDERER
Keep calm, young fellow!
If I seem old,
then show me honor, respect me.

SIEGFRIED
That is a good one!
My whole life long
there stood in my path
an ancient fellow;
now I have swept him away.
If you stand longer
barring me my pathway,
then take care, old one,
lest that you perish, like him.
(*steps nearer the* WANDERER)
How odd you appear!
Why do you wear
such a monstrous hat?
Also, why does it cover your face?

SIEGFRIED
Das wär' nicht übel!
So lang' ich lebe,
stand mir ein Alter
stets im Wege:
den hab' ich nun fortgefegt.
Stemmst du dort länger
dich steif mir entgegen—
sieh' dich vor, mein' ich,
dass du wie Mime nicht fähr'st!
Wie siehst du denn aus?
Was hast du gar
für 'nen grossen Hut?
Warum hängt der dir so ins Gesicht?

WANDERER (*without changing his position*)
Thus does the Wanderer wear it
when he goes against the wind.

WANDERER
Das ist so Wand'rers Weise,
wenn dem Wind entgegen er geht.

SIEGFRIED (*examining him still more closely*)
But an eye beneath it is lacking!
So doubtless someone
once put it out
when you were stubborn
and barred his way.
Make yourself scarce,
or else you may quickly
lose your other eye also.

SIEGFRIED
Doch darunter fehlt dir ein Auge!
Das schlug dir einer
gewiss schon aus,
dem du zu trotzig
den Weg vertrat'st?
Mach' dich jetzt fort!
sonst möchtest du leicht
das and're auch noch verlieren.

WANDERER
Although you know
nothing, my son,
you know at least your cocksureness!
With the one eye
that is missing in me,
you look yourself on the other
that still is left me for sight.

WANDERER
Ich seh', mein Sohn,
wo nichts du weisst,
da weisst du dir leicht zu helfen.
Mit dem Auge,
das als and'res mir fehlt,
erblickst du selber das eine,
das mir zum Sehen verblieb.

SIEGFRIED
Ha—ha—ha—ha!
You make me laugh with your nonsense!
Yet hear, I trifle no longer;
be quick, show me the way,
then pursue your own way yourself!
For that's all
you're good for, I think.
So speak, or out of my path!

SIEGFRIED
Ha ha ha ha!
Zum Lachen bist du mir lustig!
Doch hör', nun schwatz' ich nicht länger;—
geschwind zeig' mir den Weg,
deines Weges ziehe dann du!
Zu nichts and'rem
acht' ich dich nütz':
d'rum sprich, sonst spreng' ich dich fort!

WANDERER (*gently*)
Child, if you knew
who I am
your scoff—would have been spared!
Painful it is
when a dear one so threatens!
Long have I loved

WANDERER
Kenntest du mich,
kühner Spross,
den Schimpf—spartest du mir!
Dir so vertraut,
trifft mich schmerzlich dein Dräuen.
Liebt' ich von je
deine lichte Art,—

Grauen auch zeugt ihr
mein zürnender Grimm:
dem ich so hold bin,
allzu hehrer,
heute nicht wecke mir Neid,
er vernichtete dich und mich!

SIEGFRIED
Bleib'st du mir stumm,
störrischer Wicht?
Weich' von der Stelle!
Denn dorthin, ich weiss,
führt es zur schlafenden Frau:
so wies es mein Vöglein,
das hier erst flüchtig entfloh.

WANDERER
Es floh dir zu seinem Heil;
den Herrn der Raben
errieth es hier;
weh' ihm, holen sie's ein!—
Den Weg, den es zeigte,
sollst du nicht zieh'n!

SIEGFRIED
Hoho! du Verbieter!
Wer bist du denn,
dass du mir wehren willst?

WANDERER
Fürchte des Felsens Hüter!
Verschlossen hält
meine Macht die schlafende
Maid:
wer sie erweckte,
wer sie gewänne,
machtlos macht' er mich ewig!—
Ein Feuermeer
umfluthet die Frau,
glühende Lohe
umleckt den Fels.
Wer die Braut begehrt,
dem brennt entgegen die
Brunst.
Blick' nach der Höh'!
erlug'st du das Licht?
Es wächst der Schein,
es schwillt die Gluth;
sengende Wolken,
wabernde Lohe
wälzen sich brennend
und prasselnd herab.
Ein Lichtmeer
umleuchtet dein Haupt:
bald frisst und zehrt dich
zündendes Feuer:—
zurück denn, rasendes Kind!

your radiant face,
though it felt fear
at my furious wrath.
You, whom I love so—
all too noble—
do not waken my wrath;
it would ruin both you and me!

SIEGFRIED
Still you won't tell,
stubborn old man?
Out of my way, then;
for that way, I know,
leads to the maid on the rock.
The wood bird has shown me,
who right here took off in flight.

WANDERER (*breaking out in anger*)
It fled you to save its life!
It thought the ruler
of ravens near.
Too bad, should he get caught!
The way he directed,
shall you not take!

SIEGFRIED (*surprised, steps back defiantly*)
Hoho! you forbidder!
Who are you then
that you would bar my way?

WANDERER
Guard yourself from the guardian!
The sleeping maid
of the rock is chained by my might.
He who would wake her,
he who would win her,
mightless makes me forever!
A flaming sea
encircles the maid.
Flickering fires
lick round the rock.
He who craves the bride
must walk through flames to the rock.
(*points with his spear*)
Look toward the heights
and gaze at that light!
Its splendor grows,
its glowing swells,
clouds there are scorching,
fires there are flick'ring,
rolling and burning,
and raging this way.
A light sea
illumines your head;
enkindling flames

can seize and devour you.
Go back then, foolhardy boy!

SIEGFRIED
Go back, you babbler, yourself!
There, where the blaze is burning,
is Brunnhilda, whom I must find.
(*moves onward. The* WANDERER *bars his way*)

SIEGFRIED
Zurück, du Prahler, mit dir!
Dort, wo die Brünste brennen,
zu Brünnhilde muss ich jetzt hin!

WANDERER
Have you no fear of the fire?
Why then I must hinder your way!
For still do I hold
the mighty haft.
The sword that you swing
once broke upon this shaft;
yet once again
let it splinter upon this spear!
(*stretches out his spear*)

WANDERER
Fürchtest das Feuer du nicht,
so sperre mein Speer dir den Weg!
Noch hält meine Hand
Der Herrschaft Haft;
das Schwert, das du schwing'st,
zerschlug einst dieser Schaft:
noch einmal denn
zerspring' es am ewigen Speer!

SIEGFRIED (*drawing his sword*)
So my father's foe
faces me here?
Sweet is the vengeance
that comes my way!
Swing with your spear,
and let it split on my sword!
(*with one stroke he hews the spear in two pieces, from which a flash of lightning shoots up toward the rocky heights, where the ever-brightening flames begin to be visible. A loud thunderclap accompanies the stroke. The* WANDERER *quietly picks up the pieces, which have fallen at his feet*)

SIEGFRIED
Meines Vaters Feind!
Find' ich dich hier?
Herrlich zur Rache
gerieth mir das!
Schwing' deinen Speer:
in Stücken spalt' ihn mein Schwert!

WANDERER
Fare on! I cannot prevent you!
(*disappears into the darkness*)

WANDERER
Zieh' hin! ich kann dich nicht halten!

SIEGFRIED
When his spear is done for,
see how he flees me!

SIEGFRIED
Mit zerfocht'ner Waffe
wich mir der Feige!

(*the growing brightness of the clouds meets his sight*)
Ha! gladdening glow!
glorious light,
lighting my pathway
clearly before me!
I'll bathe in the fire!
I'll go through the flames to my bride!
Ho-ho! Ha-hei!
Again let me call you mate!
(*puts his horn to his lips and plunges into the waving fire that flows down from the heights. He is soon out of sight, and is apparently ascending the mountain*)

Ha, wonnige Gluth!
leuchtender Glanz!
Strahlend offen
steht mir die Strasse.—
Im Feuer mich baden!
Im Feuer zu finden die Braut!
Hoho! Hoho!
hahei! hahei!
Lustig! lustig!
Jetzt lock' ich ein liebes Gesell!

THIRD SCENE

(*The glow sinks to a fine transparent veil, which also clears off, revealing a lovely blue sky and bright weather. The scene, from which all the vapors have fled, represents the summit of a rocky mountain peak: left, the entrance to a natural rocky hall; right, spreading fir trees; foreground, beneath the shade of a spreading fir tree, lies* BRUNNHILDA *in deep sleep. She is in complete armor.*

SIEGFRIED *has now reached the rocky heights in the background. He looks around, astonished.*)

SIEGFRIED
Selige Oede
auf sonniger Höh'!—
Was ruht dort schlummernd
im schattigen Tann?—
Ein Ross ist's,
rastend in tiefem Schlaf!
Was strahlt mir dort entgegen?—
Welch' glänzendes Stahlgeschmeide!
Blendet mir noch
die Lohe den Blick?—
Helle Waffen!—
Heb' ich sie auf?
Ha! in Waffen ein Mann:
wie mahnt mich wonnig sein Bild!—
Das hehre Haupt
drückt wohl der Helm?
leichter würd' ihm,
löst' ich den Schmuck.

Ach!—wie schön!—
Schimmernde Wolken
säumen in Wellen
den hellen Himmelssee:
leuchtender Sonne
lachendes Bild
strahlt durch das Wolkengewölk!
Von schwellendem Athem
schwingt sich die Brust:—
brech' ich die engende Brünne?
Komm', mein Schwert,
schneide das Eisen!

SIEGFRIED
Blessed this haven
on sun-brightened height!
(*mounts to the top of the height, then looks into the wood and comes forward*)
What rests there sleeping
mid shades of the firs?
A charger,
lying in heavy sleep.
(*coming nearer he stops in surprise*)
What flashes there upon me?
What glistening steel is that?
Maybe the flames
still dazzle my sight.
Shining armor?
Here, let me see.
(*lifts up the shield and sees* BRUNNHILDA'S *form*)
Ha! in armor—a man?
The sight is pleasant to see!
His helmet's tight,
pressing his head.
He would rest
the easier thus.
(*carefully loosens the helmet and lifts it from the head of the sleeper; long curling hair breaks forth.* SIEGFRIED *starts*)
Ah! how fair!
Shimmering clouds
encircle in fleeces
a radiant, heavenly sea;
laughing, the dazzling
face of the sun
streams through the billowy clouds.
(*bends lower over the sleeper*)
The labor to breathe
is heaving his breast,
so let me loosen his corslet.

(*tries*)
Come, my sword!
Cut through the iron.
(*drawing his sword, he gently cuts through the rings, then lifts off the breastplate, so that* BRUNNHILDA *lies before him in a soft woman's dress. Startled and astonished, he draws back*)
That is no man!
Burning bewitchment
pierces my heart!
Fiery pangs
rivet my eyesight!
My thoughts are reeling from fear!
Now whom shall I call,
that he may help me?
Mother! Mother!
Remember me!

Das ist kein Mann! — —
Brennender Zauber
zückt mir in's Herz;
feurige Angst
fasst meine Augen:
mir schwankt und schwindet
der Sinn!—
Wen ruf' ich zum Heil,
dass er mir helfe?—
Mutter! Mutter!
Gedenke mein'!

(*sinks as if fainting on* BRUNNHILDA's *bosom, then starts up, sighing*)
How waken the maid,
to see her eyes when they open—
those eyes, when they open?
(*tenderly*)
Might not her look make me blind?
How could I dare
endure such a light?
All swims, and rocks,
and staggers, and whirls!
Anguish of longing
weakens my spirit!
My hand on my heart
is trembling with fear!
What ails me, coward!
Is this what fear means?
O Mother! Mother!
Your dauntless child!
(*very gently*)
A woman, resting asleep
has taught him the meaning of fear!
And now I'd unknow
the fear I know!
So, if I'm to waken,
then the maid must be wakened.

Wie weck' ich die Maid,
dass sie die Augen mir öff'ne?—
Das Auge mir öff'ne?
blende mich auch noch der
Blick?
Wagt' es mein Trotz?
Ertrüg' ich das Licht?—
Mir schwebt und schwankt
und schwirrt es umher;
sehrendes Sengen
zehrt meine Sinne:
am zagenden Herzen
zittert die Hand!
Wie ist mir Feigem?—
Ist es das Fürchten?—
O Mutter! Mutter!
dein muthiges Kind!
Im Schlafe liegt eine Frau:
die hat ihn das Fürchten
gelehrt!—
Wie end' ich die Furcht?
Wie fass' ich Muth?—
Dass ich selbst erwache,
muss die Maid ich erwecken!——

(*he is overcome with tender emotions, bends down deeper*)
Sweetly quivers
her blossoming mouth!
Its gentle trembling
has banished my fear.
Ah! and the warm
and blissful scent of her breath!

Süss erbebt mir
ihr blühender Mund:
wie mild erzitternd
mich Zagen erreizt!—
Ach, dieses Athems
wonnig warmes Gedüft!—
Erwache! erwache!
heiliges Weib!—

(as if in despair)
Awaken! Awaken!
Holiest maid!
(gazes at her)

Sie hört mich nicht.—
So saug' ich mir Leben
aus süssesten Lippen,
sollt' ich auch sterbend
vergeh'n!

She hears me not.
But life I will gather
as bees gather honey;
what though I die for the deed!
(sinks, as if dying, on the sleeping figure, and fastens his lips on hers. BRUNNHILDA *opens her eyes.* SIEGFRIED *rises and remains standing before her. Slowly she rises to a sitting position. As her consciousness returns she greets heaven and earth with stately gestures)*

BRÜNNHILDE
Heil dir, Sonne!
Heil dir, Licht!
Heil dir, leuchtender Tag!
Lang war mein Schlaf;
ich bin erwacht:
wer ist der Held,
der mich erweckt'?

BRUNNHILDA
Hail, O sun-lord!
Hail, O light!
Hail, O radiant day!
Long was my sleep;
I am awake.
Who is the hero
that broke my sleep?

SIEGFRIED
Durch das Feuer drang ich,
das den Fels umbrann;
ich erbrach dir den festen
Helm:
Siegfried heiss' ich,
der dich erweckt'.

SIEGFRIED
It was I who reached the rock
through walls of fire.
It was I who undid your helm,
Siegfried it was
who broke your sleep.

BRÜNNHILDE
Heil euch, Götter!
Heil dir, Welt!
Heil dir, prangende Erde!
Zu End' ist nun mein Schlaf;
erwacht seh' ich:
Siegfried ist es,
der mich erweckt'!

BRUNNHILDA
Gods, I hail you!
Hail, O world!
Hail, O earth in your glory!
My sleep is at an end;
my life wakens.
Siegfried is it
through whom I wake.

SIEGFRIED
O Heil der Mutter,
die mich gebar;

SIEGFRIED
Oh hail to her
who gave me my birth!

BRÜNNHILDE
O Heil der Mutter
die dich gebar.

BRUNNHILDA
Oh hail to her
who gave you your birth!

SIEGFRIED
Heil der Erde,
die mich genährt;

SIEGFRIED
Hail to earth
that fostered my life!

BRÜNNHILDE
Heil der Erde,
die dich genährt:

BRUNNHILDA
Hail to earth
that fostered your life.

SIEGFRIED
Dass ich das Auge erschaut,
das jetzt mir Seligem strahlt!

SIEGFRIED
Letting me see those eyes
that kindly bless as they laugh!

BRUNNHILDA
Your gaze alone dared behold me,
for none could wake me but you!
(*both remain filled with glowing ecstasy, lost in mutual contemplation*)
O Siegfried, Siegfried!
Glorious youth!
O waker of life,
victorious light!
Oh, did you know, joy of the world;
how I have always loved you!
You were my gladness,
my watchful care!
Your life was sheltered
before it was yours.
My shield was your buckler
before you were born.
So long was my love, Siegfried.

SIEGFRIED
My mother did not die then?
Was she only asleep?

BRUNNHILDA (*smiles, stretching forth her hand to him in a friendly manner*)
You wonderful child,
no more your mother will greet you.
We are as one,
if I am blessed by your love.
What you would know
lies in my soul;
yet only with my love
rises my wisdom!
O Siegfried! Siegfried!
I loved you always,
for I alone
divined my father's intention:
though I never dared to think
or to name it,
I guarded silence,
feeling it only;
and for it fought,
battled and strove;
and for it flouted
him who conceived it;
and so I suffered
penance in sleep;
yet I did not think it,
but only felt!
For, what the thought was—
might you discern it—
was only my love for you!

BRÜNNHILDE
Nur dein Blick durfte mich
schau'n,
erwachen durft' ich nur dir!—
O Siegfried! Siegfried!
seliger Held!
Du Wecker des Lebens,
siegendes Licht!
O wüsstest du, Lust der Welt,
wie ich dich je geliebt!
Du warst mein Sinnen,
mein Sorgen du!
Dich Zarten nährt' ich,
noch eh' du gezeugt;
noch eh' du geboren,
barg dich mein Schild:
so lang' lieb' ich dich, Siegfried!

SIEGFRIED
So starb nicht meine Mutter?
schlief die Minnige nur?

BRÜNNHILDE
Du wonniges Kind,
deine Mutter kehrt dir nicht
wieder.
Du selbst bin ich,
wenn du mich Selige liebst.
Was du nicht weisst,
weiss ich für dich:
doch wissend bin ich
nur—weil ich dich liebe.—
O Siegfried! Siegfried!
siegendes Licht!
dich liebt' ich immer;
denn mir allein
erdünkte Wotans Gedanke.
Der Gedanke, den nie
ich nennen durfte;
den ich nicht dachte,
sondern nur fühlte;
für den ich focht,
kämpfte und stritt;
für den ich trotzte
dem, der ihn dachte;
für den ich büsste,
Strafe mich band,
weil ich nicht ihn dachte
und nur empfand!
Denn der Gedanke—
dürftest du's lösen!—
mir war er nur Liebe zu dir!

SIEGFRIED
Wie Wunder tönt
was wonnig du singst;
doch dunkel dünkt mich der Sinn.
Deines Auges Leuchten
seh' ich licht;
deines Athems Wehen
fühl' ich warm;
deiner Stimme Singen
hör' ich süss:
doch was du singend mir sagst,
staunend versteh' ich's nicht.
Nicht kann ich das Ferne
sinnig erfassen,
da all' meine Sinne
dich nur sehen und fühlen.
Mit banger Furcht
fesselst du mich:
du Einz'ge hast
ihre Angst mich gelehrt.
Den du gebunden
in mächt'gen Banden,
birg' meinen Muth mir nicht mehr!

SIEGFRIED
How joyful sounds
your wonderful song!
And yet the meaning seems dark.
I can see your shining
lustrous eyes;
I can feel your warm and gentle breath,
and the song you sing
is sweet to hear:
yet what you say as you sing,
wondering I cannot grasp.
I cannot grasp clearly
thoughts in the distance,
when all my senses
feel and see you only!
A heavy fear
fetters my heart:
a fear that you only
taught me to know;
so you, who bound me
in mightiest fetters,
give me my courage again!

BRÜNNHILDE
–Dort seh' ich Grane,
mein selig Ross:
wie weidet er munter,
der mit mir schlief!
Mit mir hat ihn Siegfried erweckt.

BRUNNHILDA (*looking toward the wood*)
I see my Grane,
my sacred steed:
he slept by my side,
now he grazes there.
He too was awakened by you.

SIEGFRIED
Auf wonnigem Munde
weidet mein Auge:
in brünstigem Durst
doch brennen die Lippen,
dass der Augen Weide sie labe!

SIEGFRIED
My eyes love to graze
on lips that are lovely:
my own are athirst
to taste of their sweetness,
and to know the joys of that pasture!

BRÜNNHILDE
Dort seh' ich den Schild,
der Helden schirmte;
dort seh' ich den Helm,
der das Haupt mir barg:
er schirmt, er birgt mich nicht mehr!

BRUNNHILDA (*indicating her weapons*)
I see there the shield
that guarded heroes.
I see there the helmet
that hid my head:
it shields, it guards me no more.

SIEGFRIED
Eine selige Maid
versehrte mein Herz;
Wunden dem Haupte
schlug mir ein Weib:–
ich kam ohne Schild und Helm!

SIEGFRIED
A heavenly maid
has wounded my heart;
wounds from a woman
throb in my head.
I came without shield or helm!

BRÜNNHILDE
Ich sehe der Brünne
prangenden Stahl:
ein scharfes Schwert
schnitt sie entzwei;
von dem maidlichen Leibe

BRUNNHILDA (*sadly*)
I see there the corslet's
shimmering steel:
a keen-edged sword
cut it in two;

with its glittering edge
you loosened the mail.
No corslet or shield is left
to the weak, the sorrowful maid!

löst' es die Wehr:—
Ich bin ohne Schutz und Schirm,
ohne Trutz ein trauriges Weib!

SIEGFRIED

I battled through fire,
to get to your side;
no corslet or armor
guarded my life:
and now the flames
have pierced to my breast.
My blood runs hot
in turbulent streams;
a ravening fire
is kindled within me.
The flame that shone
round Brunnhild's rock
is burning now in my breast!
O maid! extinguish the fire!
Quiet its simmering rage!
(*embraces her impetuously*)

SIEGFRIED

Durch brennendes Feuer
fuhr ich zu dir:
nicht Brünne noch Panzer
barg meinen Leib:
mir in die Brust
brach nun die Lohe.
Es braust mein Blut
in blühender Brunnst;
ein zehrendes Feuer
ist mir entzündet:
die Gluth, die Brünnhilds
Felsen umbrann,
die brennt mir nun in der Brust.—
Du Weib, jetzt lösche den Brand!
schweige die schäumende Gluth!

BRUNNHILDA (*resisting him with the utmost strength of terror, and flying to the other side of the stage*)

No god neared me then!
The heroes showed
obeisance to Brunnhild:
holy came she from Valhall.
Woe's me! Woe's me!
Woe for the shame,
the bitter disgrace!
For he who woke me
gives me the wound!
He has broken corslet and helm:
Brunnhilda am I no more!

BRÜNNHILDE

Kein Gott nahte mir je:
der Jungfrau neigten
scheu sich die Helden:
heilig schied sie aus Walhall!—
Wehe! Wehe!
Wehe der Schmach,
der schmählichen Noth!
Verwundet hat mich,
der mich erweckt!
Er erbrach mir Brünne und Helm:
Brünnhilde bin ich nicht mehr!

SIEGFRIED

You still are
but the slumbering maid:
Brunnhilda lies
still in her sleep.
Awaken! Be now a wife!

SIEGFRIED

Noch bist du mir
die träumende Maid:
Brünnhildes Schlaf
brach ich noch nicht.
Erwache! sei mir ein Weib!

BRUNNHILDA

My senses are reeling,
my reason fails:
shall all my wisdom vanish?

BRÜNNHILDE

Mir schwirren die Sinne!
Mein Wissen schweigt:
soll mir die Weisheit schwinden?

SIEGFRIED

Did you not sing
that wisdom was
your glorious love for myself?

SIEGFRIED

Sang'st du mir nicht,
dein Wissen sei
das Leuchten der Liebe zu mir?

BRUNNHILDA

Deepening darkness
troubles my sight;

BRÜNNHILDE

Trauriges Dunkel
trübt mir den Blick;
mein Auge dämmert,

das Licht verlischt:
Nacht wird's um mich:
aus Nebel und Grau'n
windet sich wüthend
ein Angstgewirr:
Schrecken schreitet
und bäumt sich empor!

my eyes are dimming.
My light dies out,
night fills my heart.
Through horror and gloom,
writhing and raging,
comes frenzied fear;
terror screeches and rears itself high!
(*impetuously hides her eyes with her hands*)

SIEGFRIED
Nacht umbangt
gebundene Augen;
mit den Fesseln schwindet
das finst're Grau'n:
tauch' aus dem Dunkel und sieh'—
sonnenhell leuchtet der Tag!

SIEGFRIED (*gently taking her hands away from her eyes*)
Night enfolds
imprisoned eyes.
When the fetters vanish,
the fears do too.
Dive through the darkness and see:
bright with the sun blazes the day!

BRÜNNHILDE
Sonnenhell
leuchtet der Tag meiner Noth!—
O Siegfried! Siegfried!
Sieh' meine Angst!
Ewig war ich,
ewig bin ich,
ewig in süss
sehnender Wonne—
doch ewig zu deinem Heil!
O Siegfried! Herrlicher!
Hort der Welt!
Leben der Erde!
Lachender Held!
Lass', ach lass'!
lasse von mir!
Nahe mir nicht
mit der wüthenden Nähe!
Zwinge mich nicht
mit dem brechenden Zwang!
Zertrümm're die Traute dir nicht!—
Sahst du dein Bild
im klaren Bach?
Hat es dich Frohen erfreut?
Rührtest zur Woge
das Wasser du auf;
zerflösse die klare
Fläche des Bach's:
dein Bild sahst du nicht mehr,
nur der Welle schwankend Gewog'!
So berühre mich nicht,
trübe mich nicht:
ewig licht
lachst du aus mir
dann selig selbst dir entgegen,
froh und heiter ein Held!—
O Siegfried! Siegfried!
leuchtender Spross!
Liebe—dich,
und lasse von mir:
vernichte dein Eigen nicht!

BRUNNHILDA
Bright with the sun
blazes the day of my shame!
O Siegfried! Siegfried!
See how I fear!
(*her manner shows that a pleasing picture has come to her mind. She looks tenderly on* SIEGFRIED)
Life was given me,
life eternal,
endless in sweet
rapturous longing—
yet only to make you blest.
O Siegfried! Glorious!
Hoard of the world!
Hero most holy!
Light of the world!
Leave, ah, leave,
leave me alone!
Come not to me
with your mastering might!
Oh, bring me not ruin and shame!
Have you not felt
an eager joy
to see your face in the brook?
Yet if you trouble
the slumbering waves,
and shatter the quiet smile
of the brook,
your face then must be lost—
nothing left but turmoil of waves.
So inflict not your will,
trouble me not!
Like the brook
let me mirror back
your picture in beauty,
brave and joyous young man!

O Siegfried! radiant child!
Love yourself,
and leave me alone;
destroy not the one you own!

SIEGFRIED
I love you.
Oh, might you love me!
No more am I mine:
Oh, would you were mine!
Before me
a wondrous river rolls:
with all my senses
I only see
its joyous, billowing waters.
If it will not
reflect back my face,
still would I plunge
in the cooling water,
myself, as I am,
ending my pains:
Oh that its billows
might drown me in bliss,
and quench my fire with its waves!
Awaken, Brunnhilda!
Waken, O maid!
laughing and living,
sweetest delight!
Be mine! be mine! be mine!

BRUNNHILDA
O Siegfried! yours
ever I've been!

SIEGFRIED
Mine have you been,
then be mine now!

BRUNNHILDA
Yours always
will I be!

SIEGFRIED
What you will be,
be to me now!
Tight in my arms
I hold you embraced,
thus with my breast
feeling your heartbeats;
glances are kindling,
gently we mingle breath,
eyes to eyes
and mouth to mouth!
Then are you to me
what always you were and will be!

SIEGFRIED
Dich—lieb' ich:
o liebtest mich du!
Nicht hab' ich mehr mich,
o hätte ich dich!—
Ein herrlich Gewässer
wogt vor mir;
mit allen Sinnen
seh' ich nur sie,
die wonnig wogende Welle:
brach sie mein Bild,
so brenn' ich nun selbst,
sengende Gluth
in der Fluth zu kühlen;
ich selbst, wie ich bin,
spring' in den Bach:—
o dass seine Wogen
mich selig verschlängen,
mein Sehnen schwänd' in der Fluth!—
Erwache, Brünnhilde!
Wache, du Maid!
Lebe und lache,
süsseste Lust!
Sei mein! sei mein! sei mein!

BRÜNNHILDE
O Siegfried! dein—
war ich von je!

SIEGFRIED
Warst du's von je,
so sei es jetzt!

BRÜNNHILDE
Dein werde ich
ewig sein!

SIEGFRIED
Was du sein wirst,
sei es mir heut'!
Fasst dich mein Arm,
umschling' ich dich fest;
schlägt meine Brust
brünstig die deine;
zünden die Blicke,
zehren die Athem sich;
Aug' in Auge,
Mund an Mund;
dann bist du mir,
was bang du mir warst und wirst!
Dann brach sich die brennende Sorge,
ob jetzt Brünnhilde mein?

The fear and the passion would vanish,
if now Brunnhild were mine.

BRÜNNHILDE
Ob jetzt ich dein?—
Göttliche Ruhe
rast mir in Wogen;
keusches Licht
lodert in Gluthen;
himmlisches Wissen
stürmt mir dahin,
Jauchzen der Liebe
jagt es davon!
Ob jetzt ich dein?
O Siegfried! Siegfried!
siehst du mich nicht?
Wie mein Blick dich verzehrt,
erblindest du nicht?
Wie mein Arm dich presst!
entbrennst du nicht?
Wie in Strömen mein Blut
entgegen dir stürmt,
das wilde Feuer,
fühlst du es nicht?
Fürchtest du, Siegfried—
fürchtest du nicht
das wild wüthende Weib?

BRUNNHILDA
If I were yours?
Godlike repose
is tossing in tumult;
chastity's light
blazes to passion:
heavenly wisdom
flees far away;
jubilant love
is driving it hence!
If I am yours?
Siegfried! Siegfried!
Do you not see?
Does the fire of my eye
not blind you with light?
When I hold you close
are you not burned?
When my turbulent blood
is surging toward you,
the raging fire,
can you not feel?
Do you not, Siegfried—
do you not fear
the wild, amorous maid?

SIEGFRIED
Ha!—
Wie des Blutes Ströme sich zünden;
wie der Blicke Strahlen sich zehren;
wie die Arme brünstig sich pressen—
kehrt mir zurück
mein kühner Muth,
und das Fürchten, ach!
das nie ich gelernt;
das Fürchten, das du
kaum mich gelehrt:
das Fürchten—mich dünkt—
ich Dummer vergass es schon wieder!

SIEGFRIED
Ha!
As my glowing blood is enkindled,
as our burning glances are meeting,
as I clasp you, blazing with ardor,
surely my courage
comes again;
and the fear, ah!
I had failed to learn,
the fear you had
hardly skill to teach,
that terror—that fear,
has vanished and left me a fool!

BRÜNNHILDE
O kindischer Held!
O herrlicher Knabe!
Du hehrster Thaten
thöriger Hort!
Lachend muss ich dich lieben;
lachend will ich erblinden;
lachend lass' uns verderben—
lachend zu Grunde geh'n!

BRUNNHILDA
O valorous child,
O wonderful hero!
you simple lord
of glorious deeds!
Laughing must I love you,
laughing let me be blinded,
laughing let us be lost,
and laughing descend to doom!

SIEGFRIED
Lachend erwachst
du Wonnige mir:

SIEGFRIED
Laughing awake
in gladness to me!

BRUNNHILDA
Farewell, Valhall's
radiant world!
Let fall your glittering
towers to dust!

SIEGFRIED
Brunnhilda lives,
Brunnhilda laughs!
Hail, O day
that shines all around us!

BRUNNHILDA
Farewell, glistening
pomp of the gods!

SIEGFRIED
Hail, O sun
that gives us the day!

BRUNNHILDA
End in rapture,
you eternal race!

SIEGFRIED
Hail, O light,
that have burst from night!

BRUNNHILDA
Now rend, you Norns,
your rope of runes!

SIEGFRIED
Hail, O world,
where Brunnhilda lives!

BRUNNHILDA
Dusk of gods,
enfold us around!

SIEGFRIED
She wakes! she lives!

BRUNNHILDA
Night of their downfall,
come with the mist!

SIEGFRIED
She greets me with laughter.
Proudly shines
my Brunnhilda's star!

BRUNNHILDA
I see, still shining,
Siegfried's star!

SIEGFRIED
She is mine always
and forever mine,
and mine alone—my all!

BRUNNHILDA
He is mine always
and forever mine,
and mine alone—my all!

BRÜNNHILDE
Fahr' hin, Walhalls
leuchtende Welt!
Zerfall' in Staub
deine stolze Burg!

SIEGFRIED
Brünnhilde lebt!
Brünnhilde lacht!—
Heil dem Tage,
der uns umleuchtet!

BRÜNNHILDE
Leb' wohl, prangende
Götter pracht!

SIEGFRIED
Heil der Sonne,
die uns bescheint!

BRÜNNHILDE
End' in Wonne,
du ewig Geschlecht!

SIEGFRIED
Heil dem Licht,—
das der Nacht enttaucht!

BRÜNNHILDE
Zerreisst ihr Nornen
das Runen Seil!

SIEGFRIED
Heil der Welt,
der Brünnhilde lebt!

BRÜNNHILDE
Götterdämm'rung
dunkle herauf!

SIEGFRIED
Sie wacht, sie lebt!

BRÜNNHILDE
Nacht der Vernichtung
neb'le herein!

SIEGFRIED
Sie lacht mir entgegen:
prangend strahlt mir
Brünnhildes Stern!

BRÜNNHILDE
Mir strahlt zur Stunde
Siegfriedes Stern:

SIEGFRIED
Sie ist mir ewig
ist mir immer
Erb' und Eigen, Ein und All'!

BRÜNNHILDE
Er ist mir ewig,
ist mir immer, Erb' und Eigen,
Ein und All':
leuchtende Liebe,

lachender Tod!
leuchtende Liebe,
lachender Tod!

Love that enlightens!
Death that is joy!
Love that enlightens!
Death that is joy!
(*throws herself in* SIEGFRIED'*s arms*)

SIEGFRIED
Leuchtende Liebe,
lachender Tod!
Leuchtende Liebe,
lachender Tod!

SIEGFRIED
Love that enlightens!
Death that is joy!
Love that enlightens!
Death that is joy!

TOSCA

by Giacomo Puccini (1858–1924)

LIBRETTO BY
LUIGI ILLICA AND GIUSEPPE GIACOSA

Translated by JOSEPH MACHLIS

Based on Victorien Sardou's drama *La Tosca.*

CHARACTERS

CESARE ANGELOTTI, *an escaped political prisoner*	*Bass*
A SACRISTAN	*Baritone*
MARIO CAVARADOSSI, *a painter*	*Tenor*
FLORIA TOSCA, *a famous opera singer*	*Soprano*
BARON SCARPIA, *chief of the Roman police*	*Baritone*
SPOLETTA, *a police officer*	*Tenor*
SCIARRONE, *a gendarme*	*Bass*
A YOUNG SHEPHERD	*A Boy*
JAILER	*Bass*

CARDINAL, THE EXECUTIONER ROBERTI, JUDGE, CLERK, SERGEANT, INFANTRYMEN, SWISS GUARDS, TOWNSPEOPLE

Place: Rome
Time: June 1800
First performance: Teatro Costanzi, Rome, January 14, 1900

COPYRIGHT 1956 BY G. RICORDI & CO., NEW YORK
BY PERMISSION OF G. RICORDI & CO.

ACT I

(*The Church of Sant' Andrea Della Valle. To the right, the Attavanti Chapel. To the left, a scaffold. Upon it, a large painting covered with a cloth. The painter's implements. A basket. Enter* ANGELOTTI *from the side door, in prison garb, ragged, exhausted, and trembling with fear. He is breathless and almost running. He casts a hasty glance about him.*)

ANGELOTTI

Ah! Safe at last . . .
Hunted and tormented,
I saw phantoms of fear in every corner.

(*he shudders. Then he again looks about him, intently and—as he recognizes the place—more calmly. Heaves a sigh of relief as he catches sight of the column with its font of holy water and a statue of the Madonna*)

The column . . . and the statue . . .
My sister wrote I'd find it at the foot of the Madonna.

(*approaches the column, searches for the key at the foot of the Virgin's statue. Not finding it, he searches anew in great agitation. Makes a gesture of discouragement, resumes his search. Finally, stifling a cry of joy, he finds the key. Pointing quickly to the Attavanti Chapel*)

Here is the key . . . and there, the chapel!

(*he is again terrified at the thought that he has been followed. He looks apprehensively about him, approaches the chapel, and with the utmost caution inserts the key in the lock. He opens the gate, enters, locks the gate behind him, and disappears within*)

(*the* SACRISTAN *enters from the rear, crossing from left to right toward the nave of the church, intent upon his chores. He holds a bundle of paint brushes in his hand, approaches the scaffold, speaking in a loud voice as though he were addressing someone. A nervous tic shows itself in the twitching of his neck and shoulders*)

SACRISTAN

All day long I'm cleaning! Pots and paints and brushes.
Merciful saints, protect us from those artists!
Most noble painter . . . here!

(*looks toward the scaffold and is surprised to find it deserted*)

Where is he? I could have sworn
That I heard him just returning
To scrawl his strange designs and figures.

(*puts down the brushes and mounts the scaffold, looks inside the basket*)

No, I was mistaken.
Nothing has been touched here.

ANGELOTTI

Ah! . . . Finalmente! . . .
Nel terror mio stolto
vedea ceffi di birro in ogni volto.

La pila . . . la colonna . . .
"A' piè della Madonna" mi scisse mia sorella . . .

Ecco la chiave . . . ed ecco la capella! . . .

IL SAGRESTANO

E sempre lava! . . . Ogni pennello è sozzo
peggio d'un collarin d'uno scagnozzo.
Signor pittore . . . Tò! . . .
Nessuno.—Avrei giurato
che fosse ritornato
il cavalier Cavaradossi.
No, sbaglio.
Il paniere è intatto.
Angelus Domini nuntiavit Mariae, et concepit Spiritu Sancto.
Ecce ancilla Domini; fiat mihi secundum verbum tuum
Et verbum caro factum est et habitavit in nobis.

(*steps down from the scaffold. The Angelus sounds. The* SACRISTAN *kneels down and prays*)

Angelus Domini nuntiavit Mariae, et concepit Spiritu Sancto.
Ecce ancilla Domini; fiat mihi secundum verbum tuum
Et verbum caro factum est et habitavit in nobis.

CAVARADOSSI
Che fai?

CAVARADOSSI (*enters from the side and sees the* SACRISTAN *on his knees*)
What now?

SAGRESTANO
Recito l'Angelus.
Sante ampolle! Il suo ritratto! . . .

SACRISTAN (*rising*)
Saying the Angelus.
(CAVARADOSSI *mounts the scaffold and uncovers the picture, which shows a Mary Magdalen with great blue eyes and golden hair. He scrutinizes the canvas in silence. Turning to speak to* CAVARADOSSI, *the* SACRISTAN *catches sight of the uncovered painting and utters a cry of amazement*)
God in heaven! This is her portrait!

CAVARADOSSI
Di chi?

CAVARADOSSI
You know her?

SAGRESTANO
Di quell'ignota
che i dì passati a pregar qui venia
tutta devota—e pia.

SACRISTAN
That gentle lady
Who comes here daily to offer her prayers.
(*pointing unctuously to the statue of the Madonna*)
Humbly she kneels at the Virgin's feet.

CAVARADOSSI
È vero. E tanto ell'era
infervorata nella sua preghiera
ch'io ne pinsi, non visto, il bel sembiante.

CAVARADOSSI (*smiling*)
Ah, truly! She was so deep in meditation,
Pure and tender vision,
That, unknown to her, I painted her lovely features.

SAGRESTANO
Fuori, Satana, fuori!

SACRISTAN (*scandalized*)
Satan, get thee behind me!

CAVARADOSSI
Dammi i colori!

CAVARADOSSI
Give me the palette!
(CAVARADOSSI *paints rapidly, stopping now and again to look at his work. The* SACRISTAN *comes and goes, then picks up the brushes and rinses them in a bucket at the foot of the scaffold. Suddenly* CAVARADOSSI *stops painting. He takes from his pocket a medallion containing a miniature, and his eyes move from that to the painting*)

Recondita armonia
di bellezze diverse!
È bruna Floria,
l'ardente amante mia,
e te, beltade ignota,
cinta di chiome bionde!
Tu azzurro hai l'occhio,
Tosca ha l'occhio nero!
L'arte nel suo mistero
le diverse bellezze insiem confonde:
ma nel ritrar costei
il mio solo pensiero,
ah! il mio sol pensier sei tu!
Tosca sei tu!

Mysterious resemblance,
Yet what contrast in beauty!
My Tosca proudly smiles
In all her dark-eyed splendor.
And you so pure, my fair unknown,
Blond enchantress with eyes of blue!
But no less fair than Tosca,
Yet how unlike in beauty!
Strange pow'r of art, whose magic
Unites all charms in one sweet vision.
While painting those fair tresses

I thought only of Tosca.
You alone possess my heart!
Tosca, my love!
(continues to paint)

SACRISTAN *(during the preceding aria, muttering under his breath)*
I jest with fools, but fear the saints in heaven.
(he goes to fetch materials for cleaning the brushes. Returning from the rear, he begins again to clean them and, still scandalized, mutters)
He scorns the saints and shirks his sacred duty!
These females so seductive,
Who tempt the souls of men
And seek to lead them to eternal damnation . . .
I jest with knaves, but fear the saints in heaven.
These impious dogs who deny religion,
And defy all sacred law and order:—
No use to try to save them!
(he puts the bucket under the scaffold and the brushes in a vase near the painter)
He scorns the saints and mocks at all things holy.
Such heretics and scoundrels will be punished!
Praise be the Lord who saves the meek and lowly.
(to CAVARADOSSI*)*
Your Excellency, I'm going.

SAGRESTANO
Scherza coi fanti e lascia stare i santi.
Scherza coi fanti e lascia stare i santi!
Queste diverse gonne
che fanno concorrenza alle Madonne
mandan tanfo d'inferno . . .
Scherza coi fanti e lascia stare i santi.
Ma con quei cani di volterriani
nemici del santissimo governo
non c'è da metter voce! . . .
Scherza coi fanti e lascia stare i santi,
Già, sono impenitenti tutti quanti!
Facciam piuttosto il segno della croce.
Eccellenza, vado.

CAVARADOSSI
Do as you please!

CAVARADOSSI
Fa il tuo piacere! . . .

SACRISTAN
Plenty of food here. Are you not eating?

SAGRESTANO
Pieno è il paniere . . . Fa penitenza?

CAVARADOSSI
I am not hungry.

CAVARADOSSI
Fame non ho.

SACRISTAN *(he rubs his hands, is unable to repress a gesture of joy and a greedy glance at the basket, which he picks up and deposits a little to one side)*
Oh! . . . What a pity!
(takes two pinches of snuff)
Lock the doors when leaving.

SAGRESTANO
Oh! . . . mi rincresce! . . .
Badi, quand'esce chiuda.

CAVARADOSSI
Yes.

CAVARADOSSI
Va!

SACRISTAN
Good!
(exists to the rear; CAVARADOSSI *continues to work, his back to the chapel.* ANGELOTTI, *believing the church to be empty, appears behind the gate and uses the key to open it.* CAVARADOSSI, *hearing the lock creak, turns around)*

SAGRESTANO
Vo!

CAVARADOSSI
Someone's within!
*(*ANGELOTTI, *terrified, stops short as though he would seek refuge again inside the chapel. Glancing up, a*

CAVARADOSSI
Gente là dentro!

ANGELOTTI
Voi! Cavaradossi!
Vi manda Iddio!
Non mi ravvisate?
Il carcere m'ha dunque assai mutato!

CAVARADOSSI
Angelotti!
Il Console della spenta repubblica romana.

ANGELOTTI
Fuggii pur ora da Castel Sant' Angelo.

CAVARADOSSI
Disponete di me.

TOSCA
Mario!

CAVARADOSSI
Celatevi!
È una donna . . . gelosa.
Un breve istante e la rimando.

TOSCA
Mario!

CAVARADOSSI
Eccomi!

ANGELOTTI
Sono stremo di forze, più non reggo . . .

CAVARADOSSI
In questo panier v'è cibo e vino.

ANGELOTTI
Grazie!

CAVARADOSSI
Presto!

TOSCA
Mario! Mario! Mario!

CAVARADOSSI
Son qui!

half-stifled cry of joy escapes him as he recognizes the painter. He holds out his arms to him as if he had found unlooked-for aid.)

ANGELOTTI
You! Cavaradossi!
You were sent by heaven!
(CAVARADOSSI *does not recognize* ANGELOTTI *and remains on the scaffold, amazed.* ANGELOTTI *draws near so that* CAVARADOSSI *may recognize him*)
You do not know me? Have the months in prison
Changed me so completely?

CAVARADOSSI (*recognizing him,* CAVARADOSSI *quickly puts down his palette and brushes and comes down from the scaffold, peering cautiously around him.*)
Angelotti!
The consul of the outlawed Roman Republic!
(*hastens to shut the side door of the church*)

ANGELOTTI (*going toward* CAVARADOSSI . . . *secretive*)
I've just escaped from the Fortress Sant' Angelo . . .

CAVARADOSSI
Can I help in any way?

TOSCA (*from the outside*)
Mario!

CAVARADOSSI (*on hearing* TOSCA'S *voice motions quickly to* ANGELOTTI *to be silent*)
Now hide yourself!
She's suspicious and jealous.
I will be brief and she will leave us.

TOSCA
Mario!

CAVARADOSSI (*in the direction of* TOSCA'S *voice*)
Here I am!

ANGELOTTI (*overcome by weakness, leans against the scaffold and says sorrowfully*)
I am weary, my friend, and faint with hunger.

CAVARADOSSI (*quickly mounts the scaffold and returns with the basket, which he gives to* ANGELOTTI)
In this basket there's food and wine.

ANGELOTTI
Thank you!

CAVARADOSSI (*encouraging* ANGELOTTI, *he urges him toward the chapel*)
Hurry!
(ANGELOTTI *goes into the chapel*)

TOSCA (*irritated*)
Mario! Mario! Mario!

CAVARADOSSI (*pretending calm as he opens the door*)
My love!
(TOSCA *enters with a kind of violence, looking about her suspiciously. He approaches to embrace her. She thrusts him aside brusquely*)

TOSCA
Why lock the door?

CAVARADOSSI (*with feigned indifference*)
The sacristan desired it.

TOSCA
You spoke to someone.

CAVARADOSSI
To you!

TOSCA
Oh no! You whispered. I heard you.
Where is she?

CAVARADOSSI
Who?

TOSCA
Confess! Where's that woman?
I heard her footsteps plainly,
I sense her hidden presence.

CAVARADOSSI
Nonsense!

TOSCA
You're lying!

CAVARADOSSI (*with passion*)
You know I love you!
(*tries to kiss her*)

TOSCA (*gently reproving him*)
Oh! In front of the Madonna.
No, my beloved,
Let me kneel first in prayer
And offer my flowers.
(*she slowly approaches the statue of the Madonna and tastefully arranges around it the flowers she brought, kneels and prays devoutly; crosses herself, and rises. To* CAVARADOSSI, *who meanwhile is ready to resume his work*)
Listen closely, my dear. Tonight I am singing,
But my part is a short one.
You will wait at the usual place,
And later we will steal away together to your little villa.

CAVARADOSSI (*his thoughts elsewhere*)
This evening?

TOSCA
The night is fragrant.
Sweet perfumes intoxicate the air
And warm the heart. You are not eager?
(*seating herself on the step of the scaffold close to him*)

CAVARADOSSI (*absently*)
Very!

TOSCA (*struck by his coldness*)
Say it again!

TOSCA
Perchè chiuso?

CAVARADOSSI
Lo vuole il Sagrestano.

TOSCA
A chi parlavi?

CAVARADOSSI
A te!

TOSCA
Altre parole bisbigliavi.
Ov'è?

CAVARADOSSI
Chi?

TOSCA
Colei! Quella donna! . . .
Ho udito i lesti
passi e un fruscio di vesti.

CAVARADOSSI
Sogni!

TOSCA
Lo neghi?

CAVARADOSSI
Lo nego e t'amo!

TOSCA
Oh! innanzi la Madonna.
No, Mario mio,
lascia pria che la preghi,
che l'infiori . . .

Ora stammi a sentir—stassera canto,
ma è spettacolo breve.—Tu m'aspetti
sull'uscio della scena
e alla tua villa andiam soli, soletti.

CAVARADOSSI
Stassera?!

TOSCA
È luna piena
ed il notturno effluvio floreal
inebria il cor.—Non sei contento?

CAVARADOSSI
Tanto!

TOSCA
Tornalo a dir!

CAVARADOSSI
Tanto!

CAVARADOSSI
Very!

TOSCA
Lo dici male, lo dici male:
Non la sospiri la nostra casetta
che tutta ascosa nel verde ci aspetta?
nido a noi sacro, ignoto al mondo inter,
pien d'amore e di mister?
Al tuo fianco sentire,
per le silenziose
stellate ombre, salire
le voci delle cose!
Dai boschi, dai roveti,
dall'arse erbe, dall'imo
dei franti sepolcreti
odorosi di timo,
le notte escon bisbigli
di minuscoli amori
e perfidi consigli
che ammolliscono i cuori.
Fiorite, o campi immensi,
palpitate aure marine,
aure marine nel lunare albor,
ah, piovete voluttà, volte stellate!
Arde in Tosca un folle amor!

TOSCA (*annoyed*)
You say it badly, you say it badly.
Do you not yearn for our gay little cottage,
That stands demurely surrounded by flowers?
Dear little nest, hidden shrine of love,
Scene of joy and stolen hours . . .
Hand in hand we shall soon recapture
Love's elusive rapture,
Our souls released from care,
While songs of the nightingale fill the air!
From dark secluded groves
Filled with ancient sorrow,
Where shadows of yesterday
Now welcome the hopes of tomorrow,
The night, the magic night
Reveals its secret enchantment
With promise so tender,
Our foolish hearts at once surrender.
O wondrous world! Aflame with the joy
And the passion of living,
You thrill my senses with your golden fire!
Come, my beloved, let me know the ardor of your kiss—
Tosca yields to love's desire!

CAVARADOSSI
Ah! M'avvinci ne'tuoi lacci, mia sirena.

CAVARADOSSI
Ah! . . . You conquer once again!
I remain your slave, enchantress!

TOSCA
Arde a Tosca nel sangue il folle amor!

TOSCA (*with abandon*)
While your Tosca submits to love's desire! . . .

CAVARADOSSI
Mia sirena, verrò!

CAVARADOSSI
Ah, my love, till tonight!

TOSCA
O mio amore!

TOSCA (*resting her head on his shoulder*)
My beloved!

CAVARADOSSI
Or lasciami al lavoro.

CAVARADOSSI (*suddenly draws back a little and glances toward* ANGELOTTI's *hiding place*)
Now leave me to my work . . .

TOSCA
Mi discacci?

TOSCA (*surprised*)
You dismiss me?

CAVARADOSSI
Urge l'opra, lo sai!

CAVARADOSSI
It is urgent. You know it!

TOSCA
Vado, vado!
Chi è quella donna bionda lassù?

TOSCA (*irritated, gets up*)
I'm going, I'm going! . . .
(*she moves slightly away from him, then turns in order to look at him. She sees the portrait and in greatest agitation goes back to him*)
But who is that blond-haired woman there?

CAVARADOSSI
La Maddalena. Ti piace?

CAVARADOSSI (*calmly*)
I did a Magdalen. You like it?

TOSCA
È troppo bella!

TOSCA
She is far too lovely!

CAVARADOSSI (*laughing, with a bow*)
That's praise indeed . . .
TOSCA (*suspicious*)
Wait now.
It seems to me I've seen those blue eyes somewhere.
CAVARADOSSI (*indifferently*)
They are by no means uncommon! . . .
TOSCA (*trying to remember*)
One moment . . . one moment . . .
(*ascending the scaffold . . . triumphant*)
The Attavanti! . . .
CAVARADOSSI (*laughing*)
Perfect!
TOSCA (*devoured by jealousy*)
She came here? She loves you?
(*weeping*)
You love her? You love her?
CAVARADOSSI (*tries to calm her*)
You are mistaken . . .
TOSCA (*not listening, and with jealous rage*)
Those footsteps, and that strange whisp'ring . . .
Now I know! All my faith is shaken! . . .
CAVARADOSSI
Ah, Tosca!
TOSCA (*menacingly*)
She is so hateful!
And yet, you love her!
CAVARADOSSI (*gravely*)
I saw her yesterday, it was by merest chance.
She came alone to pray here,
She never saw the portrait.
TOSCA
Swear it!
CAVARADOSSI (*gravely*)
I swear it!
TOSCA (*with her eyes fastened on the picture*)
See how she gazes upon me!
CAVARADOSSI
What nonsense!
TOSCA
As if she mocked my torment.
CAVARADOSSI (*gently urges her to come down the steps*)
What folly!
TOSCA (*backs away, holding his hands in hers and never taking her eyes off the picture. They descend from the scaffold. Gently reproving him*)
Ah! those eyes! . . .
CAVARADOSSI (*holds her close to him, affectionately looking into her eyes*)
What eyes so fair can ever compare
With your own in radiance and beauty? . . .

CAVARADOSSI
Prezioso elogio.
TOSCA
Ridi?
Quegl'occhi cilestrini già li vidi . . .
CAVARADOSSI
Ce n'è tanti pel mondo!
TOSCA
Aspetta . . . aspetta . . .
È l'Attavanti!
CAVARADOSSI
Brava!
TOSCA
La vedi? T'ama?
Tu l'ami? tu l'ami?
CAVARADOSSI
Fu puro caso . . .
TOSCA
Quei passi e quel bisbiglio . . .
Ah! Qui stava pur ora!
CAVARADOSSI
Vien via!
TOSCA
Ah! la civetta!
A me, a me!
CAVARADOSSI
La vidi ieri, ma fu puro caso.
A pregar qui venne . . .
Non visto la ritrassi.
TOSCA
Giura!
CAVARADOSSI
Giuro!
TOSCA
Come mi guarda fiso!
CAVARADOSSI
Vien via . . .
TOSCA
Di me, beffarda, ride.
CAVARADOSSI
Follia!
TOSCA
Ah, quegli occhi!
CAVARADOSSI
Qual'occhio al mondo può star di paro
all'ardente occhio tuo nero?
È qui che l'esser mio,

che l'esser mio s'affisa
intero . . .
occhio all'amor soave,
all'ira fiero . . .
qual altro al mondo può star di
paro
all'occhio tuo nero?

TOSCA
Oh come la sai bene
l'arte di farti amare!
Ma . . . falle gli occhi neri!

CAVARADOSSI
Mia gelosa!

TOSCA
Sì, lo sento . . . ti tormento
senza posa.

CAVARADOSSI
Mia gelosa!

TOSCA
Certa sono del perdono
se tu guardi al mio dolor!

CAVARADOSSI
Tosca idolatrata,
ogni cosa in te mi piace;
l'ira audace
e lo spasimo d'amor!

TOSCA
Dilla ancora
la parola che consola . . .
dilla ancora!

CAVARADOSSI
Mia vita, amante inquieta,
dirò sempre: "Floria, t'amo!"
ah, l'alma acquieta,
sempre "t'amo!" ti dirò!

TOSCA
Dio! quante peccata!
M'hai tutta spettinata.

CAVARADOSSI
Or va, lasciami!

TOSCA
Tu fino a stassera
stai fermo al lavoro. E mi
promettì,
sia treccia bionda o bruna,
a pregar non verrà,
donna nessuna?

CAVARADOSSI
Lo giuro, amore! Va!

TOSCA
Quanto m'affretti!

You are my sole desire.
To you my heart ever turns in its yearning. . . .
Eyes now alight with love,
Now with anger burning bright!
Who shall compare with your midnight splendor?
My Tosca, I love you! . . .

TOSCA (*carried away and resting her head on his shoulder*)
Ah! well you know your power,
With words tender and beguiling!
(*maliciously*)
But . . . let her eyes be black! . . .

CAVARADOSSI (*tenderly*)
Ah, still jealous?

TOSCA
Yes, I know
That I cruelly torment you without reason.

CAVARADOSSI
Ah, still jealous!

TOSCA
You would soon forgive me once again,
If you knew my sorrow and pain!

CAVARADOSSI (*while she repeats the preceding lines*)
Tosca, my adored one,
I yield to your moods, your whims and fancies,
Whether you flame with anger
Or yield to the rapture of love!

TOSCA
Let me hear once more
Those sweet consoling words
That soothe my anguish!

CAVARADOSSI
My love, my darling, banish your fears,
Believe I love you only!
Ah! calm your troubled spirit,
Believe—for indeed I do!

TOSCA (*breaking away from him*)
Oh! how disgraceful!
My hair is all disheveled.

CAVARADOSSI
Now go. Let me work!

TOSCA
Then stay, and continue to paint until evening.
But promise me one thing:
No more fair ladies, neither blond nor brunette,
Who come to say their prayers—
None will distract you!

CAVARADOSSI
My love, I swear it! Now go!

TOSCA
And why this hurry?

CAVARADOSSI (*reproving her gently*)
Still jealous?

TOSCA (*falls into his arms and offers him her cheek*)
No, dear Mario!

CAVARADOSSI (*jesting*)
In front of the Madonna?

TOSCA (*indicating the Madonna*)
She's so forgiving!
(*they kiss.* TOSCA *is about to leave. Still looking at the picture, she turns and says maliciously*)
But let her eyes be black! . . .
(*she hurries away*)
(CAVARADOSSI *remains pensive, deeply moved. He remembers* ANGELOTTI *and listens to* TOSCA's *retreating footsteps, then goes to the half-open door and looks outside. Assuring himself that all is quiet, he hurries to the chapel.* ANGELOTTI *appears behind the gate.* CAVARADOSSI *opens the gate for him. They shake hands warmly*)

CAVARADOSSI (*to* ANGELOTTI *who, of course, has overhead the preceding conversation*)
My Tosca is devoted and loyal, but when she goes
To confession, she holds back no secrets.
I told her nothing. We must be very careful!

ANGELOTTI
Are we alone here?

CAVARADOSSI
Yes. And now, what is your plan?

ANGELOTTI
Within a week I will steal across the border.
Till then I stay in hiding. And my sister . . .

CAVARADOSSI
The Attavanti?

ANGELOTTI
Yes! She secretly prepared a woman's costume
There, under the altar,
Complete with veil, scarf, and fan . . .
In this disguise I'll make my way to safety.
(*looks about him in fear*)

CAVARADOSSI
Now I see it clearly!
She looked so sad, oppressed with care . . .
As she knelt in prayer,
I pitied her, that maid so fair,
I felt her secret sorrow
And thought she mourned her love! . . .
Now I see it clearly!
Hers was a sister's devotion!

CAVARADOSSI
Ancora?

TOSCA
No, perdona!

CAVARADOSSI
Davanti la Madonna?

TOSCA
È tanto buona!
Ma falle gli occhi neri!

CAVARADOSSI
È buona la mia Tosca, ma credente
al confessore nulla tien celato,
ond'io mi tacqui. È cosa più prudente.

ANGELOTTI
Siam soli?

CAVARADOSSI
Sì. Qual'è il vostro disegno?

ANGELOTTI
A norma degli eventi, uscir di Stato
o star celato in Roma. Mia sorella . . .

CAVARADOSSI
L'Attavanti?

ANGELOTTI
Sì . . . ascose un muliebre
abbigliamento là sotto l'altare . . .
vesti, velo, ventaglio, Appena imbruni indosserò quei panni . . .

CAVARADOSSI
Or comprendo!
Quel fare circospetto
e il pregante fervore
in giovin donna e bella
m'avean messo in sospetto
di qualche occulto amore! . . .
Or comprendo!
Era amor di sorella!

ANGELOTTI
Tutto ella ha osato
onde sottrarmi a Scarpia scellerato!

CAVARADOSSI
Scarpia?
Bigotto satiro che affina
colle devote pratiche—la foia
libertina—e strumento
al lascivo talento
fa il confessore e il boia!
La vita mi costasse,
vi salverò!
Ma indugiar fino a notte è mal sicuro.

ANGELOTTI
Tremo del sole!

CAVARADOSSI
La cappella mette
a un orto mal chiuso—poi c'è un canneto
che va lungi pei campi a una mia villa.

ANGELOTTI
M'è nota . . .

CAVARADOSSI
Ecco la chiave—innanzi sera
io vi raggiungo. Portate con voi
le vesti femminili.

ANGELOTTI
Ch'io le indossi?

CAVARADOSSI
Per or non monta, il sentiero è deserto.

ANGELOTTI
Addio!

CAVARADOSSI
Se urgesse il periglio, correte
al pozzo del giardin. L'acqua è nel fondo,
ma a mezzo della canna un picciol varco
guida ad un antro oscuro,
rifugio impenetrabile e sicuro!

ANGELOTTI
Il cannon del castello!

CAVARADOSSI
Fu scoperta
la fuga! Or Scarpia i suoi sbirri sguinzaglia!

ANGELOTTI
Addio!

CAVARADOSSI
Con voi verrò. Staremo all'erta!

ANGELOTTI
Heedless of danger,
She tries to rescue me from Scarpia!

CAVARADOSSI
Scarpia?
That treach'rous hypocrite who mingles
Cruelty and lust with the practice of religion!
Steeped in vice, yet most pious,
He wends his evil way,
Loathsome and lech'rous hangman!
I'll save your life, I vow it,
Though it cost my own!
But to wait here till dark is fraught with danger.

ANGELOTTI
I fear the light of day!

CAVARADOSSI (*pointing*)
From the chapel door you enter a garden.
Follow the path that runs through the meadow,
It leads to my villa.

ANGELOTTI
I've been there.

CAVARADOSSI
Here is the key, my friend.
I will join you at nightfall! And now take
This dress that will help to gain your freedom.

ANGELOTTI (*takes the bundle of clothes hidden under the altar*)
Shall I wear it?

CAVARADOSSI
Not at present, for the path is deserted.

ANGELOTTI
Farewell!

CAVARDOSSI (*hurrying back to* ANGELOTTI)
If danger should threaten, run to the well in the garden.
Deep is the water;
But halfway down the wall is a passage
That connects with a secret chamber.
There you may remain in perfect safety!
(*a cannon shot. The two men look at each other in greatest alarm*)

ANGELOTTI
Hear the cannon of the fortress!

CAVARADOSSI
Your escape is discovered!
Now Scarpia unleashes his bloodhounds!

ANGELOTTI
I go now!

CAVARADOSSI (*resolutely*)
And I with you! It will be safer!

ANGELOTTI
I hear footsteps!

CAVARADOSSI (*with enthusiasm*)
If they attack, we will fight them!
(*They leave the chapel hastily.*)

SARCRISTAN (*enters running and all excited, shouting*)
Splendid news, Your Excellence!
(*extremely surprised not to find the painter on the scaffold*)
But he's gone! Now that's a pity!
He who brings sorrow to an atheist
Earns a double indulgence!
(*Boys rush in noisily from all sides. Enter* PRIESTS, ACOLYTES, PUPILS *and* SINGERS *of the choir*)
Call together all the choir! Hurry!

PUPILS (*in the greatest confusion*)
Tell us . . .

SACRISTAN
Now listen closely!
(*herding them toward the sacristy*)

SOME PUPILS
Tell—what happened?

SACRISTAN
Glorious tidings! . . .
Bonaparte . . . That scoundrel . . .
Bonaparte . . .

OTHER PUPILS
What now? Pray, tell!

SACRISTAN
He was crushed, his army defeated.
May the devil take his soul!

ALL
Is it true? Or but a rumor?

SACRISTAN
'Pon my soul, I tell you truly.
Soon the news will spread through the city!

ALL
Hail the tidings of our glory!

SACRISTAN
Later we'll witness a torchlight parade,
A grand celebration and ball at the palace,
With an appropriate new cantata
Sung by Tosca! In every church,
A hymn to the Lord!
Now take your vestments, without delay!
(*shouting*)
Go, go quickly away!

ALL (*guffawing, laughing and shouting with joy, paying no attention to the* SACRISTAN, *who tries in vain to push them into the sacristy*)
We'll be paid double! . . . Te Deum . . . Gloria!

ANGELOTTI
Odo qualcun!

CAVARADOSSI
Se ci assalgon, battaglia!

SAGRESTANO
Sommo giubilo, Eccellenza! . . .
Non c'è più! Ne son dolente!
Chi contrista un miscredente
si guadagna un'indulgenza!
Tutta qui la cantoria! Presto!

ALLIEVI
Dove?

SAGRESTANO
In sagrestia . . .

ALCUNI ALLIEVI
Ma che avvenne?

SAGRESTANO
Nol sapete?
Bonaparte . . . scellerato . . .
Bonaparte . . .

ALTRI ALLIEVI
Ebben? Che fu?

SAGRESTANO
Fu spennato, sfracellato
e piombato a Belzebù!

ALLIEVI, CANTORI
Chi lo dice? È sogno! È fola!

SAGRESTANO
È veridica parola
or ne giunge la notizia!

TUTTI
Si festeggi la vittoria!

SAGRESTANO
E questa sera gran fiaccolata,
veglia di gala a Palazzo Farnese,
ed un'apposita nuova cantata
con Floria Tosca! E nelle chiese
inni al Signor!
Or via a vestirvi, non più clamor!
Via . . . via . . . in sagrestia!

TUTTI
Doppio soldo . . . *Te Deum* . . . *Gloria!*
Viva il Re! . . . Si festeggi la vittoria!
Questa sera gran fiaccolata!

Long live the King! Hail the news of our great glory!
Later we'll witness a torchlight parade.

SAGRESTANO
Or via a vestirvi!

SACRISTAN
Now put on your vestments.

TUTTI
Serata di gala!
Si festeggi la vittoria!
Viva il Re! Te Deum . . .
Gloria!
Si festeggi la vitto—!

ALL
A grand celebration and ball at the palace.
Long live the king!
Te Deum . . . Gloria!
Hail the news with loud rejoi—!

SCARPIA
Un tal baccano in chiesa! Bel rispetto!

SCARPIA (*appears unexpectedly in the doorway followed by* SPOLETTA *and several police agents. With great authority*)
What sacrilege in church! Fine behavior!
(*at sight of* SCARPIA *all are stricken dumb, as by a spell*)

SAGRESTANO
Eccellenza, il gran giubilo . . .

SACRISTAN (*stammering with fear*)
Your Excellence, we were overjoyed . . .

SCARPIA
Apprestate per il *Te Deum.*
Tu, resta!

SCARPIA
Now make ready for the Te Deum.
(*shamefaced, they slink away. The* SACRISTAN *tries to follow them but* SCARPIA *brusquely detains him*)
You—stay here!

SAGRESTANO
Non mi muovo!

SACRISTAN (*overcome with fear*)
Oh indeed, sir!

SCARPIA
E tu va, fruga ogni angolo, raccogli
ogni traccia!

SCARPIA (*to* SPOLETTA)
And you go search every corner.
Make note of each clue!

SPOLETTA
Sta bene!

SPOLETTA
I will, sir!
(*motions to two agents to follow him*)

SCARPIA
Occhio alle porte, senza dar sospetti!
Ora a te. Pesa
le tue risposte. Un prigionier di Stato
fuggì pur ora da Castel Sant' Angelo . . .
s'è rifugiato qui.

SCARPIA (*to the other agents, who hasten to obey*)
Watch every exit, arousing no suspicion!
(*to the* SACRISTAN)
As for you—answer my questions clearly.
A prisoner of state has just escaped
From the Fortress Sant' Angelo . . .
He's taken refuge here!

SAGRESTANO
Misericordia!

SACRISTAN
Good Lord, have mercy!

SCARPIA
Forse c'è ancora.
Dov'è la cappella degli Attavanti?

SCARPIA
He may be still here.
Where is the Attavanti Chapel?

SAGRESTANO
Eccola!
Aperta! Arcangeli!
E . . . un'altra chiave!

SACRISTAN
Here, sir.
(*he goes to the gate and finds it half open*)
But open! Oh Mother of God!
The key is not mine!

SCARPIA
Buon indizio . . . Entriamo.

SCARPIA
There's a clue. Let us enter.
(*they enter the chapel and soon return.* SCARPIA, *obviously annoyed, holds in his hand a closed fan, which he waves nervously. To himself*)

We made a blunder in firing that cannon.
The bird took warning and flew from the cage.
But he left behind him precious booty:
This dainty fan.
(waving it in the air)
What accomplice has aided his escape?
(he remains deep in thought, then carefully examines the fan. He suddenly notices a coat of arms and exclaims)
The Marchesa Attavanti! Here is her crest . . .
(looks about, scrutinizing every corner of the church. He catches sight of the scaffold, the painter's easel and the portrait, in which the face of the Magdalen seems to reproduce the well-known features of the Marchesa Attavanti)
And there's her portrait!
(to the SACRISTAN*)*
Who is the painter?

SACRISTAN *(still overcome with fear)*
Mario Cavaradossi.

SCARPIA
He!

SACRISTAN *(noticing an agent who comes out of the chapel carrying the basket)*
Heavens! The basket!

SCARPIA *(continuing his train of thought)*
He! The lover of Tosca! We suspect him!
He's for the republic!

SACRISTAN *(looking inside the basket and exclaiming in great surprise)*
Empty? Yes!

SCARPIA *(catching sight of the man with the basket)*
What is it? Speak up!

SACRISTAN *(takes the basket from the agent)*
This basket was found in the chapel, hidden away.

SCARPIA
Have you seen it before?

SACRISTAN
Surely!
The painter brought it here.
(stammering with fear)
But—if I may say so . . .

SCARPIA
Come now, spill all you know!

SACRISTAN *(more and more cowed and almost tearful as he holds up the empty basket)*
I left it filled with food,
A most tempting assortment.
The painter's midday meal!

SCARPIA *(deliberately seeking further details)*
He must have eaten!

Fu grave sbaglio quel colpo di cannone.
Il mariolo spiccato ha il volo,
ma lasciò una preda preziosa . . .
un ventaglio.
Qual complice il misfatto preparò?

La marchesa Attavanti! . . .
Il suo stemma . . .

Il suo ritratto!
Chi fe' quelle pitture?

SAGRESTANO
Il cavalier Cavaradossi.

SCARPIA
Lui!

SAGRESTANO
Numi! Il paniere!

SCARPIA
Lui! L'amante di Tosca! Un uom sospetto!
Un volterrian!

SAGRESTANO
Vuoto? Vuoto! . . .

SCARPIA
Che hai detto? Che fu?

SAGRESTANO
Si ritrovò nella cappella questo panier.

SCARPIA
Tu lo conosci?

SAGRESTANO
Certo!
È il cesto del pittor . . .
ma . . . nondimeno . . .

SCARPIA
Sputa quello che sai.

SAGRESTANO
Io lo lasciai ripieno
di cibo prelibato . . .
il pranzo del pittor! . . .

SCARPIA
Avrà pranzato!

SAGRESTANO
Nella cappella?
Non ne avea la chiave
nè contava pranzar . . . disse egli stesso.
Ond'io l'avea già messo . . .
al riparo.

SACRISTAN
Not in the chapel,
(*his hand motions no*)
For he had not the key.
Nor did he wish to eat at all, he said so himself.
Therefore I placed it here, sir . . .
(*shows where he had left the basket, and now deposits it there*)
Near the portrait.
(*intimidated by* SCARPIA'*s stern silence, aside*)

(Libera me Domine!)

Libera me Domine!

SCARPIA
Or tutto è chiaro . . .
la provvista—del sacrista
d'Angelotti fu la preda!

SCARPIA (*to himself*)
Now all is clear: . . .
The provisions of the sacristan
Served to feed that scoundrel Angelotti!
(TOSCA *enters in great agitation. She goes straight to the scaffold but, not finding* CAVARADOSSI *there, looks for him in the central nave of the church. When* SCARPIA *sees her enter he hides behind the column where the font is, and with an imperious gesture motions to the* SACRISTAN *to stay where he is. The latter, trembling and confused, remains by the scaffold*)

Tosca? Che non mi veda.
(Per ridurre un geloso allo sbaraglio
Jago ebbe un fazzoletto—ed io un ventaglio!)

Tosca? She must not see me.
(To arouse the flames of jealous passion,
Iago used a kerchief, and I this fan!)

TOSCA
Mario?! Mario?!

TOSCA (*returning to the scaffold, calling loudly and impatiently*)
Mario! Mario!

SAGRESTANO
Il pittor Cavaradossi?
Chi sa dove sia?
Svanì, sgattaiolò
per sua stregoneria.

SACRISTAN (*approaching* TOSCA)
You seek Cavaradossi?
Where he went, who shall say?
As if by magic spell,
He vanished clean away.
(*slips away*)

TOSCA
Ingannata? No . . . no . . .
tradirmi egli non può,
tradirmi egli non può!

TOSCA
Has he deceived me? No . . . no!
He could not be so untrue,
(*almost weeping*)
He could not be so untrue!

SCARPIA
Tosca divina
la mano mia
la vostra aspetta—piccola manina,
non per galanteria
ma per offrirvi l'acqua benedetta.

SCARPIA (*steps from his hiding place, dips his fingertips in the holy water and, approaching* TOSCA *with hand outstretched, says to her gently and winningly*)
Heav'nly Tosca,
With humble heart I take your hand,
Your little white hand,
Yet not because of gallantry,
But only to offer you the holy water.

TOSCA
Grazie, signor!

TOSCA (*touches* SCARPIA'*s fingers and makes the sign of the cross*)
Thank you very much.

SCARPIA
How noble your heart and free from guile.
Inspired by heaven and filled with holy zeal,
You command the sacred fire, you reveal
Such beauty as restores our faith in God!

TOSCA (*her thoughts elsewhere*)
You are very kind.
(*people begin to enter the church and move toward the rear*)

SCARPIA
Pious women who can find?
You belong to the theater,
(*deliberately*)
Yet you go to church each day,
And pray with true devotion . . .

TOSCA (*surprised*)
What do you mean?

SCARPIA
Quite unlike
Those wanton creatures
(*points to the portrait*)
Who come here shamelessly
To pose in garments of virtue,
(*with marked emphasis*)
Only to seek forbidden pleasure!

TOSCA (*with a start*)
No! Is it true? Then prove it—yes, prove it!

SCARPIA (*showing her the fan*)
Is this of any use to a painter?

TOSCA
(*seizing it*)
A lady's fan? Where did you find it?
(*some peasants enter*)

SCARPIA
On that easel.
Someone surprised the cooing lovebirds—
And when she took flight, she dropped some feathers!

TOSCA (*examining the fan*)
A crest! And coronet! The Attavanti!
As I suspected!

SCARPIA (*aside*)
My design has succeeded!

TOSCA (*with great feeling, struggling to restrain her tears and oblivious of her surroundings*)
And I came regretful and dejected,
Because I could not be with him this evening . . .
I came with love in my heart
To tell of my sorrow . . .

SCARPIA (*aside*)
Now the poison is working!

SCARPIA
Un nobile esempio è il vostro—
al cielo piena di santo zelo
attingete dell'arte il magistero
che la fede ravviva!

TOSCA
Bontà vostra . . .

SCARPIA
Le pie donne son rare . . .
Voi calcate la scena . . .
ma in chiesa ci venite
per pregar.

TOSCA
Che intendete?

SCARPIA
E non fate
come certe sfrontate
che han di Maddalena
viso e costumi . . .
e vi trescan d'amore!

TOSCA
Che? D'amore? Le prove! Le prove!

SCARPIA
È arnese di pittore questo?

TOSCA
Un ventaglio? Dove stava?

SCARPIA
Là su quel palco. Qualcun venne
certo a sturbar gli amanti
ed essa nel fuggir perdè le penne!

TOSCA
Presago sospetto!

SCARPIA
(Ho sortito l'effetto!)

TOSCA
Ed io venivo a lui tutta dogliosa
per dirgli: invan stassera il ciel s'infosca
l'innamorata Tosca
è prigioniera . . .

SCARPIA
(Già il veleno l'ha rose . . .)

TOSCA
. . . dei regali tripudi,
prigioniera! . . .

TOSCA
Since I must sing at the palace,
We'll be parted till tomorrow!
(enter a group of shepherds)

SCARPIA
(Già il veleno l'ha rosa.)
O che v'offende, dolce signora?
Una ribelle lacrima scende
sovra le belle guancie e le irrora;
dolce signora, che mai v'accora?

SCARPIA *(aside)*
Ah! The poison goes deeper.
(in a honeyed tone)
O gentle lady, what grieves your spirit?
Why does a lonely tear now appear,
To sadden your rare and radiant beauty?
Sweet lovely lady, what has caused your anguish?

TOSCA
Nulla!

TOSCA
Nothing!
(enter several noble gentlemen accompanied by their ladies)

SCARPIA
Darei la vita
per asciugar quel pianto.

SCARPIA *(with great intensity)*
I'd give my life,
Could I but assuage your torment.

TOSCA
Io qui mi struggo e intanto
d'altra in braccio le mie smanie deride!

TOSCA *(not listening to* SCARPIA*)*
In my grief, here I languish
While Mario in her arms now betrays me!

SCARPIA
(Morde il veleno.)

SCARPIA *(aside)*
Soon I shall conquer!

TOSCA
Dove son?
Potessi coglierli i traditori.
Oh qual sospetto!
Ai doppi amori
è la villa ricetto.

TOSCA *(with great bitterness)*
Where can they be?
(some townsfolk saunter in)
If only I could find the traitors!
(more and more bitterly)
O dreadful thought!
The villa we shared
Now welcomes my rival.

Traditor . . . traditor!
Oh mio bel nido insozzato di fango!
Vi piomberò inattesa.
Tu non l'avrai stassera.

(with great sorrow)
The traitor . . . the traitor!
My little nest is defiled forever!
(with sudden decision)
I will hurry there and surprise them!
(turns threateningly to the portrait)
You shall not have him tonight.

Giuro!

(with a loud and desperate cry)
I swear it!

SCARPIA
In chiesa!

SCARPIA *(scandalized, and almost reproving her)*
In church!

TOSCA
Dio mi perdona.
Egli vede ch'io piango!

TOSCA *(weeping)*
God will forgive me.
He sees how I suffer!
(Weeps bitterly; SCARPIA *accompanies her to the door, supporting her and pretending to reassure her. Scarcely has* TOSCA *left when the church begins to fill with people.* SCARPIA *returns. At a sign from him* SPOLETTA *appears from behind a column. The crowd gathers in*

the rear, waiting for the CARDINAL. *Some kneel and pray)*

SCARPIA Take three men and a carriage. Quickly! Follow ev'rywhere she goes. Let nothing escape you!	SCARPIA Tre sbirri . . . Una carrozza . . . Presto! Seguila dovunque vada . . . Non visto . . . provvedi!
SPOLETTA Very well, sir. And later?	SPOLETTA Sta bene. Il convegno?
SCARPIA Report at the palace! (SPOLETTA *leaves hurriedly.* SCARPIA, *with a sardonic smile*) Go, Tosca! Into your life now enters Scarpia. Go, Tosca!	SCARPIA Palazzo Farnese! Va, Tosca! Nel tuo cuor s'annida Scarpia. Va, Tosca!
CHORUS Adjutorum nostrum in nomine Domini Qui fecit coelum terram Sit nomen Domini benedictum Et hoc nunc et usque in saeculum.	CORO Adjutorum nostrum in nomine Domini Qui fecit cœlum terram Sit nomen Domini benedictum Et hoc nunc et usque in sæculum.
SCARPIA Two goals now lure me, both rouse my desire: To see the rebel hanging is but half the prize I seek. Ah! In those wondrous eyes To kindle the flame of passion! (*with erotic passion*) Could I but taste, in Tosca's fiery embrace, Rapture unending, fierce delight of love! (*savagely*) One to the gallows, And the other to crush in my arms. (*the worshipers turn toward the high altar. Some kneel*)	SCARPIA A doppia mira tendo il voler, nè il capo del ribelle è la più preziosa. Ah di quegli occhi vittoriosi veder la fiamma illanguidir con spasimo d'amor fra le mie braccia illanguidir d'amor! L'uno al capestro, l'altra fra le mie braccia . . .
CHORUS Te Deum laudamus: te Dominum confitemur! (SCARPIA *remains motionless, lost in thought. Then, starting as though from a dream*)	CORO Te Deum laudamus: te Dominum confitemur!
SCARPIA Tosca, You lure my thoughts away from God! (SCARPIA, *with religious fervor, joins the throng in the finish of the* Te Deum)	SCARPIA Tosca, mi fai dimenticare Iddio!
SCARPIA, CHORUS Te aeternum Patrem omnis terra veneratur!	SCARPIA, CORO Te æternum Patrem omnis terra veneratur!

SCARPIA
Tosca è un buon falco!
Certo a quest'ora
i miei segugi le due prede
azzannano!
Doman sul palco
vedrà l'aurora
Angelotti e il bel Mario al
laccio pendere.

Tosca è a palazzo? . . .

SCIARRONE
Un ciambellan ne uscia
pur ora in traccia.

SCARPIA
Apri.

Tarda è la notte.
Alla cantata ancor manca la
Diva,
e strimpellan gavotte.
Tu attenderai la Tosca in sull'
entrata;
le dirai ch'io l'aspetto
finita la cantata . . .
o meglio . . .
le darai questo biglietto.
Ella verrà . . .

per amor del suo Mario!
Per amor del suo Mario al
piacer mio
s'arrenderà. Tal dei profondi
amori
è la profonda miseria.

Ha più forte
sapore la conquista violenta
che il mellifluo consenso. Io di
sospiri
e di lattiginose albe lunari
poco m'appago. Non so trarre
accordi
di chitarra, nè oròscopo di fior,
nè far l'occhio di pesce,
o tubar come tortora!

ACT II

The Farnese Palace. Scarpia's apartment on an upper floor. The table is set. A large window overlooks the courtyard of the palace. It is night.

SCARPIA (*seated at the table, supping. He interrupts his meal now and again to meditate. He looks at his watch, displaying intense restlessness and a feverish anxiety.*)
Tosca is useful!
Without knowing,
She leads my trusty men to their prey.
Tomorrow at sunrise
Angelotti and handsome Mario
Will be swinging from the gallows!
(*Rings a bell.* SCIARRONE *enters*)
Is Tosca in the palace?

SCIARRONE
I sent a chamberlain
To bring her here.

SCARPIA (*to* SCIARRONE, *pointing to the window*)
Open it.
(*the sound of an orchestra is heard from the lower floor, where the Queen of Naples is giving a grand ball in honor of the recently announced victory.*)
The hour is late.
(*to himself*)
Eager the crowd and gay, impatient for Tosca.
Meanwhile they dance the gavotte.
(*to* SCIARRONE)
You'll wait for Tosca by the palace gate.
Say that I will expect her
After the cantata.
(SCIARRONE *is about to leave.* SCARPIA, *recalling him*)
Or better . . .
(*he rises, goes to the desk, and hastily writes a note*)
She will come . . .
(*returns to the table and, pouring himself a drink, says*)
For the sake of her Mario!
For the sake of her Mario she will submit
To my desire. Love such as hers runs deep,
And brings grief in its wake.

Give me rather the pleasure
Of a violent conquest
Than an easy surrender!
I've little taste for tender sighing
'Neath the silvery moon that shines above,
Or romantic tinkling on guitars and murmurings of love.
I lack the gift for flirting,
Nor do I coo like a turtledove!

Power!—The thing I desire I must conquer!
I possess it and soon discard it,
Seeking other pleasure.
God created many wines, many women.
I fain would taste his works divine
In fullest measure.
(*he drinks*)

Bramo.—La cosa bramata
perseguo, me ne sazio e via la getto
volto a nuova esca.
Dio creò diverse
beltà, vini diversi. Io vo' gustar
quanto più posso dell'opra divina!

SCIARRONE (*enters*)
Spoletta's waiting.

SCIARRONE
Spoletta è giunto.

SCARPIA (*cries excitedly*)
Show him in at once.
(SCIARRONE *goes out to call* SPOLETTA, *whom he accompanies into the room.* SCARPIA *seats himself and, busy eating, questions* SPOLETTA *without looking at him*)
Well, my good fellow, how went the chase?

SCARPIA
Entri. In buon punto.
O galantuomo, com'andò la caccia? . . .

SPOLETTA (*coming forward a little, fearful*)
(St. Ignatius protect me!)
Swiftly we followed the trail of the lady.
Soon we arrived at a little villa
Surrounded by forest.
She went within and departed soon after.
Then I lightly leaped
Over the garden wall with my companions
And entered the house.

SPOLETTA
(Sant'Ignazio m'aiuta!)
Della signora seguimmo la traccia.
Giunti a un'erma villetta
tra le fratte perduta
ella v'entrò. N'escì sola ben presto.
Allor scavalco lesto
il muro del giardin coi miei cagnotti
e piombo in casa . . .

SCARPIA
Well done, Spoletta!

SCARPIA
Quel bravo Spoletta!

SPOLETTA (*hesitantly*)
We looked everywhere, searching!

SPOLETTA
Fiuto! . . . razzolo! . . . frugo . . . !

SCARPIA (*notices* SPOLETTA's *hesitancy and rises abruptly, pale with anger and frowning darkly*)
Well? Angelotti?

SCARPIA
Ah! l'Angelotti? . . .

SPOLETTA
We could not find him!

SPOLETTA
Non s'è trovato!

SCARPIA
You scoundrel! Blundering idiot!
Snout of an ape!
(*furious*)
I'll send you to the gallows!

SCARPIA
Ah cane! Ah traditore!
Ceffo di basilisco,
alle forche!

SPOLETTA (*trembling, seeks to assuage* SCARPIA's *anger*)
Oh Lord!
(*timidly*)
The painter was there.

SPOLETTA
Gesù!
C'era il pittor . . .

SCARPIA (*interrupting him*)
Cavaradossi?

SCARPIA
Cavaradossi?

SPOLETTA (*nods yes and suddenly adds*)
He knows where the other is hidden.
His every move, every word and gesture
Showed such scorn and defiance,
I thought it best to arrest him.

SPOLETTA
Ei sa dove l'altro s'asconde.
Ogni suo gesto
ogni accento, tradìa
tel beffarda ironia,
ch'io lo trassi in arresto!

SCARPIA
Meno male!

SPOLETTA
Egli è là.

SCARPIA
Introducete il Cavalier.
A me Roberti
e il Giudice del Fisco.

CAVARADOSSI
Tal violenza!

SCARPIA
Cavalier, vi piaccia accomodarvi.

CAVARADOSSI
Vo' saper . . .

SCARPIA
Sedete.

CAVARADOSSI
Aspetto.

SCARPIA
E sia!
V'è noto che un prigione . . .

CAVARADOSSI
La sua voce! . . .

SCARPIA
V'è noto che un prigione
oggi è fuggito da Castel
Sant' Angelo?

CAVARADOSSI
Ignoro.

SCARPIA
Eppur si pretende che voi
l'abbiate accolto in Sant' Andrea, provvisto
di cibo e vesti . . .

CAVARADOSSI
Menzogna!

SCARPIA (*obviously relieved*)
Now that is better!
(*he walks to and fro, thoughtful. Suddenly he stops. Through the open window is heard the cantata* performed by the choristers in the Queen's apartments, which means that* TOSCA *has arrived at the palace and is directly below*)

SPOLETTA (*pointing to the antechamber*)
He is there.

SCARPIA (*a thought occurs to him and he suddenly says to* SPOLETTA:)
Will you bring in Cavaradossi?
(SPOLETTA *leaves; to* SCIARRONE)
And you go summon
Roberti and the judge.
(SCIARRONE *leaves;* SCARPIA *resumes his seat at the table.* SPOLETTA *and three agents bring in* CAVARADOSSI. *Enter* ROBERTI, *the executioner, the* JUDGE, *a* CLERK, *and* SCIARRONE)

CAVARADOSSI (*haughtily, coming forward impetuously*)
What an outrage!

SCARPIA (*with studied courtesy*)
Noble sir, I beg you to be seated.

CAVARADOSSI
I wish to know—!

SCARPIA (*pointing to a chair at the opposite side of the table*)
Will you be seated?

CAVARDOSSI (*refusing*)
I'll stand.

SCARPIA
As you please.
(*looks fixedly at* CAVARADOSSI *before questioning him*)
Did you know that a prisoner . . .
(*he breaks off as he hears* TOSCA *in the cantata*)

CAVARADOSSI (*hearing* TOSCA's *voice, exclaims with emotion*)
She is singing! . . .

SCARPIA (*resuming*)
Did you know that this morning
A prisoner escaped from the Fortress Sant' Angelo?

CAVARADOSSI
I did not.

SCARPIA
And yet we have reason to believe
That you concealed him in St. Andrew's Church,
And provided him with food and with clothing . . .

CAVARADOSSI (*boldly*)
Sheer falsehoods!

* See page 1015 for cantata.

SCARPIA (*maintaining his calm*)
—And that later
You brought him to your villa in the country.
CAVARADOSSI
Lies! Who says this?
SCARPIA (*sweetly*)
A loyal subject.
CAVARADOSSI
What nonsense! Who is my accuser?
(*with irony*)
Your spies looked everywhere but could not find him.
SCARPIA
Proving that he's well hidden.
CAVARADOSSI
Your spies were quite thorough!
SPOLETTA (*offended, interrupts*)
Scornful and mocking, he laughed at all our endeavors.
CAVARADOSSI
And I still laugh!
SCARPIA (*rising grimly*)
This is no place for laughter!
(*threateningly*)
I warn you . . .
(*tensely*)
Enough!
Will you answer?
(*Irritated and disturbed by the singing below, he goes to close the window. Then, imperiously to* CAVARADOSSI)
Where's Angelotti?
CAVARADOSSI
I do not know.
SCARPIA
You deny that you furnished him with food?
CAVARADOSSI
Never!
SCARPIA
And clothing?
CAVARADOSSI
Never!
SCARPIA
And shelter in your villa,
Where still he lies hidden?
CAVARADOSSI (*vehemently*)
Never! Never!
SCARPIA (*becoming calm again, and almost fatherly*)
My dear sir, reflect a moment:
Your stubborn behavior is most unwise, believe me.
If you confess, you save yourself much trouble and great pain!
Take my advice, tell us:
Where is Angelotti?

SCARPIA
. . . e guidato
ad un vostro podere suburbano.
CAVARADOSSI
Nego.—Le prove?
SCARPIA
Un suddito fedele . . .
CAVARADOSSI
Al fatto. Chi m'accusa? â
I vostri birri invan frugar la villa.
SCARPIA
Segno che è ben celato.
CAVARADOSSI
Sospetti di spia!
SPOLETTA
Alle nostre ricerche egli rideva . . .
CAVARADOSSI
E rido ancor, e rido ancor.
SCARPIA
Questo è luogo di lacrime!
Badate!
Or basta!
Rispondete!
Ov'è Angelotti?
CAVARADOSSI
Non lo so.
SCARPIA
Negate d'avergli dato cibo?
CAVARADOSSI
Nego!
SCARPIA
E vesti?
CAVARADOSSI
Nego!
SCARPIA
E asilo nella villa?
E che là sia nascosto?
CAVARADOSSI
Nego! nego!
SCARPIA
Via, Cavaliere, riflettete:
saggia non è cotesta ostinatezza vostra.
Angoscia grande, pronta confessione eviterà!
Io vi consiglio, dite:
dov'è dunque Angelotti?

CAVARADOSSI Non lo so.	CAVARADOSSI I do not know.
SCARPIA Ancor, l'ultima volta. Dov'è?	SCARPIA Once more, and for the last time: Tell me!
CAVARADOSSI Nol so!	CAVARADOSSI I do not know!
SPOLETTA (O bei tratti di corda!)	SPOLETTA (Maybe he needs some urging!)
SCARPIA (Eccola!)	SCARPIA (*catching sight of* TOSCA—*aside*) Here she comes!
TOSCA Mario, tu qui?!	TOSCA (*enters, anxious. She sees* CAVARADOSSI *and runs to embrace him*) Mario, why here?
CAVARADOSSI (Di quanto là vedesti, taci, o m'uccidi!)	CAVARADOSSI (*under his breath to* TOSCA, *who signifies that she understands*) Not a word of what you saw, Or you destroy me!
SCARPIA Mario Cavaradossi, qual testimone il Giudice v'aspetta.	SCARPIA Mario Cavaradossi, You will now bear witness. Your judge awaits you. (*he motions to* SCIARRONE *to open the entrance to the torture chamber. Turning to* ROBERTI)
Pria le forme ordinarie. Indi . . . ai miei cenni . . .	First the usual questions. Then—as I instruct you. (*the* JUDGE *goes into the torture chamber. The others follow, only* TOSCA *and* SCARPIA *remain behind.* SPOLETTA *withdraws to the door in the rear of the room.* SCIARRONE *shuts the entrance to the torture chamber.* TOSCA *looks greatly surprised.* SCARPIA, *studiously polite, reassures her. Gallantly*)
Ed or fra noi parliam da buoni amici. Via quell'aria sgomentata . . .	Now let us have a friendly chat together. You have no cause to be alarmed. (*motions to* TOSCA *to sit down*)
TOSCA Sgomento alcun non ho.	TOSCA (*sits down with affected calm*) I'm not, you may be sure.
SCARPIA La storia del ventaglio? . . .	SCARPIA (*he walks behind the sofa on which* TOSCA *is sitting, and leans over it*) Your fears about the fan?
TOSCA Fu sciocca gelosia.	TOSCA (*feigning indifference*) Mere jealousy and folly.
SCARPIA L'Attavanti non era dunque alla villa?	SCARPIA So the Attavanti was not at the villa?
TOSCA No: egli era solo.	TOSCA No. He was quite alone.
SCARPIA Solo? Ne siete ben sicura?	SCARPIA Really? (*inquiring maliciously*) You seem to be quite certain.
TOSCA Nulla sfugge ai gelosi. Solo! Solo!	TOSCA Nothing escapes those who love. (*insisting angrily*) There was no one!

SCARPIA (*places a chair in front of* TOSCA *and sits down, staring at her intently*)
Indeed?

TOSCA (*very much annoyed*)
Indeed!

SCARPIA
Why so angry? Is there something
You fear you might betray?
(*He turns toward the entrance to the torture chamber and calls:*)
Sciarrone, what says the witness now?

SCIARRONE (*appears on the threshold*)
Nothing.

SCARPIA (*in a louder voice*)
You must urge him.
(SCIARRONE *goes back, closing the door behind him*)

TOSCA (*laughing*)
Oh! it's useless!

SCARPIA (*gravely rises and walks about*)
We shall soon see, dear lady.

TOSCA (*slowly, with an ironic smile*)
Then if he is to please you he must feed you with lies?

SCARPIA
No. But the truth will help him escape an hour
Of pain and anguish.

TOSCA (*surprised*)
Of pain and anguish? What does this mean?
What happens in that chamber?

SCARPIA
The law must be enforced
With all firmness.

TOSCA
Oh God! What now?!

SCARPIA (*with a fierce expression and mounting vehemence*)
Bound hand and foot, your lover lies helpless,
A band of steel round his temples.
And each denial, stubborn and false,
Is sealed with his blood!

TOSCA (*leaping to her feet*)
Oh no! Oh no! Those merciless demons!
(*she listens anxiously, her hands nervously clutching the back of the sofa*)

CAVARADOSSI
Ah!
(*a prolonged groan*)

TOSCA (*almost spoken*)
They torture him! Have pity . . . have pity!

SCARPIA
But you can save him.

SCARPIA
Davver?!

TOSCA
Solo! sì!

SCARPIA
Quanto fuoco! Par che abbiate paura
di tradirvi.
Sciarrone: che dice il Cavalier?

SCIARRONE
Nega.

SCARPIA
Insistiamo.

TOSCA
Oh! è inutil!

SCARPIA
Lo vedremo, signora.

TOSCA
Dunque per compiacervi si dovrebbe mentir?

SCARPIA
No: ma il vero potrebbe abbreviargli un'ora
assai penosa . . .

TOSCA
Un'ora penosa? Che vuol dir?
Che avviene in quella stanza?

SCARPIA
È forza che s'adempia
la legge.

TOSCA
Oh! Dio! . . . che avvien?!

SCARPIA
Legato mani e piè
il vostro amante ha un cerchio uncinato alle tempia,
che ad ogni niego ne sprizza sangue
senza mercè.

TOSCA
Non è ver, non è ver! Sogghigno di demone . . .

CAVARADOSSI
Ahimè!

TOSCA
Un gemito? Pietà . . . pietà!

SCARPIA
Sta in voi salvarlo.

TOSCA Ebben . . . ma cessate, cessate!	TOSCA Very well. But stop it, stop it!
SCARPIA Sciarrone, sciogliete.	SCARPIA (*moving closer to the entrance and opening it*) Sciarrone, untie him.
SCIARRONE Tutto?	SCIARRONE (*appearing at the threshold*) Completely?
SCARPIA Tutto. Ed or la verità . . .	SCARPIA Yes. (SCIARRONE *re-enters the torture chamber, shutting the door*) And now I want the truth.
TOSCA Ch'io lo veda!	TOSCA Let me see him!
SCARPIA No!	SCARPIA No!
TOSCA Mario!	TOSCA (*gradually manages to approach the doorway*) Mario!
CAVARADOSSI Tosca!	CAVARADOSSI (*within, sorrowfully*) Tosca!
TOSCA Ti straziano ancora?	TOSCA Are they hurting you still?
CAVARADOSSI No—corragio—Taci, taci! Sprezzo il dolor!	CAVARADOSSI No. Take courage. Be silent, silent! I will not yield!
SCARPIA Orsù Tosca, parlate.	SCARPIA (*moving toward* TOSCA) And now . . . speak out, fair Tosca.
TOSCA Non so nulla!	TOSCA (*heartened by* MARIO'S *words*) I know nothing!
SCARPIA Non vale quella prova? Roberti, ripigliamo . . .	SCARPIA You've not yet been persuaded? (*walks toward the entrance*) Roberti, we continue.
TOSCA No! fermate!	TOSCA No! You shall not! (*Thrusts herself between* SCARPIA *and the entrance, to prevent him from giving the order*)
SCARPIA Voi parlerete?	SCARPIA Will you then speak?
TOSCA No! no! . . . Ah! mostro! lo strazi, ah! mostro, lo strazi, l'uccidi . . . ah, l'uccidi!	TOSCA No! No! Ah, you monster, You will crush him. You fiend of hell, You will destroy my Mario. Ah yes, you will kill him!
SCARPIA Lo strazia quel vostro silenzio assai più.	SCARPIA You harm Mario with your stubborn silence More than I do. (*laughs*)
TOSCA Tu ridi . . . all'orrida pena?	TOSCA You laugh, brute? You laugh at his torment?
SCARPIA Mai Tosca alla scena più tragica fu!	SCARPIA (*with enthusiasm*) But Tosca was never so great On the stage!

(TOSCA, *horrified, retreats from* SCARPIA, *who turns to* SPOLETTA *in a sudden access of sadism, shouting*)
Open wide the door.
Let her hear his groaning!
(SPOLETTA *flings open the door and plants himself on the threshold*)

Aprite le porte
che n'oda i lamenti!

CAVARADOSSI (*from within*)
I defy you!

CAVARADOSSI
Vi sfido!

SCARPIA (*shouting to* ROBERTI)
Now force him! Now force him!

SCARPIA
Più forte! più forte!

CAVARADOSSI
I defy you!

CAVARADOSSI
Vi sfido!

SCARPIA (*to* TOSCA)
Will you speak?

SCARPIA
Parlate . . .

TOSCA
What can I say?

TOSCA
Che dire?

SCARPIA
You know.

SCARPIA
Su, via . . .

TOSCA (*in despair*)
Ah! But I know nothing!
Oh, must I lie to you?

TOSCA
Ah! non so nulla!
Ah! dovrei mentir?

SCARPIA (*insistent*)
Tell where is Angelotti!

SCARPIA
Dite dov'è Angelotti?

TOSCA
No! No!

TOSCA
No! no!

SCARPIA (*pressing* TOSCA)
Tell me where is Angelotti!
Reveal where he lies hidden. Now tell the truth at last.
Speak out, now tell me: where is he?

SCARPIA
Dite dov'è Angelotti?
parlate su, via, dove celato sta?
Su, via parlate. Ov'è?

TOSCA
How shall I bear it? How bear this torment?
Ah, stop this torture, I beg! I cannot endure it!
(*she turns pleadingly to* SCARPIA, *who motions to* SPOLETTA *to allow her to draw near. She goes to the open passageway and, overwhelmed by the horror of the scene, appeals to* CAVARADOSSI)
I can bear no more . . . I can bear no more!

TOSCA
Ah! Più non posso! Ah! che orror!
Ah! cessate il martir! è troppo soffrir!
Ah! non posso più . . . ah! non posso più!

CAVARADOSSI (*from within, with a loud cry*)
Ah!

CAVARADOSSI
Ahimè!

TOSCA (*near the door of the torture chamber, in anguish*)
Mario, permit me to tell them . . .

TOSCA
Mario, consenti ch'io parli?

CAVARADOSSI (*in a broken voice*)
No! No!

CAVARADOSSI
No! No!

TOSCA
I beg you! I cannot bear it.

TOSCA
Ascolta, non posso più . . .

CAVARADOSSI
Tosca, you know nothing. What could you tell?

CAVARADOSSI
Stolta, che sai? . . . che puoi dir? . . .

SCARPIA (*infuriated by* CAVARADOSSI'S *words, and fearful lest* TOSCA *be encouraged to maintain silence, shouts violently at* SPOLETTA)

SCARPIA
Ma fatelo tacere!

Silence him, you fools!

(*SPOLETTA enters the torture chamber, from which he soon emerges, while TOSCA, overcome by emotion, falls prostrate on the sofa and appeals in a sobbing voice to SCARPIA, who remains impassive and silent*)

TOSCA
Che v'ho fatto in vita mia?!
Son io che così torturate!
Torturate l'anima . . .
sì, l'anima mi torturate!

TOSCA
What wrong have I ever done you
That you so cruelly torture my spirit
And rack me with pain beyond bearing . . .
(*bursts into convulsive sobbing, murmuring*)
Pain and grief past all enduring!

(*SPOLETTA, in an attitude of prayer, mutters: "Judex ergo cum sedebit quidquid latet apparebit nil inultum remanebit." SCARPIA, profiting from the fact that TOSCA is near breaking point, goes toward the torture chamber and gives a sign to begin the punishment anew.*)

CAVARADOSSI
Ah!

CAVARADOSSI (*emitting a prolonged cry of pain*)
Ah!

TOSCA
Nel pozzo . . . nel giardino . . .

TOSCA (*upon hearing CAVARADOSSI groan, leaps up and in a choked voice says quickly to SCARPIA*)
The well . . . in the garden . . .

SCARPIA
Là è l'Angelotti?

SCARPIA
There? Angelotti?

TOSCA
Sì! . . .

TOSCA (*choking*)
Yes!

SCARPIA
Basta, Roberti.

SCARPIA (*loudly, toward the torture chamber*)
Enough, Roberti.

SCIARRONE
È svenuto!

SCIARRONE (*appearing at the door*)
He has fainted!

TOSCA
Assassino!
Voglio vederlo . . .

TOSCA (*to SCARPIA*)
You murd'rer!
Now let me see him.

SCARPIA
Portatelo qui!

SCARPIA (*to SCIARRONE*)
Bring him here!

(*SCIARRONE re-enters. CAVARADOSSI, in a faint, is carried in by the agents and laid on the sofa. TOSCA runs to him, but is stricken with horror at the sight of his bleeding face and stops, covering her eyes with her hands. Then, ashamed of her weakness, she kneels beside him, showering upon him kisses that mingle with her tears. Exit SCIARRONE, the JUDGE, ROBERTI and the CLERK, at the back. At a sign from SCARPIA the agents and SPOLETTA remain*)

CAVARADOSSI
Floria!

CAVARADOSSI (*reviving*)
Tosca!

TOSCA
Amore . . .

TOSCA
Beloved . . .

CAVARADOSSI
Sei tu? . . .

CAVARADOSSI
My own!

TOSCA (*warmly*)
How you have suffered, oh Mario mine.
But that cruel tyrant shall suffer too!

CAVARADOSSI
Tosca, did you tell them?

TOSCA
No, my love . . .

CAVARADOSSI
But truly?

TOSCA
No!

SCARPIA (*to* SPOLETTA, *with authority*)
The well in the garden. Go, Spoletta!
(SPOLETTA *leaves*)

CAVARADOSSI (*rises against* TOSCA, *menacingly*)
You've betrayed me!
(*falls back, exhausted*)

TOSCA (*impulsively embracing* CAVARADOSSI)
Mario!

CAVARADOSSI (*thrusting her from him*)
You've betrayed me!

TOSCA
Mario!

SCIARRONE (*rushing in, excited*)
Sir, I bring you dreadful tidings!

SCARPIA (*surprised*)
What has happened? Why so gloomy?

SCIARRONE
Our troops have been defeated . . .

SCARPIA
How defeated? Where? And when?

SCIARRONE
At Marengo . . .

SCARPIA (*cries impatiently*)
Speak, you idiot!

SCIARRONE
Bonaparte has conquered all.

SCARPIA
And we?

SCIARRONE
Alas, our men are fleeing! . . .

CAVARADOSSI (*has listened to* SCIARRONE'S *words with mounting anxiety. From sheer exultation he now finds the strength to leap up and confront* SCARPIA *threateningly:*)
We triumph! We triumph!

Now let freedom awake,
Let all tyrants now quake!
As the dawn of a new day brings
Deliverance!
In my pain, my despair,

TOSCA
Quanto hai penato anima mia!
Ma il giusto Iddio lo punirà!

CAVARADOSSI
Tosca, hai parlato?

TOSCA
No, amor . . .

CAVARADOSSI
Davvero? . . .

TOSCA
No!

SCARPIA
Nel pozzo del giardino.—Va,
Spoletta.

CAVARADOSSI
M'hai tradito! . . .

TOSCA
Mario!

CAVARADOSSI
Maledetta!

TOSCA
Mario!

SCIARRONE
Eccellenza, quali nuove! . . .

SCARPIA
Che vuol dir quell'aria afflitta?

SCIARRONE
Un messaggio di sconfitta . . .

SCARPIA
Qual sconfitta? Come? Dove?

SCIARRONE
A Marengo . . .

SCARPIA
Tartaruga!

SCIARRONE
Bonaparte è vincitor . . .

SCARPIA
Melas!

SCIARRONE
No. Melas è in fuga! . . .

CAVARADOSSI
Vittoria! Vittoria!

L'alba vindice appar
che fa gli empi tremar!
Libertà sorge, crollan tirannidi!
Del sofferto martir
me vedrai qui gioir . . .
il tuo cor trema, o Scarpia,
carnefice!

I see joy everywhere,
While your heart sinks with fear, oh Scarpia,
Your doom is near!

TOSCA
Mario, taci, pietà di me! pietà! taci!
non l'ascoltate!
Pietà! pietà di me!

TOSCA (*clinging desperately to* CAVARADOSSI, *trying to calm him*)
Mario, quiet! Oh pity me! My love—quiet!
(*to* SCARPIA)
Ah, do not heed him!
Have pity! Oh pity me!

SCARPIA
Braveggia, urla!—T'affretta
a palesarmi il fondo
dell'alma ria!
Va!—Moribondo,
il capestro t'aspetta!
Portatemelo via!

SCARPIA (*during the proceedings stares cynically at* CAVARADOSSI, *then he smiles sarcastically*)
Keep boasting, villain!—revealing
The hideous dregs
Of your accursed soul!
Now death awaits you.
Soon the gallows will end your treason!
(*infuriated by* CAVARADOSSI'S *words, he shouts to the agents*)
Take this fool away!
(SCIARRONE *and the agents seize* CAVARADOSSI *and drag him toward the door*)

TOSCA
Mario . . . con te . . .
No, no!

TOSCA
Mario . . . with you . . .
(*opposing them with all her strength*)
No, no!

SCARPIA
Va moribondo! Va, va!

SCARPIA
Go to your doom! Go, go!

TOSCA
Ah! Mario . . . Mario!
con te . . . con te!

TOSCA (*clinging to* MARIO, *and resisting the agents with all her might*)
Ah! Mario . . . Mario!
(*she tries to force her way past* SCARPIA)
With you . . . my love!

SCARPIA
Voi no!

SCARPIA (*holds her back and shuts the door*)
Not you!

TOSCA
Salvatelo!

TOSCA (*moaning*)
Oh, save him!

SCARPIA
Io? . . . Voi!
La povera mia cena fu interrotta.
Così accasciata? . . . Via, mia bella signora
sedete qui.—Volete che cerchiamo
insieme il modo di salvarlo?
E allor sedete . . . e favelliamo . . . E intanto
un sorso.
È vin di Spagna . . .
Un sorso per rincorarvi.

SCARPIA
I? . . . You!
(*he approaches the table, notices his interrupted supper. Once again he is calm and smiling*)
You see, my lonely meal was interrupted.
(*seeing that* TOSCA *remains by the door, motionless and downcast*)
Why so disheartened? Come, my sweet and gentle lady,
And sit by me! Shall you and I together
Seek some way of saving Mario?
(*sits down, motioning to* TOSCA *to do the same*)
Come here . . . be seated. Let's talk this over.
Some wine, fair lady?
(*polishes a wineglass with his napkin, then looks at it against the light of the candelabrum*)

A splendid vintage . . .
(*he pours. Graciously*)
Please have some, to raise your spirit.

TOSCA (*sits down facing* SCARPIA, *looking at him fixedly. Leaning her elbows on the table, her hands against her face, and with the deepest possible contempt in her voice, she asks*)
How much?

TOSCA
Quanto?

SCARPIA (*imperturbable, and pouring himself a drink*)
How much?

SCARPIA
Quanto?

TOSCA
Your price!

TOSCA
Il prezzo! . . .

SCARPIA (*laughs*)
True, they say I can be bought. They say I have my price.
But to lovely women
I do not sell my favors for paltry sums of money.
No . . . No!
(*suggestively, and with meaning*)
To charming women
I do not sell myself for paltry sums of money.
If I must betray my honor and trust,
I'll choose more pleasant payment;
Ah yes, more delightful payment.
This hour I've long awaited!

Fierce desire consumes my heart,
Ah Tosca divine,
As you stood before me trembling with anger,
I vowed you would soon be mine!
Ah! Your tears rouse strange excitement,
I long to caress you.
All the hate you bear me only enhances
My craving to possess you!
Oh! So graceful and lithe,
You entwined your arms round your lover.
In that moment, Tosca,
I vowed to make you mine!
Mine!
(*approaches* TOSCA *with open arms*)

SCARPIA
Già.—Mi dicon venal, mi dicon venal,
ma a donna bella
non mi vendo a prezzo di moneta . . .
no! no!
A donna bella
io non mi vendo a prezzo di moneta.
Se la giurata fede
debbo tradir, ne voglio altra mercede,
ne voglio altra mercede.
Quest'ora io l'attendeva!

Già mi struggea
l'amor della diva! . . .
Ma poc'anzi ti mirai
qual non ti vidi mai!
Quel tuo pianto era lava
ai sensi miei—e il tuo sguardo
che odio in me dardeggiava,
mie brame inferociva!
Agil qual leopardo
t'avvinghiasti all'amante—
Ah! In quell'istante
t'ho giurata mia!
Mia!

TOSCA (*who has listened without stirring, horrified by his lascivious proposal, jumps up and seeks refuge behind the sofa*)
Ah!

TOSCA
Ah!

SCARPIA (*following her*)
You'll be mine . . . You'll be mine!

SCARPIA
Si, t'avrò . . . Si, t'avrò!

TOSCA (*in horror, rushes to the window*)
Ah! I leap if you approach me!

TOSCA
Ah! Piuttosto giù m'avvento!

SCARPIA (*coldly*)
But Mario stays behind as hostage.

SCARPIA
In pegno il Mario tuo mi resta! . . .

TOSCA
Ah! miserabile . . .
l'orribil mercato!

TOSCA
Oh, how can human heart
Encompass such evil!
(it occurs to her to appeal to the Queen. She runs toward the door)

SCARPIA
Violenza non ti farò.
Sei libera. Va pure.
Ma è fallace speranza: la Regina
farebbe grazia ad un cadavere!

SCARPIA *(divining her intention, draws aside)*
I shall not hold you by force.
You are free to go, I assure you.
(TOSCA, *with a cry of joy, is about to escape.* SCARPIA, *laughing ironically, restrains her with a gesture.*)
But if you run to the Queen,
Her help will come much too late to save your Mario!
(TOSCA *returns, frightened, and drops onto the sofa, staring at* SCARPIA. *Then she averts her eyes, with a gesture of supreme disgust and loathing.* SCARPIA, *in an assured and complacent tone*)

Come tu m'odii!

How you despise me!

TOSCA
Ah! Dio! . . .

TOSCA *(with all possible loathing and disgust)*
You beast!

SCARPIA
Così, così ti voglio!

SCARPIA *(drawing closer to her)*
But this is just how I want you!

TOSCA
Non toccarmi, demonio! T'odio, t'odio,
abbietto, vile!

TOSCA *(desperate)*
Do not touch me, you demon! I loathe you, loathe you,
You ruthless villain!
(flees from SCARPIA *in horror)*

SCARPIA
Che importa?!
Spasimi d'ira, spasimi d'amore!

SCARPIA
Does it matter?
(coming still closer to her)
Hatred and love are never far apart!

TOSCA
Vile!

TOSCA
Villain!

SCARPIA
Mia!

SCARPIA *(tries to seize her)*
Mine!

TOSCA
Vile!

TOSCA *(takes refuge behind the table)*
Villain!

SCARPIA
Mia!

SCARPIA
Mine!
(pursues TOSCA*)*

TOSCA
Aiuto!

TOSCA
Oh, help me!

SCARPIA
Mia!

SCARPIA *(cries out)*
Mine!

TOSCA
Aiuto!

TOSCA
Oh, help me!

SCARPIA
Mia!

SCARPIA *(shouting)*
Mine!

TOSCA
Aiuto!

TOSCA
Oh, help me!
(Drums from afar, gradually drawing closer. Both stop)

SCARPIA
Odi?
È il tamburo. S'avvia. Guida

SCARPIA
Listen!

Hear the drums beat . . . Drawing closer. Those about to die
Have come to the end of their journey.
Your time runs out!
(TOSCA, *having listened with terrible anxiety, leaves the window and leans wearily on the sofa.*)
See! The fearsome preparations are now completed.
Look! How high stand the gallows!
(TOSCA *shudders in fear and despair.* SCARPIA, *approaching her*)
Because of you—yes, because of you!—
The final hour now approaches for your Mario.
(TOSCA *drops wearily on the sofa, overcome with grief. Coldly* SCARPIA *leans on a corner of the table, pours himself coffee and drinks it, his eyes fastened on* TOSCA)

la scorta ultima ai condannati.
Il tempo passa!
Sai quale oscura opra laggiù si compia?
Là si drizza un patibolo.
Al tuo Mario, per tuo voler,
non resta che un'ora di vita.

TOSCA

Love and beauty, life's fairest treasures,
These humbly I served and dearly cherished.
Kindness and pity
Gladly I gave to the poor and afflicted.
Ever with fervent devotion,
I prayed to God,
Trusting fully in His truth divine.
With simple joy, I brought
Bright flowers to the sacred shrine.
In this my hour of sorrow,
I stand alone, forsaken.
Is this, O Lord, to be my just reward?
Rare gifts I gave,
And jewels for the Madonna;
My songs I offered to stars and sky
In praise of their beauty.
And now, in time of grief,
Is this my just reward, O Lord!
Oh why am I forsaken now? Oh why?
(*she sobs*)

TOSCA

Vissi d'arte, vissi d'amore, non feci mai
male ad anima viva!
Con man furtiva
quante miserie conobbi, aiutai . . .
Sempre con fè sincera
la mia preghiera
ai santi tabernacoli salì.
Sempre con fè sincera,
diedi fiori agli altar.
Nell'ora del dolore
perchè, perchè, Signore,
perchè me ne rimuneri così?
Diedi gioielli
della Madonna al manto,
e diedi il canto
agli astri, al ciel, che ne ridean più belli.
Nell'ora del dolor
perchè, perchè, Signor,
Ah, perchè me ne rimuneri così?

SCARPIA

Make your choice!

SCARPIA

Risolvi!

TOSCA

At your feet I beg for mercy.
(*kneels before* SCARPIA)
Hear me . . .
(*sobbing*)
With hands outstretched I implore you!
(*raising her clasped hands*)
Scarpia—hear me . . .
(*in desperation*)
Grant my entreaty!
Do not crush
My anguished spirit.

TOSCA

Mi vuoi supplice a tuoi piedi?
Vedi . . .
le man giunte io stendo a te!
Ecco—vedi,
e mercè . . .
d'un tuo detto,
vinta aspetto.

SCARPIA
Sei troppo bella, Tosca, e troppo amante.
Cedo.—A misero prezzo;
tu, a me una vita, io, a te chieggo un'istante!

TOSCA
Va! va! Mi fai ribrezzo!
Va! va!

SCARPIA
Chi è là?

SPOLETTA
Eccellenza, l'Angelotti al nostro giungere s'uccise!

SCARPIA
Ebben lo si appenda
morto alle forche! E l'altro prigionier?

SPOLETTA
Il cavalier Cavaradossi? È tutto pronto, Eccellenza!

TOSCA
Dio m'assisti!

SCARPIA
Aspetta.

Ebbene?

Odi . . .

TOSCA
Ma libero all'istante lo voglio!

SCARPIA
Occorre simular. Non posso
far grazia aperta. Bisogna che tutti
abbian per morto il cavalier.
Quest'uomo fido provvederà.

TOSCA
Chi m'assicura?

SCARPIA
L'ordin ch'io gli darò voi qui presente.
Spoletta: chiudi.
Ho mutato d'avviso.
Il prigionier sia fucilato. Attendi . . .
Come facemmo del conte Palmieri.

SCARPIA
You are far too lovely, Tosca, and far too devoted.
I yield!—My price you'll find quite modest:
I grant you Mario, you grant me but an instant!

TOSCA (*rises, with an expression of intense disgust*)
Go, go! You disgust me!
Go, go!
(*a knock on the door*)

SCARPIA
Who's there?

SPOLETTA (*enters breathless and excited*)
Noble Baron, as we approached,
Angelotti swallowed poison!

SCARPIA
Then tell them to hang his corpse
On the gallows. And how fares the other?

SPOLETTA
You mean Cavaradossi?
All is prepared, noble Baron!

TOSCA (*aside*)
Heaven help me!

SCARPIA (*to* SPOLETTA)
One moment.
(*softly to* TOSCA)
Your decision?
(TOSCA *nods assent; then, weeping for shame, she buries her head in the cushions of the sofa.* SCARPIA, *to* SPOLETTA)
Listen . . .

TOSCA (*interrupting* SCARPIA)
But you must set him free at once!

SCARPIA (*to* TOSCA)
We must be very cautious.
I cannot release him openly. It must be so arranged
That everyone believes he is dead.
(*points to* SPOLETTA)
This worthy fellow will see to it.

TOSCA
How can I be certain?

SCARPIA
By the orders I give him in your presence.
(*turning to* SPOLETTA, *points to the door*)
Spoletta: close it.
(SPOLETTA *quickly shuts the door and comes back.* SCARPIA *looks significantly at* SPOLETTA, *who, divining* SCARPIA'*s meaning, nods repeatedly that he understands*)
I have changed the sentence.
Cavaradossi will be shot. Mark me well:
Just as we did with Count Palmieri!

SPOLETTA
An execution . . .

SCARPIA (*suddenly with marked emphasis*)
But not a real one! . . . The same
As with Palmieri! You understand me?

SPOLETTA
I understand you.

SCARPIA
Go.

TOSCA (*who has listened eagerly, interrupts*)
I wish to tell him myself.

SCARPIA
You may.
(*to* SPOLETTA, *indicating* TOSCA)
You will admit her. Remember:
(*deliberately emphasizing*)
At four o'clock.

SPOLETTA (*with meaning*)
Yes. As with Palmieri . . .
(*exit*)

SCARPIA (*close to the door, listens to* SPOLETTA*'s receding footsteps. Then, completely changing his expression, he approaches* TOSCA *with passion*)
You see, I've kept my promise.

TOSCA (*restraining him*)
Not entirely.
Mario and I will need a safe-conduct,
So that we may quit Rome together.

SCARPIA (*gallantly*)
You really mean to leave us?

TOSCA (*with conviction*)
Yes. Forever!

SCARPIA
Your wish shall now be granted.
(*he goes to the desk and begins to write, breaking off in order to inquire of* TOSCA:)
What road will you travel?

TOSCA
The shortest!

SCARPIA
By the north gate?

TOSCA
Yes.
(*while* SCARPIA *is writing,* TOSCA *approaches the table and with trembling hand takes the glass that* SCARPIA *had filled. As she raises it to her lips, she notices on the table a knife with a sharp point. She glances quickly at* SCARPIA, *who is still busy writing. With infinite caution she gains possession of the knife, which she hides behind her, leaning on the table as she carefully watches* SCARPIA. *He finishes writing the safe-conduct,*

SPOLETTA
Un'uccisione . . .

SCARPIA
. . . simulata! . . . Come
avvene del Palmieri! . . . Hai
ben compreso?

SPOLETTA
Ho ben compreso.

SCARPIA
Va.

TOSCA
Voglio avvertirlo io stessa.

SCARPIA
E sia.
Le darai passo. Bada:
all'ora quarta.

SPOLETTA
Sì. Come Palmieri . . .

SCARPIA
Io tenni la promessa.

TOSCA
Non ancora.
Voglio un salvacondotto onde
fuggir
dallo Stato con lui.

SCARPIA
Partir dunque volete?

TOSCA
Sì, per sempre!

SCARPIA
Si adempia il voler vostro.
E qual via scegliete?

TOSCA
La più breve!

SCARPIA
Civitavecchia?

TOSCA
Sì.

SCARPIA
Tosca, finalmente mia!
Maledetta!!

TOSCA
Questo è il bacio di Tosca!

SCARPIA
Aiuto! Muoio!
Soccorso! Muoio! Ah! . . .

TOSCA
Ti soffoca il sangue?

SCARPIA
Soccorso!

TOSCA
Ti soffoca il sangue?

SCARPIA
Aiuto! . . .

TOSCA
Ah! . . .

SCARPIA
Muoio, muoio!

TOSCA
E ucciso da una donna!

SCARPIA
Aiuto!

TOSCA
M'hai assai torturata! . . .

SCARPIA
Soccorso! muoio!

TOSCA
Odi tu ancora? Parla! . . .
Guardami! . . .
Son Tosca, o Scarpia!!

SCARPIA
Soccorso, aiuto!

TOSCA
Ti soffoca il sangue?

SCARPIA
Muoio!

TOSCA
Muori dannato!
Muori, muori, muori!

SCARPIA
Ah! . . .

affixes his seal, and folds the document, then, with open arms, he goes to TOSCA *in order to embrace her)*

SCARPIA
Tosca, now at last you are mine!
(but his voluptuous tone changes abruptly into a terrible cry as TOSCA *stabs him full in the chest. He cries out)*
God damn you!

TOSCA *(crying out)*
This is the kiss of Tosca!

SCARPIA *(in a choked voice)*
Help! I am dying!
(staggering, he clutches in vain at TOSCA, *who draws back in terror)*
Help me! I am dying! Ah . . .

TOSCA *(with loathing)*
May your blood now choke you!

SCARPIA *(choking)*
Oh, help me!

TOSCA
May your sins now devour you!

SCARPIA *(struggles in vain and tries to pull himself up, clutching at the sofa)*
Oh, help me!

TOSCA
Ah! . . .

SCARPIA
Dying! I am dying!

TOSCA
And slain by a woman!

SCARPIA
Please help me!

TOSCA
Did you torture me enough!

SCARPIA *(growing weaker)*
Please help me! I die!
(makes a final attempt and falls, turning over)

TOSCA
Can you still hear me? Speak! Look at me!
I am Tosca, O Scarpia!

SCARPIA *(suffocating)*
Help . . . help!

TOSCA
You drown in your blood . . .

SCARPIA *(breathing his last)*
Death!

TOSCA *(bending over* SCARPIA*'s face)*
Die with my curse!
Die . . . die . . . die!

SCARPIA *(without voice)*
Ah! . . . *(dies)*

TOSCA

He is dead. Now I forgive him!

(without removing her eyes from SCARPIA'S *body, she goes to the table, takes a bottle of water, and, wetting a napkin, washes her fingers. Then she straightens her hair before the mirror. She remembers the safe-conduct and looks for it on the desk but does not find it. She searches anew, finally spies it in the dead man's clenched fist. She raises* SCARPIA'S *arm slightly and lets it fall limply after having taken the safe-conduct, which she hides in her bosom)*

And before this man all Rome trembled!

(she is on the point of leaving but reconsiders. She takes two candles that stand on a little table to the left and lights them from the candelabrum on the table, which she then extinguishes. She sets down one candle to the right of SCARPIA'S *head, and places the other candle to the left. She looks about and, seeing a crucifix on the wall, takes it down. She kneels beside the corpse and lays it reverently on* SCARPIA'S *breast. She rises quietly and steals out, shutting the door carefully behind her)*

TOSCA

È morto! Or gli perdono!

E avanti a lui tremava tutta Roma!

THE CANTATA *(heard in Act II during the scene between* SCARPIA *and* CAVARADOSSI*)*

Gently sing we a hymn of praise to the Lord of Hosts.
Soaring skyward, sweet tender music,
 Through the blue empyrean.
Ever rising, while the spheres praise
 The Almighty King of Kings!
May this hymn now soar aloft to Thee!
This hymn of glory now ascends to Thee,
 Almighty God of glory,
Who created heaven and earth . . .
Thou wert mighty ere the angels first sang their songs.
 This hymn to Thy glory
 Now soars aloft to Thee!
Gently sing we a hymn of praise to the Lord of Hosts.
Soaring skyward, sweet tender music,
 To Thy glory, mighty Lord, O King of Kings!

LA CANTATA

Sale, ascende l'uman cantico
varca spazi, varca cieli,
per ignoti empirei,
profetati dai Vangeli
a Te giunge, o Re dei Re!
Questo canto voli a Te . . .
quest'inno di gloria voli
sommo Iddo della vittoria,
Dio che fosti innanzi ai secoli,
alle cantiche degli angeli
quest'inno di gloria,
or voli a Te!
Sale, ascende l'uman cantico
varca spazi, varca cieli,
a Te o Re dei Re!

ACT III

(A platform of the Fortress Sant' Angelo. To the left, a casemate. A table with a lamp, writing materials, and a large register. A bench. A chair. On one wall of the casemate hangs a crucifix, with a lamp suspended before it. To the right, the opening of a little staircase that leads to the platform. The Vatican and St. Peter's are visible in the background. Night. A clear sky, brilliant with stars. Sheep-bells tinkle in the distance and gradually recede.)

UN PASTORE Io de' sospiri, Te ne rimanno tanti . . . Pe' quante foje Ne smoveno li venti. To me disprezzi Io me disprezzi Lampena d'oro Me fai morir!	A SHEPHERD Weeping and sighing Because you do not love me . . . Gray dawn and sorrow, And oh! My heart is crying. Joy has fled my soul Forever. Light of my life, Ah, would I were dying! *(the gray uncertain light just before dawn. Church bells, at various distances, ring Matins. A* JAILER *carrying a lantern comes up the stairs, goes to the casemate, and lights the lamp hanging before the crucifix, then the one on the table. He goes to the rear of the platform and, leaning over the parapet, surveys the courtyard below, to see if the squad of soldiers escorting the condemned man has yet arrived. He meets the sentry who is patrolling the platform and exchanges some words with him. Returning to the casemate, he sits down and waits, half asleep. A squad led by a* SERGEANT *escorts* CAVARADOSSI *onto the platform. The squad halts, the* SERGEANT *leads* CAVARADOSSI *to the casemate. On seeing the* SERGEANT *the* JAILER *rises and salutes. The* SERGEANT *hands him a paper, which the* JAILER *examines. Seating himself at the table, the* JAILER *opens the register and writes in it while questioning* CAVARADOSSI*)*
CARCERIERE Mario Cavaradossi?	JAILER Mario Cavaradossi? *(*CAVARADOSSI *nods. The* JAILER *hands the pen to the* SERGEANT*)*
A voi.	Sign here. *(the* SERGEANT *signs the register and goes down the stairs, followed by the soldiers)* *(to* CAVARADOSSI*)*
Vi resta un'ora. Un sacerdote i vostri cenni attende.	You have still an hour. If you like, A priest will come to attend you.
CAVARADOSSI No. Ma un'ultima grazia io vi richiedo.	CAVARADOSSI No. But may I ask you For one last favor?

JAILER
What is it?

CAVARADOSSI
I leave behind me
One whom I cherish dearly.
Would you permit me to write her briefly.
(*draws a ring from his finger*)
All that is left
Of my possessions . . . this ring.
If you promise
That you will give her
My last farewell,
You may have it.

JAILER (*after some hesitation accepts the ring and motions to* CAVARADOSSI *to sit down at the table*)
Write your letter.
(*seats himself on the bench*)

CAVARADOSSI (*remains lost in thought, from which he rouses himself to write. After a few lines, engulfed by memories, he leaves off writing. Thinking aloud*)
And the stars shone brightly,
And the air mild and fragrant . . .
The garden gate was opened,
And footsteps approached so lightly.
She stood before me, radiant.
In my arms I held her . . .
O fond embrace, o languorous caresses.
My heart was trembling,
Enraptured by the wonder of her glorious beauty!
My dream of love is now destroyed forever.
My hour is fleeting,
And I must die, despairing!
And I must die, despairing!
How cruel is death!
Ah, life was never sweeter—
Never sweeter!
(*he bursts into tears, covering his face with his hands*)
(SPOLETTA *comes up the stairs, accompanied by the* SERGEANT *and followed by* TOSCA. *The* SERGEANT *carries a lantern.* SPOLETTA *points out to* TOSCA *where she will find* CAVARADOSSI, *and calls the* JAILER *to him.* SPOLETTA *goes down the stairs, after having given orders to a sentry at the back to keep close watch over the prisoner. The* SERGEANT *and the* JAILER *follow. In the meantime* TOSCA, *in a state of extreme agitation, sees* CAVARADOSSI *weeping. She rushes over to him. Unable to speak because of her emotion, she lifts his head, then gives him the safe-conduct. On seeing* TOSCA, CAVARADOSSI *leaps to his feet in astonishment. He reads the document that* TOSCA *has given him*)

CARCERIERE
Se posso. . . .

CAVARADOSSI
Io lascio al mondo
una persona cara. Consentite
ch'io le scriva un sol motto.

Unico resto
di ma ricchezza è questo
anel . . . Se promettete
di consegnarle il mio
ultimo addio,
esso è vostro . . .

CARCERIERE
Scrivete.

CAVARADOSSI
E lucevan le stelle
e olezzava la terra—
stridea l'uscio dell'orto—
e un passo sfiorava la rena.
Entrava ella, fragrante,
mi cadea fra le braccia . . .
Oh! dolci baci, o languide carezze,
mentr'io fremente
le belle forme disciogliea dai veli!
Svanì per sempre il sogno mio d'amore . . .
L'ora è fuggita
e muoio disperato!
e muoio disperato!
E non ho amato
mai tanto la vita,
tanto la vita!

CAVARADOSSI
Ah! *Franchigia a Floria Tosca . . .*

TOSCA, CAVARADOSSI
e al Cavaliere che l'accompagna.

TOSCA
Sei libero!

CAVARADOSSI
Scarpia! Scarpia che cede?
La prima sua grazia è questa . . .

TOSCA
E l'ultima!

CAVARADOSSI
Che dici? . . .

TOSCA
Il tuo sangue o il mio amore
volea. Fur vani scongiuri e pianti.
Invan, pazza d'orror,
alla Madonna mi volsi e ai Santi . . .
L'empio mostro dicea: Già nei cieli
il patibol le braccia leva!
Rullavano i tamburi . . .
Rideva, l'empio mostro . . . rideva . . .
già la sua preda pronto a ghermir!
"Sei mia?"—"Sì."—Alla sua brama
mi promisi. Lì presso
luccicava una lama . . .
Ei scrisse il foglio liberator . . .
venne all'orrendo amplesso . . .
Io quella lama gli piantai nel cor.

CAVARADOSSI
Tu? . . . di tua man l'uccidesti?—tu pia,
tu benigna—e per me!

TOSCA
N'ebbi le man tutte lorde di sangue! . . .

CAVARADOSSI
O dolci mani mansuete e pure,
o mani elette a bell'opre e pietose,
a carezzar fanciulli, a coglier rose,
a pregar, giunte per le sventure,
dunque in voi, fatte dall' amor secure,
giustizia le sue sacre armi depose?
Voi deste morte, o man vittoriose,
o dolci mani mansuete e pure! . . .

TOSCA
Senti . . .
l'ora è vicina; io già raccolsi

CAVARADOSSI
Ah! "Permission for Floria Tosca . . ."

TOSCA (*joins* CAVARADOSSI *in reading the document*)
"And for the gentleman who is with her."
(*with enthusiasm*)
You are safe at last!

CAVARADOSSI (*looks at the paper and reads the signature*)
Scarpia! Scarpia so friendly?
(*looking at* TOSCA *with meaning*)
The first time he ever showed mercy.

TOSCA (*takes back the safe-conduct and puts it in her purse*)
And the last!

CAVARADOSSI
You mean—?

TOSCA (*with a start*)
He demanded your life or my love.
In vain, all my tears, my entreating.
In vain, frozen with horror,
I called on God above to pity and save me!
The villain sneered at my anguish. Gaily he showed me:
There, in the courtyard, the gallows waited!
And now the drums were beating.
That monster laughed in heartless derision,
Ready to pounce on his helpless prey!
"You'll be mine now"—"Yes!"
In despair I gave my promise.
And then a gleaming blade flashed across my vision.
He signed the paper that lets us depart,
And approached to embrace me.
I plunged that knife into his treach'rous heart!

CAVARADOSSI
You? So gentle, so kindly!
Unflinching you did this . . . and for me!

TOSCA
My hands were crimson and reeking with his blood!

CAVARADOSSI (*lovingly takes* TOSCA'*s hands between his own*)
O hands so gentle, delicate and tender,
O lovely hands meant for kindness and blessing,
To fondle children, to gather roses,
To pray for needy friend, or clasp in fond caress.
Came the hour, love gave you strength and power
And noble courage to smite the vile offender.
The fearful stroke of death you dared to render!
O hands so gentle, delicate and tender . . .

TOSCA
Listen: the hour approaches.

I brought my jewels and gold
For the journey. A carriage will be waiting.
But first—now smile, Mario dear . . . First you must
Face execution. Not really—with empty rifles.
They will shoot but in pretense. At the shot, you fall.
The soldiers will leave us. And then, to safety!
We go to safety!
Swiftly to the seacoast . . . we board a vessel . . .
And off to sea!

CAVARADOSSI
Free at last!

TOSCA
Safe at last!

CAVARADOSSI
Off to sea!

TOSCA
There is no more grief on earth . . .
See where beckons the rosy dawn.
In this breathless silence, all living things
Awake and love, and hail the rising sun.

CAVARADOSSI (*with the most tender emotion*)
Ah! Bitter was the thought of dying,
Because of you who lend my life its meaning.
From you my soul takes fire and joy and passion,
Hope and desire, and tender sighing.
The universe, in all its splendor,
Your eyes reflect, so lovely and revealing;
And all things borrow from you their pow'r
To charm my heart! . . . From Tosca their beauty stealing.

TOSCA
May love, whose magic rescued you from danger,
Brighten our path on land and over the water;
And light with its flame the smiling world before us . . .
Until, united in spheres celestial,
We shall soar aloft and float high over the ocean
Like sunset clouds in endless motion . . .
Endless motion . . . endless motion!
(*they gaze before them raptly, as in a dream. They remain profoundly moved, silent.* TOSCA, *recalled to reality, looks around her restlessly*)
Are they coming?
(*to* CAVARADOSSI, *with tender anxiety*)
Remember:
When you hear the sound of the shooting,
You fall down abruptly.

CAVARADOSSI (*sadly*)
Do not fear.
I shall fall down at once—in most natural fashion.

oro e gioielli . . . una vettura è pronta.
Ma prima . . . ridi amor . . . prima sarai
fucilato—per finta—ad armi scariche.
Simulato supplizio. Al colpo . . . cadi.
I soldati sen vanno—e noi siam salvi,
e noi siam salvi!
Poscia a Civitavecchia . . . una tartana . . .
e via pel mar!

CAVARADOSSI
Liberi!

TOSCA
Liberi!

CAVARADOSSI
Via pel mar!

TOSCA
Chi si duole
in terra più? Senti effluvi di rose? . . .
Non ti par che le cose
aspettan tutte innamorate il sole? . . .

CAVARADOSSI
Amaro sol per te m'era il morire,
Da te la vita prende ogni splendore,
all'esser mio la gioia ed il desire
nascon di te, come di fiamma ardore.
Io folgorare i cieli e scolorire
vedrò nell'occhio tuo rivelatore,
e la beltà delle cose più mire
avrà sol da te voce e colore.

TOSCA
Amor che seppe a te vita serbare
ci sarà guida in terra, e in mar nocchier
e vago farà il mondo riguardare.
Finchè congiunti alle celesti sfere
dileguerem, siccome alte sul mare
a sol cadente, nuvole leggere,
nuvole leggere, nuvole leggere! . . .
E non giungono . . .
Bada! . . .
al colpo egli è mestiere
che tu subito cada.

CAVARADOSSI
Non temere
che cadrò sul momento—e al naturale.

TOSCA
Ma stammi attento—di non farti male!
Con scenica scienza
io saprei la movenza . . .

CAVARADOSSI
Parlami ancor come dianzi parlavi,
è così dolce il suon della tua voce!

TOSCA
Uniti ed esulanti
diffonderan pel mondo i nostri amori
armonie di colori . . .

TOSCA, CAVARADOSSI
Armonie di canti
diffonderem!

Trionfal
di nova speme
l'anima freme
in celestial
crescente ardor.
Ed in armonico vol
già l'anima va
all'estasi d'amor.

TOSCA
Gli occhi ti chiuderò con mille baci
e mille ti dirò nomi d'amor . . .

CARCERIERE
L'ora!

CAVARADOSSI
Son pronto.

TOSCA
Tieni a mente: al primo
colpo, giù . . .

CAVARADOSSI
Giù.

TOSCA
Nè rialzarti innanzi
ch'io ti chiami.

CAVARADOSSI
No, amore!

TOSCA
E cadi bene.

TOSCA (*insisting*)
But be careful you do yourself no harm!
It's an old stage trick—
I have done it often.

CAVARADOSSI (*interrupts her, drawing her to him*)
Tell me once more that you love me forever!
To me your voice is like enchanting music!

TOSCA (*with ecstatic abandon and ever more passionately*)
Together we shall wander,
Lost in a world of golden dreams and beauty,
Resplendent with color . . .

CAVARADOSSI (*joins in, exultantly*)
Resounding with music,
Radiant with light!
(*with great enthusiasm*)
Glorious light!
With fervent hope
And faith and joy,
Our souls now scale
The heights above!
And in this luminous flight
Our hearts attain
The rapturous bliss of love!

TOSCA
Ah, when you shut your eyes I shall kiss them lightly,
And call you by the thousand names of love . . .
(*enter, from the stairs, a squad of soldiers. The* OFFICER *in charge marches the squad to the rear.* SPOLETTA, *the* SERGEANT, *and the* JAILER *follow.* SPOLETTA *gives the necessary instructions. The sky grows bright. It is dawn. The hour of four strikes.*)

JAILER (*approaches* CAVARADOSSI *and, taking off his cap, indicates the* OFFICER)
Come now!

CAVARADOSSI
I am ready.
(*the* JAILER *takes the register of the condemned and goes down the stairs.*)

TOSCA (*to* CAVARADOSSI *in a low voice, stifling her laughter*)
Now remember:
At the first shot . . . down!

CAVARADOSSI (*in a low voice, as he too laughs*)
Down . . .

TOSCA
Do not move, dearest,
Till you hear me call you.

CAVARADOSSI
No, beloved!

TOSCA
And fall down lightly.

CAVARADOSSI (*smiling*)
Just like Tosca on the stage.

TOSCA (*seeing him smile*)
Be serious!

CAVARADOSSI (*gravely*)
Like this?

TOSCA
Like this.

(CAVARADOSSI *follows the* OFFICER *after taking leave of* TOSCA, *who goes to the left side of the casemate, so as to be able to see what takes place on the platform. She watches as the* OFFICER *and the* SERGEANT *lead* CAVARADOSSI *to the wall facing her. The* SERGEANT *offers to bandage* CAVARADOSSI'S *eyes; but he refuses with a smile. These lugubrious preparations exhaust* TOSCA'S *patience*)

Ah, how fearful this waiting!
Why this stupid delay? . . . The sun is rising . . .
(*It is almost day*)
Why do they move so slowly? . . . It is a comedy,
I know . . . And yet this agony seems endless!
(*The* OFFICER *and* SERGEANT *draw up the firing squad, giving the necessary instructions*)
At last! They raise their rifles.
How handsome is my Mario!
(*seeing that the* OFFICER *is about to lower his sword, she covers her ears with her hands so as not to hear the shots. The* OFFICER *lowers his sword. The soldiers fire.* TOSCA *signals to* CAVARADOSSI *to fall, saying*)
There! Down!
(*admiring his performance, she kisses her hand to him*)
Ah, what an actor!
(*the* SERGEANT *inspects the body.* SPOLETTA *approaches and draws away the* SERGEANT, *preventing him from giving the coup de grâce. The* OFFICER *lines up his men in single file. The* SERGEANT *recalls the sentry at the back. All, preceded by* SPOLETTA, *march down the stairs;* TOSCA *has watched their every move with greatest agitation, fearful that* CAVARADOSSI, *through impatience, may move or speak too soon*)
Oh Mario, do not move yet . . . They're going now.
Quiet! Now then . . . off they go . . . off they go.
(*thinking that the soldiers are returning to the platform, she warns* CAVARADOSSI *anew*)
Be still! Oh do not move yet . . .
(*she runs to the parapet and, leaning over cautiously, looks below. As she goes back to* CAVARADOSSI)
Now away! Mario! Mario! Come quickly! Away!
(*perturbed, she touches him*)
Up, up!
(*uncovering him*)

CAVARADOSSI
Come la Tosca in teatro.

TOSCA
Non ridere . . .

CAVARADOSSI
Così?

TOSCA
Così.

Com'è lunga l'attesa!
Perchè indugiano ancor? . . .
già sorge il sole . . .
Perchè indugiano ancora? . . .
è una commedia,
lo so . . . ma questa angoscia
eterna pare! . . .
Ecco! . . . apprestano l'armi
. . . com'è bello
il mio Mario! . . .

Là! muori!
Ecco un artista! . . .

O Mario, non ti muovere . . .
s'avviano . . . taci! vanno . . .
scendono . . . scendono.
Ancora non ti muovere . . .
Presto, su! Mario! Mario! Su,
presto! Andiam!
Su, su!
Mario! Mario!
Ah!
Morto! . . . morto! . . .
morto! . . .
O Mario . . . morto? . . .
tu? . . . così? . . .
Finire così? finire così!

Tu, morto . . . morto? Mario . . . povera Floria tua! Mario! Mario!	Mario! Mario! *(a loud cry)* Ah! *(in despair)* Dead! . . . Dead! . . . Murdered! Oh Mario . . . dead? You? . . . Like this? . . . To end like this? . . . to end like this! You—dead . . . dead! Mario! Ah, what is left for Tosca! Mario! Mario! *(weeping bitterly, she falls prostrate on* CAVARADOSSI'S *body)* *(from below—a prolonged cry, from a distance: the voices of* SCIARRONE, SPOLETTA *and some soldiers, drawing closer)*
LA VOCE DI SCIARRONE Vi dico, pugnalato!	SCIARRONE'S VOICE I tell you, stabbed to death!
VOCI DI SPOLETTA, ALTRI Scarpia?	VOICES OF SPOLETTA *and* OTHERS *(crying out)* Scarpia?
LA VOCE DI SCIARRONE Scarpia!	SCIARRONE'S VOICE Scarpia!
VARIE VOCI Ah!	THE OTHERS Ah!
LA VOCE DI SPOLETTA La donna è Tosca!	SPOLETTA'S VOICE The woman was Tosca!
VARIE VOCI Che non sfugga!	THE OTHERS We shall find her!
SPOLETTA, SCIARRONE, ALTRI Attenti agli sborchi delle scale!	SPOLETTA, SCIARRONE, OTHERS *(drawing closer)* Keep watch at the foot of the stairway! *(a great tumult is heard from below.* SPOLETTA *and* SCIARRONE *appear on the staircase.)*
SCIARRONE È lei!	SCIARRONE *(pointing out* TOSCA *to* SPOLETTA, *cries)* She's there!
SPOLETTA Ah! Tosca, pagherai ben cara la sua vita . . .	SPOLETTA Oh! Tosca, You shall pay dearly for his life.
TOSCA Colla mia! O Scarpia, avanti a Dio!	TOSCA With my own! *(*SPOLETTA *rushes at* TOSCA. *But she leaps to her feet and pushes him so violently that he almost falls backward down the stairs. She runs to the parapet and, springing upon it, cries)* Oh Scarpia, we meet before God! *(she leaps into space.* SCIARRONE *and the soldiers rush in confusion to the parapet and look down.* SPOLETTA *stands terrified, stricken with amazement)*

LA TRAVIATA

by Giuseppe Verdi (1813–1901)

LIBRETTO BY

FRANCESCO MARIA PIAVE

Translated by RUTH and THOMAS MARTIN

Based on Alexandre Dumas' play *La Dame aux Camélias*

CHARACTERS

VIOLETTA VALERY, *a courtesan*	*Soprano*
DR. GRENVIL, *Violetta's physician*	*Bass*
MARQUIS D'OBIGNY, *a nobleman*	*Bass*
FLORA BERVOIX, *friend of Violetta*	*Mezzo-soprano*
BARON DOUPHOL, *rival of Alfredo*	*Baritone*
GASTON, *Viscount of Letorieres*	*Tenor*
ALFREDO GERMONT, *lover of Violetta*	*Tenor*
ANNINA, *Violetta's maid*	*Mezzo-soprano*
GEORGE GERMONT, *father of Alfredo*	*Baritone*
JOSEPH, *Violetta's servant*	*Tenor*
SERVANT *to Flora*	*Bass*
MESSENGER	*Bass*

SALON GUESTS, MASQUERADERS, DANCERS, AND SERVANTS

Place: In and near Paris

Time: About 1850. The first act takes place in Winter, the second in Summer, the third in February.

First performance: Teatro La Fenice, Venice, March 6, 1853.

COPYRIGHT, 1946, 1961, BY G. SCHIRMER, INC.

ACT I

Chorus and Scene

(*Salon in* VIOLETTA'S *house. In the rear is a door that leads into another room. Two other doors at the sides. At left a fireplace over which is a mirror. In the center a table, lavishly set.* VIOLETTA, *seated on a divan, is conversing with the* DOCTOR *and other friends, while still others go to welcome arriving guests, among them the* BARON *and* FLORA, *on the arm of the* MARQUIS.)

1ST CHORUS
You are late, we expected you sooner—
What delayed you?

2ND CHORUS
We all were at Flora's
We were gambling and time seemed to fly!

VIOLETTA (*goes to meet the newcomers*)
Flora, and you friends,
I'm happy to see you!
Won't you join me, the night will be gay!
With champagne let's enliven the party!

FLORA, MARQUIS
You don't think it will harm you?

VIOLETTA
Of course not!
I believe that enjoyment alone can cure
All troubles and brighten our life.

ALL
Yes, enjoyment will brighten our life!

GASTON (*entering with* ALFREDO)
This is Alfredo Germont, dear Violetta,
He is one of your ardent admirers.
As a friend, he is one in a thousand.

VIOLETTA
Any friend of yours is always more than welcome.

MARQUIS
Why, here's Alfredo!

ALFREDO
Delighted!
(*they shake hands; the servants have served drinks in the meantime*)

GASTON
(*to* ALFREDO)
I told you: you will meet many friends at Violetta's!

VIOLETTA (*to the servants*)
Are we ready?
(*a servant nods "yes"*)
My friends and companions,
Come fill your glasses
With sparkling champagne!

CORO I.
Dell'invito trascorsa è già l'ora,
Voi tardaste.

CORO II.
Giocammo da Flora,
E giocando quell'ore volâr.

VIOLETTA
Flora, amici, la notte che resta
D'altre gioie qui fate brillar.
Fra le tazze è più viva la festa.

FLORA, MARCHESE
E goder voi potrete?

VIOLETTA
Lo voglio;
Al piacere m'affido, ed io soglio
Con tal farmaco i mali sopir.

TUTTI
Sì, la vita s'addoppia al gioir.

GASTONE
In Alfredo Germont, o signora,
Ecco un altro che molto v'onora;
Pochi amici a lui simili sono.

VIOLETTA
Mio Visconte, mercè di tal dono.

MARCHESE
Caro Alfredo!

ALFREDO
Marchese!

GASTONE
T'ho detto:
L'amistà qui s'intreccia al diletto.

VIOLETTA
Pronto è il tutto?
Miei cari sedete:
È al convito che s'apre ogni cor.

TUTTI
Ben diceste, le cure segrete
Fuga sempre l'amico licor.
È al convito che s'apre ogni cor.

ALL
A delightful suggestion!
Let's drown all cares
In a glass filled with sparkling champagne!
(they sit down. VIOLETTA *between* ALFREDO *and* GASTON, *in front* FLORA *between the* BARON *and the* MARQUIS. *The others sit down at their pleasure)*
Come, fill your glasses and drink once again.

GASTONE
Sempre Alfredo a voi pensa.

GASTON *(addressing* VIOLETTA*)*
Alfredo never forgot you . . .

VIOLETTA
Scherzate?

VIOLETTA
You're joking?

GASTONE
Egra foste, e ogni dì con affanno
Qui volò, di voi chiese.

GASTON
Ev'ry day of your illness he came to ask
How you were feeling.

VIOLETTA
Cessate,
Nulla son io per lui.

VIOLETTA
Why should he? What can I mean to him?

GASTONE
Non v'inganno.

GASTON
Why not ask him?

VIOLETTA
Vero è dunque? onde ciò? nol comprendo.

VIOLETTA *(to* ALFREDO*)*
Did you really? Tell me why!
How unusual!

ALFREDO
Sì, egli è ver.

ALFREDO *(sighing)*
Yes, it is true.

VIOLETTA
Le mie grazie vi rendo.
Voi, barone, non feste altrettanto . . .

VIOLETTA
Then I thank you sincerely.
(to the BARON*)*
Tell me, Baron, did *you* do as he did?

BARONE
Vi conosco da un anno soltanto.

BARON
It is only a year since I met you.

VIOLETTA
Ed ei solo da qualche minuto.

VIOLETTA
Yes, but he was no more than a stranger.

FLORA
Meglio fora se aveste taciuto.

FLORA *(softly to the* BARON*)*
Your remark did not do you any credit.

BARONE
M'è increscioso quel giovin.

BARON *(softly to* FLORA*)*
I dislike this young man.

FLORA
Perchè?
A me invece simpatico egli è.

FLORA
You do?
I must say, he is charming and nice.

GASTONE
E tu dunque non apri più bocca?

GASTON *(to* ALFREDO*)*
Won't you help us to make conversation?

MARCHESE
È a madama che scuoterlo tocca.

MARQUIS *(to* VIOLETTA*)*
He's only waiting for your invitation.

VIOLETTA
Sarò l'Ebe che versa.

VIOLETTA *(pouring for* ALFREDO*)*
Would champagne give you courage?

ALFREDO
E ch'io bramo
Immortal come quella.

ALFREDO
Yes, to drink to my beautiful hostess!

TUTTI
Beviamo.
Beviamo, beviam!

ALL
We join you!
Good health to you all!

GASTON
While we are all so gaily together,
Will the Baron oblige with a song?
(*the* BARON *declines; to* ALFREDO)
Then will you?

GASTONE
O barone, nè un verso, nè un viva
Troverete in quest'ora giuliva?
Dunque a te . . .

ALL
Ah yes! A drinking song!

TUTTI
Sì, sì, un brindisi.

ALFREDO
I fear, I'm not inspired.

ALFREDO
L'estro non m'arride . . .

GASTON
But we'd all love to hear you!

GASTONE
E non sei tu maestro?

ALFREDO (*to* VIOLETTA)
Would it please you?

ALFREDO
Vi fia grato?

VIOLETTA
Yes.

VIOLETTA
Sì.

ALFREDO
Yes? Then I'll sing!

ALFREDO
Sì? . . . L'ho già in cor.

MARQUIS
Your attention!

MARCHESE
Dunque attenti!

ALL
Let us all hear his song!

TUTTI
Sì, attenti al cantor.

ALFREDO
Companions, in wine lies the merry abandon
Which makes ev'ry heart bloom and flower.
Its magic enhances the fleeting hour,
We taste it with eager delight.
In wine lies joyous ecstasy
It mellows hearts to surrender.
Amid this festival splendor
We sense its tempting might!
Companions, in wine you find love and happiness,
Let us enjoy them tonight!

ALFREDO
Libiamo ne' lieti calici
Che la bellezza infiora,
E la fuggevol ora
S'inebrii a voluttà.
Libiam ne' dolci fremiti
Che suscita l'amore,
Poichè quell'occhio al core
Onnipotente va.
Libiamo, amore, amor fra i calici
Più caldi baci avrà.

ALL (*except* VIOLETTA *and* ALFREDO)
Ah, so let us enjoy them tonight.
Come, fill your glass and enjoy them tonight.

TUTTI
Ah! libiam, amor fra calici
Più caldi baci avrà.

VIOLETTA (*rises*)
I share the spirit of love and friendship
You all are so freely giving,
Life holds no meaning, and is not worth living
If not for pleasure alone.
So come, enjoy your happiness
In breathless crowded hours,
For love, like tender flowers,
Is swiftly dead and gone.
My friends, embrace this alluring occasion,
Let's revel and laugh until dawn.

VIOLETTA
Tra voi, saprò dividere
Il tempo mio giocondo;
Tutto è follia nel mondo
Ciò che non è piacer.
Godiam, fugace e rapido
È il gaudio dell'amore,
È un fior che nasce e muore,
Nè più si può goder.
Godiam . . . c'invita un fervido
Accento lusinghier.

ALL (*except* VIOLETTA *and* ALFREDO)
Ah, companions, don't waste this alluring occasion!
Let's all spend a night of enjoyment,
Our friends are congenial,

TUTTI
Ah! godiamo la tazza e il cantico
La notte abbella e il riso;

In questo paradiso
Ne scopra il nuovo dì.

VIOLETTA
La vita è nel tripudio.

ALFREDO
Quando non s'ami ancora.

VIOLETTA
Nol dite a chi l'ignora.

ALFREDO
È il mio destin così . . .

TUTTI
Ah! godiamo la tazza e il cantico
La notte abbella e il riso;
In questo paradiso
Ne scopra il nuovo dì.

Che è ciò?

VIOLETTA
Non gradireste ora le danze?

TUTTI
Oh, il gentil pensier! . . . tutti accettiamo.

VIOLETTA
Usciamo dunque.
Ohimè!

TUTTI
Che avete?

VIOLETTA
Nulla,
Nulla.

TUTTI
Che mai v'arresta?

VIOLETTA
Usciamo.
Oh Dio!

TUTTI
Ancora!

ALFREDO
Voi soffrite?

TUTTI
O ciel! ch'è questo?

VIOLETTA
Un tremito che provo . . . Or là passate . . .
Fra poco anch'io sarò . . .

The wine is delicious,
Let's revel and laugh until dawn.

VIOLETTA (*to* ALFREDO)
We live and love for pleasure—

ALFREDO (*to* VIOLETTA)
Until we love sincerely—

VIOLETTA
A most romantic theory—

ALFREDO
And one that I believe.

ALL
Come, let's embrace the occasion,
The friends are congenial,
The wine is delicious,
Let's all spend a night of enjoyment,
Let's laugh and drink until dawn.

Waltz and Duet

(*music is heard from the adjoining room*)

A dance!

VIOLETTA
May I suggest we go to the ballroom?

ALL
What a charming thought!
That would be nice indeed!

VIOLETTA
Let us go in then.
(*they start for the ballroom, but* VIOLETTA *has a sudden fit of weakness*)
I can't!

ALL
What is it?

VIOLETTA
Nothing, nothing!

ALL
Oh, what has happened?

VIOLETTA (*tries to walk*)
Don't worry,
(*she is forced to sit down again*)
Forgive me!

ALL
Good heavens!

ALFREDO
You are suff'ring?

ALL
Do you feel better?

VIOLETTA
I just felt weak a moment—
Go to the ballroom
And I will follow you soon.

ALL (*except* ALFREDO)
As you prefer then.
(*all guests, except* ALFREDO *go to the ballroom*)

VIOLETTA (*rises and looks into the mirror*)
I am so pale!
(*she turns and notices* ALFREDO)
You here?

ALFREDO
I came to ask you how you feel.

VIOLETTA
Much better.

ALFREDO
You must abandon this way of living—
Your health is precious,
You can't afford to lose it.

VIOLETTA
You really think so?

ALFREDO
If you were mine,
How gladly I would care for you
And keep you safe from harm.

VIOLETTA
How flatt'ring!
Who ever thought of caring for me?

ALFREDO
That's because no one ever loved you!

VIOLETTA
Indeed?

ALFREDO
No one as I do!

VIOLETTA
Why surely
(*laughing*)
Such a great love I almost had forgotten!

ALFREDO
You're laughing?
How cold your heart is!

VIOLETTA
My heart? Yes—maybe—
But why does that concern you?

ALFREDO
If you could know that,
You would never jest at my love.

VIOLETTA
Are you in earnest?

ALFREDO
My word of honor!

VIOLETTA
How long then is it you love me?

TUTTI
Come bramate.

VIOLETTA
Oh qual pallor!
Voi qui!

ALFREDO
Cessata è l'ansia
Che vi turbò?

VIOLETTA
Sto meglio.

ALFREDO
Ah, in cotal guisa
V'ucciderete . . . aver v'è duopo cura
Dell'esser vostro.

VIOLETTA
E lo potrei?

ALFREDO
Oh! se mia
Foste, custode io veglierei pe' vostri
Soavi dì.

VIOLETTA
Che dite? ha forse alcuno
Cura di me?

ALFREDO
Perchè nessun al mondo
V'ama!

VIOLETTA
Nessun?

ALFREDO
Tranne sol io.

VIOLETTA
Gli è vero!
Sì grande amor dimenticato avea . . .

ALFREDO
Ridete? e in voi v'ha un core?

VIOLETTA
Un cor? . . . sì . . . forse . . . e a che lo richiedete?

ALFREDO
Ah, se ciò fosse, non potreste allora celiar.

VIOLETTA
Dite davvero?

ALFREDO
Io non v'inganno.

VIOLETTA
Da molto è che mi amate?

ALFREDO
Ah sì, da un anno.
Un dì felice, eterea,
Mi balenaste innante,
E da quel dì tremante
Vissi d'ignoto amor.
Di quell'amor ch'è palpito.
Dell'universo intero,
Misterioso, altero,
Croce e delizia al cor.

ALFREDO
Since I first saw you!
You were so radiant, so heavenly,
Like an angelic vision,
And from that day I loved you,
Loving as never before.
Never before have I known such happiness,
Never before have I felt such deep emotion,
Mysterious power, marvelously embracing
Sorrow and rapture,
Pain and delight.

VIOLETTA
Ah, se ciò è ver, fuggitemi,
Solo amistade io v'offro:
Amar non so, nè soffro
Un così eroico amore.
Io sono franca, ingenua;
Altra cercar dovete;
Non arduo troverete
Dimenticarmi allor.
Non arduo troverete
Dimenticarmi allor.

VIOLETTA
You're taking love too seriously,
Friendship is all I offer.
For love so deep, I'm not the woman.
You must forget me.
I speak in all sincerity,
You must forget this passion,
It won't be hard for you.
Pretend you never met me,
You must forget me,
I was not meant for you.

ALFREDO
Croce è delizia,
Delizia al cor,
Croce è delizia al cor!

ALFREDO
Sorrow and rapture,
Pain and delight,
I want to live for you.

GASTONE
Ebben? che diavol fate?

GASTON (*appearing at the door*)
Still there? Why don't you join us?

VIOLETTA
Si folleggiava . . .

VIOLETTA
In just a moment . . .

GASTONE
Ah! ah! . . . sta ben! restate.

GASTON
Ha, ha, that's fine, till later!
(*exit*)

VIOLETTA
Amor dunque non più . . . Vi garba il patto?

VIOLETTA
And now, no more of love,
Is that a promise?

ALFREDO
Io v'obbedisco . . . Parto . . .

ALFREDO
Then I must leave you, forgive me.

VIOLETTA
A tal giungeste?
Prendete questo fiore.

VIOLETTA
In such a manner?
(*she takes a camellia from her corsage*)
At least take this camellia.

ALFREDO
Perchè?

ALFREDO
And why?

VIOLETTA
Per riportarlo.

VIOLETTA
You may bring it back to me.

ALFREDO
Quando?

ALFREDO
How soon?

VIOLETTA
Quando sarà appassito.

VIOLETTA
When it begins to wither.

ALFREDO
You mean—tomorrow?

VIOLETTA
Well then, tomorrow!

ALFREDO (*takes the flower delightedly*)
I never was so happy!

VIOLETTA
You still are sure you love me?

ALFREDO
I love you more than words can tell,
I love you, Violetta.

VIOLETTA
You're leaving?

ALFREDO
Till tomorrow.
(*he is about to leave*)

VIOLETTA
Good-by then.

ALFREDO
I am so happy.

VIOLETTA, ALFREDO
Tomorrow.
(ALFREDO *has left*)

ALL (*returning, animated from dancing*)
In a little while the day will break;
It is time, we must be going.
Many thanks to you, dear lady,
For a most delightful time.
It is getting on to morning
And the day is almost dawning,
So we really cannot stay,
And we must be on our way.
Thank you for the lovely evening.
It is time that we are leaving.
It has been a real delight
And a truly splendid night.
This has been a merry party,
It has been the season's best.
Thank you for your invitation,
It was quite a celebration
And the hours seemed to fly.
Ah yes, we thank you once again,
And say good-by.
It was a most delightful party,
It was easily the season's best!
But now it's time that we are leaving.
We'll go home to get some rest.
(*all guests leave*)

Scene and Aria

VIOLETTA
He loves me, he loves me!

ALFREDO
Oh ciel! domani.

VIOLETTA
Ebben . . . domani.

ALFREDO
Io son, io son felice!

VIOLETTA
D'amarmi dite ancora?

ALFREDO
Oh, quanto v'amo!

VIOLETTA
Partite?

ALFREDO
Parto.

VIOLETTA
Addio.

ALFREDO
Di più non bramo.

VIOLETTA, ALFREDO
Addio, addio.

TUTTI
Si ridesta in ciel l'aurora,
E n'è forza di partir;
Mercè a voi, gentil signora,
Di sì splendido gioir.
Si ridesta in ciel l'aurora,
Si ridesta in ciel l'aurora,
E n'è forza di partir;
E n'è forza di partir;
Mercè a voi, gentil signora,
Mercè a voi, gentil signora,
Di sì splendido gioir.
La città di feste è piena,
Volge il tempo dei piacer;
Nel riposo ancor la lena
Nel riposo ancor la lena
Si ritempri per goder.
Ah! si, ritempri,
Si ritempri per goder. Sì,
Nel riposo ancor la lena,
Si ritempri, si ritempri,
Si ritempri per goder.

VIOLETTA
È strano! è strano!
in core

Scolpiti ho quegli accenti!
Saria per me sventura un serio amore?
Che risolvi, o turbata anima mia?
Null'uomo ancora t'accendeva . . . O gioia
Ch'io non conobbi, esser amata amando!
E sdegnarla poss'io
Per l'aride follie del viver mio?

Ah, fors'è lui che l'anima
Solinga ne' tumulti
Godea sovente pingere
De' suoi colori occulti!
Lui che modesto e vigile
All'egre soglie ascese,
E nuova febbre accese,
Destandomi all'amor?
A quell'amor ch'è palpito
Dell'universo intero
Misterioso, altero,
Croce e delizia al cor.

And strangely, I feel my heart responding!
But would it be ill-fortune to love sincerely?
Who can guide me in making this decision?
No love has ever touched me deeply.
Oh joy beyond all measure,
Being beloved in loving!
Could I coldly reject it
For all the shallow folly
Of my existence?
Could it be he who stirred my heart,
Lonely in life's confusion?
He the ideal of all my dreams,
And of my fond illusion?
He who with modest vigilance
During my illness waited,
And with his youthful fervor,
Wakened my heart to love?
Never before have I known such happiness,
Never before have I felt such deep emotion,
Mysterious power, marvelously embracing
Sorrow and rapture,
Pain and delight.

Follie! . . . follie! delirio vano è questo!
Povera donna, sola, abbandonata.
In questo popoloso deserto
Che appellano Parigi,
Che spero or più? Che far degg'io! Gioire,
Di voluttà nei vortici perir.

(*suddenly waking from her meditation*)
It's madness!
A futile, vain illusion!
How could I do it!
Lonely, in all this splendor,
Devoted to a life of amusement
And meaningless adventures,
What more to hope,
What course to follow?
Forget him!
Enjoy what life will offer me
And live from day to day!
Ah!—

Sempre libera degg'io
Folleggiare di gioia in gioia,
Vo' che scorra il viver mio
Pei sentieri del piacer.
Nasca il giorno, o il giorno muoia,
Sempre lieta ne' ritrovi
A diletti sempre nuovi
Dee volare il mio pensier.

Let me live for pleasure only
In a world of radiance and splendor;
Never sorry, never lonely,
Always carefree, always gay.
I shall wander the path of folly,
Ever seeking new delight.
Let me love in freedom only,
Live for pleasure day and night.
Night and day, night and day,
Let my star lead the way!

ALFREDO
Amor, amor è palpito dell'universo,
Dell'universo intero, misterioso,
Misterioso, altero,
Croce croce e delizia, delizia al cor!

ALFREDO'S VOICE (*heard from outside*)
Now at last I know true happiness,
Love such as mine fills the heart
With deep emotion,
Mysterious power, marvelously embracing

Sorrow and rapture,
Pain and delight.

VIOLETTA

Forget him, forget him, forever!
Ah—
Let me live for pleasure only
In a world of radiance and splendor;
Never sorry, never lonely,
Always carefree, always gay.
I shall wander the path of folly,
Ever seeking new delight.
Let me love in freedom only,
Live for pleasure day and night.
Night and day, night and day,
Let my star lead the way.

VIOLETTA

Follie! follie! follie!
gioir, gioir!
Sempre libera degg'io
Follegiare di gioia in gioia,
Vo' che scorra il viver mio
Pei sentieri del piacer.
Nasca il giorno, o il giorno
muoia,
Sempre lieta ne' ritrovi,
A diletti sempre nuovi
Dee volare il mio pensier.

ACT II

Scene 1

(*Country house near Paris. Room on the ground floor. In the rear, facing the audience, is a mantelpiece, on it a mirror and a clock. On both sides glass doors leading into the garden. Two other doors in front. Chairs, small tables, and writing utensils.*)

Recitative and Aria

ALFREDO
Lunge da lei per me non v'ha diletto!
Volaron già tre lune
Dacchè la mia Violetta
Agi per me lasciò, dovizie, amori,
E le pompose feste
Ov', agli omaggi avvezza,
Vedeva schiavo ciascun di sua bellezza . . .
Ed or contenta in questi ameni luoghi
Tutto scorda per me. Qui presso a lei
Io rinascer mi sento,
E dal soffio d'amor rigenerato
Scordo ne' gaudi suoi tutto il passato.
De' miei bollenti spiriti
Il giovanile ardore
Ella temprò col placido
Sorriso dell'amor, dell'amor!
Dal dì che disse: "vivere
Io voglio a te fedel,"
Dell'universo immemore
Io vivo, io vivo quasi in ciel.

ALFREDO (*enters in hunting clothes*)
Life is so idle, away from Violetta!
(*he puts his gun down*)
Three months have passed already
Since she deserted Paris,
Abandoning for my sake her pleasures,
Her lovers, and all those brilliant parties,
Where like a queen of beauty, she reigned
Over the hearts of countless admirers.
Now she is happy in this delightful country,
Living only for me.
With her beside me my life has new meaning,
And reborn through her love and her devotion,
Now I may live enjoying happiness true and lasting.
All my exalted fantasy—
Dreams born of youthful ardor
She brought to happy harmony
When lovingly she smiled, just for me.
And when she told me, tenderly:
"Forever, you are my only love"—
Then I became a happy man,
My life began to seem like heaven,
Like heaven above.

Scene

(ANNINA *enters worriedly*)

ALFREDO
Annina, donde vieni?

ALFREDO
Where have you been, Annina?

ANNINA
Da Parigi.

ANNINA
I've come from Paris.

ALFREDO
Chi tel commise?

ALFREDO
Who sent you there?

ANNINA
Fu la mia signora.

ANNINA
It was the mistress.

ALFREDO
Perchè?

ALFREDO
And why?

ANNINA
Per alienar cavalli, cocchi,
E quanto ancor possiede.

ANNINA
To sell the carriage and the horses
And her own possessions.

ALFREDO
Che mai sento!

ALFREDO
I can't believe it!

ANNINA
Lo spendio è grande a viver qui solinghi . . .

ANNINA
We need the money to meet the expenses.

ALFREDO
And you said nothing?

ANNINA
Because I was forbidden.

ALFREDO
Forbidden? How much do we need?

ANNINA
More than a thousand.

ALFREDO
All right then, I'll go to Paris,
With my own money recover her possessions,
And pay the debts before the day is over!
Go, go!
(ALFREDO *rushes off*)

Recitative and Duet

VIOLETTA (*enters from the garden*)
Where's Alfredo?

ANNINA
He just has left for Paris.

VIOLETTA
And he'll return?

ANNINA
Before the day is over—
That was his message.

VIOLETTA
I wonder—

JOSEPH (*entering with a letter*)
For you.

VIOLETTA
Thank you. A gentleman will call on me this morning. I wish to see him.
(ANNINA *and* JOSEPH *leave.* VIOLETTA *opens the letter.*)
Ha, ha! So Flora knows where I am hiding and invites me to a dance this very evening.
(*she throws the letter on the small table and sits down*)
She'll wait for me in vain.

JOSEPH
Your guest, my lady.

VIOLETTA
I will receive him.

GERMONT (*enters, ushered in by* JOSEPH)
Mademoiselle Valery?

VIOLETTA
Come in, sir.

GERMONT (*with emphasis*)
I am George Germont, Alfredo's father.

VIOLETTA (*surprised, motions him to be seated*)
Oh!

ALFREDO
E tacevi?

ANNINA
Mi fu il silenzio imposto.

ALFREDO
Imposto!
or v'abbisogna?

ANNINA
Mille luigi.

ALFREDO
Or vanne andrò a Parigi.
Questo colloquio non sappia la signora.
Il tutto valgo a riparare ancora.
Va, va!

VIOLETTA
Alfredo?

ANNINA
Per Parigi or or partiva.

VIOLETTA
E tornerà?

ANNINA
Pria che tramonti il giorno
Dirvel m'impose.

VIOLETTA
È strano!

GIUSEPPE
Per voi.

VIOLETTA
Sta bene. In breve
Giungerà un uom d'affari,
entri all'istante.

Ah ah! scopriva Flora il mio ritiro!
E m'invita a danzar per questa sera!
Invan m'aspetterà.

GIUSEPPE
È qui un signore.

VIOLETTA
Sarà lui che attendo.

GERMONT
Madamigella Valery? . . .

VIOLETTA
Son io.

GERMONT
D'Alfredo il padre in me vedete!

VIOLETTA
Voi!

GERMONT
Sì, dell'incauto, che a ruina corre,
Ammaliato da voi.
VIOLETTA
Donna son io, signore, ed in mia casa;
Ch'io vi lasci assentite,
Più per voi che per me.
GERMONT
(Quai modi!)
Pure . . .

VIOLETTA
Tratto in error voi foste.

GERMONT
De' suoi beni
Dono vuol farvi . . .
VIOLETTA
Non l'osò finora . . .
Rifiuterei.
GERMONT
Pur tanto lusso . . .
VIOLETTA
A tutti
È mistero quest'atto,
A voi nol sia.
GERMONT
Ciel! che discopro! D'ogni vostro avere
Or volete spogliarvi?
Ah, il passato perchè, perchè v'accusa?
VIOLETTA
Più non esiste . . . or amo Alfredo, e Dio
Lo cancellò col pentimento mio.
GERMONT
Nobili sensi invero!
VIOLETTA
Oh, come dolce
Mi suona il vostro accento!
GERMONT
Ed a tai sensi
Un sacrifizio chieggo.
VIOLETTA
Ah no, tacete!
Terribil cosa chiedereste certo!
Il previdi, v'attesi,
era felice troppo . . .
GERMONT
D'Alfredo il padre
La sorte, l'avvenir domanda or qui
De' suoi due figli.
VIOLETTA
Di due figli!
GERMONT
Sì.
Pura siccome un angelo
Iddio mi diè una figlia;

GERMONT
Yes, I'm the father of the son you have misguided and are leading to ruin.
VIOLETTA (*with dignity but firmly*)
Sir, I am a woman, and in my own house. Please allow me to leave you, more for your sake than for mine.
(*about to leave the room*)
GERMONT (*to himself*)
What dignity!
(*aloud*)
However—
VIOLETTA
You are indeed mistaken . . .
(*returns to her seat*)
GERMONT
He is planning to give you his fortune . . .
VIOLETTA
He hasn't dared to do so . . . I would refuse.
GERMONT (*indicating the room*)
But all this luxury . . .
VIOLETTA (*gives him a document*)
This document no one has seen yet. But you shall see it.

GERMONT (*reading the paper*)
Lord! This is shocking!
All your possessions are you planning to sacrifice?
(*in a milder tone*)
What a pity your past will speak against you!
VIOLETTA
It's gone forever! Now I love Alfredo—I started life once more through my sincere repentance.
GERMONT
Your words show noble feeling—
VIOLETTA
How it relieves me to hear you speak so kindly!
GERMONT (*rising*)
But I must ask for a sacrifice to prove it.
VIOLETTA (*rising too*)
Ah, don't ask me. I am afraid I would not have the courage—I foresaw it, I felt it . . . oh, I was far too happy!
GERMONT
I must demand it, for my sake, for the sake of my two children's happy future.
VIOLETTA
Your *two* children?
GERMONT
Yes.
God in his great benevolence

Gave me a lovely daughter;
She is engaged most happily
To wed a fine young suitor.
But since my son has gone away,
Leaving his home and family,
Her suitor will now withdraw his pledge
That would have made us all so happy.
Ah, do not turn to misery
Youthful and happy love.
I pray to God above
That you may not deny
A father's anxious plea.

VIOLETTA
Ah, I see now—
Until your daughter's marriage
I should not live with Alfredo!
That would be painful,
But if you wish—I—

GERMONT
That's not what I'm asking!

VIOLETTA
Heavens! What can it be, then?
No more is needed!

GERMONT
More is needed!

VIOLETTA
You want me to renounce your son forever?

GERMONT
It must be!

VIOLETTA
Ah no! Never!
You don't know yet how I love him,
That he has all my affection,
That I'm friendless, sad and lonely,
With not one soul for protection!
And that Alfredo is the only one
I have in all this world.
You don't know yet that I suffer
From a dreadful mortal illness,
That I never shall recover—
And I should renounce my lover?
What you ask me is so cruel,
So heartless and inhuman,
That I prefer a thousand times to die!

GERMONT
The sacrifice is bitter;
But let us reason quietly.
You are so young yet and beautiful;
A new love . . .

VIOLETTA
No more, I beg you!

Se Alfredo nega riedere
In seno alla famiglia,
L'amato e amante giovine,
Cui sposa andar dovea,
Or si ricusa al vincolo
Che lieti ne rendea.
Deh, non mutate in triboli
Le rose dell'amor.
A prieghi miei resistere
Non voglia il vostro cor.

VIOLETTA
Ah, comprendo . . . dovrò per alcun tempo
Da Alfredo allontanarmi . . . doloroso
Fora per me . . . pur . . .

GERMONT
Non è ciò che chiedo.

VIOLETTA
Cielo, che più cercate! offersi assai!

GERMONT
Pur non basta.

VIOLETTA
Volete che per sempre
A lui rinunzi?

GERMONT
È d'uopo!

VIOLETTA
Ah no! giammai! no mai!
Non sapete quale affetto
Vivo, immenso m'arda in petto,
Che nè amici, nè parenti
Io non conto tra' viventi?
E che Alfredo m'ha giurato
Che in lui tutto io troverò?
Non sapete che colpita
D'atro morbo è la mia vita?
Che già presso il fin ne vedo?
Ch'io mi separi da Alfredo?
Ah, il supplizio è sì spietato,
Che a morir preferirò.

GERMONT
È grave il sacrifizio,
Ma pur tranquilla uditemi.
Bella voi siete e giovine . . .
Col tempo . . .

VIOLETTA
Ah, più non dite . . .

V'intendo . . . m'è
impossibile,
Lui solo amar vogl'io.

GERMONT
Sia pure . . . ma volubile
Sovente è l'uom . . .

VIOLETTA
Gran Dio!

GERMONT
Un dì, quando le veneri
Il tempo avrà fugate,
Fia presto il tedio a sorgere . . .
Che sarà allor? . . . pensate . . .
Per voi non avran balsamo
I più soavi affetti!
Poichè dal ciel non furono
Tai nodi benedetti . . .

VIOLETTA
È vero! È vero!

GERMONT
Ah, dunque sperdasi
Tal sogno seduttore . . .

VIOLETTA
È vero! È vero!

GERMONT
Siate di mia famiglia
L'angiol consolatore . . .
Violetta, deh, pensateci,
Ne siete in tempo ancor.
È Dio che ispira, o giovine,
Tai detti a un genitor.

VIOLETTA
(Così alla misera ch'è un dì
caduta,
Di più risorgere speranza è
muta!
Se pur benefico le indulga
Iddio,
L'uomo implacabile per lei
sarà. Ah!)

GERMONT
Siate di mia familia
L'angiol consolator,
Siate l'angiol consolator.

VIOLETTA
Dite alla giovine sì bella e
pura
Ch'avvi una vittima della
sventura,
Cui resta un unico raggio di
bene
Che a lei il sacrifica e che
morrà!

Whatever you may say,
I never could love another . . .

GERMONT
That may be.
But who knows how long his love will last?

VIOLETTA (*startled*)
Oh heaven!

GERMONT
The day when grace and loveliness,
The bloom of youth have faded,
Your present state of happiness,
Where will it be?—Consider!
You would not have the solace
Of sweeter, deep affection,
For love cannot endure
Without the blessing of the Lord above.

VIOLETTA
It's true, it's true!

GERMONT
I beg you to abandon
Such vain and hopeless dreaming.

VIOLETTA
It's true, it's true!

GERMONT
Do not destroy the happy future
Which we all so are desiring;
Violetta, it is not too late
To do what I implore!
If you will grant a father's plea,
I shall be grateful to you
Forevermore.

VIOLETTA (*to herself, with great sadness*)
Gone is my last ray of hope for salvation,
This is the last and the hardest privation!
Though heaven smiled on my love in compassion,
Man is relentless and I must yield.

GERMONT
Do not destroy the future
Which we so much desire.
Make my family glad again.

VIOLETTA
(*to* GERMONT, *very softly and moved*)
Go tell your daughter who is so dear to you,
Never because of me will she have to suffer.
I shall accept my fate,
But one ray of hope is remaining—
That through my sacrifice I have atoned,
And I may die in peace.

GERMONT
Bitter tears will ease your despair,
Bitter tears will bring you solace!
I have at last a true understanding
How great a sacrifice I am demanding.
You have my gratitude in all your suff'ring,
Have courage, your noble heart will prevail
And reward you at last.

VIOLETTA
What shall I do then?

GERMONT
Tell him you don't love him.

VIOLETTA
He won't believe it.

GERMONT
Desert him . . .

VIOLETTA
He will follow me.

GERMONT
That's true.

VIOLETTA
Embrace me as a father would his daughter!
Then I shall have the strength!
(they embrace)
He soon will be restored to you,
But hurt beyond description.
I ask your promise to wait there
And console him.
(indicating the garden)

GERMONT
What are you planning?

VIOLETTA
I fear you would oppose me
If I should tell you.

GERMONT
Yes, I know it.
In what way can I repay you,
Repay you ever the debt I owe you!

VIOLETTA
I'll die! And then let him remember me
Without bitter malediction;
Reveal my hopeless suffering,
My anguish and affliction.

GERMONT
No, you will live and happily,
A joyous fate accorded!
What you have done for all of us
By heaven will be rewarded.

VIOLETTA
Oh let him know the sacrifice
I made because I loved him—

GERMONT
Piangi, piangi, piangi, o misera,
piangi, piangi, piangi.
Supremo, il veggo,
È il sacrifizio ch'ora io ti
chieggo.
Sento nell'anima già le tue
pene;
Coraggio . . . e il nobile cor
vincerà.

VIOLETTA
Imponete.

GERMONT
Non amarlo ditegli.

VIOLETTA
Nol crederà.

GERMONT
Partite.

VIOLETTA
Seguirammi.

GERMONT
Allor . . .

VIOLETTA
Qual figlia m'abbracciate . . .
Forte così sarò.
Tra breve ei vi fia reso,
Ma afflitto oltre ogni dire. A
suo conforto
Di colà volerete.

GERMONT
Che pensate?

VIOLETTA
Sapendol, v'oppporeste al pensier
mio.

GERMONT
Generosa! e per voi che
far poss'io?
Che far poss'io? o generosa!

VIOLETTA
Morrò! . . . la mia memoria
Non fia ch'ei maledica,
Se le mie pene orribili
Vi sia chi almen gli dica.

GERMONT
No, generosa, vivere,
E lieta voi dovrete,
Mercè di queste lagrime
Dal cielo un giorno avrete.

VIOLETTA
Conosca il sacrifizio
Ch'io consumai d'amore . . .

Che sarà suo fin l'ultimo
Sospiro del mio cor.

That all my heart and ev'ry thought
Are his forevermore,
And that I love him with all my heart,
That all my thoughts are his,
Are his forevermore.

GERMONT
Premiato il sacrifizio
Sarà del vostro amore,
D'un' opra così nobile
Sarete fiera allor.
Premiato il sacrifizio,
Premiato il sacrifizio
Sarà del vostro cor, ah sì.
D'un'opra così nobil,
D'un'opra così nobil
Sarete fiera allor.

GERMONT
You will be always very proud,
And such a noble deed
Will bring reward at last.
I always will be grateful
For your heroic action
Which saved my fam'ly's pride and name.
You won't regret your kindness,
And soon your present sorrow
Will fade into the past.
My thanks for your heroic deed
Are yours forevermore.
(*steps are heard outside*)

VIOLETTA
Qui giunge alcun! partite! . . .

VIOLETTA
Now you must go, I beg you.

GERMONT
Ah, grato v'è il cor mio!

GERMONT
Oh, I am deeply grateful!

VIOLETTA
Partite!
Non ci vedrem più forse . . .
Siate felice . . . Addio!

VIOLETTA
Go now!
This is farewell forever.
(*they embrace*)
May you be happy! Good-by!

GERMONT
Siate felice.
Addio.

GERMONT
May you be happy!
(GERMONT *goes toward the door*)
God bless you.

VIOLETTA
Conosca il sacrifizio
Che consumai d'amore.

VIOLETTA (*after a pause, weeping*)
Oh let him know the sacrifice
I made because I love him!

GERMONT
Sì.

GERMONT (*very softly*)
Yes.

VIOLETTA
Che sarà suo fin d'ultimo.
Addio!

VIOLETTA
Tell him, my heart is his alone . . .
(*under tears*)
Farewell . . .

GERMONT
Addio!

GERMONT
Farewell . . .

VIOLETTA, GERMONT
Felice siate.
Addio!

BOTH
May you be happy,
God bless you!
(GERMONT *leaves by the door leading to the garden.*)

VIOLETTA
Dammi tu forza, o cielo!

VIOLETTA (*sitting down at the writing table*)
Give me the strength, oh heaven!
(*rings a bell*)

ANNINA
Mi richiedeste?

ANNINA (*entering*)
Did you call me?

VIOLETTA
Yes; go and deliver this in person.

ANNINA (*seeing the address, surprised*)
Oh!

VIOLETTA
Say nothing. Go immediately.
(ANNINA *leaves*)
And now to write to Alfredo.
What shall I say?
How shall I find the courage?
(*she writes, then seals the letter*)

ALFREDO (*enters*)
Violetta!

VIOLETTA (*hiding the letter*)
Alfredo!

ALFREDO
You're writing?

VIOLETTA (*confused*)
Yes . . . no . . .

ALFREDO
You seem so troubled!
Whom were you writing?

VIOLETTA
To you.

ALFREDO
Then let me read it.

VIOLETTA
Not till later.

ALFREDO
Please forgive me,
I am disturbed and worried.

VIOLETTA (*rising*)
What happened?

ALFREDO
My father has been here . . .

VIOLETTA
Did you see him?

ALFREDO
Not yet; he left a stern, reproachful letter.
But I shall wait for him . . .
When he sees you, he will love you.

VIOLETTA (*excitedly*)
I don't want him to find me . . .
I'll go away till later . . .
You will calm him; then on my knees
I will implore
That he will never make us part!
(*hardly able to conceal her tears*)
We shall be happy, so very happy,
Because you love me, oh Alfredo,

VIOLETTA
Sì, reca tu stessa
Questo foglio . . .

ANNINA
Ah!

VIOLETTA
Silenzio . . . va all'istante.
Ed or si scriva a lui . . .
Che gli dirò? Chi men darà il coraggio?

ALFREDO
Che fai?

VIOLETTA
Nulla.

ALFREDO
Scrivevi?

VIOLETTA
Sì . . . no . . .

ALFREDO
Qual turbamento! . . . a chi scrivevi?

VIOLETTA
A te . . .

ALFREDO
Dammi quel foglio.

VIOLETTA
No, per ora . . .

ALFREDO
Mi perdona . . . son io preoccupato.

VIOLETTA
Che fu?

ALFREDO
Giunse mio padre . . .

VIOLETTA
Lo vedesti?

ALFREDO
Ah, no: severo scritto mi lasciava . . .
Però l'attendo, t'amerà in vederti.

VIOLETTA
Ch'ei qui non mi sorprenda,
Lascia che m'allontani . . . tu lo calma . . .
Ai piedi suoi mi getterò . . . divisi ei più
Non ne vorrà . . . sarem felici . . . sarem felici.
Perchè tu m'ami, Alfredo,
Tu m'ami non è vero?
Tu m'ami? Alfredo, tu m'ami, Alfredo,

Non è vero?

You love me, do you really?
Oh don't you? My Alfredo, you love me?

ALFREDO
Oh, quanto . . . Perchè piangi?

ALFREDO
Forever! Why are you crying?

VIOLETTA
Di lagrime avea d'uopo . . . or son tranquilla . . .
Lo vedi? . . . ti sorrido . . .
Lo vedi? or son tranquilla, ti sorrido.
Sarò là, tra quei fior presso a te sempre.
Amami, Alfredo, amami quant'io t'amo . . .
Amami, Alfredo, quant'io t'amo, quant'io t'amo.
Addio!

VIOLETTA
The tears just seem to overcome me!
But now it's over, you see it?
Now I'm smiling, you see it?
I am much calmer, I am smiling,
I'll be there . . . close to you . . .
There in the garden,
Always, always close to you—
Ah, my beloved, promise to love me always!
Ah, my Alfredo, always love me
As I love you . . . Farewell, my love.
(*she runs into the garden*)

Scene and Aria

ALFREDO
Ah, vive sol quel core all'amor mio!
È tardi: ed oggi forse
Più non verrà mio padre.

ALFREDO
She loves me so sincerely, my Violetta!
(*sits down, opens a book*)
It's late now; perhaps my father
Won't come until tomorrow.

GIUSEPPE
La signora è partita . . .
L'attendeva un calesse, e sulla via
Già corre di Parigi . . .
Annina pure prima di lei spariva.

JOSEPH (*enters hurriedly*)
The mistress has left . . .
A carriage was waiting
And drove off in the direction of Paris . . .
I think Annina must have left before her . . .

ALFREDO
Il so, ti calma.

ALFREDO
I know, don't worry.

GIUSEPPE
(Che vuol dir ciò?)

JOSEPH (*while leaving*)
What does he mean?

ALFREDO
Va forse d'ogni avere
Ad affrettar la perdita . . . Ma Annina lo impedirà.

Qualcuno è nel giardino!
Chi è là? . . .

ALFREDO
Perhaps she was anxious to dispose of her property.
But Annina will be in time.
(*some noise is heard outside*)
Someone is in the garden . . . Who's there?

COMMISSIONARIO
Il signor Germont?

MESSENGER
Monsieur Germont?

ALFREDO
Son io.

ALFREDO
What is it?

COMMISSIONARIO
Una dama
Da un cocchio, per voi, di qua non lunge,
Mi diede questo scritto . . .

MESSENGER
A lady in a carriage, not far from here, asked me to bring you this letter.
(*he gives a letter to* ALFREDO, *who pays him some money, and leaves*)

ALFREDO
Di Violetta! Perchè son io commosso?
A raggiungerla forse ella m'invita . . .

ALFREDO
From Violetta? Why am I so excited?
It could be that I am to join her later!
I'm trembling! Oh Lord! Courage!

(*he opens the letter*)
"Dear Alfredo, by the time you read this letter—"
Ah!
(*he turns and finds himself in the arms of his father*)
Oh, my father!

GERMONT
My Alfredo! How you must suffer!
Let me console you;
Return to your home and fam'ly,
The pride of your father!
(ALFREDO, *in despair, sits down by the small table, his hands covering his face*)
Can your heart be dead and cold
To all memories of home,
Of the land you loved to roam
In your childhood days of old?
What illusion could it be
That has made you break your ties
With your sunny native skies
And the blue and shining sea?
Now remember what you owe
To all those who hold you dear.
In their midst, you always know
Their affection is sincere,
And the peace of long ago
Will return when they are near.
God wills it so!
From the time you went away,
Of our joy we were bereaved.
Your poor father's heart was grieved,
And he suffered day by day!
I have never ceased to pray
That my hopes be not in vain,
And that you would see your way
To come home to us again.
If at last the gracious Lord
Has restored my son to me,
If inside his breast a chord
Still responds to pride's decree,
No more welcome a reward
For my prayers could there be!
And if my son returns to me,
God heard my plea!
(ALFREDO *remains unmoved*)
Don't you have a single word for your father?

ALFREDO
I am tortured by doubts and wild suspicion!
I must find her!

GERMONT
Don't do it!

Io tremo! . . . Oh ciel! . . . Coraggio! . . .
Alfredo, al giungervi di questo foglio . . .
Ah!
Padre mio!

GERMONT
Mio figlio! . . .
Oh, quanto soffri! oh, tergi il pianto,
Ritorna di tuo padre orgoglio e vanto.

Di Provenza il mar, il suol
Chi dal cor ti cancellò?
Chi dal cor ti cancellò
Di Provenza il mar, il suol?
Al natio fulgente sol
Qual destino ti furò?
Qual destino ti furò
Al natio fulgente sol?
Oh rammenta pur nel duol,
Ch'ivi gioia a te brillò,
E che pace colà sol
Su te splendere ancor può,
E che pace colà sol
Su te splendere ancor può.
Dio mi guidò! Dio mi guidò! Dio mi guidò!
Ah il tuo vecchio genitor
Tu non sai quanto soffrì,
Tu non sai quanto soffrì
Il tuo vecchio genitor!
Te lontano, di squallor
Il suo tetto si coprì,
Il suo tetto si coprì,
Di squallore, di squallor.
Ma se alfin ti trovo ancor,
Se in me speme non fallì,
Se la voce dell'onor
In te appien non ammutì,
Ma se alfin ti trovo ancor,
Se in me speme non fallì.
Dio m'esaudì, Dio m'esaudì, Dio m'esaudì,
Dio m'esaudì,
Ma se alfin ti trovo ancor, Dio m'esaudì,
Dio m'esaudì!

Nè rispondi d'un padre all'affetto?

ALFREDO
Mille furie divoranmi il petto . . .
Mi lasciate.

GERMONT
Lasciarti!

ALFREDO
(Oh vendetta!)

GERMONT
Non più indugi; partiamo . . . t'affretta . . .

ALFREDO
(Ah, fu Douphol!)

GERMONT
M'ascolti tu?

ALFREDO
No.

GERMONT
Dunque invano trovato t'avrò!

ALFREDO
Ah! . . . ell'è alla festa! volisi
L'offesa a vendicar.

GERMONT
Che dici? ah ferma!

FLORA
Avrem lieta di maschere la notte:
N'è duce il viscontino.
Violetta ed Alfredo anco invitai.

MARCHESE
La novità ignorate?
Violetta e Germont sono disgiunti.

FLORA, DOTTORE
Fia vero?

MARCHESE
Ella verrà qui col barone.

DOTTORE
Li vidi ieri ancor, parean felici.

FLORA
Silenzio . . . udite?

TUTTI
Giungono gli amici.

ALFREDO
I'll avenge this!

GERMONT
We must leave now—
I beg you, come with me!

ALFREDO
She loves the baron!

GERMONT
You'll come with me?

ALFREDO
No!

GERMONT
Then your father has pleaded in vain?

ALFREDO (*turns, notices the letter of* FLORA *on the table, runs through it and exclaims*)
Ah! She went to Flora's . . .
This outrageous shame I will avenge!
(*he rushes away, followed by* GERMONT)

GERMONT
Don't do it! I beg you!

Scene 2

(*Richly furnished and illuminated room in* FLORA'*s house. A door in the rear and two side doors. At right, more to the foreground, a large gambling table. At left, a table elaborately set with flowers, refreshments. Several chairs, and a divan.* FLORA, *the* MARQUIS, *the* DOCTOR, *and other guests enter from the left, conversing.*)

FLORA
A masquerade is the evening's entertainment; the count will lead the maskers.
Violetta and Alfredo also will come.

MARQUIS
Haven't you heard what happened?
Violetta and Alfredo just have parted.

FLORA, DOCTOR
Not really?

MARQUIS
And tonight she'll come with the baron.

DOCTOR
I saw them both last night,
They seemed very happy.
(*noise of arriving guests is heard*)

FLORA
Be quiet and listen.

ALL THREE
The party is beginning.

(a group of guests, dressed as gypsies enter, also dancers, in gypsy costumes)

Chorus of Gypsies

GYPSY GIRLS
From far-off Eastern countries
We gypsy girls have drifted;
Each one of us is gifted—
We'll read your open hand.
When we consult the planets and the stars in heaven,
There's nothing we don't know about your history and past.
The future has no myst'ry we do not understand.
Your former indiscretions we truly can depict,
Your future love and luck we most gladly will predict.
We are good at reading omens and what pleasures lie in wait;
We describe your joys and sorrows and tell your fate.
All we tell you is prophetic—
When to buy and when to sell.
The first one.
(a group is examining FLORA'S *hand)*
You, my lady have sev'ral pretty rivals.
(another group looks at the hand of the MARQUIS*)*
And you, Marquis, it's clear as day,
Are quite a lady's man.

FLORA *(to the* MARQUIS*)*
Aha, so you deceive me!
Well then, I must do likewise!

MARQUIS *(to* FLORA*)*
Why will you not believe me?
That story is not true!

FLORA
Chameleons change their colors,
But never change their habits;
My dear Marquis, be careful,
Or I'll make you repent,
My dear Marquis, beware, I am not yet content,
I'll pay you back at once
And you will soon repent.

DOCTOR, CHORUS OF GYPSIES
Enough, we draw a curtain
Upon what's past and ended.
What's done cannot be mended,
Let's rather look ahead.

FLORA, DOCTOR, MARQUIS, CHORUS
Let our errors be forgotten
And our cares be light and few.
May the future bring us joy
And the best of luck—
May life begin anew!
*(*FLORA *and the* MARQUIS *are reconciled and clasp each*

ZINGARE
Noi siamo zingarelle
Venute da lontano;
D'ognuno sulla mano
Leggiamo l'avvenir.
Se consultiam le stelle,
consultiam le stelle,
Null'avvi a noi d'oscuro, no,
null'avvi a noi d'oscuro,
E i casi del futuro
Possiamo altrui predir.
Se consultiam le stelle null'avvi a noi d'oscur,
E i casi del futuro possiamo altrui predir.
Vediamo!

I. ZINGARA
Voi, signora,
Rivali alquante avete.

II. ZINGARA
Marchese, voi non siete
Model di fedeltà.

FLORA
Fate il galante ancora?
Ben, vo' me la paghiate.

MARCHESE
Che diamin vi pensate?
L'accusa è falsità.

FLORA
La volpe lascia il pelo,
Non abbandona il vizio.
Marchese mio, giudizio
O vi farò pentir.
Marchese mio giudizio,
o vi farò pentir.
Marchese mio, giudizio,
O vi farò pentir.

DOTTORE, CORO
Su via, si stenda un velo
Sui fatti del passato;
Già quel ch'è stato è stato,
Badate all'avvenir.

FLORA, DOTTORE, MARCHESE, CORO
Su via, si stenda un velo
Sui fatti del passato;
Già quel ch'è stato è stato,
Bad ate/iamo all'avvenir.

other's hands; GASTON *and other masqueraders dressed as matadors and picadors enter briskly from the right)*

Chorus of Spanish Matadors

GASTONE, MATTADORI
Di Madride noi siam mattadori,
Siamo i prodi del circo dei tori,
Testè giunti a godere del
chiasso
Che a Parigi si fa pel Bue
grasso;
E una storia se udire vorrete,
Quali amanti noi siamo saprete.

GASTON, MATADORS
We are matadors of bravest demeanor,
Straight from triumphs in Spain's great arena,
Here in Paris by your invitation,
For the carnival's renowned celebration.
In the bull ring, courageous and fearless,
In affairs of the heart we are peerless!

GLI ALTRI
Sì, sì, bravi; narrate, narrate:
Con piacere l'udremo . . .

FLORA, DOCTOR, MARQUIS, CHORUS
Gallant heroes, we grant you permission!
Please begin your rendition!

GASTONE, MATTADORI
Ascoltate.
È Piquillo un bel gagliardo
Biscaglino mattador:
Forte il braccio, fiero il guardo,
Delle giostre egli è signor.
D'andalusa giovinetta
Follemente innamorò;
Ma la bella ritrosetta
Così al giovine parlò:
Cinque tori in un sol giorno
Vo' vederti ad atterrar;
E, se vinci, al tuo ritorno
Mano e cor ti vo' donar.
Sì, gli disse, e il mattadore,
Alle giostre mosse il piè;
Cinque tori, vincitore,
Sull'arena egli stendè.

GASTON, MATADORS
You shall hear it!
Once there was a young torero,
Don Piquillo was his name.
Bold and proud, this handsome hero
Quickly rose to heights of fame.
But the girl that he proposed to—
Haughty Andalusian maid—
Told him she was not disposed to
Wed him till she was obeyed.
"If you kill five bulls in one day,
Then I'll say you are a success!
If you do it, then next Monday
I can promise, I'll say 'yes.' "
Said Piquillo: "I will do it,
That will not be hard for me!"
And before his sweetheart knew it,
He had done it, one, two, three!
Five bulls dead, like nothing to it!
What a mighty man was he!

GLI ALTRI
Bravo bravo il mattadore,
Ben gagliardo si mostrò,
Se alla giovine l'amore
In tal guisa egli provò.

FLORA, DOCTOR, MARQUIS, CHORUS
Good for him, the gallant fighter,
Gave his sweetheart quite a show!
But his deeds, did they delight her?
That's the thing we want to know.

GASTONE, MATTADORI
Poi, tra plausi, ritornato
Alla bella del suo cor,
Colse il premio desiato
Tra le braccia dell'amor.

GASTON, MATADORS
Yes, the lady met her equal,
So she smiled a willing "yes."
And as joyous, tender sequel,
They lived long in happiness.

GLI ALTRI
Con tai prove i mattadori
San le belle conquistar!

FLORA, DOCTOR, MARQUIS, CHORUS
Matadors are full of passion
And their loves are fiercely won.

GASTONE, MATTADORI
Ma qui son più miti i cori;
A noi basta folleggiar.

GASTON, MATADORS
We're more peaceful in our fashion,
We're content with joy and fun.

ALL
Let us see if luck is gracious,
Let us tempt the whirling wheel;
Fortune smiles on the audacious,
Come, let's try a daring deal!

Gaming Scene and Chorus

(ALFREDO *enters, seemingly unconcerned*)
Why, Alfredo, you!

ALFREDO
Yes, good evening.

FLORA
Violetta?

ALFREDO
I don't know!

ALL OTHERS (*among themselves*)
Quite unembarrassed, bravo!
(*aloud*)
And now, let's have a game!
(GASTON *deals,* ALFREDO *and others are playing*)
(VIOLETTA *enters on the arm of the* BARON. FLORA *goes to meet them*)

FLORA
How very nice to see you!

VIOLETTA
So kind of you to ask me!

FLORA
I am so glad, dear Baron,
That you are here this evening.

BARON (*softly to* VIOLETTA)
Germont is here, have you noticed?

VIOLETTA (*to herself*)
Heavens, it's true!
(*to the* BARON)
I see him.

BARON
One thing I do insist on:
You must not speak to Alfredo!
I forbid it.

VIOLETTA (*aside*)
Ah, why did I ever come here,
Protect me now in my distress, oh, Lord!

FLORA (*sits down next to* VIOLETTA *on the divan. The* DOCTOR *stands near them. The* MARQUIS *remains at a distance with the* BARON. ALFREDO *and* GASTON *go on playing cards*)
Let us sit down here. Tell me,
What has gone wrong between you?

ALFREDO
A seven!

GASTON
You are the winner!

TUTTI
Sì, allegri, or pria tentiamo
Della sorte il vario umor;
La palestra dischiudiamo
Agli audaci giocator.

Alfredo! Voi!

ALFREDO
Sì, amici.

FLORA
Violetta?

ALFREDO
Non ne so.

TUTTI
Ben disinvolto! . . . Bravo! . . .
Or via, giocar si può.

FLORA
Qui desiata giungi.

VIOLETTA
Cessi al cortese invito.

FLORA
Grata vi son, barone, d'averlo pur gradito.

BARONE
(Germont è qui! il vedete?)

VIOLETTA
(Cielo! . . . gli è vero.)
Il vedo.

BARONE
Da voi non un sol detto si volga a questo Alfredo.
Non un detto.

VIOLETTA
(Ah, perchè venni, incauta!
Pietà, gran Dio,
Pietà, gran Dio, di me!

FLORA
Meco t'assidi; narrami . . . quai novità vegg'io?

ALFREDO
Un quattro!

GASTONE
Ancora hai vinto!

ALFREDO
Sfortuna nell'amore
Fortuna reca al gioco! . . .

ALFREDO
Bad luck in love is always
Good fortune for a gambler!
(*he takes a trick and wins*)

TUTTI
È sempre vincitore! . . .

GASTON, MARQUIS, GUESTS
He is again the winner!

ALFREDO
Oh, vincerò stasera: e l'oro guadagnato
Poscia a goder tra' campi ritornerò beato.

ALFREDO
Oh, I shall win all evening
And then I'll take this treasure
Back with me to the country
And spend it there, for pleasure!

FLORA
Solo?

FLORA
Alone?

ALFREDO
No, no, con tale che vi fu meco ancor,
Poi mi sfuggia . . .

ALFREDO
No, no! With someone who lived with me before there,
And now has betrayed me.

VIOLETTA
(Mio Dio! . . .)

VIOLETTA (*aside*)
Good heavens!

GASTONE
(Pietà di lei!)

GASTON (*to* ALFREDO)
You go too far!

BARONE
Signor!

BARON (*to* ALFREDO *with badly concealed fury*)
Monsieur!

VIOLETTA
(Frenatevi, o vi lascio.)

VIOLETTA (*softly to the* BARON)
Be courteous or I'll leave you!

ALFREDO
Barone, m'appellaste?

ALFREDO (*indifferently*)
What were you saying, Baron?

BARONE
Siete in sì gran fortuna, che al gioco mi tentaste.

BARON (*ironically*)
Your luck is so amazing
That I should like to play you.

ALFREDO
Sì? . . . la disfida accetto . . .

ALFREDO (*ironically*)
Yes? I accept the challenge.

VIOLETTA
(Che fia? morir mi sento!
Pietà, gran Dio, pietà, gran Dio, di me!)

VIOLETTA (*aside*)
Dear God, I wonder what will happen!
Protect me now in my distress, oh Lord!

BARONE
Cento luigi a destra.

BARON
I'll stake a hundred Louis d'ors!

ALFREDO
Ed alla manca cento.

ALFREDO
I put a hundred against it!

GASTONE
Un asso . . . un fante . . . hai vinto!

GASTON (*dealing*)
An ace . . . a jack . . .
(*to* ALFREDO)
You won it.

BARONE
Il doppio?

BARON
Two hundred?

ALFREDO
Il doppio sia.

ALFREDO
Well then, two hundred.

GASTONE
Un quattro, un sette.

GASTON (*dealing*)
A four, a seven . . .

TUTTI
Ancora!

DOCTOR, MARQUIS, GUESTS
He won it!

ALFREDO
I am again the winner!

ALL
Lucky indeed! Good fortune
Is once again with Alfredo!

FLORA
And for his rustic pleasures
The baron is providing!

ALFREDO (*to the* BARON)
Another deal!

SERVANT (*enters and announces*)
Supper is served.

FLORA
Let's go in then!

ALL OTHERS
With pleasure!

FLORA
Please follow!

ALL OTHERS
At once!
(*All leave except* ALFREDO *and the* BARON)

VIOLETTA (*aside*)
Dear God, I wonder what will happen!
Protect me now in my distress, oh Lord!

ALFREDO
Should you wish to continue—

BARON
Not now, but after supper.
And we shall see who's lucky then!

ALFREDO
Whatever is your pleasure.

BARON
Let's follow the others . . .
Later . . .

ALFREDO
I am at your disposal.
(*they leave the room*)
Till then.

BARON
Till then.

VIOLETTA (*returns, in great excitement*)
I sent word to him to meet me.
Will he do it? Can I persuade him?
He will come. I must prevail on him
To listen to my warning . . .

ALFREDO (*enters*)
You have called me? Well, what is it?

VIOLETTA
You must lose no time in leaving!
If you stay here, you're in danger!

ALFREDO
Pur la vittoria è mia!

TUTTI
Bravo davver! la sorte è tutta per Alfredo!

FLORA
Del villeggiar la spesa farà il baron, già il vedo.

ALFREDO
Seguite pur.

SERVO
La cena è pronta.

FLORA
Andiamo.

CORO
Andiamo.

FLORA
Andiamo!

CORO
Andiam!

VIOLETTA
(Che fia? morir me sento.
Pietà, gran Dio, pietà, gran Dio, di me!

ALFREDO
Se continuar v'aggrada . . .

BARONE
Per ora nol possiamo:
Più tardi la rivincita.

ALFREDO
Al gioco che vorrete.

BARONE
Seguiam gli amici; poscia . . .

ALFREDO
Sarò qual bramerete, Andiam.

BARONE
Andiam.

VIOLETTA
Invitato a qui seguirmi,
Verrà desso? . . . vorrà udirmi?
Ei verrà, chè l'odio atroce
Puote in lui più di mia voce!

ALFREDO
Mi chiamaste? che bramate?

VIOLETTA
Questi luoghi abbandonate!
Un periglio vi sovrasta . . .

ALFREDO
Ah, comprendo! . . . Basta, basta . . .
E sì vile mi credete?

VIOLETTA
Ah, no mai . . .

ALFREDO
Ma che temete?

VIOLETTA
Temo sempre del barone . . .

ALFREDO
È fra noi mortal quistione . . .
S'ei cadrà per mano mia
Un sol colpo vi torria
Coll'amante il protettore . . .
V'atterrisce tal sciagura?

VIOLETTA
Ma s'ei fosse l'uccisore!
Ecco l'unica sventura . . .
Ch'io pavento a me fatale!

ALFREDO
La mia morte! Che ven cale?

VIOLETTA
Deh, partite, e sull'istante.

ALFREDO
Partirò, ma giura innante
Che dovunque seguirai
I passi miei . . .

VIOLETTA
Ah, no, giammai.

ALFREDO
No! giammai!

VIOLETTA
Va, sciagurato.
Scorda un nome ch'è infamato.
Va . . . mi lascia sul momento
Di fuggirti un giuramento
Sacro io feci.

ALFREDO
A chi? dillo!
e chi potea?

VIOLETTA
A chi dritto pien n' avea.

ALFREDO
Fu Douphol?

VIOLETTA
Sì.

ALFREDO
Dunque l'ami?

VIOLETTA
Ebben . . . l'amo . . .

ALFREDO
Or tutti a me!

ALFREDO
Oh I see it, what an insult!
And you think me such a coward?

VIOLETTA
Ah no, believe me!

ALFREDO
Then why be frightened?

VIOLETTA
I'm afraid Douphol might harm you!

ALFREDO
Do not let the thought alarm you!
But of course, if I should kill him,
With one blow I would deprive you
Of your lover and protector!
Does that prospect make you tremble?

VIOLETTA
But if he instead should kill you,
That would be the one misfortune
I would dread above all others.

ALFREDO
If he killed me? Why would you care?

VIOLETTA
Do not stay here! Depart this instant!

ALFREDO
I shall go but not until you promise on your word of honor
To return to the country.

VIOLETTA
Ah no, I cannot!

ALFREDO
So you cannot?

VIOLETTA
You must believe me and forget me!
Go and leave me, at this moment! I implore you,
For I gave my word that I will leave you.

ALFREDO
To whom? Tell me! Who could ask it?

VIOLETTA
One who had the right to ask it.

ALFREDO
It's the baron?

VIOLETTA (*with utmost will power*)
Yes.

ALFREDO
Then you love him?

VIOLETTA
Yes . . . I love him . . .

ALFREDO (*runs furiously toward the door and calls*)
Come here at once!

(*everybody enters in confusion*)

ALL
Here we are! Well, what is it?

ALFREDO (*indicating* VIOLETTA, *who stands exhausted, supporting herself at the table*)
Do you all here know this woman?

ALL
Who, Violetta?

ALFREDO
What she did, you do not know yet?

VIOLETTA (*softly to* ALFREDO)
Don't say it!

ALL
No!

ALFREDO
All she possessed, this woman here
Squandered on me unsparing . . .
And blindly, vilely, recklessly,
I took it all, uncaring!
But there is time to clear myself,
Time to repay such kindness!
I call you all to witness,
I call you all to testify
That I have paid her back in full!
(*with furious contempt he throws a purse at* VIOLETTA'S *feet. She faints into the arms of* FLORA)

ALL OTHERS (*except* VIOLETTA)
Oh, what an infamous act you committed!
To shameless slander and lies you descended!
(*at this moment* GERMONT *enters*)
You have insulted and deeply offended
A person whom we respect and esteem!
Go, go, go, go! Leave this house at once!
Such shameless conduct we never have witnessed,
Such low brutality we never saw!
You are no longer one of us,
Depart at once and leave this house!

GERMONT (*with dignified fire*)
No man of honor insults a woman,
Whatever reason might rouse his anger!
How could you ever forget your dignity?
My son, my son, my Alfredo,
How could you fall so low?
Are you my Alfredo whom I respected?
This is not you, not my son,
You are no more the Alfredo I know.

ALFREDO (*to himself*)
Whatever caused me to act so blindly!
My life was shattered, I was unhappy!
My heart was broken. I lost my reason,

TUTTI
Ne appellaste? Che volete?

ALFREDO
Questa donna conoscete?

TUTTI
Chi? Violetta?

ALFREDO
Che facesse
Non sapete?

VIOLETTA
Ah, taci . . .

TUTTI
No.

ALFREDO
Ogni suo aver tal femmina
Per amor mio sperdea . . .
Io cieco, vile, misero,
Tutto accettar potea,
Ma è tempo ancora! tergermi
Da tanta macchia bramo
Qui testimon vi chiamo
Che qui pagata io l'ho.

TUTTI
Oh, infamia orribile
Tu commettesti!
Un cor sensibile
Così uccidesti!
Di donne ignobile insultatore,
Di qua allontanati,
Ne desti orror.

Va, va, va, va,
Ne desti orror.
Di donne ignobile insultatore,
Di qua allontanati,
Ne desti orror.

GERMONT
Di sprezzo degno sè stesso rende
Chi pur nell'ira la donna offende.
Dov'è mio figlio? . . . più non lo vedo:
In te più Alfredo—trovar non so.

ALFREDO
(Ah sì . . . che feci! . . . ne sento orrore.
Gelosa smania, deluso amore
Mi strazian l'alma . . . più non ragiono.

Da lei perdono—più non avrò.
Volea fuggirla . . . non ho potuto!
Dall'ira spinto son qui venuto!
Or che lo sdegno ho disfogato,
Me sciagurato! . . . rimorso n'ho).

TUTTI
Ah, quanto peni! . . . Ma pur fa cor . . .
Qui soffre ognuno del tuo dolor,
Fra cari amici qui sei soltanto;
Rasciuga il pianto che t'inondò.

BARONE
A questa donna l'atroce insulto
Qui tutti offese, ma non inulto
Fia tanto oltraggio . . . provar vi voglio
Che tanto orgoglio fiaccar saprò.

GERMONT
(Io sol fra tanti so qual virtude
Di quella misera il sen racchiude . . .
Io so che l'ama, che gli è fedele,
Eppur, crudele tacer dovrò!)

VIOLETTA
Alfredo, Alfredo, di questo core
Non puoi comprendere tutto l'amore;
Tu non conosci che fino a prezzo
Del tuo disprezzo—provato io l'ho!
Ma verrà tempo in che il saprai . . .
Come t'amassi confesserai . . .
Dio dai rimorsi ti salvi allora
Ah! io spenta ancora t'amerò.

TUTTI
Sì, rasciuga il pianto
Che t'inondò!
Fa cor, fa cor, qui soffre ognun del tuo dolor,
Rasciuga il pianto che t'inondò!

ALFREDO
Che feci, ohimè!
Ne sento orrore
Da lei perdono più non avrò.
Gelosa smania, deluso amor!
Or che lo sdegno ho disfogato,
Rimorso n'ho, rimorso n'ho!

No hope of pardon is left to me!
My pride was wounded. I could not bear it.
In raging hatred I wanted vengeance!
Now that my anger has lost its fury,
I am in mis'ry, full of remorse.

ALL (*except the* BARON, GERMONT, *to* VIOLETTA)
Oh, how you suffer, you must take heart!
We all know you, will take your part.
We love you dearly, we stand beside you,
He is unworthy of your despair.

BARON (*softly to* ALFREDO)
The insult to this lady
Is so outrageous
That it demands instant satisfaction!
And to this purpose I shall take action!
Here is my challenge! I am determined,
There shall be justice in this affair!

GERMONT (*aside, to himself*)
I only know the truth she is hiding,
All of the anguish she is not confiding.
I know she loves him, that she is faithful,
But I must cruelly conceal the truth!

VIOLETTA (*reviving; in a very weak but passionate tone*)
Beloved Alfredo, you can't imagine
What you have been to me,
And how I love you!
You do not know yet how much you mean to me,
How much I suffer beneath your disdain!
The day will come though, when you will realize,
How much I loved you
And will always love you.
May God preserve you from sad repentance,
May God preserve you from remorse.

ALL OTHERS (*except* BARON, GERMONT, ALFREDO)
Dry your tears and take heart!
Do not weep any more,
You are among dear friends!
He is not worthy of your despair,
Dry your tears and take heart!

ALFREDO
I am in mis'ry, full of remorse!
My jealous hatred has made me blind!
Now that my anger has lost its fury,
Bitter remorse fills my heart!

(GERMONT *draws* ALFREDO *with him. The* BARON *follows him.* VIOLETTA *is led by* FLORA *into another room. The others disperse.*)

ACT III

(*Bedroom of* VIOLETTA. *In the rear a bed, with curtains half drawn. A window with closed shutters. Near the bed, a stool on which are a bottle of water, several medicines. In the center, a dressing table; nearby a sofa. Farther away another piece of furniture on which a night light is burning. Several chairs and other pieces of furniture. A door at left. In front a fireplace with a fire burning.* VIOLETTA *is sleeping on the bed.* ANNINA, *sitting near the fireplace, is also asleep.*)

Scene and Aria

VIOLETTA (*awakening*)
Annina?

ANNINA (*rising, confused*)
Did you call me?

VIOLETTA
I woke you? You were sleeping.

ANNINA
Yes, please forgive me.

VIOLETTA
May I have some water.
(ANNINA *gives her water*)
And tell me, it must be morning.

ANNINA
It's past seven.

VIOLETTA
Make the room a little lighter.

ANNINA (*opens the shutters and looks out into the street*)
Here comes Doctor Grenvil.

VIOLETTA
He never fails me!
I will get up. Please help me.
(*she tries to rise, but falls back, then, supported by* ANNINA, *she goes slowly toward the sofa. The* DOCTOR *arrives in time to assist her*)
You are so good!
What would I do without you?

DOCTOR (*feeling her pulse*)
Well, how do you feel this morning?

VIOLETTA
Although I'm suff'ring, my mind is peaceful.
A priest heard my confession
And brought me comfort.
Ah, religion lightens and consoles the troubled spirit.

DOCTOR
How did you sleep?

VIOLETTA
Calmly, without awaking.

DOCTOR
Then do not worry,
You are on the way to convalescence.

VIOLETTA
Annina?

ANNINA
Comandate?

VIOLETTA
Dormivi, poveretta?

ANNINA
Sì, perdonate.

VIOLETTA
Dammi d'acqua un sorso.

Osserva, è pieno il giorno?

ANNINA
Son sett'ore.

VIOLETTA
Dà accesso a un po' di luce . . .

ANNINA
Il signor di Grenvil! . . .

VIOLETTA
Oh, il vero amico! . . .
Alzar mi vo' . . . m'aita.

Quanta bontà! . . . pensaste a me per tempo! . . .

DOTTORE
Sì, come vi sentite?

VIOLETTA
Soffre il mio corpo, ma tranquilla ho l'alma.
Mi confortò ier sera un pio ministro.
Religione è sollievo ai sofferenti.

DOTTORE
E questa notte?

VIOLETTA
Ebbi tranquillo il sonno.

DOTTORE
Coraggio adunque . . . la convalescenza
Non è lontana . . .

VIOLETTA
Oh, la bugia pietosa
Ai medici è concessa . . .

DOTTORE
Addio . . . a più tardi.

VIOLETTA
Non mi scordate.

ANNINA
Come va, signore?

DOTTORE
La tisi non le accorda che poche ore.

ANNINA
Or fate cor.

VIOLETTA
Giorno di festa è questo?

ANNINA
Tutta Parigi impazza . . . è carnevale . . .

VIOLETTA
Oh, nel comun tripudio, sallo Iddio.
Quanti infelici soffron! . . . Quale somma
V'ha in quello stipo?

ANNINA
Venti luigi.

VIOLETTA
Dieci ne reca ai poveri tu stessa.

ANNINA
Poco rimanvi allora . . .

VIOLETTA
Oh, mi saran bastanti;
Cerca poscia mie lettere.

ANNINA
Ma voi? . . .

VIOLETTA
Nulla occorrà . . . sollecita, se puoi.

VIOLETTA
Teneste la promessa . . . la disfida
Ebbe luogo! il barone fu ferito,
Però migliora . . . Alfredo
È in stranio suolo; il vostro sacrifizio
Io stesso gli ho svelato;
Egli a voi tornerà pel suo perdono;
Io pur verrò . . . Curatevi . . . mertate
Un avvenir migliore.
Giorgio Germont.
È tardi! . . .
Attendo, attendo . . . nè a me giungon mai! . . .

VIOLETTA
You say that out of kindness
Because you want to cheer me!

DOCTOR (*pressing her hand*)
Good-by then, till this evening.

VIOLETTA
You won't forget me?
(*the* DOCTOR *leaves.* ANNINA *escorts him*)

ANNINA (*softly and quickly*)
How is she, Doctor?

DOCTOR
I think that by tonight it will all be over.
(*he leaves*)

ANNINA (*hiding her shock and grief, returning to* VIOLETTA)
You must take heart.

VIOLETTA
Isn't today a holiday?

ANNINA
Paris is wild with excitement,
Because it's carnival!

VIOLETTA
And while the crowd rejoices,
God alone knows how many poor are suff'ring!
How much money is there left now?

ANNINA (*opens a box and counts*)
Just twenty Louis d'ors.

VIOLETTA
Ten of them give to the poor and needy.

ANNINA
That will leave you little.

VIOLETTA
Oh, I shall never need it!
Will you go for my letters now?

ANNINA
But you?

VIOLETTA
I'm quite all right, but try your best to hurry.
(ANNINA *leaves.* VIOLETTA *takes a letter from her bosom and reads in a soft voice*)
"You have kept your promise. The duel took place—the baron was wounded, but not seriously. Alfredo is on foreign soil. I myself revealed your sacrifice to him. He is returning to beg your forgiveness. I will come with him. May you soon recover and a happier future be yours. George Germont."
Too late!
(*she rises*)
I waited and waited—but my days are numbered.
(*she looks into the mirror*)

Ah, how my illness changed me!
Yet the doctor gave me hope of recov'ry!
Ah, with such an illness I know that all is hopeless.

Farewell then, to illusions,
To hoping and dreaming.
The joys I so longed for
Are gone past redeeming.
How lonely without my beloved beside me,
His loving affection forever denied me.
How lonely to die, ah—
Grant me Thy blessing, dear Father in Heaven,
Console and absolve me,
To enter Thy Kingdom.
Ah, ended, ended,
All dreams, all hope is lost and dead!
(from the street the singing of a merry carnival crowd is heard)

Oh, come son mutata!
Ma il dottore a sperar pure m'esorta!
Ah, con tal morbo ogni speranza è morta.
Addio, del passato bei sogni ridenti,
Le rose del volto già sono pallenti;
L'amore d'Alfredo perfino mi manca,
Conforto, sostegno dell'anima stanca
Ah, della traviata sorridi al desio;
A lei, deh perdona; tu accoglila, o Dio.
Ah! tutto, tutto finì,
Or tutto, tutto finì.

Bacchanal Chorus

CHORUS
Hail to His Highness, we bow to his powers,
Let us adorn him with garlands of flowers.
Hail to King Carnival!
Hail to His Majesty!
Greet him with piccolo, tambourine, and tuba!
Gather one and all and join the merry carnival procession!
Hail to His Highness, we bow to his powers,
Let us adorn him with garlands of flowers.
Hail to him,
The mighty King.
(the sound fades away)

CORO DI MASCHERE
Largo al quadrupede
Sir della festa,
Di fiori e pampini
Cinta la testa . . .
Largo al più docile
D'ogni cornuto,
Di corni e pifferi
Abbia il saluto.
Parigini, date passo
Al trionfo del Bue grasso.
Largo al quadrupede
Sir della festa,
Di fiori e pampini
Cinta la testa;
Largo al quadrupede
Sir della festa,
Largo, largo, largo.

Scene and Duet

ANNINA *(returns hurriedly)*
My Lady!

ANNINA
Signora!

VIOLETTA
What has happened?

VIOLETTA
Che t'accadde?

ANNINA
This morning, you told me
You were feeling better?

ANNINA
Quest'oggi, è vero? vi sentite meglio? . . .

VIOLETTA
Yes, but why?

VIOLETTA
Sì, perchè?

ANNINA
And you won't be too excited?

ANNINA
D'esser calma promettete?

VIOLETTA
No, won't you tell me?

VIOLETTA
Sì, che vuoi dirmi?

ANNINA
I hurried back to tell you
That a great surprise awaits you.

ANNINA
Prevenir vi volli . . .
Una gioia improvvisa . . .

VIOLETTA
Do you mean it? Is it really?

VIOLETTA
Una gioia! . . . dicesti? . . .

ANNINA
Sì, o signora . . .

VIOLETTA
Alfredo! . . . Ah, tu il vedesti?
Ei vien! . . . l'affretta.
Alfredo!
Amato Alfredo! Amato Alfredo!
Amato Alfredo, oh gioia!

ALFREDO
Oh mia Violetta! . . . oh, mia Violetta!
Oh, mia Violetta, oh, gioa!
Colpevol sonno . . . so tutto, o cara.

VIOLETTA
Io so che alfine reso mi sei! . . .

ALFREDO
Da questo palpito s'io t'ami impara,
Senza te esistere più non potrei.

VIOLETTA
Ah, s'anco in vita m'hai ritrovata,
Credi che uccidere non può il dolor.

ALFREDO
Scorda l'affanno, donna adorata,
A me perdona e al genitor.

VIOLETTA
Ch'o ti perdoni? la rea son io;
Ma solo amor tal mi rendè.

ALFREDO
Null'uomo o demon, angiol mio,
Mai più dividermi potrà da te.

VIOLETTA
Null'uomo o demon, angiol mio,
Mai più dividermi . . .

ALFREDO
Parigi, o cara, noi lasceremo,
La vita uniti trascorreremo:
De' corsi affanni compenso avrai,
La tua salute rifiorirà.
Sospiro e luce tu mi sarai,
Tutto il futuro ne arriderà.

VIOLETTA
Parigi, o cara, noi lasceremo,
La vita uniti trascorreremo:
De' corsi affanni compenso avrai,
La mia salute rifiorirà.
Sospiro e luce tu mi sarai,
Tutto il futuro ne arriderà.
Ah, non più, a un tempio . . . Alfredo, andiamo,

ANNINA
Yes, dearest lady.

VIOLETTA
He's coming! You saw my Alfredo?
At last, at last! He's coming!
(ALFREDO *appears*)
My Alfredo!
Oh my beloved, oh my Alfredo,
Dearest love, oh joyful day!

ALFREDO
Oh, my Violetta, oh Violetta,
Dearest love, oh joyful day!
(*they embrace*)
How could I hurt you and ever doubt you?

VIOLETTA
To have you near me is such a blessing!

ALFREDO
I lived in misery, alone without you,
And how I longed for you is past expressing!

VIOLETTA
If to this moment the Lord has spared me,
He will be merciful and let me live.

ALFREDO
All bitter suff'ring I must have caused you,
I came to beg that you forgive!

VIOLETTA
I should forgive you, when I am guilty?
Though it was love that made me so.

ALFREDO
No force on earth, beloved, ever
Shall be strong enough to part us now.

VIOLETTA
No force on earth, beloved, ever
Shall be strong enough to part us now.
(*he leads* VIOLETTA *gently to the sofa*)

ALFREDO
Nothing, my dearest, shall now remind us
Of all the suff'ring we leave behind us;
Far from Paris, far from intrusion
You shall recover, free from the past.
Living united in sweet seclusion,
Our love will bring us happiness at last.

VIOLETTA
Nothing, my dearest, shall now remind us
Of all the suff'ring we leave behind us;
Far from Paris, far from intrusion
I shall recover, free from the past.
Living united in sweet seclusion,
Our love will bring us happiness at last.
(*getting up from the sofa*)

Come, we'll go to church now,
And, reunited before the altar,
Thank God in Heaven.
(*she has a spell of weakness*)

ALFREDO
You are trembling!

VIOLETTA
It's really nothing, the joyous moment,
So long awaited, made me so happy,
It overwhelmed me.
(VIOLETTA *sinks utterly exhausted upon a chair*)

ALFREDO (*frightened, supporting her*)
Good heavens, Violetta!

VIOLETTA
It is not serious, a passing weakness,
Already I'm better, you see it?
(*forcing herself to smile*)
I'm smiling . . .

ALFREDO (*disconsolately*)
Ah, what misfortune!

VIOLETTA
It's nothing! Annina, help me get ready!

ALFREDO
How can you? Be patient!

VIOLETTA (*rising*)
No, I want to go with you!
(ANNINA *hands* VIOLETTA *a jacket, which she tries to put on, but, unable to do so, she throws it to the floor and exclaims*)
Great heavens! I cannot!
(*falls back on the chair*)

ALFREDO
God! I see it.
(*to* ANNINA)
Go for the doctor!

VIOLETTA (*to* ANNINA)
Yes, tell him that Alfredo has come to join me,
That he is with me, and that he loves me;
Tell him that now I must live for him
And that I must recover.
(ANNINA *leaves*)
(*to* ALFREDO)
But if your coming does not restore me
No earthly power can save me ever!
Ah, dear Lord! How sad to die so young,
How tragic and ill-fated!
To die so close to happiness
I have so long awaited!
It was a vain delusion
Which made me keep on hoping!

Del tuo ritorno grazie
rendiamo . . .

ALFREDO
Tu impallidisci!

VIOLETTA
È nulla, sai!
Gioia improvvisa non entra mai
Senza turbarlo in mesto
core . . .

ALFREDO
Gran Dio! . . . Violetta!

VIOLETTA
È il mio malore!
Fu debolezza! ora son forte,
Vedi? . . . sorrido . . .

ALFREDO
(Ahi, cruda sorte!)

VIOLETTA
Fu nulla . . . Annina, dammi
a vestire.

ALFREDO
Adesso? Attendi.

VIOLETTA
No! voglio uscire.

Gran Dio! non posso!

ALFREDO
(Cielo! che vedo!)
Va pel dottore . . .

VIOLETTA
Ah! Digli che Alfredo
È ritornato all'amor mio . . .
Digli che vivere ancor
vogl'io . . .
Ma se tornando non m'hai
salvato,
A niuno in terra salvarmi è
dato.
Ah! Gran Dio! morir sì giovine,
Io che penato ho tanto!
Morir sì presso a tergere
Il mio sì lungo pianto!
Ah, dunque fu delirio
La credula speranza;
Invano di costanza
Armato avrò il mio cor!

In vain I made a solemn vow
To arm my loving heart!

ALFREDO
Oh mio sospiro e palpito
Diletto del cor mio!
Le mie colle tue lacrime
Confondere degg'io
Ma più che mai, deh, credilo,
N'è d'uopo di costanza.
Ah! tutto alla speranza
Non chiudere il tuo cor.

ALFREDO
You are my life and happiness,
My joy and inspiration!
My tears with yours are flowing
In this hour of tribulation.
I beg you to have faith again
You must go on believing.
Ah, do not close your mind to hope—
Bereaving so your heart.

VIOLETTA
Oh, Alfredo! il crudo termine
Serbato al nostro amor!

VIOLETTA
Oh tragic fortune and cruel, bitter irony—
So soon again to part!

ALFREDO
Ah! Violetta, m'uccide il tuo dolor,
Deh! calmati!

ALFREDO
Oh, Violetta you must not yet lose hope,
You break my heart!

VIOLETTA
Morir sì presso a tergero.

VIOLETTA
Alas, so soon to part!

ALFREDO
Violetta, deh, calmati!

ALFREDO
Violetta, do not lose heart!
(VIOLETTA *sinks upon the sofa*)

Finale—Quintet

GERMONT
Ah, Violetta! . . .

GERMONT (*entering, followed by the* DOCTOR *and* ANNINA)
Ah! Violetta!

VIOLETTA
Voi, signor! . . .

VIOLETTA
You have come!

ALFREDO
Mio padre!

ALFREDO
My father!

VIOLETTA
Non mi scordaste?

VIOLETTA
You did remember?

GERMONT
La promessa adempio . . .
A stringervi qual figlia vengo al seno,
O generosa . . .

GERMONT
I have kept my promise and came here to embrace you
As a father would his daughter!

VIOLETTA
Oimè, tardi giungeste!
Pure, grata ven sono . . .
Grenvil, vedete? fra le braccia io spiro
Di quanti cari ho al mondo . . .

VIOLETTA
Alas! That is too late now.
Just the same I am grateful.
Grenvil, you see this?
I shall die, surrounded
By those I love and cherish.

GERMONT
Che mai dite!
(Oh cielo . . . è ver!)

GERMONT
What are you saying?
(*observing* VIOLETTA, *aside*)
Oh, heaven, it's true!

ALFREDO
La vedi, padre mio?

ALFREDO
My father, do you see her?

GERMONT
Di più non lacerarmi . . .
Troppo rimorso l'alma mi divora . . .

GERMONT
My son, do not reproach me,
For my remorse is great enough already!
As if lightning had struck me,

Her words overwhelm me.
(VIOLETTA *opens a drawer and takes a medallion from it*)
How misguided a father!
The wrong I did her
Now is apparent.

VIOLETTA
Come here beside me and listen,
Beloved Alfredo!
Dearest, on this medallion
You see my past resemblance,
To keep as a remembrance
Of her, who loved you so!

ALFREDO
You must not die, but live for me,
No, you shall live, believing!
Almighty God would never
Make me sustain such anguish,
Such hopeless grieving!

GERMONT
Can you forgive me
For all the suffering
Your sacrifice has caused you?
Forgive me for the anguish
Your noble heart has borne.

VIOLETTA (*softly and calmly*)
Someday you'll learn to love again
One who will give her heart to you,
Innocent, pure and worthy,
Then you should marry—I wish it.
Then give her this medallion.
Say that it came from me
Who then will be in heaven above,
Praying for her, for you.

ALFREDO
God will not part us now
So close to happiness.
Death must not tear you thus away from me.

ANNINA, GERMONT, DOCTOR
As long as I have tears to shed,
I'll always weep for you.
The angels will be with you,
God calls you to His side.

VIOLETTA
How strange—all at once—
The dreadful pain is gone.
I am reviving . . . Suddenly . . .
I feel I am reborn!
Ah, once more I feel my health returning!
Oh joy!
(*she rises joyfully, then, with the last word, falls dead*

Quasi fulmin m'atterra ogni suo detto . . .

Oh, malcauto vegliardo!
Il mal ch'io feci ora sol vedo!

VIOLETTA
Più a me t'appressa,
Ascolta, amato Alfredo:
Prendi; quest'è l'immagine
De' miei passati giorni;
A rammentar ti torni
Colei che sì t'amò.

ALFREDO
No, non morrai, non dirmelo . . .
Dêi viver, amor mio . . .
A strazio sì terribil
Qui non mi trasse Iddio . . .

GERMONT
Cara, sublime vittima
D'un disperato amore,
Perdonami lo strazio
Recato al tuo bel cor.

VIOLETTA
Se una pudica vergine
Degli anni suoi sul fiore
A te donasse il core . . .
Sposa ti sia . . . lo vo'.
Le porgi quest'effigie:
Dille che dono ell'è
Di chi nel ciel fra gli angeli
Prega per lei, per te.

ALFREDO
Sì presto, ah no, dividerti
Morte non può da me.
Ah, vivi, o solo un feretro
M'accoglierà con te.

ANNINA, GERMONT, DOTTORE
Finchè avrà il ciglio lacrime
Io piangerò per te.
Vola a' beati spiriti;
Iddio ti chiama a sè.

VIOLETTA
È strano! . . .
Cessarono
Gli spasimi del dolore.
In me rinasce . . . m'agita
Insolito vigore!
Ah! ma io ritorno a viver . . .
Oh gioia!

ANNINA, GERMONT, DOTTORE
Oh cielo! muor!

ALFREDO
Violetta?

ANNINA, GERMONT
O Dio, soccorrasi!

DOTTORE
È spenta!

ANNINA, ALFREDO, GERMONT
Oh rio (mio) dolor!

upon the sofa. ALFREDO, GERMONT, *the* DOCTOR, *and* ANNINA *remain near her, grief-stricken)*

ANNINA, GERMONT, DOCTOR *
Oh heaven, Ah!

ALFREDO
Violetta!

ANNINA, GERMONT
O God, be merciful!

DOCTOR
It's over.

ANNINA, ALFREDO, GERMONT
May she rest in peace!

* These last lines are usually omitted in performance.